SEA POWER

A Naval History

Editor

E. B. POTTER, U.S. Naval Academy

Associate Editor

CHESTER W. NIMITZ, Fleet Admiral, USN

Assistant Editors

J. R. Fredland
Henry H. Adams

Authors

Henry H. Adams
James A. Arnold
William M. Belote
Ellery H. Clark, Jr.
J. R. Fredland
Edwin M. Hall
Neville T. Kirk
Winston B. Lewis
Philip K. Lundeberg
E. B. Potter
W. H. Russell
H. O. Werner

S E A

1960 : *Englewood Cliffs, N. J.*
PRENTICE-HALL, INC.

POWER

A Naval History

SEA POWER — A Naval History. E. B. Potter, Editor

© 1960 by Prentice-Hall, Inc., Englewood Cliffs, N. J.

Library of Congress Catalog Card Number: 60–14957

Printed in the United States of America

79687–C

Foreword

Sea Power contains an extraordinary amount of information about navies and naval warfare, expressed in language that the seaman will appreciate and that the civilian will easily understand. The book also contains a fast-moving narrative of war at sea from the earliest times to the present. Lastly, it truly demonstrates the importance of a navy, and of the United States Navy in particular, as an instrument of national policy.

The historical approach used in this work permits the reader to observe navies in action, first under the simple conditions of early times, then under the growing complexity of the age of sail and of the age of steam, and at last in the tri-elemental present, when navies are no longer mere fleets of ships but extraordinarily complicated systems for projecting power at a distance. By observing the evolution of navies and sea power, both seaman and civilian readers will become better able to understand current naval practices, techniques, and functions, and to appreciate the continuing value of the Navy to the nation.

One fact that cannot escape the attentive reader is that underlying the changing elements of naval warfare, which reflect the constant changes in weapons, there are unchanging principles as applicable to missile warfare as to warfare under oar. The reader will perceive that command of the sea is as important today, when command extends to the air above the surface and to the waters below, as it was in early days when command was limited to the surface of inland waterways. He will see that the United States is the logical inheritor of the trident from the great sea powers of the past. As Britain for centuries stood off Western Europe, and maintained the balance of power therein, largely by means of her Royal Navy, so the United States now stands at the very center of the world's sea power complex, maintaining the balance of power in the rest of the world. Let the reader study the map on page 884. From this it is clear that the tangle of international alliances to which the United States is now committed—NATO, ANZUS, SEATO, and the rest—is actually an association of powers militarily connected by sea. So long as the nations thus banded together find it necessary to join hands for their mutual interests and safety, so long will it be necessary for them to make use of the sea—to transport troops, munitions, and supplies to the places where they are most needed, to put forces ashore where least expected by a real or potential enemy, and by virtue of the mobility of forces at sea to provide aircraft and missile platforms in ever-changing locations, difficult to locate and hence difficult to destroy or to defend against.

It is the duty of every person interested in the national defense to read and understand such a book as *Sea Power*.

Chester W. Nimitz
Fleet Admiral, USN

Preface

The term *sea power* comprises all those elements that enable a nation to project its military strength seaward and to project and maintain it beyond the seas. The elements of sea power are by no means limited to combat craft, weapons, and trained personnel but include the shore establishment, well-sited bases, commercial shipping, and advantageous international alignments. The capacity of a nation to exercise sea power is based also upon the character and number of its population, the character of its government, the soundness of its economy, its industrial efficiency, the development of its internal communications, the quality and number of its harbors, the extent of its coastline, and the location of homeland, bases, and colonies with respect to sea communications. Full historical treatment of all these elements is impossible within the covers of a single book. The authors of *Sea Power* have chosen to emphasize the naval aspect, without however neglecting the other elements.

Sea Power is in a sense four books in one: a history of the United States Navy and of American naval power, a history of the world's navies, a study of the evolution of naval warfare, and a study of the part that sea power has played in the exercise of national power. Beginning with a brief study of the age of galley warfare, with successive emphasis upon ancient Greece, ancient Rome, and Renaissance Venice, *Sea Power* next devotes ten chapters to the age of sail, with emphasis upon the rise of Great Britain to her century-long position of pre-eminence as Mistress of the Seas. Thereafter the book is increasingly concerned with the development of the United States Navy and with the rise of American naval power. The authors have thus placed their emphasis in proportion to the actual power situation in succeeding historical periods.

Sea Power develops six main themes: (1) the influence of sea power upon history, (2) the reasoning behind strategic decisions, (3) the characteristics of successful leadership, (4) the evolution of naval weapons, (5) the evolution of naval tactics, and (6) the evolution of amphibious doctrine. Within these categories, emphasis is placed on the problems posed in each period of history by new weapons and new conditions, and on the solutions worked out for each by the navies of the world. Modern techniques of naval warfare and modern applications of naval power are shown as the products of a long evolution. To demonstrate this development most clearly, the authors have not hesitated to be highly selective in their recording of more remote historical periods, and to devote more than half the book to recent events.

Every page of *Sea Power* reflects the influence of Fleet Admiral Chester

W. Nimitz USN, who was closely associated with the project from beginning to end. It was he who set the general tone of the work, and it was he chiefly who steered the civilian writers away from the pitfalls of amateur military analysis. Guided by Admiral Nimitz' experience and professional insight, the authors have boldly developed certain concepts that they otherwise would have been hesitant to expound.

Another important influence on the book has been the writings of Alfred Thayer Mahan. The authors have in general adopted Mahan's analysis of naval history from the beginnings of the age of sail to the early 20th century, and where applicable they have also applied his concepts to more recent events.

Though *Sea Power* is a multi-author work, it is in no sense a symposium. The writers believe they have achieved organic unity in style and treatment. This has been possible, first, because the writers have similar professional backgrounds. All saw service in World War II, mostly in the naval reserve. Since then they have been closely associated as teachers of naval history at the United States Naval Academy. Here they have tested their ideas on each other through several years of discussion and of writing together. Most of the authors were associated in an earlier, preliminary study, *The United States and World Sea Power* (Prentice-Hall, Inc., 1955), parts of which have been incorporated into the present book. Second, the efforts of each author have been subjected to intensive analysis and criticism by his colleagues and by professional officers. Third, the authors, eschewing pride of authorship, have submitted their work to unlimited editing where necessary to achieve continuity, unity of style, and unity of treatment.

Though there are numerous instances where it would be difficult to specify where one writer's work leaves off and another's begins, or to separate editorial work from original composition, the authors take primary responsibility for the various chapters as follows: Henry H. Adams, chapters 8, 27, 28, 44, and 45; James A. Arnold, 18; Ellery H. Clark, Jr., 20 and 22; J. R. Fredland, 3, 13, 14, 21, and 26; Neville T. Kirk, 19 and 24; Winston B. Lewis, 4, 5, 35, and 36; E. B. Potter, 1, 2, 37–41, and 43; W. H. Russell, 23; and H. O. Werner, 10, 11, 15, and 16. Chapter 6 is by Clark and Kirk; 7, by Adams, Clark, and Potter; 9, by Adams and Kirk; 12, by Clark and Hall; 17, by Fredland and Werner; 25, by Adams and Clark; 29, by Adams and Arnold; 30, by Adams and Lundeberg; 31 and 32, by Belote and Werner; 33, by Adams and Potter; 34, by Adams, Potter, and Russell; 42, by Adams and Hall; and 46, by Adams and Fredland.

While taking full responsibility for errors of fact and interpretation, the authors wish to express their gratitude to all who have helped them complete this work.

The following officers have read in manuscript portions of *Sea Power* covering their own experiences and have provided the writers with detailed comment and marginal notes: the late Fleet Admiral William F. Halsey USN (Ret.), Admiral Raymond A. Spruance USN (Ret.), Admiral H. Kent Hewitt USN (Ret.), Admiral Thomas C. Kinkaid USN (Ret.), Admiral Robert B. Carney USN (Ret.), Lieutenant General Julian C. Smith USMC (Ret.), Vice Admiral A. Stanton Merrill USN (Ret.), and Captain Ralph Weymouth USN.

This project is perhaps unique in that it has thus been reviewed and criticized by so many of the participants in the operations described.

The following have read portions of the manuscript, as indicated, and gave helpful advice: Professor Richard S. West of the Naval Academy faculty—the Civil War; Commander F. Barley RN (Ret.), Commander M. G. Saunders RN (Ret.), and Lieutenant Commander D. W. Waters RN (Ret.), all of the Historical Section, British Admiralty—chapters 25 and 30; Dr. Philip H. Crowl of the United States State Department—chapter 34; the late Vice Admiral Eliot H. Bryant USN (Ret.) and Rear Admiral Walter C. Ansel USN (Ret.)—World War II; Vice Admiral Bernard L. Austin USN and Mr. William M. Franklin of the U.S. Department of State—chapters 44 and 46.

Useful editorial assistance was provided by Commander Micajah R. Wyatt USN, by Mr. John Jeffries, and by Mr. David Vanderburgh of Prentice-Hall.

So many persons have been helpful in supplying information that a comprehensive listing is impossible, but prominent among them are General of the Army Douglas MacArthur USA; Grand Admiral Erich Raeder, formerly Commander in Chief of the Germany navy; Admiral Arleigh A. Burke, Chief of Naval Operations, U.S. Navy; General Thomas Holcomb USMC (Ret.); Vice Admiral Friedrich Ruge, Chief of Naval Operations, German Federal Navy; Vice Admiral Giuseppe Fioravanzo, Director of the Historical Division of the Italian Navy; Major General R. W. Keyser USMC (Ret.); Commodore Howard H. J. Benson USN (Ret.); Lieutenant Commander P. K. Kemp RN (Ret.), Archivist and Head of the Historical Section, British Admiralty; Commander G. A. Titterton RN (Ret.), Historical Section, British Admiralty; M. Jacques Mordal, Historical Section, Ministry of the French *Marine*; Professor Wilhelm Hadler; Herr Erich Gröner; Herr Jurgen Rohwer; Mrs. Robert Dunlap; and Mr. Charles Fox, Jr.

Professor Vernon D. Tate, Head Librarian of the United States Naval Academy, his predecessor, the late Professor Louis H. Bolander, and their staffs have been unstintingly helpful, as have Rear Admiral Ernest M. Eller USN (Ret.), Director of Naval History, and his staff. Thanks are due also to the Historical Branch G-3, Headquarters U.S. Marine Corps, which arranged for Professor Russell to have access to records at the Marine Corps Schools, Quantico, and at the Naval War College, Newport.

The charts and diagrams were drawn, largely from authors' sketches, by Mr. William M. Shannon and Mr. Albert R. Jones, both of the U.S. Naval Academy.

Mention should be made of the extensive use of *History of United States Naval Operations in World War II,* by Samuel Eliot Morison, and of *The War at Sea,* by S. W. Roskill RN (Ret.). These books were basic sources of information for the World War II chapters.

The authors and Admiral Nimitz wish to emphasize that *Sea Power* is in no sense an official history. It was conceived and written as a private enterprise. The opinions expressed are the writers' own.

E. B. Potter

Contents

Illustration Acknowledgments

The maps, charts, and diagrams used in this book are necessarily compiled from information drawn from many sources. In some instances one source has been the primary basis for an illustration. The authors therefore wish to acknowledge these sources for the illustrations appearing on the following pages: pages 155, 157, and 459, adapted from William Oliver Stephens and Allan Westcott, *A History of Sea Power* (Garden City, New York: Doubleday & Company, Inc., 1942); pages 210 and 650 adapted from Allan Westcott, ed., *American Sea Power since 1775* (Chicago: J. B. Lippincott Company, 1952); page 333 adapted from H. W. Wilson, *Ironclads in Action,* vol. II (Boston: Little, Brown & Company, 1896); page 350 adapted from H. W. Wilson, *Battleships in Action,* vol. I (Boston: Little, Brown & Company, 1928); the inset on page 423 adapted from Alan Moorehead, *Gallipoli* (New York: Harper and Brothers, Publishers, 1956); pages 440 and 447 adapted, with permission, from Langhorne Gibson and Vice-Admiral J. E. T. Harper RN, *The Riddle of Jutland* (New York: Coward-McCann, Inc., 1934); pages 468 and 560 adapted from David W. Waters, "The Philosophy and Conduct of Maritime War," *Journal of the Royal Naval Scientific Service,* July 1958; page 506 adapted from Antony Martienssen, *Hitler and His Admirals* (New York: E. P. Dutton & Co., Inc.); page 513 adapted, with permission of the Controller of H.M. Stationery Office, from Captain S. W. Roskill RN, *The War at Sea, 1939–1945* (London: Her Majesty's Stationery Office, 1956); pages 567 and 624 adapted from Dwight D. Eisenhower, *Crusade in Europe,* copyright 1948 by Doubleday and Company, Inc.; pages 557, 573, 660, 703, 762, and 763 adapted with the permission of the author from Samuel Eliot Morison, *History of United States Naval Operations in World War II,* vols. II, III, V, and VIII (Boston: Little, Brown & Company, 1948–1953); pages 607 and 609 adapted from Chester Wilmot, *The Struggle for Europe* (New York: Harper and Brothers, Publishers, 1952); page 613 adapted from Department of Military Art and Engineering, United States Military Academy, atlas for *A Military History of World War II* (West Point, 1953); page 617 adapted from Alfred Stanford, *Force Mulberry* (New York: William Morrow and Company, 1951); page 746 adapted from Philip A. Crowl and Edmund G. Love, *Seizure of the Gilberts and Marshalls* (Washington: Office of the Chief of Military History, Department of the Army, 1955); page 884 reproduced from Commander Burdick H. Brittin USN, *International Law for Seagoing Officers* (Annapolis, Md.: United States Naval Institute, 1956).

1:

The Age of Galley Warfare

When man ceased to look upon streams, rivers, and seas as barriers and learned to use them as highways, he made a giant stride toward civilization. The waterways of the world provided a new mobility—to man himself, later to the products of his toil and skill, and at all times to his ideas.

The mobility provided by rivers and seas both enriched and enlightened their users. River-faring and seafaring peoples could barter their products with other peoples far and near, trading those goods which they were best equipped to produce in exchange for the agricultural and industrial specialties of other lands. They could act as carriers or middlemen, exchanging the produce of one region for that of another. Because the seas required no fixed routes, they permitted an almost unlimited variety of contact between peoples bordering their shores, and early seafarers were able to work out trading combinations that earned them a wealth-producing surplus, or profit. In the process they also brought home in their heads an invisible cargo of ideas and information, a form of wealth oftentimes more precious than the trade goods they carried in their ships' holds.

The prosperity of sea-using nations gave them leisure to foster the arts and sciences, and power to make their influence felt in distant places. In every epoch the sea powers have been beacons of enlightenment, spreaders of civilization, explorers of distant coasts, and founders of colonial empires. It was the seafaring Phoenicians who disseminated the alphabet and who carried civilization into the western Mediterranean and beyond. It was the seafaring Greeks who developed and gave to the world patterns of thought and expression which are basic to our Western Civilization. It was the seafaring Romans who evolved and spread enduring concepts of law, order, and justice, and it was within the Roman Empire that Christianity was first propagated. It was seafaring Portugal that first joined Europe and the Orient, seafaring Spain that permanently joined the New World to the Old, seafaring England that was most instrumental in launching the Industrial Revolution and spreading the concept of representative government. All were founders of overseas empires.

Western man first began to use the broad seas in and around the Mediterranean basin. In the Middle East and in North Africa, deserts facilitated the establishment of caravan routes between populated areas, but in general water transportation was so much swifter, cheaper, and in general safer than transport over land that major nations and city-states tended to rise in areas that had access to navigable rivers and seas.

Most of the basic institutions of our Western culture had their origins in the ferment of ideas that exercised the Mediterranean peoples within a few centuries before and after the advent of the Christian era. If we look for the cause of this productive ferment, this tremendous churning and upsurging of ideas, we must consider the peculiar conditions of the area. The Mediterranean basin has been a principal area of contact, whether for trade or conquest, among the vigorous civilizations of Asia, Europe, and Africa. At the period of the great ferment of ideas, all the major centers of culture impinging upon the Mediterranean and its tributaries had reached such a state of development that each had something of value to offer. Hence each, chiefly through overseas contacts, had a civilizing effect upon the others.

Early Navies

The appearance of wealth on the seas in the form of trade goods inevitably produced piracy, and increase of overseas commerce led to clashes between rival trade interests. The first battles afloat were merely unorganized skirmishes between traders and predatory seafarers out to capture booty. Because merchant vessels loaded with goods and manned by their regular crews were ill prepared to defend themselves, organized communities early set aside certain vessels carrying marines (soldiers assigned to sea duty) to patrol and to guard the commercial ships at sea.

Specialization of function soon led to specialization of type, as marine architects devised craft especially designed for fighting. Hence at the very dawn of history in the Mediterranean world we find two sorts of vessels: the broad, clumsy cargo carrier, driven primarily by sails; and the long, narrow man-of-war, or *galley*, propelled by oars in battle and in calms but provided with masts and sails for cruising in a good wind or to aid in flight. Thus navies came into being to protect sea commerce, and the history of sea power is to a great extent the story of rivalries among nations resulting from their conflicting commercial interests.

Even when conflict between nations came about from other causes, warships retained as their principal function the task of patrolling and escorting to protect their own shipping and to attack the enemy's. To put it a little differently, the primary task of navies, especially in war, has been to safeguard their own shipping and to deny to the enemy the use of the sea. To the extent that a fleet has achieved this goal in any given area, it is said to have command (or control) of the sea in that area.

The whole complex of routes and transport is called *communications*.[1] The primary function of navies, then, has been to control sea communications, that is, to defend one's own and to disrupt the enemy's. Such control is generally attained by destruction of enemy sea forces; and often it has been achieved by a single decisive naval battle, in which one fleet by shattering the opposing fleet secured command of the sea at a stroke. Securing command of the sea, as we shall see, underlies and provides the means whereby navies have been able to perform their other wartime functions: defending the state against seaborne attack,

[1] Not to be confused with another word of the same spelling which refers to the dissemination and exchange of information by whatever means—messenger, post, telegraph, radio, flag hoist, and the rest. Without this second sort of communications, there can of course be no effective control of forces.

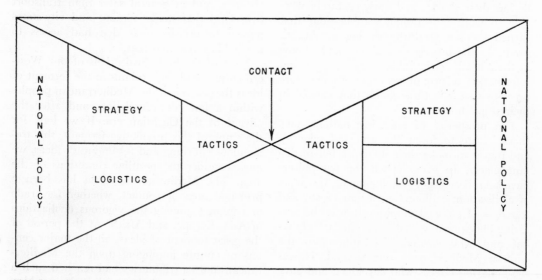

THE ELEMENTS OF WARFARE

isolating the enemy, and carrying the attack across the sea to the enemy.

By the 5th century BC, when the naval history of the Mediterranean came to be recorded with some degree of accuracy, the leading nations in that area had long since outgrown the mere piratical raiding that characterized the dawn of sea power. They had, in fact, mastered the basic elements of warfare as we know them today. They knew that the foundation for the successful conduct of war is what we call *logistics*, the science of supply, transportation, and maintenance. They had a firm grasp of the large-scale planning, deciding what forces to use and where to use them, that the early Greeks called *strategia*, or generalship, and we call *strategy*. And on land and sea they had developed systems of *tactics*, that is, organized handling of forces in battle. To be sure, naval operations of the 5th century were crude by later standards, partly because the same general officers commanded both ashore and afloat, with their chief interest devoted usually to land operations. The fleet was regarded merely as a seagoing army and in fact usually operated in conjunction with infantry ashore.

In tactics particularly the early navies revealed their dependence upon the examples of land warfare. The common battle formation for infantrymen was the phalanx, a rectangle of men usually eight ranks deep. Like infantrymen en route to the field of battle, the galleys cruised in column (line ahead), generally several columns abreast, but on making contact with the enemy or assuming a defensive position they deployed into line abreast, normally several ranks deep, a kind of seagoing phalanx. Though one may question the wisdom of deploying in ranks, a formation that was early abandoned, it cannot be doubted that line abreast was certainly the most logical arrangement for galleys. In line abreast each galley protected its neighbors' vulnerable sides, where the banks of oars were exposed, and at the same time presented to the enemy its fighting part, the bow with its ram, its grappling irons, and its missile-hurling devices.

The weakness of the early naval tactics lay in their lack of flexibility, a fault shared with the infantrymen's phalanx. While sideswiping and flanking were not unknown in early sea battles, strong emphasis was placed upon maintaining an unbroken front for mutual support. As opposing fleets of galleys approached each other, oars stroking in unison, archers stationed in the bows fired volleys of arrows. Then the lines collided, metal-shod underwater rams crunched into wooden hulls, the galleys grappled one another, and marines armed with swords and spears swarmed across decks, turning the sea fight into an infantry battle.

To attain the degree of speed and striking power required for this sort of combat, early navies developed special galleys, notably the *trireme*, which by the 5th century had become the capital ship of the Mediterranean. Compared to later triremes and their successors, these early combat vessels were small, probably not longer than 75 feet, with a beam of 13 feet at the water line. Normally carrying four officers, 12 sailors, perhaps 18 marines, 90 rowers, who manned oars in three banks, and a flute player or drummer to set the stroke, the trireme could achieve speeds above seven knots.[2] Like all galleys it was a fragile craft, unseaworthy, unable to weather storms. By day fleets of triremes hugged the coast and by night or in foul weather they were usually hauled ashore. Even if there had been a better understanding among the ancients of the potentialities of naval power, these frail vessels could scarcely have carried them out. Extended blockade duty or assaults on distant defended coasts were quite beyond their capabilities. Yet they played an important, indeed an indispensable role in shaping the history of the world. The wonder is that they accomplished so much.

It is difficult to say what people first exercised extensive sea power, but clearly Crete (c. 2,500-1,200 BC) was one of the earliest and most powerful. The reasons are obvious, for

[2] Later triremes were considerably larger, more than 100 feet long and carrying about 160 rowers. The quinquereme, octireme, decireme, and so on, used in Roman naval warfare, were formerly thought to have carried from five to forty banks of oars. Recent study and experiment, however, have shown that such multi-banked galleys would have been inefficient if not impossible. Evidently the system of nomenclature varied. The quinquereme, for example, probably carried a single bank of oars with five men to an oar.

given a population of sufficient density, the Cretans must early have been forced by the mountainous, inhospitable geography of their island to seek their living on the sea. Here geography was more in their favor, for Crete sits squarely athwart the major sea routes of the eastern Mediterranean. She was thus strategically placed not only as a commerce carrier but also for attacking and limiting the operations of her commercial rivals.

The Phoenicians (c. 2,000-300 BC) were the next wielders of pre-eminent sea power. They established a flourishing maritime trade that carried their ships into all the inland seas in their part of the world and even beyond the Pillars of Hercules (Straits of Gibraltar) to seek the tin of Britain, the amber of the Baltic, and the slaves and ivory of western Africa to exchange for the spices, gold, and precious stones of India. This East-West trade enabled them to establish the mighty ports of Sidon and Tyre at the termini of caravan routes from the Orient, and the search for new customers and new sources of raw materials impelled them to become the first great colonizers of ancient times. Their trading stations on the shores and islands of the Mediterranean became new centers of civilization, some of which outlasted the influence of the parent state. Carthage is a notable example. In the course of time this Phoenician colony came to dominate the western Mediterranean and founded an empire embracing North Africa, Sardinia, Corsica, half of Sicily, and much of Spain.

It is of early Greek sea power that we are able to attain the clearest and most accurate picture, thanks to Herodotus and Thucydides, who wrote excellent contemporary histories of the Greco-Persian and Peloponnesian wars. Even before an accurate history of Greece was put into writing however, Greece's naval traditions were old and her sea trade was well developed. Indeed, there is reason to believe that Homer's *Iliad* is really a poetic description of prehistoric Greek sea power at work— that the siege of Troy was a commercial war, to secure control of the Hellespont (modern Dardanelles) and thus of the Black Sea trade. At any rate, the Greeks had by the 5th century BC excluded the Phoenicians and the Carthaginians from the Black and Aegean seas and held a virtual monopoly on shipping in the eastern Mediterranean. From their own mountainous, unfertile peninsula they could export few agricultural products but olive oil and wine; these however were of the best and much in demand. Moreover, the work of their artisans (pottery, rugs, swords, tiles, and metal work) and their artists (jewelry, painted vases, and statues) gave them a highly favorable balance of trade. As their trading stations

EASTERN MEDITERRANEAN SEA

developed into colonies, the coasts of Asia Minor to the east, Thrace to the north, and Sicily and southern Italy to the west had become virtual extensions of Greece. Other Greek settlements existed as far away as the northern shores of the Black Sea and the Mediterranean coasts of Spain and Gaul (France). All that prevented the ancient Greeks from founding one of the mightiest maritime empires of history was the fatal defect of disunity. Within the Hellenic peninsula the Greek peoples were split up into separate little city-states—Athens, Sparta, Corinth, Thebes, and the rest—more often than not at odds with each other. The overseas Greek settlements were for the most part no true colonies at all but independent communities, attached to the mother cities of Greece by sentiment, tradition, and commercial ties. This dispersion of power, as much as anything else, was at length to cost the Greeks their freedom.

The Greco-Persian War

The dawn of recorded naval history coincides with one of the great crises in the history of mankind. As viewed from later times, it can be seen as nothing less than an attack by Asia on Europe. Had the hordes out of the Middle East succeeded in subduing peninsular Greece, the cradle and first home of Western Civilization, we may be sure that subsequent world history would have been very different.

The instrument of the attack was Persia, a true empire, tightly knit and centrally controlled, one of a series of empires which through the centuries dominated Western Asia. Expanding out of the Iranian highlands, Persian control had by the 6th century BC reached the Mediterranean and the Aegean seas. The Phoenicians, having no solidarity as a nation or prospect of assistance, submitted easily—as they had earlier submitted to Egyptians, Assyrians, and Babylonians—and provided fleets for the overseas conquests of their new masters. But the Greek cities of Asia Minor resisted, and even when conquered, rose against their conqueror with naval aid from Athens and Eretria across the Aegean. The Persians recaptured the rebellious cities, but suppressing the revolt cost them several years and gave the city-states of the Hellenic peninsula time

to prepare for the inevitable attack. Herodotus explains the Persian assault on Greece as reprisal for the assistance that Athens gave the rebels in Asia Minor, but the fact is that Persia's absorption of populations with maritime trade interests had long since brought her into direct competition with Greece. Hence a struggle for commercial domination of the eastern Mediterranean was sure to come. Besides, the expanding Empire had already spread across the Hellespont and through Thrace and Macedonia as far as Thessaly. Evidently the Persians, having already absorbed so many recalcitrant Greeks, would have to conquer *all* the Greeks if they expected to have peace within their domains.

The first Persian expedition against Greece, in 492 BC, succeeded in subduing revolt in Thrace and Macedonia, but the fleet of fighting ships that accompanied the army as it marched around the northern shores of the Aegean, was heavily damaged in a storm off the promontory of Mt. Athos. With the fleet out of action, cargo vessels could not be protected while supplying the troops; hence further advance was out of the question. The army was too large either to live off the land or to subsist upon supplies hauled in driblets by land transport. Loss of its overseas communications thus stopped the first expedition in its tracks.

The second Persian expedition, two years later, came to an even more inglorious end. This was an amphibious operation, an attack by sea directly across the Aegean. As it turned out, the ships and techniques of the period were entirely inadequate for this sort of thing. The small transport vessels then in use could not land and reinforce troops fast enough to make a frontal assault against forces that the Greeks could assemble overland. When the first Persian echelon, some 15,000 strong, landed on the plain of Marathon, 10,000 Athenians marched the 20 miles to the beachhead and hurled them into the sea without waiting for tardy reinforcements from their Spartan allies.

The Persians did not attack Greece again for ten years, partly because the new Persian ruler, King Xerxes, undertook elaborate preparations to assure that the third expedition would be a success. Choosing the less vulnerable of the two difficult lines of approach,

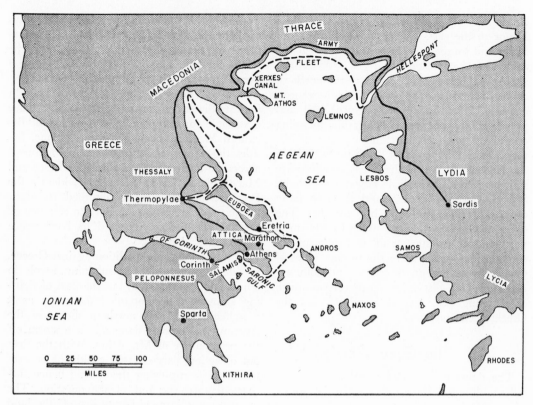

ROUTES OF XERXES' FLEET AND ARMY, 480 BC

Xerxes in 480 BC assembled 180,000 troops at Sardis in Asia Minor and marched them overland to the Hellespont, which they crossed by means of two pontoon bridges. The new expedition perforce followed the example of the first by proceeding along the Aegean coast while hundreds of cargo vessels kept it supplied from Asiatic bases. About 1,300 fighting ships, manned by some 175,000 seamen, rowers, and marines, covered the flank of the advancing army and protected the cargo vessels. To avoid the disaster that had befallen the earlier expedition along this route, Xerxes had a canal dug across the peninsula of Athos so that his fleet could avoid rounding it in stormy weather.

Aware of the Persian preparations, the peninsular Greeks had for once united and set up a Panhellenic Congress to direct the defense. Luckily, Athens had produced an exceptional leader in Themistocles, who correctly saw that the Persian army was no stronger than the fleet that protected its communications back to base. He persuaded his fellow Athenians to invest in an enlarged fleet, which with ships of the other city-states gave the Greeks a naval force of 380 triremes. By means of this force Themistocles expected at least to prevent the Persians from using their navy to outflank and put troops behind his army's defense lines. With luck he hoped to win a naval victory that would expose the Persian communications to attack. Not all the Greek leaders perceived so clearly the crucial role to be played by the fleet, but all were agreed that resistance to the Persian hordes would be futile on an open plain. Their only chance lay in meeting them in some narrow passage, where the Greek army might hold back the invaders in Horatius-at-the-bridge fashion. The Spartans and other Peloponnesians favored the Isthmus of Corinth, but in the end the Congress elected to take a stand at the coastal pass of Thermopylae. Here mountains would cover the Greek left flank, while the Greek fleet in the narrow strait between Euboea and the mainland would cover their right.

Xerxes' strategy, like his logistics, was on a grand scale. He had little doubt that he could overcome the Greeks of the Hellenic Peninsula. But what if they should greatly increase their numbers by bringing in additional Greeks from Sicily and southern Italy? It is possible that Xerxes had intelligence that the Panhellenic Congress was negotiating with Syracuse for just such assistance. At any rate, he induced the Carthaginians, probably through their Phoenician kinsmen, to stage an attack on Greek Sicily timed to coincide with his invasion of Greece. The Carthaginians were only too glad of such an opportunity to crush their competitors. So, as the Persians poured into Thessaly, an army of mercenaries from North Africa landed in Sicily and thrust westward toward the Greek cities there. Xerxes was thus using the strategy of *exterior position*, which we shall see used many times again, particularly in World War II.[3]

At first glance the Greeks and the Persians appear to have chosen entirely different strategies. Basically however the object was the same: to defeat the enemy in fractions, to bring decisive strength against *part* of the enemy forces while the rest of the enemy was held in check. Xerxes saw his advance into Greece as the main attack, the striking arm of his strategic plan. For him, the Carthaginian advance was a diversion, intended to hold the Sicilian Greeks in check while he defeated the Hellenic Greeks on the peninsula. For Themistocles and his fellow Greeks, the pass, strait, or isthmus in which they elected to do their fighting would permit the enemy to present only a narrow fighting front and at the same time hold his rear out of battle. In both strategies, then, there was a *hitting* and a *holding*

[3] The *exterior position* is attained by partly or wholly surrounding the enemy. The force thus surrounded has the *interior position*. Either position may be the more advantageous, depending upon circumstances. The weaker power however will normally prefer the interior position, because he may be able to use his short *interior lines* to strike with his full strength at successive segments of the surrounding enemy force faster than the enemy can bring reinforcements via his longer *exterior lines*.

element. While one element hit a part, or fraction, of the enemy, the rest of the enemy was to be held outside the area of the main attack. Securing this advantage of defeating the enemy piecemeal is a major technique of all warfare whether on land or sea, on the tactical or the strategic level. Achieved by a score of different combinations, it is an important object of all military planning and maneuver. It is part of what Mahan called "the one great principle of concentration."[4]

The Greek stand at Thermopylae was a failure. The Persians, sending a part of their force around the Greek left flank by way of a mountain path, clamped the pincers on the defending infantry and annihilated them. That path, revealed to the Persians by a Greek traitor, was the flaw in the strategic defensive. Once the Persians learned of it, the capacity of the Pass of Thermopylae to hold the enemy rear was lost. The allied fleet, which had steadfastly covered the Greek right despite attacks from Persian triremes, now retired south to the narrow waters between the island of Salamis and the mainland not far from Athens. At the same time Xerxes pressed with his army into Attica, laying waste everywhere and at length plundering the abandoned city of Athens. His fleet however had encountered a succession of storms that cost him some 400 of his galleys, ". . . the gods so contriving," wrote Herodotus, "that the Persian fleet might not greatly exceed the Greek, but be brought nearly to its level."

When Xerxes' remaining 800 ships entered the Bay of Phalerum, the port of Athens, the Peloponnesians were for withdrawing the 300 surviving Allied ships to the Isthmus of Corinth, where the Greek armies had taken a new stand. But Themistocles, exercising all his force of intellect and powers of persuasion, argued in favor of keeping them where they were instead of exposing them to superior numbers in the open sea. Xerxes, equally anxious to fight before bad weather could further cut down his naval advantage, settled the matter by sending 200 ships south around Salamis to block any attempt of his opponents to escape. The Greek admirals now had no choice but

[4] Capt. Alfred Thayer Mahan usn, *Naval Strategy* (Boston, 1918), 49.

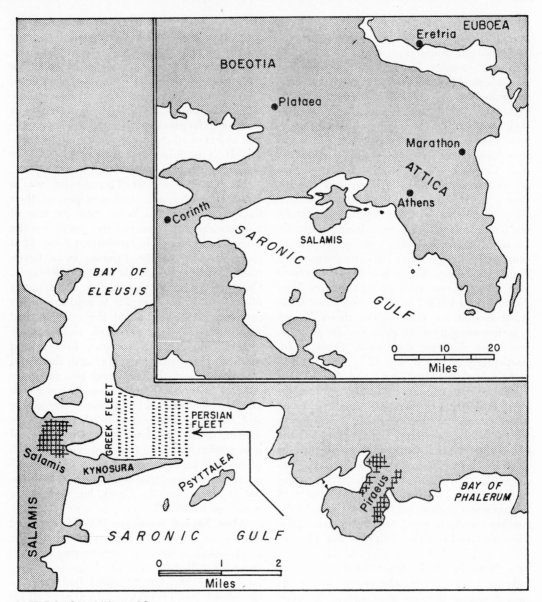

BATTLE OF SALAMIS, 480 BC

to fight where they were, for the other 600 Persian ships were already advancing on the eastern entrance to the strait.

Under the eyes of Athenian evacuees watching from the heights of Salamis, and of King Xerxes enthroned on the opposite shore, the Persian galleys moved north, presumably in several columns, past the island of Psyttalea. They then must have executed ships left and advanced in line abreast, ultimately six to eight ranks deep, against the Greeks, who we may suppose were in line abreast three or four ranks deep, with their flanks covered by the shorelines to avoid envelopment by the opposing fleet.

The Persians could thus present no more front-line bows and rams to their enemy than the Greeks could, and though they possessed greater strength in depth, their rear ranks could do little more than feed fresh troops forward. The fact that the Persians had twice as many ships as the Greeks made no difference at all. They could actually use no more ships as weapons than the Greeks could, for most of their galleys were held out of battle by the narrow strait. To be sure, the Persians had more marines, but this advantage too was offset by the fact that the Greek sailors and oarsmen were mostly freemen who could when needed seize sword and shield and join the fight across decks. Among the Greeks moreover there were no unwilling levies but men fighting for their lives and homes, whereas the Persian forces were made up largely of conscripts and mercenaries. Lastly, the Greeks wore metal breast plates in battle and the Persians did not. In the daylong infantry engagement that the Battle of Salamis turned out to be, the Greeks thus had the advantage in numbers, in aggressiveness, and in armor. These explain the overwhelming Greek victory, with no need to look for tactical subtleties that almost certainly did not occur. By nightfall, every Persian vessel that could extricate itself from the massed confusion in the strait had fled the area. No more than half got away. Greek losses were 40 ships.

With his naval force thus cut to shreds, Xerxes recognized that his seaborne communications were no longer secure, and that his army was stranded with insufficient supplies for an extended campaign. So he dispatched what was left of his fleet to Asia Minor and returned the way he had come, leaving behind some 50,000 troops to winter in Thessaly, where grain enough could be found to feed that many but no more. The following summer, land forces of the Panhellenic League—at last operating in unison as the combined fleet had operated at Salamis—attacked and annihilated Xerxes' 50,000 at Plataea, 40 miles northwest of Athens. In Sicily, meanwhile, Greeks under Gelos of Syracuse had decisively defeated the Carthaginian expedition. The Carthaginians did not renew the attack. Probably the news of Salamis left them with no stomach for operations requiring supply via vulnerable sea communications. No Persian invader ever again entered Greece; the Sicilian Greeks were left undisturbed by Carthage for 70 years.

The wars between Greece and Persia illustrate as clearly as any in history the truth of Mahan's axiom: "Communications dominate war."[5] Themistocles perceived that an army which cannot live off the land is no stronger than its line of supply and that when supplies must come across water, a victory at sea can set the stage for a victory on land. In centuries to come, many another army commander—Montcalm at Quebec, Cornwallis at Yorktown, Napoleon in Egypt, Lee at Petersburg, Blanco at Havana, and Yamashita in the Philippines, to name a few—was to find himself isolated like Xerxes in Attica by naval operations that decisively cut his communications.

The history of Greece in the century following Salamis demonstrates that war, when not too destructive, can be a stimulating and a civilizing influence. For warfare, along with its undoubted evils, shatters the restrictions of entrenched custom and tradition and compels nations to reassess their ideas and institutions. It gives the victor a sense of accomplishment and a new confidence in his own powers. Certainly no people in history have been electrified into greater creative activity than the Greeks were after their triumph over mighty Persia. Out of the ruins left by the war, the Athenians erected a new and greater Athens, a city of surpassing grandeur, whose magnificent ruins excite the imaginations of men to this day. Under the enlightened leadership of Pericles, Athens became "the teacher of Hellas," attracting artists and thinkers from the whole Greek world. During the Golden Age of Greece, in which the Athenians retained the intellectual and artistic pre-eminence, Aeschylus, Sophocles, and Euripides virtually created the art-form of tragic drama; Herodotus, Thucydides, and Xenophon wrote the first true histories, as distinguished from legendary and semi-legendary accounts; Myron, Phidias, and Praxiteles carried realistic sculpture to heights never surpassed; and Socrates, Plato, and Aristotle developed the technique of systematic thinking which is a principal basis of all science and philosophy. These are the men who, along with other Greeks of their time, laid the foundations of Western Civilization.

But the Greeks for all their brilliance could

[5] Mahan, *Naval Strategy*, 166.

not, or would not, maintain a necessary degree of unity. After bleeding themselves white in the bitter Peloponnesian War (431-404) BC), in which Greek fought Greek, they were overrun by Philip II of semibarbaric Macedonia. Philip at last unified most of Greece under his leadership in a Hellenic League which he passed on to his son, known to history as Alexander the Great. Alexander, a student of Aristotle, made the Greek cause his own and at 22 years of age set out to achieve the fixed ambition of all patriotic Greeks since Salamis. This was nothing less than the conquest of the Persian Empire—only to Alexander it was less a plan of military conquest than an attempt to unite all nations in a brotherhood of men founded upon Greek institutions.

Crossing the Hellespont in the spring of 334 BC with 35,000 disciplined troops, Alexander administered a stinging defeat to a numerically superior Persian army. He then advanced into Asia Minor and captured Sardis. Behind him in the Aegean however, a large Persian fleet denied him direct overseas communication with Macedonia, threatened to land an invasion force in Greece, and interdicted the seaborne trade of any ports that submitted to him. Alexander could not hope to eliminate this nuisance by means of a decisive battle at sea, for he had no fleet to speak of. So he undertook to solve this problem through the extraordinary measure of conquering sea power by use of land power—in effect a reversal of the strategy of Salamis. He reasoned that since fleets are dependent upon bases, he had only to occupy their bases and the hostile fleets must surrender or perish.

Accordingly he set out to seize all the ports rimming the eastern Mediterranean. The Greek cities of Asia Minor, for the most part, submitted willingly. Phoenician Sidon capitulated to threats and persuasion, but Phoenician Tyre fell into Alexander's hands only after a difficult seven-month siege which so annoyed the conqueror that he caused the city to be plundered and destroyed. Gaza submitted after a two-month assault, and Alexander marched into Egypt. Here he founded the port of Alexandria, which he made the principal entrepôt for the East-West trade. As a result of these operations Persian sea power was extinguished and the Phoenicians disappeared from history.

By means of land campaigns, Alexander had secured command of the sea and made Macedonia the world's greatest naval power.

The paradox of the situation is that Alexander, having captured a mighty fleet by the back-door approach, had little use for it. The eastern Mediterranean, in the phrase of Sir Halford J. Mackinder, proponent of the land-power theory, had become a "closed sea," that is, a sea over which commerce could move without strong naval protection because the shores were all held by one and the same power. With his rear covered and his military communications assured, Alexander now turned east and advanced confidently into the heart of the Persian Empire and beyond. In his wake came Greek ideas, illuminating the whole Middle East—ideas that might never have reached fruition had the Persians won at Salamis.

The Rise of Rome

Meanwhile, the supreme struggle for control of the *western* Mediterranean was about to begin. For two centuries after Salamis, Carthage and the Greeks of southern Italy and Sicily had held each other in check. The Carthaginians controlled the waters west of the Mediterranean narrows as their private lake, but the Greeks consistently blocked their attempts to advance eastward. In 275 BC however the Romans, expanding from the Tiber basin, conquered southern Italy, engulfing the Greek cities.

The Carthaginians at first saw Rome's conquest of the Italian Greeks as their own opportunity and promptly renewed their pressure on the Greeks of Sicily. What they did not realize was that they were thereby coming to grips with a rival far more formidable than any they had ever encountered. The Romans, sturdy and resolute, originally of farming stock, had developed a genius for administration and the arts of war. Their special gifts are nowhere better displayed than in their invention of the flexible legion to replace the unwieldy phalanx. When the Carthaginians in 264 BC threatened to send troops into Messana (modern Messina), just across the straits from the toe of the Italian boot, the alarmed Romans sent their legions into Sicily and quickly bot-

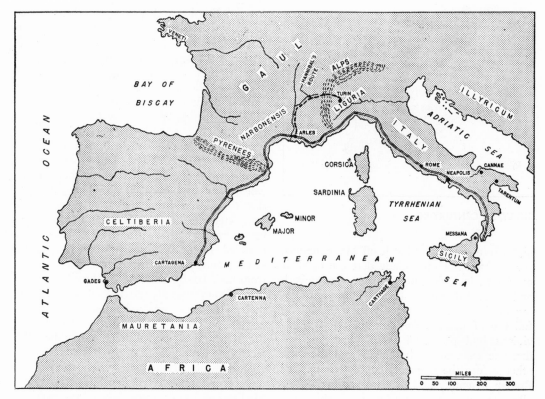

WESTERN MEDITERRANEAN SEA, 3rd CENTURY BC

tled up the Carthaginians in their fortified cities at the western end of the island. They thereby launched the first of three Punic Wars (so called from the Latin word for Carthaginian) and took the initial step toward overseas conquest.

Rome's first major problem in her century-long conflict with Carthage was how to deal with the Punic navy, which not only guarded Carthage from Roman attack but promptly interdicted Rome's maritime commerce and began to plunder her coasts. The problem was twofold: how to acquire a fleet, and how to handle it. Solving the first proved not too difficult; Rome's subject and allied Greek cities provided galleys and also shipbuilders to build more galleys. More perplexing was how to deal with the highly evolved Carthaginian mode of sea fighting, which included ramming, sideswiping, flanking, and breaking the line—distinctively naval tactics, designed to concentrate ships against ships. Rome's only hope was to force a return to the "old tactics"

used at Salamis, tactics which concentrated men against men. Rome then would have the advantage of confronting the Punic mercenaries with her own specialty, the well-disciplined legionary. The crux of the problem was how to get close enough to the agile foe to throw men aboard his ships.

The ingenious Roman solution was the corvus, or "crow," an 18-foot gangway bearing a pointed iron beak under the outboard end. Pivoted from a mast by a topping lift, it could be dropped forward or on either side to grip any unwary enemy vessel that approached close enough to ram or sideswipe. Over the gangway, foot soldiers then surged to convert a naval battle into an infantry battle across decks. The corvus first proved decisive off Mylae in 260, when the Carthaginians, despising their lubberly foe, bore down without bothering to assume a formation. The crashing corvi and the expert legionaries promptly disposed of nearly half the enemy ships and sent the rest scurrying in bewildered

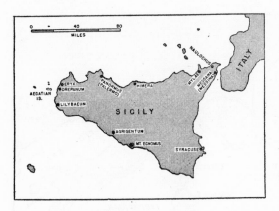

SICILY, 3rd CENTURY BC

flight. In a subsequent battle off Mt. Ecnomus, the Romans not only made deft use of their corvi but, in a dazzling display of teamwork and command control, turned Punic enveloping tactics to their own advantage. Making full use of the *interior position* the Carthaginians had presented them, they smashed first one segment of the enemy and then the other before the segments could reunite. But Roman ingenuity and teamwork proved after all no adequate substitute for seamanship. Admonished by a defeat and the loss in storms of several mishandled fleets, the Romans by dogged perseverance at length made themselves such skillful sailors that they brought the First Punic War to a close with a naval battle in which they defeated the enemy through sheer shiphandling.

Such was the ascendancy the Romans had won at sea that in the Second Punic War, the Carthaginian general, Hannibal, chose to attack Rome overland from Spain via the Alps. Though he managed to maintain himself in Italy for 15 years, he did so only by ravaging farm lands to sustain his army, thereby incurring the wrath of the disaffected Roman subject states on whom he had counted for aid. At length when Rome, by virtue of her sea command, carried the war to Africa, Hannibal hastened home to the defense, only to be defeated in the Battle of Zama. The Third Punic War began with a Roman seaborne invasion of Africa and concluded with the razing of Carthage and the utter destruction of Carthaginian power.

The Punic Wars stimulated the rise of the Roman Empire and also sowed the seeds of its ultimate destruction. Rome's first war with Carthage gave her Sicily as a province, the second gave her Spain, and the third gave her North Africa. The struggle and the final victory provided the warlike experience that carried Roman armies eastward through the Hellenic Peninsula and the Middle East to the Caspian Sea and the Persian Gulf and northward through Gaul to Britain. But Hannibal's devastation of Italy had broken up the small-farm economy upon which the republican power had been based. The influx of slaves resulting from the Roman conquests completed the process. The small farms were never re-established. In their place were founded huge cash-crop estates farmed by slave labor. A pauperized peasantry, driven from their lands, ceased to produce large families as they moved into the cities, a restless mob. The result was a land problem and a population problem. The first contributed to the downfall of the Roman Republic; the second, to the downfall of the Roman Empire.

During the period of expansion, the Roman navy, ever the neglected stepchild, cleared the Mediterranean of pirates, covered the overseas transport of the invincible legions, and successfully challenged any hostile fleet that had the temerity to contest Rome's command of the seas. In the process Rome completed her naval education. The legionaries remained her principal weapon on the sea as on land, but these she learned increasingly to support by judicious use of ship tactics and, later, missile tactics—employment of catapults and ballistae to hurl stones, javelins, and combustibles. Out of this combination the methodical Romans developed a fighting team as irresistible at sea as their infantry proved on land.

Rome's naval flexibility is nowhere better illustrated than in the two sea battles that paved the way for the conclusion of the long-drawn-out Roman Civil War (133-31 BC). The last stage of the war, following the assassination of Julius Caesar and the defeat of his assassins at Philippi, saw Caesar's grand-nephew Octavius opposed by two powerful adversaries in his drive for control of the Roman world. Sextus Pompey, from his base in Sicily, had secured naval control of the western Mediterranean and cut off Rome's overseas food supply. Mark Antony, based on Egypt, aroused fears that he planned to subdue Rome and make Alexandria the capital of the Empire.

To deal with Pompey's light, swift vessels, designed for semi-piratical operations, Octavius' naval commander, Agrippa, built a fleet of comparatively heavy vessels. Pompey's fleet thus had the advantage of speed and maneuverability in naval tactics, but at the showdown Battle of Naulochus Agrippa unveiled a secret weapon which enabled him to use infantry tactics. This was the *harpago*, as much an advance over the corvus as the corvus had been over the simple grappling iron. It consisted of a heavy timber with an iron claw at one end and a long line attached to the other. Retaining one end of the line on board, the Romans fired the harpago from a catapult, and when it hooked an enemy vessel, they hauled her in by means of a winch and then dashed aboard. Seeing their ships being reeled in like so many hooked fish, Pompey's surviving captains took to flight, as the Carthaginians had fled before the corvus at Mylae. His sea power destroyed, Pompey escaped to Asia.

Octavius and Agrippa combined skills for the overthrow of Antony. Their strategy was to isolate him and his wife Cleopatra, Queen of Egypt, in their advanced headquarters in Greece, near Actium on the Gulf of Amvrakia. Octavius set up an army base on the high healthful ground north of Antony's position while Agrippa, using the ships that had defeated Pompey, tightly blockaded Antony's remaining fleet and sea communications. Octavius next encouraged the Greeks, disaffected by Antony's high taxes, to cut his overland communications. He then simply remained in his fortified position, declining Antony's offers of battle.

Octavius could afford to wait, for, as he had surmised, time was on his side. In Antony's camp food became scarce, malaria struck, and his Roman followers fell to quarreling with Cleopatra's Egyptians. Antony's Romans, perceiving at last that they were serving an alien cause, began deserting to Octavius. So Antony was forced to seek a battle at sea, since he could not have one on land except under impossible disadvantages. If he were to win at sea, he might turn the tables and blockade Octavius. If the battle went against him, he

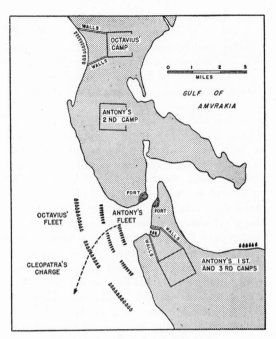

BATTLE OF ACTIUM, 1st CENTURY BC

might at least escape to Egypt with the bulk of his fleet, leaving the army to follow as it could.

The fleet of 200 vessels which Antony took out of the Gulf to face Agrippa's 260 was burdened with troops and stores—and with sails for flight in event of defeat. They were enormous vessels, for Antony, attributing the Roman victory at Naulochus to Agrippa's bigger ships, had built still bigger ships to meet Agrippa. Now, in the Battle of Actium, the Roman vessels that had overawed Pompey's by their size were dwarfed by their new opponents. Agrippa was not awed. Aware that the enemy had legionaries aboard every bit as good as his, he had discarded the harpago and planned to oppose naval tactics and maneuver to Antony's infantry and missiles.

Through the morning the two fleets remained inactive facing each other, Agrippa's in three squadrons abreast, Antony's in a similar formation, with 60 vessels under Cleopatra in reserve to the rear. At noon a breeze set Antony's left flank in motion and soon the fleets were engaged all along the line. Agrippa's ships, in a fine display of naval concentration, avoided compact formations of the enemy and attacked isolated units, darting in to sweep away oars and rudders and then, without pausing to permit boarding, backing off and striking swiftly again. At a crucial moment Agrippa released a terrifying fire of blazing arrows and pots of flaming charcoal that had considerably greater range than his opponent's catapulted stones.

Seeing the battle turning against Antony, Cleopatra came charging through the center of both lines with the wind at her back and her reserve squadron under sail. The agile Roman ships seem merely to have drawn aside and let her pass, leaving her separated from the main body of Antony's fleet. Since the wind did not permit her to reverse course and repeat her maneuver, she headed south and sailed away to Egypt. Antony boarded one of his smaller craft and managed to join her, but the rest of his fleet, under attack by Agrippa's fiery missiles, could not disengage and follow according to plan. Instead, they fought on until the flaming arrows and fire pots decided the issue in Agrippa's favor. At nightfall what was left of Antony's navy withdrew within the Gulf, whereupon the Roman blockade again closed down. A week later fleet and army surrendered to Octavius. His victories at Naulochus and Actium gave Octavius command of the whole Mediterranean, an indispensable preliminary to his subsequent conquest of Egypt and his assumption of imperial power as Caesar Augustus.

We are likely to think of imperial Rome as a land power, its parts linked together by the finest highway system of ancient times. This concept is only partly true. Far more important than any overland communications in binding the Empire together were the Mediterranean Sea and the other waters that lapped its shores. The story of the sea and its part in imperial history is neither dramatic nor dynamic and hence tends to escape notice. Yet the humble merchantman, distributing the products of every part of the Empire to all parts, transporting the proconsuls and their supporting legions to their overseas domains, conveying the Apostles and their successors with the message of Christianity, played an indispensable part in forming and preserving the greatest empire of antiquity. For five centuries after Actium, commercial vessels moved from the Black Sea to the Atlantic front protected only by small fleets of police vessels to keep down piracy. The entire Mediterranean and its tributary waters had become a "closed sea," with all coasts and naval bases controlled by Rome. On land and sea the *Pax Romana* was established, the longest period of comparative peace in history.

The Decline of Rome and the Rise of Europe

The heavy influx of slaves, which for centuries had offset Rome's declining birth rate, came to an end as the Roman conquest reached its limits. Into the resulting manpower vacuum at first seeped, then poured, the Germanic peoples of northern and eastern Europe—originally by invitation, as farmers and soldiers; then by permission, to escape the inroads of the nomadic Huns out of Central Asia; and at last as conquerors. Under these stresses, the Empire split into two parts, each under its own emperor: the Western Roman Empire, with its capital at Rome, and the Eastern or Byzantine Empire, with its capital at Constantinople. By the end of the 5th century AD the Western Empire had disappeared as a political entity. Angle and Saxon invaders from the Continent shared Britain with the original Britons; Franks and Burgundians ruled Gaul, Goths controlled Spain and Italy, and Vandals dominated North Africa. Vandal fleets from the port of Carthage had seized command of the Mediterranean, crushed Roman sea power, raided all the shores, and even sacked Rome. Expeditions sent by the Eastern Emperor against the Goths and the Vandals resulted in mere devastation of the Italian peninsula and the North African coast. In the ensuing chaos, wild Lombards from the north invaded Italy, and the indigenous Berber tribesmen overwhelmed North Africa.

In the next century, the rise of Islam threatened all Roman and former Roman territories. Nomadic Arabs, filled with religious fervor by the eloquence of Mohammed, poured out of the Arabian desert and attacked the neighboring empires. The Persians and the Byzantines quickly gave way as Moslem forces advanced eastward to the Indus and westward to the Bosporus.[6] Arab conquest of Egypt soon followed. Based securely on the whole Middle East, the Moslems took to the sea, overrunning Cyprus and Rhodes and raiding southern Italy and Sicily. At the same time they pushed westward across North Africa, conquering by the sword and then winning adherents through their policy of low taxes and religious toleration. By the year 700 AD the movement had reached the Straits of Gibraltar, across which Berber converts to Islam advanced to conquer the Gothic kingdom of Spain and to invade Gaul. It appeared that Moslem power was about to engulf the whole Christian world. In the East however, Constantinople held firm. An assault by 80,000 Moslems in 717 failed to breach the city walls, and Byzantine galleys scattered the blockading fleet with a new incendiary weapon, the practically inextinguishable Greek fire. In the West, the Moslem thrust into Gaul was hurled back in 732 by a Frankish army.

The Franks under Charlemagne, in cooperation with the Papacy, briefly restored order in Western Europe, but the Frankish empire fell apart under fresh attacks by the Moslems in the South, by Slavs and kindred peoples in the East, and by Vikings out of Scandinavia in the North. Thus while the Islamic and Byzantine empires reached peaks of culture and enlightenment, the West entered the period of disorder and confusion known as the Dark Age.

From this slump Western Europe at length extricated itself under the leadership of the Church and by means of the politico-military system of feudalism. Out of the ruins of the Frankish empire rose the Holy Roman Empire, embracing Germany and most of Italy. The Vikings ceased their raids and blended with the peoples whose lands they had penetrated. The Slavs settled down in the areas east of the new Empire. Only the Moslems continued to pick at the frontiers of Christendom, while their fleets dominated the Mediterranean. By the 11th century however Christendom was ready to strike back. Christian forces expelled the Moslems from Sardinia and Sicily and thrust them back into southern Spain. In 1095 Pope Urban II preached the First Crusade. By the end of the century, the Arabs had been very nearly swept from the seas, and the Christians had captured Jerusalem.

The Crusades, which fired Western imagination for 250 years, were responsible for a prodigious growth of the Italian commercial cities, which took over the bulk of the carrying trade between East and West. Their merchant fleets picked up spices and fine goods at the termini of the Oriental caravan routes in the Middle East and transported them to the coastal cities of southern and western Europe. Venice was especially fortunate in her central position. Situated at the head of the Adriatic, her merchants had ready access to the passes of the Alps, through which they conducted a lucrative commerce with northern Europe. During the Crusades the Venetians profited handsomely by keeping a foot in both the Christian and the Moslem camps—alternately hiring out their ships to the crusaders and then coming to terms with the Arabs to obtain commercial advantages. As a result of the sack of Constantinople by the Fourth Crusade, partly instigated by the Venetians, Venice acquired possession of Crete. Subsequently she increased her control over the sea traffic by annexing Cyprus. The great Arsenal of Venice, a sort of assembly-line shipbuilding yard, provided the fleets of galleys whereby she enforced her monopoly. By the year 1400, when Venice was at the height of her power and grandeur, she had 3,000 ships, and 38,000 seamen out of a population of 200,000.

From Venice and other Italian cities, goods of the Orient and Mediterranean were transported over the Alpine passes and down the rivers of Germany. Here commercial cities sprang up to distribute the merchandise to all northwest Europe. The merchant guilds of these cities (Cologne, Hamburg, Bremen, Lübeck, Danzig, and some 70 others) pooled their resources to maintain their independence and to open the eastern Baltic to trade. From this early association developed commercial combinations which merged into the Hanse, or Hanseatic League, of north German cities.

---

[6] *Moslem*: believer in the faith taught by Mohammed. *Islam*: the whole body of Moslems; also the religion.

During the two hundred years in which the Hanse dominated north and west European economic development, the Baltic and North Seas together became a sort of Mediterranean of the North, serving to link the adjacent areas intellectually as well as commercially. By 1400 the Hanse, like Venice, was at the height of its power and prestige.

But prospering Christendom was already under attack by a new surge of Moslem aggression. Political and religious feuds among the Arabs opened the way for the Ottoman Turks, coming down out of the hills of central Asia, to take over the Arab world and its religion. By 1400 the Turks had swept across the Dardanelles and advanced to the Danube. In 1453 surrounded Constantinople fell before a Turkish siege backed by guns. The Byzantine Empire, which for a thousand years after the fall of Rome had been a bastion of Europe and a preserver of the ancient culture, had at last been extinguished. Thereafter the Turks overran eastern Europe as far as Vienna, and from their bases in North Africa and the Middle East, increasingly dominated the Mediterranean. Like the Arabs, they gladly served in the profitable capacity of middle-man for the trade between Europe and the Orient, but this did not in the least hinder their sea-rovers from capturing Christian merchant ships and enslaving their crews or from raiding and pillaging the Mediterranean coasts of western Europe.

The Campaign of Lepanto

Against the menace of the Ottoman Empire there was never any such spontaneous uniting of the forces of Christendom as had carried European armies and navies into the Middle East during the Crusades. The main reason was the rising spirit of nationalism, which broke Europe into mutually distrustful segments with conflicting interests. Some governments, to the disgust of their neighbors, found it commercially or politically useful to come to terms with the Turk. Even the Papacy and the Holy Roman Empire, both of which maintained an anti-Moslem policy, were more often than not at odds. Emperor Charles V, who happened also to be King of Spain, could use his German army against the Turk in central Europe and his Spanish navy against the Turkish satellite states in the Mediterranean. But when he tried to combine his naval forces with those of Venice against the main Turkish fleet, the results were so indecisive that the alliance soon broke up in a spate of reciprocal accusations. A Turkish invasion of Cyprus in 1570 at length provided the atmosphere of urgency and alarm that drew the Christian Mediterranean powers together. Pope Pius V, with deft diplomacy and crusading zeal, urged the creation of an anti-Moslem Holy League. Neither Portugal nor the Empire would have any part of the alliance, but Spain and the Italian states agreed and dispatched their fleets for a grand concentration at Messina, for it was clear that the Christians would have to defeat the Turks at sea before Christian armies could land on Cyprus.

The Christian fleet comprised some 200 galleys, mostly Venetian and Spanish, with a few from the Pope and from Genoa, Savoy, and Malta. Their total complement must have numbered at least 44,000 seamen, including rowers. In addition there were some 28,000 soldiers aboard, about two thirds of whom were supplied by Spain. The Ottoman fleet, commanded by Ali Pasha, numbered about 250 galleys, manned by 50,000 seamen and 25,000 marines. The capital ships on both sides were long, slim, flat-bottomed craft like the galleys of ancient Greece and Rome, but they carried an 18-foot spur above the water line in place of the classic underwater ram. While the Turks still clung to the bow and arrow, many of the Christian soldiers aboard were armed with the arquebus, precursor of the musket. And whereas the Turks carried only three guns at the bow, the Christians carried five, firing shot ranging from 4½ to 36 pounds. The Holy League galleys for the most part also mounted smaller guns along the sides to repel boarders. In addition to galleys, the Venetians brought along six galleasses—heavy, sluggish vessels with a deck above the oarsmen and carrying up to 30 guns each, mostly in broadside. Lastly, because it had to seek out the enemy in his overseas lair, the Holy League fleet was attended by a train of 24 sailing cargo vessels.

The inevitable suspicions and cross-purposes of the Christian allies were somewhat mitigated by the appointment of Don John of

Austria as Captain-General of the fleet. Though the choice was dictated by his half brother, Philip II of Spain, the principal contributor to the armada, it was not an unpopular one, for at the age of 24 Don John was known as an experienced and successful campaigner on land and sea. Fired with zeal for the Christian cause, he aroused general enthusiasm, not unmixed with some uneasiness among his senior lieutenants lest he act rashly against the wily Turk.

Ali Pasha, in the summer of 1571, took his fleet raiding into the Adriatic to capture oarsmen and to overawe the Holy League fleet into breaking up or tempt it into a premature sortie. But the Christians remained steady, and Ali in mid-September fell back upon his advanced base within the Gulf of Lepanto (or Corinth) to revictual and replace casualties.

At last fitted and fully assembled, the ships of the Holy League set out from Messina, a special envoy from the Pope blessing each as it put out to sea. After crossing over to the coast of Greece, the armada worked its way south—galleys towing the galleasses, which could make no respectable speed whether under sail or being rowed. Early in the morning of October 7, the Christians rounded Cape Schropha and entered the Gulf of Patras, of which the Gulf of Lepanto is an extension. Almost at once lookouts sighted Ali Pasha's fleet approaching from the east, for the Turks had decided to fight in open water. Some of Don John's counselors advised him to retire, but to this timorous advice the young commander replied, "It is too late for council; it is now time for battle."[7]

The Battle of Lepanto is especially significant as the first great galley action since Actium, and also the last. As in the Battle of Actium, fought 16 centuries earlier only a few miles north of the scene of Lepanto, the ships of the opposing fleets were in three squadrons abreast, each squadron in line abreast. Both Turks and Christians held an additional squadron in reserve in the rear. Don John made an innovation in the ancient battle plan by placing the four galleasses that arrived on time ahead of his squadrons of galleys. When the Turks advanced to attack, they were obliged

[7] Vice Admiral William L. Rodgers USN, *Naval Warfare under Oars* (Annapolis, 1939), 190.

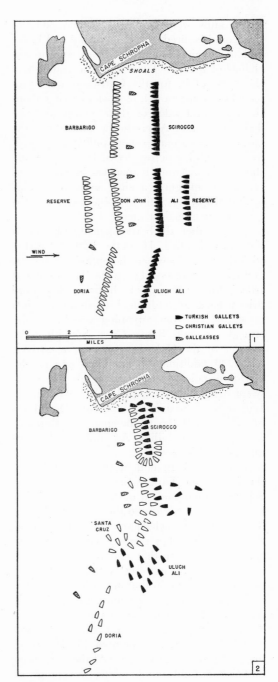

BATTLE OF LEPANTO,
OCTOBER 7, 1571

to sweep around these floating fortresses, taking heavy losses from their broadside guns.

As the opposing lines came together, each galley fired its bow guns two or three times.

These guns were rarely used thereafter for they could be fired only dead ahead and hence had to be aimed with the helm. In this exchange of fire, the Turks almost certainly had the worst of it, for the Christians were protected by an armor belt of thick planking about the bows and sides of their galleys and the Turks were not. After the opening shots, the battle became a matter of grappling and boarding and fighting across decks. In other words, though the opening maneuvers involved concentration of guns against guns and ships against ships, the ultimate object was to concentrate men against men.

At the center, the battle opened with a clash all down the line. Here the hottest fighting soon developed between the opposing flagships and their supporters. Twice the Turks entered Don John's ship, and both times they were driven back as additional Christian soldiers came aboard from adjoining vessels. At the crucial moment, Santa Cruz, Spanish commander of the Holy League reserve, arrived with 200 additional men. Then one of the Christian galleys, ranging alongside the Turk, swept her deck with arquebus fire, whereupon Italians and Spaniards, including Don John himself, poured aboard the enemy flagship and took possession, killing Ali and all that remained of his crew.

At the northern end of the line of battle, the ships of the Turkish right squadron, under Scirocco, attempted to outflank the Christian left by putting in close to the shore, exploiting their superior knowledge of the shallows. Had they succeeded, they might have grappled the Christian ships at that end of the line fore and aft, thereby massing two units of manpower against one in that area. But Barbarigo, the Christian squadron commander, concluding that where there was enough water for Turks there was enough for Christians, also closed the beach and planted his left wing impassably against the shore. At the same time Barbarigo's right wing, taking advantage of the Turkish shift to shoreward, enveloped Scirocco's left flank like a closing door. The Turks, thus surrounded and forced against the coast, were defeated in an hour of fierce fighting.

A Turkish attempt to envelop at the opposite end of the line of battle came nearer success. Uluch Ali made a feint at the right flank of his opponent, Doria, who to avoid being enveloped edged south. He thereby opened a broad gap between his squadron and the Christian center. Uluch Ali, seeing his opportunity, shifted course to northwest and headed for the opening in order to outflank the right wing of Don John's center squadron. In this he partially succeeded, doing fearful carnage among the Christians in that area. But by now Don John's squadron was so near victory that it could swing bows around toward the point of attack. Before Doria, having realized his blunder, could get back into the battle, Santa Cruz had thrown his reserve squadron into the breach, and Uluch Ali was in flight.

When the battle ended late in the afternoon, the Gulf was red with blood. According to contemporary Christian accounts, possibly exaggerated, 30,000 Turks lost their lives and all but 60 of their ships were captured or destroyed. The Christian losses were 12 ships and 7,700 men.

Like most purely naval victories, the triumph of the Holy League at Lepanto was both decisive and indecisive. The Christians had won the moral ascendancy; their dread of the Turk was never again so great as it had been, and the Turks thereafter operated with a prudence that kept their incursions within bounds—they and their subsidiary states of North Africa never again threatened to dominate the Mediterranean.

On the other hand, because the Holy League soon broke asunder and the Christians did not follow up their success at sea with combined intervention ashore, the Turks retained possession of Cyprus, and armed Moslem vessels continued to create an almost intolerable nuisance. The "Barbary System" of piratical excursions and extortion of tribute and ransom from Christian powers continued for centuries.[8] Even when certain European states developed navies powerful enough to put an end to the system, they tolerated the corsairs for the damage they could do to their commercial rivals. The United States in due course was to pay tribute, ransom captives, and become involved in two naval wars with the Barbary powers. The inconclusive results of these wars merely

[8] Barbary: land of the Berbers.

underlined what had been demonstrated at Lepanto: that while naval victories often make a decision possible, the final decision is usually reached on land.

Summary

We are now ready to define *sea power*. It is clearly more inclusive than *naval power*. It comprises not only combat craft and weapons but also auxiliary craft, commercial shipping, bases, and trained personnel. It is measured in terms of ability to use the sea in defiance of rivals and competitors. The phrase is also applied to a nation possessing a high degree of such ability: a sea power is a nation capable of exercising sea power. The capacity of a nation to use the sea is based upon the character and numbers of its population, the character of its government, the soundness of its economy, the quality and numbers of its harbors, the extent of its coastline, its colonies, and the location of homeland, bases, and colonies with respect to sea traffic.

A warring nation that has achieved a predominant capacity to use the sea is said to have *command* (or *control*) *of the sea*. Specifically, command of the sea consists of (1) the ability to defend one's own sea communications and (2) the ability to deny to the enemy the sea communications he requires to carry on the war. When sea warfare was confined to the surface, a clear-cut naval victory often conferred command upon the victor. Having eliminated the enemy's main fleet, he could supply himself by sea, and he could carry the attack across the sea to the enemy. If the vanquished attempted to do these things, it had to be by stealth, for he no longer had the means to defend his transports.

In a war involving use of the sea, securing command sets up the conditions for a decision, but the final decision is usually reached on land. Salamis had to be followed by Plataea and ultimately by the land campaigns of Alexander the Great before the Persian menace was removed. Rome's naval victories in the Punic Wars had to be followed by the Battle of Zama and ultimately by the razing of Carthage. Actium had to be followed by the Roman invasion and conquest of Egypt. If Lepanto proved less than decisive, it was because the Europeans failed to follow up their victory with operations ashore.

Bases are indispensable to naval operations, for both logistic and strategic reasons. That is to say, bases are needed to replenish, repair, and protect fleets and also to maintain them near important communication routes. Lack of a secure base near the scene of operations obliged Xerxes' fleet after Salamis to retire all the way to Asia. Alexander defeated and captured the Persian fleet merely by seizing its bases. Carthage capitulated in the First Punic War when her base in Sicily became untenable. When Mark Antony's base in Greece became untenable, he was obliged to fight a battle for which he was ill prepared and then retreat to Egypt. Securing and exercising command of the sea is greatly facilitated by possession of *strategic bases*, that is, positions near waters where shipping converges or across which armies can be readily transported and supplied. These are positions on narrow seas, such as the Bosporus, the Hellespont, the Straits of Gibraltar, and the channel between Sicily and North Africa; or centrally located positions, such as Crete, Sicily, Malta, and Sardinia; or positions near major ports, such as Cyprus and Rhodes. As we have seen, possession of these bases has been an important objective of all sea powers having interests in the Mediterranean. Attempts to seize one or another of them have several times brought on major wars. Even in the Age of the Galley, bases were the fixed positions of naval warfare.

In any form of warfare, the commander endeavors to defeat the enemy in fractions. He does not, if he can avoid it, send his force spread thin against the whole of the enemy force at one time. Instead, he endeavors (1) to bring his chief attack against part of the enemy force while (2) the rest of the enemy force is being held out of the main action. Mahan described this technique as "the specific method of so distributing your own force as to be superior to the enemy in one quarter, while in the other you hold him in check long enough to permit your main attack to reach its full result."[9] We have already observed examples of the numerous ways in which part

[9] Mahan, *Naval Strategy*, 49.

of the enemy force can be held in check: by allied forces, in the third Persian expedition against Greece; by a narrow strait, at Salamis; by getting between divisions of the enemy (interior position), at Ecnomus; by taking advantage of superior mobility in order to mass on isolated units, at Actium; by envelopment and a feint, at Lepanto. Even the corvus and the harpago were instruments to this end, for they enabled their user to bring his marines against the enemy's fewer or inferior marines while alarming part of the enemy's ships into abandoning the area of contact. This dual operation, involving hitting one fraction of the enemy force while holding the other, is part of what Mahan understood by *concentration*. To be perfectly concentrated however, the force must also be under unified command, its elements must be mutually supporting, it must be in pursuit of a single main objective, and it must be disposed with regard to the strategic center. In due course, we shall encounter examples, good and bad, of all these essentials.

In studies of warfare, much emphasis is likely to be placed on method and material, on technique and weapons, for these are tangible matters about which something definite and clear-cut can be stated. The characteristics that make men aggressive fighters and inspiring leaders are less easily analyzed. They cannot readily be described, much less systematized; they can only be illustrated and suggested. We know that free men fighting for their homes or for a cause they understand are apt, all other things being equal, to outfight unwilling conscripts and mercenaries, but we cannot be dogmatic about the matter, any more than we can measure the contributions of Themistocles, of Agrippa, or of Don John of Austria. Yet the student of warfare must never lose sight of the fact that the ultimate key to victory is neither techniques nor weapons but men. Even Napoleon, perhaps history's greatest master of techniques and weapons, could state with conviction based on unparalleled experience in warfare: "The moral is to the material as three to one."

The Mediterranean, by serving both as a civilizer for Europe and as a shield for maturing European culture, played an indispensable part in the development of Western Civilization. Its period of greatest influence coincided with the Age of the Galley. Even before Lepanto however the Mediterranean was becoming a backwater. Sailing ships had crossed the Atlantic to the New World and around Africa to the Orient. Maritime interests were shifting from the seas to the oceans.

2:
The Rise of English Sea Power

Rising commercial interests along the Atlantic seaboard of Europe looked with envy on the Italian and German monopoly of the rich carrying trade from the Orient. The cottons, silks, spices, dyes, perfumes, and gems of the East found a ready market in the West, even though prices quadrupled in transit— chiefly as a result of costly caravan transport from the Persian Gulf or the Red Sea to the Mediterranean. Toward the end of the medieval period, Europeans dwelling on the Atlantic front began to consider old legends and quasi-historical accounts of unbroken water routes to the Orient. The invention of printing made widely available ancient ideas of a spherical world, so that daring thinkers and explorers dreamed of reaching the Far East either around Africa or across the mysterious Atlantic.

Such distant voyages had at last become possible. The ancient, relatively frail cargo carrier with one mast and one sail evolved in the 15th century into a full-rigged ship with three or four masts, a bowsprit, and five or more sails—a vessel at last strong enough to cope with Atlantic gales and swift and seaworthy enough to cross vast stretches of ocean without replenishment or repair. Progress in the art of navigation enabled the new ships to abandon the old practice of hugging the coasts. The compass, brought to Europe from

CARAVEL, LATE 15th CENTURY

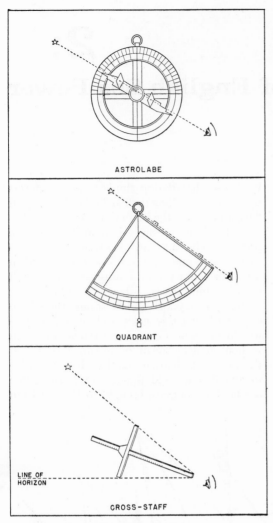

ASTROLABE

QUADRANT

LINE OF
HORIZON

CROSS-STAFF

LATE MEDIEVAL INSTRUMENTS FOR
FINDING LATITUDE AT SEA

China via the Arabs and the Crusaders, now gave the seafarer his approximate direction in any sort of weather. He had learned to measure his approximate speed by observing the time it took his ship to pass a bubble or a bit of flotsam. Using these two factors, he was able to find his way reasonably well by dead reckoning.

Though dead reckoning enabled the mariner to guess intelligently, once out of sight of land he was never really sure of his course or position. Contemporary instruments for finding latitude all required a steady platform and some knowledge of mathematics; the sea-tossed mariner rarely had either. In general, he found it wise to sail north or south along the coast to the latitude of his destination and then strike out due east or west, hoping to make a recognizable landfall on the far shore. Finding longitude was utterly beyond his means because he had no sure way of measuring time. Development of the accurate chronometer and the reflecting quadrant, which would solve his navigation problems, was still centuries away.

Nevertheless, ships out of Western Europe ventured farther and farther afield. Explorers sponsored by Prince Henry "the Navigator" of Portugal inched their way down the west coast of Africa, capturing Negroes and re-establishing the old African slave trade. In 1487 Bartholomeu Diaz raised to a near-certainty the belief in an all-water route to the Orient by rounding the Cape of Good Hope. In 1492 Christopher Columbus, sponsored by the Queen of Spain, crossed the Atlantic in search of a competing route and instead discovered the New World. Six years later Vasco da Gama completed the work of Diaz by sailing from Portugal around Africa all the way to India.

Results flowing from these discoveries ushered in the modern period, sometimes known as the Oceanic Age. Portuguese fleets, following in the wake of da Gama, easily defeated the Arab traders in the Indian Ocean, established a trade empire stretching from East Africa to Japan, and secured a monopoly of the rich spice trade of the East Indies. Spanish conquest of Mexico and Peru made available to Spain wealth accumulated over the centuries by the Indian civilizations, and the working of American gold and silver mines assured an apparently inexhaustible flow of precious metal into the Spanish treasury. These changes were bound to have a shattering effect upon Old World economy.

Europe was already in ferment. The vague internationalism of the feudal system was giving way to national feudalisms with a dominant monarch. National monarchs were abetted in the increase of their power by a rising merchant class that wanted domestic peace, uniform coinage, and a centralized government favorable to commerce and industry. The Church, for centuries a unifying influence, was itself beginning to break asunder in the Protestant Reformation. The new maritime discov-

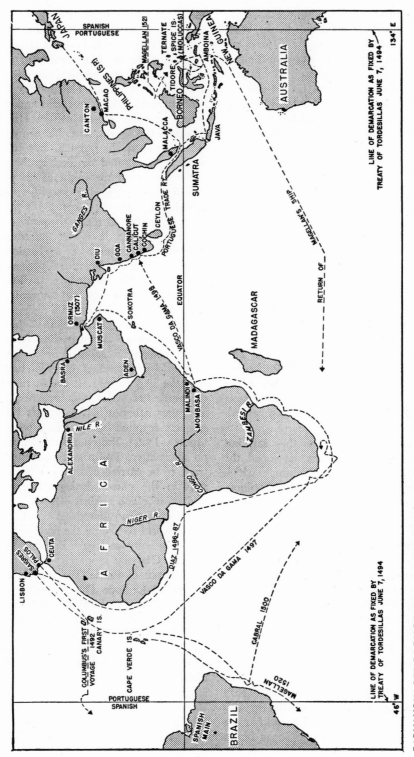

EARLY VOYAGES OF DISCOVERY AND THE PORTUGUESE TRADE EMPIRE

eries hastened the breakup of medieval unity by shifting European interests from the East, so long the focus of trade and the source of recurrent threats of conquest, to the West, where nationalism had made its greatest advances. With loss of trade, the Ottoman Empire gradually weakened and the commercial cities of Italy and Germany went into a decline. The inland seas of Europe and the Middle East, from the Baltic to the Red Sea and from the Mediterranean to the Persian Gulf, became backwaters. The major states of Europe's Atlantic seaboard—Spain, Portugal, France, the Netherlands, and England—began to rise as rival oceanic powers.

The new situation imposed unprecedented problems. The influx of precious metal from Spanish America debased the value of European currencies. At the same time raw materials from East and West came into competition with European farm products. As a result, income from agriculture declined relative to the costs of services and manufactured articles. This shift worked to the advantage of the city commercial classes but tended to undermine the land-owning aristocracy. The Age of Discovery thus set in motion economic forces that were to transfer the wealth, and hence the power, from the nobility to the bourgeoisie and change Europe from a feudal to a capitalist society.

To account for the changes they saw but could not explain, Europeans developed the economic theory of "mercantilism," which measures national wealth in terms of bullion. Since precious metal was limited in amount, it apparently followed that available wealth was limited and that a nation could grow richer only in proportion as it made some other nation poorer through capture of part of its trade or possessions. This remorseless logic accounts as much as anything else for the post-medieval division of Europe into competing states. It accounts for the trade and colonial wars which, along with other causes, kept the rivals in almost continuous conflict from the beginning of the modern age until after 1800.

To a late 16th century "mercantilist," Spain seemed strong beyond rivalry and the Spanish King, Philip II, uncontestably the world's most powerful monarch. In addition to Spain, Philip had inherited the Netherlands (Belgium and Holland), Franche Comté (eastern France), Milan, the Kingdoms of Naples, Sicily, and Sardinia, Spanish North Africa, and all of Spain's farflung transoceanic possessions. To these in 1580 he added Portugal and all of Portugal's overseas empire, thereby acquiring a claim, with Papal blessing, to the entire heathen world. American gold and silver continued to pour into his coffers. His fleet had defeated the Turks, and his army and fleet had chastened the French. His infantrymen were justly reputed the best in the world.

Yet Philip, in the midst of his power and grandeur, was growing steadily poorer. His mistakes and the mistakes of his predecessors were beginning to make themselves felt. The expulsion of the Jews and the Moslems had injured Spain's commerce and ruined her industry. Conquering Spanish America and maintaining Spanish dominance in Europe had been too costly in men and treasure. American silver and gold had proved a curse: the influx of bullion had set off uncontrollable inflation in Spain; diversion of her ships from carrying trade goods to transporting precious metal had so nearly extinguished her merchant marine that she had to rely on Dutch merchantmen to handle her overseas commerce. This led to a curious situation when Philip's Netherlands subjects revolted against his bloody drive to suppress Dutch Protestantism. Because he had no alternative, Philip still permitted Spanish trade to be carried in Dutch bottoms. He was thus in the paradoxical position of helping finance rebellion against himself.

Philip was no less deceived than the rest of the world regarding the condition of Spain. He took very seriously his role as leading Roman Catholic monarch and champion of the Church of Rome. We have seen how he responded to Pope Pius V's proclamation of 1570 against the Moslems and the part his galley fleet played in the Battle of Lepanto. In 1570 also, the Pope, despairing of reclaiming Protestant England, excommunicated England's Queen Elizabeth I, branded her a heretic and usurper, and called on Philip to launch a crusade against her as well as the Turks. To the Spanish monarch, northern Europe's heretical Protestantism was every bit as detestable as infidel Islam, but against Elizabeth he was not prepared to move. For the moment, he had his hands full with the war against the Turks and with the Dutch revolt. Elizabeth realized however that this was only a reprieve. When Philip's hands were freed he would unquestionably try to oust her from her throne. She therefore set about strengthening England's defenses and undermining the power of Spain. In 1572 she achieved a master stroke by allying herself with the King of France. Then she secretly released her gold-hungry seamen against Philip's treasure ships and with equal secrecy encouraged her subjects to aid the Dutch. More to the point, she began rebuilding her neglected navy.

The English Navy

Though the Vikings employed combat craft using oars as well as sails, galley warfare did not develop to any great extent in Atlantic waters. Slim, shallow-draft galleys, adequate for the choppy waters of the Mediterranean, were too easily capsized by the long ocean swells. Besides, the King of England and his royal neighbors were necessarily frugal men who in the early days felt that they could not afford ships specially designed for fighting. When they wished to contest the seas with their rivals, they usually called on their merchants for cargo sailing vessels—crank, broad-beamed Round Ships—and sent them out loaded with soldiers to do the work.

Battle in the earliest days of sailing warfare was mere bunched confusion, every ship for itself. Fighting consisted mostly of grappling and boarding, and action ended when crews of captured vessels were tossed over the side. Fleet tactics under sail began to emerge when some observant sailor noticed that getting upwind of the enemy conferred enormous advantages. A naval force having the *weather gage* could stand off out of reach of its leeward adversary, for the cumbersome Round Ship could sail only down wind. From the windward position, a fleet could send fireships drifting down upon the enemy. At a moment of its own choosing it could attack, overwhelming the enemy's weathermost ships, which his leeward ships were helpless to succor. The windward fleet thus had the initiative. It could apply tactical concentration, bringing its main

attack against part of the enemy's fleet, while the rest of his fleet was held in check by the wind. The introduction of naval gunfire conferred additional advantages on the possessor of the weather gage. The windward fleet could choose the ranges, and black smoke from its guns drifted into the enemy's eyes. Despite these clear benefits, not every commander wanted the weather gage. If his force were clearly inferior, he might deliberately accept the lee gage in order to keep open a line of retreat down wind. In general however, engagements between fleets of anything like equal strength began with maneuvers to "get the wind" of the adversary.

The first structural refinement in men-of-war under sail was the addition of temporary towers fore and aft, called forecastles and aftercastles. When the enemy succeeded in boarding, the defenders retreated into these towers and rained down stones, arrows, hot pitch, and, later, shot upon the intruders in the waist of the ship. From the towers too, missiles could be fired and stones dropped upon the enemy in ships alongside. The towers, or castles, proved so useful that the merchant owners at length had them built permanently into new construction, for one never knew when he might have to deal with pirates or other raiders. This is only one of many struc-

13th CENTURY WARSHIP
(FROM SEAL OF WINCHELSEA)

tural changes resulting from the occasional use of cargo carriers as men-of-war. The great advances in ship design in the early 15th century doubtless owed much to this dual employment.

The introduction of the gun brought about considerable strengthening and enlargement of the castles. The guns were originally placed here because, like all earlier weapons, they were aimed at men and not at ships—indeed, the early naval guns were too small and feeble to do serious damage to ships even at close range.

Guns were received with some trepidation by seamen, for their recoil was difficult to check and they had a bad habit of blowing up, especially during the period before breech loading was given up as hopeless. The only really safe method of attaching the breech to the gun was by screwing the one onto the other, but then the heat of the explosion so expanded the threads that the breech could not be unscrewed until it had cooled off. Not for centuries would anyone hit upon the simple device of the interrupted screw, which permitted the breech to be engaged or disengaged by a quarter turn or less. Meanwhile fleets eliminated breech loaders from their main batteries. The muzzle loader, with a touchhole in the breech to ignite the charge, became universal on the high seas.

When peace was restored at last in England following the Hundred Years' War and the long-drawn-out civil Wars of the Roses, the nation began to prosper to the extent that King Henry VIII was able to build a few ships of his own, intended exclusively for fighting. His first battleships were huge, high-towered Great Ships such as the *Henry Grâce à Dieu* or, as she was generally called, the *Great Harry*. But the *Harry* was already obsolescent when she was built, for the big guns that became possible with the general acceptance of muzzle loading made ships top-heavy when they were mounted in the castles. Puzzling over the problem, King Henry's carpenters cut gunports in the sides and mounted most of the guns on the "cargo deck." Thus the first broadsides came into being. When Lord Lyle after an action off Shoreham in 1545 reported to Henry that the broadsides had proved ship destroyers and not man killers only, he was announcing a new sort of warfare. "Off-fighting" had become possible; ships no longer had to be in physical contact in order to "engage."

With the introduction of guns in broadside and King Henry's decision that he would have a fighting fleet apart from the merchant marine, England began to forge ahead of all other nations in warship design. Progress slackened during the brief reigns of Edward VI and Mary Tudor. Under Queen Elizabeth it came to a standstill, until the Spanish threat impelled her to resume Henry's naval policy. The English ships built or rebuilt during the 20 years preceding the Spanish attack reflected the influence and experience of the privateers and semi-pirates that the Queen had turned loose against Spanish colonies and shipping. Foremost among these were John Hawkins and his cousin and protégé Francis Drake.

Hawkins' position as chief sea commander of England made his opinions respected long before he was appointed Treasurer and Controller of the Navy in 1577. A prosperous merchant shipowner of Plymouth, he had interspersed peaceful business pursuits with periods of free-booting and slave-running in Spanish-American waters, sometimes with royal connivance and profit. His experiences at sea, which included some hot fighting, had imbued him with a dislike for boarding tactics and an unshakable respect for guns and maneuver. By his advice and, later, under his stewardship, royal combat vessels became floating gun platforms emphasizing speed and mobility. The lofty fore- and aftercastles were cut down,[1] keels were deepened, and length was increased relative to beam. Though a certain proportion of Great Ships were built, to overawe the enemy and for close work when it could not be avoided, the flush-decked (or nearly flush-decked), low-freeboard ship of three or more beams' length became standard in the Queen's navy.

A revolution in naval ordnance kept pace with the revolution in English ship design. Though armament was outside Hawkins' responsibility, his influence can be detected in this department also. If the new fashion was to eschew hand-to-hand fighting for long-range

[1] A vestige of the aftercastle was retained or restored as the raised quarterdeck, useful for observation and command.

gunnery, then the longest range guns would appear to be in order. So we find in English ships fewer and fewer *cannon*, which could throw a 32-pound iron ball one mile, and *periers*, which could throw a 24-pound ball three-quarters of a mile, and an increasing proportion of long *culverins*, which could throw a 17-pound ball 1¼ miles.

One priceless advantage that Elizabeth possessed was her seamen. They had little opportunity to develop tactical niceties, but their freebooting excursions had endowed them with an incomparable knowledge of ships and the sea. If Philip of Spain could boast that he had the finest infantrymen in the world, Elizabeth could assert with equal justice that her sailors were without equal.

The Challenge of Spain

Nothing infuriated Philip II more than the raiding of Spanish bases and shipping by English privateers, whom the irate Spaniards considered mere pirates. The most famous of such expeditions was that of Drake's *Golden Hind*, which entered the Pacific through the Straits of Magellan in 1578 and raided Spanish cities and shipping up and down the west coast of South America. Drake returned to England via the Cape of Good Hope, arriving in 1581 with gold, silver, and jewels valued at half a million pounds sterling. Queen Elizabeth openly acquiesced in the enterprise by sequestering the bulk of the treasure and knighting Drake on his own quarterdeck. Though Philip raged, he was not yet prepared to risk open warfare. Instead he began secretly conspiring with the large Roman Catholic faction in England to assassinate Elizabeth. Her death would vacate the throne in favor of her Catholic cousin, Mary Stuart, Queen of Scots, whom Elizabeth had held captive since 1568, when Mary had been driven out of Scotland by the Calvinist hierarchy.

Two events in 1584 at length brought this clandestine warfare into the open. France was plunged into civil war by the death of the Catholic heir and the succession of a Protestant claimant to the throne. An assassin in Spanish pay struck down William "the Silent," Stadtholder of the newly-proclaimed Dutch republic. The war in France destroyed the effectiveness of the Anglo-French alliance that had restrained Philip for twelve years. The assassination of the Stadtholder paved the way for Spanish subjugation of the Netherlands, which would undoubtedly be followed by an invasion of England. Philip now began seizing English merchantmen peacefully trading in his ports. Elizabeth promptly retaliated. To cut down still further the flow of precious metal to Spain, she sent Drake with a fleet of 19 ships to raid the Spanish Indies. She formed an alliance with Philip's rebellious Dutch subjects and dispatched an army to Holland. If there was to be war, she considered, it was better to fight on foreign soil with an ally than alone in her own realm. The Spanish king now stepped up his campaign for the assassination of Elizabeth. To remove the focus for such plots, Elizabeth early in 1587 reluctantly signed the death warrant of Mary Stuart. Philip thereupon openly claimed the crown of England, alleging his descent from Edward III and his marriage to Mary Tudor, Elizabeth's half-sister and predecessor on the English throne.

The Spanish monarch proposed nothing less than a descent upon England out of the ports of Spain with an army carried and supported by a great naval armada. In the end he had to compromise by drawing most of his invasion troops from those engaged in Flanders against the Dutch, but his general concept remained. If Philip had any hope of conquering the English fleet with the weapons he had used in 1571 against the Turks, he was presently disabused, for in April 1587 Drake sailed boldly into the Spanish port of Cadiz with 23 ships, easily thrust aside the defending galleys, and destroyed some 18 cargo vessels. The vaunted galleys were clearly no match for England's sailing fleet with its long-range broadside batteries.

Luckily for Philip, he now had at his disposal the warships and armed merchantmen of Portugal and the services of Portuguese marine constructors, men well acquainted with Atlantic naval shipbuilding practices. He adopted the sailing man-of-war and the broadside, somewhat grudgingly we may assume, for he could not forget Lepanto. Once more, as at Lepanto, he would rely on his famous infantry for victory at sea. To give his soldiers the advantage of height, he impaired the sailing qualities of his warships by specifying lofty fore- and aftercastles, and he cut into their operational efficiency by cluttering their decks with troops. To cripple the English vessels so that they could not maneuver out of reach of his boarders, he armed his ships with the biggest naval guns he could find, including cannon firing 50-pound shot.

The Grand Armada, as finally assembled and dispatched against England in July 1588, consisted of 124 vessels carrying 1,100 guns and 27,000 men, more than half of whom were soldiers. In command was the Duke of Medina Sidonia, whose chief qualifications were noble rank and reputation for piety. Begging to be excused from so novel an undertaking, Medina had gloomily accepted only at Philip's insistence. His assignment was to proceed via the English Channel to Flanders, add 6,000 troops to the 17,000 already there under the Duke of Parma, and then cover Parma's invasion force as it crossed in small craft from the Flemish port of Dunkirk to Margate at the mouth of the Thames. The English fleet was of course expected to give battle, probably before Parma's crossing could be carried out. Though Philip knew that the Englishmen intended to fight with guns alone, he specifically directed his Spaniards to "grapple and board and engage hand to hand."

Meanwhile the Queen's navy of 34 men-of-war had been heavily reinforced. Armed merchantmen from the seaport towns and artillerymen from all over England had brought it up to the respectable strength of 197 vessels carrying 16,000 men and 2,000 guns. Mere numbers however fail to point up the really important differences between the opposing fleets. Though the English ships were in general lighter than the Spanish, they were incomparably handier and better handled. Moreover, they carried no infantrymen, only sailors and gunners. The Armada, with fewer guns, was superior in total weight of broadside, about 17 pounds per gun as compared to an English average of around seven pounds. But most of the Spanish guns were heavy, medium-range cannon and light, short-range border-repelling pieces, while 95 per cent of the English guns were long-range intermediate culverin types. Thus the Spaniards had the advantage in strik-

ing power; the English, in maneuverability, relatively clear decks, and range.[2]

Like the Armada, the Queen's fleet was officially headed by an aristocrat, Charles Howard of Effingham, Lord Admiral of England. An intelligent administrator, Lord Howard had the good sense to take the advice of his subordinates, old sea dogs Drake, Hawkins, and Martin Frobisher. At crucial moments in the campaign, Drake virtually exercised command. At government insistence, over Drake's protests, the fleet was divided. The main body took station at Plymouth to cover Ireland and the southwest coast, while a detached force under Lord Henry Seymour watched Parma from Dover.

The southwest wind that brought the Spanish Armada into the English Channel caused Howard considerable embarrassment in beating out of Plymouth Sound. Had Medina Sidonia attacked then, the result might have been disastrous for England. Instead, he sailed majestically past Plymouth, and Howard fell in behind, seizing the weather gage and blocking his line of retreat back to Spain. For a week the Armada moved slowly up the Channel while the English fired at its weathermost ships and forced three general engagements. At first, the Spanish men-of-war were in three squadrons roughly abreast, each in line abreast, a formation somewhat like that employed by the galleys at Lepanto. As the running battle progressed, the Spaniards drew defensively together, first into a crescent, then into a roughly circular mass. Meanwhile the English, to attain greater flexibility, began to operate in four squadrons, under Howard, Drake, Hawkins, and Frobisher.

Within their squadrons, the English ships were as badly bunched as the Spanish. But the Queen's fleet had a tactical doctrine that brought order out of apparent disorder. To engage the Spaniards, a squadron commander would head for the enemy's weathermost units, other ships of his squadron following in single file. As each English vessel came within a certain prescribed range, she fired a broadside and hauled off. When the entire line had completed firing, it circled back in follow-the-

[2] Michael Lewis, "Armada Guns," *The Mariner's Mirror* (April 1943).

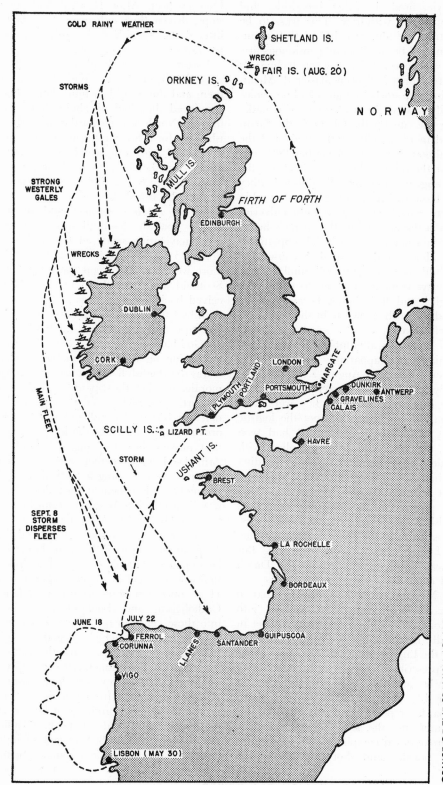

COLD RAINY WEATHER

SHETLAND IS.

WRECK
FAIR IS. (AUG. 20)

ORKNEY IS.

STORMS

NORWAY

STRONG
WESTERLY
GALES

MULL IS.

FIRTH OF FORTH

EDINBURGH

WRECKS

DUBLIN

CORK

LONDON

MARGATE

PLYMOUTH
PORTLAND
PORTSMOUTH

DUNKIRK
ANTWERP
GRAVELINES
CALAIS

MAIN FLEET

SCILLY IS.
LIZARD PT.

STORM

USHANT IS.

HAVRE

BREST

SEPT. 8
STORM
DISPERSES
FLEET

LA ROCHELLE

BORDEAUX

JUNE 18

JULY 22

FERROL
CORUNNA
LLANES
SANTANDER
GUIPUSCOA

VIGO

LISBON (MAY 30)

CRUISE OF THE SPANISH ARMADA, 1588

leader style, fired the other broadside, and then temporarily withdrew. This was, to be sure, no true line ahead; it lacked the advantages of massed broadsides and continuous fire. All that was to come later, when techniques of rapid reloading had been mastered. Meanwhile, ships with unshotted guns had no choice but to withdraw well out of range to reload.

During the run up the Channel, the Spaniards fired more than 100,000 rounds and the English almost as many, yet neither fleet seriously hurt the other. The reason is clear: the selected range was too great. Established policy required Howard's fleet to engage only within the "safety zone," where their light culverins could reach the enemy but the enemy's heavy cannon could not reach them. The Spaniards achieved almost nothing at all because they simply could not get at Howard's nimble ships, which always managed to keep to windward. The English did little better because at the prescribed range their own light shot was generally ineffective.

For all Howard's attempts to thwart them, the Spaniards had apparently achieved their first objective when on August 7 the Armada, practically intact, dropped anchor in the neutral port of Calais. Actually they were in a poor situation, for Calais was not the logistic base they sorely needed. Howard had won after all, for he could be re-supplied with ammunition from England, whereas Medina Sidonia had fired off all his heavy shot and could get no more. In the dubious hope that the mere presence of the Armada would hold the English fleet in check, Medina sent a messenger post haste to the Duke of Parma urging him to launch the invasion forthwith. But Parma was tightly blockaded by the Dutch fleet and could not move.

While Medina was still wondering what to do next, Howard sent eight fireships into Calais Roads, forcing out the Spanish fleet in the middle of the night. Off Gravelines the next day the English attacked. They now abandoned "prescribed range" and closed with impunity because the Spaniards, lacking shot for their big guns, could reply only with small boarder repellers and muskets. At this critical moment, the shaky English logistic system broke down completely. No more shiploads of powder and shot arrived for the

Queen's fleet. After Howard had sunk two ships, driven three others on the shoals, and littered the Spanish decks with casualties, he too ran out of ammunition.

Fortunately for England, the Spaniards were already on the run. With the wind against them and the English behind them, they were convinced they had no choice but to retreat into the North Sea. Howard plowed the Spanish wake for a few days, spurring the fugitives northward with a brave show of wanting to attack. But the Grand Armada was already en route back to Spain—the long way, north and west of the British Isles.

In the Atlantic, hunger and thirst completed Spanish demoralization. Storms and inept navigation scattered the Spanish ships. Some 35 or 40 foundered at sea; at least a score were wrecked upon the rocky shores of Scotland and Ireland. In October Philip received back into the ports of Spain no more than half the naval and military power he had sent so confidently against England.

"God blew and scattered them," so went the inscription on the Dutch victory medal. Yet it was the English fleet that wore down Spanish morale, mauled the Spanish vessels into unseaworthiness, and forced the Spaniards, in a defeatist frame of mind and with insufficient provisions, to undertake the long voyage home that proved their undoing. In repulsing the Armada, English seamen also took the first major step in devising a tactical doctrine for sailing fleets. For them at least, decisions at sea were henceforth to be reached not by hand-to-hand combat but with the gun.

Historians of later times recognized that the catastrophic failure of the Armada marked the beginning of Spain's decline. The true situation was not so clear to contemporaries. Philip II at once lost some credit as defender of Catholicism, and England was stimulated into those ventures in commerce, exploration, and colonization which, together with the flourishing of the arts, mark the Elizabethan Age. Neither Englishmen nor other Europeans perceived that Spain was no longer a first class power, that bullion from America was neither wealth itself nor a producer of lasting wealth, or that the spice trade of the East Indies was not enough to offset Spain's lack of industries and poverty of internal resources. Spain survived, and even retained some of her colonies for three more centuries, mainly because her enemies failed to take advantage of her inherent weakness.

The Anglo-Spanish conflict became a desultory raiding war, neither side daring to take decisive measures against the other. It ended at last in 1603 with the death of Queen Elizabeth and the accession of James I, king also of Scotland and son of Mary Stuart. James, even more hypnotized than Elizabeth by the Spanish myth, soon sealed an alliance with England's erstwhile enemy. In so doing he abandoned the struggle for Dutch independence and sowed the seeds of future hostilities between England and Holland.

The Challenge of Holland

Not even King James took Spain's claim to the entire heathen world seriously. Before the Armada campaign, non-Spanish seafarers had limited themselves to smuggling in the Spanish colonies, to quasi-military, quasi-piratical attacks on Spanish shipping in the manner of Hawkins and Drake, or to hopeful searches for northeast and northwest passages to rival Spain's southeast and southwest passages to the Orient. After the Armada, all that was changed. Englishmen, Frenchmen, and Dutchmen, at first circumspectly and then more and more boldly, infringed on lands and trade that the King of Spain claimed as his own.

England planted the most stable and flourishing colonies, not because of any intentional encouragement from the King but mainly because most English colonists were true homeseekers. Some were in flight from economic distress; more were refugees from religious and political intolerance. The practice of "salutary neglect" by the London government left them mainly to their own devices and bred in them self-sufficiency and a spirit of independence. During the 1600's, Englishmen settled the Atlantic seaboard of North America from Nova Scotia and the valley of the St. Lawrence, which the French staked off for themselves, to Florida, which Spaniards occupied. Until past the middle of the century however, the Dutch claimed the Hudson Valley and maintained on Manhattan Island their prosperous colony of New Amsterdam. In the West Indies English, French, and Dutch adventurers rushed to seize islands that were not firmly in the hands of the Spaniards. The French and Dutch, moreover, obtained footholds in South America; and the English, in Central America.

In the competition for maritime trade, Holland quickly outstripped her rivals. Her long war with Spain, by which she won *de facto* independence in 1609, had actually nourished Dutch commerce and provided Holland with a formidable fleet to extend and protect it. But her decisive advantage was a business-minded government that steadily encouraged and supported commercial ventures. While England was torn internally by a struggle between King and Parliament; and France, by a struggle between King and nobility, Holland more and more dominated commerce in the Baltic, the Middle East, and the Far East, and at the same time by legal and illegal means took over a large part of the American trade. Concurrently Dutchmen made themselves the chief whalers, fishermen, and carriers of Europe. Wherever the English and French turned to enrich themselves on the seas, they met ruinous competition from the enterprising seamen and traders of Holland. When they sought to participate in the spice trade, they found the Dutch so unshakably established in the East Indies that they were obliged to shift their interests to India. Holland's ruthless monopoly turned her seafaring competitors into enemies. The monopoly would have to be broken, insisted the mercantilists, if other sea powers hoped to prosper.

England was first to issue the challenge. It came late, for want of means to back it up. Elizabeth's navy had wasted away under James's mismanagement. When James's son and successor, Charles I, called for "ship money" to restore the fleet, his domestic enemies made his demand an issue in the civil war that broke out in 1642. Only after Charles had been defeated and beheaded by his own subjects, and Oliver Cromwell and the commercial interests had taken over the reins of government, did England seriously prepare to act. The new Commonwealth greatly enlarged the neglected navy, mostly through the sale of estates seized from the aristocracy. It improved the pay and victuals of the sailors, introduced an incentive system of "prize money" for captures or sinkings of enemy vessels, and reorganized and strengthened the naval establishment in every department. At length, armed with a powerful and disciplined fleet, Parliament threw down the gantlet to Holland. It passed the famous Navigation Act of 1651, which stipulated that goods could be brought into England or English possessions only by English ships or by ships of the country where the goods originated. This Act, aimed directly at the Dutch carrying trade, brought about the first of three naval wars between Holland and England.

These wars revealed the fatal weaknesses underlying Holland's pretensions. First, she was absolutely dependent upon the sea for a livelihood, yet England dominated the sea approaches to her coast. Second, because Holland had a land as well as a sea frontier to guard, she was obliged to divert much of her wealth and manpower to building fortresses and maintaining a standing army. Third, the Dutch fleet, though formidable in numbers of ships, was composed of small, unhandy, flat-bottomed craft built to enter the shallow Dutch harbors. Lastly, the English navy usually managed to keep a tactical step ahead of the Dutch.

This last is surprising, for the Dutch admirals were reputed the best in the world. The English navy, on the other hand, was initially headed not by admirals at all but by army officers called Generals-at-Sea. Cromwell had put them in command of the fleet because of the suspected monarchism of his naval officers. The sea-going generals had had no previous experience with naval operations or naval warfare. Yet two of them, Robert Blake and George Monk, quickly earned places for themselves among the top rank of the world's sea fighters.

The first year of the First Anglo-Dutch War (1652-54) was a see-saw affair, but in the second year the new English fleet and the maritime generals caught their stride, roundly trounced the Dutch fleet twice in succession, and then blockaded Holland into submission. Cromwell was glad to let the Dutch off with payment of an indemnity and an agreement to admit the English on equal terms to the East Indies trade. He had no stomach for warring against fellow Protestants. Besides, he had other scores to settle.

The Moslem states of North Africa had taken advantage of England's involvement to capture English ships and to enslave Englishmen. Catholic Spain persistently barred English merchants from the West Indies trade. To deal with the Barbary states, Cromwell sent General Blake with 20 ships to the Mediterranean. To chastise Spain, he sent Vice Admiral William Penn[3] and General Robert Venables with a fleet and army to the West Indies, where they seized Jamaica.

In the wars against the Moslems and the Spaniards, Blake won his greatest claim to fame. This former merchant, turned soldier at the age of 43 and sailor at 50, astonished the world by taking his fleet into the supposedly impregnable Tunisian harbor of Porto Farina, where he silenced the forts and burned the Moslem ships, and then brought his fleet out again almost unscathed. Two years later, he sailed his fleet to the Canary Islands, took it into the narrow-mouthed harbor of Santa Cruz, and there repeated his exploit of Porto Farina by destroying a fleet of six Spanish treasure galleons and ten escorting warships. His health failing from the rigors of blockading Cadiz, he headed at length for home, but died as he arrived within sight of England.

The Second Anglo-Dutch War (1665-67) broke out five years after Charles II, son of Charles I, had been restored to the English throne.[4] Like the earlier war, it grew out of trade and colonial rivalries. In the opening naval engagement, the English under the Duke of York, Lord High Admiral and brother of the king, won a limited victory. The next year, a segment of the English fleet under Monk was defeated in the drawn-out Four Days' Battle by a much more powerful enemy force. Monk soon turned the tables however by decisively defeating the Dutch and following up his victory by a raid along the coast of Holland, in which his fleet made numerous captures and burned scores of merchantmen.

The Dutch now requested terms, but King Charles dragged out the negotiations and at the same time, over Monk's strong protests,

[3] Father of the founder of Pennsylvania.
[4] Under Charles II the fleet became the Royal Navy, the title it has borne ever since.

laid up most of his ships and discharged the crews. This short-sighted action exposed England to humiliating counterattack. In June 1667, a powerful Dutch fleet entered the Thames Estuary unopposed, seized a large supply of naval stores at Sheerness, proceeded up the Medway River, bombarded Chatham, burned seven large men-of-war, and captured the *Royal Charles,* flagship of the English navy. Departing as suddenly as it had arrived, the enemy fleet clapped so tight a blockade upon English shipping that in a few weeks the London government was ready to discuss peace. This time both sides gained and lost something at the peace table. England relinquished all claims to the East Indies and modified the Navigation Act. The Dutch recognized the West Indies as an English sphere of influence and ceded the Hudson Valley and the colony of New Amsterdam, which the English re-named New York.

The Third Anglo-Dutch War (1672-74) was a senseless struggle, contrary both to English interests and to English public sentiment. Louis XIV of France (1643-1715), desiring to annex Holland, bribed King Charles into participation. He then invaded the Netherlands while Charles's navy launched a sudden attack on Dutch sea commerce. In Holland, William of Orange, the Stadtholder, checked the French invasion by opening the dikes and flooding the countryside. At sea, Admiral de Ruyter more than held his own against the English in two skirmishes and two indecisive battles. The poor showing of England's vaunted fleet and the French navy's reluctance to fight turned English dissatisfaction into disgust. Accepting the inevitable, Charles not only made peace but sealed an alliance with Holland by giving the Duke of York's daughter Mary in marriage to William of Orange.

Fear of imperialistic France had drawn Spain and several German states to the Dutch cause. King Louis, finding himself isolated against a growing coalition, in 1678 acknowledged his failure and made peace with the Dutch, from whom he had not extracted a foot of territory. England turned out to be the only beneficiary of the war, for more and more of the lucrative carrying trade had passed from exhausted Holland to English merchants.

The battles of the Anglo-Dutch Wars were as fierce as any in history, for the English, always aggressive fighters, never found on the seas a more determined and hard-hitting enemy than the sailors of Holland. As many as a hundred vessels fought on each side. These included everything from men-of-war carrying a hundred guns down to six-gun converted merchantmen commanded by merchant skippers. All fought together with little regard for fleet homogeneity or even for the old naval maxim that "like fights like." Both fleets were worked in squadrons, but in the earliest battles the individual vessels of each squadron merely bunched around the flagship, endeavoring by sheer seamanship to keep out of each other's line of fire.[5] Action was in general much closer than during the Armada campaign, when the English learned that they could not hold off at a safe distance and still hurt the enemy. With improved techniques and more gunners per gun, crews reloaded more rapidly and hence kept up a more nearly continuous fire than in Armada times.

At the opening of the First Anglo-Dutch War, the only fleet tactical maneuvers seem to have been the old opening gambit of getting the wind and then massing fire on the weathermost ships of the enemy. The chief tactical aim was to throw the enemy into confusion and profit by his mistakes. To the seagoing English generals that was all well and good, but they must have been appalled by the formlessness of naval warfare as they found it. At any rate, they early experimented with more orderly tactics. As a result, in March 1653, less than a year after the outbreak of war, they issued a new set of Fighting Instructions. Included was the epochal Article 3: "All ships of every squadron shall endeavour to keep in line with the chief . . . ." This article did away with bunching and follow-the-leader tactics and established the column as the standard battle formation.

The column, or line ahead, is the logical corollary of the broadside, and the new, faster rate of fire had made it practical. In column,

[5] The English fleet was organized in three squadrons—the White, the Red, and the Blue, commanded respectively by a general or an admiral, a vice admiral, and a rear admiral. Very large squadrons were subdivided into first, second, and third divisions, commanded respectively by a general or an admiral, a vice admiral, and a rear admiral.

no broadside is masked by a friendly ship—all have a clear line of fire. Ships are mutually supporting and hence difficult to board or to defeat in detail. Enemy vessels cannot readily get across their bows or sterns, where they are out of reach of the broadside guns and whence they can send deadly raking fire the length of the ship. Article 3 marked a final break with galley tactics—and with imitation of infantry tactics as well. Galleys and infantrymen fire in the direction of their advance; ships in column fire at right angles to their line of advance. Tactically speaking, the van and rear of a column of ships are its flanks. This 90-degree shift was bound to require a long period of assimilation and tactical adjustment.

The English did in fact make two important adjustments before the end of the First Anglo-Dutch War. Ships were required to assume regular intervals of about half a cable's length (100 yards) between ships. The entire column when in battle undertook to sail close hauled, that is, as close as possible into the wind, which for English square-riggers was about six points—a little closer than at right angles. Both refinements strengthened the line ahead, making it easier to handle and more difficult to penetrate. The Dutch, recognizing a good thing when they saw it, followed the English lead, but with indifferent success. Their captains lacked the necessary discipline, and their shallow-draft ships were too leewardly. They rarely attained an orderly line, and close hauling was quite beyond their means.

Far from repudiating the innovations of the Commonwealth Navy, the Duke of York adopted them all in the Fighting Instructions under which the Second Anglo-Dutch War was fought. Nevertheless there arose a sharp division of opinion about how the Instructions were to be applied. The crux of the dispute had to do with the fleet line ahead. Nobody disparaged its value, at least for the approach, but there arose two rival schools of thought concerning what to do after contact with the enemy.

These groups have been called the Formal School and Melee School, and the names aptly suggest the point of view held by each. The *formalists,* a strictly naval group headed by the Duke of York, insisted upon maintaining the line throughout the battle. Thus only would the fleet continue as a unit in the hands of the admiral; despite obscuring clouds of gunsmoke, he could hope to retain a fairly tight control. If the battle turned against him, he could extricate his fleet with minimum risk. The *meleeists* were ready, at a favorable opportunity, to unleash their squadron and ship commanders from the line and send them in on their own initiative to overpower the enemy in a massed attack. This would bring on a melee in which control would slip from the hands of the admiral and from which it might be impossible to retreat, but it would produce a greater preponderance of gunfire at the decisive point than could ever be achieved by a battle line stretched out twelve miles or more, with a good many ships out of range of a disorderly enemy. The question at issue was the relative emphasis to be put on the defensive and the offensive, of risks to be avoided to escape defeat and risks to be taken as the price of victory.

In the Second and Third Anglo-Dutch Wars, each school had opportunities to try out its theories. The meleeists were of course more aggressive, sometimes rash. The formalists, as might be expected, tended to be over-cautious, much given to maneuver for maneuver's sake. By the end of the wars, the formalists were in the ascendant, but they had learned something from their rivals. They no longer insisted upon maintaining the line in any and all circumstances. The Duke of York's last Fighting Instructions, issued in 1673, even provided for a fleet to leeward breaking through the enemy's line in order to weather some of his ships and contain the rest. This provision might even be interpreted as the first step in line concentration tactics. The stiff formalism that largely nullified concentration and hampered English naval tactics for generations had not yet crystallized. That came later, during England's long struggle with France.

The Challenge of France

The continuing aggressions of Louis XIV so alarmed his continental neighbors that Austria, Spain, Sweden, and several German states banded defensively together in the anti-French

League of Augsburg. Into this league England and Holland were soon precipitated as the closest of allies. The Duke of York had succeeded his brother Charles on the English throne as James. II. An avowed Catholic, James undertook to Catholicize England, thereby so outraging Parliamentary leaders that they invited William of Orange and his wife Mary (James's daughter) over from Holland to be joint sovereigns. William and Mary came, James fled to France, and England and Holland joined hands under a single head of state. Attempts by Louis XIV to restore the deposed king brought about the War of the English Succession, which merged into the War of the League of Augsburg.

This was only the first of seven successive wars in which England and France were antagonists. In the War of the English Succession (1689-97) and the War of the Spanish Succession (1703-13), England's chief objective was to maintain the balance of power on the Continent by containing French aggression. In the War of the Austrian Succession (1740-48), the Seven Years' War (1756-63) and the War of the American Revolution (1775-83), England was chiefly concerned with expanding and defending her overseas colonial and trade empire. In the Wars of the French Revolution (1793-1802) and Empire (1803-15), she was again striving to contain French aggression. Throughout the long, intermittent struggle, sea power played a major role.

Ironically, the single useful legacy that James II left behind when he fled England in 1688 was a fleet powerful enough to bar his return. At the restoration of his brother in 1660, James had received with delight his appointment as Lord High Admiral, a position for which he had been trained since childhood. Aided by Samuel Pepys, that most efficient of naval secretaries, he had reorganized and refurbished the Royal Navy from top to bottom. As a step toward establishing a permanent officer corps in place of the prevailing system of temporary appointees, he introduced the new rank of Volunteer-per-Order or King's Letter Boy,[6] to which young gentlemen were appointed by the Admiralty to grow up with the

[6] So called because they were issued a royal letter in lieu of a commission.

fleet in preparation for command at sea. James watched with dismay as his work was undone and the fleet allowed to deteriorate as a result of the King's misplaced economies. After the Third Anglo-Dutch War an ascendant Parliament took the Navy into its own hands, and a series of parliamentary boards, through politics, mismanagement, and sheer ignorance, very nearly ruined what was left of it. On coming to the throne, James set out to repair the damage, again with the assistance of the indefatigable Pepys. In the four years of James's reign, much was accomplished. The Royal Navy regained its former efficiency though by no means its former strength. Luckily for England, the accession of William and Mary brought the Dutch and English fleets into combination, for France had built the world's most powerful navy.

The chief architect of French sea power was Jean Colbert, Louis XIV's mercantilist minister of finance. Trusted and given wide latitude by his sovereign, Colbert set out to increase his country's wealth and prestige. He fostered agriculture, manufacture, and commerce, and stimulated colonial progress in Canada, India, and the West Indies. To develop and protect France's growing commercial and colonial empire, he enlarged both the merchant marine and the navy, established shipyards and bases in major ports, and set up naval officer training schools. Under his patronage, French ship design became a science, far superior to the rather casual practices of the English. By the time of Colbert's death in 1683, the *Marine Française* was the equal of any navy on the high seas. By 1689 it was numerically equal to the combined fleets of England and Holland.

French naval superiority was to a large extent offset by two serious handicaps. Because France was a continental power, the *Marine* had to compete with the army for military funds; in a long war it could not count on adequate replacements of men or material. Because France had two coasts, the Paris government felt obliged to divide its sea forces between the Atlantic and the Mediterranean, basing them on Brest and Toulon. The obvious English strategy was to keep France expensively campaigning in Europe and to prevent the two parts of the French fleet from uniting.

During most of the Anglo-French wars, England achieved these objectives by encouraging, and even subsidizing, European allies, and by maintaining a fleet off Toulon or near the Straits of Gibraltar.

Early in the War of the English Succession (1689-97) however the Toulon fleet eluded English vigilance and united with the Brest fleet while English naval forces were divided several ways. As a result, in June 1690 the Comte de Tourville with 74 French ships challenged an Anglo-Dutch Channel force of 57 under Lord Torrington. The English admiral skillfully evaded action, arguing that in the circumstances he should maintain his force as a "fleet-in-being" until his detached squadrons could rejoin. But on peremptory orders from the Crown Torrington reluctantly accepted the French challenge and was overwhelmed in the Battle of Beachy Head. Two years later, at the Battle of Barfleur, the situation was almost exactly reversed. This time a united Allied fleet defeated the Brest fleet under Tourville while the French Mediterranean fleet was far away at Toulon.

For the French navy, Barfleur marked the end of offensive operations against fleets. King Louis, recognizing that he could not maintain both a powerful army and a formidable navy, sacrificed his fleet to his continental ambitions. Rotting ships were not replaced, others were laid up, still others joined swarms of French privateers in disputing the allied command of the sea by *guerre de course*— raiding the enemy's sea commerce. Though France's raiding strategy proved a serious nuisance to English shipping, it was far from decisive. England actually prospered. France, on the verge of financial ruin, was obliged to capitulate. By the terms of the peace treaty, Louis was forced to abandon all his continental conquests and to acknowledge William of Orange as King of England.

In the War of the Spanish Succession (1703-13) which broke out six years later, the English began to add to their domains at the expense of France and her allies. England's great strategic acquisition was Gibraltar, taken in 1704 by English and Dutch marines and English seamen, backed by an Anglo-Dutch fleet under Admiral Sir George Rooke. England's possession of Gibraltar apparently guaranteed that the Toulon and Brest fleets should never again unite in time of war. Louis, recognizing the extreme gravity of the situation for France, dispatched his Toulon naval squadrons with orders to oust the invaders. But Rooke's force barred the way. Having the wind, Rooke bore down on the French and stretched his line alongside theirs. The ensuing engagement, called the Battle of Malaga, was tactically indecisive in that neither line broke and neither could gain any serious advantage over the other. Nevertheless, the English were the strategic victors, for the French flinched under bombardment and slipped back to port under cover of darkness, and Rooke retained his grip on the Rock. Four years later the Royal Navy buttressed Gibraltar by capturing Minorca and its fine harbor of Port Mahon, an excellent base for blockading Toulon. The long war brought France nothing but financial prostration. England, on the other hand, acquired Nova Scotia, Newfoundland, and the Hudson Bay Territory from France; Gibraltar, Minorca, and a share of the Spanish-American trade, from Spain. Moreover, despite the continued efforts of French sea raiders, she had taken a strong lead in maritime commerce and made good her self-conferred title of Mistress of the Seas.

During the Wars of the English and Spanish Succession, English tacticians revived the old formalist-meleeist controversy. The new melee school interested itself particularly in the problem of how to bring more of one's guns against fewer of the enemy's guns at some selected point in the enemy line—in short, how to *mass* on the enemy. The obvious means, assuming one had the wind, was to decrease intervals between one's ships and bring the massed force against part of the enemy line. (See diagram page 37.) The objections to this simple form of massing was that the enemy could always elude or counteract it. If one massed anywhere but on his rear, he could bring his rear ships forward on their original course and offset the advantage. If one massed on his rear, he had three choices: he could make a simultaneous reversal of course and bring forward his new rear, he could double back and put his attacker's van between two fires, or he could escape merely by putting his helm over and falling off down wind.

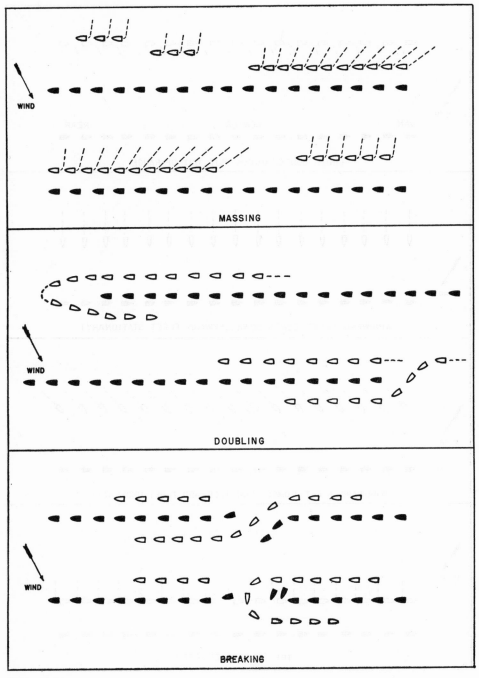

MASSING

DOUBLING

BREAKING

WIND

MELEE TACTICS

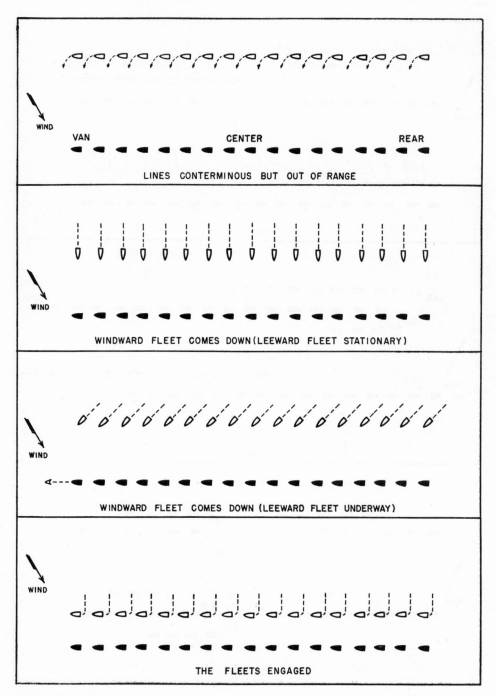

VAN CENTER REAR

LINES CONTERMINOUS BUT OUT OF RANGE

WINDWARD FLEET COMES DOWN (LEEWARD FLEET STATIONARY)

WINDWARD FLEET COMES DOWN (LEEWARD FLEET UNDERWAY)

THE FLEETS ENGAGED

FORMAL TACTICS

To prevent the enemy from reversing course or abandoning the field of battle, one would have to maneuver some of one's ships to the far side of his line. This could be achieved by special forms of massing known as *doubling* and *breaking*. Doubling consisted of steering one's ships to both sides of the enemy van or rear. Breaking, or "breaking the line," attained the same effect by thrusting part of one's column *through* the enemy column. Both maneuvers put the enemy between two fires.[7] In the area of the doubling or breaking, he would be outgunned perhaps as much as two to one. The guns on his formerly disengaged side would probably be secured and the gunports closed, and even if he managed to get these guns into action, he could not carry enough gunners to keep up anything like continuous fire with both broadsides. A fleet planning to break the enemy's line however might enter battle with all guns shotted and run out and thus be prepared to fire one complete double broadside while passing through.

The Battles of Beachy Head and Barfleur threw the meleeist innovations into disrepute. At Beachy Head, the outnumbered allies massed on the French rear, whereupon the French van doubled back on the allied van and crushed it. At Barfleur, the French attempted to mass on the allied rear, but their line was so stretched out elsewhere with long intervals between ships that the allies were able to break through the French center. Evidently, unless one had overwhelming superiority in numbers, any attempt to mass, double, or break so shortened or stretched out one's line that the enemy could easily break through or double around the ends. Every thrust seemed to invite a counterthrust.

The meleeists had solved the hitting aspect of tactical concentration but not the holding aspect. They knew how to bring their main attack against part of the enemy force, but they had not found any way to hold the rest of the enemy force in check while their main attack succeeded. In the English fleet—the British fleet after 1707—the problem was compounded by lack of a rapid and flexible signal

---

[7] The doubler or breaker had of course to accept the risk of hitting his own ships on the far side of the enemy line.

system to facilitate command. Practically the only available signals directed compliance with one or another of the articles of the Fighting Instructions.

The new formal school, taking as its ideal the Battle of Malaga, eschewed massing altogether. True, Malaga was a tactical stalemate, but it had saved Gibraltar. The perfect battle, as envisioned by the formalists, would be something like this. The British fleet, in line ahead, would seize the weather gage and then come opposite but out of range of the enemy column, adjusting intervals until the lines were conterminous, that is, van opposite van, center opposite center, and rear opposite rear. Then on signal the entire British column would put helms over and bear down on the enemy in line abreast—or if the enemy had way on, in line of bearing. As the British came within gun range, they would turn together once more into line ahead, paralleling the enemy, and open fire. (See diagram page 38.) Such a battle would keep control firmly in the hands of the admiral, but it could be won only by superior gunnery and stamina. In seeking to be equal to the enemy all down the line, the formalists forfeited all chance of bringing superior power to bear against any portion of his line. Even possession of the weather gage was offset by the price the British had to pay: the raking fire they were obliged to endure while closing the enemy in line abreast.

Ironically, as Malaga demonstrated, the perfect formal battle was an unattainable ideal. For one thing, the attacking ships could never manage to come down on the enemy together. In the turn from line ahead to line abreast, the helmsman in the second ship in line would put his helm over only as he saw the first ship coming around. The third ship would turn after the second, and so on down the line. As a result, the windward fleet generally arrived within gun range of the enemy van-first, with the rest of the line arriving a ship at a time. (See diagram page 40.)

As experience was to prove, this awkward situation was made to order for the French. British naval policy and the weight of British naval tradition required admirals of the Royal Navy to keep foremost in mind the *tactical objective* of destroying the enemy fleet. French

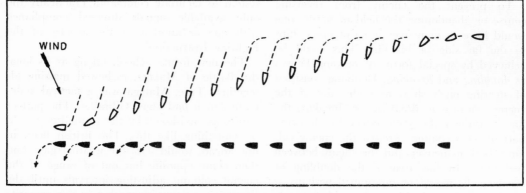

TENDENCY OF WINDWARD SHIPS TO COME SINGLY INTO ACTION

admirals, serving a numerically inferior navy and sternly enjoined to conserve ships, used their fleets only as supporting forces to assist in attaining *strategic objectives*. However offensive their strategic aims might be, they were invariably on the tactical defensive. Hence French fleet commanders deliberately accepted the lee gage, from which escape was possible. In this downwind position they backed their sails and lost way in order to force the British attacker into a perpendicular approach that would deny him the use of his broadsides. They would then rake him while he bore down, massing fire on his van as his ships came into action one at a time.

The French fired on the upward roll, aiming high at the enemy's masts, yards, and rigging so as to impair his ability to pursue. They then fell off down wind out of range, usually in succession beginning with the van. This piecemeal falling off could be carried out with impunity because British men-of-war, even if they could still work their sails, were restrained from pursuit by Article 21 of the 1703 Fighting Instructions, which read: "None of the ships of the fleet shall pursue any small number of the enemy's ships till the main body be disabled or run." English formalism thus permitted the *Marine* to mass, while avoiding being massed upon. This sort of concentration tactics often cost a good many French lives, for the English usually managed to get in a few blows of their own, and they fired on the downward roll, aiming at hulls with the intent to capture or destroy and not merely to cripple. Nevertheless, such a clash sometimes so mismasted the British

van that the Britons were obliged to return to base for repairs. During their absence, the French made use of their temporary command of the sea to gain a foothold on some bit of British territory or to isolate some British army that depended on overseas communications.

This French tactical riposte was the result of no sudden inspiration; it evolved slowly out of battle experience. Certainly it was not foreseen by British naval theorists of the early 18th century, who had before them in recent history only the examples of Beachy Head, Barfleur, and Malaga. As they saw the matter, melee tactics had been tried and found wanting; formal tactics had repulsed the enemy. So official opinion came out unequivocally in favor of formalism. Rooke's Fighting Instructions of 1703 requiring a line conterminous with the enemy (the Instructions he had used at Malaga), were adopted by the Admiralty as Permanent Fighting Instructions. They thus had the force of Standing Orders. During the long peace from 1713 to 1740, while top-ranking naval officers grew old and conservative, formalism acquired the added sanction of tradition. Formal doctrine became dogma; melee tactics were forgotten. If anyone doubted that the conterminous line had become inviolate, he was disabused by official reaction to the first fleet engagement of the War of the Austrian Succession (1740-48). This was the curious Battle of Toulon.

Pursuing a Franco-Spanish fleet off Toulon in February 1744, Admiral Thomas Mathews with a fleet of equal size but with bottoms fouled by long blockade duty, could not overtake the enemy van with his own van. Rather than let the enemy escape, he bore down as he was and engaged while still flying the signal for Line Ahead. This brought his van against the enemy center and his center against the enemy rear. Mathews had expected Vice Admiral Richard Lestock, commanding the British rear, to do the obvious and common-sense thing: press on all sail and advance into the battle, joining the British center in massing on the enemy rear. But Lestock did nothing of the sort. In literal obedience to Mathews' line signal, he brought his rear squadron down against an open sea and so remained out of battle. After the engagement, in which ships in the British van and center were severely battered, Mathews placed Lestock under arrest, but in the subsequent courts-martial the tables were turned—Lestock was acquitted and Mathews was cashiered.

Few officers appreciated that these strange findings were at least partly dictated by politics. For a good many years after the trials, it was a bold officer indeed who would risk disgrace by failing to maintain a conterminous battle line. Certainly Admiral Sir John Byng, who had sat as a judge in Mathews' court-martial, was no such officer—as we shall presently see. Thus formalism, already well entrenched, fixed itself all the more firmly in the Royal Navy, and tactical initiative was suppressed. A few daring commanders, intending to offset the extreme rigidity of the Permanent Fighting Instructions, issued Additional Instructions to their fleets, but these did little to relieve the situation. Between the Battle of Toulon and the Battle of the Saints in 1782, British admirals fought 13 battles using the conterminous line; every one was a tactical draw—no ship was captured or destroyed on either side. In the same period however, British fleets won six victories; all six were won by admirals who had the courage and the tactical acumen to abandon the conterminous line.

Abandonment of the line was sanctioned by Article 25 of the Permanent Instructions, which permitted pursuit when the enemy fleet as a whole was "put to the run." The onus of course was placed on the admiral, for it was up to him to decide (1) whether the enemy was actually in flight and (2) whether the chances for success warranted the risk of break-

ing formation. If he signaled General Chase and won a victory, nobody was going to inquire too closely about the state of the enemy when the signal was given. But if he signaled Chase and lost, he would have to convince a skeptical court-martial that the enemy had indeed been on the run. Thus the decision for a chase was the touchstone distinguishing those British admirals possessing merely physical courage, which seems to have been the common possession of the breed, from those possessing the rarer quality of moral courage.

Two such admirals were George Anson and Edward Hawke, who possessed also the steadiness and tactical skill to deal with the risks involved. Each, in 1747, defeated French fleets by discarding line tactics and giving the chase signal. These engagements, known as the First and Second Battles of Finisterre, provided the experience that converted pursuit from a mere free-for-all to something more orderly. Some time after Second Finisterre, there appeared a new set of Additional Instructions with articles devoted to controlling fleet movements during pursuit. These articles, which carefully avoided the rigidity of the Permanent Instructions, were available and in use when England and France again came into conflict in the Seven Years' War (1756-63). They provided the tactical flexibility that enabled the Royal Navy to banish the major French fleets from the seas and lay the foundation for Britain's world-wide empire.

Eighteenth Century Ships and Guns

When fleets abandoned bunching tactics for fighting in line ahead, small, lightly armed warships and armed merchantmen too often found themselves opposite men-of-war many times more powerful than themselves. This sort of thing had to be avoided because the strength of a column of ships lies in its coherence. Like a chain, it is no stronger than its weakest link. The obvious, and only practical, solution to this dilemma was to eliminate the weaker vessels from the line. So, before the end of the 17th century, the smaller types were detached for cruising and patrol duty, became in fact the cruisers of the navy, and merchantmen

74-GUN SHIP OF THE LINE

went back to transport and cargo hauling. The tendency thereafter was toward shorter, more homogeneous battle lines containing only heavily gunned men-of-war considered "fit to lie in the line." Such ships were called *ships of the line.*[8]

In the early 18th century, the division between ships of the line and cruisers was fixed at 50 guns. This arbitrary division proved unsatisfactory however, for 50-gun ships were found not fit to lie in the line with ships of 100 guns. Not until mid-century were types clearly categorized, with standards of size, tonnage, and armament fixed for each. This was the work chiefly of Admiral Anson, who became First Lord of the Admiralty in 1754. Besides introducing standardized uniforms for officers and pulling the Royal Navy out of the material and administrative doldrums into which it had again declined, he made a practical distinction between line ships and cruisers and established rates in each category. Since other countries generally followed the lead of Britain in naval matters, Anson's plan of or-

[8] Called also *line ships, line-of-battle ships, battleships,* or in naval parlance, simply *ships.*

ganization, with some modifications, was adopted elsewhere.

In brief, Anson divided all men-of-war into six rates according to the number of guns carried, First, Second, and Third Rates being designated ships of the line, and the rest, cruisers. We need not concern ourselves with the details, for Anson's system of rates, though not his basic plan, was largely discarded toward the end of the century for a designation by rated number of guns, a system that prevailed until the end of the age of sail and even a little beyond. Thus we read of a 74-gun ship or a 36-gun frigate, though the number of guns actually carried might be somewhat more or less than the rated number. We also find men-of-war named with rated number of guns following, as *Victory,* 100; *Constitution,* 44; or *Wasp,* 18. To the initiated these figures indicated that the first was a ship of the line; the second, a frigate; and the third, a sloop-of-war.

Flagships of the line carried from 80 to more than 100 guns. In later periods some huge ships managed to crowd up to 140 aboard. Ships of 80 guns and upward, Anson's

First and Second Rates, were three-deckers, that is, they carried their guns on three complete decks, with additional guns on the forecastle and quarterdeck. A typical 100-gun ship had the following measurements: burden, 2,200 tons (about 3,500 tons displacement); length of gun deck, 190 feet; beam, 52 feet; depth of hold, 22 feet; draft, 21 feet. Her full complement was 900 men. On her lower gun deck she carried 32-pounders (guns firing shot weighing 32 pounds); on her middle deck, 24-pounders; on her upper deck, 18-pounders; on her forecastle and quarterdeck, 12-pounders, or later in the century, stubby, heavy-shotted carronades. By way of comparison, the largest United States battleships of World War II displaced more than ten times as much, and post-World War II United States carriers displace up to 16 times as much. A post-World War II United States frigate (large destroyer) has the same displacement, beam, and depth of hold as a 100-gun ship of the line, but is considerably more than twice as long and carries fewer than half as many men.

Most of the "private," or non-flag, ships in the line were two-deckers (Third Rates) carrying 74 guns. These had a full complement of about 650 men and generally omitted the 24-pound battery. A good many 64's also were built and some continued in use in the 19th century, but these economy-sized ships generally proved inadequate for service in the line.

An in-between and relatively rare type was the 50 (Fourth Rate), which served mainly as

SLOOP-OF-WAR

flagship in cruiser squadrons. The Fifth and Sixth Rates were the cruisers themselves. The most famous and numerous of these were the frigates, which in Anson's time carried 28 to 30 guns but were later standardized at 36 and 44. They were ship-rigged (square-rigged on three masts) single-deckers carrying a main battery of 12- or 18-pounders, with a secondary battery of 6-pounders on the quarterdeck. The most versatile of men-of-war, the frigate carried out functions varying from commerce raiding to scouting for the fleet. In action they normally took station on the unengaged side of the line to repeat signals and take disabled ships in tow. Smaller types were sloops-of-war —single deckers, usually ship-rigged, with no secondary battery; brigs—square-rigged vessels with two masts; and schooners—fore-and-aft-rigged vessels with two masts.

Eighteenth century men-of-war carried huge complements of seamen, partly to work the great cloud of sail needed to drive such broad-beamed vessels at an acceptable speed[9] but chiefly to manhandle the awkward guns of the period. A dozen men were required to secure, load, run out, and lay a long 32-pounder. Well trained gun crews in the Royal Navy could fire a broadside every two or three minutes and get off three or four broadsides before exhaustion slowed them down. A few British captains toward the end of the century trained their crews to fire five broadsides in five minutes. French and Spanish gunners did well to get off one broadside every five minutes. The contrast

[9] In average winds, a ship of the line could make five or six knots before the wind. Frigates could make eight to ten knots.

FRIGATE

in rate of fire was a result partly of superior British training and discipline and partly of differences in objective. Because the British usually reserved their fire for close range action —under 600 yards—and fired at hulls, they rarely bothered with the niceties of accuracy. Frenchmen and Spaniards, on the contrary, took careful aim in order to hit masts and spars —at long range if possible. As formalism waned and Englishmen again sought to bring on a melee, rate of fire proved decisive over aim— or at least over the aim that their opponents generally achieved. That is why the great British meleeists of the last days of sail seldom hesitated to tackle enemy fleets far superior in numbers to their own.

Though the British fleet by the mid-1700's surpassed all others in organization, shiphandling, and gunnery, nothing could shake the Royal Navy loose from its traditional guesswork in ship design. French and Spanish ships were swifter and more maneuverable than British ships, not because they were better built but because they were more scientifically designed. British admirals were only too glad to capture them intact and incorporate them into their own fleets, where more often than not they were appropriated as flagships.

As in times past, the merchantman tended to follow the structural lead of the man-of-war. She needed the speed conferred by clean lines to meet the competition of trade, and she still carried guns to protect herself from commerce raiders and from pirates that abounded in distant seas. The cargo ship, moreover, still served occasionally as warship, not incorporated into the line as of old, but as a privateer, issued a letter of marque by the government to prey on enemy commercial shipping. Such armed merchantmen, through sheer numbers, sometimes outdid naval vessels in the shadowy operations of *guerre de course*.

Summary

The voyages of exploration and discovery in the late 15th and early 16th centuries reoriented the interests of Europe toward the oceans and involved the oceanic powers in a long and often bitter rivalry for trade and colonies. In this competition England took a strong lead after meeting the challenges successively of Spain, Holland, and France. Early in the 18th century she had become the world's greatest trader on the seas, she possessed the world's largest navy, and she had laid the foundations of a vast overseas empire.

The chief reason for England's success was her almost exclusive reliance upon her navy, and that in turn grew out of her unique fitness for the role of sea power and colonizer. Her comparatively sparse internal resources together with her burgeoning population provided the impetus and the manpower for developing overseas commerce and planting colonies. Englishmen had an outstanding capacity for colonization, trade, and industry, all three of which nourish sea power. The government of England, unlike those of Spain and France, more and more favored industrial, commercial, and naval progress. Unlike France, England had a continuous coastline that permitted her to keep her naval forces concentrated. Uniquely among her rivals, she had no land frontier to tempt her into continental expansion or oblige her to maintain a defensive standing army. She could therefore devote her wealth to fleets for extending and protecting her trade, seizing and defending new colonies, and blockading and destroying the fleets of her enemies. Lastly, her position athwart the sea approaches to Western Europe enabled her easily to blockade enemy ports and disrupt seaborne enemy commerce.[10]

Partly by chance, partly by policy, England supported a balance of power in Europe by allying herself in each period with secondary powers against the strongest and most aggressive power. At peace conferences she demanded trade concessions, overseas colonies, and on the advice of the Admiralty, strategic bases near terminal points (major ports) and focal areas (waters near capes and straits), where shipping tends to converge. Her strategic-base policy enabled her at length, as the old phrase has it, to "lock up the seven seas of the world." In the early 18th century her acquisition of Gibraltar and Minorca had already given her virtual control of the western Mediterranean. These bases also facilitated blockades of Cadiz and Toulon and made it next to impossible for France to

[10] Based on Capt. Alfred Thayer Mahan USN, *The Influence of Sea Power upon History* (Boston, 1890), 25–89. (See page 341f., below.)

combine her Brest and Toulon fleets for wartime operations in the English Channel.

The isolation that had enabled England to hold aloof from continental disputes, picking her time and allies, was interrupted during the period (1689-1701) when the Dutch Stadtholder was also King of England. It was interrupted again in 1714 when the Elector of Hanover acceded to the English throne as George I. While the Hanoverian Electors were also Kings of England, their little German state was likely to be a millstone hung on British foreign policy and military strategy.

In seamanship and gunnery, Englishmen consistently outdistanced their rivals. For a long while too they remained a step ahead in ship design and tactical doctrine. They were the first to use broadsides and the first to stress maneuverability in their warships. They were the first to abandon grappling and boarding and the first to improve upon the old bunching tactics. By the end of the 17th century however, traditionalism in ship construction and formalism in tactics began to put the Royal Navy at a disadvantage. England's enemies were quick to profit by these self-imposed handicaps by designing ships more scientifically and by inventing suitable counter-tactics.

After any drastic change in naval weapons, such as the introduction of the sailing warship, five basic questions have to be answered: (1) What weapons are suitable for use in the main battle formation? (2) What battle formation gives fullest play to the weapons in use? (3) How can one mass one's fleet against the enemy fleet? (4) How can the enemy fleet be prevented from massing against one's own? (5) How can the enemy be prevented from escaping? The first two questions must be answered before an effective tactical doctrine can be worked out. Working out the doctrine involves finding a simultaneous solution to questions 3, 4, and 5. In meeting the challenge of Spain in the Spanish Armada campaign, England answered question 1 for herself: the gun was to be her primary naval weapon. In meeting the challenge of Holland in the Anglo-Dutch Wars, England answered question 2: the line ahead gave fullest play to the gun. By the middle of the 18th century neither the melee nor the formal school of tactics in England had found a complete and simultaneous set of answers for the rest of the tactical questions. The meleeists proposed the devices of *massing*, *doubling*, and *breaking* as answers to question 3, and *doubling* and *breaking* as answers to question 5, but they found no answer for question 4. The formalists proposed the *conterminous line of battle* as an answer to question 4, but found no answer to questions 3 and 5. When opposing fleets are equal or nearly so, solutions to 3 and 5 may provide the key to victory, but a solution to 4 is likely to prevent defeat. Hence a choice between melee and formal tactics boils down to whether one wishes to emphasize the offensive or the defensive. Early in the 18th century, English naval tacticians chose a formal defensive doctrine and wrote it into the Permanent Fighting Instructions. A naval service grown old and conservative in a long period of peace raised the formal doctrine into inviolate dogma. The formalists, as it turned out, won no decisive victories but neither did they suffer any decisive defeats.

Clear-sighted admirals like Anson and Hawke were far from satisfied. Scorning the paper tacticians and their precise solutions, they set out to free the Royal Navy from its tactical chains. They were prepared if necessary to jettison the line, and dogmatic tactics in general, and submit the issue to the fortunes of chase. In such a free-for-all something was lost and much was risked, but individual initiative, skill, and spirit were given a chance to weigh in the balance. Chase tactics won the clear victories that Englishmen had almost ceased to expect, but they did not provide the final solution. That was to come later, when initiative and doctrine were brought into balance and united by an efficient signal system. The combination at length produced the victories of Howe, Jervis, Duncan, and Nelson in the golden age of sail.

3:

The Seven Years' War

The Seven Years' War (1756–63), more than any of the preceding wars in the long struggle between England and France, is of special interest to the student of naval history. Important military operations occurred in the German states, in the Mediterranean, in Canada, in the West Indies, in India, in Africa, and in the Philippines. It was thus genuinely a world war. It has its object lessons in tactics, both in fleet actions and in amphibious operations. It is a mine of examples both of faulty and of superb strategic planning and execution. In Pitt and Choiseul, war ministers of England and France, in Frederick the Great of Prussia and his ally Ferdinand of Brunswick, in Boscawen and Hawke, in the amphibious team of Wolfe and Saunders, this war produced some of the finest leaders in their countries' histories.

But above all else the Seven Years' War is the archetype of wars between a strong land power and a strong sea power. Britain's sweeping victories and the Carthaginian peace she was able to dictate established for the first time Britain's position as the primary world power. It was Pitt's strategic insight, and particularly his sure hand in disposing the British fleet, that made the far-flung British Empire a reality. Never has there been a better exemplification of the "influence of sea power upon history."

The Peace of Aix-la-Chapelle (1748), which ended the War of the Austrian Succession, satisfied no one. A renewal of hostilities was inevitable. There were two focal points of dissension. In America, the British colonists and the French had conflicting claims to the land beyond the Appalachians, especially the Ohio Valley and the area south of the Great Lakes. In Central Europe, Austria smarted at the loss of Silesia to Prussia, and schemed to get it back. Great Britain was potentially involved in any German quarrel, since George II of England was also Elector of Hanover, his ancestral patrimony.

Hostilities broke out in America. What the colonists called the French and Indian War was simply the American phase of the Seven Years' War. In the spring of 1754 a rawboned young colonel of Virginia militia named George Washington was sent with a battalion to establish an outpost near the confluence of the Allegheny and Monongahela rivers in what is now western Pennsylvania. Defeated by superior French and Indian forces at Fort Necessity, Washington was obliged to surrender. The following year the British ministry sent a column of regulars under Major General Edward Braddock. This force, supplemented by Colonel Washington's militia, undertook to capture Fort Duquesne, the French outpost at what is now Pittsburgh. Ambushed at Great Meadows, this command also was defeated, and General Braddock was killed.

In the context of the 18th century, it might have been possible to circumscribe the area of conflict, to fight a war of limited objectives entirely in the colonies. But dramatic things were happening in Europe.

The Diplomatic Revolution

For the better part of a century the Bourbon house of France and the Hapsburgs of Austria had nursed a hostility based on a cleavage of dynastic and territorial interests. French expansionism from the time of Louis XIV had periodically threatened the Rhenish principalities and the Austrian Netherlands. Not only were

England and France chronically at war; France and Austria had come to be "traditional enemies" as well.

But now the pretensions of the poverty-stricken kingdom of Prussia to military power of the first rank altered the "balance of power" on the continent. King Frederick's bare-faced theft of Silesia from Austria still rankled. Austria therefore shifted camps. So recently France's enemy and Britain's ally, she now became France's ally. She thus doomed herself to becoming England's enemy as well as Prussia's.

For it was basic in Britain's foreign policy that the strongest continental power must not become established in the Netherlands. London was a bare day's sail from the mouths of the Scheldt. With a French garrison in Antwerp, the Scheldt estuary became a pistol pointed at the heart of England. Besides, there was the matter of Hanover. Connected to England only by a common crown, Hanover became a hostage to fortune with its two powerful neighbors allied. England must then have a continental ally, and this could only be Prussia.

France and Austria were to draw into their coalition Sweden, then a respectable military power, and later Russia. Only by virtue of great military genius was Frederick the Great able, with the help only of allied minor German states and a British subsidy, to survive and keep his nation intact through seven years of war.

It is impossible in an account predominantly naval to review the complicated campaigning of the land war. But it must not be forgotten that Britain's grand strategy and her distribution of forces was throughout the war strongly influenced by these land campaigns. Though British cooperation was seldom of a "shoulder-to-shoulder" variety, Prussia and Britain formed an effective alliance against their powerful common enemy—France.

Belleisle's Plan

Not until 1756 was war officially declared. But depredations by English privateers and naval units, and the public announcement of the secretly negotiated treaty between England and Prussia had made an overt declaration of war and a spreading of hostilities inevitable.

In the past, when England had been allied with Austria, France could by striking at the Austrian Netherlands (now Belgium) secure a *quid pro quo* to exchange for any colonies she might lose to superior British sea power. The new alliance system made this impossible. France could strike at Hanover, to be sure, but England's alliance with Frederick made this strategy less certain. The obvious remaining alternative was a cross-Channel invasion of England herself, a blow struck before England could fully marshal her naval resources or prepare adequate land defenses.

To the refinement of such a plan the gifted Marshal Charles Fouquet de Belleisle applied his genius. In essence, Belleisle's plan envisioned three simultaneous invasions: one in Ireland, one in Scotland, and one in England. A "second wave" was to reinforce the main attack after a foothold was won—presumably in England. At about the same time, an amphibious diversionary attack was to be made on Minorca, England's only naval base within the Mediterranean. For the invasion of England, flatboats to carry the troops were built in quantity, and military detachments were moved to Channel and Biscayan ports.

Through diplomatic channels and intelligence reports, the British Cabinet and the British people were apprised of these preparations and of the invasion scheme. With England's tiny professional army widely scattered, and a large part of her navy dispersed on foreign stations, there was something very like a panic in London. To the Duke of Newcastle, then chief minister, and his advisers, it seemed self-evident that no effort should be spared to strengthen military defenses at home, and most particularly to enlarge the Channel fleet at the expense of all other prospective theaters of war whatever. In the context of more recent history it seems quixotic to plan a sea-borne invasion without effective naval supremacy (for which the French had no real prospect or plan). But in 1755 an invasion by evading the British navy was still thought possible.[1] It is against

[1] As recently as 1745 such an invasion had been partially successful. As will be seen, fears of invasion from France would on occasion dominate British strategic thinking, particularly during the wars of the French Revolution and Empire (1793–1815).

this background that the Minorca operation must be examined.

The French Capture Minorca

It was soon evident that the French government and the French navy lacked the aggressive spirit of Belleisle, and lacked material means as well. If England was unready to defend against an invasion, France was equally unready to mount it. When the French commanders reached the point of translating the bold plan into an effective operational blueprint, they shied away. But in throwing into confusion the defensive strategy of Britain, the French gained the priceless advantage of surprise in the Mediterranean theater of operations. One hundred and fifty transports carrying 15,000 troops under the Duc de Richelieu and twelve ships of the line under the Marquis de la Galissonière were assembled at Toulon. The diversion against Minorca had now become the main operation.

The French effected a landing on Minorca in mid-April 1756 and quickly drove the 3,000-man garrison into the stronghold of Fort St. Philip, which covered the main city, Port Mahon. The French fleet stood by under light sail, blockading the island and maintaining readiness to intercept any British reinforcements.

British strength in the Mediterranean at this time consisted of a tiny squadron-of-observation under Commodore George Edgecumbe—one 60, two 50's, and four frigates. Acting belatedly on conflicting intelligence reports, the Admiralty finally dispatched Admiral Sir John Byng with ten of the line to proceed to the Mediterranean. His instructions were complicated, taking into consideration many possible contingencies, including a splitting of his force at Gibraltar if there seemed good evidence that French reinforcements had been sent to North America. Otherwise he was to proceed to Minorca in full force. If the French had attacked it, he was to use "all possible means in [his] power for its relief." If Minorca had not yet been attacked, he was to blockade Toulon. And in any circumstances, he was to cover Gibraltar.

Reaching Gibraltar on May 2, 1756, Byng was informed of the true situation by Commodore Edgecumbe, whose ships were a welcome reinforcement. After a week's delay he sailed with a regiment of fusiliers he had brought out from England and 13 line-of-battle ships to attempt to raise the siege.

Byng sighted Minorca on May 19, and sent frigates ahead to reconnoiter Port Mahon and to try to communicate with the British garrison ashore. The appearance of the main French fleet to the southeast frustrated this mission. The battle lines soon came into sight of each other on intercepting courses, but the wind dropped off, and night fell before action could be joined.

As the morning mists cleared the following day, the French were reported to the south and east, about 12 miles distant. There was a moderate SSW wind. Recalling his frigates, which had been chasing small craft presumed to be hostile, Byng tacked his fleet southeast toward Galissonière's, and signaled for line-of-battle at two cables' length. His squadron was organized in two divisions, Byng himself commanding the van, of seven ships, and Rear Admiral Temple West, his second-in-command, commanding the six of the rear. The French presently appeared, on a WNW course, carrying all plain sail. Byng spread more canvas, and raced to cross the enemy course and thereby secure the weather gage.

For an hour or more the adversaries continued on near collision courses. Shortly after noon the wind veered to the southwest, favoring Byng's maneuver. Seeing it would be impossible to weather the British, Galissonière shortened sail and fell off the wind to starboard, in effect accepting the lee gage. Byng eased off a little, and the fleets came abreast on nearly reciprocal courses in not quite parallel columns, the French on the port tack, the British on the starboard.

The orthodox course prescribed for Byng in the Permanent Fighting Instructions would have been to hold course until his van ship was opposite the enemy rear ship, then to tack together, and attack the enemy ship to ship. As we have seen, the weakness of this style of attack was that the aggressors thereby approached the broadsides of the enemy almost bows-on and were consequently exposed for many minutes to a raking fire to which they could make no effective reply.

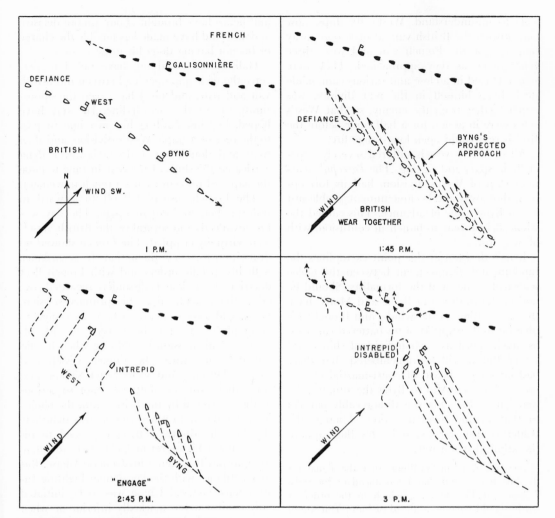

THE BATTLE FOR MINORCA, MAY 18, 1756

Byng had therefore planned a slight but significant tactical innovation: he would hold course until his van was well past the rear of the French line, and *then* come about and make his approach on a line-of-bearing—a diagonal or angling course on the enemy's quarter, which would allow the exercise of his own guns.[2]

At what he judged to be the right moment, Byng backed topsails to kill way. Galissonière

[2] Though not usual at the time, this approach was not wholly original with Byng. It was enjoined by Lord Dartmouth as an addition to the Duke of York's instructions as early as 1688. Cf. Sir Julian S. Corbett, *England in the Seven Years' War*, I (London, 1907), 118–119.

parried by the same maneuver. Byng signaled to tack, intending that when the line re-formed on the northwesterly course the *Defiance* (which would then be the van ship) would at once fall off to starboard to engage the leading ship in the French line, thus initiating the action. This the *Defiance* failed to do, holding to a course nearly parallel to that of the enemy with West's whole division following. Hampered by an inadequate signal system, Byng was delayed in communicating his intention. He thereby missed the critical moment for which his tactics up to now had been a skillful preparation.

In desperation Byng finally signaled for general action. Here at last was an order impossible to misunderstand. West's six ships, now constituting the British van, at once bore away bows-on for the French van and were three times raked as they approached. They were soon engaged in a close and furious cannonade duel. Byng himself in the rear division was much farther from the enemy, so that West's ships were in action for a half hour before the British rear could open long-range fire.

All of West's vessels suffered severely, especially in spars and rigging. The *Intrepid*, rearmost ship of West's division, had its foretopmast shot away and became unmanageable just across Byng's line of advance. This caused the whole British rear to bunch in confusion, with all way lost.

Byng's decision at this point exemplifies the fundamental disagreement between the melee school of tactics and the formalists. Should he not, in the tradition of Blake and Monk, have thrown caution to the winds, and brought his division to the support of his battered van with as much speed as each individual ship could show? But it will be remembered that Byng had sat on the board of court-martial of Admiral Mathews. And to Byng the situation he found himself facing was disagreeably parallel to that at the Toulon action. Though the bolder course was urged by his flag-captain, the admiral demurred:

> You see, Captain Gardiner, that the signal for the line is out, and that I am ahead of the ships *Louisa* and *Trident* . . . [which in the order of battle should have been ahead of him]. You would not have me, as admiral of the fleet, run down as if I were going to engage a single ship. It was Mr. Mathews' misfortune to be prejudiced by not carrying down his force together, which I shall endeavor to avoid.[3]

And in fact he delayed in order to re-form a column of sorts, only to find the French breaking off the action. Byng's own ships were never seriously engaged. It cannot certainly be known if Byng's rigid adherence to the close column cost him his reputation and his life by denying him a victory. Galissonière was far too capable an officer to make a British victory certain under any possible circumstances. But for Byng to have precipitated a general melee

and hence have brought about a more decisive action would have made less tenable the charge of his not having done his utmost.

Galissonière could not have failed to perceive the wide gap opening between the British van and rear, and must have seen the opportunity to cut the British line. He may have hoped, by close-hauling his own line to pass to the rear of Temple West's division, and then wear and double on it. If so however Byng extricated the ships of the rear in time to close the gap and prevent such a French movement. The French instead fell off to leeward to re-form their line out of range. The day was far advanced, and several of the British vessels were virtually crippled. The French showed no disposition to renew the action. In accordance with his specific orders and with French fleet doctrine of the time, Galissonière regarded covering the beachhead as his primary mission. He would accept action where necessary to accomplish this. But he refused to risk his ships and his mission by fighting when he did not have to. Since the French vessels had cleaner bottoms and were faster sailers, and since their injuries aloft were not so serious as those suffered by the British van, the choice of when and if to renew action was definitely the French admiral's. Byng expressed to his flag captain his regret at lacking an adequate force to justify a signal for General Chase. But in accordance with the Permanent Fighting Instructions, General Chase was to be initiated only against a foe markedly inferior or when ". . . the main body be disabled or run."[4] Neither of these conditions applied to Galissonière's well-handled force. Byng instead set easy sail to cruise in the area, while West's crews juryrigged their damaged top hamper.

Byng was now in a quandary. He was unable to attack Galissonière, who was so uncooperative as not to attack him. While still at Gibraltar, he had already despaired of raising the siege of Fort St. Philip. Certainly such poor reinforcements as he could provide could hardly save Blakeney's garrison—outnumbered five to one. The British fleet was still spread all over the world, and the loss of many of his battered ships would seriously compromise the whole

---

[3] Quoted in Capt. Alfred Thayer Mahan USN, *The Influence of Sea Power upon History, 1660–1783* (Boston, 1890), 287.

[4] Permanent Fighting Instructions, Article 21. Sir Julian S. Corbett, ed., *Fighting Instructions, 1530–1816* (London: Navy Records Society, 1905).

British position in the Mediterranean. His orders included support for Gibraltar. So the Admiral's mind worked.

But with his natural reluctance to relinquish all hope of succor for the British force on the island, some four days after the action Byng sought advice from a formal council of war composed of Rear Admiral West and the senior army and naval officers in the squadron. They concurred in his defeatist views, and Byng withdrew his fleet to Gibraltar. General Blakeney held out for over a month longer, but by the time Admiral Sir Edward Hawke arrived to supersede Byng as commander in chief in the Mediterranean, the doughty British garrison had finally surrendered. Minorca remained in French hands for the rest of the war.

The Fate of Byng

The news of the loss of Minorca, coming as it did on the heels of Braddock's defeat, was very badly received in England, and threatened the government of the Duke of Newcastle and his political coterie. A scapegoat was needed.

Poor John Byng was born for such a role. Mild and amiable of disposition, overcome by self-doubt and an excess of conscientiousness, he lacked the tough resoluteness of an Anson or a Hawke. He had not, in a tactical sense, lost a battle. But he had done worse: he had failed to win one when a victory was psychologically necessary.

He was ordered home to face court-martial. After an exhaustive hearing, he was formally exonerated of the charge of cowardice in the face of the enemy, but was held guilty of failing to "do his utmost" to defeat the enemy—either to destroy the French fleet or to relieve the garrison on Minorca. For this offense a recent revision of the Articles of War made a death penalty mandatory. King George II declined a petition of pardon from members of the court itself and from several of his ministers. Byng was accordingly shot.

Byng's trial and execution were a public *cause célèbre* and the talk of the naval service for many months. Though in fact he was not punished for any purely tactical mistake, but rather for not persisting in his effort to succor the garrison on Minorca, it was evident that in his attempt to restore the line at the crisis of the naval action he had rejected a chance for victory and honor. The painstaking detail with which the engagement off Minorca was reconstructed by the court helped to re-focus an interest in tactics as such, and to bring into question the inflexible rules of the Permanent Fighting Instructions. If for no other reason, it may not be too much to say that Byng by his death accomplished more for his service than by his living deeds.

Pitt's Plan

The unrelieved British disasters of 1756, seen in the perspective of history, were a blessing in disguise. For they forced a cabinet shuffle by the incompetent Duke of Newcastle and his "government-by-crony." The elder William Pitt, darling of the House of Commons and of the English people, anathema to King George[5] and rival to Newcastle, had to be invited to join the government. Such was the desperation of Newcastle and his party that they were obliged to accept Pitt on his own hard terms—that he be principal Secretary of State for War, with virtually dictatorial power over troop and ship movements. Such were Pitt's energies and strategic genius that he became in effect the creator of the greatest chain of victories in all British history.

Since England was allied with Frederick, and since the protection of Hanover was a major objective of the war, it is obvious that any British government could easily find itself expending the bulk of its military forces on the continental war. There was in fact what might be termed a "continental school" of strategy within the British government, of which the King himself was the ranking member.

Pitt strongly disagreed. To aid Frederick with a subsidy, to support the Hanoverians with token forces and the presence of a prince of the blood, to relieve Frederick by drawing off French forces to the coastlines by hit-and-run raids—these actions Pitt could approve as subserving his main plan. But the great prizes

[5] In political in-fighting against Lord John Carteret (later the Earl of Granville) in Parliament, Pitt had excoriated Lord John's Hanoverian sympathies, and thereby had mortally offended George II's German patriotism.

were overseas—North America, the "sugar islands" of the Caribbean, India. To Pitt the securing of these, permanently and irrevocably, was the great end of the war. Pitt was by temperament first and last an empire-builder.

His reasoning was simple. England throve on trade. The Empire nourished trade. Trade made for wealth. Wealth enhanced military strength. At that very time Frederick was in effect fighting England's battles by virtue of the chests of specie England could send to pay his troops.

Furthermore, on the battlefields of Europe England's outnumbered little army could scarcely hope to be more than a pawn. In overseas war her naval preponderance could be utilized to best advantage. In terms of field strategy her navy must first cork up the French

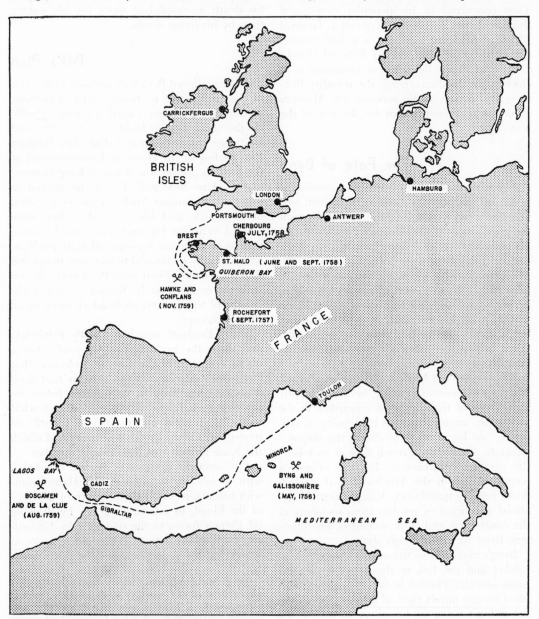

THE SEVEN YEARS' WAR IN EUROPEAN WATERS

ports by blockade, keeping the French fleet segmented. Then any naval margin could be employed to convoy overseas expeditions and support amphibious operations in the four corners of the earth. And the British navy would of course cut off support from France to her colonies.

European Coastal Operations

The military successes of Prussia early in the war simply stimulated greater efforts by the French and the Austrians, who together had an overwhelmingly greater force. Not unnaturally, Frederick demanded of his British allies more material assistance than the subsidy and the dubious support of a small English force under the Duke of Cumberland. A part of England's answer was the "conjunct operations"—amphibious raids against French ports. These campaigns were aimed incidentally at cleaning out nests of troublesome privateers that preyed on English coastal shipping, but their primary object was, by attracting concentrations of French troops from the eastern battlefront, to relieve the pressure on Frederick in Middle Europe.

The first "conjunct operation" was directed against Rochefort in the fall of 1757. In spite of the investing and subsequent capture of the island of Aix, lying just offshore, this expedition was correctly accounted a failure. A lack of adequate planning led the commanders to conclude that a landing was impossible. The undertaking did however offer a negative object lesson to Lieutenant Colonel James Wolfe, who was serving as chief of staff. Apropos of the ill-starred Rochefort campaign, he remarked in a famous letter:

I have found out an Admiral should endeavour to run into an enemy's port immediately . . .; that previous directions should be given in respect to landing the troops, and a proper disposition made for the boats of all sorts, . . . that pushing on smartly is the road to success . . .; that nothing is to be reckoned an obstacle to your undertaking which is not found really so upon trial; that in war something must be allowed to chance and fortune, seeing that it is in its nature hazardous, and an option of difficulties; that the greatness of the object should come under consideration, opposed to the impediments that lie in the way; that the honour of one's country is to have some weight; and that, in particular circumstances and times, the loss of a thousand men is rather an advantage to a nation than otherwise, seeing that gallant attempts raise its reputation and make it respectable. . . .[6]

As Wolfe was to demonstrate at Louisburg and Quebec, the lesson was not lost on him.

The British scored a somewhat larger measure of success at St. Malo, on the Bay of St. Michel between the Breton and the Norman peninsulas. St. Malo was home port for many small craft whose owners in wartime turned naturally from fishing and the coasting trade to privateering. Here in June 1758 some 13,000 British troops landed and spent a week ashore, burning more than a hundred privateers. The following August the British took temporary possession of Cherbourg and destroyed fortifications and shipping. A renewed attack on the St. Malo area achieved limited success, but a speedy French concentration drove the expedition back to its ships and destroyed the British rear guard ashore.

These were all relatively small-scale coastal raids, with no design to hold the territory captured. Though they did in fact contribute to the strategic ends noted above, their importance was mainly psychological. They encouraged Frederick to believe in the reality of British military assistance. Their effect on the outcome of the war on land was no more decisive than the *guerre de course* at sea.

Fleet Actions in the European Theater

Once Pitt had perfected his strategic dispositions and strengthened the Channel fleet and both the Brest and Toulon blockading squadrons, he was prepared to push his empire-building plans overseas. He did not feel it necessary to wait for the total destruction of France's divided, land-locked fleet. So in 1757, in 1758, and in 1759 were mounted important British expeditions, whose fortunes will be developed presently. To maintain geographic unity however, it is here convenient to describe two fleet actions in European waters which in 1759 destroyed France's last naval hopes.

Undoubtedly the annoyance of the British

[6] Robert Wright, *The Life of Major General James Wolfe* (London, 1864), 396-7.

"conjunct operations" helped to stimulate the French government to revive the discredited scheme of invasion of England considered earlier in the war. The bold and able Duc de Choiseul had become the war minister for Louis XV. He openly planned to put a French army ashore across the Channel. As in 1756, the prerequisite of success was to secure at least temporary naval supremacy in the "Narrow Seas" by concentrating there the entire French fleet. This involved bringing the Toulon squadron to Brest.

When, in the late summer of 1759, Admiral Edward Boscawen temporarily abandoned the close blockade of the French Mediterranean ports to recondition at Gibraltar, French Admiral Sabran de la Clue with ten of the line took this opportunity to attempt escape to the Atlantic. Though de la Clue weathered the Straits of Gibraltar, Boscawen was alerted by his watch-frigates and gave chase with his more heavily-gunned fleet of 13 of the line and many frigates. De la Clue conceived it his proper mission to avoid action, and fled precipitately. Boscawen cracked on all sail, and by accident of wind and weather brought the French to bay off the Portuguese coast.

Since the French would not stand and fight, there was no question of formalist line tactics here. It was General Chase and devil take the hindmost! By sheer hard fighting the British defeated the French squadron, and drove the survivors into Lagos Bay, which gives the battle its name. There de la Clue deliberately grounded his flagship, and Boscawen, in violation of Portuguese territorial waters, captured three French two-deckers. Another French 74 was burned. The sortie of the Toulon fleet had ended in utter disaster.

In the fall of 1759, Admiral Hubert, Comte de Conflans, commanding in Brest, seized an opportunity to dodge Sir Edward Hawke's persistent blockade. When a northwest gale made the Breton coast a lee shore, the British blockading squadron clawed back into their own Channel ports. Alerting his force, Conflans prepared to up anchor as soon as the wind moderated. He hoped first to defeat a small British squadron operating in the vicinity of Belle Île, and then by dodging the Channel fleet possibly to support a landing in Scotland.

But Hawke was too shrewd to be deceived.

As he came down close-hauled from Torquay and Plymouth on the westerly wind, his frigates reported the sortie of the French fleet from Brest. The English admiral correctly guessed that Conflans must have entered the Bay of Biscay. He sighted the French fleet off the Quiberon Peninsula, and swooped down like a falcon on his prey.

Like de la Clue, Conflans had no intent to stand and fight even a slightly superior British force. Relying on a rising gale and approaching darkness, he signaled a retirement into Quiberon Bay, a reef-strewn difficult anchorage, into which he could not believe the British would dare to follow. Seeing his quarry in full flight, Hawke, like Boscawen at Lagos Bay, felt free to fire a General Chase signal. Setting as much sail as he dared in the heavy weather, each captain sought the honor of first engaging. As the pursuit became protracted, the resultant formation was a straggling line with ships arrayed according to their sailing qualities. The British followed in the French wake, their van engaging the French rear. Both fleets skirted the breakers on the rocks lining the bay entrance, firing when a target presented. Lower deck gunports rolled under water in the heavy seas; one French vessel foundered when she opened them. Hawke finally anchored when nightfall made further chase suicidal. Two British vessels were lost by grounding. The French lost one by gunfire, besides the one that capsized. During the night seven of the French ships jettisoned their guns and, thus lightened, escaped over the bar into the shallow Vilaine River. Seven others slipped their cables and under cover of darkness made their escape to

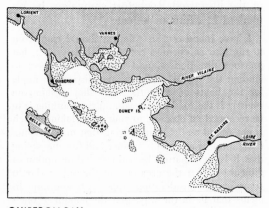

QUIBERON BAY

Rochefort. The following morning Conflans ordered his flagship—the only remaining French vessel—purposely beached to avoid capture.

Thus was destroyed or scattered the last substantial French naval forces. Not again in the war would there be a French invasion threat to England. Not again could there be a substantial challenge to British naval supremacy. Lagos and Quiberon Bay may be thought of as "twin actions" in that each was a decisive British victory, and in that each was won by melee tactics initiated by a General Chase signal by the British commander. Since they did not affect Pitt's major strategy, they were not of great strategic significance. They did however materially reduce the burden of the blockades of Brest and Toulon for the British fleet, and they have an obvious significance in the history of tactics.

The British Capture Louisburg

In America, meanwhile, Pitt had already put his plans in motion. In 1757 an unsuccessful expedition had been mounted from Halifax against Louisburg, the French bastion on Cape Breton Island, which flanked the approaches to the Gulf of St. Lawrence. In 1758 a larger and better-commanded amphibious force, nominally under the superannuated Major General James Abercromby, but effectively under the field command of Lord Jeffrey Amherst, set out to accomplish the same objective. This time Admiral Boscawen held the naval command, and the redoubtable James Wolfe was one of the brigadiers of the assault force.

In a well-planned amphibious assault, the fleet's boats took the troops in under fire to the rocky open coast west of the city. Many boats capsized in the heavy surf, but a contingent of Wolfe's redcoats on the left of the line made a precarious beachhead, which their commander was quick to perceive and exploit. As quickly as they landed, the superbly conditioned British troops wheeled into a bayonet-studded line, charged and cleared the coastal batteries. As reinforcements poured ashore, the English infantry rapidly forced the now-outnumbered French back into the fortifications of the city.

Satisfied that superior British sea power would now cut off French reinforcements and

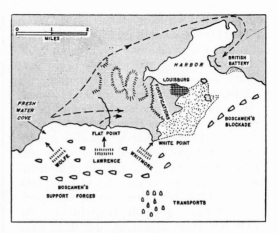

ASSAULT ON LOUISBURG, 1758

supplies, Amherst refused the temptation to assault and settled down to siege. With Boscawen's ships coasting back and forth hull-down on the horizon, there was no likelihood of relief for the besieged. On short rations and without hope, the French garrison finally surrendered in late July, after a six-weeks' investment.

The Quebec Campaign

If Louisburg was the "key to the St. Lawrence," then Quebec was the key to North America. Situated almost a thousand miles within the heartland of the continent, Quebec is located at the point where the St. Lawrence begins to broaden into a great tidal estuary. With the ordnance of the 18th century, the range of shore batteries was adequate to command the river above Quebec, but not below. Protected by the turbulent Montmorency River to the east, and by the cliff-like shore line to the west, the rocky bastions of the "Upper City" were deemed to be virtually impregnable to assault. Yet to control Quebec was to control the upper St. Lawrence, the natural water-highway to the Great Lakes and the whole interior of the continent. To Pitt's perceptive eye, here was a prize worth any cost. Thus the major British overseas effort in 1759 was a three-pronged campaign against Quebec.

Lord Jeffrey Amherst with 12,000 men would strike from the south, using the natural waterway provided by Lake Champlain and the Richelieu River (later to figure importantly in both the American Revolution and the War of 1812). This would entail the capture of French outposts at Fort Ticonderoga and Crown Point. A smaller British force would capture Fort Niagara and converge on Quebec from the west, following the valley of the St. Lawrence.

An amphibious force would meanwhile ascend the St. Lawrence from the sea and operate against Quebec directly, isolating it from seaborne reinforcement and supply. This was a substantial command, consisting of 26 fighting vessels, besides auxiliaries and transports. It ferried 9,200 British regulars, at this epoch of history quite possibly the best soldiers in the world. But most important, the ships were commanded by Admiral Charles Saunders, and the troops by Major General James Wolfe. Together, Wolfe and Saunders proved to be one of the great amphibious partnerships of history.

The campaign plan of the British was well conceived, and their forces, by the standards of colonial war at this time, were exceedingly formidable. The French position, on the contrary, was weakened by a fatal feud between the Marquis de Vaudreuil, the Governor of French North America, and the Marquis de Montcalm, the military commander.

But the French had the benefit of "holding the ground," and geographically Quebec is a very strong position. They had, besides, the advantage of being in the midst of a French colony, with a friendly civilian population scattered up and down the river. They had a potential garrison of 14,000 men and over 300 guns for the defense of their strong point. Furthermore they had in Louis Joseph de Montcalm a talented and experienced commanding officer, altogether unlikely to be fooled by any elementary subterfuge. The French had also been successful in winning the allegiance of most of the Indians. The natural difficulties imposed on a military advance through the trackless wilderness would in any event have delayed the southern and western columns invading Canada, but harassing guerrilla operations by small French forces powerfully reinforced by Indian war parties helped to guarantee that neither of these British commands would reach its goal in time to assist Wolfe and Saunders.

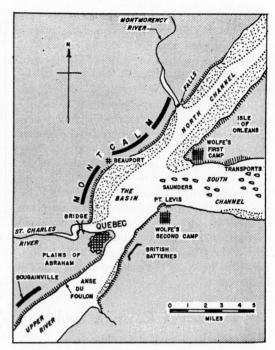

SIEGE OF QUEBEC, 1759

Admiral Saunders meanwhile was bringing Wolfe's army to the threshold of Quebec City. By dint of boat surveys made by British squadrons earlier, and through the grudging aid of captured French-Canadian pilots, he took his whole armada of over a hundred sail up the difficult channel without loss. He anchored just out of cannon shot of Quebec in the South Channel between the Isle of Orleans and Point Lévis. Disembarking the troops from the overcrowded transports, Wolfe first occupied the undefended, low-lying Isle of Orleans and encamped at the extreme western end. Subsequently he sent a column of troops to seize the lightly defended heights of Point Lévis, and emplaced heavy guns there to fire into the "Lower City" across the river. The investing of Quebec had begun.

On several occasions the French attempted to drift down fireships and firerafts on the ebb tide to destroy the anchored British men-of-war, but the ever-watchful Saunders had ships' boats patrolling nightly upriver, and these had little trouble in boathooking the flaming hulks harmlessly to shore. For the most part Montcalm was content to hold a tactical defensive, and depend on his entrenched troops to hold all of the north bank of the river.

By raid and by personal reconnoitering, Wolfe endeavored to find a weak spot in Montcalm's troop dispositions. But there appeared to be none. Leaving the strong walled city lightly garrisoned, the French commander had arrayed the bulk of his force in earthworks along the high ground back of the beach all the way from the St. Charles River to the Montmorency River. The lower reaches of the St. Charles River were covered by two armed hulks sunk athwart it. Thus all the beaches that looked practicable for assault were covered. Westward of the city the river bank was virtually cliff. At those few spots where landing even a single boat was possible, there was an outpost, able to give a prompt alarm. A mobile force under Montcalm's able lieutenant, Louis Antoine de Bougainville, operated upriver also, able to reinforce any threatened picket.

The narrow channel above Quebec made it infeasible for Saunders to take his big ships farther up the river, but flatboats, sloops of war, and even frigates passed under the guns of the city at night. From these, various probing raids were made against positions on the north bank, establishing beyond doubt that the French were alert and ready for any contingency.

After mature consideration of this choice of difficulties, Wolfe elected to prepare his major assault on the French left flank, where it rested on the Montmorency River. Pursuant to this design, he landed two brigades on the east bank of the Montmorency, planning to protect their fording of the stream by a simultaneous frontal assault from boats. Meanwhile the Admiral helped perfect the plan. The offshore shoals and ledges would generally prevent running frigates close enough inshore to give effective fire support, though possibly one well-handled vessel might work its way up the channel carved out by the rapid currents of the Montmorency. To supply at least a minimum of artillery backing for the left and center boat squadrons, Saunders improvised gunboats (called "cats") out of shallow-draft transports, which he intended to beach broadside as close to shore as possible.

On July 31, Wolfe set the scheme in motion. It was a dangerous, almost desperate gamble. To achieve success, everything had to work perfectly, a very rare occurrence in amphibious war.

In fact, the assault worked out very badly. The boats started in brave alignment, but most of them beached on flats well offshore, or had to grope their way through irregular channels in the mudbanks. The grenadier companies, who were among the first troops ashore, broke discipline under the galling fire from the heights to charge the enemy line in driblets before they could be supported either from the boats or from the ford. By the time they could be recalled and re-formed, the day was already far advanced. A severe storm, threatening earlier, now burst, dampening both spirits and primers.

Abruptly deciding to cut his losses before defeat became disaster, Wolfe evacuated his troops under cover of protective fire from Saunders' stranded "cats" and the frigate *Centurion*. The whooping savage allies of the French came pouring down from the heights to butcher the wounded and scalp the dead. Wolfe had left 500 irreplaceable soldiers on the beach.

With the benefit of hindsight, military scholars condemn the Montmorency attack as badly conceived—a misuse of the mobility of sea power, since it involved a frontal assault on a carefully prepared, fixed position. Though the British hoped also to attack the French flank, it was not an *exposed* flank, for it was protected by the swift-flowing Montmorency River, fordable at only one place. The shoals that prevented the fleet from sending its big ships in close enough to lend effective fire support were a crucial factor. For only when seaborne artillery can lay down a crushing barrage just ahead of the infantry as it lands, will a frontal assault on a defended beach have much chance of success. Furthermore, Montcalm's interior lines made reinforcement of any threatened point easy. Only panic among the French defenders or some grievous blunder by Montcalm could have enabled the British to gain their objectives. In weighing risks against the probability of success, the balance was clearly for not making the effort at this location.

Wolfe however at this time could see no alternative. Haunted by the memory of the Rochefort fiasco, he preferred a gallant failure to inaction. As he wrote to Pitt,

. . . the desire to act in conformity to the King's intentions, induced me to make this trial, persuaded that a victorious army find no difficulties.[7]

Soon afterward Wolfe himself became seriously ill of fever. It appeared the campaigning season would end with Saunders having to take his ships out of the river before a decisive blow could be struck. Now the qualities of Wolfe's leadership were put to the test. He had tried a bold stroke and failed. Though perforce the attacker, he was greatly outnumbered. He had not received the reinforcements and relief he had been led to expect from Amherst. His ailing body refused the demands of his soaring spirit. He could, indeed, have sailed for Halifax secure in the reputation of an honorable effort.

But the record shows that neither Wolfe nor Saunders nor any of their principal subordinates had any idea of quitting while they had any resources remaining. Even as Wolfe tossed in delirium, his brigadiers pushed boat expeditions up the river, ever probing for a soft spot. Somewhat concerned by this possible threat to his right flank, Montcalm detached 3,000 men from his garrison and the Montmorency defenses to reinforce Bougainville's guard force. Bougainville, whose role was to protect the whole north bank of the river above Quebec by moving troops to any threatened point, now mustered nearly 4,000 men.

Wolfe was well enough to resume active command in early September, and eager to try a new line of attack. While Saunders feinted a landing at the old beachhead, he would try a surprise attack at the Anse du Foulon, a little boat landing a bare mile and a half upriver from the city walls. The movement was to begin the evening of September 12.

Saunders played his role to perfection, bombarding the ruined lower town and the Beauport beach with every gun that could be brought to bear, ostentatiously loading the ships' boats with marines and seamen as if a

[7] Quoted in R. Beatson, *Memoirs of Great Britain* (London, 1804), II, 290.

new landing were imminent. Meanwhile a strong infantry force in flat-bottomed boats, supported by frigates and sloops-of-war, worked upriver with the tide as if to effect a lodgment far above the city. It was a fine moonlit night, and Bougainville marched the bulk of his force along the shore to parallel this cleverly visible movement.

But when the tide turned, the British boat force began rowing furiously down river. Aided by the tidal current it quickly outdistanced Bougainville's exhausted foot soldiers. The lead boat scraped ashore shortly before dawn at the foot of the narrow rocky path up the bluff at Anse du Foulon. The light infantry swarmed up the slope, and bayoneted the picket force before an alarm could be sounded. Working against time, the officers swiftly disembarked their troops, and sent the boats to help bring reinforcements across from Point Lévis, the British post directly across the river. By clear daylight, Wolfe had spirited 4,500 men up to the Plains of Abraham and had them arrayed in battle order in sight of the walls of Quebec.

The shock of Wolfe's sudden appearance virtually at the city's gates and the chagrin of seeing his nearly perfect defenses so readily breached caused Montcalm for once to abandon his steady good judgment. After all, his immediate command could readily be drawn in behind solid walls built to withstand siege, and somewhere off to the west was Bougainville, with nearly 4,000 stout troops. With a little patience a sortie coordinated with an assault by Bougainville on the British rear might be effected. In such a battle the odds would scarcely favor the outnumbered British, caught in a powerful pincers.

But Montcalm did not wait. He marched out his garrison pell-mell, forming a battle line as it advanced, its front covered by a swarm of skirmishers and marksmen. The British lines waited stolidly, while the French regulars marched steadily to a drumbeat. A six-pounder which some sailors had wormed up the cliff began rapid fire, and cut swathes in the white-clad French column. But the disciplined troops closed ranks and came on. As they approached small arms range, they began to fire, individually and by companies. The British accepted the fire without returning it.

When the French were within 30 yards, the swords of the British officers flashed up. Then down. "Fire!" That great double-shotted volley may be said to have won Canada for Britain. It swept great windrows of French soldiery to the earth. Exercising superb fire-discipline, the British infantry rapidly reloaded, and delivered another volley before the French could recover from the shock of the first. After that it was a disorganized melee, rapidly turning into a rout. While the bagpipes of the highland regiments skirled madly, the demoralized French fled the field before the British bayonets and Scottish broadswords.

Montcalm was mortally wounded; his second and third in command were killed outright. The British lost their quartermaster-general and one of their brigadiers. Wolfe, leading a charge of the Louisburg Grenadiers, was himself fatally injured, and was dead in the hour of victory.

The command devolved upon Brigadier George Townshend, who quickly re-formed the troops. He had hardly done so when the advance guard of Bougainville's force appeared in the British rear. But Bougainville deemed it prudent to withdraw without a fight. Townshend rapidly put out siege lines around the city and began the laborious work of building redoubts and siting batteries. Before this could be far advanced, the garrison recognized the hopelessness of its position and surrendered.

This durable triumph of British arms is a monument to excellent interservice cooperation, rather rare in military and naval annals until World War II. This unity of purpose and achievement is reflected in Townshend's report to Pitt, in which he says:

I should not do justice to the Admirals, and the naval service, if I neglected this occasion of acknowledging how much we are indebted for our success to the constant assistance and support received from them, and the perfect harmony and correspondence which has prevailed throughout all our operations, in the uncommon difficulties which the nature of this country, in particular, presents to military operations of a great extent, and which no army can itself solely supply; the immense labour in artillery, stores, and provisions; the long watchings and attendance in boats; the drawing up our artillery by the seamen, even in the heat of action. It is my duty, short as my command has been, to acknowledge, for that time, how great a share the navy has had in this successful campaign.[8]

Events in India

The winning of India for the British *raj* is a saga in itself—the most decisive chapter of which was written during the Seven Years' War. The prime contestants in this theater of war were the great trading companies—the French and the British East India companies, each almost a sovereign power with its own fleet and army. But the prizes of success were so obvious and considerable that each was able to secure the aid of royal forces. Ultimate British victory was due in part to a slight preponderance in Indian waters, in part to the genius of Robert Clive, commander of the British East India Company's troops, in part to the professional skill of the Royal Navy's admirals, Charles Watson in the early part of the campaign and, after Watson's death in 1757, Sir George Pocock.

The French naval commander, the Comte d'Aché, was a competent tactician, whom Pocock in several engagements failed to defeat decisively. But, after the fall of Chandernagor, d'Aché was handicapped by having no base for refitting nearer than Mauritius, some 2,000 miles to the southwest, across the Indian Ocean. Pocock could refit and wait out the monsoon season in Bombay. Furthermore, d'Aché failed to receive from France needed reinforcements and supplies.

The major naval phase of the Indian campaign occurred between April 1758 and October 1759, when d'Aché sailed his battered fleet away from India for the last time.

The first major fleet engagement occurred on April 29, 1758, when Pocock sailed his squadron to the relief of Fort St. David, a British post on the Coromandel (southeastern) Coast of India. With seven ships, Pocock gained the weather gage of d'Aché's eight, and attempted a conventional attack in formal column. The three rear ships of Pocock's column straggled behind the van. The lead ships suffered the concentrated fire of the French line when d'Aché's force wore ship and defiled past

[8] Beatson, *Memoirs of Great Britain,* II, 306.

the British flagship. The French withdrew as the British rear finally came to the support of its van ships. The British ships that had been engaged were far too crippled through injuries aloft for Pocock to attempt pursuit. Fort St. David was obliged to surrender to French forces ashore.

A second engagement took place in August under much the same conditions and with similar results. Pocock was bold enough in seeking out his adversary, but in attack he was firmly committed to the conterminous line. D'Aché was chary in accepting action, always aware that his adversary had better local logistic support and could more readily repair damages. But he handled his ships skillfully and parried Pocock's attacks.

A final major action took place after the monsoon season in September 1759, when Pocock sought out the French off Pondicherry. After considerable prior maneuvering, d'Aché, with eleven ships to Pocock's nine, once more accepted the British attack. Though this too was a conventional line-against-line action, it was fought at close range and with uncommon fury by both sides. The British in this single engagement suffered 569 casualties, and the French losses were of the order of 1,500 killed and wounded. Here again the French withdrew, and the British were too severely damaged in rigging to give chase.

These battles were all tactical draws. In only one of them was even one ship lost, a French vessel that had to be beached after the action to save her personnel. These encounters were object lessons in the indecisiveness of formalist tactics. Yet they had great strategic importance. From the British point of view, since Clive was winning the war ashore, and since reinforcements and supplies could be sent freely from Britain and only with great difficulty from France, for Pocock merely to continue *contesting* the seas around the subcontinent was enough to insure ultimate British victory.

Presently d'Aché abandoned the whole area to the British, perhaps in part because he was informed of a four-ship reinforcement being sent out to the British squadron. In the peninsula Clive profited from this sea supremacy and destroyed the remaining French forces. Though Pondicherry and some other minor enclaves were restored at the peace, India was to remain substantially British until after World War II.

Operations in the West Indies

In the mid-18th century, the islands of the Caribbean enjoyed an economic importance hard to realize today. Enormous fortunes were made by the sugar planters. Indeed, except for the tea and spices of the Far East, the West Indies supplied nearly all the tropical products taken by the European market. As buyers these islands were also important in the cruel but profitable African slave trade. As will be apparent in subsequent chapters, their trade relationships with the 13 English colonies on the North American seaboard were also significant, though largely illicit.

As we have seen, many of the Antilles had changed hands from time to time in earlier wars. But by the time of the Seven Years' War, tradition had sanctified Spain's claim to Cuba and Puerto Rico; England's, to Jamaica, Antigua, and Barbados; France's, to Martinique and Guadaloupe. The Netherlands also had some small possessions in the area—Curaçao, Aruba, and the tiny island of St. Eustatius. Santo Domingo was divided between France and Spain.

Since "filching sugar islands" had become established practice in maritime war, Pitt at the earliest convenient opportunity set about uprooting France from her valuable Caribbean possessions. Apart from his general empire-building objective, Pitt was motivated by the depredations of privateers based on Martinique and Guadaloupe. From the beginning of the war, these had raised havoc with English commercial shipping in the area, particularly where the trade routes converged on passes in the island barrier offered by the Lesser Antilles.

In early 1759 Commodore John Moore with nine ships of the line and a frigate escorted a military force under Major General Peregrine Hopson, a courageous but elderly and infirm veteran, to attack Martinique. Operations against Fort Royal, and later against St. Pierre, though bravely sustained by the rank and file, were unsuccessful—partly because of the strength of the defense, but also because of the vacillation, lack of thorough planning, and

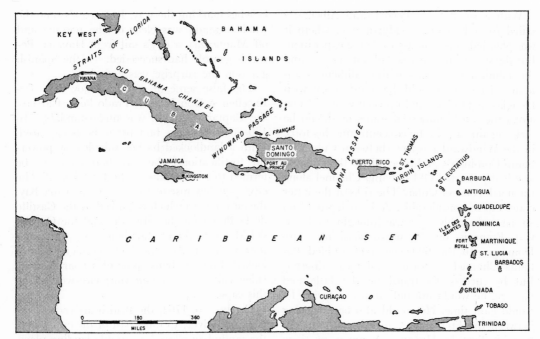

THE WEST INDIES

faulty cooperation between the military and the naval command. The expedition was then diverted to less heavily defended Guadaloupe.

Here in the face of discouraging advice from his chief engineer, Moore proceeded to bombard and silence the fortifications of Basse-Terre, the capital. The troops were able to occupy the town and forts without opposition. But the French troops made a campaign of it in the interior of the island, so that it was three months before the whole of Guadaloupe was secured. Major General John Barrington, who succeeded to the military command on the death of Hopson in February, showed a vigor and imagination lacking in his former chief. Though outnumbered, he maintained a calculated program of small attacks, utilizing boats and small craft to get behind enemy strong points by water. The French finally surrendered just a day too soon. One day after the capitulation, a relief force under Commodore de Bompart appeared, now too late to undo Barrington's skillful work.

In 1760 Commodore James Douglas and Lord Rollo stormed Dominica. In 1762 a very strong force under Admiral George Rodney and General Moncton captured Martinique in a three weeks' campaign. Grenada fell simul-taneously. Captain Augustus John Hervey was at once dispatched to St. Lucia. Both it and St. Vincent's were presently in British hands— a clean sweep of all the French possessions in the Lesser Antilles.

Spain entered the war in January 1762. Earlier the combination of the Spanish and French fleets could well have presented a mortal danger to England. But by now the French fleet had been broken, and Spain's involvement at this time spelled to England merely opportunity. For Spain's treasure-laden convoys were an open invitation to depredation by the cruisers of the British navy, and Spain had enormously rich dependencies in the West Indies and the Far East.

Since England already had squadrons and soldiers in the West Indies, an operation against Havana was put in train almost at once. It was hoped that with reinforcements from England and America, it would be possible for the Earl of Albemarle to take at least 15,000 effectives against Spain's Caribbean bastion. Admiral Sir George Pocock would have 50-odd fighting ships (including 22 rated at 60 guns or more). With transports and auxiliaries the invading armada would amount to about 200 sail.

With a small force Pocock and Albemarle sailed from England to Martinique, where it was planned at first to assemble the expedition. But the supporting vessels had not arrived, and the admiral was faced with a difficult command decision. Should he rendezvous with Douglas in Jamaica and proceed west of Cuba along the safe commercial route, or should he seek to gain surprise by concentrating his force in the Windward Passage (between Cuba and Santo Domingo), and proceed via the tortuous and badly charted Old Bahama Channel along the north coast of Cuba? The risks of the latter course were considerable. A French squadron stronger than his own was thought to be at Cap Français, on the north coast of Santo Domingo. In the 600-mile, reef-studded Bahama Channel, a storm could mean disaster. But by successfully transiting the little-used passage, he would not only insure surprise; he would gain time. He would also be operating between the French at Cap Français and the Spanish fleet in Havana. A union of these forces would thereby be made less likely. Furthermore his route would favor a speedier meeting with the transport force expected from America.

Pocock considered that the advantages of assembling off Cape St. Nicholas outweighed the dangers. Dispatches were sent to Hervey and to Rear Admiral Sir James Douglas, commanding the Jamaica squadron. Pocock then moved his convoy north, through the Mona Passage (between Santo Domingo and Puerto Rico), and coasted westward along Santo Domingo. When he reached a point where a French sally from Cap Français might endanger his force, the admiral was reassured to find Hervey with seven of the line already blockading the roadstead.

Sending a frigate ahead to survey, Pocock awaited Douglas off Cape St. Nicholas for a week. When Douglas' nine ships appeared, the British set out at once to thread their way through the Old Bahama Channel. Local pilots were procured, but their value was slight. An old Spanish chart given to Pocock by Lord Anson and the survey work of Captain Elphinstone in the frigate *Richmond* were however sufficient. The most dangerous narrows was transited at night, with beacon fires on the beaches marking the way. In a week's time the whole armada was clear of the passage and off Mantanzas, a day's sail from Havana. Pocock's gamble had succeeded. To the Spanish garrison the surprise was complete.

The false sense of security enjoyed by His Excellency, Don Juan de Prado Porto Carrero, the Captain-General, was understandable. In 150 years Havana had never been captured. With a landlocked harbor shielded by powerful fortifications, the city had come to be termed the "Gibraltar of the Caribbean." The city itself lies just to the west of Havana Bay, the entrance to which is flanked by the Castillo de la Punta on the city side, and the Castillo del Morro to the east at the end of a promontory which makes the bay completely landlocked. Like the bony spine of a boar, a rocky ridge called *la Cabaña* runs east-west along this cape.

On June 6, 1762, the British arrived off the Coximar River, 15 miles east of the city, where the sandy bay offered a suitable landing place. After battering down the blockhouses with cannon fire, Pocock set the troops ashore at this point, and then proceeded to threaten the city by a feinted landing to the west of it.

Had Albemarle fully exploited the advantage of tactical surprise, he might well have taken Havana by a *coup de main* without a costly siege of the Morro. But Albemarle was a continental general, trained in the school of formalism. He was determined to invest the Morro and take it by storm if necessary.

So for nearly two months the rank-and-file suffered agonies in the tropical summer. Guns from the fleet were laboriously winched into position. Above-ground works had to be built on the rocky ledges since there was too little earth for entrenchments. The fascines took fire from enemy shot. There was no water on the whole peninsula; it had to be brought by boat from the fleet, and there was never enough. Spanish resistance was stubborn and unremitting.

Pocock's task of blockade was rendered almost needless by the Spaniards themselves. In spite of the very strong fortifications on each side of the half-mile-wide entrance to the harbor, they deliberately sank three of their ships of the line as blockships in the channel, thereby locking in their remaining nine, and incidentally freeing Pocock from the responsibility of guarding against a sortie.

As in all West Indian operations, the most severe toll of casualties was from disease, especially yellow fever, which struck down many times the number lost in battle. The reinforcements from Lord Amherst were slow in arriving, and for a time in July it began to look as though the expedition would fail.

But though a mediocre tactician, Albemarle had perseverance. Sappers finally completed a tunnel under the shoreward walls of the Morro, where a mine was exploded, and the redcoats swarmed through the narrow gap it blew out. They hunted down the defenders in the stone corridors of the fortress in a matter of minutes. With the Morro in British hands, the city also was obliged to surrender.

Few conquests of any war have had the immediate cash value of the capture of Havana. Spain lost a fifth of her fleet—in a nearly undamaged condition. Over a hundred major pieces of ordnance and great quantities of other war materials and commercial valuables (including chests of specie) fell into British hands. Both the commanding general and the admiral received £122,000 in prize money.[9]

In the Havana operation the role of the fleet was indispensable—both in fighting and in logistic support. Like Saunders at Quebec, Pocock at Havana set an example of selfless cooperation for subsequent naval commanders. Albemarle himself wrote:

. . . Sir George Pocock, and Commodore Keppel have exerted themselves in a most particular manner; and I may venture to say, that there never was a joint undertaking carried on with more harmony and zeal on both sides. . . .[10]

Other Operations

Because control of the seas gave the British a virtually free choice of where and when to strike, Britain was able not merely to conduct those major operations which would contribute materially to the outcome of the war. She was also from time to time capable of investing a fraction of her power in "sideshow operations," which had but commercial importance, or which might slightly improve her bargaining position at the peace table. Her seizure in 1758 of the French slave-trading stations of Goree and Senegal in the Guinea Gulf is an example. And in 1760 Pitt renewed "conjunct operations" against the French coast, sending a considerable force to seize Belle Île.

In 1762 a group of private English adventurers equipped a shoestring expedition to Buenos Aires. With two frigates purchased from the British government and two small Portuguese men-of-war, and 500 Portuguese troops, they set out from Rio de Janeiro to try to do in Spain's vast mainland colony what Clive with his little handful had done at Plassey and Windewash. Through poor piloting in the Plata estuary and through the mischances of war this effort came to disaster.

The capstone of the British war effort overseas was the Manila expedition, undertaken by East India Company troops under Brigadier William Draper and an eight-ship squadron commanded by Vice Admiral Samuel Cornish. After bombardment and siege, Manila fell in less than two weeks. The Governor surrendered the entire Philippines and ransomed Manila for $4,000,000 (Spanish). Since the squadron also captured the Acapulco galleon with $3,000,000 in specie and bullion, the prize money rivaled that in the capture of Havana.

The End of the War

The complicated patterns of European power politics shifted with bewildering rapidity in the last stages of the Seven Years' War. With victorious peace almost in sight, Pitt resigned when the Cabinet refused his demand for an immediate declaration of war against Spain.[11] Spain attempted invasion of Portugal, England's ancient ally, only to be frustrated by a British fleet and expeditionary force. Pitt's bumbling successor in the Cabinet, Lord Bute, alienated Frederick the Great and destroyed

[9] There is an instructive sidelight on the social hierarchy of the 18th century in the fact that a private's share was £4.1s.8½d; an able seaman's, £3.14s.9¾d.

[10] Letter to Lord Egremont, quoted in Beatson, *Memoirs of Great Britain*, II, 566.

[11] Pitt's resignation is ironic in that events made the declaration inevitable soon thereafter in any case.

the Prussian alliance. The Russian Czarina died, and was succeeded by the nearly idiotic Prussophile Peter III, who signed an immediate peace with Frederick. Peter III was presently assassinated, but Catherine II, who succeeded him, would not renew the war. Sweden withdrew from the Grand Coalition. Their allies gone, nearly exhausted, and without further expedient, France and Austria both sued for peace.

The Peace of Paris (1763) represented the high-water mark of Britain's "Old Empire." Everywhere victorious, the British might well have demanded even more than they took. And they took the lion's share. Britain received Canada and a cession of French claims to all territory east of the Mississippi. She thereby unwittingly defined the boundaries of the then undreamed-of United States of America, to be established 13 years later. From France Britain also received Senegal. From Spain she received Florida in exchange for Cuba. She had Minorca returned to her. To France were restored Belle Île, Guadaloupe, Martinique, St. Lucia, Goree, the French trading stations in India (which France promised not to fortify), and the little North Atlantic islands of Miquelon and St. Pierre. To Spain were restored Cuba and the Philippines. France helped to make the treaty more acceptable to Spain by ceding to her New Orleans and the Louisiana Territory, a primeval empire of unsurveyed dimensions to the west of the Mississippi River.

Summary

The Seven Years' War was the first of the world wars. It is the archetype of wars between a strong land power and a strong sea power. In it Britain followed the pattern she had employed earlier against Spain, Holland, and France of allying with other continental powers against a major continental power. The distinctive strategic feature of the Seven Years' War, from the British point of view, was Pitt's Plan, a strategy toward which Britain had been groping since the Anglo-Dutch Wars.

On the worldwide scale, Pitt's strategy, like all strategies that achieve true concentration, had both a *hitting* and a *holding* aspect. The main British offensive, the hitting aspect, was carried out beyond the seas—using England's naval preponderance to support attacks on the colonies of France and Spain. Capture of these colonies expanded the British Empire, promoted trade, and thereby produced wealth. A part of this increased wealth went to subsidize Britain's allies on the continent of Europe. The holding aspect consisted of 1) the efforts of the Royal Navy in first blockading and then destroying the French fleet and 2) the efforts of Britain's allies, chiefly Frederick the Great of Prussia, in absorbing French wealth and containing French manpower that might otherwise have been used to build up the French navy, break the British blockade, and succor France's overseas possessions.

Within the European theater also, Pitt's Plan had a hitting and a holding aspect. Here Frederick's army was the principal hitting element, while British "conjunct expeditions" along the coast of France were intended in part to make the French sufficiently fearful of an invasion to hold back troops that might otherwise have been sent against Frederick.

France's counter-strategy against Britain consisted of 1) raids on British maritime commerce, 2) attempts to defend French colonies, and 3) attempts to invade England. Britain's naval preponderance rendered all such efforts futile. Belleisle's scheme for invading the British Isles by eluding the Channel fleet died in the planning stage, but his Mediterranean diversion resulted in the repulse of Byng's fleet and the capture of Minorca (1756). Later French invasion plans, requiring the combining of the Toulon and Brest fleets in the English Channel, were nullified when the former was destroyed by Boscawen in the Battle of Lagos Bay (1759) and the latter by Hawke in the Battle of Quiberon Bay (1759).

While France was expending her strength and treasure in the fruitless war in Europe, relatively minor British forces were capturing French possessions all around the world. In 1758 Amherst and Boscawen opened the St. Lawrence River by capturing Louisburg. In 1759 Wolfe and Saunders assured the British conquest of Canada by capturing Quebec. At the same time Clive, with the naval cooperation of Watson and Pocock, was winning control over India, and such army-navy teams as those of Barrington and Moore, Rollo and Douglas, and Moncton and Rodney were seizing French possessions in the West Indies. When Spain allied herself with France in 1762, she was promptly dispossessed of Havana by Albemarle and Pocock, and of Manila by Draper and Cornish. Such conquests were rendered possible by French preoccupation with the European war and by the sea control of the Royal Navy that isolated the colonies, denying them assistance from the homeland.

All wars have their object lessons for the thoughtful student. The Seven Years' War, more than most, is replete with lessons and examples. The following are among those most evident.

The strict adherence to line tactics, as enjoined by the Permanent Fighting Instructions, prevented decisive victory, since it rendered tactical concentration nearly impossible. The Minorca action and the several engagements of Pocock and d'Aché in Indian waters exemplify this. On the other hand melee tactics, initiated by General Chase, won smashing victories at Lagos and at Quiberon Bay.

In amphibious war, careful planning, unstinted interservice cooperation, boldness of leadership, and perseverance are essential. These were lacking in the Rochefort operation and in the first Martinique invasion, both of which failed. Wolfe and Saunders at Quebec, Moore and Barrington at Guadaloupe, and Albemarle and Pocock at Havana showed the qualities necessary to accomplish this most difficult of military tasks—assault on land positions from the sea.

Pitt is the model of the Commander in Chief, characterized by unity of purpose, consistency, and decisiveness. In the chess game of war, he saw the board as a whole. He disposed his pieces so that each aided all the others. The ineptness of the British conduct of the war before Pitt came to power, and its lessened efficiency after he left the government, evidenced his indispensability. Because Pitt thought naturally in grand strategic terms, he could insure not merely victory, but a chance for England to secure all her war aims.

Above everything else the great lesson of the Seven Years' War is the pervasive and inexorable power of naval preponderance in a world war. The British navy at once kept the tight little island secure from invasion and made possible winning half the world for empire. Pitt's vision, in which the continental war became secondary, was based on his perception of the potential of sea power. It is natural that the great American naval historian, Alfred Thayer Mahan, should have turned to the history of England between 1660 and 1783 to mine object-lessons to support his sea power thesis. In his chapter on the Seven Years' War he concludes,

[Sea power] . . . made [England] rich, and in turn protected the trade by which she had her wealth. With her money she upheld her few auxiliaries, mainly Prussia and Hanover, in their desperate strife. Her power was everywhere her ships could reach, and there was none to dispute the sea to her. Where she would she went, and with her went her guns and her troops. By this mobility her forces were multiplied, those of her enemies distracted. Ruler of the seas, she everywhere obstructed its highways. The enemies' fleets could not join; no great fleet could get out, or if it did, it was only to meet at once, with uninured officers and crews, those who were veterans in gales and warfare. Save in the case of Minorca, she carefully held her own sea-bases and eagerly seized those of the enemy. What a lion in the path was Gibraltar to the French squadrons of Toulon and Brest! What hope for French succor to Canada, when the English fleet had Louisburg under its lee?

The one nation that gained in this war was that which used the sea in peace to earn its wealth, and ruled it in war by the extent of its navy, by the number of its subjects who lived on the sea or by the sea, and by its numerous bases of operations scattered over the globe.[12]

[12] Mahan, *Influence of Sea Power upon History*, 328–9.

4:

The War of the American Revolution, I

By the close of the Seven Years' War the Duc de Choiseul, France's Minister of Foreign Affairs, had come to understand what Pitt had known from the beginning—that sea power was the key to colonial conquest. It was then too late to save Canada and India, but immediately after the peace Choiseul added the post of Minister of Marine to his duties and began to rebuild the French navy.

Of the 60 ships of the line with which France had begun the war, she had lost 37 by wreck or capture. To replace these, Choiseul persuaded the cities and provinces of France to raise money for gifts of ships to the navy. Eighteen were provided in this manner, including the famous *Ville de Paris,* the finest of her day. Choiseul also reorganized the Department of Marine, improved dockyards and arsenals, formed a corps of engineers from among the most skilled workmen, and revived the manufacture of cannon, of which the French navy had been almost fatally short during the war.

While the French were thus purposefully rebuilding their navy, the British allowed theirs to decline in strength and efficiency. Although appropriations were far larger than they had been even at the height of the war, inordinate amounts were consumed in the maintenance of vessels that had been hastily built of imported oak, which quickly decayed. More serious, the corruption prevalent in British politics had penetrated the Admiralty. Here it appears to have been condoned, if not actually fostered, by the able but worldly Earl of Sandwich, who became First Lord in 1771. Large sums voted for the repair and refitting of ships disappeared while the vessels rotted in the docks. Money for rations was regularly appropriated for a larger number of seamen than were actually serving. As a result of such practices, the official lists ceased to bear any relation to the actual strength of the navy. When war broke out in America, there were not enough ships ready to provide even the modest strength required on the American station.

The Outbreak of the American Revolution

Choiseul was astute enough to foresee the most likely opportunity for using the navy he had revivified. Writing soon after the Seven Years' War, he observed, concerning Britain's American colonies:

As long as the vast American possessions contribute no subsidies for the support of the mother country, private persons in England will still grow rich for some time on the trade with America, but the state will be undone for want of means to keep together a too-extended power; if, on the contrary, England proposes to establish imposts in her American domains, . . . they will easily part from her, without any fear of chastisement, for England could not undertake a war against them to chastise them.[1]

As Choiseul had prophesied, it was the tightening up of the mercantilist system and the reassertion of British authority in the colonies after the Seven Years' War that led to the defection of the Americans. The Revenue Act of 1764, with its threat of actual collection of a threepence-a-gallon molasses duty, appalled merchants and distillers who had habitually evaded the previous sixpence duty. The Stamp Act of 1765, by asserting Parliament's internal taxing power, united in opposition colonies that had grown accustomed to a large measure of practical independence.

[1] Quoted in François Guizot, *History of France,* trans. Robert Black, V (New York, n.d.), 259.

Although the Stamp Act was repealed, the Townshend Acts of 1767, providing for import duties on paper, lead, and tea, indirectly brought about the "Boston Massacre" of 1770. "Have a care," Pitt warned the British government soon after Lord North became Prime Minister in 1770. "Foreign war is suspended over your heads by a thin and fragile thread. Spain and France are watching your conduct, waiting for your blunders; they have their eyes fixed on America."

The Boston Tea Party of 1773 began a chain of events that led to war. This act of defiance caused Parliament to pass the Coercive Acts, which among other things closed the port of Boston and abolished the long-established liberties of Massachusetts, taking from the people the right of selecting their Council. "The die is cast:" wrote George III, "the colonies must either triumph or submit."[2] British attempts to enforce the Coercive Acts led to shooting at Lexington and Concord in April 1775. After that there was little room for moderation or reconciliation.

For Britain the war presented peculiar difficulties. Eighteenth-century logistics were weak at best, and many overseas expeditions of the era failed primarily because the invader was unable to organize, transport, and supply a suitable force. Moving troops and supplies in quantity across the Atlantic, a passage that might easily take two months, was a stupendous task. Recognizing the difficulty, Lord Barrington, British Secretary of State for War, suggested a naval blockade to bring the colonists to terms. But Lord George Germain, the Colonial Secretary, who was to direct the war, seems scarcely to have considered such a strategy. The temptation to punish the colonies by conventional occupation was reinforced by a desire to protect the loyalists ("Tories"), who were expected to assist. Britain was thus committed to a course that ultimately proved disastrous.

The American Offensive, 1775

Although the fray at Lexington and Concord had precipitated hostilities, more than a year passed before the colonies declared their

[2] Quoted in John Richard Green, *History of the English People* (London, 1885–86), IV, 253.

independence. While the British were still gathering their forces, the colonials seized the opportunity and initiated a series of military operations that amounted to an American offensive.

Less than a month after Concord, Ethan Allen took Fort Ticonderoga on Lake Champlain, key to communications between the rebellious colonies and Canada. In the autumn of 1775, colonial forces invaded Canada, hoping that the Canadians might join them in resistance to Britain. General Richard Montgomery, leading a thousand men by the Hudson River-Lake Champlain route, took Montreal in November. Then, joined by Benedict Arnold, who had led 600 men across northern Maine, he assaulted Quebec on the last day of the year. With Montgomery killed and Arnold wounded, the attack failed, but Arnold maintained a siege of the city till spring, when melting ice permitted the British to bring in reinforcements via the St. Lawrence River.

In Boston, center of hostilities, the British found themselves besieged by 16,000 American militia who had swarmed to the city from the surrounding colonies. The defenders were virtually helpless until the arrival in May 1775 of Major General Sir William Howe, accompanied by Generals Clinton and Burgoyne and 10,000 troops. General George Washington took command of the American forces in July and undertook to organize the raw militia into an army, but he had so little gunpowder that his troops could scarcely return the British fire. In early March 1776 he emplaced cannon from Fort Ticonderoga on Dorchester Heights, overlooking Boston from the south. General Howe, having had enough of storming American-held heights at Bunker Hill the year before and finding his position untenable, evacuated Boston by sea and retired to Halifax, Nova Scotia, where he waited till early June for reinforcements from England.

If Washington had needed any lesson on the importance of sea power, the unopposed withdrawal of the British from Boston would have supplied it. So long as the British had free use of the sea, the Americans were helpless either to prevent the evacuation of a beaten army or to prevent seaborne forays along the coast.

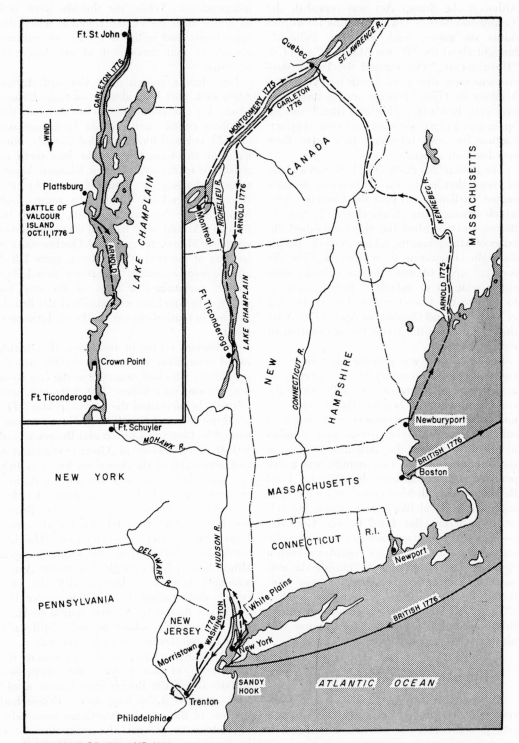

CAMPAIGNS OF 1775 AND 1776

The Americans on the Defensive, 1776

In 1776 the British, having assembled their forces, took the initiative. In the north, Sir Guy Carleton, Governor General of Canada, now reinforced by British regulars under General Burgoyne, planned to penetrate the colonies by the Champlain-Hudson route. A second British expedition was to attack a point in the southern colonies as a diversion, while the main British army under General Howe seized New York City as a base and began operations against Washington's army. Each portion of this plan required some sort of naval support.

In the spring of 1776 Arnold retreated to Lake Champlain, where he began the rapid expansion of the tiny American fleet already on the lake, thereby forcing the pursuing British to stop and build a superior fleet. For obviously Carleton could not maintain his line of supply with an undefeated enemy naval force in his rear. With materials brought overland and by small boats up the Richelieu River, the British constructed a 180-ton ship. In addition, they dismantled two schooners on the St. Lawrence and reassembled them on the lake. These vessels easily gave them superiority over Arnold's motley collection of smaller craft.

When the British squadron was finally ready, on October 11, it moved down the lake before a north wind. Arnold's force, concealed behind Valcour Island, let it pass, thus obliging the enemy to beat back upwind to attack him. Despite this advantage, the Americans suffered so severely in the ensuing battle that they were fortunate to succeed that night in slipping past the British squadron toward Crown Point. The British pursued, and in a running two-day battle most of the American vessels were either captured or beached and burned, while the survivors took to the woods.

While the British could congratulate themselves that they had rendered Canada secure, their months of shipbuilding had cost them their strategic opportunity, for mid-October was too close to winter for them to resume their advance. "If we had begun our expedition four weeks earlier," lamented one of Carleton's officers, "I am satisfied that everything would have ended this year." In the circumstances however there was nothing for the British to do but retire to Canada.

American naval power had scored its first and, as events were to prove, its most important success, for it had delayed the invasion when there was little else to do it. The colonists were thereby granted time to gather forces which in 1777 would win the victory that brought France into the war and tipped the balance in their favor.

The second British operation of 1776, the diversion to the south, was a failure. A squadron attempting to land troops at Charleston, South Carolina, was repulsed by fire from Fort Moultrie, a hastily erected sand-and-log fortification, with heavy casualties in the bombarding vessels.

Only the expedition against New York was a success. Washington had fully anticipated this British move, for New York's harbor occupied a central position on the American coast, and the city secured the southern terminus of the Hudson-Champlain route to Canada, which in British hands would split New England from the southern colonies. Hence he promptly moved troops from Boston to Long Island despite the obvious vulnerability of Long Island to sea power. Here he was at first puzzled and then alarmed by the failure of the British to appear.

Finally at the end of June General Howe arrived, escorted by a fleet under the command of his brother, Admiral Richard Lord Howe. Even then General Howe marked time on Staten Island until the arrival of a convoy of Hessian troops and the return of the inglorious Charleston expedition gave him some 30,000 men to oppose Washington's 10,000. Then, on August 27, Howe crossed to Long Island and began a leisurely advance. Washington slowly withdrew, aided by winds that prevented British frigates from supporting Howe's left flank and by a fog that enabled him to slip across to Manhattan on the night of the 30th. Within two months he was forced north to White Plains, whence he crossed the Hudson into New Jersey. In another month he was forced across the Delaware into Pennsylvania.

By this time Washington's army had dwin-

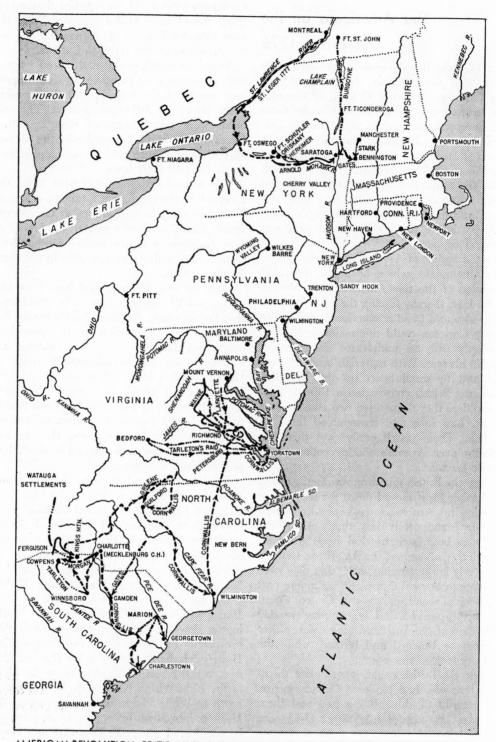

AMERICAN REVOLUTION: BRITISH INVASIONS FROM NORTH AND SOUTH

dled to a mere 3,000 men, and only the lateness of the season prevented Howe from advancing on and taking Philadelphia, seat of the Continental Congress. It was at this point, when the colonial cause seemed hopeless, that Washington demonstrated his greatness as a general by his dramatic crossing of the Delaware and capture of Trenton on Christmas Day. After a series of attacks on British outposts, by which he regained control of the greater part of New Jersey, Washington took a position at Morristown, from which he could threaten any British move toward Philadelphia or up the Hudson.

Early American Naval Efforts

Although Washington had no naval experience, he was quick to understand the importance of sea power. Even while conducting the siege of Boston in 1775 he had on his own initiative and without authorization from Congress begun to ready vessels to prey upon British shipping—with the dual objective of embarrassing the enemy and relieving his own army's acute shortage of powder. These vessels he manned with troops from maritime areas, particularly Salem, Marblehead, and Beverly. The first, the schooner *Hannah,* sailed in early September and soon returned with a prize. By the end of October Washington had half a dozen vessels in operation, but the results were far from satisfactory. The crews were unruly and the officers often incompetent. Only Captain John Manly showed the qualities requisite for successful command; at the beginning of 1776 Washington made him Commodore of the fleet. After Washington moved to New York, the little squadron continued for a while to cruise Massachusetts Bay, but early in 1777 it was broken up and the vessels were disposed of by order of the Marine Committee of the Continental Congress, whereupon some of its officers transferred to the new Continental Navy. In its short existence "Washington's navy" had taken some 35 prizes, which considerably eased the American logistic problem.

Congress had taken the first steps toward creating a Continental Navy by establishing in October 1775 a "Naval Committee" to acquire and fit out vessels for sea and to draw up regulations. The following month the committee purchased two ships, two brigs, and subsequently two sloops and two schooners, and Congress established a Marine Corps by authorizing the raising of two battalions of marines. Esek Hopkins, brother of the Rhode Island member of the Naval Committee, was appointed "Commander in Chief of the Fleet." Despite the obvious nepotism, Hopkins was a reasonable choice. He had gone to sea at the age of 20 and had become the prosperous commodore of a fleet of 17 merchantmen. In the Seven Years' War he had proved himself a daring privateersman.

Taking advantage of a discretionary clause, Hopkins disregarded his orders to clear the Virginia and Carolina coasts of enemy forces, and sailed instead for the Bahamas, where there was reportedly a supply of powder. He landed a force on New Providence in early March, 1776, took the two forts guarding Nassau after only token opposition, and then spent two weeks loading the captured munitions.

This was the squadron's only cruise. Partly because of deficiencies in the vessels themselves, partly because of the impossibility of enlisting adequate crews. Hopkins found himself unable to obey orders to go to sea and attack the Newfoundland fisheries. He was called before Congress to explain his conduct and, despite an able defense by John Adams, he was censured. Individual vessels however made successful cruises. Captain Nicholas Biddle, in the brig *Andrew Doria,* took several prizes, while Captain John Paul Jones in the sloop *Providence* captured 16 merchantmen off Nova Scotia. In a subsequent cruise in the *Alfred,* Jones took several more, including an armed vessel laden with winter clothing for Burgoyne's army.

After Hopkins' raid on New Providence, the Continental Navy participated in only one major operation—the so-called Penobscot Expedition of 1779. This was primarily a Massachusetts enterprise against the British-Tory base at Castine, Maine, but the 16 fighting ships that accompanied the transports were stiffened by three vessels of the Continental Navy, of which the most powerful was the frigate *Warren,* 32, under Captain Dudley

Saltonstall, who commanded the expedition. Arriving at Castine in the latter part of July, the ill-managed force made such slow progress that a British relief squadron had time to arrive from New York in mid-August, whereupon the Americans fled ignominiously up the river and beached their vessels.

All the 13 colonies except New Jersey and Delaware created state navies during the war, but these consisted principally of small craft and conducted few operations of significance. Rhode Island led the way when, in June 1775, she fitted out two sloops to deal with a British vessel that had been patrolling Narragansett Bay. Connecticut followed by fitting out two vessels in July of the same year—a force eventually increased to twelve. Pennsylvania concentrated chiefly on small craft to defend the Delaware River. Virginia created a large fleet of light craft to stop the depredations of a squadron formed by Tory Governor Dunmore. South Carolina provided one of the larger navies, having 15 seagoing vessels.

Privateers made by far the most effective contribution to the American naval effort. In the spring of 1776 Congress authorized privateering, and adopted a form of commission to be issued by the colonial governments and by American agents abroad. Massachusetts had already authorized privateers and prize courts, and some of the other colonies followed suit, issuing both their own and the Congressional commissions. While the individualistic American seaman took rather badly to the disciplined life of a regular navy, his ingenuity and resourcefulness fitted him admirably for the life of a privateer, and the opportunity for profit was so attractive that the Continental Navy found itself unable to compete with privateersmen for crews. After some decline in 1777 as the Royal Navy's frigates took to sea to protect British commerce, American privateering revived in 1778, when France's entry into the war obliged the British to concentrate their naval forces. Thereafter the number of vessels engaged in privateering increased and their quality and effectiveness improved each year until the end of the war. Altogether there were nearly 800 American privateersmen during the Revolution, and they captured some 600 British merchant vessels.

The most remarkable accomplishment of the Continental Navy was carrying the war into British waters. The use of French bases for this unneutral purpose presented some inconveniences, for the French occasionally had to make concessions to British protests, but the net effect was to embroil France with England. The first Continental vessel in European waters was the brig *Reprisal,* commanded by Lambert Wickes, who brought Franklin to France at the end of 1776. Sailing from Nantes in January 1777, Wickes took five prizes; his bringing them into French ports raised a storm of British protest. The fitting out of the cutter *Dolphin* and the arrival in France of the Continental brig *Lexington* created a little squadron which Wickes led in a month's cruise around Ireland, netting 18 prizes. On the return voyage to America in the fall, the *Reprisal* foundered in a storm off the Grand Banks, taking her captain with her.

Meanwhile American agents in France had purchased the lugger *Surprise,* command of which was given to Gustavus Conyngham. Sailing from Dunkirk in May, Conyngham soon returned with two prizes. British protests caused the French government to release the captured vessels, seize the *Surprise,* and imprison Conyngham and his crew. But Benjamin Franklin procured his release in time for him to take command of the cutter *Revenge.* Operating first from French and later from Spanish bases, he contributed not a little to increasing tension between the Bourbon powers and England.

If Hopkins' squadron of converted merchantmen was the first Continental Navy, 13 frigates authorized by Congress at the end of 1775 may be considered the second. These were to be real men-of-war from the keel up, not mere conversions. To supervise their construction Congress created a Marine Committee composed of a member from each of the 13 colonies. But the promise of an effective fleet of genuine combat vessels was never realized. Six of the frigates for various reasons never got to sea at all, and of the remainder, four had only short careers. The *Hancock,* 32, an exceptionally fine, fast vessel, was taken in 1777 by a British 64. The *Raleigh* was lost when Captain John Barry was driven ashore in Penobscot Bay by superior forces in September 1778. The *Warren* was lost in the

Penobscot Expedition. Only the *Randolph,* 32, died with glory. Her captain, Nicholas Biddle, had commanded the *Andrew Doria* under Hopkins and had made a successful cruise afterward. He was fortunate in being able to take the *Randolph* out of the Delaware and to sea early in 1777, before the British moved on Philadelphia. Returning in the spring of 1778 from a cruise to France, Biddle was given a small squadron headed by the *Randolph* to hunt down British cruisers off the Carolina coast. In March he encountered the 64-gun *Yarmouth* near Barbados. Biddle engaged her and, although unsupported by the rest of his squadron, appeared near victory when the *Randolph's* magazine exploded. "Biddle's death deprived America of one of her most promising officers."

Thus by 1780 only three of the 13 frigates survived. The *Boston* and the *Providence* after a cruise to the south put in at Charleston, shared in the defense of the city, and were lost when it fell to the British in May 1780. The *Trumbull* alone survived into 1781, principally because she was unable to get over the Connecticut River bar and to sea before 1780.

Greatest of the Continental naval officers was John Paul Jones. Equal to the others in courage and resourcefulness, he surpassed them all in his high concept of the naval profession and his understanding of the strategic use of naval power. After serving as lieutenant in the *Alfred* under Hopkins and making successful cruises in command first of the *Providence* and then of the *Alfred,* he was in June 1777 given the new 18-gun *Ranger.* Sailing her to France in the autumn, he was in that country when she signed her treaty of alliance with the colonies and a week later had the satisfaction of receiving a salute from LaMotte-Picquet's squadron at Quiberon Bay. Disappointed in his hope of commanding a squadron to carry the war into British waters, Jones took the *Ranger* alone on a cruise around England, Scotland, and Ireland in the spring of 1778. At Whitehaven he burned some shipping and spiked cannon, at St. Mary's Isle he raided ashore, and outside Carrickfergus he captured H.M.S. *Drake,* 20, the first vessel of the Royal Navy to become an American prize.

For a year after this remarkable cruise Jones remained in France, repeatedly disappointed in his expectation of a new command. Finally he was given an old, half-rotten East Indiaman, which he armed with 42 assorted 9-, 12-, and 18-pounders, mostly secondhand, and named the *Bonhomme Richard* in compliment to Franklin. He sailed in mid-August 1779 in command of a motley squadron. Included besides his *Bonhomme Richard* was the newly-built American frigate *Alliance,* 32, commanded by a Frenchman, Captain Pierre Landais, and three French vessels, the *Pallas,* 32, the *Cerf,* 18, and the *Vengeance,* 12. In a clockwise circuit of the British Isles Jones picked up several prizes, and on September 24 off Flamborough Head, on the east coast of England, he fought his most famous battle.

The Franco-American squadron, reduced to four vessels by the separation of the *Cerf,* was stalking a British convoy when just at twilight its two escorts approached. These proved to be the 50-gun frigate *Serapis,* Captain Richard Pearson, and the *Countess of Scarborough,* 22. While the *Pallas* engaged the *Countess,* Jones headed for the *Serapis,* which was superior to the *Bonhomme Richard* in both maneuverability and firepower. Jones canceled the first of these British advantages when he succeeded personally in lashing the two vessels side by side, but the disparity in firepower increased as Jones had to forgo the use of his 18-pounders after two of them burst on the first round. Soon the *Bonhomme Richard* was so riddled that British balls were passing unimpeded through her hull, and only three American 9-pounders remained in action. To all appearances she was a sinking ship and might have been surrendered with honor. The master-at-arms released the prisoners, and a gunner made an unauthorized call for quarter. When Captain Pearson asked if the American had in fact struck, Jones made his famous reply, "I have not yet begun to fight."[3]

The French marines and a few Americans had by this time captured control of the tops of both vessels, and from that vantage had cleared the weather decks of the *Serapis.* About 9:30 PM a grenade thrown from the rigging entered a hatch of the British frigate,

[3] So reported by Jones's first lieutenant and certainly Jones's meaning if not his precise words.

ignited powder on the main gun deck, and set off an explosion that marked the turning point of the battle.

Throughout the action the *Bonhomme Richard* had been unsupported by her squadron, but at this point Landais brought up the *Alliance* and fired a few broadsides indiscriminately into the combatants, apparently doing more damage to friend than to foe. His presence however may have been a factor in Pearson's decision to strike. The battered *Bonhomme Richard* sank the next day, and Jones transferred his flag to the *Serapis*.

Saratoga, the Turning Point

In 1777 the British undertook to complete the campaigns that had been postponed by winter. Washington's judgment told him that the logical British objective was a junction of Howe's and Burgoyne's forces on the Hudson-Champlain route, but the withdrawal of Howe's forces from New Jersey and their embarkation in early July suggested the possibility of a movement on Philadelphia by sea. For almost two months Washington was in grave doubt as to the proper disposition of his troops, whether to move to the north or to cover Philadelphia. The dilemma imposed upon him was a striking demonstration of the mobility and initiative conferred by British sea power.

As Washington had suspected, the British plan did in fact envisage Burgoyne's moving south via Lake Champlain and the Hudson to join Howe. Incredibly enough, it specified no cooperation from the south, for the idea of coordinating the two armies seems to have occurred neither to Burgoyne nor to Colonial Minister Lord Germain at that time. In the spring of 1777, Germain approved Howe's plan for moving on Philadelphia. It was not till summer that he thought of ordering Howe to cooperate with Burgoyne, and by the time his letter reached America, Howe was already en route by sea to Philadelphia and could do no more than order General Clinton, whom he had left at New York, to make what diversion he could in favor of Burgoyne.

The British moved on Philadelphia by the roundabout route of the Chesapeake rather than by the obvious way of the Delaware partly because of exaggerated reports of American defenses on the river. Washington's forces, exhausted by their marches and countermarches in an attempt to anticipate British movements, could do little more than harry the British as they advanced on the city, which surrendered at the end of September. However, in an effort to make the British communications as costly and as vulnerable as possible, the Americans tenaciously defended the Delaware forts, which did not fall until the middle of November.

Meanwhile Burgoyne, who had retained the control of Lake Champlain, won the previous autumn, moved down the lake in June and captured Ticonderoga in early July. By the end of the month he was on the upper Hudson despite the obstructions put in his path by General Schuyler. But in early August British General St. Leger, who was advancing from Lake Ontario by the Mohawk Valley to join Burgoyne, was stopped in a bloody battle at Oriskany, near Fort Stanwix, and retreated to Canada upon news that General Arnold was approaching with American reinforcements.

At the same time Burgoyne was finding his long line of communications through the wilderness inadequate to supply his army. He therefore dispatched over 700 men to cross the Green Mountains near Bennington, seize the stores reported to be in that town, and then raid the Connecticut Valley for supplies, cattle, and draft animals. This detachment got no farther than Bennington, where the Green Mountain Boys destroyed or captured the entire force in mid-August. After these disasters Burgoyne pressed on against growing opposition. Finally, surrounded by American militiamen, now stiffened by regulars under General Horatio Gates, Burgoyne surrendered his army of more than 5,000 men at Saratoga on October 17, 1777.

This American victory was a turning point, for by demonstrating that the colonies had a chance of success it was to bring France into the war—and French assistance was to be decisive. But that result could not be foreseen in the autumn of 1777. While Howe's army settled down for a comfortable winter in Philadelphia, the despairing remnants of Washington's army endured cold and hunger at Valley Forge.

France Enters the War

Since the beginning of the Revolution, the French had supplied some indirect and secret aid to the Americans. After the news of Saratoga, fearful that England might make concessions that would bring peace with the colonies, they concluded with Benjamin Franklin on February 6, 1778, treaties of commerce and alliance. The entry of France into the war completely altered its character. From a sort of civil war, in which British opinion had been divided, it was transformed into an international war, soon to involve Spain and Holland, in which all Englishmen rallied to defend England against her traditional enemies.

In the American theater the center of military operations was to shift from the colonies to the West Indies, and in the colonies themselves the fighting was to shift to the South. In practical military terms, Britain now found herself committed to an overseas operation without secure control of the seas. Washington, who had been frustrated when sea power enabled the British to escape him at Boston, and who had exhausted his army in an attempt to anticipate Howe's movement by sea in the summer of 1777, at last had the prospect of the support of a first-class navy. From this point on, the history of the Revolution from the American point of view becomes the story of Washington's attempts to secure the cooperation of the French fleet for a decisive action, for he saw clearly that in a combined operation lay the best hope of American victory.

In Europe, Britain found herself on the defensive, for in this war France's position differed in one significant respect from the position she usually held in fighting Britain. This time France had no enemy on the Continent, no land warfare to tax her resources, no threat to her own frontiers to distract her attention. This time she was free to concentrate on Britain. She intended to exploit this freedom by seizing control of the Channel and invading the British Isles. A successful invasion would even old scores, regain her lost West Indies possessions, and free America at a single stroke. Her own naval resources appeared sufficient for the task, and if Spain should join her she would have a superfluity of power.

The French navy of 1778 was probably the world's best, equal to the British in most respects and superior to it in many, for the renaissance begun by Choiseul had been continued by his successors in the Ministry of Marine. The *Marine* was superior to the Royal Navy in numbers of ships ready for action, in quality of ships, in gunnery, and in tactical skill. By 1778 France had 63 ships of 64 guns or more. While the British lists showed a larger number, those actually fit for sea were considerably fewer. Hence the French, with about 45 ships ready for action, had the advantage, and this superiority was increased, at least on paper, by the entry of Spain into the war the following year.

French ships, scientifically designed, still had cleaner lines and were faster and heavier rate for rate than British ships. The British however soon offset much of the French superiority in design by copper-sheathing the underwater hulls of more and more of their vessels, a practice the French were slow to follow. Coppering conferred a speed advantage that increased during a campaign as marine growth fouled wooden hulls. This consideration was especially important in the West Indies, where the climate and sea organisms were particularly destructive to wood and where there were few facilities for cleaning and repair.

At the outbreak of the American Revolution, the French corps of seaman gunners were probably the most accurate marksmen in the world, clearly outshooting the British at long ranges. This French advantage the Royal Navy at last offset in the final year of the war, partly by gunnery reforms and partly through the introduction of the carronade[4] to supplement the regular battery. Short and light, the carronade threw a heavy ball with terrific smashing effect at short range, and it could be worked by fewer men than the long guns. The British thus belatedly acquired greater fire power with little increase in weight.

Lastly, the French led the British in the theory and practice of naval tactics. Bigot de Morogues' famous *Tactique Navale,* published in 1763, not only expounded the various methods of achieving tactical concentration but

[4] So called because this type of gun was first cast by Scotland's Carron Iron Works.

also spurred the development of a practical signal system, toward which the French *Marine* had been groping for nearly a century. Both theory and signals were put into practice in "Squadrons of Evolution," in which most of the French naval leaders of the war had been trained.

The British, on the other hand, had only the Permanent Fighting Instructions. "That we have no regular system of tactics you know," wrote British Admiral Richard Kempenfelt in 1779.[5] But officers like Kempenfelt and Howe were interested in the subject, and one of the significant developments of the American Revolution was their creation for the British Navy of an efficient system of signals and of flexible tactics, for which they borrowed heavily from the French. Signals and tactics were inseparable, for so long as an admiral could signal only to execute a given article of the Fighting Instructions, it was obviously impossible to escape the Instructions.

Although the Permanent Fighting Instructions remained the only order authorized for general use till 1793, it had become customary for admirals to issue Additional Instructions applicable to their specific commands. It was this practice that made possible some progress and reform, and Lord Howe exploited it to the fullest. In July 1778, as he was about to transfer his brother's army from New York to the Chesapeake for the march on Philadelphia, he issued a set of Additional Instructions that entirely superseded the Permanent Fighting Instructions within his command and to which was attached a complete signal book of his own.

The Battle of Ushant, July 27, 1778

One of the first acts of the French on forming an alliance with the colonies was to ready a fleet at Toulon for use in American waters. After many delays, twelve ships of the line sailed in April 1778 under the command of Vice Admiral the Comte d'Estaing, a former brigadier general in the army. The English were aware of the French preparations and recognized the absolute necessity of getting

[5] Kempenfelt, quoted in Sir Julian S. Corbett, ed., *Signals and Instructions 1776–1794* (Navy Records Society, 1908), Introduction, 2–3.

prompt reinforcements to Admiral Lord Howe if the British position in America was to be preserved, but they experienced the greatest difficulty in assembling a suitable force. It was only by taking men and supplies from Admiral Augustus Keppel's Channel fleet and thus delaying its sailing that the Admiralty was able to provide 13 of the line for Vice Admiral John Byron, who sailed early in June.

Furnishing Byron's needs delayed full-scale operations in the Channel. At length, however, after a brief sortie perilously under strength, Keppel put to sea on July 9 with 30 of the line. It so happened that Admiral the Comte d'Orvilliers had sailed with the Brest fleet of 29 ships the preceding day on what was intended as a training cruise. In the afternoon of July 23 the two sighted each other a hundred miles west of Ushant, an island off the tip of Brittany. Keppel was the more ardent for battle, for if he could remove the Brest fleet from the board, England would be saved from the danger of invasion, and the chances of losing her American colonies would be considerably lessened. D'Orvilliers, less interested in combat than in getting his fleet safely back to Brest, for three days eluded Keppel's every attempt to engage. In the course of these maneuvers, d'Orvilliers' fleet dwindled through separations to 27 ships; Keppel retained his 30.

At length on July 27, Keppel saw his opportunity and signaled General Chase, sacrificing an orderly line for an opportunity to mass ships on d'Orvilliers' rear. But d'Orvilliers suddenly wore his fleet together and headed toward the pursuing British for a passing engagement on opposite courses. Such an action was rarely decisive, but in this instance d'Orvilliers hoped to take advantage of British disorder to mass fire on a few enemy ships while remaining out of range of the others.

Keppel, perceiving d'Orvilliers' intention, had the option of falling off and re-forming his line. This he rejected, since it might mean no battle at all and might even permit the French to escape. Without hesitation he hoisted the signal to engage, not taking time to order his line. The result was as d'Orvilliers had foreseen. Firing on the upward roll, he dismasted several ships of the British van and center before the others could come to their support. But Sir Hugh Palliser's British rear division, having had time to attain some order before coming under attack, took the fire of the entire French line and was heavily damaged in the rigging.

That one inconclusive pass ended the battle. D'Orvilliers, coming about again, desired to pass between Keppel's main body and several damaged British ships, but the French van commander either misunderstood or disregarded his intention. Keppel tried to re-form his line and cover his cripples, but Palliser remained to windward and would not rejoin with his rear division. At length, when neither signals nor a message sent by frigate produced action from Palliser, Keppel by-passed his subordinate and ordered the rear ships by individual signal to rejoin the line. By then night had fallen and Keppel reluctantly postponed further action till morning. But d'Orvilliers, considering that he had done well enough, took advantage of the darkness to shape course for Brest. Although the French had suffered the greater number of casualties, they had clearly outmaneuvered the British. Moreover, they enjoyed the unusual experience of bringing home all their ships from an engagement with the Royal Navy. For the underdogs of the Seven Years' War, that was no small victory.

In a subsequent court-martial, Keppel was charged on a number of counts that amounted to two mutually contradictory accusations: 1) that he had engaged in the first place without waiting to order his line, and 2) that, delaying in order to re-form his line, he had failed to resume the engagement and thus had failed to "do his utmost." For the first offence, it will be recalled, Admiral Mathews had been cashiered after the Battle of Toulon in 1744. Time lost by Admiral Byng in ordering his line twelve years later had cost Britain Minorca and Byng his life before a firing squad. Now Keppel was being charged simultaneously with the offenses of Mathews and Byng. Having sat on Byng's court-martial, Keppel felt that he was fighting for his life. But by this time both the Permanent Fighting Instructions and the Line had lost their sacrosanct character, and common sense sat in judgment. Keppel was exonerated with immense popular acclaim. For the officers of the Royal Navy the inference was clear—an admiral could now conduct a battle according to his own best judgment.

The First French Fleet: D'Estaing

Philadelphia, as George Washington remarked on learning of the French alliance, had become "an ineligible situation" for the British army in America. General Clinton, who had succeeded to over-all command, was ordered to evacuate the position forthwith and return to New York. Aware that a French fleet was probably on the way to America, he marched his army overland, leaving his supplies and artillery for Lord Howe to bring by sea. Howe cleared the Delaware with his little fleet on June 28, reached New York the next day, and immediately stationed frigates to warn of the approach of French naval forces.

D'Estaing, who had proclaimed, "Speed is the foremost of military virtues; to surprise is almost to have conquered," honored his own precept in the breach rather than the observance. With a prompt crossing of the Atlantic, he could have caught Howe's fleet still in the Delaware and destroyed it along with Clinton's artillery. As it was, he spent 85 days getting from Toulon to the Capes of the Delaware, where he arrived on July 6. He was lucky that "Foul Weather Jack" Byron's reinforcements, having been completely scattered by a storm, did no better. Howe was thus left to face a French fleet mounting nearly twice as many guns as his own.

Howe prepared with great gallantry for what promised to be a fight against hopeless odds. He placed his ships in a close line across the main channel into New York harbor, while Clinton mounted a battery at the end of Sandy Hook. D'Estaing arrived on July 11 and anchored about four miles distant. Washington sent him a member of his staff with an offer of full cooperation in an attack on New York, but American pilots did not arrive on board till the 16th. The pilots, on learning that the larger French ships drew 23 to 25 feet, refused to assume responsibility for taking them across the bar, over which there was only 22 feet of water. After vainly offering a reward of 50,000 crowns to any pilot who would take his ships across, d'Estaing abandoned the enterprise.[6] On the 22nd, when the French made sail, the British fully expected attack. The tide was high and the wind right for crossing the bar, but as they watched, the French fleet moved off to sea and disappeared.

Washington accepted d'Estaing's decision with good grace. Although he preferred New York as the object of a coordinated land and sea attack, he was willing to accept any other theater where decisive results could be achieved. When d'Estaing decided to shift his attack to Newport, Rhode Island, Washington fully concurred.

Newport, with a harbor second only to that of New York in strategic value, had been occupied by the British since the end of 1776. Although the American General Sullivan, who was watching the British there, had been providently reinforced by Washington, he was not ready to move until a week after d'Estaing arrived off Narragansett Bay. The delay was to prove fatal to the enterprise, for just when the position of the British, besieged by an immensely superior force and blockaded by a strong fleet, seemed hopeless, Admiral Howe appeared off Newport on August 9. It was a bold move, since even the four reinforcements which had recently arrived gave him only eight of the line to oppose d'Estaing's twelve, but it saved Rhode Island for the British. Had d'Estaing kept his position in the Bay, the British could hardly have dislodged him, and Newport's fate would have been sealed. Moreover, the local fishermen could have told him that all signs indicated the approach of an "August gale"—a hurricane from the West Indies. But d'Estaing accepted the British challenge, took aboard the troops already landed, and sailed forth to fight.

D'Estaing had the advantage of the wind, but it was not till evening of the following day that the superior sailing qualities of the French ships enabled him to come up to Howe, who quite sensibly preferred to avoid a decisive action. By then light was waning, visibility was further reduced by rain squalls, and the wind was freshening dangerously. That night the hurricane scattered the two fleets. All thoughts of battle vanished in the struggle for survival.

The battered British sailed for Sandy Hook, while d'Estaing, his dismasted flagship in tow, fulfilled his promise to return to Narragansett Bay. On the way he sighted the *Princess Royal*, Byron's flagship, just arriving after her stormy crossing of the Atlantic. During the fleet's absence Sullivan had made excellent progress in his siege of Newport and wanted only the French to take up the right flank. D'Estaing however would have nothing further to do with the Newport operation. He now knew of Byron's arrival and, fearful of finding himself blockaded by the combined British forces, insisted on withdrawing to Boston to refit.

His retirement ended the Newport enterprise. The departure of the French, General Nathanael Greene wrote Washington, "struck such panic among the militia and volunteers that they began to desert by shoals. . . ."[7] Indeed, Sullivan was fortunate to effect his withdrawal before the indefatigable Howe reappeared with 13 of the line and 5,000 troops under General Clinton. On learning of d'Estaing's departure, Howe made a vigorous effort to overtake him, but he was too late to catch the French at sea, and he did not dare attempt to force Boston harbor. Having done all he could, he returned to New York, where he surrendered command of his squadron, declaring that he could serve no more "so long as the present Ministers remained in office."

Washington was severely disappointed at the French withdrawal. He understood the strategy of victory and had done everything within his

---

[6] D'Estaing has been criticized for this abandonment. The disappointment of the Americans is understandable. There is no doubt however that the heavier ships could not cross the bar. When Hood was being sent to the American coast in 1781 in pursuit of de Grasse, Rodney decided against sending the *Gibraltar* because "her great draught of water, which was twenty-seven feet, prevented her being sent to New York, as she could not cross the bar of Sandy Hook." (Major General Godfrey Basil Mundy, *The Life and Correspondence of the Late Admiral Lord Rodney* [London, 1830], II, 144.) Similarly, when Hood arrived, Graves sent him a note: "The *Princessa*, I understand, draws twenty-six feet water; it is too much to come over the bar. Therefore I have sent up two transports to come down for her guns." (Sir John Knox Laughton, ed., *Letters and Papers of Charles, Lord Barham, Admiral of the Red Squadron, 1758–1813,* [Navy Records Society, 1907–11], I, 122.)

[7] Letter of August 28–31, John C. Fitzpatrick, ed., *Writings of George Washington* (Washington, 1931–1944), XII, 368 *n.*

power to put it into effect. As he no doubt sus-pected, it would be a long time before he would have another such opportunity, but he at once turned his efforts to healing the rift between the French and Americans, to pre-serving the alliance, and to protecting the French fleet in Boston.

Early in November d'Estaing sailed for the West Indies. The British at the same time sent 5,000 troops from New York thither, and early in January 1779 the main British fleet left Newport to follow. The winter season was about to begin.

The West Indies, 1779

Although the French had made the invasion of England the principal objective in their strategy, they could not resist the temptation to disperse their fleet by sending squadrons to various areas of interest. The most impor-tant of these was the West Indies, which ac-counted for about one-third of all French trade. France now possessed only St. Lucia, Martinique, and Guadeloupe among the Windward Islands, and Haiti in the Leewards. Spain owned Puerto Rico, Santo Domingo, and Cuba, all to leeward. The British con-trolled a chain of Windward Islands running from St. Kitts to Tobago, including Dominica, St. Vincent, and Grenada, Barbados still fur-ther to the east, and Jamaica to the west. The distinction between windward and lee-ward was important. With the prevailing easterly wind, a windward position at Mar-tinique or St. Lucia conferred initiative. From Jamaica a sailing ship had to beat a thousand miles into the wind to reach the Windward Islands. (See map page 61.)

The hurricane season in the West Indies lasted from July to October. During that period major forces in the area usually cleared for home or for the North American theater. Similarly, convoys from Europe ordinarily ar-rived in the spring and returned in May or June, or sometimes in November. These con-voys, necessary for the inhabitants of the islands, vital for the military forces, and eco-nomically important to the home countries, were the objects of much of the naval action in the West Indies.

Before the end of 1778 the French and British in the West Indies made an exchange of territory which was not to be reversed dur-ing the war. In early September the Marquis de Bouillé, Governor of Martinique, captured lightly garrisoned Dominica while British Rear Admiral Samuel Barrington sat at Barbados with two ships of the line awaiting orders. When reinforcements arrived in December from New York, the British at once attacked St. Lucia. D'Estaing, who had left Boston at about the same time the British forces had left New York, came to its relief; but his fleet, though much superior, failed to break the line of British ships anchored across the Grand Cul de Sac, the troops he landed were re-pulsed with heavy casualties, and the island fell. It was a significant event, for the British thus acquired an excellent harbor only 30 miles from Fort Royal, Martinique, the prin-cipal French base.

At the beginning of 1779 both Britain and France increased their forces in the West Indies. Byron's arrival from New York in January brought the British West Indian fleet up to 21 of the line. But in February the Comte de Grasse arrived from France with four of the line for d'Estaing; in April de Vaudreuil, fresh from retaking Senegal for France, arrived with two of the line and two frigates; and in June La Motte-Picquet brought a convoy of 45 transports escorted by four of the line and three frigates. While Byron was out in a vain attempt to intercept La Motte-Picquet's convoy, d'Estaing sent out a small force which took St. Vincent, just south of St. Lucia, in mid-June.

D'Estaing, now well supplied with troops and with 24 of the line, sailed on June 30, scarcely giving La Motte-Picquet's vessels time to land their sick and to reprovision. His in-tention was to take Barbados, to the east, which with Martinique and St. Vincent would effectively box in the British at St. Lucia, but a persistently contrary wind forced him to transfer his attack to Grenada, which he easily took on July 4. On the afternoon of the next day a fleet was reported approaching Grenada. It was Byron, who had learned of the French attack and was belatedly coming to the relief of the island with several transports of troops and 21 ships of the line. The resulting Battle of Grenada, like the Battle of Ushant, demon-

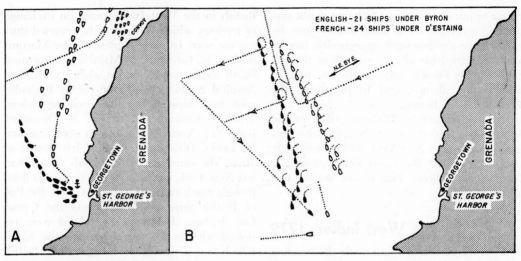

BATTLE OF GRENADA, JULY 6, 1779

strates the danger of falling in the disarray of a General Chase upon a competently handled force that intends to stand and fight.

Long before dawn on the 6th, d'Estaing ordered his fleet to get under way from St. George's Harbor, but he was frustrated by the morning calm. The French van was scarcely clear and not yet in formation when first light disclosed the British bearing down. Byron, eager to catch the French in disorder as they straggled from the harbor, ordered General Chase. His faster sailers drew ahead and, rushing pell-mell upon the French, suffered severe damage from the combined fire of shore batteries and of the French van, which had formed into line just in time to receive them. The quickening breeze enabled the rest of the French to fall into line of battle, whereupon Byron was forced to order his ships to wear into a parallel line. At this point two of the British ships which had been to windward with the transports came down and fell upon the French van, which handled them both roughly. Altogether, six of the British ships were disabled.

The battle moved to the westward with the fleets in parallel lines, but d'Estaing did not forget his strategic purpose of covering Grenada, and with that in view he tacked his fleet about 3 PM and headed for the island and for the British cripples. Byron followed, so that d'Estaing, instead of taking the cripples, was content to cannonade them in passing.

During the night the French slipped back into St. George's Harbor, and next day the battered British withdrew to St. Kitts.

Although the French as usual suffered greater casualties than the British, they had won not only a strategic victory in preserving their hold on Grenada but a neat tactical victory as well. All in all, they had not done badly in the West Indies. While the British possession of St. Lucia would continue to plague them, the French could congratulate themselves on the conquest of Dominica, St. Vincent, and Grenada.

Savannah, 1779

The Allied cause had fared less well in the Colonies, where the British had transferred their activity to the south. In May 1779 Clinton had sent 1,800 men with a strong naval escort to Virginia. This force plundered and burned Portsmouth and Norfolk, seized considerable naval stores and shipping, and forced the Americans to burn an almost completed frigate on the ways to prevent her capture.

The British had been in possession of Savannah since the end of 1778, and Governor Rutledge of Georgia had requested d'Estaing to come there when the hurricane season put an end to operations in the West Indies. Accordingly, d'Estaing arrived off Savannah on September 1 with 20 ships of the line and 3,000 troops in transports. This operation had not been concerted with Washington, who did not hear of d'Estaing's arrival on the American coast until two weeks later. Washington at once wrote the French admiral proposing a combined operation against New York, where Vice Admiral Marriot Arbuthnot, Lord Howe's successor, currently had only five of the line. General Clinton, at New York, also heard of d'Estaing's arrival, and fearing precisely what Washington was urging, ordered the hasty evacuation of Rhode Island in October in favor of a concentration at New York.

But there was no real occasion for Washington's hope or Clinton's fears. D'Estaing, who had generously undertaken the Georgia expedition after receiving orders to return to France, was anxious to get it over. At his urging, the French and Americans launched an assault on Savannah on October 9. The French suffered severely, d'Estaing himself was badly wounded, and the attack failed. D'Estaing then sailed for France, leaving bitterness and disappointment in his wake.

European Waters, 1779–1780

France had from the first expected to be joined in the war by Spain, her sister Bourbon power and sister-sufferer in the Seven Years' War. At the beginning of June 1779, d'Orvilliers put to sea from Brest with 28 of the line, a little too late to interfere with an immense British convoy bearing supplies and reinforcements to Clinton in New York. He then moved southward toward a rendezvous with the Spanish fleet, while the Spanish ambassador in London delivered a list of complaints that provoked a British declaration of war in mid-June.

Franco-Spanish plans, already drawn up, had set the summer of 1779 for a great invasion of England at the Isle of Wight and Portsmouth. The prospects for success were excellent, for the French could muster 62 and the Spanish 40 of the line, against a maximum British strength of 80. In this crisis the dearth of leadership in Britain became evident. Howe and Keppel had resigned in disgust. To take command of the vital Channel fleet the Ministry could find only Sir Charles Hardy, the 63-year-old Governor of the Veterans' Home at Greenwich. Kempenfelt, the signal

expert, who was fleet captain (chief of staff), wrote in despair to a friend, "Does the people at home think the nation is in no danger? Where is Lord Howe at this alarming period?"[8]

The English were hurrying preparations to met the expected invasion, but there was no need for their haste. Because d'Orvilliers had to wait a month for the Spaniards to join him, the huge armada of 67 ships was not assembled till late July. By mid-August it lay becalmed off Plymouth. Hardy with his 35 ships had been in and out of port without offering any real challenge, but aboard the French and Spanish vessels water and provisions were running short and sickness was reaching serious proportions. It was obvious that the Allies must act promptly if the operation was to succeed. Then d'Orvilliers received word that his government had altered its plans and contemplated a landing on the rocky coast of Cornwall, a change that doomed the enterprise. While his government hesitated, d'Orvilliers sighted Hardy and pursued him briefly. Finally, with his supplies exhausted, he returned exasperated to Brest in mid-September and took no further part in the war. Thus the Franco-Spanish fleet had held command of the Channel for an entire summer, and England had only the incompetence of the French high command to thank for her escape from invasion.

After their fiasco of 1779 the French and Spanish "provisionally abandoned" any plan for invading England in 1780. Rather, they would continue the blockade of Gibraltar, which Spain was eager to recover, check the British in America, and launch a major offensive in the West Indies.

Gibraltar had been under siege since Spain's entry into the war in June. Its relief was entrusted to Admiral George Brydges Rodney, who, by borrowing heavily from the Channel fleet, was able to sail with 22 of the line, 14 frigates, and a large convoy at the end of December 1779. Rodney had risen to the rank of rear admiral during the Seven Years' War. An inveterate gambler, he was in Paris to escape his creditors when the new war broke out. He was 60 years old and plagued by bad

[8] Quoted in Capt. W. M. James RN, *The British Navy in Adversity* (London, 1926), 174.

health, but he belonged to the right political party and hence was pressed into service.

The relief expedition had passed Cape St. Vincent when, on January 16, the British sighted a Spanish fleet of eleven ships commanded by Admiral Don Juan de Langara. Crowding on sail before a westerly wind, Rodney ordered General Chase. The newly coppered British ships slowly overhauled the Spaniards and by evening, as the wind freshened to a half-gale, began action with the rearmost. The fighting continued throughout the night—the famous "Moonlight Battle." One Spanish ship blew up, but six others, including de Langara's flagship, were taken. With the Straits thus cleared, Rodney had no difficulty relieving Gibraltar.

In view of what was subsequently learned of Spanish incompetence at sea, there was perhaps no great glory in Rodney's defeating a Spanish fleet of half his strength.[9] But it was the first British success of the war, won by an admiral who belonged to the ministerial party, and the government made the most of it. "You have taken more line of battle ships than had been captured in any one action in either of the last preceding wars," the First Lord wrote to him.[10]

From Gibraltar Rodney sailed in mid-February for the West Indies, detaching on the way those vessels which were to return to the Channel fleet. Although the French and Spanish occasionally combined to put to sea a fleet considerably outmatching anything the British could muster, naval actions in European waters were confined to *guerre de course* for the rest of 1780.

[9] Because Rodney was confined to his cabin with gout during this action, it appears that a considerable share of the credit belongs to his fleet captain, Walter Young. In a letter of July 24, 1780 (*Barham Papers*, I, 64–66), Captain Young says that he urged Rodney to order General Chase earlier in the action, but that Rodney refused. Young continues: "I am perfectly of your opinion that it is a dangerous practice to make the signal for a general chase after an enemy equal or superior to you, particularly if they are formed in line of battle or are near each other. . . ." This observation has particular relevance to the battles of Ushant, Grenada, and the Virginia Capes.

[10] Quoted in James, *British Navy in Adversity*, 1941.

De Guichen and Rodney in the West Indies, 1780

The principal action of 1780 took place in the West Indies, where the French planned their main offensive. In March the Comte de Guichen arrived at Martinique from France with 16 ships. Added to the ships already in the West Indies, these gave the French a fleet of 23 of the line. Since the British had only 16, de Guichen and de Bouillé, the able Governor of Martinique, thought the time opportune for an attack on St. Lucia. But discovery of the strength of British defenses on the island, together with the news of Rodney's arrival from Gibraltar with four of the line, caused them to abandon the project.

De Guichen then decided on an expedition against Barbados, where d'Estaing had been frustrated the year before. In mid-April he sailed with his entire fleet with 3,000 troops aboard. British frigates reported the movement however, and Rodney was soon in pursuit. By evening he had overtaken the French a few miles south of Dominica, and the two fleets formed for action.

Although Rodney was no innovator, he had a sound understanding of tactics and an appreciation of the value of concentration. The form of massing he particularly favored was achieved by reducing the interval between ships, thus bringing more firepower to bear on a given segment of the enemy line. The idea was of course by no means original; it was discussed in Morogue's *Tactique Navale* and, as we have seen, it had been practiced even earlier by British meleeists.

De Guichen, France's ablest tactician and former commander of a "Squadron of Evolution," was a worthy opponent and spent the forenoon of the 17th in demonstrating his skill in maneuvers. The English however had the advantage of the wind and were able to retain it. Just before noon the two fleets found themselves on the starboard tack on parallel courses, with the French line somewhat more advanced and to leeward of the British, which was at reduced intervals. Rodney, seeing the opportunity for which he had been maneuvering all forenoon, gave the signal "for every ship to bear down, and steer for her opposite in the enemy's line agreeable to the 21st article of the additional fighting instructions."[11]

Rodney's intention was for each ship to bear down on the French vessel *actually* opposite, which would have massed force on the French rear; but the captain of his van ship and several others steered instead for their *numerical* opposites, while still others hung back in confusion. The English line dissolved, and the ships attacked individually or in small groups. Seeing his van in disorder and roughly handled, Rodney brought his remaining ships into close action. His flagship, the *Sandwich*, actually passed through the French line[12] and was so badly damaged that Rodney had to transfer his flag. Soon after four o'clock the French fell off down wind to re-form, and Rodney made no attempt to follow. The French, although they had won a tactical victory, were forced to abandon their expedition against Barbados.

Rodney complained bitterly of the failure of his captains to support him, but he had only himself to blame. Haughty and aloof, he had made no effort to explain his tactical views or plans to his captains in advance, and the signal system was inadequate to convey them in action. Nor does it appear that Rodney had any interest in the attempt Howe and Kempenfelt were making to provide adequate signals. In the summer of 1780, only about three months after this Battle off Dominica, Rodney's fleet captain, who must have known his chief well, wrote Kempenfelt, "I have delivered the signal books to Sir George for his perusal, though I am apprehensive these are books he will pay little attention to."[13] Rodney was a tactical conservative, but tactical ideas had undergone such development in a generation that a conservative in the American Revolution would have been considered an innovator in the Seven Years' War.

[11] Mundy, *The Life and Correspondence of Rodney*, I, 286.

[12] Captain Young's letter (*Barham Papers*, I, 54–5) makes it clear that this was entirely accidental, occasioned by her opponent's giving way. The point is important only because some historians have attempted to find in this incident a precedent for Rodney's breaking the line at Saints' Passage.

[13] *Barham Papers*, I, 69.

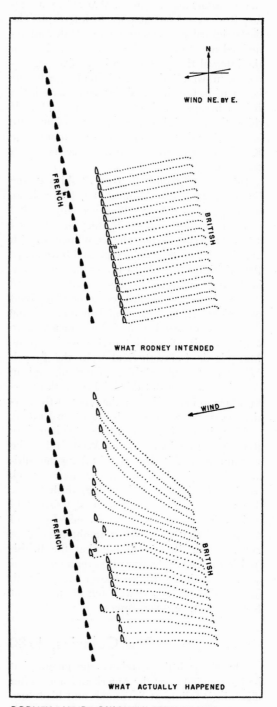

WIND NE. BY E.

WHAT RODNEY INTENDED

WHAT ACTUALLY HAPPENED

RODNEY AND DE GUICHEN, APRIL 17, 1780

In early May the French again put to sea from Basse-Terre, Guadaloupe, with the intention of attacking St. Lucia. Warned by a frigate, Rodney set out at once to intercept. The fleets sighted each other on the 10th and remained in contact for the next twelve days. In the interval there were two indecisive engagements in which the French had clearly the better of it. On the 22nd the fleets parted, the British because of the poor condition of their ships, the French because their provisions were low. Although the French had outfought the British, their attempt on St. Lucia had been thwarted.

In June a Spanish fleet of 12 ships of the line commanded by Admiral Don José Solano, escorting a convoy of 83 ships with 11,400 men, successfully evaded Rodney and arrived safely at Basse-Terre. The combined French and Spanish forces might very well have swept the British from the West Indies, but the Spaniards were suffering horribly from scurvy, and Solano showed no inclination to conduct joint operations. Instead, de Guichen escorted the Spaniards toward Havana, then turned in to Cap Français, where he found letters from the Marquis de Lafayette and from the French Minister at Philadelphia, asking his aid in American waters. But de Guichen, with orders to return to France before the onset of the hurricane season, sailed in mid-August for Europe.

Though the departure of de Guichen gave Rodney a free hand in the West Indies, he was unaware of it. Instead of taking the initiative, he anxiously anticipated a major attack by the combined French and Spanish forces. Then he learned that a French squadron had arrived in Narragansett Bay in mid-July and speculated that de Guichen might have gone north to join it. Concluding that the British position in North America was threatened and aware that the hurricane season was at hand, he set sail and arrived with ten of the line at New York in mid-September.

The Colonies, 1780

There was little to relieve the gloom that had descended upon the American leaders after d'Estaing's failure at Savannah and his return to France in the fall of 1779. Washington's army spent the winter of 1779-80 once more at Morristown, where its hardships surpassed those of Valley Forge.

Confident that Washington was too weak to threaten New York City, Clinton decided at the urging of General Lord Charles Cornwallis to make the southern colonies the object of his principal effort in 1780. At the end of December 1779, as soon as he was certain that d'Estaing was out of the way, he sailed with Cornwallis and 8,000 men for Charleston, which fell early in May. British forces soon had substantial control of South Carolina. In mid-August Cornwallis beat Gates decisively near Camden, South Carolina, and followed up this success by invading North Carolina in September. Washington was powerless to interfere with this overrunning of the South.

There was but one bright spot in the picture. Early in 1779 the Marquis de Lafayette had returned to France to advocate the cause of the Colonies. In April 1780 he arrived in America with the news that his government was sending General Rochambeau with French troops— "Dr. Franklin's soldiers," Voltaire called them. Washington at once raised the question of the cooperation of de Guichen's fleet from the West Indies, and at his instance both Lafayette and the French Minister wrote letters to the admiral which, as we have seen, he received just before his departure for France.

Meanwhile, considering that Rochambeau's transports might be escorted by a naval force sufficiently strong to establish control of American waters, Washington drew up careful plans for a combined operation against New York, with alternatives in case the French should prefer to act elsewhere. Then, upon learning of Rochambeau's arrival at Newport, he dispatched Lafayette with his plan, the first article of which read:

1st. In any operation, and under all circumstances a decisive naval superiority is to be considered as a fundamental principle, and the basis upon which every hope of success must ultimately depend.[14]

The French transports had in fact been escorted by seven ships of the line and three

[14] Fitzpatrick, *Writings of George Washington,* XIX, 174.

frigates, a force certainly adequate to deal with Arbuthnot's four of the line at New York. But its departure from Brest had not passed unnoticed by the British, who had at once sent a warning to Clinton at Charleston and dispatched Admiral Thomas Graves with six of the line to reinforce Arbuthnot. Clinton left Cornwallis in command in the South and hurried back to New York with part of his army. His arrival in mid-June introduced an unwelcome factor in the plans Washington was formulating, but Graves' arrival doomed the whole project, for the British fleet was now stronger than the French. But Washington did not cease to hope. A second division of Rochambeau's forces was to follow the first, and with it might come naval superiority. Washington did not know that the British had in the meantime blockaded Brest and that the second division was destined never to sail.

The superiority brought by Graves in fact turned the tables completely, and it was the British who went on the offensive. Their fleet arrived off Newport in late July to establish a blockade while Clinton embarked troops to follow. Washington sent a warning to Rochambeau:

Had I any prospect of arriving in time I would march to your support, but as I think there is no probability of this, the only way I can be useful to you is to menace New York, and even to attack it, if the force remaining there does not exceed what I have reason to believe. I am pressing my movements for this purpose with all the rapidity in our power.[15]

The strategy was successful. The threat to the British main base brought Clinton back from Rhode Island to New York at once, but Arbuthnot remained off Narragansett Bay to continue his blockade.

In September Washington at last met with Rochambeau at Hartford to plan a joint strategy. In response to questions posed by the French, Washington reiterated the views from which he never deviated:

1st. That there can be no decisive enterprise against the maritime establishments of the English in this country without a constant naval superiority.

2nd. That of all the enterprises which may be undertaken, the most important and decisive is the

[15] *Ibid.*, XIX, 281.

reduction of New York, which is the center and focus of all the British forces.[16]

But even as Washington was conferring with his allies, news came of Rodney's arrival at New York with ten ships of the line. This put an end to any lingering hope of a Franco-American campaign. Rather, the Allies were fortunate that the British made no effective use of their naval superiority. True, it enabled Clinton to send 2,500 troops to Virginia to stage a diversion in favor of Cornwallis, but Arbuthnot resented Rodney's assumption of command in New York, and the two men quarreled bitterly. Clinton had no inclination to renew his attempt on Rhode Island, and Rodney, who was ill and little disposed to activity, did not urge the project. Finally in mid-November he sailed again for the West Indies without having accomplished anything.

Thus the year 1780 closed on a bitter note for the Americans. The fine new French forces, which had seemed to promise so much, had remained idle, blockaded in Newport ever since their arrival. In September Washington returned from the Hartford conference to be confronted with the treason of Benedict Arnold. At the end of the year he wrote Benjamin Franklin:

Disappointed of the second division of French troops, but more especially in the expected naval superiority, which was the pivot upon which everything turned, we have been compelled to spend an inactive campaign after a flattering prospect at the opening of it and vigorous struggles to make it a decisive one on our part. Latterly we have been obliged to become spectators of a succession of detachments from the army at New York, in aid of Lord Cornwallis, while our naval weakness and the political dissolution of a large part of our army puts [sic] it out of our power to counteract them at the southward, or take advantage of them here.[17]

Summary

At the outbreak of the American Revolution, Britain's unpreparedness permitted the Americans in 1775 to make several offensive moves. Their capture of Fort Ticonderoga brought temporary control of the Champlain-Hudson

[16] *Ibid.*, XX, 76–8.
[17] Letter of December 20, 1780, *Ibid.*, XX, 507.

Valley invasion route; their attack on Quebec frightened the British into diverting forces to Canada the following year; and the siege of Boston obliged the British to withdraw to Halifax the following spring.

But in 1776 the British, having gathered their forces, seized the initiative, and they were to exercise it until the French entry into the war. Their control of the sea enabled them to seize almost any coastal point at will and to conduct harassing raids from New England to Virginia that very nearly destroyed both the American will and capacity to continue the war. But when they attempted to penetrate inland, they exposed their communications to the semi-guerrilla tactics of the Americans and courted disaster.

In the summer of 1776 General Howe took New York and made it his main base, while Carleton, after driving Arnold from Canada, undertook to penetrate the colonies by the Champlain-Hudson route. He was unable to use the lake however until he had spent the summer building a fleet to overmatch that of Arnold, so that not till October was he ready to move down the lake. Although Arnold was defeated at Valcour Island, he nonetheless scored the only significant American naval success of the war, for he had delayed the British till too late in the season for them to proceed with the campaign. Next year when Burgoyne attempted to continue Carleton's strategy, the Americans were better prepared and captured the British army at Saratoga. That victory was decisive, for it brought the French into the war, and it was French aid, and particularly French naval power, that ultimately made American victory possible.

Early in the war Washington realized that sea power was the key to the struggle in America, and the strategic aim to which he adhered firmly throughout was to secure a naval superiority that would make possible a combined sea and land operation against one of the British lodgments on the coast. He preferred an attack on New York, as the center of British military operations, but was willing to act elsewhere if necessary. The arrival of d'Estaing in 1778 offered an opportunity to put this strategy into effect and did cause the British to abandon first Philadelphia and later Rhode Island in order to concentrate their forces. However, d'Estaing failed at New York, Newport, and Savannah, leaving Washington discouraged but with unwavering faith in his own strategy.

The French exercised the initiative almost continuously from their entry, but the vacillation of the French government threw away the chance to end the war at a stroke by invading England in the summer of 1779, when the Franco-Spanish fleet held unchallenged control of the Channel. After that, French sea power was dissipated into various theaters, the most important of which was the West Indies, where the French made significant but indecisive gains. While they were thus occupied, the British regained the initiative on the American coast by taking Charleston in May 1780, after which Cornwallis undertook to conquer the Carolinas.

The Continental Navy was too weak to play a significant role, and except for the moral effect of the exploits of a few individuals, it had little influence on the war. After a minor raid on the Bahamas in 1776, it could do no more than harry British communications, principally by single cruisers.

5:

The War of the American Revolution, II

American prospects seemed at their bleakest in the winter of 1780–81. "I see nothing before us but accumulating distress," Washington wrote in October 1780. "We have been half our time without provisions and are like to continue so. We have no magazines, no money to form them, and in a little time we shall have no men, if we had money to pay them. We have lived upon expedients until we can live no longer."[1]

French aid seemed to have proved illusory. The squadron at Newport had lain blockaded since its arrival, and Rochambeau's troops had been forced to sit idle. De Guichen had not even replied to the American requests for assistance from the West Indian fleet. The British appeared to be conquering the South. Washington, barely holding together his little army of 3,500 men near West Point, could do nothing. In January 1781 the Pennsylvania and New Jersey troops mutinied. As spring came, Washington confided to his journal that he saw no prospect for a successful offensive campaign "unless we receive a powerful aid of ships, land troops, and money from our generous allies."

There were nonetheless some favorable factors in the situation. First, Britain had united the maritime nations of Europe against her. Second, she was paying too high a price for her successes in the south. And finally, the French were at last about to send really effective naval assistance to America.

Britain's seizure of neutral merchant vessels had caused Russia, Denmark, and Sweden to unite in the first Armed Neutrality of the North. Their object was to assert the right of

[1] To Brig. Gen. Cadwalader, October 5, 1780, John C. Fitzpatrick, ed., *Writings of George Washington* (Washington, 1931–44), XX, 122.

neutral vessels to carry any goods except contraband freely to any ports except those actually under blockade—the principle of "free ships, free goods," which was to play an important part in the subsequent history of neutral rights—and to limit seizures to contraband goods alone. Since the League controlled 84 ships of the line, and since Britain was dependent upon the Baltic trade for naval stores, she was forced for the moment to acquiesce.

Britain had been angered by Dutch trade with France and with the Americans and French in the West Indies. Furthermore, she looked with a covetous eye upon the weakly-held Dutch possessions. When the Dutch States General debated joining the Armed Neutrality, Britain delivered an ultimatum demanding that the Dutch honor their treaty of alliance of 1678, which obliged them to support her against France. When the Dutch rejected the ultimatum and voted to join the League, Britain seized upon the discovery of trade negotiations between an official of Amsterdam and the American colonies as an excuse and declared war on Holland in the latter part of December 1780.

The second factor favorable to the Americans was the excessive cost to the British of the campaign in the south. In this theater of the American war, General Nathanael Greene, America's ablest general next to Washington himself, had succeeded General Gates after the latter's defeat at Camden. In October 1780 a British-Tory raiding party of a thousand men had been wiped out by American backwoodsmen at King's Mountain. The following January substantial detachments from the two main armies met at Cowpens, South Carolina, where the skilled American riflemen practically annihilated the British. But Cornwallis, reinforced by troops from Virginia, pressed on after Greene, who finally made a stand in mid-March at Guilford Courthouse, North Carolina. The battle was a bloody draw in which more than a fourth of Cornwallis's army were killed or wounded.

From that time onward, Cornwallis was incapable of a real offensive. As British generals usually did when in difficulty, he retreated with his half-starved troops to the seacoast, at Wilmington, while Greene proceeded to reduce the British outposts in South Carolina and within a few months brought the greater part of the state again under American control.

The third and decisive factor in 1781 was the arrival via the West Indies of the effective French naval aid that Washington had so long sought.

The West Indies, 1780–81

Returning from New York to the West Indies at the end of November 1780, Rodney found that the islands had been devastated by an October hurricane and that the British ships that had remained there had been badly shattered. But in early January Rear Admiral Sir Samuel Hood, designated Rodney's second in command, arrived from England with reinforcements. In his mid-fifties, Hood was to prove an able and energetic, though somewhat less than loyal, subordinate. To his natural cantankerousness he soon added a detestation of Rodney, so that relations between the two were far from cordial. The eight of the line which he brought gave Rodney a fleet of 21 ships.

In January 1781 Rodney received orders to attack the Dutch West Indian Islands, most important of which at that time was St. Eustatius. Lying near the head of the Windward Islands, it had grown immensely wealthy as a neutral entrepôt in a world at war. It was a principal source of munitions for America as well as for the French West Indies, and from it the produce of both areas could be shipped in neutral bottoms to Europe. Consequently Rodney, whose greed was notorious, welcomed the opportunity for plunder. At the beginning of February he seized the island with its immense stores and with 120 merchantmen in its harbor. If the booty, running into millions of pounds, made him wealthy beyond his

dreams, it also ended for the time being his usefulness as an officer to the British navy, for he at once became too engrossed in his treasure to pursue the plan for operations against other Dutch possessions. Even word that a strong French fleet was heading for the West Indies failed to arouse Rodney, who contented himself with ordering Hood to a position from which he could both watch Fort Royal, Martinique, and cover the departure of a huge treasure convoy from St. Eustatius.

Rear Admiral the Comte de Grasse had sailed from Brest in the latter part of March 1781 with a sizable fleet escorting a large convoy of merchantmen. Aged 58, he was tall, handsome, energetic, and courageous, with a lifetime of experience at sea. Arriving off Martinique after a remarkably rapid passage of 36 days, he beat off Hood's attempt to intercept his convoy, damaging six British ships badly, and pursued the British for two days, turning back only when it became evident that he could not overtake their copper-clad vessels.

Immediately on reaching Martinique, de Grasse organized expeditions against the British. After an unsuccessful attempt to surprise St. Lucia, he turned to Tobago, which fell on the first of June. Rodney arrived three days too late, furious at the island's surrender and "determined, as he told everybody, to give the enemy battle wherever he should meet them." But next day, when he sighted the French nine or ten miles to leeward, he found an excuse not to attack.

De Grasse returned to Fort Royal to repair and replenish his ships. In early July he sailed with his entire fleet of 23 of the line and a convoy of 160 merchant vessels for Cap Français. Here he was joined by four additional ships, and here too he found letters from Rochambeau and from the French minister in Philadelphia requesting his aid in America.

The War in the Colonies, 1781

While de Grasse was winning successes in the West Indies, the Allied cause was faring less well in America. In December 1780 Clinton had sent Benedict Arnold with 1,600 men to ravage Virginia and incidentally to threaten Greene's communications. Landing at Portsmouth at the end of the month, Arnold cut a path of destruction across the state and ended by partially burning Richmond in January before returning to Portsmouth.

At Washington's urging, in early March 1781, the French Newport squadron eluded the British blockaders and sailed with a thousand of Rochambeau's troops for the Chesapeake to operate against Arnold. Washington had already sent Lafayette with 1,200 men overland to the head of the Bay to be in a position to cooperate. But the pursuing British beat the French to the Chesapeake and met them off Cape Henry on March 16. Although the French outmaneuvered and outfought the superior British squadron in the ensuing battle, they forfeited the strategic victory by returning to Newport, leaving the British in control of the Chesapeake.

General Clinton took advantage of this newly-confirmed control by sending General Phillips with 2,600 men to reinforce and supersede Arnold. Arriving at Portsmouth at the end of March, these forces spent two months ravaging Virginia, then in the latter part of May joined Cornwallis, who had marched north from Wilmington, North Carolina to Petersburg, Virginia. Lafayette with his 1,200 men found himself in grave danger. "I am not strong enough even to get beaten," he wrote Washington, while Cornwallis boasted, "The boy [Lafayette] cannot escape me."

Early in May a French frigate arrived at Boston bringing Admiral de Barras to take command of the Newport squadron, and news that France would send money but would commit no more troops to the American struggle. But a letter for Rochambeau in some paragraphs "not to be communicated to General Washington" contained more important information: in the latter part of the summer the French West Indian fleet would arrive to liberate and join the Newport squadron.

To determine Allied strategy for the campaign of 1781, Washington met in the latter part of May with the French leaders at Wethersfield, Connecticut. Washington had no official information regarding de Grasse's coming, and Rochambeau was not free to reveal what he knew. Admiral de Barras had already declared it impractical for his fleet to escort the French troops to Virginia, and a march overland was, in Washington's opinion, even more impracticable. An operation against New York was the only alternative, and it might still save Lafayette in Virginia by forcing Clinton to recall troops from the South. If de Grasse should appear with his fleet, the memorandum of the meeting stated, "the force thus combined may either proceed in the operation against New York or may be directed against the enemy in some other quarter, as circumstances may dictate."

Recognizing that naval superiority was of "essential importance in any offensive operation," Washington wrote the French minister in Philadelphia, asking him to urge de Grasse to come north to join in the operation against New York. Rochambeau wrote directly to de Grasse. He had agreed at Wethersfield to the New York campaign, but he had from the beginning entertained a certain skepticism regarding it. Moreover, he had information that the British planned to center operations in the South and was deeply concerned for his countryman Lafayette. He therefore told de Grasse:

There are two points at which an offensive may be made against the enemy: Chesapeake Bay and New York. The southwesterly winds and the state of distress in Virginia will probably make you prefer Chesapeake Bay, and it will be there where we think you may be able to render the greatest service.[2]

In a second letter he strongly urged the Admiral to bring not only his fleet but also troops and money.

In early July the main French and American armies met at Northcastle, near White Plains, for the campaign against New York. Rochambeau was not reassured by the sight of his allies. "The army of our neighbors," he reported to France, "has not four thousand men under arms." His own army numbered about 3,600, while Clinton had nearly 13,000 well-supplied, well-equipped troops in New York. To assault a city with a force substantially smaller than its garrison was not a promising enterprise. Washington, who now knew of de Grasse's impending arrival, saw no alternative

[2] French original in Henri Doniol, *Histoire de la Participation de la France à l'Etablissement des Etats-Unis d'Amérique*, (Paris, 1886–1892), V, 475; English translation in Charles Lee Lewis, *Admiral de Grasse and American Independence* (Annapolis, 1945), 120.

but to await his coming. If de Grasse brought sufficient troops to make the New York campaign practicable, he preferred to continue it. If not, they might look to the Chesapeake. Recognizing the latter possibility, Washington wrote General Knox "to suspend the transport of heavy cannon and stores from Philadelphia lest we should have them to carry back again," and two days later wrote Robert Morris to find what shipping would be available in Philadelphia, Baltimore, and elsewhere, "should we obtain a naval superiority, of which I am not without hope, and be able to carry a body of men suddenly round by water."

Meanwhile the opportunity was being created in the South. Cornwallis, under orders from Clinton, was withdrawing down the York Peninsula. Lafayette, now reinforced by Wayne from the North and by Steuben from the Carolinas, had suffered a defeat in early July when he attacked the British rear guard at Green Spring, near Jamestown, but he continued to follow as if he were pursuing.

Washington surmised that Cornwallis would establish himself at Portsmouth, ship part of his force to New York, and take the rest to Charleston. Such a move would have effected a sensible concentration of the divided British forces, which would have made more difficult any Allied operation against them when de Grasse appeared. Indeed, such an idea had occurred to the British generals. Clinton, apprehensive of Washington's designs, had since early June been calling on Cornwallis to send troops to reinforce New York, but Cornwallis had some notion of withdrawing to Charleston.

But there was a basic failure of coordination between the two. After a visit to England in 1778-79, Cornwallis had returned to America as second in command with the expectation of succeeding Clinton and with encouragement from Germain to communicate with him directly, a short-circuiting of the chain of command that could not fail to cause trouble. The two generals moreover differed radically in their strategic views. Cornwallis felt that Virginia and the Chesapeake were the key to the colonies and had entered upon his campaign through the Carolinas without even consulting Clinton. Clinton wanted on the Bay only a base for raiding parties, which he conceived could be defended by only a few troops. Cornwallis felt that his entire army was none too strong to hold such a base. Consequently he delayed sending reinforcements to New York even when in early July Clinton's calls became more urgent. Then, feeling that he had peremptory orders to establish a base on the York Peninsula, he began with considerable misgiving to fortify Yorktown and also Gloucester, across the York River. Lafayette in reporting this move to Washington added prophetically, "If we should have a fleet arrive at this moment, our affairs would take a happy turn."

Preparations for Yorktown

Miracles do not often occur in military and naval operations, but Yorktown was a miracle. At a time when the American cause was disintegrating, it brought victory. At a time when the British could not effectively coordinate two armies in the colonies—witness Howe and Burgoyne, or Clinton and Cornwallis—it was an example of perfect coordination of a fleet with the armies of two different nations. At a time when communications were slow and unreliable, it demonstrated precise timing on the part of forces 1,500 miles apart. It was the sort of operation of which Washington had dreamed ever since the French entered the war.

The letter on which everything hinged arrived at Washington's headquarters on August 14. The essence was that de Grasse was sailing from Cap Français on August 13 with more than 3,000 troops embarked in from 25 to 29 vessels of war, and that he was also bringing the money requested. He would go directly to the Chesapeake, "the place which seems indicated . . . as that most certain to achieve the benefit which you propose." But he would be able to remain only till mid-October, for his troops had been promised for other operations. He therefore hoped to find all ready to make the best use of the precious time he could spend on the American coast.

Washington quickly adjusted his plans to embrace the opportunity. Because half the American troops would have to remain to protect West Point, he could take only 2,500 men to Virginia, but Rochambeau would take his entire force of 3,500. Accepting the difficulties of moving an army overland, which had previously deterred him from a campaign in the

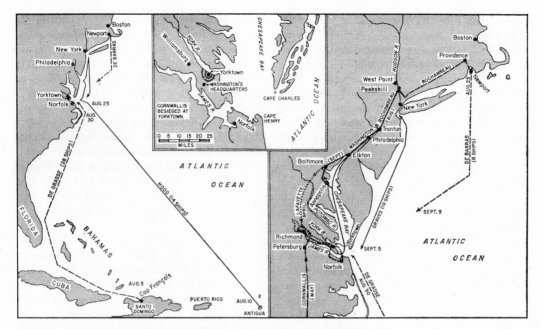

FRENCH, AMERICAN, AND BRITISH FORCES CONVERGE ON YORKTOWN, 1781

south, Washington had his men on the march within four days of receiving de Grasse's letter. To prevent the British from falling on his rear or from making any move to extricate Cornwallis, he made an elaborate pretense of preparing for an attack on Staten Island.

Although this stratagem succeeded beyond expectation, the march south marked a period of intense anxiety for Washington. Arriving at Philadelphia on the last day of August, he received news that a British fleet—actually Hood's from the West Indies—was off Sandy Hook. There seemed a real danger that it might intercept de Barras, who had just sailed from Newport, or that it might enter the Chesapeake before de Grasse, of whom there had been no further word.

By September 5 both the American and French troops had passed through Philadelphia, and Washington, after concluding his business in the city, followed at his customary hard pace. On the way he received the news that de Grasse was in the Chesapeake and at once turned back to Chester to bring the news to Rochambeau, who had been inspecting the famous Delaware forts by water. As the French general's boat approached shore he was astonished to see the usually reserved Washington waving wildly with his hat in one hand and his handkerchief in the other, and to be vigorously embraced as soon as he stepped ashore. On the evening of September 14, after a furious ride, Washington and Rochambeau approached Williamsburg to greet Lafayette and Wayne. Early the next morning came news that de Grasse had returned to the Chesapeake after a successful though inconclusive engagement, and that de Barras had arrived safely from Newport with the artillery and provisions.

The Battle of the Virginia Capes, September 5, 1781

De Grasse, after reading the appeals from North America at Cap Français, had decided to go north with his entire fleet, delaying the sailing of a great convoy for France so as not to weaken his force by providing escorts. He thereby set in train the naval operations that proved basic to the Yorktown campaign.

Sailing on August 5, he proceeded by the unfrequented Old Bahama Channel, between the north coast of Cuba and the Bahama Banks, and arrived off the mouth of the Chesapeake on August 30 without any report having reached the English. After landing the troops he had brought, he transported General Wayne and his soldiers to a position below the James to cut off Cornwallis' retreat into the Carolinas. Then, in response to a request from Washington, he was preparing to send his lighter vessels to the Head of Elk to bring French and American troops down the bay, when at about ten o'clock on the morning of September 5 his frigates posted outside the bay signaled that a fleet had been sighted. There was at first some hope that it might be de Barras' squadron from Rhode Island, but it was soon evident that there were too many sails. The fleet was obviously enemy.

When de Grasse had sailed from Fort Royal to Cap Français in early July, his movement had been reported to Rodney, who sent sloops to alert both New York and Jamaica and ordered Hood to prepare to sail for New York should the need arise. Then, being in poor health, he sailed on August 1 for England with four of the line, leaving Hood with orders to proceed to North America. Next day Hood sailed to Antigua, where he found dispatches from Clinton and Graves indicating that de Grasse was expected to come to Rhode Island to join de Barras for an attack on New York. Hood therefore sailed from St. John's on August 10, five days after de Grasse's departure from Cap Français. Outside the harbor he was joined by four of the line, to give him a total of 14 ships. That such a number might not be adequate seems never to have entered the heads of the English admirals. Both Rodney and Hood assumed that de Grasse, after detaching a number of vessels to protect the West Indian convoy to France, would go north with no more than a dozen ships.

Hastening north by the direct route, Hood looked into the Chesapeake on the 25th. Finding no trace of the French there, since he was ahead of de Grasse, he looked in at the Delaware and then hurried on to New York. There he found Clinton and Graves oblivious of the real situation, making leisurely plans for an operation against the French in Rhode Island. Hood's urgent representations, reinforced by news that de Barras had sailed from Newport, brought Graves over the bar with his five available ships—only half of what he might have

had.[3] As senior, he assumed command of the combined force of 19 of the line and set sail for the Chesapeake, where he arrived on the morning of September 5. It was a fine, fair day with a moderate breeze from the NNE. At about 9:30 British lookouts sighted the French fleet at anchor just inside Cape Henry, and Graves ordered his ships to form a line of battle. French frigates on guard outside the Bay reported the British at about the same time.

De Grasse had just detached four ships of the line to blockade the York and James rivers, so that only 24 were available for a sortie. His boats with a large part of his crews were absent landing troops, leaving his fleet seriously undermanned. The flagship *Ville de Paris*, for example, was short 200 men, while the *Citoyen*, which could hardly have been an exception, had not sufficient crew aboard to man the guns of her upper deck. Altogether, nearly 1,900 officers and men were ashore. Under these circumstances de Grasse might well have taken a defensive position across the mouth of the Chesapeake. In sailing out he ran a double risk—of being defeated, and of having the British slip into the Bay behind him. On the other hand, remaining in the Bay would sentence de Barras to almost certain capture on his arrival, with the loss of all the French siege artillery and munitions. Weighing these alternatives, de Grasse decided to leave the Bay for battle.

But to leave the Chesapeake in the face of a fresh northeasterly wind was no simple problem. Although Cape Henry and Cape Charles are some ten miles apart, the channel for large ships between Cape Henry and Middle Ground Shoal is only about three miles wide. To beat out against a flood tide was impossible. Therefore de Grasse's order was for ships to get under way at noon, when the tide would turn.

At 12:30, when the British were 12 to 15 miles northeast of Cape Henry, de Grasse ordered his ships to slip cables and form a line of battle in order of swiftness without regard

[3] He left two under repair in the East River and had detached three only a few days before. Rodney had sent one ship to Jamaica and had taken four to England, leaving Hood with five fewer than he might have had. The British fleet was thus ten ships weaker than it need have been had the British leaders felt any real urgency.

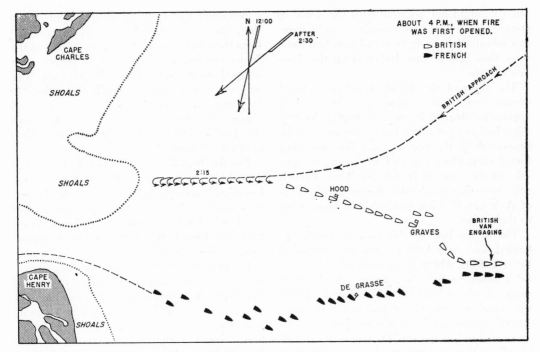

BATTLE OF THE VIRGINIA CAPES, SEPTEMBER 5, 1781

to assigned positions. They executed this command with remarkable efficiency, considering their shorthanded condition, but they could hardly avoid straggling out of the Bay. The first four vessels emerged in good order, but the next two were a mile to leeward, while the center and rear were almost another two miles to leeward.

The British, by contrast, were coming down from the northeast in a well-formed line at one cable's length. Gradually Graves changed course toward the west until the two fleets were on approximately parallel and opposite courses. At 2 PM the French van was three miles south of Graves' flagship *London*, which was at the center of the British line. Then at 2:15, as the head of the British line approached the shoals at the entrance to the Bay, Graves ordered his fleet to wear together. This maneuver of course reversed the order of his line, putting Drake's division in the van and Hood's in the rear. By this time the French center and part of the rear division were well clear of Cape Henry. Although the two fleets were now on the same tack, the lines were by no means parallel. The British tended to close by having

their van lead toward the French, leaving their rear well to windward, while, as has been said, the French rear had fallen to leeward of its van. Neither were the two lines conterminous, for the French were not only more numerous but were also in much less compact order than the British.

To correct his line, de Grasse about three o'clock ordered his van to fall off to leeward and run full, while all through the action he kept his center hugging the wind as closely as possible in order to support his leading ships. Graves meanwhile was signaling his van to lead more to starboard, that is, toward the French. At 3:46, when he had reached a suitable position, he ordered his fleet to bear down and engage the enemy closely. As we have seen, this maneuver regularly resulted in a diagonal approach with the vans making first contact. In this instance the tendency was accentuated by the "V" arrangement of the two columns. The result was that at about four o'clock the two vans came within pistol shot and began a very heavy engagement. Seeing that only his leading ships were in contact, Graves at 4:11 hauled down the signal for line ahead, in order "that it might not interfere with the signal to engage close," and flew it again for only about five minutes before 4:30 to call into line some ships that had become bunched on the *London's* beam.

The ships of the British van had suffered heavily from a near-raking fire during their approach. Meanwhile the four leading French ships had not yet fallen back sufficiently to be supported by the rest of their line and thus found themselves engaged by seven or eight ships of the compact British van. These French ships were in considerable danger until others of their van division succeeded in coming up to their relief.

The action had by this time gradually extended back to a little beyond the centers of the two fleets, where de Grasse's great *Ville de Paris* joined in, but the rears remained out of range. At about 5:30 Hood at last noticed that the signal for line ahead was not flying and started to bear up, but it was too late, and the move was only a gesture. De Grasse perceived Hood's action and prepared to tack his fleet together to the NNW, which he considered "would inevitably have thrown the British line into confusion," but Hood had already thought better of his move and canceled his order, so that there was no contact between the rear divisions. Hood's own explanation of his failure to engage is as follows:

So soon as the signal for the line was hauled down, about twenty-five minutes after five, the rear division bore up three quarters of a mile to leeward of the center division; but the French ships bearing up also, and the *London* continuing to lay to, Rear-Admiral Sir Samuel Hood called to the *Monarch* [lead ship of his division] to haul her wind, as he did not dare to separate with his division just at dark; and the signal for the line ahead at half a cable being again hoisted about ten minutes after six, and the signal for battle hauled down, Sir Samuel tacked with his division to regain his station.[4]

[4] G. R. Barnes and J. H. Owen (eds.), *The Private Papers of John, Earl of Sandwich, First Lord of the Admiralty, 1771–82* (Navy Records Society, 1932–38), IV, 191. Note the nautical term *bear up*. This means to fall off before the wind, change course so as to move downwind. The phrase derives from the fact that the wheel formerly turned opposite to the swing of the ship's bow; hence it was turned toward the wind (up) in order to swing the

Although the vans remained within pistol shot, the crews ceased firing at about 5:30 from sheer exhaustion. The cannonading in the center continued for half an hour longer, then stopped about sunset. At 6:15 Graves sent frigates to his van and rear with the order "to keep in a parallel line with the enemy and well abreast of them during the night," but with the British hugging the wind the two fleets gradually separated.

For the British it was, as Hood observed, a day of lost opportunities. Their inferiority was less than it appeared, for although the French fleet carried 384 more guns, just about that number had to be left unmanned. More important, the French had been caught straggling from harbor under an adverse wind.

It seems clear that Graves was unimaginative and conventional, bent on fighting a traditional line battle. As he wrote to Lord Sandwich, "My aim was to get close, to form parallel, extend with them, and attack all together."[5] It has been suggested that upon first sighting the French he ought to have signaled General Chase and fallen upon the French as they emerged from the Bay. But Graves in fact seems to have closed as rapidly as he could after sighting, and twice he ordered Drake's rear division to make more sail. By 2:15, the time the head of his column neared Middle Ground, which, it is reasonable to suppose, is as early as a general engagement could have been brought on under General Chase, the French vessels already clear of the Cape were at least as numerous as the English fleet, with more coming on immediately. Except for the van's being to windward, they were in fair order, whereas the British under General Chase would have been in disorder. It seems likely that had Graves given such a command, he would have fared no better than Byron off Grenada, and he might have fared a great deal worse.[6]

bow of the ship downwind. This practice, derived from the earlier tiller, made for some curious phraseology. The command "Port your helm," for example, meant "Turn to starboard." And because a fleet approaching another fleet in line of bearing to engage was said to *bear down* on the enemy, the windward fleet had to *bear up* in order to *bear down*.

[5] *Ibid.*, IV, 181.

[6] See Young's comment on General Chase, page 82, n 9, above.

The real mistake of the British, which was well enough perceived by critics on the spot, was their failure to mass on or even cut off the exposed French van. This was the burden of the criticism which Hood wrote to Lord Sandwich next day. He concluded:

Had the centre of the British line gone on to the support of the van, and the signal for the line been hauled down, . . . the van ships of the enemy must have been cut up; and the rear division of the British fleet would have been opposed to those ships the centre fired at, and at the most *proper* distance for engaging.[7]

The interesting thing about this criticism is that it is just what would have happened had Graves' signals been obeyed, for despite his conventional intention, the more compact British fleet had inadvertently massed on the forward part of the French line. All that was lacking was to make the action close. Graves repeatedly signaled for close action all along the line, he hauled down the line-ahead signal that it might not interfere, and he raised it again briefly "only to push the ships ahead of me forward and who were some of them upon my off beam." The man who failed to close for action and to bring the entire British force to bear on the French van and center was Hood himself, who chose to interpret the signal for the line as requiring the rear to remain on a geometrically straight line extended from the van through Graves' flagship. His criticism shows that he understood well enough what he ought to have done.

Bitterly disappointed at the failure of his fleet to execute his wishes, Graves next day circulated a memorandum:

When the signal for line of battle ahead is out at the same time with the signal for battle, it is not to be understood that the latter signal shall be rendered ineffectual by a too strict adherence to the former. The signal for the line of battle ahead is to be considered as the line of extension for the fleet, and the respective admirals and captains of the fleet are desired to be attentive not to advance or fall back, so as to intercept the fire of their seconds ahead and astern, but to keep as near the enemy as possible whilst the signal for close action continues out; and to take notice that the line must be preserved parallel to that of the

enemy during the battle, without regard to a particular point or bearing.[8]

The important words are "line of extension of the fleet," by which Graves meant that his line ahead signal was flown to warn ships not to overlap and mask each other's fire. His succeeding words make it clear that he did *not* intend the signal to freeze the line into a rigidity that would keep some ships out of combat. The memorandum was a pointed rebuke to Hood, who blusteringly wrote on the back of his copy, "It is the first time I ever heard it suggested that too strict an adherence could be paid to the line of battle. . . . According to Mr. Graves's Memo., any captain may break the line with impunity when he pleases."[9] Hood may have been supported by the letter of tradition; the sacrosanct conterminious line might still serve as a refuge for fools and scoundrels; but by all reasonable standards he was wrong —and he knew it.

Despite the failure to achieve the general action that both commanders obviously desired, the battle of September 5 was no mere skirmish. In the vans at least it was a close and devastating combat. The frigates sent out by Graves at 6:15 brought him, as he wrote "such a state of damages that we could only think of preserving the best appearance." The *Terrible* was so badly riddled that she had to be sunk a few days later, and at least five other ships had sustained serious damage, a good deal of it in their hulls. The French van too had suffered severely, but when Graves viewed the French fleet next morning, "they had not the appearance of near so much damage as we had sustained."[10] Nor was it a mere French "rigging shoot." The British suffered 336 casualties, the French 230.

Through the 6th, a calm day, the two fleets remained within sight of each other, repairing their damage, with neither attempting to attack. Indeed, Graves had already decided that

8 Sir John Knox Laughton, ed., *Letters and Papers of Charles, Lord Barham, Admiral of The Red Squadron, 1758–1813* (Navy Records Society, 1907–1911), I, 127.

9 *Ibid.*

10 Rear Admiral French Ensor Chadwick (ed.), *The Graves Papers and Other Documents Relating to the Naval Operations of the Yorktown Campaign, July to October 1781* (Naval History Society, New York, 1916), 63.

7 *Sandwich Papers*, IV, 189–90.

his fleet was in no condition to renew the engagement. At daybreak on the 7th de Grasse tacked in an effort to attack the British van, but Graves wore his fleet and avoided action. Later in the day squalls separated the two fleets. The 8th was stormy with a northerly wind. Since de Grasse expected de Barras from the north, he made a strenuous effort to secure the weather gage in order to protect his colleague, and succeeded a little before sunset. This seizure of the windward position was well timed, for on the morning of the 9th the sails of a squadron appeared on the horizon. De Grasse was unable to close sufficiently to make out the flag, but it was, as he suspected, de Barras, who anchored safely in the Chesapeake on the 10th. Being out of sight of the British and conscious of his strategic mission, de Grasse too set course for the Bay, where he arrived next day. With de Barras' ships, he now had 36 of the line.

Hood, on seeing the French carry "a great press of sail" on the 9th, correctly guessed de Grasse's destination and next day persuaded Graves to run for the Chesapeake to relieve Lord Cornwallis, but he added that he was afraid the opportunity had already been lost. Upon arriving off the entrance to the Bay on the 13th and finding the French at anchor inside, Graves again asked Hood's advice. Hood replied, "Sir Samuel would be very glad to send an opinion, but he really knows not what to say in the truly lamentable state we have brought ourselves."[11]

There was indeed nothing to do but return to New York to repair the fleet as quickly as possible in order to carry Clinton with 6,000 troops to the aid of Cornwallis. It is a measure of the effectiveness of French fire at Virginia Capes that despite the urgency, Graves was not ready till October 19. The British plan was somehow to slip by the French in the Bay, anchor at the mouth of the York River, and unload the troops. This desperate scheme ignored the shore batteries, the probable action of the superior French fleet, and the danger that if the British fleet reached the York it might well share the fate of Cornwallis. In that event the West Indies also would be lost. Hence it is no reflection on Graves that he had his doubts. Only Hood among the admirals enter-

[11] *Ibid.*, 89.

tained any real hope, and that rested upon the expectation that the French would come out to fight at sea.

On the 19th Graves sailed with 23 of the line, and arrived off the Chesapeake a week later. But Cornwallis, after losing two of his outer redoubts and failing in an attempt to escape across the river to Gloucester, had already surrendered his entire army of 7,600 men on October 19. The relief expedition could only return to New York.

In justice to Graves, it must be remembered that he had an inferior fleet, and few naval victories have gone to the weaker side. But the British inferiority was unnecessary, and the man most directly responsible for it was Rodney.

The War Dies Out in the Colonies

The British capitulation at Yorktown practically ended the war in the colonies. Greene, reinforced after the surrender of Cornwallis, succeeded in clearing South Carolina by the end of the year, confining the British to Charleston, while Washington lamented the departure of the sea power that might have made the success complete.

To the British the loss of a second entire army in America was stunning, but an aroused Britain might have made good the loss and continued the war. However, the disaster discredited the North ministry, and that proved decisive. Early in 1782 Lord Germain, who alone in the cabinet had been in whole-hearted agreement with the King's policy of coercion, resigned his office. At the end of February the House of Commons passed a resolution "That it is the opinion of this House that the further prosecution of offensive war on the continent of North America . . . will be the means of weakening the effort of this country against her European enemies and tends . . . dangerously to increase the mutual enmity so fatal to the interests of both Great Britain and America."[12] Three weeks later Lord North announced the resignation of his ministry, and George III seriously considered abdicating. The Marquis of Rockingham, who had earlier been responsible

[12] Quoted in Capt. W. M. James RN, *The British Navy in Adversity* (London, 1926), 318; Lewis, *De Grasse and American Independence*, 222.

for the repeal of the Stamp Act, formed a new government friendly to America and at once sent an emissary to Paris to discuss peace terms with Franklin, but not till November was the preliminary treaty signed.

Final Operations of the Continental Navy

The Continental Navy played very little part in this final phase of the war. Indeed, it had very nearly ceased to exist. At the beginning of 1781 it consisted only of the *Trumbull* of the 1775 program, the *Confederacy* and the *Alliance* of the 1776 program, the frigate *Deane* and the sloop *Saratoga*. Sailing from the Delaware on August 1781, the *Trumbull* lost her topmasts in a storm before encountering H.M.S. *Iris*, formerly the American *Hancock*, to which she was forced to strike after a stubborn resistance. The *Confederacy, Deane,* and *Saratoga,* under Commodore Samuel Nicholson, cruised in the West Indies in the early part of the year. On their return they became separated off the Delaware Capes. The *Confederacy* encountered two British frigates and surrendered, while the *Saratoga* foundered at sea.

Only the *Alliance,* commanded by Commodore John Barry, survived the war. At the beginning of 1781 he was ordered to take Washington's aide, Colonel John Laurens, to France on an urgent mission. On his return voyage Barry captured two armed British vessels—a ship and a brig—after a sharp engagement. In the latter part of 1782 he made creditable cruises off Bermuda and Newfoundland, during which he took several prizes. In the spring of 1783 Barry in the *Alliance* successfully brought money and a newly purchased vessel from Havana after fighting off a superior British force that attempted to intercept him.

The relative failure of the Continental Navy stemmed not merely from the disadvantages of semi-blockade of its home ports and superior enemy forces at sea. The difficulty or impossibility of finding crews not infrequently delayed or prevented the sailing of Continental vessels. Another handicap was lack of effective organization, efficient management, and a real high command. The Maritime Committee proved so unsatisfactory that in October 1779 Congress abolished it and created in its stead a Board of the Admiralty. But great difficulty was experienced in finding commissioners for the Board, and it was discontinued in 1781. Naval administration was then vested in an Agent of Marine, but none was appointed, so that almost by default the function was exercised by Robert Morris, who had been executive for the Continental Congress and had recently been appointed to the unenviable position of Superintendent of Finances. Thus the Navy remained administratively the stepchild of the Revolution, principally for lack of "a naval counterpart to Washington."

The Battle of the Saints, April 12, 1782

Washington had been eager to follow up the success at Yorktown with an attack on Charleston, but de Grasse felt that his commitments to the Spaniards precluded his cooperation. On November 4 he sailed for the West Indies with his 27 of the line and de Barras' seven. On arriving at Fort Royal in the latter part of the month he found that the French Governor of Martinique had taken advantage of Hood's absence to surprise and recapture St. Eustatius with a part of Rodney's booty.

While awaiting supplies for the Jamaica expedition, de Grasse used his time to advantage. After being frustrated by the weather in an attempt on Barbados, he turned in early January to St. Kitts. Although Hood, who had followed de Grasse from America to the West Indies, appeared on the scene before the island was completely in French hands, he was unable to prevent its fall in February. Meanwhile other French expeditions had captured minor islands from the British, who now retained only St. Lucia, Antigua, Barbados, and Jamaica. Having lost the war in North America, they were well on the way to losing it in the West Indies.

By April de Grasse was ready for the descent on Jamaica, largest and most valuable of the British West Indian possessions. The task facing him was not an enviable one. He had first to sail to Santo Domingo to join a Spanish force, but he would be hampered by a convoy of 150 ships, some of which carried the artillery for the projected expedition. Hood had been joined by Rodney with twelve of the line fresh from England, making the British fleet slightly superior to the French. With the British based at St. Lucia, immediately south of Martinique, and with their frigates constantly watching Fort Royal, de Grasse had little opportunity of escaping undetected.

At daybreak on April 8 de Grasse saw his convoy safely out of port and then put to sea with his fleet of 33 of the line and four frigates. By noon Rodney was at sea with 36 of the line and 20 frigates, and by evening the two fleets were within sight of each other.

That night the French fleet lay becalmed under the lee of Dominica. When dawn revealed the British to leeward, de Grasse signaled his convoy to run into Guadeloupe, while the fleet formed a line of battle to cover its retreat. During the forenoon the British van under Hood progressed sufficiently to catch a little of the NNE breeze coming around the northern end of the island and thus threatened the most leeward of the French vessels. De Grasse therefore put his fleet on the port tack in reverse order and, taking care to remain out of reach of the British carronades, engaged Hood briskly at about half cannon range, while the British center and rear lay becalmed, helpless to intervene. Four of Hood's ships were considerably injured, and the division as a whole suffered such damage and casualties that Rodney subsequently transferred it to the rear to recuperate. One French ship had to be sent into Guadeloupe for repair.

While the action was in progress, de Grasse had sent word for the convoy to leave Guadeloupe for Santo Domingo, and by evening it was out of sight. But since the copper-sheathed British fleet might easily overtake it, de Grasse remained in Dominica Channel through the 9th, keeping to windward of the British, in order to give his convoy ample time to escape, while the British lay to, making repairs. On the 10th the French worked to windward in Saints' Passage, north of Dominica, with the British in pursuit.

Up to this time things had gone well for the French. Their convoy was now safe, and the fleet was withdrawing successfully. But during the night the *Zélé* collided with another vessel, forcing the latter to retire into Basse-Terre and causing the *Zélé* to fall behind so that she and her escort at dawn were in danger of capture. With his fleet already reduced to 31, de Grasse was unwilling to lose two more vessels. Sacrificing his lead, he reversed course to cover his laggards. The leading British ships fell back to take their places in line, so that de Grasse was able to save his two ships without fighting.

That night the *Zélé* crowned her wretched career by colliding with the *Ville de Paris*. It was her fourteenth collision in 13 months, and her fourth since leaving Fort Royal. This time she lost her bowsprit and mizzen, so that she had to be taken in tow for Guadeloupe by a frigate. De Grasse now had only 30 ships to face Rodney's 36.

Dawn of April 12 found the French fleet in considerable disorder, scattered between Dominica, the Saints, and Marie Galante. The *Ville de Paris,* which had been delayed by the accident, was 10 or 15 miles from those French ships farthest to windward in the ENE breeze. Two miles to leeward of the flagship plodded the *Zélé,* towed by her frigate. Rodney, seeing the opportunity to force a battle, sent four of his fastest ships in pursuit of the *Zélé.* When de Grasse saw his ship and frigate threatened, he made the gallant decision to turn back to their support. With eight or ten days' sailing ahead of him, he could not permit his stragglers to be picked off without finding his fleet seriously depleted. Already he had twice succored trailing vessels without serious difficulty. Therefore a little before six o'clock he ordered his fleet to form line of battle in reverse order on the port tack and advanced on a SSW course to meet the British. But in his haste to save his threatened vessels de Grasse did not allow his fleet time to form up properly, for it was scattered over 12 or 15 miles. The battle started before the first four ships of the van could reach their positions, and the French line remained a succession of bunches and gaps.

Rodney had in the meantime recalled his chasers and ordered line of battle on the starboard tack. With the British advancing on a northeasterly course, the two fleets converged at an angle. A little before eight the head of the French line crossed the line of advance of the British, thus winning the windward position. The last ships of the French van division

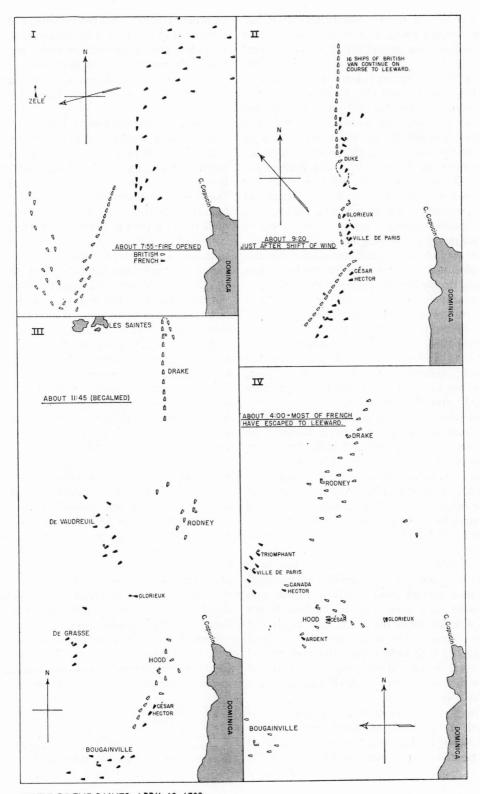

BATTLE OF THE SAINTS, APRIL 12, 1782

opened fire on the leading British ships just before eight o'clock. Soon afterward de Grasse ordered his van to fall off more to the west in order to maintain contact with the British line after passing the point of convergence.

De Grasse realized that in proceeding upon its present course his fleet would pass into the lee of Dominica with its false airs and calms. Accordingly he made two attempts within the first hour of the battle to wear his fleet onto the same tack as the British, but since the majority of his ships were already engaged at pistol shot, to have worn would have exposed them to a severe raking, and his captains refused to attempt the maneuver.

Ordinarily the passing of two fleets on opposite tacks had no significant results, but this occasion was an exception, for the battle was largely decided at this stage. In the first place, the extremely light airs made the passage slow and greatly protracted the exposure to enemy fire. In the second place, the range was extremely close. The British close-hauled to bring the lines within easy pistol shot, and the French, occupying the windward position, could not fall off to a greater distance, as they would ordinarily have done.

The closeness of the action was particularly disadvantageous to the French because the English were well equipped with carronades, while the French had none. Their effect was murderous aboard the crowded French vessels, which carried some 5,500 troops in addition to their regular crews. The carronades were well seconded by the British long guns, the effectiveness of which had been vastly increased by the gunnery reforms of Rodney's fleet captain, Sir Charles Douglas. The old rule had been "two or three quick broadsides in passing," but now special tackle enabled British gun crews to train their guns up to four points ahead or astern of the beam. The result was that a British ship could fire two or three broadsides both before and after the guns of a French ship could be brought to bear, and while they were opposite, the British were able to fire a great deal more rapidly.

The greater rapidity of British fire was effected by a series of small improvements initiated by Sir Charles. "Wedges," or inclined planes, and heavy springs and weights in the breeching absorbed the recoil of guns and made their return to battery easier. Flannel-bottomed cartridges and the use of wet wads eliminated the whole process of worming, that is, cleaning out the cannon to remove any sparks or burning fragments before recharging it with powder. Formerly, after a gun was loaded, the gun captain trickled a small stream of powder from a horn at his waist into the touchhole, then called up a boy with a slow-burning match, and lit off the gun. Sir Charles invented a quicker and safer method. He had "perforated goose quills" filled with powder in advance. The gun captain simply took a quill from his pocket, inserted it in the touchhole, and then fired it with a flintlock similar to that of a musket. Sir Charles was not exaggerating when he said after the battle that the British fire had been "so quick and so well directed, and extending so far to the right and left, that the French cannot comprehend how they came to lose so many and we so few."[13]

At any rate, it is evident that the French incurred heavy casualties and severe damage at this stage of the battle. In particular they suffered from the fire of the great three-deckers at the center of the British line. Worst hit was the *Glorieux,* which was staggered by the broadsides of the *Duke* and came reeling down toward Rodney's *Formidable.* At just this moment, about a quarter past nine, the wind veered four points toward the south, filling the British sails from the stern, but striking the bows of the already close-hauled French. Most of the French vessels swung to starboard (toward the British) in an attempt to keep their sails filled and to preserve steerage way. This tended to place them in a line of bearing and to force them down upon the British. Others, being taken aback, filled on the opposite (starboard) tack. Thus the French line, already badly formed, simply disintegrated.

One of the ships falling onto the starboard tack was immediately astern of the disabled *Glorieux.* This coincidence opened a great gap in the French line on the starboard bow of

[13] *Barham Papers,* I, 280–81. The quality of French gunnery, on the other hand, had fallen off seriously during the war as the corps of skilled seaman gunners was more and more diluted by drafts from the army to keep up its strength.

the British flagship. As the disabled *Glorieux* drifted down upon the *Formidable,* Rodney sent his physician below decks to tell the gunners to depress their guns in order to hole her near the water line. Since this action deprived us of the one reliable witness, it can never be known whether the maneuver which followed was at the suggestion of Sir Charles Douglas, as some have asserted, or on Rodney's own initiative—if, indeed, it was not either inadvertent, or inescapable in order to clear the *Duke,* which was nearly afoul of a French ship ahead. At any rate, the *Formidable* swung to starboard through the gap in the French line. There was no signal for the maneuver—that for close action to starboard was still flying. Indeed, there could have been none, for, as Sir Julian Corbett has pointed out, "there was a signal for breaking the line on every principal station except that which Rodney commanded."

Despite the lack of a signal, British ships almost simultaneously cut through the French line at two other points. The next five ships astern of the *Formidable* followed Rodney. The sixth, the *Bedford,*[14] spontaneously cut through a few ships ahead of the *Ville de Paris* and was followed by Hood's entire division, thus placing most of the French center (seven vessels, including the flagship) between the British rear and the six ships of Rodney's group. At the same time, Rodney's penetration had caused the four or five French ships astern of the gap to become badly bunched. The *Duke,* which had been just ahead of the *Formidable* in the British line, also ported her helm and passed through the French line just astern of this group, firing both broadsides into the clustered French as she went. But she was unsupported and was soon surrounded by several vessels of the French rear, which came up at once. She was forced to strike but was fortunate that the French had no opportunity to take possession. Meanwhile the 16 British vessels ahead of the *Duke* had continued on course and were soon out of the battle to leeward.

[14] The *Bedford's* captain was Thomas Graves, who, in looking over Byron's instructions in 1779, had written, "Is it not wonderful that there are no signals for breaking the enemy's line . . . ?"

"Breaking the line," far from conferring an automatic victory upon the British, brought them no obvious advantage except perhaps as the British captains were better fitted for the disorganized fighting that followed. The two fleets were equally fragmented. If de Grasse with seven ships was for the moment cut off from the rest of his fleet, so was Rodney with six cut off from his, while the *Duke* had been isolated and nearly lost. Moreover, with the 16 ships of his van out of the battle to leeward, Rodney was badly outnumbered, for the French fleet was still practically intact.

There was however very little actual fighting at this point. Rodney had hauled to windward and found no more opponents after passing through the French line. Before he could tack to rejoin the battle, the breeze, already light, failed completely. The calm also frustrated his attempt to recall his van division, which was unable to rejoin until afternoon. In the meantime de Grasse with seven ships, finding no British to leeward, had run downwind to aid the crippled *Glorieux,* and the French rear division had assembled in the same general area before the calm descended. Thus by about 10:50 most of the firing had ceased, but smoke hung heavy over the battlefield.

Only between a few ships of the British rear and the French van which were becalmed in contact did the firing continue for about an hour longer. There Hood, whose *Barfleur* was already clear of the French, noticed about 11:00 that the signal for line of battle had ben hauled down and set an example for his division by putting out his boats and towing the head of his ship around toward the enemy. Rear Admiral de Bougainville, commanding the French ships farthest to windward, held the key to the battle. He had drawn off to the westward with most of his van division after suffering substantial damage, but with his flagship rendered incapable of combat, he played no further part in the engagement.

The first phase of the battle thus ended about noon with a complete calm lying over the battlefield, on which the British and French had exchanged windward and leeward positions, and with only a few of Hood's and Bougainville's ships still in contact.

About one o'clock a light breeze sprang up and the battle came back to life. De Grasse took advantage of the opportunity to attempt to re-form his line, signaling for reverse order on the port tack—the same as that of the morning. De Vaudreuil soon had the French rear division in position, but Bougainville's van failed to join up. Realizing that his fleet was in no condition to renew the battle, de Grasse attempted to make an orderly withdrawal, sailing first west and then northwest, running generally before the wind. But the *Ville de Paris,* already badly damaged, appears to have fallen somewhat behind, while many of the French ships simply took to flight.

After waiting for his van to rejoin, Rodney came down in a leisurely fashion, though some of his ships raced Hood's for the French cripples. The swift *Canada,* from Rodney's group, was the first to overtake the dismasted *Glorieux,* in tow by a frigate. The French captain, seeing the hopelessness of his position, himself cut loose the frigate in order that she might not share the fate of his own vessel, then at about 1:30 struck to the *Canada.* Captain Cornwallis however would not wait to take possession but pressed on after the French main body. Meanwhile ships of Hood's division were pursuing two French vessels which had previously been becalmed opposite them and were now attempting to rejoin de Grasse. In mid-afternoon they took the first, but the *Canada* an hour later beat them to the second, which had almost reached the *Ville de Paris.* Again Captain Cornwallis refused to pause and pressed on after the French flagship. Nearby the British took a fourth prize when Hood's ships captured the *Ardent,* which alone of Bougainville's division was attempting to come to the support of the French flag.

When the *Canada,* which was leading the British, overtook the *Ville de Paris,* the flagship was, according to the description of Captain Cornwallis, "going before the wind with a fore sail and lower steering sail set, . . . apparently quite disabled. Our Admiral [Rodney] was at this time abreast of the *Ville de Paris,* . . . but wide [apparently to the north] and far out of gun shot, under little or no sail, with some ships about him. The body of the French fleet lay far to leeward of our ships.

. . . The *César* and *Ardent,* having been disabled in passing, were taken possession of by Sir Sam: Hood's squadron, then in the rear, but they were coming up with all sails set."[15] Rodney's failure to press on all sail in a general chase of the French at this point was the basis of considerable criticism and most probably enabled several French ships to escape that might otherwise have been captured.

With the *Ville de Paris* as the British came up were her seconds ahead and astern from the line. Close by also was de Vaudreuil's *Triomphant* with four others of his squadron. The French flagship made a most gallant defense against the British vessels which soon surrounded her. De Grasse's commanding figure was conspicuous on the quarterdeck, where he almost alone remained unwounded. A little before 6 P.M., when his situation was clearly hopeless, he released the few French vessels still endeavoring to support him.

Hood had in the meantime come up and directed the fire of his *Barfleur* against the nearby *Triomphant* of de Vaudreuil, courteously leaving de Grasse for Rodney. But when the *Ville* fired a broadside at the *Barfleur,* Hood took it as a sign that de Grasse chose to surrender to him. Stripped of her rigging and without a rudder, the French flagship was obviously in no condition to continue the fight. Her cartridges had for some time been exhausted, so that powder had to be ladled into her guns. Now there were no more shot. Returning a broadside for form, Hood had taken a position to rake when de Grasse struck at 6:30. Rodney had at last come up, and his representative boarded the French flagship at about the same time as Hood's lieutenant.

Upon the surrender of de Grasse, command of the French devolved upon de Vaudreuil. With darkness approaching, he could only fall off to leeward, rally the fugitives, and head for Cap Français. Had the English pursued, they might well have taken several more prizes, for many of the French were badly injured in the rigging, and most had so nearly exhausted their powder that they would have been incapable of serious resistance.

But Rodney refused to order pursuit. In-

15 G. Cornwallis-West, *The Life and Letters of Admiral Cornwallis* (London, 1927), 123.

stead, soon after de Grasse's surrender he signaled his fleet to lie to for the night. Only Commodore Affleck, who failed to see the signal, continued with six ships after the French all night. When at dawn not a ship was in sight, he returned to rejoin the British fleet.

In the battle the British took five ships, three of which had been seriously damaged in the first phase of the battle and had been poorly supported by their colleagues. Two more prizes fell to the British when Hood, at last released for pursuit five days after the battle, overtook two French vessels in Mona Passage. British casualties totaled slightly over a thousand; there is no reliable tabulation of the French, but it is clear that they ran to several thousand.

Hood made Rodney's failure to pursue the burden of the many critical letters he wrote after the battle, and it appears that his opinion was generally shared in the fleet. Certainly the feeling was sufficiently strong to cause Rodney to compose an elaborate, and rather weak, defense of his course. At any rate, it appears that most of his officers felt that Rodney had failed to take advantage of a glorious opportunity and had "botched his battle." Perhaps the most interesting testimony on this point is that of Captain Cornwallis:

I am perfectly convinced that even Adm. Rodney thought of it as I did—and for that reason during the three months suspense at Jamaica until the return of his dispatches he was like a man that did not know whether he was to be rewarded or punished. *I could think of nothing for a week* after the 12th of April but what could be the motive of his forbearance, having such an opportunity thrown in his way, not to take advantage of it. . . .[16]

But in England, where the details were not known and where news of victories had been scarce indeed, the capture of five ships was welcomed as a great success. Moreover, in ignorance of the truth, John Clerk of Elden, a layman who had written a book on naval tactics condemning the formal Fighting Instructions and advocating massing, conceived that he had influenced Rodney to break the line and that the victory was due to that

[16] *Ibid.*, 126.

maneuver. In this belief he has been followed by most naval historians since, who have taken the battle as marking a revolution in the history of tactics.

Yet the truth was that Rodney had not "broken the line" in any tactical sense, and that among the many able men and students of tactics in the fleet, not one appears to have considered his maneuver remarkable. Moreover, far from regarding their admiral's passing to windward of some of the French ships as the key to the victory, the men who were there considered it the means by which the opportunity for a smashing victory was thrown away. The windward position was of advantage chiefly in enabling its possessor to force an action. In this instance the French were already irrevocably committed to battle. The leeward position then became desirable from the British point of view because in it the British could hold the French to the action. As Captain Cornwallis put it, "If the *Formidable* had been kept close to the hull of her second ahead as the line was then formed [instead of passing through the French line], these [French center] ships must have passed the remainder of the English fleet very close to windward and of course been disabled."[17] But Rodney threw away that advantage, and as a consequence the greater part of the French fleet escaped.

This victory, the only significant success gained over the French in the entire war, was most timely for the British, for it went far toward retrieving their position in the West Indies. Although it was not evident at the time, the battle in fact ended the war in that theater.

De Vaudreuil's refugees from the Battle of the Saints, added to other French vessels already at Cap Français, made a total of 26. With about a dozen Spanish ships, an Allied fleet of almost 40 ships was thus available to escort the 8,000 Spanish troops for an attack on Jamaica. Hood, anxiously keeping watch with 25 ships, cannot perhaps be blamed for bitterly lamenting Rodney's failure to make the victory of April 12 complete. But the loss of De Grasse had taken the heart out of the French. The Spanish were, as ever, indisposed

[17] *Ibid.*, 121.

to act, and disease was decimating their troops. The real threat to Jamaica had been averted.

Europe, 1782

The change in the British ministry in the spring of 1782 brought Howe to the Channel fleet, where he was ably seconded by Kempenfelt. This happy combination marked the beginning of another period of British tactical progress, for Howe gave his subordinate a free hand to draw up signals for the fleet. Kempenfelt's first book contained all of Morogue's signals plus a good many innovations, but the significance of his flags still depended upon their location. It was not till summer, when preparations were being made for the relief of Gibraltar, that he composed a book based on a numerary system with signals arranged in a logical order. Issued for the entire Channel fleet by Howe, who had earlier had no scruples about setting aside the Admiralty instructions in favor of his own, this book marked the end of the Fighting Instructions far more truly than the "breaking of the line" by Rodney.

In the summer of 1782 France and Spain again assembled a great fleet, but after cruising fruitlessly in the Channel, it returned to Spain to assist in the siege of Gibraltar. The Spanish and the French had concentrated a huge force, supported by heavily protected floating batteries, for an assault on the Rock in the autumn, but the British fired the batteries with red-hot shot and eventually beat off the attack.

Howe had been ordered to relieve Gibraltar. During his fitting out Britain suffered an irreparable loss. At the end of August the *Royal George*, Kempenfelt's flagship, was being slightly careened for repairs to her bottom. Officers, crew, and visitors were aboard, and the Admiral was at his desk when the rotten bottom fell out. The ship went down so suddenly that, although she was at dockside, a thousand persons were lost, including Kempenfelt.

Howe arrived off Cape St. Vincent in early October with a convoy and 34 of the line. Despite the presence of the Allied fleet of 46, he pressed on and delivered his supplies without being seriously challenged until he reentered the Atlantic. Then the French made a distant attack on his van and the Spanish on his rear, but it was a half-hearted affair. Obviously the Allies had no desire to come to grips. The moral effect of this relief of Gibraltar was as great as that of a victory. The success was due not only to Howe's courage and the seamanship of his captains, but also to the tactical flexibility conferred by Kempenfelt's new signal system.

The War in the Far East: Suffren

The brightest chapter in the French naval history of the war was written in the Far East, too far from the main current to affect the French navy greatly and too remote to influence the terms of the peace. There France proved that in Suffren[18] she possessed an admiral of genius.

Since the Seven Years' War the British had established virtual control over Bengal. When the French entered the war in 1778, the British took Pondicherry, which was ill supported by the small French naval force in India. With the Dutch entry, they seized the Indian port of Negapatam and the Ceylonese port of Trincomalee, which provided the only good harbor near southeastern India.

Sent to India in the spring of 1781, Suffren fought five major battles with Sir Edward Hughes, the able commander of the British Indian fleet. Suffren's plans, which often provided for doubling on the enemy rear, show a thorough understanding of concentration, but bitter experience showed him that his captains were either unwilling or unable to execute such tactics; the instrument was simply not equal to his purpose. Consequently, not one of the five battles was tactically decisive; not a single ship of the line was captured by either side. Nonetheless, they were among the bloodiest, most fiercely fought battles of the war, for Suffren, fully appreciating that sea power was the key to the war in India, had as his objective nothing less than the annihilation of the British naval forces.

Although he failed to achieve that aim,

[18] Pierre André de Suffren Saint Tropez, usually known as the Bailli de Suffren, a title bestowed upon him by the Knights of Malta.

Suffren by his sound sense of strategy, his energy, and his timing did in fact reap some of the benefits of control of the sea. After his first battle with Hughes, Suffren established relations with the ruler of Mysore, France's principal ally in India. After his second, he received orders to retire to Mauritius for repairs and refit, but, realizing that the French position in India would collapse if his fleet were withdrawn, he disregarded the orders and continued the campaign. Repairing his ships quickly after a devastating third battle, he captured Trincomalee before the British could react, and subsequently fought a drawn battle to retain it. His fifth fight was also a tactical draw, but it was a French strategic victory, for Suffren was left in a position to raise the siege of Cuddalore.

Soon after this battle, news of the signing of peace in Europe brought an end to hostilities in India. On his return voyage Suffren put in at Port-Louis, Île de France, where the populace gave him a hero's welcome. At Table Bay he was paid similar honors, both by the inhabitants of Cape Town and by the captains of nine British vessels which had also put in there on their return voyage. In France he was honored by king, officials, and people. In April 1784 he was made Vice Admiral of France, an office created especially for him, while the States General of Holland bestowed on him a sword of honor and struck a medal commemorating his service to that country.

The Treaty of Paris

The Treaty of Paris closed a war in which Britain had been defeated. In America she had lost entire armies at Saratoga and Yorktown, and with them the desire to continue the conflict. In the West Indies she had seen her holdings steadily diminished. In the Mediterranean she had lost Minorca. In India Suffren was inclining the balance toward France. And at home, Ireland had taken advantage of England's embarrassment to present a demand for virtual independence, backed by an effective army of "volunteers."

That Britain fared no worse than she did at the peace table was due in part to the exhaustion of her opponents, in part to her success in dividing them, and in part to her timely defensive successes at Saints' Passage and at Gibraltar. It was, in fact, Britain's retention of Gibraltar that made peace difficult, for a secret article in the Franco-Spanish treaty of alliance bound France to continue the war till Gibraltar should be taken. The French Foreign Minister, Vergennes, desperately searching for something that might be offered Spain in place of Gibraltar, suggested that Spain might have the American territory between the Appalachians and the Mississippi. The Americans regarded this proposal as a betrayal of their interests which justified their proceeding with independent negotiations. Britain thus scored a diplomatic success by dividing her opponents.

The terms of the provisional treaty between Britain and the United States, signed November 30, 1782, were remarkably favorable to the Colonies when it is considered that Britain still held New York, Charleston, and Savannah. The Colonies received full independence and a territory stretching westward to the Mississippi, with the northern boundary following the Great Lakes substantially as at present and a southern boundary marked by Florida. Since the treaty of alliance with France forbade a separate peace, the Americans preserved the letter of the treaty by providing that these terms should not take effect until the conclusion of peace between Britain and France.

It was not till the beginning of January 1783 that the provisional articles were settled, ending hostilities between Britain and France and Spain. Spain fared well, considering her indifferent participation in the war. She kept Minorca and, as compensation for her failure to obtain Gibraltar, she received back Florida, which she had ceded to Britain in 1763 and upon which she had established only a partial hold in the War of the American Revolution. France, which had borne the brunt of the war, in a sense paid for the gains of her allies by receiving almost nothing herself. In the West Indies, St. Lucia, which she had lost to the British in 1778, was restored, and she retained Tobago, which she had captured in 1781; her other West Indian conquests were returned to Britain. In Africa she recovered her former possessions of Goree and Senegal, and in India she retained her previous holdings.

Britain's principal concessions were in North America, where she retained only Canada. All her West Indian possessions were restored except Tobago, and in India she actually improved her position somewhat at the expense of the Dutch, who had to make a separate peace. Nonetheless, the loss of the American colonies, by far her most valuable possessions, was so serious that to contemporaries it seemed to mark the end of Britain's greatness as an imperial power. Principally because of opposition in the British Parliament, the definitive treaty of peace was not signed till September 1783.

Summary

The French Navy at the time of the American Revolution was the best in the world, far different from the one that had fought in the Seven Years' War and beyond comparison to the demoralized organization that was to fight the Wars of the French Revolution and Empire. Until the last year of the war it outfought the British in every engagement, but the tradition of caution persisted and inhibited the aggressiveness which might have made French victories really decisive. Moreover, the French, being strategically on the offensive, frequently were escorting convoys for an island invasion, and, with their eyes on their strategic objectives, had sound reason for avoiding conclusive action.

But the French did not take full advantage of their naval superiority. Their most obvious error was their failure to concentrate for an invasion of Britain, which might have brought a quick and complete victory. Although they were capable of controlling the Channel at any time, they did not seriously renew their invasion project after the failure of 1779, but weakened their fleet by detachments to colonial theaters. This mistaken policy was encouraged by their Spanish allies, who demanded French assistance for their own objectives, all eccentric to the main purpose of defeating England at home.

The British, without the capability of blockading the French naval bases as they were to do in the Napoleonic Wars, were also obliged to fragmentize their fleet, and generally found themselves inferior. In the latter part of the war Britain, facing the principal naval powers of Europe—France, Spain, and Holland—as well as a hostile Baltic coalition, was consistently on the defensive. In the Mediterranean she lost Minorca and was hard pressed at Gibraltar. Nearer home she repeatedly found herself unable to match the forces that France and Spain sent into the Channel.

Only in the American colonies, where there was no effective naval opposition until late 1781, did Britain retain the initiative. There, after taking Charleston in 1780, she sent expeditions to ravage Virginia. But in attempting to penetrate inland through the Carolinas, Cornwallis very nearly repeated the experience of Burgoyne, for he was able to reach the seacoast at Wilmington with only a fraction of his original force. The single attempt of the French Newport squadron to challenge British control of American waters in the spring of 1781 produced a creditable French tactical victory off Cape Henry (one of the only two fleet actions fought off the American coast), but the strategic prize of the Chesapeake was left to the British.

The British forces, divided among several points along the American coast, were extremely vulnerable to sea power. Washington clearly perceived this, but for a considerable time his appeals for French naval aid met with no response. After d'Estaing's failure, de Guichen, who brought the second French fleet to American waters, confined his activities to the West Indies. So Washington, lacking transportation for a campaign in the South, and believing that New York was the key to the British position in America, planned a campaign against that city for 1781, but found that his army, even when joined by the French from Newport, was far too weak for the task.

At this point the American cause was saved by the arrival of de Grasse with his entire fleet from the West Indies for an operation in the Chesapeake. Hurrying south, Washington besieged Cornwallis at Yorktown from the landward side while de Grasse sailed from the Bay to fight the combined British New York and West Indian fleets. The resulting Battle of the Virginia Capes (September 5, 1781), while indecisive tactically, was in its long-range results one of the decisive battles of history, for de Grasse returned to control the Chesapeake, thus completing the isolating of

Cornwallis and forcing his surrender. This Allied victory at Yorktown substantially ended the war in the Colonies. The Continental Navy played no part in these events, and indeed had almost ceased to exist.

The war in the West Indies continued for another year, with the French taking several British-held islands. But preparations for a Franco-Spanish expedition against Jamaica led to one of the longest and bloodiest battles of modern naval history, that of the Saints (April 12, 1782). There the British demonstrated that, thanks to coppering, to the gunnery reforms of Sir Charles Douglas, and to the introduction of the carronade, they had at last regained naval ascendancy. Henceforth they could feel confident that in any close engagement they would emerge victorious.

In another respect the War of the American Revolution marked an enormous stride forward for the Royal Navy. Evidence of greatly improved skill in the French navy jarred the British into re-examining their own naval tactics. The battles of Ushant (1778) and of Grenada (1779) demonstrated that General Chase was not a safe means of by-passing the restrictions of the Permanent Fighting Instructions. Keppel's exoneration following the Battle of Ushant (1778) notified officers of the Royal Navy that henceforth professional judgment was to replace blind adherence to rules, and that even the Fighting Instructions and the well-ordered line might be discarded in appropriate circumstances. Additional Instructions provided most commands of the Royal Navy with signals for the various methods of massing, including breaking the line. Rodney's battle against de Guichen in 1780 demonstrated however that professional judgment could not be fully exercised without adequate signals. By borrowing heavily from the French *Marine,* Kempenfelt before the end of the war devised for the Royal Navy a complete system of tactics with a numerary system of signals for putting it into effect. The issuance of this work to the Channel fleet by Admiral Howe marked the beginning of a new era in British tactics.

Thanks to Britain's recovery in the last year of the conflict, the war cost her only part of her empire, and she survived to re-assert her control of the seas. Not only had France lost her best opportunity to humble her traditional enemy decisively, but she had suffered an economic strain that was to be a major factor in the downfall of her Bourbon rulers.

6:

The War of the French Revolution

Because the Treaty of Paris, concluding the War of the American Revolution, gave France comparatively little to show for her generous expenditure of men and money, some of her public men, including Navy Minister Castries, regarded the termination of hostilities as little more than a truce. In the years immediately following, Castries set out to correct abuses that had become traditional in French naval administration. Among other reforms, he made naval conscription less capricious, placed the recruitment of seamen gunners on a voluntary basis, and stiffened officer training with a view to stamping out the insubordination of juniors that had handicapped every outstanding officer from Tourville to Suffren.

Turning to strategic matters, Castries sought to provide France with a Channel base, the lack of which had thwarted French attempts to invade England in the last two wars. He vigorously set about providing Cherbourg with an arsenal and a protected fleet anchorage. Here in 1784 the first caisson of a three-mile-long breakwater was sunk in position. He began work on fortifications at Dunkirk, which faced the Thames Estuary and was thus an ideal base for raiding British shipping. In 1786 these projects came to an abrupt halt for lack of appropriations. Castries resigned in protest, but this was no mere crisis of personalities. France was approaching bankruptcy, and national revolution impended.

Across the Channel, the British government was headed by William Pitt the Younger. His coalition ministry, formed shortly after the American Revolution, when Pitt was not yet 25, was to continue with but minor interruptions for more than 20 years. Pitt's ministry was little disposed to invest large sums in the Royal Navy, for it was the heavy cost of the war more than anything else that had caused Parliament to replace Lord North's Tories with peace-minded Whigs. Partial mobilizations following war scares in 1785, 1790, and 1791 helped to maintain the material condition of the navy, but they were too brief to insure sustained training of personnel. The years of peace saw the bulk of British naval officers stagnate professionally in the forced inactivity of "half pay." Nevertheless, after 1786 the balance of power in Europe inclined steadily in Britain's favor, for the armed strength of France was being undermined, at first by insolvency and then, in 1789, by revolution and civil war.

The French navy was not immediately influenced by the political upheaval, but by the end of 1789 disaffection spreading from Paris had touched the fleets at Brest and Toulon. The unrest in the navy soon became mutiny, and for two years French naval power ceased to exist. With aristocratic officers fleeing abroad in large numbers, the government in 1791 averted complete dissolution by a decree of reorganization. The changes, in harmony with the spirit of the times, were carried out along egalitarian lines. Juniors sympathetic to the revolution were promoted, and numerous petty officers and merchant marine officers were given commissions. The corps of seamen gunners, which had come to be regarded as a privileged order of the lower deck, was banned in the name of democracy. Finally, in 1793, the Navy Minister was empowered to promote any individual to any rank. Thereafter political reliability became the principal qualification for command.

This policy, disastrous to the navy, had little detrimental effect on the army, mainly because the artillery officers, drawn largely from the middle class, supported the revolution from the beginning and hence were not touched by the reorganization. An improvised infantry, caught up with revolutionary fervor and backed by the finest artillery in Europe, was soon to work wonders. But in the navy, enthusiasm proved an inadequate substitute for training. Though French fleets would fight with great courage and captains would handle individual ships skillfully, the new flag officers lacked the time needed to master the art of the admiral. They misinterpreted orders, executed maneuvers improperly, failed to achieve mutual support among their fleet divisions, and were plagued by indecision at critical moments.

The Outbreak of War: The Rival Strategies

The rulers of Austria and Prussia, seeing in the political events in France a frightening incitement to revolt at home, proceeded to concert military countermeasures. The British however were at first inclined to applaud the revolution, which seemed to be leading France toward a constitutional monarchy like their own. Pitt declared in his budget speech of February 1792 that "unquestionably there never was a time in the history of this country when, from the situation of Europe, we might more reasonably expect 15 years of peace than at the present moment," and then proposed further reductions in the British army and navy. Less than six weeks later the French government anticipated armed attack by declaring war on Austria, Prussia, and Sardinia. The conflict would inevitably involve Great Britain and then, continuing for 20 years and taking on world-wide scope, impose on her armed forces the greatest effort of their history up to that time.

Initial defeats in the field proved too much for the stability of the French monarchy. Insurrection in Paris led to the proclamation of the First Republic in August 1792. The constitution-making National Convention made itself the effective government of France, and the radical Jacobins who dominated it proceeded to infuse fanatical energy into the conduct of the war. French armies soon rolled the Prus-

sians back across the Rhine and then counter-attacked to open the road to the Austrian Netherlands (Belgium). Reinforced by elements of the first of the modern mass armies, which the Convention was straining every resource to raise, the French poured into the Low Countries and in December 1792 occupied Antwerp.

It was now the turn of the British governing classes to take fright, for the most ancient maxim of policy at Westminster held that Antwerp must never come into the possession of a dynamic naval power. Public opinion in Britain was further alarmed by the Convention's decree establishing a system of revolutionary propaganda and conquest. The decree directed French generals in occupied areas to proclaim liberty, equality, fraternity, and the suppression of existing governments. Relations between the two countries were further embittered when the French opened the Scheldt to navigation in violation of treaty commitments. The execution of Louis XVI augmented the crisis, and on February 1, 1793, the National Convention declared war on England. Hostilities now entered the naval phase.

As a war leader, the younger Pitt concerned himself primarily with finance, leaving the strategic planning to his Secretary of State for War and closest friend, Henry Dundas. Influenced by Dundas, the British cabinet rejected the continental strategy of landing an army in France to support an allied drive on Paris. It decided instead to revive the peripheral and colonial strategy of Pitt's Plan of the Seven Years' War, in order to make optimum use of the mobility and surprise conferred by sea power. This required (1) blockading the French fleet; (2) reviving the elder Pitt's "conjunct," or amphibious, operations against French coasts and ports, with the objectives of containing military forces that might otherwise be used against Britain's allies on the Continent, assisting a formidable counterrevolution in the Vendée (in western France), and possibly destroying French naval forces or at least depriving them of bases; (3) protecting British commerce on the high seas and destroying the enemy's; (4) using the increased earnings of an expanding commerce to subsidize allies; and (5) attacking French overseas colonies.

Though Pitt and Dundas believed that bankrupt France could not long withstand the on-

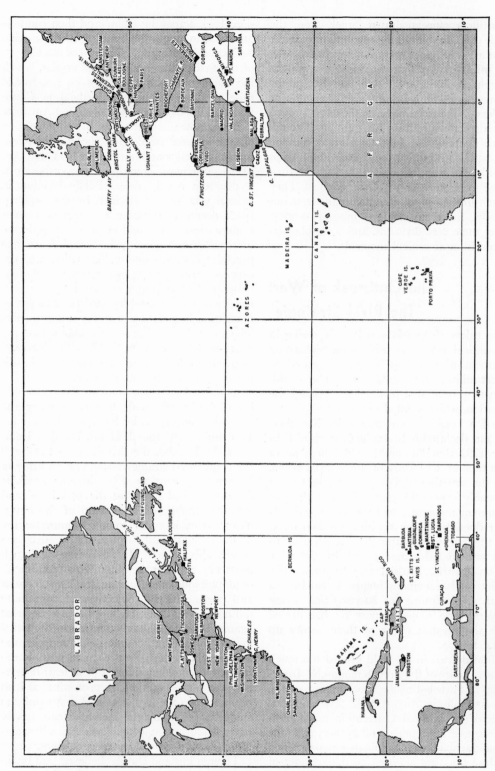

NAVAL BASES ON THE NORTH ATLANTIC, 1700-1815

slaught of Austria and Prussia, they knew that Britain had to have allies on the Continent. The hard lessons of the War of the American Revolution had driven that fact home. The British government therefore promptly concluded treaties of alliance with Austria, Russia, Prussia, Spain, Portugal, Hanover, and the Kingdom of the Two Sicilies (Naples), thereby completing the first of a series of coalitions directed against revolutionary France and the succeeding French Empire. The treaties required Britain to make cash payments in return for specified allied forces to be used in stipulated areas. Since the treaties also provided for British naval support for Austrian and Italian land forces, the command of the Mediterranean became a principal British objective.

On entering the war, Britain lost no time in putting into operation her economic weapons of warfare. Her cruisers soon hunted the French merchant marine from the high seas. Then, as escorts became available, she herded into convoys her own carriers to the North American, West Indies, and Levant trades.

Establishing a blockade off French ports required transforming a laid-up navy into an efficient war machine. Long rows of hulks, including nearly all of Britain's ships of the line, lay anchored "in ordinary" in the dockyard back channels. Stripped down to lower masts, they had to be fitted out, rearmed, and re-manned. Most of their officers had to be recalled from half-pay status, and most of their crews rounded up by press gangs. Of 113 sail of the line, 90 were found fit for commissioning. By June 1793 the Channel fleet had been brought up to 26 ships and the Mediterranean fleet to 16.

From his anchorage at Spithead, off Portsmouth, Lord Howe soon maintained a distant blockade of Brest and the French Atlantic fleet. While his frigates kept a picket line off Ushant in all weathers, he took his battle fleet on periodic sweeps to cover convoys, to count the French ships in Brest Roads, and to shake down his own ships. If westerly gales caught the battle fleet at sea, it ran for Tor Bay, a protected anchorage 20 miles east of Plymouth, assured that the same wind would hold the French two-deckers inside the rocky channel at Brest.

Lord Hood, in the Mediterranean, kept close watch on Toulon, leaving his station only to shelter from northers behind the Hyères Islands, 20 miles to the east. For provisions and water he depended on friendly Italian ports, and Gibraltar was available for anchorage, though ill-equipped for refitting. Hood prevented an enemy thrust into Italy, aimed at severing Britain from Austria, by sending his light units to attack the coastal shipping that supplied the French "Army of the Alps."

French leaders, aware that they were helpless to counter British moves by sea, decided to concentrate all their available strength in land operations on continental Europe. Their objective was nothing less than to bring the whole continent and its resources into their republican system. They believed that the British, isolated in their island fortress, would be obliged at last to yield to the threat of economic ruin. The war between France and Britain thus became, in the contemporary metaphor, a struggle between the Elephant and the Whale, each fruitlessly seeking some means of coming decisively to grips with the other.

Opening Operations Against the Continent, 1793

Believing that the war would be short, Pitt brought the British army up to a strength of barely 29,000 men. Even this modest force was fragmented in a dozen expeditions as the Cabinet undertook simultaneously to reinforce Austria in Belgium, to harass the French coasts, and to seize enemy colonies in the East and West Indies. As a result there were rarely enough British troops in any one area to exploit opportunities or reach permanent decisions.

To cooperate with the Austrians in the Netherlands, the 29-year-old Duke of York in August 1793 landed at Ostend at the head of 10,000 British soldiers. Adding an equal number of Austrians and Hanoverians, he took the initiative and moved rapidly on the commerce raiders' haven at Dunkirk. But here he found no siege artillery waiting for him off the port, as promised by the Admiralty. Instead, he faced an encirclement of superior enemy reinforcements, for his thrust at the sensitive Channel coast brought quick reaction from War Minister Lazare Carnot at Paris. The Duke, thus pressed, withdrew to the Austrian Netherlands, leaving behind all his field artillery and baggage.

This fiasco pointed up not only the defective coordination between the British army and navy but also the nearly fatal lack of cooperation among the allies. It was lack of cooperation, as much as anything else, that caused the allies to pass up the numerous openings presented by the raging counterrevolution, spreading from western to southern France, that threatened to engulf the French republican government. Britain's greatest chance came in August, the month of the Dunkirk expedition, when the entire French Mediterranean fleet passed temporarily into her hands. Had she successfully exploited this opportunity, French naval power would have been eliminated from the Mediterranean once and for all.

The French naval commander at Toulon, reflecting the royalist sentiments of his officers, had transferred to Lord Hood the city's arsenal and 31 ships of the line, 19 of which were ready for sea. Acting as technical custodian for the heir of Louis XVI, Hood took over port and ships and assumed the responsibility for the defense. He then proceeded in a leisurely manner to prepare the unready ships for sailing. A Spanish fleet of 16 ships, equal in number to Hood's, soon arrived. But the commander, Don Juan de Langara, failing to get from Hood recognition of his claim to equal authority, remained sullen and uncooperative at anchor in the outer roads.

To the British Cabinet the unexpected acquisition of Toulon opened prospects for invading southern France. But troops for such an offensive were hard to come by. Some 12,000 Spanish, Sardinian, and Neapolitan soldiers—"dastardly trash," the irascible Hood called them—were quickly assembled. Pitt added 2,000 British regulars by depleting the slender Gibraltar garrison. This combined force however was inadequate even to defend the port, for Toulon was situated in a basin with rugged heights commanding it at easy gun range. Pitt's military adviser estimated that 50,000 troops would be needed to hold the defiles.

News of Toulon's surrender to Hood created rage and dismay throughout republican France. The Committee of Public Safety, which had replaced the National Convention as the French executive agency, rushed troops thither. Before Hood had properly organized his defense forces, the Republicans stormed the passes and brought the city under heavy fire.

In desperate need of reinforcements, Hood sent his captains with their ships to the Italian coasts, instructing them to get what help they could from the Austrians and the local rulers. Captain Horatio Nelson of the *Agamemnon* alone had any measure of success. Strongly backed by British Minister Sir William Hamilton, he obtained 8,000 troops from the King of the Two Sicilies at Naples. The Austrian government, whose Italian possessions gave it the greatest stake in retaining Toulon, doomed the defense by refusing to contribute anything.

Toulon's defenders held out stubbornly for several months under round-the-clock fire from the heights. At length however Lieutenant Colonel Napoleon Bonaparte, commanding the republican artillery, felt out the critical spot in the city's defenses—the Eguilette peninsula, which divided the inner harbor from the roadstead. In mid-December, four months after the initial investment, republican infantry carried the Eguilette in a night attack, whereupon Bonaparte's artillery moved in and swept the bay, making Toulon no longer tenable by the allies.

The allied evacuation began at once, a task complicated by the moral obligation to remove the thousands of royalists from the reach of republican vengeance. Hood, postponing action beyond good judgment, barely managed to bring out four French ships and burn ten more. The remaining 17 were saved for France by republican troops who rushed the arsenal and dockyard. To this result Spanish apathy heavily contributed, for the disaffected Spaniards now wished to preserve the French naval forces to counterbalance the British.

In this campaign Austria's neglect and Hood's ineptitude in dealing with allied forces influenced the whole course of the war unfavorably for the allies. Had Toulon been held, there would have been no Italian campaign to put Bonaparte in the forefront of French leaders. Had Toulon and its fleet been destroyed, there could have been no French expedition to Egypt. With Toulon lost, Hood soon withdrew from naval history into forced retirement, and Austria braced herself for the inevitable attack.

Caribbean Operations, 1794

British troops that might have held Toulon were dispersed elsewhere. Some were in India, where they captured Chandernagore and Pondicherry. Others were in Flanders with the Duke of York. Still others were assigned to the joint command of Major General Sir Charles Grey and Rear Admiral Sir John Jervis for operations in the West Indies. This last expedition was the special brain child of Henry Dundas, who believed that the French were heavily dependent on trade with their rich West Indian sugar islands.

The arrival of Jervis and Grey at Barbados with 6,500 troops in January 1794 initiated a series of amphibious operations that would last five years and cost Great Britain 50,000 dead and a like number permanently disabled. Collectively known as Dundas' "Sugar Island Strategy," these operations seemed to revive an important essential of Pitt's Plan. But campaigning in the Caribbean, difficult at best, presented special problems in 1794. There was always the danger of yellow fever, which generally disabled half a newly arrived army the first summer, but this risk could be calculated. Less calculable was the force of the revolutionary spirit sweeping the French islands, where the Convention's representatives had roused the native populations with slogans of equality and promises of independence.

Ordered to capture Martinique, Jervis and Grey proceeded thither with their assault troops carried in three ships of the line, eight frigates, and several gunboats, and made landfall on February 5. Reconnaissance showed Grey that the local commanders, using the "cordon defense" then popular with the republican armies, had ringed the coast with isolated batteries, leaving his harbors relatively undefended. Here was a situation highly favorable to amphibious operations, which are greatly facilitated by the capture of ports for bringing in supplies.

The landings that followed incorporated amphibious lessons the British had learned in a century of costly experience. Selecting five

beaches near the northern port of St. Pierre, Jervis and Grey sent in the frigates and sloops to provide fire support for simultaneous landings, each flanking but beyond the range of fixed coastal batteries. To insure swift lodgment, the assault parties did not pause to fire on landing, but carried the beach defenses with the bayonet and on the run. Once in the covering woods, the invaders fanned out to link up behind the batteries. These they captured one at a time in night attacks "with flints out," for Grey was a great believer in the bayonet. Within a fortnight the British had captured St. Pierre, thereby acquiring control of the northern half of the island.

Jervis had meanwhile taken his heavy ships some ten miles down the coast to the vicinity of Martinique's main port, Fort de France (formerly Fort Royal), and landed troops and seamen to invest the harbor defenses. From St. Pierre, Grey now moved his troops down the coastal road in support. In a final combined operation, the British, on March 20, assaulted and captured the two forts guarding Fort de France. Martinique surrendered the next day.

Grey and Jervis went on to capture St. Lucia in three days and Guadaloupe within a month, using the same general pattern of attack—the Admiral laying his ships, as he put it, "in the good old fashioned way, within pistol shot," and the General concentrating on means to reduce the time of landing and crossing the exposed beaches. Thanks to their skillful efforts and to the operations of their small but exceedingly well handled expeditionary force, all the French West Indies except Haiti passed into the hands of the British in less than three months.

At this point in the Britons' victorious sweep, both the calculable and the incalculable elements intervened decisively. Yellow fever began to take a heavy toll among the invaders, and republican troops from France joined native and colonial militia in a counterattack on Guadaloupe. Under the leadership of the able and ruthless mulatto Victor Hugues, the French-West Indian forces quickly surrounded the British garrison. Jervis, down with the fever like many of his seamen and the majority of the troops ashore, was unable to cope with an enemy who had no visible communications and relied on infiltration from scattered points. Obliged to surrender Guadaloupe and evacuate the British troops, he and Grey returned to England in November, worn with fatigue and illness.

Hugues' followers, stirring up revolt as they advanced, drove the British out of all the Antilles except Jamaica and Barbados. By drawing on the local populations for troops and supplies and slipping from island to island, the French reduced their dependence on Europe for logistic support and nullified British sea power in the West Indies. A series of costly campaigns in 1796 convinced Dundas of the need for employing climate-seasoned native and colonial battalions. By 1799 twelve of these had been raised and the process of re-conquest was begun, but Guadaloupe, a haven for privateers, plagued the British until its final capture in 1810.

The Glorious First of June, 1794

The loss of Guadaloupe and Martinique brought the potentiality of sea power sharply to the attention of the National Convention, which had already begun to re-create the naval strength of France. Casting about for a dependable officer to wield the nation's resurrected sea arm, the Convention in January 1794 appointed Rear Admiral Louis Thomas Villaret-Joyeuse to command the Atlantic Fleet. Villaret, recently promoted to flag rank, had made a good record commanding a ship of the line. More important in the eyes of the Convention, his loyalty to the Republic was unquestioned. To back him up against turbulent seamen and shipyard workers, the Committee of Public Safety sent to Brest one of its own members, Navy Minister Jean Bon St. André, enpowered freely to use all the weapons of revolutionary terror to get the fleet to sea. St. André needed no urging. He restored a degree of order in dockyard administration, filled ships' complements and storerooms, and continually urged the deliberate Villaret to break off exercises in Brest Roads and take out the fleet to seek a decision with the British.

Meanwhile, a food shortage in southern France, resulting from bad weather and the injudicious conscription of farmers, was threatening to bring on civil war. To relieve this situation the French government purchased in the United States a large quantity of grain. This was loaded into American vessels at Norfolk and Baltimore, but getting it to France presented a problem, for the British had declared grain contraband. It happened that there were also in the Chesapeake Bay area a large number of French West Indiamen carrying revenue-producing sugar and coffee. In a hazardous attempt to get all these vessels safely across the Atlantic at one time, the French government had them assembled into a large convoy of 130 sail and sent two ships and two frigates to escort them to France. Then, fearing that the escorting vessels might not reach America in time, the government directed Rear Admiral Nielly to cruise 300 miles west of Belle Île with five ships and five frigates to meet the approaching convoy. On May 15 the government learned that Lord Howe's Channel fleet was at sea, whereupon it peremptorily ordered Villaret to put out from Brest with his entire fleet to support Nielly and protect the merchantmen.

The British had obtained information of the great Franco-American convoy, and Howe had left port on May 2 to make sure that it never reached France. First however he had to cover the departure of a hundred English merchant ships. Off the Lizard he weakened his fleet by detaching eight ships to escort the merchantmen across the Bay of Biscay. Six of the escorts under Rear Admiral Montagu were then to search for the Franco-American convoy between Cape Finisterre and Belle Île, while the main body of the Channel fleet swept a north-south line 300 miles west of Ushant. Howe himself looked into Brest on the 19th and found the roads empty. That evening a frigate from Montagu reached Howe, requesting aid against a possible combination of Nielly and the French convoy escorts. Howe thereupon steered southwest to join his subordinate but, learning from merchant ships of Villaret's position and heading, he changed to a westerly, intercepting course.

Villaret judged that the Franco-American convoy could best be safeguarded by drawing Howe away from the convoy's vicinity. His instructions were clear: "It is not naval action that we need at this moment, but our convoy. We do not need to fight, but to maintain a proud and imposing bearing which will hold up the enemy and make him lie to." First however Villaret wanted to join Nielly, whom he expected to raise momentarily. But on the morning of May 28 it was not Nielly but Howe who hove into sight in the northwest, twelve miles to leeward. Each fleet, deprived of a part of its strength, numbered 26 sail of the line and a dozen frigates.

On contact, Villaret promptly hauled into the wind and continued westward. Rain squalls from the southwest reduced visibility often to less than a mile, and the sea made it difficult to work lower deck batteries without shipping water. Howe endeavored to close the French and gain the weather gage by tacking in succession and carrying a press of sail. After some hours however he abandoned formation and ordered General Chase—his ships "to take suitable station for their mutual support, and engage the enemy as arriving up with them in succession." The French fleet at about the same time fell into disorder, and Villaret lost some ground in coming about to cover his stragglers.

Late in the afternoon the leading British ships came within range of the *Révolutionnaire*, 120, at the rear of the French formation. In yawing to fire broadsides they ceased to gain on this target, but gradually reduced her to a wreck—commanded by her third lieutenant, her senior surviving officer. In the gathering darkness Howe recalled his van ships and formed up the fleet for the night. Because their signal books contained only tactical messages, his captains were unable to inform him that a fine French three-decker was his for the taking. Nor could the British *Audacious* inform the Admiral that she had been battered into helplessness. Both the *Révolutionnaire* and the *Audacious* were left to make their way home as best they could.[1]

The next day, May 29, Howe continued his efforts to weather the French, this time hoisting Signal 34, "to pass between them for obtaining the weather gage."[2] The first tack fell short and resulted only in an exchange of broadsides in passing. A similar tack in the afternoon also failed to carry the British fleet through the French, but by threatening the French rear it obliged Villaret to wear in succession and so relinquish the weather gage to Howe. Only a heavy sea and loss of all formation by both fleets prevented decisive action at this point. In the melee one French 74 was so damaged that she had to be sent back to Brest, towed by a frigate and escorted by another 74. A third French 74 lost all upper masts and had to be towed by a consort, thus hobbling Villaret with a cripple. Howe had achieved the remarkable feat of very nearly forcing a decision on the enemy while to leeward. Now that he had the wind, he intended to engage at the first opportunity.

During the next two days however Howe was unable to bring about an engagement. Battle lines were formed and crews beat to quarters, but thick weather and a succession of gales hampered maneuvering and kept the fleets from closing. On the evening of the 30th Nielly joined Villaret with three ships, and soon afterward a fourth arrived independently from France. Thus the French, despite heavier losses, had gained a slight numerical advantage over their opponents, 26 ships to 25. Many of the French ships moreover were larger, sailed better, and were more heavily armed. But on board the 120-gun flagship *Montagne*, considered to be the finest warship in the world, Jean Bon St. André was noting in his report to the Convention that in sea warfare there is no substitute for training and experience.

June 1, the fifth day of contact, dawned cloudy with strong breezes, but visibility was good. The fleets lay about four miles apart, the French to leeward, still leading the British

[1] The crew of the *Audacious*, working through the night, put her under a jury rig and on a homeward course. The *Révolutionnaire*, with mizzen shot away, rolled her other masts overboard. She was found at dawn by one of Nielly's ships, which towed her to Brest. Here her remaining officers were thrown into jail for "leaving the fleet without orders."

[2] Signal 34 appeared in Howe's signal book as follows: "If when having the weather gage of the enemy the admiral means to pass between the ships of their line for engaging them to leeward, or being to leeward, to pass between them for obtaining the weather gage. N.B.—The different captains and commanders not being able to effect the specified intention in either case are at liberty to act as circumstances require." Sir Julian S. Corbett (ed.), *Signals and Instructions, 1776–1794* (Navy Records Society, 1908), 70–1.

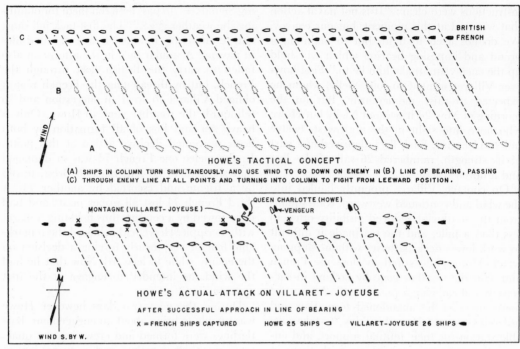

HOWE'S TACTICAL CONCEPT

(A) SHIPS IN COLUMN TURN SIMULTANEOUSLY AND USE WIND TO GO DOWN ON ENEMY IN (B) LINE OF BEARING, PASSING
(C) THROUGH ENEMY LINE AT ALL POINTS AND TURNING INTO COLUMN TO FIGHT FROM LEEWARD POSITION.

HOWE'S ACTUAL ATTACK ON VILLARET-JOYEUSE

AFTER SUCCESSFUL APPROACH IN LINE OF BEARING

X = FRENCH SHIPS CAPTURED   HOWE 25 SHIPS ◁   VILLARET-JOYEUSE 26 SHIPS ◀

WIND S. BY W.

BATTLE OF THE FIRST OF JUNE, 1794

on a northwest course. Shortly after seven, Howe ordered his fleet to form line of battle, and ten minutes later indicated his tactical plan by again hoisting Signal 34—to pass through the enemy line, this time to leeward.

Howe's hoisting of Signal 34 on June 1 has puzzled some students of naval warfare, to whom it appeared that the British admiral was ready to throw away the wind advantage he had won in two days of maneuvering. It has been suggested that Howe's intention was to pass his ships through the intervals in the enemy column and then to form a line to leeward from which the enemy, or at least his cripples, would have difficulty escaping. But passing through an enemy column ship for ship, when opposed by a determined foe, was an impossible feat of seamanship, and it was rendered further unlikely by the escape clause following Signal 34: "The different captains and commanders not being able to effect the specified intention . . . are at liberty to act as circumstances require." Howe never set down or discussed his tactical reasoning for posterity, but evidence indicates that after four days of inconclusive contact with the enemy, he meant now to force a decision by bringing on a melee, in which superior British gunnery at close range would give him the advantage. His maneuver, besides being a superb shock tactic, would enable his ships (1) to rake opponents on either hand in passing through their column; (2) to break the French formation and thereby jeopardize Villaret's tactical control; and (3) to reap the advantage of tactical surprise, for the French lee batteries and gunports might be expected, and in fact were found, to be secured.

When Howe had closed his line to his satisfaction, he made hoist shortly after 8 AM "to engage the enemy." Ten minutes later a signal gun was fired, the preparatory flag was hauled down, and each British captain put his ship's helm to the wind and ran down to engage his opposite number. The 68-year-old Admiral, who had been sleepless for four days save for an occasional armchair doze, was haggard from fatigue but still vigorous. Closing his pocket signal book, he turned to his staff with the remark, "Now, gentlemen, no more book, no more signals. I look to you to do the duty of the *Queen Charlotte*. I don't want the ships to be bilge to bilge, but if you can lock the yardarms, so much the better; the battle will be the quicker decided." Only ten of Howe's 25 ships kept on into the French line; the others came round to engage in the traditional manner on the windward side. The escape clause in Signal 34 had well-nigh stultified the order.

As the British maneuver became apparent, Villaret's ships, already in close order line of battle, endeavored to prevent or offset it. They strove to close the intervals or, failing in this, to support their consorts under attack by coming up on the lee side of such British as had broken through, putting them between two fires. Thus Howe's *Queen Charlotte*, passing through astern of Villaret's *Montagne*, was forced so close by the *Jacobin* next astern, that the *Montagne*'s ensign swept her entire length. In these close quarters the *Queen Charlotte* fired a broadside that struck down 200 of the *Montagne*'s men with raking fire. With another broadside she smashed in the bow frames of the *Jacobin*, forcing her to bear up to leeward. The two Frenchmen immediately astern of the *Jacobin*, shaking off their antagonists, then closed the *Queen Charlotte*, which had lost her foretopmast in sheering up alongside Villaret.

By ten o'clock the engagement had become general, with the British hammering on both sides of the French line. Villaret, noticing a group of his van ships out of action well to windward, left the *Queen Charlotte* to her new opponents. Joining his detached van, he promptly tacked it about in support of his hard-pressed center. To meet this fresh onslaught, Howe ordered his line re-formed. But the French admiral, in the spirit of his orders to observe "a proud and threatening immobility," was now endeavoring only to disengage and to shield his cripples.

Bringing his fleet into column to leeward, Villaret towed three of his dismasted ships to its shelter. The other seven he left engaged with the enemy, believing a false report that they had already struck. Ever thinking of the convoy, he shortly afterward bore up, and soon cleared the battle area. Of the seven ships he left in British hands, the shattered *Vengeur du Peuple* fought a four-hour duel with the *Brunswick* that has become a naval classic.

As the two ships grappled side by side, the *Vengeur* swept the *Brunswick*'s upper decks with langridge, but the British, blowing out their own gunports, hulled their opponent till she went down, carrying 300 men. The other six abandoned ships were taken to England as prizes of war.

The British had suffered some 1,100 casualties, including nearly 300 killed; French casualties were more than four times as great. Only Howe's physical exhaustion saved Villaret's fleet from annihilation. Nevertheless Howe's victory became the "Glorious First of June" to the British nation, which had waited 18 months for its first success against the French fleet. The victors were voted medals and prize money to the accompaniment of a generous award of titles, Howe himself receiving an earldom.

The National Convention also proclaimed victory, for the convoy passed over the battle site on June 3 without raising a sail and proceeded unhindered to its dispersal point. The French, as usual, had fought with an eye to ultimate objectives, which in this instance was supplying the French treasury with gold and the French people with food. The British, as usual, had fought with the immediate objective of destroying the enemy's fighting force, in the belief that this was the surest means to ultimate victory.

Though Howe had failed to take full advantage of his opportunities on the field of battle, he had done better than he realized. He had demonstrated to the French sailors that they could not stand up to better trained and more experienced opponents. Confined in Brest Roads, Villaret's fleet suffered a decline in morale, and this was aggravated by shortages of supplies, including daily rations. In logistic matters the French army chiefs had been forced to improvise and had done so brilliantly. The Committee of Public Safety failed to comprehend that similar makeshifts were impractical in naval warfare, that fleet training depended on the quantity and quality of material, and that naval history records few instances of victory by materially inferior forces. The Brest fleet sortied on a few escort missions but always withdrew promptly on the approach of the Channel fleet. Gradually it ceased to exist as an effective fighting force.

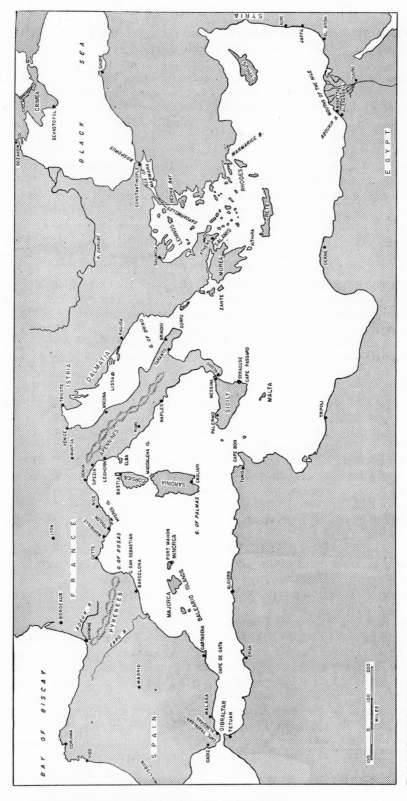

THE MEDITERRANEAN

The Mediterranean Stalemate, 1794-1796

The main focus of naval activities had in fact shifted to the Mediterranean, for with French armies occupying Belgium and the left bank of the Rhine, Paris considered the northern frontier secured. Brest fell into neglect as the government proceeded to build up and equip the fleet at Toulon. Thither the Committee of Public Safety dispatched the indefatigable St. André to resurrect French naval power within the Straits.

The British Mediterranean fleet, deprived of Toulon, found itself again blockading the port and seeking adequate base facilities. Spain's increasing coolness made Minorca unavailable, and Gibraltar was too far away to provide support. Lord Hood, in his last campaign before retirement, set out to remedy this situation by occupying Corsica, where patriot partisans were revolting against the French. For lack of sufficient soldiers, British seamen did much of the fighting ashore, in the course of which Captain Horatio Nelson was wounded in the face, losing the sight of his right eye. By June 1794 Corsica was in the hands of the British, providing them with an important base, and depriving the French in Toulon of a principal source of ship timber.

Despite these elaborate preparations, neither France nor England was able to achieve anything decisive in the Mediterranean. Rear Admiral Pierre Martin, commanding the Toulon fleet, was too painfully aware of the inexperience of his crews to take any chances. Rear Admiral Sir William Hotham, Hood's successor, permitted himself to become so impressed with the rapid French buildup that his caution came to match that of his opponent. At his first encounter with the Toulon fleet, in May 1795, Hotham's aggressive captains, well schooled under Hood, captured an 80 and a 74, and separated two other ships from Martin, but were then ordered to rejoin the British main body in accord with Hotham's "no risks" policy. Nelson went aboard the flagship to urge pursuit, only to be told that the fleet had done very well. "Now, had we taken ten sail," he commented bitterly to a friend, "and allowed the eleventh to escape, when it had been possible to have got at her, I could never have called it well done."

By now the Austrians had crossed the Apennines and were establishing themselves at Savona, on the Italian coast near Genoa. Their further advance, and indeed their security, depended on the British navy's ability to cut coastal communications from Toulon. This task was entrusted to Nelson, who was given the inshore squadron of five frigates in addition to his 64-gun *Agamemnon*. It was soon apparent that only ships of the line could deal with the numerous fortified harbors that gave coastal craft easy refuge, but Hotham kept his heavy ships in his own hands, alternating them between the waters off Toulon and his Corsican base. Nelson's urgent appeals went unheeded, and the communications of the French Army of Italy remained intact. In November the French launched a counterattack that thrust the Austrians back across the Apennines. Nelson looked on helplessly, but his torment at inaction was short lived. That same month Vice Admiral Sir John Jervis hoisted his flag in the *Victory*. One of the Royal Navy's soundest professionals, and its sternest drillmaster, had come to the Mediterranean.

Breakup of the First Coalition, 1795-1797

Jervis could hardly have arrived at a time less favorable to allied fortunes. Prussia had liquidated an unsuccessful campaign on the Rhine and made peace the preceding May. Occupied Holland had then formally joined France as an ally, and Spain retired from the war in July. The British responded by seizing the Cape of Good Hope, Ceylon, and other Dutch holdings—in India and the West Indies. They also put a North Sea fleet off Texel under Vice Admiral Adam Duncan to watch the Dutch navy and to interdict the passage of Baltic timber and hemp to France. On balance however, the end of 1795 saw the French military position immeasurably improved and the First Coalition reduced to only two major powers—Britain and Austria.

The five-man Directory, recently made the French national executive, resolved to obtain a military decision by striking simultaneously at both remaining enemies. To command this dual attack they appointed France's two most brilliant young generals, Napoleon Bonaparte to head the Army of Italy and the anglophobic Lazare Hoche to head the Army of England. Bonaparte was to drive across Lombardy, with Vienna as his objective. Hoche was to launch an amphibious thrust into the British Isles directed at London. To provide efficient fleet support for both campaigns, the Directory appointed the able Vice Admiral Laurent Truguet to the Navy Ministry, giving him a free hand. A veteran of the pre-revolutionary navy, Truguet made it his first business to restore the authority of line officers in all branches of administration, thereby eliminating the influence of the political agents who had been omnipotent during the Jacobin regime. He then set out to reinvigorate the Brest fleet and ready it for sea. At the same time, he fragmented the Toulon fleet, sending it to raid British commerce in all parts of the world as a means of diverting the Royal Navy.

General Bonaparte took command of the Army of Italy in February 1796 and launched his classic six-weeks' campaign that cleared the Austrians from Lombardy. Then, turning southward, he entered Livorno in June to deprive the Royal Navy of its chief victualing base inside the Straits. The British lost the use of Palermo and Naples shortly afterward when French pressure forced the King of the Two Sicilies to close his ports to belligerents. Not even Corsica remained secure, for French successes turned the islanders against the British, and Bonaparte at Livorno assembled an amphibious force to infiltrate across the 60-mile-wide sea passage.

Spain's expected declaration of war against Great Britain came in August. The Spanish ships, as regards design and sailing qualities, were unexcelled, but their conscript crews were led by officers who disdained professional study and training in their reliance on raw physical courage. The British cabinet, counting numbers rather than quality, ordered Corsica and Elba evacuated. Jervis, with 15 ships to face 36 Spanish and French, shifted his fleet to Gibraltar and then to Lisbon, where he arrived in December 1796, having lost four ships to storms and grounding enroute. The Mediterranean now became a Franco-Spanish lake.

The Admiralty could send Jervis's depleted fleet no reinforcements because every disposable ship was deployed to meet the threat of invasion at home. The Brest fleet lay ready for sea, and General Hoche's army of 14,000 was fully embarked. More than 50 vessels were observed in Brest Roads. On December 16 Hoche slipped to sea with his whole force and headed for Bantry Bay, Ireland. But gale succeeded gale for three weeks, scattering the invasion armada, which straggled back piecemeal into French ports. Not a soldier had managed to land, but Hoche could count himself lucky—the bad weather that spoiled his plans had also saved him from Britain's Channel fleet.

The Spanish fleet meanwhile had utterly failed to carry out its assigned mission of drawing British naval forces away from the Channel. From Paris, accordingly, came demands that it go forthwith to Cadiz. This was to be the first step in a move to Brest for a renewal of Hoche's invasion attempt, to be supported this time by the combined fleets of Holland, France, and Spain. Complying with the French demand, Admiral Don José de Cordoba left Cartagena on February 1, 1797, and passed into the Atlantic with 24 ships and a Cadiz-bound convoy in company.

The Battle of Cape St. Vincent, February 14, 1797

When Jervis learned of Cordoba's departure, he immediately put to sea from Lisbon and, with his ten available ships, proceeded to Cape St. Vincent to watch the Straits. Here a welcome reinforcement of five more of the line reached him on February 6. Easterly gales then drove him from the coast. A week later Jervis was regaining his position when a frigate, bringing Nelson from the evacuation of Elba, reported that Cordoba had left the Mediterranean. Another frigate that afternoon reported an enemy contact to the southwest. This was the Spanish fleet and convoy, which had also been blown out into the Atlantic and were now taking advantage of the westerly wind to bear up for Cadiz.

Cordoba, believing that Jervis had no more than his original ten ships, was convinced that the British would avoid action. Some of his own warships had become widely scattered in capturing a few merchantmen prizes. Early February 14, on report of a suspicious sail, he belatedly endeavored to assemble fleet and convoy, ordering his warships into escort formation. Since the frigates and many of the convoy were off to the southwest, Cordoba detached two ships of the line for their protection. At 9 AM reports of contacts in the northeast came in from ships on his left flank, whereupon he sent Rear Admiral Moreno's squadron of five heavy ships to investigate. When the mist lifted shortly afterward, Cordoba was amazed to see Jervis's battle force of 15 sail advancing from the north cleared for action. The Spanish fleet had been caught divided, with Moreno's ships isolated to leeward in the northeast.

The British approached closehauled and at 11 AM formed a line of battle, with Admiral Jervis in the *Victory* at the center, and Commodore Nelson in the *Captain* commanding the rear. Jervis, resisting the temptation to fall on Moreno's detached squadron, kept on for the main body. Cordoba could have stretched across the British line of advance to join Moreno, whom he had recalled. But he vacillated and then hauled to the wind northward, trying to form his 17 ships into a closehauled line of battle. This was too much for his partially trained crews, and the main body bunched in several groups.

Moreno tried to cooperate with his chief by wearing round to join Cordoba's rear, but Jervis, making signal to "pass through the enemy line," beat him into the gap. The confusion in Cordoba's line enabled the British fleet to mass fire on his six rear ships, including the flagship *Santisima Trinidad*, pouring in point-blank broadsides from leeward as it passed on the opposite tack. Moreno tried to cut through the British line, but a few broadsides turned his ships away—one running down the length of the British line to cross over its rear, the others wearing round to rejoin Cordoba by doubling around the enemy van.

When Jervis had passed clear of the last Spanish ship, thereby gaining the weather gage, he signaled his fleet to tack round in succession in order to fall once more on the enemy. Thomas Troubridge in the *Culloden* led the van division up the lee side of the nearest Spanish ships. Jervis, instead of following, brought the rest of his line up to windward of the enemy, thus achieving a double envelopment of the Spanish rear.

The foremost British ships, on arriving up with their targets, found a fierce engagement in progress. Nelson had already thrown himself on the *Santisima Trinidad*. During the initial British cannonade, the huge Spanish flagship had been heavily hammered and began to drift to leeward. Nelson, observing this from his position near the end of the line, interpreted it as an attempt by the Spanish admiral to lead his main body around the British rear in order to unite his forces. To head off such a move, Nelson promptly wore his 75-gun *Captain* out of the line and cut back between his two rear ships. Engaging the 130-gun fourdecker, he forced her into the wind. The rest of the Spanish rear was soon swarming around, and the *Captain* became the target of the *San José*, 112, the *Salvador del Mundo*, 112, and the *San Isidro*, 74. Nelson's courage in challenging the whole Spanish rear with his single ship was surpassed by his audacity in disregarding signals and disobeying the firmest regulation of the Royal Navy, which forbade commanding officers on pain of court-martial and disgrace to leave the line during battle without specific orders. Nelson had in fact assumed a responsibility that belonged to the commander in chief alone.

The arrival of Troubridge and Jervis with the rest of the British fleet confronted the Spanish rear with a concentration of more than twice its strength. Cordoba, overwhelmed, signaled vainly to his center and van to come down in support. Smoke clouds partially obscured his hoists, and shortly afterward the flags came down with his topmasts. The British commander, intent on smashing all formation in the Spanish rear, ordered his windward ships to pass through the enemy and himself set the example with the *Victory*. The six Spanish ships lay helpless under the attack. Clouds of canvas draped the sides of the partially dismasted *San José* and *San Nicolas*, masking their batteries. Cuthbert Collingwood, bringing the *Excellent* through in response to Jervis's signal, closed to pistol range and steered between the heavily damaged *Captain* and the

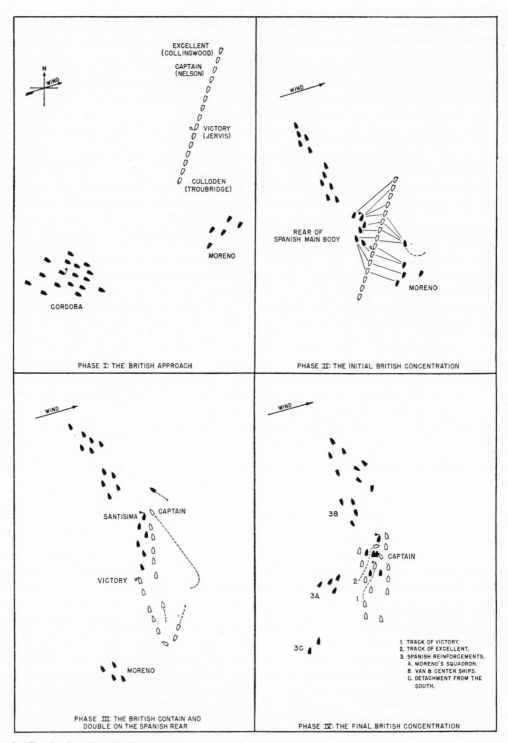

PHASE I: THE BRITISH APPROACH

EXCELLENT
(COLLINGWOOD)

CAPTAIN
(NELSON)

N

WIND

VICTORY
(JERVIS)

CULLODEN
(TROUBRIDGE)

MORENO

CORDOBA

PHASE II: THE INITIAL BRITISH CONCENTRATION

WIND

REAR OF
SPANISH MAIN BODY

MORENO

PHASE III: THE BRITISH CONTAIN AND
DOUBLE ON THE SPANISH REAR

WIND

SANTISIMA   CAPTAIN

VICTORY

MORENO

PHASE IV: THE FINAL BRITISH CONCENTRATION

WIND

3B

CAPTAIN

3A   2

1

3C

1. TRACK OF VICTORY.
2. TRACK OF EXCELLENT.
3. SPANISH REINFORGEMENTS.
   A. MORENO'S SQUADRON.
   B. VAN & CENTER SHIPS.
   C. DETACHMENT FROM THE
      SOUTH.

BATTLE OF CAPE ST. VINCENT, FEBRUARY 14, 1797

San Nicolas, his broadsides driving the Spanish seamen from their guns. The *San Nicolas* luffed, only to fall foul of the *San José*, while the *Captain* fetched up on her quarter, grinding bulwarks into her quarter galleries.

Nelson now called away boarders, and himself went into the *San Nicolas* through a stern window. After a scuffle in the cabin, he reached the deck, where he found shipmates pausing to haul down the Spanish colors before going up the chains of the adjacent *San José*. Shouting "Westminster Abbey or victory!" Nelson boarded the second enemy. Soon afterward, at 4 PM, he received the formal surrender of both ships.

Five of the six ships of the Spanish rear had now struck. The action however increased in intensity as Spanish reinforcements closed in. Moreno completed his circuit of the British fleet, the two Spanish ships detached in the morning came up from the south, and elements of the Spanish center and van at last were entering the battle. These developments distracted the British from taking possession of the surrendered *Trinidad* and enabled Cordoba to gain the shelter of his reinforcements. As sunset came on, Jervis grew anxious to cover his remaining four prizes. He wore the *Victory* at 5:45 and signaled close order of battle. This directive caused the British to disengage and permitted Cordoba to haul off to the north.

During the night Jervis closed Cape St. Vincent. He had his victory; he also had nine cripples in tow. Typical entries in the British logs record: "All the night employed knotting and splicing rigging", and "Served an extra allowance of grog to the ship's company." Throughout most of the next day the two fleets remained in sight of each other. Though Cordoba still had 20 ships, at least half of which had not participated in the battle, he made no attempt to close. His ships made a leisurely return to Cadiz, on which Jervis, in response to the First Lord's instructions "never if possible to suffer the main body of the fleet of Spain to be between you and us," soon clapped a blockade.

For his victory, which lifted the spirits of all Englishmen at a time of profound depression and near bankruptcy, Jervis was created Earl of St. Vincent and granted an annual pension of £3,000. Nelson was promoted to rear admiral, and each captain of the fleet received a medal.

The main tactical significance of the Battle of Cape St. Vincent lies in the manner in which Nelson's single ship, the British van led by Troubridge, and the rear and center led by Jervis independently closed in on a portion of the Spanish fleet, enveloping and crushing it before the rest of the enemy ships could arrive to lend support. While this concentration of force was merely an extension of chase tactics, it demonstrated that the Royal Navy had now fully regained the tactical flexibility lost since the Anglo-Dutch wars. It also introduced a new principle into naval warfare, that of dividing one's force in order to move each segment with the greatest facility to the point where it is most needed. Nelson further developed this principle in his victorious battles of the Nile and of Trafalgar, which became the study of later generations of naval officers. The divided Japanese forces that the Americans and their allies met time and again in World War II thus had their origin in the spontaneous tactical innovations at Cape St. Vincent.

The battle brought Nelson fame. The British public acclaimed his daring in leading boarders over the heavily armed *San Nicolas* ("Nelson's Patent Bridge for Boarding First Rates") to capture the still stronger *San José*. Within the Royal Navy however Nelson had his critics. Had he not abandoned the line without orders? But Jervis praised his initiative, which, had it failed, would have been insubordination. When Jervis's fleet captain, Robert Calder, pointed out that Nelson had disregarded signals, the Admiral snapped, "It certainly was so, and if ever you commit such a breach of your orders, I will forgive you also."

Cordoba's defeat cost him his command and destroyed the morale of the Spanish navy. There would be no Spanish support for any further French invasion schemes—at least not for several years. But this advantage, from the British point of view, was quickly offset by the victories of General Bonaparte. On February 2 he had captured Mantua. On March 23 he led his triumphant troops into Trieste. On April 18 he took Austria out of the war by forcing on her the Truce of Leoben, a preliminary to the Treaty of Campo Formio. England now stood virtually alone against the

Atlantic alliance of France, Holland, and Spain. Her only remaining ally was Portugal, whose sole contribution was permission to use Lisbon as a base for blockading Cadiz.

Prudent statesmanship required that the Directory, having gained its military objectives on the Continent, now secure a peace with England in order to gain a breathing space for reconstruction of its neglected navy. Only by commanding the sea could France check British influence and preserve her newly-won dominions in western Europe. But caution did not commend itself to men whose policy of all-out offensive had unfailingly produced success in every corner of the Continent. They showed little understanding of sea power and total ignorance of its influence in European affairs. For the moment indeed the potency of the Royal Navy appeared on the wane. Four days before the peace at Leoben, the seamen of the Channel fleet had refused to go to sea. During the next month the mutiny spread from Spithead to the Nore and to the fleets off Texel and Cadiz.

The British Naval Mutinies, 1797

Long-standing discontent among the seamen of the Royal Navy found vent early in 1797 in respectful remonstrance. Failure in official quarters to heed the obvious danger signals permitted the situation to develop into a large-scale mutiny that immobilized the British fleets in home waters in the face of threatened enemy invasion.

In March, crews of the Channel fleet sent a petition for redress of grievances to Lord Howe, their ailing commander in chief, who was taking the waters at Bath. Howe, widely known as "the Sailors' Friend," made no reply. A similar petition sent to the Admiralty at the same time brought peremptory orders to Lord Bridport, Howe's deputy, to take the ships to sea. The crews refused point-blank and proceeded to elect delegates to a General Assembly that shortly afterward assumed authority over the fleet.

Inadequate pay was foremost among the sailors' grievances. For able bodied seamen this had stood at 22s. 6d. a month since the reign of Charles II, and it was but a fraction of current wages in the merchant marine. The men were paid only in home ports and at six months' intervals. Even then the payment was by warrant, a form of check which could be cashed at face value only in naval offices. Particularly galling was the fact that all pay ceased during any period of disability from duty—even when resulting from wounds incurred in combat. Prize money proved an irregular source of income, and the share allocated to seamen was disproportionately small.

Food aboard men-of-war was both scanty and bad. Rations were reduced by the use of 14-ounce ("purser's") pounds to allow for mythical "leakage." The generally poor quality of provisions was hardly compensated by the daily issue to every member of the ship's company of one gallon of beer and a half pint of rum, which when watered was called "grog." Despite experiments with fresh vegetables that had kept West Indies squadrons healthy, the Admiralty issued only flour, dried peas and beans, and salted meat. Hence even Duncan's officers and crews, operating close to home, suffered from scurvy.

A principal complaint concerned inadequate shore leave. During hostilities this was curtailed at home and abroad, liberty being confined to dockyard precincts. Though in home ports women and families were usually permitted to live on the berth decks, the men themselves might spend years without setting foot on shore. In practice the system amounted to virtual imprisonment.

It is significant that the seamen made no demand for mitigating flogging and other brutal punishments. The threat of the cat at sea was after all no more terrifying than the harsh laws ashore. Among British naval officers there were a few brutes and sadists, and their misdeeds have somewhat obscured the work of such officers as Nelson, Collingwood, Howe, St. Vincent, and many others who without relaxing discipline spared no pains to see that their men received justice and got decent food.

As the war expanded and the demands for naval crews exceeded the returns by impressment, Parliament in 1795 passed the Quota Act requiring all parts of Great Britain to furnish naval conscripts. Local authorities took advantage of the act to ship off their undesirable characters to the navy. While these, together with debtors and petty criminals whom the magistrates had offered the choice of sea service or prison, probably did not exceed 15 per cent of the average ship's crew, their influence was disproportionate. Often men of some education, possessing every talent perhaps but the ability to keep out of trouble, they provided the leadership below decks that brought long standing resentments to a head.

After three weeks of parleying, the Admiralty commissioners gave way on all important points and agreed to a seamen's pay raise of 5s. 6d. Having accommodated the major issues, they permitted bureaucratic inflexibility to wreck the negotiations on the minor demands for fresh vegetables and a guarantee of pardon for the seamen's delegates. There was also delay in Parliament in enacting legislation to formalize the concessions. This led the seamen, ever suspicious, again to refuse to take the ships to sea. The incident involved some violence—Bridport was locked in his cabin and unpopular officers were put ashore.

Parliament now moved with alacrity and Howe took personal command at Spithead, going through the fleet with a copy of the ratified act and explaining its provisions to each ship's company. He also exerted his influence to obtain the Admiralty's acquiescence in the removal of the beached officers. For this action he was criticized in naval quarters, but it was probably the course of wisdom, and necessary for restoring the seamen's confidence in governmental sincerity.

The Spithead mutiny formally ended on May 15, and Bridport weighed anchor the next day. Though the concessions applied to the navy generally, the Admiralty had scarcely begun to implement them when a more serious mutiny broke out at the Nore, an anchorage at the mouth of the Thames Estuary. From here it spread to Duncan's North Sea fleet. The spirit at the Nore was markedly different from that at Spithead. Here the mutineers ran up the red flag and established connections with the pro-French republican societies in London.

For leader and spokesman, the Nore mutineers chose Richard Parker, a former naval officer but a natural rebel. Cashiered for insubordination, he had later been thrown into jail for debt, whence he had been conscripted back into the navy as a seaman. Some of the demands made by Parker and his followers were reasonable but many were not, and the mutineers alienated public sympathy by blockading the Thames. At Spithead the leaders had announced that they would return to duty should an enemy put to sea; Parker's followers threatened to carry the fleet to France.

In the North Sea, Duncan's personal influence steadied the crew of his flagship *Venerable*. With the *Venerable*, the *Adamant*, and a frigate, he maintained the blockade of the Dutch squadrons virtually singlehanded.[3] Signals he made to his frigate, stationed on the horizon, were transmitted on to imaginary forces beyond. The ruse was apparently effective, for the Dutch continued to swing at their anchors during the three weeks it took the British government to suppress the Nore mutiny and hang Parker and 13 of his associates.

St. Vincent, off Cadiz, repressed incipient mutiny with an iron hand. In one famous incident he forced the seamen of a mutinous ship to hang their own leader by threatening to sink the vessel with gunfire, crew and all. But, balancing severity with humanity, he was ever watchful to see that his men were well fed, justly treated, and kept busy. As diversions in the touchy summer of 1797 he twice bombarded Cadiz and, in a moment of lapsed judgment, consented to a scheme of Nelson's and Troubridge's for capturing a cargo of Manila silver rumored to be at Santa Cruz in the Canary Islands. The Santa Cruz expedition was a complete fiasco—200 Englishmen were killed and Nelson lost his right arm.

The Battle of Camperdown, October 11, 1797

While mutiny held his fleet helpless at home, Duncan was able to maintain a skeleton force off Texel because the Dutch squadrons were not fully shaken down for operations, and he had, besides, the occasional assistance of a half dozen Russian warships. By the time

[3] A huge man, still powerful at 66, Duncan quelled mutiny in the *Adamant* by dangling the leader over the side by one arm. In the frigate, the captain and the first lieutenant gave orders with loaded carbines in their hands.

15,000 French troops were embarked in the Zuider Zee, the peak of the mutiny had passed and Duncan was again blockading in full strength. Still graver for the French, preparation of the Brest fleet continued to lag. This caused postponement, then modification, and finally abandonment of the plan to invade England. But the Dutch government, having gone to the expense of fitting out a fleet, ordered Admiral Jan de Winter to use it to clear the home coasts of the enemy. An opportunity presented itself in October when Duncan, low in stores, put back to Yarmouth Roads with the bulk of his ships to revictual.

De Winter took his squadrons out through the Texel channel on October 8 and shaped a southerly course for the Meuse estuary, where he expected to pick up an additional ship. The expected reinforcement was not to be found, but his ships were sighted by British patrols, and a fast cutter carried the report to Yarmouth. Duncan received the word next morning; by noon he was steering for the Dutch coast. Numerically the opposing battle lines were equal, 16 ships in each, with accompanying frigates and smaller craft. The British however were superior in guns and tonnage, with seven 74's, seven 64's, and two 50's to their opponents' four, seven, and five respectively, the smallest of the Dutch ships actually carrying 54 guns. On the other hand, the shallow draft of de Winter's vessels, a handicap in the open sea, had obvious advantages with shoal water hard by. The wind being from the northwest, the Dutch admiral could avoid battle merely by falling off downwind, or he could accept battle and then withdraw safely when hard pressed.

British scouts, at 9 AM on October 11, signaled "enemy to leeward," at which Duncan ordered General Chase, for he was determined not to let the Dutch gain the security of the shoals. His fleet came down in two divisions from the northwest. With all sails set, his ships fell into increasing disorder as the swifter ships took the lead. After two hours Duncan sighted his opponent some nine miles off the coastal town of Camperdown. Observing that de Winter had backed his topsails and was preparing to make a stand, he ordered his ships to shorten sail and re-form the line. To insure that the battle should be orthodox,

he made the general signal for each ship to attack its opposite number. Before he could get his ships back into column however, the Dutch began edging toward the shoals. Noting this, Duncan threw formalism to the winds and ordered all ships to up helm and run down to engage the enemy rear and center. This decision was crucial. "Your not waiting to form line ruined me," de Winter told him later. "If I had got nearer to the shore and you had attacked, I should probably have drawn both fleets on to it, and it would have been a victory to me, being on my own coast."[4]

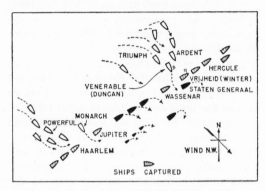

BATTLE OF CAMPERDOWN, OCTOBER 11, 1797

To grapple the enemy effectively and prevent him from passing into shoal water, Duncan next hoisted the signal (Howe's No. 34) to pass through the enemy line. Then, suspecting that the signal might not be understood or that his disordered squadrons might find it impossible to execute, he signaled for close action. Though the numerous hoists had bewildered most of Duncan's captains, not one had any thought of not engaging the enemy closely. Typical was the reaction of one captain, a fellow Scot, who hurled the signal book to the deck with an oath. "Up wi' the hel-lem," he roared to the master, "and gang into the middle o't!"[5]

In the same spirit most of the other British ships kept on through raking fire and sought an opponent where the action was thickest. But Vice Admiral Richard Onslow, commanding the rear squadron, correctly executed Signal 34, taking the *Monarch* through the enemy

[4] James R. Thursfield, *Nelson and Other Naval Studies* (New York, 1920), 158.
[5] *Ibid.*

line and luffing up to leeward of the *Jupiter*, flagship of the Dutch rear. A few minutes later, Duncan brought the *Venerable* through astern of de Winter's *Vrijheid* and engaged her from leeward. These penetrations, at van and rear, effectively gripped the whole fleet, for the rest of the Dutch vessels could not honorably desert their flagships.

As units of both fleets maneuvered to support their admirals, the action developed into two melees. Unlike the French and Spanish, the Dutch followed the British example of firing at hulls; scarcely a mast or spar of the North Sea fleet was damaged, but casualties of men and guns mounted rapidly on both sides. One English ship was hulled 98 times; most of the Dutch vessels in the two centers of action were so badly shattered as to be worthless for further service.

Englishmen had not met such stubborn antagonists in any fleet battle since the Anglo-Dutch wars. It was only a matter of time however before weight of British shot and larger British hulls prevailed. When both Dutch flagships struck, seven of their line—mostly from the center squadron, which had not been heavily engaged—slipped away into shoal water out of British reach. The other nine, with two frigates in addition, were prizes of war. The battle cost the North Sea fleet some 200 killed and more than 600 wounded—or about ten per cent of its complement. The smaller Dutch fleet had as many wounded and more than double the number killed. "It is a matter of marvel," said de Winter, a huge man like his opponent, "that two such gigantic objects as Admiral Duncan and myself should have escaped the general carnage of this day."[6]

Following hard upon the crisis of the mutinies, the victory over the Dutch served to renew public confidence in the Royal Navy. Bonfires and oratory blazed from Scotland to Devon, and in the general enthusiasm the fleet commander became Viscount Duncan of Camperdown. The professional-minded St. Vincent was less affected and commented that the battle "was fought pell-mell, without plan or system." This observation was less than fair to Duncan, who had stated clearly in his official report the imperative need of holding

the Dutch where they could be attacked, adding that "finding there was no time to be lost in making the attack, I made signal to bear up, break the enemy's line, and engage them to leeward, each ship his opponent; by which I got between them and the land, whither they were fast approaching."[7]

The battle demonstrated beyond question that the British profited by a melee, even when facing such determined antagonists as the Dutch. Steady improvements in gunnery not only gave them a faster rate of fire than their opponents but, by reducing the number of men required to work each gun, enabled them to fight port and starboard broadsides simultaneously. Thus, being caught between two fires, long considered a major hazard of melee tactics, gave the British a positive advantage. The melee moreover put a premium upon close range fire and mutual support among ships, in both of which British captains were especially indoctrinated. Like the Scottish commanding officer who threw down his signal book and ordered the master to "gang into the middle o't," British captains everywhere knew that they could advance into the heat of battle with assurance that they would be fully supported.

Even after his clear-cut victory over the Dutch, Lord Duncan continued to maintain his blockade off Texel, just as Lord St. Vincent continued to blockade Cadiz after his victory over the Spaniards. But there would not be any further attempt at combining French, Dutch, and Spanish fleets. For the time being, at least, there would be no further attempt at invading the British Isles. Napoleon Bonaparte, four months after the Battle of Camperdown, studied the strategic situation and reported to the Directory: "We must really give up the expedition against England."

Summary

The War of the French Revolution, on the grand strategic level, is a classic example of how coalition warfare should not be conducted. The Allies could never put common objectives above national objectives. The re-

---

[6] Michael Lewis, *The Navy of Britain* (London, 1948), 556.

[7] T. Sturges Jackson, ed., *Logs of the Great Sea Fights, 1794–1805*, I (Navy Records Society, 1899), 200.

sult was a series of uncoordinated military operations that proved generally ineffective against a dynamic and determined enemy. The Austrians, preoccupied with relatively petty issues in Bavaria, failed to provide support for the Allied occupation of Toulon, which held promise of being decisive in the outcome of the war. For the British, a revival of Pitt's Plan failed to yield the results of 1763 because they placed too much stress on conquering colonies and too little on supporting allies on the Continent. The French, while dominating Europe, could never come successfully to grips with Britain because, failing to understand the significance of sea power, they neglected their navy. So long as the commercial and maritime dominance of Britain remained unchallenged, she could raise up coalition after coalition to restore the balance of power on the Continent.

The strategic picture reflected the grand strategic stalemate. While France exerted her main military strength on the Continent, British objectives centered on (1) sending expeditions for colonial conquest in distant seas, (2) commanding the Atlantic coastal waters off Europe to safeguard the homeland from invasion, and (3) keeping the Mediterranean open for trade and for liaison with allies. The British victory in the Battle of the First of June, 1794, set in train a decline of France's Brest fleet that rendered it incapable of serving as a nucleus for naval forces to support an invasion of England. In 1796, Bonaparte's victories in Italy, combined with the Spanish declaration of war against Great Britain, forced the British out of the Mediterranean. The year 1797 saw Britain, despite a period of naval mutiny, recovering her ascendancy on the seas

by defeating the Spanish fleet off Cape St. Vincent in February and shattering the Dutch fleet off Camperdown in October. But these gains were more than offset by French victories ashore, for Bonaparte had rounded out his breathtaking conquest of northern Italy by forcing on Austria first the Truce of Leoben and finally the Treaty of Campo Formio. France was now at peace with all her former enemies except England. Yet England had the capacity, by virtue of her unimpaired sea power, to strike a blow that would reverse the whole picture. The opportunity was to come in 1798.

While strategically the war between England and France moved from stalemate to stalemate, the British were making strides in naval tactics and amphibious techniques that boded ill for their enemy. In the battles of the First of June, Cape St. Vincent, and Camperdown, the British commanders passed through the enemy's line to break it up and, at Camperdown, to cut off his retreat. Such line-breaking tactics inevitably brought on a melee, and this the British turned to their advantage through improved close-range gunnery, using both broadsides, and by indoctrination for dependable mutual support of ships under any conditions. In the West Indies the forces under Grey and Jervis successfully combined coordinated naval gunfire support, simultaneous landings to distract the enemy, speed in the seizure of beaches, quick envelopment of defensive strongpoints, and the rapid exploitation of initial gains. Advances such as these led ultimately to the victory at Trafalgar that removed the Napoleonic fleet from the seas, and to the Peninsular campaign that fatally undermined the French Empire.

7:

Nelson and Bonaparte

Neither the defeat of the Spanish fleet off Cape St. Vincent in February 1797 nor the shattering of the Dutch fleet off Camperdown the following October deterred the French Directory from its plan of invading the British Isles. Troops made available by the cessation of hostilities on the Continent were shifted into a new and more formidable Army of England. General Hoche, the architect of the invasion plan, was now dead, but the Treaty of Campo Formio had made General Bonaparte available. Into his hands the Directors placed their cherished project, with orders to prepare for a full-scale cross-Channel attack.

Arriving in Paris early in December 1797, Bonaparte soon plunged into his new assignment, energetically inspecting the Channel coast. But the more he studied the problem of conquering Britain by frontal assault, the less he liked it. Besides, his thoughts were elsewhere. Having played Caesar in Italy, he now dreamed of playing Alexander in the East. While going through the routine of preparing to invade England, he was secretly planning to invade Egypt. His personal reasons were mainly romantic and egotistical, the desire for exotically named victories to crown his fame and to enhance his drive to power, but the reasons he adduced to the Directors were of another sort and won their grudging support.

Bonaparte spoke, on the one hand, of commercial advantages, of the opportunity to obtain a base athwart the lifeline of the British Empire, of an eventual expedition against India. On the other, he assured the Directors that it would be impossible to invade England before the following autumn, that by then he would have completed his conquest of Egypt and returned to France. The expedition would thus serve as a giant diversion, attracting British warships to the defense of India and thereby simplifying the problems of the cross-Channel assault, which might be impossible with the Royal Navy concentrated in European waters. He scouted the Directors' fears that the invasion would make an enemy of Turkey, pointing out that not the Sultan but the military caste of Mamelukes controlled Egypt. Doubtless the sultan would prefer sharing control with France to remaining deprived of all authority in Egypt by the arrogant Mamelukes.

The Campaign and Battle of the Nile

With some reluctance the Directory finally approved Bonaparte's proposal. Though the immense preparations that were immediately set afoot could not be concealed, their purpose was a well guarded secret. All Europe soon knew that a great sea-borne expedition was in the making, but few besides Bonaparte and the five Directors were aware that its destination was Egypt. Bonaparte seemed tireless, his enthusiasm without bounds. Working night and day, he alerted Vice Admiral François Paul Brueys' fleet at Toulon, contracted for French and Italian merchantmen to serve as transports, collected artillery and cavalry, and out of his Army of Italy assembled an Army of the East, which as a subterfuge he temporarily labeled "the left wing of the Army of England."

Escorted by Brueys' fleet, the main body departed Toulon on May 19, 1798. On the following night a gale threatened to wreck the enterprise at the outset. But Bonaparte's famous luck held; not a ship was lost. In the ensuing days the expedition picked up contingents from Italian ports until the armada comprised 280 transports, escorted by 13 sail of the line, seven frigates, and 35 lighter vessels. Aboard were more than 50,000 men, including the cream of the French army, with Bonaparte in command. On June 9, the armada put in at Malta, which quickly capitulated after a token show of resistance. Bonaparte thereupon turned over the island base to an occupation force of 4,000 French troops and on June 19 set out for Alexandria.

In retrospect, Bonaparte's Egyptian expedition appears even more quixotic than Medina Sidonia's Spanish Armada against England two centuries earlier. A man less supremely confident of his own invincibility would have been appalled at the risks. He was undertaking to transport an army across a sea he did not control to a hostile coast where he had no base. His escorting fleet of warships was far too weak to support his landing and at the same time afford cover against attack from an enemy fleet. By secrecy and evasive routing he hoped to attain the surprise which alone could bring success. He succeeded by the narrowest of margins, for just over the horizon sailed a British fleet under Rear Admiral Sir Horatio Nelson, a name Bonaparte would come to respect and fear.

Nelson, back at sea after months ashore convalescing from the loss of his arm, had been ordered by Lord St. Vincent to take three 74's and three frigates to reconnoiter Toulon and to gain intelligence of the immense French expedition there assembled. The severe gale of May 20 that had threatened Bonaparte's enterprise hit Nelson's little observation squadron with full force. His flagship *Vanguard* was partially dismasted, and his frigates were so scattered that they retired to Gibraltar. In the lee of Sardinia he succeeded by prodigious efforts in repairing the damaged flagship in four days. On May 28 he learned from a passing merchantman that the French armada had sailed, whereupon he hastened to the appointed rendezvous off the French coast in the hope of finding his frigates. Instead he found a contingent of ten of the line, a 50, and a brig, under Rear Admiral Sir Thomas Troubridge, sent by St. Vincent to give Nelson

a force sufficient to handle the French, wherever they might be. Unfortunately Nelson's new force had no frigates either.

Thus reinforced to 13 of the line, Nelson headed east around Corsica to the coast of Italy, lamenting his lack of frigates, without which he was almost fatally hampered in search and scouting operations. Off Naples on June 17, he learned that the French had attacked Malta. Thither he proceeded by the shortest route, through the Straits of Messina.

Nelson reached Cape Pessaro, Sicily on June 22. Here a passing brig informed him that Malta had fallen and that the French armada had sailed again on the 16th. This was to prove a fateful piece of misinformation. On that date, as we have noted, Bonaparte was still at Malta, not sailing for Egypt until the 19th. The steady wind from the northwest convinced Nelson that the only likely goal of the French was Alexandria, and thither he promptly shaped his own course. Unhampered by wallowing transports and anticipating early action, he formed his fleet into three parallel columns, on the principle—afterwards written into his famous Trafalgar Memorandum—that the order of sailing should be the order of battle. Two of his columns were to attack the French men-of-war; the third would pursue the transports.

It is fascinating to speculate upon what might have happened had the two forces actually met. In all probability either Nelson or Bonaparte, the great masters respectively of sea and land warfare, would have been removed from the stage of history, with far-reaching effects upon subsequent events. But Nelson had no frigates to stretch out in a scouting line to provide far-ranging eyes for his fleet, and Bonaparte was heading almost due east for the southern coast of Crete, whence he intended to cross the Mediterranean narrows and then move along the African coast to Alexandria. As Nelson's compact formation and Bonaparte's tight convoy moved on converging courses, the mists thickened unseasonably. In the evening of June 22 the two forces actually crossed paths within what in clearer weather would have been visual range. That night Brueys was alarmed to hear British signal guns in the distance.

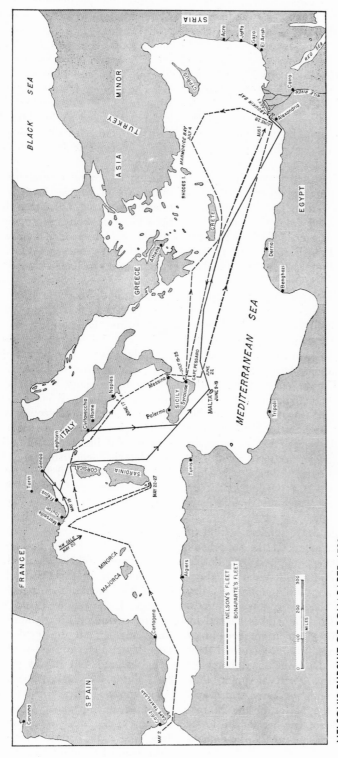

NELSON'S PURSUIT OF BONAPARTE, 1798

Nelson, taking a direct route, reached Alexandria first, on June 28. Finding no French ships in the harbor, he bitterly concluded that he must have guessed wrong. Still laboring under the misapprehension that Bonaparte had departed Malta on the 16th, he could not believe that he had outsped the French by six days. His impatience and restless energy now betrayed him into a false move. Scarcely pausing, he set sail to find the enemy wherever he might be. From the Pharos outside the harbor of Alexandria, lookouts within a few hours saw the last of Nelson's sails disappearing northward over the horizon as they caught their first glimpse of French sails arriving from the west.

Reaching Alexandria on July 1, Bonaparte received from the French consul the electrifying information that Nelson had touched there only three days before. In the circumstances a lesser man might have withdrawn, at least temporarily, but Bonaparte characteristically chose the bold course of landing at once, even though the hour was late and the sea heavy. Moving westward some miles along the coast, the transports began hoisting out boats, while Brueys gave cover. Despite the perils of collision and foaming reefs, some 4,000 troops managed to struggle onto the beach that evening, and at the head of these Bonaparte marched through the night upon Alexandria, which fell the next day. The transports thereupon entered the harbor, while Brueys anchored his 13 of the line and four frigates in the deeper water of Aboukir Bay, some twelve miles northeast of the city.

Bonaparte, leaving 3,000 soldiers behind to garrison Alexandria, ascended the west bank of the Nile with 30,000, followed by a flotilla bringing supplies and artillery. After three weeks he reached a position opposite Cairo and almost in the shadow of the Pyramids. Here 10,000 mounted Mamelukes backed by 24,000 foot were drawn up in gorgeous array to contest his advance. The French held their fire in the face of the impetuous charge of the Egyptian cavalry. Then at point-blank range they opened with musketry and grape. That volley broke the power of the Mamelukes and made Bonaparte master of lower Egypt. Two days later, on July 23, he entered Cairo.

Nelson meanwhile had been combing the Mediterranean in an agony of frustration and apprehension. From Alexandria he steered north to the coast of Asia Minor. Gleaning no information there, he began beating back toward Sicily and put into Syracuse on July 19. The almost intolerable tension was somewhat relieved by the news that the French had not attacked Sicily or Naples, but beyond that he could learn nothing. "If they are above water, I will find them out," he said grimly, "and if possible bring them to battle." Pausing only long enough to take on provisions, Nelson was again at sea on the 25th, steering eastward. Off Greece he at last picked up a piece of useful information. The French armada had been seen four weeks earlier off Crete steering southeast. On this intelligence, Nelson at once shaped course again for Alexandria.

The month-long search, while trying Nelson's nerves to the utmost, was by no means wasted time. Unlike many naval commanders of his day, he refused to hold himself aloof. Scarcely a calm day passed that he did not have one or more of his captains aboard the *Vanguard* to share his meals and, more important, his views. Every conceivable circumstance was reviewed—combats at sea and at anchor, by day or by night. Nelson never relinquished his command or his responsibilities, but his leadership and his professional judgment so unified his captains that their minds became extensions of his own, his decisions theirs. "I had the happiness," Nelson later wrote, "to command a Band of Brothers."

The passage of time had served the French admiral quite otherwise. As the days went by with no signs of the British, he gradually relaxed his precautions. Anchored in the open roadstead, he allowed his men to forage ashore, permitted his frigates to neglect picket duty, and left off the regular drill needed to keep his gunners combat-ready. He did make a battle plan, but it was perfunctory, based on habit rather than expectation of attack. Assuming a fortress mentality, he proposed to meet any possible British onslaught at anchor in the treacherous waters of Aboukir Bay, where the British superiority in seamanship would be nullified by a static battle. He drew up his fleet in a north-northwest, south-southeast line hugging a shoal on the westward side. Believing that the puny battery on Aboukir Island a mile and a half away to the northeast would protect his van, he stationed his strongest ships in the center and rear out of respect to the British custom of massing on these divisions. He forgot that such a practice was employed by the British in actions *at sea*, since it was difficult for the van to succor the rear against the wind that gave the fleet headway. At anchor it was a different story.

His situation was in several respects fatally weak. His ships were anchored by the bows only, with excessive intervals between ships, an obvious defect he planned to remedy in the event of impending attack by rigging stern anchors and springs[1] and passing cables between ships. The most serious flaw in Brueys' disposition was that it depended for defensive strength mainly on an offshore wind blowing into the teeth of any approaching enemy. But winds in the Mediterranean are not readily predictable. In fact, when Nelson again reached Egypt, a stiff breeze was blowing directly down the French line, van to rear, permitting the British to attack as they chose and preventing French ships from moving forward to assist their neighbors ahead. Brueys, in short, through negligence, miscalculation, and inadequate understanding of tactics, had made his fleet extraordinarily vulnerable to attack by seamen who knew their business—and Nelson and his captains knew their business.

The British fleet passed the transport-filled harbor of Alexandria in the early afternoon of August 1 and steered for the French men-of-war, whose masts were visible in the distance across the coastal flats. Despite the presence of the 120-gun flagship *Orient* and three 80's in the French line, the hazards of entering an unfamiliar roadstead without dependable charts, and the lateness of the hour, Nelson decided to attack without delay.

The French fleet meanwhile was all con-

[1] The term *spring*, as used here, refers to a cable run from the anchor through a stern or quarter port to the capstan. Taking up or paying out on this cable enabled a ship to be turned to direct her broadsides wherever desired.

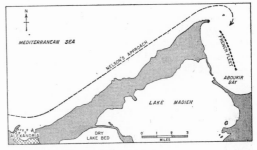

BATTLE OF THE NILE (APPROACH)

fusion. Brueys, appalled by the celerity of the British approach despite unfamiliar shoals and oncoming darkness, wavered between remaining at anchor and flight. He cleared for action, but only on the seaward side, and he failed to get stern anchors out or to rig springs and cables before the enemy was upon him.

Nelson's plan, with which his captains were perfectly familiar, was for each British ship to anchor by the stern as it came alongside the French line. The following British ship would pass on the disengaged side of the first one and anchor next ahead, so that the first fire from each French broadside would be met by first fire from a fresh British broadside. One British ship would take station off the bow and another off the quarter of each of the leading French ships, giving the British a two-to-one advantage in the sector under attack. From these positions the English men-of-war would be in small danger of broadsides from the uncontrollably swinging enemy ships, while by use of their springs they could direct their own broadsides where they willed.

Nelson probably expected all his captains, to anchor along the seaward side of the enemy van and center, since he must have assumed that Brueys would take the elementary precaution of anchoring so close to the shoal that no ship could pass on his landward side. But Captain Thomas Foley, from his position in the leading British ship *Goliath*, saw an opportunity for an even better method of attack. Noting that the French ships were swinging freely at their bow anchors, without a moment's hesitation he crossed the bows of the *Guerrier* at the exposed head of the enemy column. Delivering a murderous raking fire, he came to anchor on the landward

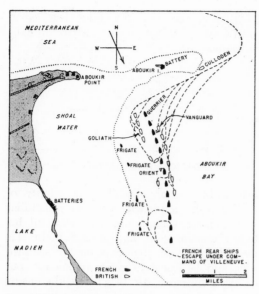

BATTLE OF THE NILE, AUGUST 1, 1798

the last two ships safely. These, arriving as a timely reserve, advanced to the relief of two English 74's opposite the French center, where they were taking heavy punishment from the huge *Orient* and an 80-gun ship next astern.

As the ships of the French van, shattered by overwhelming gunfire, surrendered one at a time, Nelson's ships moved methodically down both sides of the enemy line, enveloping the center and part of the rear. The *Orient,* under fire from several directions, burst into flames which crackled up her rigging and slowly ate into her hull. At ten o'clock, as the fire reached her magazines, the great flagship blew up with a force that opened the seams of nearby vessels. Awestruck by this appalling spectacle, battle-hardened seamen left off working their guns, and dead silence reigned for many minutes. Then the roar of battle resumed, and ships of the French center and rear began to strike their colors.

Dawn of August 2, 1798 revealed an unparalleled scene of triumph on the one hand and of devastation on the other. The British had not lost a single ship, and while their casualties amounted to nearly 900 men, French losses were almost six times as great. All the French ships except the three at the rear of the line had been taken or destroyed. Of these, one was deliberately grounded and burned by her crew. With the other two and the two remaining French frigates, Rear Admiral Pierre Villeneuve managed to slip out of the bay and escape to Malta.

From the quarterdeck of the *Vanguard,* Nelson surveyed his nine prizes with satisfaction. "Victory," said he, "is not a name strong enough for such a scene." The night's work had destroyed France's Toulon fleet, given Britain uncontested command of the Mediterranean, and isolated Bonaparte and his army in hostile Egypt. Even those who escaped in the fleeing ships were psychologically beaten men; the "horror of the Nile" was to cloud their judgment and to fill them with premonitions of defeat in future engagements with the British. Bonaparte himself was chastened by his first contact with triumphant sea power, and though he was never fully to grasp the significance of naval operations, the tall ships

side of the French line. Four more British ships followed.

Foley's instant decision was probably based on Nelson's remark that "wherever an enemy ship can swing, one of ours may anchor." Nelson, at any rate, tacitly applauded his subordinate's initiative by carrying out its tactical counterpart. Arriving sixth in the *Vanguard,* he anchored outside the enemy line, and so did the next few arrivals. The British thus doubled the weak French van and part of the center, placing them between two fires, while the rest of the French line, held by the wind, looked on helpless. Soon after seeing his fleet in position, Nelson was struck on the forehead by a piece of langridge and was out of the battle for some hours. But his task was done—he had brought his fleet to action; his Band of Brothers could carry on.

Nightfall threw the baffled French into increasing confusion without greatly incommoding the English, who by Nelson's prior direction had lighted recognition lanterns in the tops. Three British stragglers at last reached the bay, led by Troubridge's *Culloden,* but Troubridge, ardent for battle, cut the reef too closely and grounded hard. While captain and crew raged in frustration the *Culloden* tamely served as a buoy to guide of England had won his lasting respect and would influence all his future campaigns.

Tactically Nelson's Nile victory was unique in that he had at last found a solution to the problem over which naval theorists had been puzzling since the earliest days of the formalist-meleeist controversy—how to mass on part of the enemy force while containing the rest; in short how to attain tactical concentration. While Brueys' faulty disposition had provided the British with the opportunity of massing on his van and center, and a fortuitous wind had held the French rear out of action, Nelson deserves credit for instantly perceiving the possibilities and acting upon them. When at Trafalgar he again met a French fleet in battle, he would demonstrate that he could work the same combination with no special advantages of wind or shoals.

More significant than its tactical implications were the strategic results of the battle. Like all decisive naval victories, it exercised a powerful influence far beyond the scene of action. It had an impact on concurrent operations in three major theaters of war.

The Second Coalition

Nelson's victory reignited the war in Europe. Heartened by the isolation of Bonaparte and his army, France's enemies were soon once more on the march. William Pitt the Younger was at last able to achieve his Second Coalition. Yet in spite of all the hopes with which it began, the coalition fell apart under the follies and jealousies of its members until once again England stood alone.

The loss of her fleet at the Nile found France hopelessly overextended, an army deep in Italy, one in central Europe, and one in Egypt, cut off from home. The British and their allies lost no time in exploiting their newly-won command of the Mediterranean. Combined Russian-Turkish naval forces operated near the mouth of the Adriatic, attacking the Ionian Islands recently captured by France. Most of the islands fell quickly, but the main French base at Corfu held out until March of the following year. The bulk of the British Mediterranean fleet remained perforce outside the Straits blockading Cadiz, but Lord St. Vincent detached a squadron under Rear Admiral Sir John Duckworth against Minorca, which capitulated in mid-November 1798.

Back at Naples, Nelson, exhilarated by the adulation he was everywhere accorded, and his judgment possibly clouded by his head wound, fell into two major errors. Accepting the hospitality of Ambassador Sir William Hamilton, he soon succumbed to the charms of Emma, Lady Hamilton. This passionate liaison lasted until the end of Nelson's life, to the scandal of his friends, the wreck of his marriage, and the near-ruin of his career.

Emma Hamilton, a close friend of Queen Maria Carolina, soon enlisted Nelson in Her Majesty's cause. This remarkable woman was the real ruler of the Kingdom of the Two Sicilies, her husband, King Ferdinand IV, being little more than a figurehead. Sister of the unhappy Marie Antoinette of France, Maria Carolina intensely hated everything republican and longed to strike out with all her strength, now that, as she fancied, France's head was in the dust. In seeking to please Her Majesty, Nelson urged an attack on the Papal States, which he would support from the sea with his ships. Command of this operation fell to the Austrian General Mack, whose incompetence was exceeded only by his zeal. In November 1798 Mack's force entered the Papal States with Nelson landing troops at Leghorn in the enemy rear. But on land France's head was by no means in the dust, and she retaliated swiftly. Mack's army came streaming back. "The Neapolitans have not lost much honour," wrote Nelson ruefully, "for God knows they have but little to lose; but they lost all they had." As the French closed on Naples, Nelson spirited the Royal Family aboard the *Vanguard,* in which he took them and the Hamiltons to Palermo.

By January 1799, Russia, Turkey, Portugal, Austria, the Kingdom of the Two Sicilies, and the Papal States had joined England in the Second Coalition. The immediate opportunity was in Northern Italy, weakened by the French counterattack on the Neapolitan armies. Into this area plunged an Austro-Russian army under the hard-hitting Russian Marshal Alexander Suvorov, who by the middle of the year had expelled the French from all of Italy except the area around Genoa and threatened France herself with invasion. At the same time France faced peril in Central Europe, where Austrian armies under Archduke Charles outnumbered the French. At home, the threat of civil war boiled up. The prestige of the Directory reached its nadir.

In a desperate effort to retrieve their fortunes, the Directory ordered the young Minister of Marine, Admiral Eustache Bruix, to put to sea from Brest, add to his command any Spanish ships that could escape their blockaders, smash the British Mediterranean fleet and so regain supremacy within the Straits, and finally rescue Bonaparte and his army from Egypt. In this crisis, the Directors forgot their jealousies and saw Bonaparte as the one man who could save France.

Bruix found his opportunity because Lord Bridport, commanding the British Channel fleet, imperfectly understood the meaning of blockade. He conserved ships and crews against future requirements, allowing them frequent stays in port for refit. On blockade, he kept his fleet well out, avoiding the treacherous coast of France. On April 25 a northeast wind drove him some miles west of Ushant, and the same wind filled the sails of Bruix's 25 of the line and ten frigates as they set out for the Mediterranean. Bridport, attempting to close the proverbial stable door, collected every available ship for the defense of Ireland, whither he assumed the French fleet was headed.

Having made good his escape from the befuddled Bridport, Bruix also eluded Lord Keith off Cadiz and passed through the Straits in a gale on May 5. Now, had he chosen, he might have made himself master of the Mediterranean, for half the British fleet was outside guarding Cadiz, and the other half was scattered—at Minorca, Naples, Sicily, Malta, and the Levant. But the "horror of the Nile" had clouded his judgment. Fancying himself already under British guns, he abandoned his mission and made all haste for Toulon. Lord St. Vincent, who could not know that Bruix had thrown away his once-in-a-lifetime opportunity, in great alarm summoned Keith's ships from before Cadiz and added them to those at Gibraltar. This massing of British forces freed the Cadiz fleet

of 17 ships under Admiral Mazarredo, who at once quitted port and proceeded through the Straits to Cartagena. St. Vincent then divided his fleet with Nelson, who with 16 of the line was to oppose any enemy advance toward Malta or Egypt, while St. Vincent with 21 stood between Cartagena and Toulon to prevent a juncture of the enemy fleets. Both St. Vincent and Nelson risked defeat, but each counted on so crippling the foe in any encounter that the other British force could easily overtake and destroy him.

At Toulon Bruix found new orders. Suvorov was now threatening France itself. The Directors therefore dropped their plan to rescue Bonaparte and sent Bruix's fleet with supplies and reinforcements to the besieged French army at Genoa. St. Vincent was soon plowing Bruix's wake, but increasing poor health obliged him to relinquish his command to Keith. On June 6, as Bruix departed Genoa, his mission completed, Keith was just 80 miles away, frustrated by the wind. Worried about the intentions of the enemy, he warned Nelson and then fell back to defend Minorca. This move, contrary to St. Vincent's parting injunction to keep at all costs between Mazarredo and Bruix, permitted the French fleet to get past him. Hugging the coasts of France and Spain, Bruix picked up the Spanish fleet at Cartagena, and with a combined force of 40 of the line, headed for the Atlantic. Keith, his fleet built up to 32 ships by reinforcements from England, passed through the Straits of Gibraltar on July 29, staying grimly on Bruix's trail. The Franco-Spanish fleet entered Brest on August 13, just one day ahead of the British.

Bruix's long cruise had not been altogether fruitless, for the Spanish ships remained in Brest as hostages, stiffening the wavering loyalty of Spain. Moreover he had deprived Britain's Mediterranean Fleet of sorely needed ships, for Keith was obliged to remain in England until the end of 1799 to quiet British fears that the arrival of so many enemy ships at the Channel presaged a new invasion attempt.

Even while Bruix was in the Mediterranean, disaster seemed to be threatening France from all sides. At the end of May Suvorov captured Turin, winning a large haul of guns and ammunition, and a few days later was poised in the Alpine passes to France. In the north, Archduke Charles defeated Masséna at Zurich. Meanwhile patriots, supported by British sea power, had recaptured Naples, to which the King made a state visit with all pomp and ceremony, returning to Sicily a few days later. As Nelson divided his time thereafter between Naples and Palermo, it seemed to his fellow officers that he was more interested in Emma Hamilton than in his duty. Yet Nelson recognized that the Kingdom of the Two Sicilies afforded the only places in the Mediterranean where the navy might expect to find support. Thus when Keith, on leaving to pursue Bruix, sent him peremptory orders to leave Italian waters and cover Minorca, Nelson flatly disobeyed, an act of insubordination that earned him a letter of censure from the Admiralty. "I have no scruple in deciding that it is better to save the Kingdom of Naples and risk Minorca," he said, "than to risk the Kingdom of Naples and save Minorca."

During the months that Keith remained in England, Nelson acted as commander in chief in the Mediterranean. It was a frustrating experience, for with never enough ships or men he was responsible for cooperating with the Austro-Russian army in Italy, protecting Gibraltar and Minorca, continuing the blockade of Malta, and keeping Bonaparte and his army isolated in Egypt. In September 1799 a few ships and their crews under Troubridge assisted in the capture of Civitavecchia and Rome. Lord Keith's arrival in January 1800 greatly eased the problems of British naval control but only added to Nelson's discontent, for Nelson believed that he and not Keith should have been appointed commander in chief. He was particularly galled when Keith, in assigning him to the Malta blockade, stipulated that he was to base his squadron on Syracuse or another port on the east coast of Sicily. Keith's intention, as Nelson suspected, was in part to keep him away from the influence of the Hamiltons and the Queen.

Keith's well-meaning plan did not succeed, for Nelson, whose complex personality combined the sensitive artist with the fearless warrior, simply went to pieces with frustration and resentment. His health became so affected that he asked and received permission to return to England. He and the Hamiltons proceeded in a triumphal procession across Germany and so back home, landing at Yarmouth in November 1800. The people of England received back the hero of the Nile with demonstrations of enthusiasm, but in society Nelson experienced a certain coldness, occasioned by his continued open association with Lady Hamilton.

Nelson's Mediterranean assignment was completed by others. Scarcely had he left Malta before the blockading fleet captured the *Guillaume Tell*, last of the survivors of the Nile, as she was attempting to escape from Valetta by night. The starving French garrison at last capitulated in September 1800.

To share in the land operations in Europe, the only kind of military enterprise her allies appeared to understand, Britain made the decision to invade the Low Countries. The strategic aim was three-fold: (1) to eliminate the Dutch fleet, regardless of any other outcome of the campaign; (2) to reestablish the House of Orange on the Dutch throne; and (3) to have a successful army on the Continent as a make-weight against Austria's demands in the carving up of Europe following what appeared to be the impending defeat of France. Britain however had only 10,000 regulars available for foreign service. Czar Paul, approached by Cabinet representatives, agreed to furnish 18,000 Russian troops for the expedition, with the proviso that Britain foot all the bills. The British government filled out the expeditionary force with 20,000 raw militia from the English counties. This heterogeneous collection of troops was hardly expected to surmount stout resistance, but the British nursed the illusion that the Dutch would receive them as liberators from the French and flock to the standard of the deposed Prince of Orange, who would accompany the army.

The actual assault, an exclusively British affair, was placed in the steady hands of a formidable old veteran, Lieutenant General Sir Ralph Abercromby. Cover for the invasion was to be provided by Lord Duncan's North Sea blockading fleet. Close support would be furnished by a squadron of eleven ships, including two Russian, and several frigates under Vice Admiral Andrew Mitchell. Abercromby, who had no faith in the expedition, did the best he could in view of his vague orders—to land somewhere and do something. Choosing the Helder Peninsula in North Holland as his point of attack, he landed in considerable confusion on the morning of August 27, 1799, supported by Mitchell's squadron.

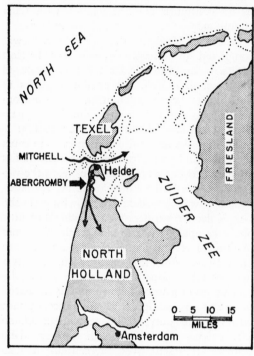

HELDER EXPEDITION, 1799

Once ashore, Abercromby at first made rapid advances. Then he made a fatal mistake —he stopped. Underestimating his opponent's difficulties and overestimating his own, he dug in to await reinforcements. As a result, the French were able to bring up reserves and counterattack. Upon the arrival of the Russian contingent, over-all command devolved upon the Duke of York, who had sufficient rank but insufficient skill or resolution to lead an international army. From that moment, all success left the enterprise. When the onset of winter weather in mid-October made supply over open beaches impracticable, the army was obliged to withdraw from Holland.

Still, the expedition was far from a failure, for the British had achieved their military objective, which in the long run outweighed all the rest. Capture of the Helder batteries

by Abercromby's troops had enabled Admiral Mitchell to make a daring penetration of the Zuider Zee, where he surprised the Dutch fleet and forced it to surrender. This cancellation of Dutch naval power permitted Britain to end her long blockade of Holland and to assign the ships, her own and the captured Dutch, to other operations.

The bright prospects of the summer of 1799, when victory seemed at hand, suddenly faded as the jealousy of the near-victors led to suspicion, suspicion to blunder, and blunder to disaster. Half-mad Czar Paul called upon Christendom to liquidate the Revolution and to restore all conquests to those who had held them in 1798. This accorded ill with the desires of Austria, who had expanded her borders considerably in recent months. At Britain's suggestion, to relieve tensions in Italy, the Czar ordered Suvorov to shift his forces over the Alps and join the Russian army under General Korsakov, then operating with the Austrians in Switzerland. This proved a fatal move. Scarcely had Suvorov's Russians separated from the Austrians in Italy when the Archduke Charles withdrew his Austrians from Korsakov's Russians in Switzerland. Thus where there had been two formidable Austro-Russian armies on the eastern frontiers of France, there were now two weak Austrian armies on the flanks and two weak Russian armies trying to make contact at the center. Before the Russians could unite, the French army in Switzerland routed Korsakov and then forced Suvorov to retreat into Germany. On October 23, five days after the Duke of York had agreed to evacuate Holland, the Czar notified the Emperor that the alliance was at an end and recalled Korsakov and Suvorov to Russia. Thus the Second Coalition fell asunder, and on all fronts save in Italy the French had hurled back their enemies.

Almost as though on signal, there arrived the man who could restore to France the grandeur she had lost. Napoleon Bonaparte came ashore at Fréjus on October 9, 1799.

The Return of Bonaparte

The smashing defeat at the Nile had left Bonaparte a badly shaken man. Instead of a dangerous threat to Britain's empire, he was now a virtual exile, cut off from all hope of succor from France. The only way out for him and his army was the long route around the Mediterranean through Turkey. But the Sultan had not been convinced by Bonaparte's assurances, and encouraged by the promise of military assistance from Russia and Great Britain, Turkey prepared to crush Bonaparte's stranded army in a gigantic pincers. One Turkish army would advance on Egypt overland through Syria; a second would attack via the sea from the Island of Rhodes.

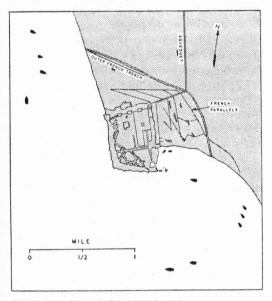

SIEGE OF ACRE, MARCH-MAY, 1799

Bonaparte, informed of the Turkish plan, characteristically decided to strike first, taking advantage of his interior position. He would attack overland and then return to Egypt to throw back the assault from the sea. Counting on foul winter weather to delay the seaborne expedition, he marched on Syria in February 1799 with 13,000 troops, easily captured the advanced Turkish outpost of El Arish, and then proceeded northward up the Syrian coast, seizing Gaza and Jaffa. Like Alexander the Great, he was obliged to capture every seaport on his route, lest a hostile army be landed in his rear. This necessity, plus a touch of British sea power, brought his expedition ingloriously to a halt at Acre.

Commodore Sir Sydney Smith, who had succeeded to the command of the Alexandria blockade, had correctly identified Acre as the point where the French army could best be stopped, for the city, roughly square, stood on a point of land with two faces on the sea and the approaches to the other two accessible to naval gunfire. Here sea power could come to grips with land power. So he proceeded to Acre with two of the line and several smaller vessels. Almost at once he captured a flotilla from the Nile bearing Bonaparte's siege guns, which Smith promptly added to the city's defenses. He then stationed his two ships in position to enfilade the approaches to the landward walls. Thus supported, the 3,000 defending Turks, to whom Smith added 500 of his own seamen and marines, held out until reinforcements could be brought in by sea from the Turkish army on Rhodes. The baffled French, after 63 days of siege, at last acknowledged defeat and retreated hastily to Egypt, leaving 5,000 casualties behind. "If it had not been for you English, I should have been Emperor of the East," Bonaparte afterward declared angrily to an English sea captain, "but wherever there is water to float a ship, we are sure to find you in the way."

The long-delayed Turkish attack by sea finally came in July 1800. Supported by thirteen 74's and numerous smaller vessels, 12,000 infantry came ashore at Aboukir Bay and there entrenched in the vain expectation of reinforcements from Syria. Mameluke cavalry from the south supported a general uprising of natives all over Egypt. Before any sort of help could arrive however, Bonaparte was at Aboukir with cavalry, artillery, and 8,000 troops. Under a steady fire of grape, the Turkish line gave way and was enveloped by infantry on both flanks, while French cavalry attacked from the rear. In mad panic hundreds of Turks threw themselves into the sea. The last of the survivors, 3,000 who had shut themselves up in Aboukir castle, surrendered on August 1, 1799, the anniversary of Nelson's victory on the same scene. The French had suffered 200 killed and 750 wounded.

Crowned with a decisive victory to offset Brueys' defeat and his own repulse from Acre, Bonaparte prepared to carry out his long-cherished intention of returning to France to make a bid for power. Handing over his Army of the East to General Jean Baptiste Kléber, on

August 23 he left Alexandria with two swift frigates and two smaller vessels while Smith was off station. The little squadron, by hugging the African coast, slipped through Nelson's inadequate screen of frigates and reached France safely.

Disgusted by Bonaparte's desertion, Kléber early in 1800 signed an agreement with the Turks whereby his army was to evacuate Egypt and return to France. Though Sir Sydney Smith, exceeding his powers, assented to the agreement, it was nullified by orders from London that not a single French soldier should leave Egypt except as a prisoner of war. Britain could hardly have acted otherwise at that time, for Bonaparte was then with great difficulty gathering troops for a campaign against the Austrians in Italy. For the British to have countenanced the transfer to France of Bonaparte's veterans of the Army of the East would have meant betraying an ally.

Bonaparte, on his return to France, found himself the man of the hour. His amazing luck had brought him home at precisely the right moment to attain his ends. France was no longer in serious danger, to be sure, for the coalition of her enemies was already falling apart. But to most Frenchmen it was not apparent that the crisis had passed. They saw only that the Directors had thrown away Bonaparte's brilliant, peace-crowned victories of 1797 and plunged the country into a disastrous war. No one seemed to realize that it was Bonaparte's own Egyptian expedition that set the stage for the new war. Beguiled by propaganda out of Egypt, they saw Bonaparte as France's only consistently victorious general. Now the victor had returned to save France. It was all the sheerest illusion, but politicians in Paris were ready to make use of the illusion to further their own ambitions.

Bonaparte, with the assistance of his brother Lucien, engineered a series of decrees that cleared the way for a *coup d'état*. Sensing that after ten years of internal strife France would gladly accept a strong executive, Bonaparte drafted a new constitution that provided for a head of state with extraordinary powers. It was overwhelmingly accepted in a plebiscite on December 15, 1799, and Bonaparte, then 30 years old, was acclaimed First Consul. As such he was virtual dictator of France.

In order to establish himself among his war-weary people as a man of peace, Bonaparte offered England and Austria terms that he knew they would reject. While his captive newspapers were creating propaganda out of this situation, he set out with considerable success to shore up the national finances. At the same time he took the French army and navy under his direct command. By spring he felt ready to deal militarily with the remnants of the Second Coalition. He elected to act first against Austria, as the most accessible. In May 1800 he led an army across the Alps, dragging his guns through snow over the difficult Great St. Bernard Pass, and descended into Italy. The main Austrian army, its communications cut, abandoned its strong position on the French border and marched hastily eastward, only to be overwhelmed by Bonaparte's forces in mid-June at the Battle of Marengo. Six months later General Jean Victor Moreau decisively defeated the Austrians at Hohenlinden in Germany, whereupon the War of the Second Coalition collapsed as Austria accepted the Peace of Lunéville.

Britain Strikes Back in the South—Aboukir

Once more virtually without an ally, Britain was again driven to exploit her sea power. Bonaparte showed evidence that he was ready to close the Continent to British forces and to British trade. Because Spain seemed the weakest link in the defense of Europe, the British Cabinet decided to attempt the capture of Cadiz. An army of 22,000 soldiers under Abercromby, transported and covered by Keith, sailed from Gibraltar early in October at the height of the hurricane season to attempt to make a descent on one of the most strongly held ports in Europe. When he could not secure Keith's unequivocal promise of logistic support regardless of weather or other circumstances, Abercromby abruptly abandoned the venture. He and Keith returned sheepishly to Gibraltar to find new orders from England.

With Austria again forced out of the war, conclusion of peace between France and Britain appeared imminent. The presence of French soldiers in Egypt might establish French claims there, or serve as a bargaining point for bolstering French pretensions elsewhere. At all costs the Army of the East had to be evicted. This was the task Abercromby and Keith were ordered to undertake. As a result of their unhappy recent experience at Cadiz and of Abercromby's misfortunes at the Helder, the two commanders determined that this time there would be no mistake. They gave unstinted pains to their plans—and incidentally worked out many of the techniques of modern amphibious warfare.

Underestimating the number of French troops in Egypt, the War Ministry provided Abercromby with only 16,000 men. As usual the British troops were poorly equipped and, as usual, Abercromby's orders were vague in the extreme. The little army, carried in 28 transports and escorted by seven of the line and twelve smaller vessels, proceeded to Marmorice Bay, 40 miles north of Rhodes, arriving in December 1800. Here Britain hoped to concert operations with the Turks, who had been lavish in promises. But it quickly appeared that little was to be had from Turkey except horses, mostly of poor quality, and transports to carry them.

The six weeks it took to assemble the animal transports proved the most fruitful of the campaign, for during this period the British soldiers and sailors engaged in intensive and realistic rehearsals, something that had been lacking in all previous amphibious assaults. The repeated landing drills and the exercises ashore anticipated as closely as possible the conditions that the participants would find in the Aboukir Bay area, the only practical spot near Alexandria for an invasion with fleet support. Every man was put through the intended operations until each motion became a habit. The goal of the rehearsals is best expressed by paraphrasing Nelson—the order of landing was to be the order of battle.[2]

When the British reached Egypt on March 1, 1801, General Menou, who had succeeded to command, was in Cairo with his main army. Contemptuously he made no move to defend the beach during the week that Keith's fleet rocked in Aboukir Bay awaiting suitable weather for landing operations. When the as-

[2] Extracts from the landing orders can be found in Sir Henry Bunbury, *Great War with France* (London, 1927), 103–6.

sault came on March 8, fewer than 2,000 troops opposed the landings.

Active British operations were initiated by a signal rocket from Keith's flagship at 2 AM. From the transports, anchored seven miles out in deep water, the soldiers of the first division were rowed to the line of departure, marked by two shallow-draft vessels moored two miles offshore. By 9 o'clock the landing force was aligned in three waves facing the mile-wide beach, with gunboats at their flanks and rear. On signal, the gunboats opened fire on the shore as the landing craft started in. The first wave consisted of 58 flatboats, carrying 3,000 infantrymen, with 50-foot intervals between boats; the second was composed of 84 ships' cutters carrying 2,700 infantrymen; the third, of 37 launches in which seamen towed 14 more launches bearing field guns and gunners. As the three waves advanced they were met first by a cross-fire of shot and shell that did but little damage, then by grape and langridge that caused numerous casualties, and finally by musketry.

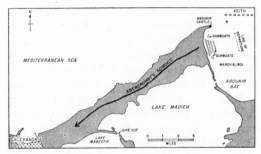

BRITISH AMPHIBIOUS ASSAULT AT ABOUKIR, MARCH 8, 1801

As the first wave touched bottom, the second and third slipped into the intervals, and 6,000 men stepped ashore already organized in companies and battalions. Thrusting aside attacks by infantrymen and by mounted dragoons, the British followed Major General Sir John Moore up the sandhills. By nightfall they had advanced two miles along the peninsula toward Alexandria, and the rest of Abercromby's army had landed. British casualties by that time amounted to 700, of whom a hundred were navy. French losses were something over 400.

An engagement on March 13 forced the

French back to Alexandria. Taking alarm at last, General Menou brought reinforcements to Alexandria on the 19th, reaching the city via the dry bed of Lake Mareotis to the south. This action brought the defense forces up to 10,000, but Menou had unaccountably left half his army in Cairo. In a fierce battle on the 21st, Abercromby was killed, and command devolved upon Major General John Hely-Hutchison, who isolated Alexandria by cutting the dike and flooding Lake Mareotis. Then, leaving 6,000 troops to invest the city, he marched with 5,000 on Cairo. En route he was dismayed to learn that French reinforcements were arriving by sea.

With Keith's squadron standing cover off the Egyptian coast, he need not have worried. Rear Admiral Honoré Ganteaume, on Bonaparte's orders, had slipped out of Brest in a gale the preceding January with 5,000 troops aboard seven sail of the line and two frigates. Like Bruix, he had eluded British squadrons and passed safely through the Straits. Once inside the Mediterranean however, he took alarm and steered for Toulon. Twice ordered out of port by a much annoyed Bonaparte, he finally got under way for Egypt in May. On June 7, some 200 miles west of Alexandria, he sent in a corvette to reconnoiter. When the corvette failed to return, having been chased into port by the British, Ganteaume retreated to Benghazi, with the absurd idea of landing his troops to march 600 miles across the desert sands to Alexandria. Keith meanwhile had come westward to investigate. At the first sight of British sails, Ganteaume fled once more to Toulon. He had shown remarkable skill in eluding capture, but not much else. Nevertheless, Bonaparte was convinced that despite British vigilance French fleets could pass through the Straits whenever needed, a notion that was to lead to the Trafalgar campaign four years later.

Hely-Hutchison, approaching Cairo, was joined at last by the long-promised Turkish force of 4,000 troops and by a body of 1,200 Mamelukes. At the same time 6,000 British troops from India had reached Egypt by way of the Red Sea and were advancing on Cairo from the southeast. This massing of force proved unnecessary, for the 13,000 homesick French soldiers at Cairo quickly surrendered

on being assured that they would be evacuated to France. Alexandria, after some desultory fighting, capitulated on September 2.

After eight years of poor showing against the French, the British army had achieved a brilliant victory against superior numbers. The desire of the French soldiers to go home played its part, but Bonaparte's veterans fought as sturdily as ever until the incompetence of General Menou was fully revealed. Menou's ineptitude, first demonstrated by his failure to send defending forces to the Aboukir beachhead, became ludicrous when he divided his army to no purpose and thereby presented the British with the opportunity to defeat him in detail.

The whole Egyptian adventure reveals Bonaparte's gambling instinct at its unluckiest. It deprived France of her Toulon fleet and tied up a valuable army while France's enemies brought her to the brink of ruin, from which she was saved mainly by the follies of her foes.

Britain Strikes Back in the North—Copenhagen

In the fall of 1800, Bonaparte, flushed with the victory of Marengo, prepared to wipe out the bitter memory of the Nile with another drive to the Orient. That would require him again to use the sea, but on the sea he could not stir without first neutralizing the power of England. For Lord Bridport's easy-going watch over the Channel ports had given way to a relentless vigil under Lord St. Vincent. This stern old admiral, not sparing himself, his ships, or his captains, established a year-round blockade that drove even the strongest of his commanders to complain. The rigors of the Channel blockade, hard on the blockaders, ruined French maritime commerce and wrought physical and moral decay in the French navy.

To counter Britain's sea power, Bonaparte set out by devious means to stir up trouble in the Baltic. Playing on the vanity of the addled Czar Paul of Russia and on the economic interests of Sweden and Denmark, he eventually induced them, together with Prussia, to form a new Armed Neutrality of the North. The purpose of the Armed Neutrality was to exclude British trade from the Baltic Sea and to undermine the Royal Navy by depriving Brit-

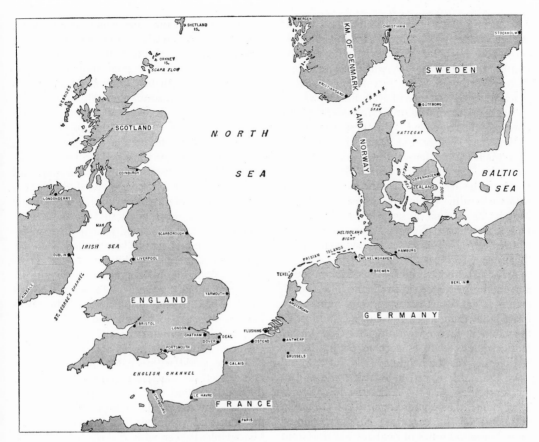

THE NORTH SEA AND THE BALTIC APPROACHES

ain of masts, spars, and other vital naval stores. To forestall such an intolerable situation, the British government acted quickly, assembling a fleet at Yarmouth for operations in the Baltic.

Assuming command at Yarmouth in February 1801 was Admiral Sir Hyde Parker, aged 62, a man long on seniority but short on experience. Parker had been selected because the Ministry thought the Danes might be persuaded to withdraw from the League without fighting. As second-in-command the Admiralty named Baron Nelson of the Nile, apparently in order to have a fighting admiral on the scene should fighting be necessary. No one stopped to consider the difficulties this arrangement would raise for both admirals, or Nelson's record of non-cooperation with less talented superiors. Nelson, resented by many as the spoiled darling of St. Vincent, would in event of hostilities have to persuade Parker to let himself be superseded by an officer 20 years his junior.

Remarkably enough, that is exactly what happened.

At the beginning however the command situation was tense. While Nelson fretted at the delay, Parker swung placidly at anchor, simply ignoring his second in command. But time was not to be wasted, for the coming of spring would soon free the Baltic ports of ice, permitting the Northern Allies to combine their fleets. At length Nelson, more aware than most men of the importance of time, seems to have dropped a hint to his old friend St. Vincent, who had just taken over as First Lord of the Admiralty. At any rate, the force suddenly sailed on March 12, with relations between the two admirals something less than cordial.

The fleet that arrived off the Skaw on March 19 included 23 sail of the line, with Parker's flag in the *London*, 98, and Nelson's in the *St. George*, 98. Besides these three-deckers, there were fourteen 74's, five 64's, and one 50, plus eleven frigates and 23 smaller vessels. Parker sent a frigate ahead carrying the British envoy, Nicholas Vansittart, with an ultimatum to the Danes to withdraw from the League forthwith. The fleet followed slowly, much to the annoyance of Nelson, who wanted to back up the ultimatum with ships of the line, which he called "the best negotiators in Europe," before the Danes had time to strengthen their defenses. But, Parker deeming otherwise, the fleet on March 20 anchored north of the Island of Zealand to await Vansittart's return. When the envoy arrived on March 23 bearing a negative reply, Parker at last summoned Nelson. "Now we are sure of fighting," Nelson wrote to Lady Hamilton, "I am sent for."

Arriving on board the *London,* Nelson found a council of war steeped in gloom. The Danish defenses, Vansittart reported, were much more formidable than had been supposed. Most of the council favored waiting for the united Baltic squadrons to emerge to do battle. To Nelson this was the height of folly, for it would leave the Baltic closed to British trade and at the same time give the Allies the initiative to attack when they chose. Eager to hit at Russia, the heart of the coalition, Nelson proposed slipping around south of Zealand, via the Great Belt, and descending on the Russian fleet at Reval before melting ice permitted it to retire to the strong defenses of Kronstadt. This course had the "Nelson touch" of striking where the enemy least expected. It would permit the British to defeat the Allied fleets in detail.

This plan proving too bold for the unimaginative Parker, Nelson proposed an attack on Copenhagen. The city's defenses, according to Vansittart, were oriented to the north, with the harbor entrance protected by the powerful Trekroner Battery. Nelson therefore recommended an attack from the south. As he talked, his enthusiasm began to infect the council, which at length adopted his general plan.

Parker at first intended to reach Copenhagen from the south by going west around Zealand, but learning more of the intricacies of the Great Belt route, he decided to brave the narrow gantlet between Zealand and Sweden. (See map, page 143.) This he did on March 30, hugging the eastern shore to avoid the fire of Danish batteries, and anchored five miles

northeast of Copenhagen in the body of water known as the Sound. Nelson now led a boat party to examine the Danish defenses.

East of the Trekroner Battery, the Sound was divided by the Middle Ground Shoal into two roughly north-south channels. In the western passage, King's Channel, the Danes had anchored a row of blockships to cover the southern approaches to the city. These comprised ten dismasted ships and ten lighter floating batteries, all mounting powerful guns and with the more heavily armed vessels distributed fairly evenly along the line. On the shore, some distance away, were additional batteries. Nelson's inspection confirmed him in his conviction that the city should be attacked from the south, not directly into the guns of the Trekroner—which, as he expressed it, would be "taking the bull by the horns"—but via King's Channel and the line of blockships. This opinion he reported to a second council of war, meeting that evening on board the *London.*

Nelson found that in his absence pessimism had once again set in, but again his enthusiasm carried the day. He urged the attack from the southern end of the line of blockships to be made by ten of the lightest draft ships of the line and volunteered to lead it himself. Meanwhile Parker with the rest of the force would demonstrate to the north of Copenhagen to hold the Danes from reinforcing the southern extremity of their defenses. Once the blockships had been destroyed, bomb ketches could be placed in position to bombard the city. Parker allowed himself to be persuaded to accept this course of action and, on an impulse of generosity, gave Nelson twelve ships instead of the ten he asked for. His Journal states his decision baldly: "Ordered Vice-Admiral Nelson to take the ships, frigates, bomb-vessels, fire-ships and gun vessels therein mentioned under his command for the purpose of attacking the enemy line, &c. &c."[3]

Nelson first shifted his flag from the *St. George* to the lighter draft *Elephant,* 74. Then, in contrast to the Nile, where he gave his captains only general instructions, he made the most careful preparations. Moving his fleet to a position southeast of the lower end of the

[3] "The Journal of Sir Hyde Parker," *Logs of the Great Sea Fights, 1794–1805,* II (Navy Records Society, 1900), 88.

blockship line, he studied the situation minutely. In his orders he listed the 20 vessels opposing him, giving the estimated number of guns in each. To each of his own ships he assigned one or more Danish ships as targets. Because the blockships were backed by shore batteries and were anchored bow and stern on the very edge of shoal water, he made no plans to double as he had done at the Nile. Nor did he expect to mass on the southern end of the enemy line, for this would permit the carefully prepared Danish vessels to use their springs to swing ship and rake the British. This possibility Nelson planned to counter by a nearly simultaneous engagement of the entire line, relying on sheer gun power to crush the enemy. He so arranged his own line as to bring a superior number of guns against nearly every Danish ship or combination. The sole exception was H.M.S. *Isis*, which would face the slightly more powerful Ship Number Two in the enemy line, but Nelson arranged for Ship Number Two to be weakened by fire from another British ship in passing before the *Isis* came opposite. Estimating the enemy guns at 369, he proposed to overwhelm it with 443 guns, a 6-to-5 superiority. In addition he assigned six gunboats to work over Danish Ship Number One, at the southern end of the line. When she struck, the gunboats would take on Ship Number Two, while the *Isis*, and the *Agamemnon* next astern, were to move forward to support ships ahead. Meanwhile frigates under Captain Edward Riou were to demonstrate to the north of the line, and Parker's remaining force was to stand toward Copenhagen to be available as a mobile reserve.

During the night of April 1-2, as Nelson expected, the wind shifted to the south-southeast, and all was in readiness for the attack. At 7:30 the following morning he held a final conference. Between 9:45 and 10:15 all ships were under way and forming into line of battle in close order at 300 yards distance. As the fleet began the approach for the attack, the Baltic pilots became panicky at the prospect of coming under fire and refused to conn the ships. One of the sailing masters of the fleet volunteered to lead the column, but while confusion still reigned, two British ships went aground. A third found herself unable to weather the Middle Ground Shoal. Thus at the outset Nelson's force was reduced by a quarter, and his gun superiority was cut down from 6 to 5 to an inferiority of 5 to 5½. Undaunted, the British advanced in silence as was their custom when standing into battle. To the north Parker's force was able to make little headway against the wind, but Riou got his frigates into position northeast of the Trekroner, where he heavily damaged the northernmost ship of the Danish line.

The loss of the three ships required a last-minute revision of Nelson's plans. The *Edgar* now led the line in, and then each ship passed outboard of her leader and anchored ahead of her, so that the order of the line was reversed. Thus no British ship had to take the fire of the whole enemy line and, as at the Nile, the first fire of each enemy ship was met by the first fire of each British ship. The firing, opened by the Danes, reached a bloody crescendo by 11:30 AM and continued with little abatement until 2:00 in the afternoon. "Here," Nelson wrote, "was no maneuvering: it was downright fighting."

Watching the mutual slaughter from the *London*, Parker became increasingly alarmed and discussed with Captain Otway, his flag captain, whether he should call off the action. Captain Otway strongly opposed any such move and volunteered to go by boat to consult Nelson before a decision was made. To this Parker agreed. Yet before Otway had time to reach the *Elephant*, Parker at 1:30 hoisted the signal "Discontinue the action." Nelson at first appeared to take no notice of it, and then directed that a mere acknowledgment be sent and inquired whether his own for close action was still flying. Assured that it was, Nelson put his telescope to his blind eye, remarking to the *Elephant*'s captain, "You know, Foley, I have only one eye—I have a right to be blind sometimes. I really do not see the signal." None of the ships in Nelson's line either repeated or obeyed Parker's signaled order. To the north, Riou, exercising a semi-detached command, felt obliged to obey and regretfully began to withdraw, saying, "What will Nelson think of us?" A moment later a cannon ball cut him in two.

In the circumstances, Nelson had every right to be blind. It would have been physically impossible for his ships to retreat the way they

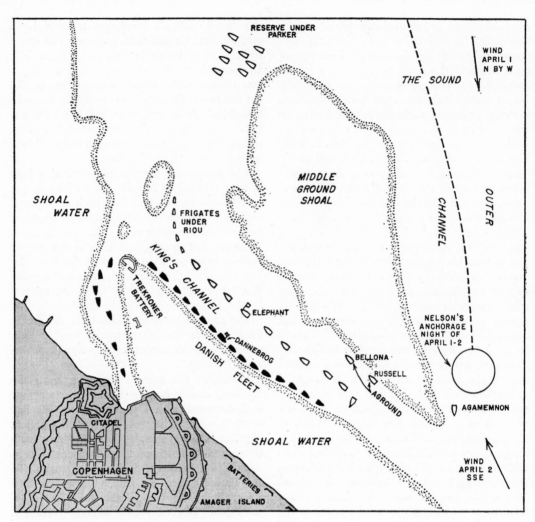

THE BATTLE OF COPENHAGEN, APRIL 2, 1801

had come, for in that direction the wind was dead foul. The only way out was past the entire blockship line and the Trekroner battery, considered by all too dangerous to attack. Nelson's force was thus in a position from which only victory could extricate it.[4]

[4] Apologists for Parker have suggested that his signal was permissive and that Otway carried a verbal message to that effect. If so, we may wonder why Parker did not wait until Otway reached the *Elephant* before hoisting the signal, or why, since Otway could carry the message, a signal was necessary at all. There is no evidence to support this charitable view; it seems more likely that Parker was hastening to clear his own skirts. If, as seemed probable to him at that point, Nelson's force should meet with disaster, then the record would show that the action had been fought contrary to orders. Nelson

About two o'clock the Danish fire began to slacken, and soon thereafter Nelson sent an ultimatum ashore: "To the Brothers of Englishmen, The Danes. Lord Nelson has directions to spare Denmark, when no longer resisting; but if the firing is continued on the part of Denmark, Lord Nelson will be obliged to set on fire all the Floating-batteries he has taken, without having the power of saving the brave Danes who have defended them."[5] To

did not consider the order permissive, for he said some hours after the battle, "Well, I have fought contrary to orders, and I shall perhaps be hanged; never mind, let them."

[5] Quoted in Carola Oman, *Nelson* (London, 1947), 391.

the preparation of this note, Nelson gave great care, even sealing it with his own signet—rather than a wafer, which would have implied haste. Although his antagonists were by no means in the hopeless position the note suggested, Nelson's bluff worked—perhaps because the Danes had just received news of the assassination of Czar Paul and realized that Russia might soon be pulling out of the Armed Neutrality. The Danes agreed to supply the British fleet for 14 weeks, during which time they would not ready any ships for sea. They also agreed to quit the Armed Neutrality.

Nelson urged Parker to proceed at once against the Russian ships at Reval. He even offered to take a small detachment to seek out the Russian and Swedish fleets. When it was objected that they might mass against him, he replied, "I wish they were twice as many: the more numerous, the easier the victory!" By this he apparently meant that a large bi-national fleet, unused to joint operations, should prove unmanageable and easy prey to the disciplined, well-trained British. It was to no avail. All enterprise seemed to have gone out of Parker, who insisted on waiting for additional instructions from England.

At length the frustrated Nelson applied for leave to return home. Parker gladly consented, relieved at the prospect of ridding himself of his uncomfortably demanding subordinate. Then on May 5, a month after the battle, the new instructions came. Both admirals were thunderstruck. Parker was recalled to England and Nelson was left in command in the Baltic.

The next day Nelson sailed for Reval. But Parker's delay had spoiled his opportunity. The ice had gone out three days before, and the Russians reached Kronstadt in safety.

The Peace of Amiens

Although Nelson's move against the Russians came too late for the destruction of the Russian fleet, it did not much matter. With the new Czar, Alexander I, Russian sympathies changed, and the Armed Neutrality was dead. When Nelson went ashore at Reval, he was welcomed as the "young Suvorov," and on his return to England, he was again the hero of the hour, being raised a degree in the Peerage to become Viscount Nelson.

With the collapse of the Armed Neutrality and with Abercromby's victories in Egypt, England once again blocked Bonaparte. He had lost the initiative, and Britain's sea power had grown ever stronger. At the opening of the war, the Royal Navy had 15,000 men enrolled; at the end of 1801, 133,000 manned its ships. The navy had grown from 135 to 202 ships of the line and from 133 to 277 frigates. At the same time, the French navy had been reduced by more than 50 per cent, and few of the remaining ships were fit to take to sea. The impact of the war had wrought profound changes in the economic life of both countries. In many places in England, the people were in want. Almost everyone was heartily tired of war. Henry Addington's new ministry was eager to consummate a peace, having no idea how a continuation of the war might lead to ultimate victory.

Bonaparte was equally anxious for peace, but for other reasons. He hoped to gain at the conference table what he had been unable to win by force of arms. Thus, when Britain's secret overtures came to his attention, he was ready to receive them. Like a good negotiator however, he exploited his enemy's weaknesses while concealing his own—the First Consul proved as adept in diplomacy as in commanding armies. After a preliminary agreement was signed on October 1, 1801, the British began speedily disarming. In later negotiations Bonaparte blandly denied verbal agreements made in former discussions. As a result Britain, having lost her bargaining power by her too-hasty disarmament, had to restore many of her hard-won overseas conquests. While wits might quip about "the peace which passeth understanding," the general rejoicing drowned the voices of the Jeremiahs. Englishmen returning to the joys of peaceful living had no use for "Ancestral voices prophesying war."

Summary

The Treaty of Campo Formio and the consequent isolation of England in the fall of 1797 brought clearly into focus the old problem of the Elephant and the Whale—how could the greatest land power come to grips with the greatest sea power? Napoleon Bonaparte, seeing little promise of success in a frontal attack on Britain via the Channel, substituted in 1798 an expedition to Egypt. This was a fatal mistake, for in using the sea he exposed himself to attack by British sea power. In the Battle of the Nile (August 1, 1798), Nelson not only destroyed France's Mediterranean fleet and isolated Bonaparte and his army far from the strategic center; he also set the stage for the War of the Second Coalition against France. Bruix's seaborne attempt to rescue the French army in Egypt, like Ganteaume's two years later, merely proved that while it was not impossible for French fleets to elude British vigilance and pass through the Straits of Gibraltar, they were not likely to be effective in an area controlled by the Royal Navy.

In the War of the Second Coalition, England continued with some modification the strategy she had inherited from the elder Pitt. She subsidized allies to employ continental strategy, driving at the heart of the enemy, while she used her own military and naval forces to maintain command of the sea, to blockade enemy ports, and for peripheral strategy, the indirect approach of striking around the edges of the enemy's continental position and at his overseas possessions. While Austria pleaded for a British army in Italy, Britain preferred to expend her military strength in amphibious pinpricks along the Atlantic coast —in North Holland, at Cadiz, and elsewhere. Every attempt was a failure and none achieved even the advantage of drawing French forces from contact with the Austro-Russian armies on France's eastern border. In attempting to go ashore, the Whale was only too clearly out of its element. In the Mediterranean, the British captured Minorca and Malta, but their support of the coalition in Italy and the Middle East was largely limited to such purely naval operations as blockade and control of sea communications. A brilliant exception was

Sir Sydney Smith's participation in the defense of Acre, which ended Bonaparte's advance against Turkey. Only after the defeat of Austria did the British army and navy devise effective means of operating together. In the Egyptian campaign of 1801, Keith and Abercromby at last developed the amphibious doctrine and the inter-service cooperation that Britain needed to project her power onto the land. At the same time the British army began to regain the prestige and confidence that had declined steadily since the Seven Years' War. The Peninsular Campaign, that eventually was to bring about Napoleon's downfall, had become possible.

On the Continent, France was able to repulse all her enemies, partly, to be sure, because of the ineptitude and divided aims of the anti-French coalition, and Bonaparte as First Consul succeeded in restoring the conditions of 1797. Britain however, while strangling French overseas commerce and taking her pick of French overseas possessions, remained as inaccessible as ever. The French could not bring effective force to bear against the British Empire by direct assault on England, by the back door approach through Egypt, or by attacking her commerce at sea. Bonaparte's attempt to strike at the foundations of British sea power through the Armed Neutrality merely resulted in the chastisement of Denmark in Nelson's Battle of Copenhagen (April 2, 1801)—a lesson that the Baltic states would not forget. The Elephant proved as awkward in attempting to project its strength upon the seas as the Whale had been clumsy in operations ashore.

Britain and France at last conceded that the problem was insoluble, for the time at least, by signing peace preliminaries in October 1801 and concluding a formal peace treaty at Amiens in March 1802.

8:

The Campaign of Trafalgar

Englishmen rejoiced at the treaty signed in Amiens in the spring of 1802, ending the nine-year-old war with France. Prime Minister Henry Addington was hailed as the peacemaker. Seamen again pursued their trade without fear of the press gang or French privateers, and Englishmen for the first time in over a decade resumed acquaintance with the *divertissements* of Paris. To win this peace, England had to pay, but the price seemed reasonable. To prove their good faith and desire for everlasting peace, Addington's negotiators had ceded all overseas conquests except Ceylon and Trinidad. Thus Spain regained Minorca; Holland, the Cape Colony, the Spice Islands, Malacca, Demerera, and Berbice. Egypt was to be returned to Turkey, and Malta to the Knights of St. John. To France the Treaty restored her West Indian, African, and Indian colonies. In return for all this, the First Consul promised the *status quo* in Europe.

Confident that Napoleon had been appeased, the English disarmed in haste. The income tax law was the first to go. The navy was reduced from over 100 ships of the line to not quite 40. Over 40,000 experienced seamen were paid off, and half-pay officers by the hundred vied for the few vacancies in the peacetime fleet. Army cuts were as vigorous as those inflicted on the navy.

Visitors to France proclaimed themselves charmed by the fine, handsome, statesmanlike First Consul. The caricatured "Boney" disappeared from men's ken; in his place appeared Consul Bonaparte, suave, Byronic, brooding, good humored, and intelligent. He deliberately set out to captivate the visiting English by a grand whirl of balls, reviews, and *Te Deums*. These were followed by more than a hint of things to come, foreshadows of imperial grandeur—levées, and his habit of calling himself by his first name alone: Napoleon.

The Rupture of the Peace of Amiens

Only briefly were the English deceived. They had disarmed; Napoleon had not. His shipyards hummed with activity. He planned to build 25 ships of the line a year. In a few years, with two hundred of the line, he could laugh at England's domination of the sea. He had signed the treaty to accomplish by peace what he had been unable to win at war, for he had not been able to break the British stranglehold on his overseas lines of supply. With his new ships he need no longer fear the crushing blockade of the Royal Navy. All he needed was time. Had Napoleon been content to wait, it is possible that England would have become so entrenched in the ways of peace that it would have been difficult for her to meet the vastly greater challenge Napoleon was preparing. But Napoleon was a vain man. For various reasons insulting stories and caricatures began appearing in the British papers. These infuriated Napoleon, and he was even more enraged to learn that the British government could do nothing about them. To him it seemed "would not," for he could not conceive of a free press.

Vastly more important to the British, Napoleon promptly began to violate the terms of the Treaty of Amiens. The only concession he had given was to promise to respect territorial boundaries in Europe and overseas. Yet even before the treaty had been signed, he had sent a force to the West Indies, ostensibly to put down a rising of the Negroes in Haiti (Santo Domingo Island), but actually to claim Louisiana under provisions of a secret treaty with Spain. In Europe he took the bloodless offensive, becoming President of what he called the Republic of Italy. To secure the independence of Italy, Britain had yielded Porto Ferraro and Minorca and agreed to evacuate Egypt and Malta. During the autumn, Piedmont, Parma, and the Canton of Valois became a part of the dominions of the Corsican. French troops remained in Holland in spite of his promise, and agents there stirred disaffection against the British.

Britain at first made no protest. Emboldened, Napoleon set his designs on Switzerland, and taking as an excuse violence that his own agents stirred up in the Cantons, he decided he was under no further obligations to respect the territorial integrity of the Swiss. Ordering General Ney to invade, he called upon the Helvetic Republic to submit. The Swiss promptly turned to England for assistance. Well-meaning but weak-willed, the Addington Government sent a remonstrance to Paris claiming the right of the Swiss to settle their affairs "without the intervention of any foreign Powers." The only result of this note was to drive Napoleon to further exertions for the conquest of Switzerland. Realizing that the Royal Navy could not help them, and receiving no support from continental powers, the Swiss submitted.

England's vain espousal of the Swiss cause cast grave doubts on Addington's policy of "Peace and Plenty." Men who, a few months before, tired of the "confounded men of genius" of Pitt's party, had eagerly welcomed Addington's cabinet of nonentities, now seriously questioned his ability to preserve the peace he had bought with "unnecessary and degrading concessions." As Napoleon hastened from one outrage to another, thoughts of Englishmen turned to Pitt, now almost retired from politics. "Whether Pitt *will* save us, I do not know:" wrote George Canning, "but surely he is the only man that *can*." Pitt however had promised loyalty to Addington's ministry, and he intended to keep his promise. He refused to allow a coalition plot to unseat the Prime Minister. But enough of the background rumblings reached Addington, so that, faced with new ominous intelligence of Napoleon's activ-

ity, he was forced to stiffen his position. New instructions went to Lord Whitworth, Ambassador in Paris, that henceforth Britain would insist on her right to intervene in the affairs of the Continent. At the same time Whitworth hinted at reparations for breaches of the *status quo* already committed by France.

These representations could not have come as a surprise to Napoleon, for he had always known that a point would be reached where the British government would be forced to take a stand. Even so, the timing was awkward. He had not had sufficient time to fill his storehouses depleted by years of blockade, and his ambitious naval building program was barely underway. His effective ships were mostly in the Caribbean dealing with the Haitian revolt, and the troops that had sailed in them had succumbed in huge numbers to yellow fever.

To play for time, Napoleon turned to the counter-offensive, demanding the British evacuation of Egypt and Malta under the terms of Amiens. The British made no objections over Egypt, but over Malta, Napoleon encountered the traditional British bulldog tenacity. To evacuate Malta while the French had violated every provision for which the British had agreed to yield the island was impossible. Until Britain received guarantees from other continental powers that Malta would be independent, the British garrison would remain.

The inhospitable island was of no possible value to Napoleon except to deny its use to the British, to whom it was of inestimable worth as a base. So long as England had to maintain a fleet in the Mediterranean, she needed a base nearer to the scene of action than Gibraltar. Minorca, a possible alternate, had already been given up. No government faced with gathering war clouds could agree to evacuate the island that gave them the means to command the Mediterranean. In a stormy interview with Lord Whitworth, Napoleon threatened war, gibing at the divisions of English politics. Nothing could have been more calculated to unite the British. While Whitworth played the game out to the last, the British began to rearm. On May 16, 1803, Britain declared war.

The Addington ministry had no plans for the strategic direction of the war. It had come to power to conclude a peace, and when events again forced war, its program collapsed. Yet there was one thing that any British Cabinet would do almost automatically; it issued orders to the Navy to re-establish the blockade of French ports. Upon the declaration of war, five of the line sailed from Tor Bay under veteran Vice Admiral Sir William Cornwallis. Three days later they appeared at their old station off Ushant. Also on the 16th, Keith hoisted his flag at the Nore, and that same evening Nelson boarded the *Victory* at Portsmouth and was quickly away to take up command of the Mediterranean station.

Napoleon's Strategy

At the resumption of war, Napoleon found himself in a difficult position. On land he was as formidable as ever, but at sea his evasions of the Treaty had left him badly over-extended. In addition to his fever-racked army at Haiti, there were more than 50 French ships in the Caribbean and others scattered over the oceans of the world. His ships in port were few, ill-kept, ill-found, and manned by ill-disciplined and untrained crews. When, on the 18th, the British captured two French ships at sea, Napoleon ordered the imprisonment of all British civilians caught in France by the sudden outbreak of hostilities. He closed the Continent to British ships, including the free towns of

Hamburg and Bremen, recently overrun by his troops. Yet nothing but invasion could satisfy the First Consul. A blow at Britain's very heart was the proper reply to Perfidious Albion, and this could only be done by crossing the Channel. "They want us to jump the ditch, and we *will* jump it!" he cried.

Napoleon, though a military genius, was no naval strategist. He made the fundamental mistake of assuming that naval forces could be handled like armies, and that they could seize and hold positions at sea. He believed he could force Britain to act in accordance with his plans rather than in support of her own strategy and national policy. Admirals of the Royal Navy had been so long at the game they played and possessed such a sure habit of thought that routine actions to protect sea communications and to guard the homeland and overseas possessions came automatically. This was fortunate, for Addington's ministry was unable to give direction to the British war aims. Obsessed with fear of Napoleon, the government made no plans at all for the offensive, instead directing their energies toward repelling the French legions in the Kentish and Sussex meadows. Impatient, improvident, ill-considered directives went out urging men to enlist in the Volunteers, but the chief result was to dry up the source of men for the regular army, the only force that could be used abroad. The reconstituted "Sea Fencibles," coast-guard mi-

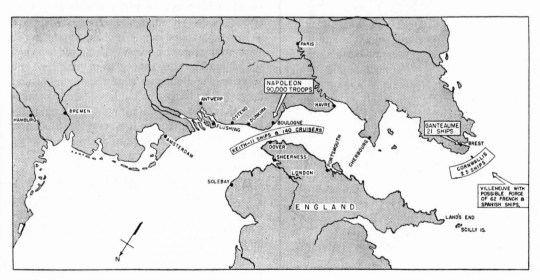

THE INVASION FRONT, 1805

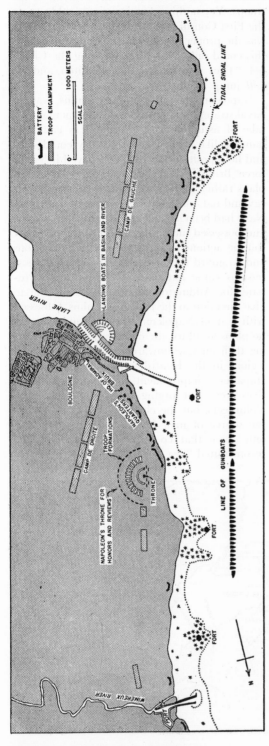

THE CAMP AT BOULOGNE, 1803-1805

litia, ate into the store of men who might have manned the ships of the navy. The Volunteers enrolled some of the most illustrious names in the land: Sir Walter Scott, Pitt, Fox, the Duke of Clarence. Addington himself wore a uniform into the Commons.

Across the Channel Napoleon sneered pityingly at these preparations. Not for a minute could these enthusiastic amateurs withstand the victors of Marengo. All that remained was to "jump the ditch." All this time, almost forgotten by both attackers and defenders alike, the ditch was guarded by the ships of the Royal Navy, which controlled the situation so thoroughly that all preparations on both sides were futile.

At Boulogne and Calais, at Dunkirk and Le Havre, at every Channel port and inland river town, French shipwrights toiled at building the invasion flotilla of 2,000-odd craft. Odd indeed they were, of several types, but generally flat-bottomed, so that in a tideway they became unmanageable. Tides in the Straits of Dover are notorious. These barges were designed to carry the maximum load without regard for sea-keeping qualities. The preparations were so frenzied that everyone hourly expected Bonaparte to make the attempt. The blockading fleet off Brest looked for the opportunity to close action with the invasion barges. Yet the summer, fall, and winter dragged on, and still Napoleon did not come. Several things stood in his way: he was not able to get his flotilla built fast enough, and everywhere the British navy foiled him. Watchful frigates noted what went on in the invasion ports and snapped up his craft as they moved from their building ways to the Boulogne area for assembly and staging. The harbor at Boulogne needed extensive dredging and enlarging. This being accomplished at tremendous cost in time and effort, it was found impossible to effect sortie of the whole flotilla on a single tide. Thus something over twelve hours would elapse before the second part could follow the first. The French would be committed piecemeal. The delay would permit British forces to concentrate in order to wipe out the crowded barges laden with the seasick victors of Marengo. So preposterous was the flotilla that keen-minded naval officers such as Pellew and St. Vincent wondered whether the whole thing were not a gigantic feint designed to cover a real threat elsewhere.

But Napoleon was not feinting. He was deadly serious; he meant to invade with those barges. Yet he stood helpless gazing across the Channel at the chalk cliffs near Dover so long as the British squadrons mounted blockade. And these ships kept station through winter and summer, stations dictated by the enemy's bases, not by his invasion flotilla. As Napoleon's ships struggled back from the Caribbean and took refuge in the neutral Spanish port of Ferrol, Admiral Alexander Cochrane quietly sealed them in. The English battleships checked Napoleon's every move at sea. As Mahan put it, "Those far distant, storm-beaten ships upon which the Grand Army never looked stood between it and the dominion of the world."

In spite of this, the capabilities of the British navy were only partially employed. The blockade required the utmost exertion, but as Pitt the Elder had shown in the Seven Years' War, and as his son had shown before the Treaty of Amiens, the navy's mobility gave unequalled opportunity for sudden, damaging blows at the enemy. The navy could support, supply, and cooperate with continental allies, and could wrest overseas possessions from a foe that depended on land communications. For England to remain on the defensive was to abandon the Continent to Napoleon and possibly risk her whole position in the Orient. To assume the offensive at this moment of greatest danger was her most prudent course.

Pitt Returns as Prime Minister

It was to grasp this flower safety out of the nettle danger that Pitt once again assumed the reins of government. He had loyally supported his friend Addington during the year that had elapsed since the declaration of war. But concluding at length that Addington's policies gave no prospect of victory, Pitt reluctantly, on April 26, St. George's Day, assailed in the Commons the dragon of despair. Addington resigned, and on May 7, the King sent for Pitt. Thus the human embodiment of the offensive spirit was once more leading the British.

On the same day that Pitt undertook his duties, Napoleon had himself declared Emperor of the French. He immediately made use of his new power by executing on trumped up charges of treason the young Duc d'Enghien. This murder opened the eyes of the monarchs of Europe to the fact that they were dealing with a Jacobin in ermine, a Terror in purple. They were prepared to listen when Pitt's ambassadors proposed an alliance against the bloody Corsican. Thus was conceived the Third Coalition. Never completely successful, it nevertheless seized the initiative from Napoleon. Pitt's first act was to open negotiations with Russia, hoping for joint Anglo-Russian activity in the Mediterranean. With Austrian assistance, he planned to attack what Winston Churchill was later to call the "soft underbelly of Europe."

In the meantime Napoleon had realized that he could not cross the Channel by barges alone. Hence he conceived the notion of massing ships in the English Channel to drive off or destroy the blockading fleets. During the summer of 1804, he attempted to ready his ships for this enterprise. He ordered his most skilled admiral, Latouche-Tréville, to escape from Toulon, release the French ships at Ferrol and Rochefort, evade Cornwallis at Brest, and appear at Boulogne in September with the combined fleet, which by this time would consist of 16 of the line and 11 frigates. This scheme seemed so plausible to him that he had a victory medal struck which bore the inscription: "*Descente en Angleterre, frappé à Londres en 1804.*"

It takes small reflection to see the inherent weakness of Napoleon's plan. First, Latouche-Tréville had to evade Nelson. This was perhaps his easiest task, since Nelson favored a loose blockade in the hope of drawing his enemy out to destruction. Next the French admiral had to release blockaded ships at Ferrol and Rochefort; this certainly meant a battle with the blockaders. In addition, a wind that would be fair for him to force the blockade would be foul for the blockaded ships to come out of port. Finally, at Brest he had to evade Cornwallis, who had the advantage of interior position, and if he succeeded in escaping him, he would be subject to almost certain destruction with a vastly superior, undefeated enemy across his line of retreat. He would find himself in the position of Medina-Sidonia 216 years before. He would be too busy fighting for his life to protect the invasion flotilla. Napoleon never realized that the principal objective of Cornwallis and the others was not blockade but protection of the Channel. In time of crisis they headed there like iron drawn to a magnet.

Once that summer Latouche-Tréville did emerge from Toulon, but realizing that he was running into a trap, hastily returned to port. This was the only result of Napoleon's first naval scheme. By September, the Emperor realized that the attempt would have to be deferred until the next year.

The Third Coalition

All summer Pitt had worked to create the new coalition against Napoleon. By November, the Russians, in conjunction with Austria, were prepared to sign a treaty for an Armed League to be led by Russia but paid for by Britain. This league was to insist on the evacuation of Italy, Germany, and Holland. In return for this support on the Continent, Britain had to make a show of force in the Mediterranean, and this show of force had to be one comprehensible to the land-minded rulers of Europe. Accordingly, Pitt began to prepare for an army to be sent to that area.

However, before he could risk an army so far from home, he had to insure the safety of his communications between England and her bases at Gibraltar and Malta. The position of Spain was anomalous. Few Spaniards desired another war with England. On the other hand Manuel de Godoy, whose title was Prince of the Peace, but who in actuality was dictator of Spain, was little more than a puppet of Napoleon. When the British cabinet learned that the Corsican had demanded the active support of the Spanish navy, they knew it would be forthcoming. In September, with Godoy's consent, 1,500 French troops marched from Bayonne into Spain to man the French ships at Ferrol.

Immediately Pitt decided on action. He directed his ambassador in Madrid to demand an accounting and the demobilization of the Spanish fleet. At the same time he ordered Cornwallis to send four frigates to intercept the homecoming Spanish treasure fleet from Mexico. Both schemes fell afoul of Spanish pride, for Godoy rejected Britain's representations, and the small size of the attacking frigate force led the admiral of the treasure fleet to believe he could not surrender with honor. In the ensuing fight, the Spanish flagship blew up with a loss of 300 lives. As a consequence, the Spaniards declared war on December 12, 1804. At once the British blockade was extended to cover Cadiz and Cartagena.

Turning his eyes on Britain's colonial possessions, Napoleon directed Admiral Comte de Missiessy, in charge of the fleet at Rochefort, and Admiral Villeneuve, who had succeeded to the command of the Toulon fleet on the death of Latouche-Tréville, to raid British colonies and commerce in the West Indies. On January 11, 1805, in the temporary absence of the blockading squadron of Sir Thomas Graves, Missiessy sailed with five of the line and an equal number of frigates for Martinique. Six days later Villeneuve attempted to depart Toulon but was driven back by weather.

As Missiessy approached the West Indies, Napoleon's fertile brain produced a new invasion scheme. He now conceived what he called his "Grand Design." Austria's growing subservience seemed to him to have wrecked Pitt's coalition. He felt he could afford to make the year 1805 the great year for crushing England. Hence he turned definitively and seriously to his task.

Napoleon's Grand Design

Invasion had failed in 1803 and again in 1804 because British sea power controlled the Channel. These failures caused Napoleon to look foolish in the eyes of the world. English wits had jested about Don Quixote "de la Manche." Now it would be different. Since British sea power in the Channel blocked his schemes, let the sea power be removed. This, as Bonaparte saw it, could be accomplished in either of two ways or both ways in combination. His navy could defeat Britain's, or the British sea dogs could be tricked into sending their fleets to the wrong place.

In barest outline, the plan was to work as follows: Villeneuve was to break loose from Toulon, and sailing westward, release the Spanish ships at Cartagena. Then, passing Gibraltar, he was to liberate Gravina's squad-

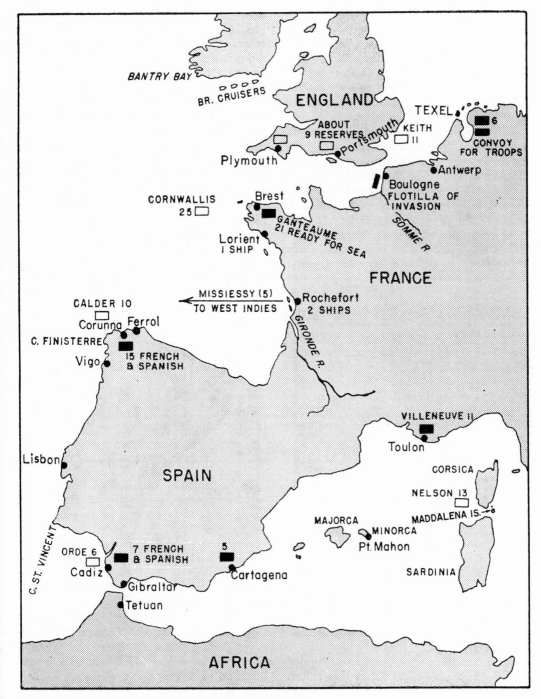

POSITIONS OF BRITISH AND OF ALLIED SHIPS, MARCH 1805

ron at **Cadiz**, and commanding the combined force, he was to sail for the West Indies, where he would join Missiessy and be joined by Ganteaume, who in the meantime would evade the Brest blockade. Then the huge Armada would sail for the Channel to cover the crossing of Napoleon's flotilla. If Ganteaume did not appear, Villeneuve was to wait 40 days and then recross the Atlantic, liberate Ganteaume, and cover the invasion.

Such was the Grand Design. It failed for many reasons, but its inherent weakness was that it did not appreciate a fact the British understood well—that the English Channel was Britain's strategic center, and that whatever other dispositions they might make, the British would never fail to make provisions for the control of its waters. There, enjoying the advantage of interior position, they were able to move rapidly to counter any threat to the strategic center.

Villeneuve Escapes from Toulon

Orders to implement the Grand Design went forth from Paris to the various commanders concerned. Missiessy was instructed to remain in the West Indies to await the reinforcement of Villeneuve. At Toulon Villeneuve received his instructions near the end of March 1805, and taking advantage of Nelson's loose blockade, sailed for Gibraltar on March 30.

Nelson's shortage of scouting frigates left him in darkness as to his enemy's movements. He could not be sure whether Villeneuve's destination lay to the east or the west. It was a situation that reveals Nelson's appreciation of Britain's strategy. His mission called for the protection of the Mediterranean station, and he knew that its most vulnerable points lay to the east—Naples, Malta, and Egypt. Additionally he knew that Pitt planned operations in the central Mediterranean. Nelson has been accused by detractors of allowing Lady Hamilton to fix his mind on Naples so that it excluded all else. Lady Hamilton was now in England, but the King of Naples was Britain's only ally in the area. It was further evident that if Villeneuve were bound for the Channel, Nelson's decision to protect his station could have no serious consequence, for the Combined Fleet would have to pass succes-

sively the forces of Sir John Orde off Cape St. Vincent, Calder off Ferrol, Graves off Rochefort, and finally Gardner off Brest,[1] before he could reach his destination. The only other point of danger would be the West Indies; thither Nelson intended to go once he was sure that his primary responsibility was secured. Accordingly he took station off the island of Ustica, in position to guard the approaches to both the Straits of Messina and the Sicilian Channel.

Meanwhile Villeneuve made his way westward. On April 7 he was becalmed off Cartagena. He signaled the Spanish ships in port to join him, but they were not ready for sea, and the specter of Nelson would not allow him to wait. The next day he passed through the Straits of Gibraltar, and making the most of an easterly breeze, rounded Cape Trafalgar and set his course for Cadiz. There he was joined by eight Spanish ships under Admiral Gravina. Together they took departure for the Canary Islands to pick up the easterly trade winds for a swift passage to the Caribbean.

His passage by Gibraltar did not go unobserved. Sir John Orde, heavily outnumbered, watched him pass, and then set out for Ushant to warn Gardner and the Admiralty. On the way he looked into Cadiz, but it was empty. Villeneuve had made good his escape, disappearing into the Atlantic.

Britain Takes the Offensive

In England the situation had been complicated by two new developments. The first resulted from Pitt's attempt to assume the offensive. On April 19, a force, known as the "Secret Expedition," under the command of Lieutenant General Sir James Craig, sailed from England in 45 transports, guarded by two ships of the line, bound for Malta, to release the garrison there for conjunct expeditions in the Mediterranean. With Villeneuve loose and unaccounted for, this force was in grave danger, for it was more than possible that Villeneuve had sailed with the express intention of intercepting and destroying Britain's only army then available for overseas operations.

[1] Gardner had temporarily relieved Cornwallis in command of the Channel fleet.

The decisions called for by the new peril had to be made by a man who had just taken over the Admiralty, for administrative scandals had brought about a Cabinet crisis, forcing Melville to resign as First Lord. Hourly Pitt's own resignation was expected. Yet the Prime Minister held on against all opposition, determined to see the fruition of his plans against Napoleon. For two weeks the Admiralty was leaderless; then, ignoring the wishes of the King and most of his own cabinet, Pitt named 78-year-old Admiral Charles Middleton, Lord Barham, to this most demanding of positions.

On April 25, as Barham, vigorous and keen-minded as ever, assumed his duties, news reached London of the escape of Villeneuve. Barham quietly issued the necessary orders. Since no one knew where Nelson had gone, Barham took steps to reinforce the West Indian station and also to insure the safety of Craig's Secret Expedition. Gardner was ordered to give Vice Admiral Collingwood a Flying Squadron of five ships which was to cross to Jamaica to bring the forces there up

to 18 of the line. At the same time, forced by the news Orde had brought, Barham took measures to reinforce Calder and Graves. He laid down as a policy that, come what might, the force off Ushant should never be brought below 18 ships, and that all other instructions Gardner might receive were to be conditional on this requirement. The situation was only slightly eased by the surprise return of Missiessy to Rochefort. He had come back to Europe on the false assumption that Villeneuve had abandoned the West Indian operation. Already the machinery of the Grand Design was beginning to creak.

Nelson's Pursuit of Villeneuve

Nelson in the meantime was fuming at his station near Ustica. With every passing day it became more evident that Villeneuve had designs to the west, not the east. On April 10, he chanced to learn that the Secret Expedition was actually about to sail, and he realized that it was in grave danger. Immediately he began to beat his way westward against head winds.

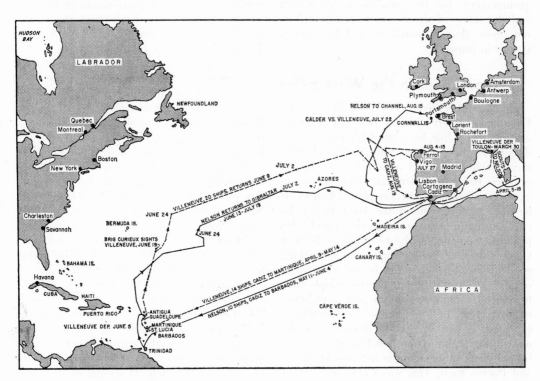

NELSON'S PURSUIT OF VILLENEUVE

In nine days he made good only 200 miles. On the 18th he learned from a neutral vessel of Villeneuve's rendezvous with Gravina off Cadiz and realized that something important was in the air. He decided that if he got no further information he would take his ships to join those of Gardner. When he finally arrived at Gibraltar on May 8, he received dispatches from the Admiralty informing him in detail of the Secret Expedition, and, to his vast relief, he learned that it had taken shelter in Lisbon. Once again Nelson began to believe that Villeneuve's destination was the West Indies. The Allies had been on a westerly course when last seen; this was suggestive but not conclusive, for they would have had to make considerable westing to weather Cape St. Vincent. Still in a quandary, Nelson took his 11 ships to Lagos Bay to provision against a long voyage. There he learned from a frigate just out of England that Villeneuve had not been reported to the north. Nelson was now convinced, and on May 9, he made his famous decision to cross the Atlantic in pursuit of his quarry. On the 11th, after completing arrangements for the security of his station and the safety of the Secret Expedition, Nelson, more than a month behind his enemy, set out in pursuit.

Operations in the West Indies

On May 14 Villeneuve reached Martinique. Here he grappled with the problem of useful employment while he waited his required 40 days before returning to Europe. French military authorities urged action against British colonies, but now Villeneuve began to appreciate the dilemma his orders placed him in. If he undertook actions in the West Indies, he risked casualties that would weaken him for his primary task, forcing the blockade at Brest if Ganteaume had been unsuccessful in making good his escape. But unless he did something, no pressure would be put on the British navy to reinforce the West Indian area, and hence no weakening of the Channel fleet could be expected. It was a knotty problem. To make matters worse, word reached him of a powerful British fleet operating near Santo Domingo and Puerto Rico. This was Cochrane's six of the line, far inferior to Villeneuve's 19. The

first action Villeneuve undertook was the reduction of a small island called Diamond Rock, garrisoned by the Royal Navy. This proved harder than had been expected and took him 15 days. Then he learned that he was to operate against British colonies in conjunction with Admiral Magon, who had escaped from Rochefort with 800 troops. Thirty-five days after Magon's arrival, if not joined by Ganteaume, Villeneuve was to sail back to Ferrol. When Magon arrived, Villeneuve decided to do the best he could and departed Martinique to attack Antigua or Barbuda.

It was as well for Villeneuve that he moved off when he did, for as Magon dropped anchor in Martinique harbor, Nelson arrived at Barbados. It was almost as though the ships had responded to their leader's eagerness, for they had made an almost record crossing of 24 days, averaging 135 miles a day. Wasting no time, Nelson embarked troops, and adding to his command two ships of Cochrane's which he found at Barbados, was off the next day—on a false scent as it happened, for he received intelligence that Villeneuve would be found at Trinidad. On arrival he learned the truth—that Villeneuve's destination had been Antigua. Thither Nelson bent his course.

In the meantime Villeneuve chanced upon and captured a British convoy of sugar ships and learned the appalling news that Nelson was on his heels. He made up his mind immediately. Gone was any idea of waiting for a concentration in the West Indies. Gone was his plan of cooperation with the Grand Design. All that Villeneuve could think of was his terrible pursuer. He had been the only flag officer to escape from the Battle of the Nile, and he had never forgotten that holocaust. Now the victor of the Nile was once again on his track. He could endure no more. The next morning he transferred his troops to frigates and set sail for Ferrol.

At Antigua Nelson found no sign of Villeneuve. He was four days too late. Once again indecision tormented him. Then the schooner *Netley* settled his doubts. She had been one of the escorts for the captured convoy, and powerless to interfere, had shadowed the Combined Fleet, now 23 strong, as they took departure for Europe. At last Nelson could act. Whether Villeneuve was headed for the Channel or for Cadiz, Nelson's responsibilities lay at his station. The night before sailing he wrote, "I am going toward the Mediterranean after Gravina and Villeneuve, and hope to catch them." He had already dispatched the brig *Curieux* to England with a warning that he believed the Combined Fleet was heading for Europe. At noon on July 13, Nelson, having spent little more than a week in the West Indies, took his fleet out of harbor and set course for Gibraltar.

In her passage, the *Curieux* justified her name. On June 19, in position 33° 12′ North, 58° 00′ West, she sighted Villeneuve's fleet still standing northward. She shadowed them long enough to be sure of her enemy's course, and then made all possible speed for Plymouth. On arrival there, her captain had rushed by post to London, only to be told that Lord Barham had retired and no one dared wake him. Early on the morning of July 8, Barham awoke and was furious, so the story goes, that he had not been informed immediately. The meaning of the *Curieux*'s intelligence was plain. From that position, and from the northerly course, Villeneuve could not be heading for Cadiz. His objective must be either the Channel or Ferrol. It became imperative to strengthen Calder at Ferrol, for there lay the point of greatest weakness. Accordingly Barham sent orders to Cornwallis, who the day before had resumed command of the Channel fleet, to send Stirling from the Rochefort blockade with eight ships to strengthen Calder off Cape Finisterre. On July 15, Stirling joined Calder.

The junction was none too soon. A week later, with a heavy mist and a gentle westerly swell, Calder's lookouts discerned a strange fleet to the westward. It was the Combined Fleet making for Ferrol. It was the business of Calder and Stirling to stop them. Calder had found the opportunity Nelson had twice crossed the Atlantic to win.

Calder's Battle with Villeneuve

Sir Robert Calder had the chance Nelson later exploited at Trafalgar. Had he been successful, he might have gone down in history as one of England's truly great admirals. In London the area between the Mall and the Strand might have been named Finisterre Square, and the *Prince of Wales* rather than the *Victory* have been preserved in the Portsmouth Naval Base. Trafalgar would never have been fought. Instead Villeneuve and Gravina escaped almost scot-free and reached Ferrol, while Calder was left to face court-martial on the same charge that had cost Byng his life half a century earlier—failure to do his utmost.

There was no question of Calder's courage. He did not hesitate to seek action against the Combined Fleet when he sighted it through the mist. His weakness was in lack of imagination, in ability to force the enemy's hand. He was indefatigable, but his perceptions did not keep pace with his energies. He could not cope with the unexpected.

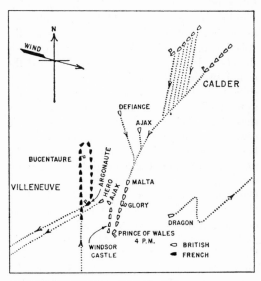

ACTION OFF FERROL, JULY 22, 1805
CALDER VS. VILLENEUVE

Calder's plan of action was a simple one. He was sailing in two divisions, close-hauled on the starboard tack on a southwesterly course. Villeneuve was on the opposite course in three divisions in order of sailing. Although the fleets sighted each other about noon, neither was able to make out much about the other for nearly two hours. Then Villeneuve formed line of battle in a single line. Calder in the meantime maneuvered to get between Ferrol and the enemy to cut off his line of retreat. Like Nelson later at Trafalgar, he planned to mass on the enemy's center and rear, leaving the Spanish van unengaged but, unlike Nelson, he made no provision to contain the van. Though Calder could count from 20 to 22 of the line opposing his 18, there was no thought in his mind but attack. About 3:30 he formed in line of battle on a course. That led him to the leeward, thus giving the initiative to the Allies, but retaining his position to intercept a dash for Ferrol. Visibility then deteriorated, and the two fleets lost sight of one another. When visibility improved, 15 minutes later, the two fleets were on opposite tacks, nearly parallel, and just out of range.

Villeneuve believed that Calder intended to double his rear, and to counter such a maneuver he ordered Gravina to lead the fleet in wearing in succession the moment he heard firing from the rear. Whether by misunderstanding or perception, Gravina, unchecked as a result of Calder's failure to hold the Allied van, wore immediately. Simultaneously the *Hero*, leading the British line, reached the center of the Allied fleet. Calder ordered his ships to tack in succession and engage on the same tack as the enemy from leeward. Six ships had tacked and were on a northerly course paralleling the enemy when the *Hero* beheld a strange ship looming up out of the mist ahead of her. Calder could not see what was happening. It was entirely up to Captain Gardner, commanding the *Hero*. If he held on, the two fleets would pass on opposite courses and nothing decisive could be accomplished. In addition, the Allied fleet would have a free run for Ferrol. On his own responsibility Gardner tacked to port, leading the fleet on a southwesterly course and forcing Gravina to adopt this course also. (See diagram.) By the time Calder was able to perceive what had happened, six ships had followed the *Hero,* and Calder had no choice but to accept the massing on the Allied van and center to which Gravina's early turn had committed him. Before any decisive results could be obtained, fog closed in, so that gunners fired at flashes and at the sound of guns. This game of blind man's death continued until after nightfall. About nine in the evening, the action finally over, the British discovered that they had captured two Spanish ships and had one of their own crippled by the loss of a foretopmast.

There is little to criticize in Calder's action. Considering the conditions, he did as well as he could. He was not one to force a melee. The diagram showing the position of the ships at the outset of the battle looks surprisingly like that of Trafalgar turned upside down. But Calder elected to fight in a formal line of battle, and this decision gave Gravina his opportunity to succor the rear. Once Gravina had turned, there was little Calder could have done, even had he been able to see and so control his fleet. And it was not for the battle that Calder was ordered to face his courtmartial. It was his action or, rather, lack of it the next day. Secondary considerations, such as preserving his prizes, repairing and reforming his fleet, took precedence over rejoining battle. In his defense, Calder claimed that Villeneuve's possession of the weather gage made it impossible for the British fleet to close. But the following day, the 24th, the wind shifted, giving Calder the weather gage, and still he made no attempt to come to grips. He later claimed he feared the 16 ships at Ferrol would come out to support Villeneuve. If they had been coming out, it would have been better for Calder to have fought the two fleets piecemeal before they could unite against him.

Villeneuve was content to leave well enough alone. At the first opportunity, he gave up the attempt to reach Ferrol and set his course for Cadiz. As the weather worsened, on Gravina's advice, Villeneuve decided to run for Vigo, which he reached on July 28. There he found that the Ferrol fleet was still at its base, so he made up his mind to join it.

The Crisis

Meanwhile Nelson had bent all sail in his crossing of the Atlantic and made landfall on Cape St. Vincent on July 17, entering Gibraltar two days later. Here, setting foot ashore for the first time in over two years, he sought intelligence of Villeneuve. Receiving none, Nelson gradually came to the conclusion that Villeneuve's destination lay to the northward, either Ireland or the Channel. While Lord Barham was penning orders directing him to return to England, Nelson made up his mind to go place his ships at the disposal of Cornwallis.

The crisis was at hand. Napoleon believed that the time was ripe for the crossing. He had collected his invasion forces and had prepared the barges. He ordered his Imperial Guard to Boulogne and proceeded there himself. Now if ever was the time. Yet the day after he had summoned the Guard, he countermanded the order. News had reached him that Nelson was back in Europe. Then, on the same day, August 8, he received word from Villeneuve, claiming victory over Calder and reporting that he was in Vigo. Napoleon at once proclaimed a victory and sent imperative orders for Villeneuve to go north, not to enter Ferrol, but to press on to the Channel to carry out the destiny of empire.

By chance Villeneuve had already left Vigo, but not with the high purpose of his Emperor. He was discouraged; his ships' stores were short, and his crews weakened by dysentery and scurvy. He left, not to fight, but to creep into Ferrol, which afforded facilities not available at Vigo. When he arrived, half his fleet had entered the port before Napoleon's prohibition reached him. He anchored his remaining ships in Corunna Bay and waited for his chance. On August 10, anxious to repair the damage done by his unwitting disobedience of orders, Villeneuve, heartsick and discouraged, sailed with 14 fresh ships from Ferrol, bringing his force up to 29 of the line. "I am sailing," he wrote to Decrès, the French Naval Minister, "and I shall make for Brest or Cadiz according to circumstances. The enemy observe us too closely here to leave any hope of concealing our movement."

As Villeneuve was struggling to leave Ferrol, the Royal Navy was concentrating, true to the reflex action of centuries, at the mouth of the Channel. Calder, finding his station vacant, raised the blockade and headed for Ushant, joining Cornwallis with ten ships a few hours after Stirling had come in with seven. To the fleet of 27 then assembled, Nelson the next day added his 12, bringing the total to 39. This was the outcome of Napoleon's plan to disperse the British fleet.

For a few days after leaving Ferrol, Villeneuve held on to the northwest, as though to gain westing for the run to the Channel. But as his letters show, as early as the 13th of August, he had decided to go instead to Cadiz. After two days of desultory movements, of shying at the sight of every strange sail, Villeneuve lost heart. On the evening of August 15 he gave the order which put his fleet on the course for Cadiz.

At the mouth of the Channel the extraordinary concentration prepared for his reception was already breaking up. Since no danger immediately threatened, it should be possible to go out from the interior position to intercept trouble at the source. On his own initiative, and just as Barham was ordering him to do that very thing, Cornwallis sent Calder with 18 of the line back to Ferrol. These provided the backbone of the force that was to blockade Villeneuve at Cadiz and that Nelson was to employ at Trafalgar. At the same time Cornwallis detached Nelson in the *Victory* to proceed to Portsmouth. The latter arrived there August 18, 1805 and struck his flag. He had been concerned about his reception after his fruitless 14,000-mile pursuit of Villeneuve. But the warmth of the crowds reassured him. The drama of his relentless chase had fired the imagination of the British public so that they made the most of "our hero of the Nile." Only in London was there a sign of coolness. Barham, apparently distrusting this impetuous young admiral—Nelson was 47—had made the almost unprecedented move of asking for his journal, a request he scarcely would have made of a man he trusted. Whatever it was Barham read, it converted him, and Nelson's personal reception by the First Lord on his arrival in London was all that he could have asked. There, too, by chance, he met a soldier who, though generally unknown at the time, was to be forever linked with his name. There the future victor at Trafalgar exchanged views on the war with the future victor in Spain and at Waterloo—Arthur Wellesley, later the Duke of Wellington.

On August 20, Villeneuve entered Cadiz. This ended once and for all Napoleon's Grand Design. At first the port could not be said to be blockaded, for Collingwood had but four ships to watch Villeneuve's 27. But Calder, finding Ferrol empty, had sailed on and closed Cadiz in tight on August 29. Villeneuve's timidity had frustrated the Grand Design, but had saved him from annihilation. Now affairs were back to normal, with the relentless British blockading Napoleon's naval strength. The concentration of the *Marine Impériale* in the Channel would never be realized.

Toward the end of August, for the first time since taking office, Pitt could look around with some degree of satisfaction; the naval threat had diminished, the danger of invasion was at an end, and best of all, his plans on the Continent were bearing fruit. The things Napoleon had believed impossible had come to pass, partly because of Pitt's endeavors and partly because Napoleon's own actions had so roused the fears of the Continent that some governments at last were showing a desperate courage and turning to face the Emperor. Russia, which had raised difficulties in the negotiations with Britain, fell into line when she received news of Napoleon's seizure of the crown of Italy and of his annexation of Genoa. Austria and Prussia both prepared to make a stand, and Craig's Secret Expedition had safely entered Valetta in Malta. Now England had in the Mediterranean a force that could exploit the mobility of sea power to strike in conjunction with Russia, Austria, and Prussia against the French in the Italian peninsula.

Inexorably the forces of circumstance were turning Napoleon's back on the English Channel and his face toward Central Europe. He still clung to the hope of a quick victory over England, but he knew it had to be quick. As early as August 13, the Emperor had informed Tallyrand that they would be in Vienna by November, prepared to deal with Russia if need arose. Believing Villeneuve to be en route to Brest to raise the blockade, Napoleon dispatched an optimistic order to Ganteaume to be prepared to sortie. "Never," he wrote, "will my soldiers of the land and sea risk their lives for a greater goal." And to Villeneuve: "I hope you are at Brest. Sail without losing a moment and enter the Channel with my reunited squadrons. England is ours! We are all ready. Everything is embarked. Appear for but twenty-four hours and all will be finished."

At this point, when all depended on the French navy, Napoleon received Villeneuve's letter written from Ferrol stating that he would make for Brest or Cadiz. It was rankest treachery, Napoleon raged, that Villeneuve could even consider Cadiz. Yet on Villeneuve's decision hung his own. If his admiral appeared off Ushant, Napoleon would invade and crush England. If he had gone to the south of Spain, then Napoleon would lead 200,000 men into Austria.

New Decisions

For two days Napoleon kept an anxious eye on the waters of the Channel. A letter from Decrès bore that minister's conviction that Villeneuve had indeed gone to Cadiz. Summoning his secretary, Napoleon ranted for five minutes, expressing his disgust for navies in general and for Villeneuve in particular. Suddenly he exclaimed, "Sit! Write!" Then for several hours he poured out with great detail and precision his whole plan for the campaign against Austria, a plan that was to lead to the victories of Austerlitz and Ulm. For a few days he held his position at Boulogne, largely to deceive the British while preparations were made, and it was during this time, on September 1, that he received final word from Villeneuve that he was in fact at Cadiz.

In view of his new plans, Napoleon had a new use for his naval forces, and fresh orders went out to Villeneuve, directing him to leave Cadiz and enter the Mediterranean to support the Austrian campaign by attacking Naples. At the same time, having had enough of Villeneuve's lack of determination, he secretly dispatched Admiral Rosily to relieve him.

As Napoleon was setting his face toward the Austerlitz campaign, Nelson was taking leave of his friends in London before departing to resume his old command. Gone were the suspicions Barham had had of him. Nelson had completely won the old man over. He spent much time at the Admiralty planning steps in the campaign in the Mediterranean. On September 13, after taking leave of his beloved Emma, Nelson proceeded to Spithead where, the next day, he was met by cheering crowds. Many wept, and not a few knelt and blessed him as he passed. That afternoon he once more hoisted his flag in the *Victory,* which sailed the next morning in company with a frigate. By September 25 he was off Lisbon. He sent urgent messages to the British Consul there and to Collingwood not to disclose his coming, for, as he wrote, "I hope to see the enemy at sea." As a result when, on September 28, the *Victory* joined Collingwood's fleet, not a gun saluted, and not a flag was broken.

Although Nelson's arrival was not marked with outward show, his spirit quickly permeated the fleet. Never had Nelson's leadership shown itself more inspired. These were not the ships of his old Mediterranean command. Few of the officers had served under him before, but he began to work to inspire others with the will to serve. Every officer and man who came under his influence soon realized that this admiral was no autocrat to demand blind obedience. He was rather a leader who inspired his subordinates to work with a will, with intelligence, and with freedom to exercise initiative to achieve a common goal. He expected his subordinates to exercise their professional competence in carrying out a plan. It was in this spirit that the famous Memorandum was written. It was in this spirit that he allowed Calder to go home in his own flagship, the 98-gun *Prince of Wales,* to face court-martial, thereby depriving himself of a three-decker on the eve of action.

Nelson's Memorandum

On taking command off Cadiz, Nelson had as his primary objective luring Villeneuve to sea so that he might destroy him. To this end he adopted the loose blockade he had favored at Toulon. Watchful frigates kept Cadiz under observation while the main fleet cruised some distance to the westward. Knowing that Villeneuve could command from 30 to 35 of the line, and further realizing that it might be a long wait before Villeneuve emerged, Nelson had to make plans for provisioning his fleet in relays while remaining at all times ready to fight. To this end he dispatched Admiral Louis with five ships to Tetuan Bay to replenish. Having no opportunity for the informal discussions with his captains that had preceded the Battle of the Nile, he set his ideas on paper as a guide for his officers. The Memorandum is worth quoting in part as an example of Nelson's tactical thinking and of his trust and confidence in subordinates.

Thinking it almost impossible to bring a fleet of forty sail of the line into line of battle in variable winds thick weather and other circumstances which must occur, without such a loss of time that the opportunity would probably be lost of bringing the enemy to battle in such a manner as to make the business decisive—

I have therefore made up my mind . . . that the order of sailing is to be the order of battle. . . .

The second in command will after my intentions are made known to him have the entire direction of his line to make the attack upon the enemy and to follow up the blow until they are captured or destroyed.

The whole impression of the British fleet must be to overpower from two to three ships ahead of their commander-in-chief, supposed to be in the centre, to the rear of their fleet. . . . Something must be left to chance; nothing is sure in a sea fight beyond all others. Shot will carry away the masts and yards of friends as well as foes but I look with confidence to a victory before the van of the enemy could succour their rear. . . .

The second in command will in all possible things direct the movements of his line by keeping them as compact as the nature of the circumstances will admit. Captains are to look to their particular line as their rallying point. But in case signals can neither be seen or perfectly understood no captain can do very wrong if he places his ship alongside that of an enemy.

This Memorandum is noteworthy especially for its spirit of aggressiveness, its trust of juniors, its simplicity, and its confidence in victory. While it in no way abandoned the Admiral's control of his ships, it left complete initiative to Collingwood, his second in command, "after my intentions are made known to him." The plan provided for flexibility and for the greatest freedom of action on the part of each captain. Briefly, Nelson's plan was to divide his fleet into three divisions, Collingwood's to the leeward to deliver the principal thrust on the enemy rear, Nelson's own windward division to contain the van and then strike at the center and force a decision before the enemy van could get back to take part in the battle. He also planned for a reserve division of eight ships to give support as needed.

The Battle of Trafalgar

On the morning of October 19, 1805, the inshore frigate hoisted Signal Number 370: "The enemy's ships are coming out of port or getting under sail." By 9:30 the news had reached Nelson. The opportunity he had worked so long for had arrived.

What caused Villeneuve to go out to face the implacable opponent who had so long blockaded him and who had twice pursued him across the Atlantic? Napoleon's orders to proceed to Naples had been most peremptory. On October 17, Villeneuve had heard that Rosily was in Madrid and on his way to take command of the Allied fleet. Rather than endure the disgrace of being relieved under conditions which suggested cowardice, Villeneuve decided he would try to make the Straits of Gibraltar before he was intercepted. If not, well then, death with honor was preferable to the alternative. He hoisted anchor the next day, but it was not until the 20th that he was able to get his ships out and formed up. Then he began a dash for the Straits.

When Nelson heard of Villeneuve's departure, he guessed it could mean only that he was bound for the Straits, and he took a course to intercept. He did not wish Villeneuve to sight him too soon and retreat to Cadiz. On October 20, the British fleet was near Gibraltar, but there was no sign of the Allies. No more was there sign of Louis and his four ships which Nelson had hoped to find there. Beating back toward Cadiz, the British learned from a scouting frigate that Villeneuve had only just completed his sortie from the port. Nelson was jubilant. That night he invited several midshipmen to dinner, promising them that the morrow would bring something for them to talk about all the rest of their lives.

Villeneuve, his ships at length formed up, set sail for the Straits of Gibraltar at noon on October 20. He did not really expect to make it without a fight, but he was determined to press on. During the night, Nelson, who had come back to within 25 miles of Cadiz had opened out again toward the southwest to allow the Allies to gain sea room, but most especially to keep them from running to Cadiz

before he could force an engagement. Villeneuve seems to have predicted the tactics Nelson would employ; at least he foresaw a concentration on his center and rear. During the night he held on for the Straits, expecting to receive at any moment the smashing broadsides of the "fougueux amiral," as the French called Nelson. Out of the dark they had struck at the Nile, and out of the dark they might strike again. But the night passed without incident.

As dawn broke on October 21, 1805, the sea was smooth, with a gentle breeze from the west-northwest. Cape Trafalgar lay to the east about 20 miles. To anxious lookouts on the British ships came the welcome sight of white patches of canvas on the eastern horizon. A little after 6 AM, Nelson began to implement his Memorandum. Because of the absence of Louis's ships, he discarded the idea of a reserve division and sent a signal for his fleet of 27 sail to form two columns on an easterly course. He, in the *Victory,* led the northern or windward column, while Collingwood in the *Royal Sovereign* headed the southern or leeward column.

About this time Villeneuve, realizing that he could not reach the Straits without engagement, gave the order to wear together and form column of battle in inverse order. This had the effect of turning the Allied fleet into a single line on a northerly course, the Third Squadron under Dumanoir leading. Yet the order came too late for the Allies to retreat to Cadiz. There was no hope of avoiding engagement. As he saw the situation, one of the Spanish captains snapped his telescope shut and exclaimed, "Perdidos!"

As Villeneuve's ships made their turn the line became slightly bowed, concave toward the British. The handier ships were forced to back sail to wait for the laggardly ones. Thus for nearly two hours the Allied fleet made good no distance at all, while the British, their two columns at an oblique angle to the Franco-Spanish line, advanced with all sail set, including studding-sails. As a result, the rearmost vessels in both columns tended to lag behind. Collingwood, in compliance with the Memorandum, was heading to cut the Allied line at the twelfth ship from the rear, while Nelson was on a course for a point two miles ahead of the enemy van. Since the Allied ships were by this time heading north, the relative movement put the *Victory* on a collision course with the *Neptuno*, Villeneuve's leading ship. The psychological pressure on the waiting French and Spanish was tremendous. No one could tell where the blow would fall. So long as Nelson held his course, the Allied van had to brace to receive the onslaught of Nelson's 12 juggernauts. Yet by simply putting the helm over, Nelson could deliver his thrust at Villeneuve's center, with the van held out of action by the wind and by the necessity of reversing course. Thus was concentration achieved at Trafalgar, for Nelson's squadron acted as a holding force on the Allied center and van to support Collingwood's attack on the rear, while Nelson's own course held the Allied van to cover his smash into the center. In this double role for his own squadron lay Nelson's brilliance. Where Calder had failed to hold the Allied van until he could force a decision, Nelson, by his knowledge of the enemy's psychology and by his threat to the van, insured that it would be out of action while he and Collingwood disposed of the center and rear.

As the morning wore on, the British continued their implacable closing on the Allies. The two British columns, their black and yellow hulls somber under their clouds of canvas, their guns run out and double-shotted, were forbidding indeed. Nelson had given considerable attention to the order of his ships in the columns. Anticipating that his leading ships might be in action before the rearmost ones could catch up, he had headed each column with his heaviest ships. Leading his own were three three-deckers, the *Victory,* 100 guns, and the *Téméraire* and *Neptune,* 98 guns each. Leading Collingwood's squadron were the *Royal Sovereign,* 100, and the *Prince,* 98. As the fleets neared one another, several of Nelson's officers pleaded with him to allow another ship to lead the column lest Nelson himself be uselessly killed or disabled. Nelson appeared to acquiesce, and signals were made for the *Téméraire* to take the lead. But when the *Téméraire,* slightly handier than the *Victory,* began to edge forward, Nelson ordered her back into position second in line.

About 11 in the morning, when it seemed

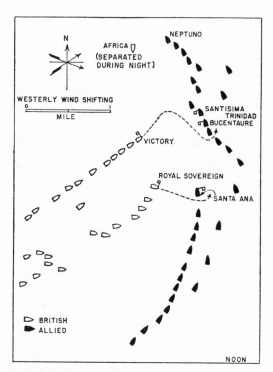

THE BATTLE OF TRAFALGAR, OCTOBER 21, 1905

battle would be joined in another hour, Nelson went below to his cabin. Here he made a codicil to his will and composed a prayer which he left as a legacy to his country:

May the great God whom I worship grant to my country, and for the benefit of Europe in general, a great and glorious victory; and may no misconduct of anyone tarnish it; and may humanity after victory be the predominant feature of the British fleet. For myself, individually, I commit my life to Him who made me, and may His blessing light upon my endeavours for serving my country faithfully. To Him I resign myself and the just cause which is entrusted to me to defend.

After he returned to the deck, Nelson was informed that Cape Trafalgar had been sighted. He then announced that he would amuse the fleet with a signal. At 11:35 there rose to the *Victory*'s yardarm, "England expects that every man will do his duty." There followed another, which remained flying until it was shot away—Number 16, "Engage the enemy more closely."

The moment was at hand. About noon, while the *Victory* was still out of range and still relentlessly steering for the Allied van,

Collingwood's division began the action. Instead of steering, as the Memorandum directed, to isolate the last 12 ships in the Allied line, Collingwood decided to cut off the last 16, thus opposing his 15 ships to a superior number. But he relied on superior British seamanship and gunnery, and in these he was not disappointed. Nelson apparently approved, for as Collingwood bore down on the *Santa Ana,* he exclaimed, "See how that noble fellow Collingwood carries his ship into action!" Collingwood's division by this time was no longer in column, but in line of bearing to the southwest. As the enemy's rear was curved toward the southwest, it made the two lines nearly parallel and brought Collingwood's ships into action much more rapidly than was possible for Nelson's, still in column. Within 15 minutes, eight of Collingwood's ships had broken through the Allied rear, and soon all were furiously engaging the enemy.

Meanwhile the French and Spanish admirals had broken their colors. Satisfied that his feint toward the van had prevented Villeneuve from interfering with Collingwood, and that it was too late for Dumanoir to counter his own attack, Nelson directed Hardy, captain of the *Victory,* to turn to starboard and make for the *Bucentaure,* Villeneuve's flagship. About 12:30, the *Victory* put her helm over and bore down. Finding the *Redoubtable* close astern of the *Bucentaure,* Hardy asked Nelson which ship he should run down, and received the reply, "Take your choice, Hardy, it does not much signify which." As the *Victory* passed astern of the *Bucentaure* she discharged her port broadside, causing over a hundred casualties and unnerving Villeneuve. Behind the *Victory* in quick succession followed the *Téméraire, Neptune, Leviathan, Conqueror, Britannia, Ajax,* and Nelson's old *Agamemnon.*

Nelson, his task accomplished, having successfully brought his fleet into action, quietly walked the quarterdeck of the *Victory* with his old friend Hardy. As was his custom in battle, Nelson wore his medals, making himself a conspicuous target. All around were scenes of horror and destruction. Blood flowed across the white decks and collected in streams in the scuppers. Nelson's secretary, standing near him, was smashed by a ball. "This is too warm

work, Hardy," Nelson remarked, "to last long." As they continued their stroll, Hardy suddenly noticed that he was alone. Turning, he saw Nelson collapsing on the deck. "They have done for me at last, Hardy," Nelson murmured. As he was borne below, he covered his medals with his handkerchief so that the men might not recognize him and be disheartened. In the cockpit the surgeon could only confirm Nelson's diagnosis. A sharpshooter in the rigging of the *Redoubtable* had picked him off, the ball passing through his shoulder, lung, and spine, and lodging in his hip. Five minutes later, Villeneuve surrendered the *Bucentaure.* By such a narrow margin was Nelson robbed of receiving the submission of his rival.

While the action continued, Nelson in the *Victory*'s cockpit was kept informed of the progress of the battle. By a little after two the action in the center was nearly over. Eight French and Spanish ships had surrendered. In another hour Collingwood's division had won out in the rear, and Hardy hastened below to speak to his dying leader. "I hope that none of our ships have struck, Hardy," Nelson inquired when Hardy had informed him of the results.

"No, my Lord, there is no fear of that."

Then Hardy was summoned back to the quarterdeck to repulse the counterattack of Dumanoir, who by almost superhuman efforts, using his ships' boats as tugs to help him around, had come down from the van. Within 20 minutes this attack had failed, and Hardy once again went below to report to Nelson that 14 or 15 of the enemy had struck. "That is well," whispered Nelson, "but I had bargained for 20." Then Nelson's seaman's instinct came to the fore. He could feel from the motion of the ship that the wind was freshening, and mindful of the crippled condition of the ships, friend and foe alike, and of the proximity of the dangerous lee shore of Trafalgar, he gave his last order. "Anchor, Hardy, anchor!"[2] Then, growing weaker, he begged Hardy not to throw his body overboard, and with some flash of childhood's affection, asked Hardy to kiss him. Shortly afterward he mur-

[2] Collingwood did not see fit to carry out this order. As a result all but five of the prizes were lost in the gale that sprang up after the battle.

mured, "Thank God I have done my duty. God and my Country." A moment later he was dead.

About the same time the battle ended. Dumanoir with four ships and the mortally wounded Gravina with ten pulled out of the fight, leaving the remainder prizes to the British. The Battle of Trafalgar was over.

Summary

Napoleon had agreed to the Treaty of Amiens to win through diplomacy and treachery objectives he had been unable to attain through military operations. Above all he sought to gain time to build naval strength to destroy England.

For a brief and illusory suspension of hostilities, Prime Minister Henry Addington, the "peacemaker," paid dearly; he yielded most of England's conquests won in nearly a decade of fighting.

Contemptuous of promises, Napoleon soon drove a reluctant England back to arms by repeated and flagrant violations of his obligations. At length even Addington could see no escape, and on May 16, 1803, wearily but doggedly, Britain once more grasped the sword. As always that sword's keenest edge was Britain's sea power. Firmly the blockade was resumed off Toulon, Rochefort, and Brest. For over a year Addington let Napoleon retain the initiative, for the mediocrities in the British Cabinet could think of nothing but Napoleon's threatening invasion. For over a year the First Consul worked feverishly to prepare his troops and complete his flotilla for a cross-Channel assault. Yet England, guarded by her fleet, remained impregnable beyond "the silver sea which serves it in the office of a wall." As the years 1803 and 1804 passed, Napoleon's impotent rage intensified. Wrathfully he worked out plans to divert a part of the British fleet and destroy the rest so that his legions could add London to the triumphs of Marengo and Hohenlinden.

Meanwhile England had assumed the offensive. Addington had given way to Pitt, whose penetrating mind had realized the necessity for attack. On the diplomatic front, Pitt struck at Napoleon by the formation of the Third Coalition. On the military front, he committed England's only available army to conjunct operations in the Mediterranean. The campaigns of Napoleon and of Pitt both matured in the summer and fall of 1805.

As the first step in the conquest of Britain, Napoleon ordered the Franco-Spanish fleets to rendezvous in the Caribbean and then, under the command of Villeneuve, to return to the Channel to cover the crossing. The contrasting traits of two men foiled what slight chance this plan ever had. The resolution of Nelson and the vacillation of Villeneuve brought the Grand Design crashing in ruins. Across the Atlantic and back Nelson relentlessly pursued Villeneuve, who, fleeing from his implacable foe, was forced into battle with Sir Robert Calder. Indecisive as this action of Cape Finisterre was, it disheartened Villeneuve, who crept first into Vigo, then to Ferrol, and finally to Cadiz, while Napoleon kept anxious watch for his sails in the Channel. Learning of Villeneuve's retreat, Napoleon realistically abandoned hope of crushing England and turned to face the menace at his back, Austria and the Third Coalition. To support this new campaign, Villeneuve took his 33 ships to sea to attack Naples. Instead he met his Nemesis, Nelson's 27 of the line, on October 21, 1805, off Cape Trafalgar. By nightfall Napoleon's navy had ceased to exist as a fighting force.

The significance of the battle was profound. For all time it ended Napoleon's threat to invade England. It meant that he was forever denied the use of the sea; henceforth all his campaigns would be land-bound. It meant that French overseas trade was at a virtual standstill while Britain's was free. It meant that Britain had the initiative to project her power via the sea to strike at any point on the coast of Europe where Napoleon might be vulnerable. It made possible the whole Peninsular Campaign, which was the beginning of Napoleon's downfall. It contributed heavily to the defeat of the Russian campaign, which completed his ruin.

9:

The Decline and Fall of the French Empire

The extent of the victory Nelson had bought with his life at Trafalgar was not at once apparent either in London or in Paris. For on October 20, 1805, Napoleon's troops at Ulm crushed the Austrian army under the incompetent General Mack, thereby striking a mortal blow at the Third Coalition.

When the news of Ulm reached London, it was scarcely credited. While Pitt contemplated the wreck of his hopes, he received Collingwood's dispatches reporting the Battle of Trafalgar. But the greatest naval victory of the days of sail was not celebrated; it was mourned. "The Combined Fleet is defeated, but Nelson is no more!" Grief over the loss of England's greatest seaman clouded the triumph.

Pitt however was not the man to waste time with useless repining. Although the Austrians had thrown away the initiative his genius had won, Pitt saw clearly that Nelson's victory was in a real sense overwhelming. It made the lengthy ship- and man-destroying blockades unnecessary, for the French navy had ceased to exist as a naval force, and the feeble units remaining could easily be dealt with by flying squadrons which would pursue and destroy any misguided enough to leave their ports. It made escorts more readily available to protect from privateers the many convoys carrying Britain's trade, her life blood. Finally it meant that the Royal Navy could be employed to hit wherever it was desirable to strike a blow, whether in support of her allies or in support of her own strategic aims.

Opportunity seemed to call in the north. Just as Craig's expedition had been sent to the Mediterranean to cooperate with the Aus-

trians, a force could also be sent to the North to support the Russians and Swedes and, it was hoped, the Prussians. On the readiness of Prussia to cooperate depended the success of the new plan. Yet while the Prussian king vacillated, Napoleon on December 2, 1805 struck again at Austerlitz, and by the end of the day, Austria had been driven out of the Third Coalition. This French triumph and the ensuing Treaty of Pressburg broke Pitt's heart. On January 9, 1806, as Nelson's body was being drawn through London to its resting place in St. Paul's Cathedral, Pitt set out for London for the last time, a sick and broken man. His last decision, the recall of the northern expeditionary force, symbolized the death of hope, the end of a vision. With Pitt passed, so far as men could see, all chance of victory.

Yet Nelson's legacy to his country was already beginning to have its effects. In spite of Napoleon's devastating victories on land, the Emperor realized that Britain through her sea power could ultimately starve him. He desperately needed overseas trade; Nelson had deprived him of all chance of winning it by force. Once before England had allowed herself to be tricked into a peace that conferred all the advantages on France. Perhaps once again guile would win where his ships had failed.

With Pitt's death, the new government, led in fact if not on paper by the enigmatic Charles Fox, was equally ready to make peace. In despair over the conquests of the Emperor and the loss of her greatest seaman and her greatest statesman, Britain saw no way to keep Napoleon from winning further victories except by giving him no further opportunities for fighting. Fox, often suspected of French sympathies, was eager to conclude peace and was able to open negotiations with the highest hopes. But in spite of the opinion of his political enemies, Fox was first and foremost an Englishman. As the summer progressed it became evident that Napoleon was engaged in double-dealing, playing England off against Russia. Fox therefore broke off negotiations. He did not long survive his disappointment, but his recognition of the impossibility of dealing with Napoleon was a lesson borne in upon all Englishmen. If not even Fox could believe in the Emperor's good faith, no one could. Resolutely the British faced the prospect of limitless war. Not until the final victory was won did Britain again consider turning aside from her task of effecting the ruin of Napoleon and all that he stood for.

Even while the peace negotiations were in progress, Britain was fumblingly attempting to exploit her command of the sea. Many opportunities beckoned to capture overseas colonies of France and her allies and to hit at weak points around the coasts of Europe. Thus an expedition under Commodore Sir Home Riggs Popham in January 1806 recaptured the Cape Colony, restored to the Dutch at the Peace of Amiens. Popham followed up this success with an ill-conceived capture of Buenos Aires the following June, but was soon forced to evacuate. In the Mediterranean, Major General Sir John Stuart on his own initiative left Sicily in late June and on July 1 landed with some 5,000 troops near the toe of Italy. Although the British won an overwhelming victory over French forces at the Battle of Maida, Stuart was soon forced to withdraw.

These and similar raids were not and could not be decisive. Superficially they appeared to be a continuation of Pitt's Plan of the Seven Years' War. But the success of Pitt's Plan depended on the existence of a powerful allied army on the Continent. Land and sea power had worked together in mutual support, alternately containing and striking enemy forces. Now the land element was lacking. No large, well-trained, well-led army faced Napoleon. Repeatedly, by means of alliances, Britain had raised coalitions on the Continent, only to see their armies fall apart as a result of divided aims and French blows. Either Britain must somehow build up a stable coalition or else husband her own land forces until they could be sent ashore where their weight could be effective. The ideal combination would of course see British sea power, British land power, and coalition armies all operating in concert against the enemy. That combination was not to be attained until 1813 and the Fourth Coalition. The years between tell the story of the discovery and forging of the decisive weapons.

The Continental System

Enraged by the breakdown of the peace negotiations and by British operations against the colonies, Napoleon countered with an attempt to exclude England from the trade of the Continent. The Kingdom of Naples and the coast of Portugal were obvious gaps through which British commerce flowed. Taking steps against Naples first, Napoleon invaded southern Italy and closed that entrepôt to British trade goods. The King and his court escaped to Sicily, establishing their government at Messina under the protection of Craig's army and Collingwood's fleet. Turning his attention to Portugal, Napoleon in August 1806 threatened invasion there. This time British sea power forestalled him, for while he and his staff were first encountering the fantastically difficult terrain of the Iberian Peninsula, Lord St. Vincent slipped into Lisbon with the entire Channel fleet. The sight of the powerful British ships of the line reassured the Prince Regent, who ceased to look apprehensively northward and resolutely reaffirmed loyalty to the English cause, proclaiming that if necessary he would transfer his fleet and his court to Brazil. St. Vincent's appearance was a dramatic demonstration of how sea power could make light of distance and terrain difficulties insurmountable for an army.

Nor was this Napoleon's only trouble in the Iberian Peninsula. Spanish sympathies were decidedly against the overbearing little Corsican, and Spaniards everywhere were sick of the war which was ruining their country, bringing only the miseries of taxation and poverty. Impressed by Britain's success at sea, especially at Trafalgar, and clearly reading the lesson of St. Vincent's appearance at Lisbon, Godoy, the Spanish dictator, suddenly cast off the shackles which had bound him to Napoleon, and in October 1806 appealed to the Spaniards to spring to arms to defend their country against the French.

When the outraged Napoleon read Godoy's proclamation, he could not afford to deal with him immediately, for his attention had been called to the north. Prussia, whom Napoleon had bribed with Hanover to close her ports to British ships, soon learned that, like all who treated with Napoleon, she had been cheated. On the heels of unkept promises, Napoleon had offered to return Hanover to England during the abortive peace discussions. When Frederick William of Prussia heard of this, he appealed to the Czar. Receiving a promise of Russian aid, he sent an ultimatum to France in September 1806.

Showing that he was still master of the land, Napoleon drove hard into Germany and in mid-October at Jena and Auerstadt shattered the Prussian armies in a single day and drove Frederick William to abject surrender. As the Royal Navy could move around the periphery of Europe, hitting where it would on the coast, Napoleon had again demonstrated that he could strike at will on the Continent. Until the British could devise some means of combining naval mobility with effective blows at the enemy, their outlook seemed bleak.

Napoleon celebrated his humbling of Prussia by setting forth the essence of his Continental System in the Berlin Decree of November 1806. Its purpose was to complete the conquest of the sea by the land. In the Berlin Decree the Emperor declared the British Isles to be blockaded, closed every port under his control to British vessels, and ordered all goods of British origin seized. Without the capability of keeping a fleet at sea, Napoleon defied the principle of international law that to be legal a blockade must be effective. To counter this new form of economic warfare, Britain retaliated in January 1807 with an Order in Council forbidding neutral ships to trade with ports closed to British ships. This order was at first leniently applied, for neutrals were allowed to carry non-contraband goods from their own countries to ports under the control of France, but they were not allowed to carry goods from one French-controlled port to another. In November the order was stiffened to declare that all French-controlled ports were automatically blockaded and that neutrals could trade with them only by calling first at an English port and there paying duty on their cargoes and buying licenses before going on to their destinations. Thus the practical British planned to make their economic war with France a paying proposition, to help defray the costs of the military war.

Napoleon's hope of starving the British Isles through the Berlin Decree proved futile. British goods were of too high quality for the Continent to do without them. The result of the decree was largely to lend respectability to smuggling. Even the Emperor was obliged to supply his armies with English overcoats and boots. Yet refusing to abandon the blockade, in December 1807 he issued the Milan Decree, outlawing any neutral ships that submitted to British search or complied with the Order in Council of November by paying duties to Britain. All such ships were, he declared, lawful prize to his ever-increasing swarm of privateers. Even though insurance rates for American ships trading with England rose from 2½ per cent to 3¾ per cent, British sea power kept the essential ships moving. The outcome of the series of Decrees and Orders in Council was to cause British products to pile up in warehouses. Although many businesses failed, the development of new overseas markets prevented ruin. As time passed, the new markets more than offset the losses resulting from the stoppage of trade to the Continent. While the Emperor could, albeit with the greatest difficulty, exclude the bulk of English trade from Europe, he was helpless to prevent colonies overseas—even French colonies—from dealing with the British. By 1810, the Caribbean had become a British lake, and in the Indian Ocean, in the Malay area, and in Australia and New Zealand, Britain opened up a new empire whose trade nourished the home islands. In the same year the annual value of British exports had risen to almost £70,000,000, as opposed to £50,000,000 before the institution of the Continental System.

In France in the meantime, as well as in those countries adhering to the decrees of Napoleon, the Continental System brought privation and ruin. The economy of Europe, including that of France herself, was geared to British trade. The stoppage of British goods meant that the wealth needed to run Napoleon's vast war machine could no longer be supplied from national income. In spite of constantly increasing taxes, the national deficit continued to mount. The average man did not understand the economic problem; he only knew that the stubborn will of one man kept from him the goods he needed. As French soldiers burned confiscated smuggled items, crowds stood sullenly watching the commodities they longed for go up in smoke. It appeared that Britain, the stronghold of rank and privilege, supplied the needs of the common man, while France, the theoretical custodian of the rights of man, denied him the necessities of life. Thus in the long run Napoleon's Continental System was a failure, for it strengthened Britain's economy by forcing her to develop new markets, while on the Continent it brought inflation, misery, despair, and ultimate collapse.

The Dardanelles Operation

To punish Russia for her support of Prussia, Napoleon set in motion new operations against her. At Russian urging, the British agreed to support their ally by undertaking an operation against Turkey, Russia's perennial enemy. After a preliminary reconnaissance, a force of eight ships of the line, two frigates, and two bomb vessels arrived at the entrance to the Dardanelles in early February 1807, under command of Vice Admiral Sir John Duckworth. His orders were to demand the surrender of the Turkish Fleet and naval stores. Failing this, he was to bombard Constantinople. Duckworth got through the Dardanelles with little difficulty, but once inside, he accomplished nothing. He captured a few ships, but allowed himself to be drawn into the trap of extended negotiations, while the Turks strengthened the Dardanelles fortifications with a view of sealing him in the Sea of Marmora. Finally, after ten days, Duckworth withdrew his force, sustaining heavy damage during the passage.

On reaching the Mediterranean, Duckworth was joined by eight Russian ships of the line under Admiral Siniavin, who urged a return to the attack on Constantinople. Admiral Duckworth however declined and retired to the west. Siniavin, lingering near the Dardanelles, defeated the Turkish Fleet as it emerged in June. On the news of the Treaty of Tilsit, Siniavin concluded an armistice with Turkey and took his fleet to Lisbon to await instructions.

The Treaty of Tilsit

Napoleon's attack on Russia at first gave presage of things to come five years later. The Emperor suffered the miseries of inadequate logistics in a barren country which his troops could not live on, and when he engaged the Russian army in February 1807 at Eylau, he took losses almost as great as he exacted. But after a winter of bringing up reinforcements, Napoleon resumed the offensive, and at Friedland in June he routed the Russians, destroying a third of their force.

A few days later, while the King of Prussia cooled his heels in the rain on the banks of the Niemen, the Emperors of France and Russia met on a raft in the river. "I hate the English as much as you do," said the Czar. "In that case," Napoleon replied, "peace is made." In July formal articles were signed at Tilsit. By this treaty France and Russia agreed to carve up the world between them. For territorial gains at the expense of Prussia, Sweden, and Finland, Russia agreed to recognize all of Napoleon's conquests and to acknowledge Western Europe as France's sphere of influence. Denmark, Portugal, and Austria were to be required to align themselves with the common cause, and an enormous Allied fleet was to be assembled in the Baltic to regain command of the sea. As a special favor Prussia was allowed to exist, but she had to close her ports to British ships. If by November the English had not recognized the inevitability of defeat and made peace, Russia would enter the war against them.

The British Against the Danes

Although Britain was left without an effective ally, the London government responded to the Treaty of Tilsit with dispatch. Certain that the Danes could not withstand pressure from France and Russia, the British determined at once on an expedition to forestall the possibility of the Danish fleet falling into Napoleon's hands. Scarcely a month after the conclusion of the treaty, Admiral James Gambier appeared off Zealand with more than 50 of the line and numerous lesser vessels, escorting an army of 50,000 under the Earl of Cathcart. Surrounding Zealand, the British fleet cut off all support. Near the end of August Sir Arthur Wellesley landed with a strong force and encircled Copenhagen. Then on September 1 the British called upon the Danes to join an alliance with Britain and to surrender their fleet in return for a yearly allowance of £100,000. The commander of the Danish defenses asked for time but was refused, and at dusk on the following day all British batteries, afloat and ashore, opened fire with mortars, Congreve's rockets, and red-hot shot. The Danes fought gallantly from their blazing city until September 7, when, further resistance being vain, they capitulated. The British removed 18 ships of the line, ten frigates, and many smaller vessels. Perhaps even more important, since only four of the Danish ships were found worth reconditioning, was the acquisition of an immense amount of naval stores—masts, yards, sails, cordage, and the like—which filled the holds of 92 vessels for the passage back to England. Although the expedition brought Denmark into the war against Britain, it stripped her of power to operate effectively with a new Northern Coalition.

The Opening of the Peninsular Campaign

Once more, to Napoleon's rage, the hated islanders had forestalled him. He threatened again to assemble 100,000 men at Boulogne, but the port had silted up. He decided to enforce the terms of Tilsit by bringing luckless Portugal to heel. Here was the one remaining corner of Europe where English merchants might vend their wares. "The English declare they will no longer respect neutrals at sea," he declared. "I will no longer recognize them on land!" The alarmed Prince Regent of Portugal declared that he must "adhere to the cause of the Continent," but he was too late, for Napoleon had already acted. He had dispatched General Androche Junot with 30,000 troops to make a forced march to capture Lisbon and seize the Portuguese ships before the British could arrive.

But again the superior speed of sea communications foiled Napoleon. The remnants of Junot's force, having marched 300 miles in two weeks, leaving some 28,000 exhausted men on the roadside, straggled into Lisbon on the last day of November 1807. The Portuguese court had fled two days before under the protection of Rear Admiral Sir Sydney Smith, who saw to it that they were provided with an escort to Rio de Janeiro. He then returned to the Tagus to blockade the Russian ships of Siniavin.

The subjugation of Portugal was only one of Napoleon's reasons for undertaking operations in the Iberian Peninsula. He also intended to punish the Spanish dictator Godoy, who had dared to show signs of independence before the Jena campaign. But, most important, the Emperor had revived his dream of conquests in the Orient. He eagerly proposed to the Czar that the Russians attack through Turkey, leading to an eventual campaign via Persia into India. To succeed, he had to drive the British from the Mediterranean, and therefore must seize Gibraltar. Thus, a number of reasons impelled Napoleon to cross the Pyrenees. Having secured the passes in February 1808, he poured 100,000 troops into Spain under his brother-in-law, Joachim Murat, who captured Madrid in April. Forcing the abdication of both Charles IV and his son Ferdinand, Napoleon installed his brother Joseph Bonaparte on the Spanish throne. With a stroke of the pen, the Emperor believed that he had subjugated his ally, won control of the Iberian Peninsula and all of Spain's overseas colonies, and insured the safety of his expedition in Portugal.

Yet Spain, so easily won, so apparently rewarding in its conquest, was to prove a cancer in Napoleon's empire. For the next five years, French lives and material were thrown away in a futile campaign to hold the territory that had come so effortlessly. The Iberian Peninsula sapped the strength of the French less dramatically than the Russian winter, but the drain was no less real. The Spanish people, misgoverned, proud, ignorant of the world outside, rose spontaneously against the invaders as a result of the forced abdication of their

THE PENINSULAR WAR, 1808-1814

king. In May 1808 a mob slaughtered the French garrison in Madrid. During the next few weeks, similar massacres took place in three other cities. Local armies sprang up in half a dozen places. During the last week in May, the British governor at Gibraltar, Sir Hew Dalrymple, received an appeal from Madrid for money and arms. This request he forwarded to Britain.

Britain's First Iberian Expedition

The Spanish appeal fell on receptive ears. While the British government pondered the best course of action, naval commanders anticipated their instructions. Collingwood seized five ships of the line, fugitives from Trafalgar, still in Cadiz. Inside the Mediterranean, Lord Cochrane raided communications from Gibraltar to the French border. When the insurrections spread to Portugal, Britain decided to act. Instead of scattering her forces in raids on overseas colonies, she would launch a main

effort in the Iberian Peninsula, coming directly to grips with the enemy. This decision marked a turning point in the war.

The expedition was entrusted to Lieutenant General Sir Arthur Wellesley, who in July 1808 sailed with 17,000 troops under vague orders to support the Spanish patriots. But the Spaniards seemed almost as reluctant to have British troops in Spain as French. Money and supplies were welcome, but troops, no. When Wellesley arrived at Corunna and attempted to cooperate with the local junta, he was met with old-world courtesy and a strong suggestion that he take his troops elsewhere, preferably to Portugal. At length, fobbed off with excuses and promises but no performance, Wellesley took his force by sea to Mondego Bay, a hundred miles north of Lisbon, which he was determined to free. On August 8 he landed his entire force and pressed south. At the little town of Roliça he encountered Junot, who had advanced from Lisbon with 13,000 troops to stop him. After heavy fighting, Wellesley carried the day. But as he prepared to follow up his success with a hard drive on Lisbon, he found himself superseded, and all advance stopped.

The British government had decided to commit its entire available army. In advance of the additional forces came two very senior lieutenant generals, Sir Hew Dalrymple, in command, seconded by Sir Harry Burrard, both of whom were better known for achievements on the parade ground and at the dining table than for handling troops in the field. On their arrival Dalrymple and Burrard viewed Wellesley's plans with exceedingly jaundiced eyes. While Junot braced himself for a British flanking attack to free Lisbon, an attack he knew he could not withstand, Dalrymple's wisdom decreed a siege. Wellesley loyally supported his new superiors although bitterly disappointed at the wasted opportunity. When the French proposed a convention for the evacuation of Portugal, Dalrymple leaped at the chance, and even Wellesley had to concede that the British position had so deteriorated that there was now no alternative. Hence was signed the Convention of Cintra, which gave the British far less than they might have won by force of arms. British transports carried Junot's army to France with no parole on their freedom to fight again elsewhere. Another provision stipulated that Siniavin's fleet should be taken to the Baltic under British escort. This however was too much for Sir Charles Cotton, commanding the blockade of the Tagus, who insisted that the Russian ships be taken to England for internment until the end of the war.

The terms of the Convention, arriving in England after the news of Wellesley's victory at Roliça, came as a shock. Although the chief blame fell on his seniors, Wellesley received more than his share. The three were recalled, Dalrymple to face a Court of Inquiry.

Sir John Moore was thus left senior British officer in the Iberian Peninsula. Commanding 30,000 troops, he had orders to help the Spaniards free their country of the French. Specifically he was to seize the key city of Burgos, which commanded French communications to Madrid. These orders did not seem unreasonable to the British ministers. The Spanish risings had swept the French from most of Spain

except the provinces of Navarre and Barcelona. Yet the campaign was doomed from the start because of certain factors the ministers had overlooked. They were mistaken in the first place in regarding Spain as a nation. The Spanish government consisted of isolated juntas, each jealous of the others, and a Supreme Junta, planning campaigns it could not coordinate to be executed by local juntas it could not control. Nor could the fighting forces be persuaded to accept the discipline of a regular army life. Should an invader enter his own territory, the Spanish peasant would fight like a demon, but so long as the French were in the next province or the next valley, he had thoughts only of his own farm. Campaigns are built around armies, and armies are built around discipline. The Spaniards had neither.

The second factor not considered by the British ministers was the reaction of Napoleon. Men less bemused by their hopes and with more understanding of the mind of the Emperor could have foreseen that he would not allow the Spanish revolt to go unpunished. He had given them as king his own brother Joseph, whom they had forced to flee. The ungrateful Spaniards would pay in blood for this insult to the Bonapartes. The country had to be subdued lest Napoleon's reputation for conquest be compromised and his splendor dulled. Finally the hated English had dared to meet him on land. They must be given a lesson.

Thus while Moore moved into Spain in accordance with his orders, Napoleon moved across the Pyrenees to chastise Spain, to regain Lisbon, and to drive the British into the sea. Moore knew the difficulties he was facing. Traversing the mountains through blinding rainstorms and a territory swept clean of sustenance, he crossed Portugal into Spain, following roughly the valley of the Tagus. While his army fought and overcame difficulties of terrain, Napoleon smashed the Spanish at Burgos and occupied Valladolid. When Moore on November 13 arrived at Ciudad Rodrigo, he heard the appalling news that Napoleon's army, far outnumbering his own, stood between him and Burgos, his objective. Worse, he had a shorter route than Moore to reach Corunna, the only possible evacuation port for the British. If Moore stayed where he was he faced almost certain annihilation. Yet for over a month he did his best to cooperate with the Spaniards, who told him little and gave him less. In the end it was Spanish folly that solved his dilemma. The Spaniards attacked Napoleon's eastern flank with the idea of cutting him off from France. Although they were soundly thrashed, they diverted the Emperor's attention long enough to open the road to Corunna for Moore, who was quick to seize his opportunity. When his enemies began to close in on him, they were too late.

Driving hard through inhospitable territory, Moore's army covered the 300-odd miles to Corunna in just over three weeks, losing some 5,000 men as casualties and stragglers. Arriving on January 11, 1809, exhausted, but still a fighting force, they found no transports to receive them. Only supply and hospital ships swung at anchor in the harbor. Adverse winds had delayed the transports at Vigo. Accordingly Moore prepared to hold until his ships could reach him. Deprived of naval gunfire support, he knew he might have to withstand siege. Some faint-hearted officers urged him to treat with Marshal Soult, who was closing in on him with 50,000 men, for a negotiated evacuation. But Moore, realizing that he had nothing to offer for negotiation, rejected the proposal, which would have amounted to surrender. At length, on January 14, the missing transports arrived, escorted by twelve of the line. Moore immediately evacuated the rest of his sick and wounded, and on the 16th fought and defeated Soult's advance force of 20,000. He lost his life in the battle, but his army escaped after a brilliant rearguard action. His campaign and retreat, disaster though they seemed, proved advantageous to England. It was Napoleon who ultimately lost. Instead of planting his eagles in Lisbon, the Emperor returned to France, recognizing that the moment had been lost through his fruitless pursuit of Moore. Thus England's foothold at Lisbon had been preserved, and her army was available to fight another day. Once again sea power had taken troops to the scene of action and pulled them out when they had to be evacuated.

Aix Roads, April 11, 1809

While Moore's veterans were recuperating in England from their Spanish ordeal, the Ad-

miralty noted that Napoleon's fleet was again growing. Ten ships were in service in the Scheldt, while another dozen or so were building at Antwerp and Flushing. As always, there remained the Brest fleet. Although direct invasion was no longer a danger, Ireland remained a likely objective. The escape of the Brest fleet under Rear Admiral Jean Baptiste Willaumez in February 1809 caused anxious moments in London. At length Willaumez's ten ships were discovered in Aix Roads near Rochefort. The blockading fleet under Lord Gambier at once closed in. But this time the Admiralty determined to end once for all the menace of the Brest fleet. They dispatched a colorful young Scottish naval officer, Captain Lord Thomas Cochrane, with special instructions to destroy or force the sortie of the French fleet by means of fireships. Although Gambier disapproved of Cochrane and his methods, he had to allow the attack.

Admiral Allemand, who had replaced Willaumez, realized that he was about to receive a fireship attack and made preparations to repel it at anchor. He bent his best efforts to reducing the risk of fire by having all ships strike topgallant and topmasts and send below all unneeded sails and cordage, and to be in readiness to get under way immediately if the occasion arose.

On the night of April 11, the weather dark and stormy, Cochrane's force started in, Cochrane leading in a vessel packed with 1,500 barrels of gunpowder. Behind came 19 fireships and two other ships laden with explosives. Although many of the fireships, stopped by an unsuspected, anchored boom, were ignited prematurely, the effect on the French was tremendous. By morning, all of the French ships were aground. Thus the attack, while it had not destroyed the fleet, had rendered it defenseless against the attack by ships of the line Cochrane now proposed. Gambier refused. Repeated signals brought nothing. Then Cochrane perceived that the French ships were being refloated and took his frigate *Impérieuse* to upset the salvage operations. He engaged the ship *Calcutta*, which soon struck her colors. This action apparently nettled Gambier, who at length dispatched three ships to take a hand. The reinforcements together with Cochrane's frigates accounted for three more

French ships of the line. The remainder made good their escape to Charente.

On their return to England, Cochrane angrily demanded the court-martial of Gambier. All that resulted was Gambier's honorable acquittal and the ruin of Cochrane's career, which deprived the navy of the services of a brilliant but erratic officer.

The Walcheren Expedition, 1809

Early in April 1809 Austria rose from the grave that had been dug for her at Tilsit, renounced the Treaty of Pressburg, and declared war on France. On learning this, the British made two major decisions. One proved abortive, but the other led to the ultimate triumph. With the second of these—to hold Portugal in order to strike at the French in Spain—we will presently be concerned. First we must look at the other, a plan to support Austria by hitting at Napoleon from the rear. The British thought they saw their opportunity at Walcheren, an island controlling the entrances to the Scheldt. By capturing Walcheren they hoped to be in a position to destroy a small French fleet in the river and also cause Napoleon to turn about to succor Antwerp.

Mindful of the fate of other expeditions where insufficient force had been provided, the British government assembled 40,000 troops for the assault on Walcheren. Ready to carry them were nearly 400 transports to be escorted by 37 ships of the line and over 160 lesser warships. The naval commander, Rear Admiral Sir Richard Strachan, flew his flag in the *Venerable*, 74. The troop commander, Lieutenant General the Earl of Chatham, had been appointed to lead the expedition in order to groom him for a ministerial position. He was noted for his leisureliness in an age that cultivated leisure. The expedition, on the contrary, demanded speed.

The orders for the operation failed to specify its purpose clearly. They provided for "the capture or destruction of the enemy's ships either building at Antwerp and Flushing or afloat in the Scheldt, the destruction of arsenals and dockyards at Antwerp, Terneuse, and Flushing, the reduction of the island of Walcheren and the rendering, if possible, the Scheldt no longer navigable for ships of war." Yet, if the

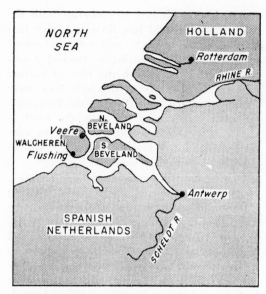

THE WALCHEREN EXPEDITION, 1809

desired diversion of Napoleon's attack on the Austrians was to be realized, nothing less than the capture of Antwerp would have served, for it guarded against any advance into either France or the Low Countries. Nor could the naval purpose well be served without the capture of Antwerp, for the ships in the Scheldt could take refuge there. As it was, the threat was useless, for while Lord Chatham dawdled in his preparations, Napoleon once again defeated the Austrians in the Battle of Wagram on July 10, 1809.

Unaware of this disaster, the British began embarking on July 20. When the news of Wagram reached them, having set their hands to the plow, they refused to abandon the expedition. The huge armada sailed on July 28, crossing so swiftly that it reached the destination area that evening. Then, while Strachan fumed at the delay, Chatham paused to consider his strategy, a process that took him three days. Admiral Missiessy promptly removed his fleet of ten ships to safety behind a boom up the river. Chatham at length decided to make the assault on Walcheren and the adjacent South Beveland Island from the north side. A force of 12,000 men under Sir Eyre Coote was safely landed on July 30 on the northwestern side of Walcheren. The force moved on to attack Veere, a strong fort commanding the passage between North Beveland and Walcheren Islands. As the troops attacked from the landward side, Sir Home Riggs Popham, with a flotilla of gunboats and bomb vessels, gave effective support from the sea. Two days later Fort Veere capitulated. The army then swung south to capture Flushing from the rear. This attack also received naval support, the climax coming on August 14, as Sir Richard Strachan, on his own responsibility, forced the Walcheren channel with seven 74's and bombarded the town. This combined army-navy assault carried the city the following day. Meanwhile another joint force had seized control of South Beveland.

Having won this far, Chatham had no plans for further action. Other than garrison troops, he had about 28,000 men at his disposal for operations against Antwerp, but his procrastination had given the French ample time to increase the defenders of the city to 35,000. Behind the boom, Missiessy's ten ships lay snug, their bare masts and yards mocking the failure of the expedition to accomplish its goals. To make matters worse, a kind of malarial fever began to attack the British troops so that soon less than half were fit for duty. Chatham, content with the destruction of the dockyards at Flushing, decided to evacuate. He attempted to keep Walcheren for a time, but soon the sickness made even this limited objective impossible. By the end of 1809, not a single British soldier remained in the Scheldt area. Procrastination, the lack of a clear-cut plan, and the fever had done their work.

Wellesley Returns to the Peninsula

In accordance with the British decision to continue operations in the Iberian Peninsula, Wellesley returned to Portugal. He went this time in undisputed command of all British forces south of the Pyrenees. His command consisted of some 20,000 British troops, 3,000 Hanoverians, and 16,000 Portuguese regulars. In their state of training, the Portuguese were more of a liability than an asset. Not even the most optimistic could have foreseen the ultimate result of Wellesley's campaign—the expulsion of the French from Portugal and Spain and the invasion of France itself—for facing him were over 250,000 French troops in various parts of the Iberian Peninsula.

As Wellesley took stock of the situation, he realized that the terrain of the Peninsula favored a strategy based on the exploitation of sea power. His own army could receive support by sea more easily than could the French through the rugged mountains of Spain. Only two roads connected France with the French headquarters in Madrid. One, along the Mediterranean coast, led from Perpignan through Barcelona, Tarragona, and Saragossa. This road could be easily interdicted by sea power and by Catalan armies. The main French supply route, then, would have to be that leading from Bayonne through Burgos to Madrid. Further, there was but one reliable route from Madrid to Lisbon—via the Merida highway south of the Tagus. Actually this road did not lead directly to Lisbon, but terminated at the south shore of the Tagus Estuary. The navy could interdict any assault from this direction. The only possible crossing was 50 miles upstream. Thus Lisbon could be made impregnable from the south, while from the east or north the natural defensive features of the Torres Vedras mountain range could well be developed into an impassable barrier running from the Tagus Estuary to the sea.

Three rivers seem to offer access from Portugal to the interior of Spain: the Guadiana, the Tagus, and the Douro. But these river valleys were nearly as impassable as the mountains through which they flowed. Only a well-trained, well-disciplined force, such as that of Moore or those of some of Napoleon's best marshals could hope to employ these difficult routes. The few frontier forts that guarded these paths afforded the keys to the Peninsula. Before Wellesley could safely advance into Spain, he needed to control Elvas and Badajoz, commanding the Merida highway, and, further north, Ciudad Rodrigo, through which passed a secondary road from Madrid to the Douro valley. If any of these were in French hands while Wellesley was in Spain, he risked having a French force get behind him to threaten Lisbon before he could retrace his steps to protect this vital base.

Landing in Lisbon late in April 1809, Wellesley had two armies opposing him. Marshal Soult at Oporto in the north commanded 23,000 veterans, while Marshal Victor with 25,000 threatened Portugal from the east. Yet the situation was not hopeless, for there was no communication between Soult and Victor. Wellesley thus had a good chance to exploit his interior position by hitting first one, then the other. He decided to strike first at Soult. Advancing to the north, Wellesley reached the south bank of the Douro on May 10 at nightfall. Then for the first time Soult realized his danger but depended on the torrent of the river, in spring flood, to protect him. His adversary however, from his wide experience in India, was an old hand at crossing rivers, and forced a passage some four miles above Oporto. Pressing the action immediately, he forced Soult to retreat into Galicia, suffering severely along the way at the hands of Portuguese and Spanish patriots. By noon on May 11, the action was over and Wellesley was sitting down to eat the dinner prepared for Soult.

On the day the news of the Douro reached England, Napoleon suffered a bloody setback at Aspern and Essling at the hands of Archduke Charles of Austria. The Emperor could ill afford to spare attention for Spain. Thus Wellesley was able to turn his thoughts to driving into the heart of the Peninsula and carrying out his orders to cooperate with the Spaniards. But before he dared leave Portugal he had to see to the safety of Lisbon. To do so he determined to build the Portuguese army into a fighting force. Hence he assigned British commissioned and non-commissioned officers to provide sound discipline and training to his allies, who had never received either. Then on May 7, 1809, he began the advance into Spain to concert operations with 70-year-old Captain-General Don Gregoria de la Cuesta. Cuesta had the idea of encircling Victor's 25,000 and driving for Madrid. At first success rewarded this effort, but on July 28 the French counterattacked near Talavera, 65 miles southwest of Madrid. Cuesta's routed troops proving no help, Wellesley realized that he had to extricate himself by his own endeavors. In a brilliant action he cleared his opposition and, refusing to listen to the Quixotic proposals of the mercurial Cuesta, resolutely began his retreat to Portugal. Twice now an English army had nearly met with disaster in the effort to cooperate with the Spaniards. Henceforth, Wellesley determined, he would operate on his own. Withdrawing to the mountains,

Wellesley, who had been created Viscount Wellington for his victory at Talavera but damned for his retreat, went into winter quarters at Badajoz. He realized that the French would employ the year 1810 in an effort to drive him into the sea.

The Lines of Torres Vedras

Since the army Wellington commanded was yet too weak to force a decision in Spain, he realized that he must secure his base at Lisbon from any French attack. As we have seen, the city was impregnable from the south so long as the British had a naval force available for its defense. He determined to make it so from the east and the north. In October 1809 he gave the order for three main defensive lines to be built in the Torres Vedras range, an enormous labor of constructing some 50 miles of trenches, breastworks, and redoubts. Thousands of Portuguese workmen labored at this gigantic task. The result of these labors were the celebrated Lines of Torres Vedras, truly impregnable to an army of that day.

In 1810, as Wellington had foreseen, the French counterattack developed. Napoleon, reluctant to leave Paris in the face of resurgent Austria and growing peril in the north, entrusted the campaign against Lisbon to his most experienced commander, Marshal Masséna. In August Masséna took the field against Wellington. Abandoning his mountain position, Wellington fell back to the west. His demands were harsh. Behind him he expected the Portuguese to destroy their crops, their livestock, their houses, everything that might provide the French with subsistence. He expected the British Cabinet to support his retreat, which seemed to abandon everything with nothing to show in return. He sacrificed all that he had gained and the livelihoods of thousands of Portuguese patriots to lead Masséna into a death trap. En route he met his adversary in a brief engagement in late September 1810, and then retreated to his prepared position behind the Lines of Torres Vedras, the French pursuing in high spirits, for they believed the victory was won. Then Masséna saw the Torres Vedras defenses. After one probing attack, he realized that a serious attempt to penetrate these thousands of trenches, palisades, parapets, and redoubts could only result in the slaughter of his troops. He therefore settled down to a siege.

The strength of the defenses of Torres Vedras was only one jaw of the death-trap Wellington had prepared for the French. As Masséna awaited his opportunity, the other jaw closed. Wellington's scorched earth policy had deprived the French of subsistence. Even French armies, masters at living off the land and at the expense of unwilling hosts, could find little of the necessities of life. As Masséna's men ate their pack animals, Wellington's army grew stronger, for it was amply supplied by regular convoys from home. Sea power enabled one army to wax strong while another, almost within eyesight, starved to impotence.

In November Masséna retreated to Santarem and in March to Ciudad Rodrigo. He had lost 27,000 men in seven months. The moral effect of his defeat spread throughout Europe. Napoleon had vowed to "drive the leopard into the sea" and had failed miserably. The French retreat from Torres Vedras was the beginning of the long road through Spain to France itself.

On to France

The next two years mark Wellington's attempts to open the doorways to Spain. French forces scattered throughout the Peninsula could annihilate him if he made a false move. Carefully, husbanding his strength, Wellington in 1811 probed at Ciudad Rodrigo and at Badajoz, taking advantage of the rivers for supply. It was no use. The French, in spite of their logistic weaknesses, were too strong. Wellington fell back to gather strength from the sea, while amphibious British raids and Spanish guerrilla attacks weakened the French. In 1812 Wellington tried again, seizing Ciudad Rodrigo and Badajoz in the early months of the year. In August he captured Madrid, rendering southern Spain untenable for the French. Then he made a serious error. Attempting to take Burgos, the key to French land communications in northern Spain, he failed to arrange adequate supplies for his forces. With three French armies closing in on him, he abandoned both Madrid and the Burgos siege and retreated to Ciudad Rodrigo to await the next year's campaigning season.

In 1813 Wellington began the decisive offensive in Spain. Bypassing Burgos and outflanking the French armies, he reached the Pyrenees. This was made possible for him by utilizing the sea for a complete logistic reorientation. He moved his seaport base from Lisbon to Santander on the Bay of Biscay, practically on the battlefield. At the Battle of Vittoria in June the French were to all intents and purposes driven out of Spain. Wellington refused to follow until he had protected his flanks by taking San Sebastian and Pamplona. This precaution consumed four months, but when it was accomplished Wellington pushed into France with confidence. Marshal Soult, recalled to oppose him, retreated slowly on Toulouse, which fell to the British on April 11, 1814. That same day, Napoleon, surrounded by hostile armies, was forced to abdicate.

Thus ended the greatest of amphibious wars before the modern period. It had made Napoleon vulnerable by sapping his strength—"the running sore," he called it. Nearly a quarter million veteran soldiers had been tied down in the Peninsula by a numerically inferior enemy who was able to exploit the advantages of sea power. In the decisive German campaign of 1813, the Emperor had had to make do with raw conscripts. The hardened legions of Soult might have enabled him to force a drawn peace.

The Baltic Campaign and the Invasion of Russia, 1809–1812

We have already noted how the Lisbon fissure in the Continental Blockade against British goods led to the operations just described. We must now turn our attention to the north, and back in time to the period following the British bombardment of Copenhagen in 1807. Denmark entered the Napoleonic camp, but neutral Sweden provided a northern door into the Continent for British trade and permitted British ships to enter the Baltic. This was a gap in the Continental Blockade that the Emperor was determined to close.

To Britain the navigation of the Baltic was essential, for here lay her chief source of timber, hemp, and tar. British statesmen therefore sought to maintain the freest trade relations

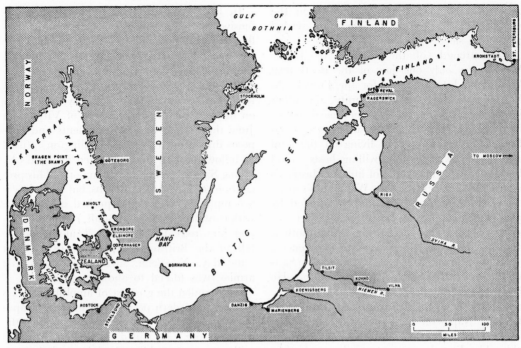

THE BALTIC AND ITS APPROACHES

with Sweden, or at least engage her benevolent neutrality. Since Sweden could be successfully invaded only from the sea, her defense became the mission of the Royal Navy. Swedish policy however did not depend alone on the security of the homeland, for she had possessions across the Baltic in Pomerania which Napoleon could threaten, and across the Gulf of Bothnia the Swedish province of Finland lay open to the encroachments of Russia. Early in 1808 the Czar moved against Finland. At the same time, a French army under Marshal Bernadotte threatened to bring Sweden completely within the Napoleonic orbit.

The British at once dispatched Sir John Moore with 10,000 troops to cooperate with the Swedes. The Royal Navy quickly established naval superiority in the Baltic, but the Swedes, to avoid open rupture with France, refused to permit Moore's men to disembark. After three months spent cooped up in their ships off Göteborg, Moore and his men departed for home—and the Peninsula.

With rare diplomatic skill, Vice Admiral Sir James Saumarez, commanding the Baltic fleet, permitted Sweden to give the appearance of an alliance with Napoleon while keeping her

ports open to the British. His principal task was to keep Baltic trade moving until winter ice closed shipping. A division of ships of the line blockaded the Russian squadron at Kronstadt. The main body of the fleet held the Sound against Bernadotte's passage and furnished merchant vessels with protection against the privateers and gunboats of the vengeful Danes. Paying lip service to Sweden's neutrality, Saumarez sheltered his fleet in the international waters of Hanö Bay and obtained provisions from the Island of Bornholm. At an island in the Kattegat the British established a fortress and another fleet base, which enabled them to keep a close watch on Zealand and the Danish mainland. By 1810 some 2,000 merchant ships were entering the Baltic annually—British ships freely, neutral ships under British license.

Napoleon had meanwhile left Spain to subordinates and turned his attention to Northern Europe. He forced Sweden to declare war on England. But Britain, not the Emperor, controlled the Baltic seaways. Sweden's new king, Napoleon's former marshal, Bernadotte, conceived his duty to lie with his adopted country rather than with his former master. Saumarez, remembering that the real enemy was France, gave Sweden a way out. He and Bernadotte reached an agreement by which Saumarez respected Swedish trade, while the Swedes enforced the prohibition on British trade in fortified ports only.

Napoleon's troubles with the Baltic trade did not stop with Sweden. The Czar saw piling up in his ports the raw materials he had promised not to sell to Britain. Since France could not supply the manufactured goods his people most needed, he had to look elsewhere. To prevent Russian gold from swelling French coffers, he imposed a tariff on French goods of all sorts. At the same time he began to wink at the smuggling of British goods and freely allowed neutral ships to bring British colonial produce to Russia. Napoleon, rather than see his blockade thus ignored, threatened war. An uneasy truce continued throughout 1811, with neither side willing to back down. Czar Alexander, encouraged by Wellington's limited successes in the Peninsula, especially by his Fabian tactics in the retreat to Torres Vedras, remained defiant. But with Wellington sealed up behind Badajoz and Ciudad Rodrigo, Napoleon considered the Spanish problem to be well in hand. He determined accordingly to turn the power of his seven kingdoms and 30 principalities on Russia. In East Prussia and the Duchy of Warsaw he assembled 427,000 troops from France, the Rhine Confederacy, and Italy. Sixty thousand Poles joined his banner in order to reunite their country, providing him with a large proportion of his cavalry. An Austrian army of 30,000 covered the southern flank. On June 23, 1812, the vanguard of the Grand Army crossed the Niemen River, Russia's boundary with Poland. In all, some 600,000 men plunged into the vastness of the Russian plains.

To open the lower Dvina River and to insure a water-borne logistic line, Napoleon sent Marshal Macdonald's mixed force of French and Prussians against Riga. They virtually starved before its fortifications while the Russian defenders drew supplies and reinforcements from Finland by sea. Raiding Macdonald's lines of support, 102 Russian and eight British gunboats cut his logistic reserve to nothing. Meanwhile Rear Admiral Sir Thomas Byam Martin made feint landings near Danzig and elsewhere to contain local garrisons and to force Macdonald to divert strength from Riga. In August Macdonald withdrew.

Napoleon's strategy was characteristic of the man. He maneuvered to force the Russian army into a decisive battle which would end the war with a single blow. This he had done at Friedland the last time he faced Russia. In 1812 however Czar Alexander's generals counseled a policy of retreat and scorched earth. The Czar's especial defense plan had certain similarities to Wellington's at Torres Vedras. The strong defensive Drissa Line and the scorched earth were similar, but he also planned to use part of his army to attack Napoleon's rear. Against the Emperor such tactics were nearly fatal, for the master of mobile war succeeded in getting between parts of the Russian army and threatened to defeat them in detail. Also the Drissa Line, unlike Torres Vedras, had no secure flanks. The Russian armies barely extricated themselves in time. Then, inflicting heavy losses on Napoleon in defensive battles at Vitebsk, Smolensk, and Borodino, they withdrew to Moscow—and beyond, leaving their capital in flames rather than provide Napoleon with anything he might use. The French reached Moscow on September 14, low on provisions with none to be had, and faced with an enemy still intact and strong. Napoleon now found his expectations confounded; Moscow was not the heart of Russia; the stroke was not fatal. Then came the news that Wellington had taken Madrid. After waiting for five weeks for a Russian surrender that never came, and with disaster facing him to the north and south, the Emperor on October 18 gave the order for the fatal retreat.

The Grand Army was shortly overwhelmed, partially by the winter weather, partially by its opponents, who seldom gave battle but never lost contact, even more by its own indiscipline in retreat, but most of all by the disaster which overtook its logistics. Before launching his Russian campaign, Napoleon had stripped Northern Europe of foodstuffs. He could not however take with him the fodder needed for the animals that hauled his provisions. What little fodder the Russians had left behind he had used on the way to Moscow. There was none for the retreat. Both men and animals faced starvation. The resulting losses were appalling. Large scale straggling and the spirit of *sauve qui peut* destroyed all organization as the army vainly sought to live off the denuded countryside. Only by water, the sea and the rivers, could the Grand Army obtain the needed quantities of provisions and supplies. Now the consequences of Macdonald's failure lay starkly revealed. Some two million pairs of boots for his barefoot army were stored at Napoleon's principal base of Danzig. There they stayed, for Russian, Swedish, and British patrol ships blocked all coastal communication from Danzig to the rivers.

The Russian campaign ended in the middle of December 1812. Of the 600,000 men who had entered Russia in June, only 20,000 half-frozen scarecrows stumbled back across the Niemen. Alexander, pressing close behind, summond allies to pursue the French across the Elbe. In March 1813, Prussia cast off the shackles that had bound her to Napoleon. Bernadotte, too, turned on his former master and in May landed with an army at Straslund. In July, Austria joined the new alliance. Taking care first to clear up conflicting territorial claims, the Allies entered into the firmest compact Europe had ever known. Each signatory pledged in effect to war to the death with Napoleon wherever he might be. As before, British subsidies, made possible by the wealth derived from maritime commerce, cemented this Fourth Coalition. Unity at last achieved, the Allies seized the initiative, which this time they never relinquished.

The Triumph of Coalition Warfare

Not even Napoleon's genius sufficed to bring victory in the two-front war now facing him. Wellington's advance through Spain in 1813 brought the French to a crisis in the south. Soult, dispatched to retrieve the situation in Spain, accomplished little, while he tied up in the Pyrenees 150,000 French troops that might have been better used in the decisive area in Saxony. Napoleon, having returned to Paris after a second time deserting an army in the east, worked miracles in raising new levies. In August he turned upon his adversaries and defeated them at Dresden. Still the Allies came on relentlessly. In September at

Leipzig he won again, but it was his last effective victory. Outnumbered two-to-one, he could no longer replace losses. In the spring of 1814 the armies of Russia, Prussia, and Austria closed on Paris as Wellington entered Toulouse. Exhausted in resource, in body, and in spirit, Napoleon abdicated on April 11, 1814 and was exiled to the Island of Elba.

While the representatives of the victorious powers assembled at the Congress of Vienna, while the restored Bourbons sought to re-establish the *ancien régime*, while the rivalries of peace replaced the solidarity of the preceding year, Europe was shaken to its foundations by the escape of the ex-Emperor from Elba and his landing in France on March 1, 1815. Quickly setting quarrels aside, the delegates outlawed Napoleon and pledged themselves to settle the Corsican ogre once and for all. The well prepared British and Prussian armies under over-all command of the Duke of Wellington took position across Belgium while the larger masses of Russia and Austria advanced slowly westward toward Alsace and Lorraine.

Napoleon, rallying an army of 200,000, planned to strike successively against the divided Allies. He turned first toward Belgium to cut Wellington off from the Prussians under Blücher. The fighting was markedly reminiscent of the Peninsular battles. Wellington held his thin lines in check until they had broken the massed French troops. Blücher arrived in time to complete the rout. In Wellington Napoleon had at last met his master. The Battle of Waterloo on June 18, 1815 saved Europe from further bloodshed, for the Allies were organized and overwhelmingly superior. The end of the "Hundred Days" found the ex-Emperor prostrate once again.

A month later the man who had held Europe at his feet but who had never understood sea power surrendered, appropriately enough, to a unit of the force that had made his defeat possible. Boarding H.M.S. *Bellerophon* off the Isle of Aix, he was received with no ceremony. "General Bonaparte" gave himself into the hands of the one nation that had opposed him throughout. This time there would be no return. His new place of exile was St. Helena in the South Atlantic. There on May 5, 1821 he died, uncomprehending to the last how he, the greatest military leader Europe had ever produced, leading the largest armies the world had ever seen, had been defeated by "the nation of shopkeepers," whose strength lay in their ability to use the sea.

Summary

In their 22-year struggle against France and her allies, the British began with two advantages they had not enjoyed in the War of the American Revolution: (1) the French navy was undermined by bankruptcy, egalitarianism, and the loss of its royalist officer corps, and (2) Britain had powerful allies on the Continent. The strategic situation in 1793 thus more closely resembled that of 1756 than that of 1778. Hence William Pitt the Younger and his cabinet reverted to the strategy of William Pitt the Elder—using naval power to seize the enemy's colonies and commerce as a means of earning income to subsidize European allies. Pitt's Plan however did not again yield the decisive results it had won for England in the Seven Years' War. Among the numerous reasons, two stand out. The first was disunity among the Allies. In the Wars of the French Revolution and Empire (or, more briefly, the Napoleonic Wars), France's enemies failed time and again to cooperate, repeatedly putting national objectives above common objectives. Three successive coalitions raised up against France fell apart, leaving Britain each time to face the enemy alone. Only the Fourth Coalition achieved the coherence and common purpose needed to attain victory. A second reason for the failures of the coalitions was inferiority of leadership. While the admirals of the Royal Navy proved themselves among the ablest in history, no counterpart of Frederick the Great appeared among Britain's allies. France, on the contrary, produced a galaxy of brilliant generals and military organizers, the brightest of whom was the incomparable Napoleon Bonaparte. After 1799 Bonaparte, as First Consul and then as Emperor, took the war against the coalitions into his own hands and humbled enemy after enemy—all except England.

French strategy against Britain sought to destroy her will to fight. If France controlled all Europe, Britain would have to trade on French terms or not at all. Thus the French believed they could bring Britain to heel without fighting her directly. But as Britain's overseas trade expanded while France's diminished, as British sea power made its weight felt around the periphery of Europe, and as British gold more and more subsidized the armies of France's enemies, the French set out to conquer Britain by invasion. The Royal Navy frustrated all such attempts. Even when France was at the apex of power, controlling the combined fleets of Europe, England stood impregnable. Napoleon, the master of land warfare, had too little understanding of the sea to develop the means of projecting his legions safely across the Channel. At length he abandoned his attempts and embarked upon the all-out economic warfare that proved his undoing. In the metaphor of the day, the Elephant could never come to grips with the Whale.

In the War of the First Coalition (1793-97), the Royal Navy early demonstrated its superiority by defending the coasts of Britain, protecting British commerce, blockading France, and defeating the French Brest fleet in the Battle of the First of June (1794). But the British army did poorly. Pitt, underestimating the enemy, had brought it up to barely 29,000 troops. These he fragmented in several simultaneous operations. As a result the British were repulsed from footholds in the Netherlands and at Toulon, and made little progress in the French West Indies, where native populations took up arms against them. At the beginning of 1797 Britain's fortunes were apparently approaching their nadir. Spain's new alliance with France and Bonaparte's drive into Italy had forced the British out of the Mediterranean. The French Directory was planning an invasion of England supported by the combined fleets of Holland, France, and Spain. Bonaparte broke up the First Coalition by forcing Austria out of the war, but Britain was preserved by her Royal Navy. The French invasion plan was foiled by Jervis's victory over the Spanish fleet in the Battle of Cape St. Vincent (February 1797) and Duncan's victory over the Dutch fleet in the Battle of Camperdown (October 1797).

The War of the Second Coalition (1798-1802) was brought about by the failure of a renewed French attempt to come to grips with Britain. Bonaparte, entrusted with the project, chose to strike at the British Empire by leading an army against India via Egypt. The attempt, requiring him to use the sea, proved disastrous, for Nelson shattered the Toulon fleet at the Battle of the Nile (August 1798), thereby isolating Bonaparte and his army in Egypt. This reversal of French fortunes encouraged Austria, Russia, and other powers to join Britain in the Second Coalition. As before, England's contribution was to subsidize her continental allies, control the sea, blockade enemy ports, and strike around the edges of the enemy's European position and at his overseas possessions. In invading the Helder (1799), Britain improved her sea power situation by capturing the remains of the Dutch fleet. But neither this nor other British invasions along Europe's Atlantic coast achieved lasting footholds or succeeded in diverting appreciable French forces from contact with the Austro-Russian armies pressing upon France's eastern border. As in the First Coalition, the allied powers failed to cooperate effectively. Quarreling over objectives, the Russian and Austrian armies drew apart, and in October 1799 Russia withdrew from the war. That same month Bonaparte returned secretly to France, where he quickly assumed control as First Consul. In 1800 his armies decisively defeated the Austrians at Marengo and Hohenlinden, forcing Austria out of the war and breaking up the Second Coalition.

Once more England stood alone against the French alliance. But as before she remained inaccessible to the might of France and by virtue of her navy retained the power to strike telling blows. To improve Britain's negotiating position vis-à-vis France, Keith and Abercromby in 1801 invaded Egypt from the sea. The British army, aided by Turks and Mamelukes, defeated and evicted Bonaparte's stranded occupation forces. At the same time, Nelson destroyed the Danish fleet at Copenhagen in sharp reaction to Bonaparte's attempt to undermine British sea power through the Armed Neutrality of Baltic nations. Such British blows however were as indecisive as French efforts to dominate Britain. Deciding that, for the time at least, the problem of the Elephant and the Whale was insoluble, Britain and France signed peace preliminaries late in

1801 and the following March concluded the short-lived Peace of Amiens.

When it became apparent that Bonaparte had no intention of abiding by the terms of Amiens, Britain in 1803 again declared war on France. Bonaparte's reaction was to make all-out preparations for invasion of England. The success of Bruix and Ganteaume during the War of the Second Coalition in eluding British vigilance to bring the Brest fleet twice into the Mediterranean convinced him that with a little trickery he could bring decisive naval forces to the Channel. As part of his Grand Design, he ordered the Franco-Spanish fleets to slip past the Royal Navy's blockade and rendezvous in the Caribbean in order to attract British squadrons away from Europe. The Combined Fleet was then to return to the Channel to cover the crossing of French troops based on Boulogne. In the spring of 1805, the Toulon fleet under Villeneuve did in fact elude Nelson's blockade, picked up Spanish ships at Cadiz, and crossed to the West Indies. The approach of Nelson in pursuit however induced Villeneuve to head back for Europe. Off Finisterre, the French admiral was discouraged by an indecisive brush with a British fleet under Calder. Instead of advancing to the Channel, Villeneuve retired into port. When Napoleon drove him out again, Nelson, on October 21, 1805, smashed his Combined Fleet off Cadiz in the Battle of the Trafalgar.

Meanwhile, Pitt had raised up still another coalition on the Continent. Bonaparte, now the Emperor Napoleon, had concluded even before Trafalgar that his fleets would not attain the concentration he needed to support an invasion of Britain. So he turned to meet the new threat in his rear, thereby precipitating the War of the Third Coalition (1805-7). Using the army he had trained to conquer England, Napoleon in 1805 drove Austria a third time out of the war by victories at Ulm and Austerlitz. In 1806 he defeated the Prussian armies at Jena and Auerstadt. In the middle of 1807 his victory over the Russians at Friedland induced the Czar to sign the Peace of Tilsit, whereby France and Russia agreed to carve up the world between them. The Third Coalition thus came to an end, and Britain was again without effective allies.

After Trafalgar, while Napoleon was bringing the Continent under his sway, the British used their sea power to send expeditions against the Cape Colony, Buenos Aires, southern Italy, and Constantinople. The Peace of Tilsit spurred them into vigorous action nearer home. To prevent Napoleon from re-assembling a navy, they bombarded Copenhagen in 1807 and seized the Danish fleet. In 1809 they attacked Aix Roads with fireships, forcing 13 French ships of the line ashore and capturing four. Later that year, a British expeditionary force captured Walcheren Island in the mouth of the Scheldt and held it for several months. Such operations irritated Napoleon but could not bring about a decision in Europe, where there were no armies adequate to cope with the French legions. Briefly in 1809 Austria had returned to the attack only to be forced out of the war a fourth time by defeat in the Battle of Wagram.

Unable to strike effectively at Britain by military means, Napoleon began putting greater emphasis upon economic warfare. By his Continental System he undertook to exclude Britain from the trade of the Continent. By his Berlin Decree, he unrealistically declared the British Isles to be blockaded. Britain countered with Orders in Council declaring all French-controlled ports blockaded. Napoleon replied with the Milan Decree, outlawing neutral ships that complied with the Orders in Council. To enforce his decrees on the high seas, Napoleon could only release a swarm of privateers that proved a nuisance but could not greatly curtail Britain's expanding maritime commerce. His economic warfare did however force Britain into ever-increasing strictures against neutral shipping that in 1812 impelled the United States to declare war on her—at a time when the British could little afford to divert strength to deal with an additional enemy.

On the other hand, the Continental System ruined Napoleon. The countries of Europe, geared to the British economy, were impoverished without British trade. The good will Napoleon had garnered as the self-styled defender of the rights of man was lost as his decrees denied the Europeans the necessities of life. Attempts to enforce his System brought him into wars in the Iberian Peninsula and on the plains of Russia that swallowed up his armies. His attempts also provided the British Whale with the opportunity to come ashore at long last in the guise of a Lion.

Preparatory to closing the ports of Portugal, which provided a gap in his Continental System, Napoleon seized control of Spain. He thereby set off a Spanish rebellion that he was never able to subdue. Britain, responding to the pleas of the Portuguese and the Spaniards, in 1808 put an army into the Iberian Peninsula. Repulsed under Moore, it returned under Wellington, the general with the professional skill needed to defeat Napoleon. During the Peninsular War, which continued until 1814, the Royal Navy at length found its true function in the post-Trafalgar struggle—supplying and reinforcing British and allied troops by sea more efficiently than the French could supply their own forces overland through guerrilla-controlled Spain.

While Britain and her Iberian allies exploited the advantages of sea power to contain nearly a quarter million of Napoleon's veteran troops, Russia more and more ignored the Continental System. Napoleon threatened war but the Czar, heartened by Wellington's success, remained defiant. In June 1812, the Emperor invaded Russia with 600,000 troops. He reached and occupied Moscow but, cut off from supplies and surrounded by scorched earth and an army that raided but would not commit itself to pitched battle, he was obliged to retreat through winter weather across the denuded Russian countryside. Only 20,000 of his troops survived the retreat.

Napoleon's setbacks in Spain and Russia encouraged Prussia, Sweden, and Austria to join Russia and Britain in the War of the Fourth Coalition (1813-15). The Fourth Coalition, at length realizing the necessity, achieved the coordination and unity of objective so conspicuously wanting in the earlier anti-French alliances. Despite setbacks and defeats, the allied armies relentlessly pushed into France, forcing the Emperor to abdicate in April 1814. His return from exile the following year found the Coalition unshaken. In June 1815, Napoleon was finally defeated at the Battle of Waterloo by the armies of Britain and Prussia.

The Napoleonic Wars taught the Royal Navy the lesson it had long practiced in smaller-scale colonial operations—that a navy exists not only to protect trade, to throw back invasion attempts, to blockade the enemy, and to destroy the enemy's ships and commerce; it exists also to project and support decisive military power beyond the seas. To carry out this function it must coordinate operations so closely with the army that the two services act as a single unit. The Allies learned that the essence of coalition warfare is cooperation. Anything less than the closest coordination in the face of a powerful and skillful foe merely invites defeat in detail. Only when the powers of Europe attained unity in their objectives as close as that attained in the joint operations of Britain's army and navy were they able at last to topple the Corsican from his throne.

10:

The Beginnings of the United States Navy

While France and Britain together with their various allies were struggling for mastery in Europe, the United States Navy came into being. During the 22 years of the Napoleonic Wars, the new navy three times engaged in extended hostilities. These wars established precedents, good and bad, reflecting the enduring strengths and weaknesses of American democracy. They formed the traditions and professional attitudes of a navy destined to become the world's most powerful. The history of the origin and early development of the United States Navy throws a revealing light on American concern with naval power and the contributions of the Navy to the national welfare.

A Decade Without a Navy

At the end of the War of the American Revolution in 1783, the weak central government of the United States had to deal with the problems of debt and depression without having the power to tax. In the circumstances, Congress concluded that the Continental Navy was an expendable luxury and ordered it disbanded. By 1785 all United States warships had been sold.

Officers and men of the Continental Navy returned to their peacetime pursuits in merchant shipping, but they soon found that in gaining independence they had forfeited the privileges they had enjoyed as British subjects. Freedom carried a price tag. Before the Revolution, American merchantmen had been major carriers for the British Empire. Fully a third of their trade had been with the West Indies, where the slave labor economy depended on continental North America for its basic foodstuffs. Colonial shipbuilders, profiting by the competitive advantage of ample timber reserves, had by the eve of the Revolution built a third of Britain's merchant ships. With American independence these sources of income were wiped out as Britain took measures to exclude her former colonies from the carrying trade within what remained of her empire. Applying the Navigation Acts to the United States, the London government issued an Order in Council that barred Americans from the British West Indies trade. Further Orders prohibited British subjects from purchasing American-built ships and severely restricted the British market for American exports carried in American bottoms.

The British restrictions, breaking up old patterns of trade, had a devastating effect on American maritime commerce. For the United States merchant marine to survive, it would have to find new markets. In search of business a few hardy Yankee skippers early found their way to China; others sought new European contacts. On the high seas the Americans found what it meant to be no longer under the protection of the British flag. The China trade proved financially hazardous but not nearly so dangerous as commerce with southern Europe. For in the Mediterranean and outside the Straits piracy existed on a scale then unmatched anywhere in the world. United States vessels had now become fair game for the Barbary corsairs operating off the North African coast.

Capture of merchantmen was part of the notorious Barbary System, which extended back to medieval times. In the 18th century the

Barbary states—Morocco, Algiers, Tunis, and Tripoli—were ruled by petty despots and loosely held in the Ottoman Empire by a kind of feudal allegiance. For all of them piracy, ransom of captives, and tribute were major sources of income. Seafaring nations could purchase immunity for their merchantmen by paying a monetary tribute. Even Britain, France, and Holland, with navies powerful enough to smash the pirate nests, paid the required protection money, partly because it was cheaper and less troublesome than going to war and partly because the System hampered commercial rivals. Ships of nations too poor to pay, and lacking power to retaliate, were liable to capture whenever they entered waters patrolled by the corsairs.

In 1784 the Moroccans seized an American ship. The following year the Algerians captured two more and enslaved the crews. Morocco in 1786 sold the United States a treaty of immunity at the bargain price of $10,000, but Algiers could not be bought off so cheaply. Rebuffed, Thomas Jefferson, then Minister to France, called for a United States Navy and a naval war on the Barbary powers. "We could not begin it in a better cause," said he, "nor against a weaker foe." Cynical London merchants meanwhile were only too happy to see growing American competition checked by Algiers. "If there were no Algiers," Benjamin Franklin reported them as saying, "it would be worth England's while to build one."

The humiliation of the Barbary captures had at least the good effect of providing an additional argument supporting advocates of a stronger central government. George Washington, who had learned to appreciate naval power during the American Revolution, was among those favoring a new federal government and the navy it would make possible. The desire for naval protection, particularly among the influential commercial classes, had a perceptible effect on the adoption of the Constitution in 1789. That year, which saw the establishment of the federal government of the United States, is memorable also as marking the outbreak of the French Revolution. Each was to exert a decisive influence on the development of American naval policy and of the United States Navy.

Under the Constitution, Congress was not only authorized "to provide and maintain a navy" but at last had the power to finance it through taxation. Naval appropriations however had to await the settling of more pressing problems, particularly the national debt. Political pressure for a fleet had diminished because war between Portugal and Algiers had sealed the corsairs in the Mediterranean, where American merchantmen could join a Spanish or Portuguese convoy.

The United States merchant marine now began to prosper. The first act of the new federal government established a revenue-raising tariff that gave American merchants preferential treatment and froze European ships out of the American tea trade. Further acts specified that United States citizens were to pay only 20 per cent of the tonnage duty charged foreigners. At the same time West Indian planters, who had seen thousands of their slaves starve when American cattle, fish, and grain had been cut off, welcomed brigs and schooners from the United States that arrived for trade in defiance of the British Orders in Council. Even the London government, perceiving the necessity, chose to wink at this profitable smuggling. Thus encouraged, American shipping and shipbuilding boomed. In the first five years under the Constitution, United States merchant tonnage rose from 124,000 to 439,000 tons. In the same period imports carried in American ships jumped from 17.5 to 91 per cent of the total; exports, from 30 to 86 per cent of the total.

Under the new government, naval affairs were administered by the Secretary of War, General Henry Knox. As early as 1790 Knox, citing the continued enslavement of Americans by Algiers, requested the first estimates for a seagoing navy. Opposition in Congress however forced a suspension of all naval shipbuilding plans until 1793. Two events that year put an entirely new complexion on the matter. A truce between Portugal and Algiers permitted a corsair fleet to sail out into the Atlantic, where it promptly captured ten American ships. France's declaration of war on Britain, Holland, and Spain imposed increasingly severe restrictions on neutral carriers. New British Orders in Council authorized stopping all neutral ships taking foodstuffs to France and all ships trading with the French West Indies, which had recently been thrown open to American trade. Retaliatory measures by the French government and captures of American merchantmen by French privateers aggravated the situation. Thus spurred, the United States Congress turned to serious consideration of establishing a navy.

The Navy Act of 1794

The move at last to build a navy brought to the fore the conflict of beliefs and interests that had appeared as early as the debate over the ratification of the Constitution. Favoring the creation of a United States Navy were the Federalists, led by President Washington's Secretary of the Treasury, Alexander Hamilton, and representing mainly the commercial interests of the Northeast. These were willing and anxious to protect their lucrative trade with the use of armed force. Their fondest hope was for a squadron of ships of the line which, together with frigates and sloops-of-war, could not only protect commerce but challenge any detachment a foreign navy was likely to venture in American waters. Because 90 per cent of American foreign trade was with Britain, the Federalists saw the proposed United States naval power as chiefly useful for halting French interference. In their public statements however they spoke mainly of the Algerian insult, which continued to rankle among the American people.

Opposing the Federalists were the Republicans,[1] representing the artisans and landholders of the South and inland districts and headed by Secretary of State Thomas Jefferson, who had shifted his ground regarding the need for a navy. The Republicans were embittered by British-inspired Indian raids, sympathetic with the French, and essentially isolationist. To them a navy was aristocratic, imperialistic, and so expensive as to imperil the national economy. They argued moreover that the creation of a navy would mean taxing the whole country for the benefit of New England merchants and shippers. They proposed, as safer and cheaper measures, continuing diplomatic protests, paying tribute to the

[1] Not to be confused with the present Republican Party of the United States, which is a lineal descendant of Hamilton's Federalist Party.

Barbary states, and subsidizing a European navy to protect American trade.

With lines so sharply drawn and debate over the issues raging in and out of Congress, the best legislation the Federalists could get passed was embodied in the Navy Act of May 27, 1794. The bill provided for a navy of six frigates "by purchase or otherwise." It carried a cancellation clause in event of peace with Algiers. Inadequate as the Act was in the opinion of most Federalists, it established the United States Navy.

The Federalists had no intention of obtaining the six frigates "by purchase." They interpreted "or otherwise" as authorizing new construction according to plans earlier worked out in Secretary Knox's War Department. To placate sectional interests, each frigate was to be built in a separate port—Portsmouth, N.H., Boston, New York, Philadelphia, Baltimore, and Norfolk—from oak, pine, and cedar cut in the Carolinas and Georgia by work gangs from New England. Other materials were to be procured so as to spread the economic advantages and political profits as widely as possible.

Knox, after correspondence with naval officers and shipbuilders of the American Revolution, had decided to interpret the word "frigate" loosely. With the Algerians in mind, he planned to build outsize 44's, able to overmatch any Barbary frigate. What he had in mind was, in fact, a new type of warship, somewhat smaller and swifter than a 64, more heavily armed than any standard frigate—capable of outrunning the one and of defeating the other. Congress approved construction of only three of this class however, specifying that the other three should be 36's.

In 1796, when work was well under way, American envoys in Algiers succeeded in getting a treaty from the Dey, at a cost of $525,000 in ransoms, a 36-gun frigate, and a $21,000 annual tribute in the form of naval stores. By law, all construction on the American warships was now to stop, but President Washington prevailed on Congress to permit completion of three of the frigates. These, launched in 1797 at Philadelphia, Baltimore, and Boston respectively, were the *United States*, 44, the *Constellation*, 36, and the *Constitution*, 44.

The plans for these vessels, incorporating

the theories and practices of many men, were worked out in accordance with War Department stipulations. Because the final designs were completed under the direction of Joshua Humphreys, a Pennsylvania shipbuilder, they are often called "Humphreys frigates." The *Constitution,* built at the cost of some $300,-000, was 175 feet over all, with a beam of 44 feet and a depth of hold of 14 feet. She was thus some 20 feet longer than British 44-gun frigates, her largest contemporaries. Her armament normally consisted of thirty 24-pounder long guns on her gun deck and twenty 32-pounder carronades on her spar deck. Her hull was "sharp" for her day, making her close-winded and fast if properly rigged and not overloaded. Her great strength derived in part from an almost complete upper deck. The *Constellation,* usually armed with twenty-eight 18-pounders on the gun deck and ten or more carronades on the spar deck, was a "reduced copy" of the *Constitution.*[2]

". . . not one cent for tribute!"

In retaliation for Britain's drastic Orders in Council of 1793, the Republicans proposed terminating all commerce with England. Hamilton, shocked at the suggestion, did his utmost to head off any such extreme measure. The financial structure of the government, his own creation, was based on revenues from trade—and most of America's trade was with England. Losses from cargo seizures were severe, he admitted, but cancellation of Anglo-American commerce would mean national bankruptcy. Partly through Hamilton's suggestion, passed quietly through diplomatic channels, the London government by late 1794 had taken a more conciliatory attitude, opening the British West Indies to American trade and indemnifying the owners of seized cargoes. The year ended with the signing of Jay's Treaty of Amity, Commerce, and Navigation, which for the next decade provided at least a *modus*

[2] Since both the armament and rigging were changed frequently by commanding officers, such details of these famous frigates varied considerably from time to time. They always however carried more than their rated number of guns. For drawings and technical data, see Howard I. Chapelle, *The History of the American Sailing Navy: The Ships and Their Development* (New York, 1949).

vivendi for Anglo-American maritime and commercial relations by establishing arbitral commissions to adjudicate grievances.

The fact was that Britain and France were coming more and more to depend on the United States for foodstuffs and on American carriers to feed their colonies. England's Prime Minister William Pitt, a master of what is now called economics, understood very well that confiscation of American merchantmen might ultimately work to the detriment of Britain. Hence the British avoided outright seizure of neutral vessels and even permitted neutrals to ship goods between French possessions and French ports, provided (1) that such trade had been normal before the war ("the Rule of 1756") and (2) that merchantmen engaged in such trade stop at a neutral port and pay duty ("broken voyage"). By such measures the British controlled and slowed down supplies to their enemy without attempting to halt it altogether.

The French were less far-seeing and less restrained, as shown by their reaction to Jay's Treaty. What aroused the wrath of the Paris government, and incidentally of the American public, was that the treaty said nothing about the supposed right of neutral carriers to transport non-contraband goods to or between ports of nations at war with Britain. In fact, by admitting foodstuffs as contraband, seizable on payment, it tacitly acknowledged Britain's right to stop ships and confiscate cargo. The French denounced the treaty as violating the "free ships, free goods" clause of the 1778 Franco-American treaties of commerce and alliance, but what particularly incensed them was the inclusion of foodstuffs as contraband —at a time when a series of poor harvests had made France heavily dependent on the United States for grain.[3] In retaliation, the Directory contemptuously refused to receive the American minister to France, ordering him to leave the country, and issued a series of decrees of increasing harshness. These culminated in the decree of January 18, 1798, which stated: "Every vessel found at sea, laden in whole or in part with merchandise coming from Eng-

[3] The Battle of the First of June (1794), it will be recalled, resulted from French determination to safeguard a large grain convoy en route from the Chesapeake.

land or her possessions shall be declared good prize." As paraphrased by a French politician, "If a handkerchief of English origin is found on board a neutral ship, both the rest of the cargo and the ship itself are subject to condemnation."

Quite apart from the insult to America's representative, the decrees and the resultant seizures of American vessels were ample justification for war. But what really aroused the public in the United States to a fighting pitch was the notorious X Y Z Affair. In an attempt to head off war, President Adams sent to Paris three commissioners with instructions to secure a treaty—a French version of Jay's Treaty. The American envoys, never officially recognized, were met by anonymous go-betweens (Messrs. X, Y, and Z) from French foreign minister Talleyrand. These demanded bribes and "loans" amounting to several million dollars as the price for opening negotiations. When this piece of effrontery became known in the United States, all but the most ardent Francophiles were disillusioned. Popular indignation was phrased in the slogan "Millions for defense, but not one cent for tribute," which caught the public's fancy in an outburst of patriotic fervor that swept Congress and country.[4]

The United States was now in a mood to take positive action. Early in 1798 Congress voted to equip the three original frigates, *Constitution, United States,* and *Constellation,* and to complete the *President,* 44, *Congress,* 36, and *Chesapeake,* 36, on which work had been stopped. On April 30, Congress created the Navy Department. In May, it passed "An Act More Effectually to Protect the Commerce and Coasts of the United States," which authorized the seizure of "armed vessels sailing under authority or pretense of authority from the Republic of France" in American coastal waters. In July, it extended authorization of

American warships or privateers to "subdue, seize and take any armed French vessel" anywhere on the high seas. Thus the United States was launched into a limited, undeclared war—the Quasi-War with France.

Stoddert's Navy

When Congress created the Department of the Navy, it specified that the Secretary of the Navy should execute the President's orders "relative to the procurement of naval stores and materials, and the construction, armament, equipment, and employment of vessels of war, as well as all other matters connected with the naval establishment of the United States." This broad directive gave the Secretary immediate control over naval administration, logistics, and operations. He thus held at one and the same time the responsibilities later assigned to the Secretary, the Bureau Chiefs, and the Chief of Naval Operations.

The first Secretary of the Navy was Benjamin Stoddert, who performed his duties with distinction throughout the Quasi-War. From the War Department he inherited the vessels and the organization of naval agents begun by General Knox. Stoddert's first task was to put the Navy on a wartime footing. His second was to build up the fleet, in the face of powerful Congressional opposition, to a strength sufficient to safeguard the interests of the nation. Looking to the future, he asked Congress for funds to build "twelve ships of 74 guns, as many frigates, and 20 or 30 smaller vessels." This was a shock to Congressmen from the South and West, who only a few years before had balked at the cost of building half a dozen frigates. But such was Stoddert's power of persuasion that he obtained a substantial part of what he requested, including a million-dollar appropriation toward the construction of six 74's.

Working with immense energy and foresight, Stoddert purchased timber reserves and land for new dockyards and encouraged the weaving of canvas and the manufacture of sheathing copper. Above all, he obtained the ships to fight the war and the crews to man them. His chief source for both was, of course, the merchant marine. By the war's end he had a fleet of 50 vessels, obtained through pur-

[4] In diplomatic circles it was generally understood that satisfaction from the corrupt French government could be had only through the generous application of *douceurs,* but the American commissioners could not meet Talleyrand's stiff price. Bribery was in fact much practiced in 18th century diplomacy and international relations. While the American public was crying, "Not one cent for tribute," the government was paying tribute to all four Barbary states.

chase, new construction, conversion, gifts from the states, and cooperation of the Treasury Department's revenue cutters.[5] By that time there were in the Navy 154 commissioned officers, more than 350 midshipmen, and some 6,000 seamen. The Marine Corps, re-established in 1798, numbered nearly 1,100.

Operations of the Quasi-War

In compliance with the act of May 1798, United States warships swept the American coasts to clear them of French privateers. Following the act passed in July, the United States squadrons concentrated operations in the West Indies. Here they had an enormous advantage over the French. British victories in the battles of Cape St. Vincent, Camperdown, and the Nile had left France and her allies cut off from their New World colonies. Few French men-of-war of any consequence could elude British vigilance and get so far from home.

On the other hand, the U. S. Navy had the free use of numerous British ports and bases—and even of French ports in Haiti, then dominated by rebellious slaves under Toussaint l'Overture. Throughout the war the American squadrons had the full support and cooperation of the Royal Navy. The British even considered lending them ships of the line, if the Americans could provide the crews to man them. To organize convoys and conduct patrols, one United States squadron was based on Dominica, another on St. Kitts, a third at Cap Français, Haiti, and a fourth briefly at Havana.

Under the shield of Britain's ships, the American squadrons easily attained their objectives. They also had the inestimable benefit, for a fledgling navy, of serving with the finest navy in the world at a time when it was at the height of its readiness. From this period of friendly contact with the British fleet, the United States Navy acquired its basic signal systems, its general plan of maneuver in formation, and the beginnings of a professional attitude.

Though never powerfully challenged, the U. S. Navy had its hands full. Out of the

[5] Ancestors of the U.S. Coast Guard, which normally serves with the U.S. Navy in time of war.

French West Indies swarmed a horde of privateers—small, shallow-draft vessels, rarely carrying more than twelve guns, able to elude capture by skipping into shoal water. Some performed their commerce raiding legitimately, according to the decrees of the French government. Others, having only the most tenuous connection with distant, blockaded France, verged on or actually practiced piracy. The only French national vessels in American waters were occasional fast frigates maintaining uncertain communication between France and her remaining West Indies colonies. It was against the privateers that the U. S. Navy directed its chief effort—hunting them down, escorting merchantmen, or recapturing captured American vessels.

The first American prize was the privateer *Croyable,* 12, taken in July 1798 off the New Jersey coast by U.S.S. *Delaware,* 20, whose commanding officer was Captain Stephen Decatur, father of a more famous son of the same name, then serving as a midshipman aboard another American vessel. The subsequent history of the *Croyable* illustrates the nature of the generally small-scale but busy operations of the war. Incorporated in the U. S. Navy as the schooner *Retaliation,* commanded by Lieutenant William Bainbridge, the ex-*Croyable* became separated from her squadron the following November and was captured by the frigates *Insurgente,* 36, and *Volontaire,* 44. Renamed the *Magicienne* by the French, the ex-*Croyable,* ex-*Retaliation* was captured once again by the Americans in June 1799.

Busiest of all the American warships was the "lucky little *Enterprise.*" Built specifically for her task, this swift, shallow-draft, 12-gun schooner outdid the frigates in protecting trade and capturing enemy ships. During one cruise she took five privateers (one a 12-gun brig), dismasted a 12-gun lugger, and freed eleven captured American merchant vessels. The most far-ranging of the American men-of-war was the frigate *Essex,* 32, Captain Edward Preble, which proceeded via the Cape of Good Hope to the East Indies. Here she recaptured several American merchantmen before escorting a merchant convoy back home. In one of the few engagements between naval vessels, U. S. frigate *Boston,* 28, forced the surrender of the corvette *Berceau,* 24, in a

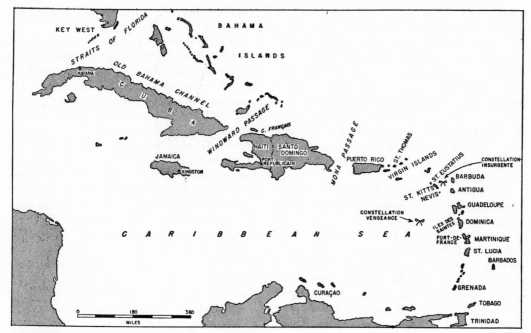

MAIN THEATER OF THE QUASI-WAR WITH FRANCE

spirited battle 600 miles northeast of Guadeloupe. The most famous actions of the Quasi-War however were the two frigate engagements fought by the *Constellation* under Commodore Thomas Truxtun.

Truxtun was an American St. Vincent and just what the new, somewhat undisciplined Navy needed. Entering the merchant marine as a boy, he had once been pressed for a brief career in a British 64. During the American Revolution, still in his early twenties, he had successively commanded two privateers, and after the war he had helped open the China trade. Appointed a captain in the U. S. Navy, he had supervised the building and launching of the *Constellation* at Baltimore. A superb navigator and shiphandler, he studied constantly to improve his professional qualifications and strove to develop professional attitudes in his subordinates. He sought to form his own navy on the British model, which he regarded as the ultimate in sea services. Autocratic, stern, dedicated, he was known as a strict disciplinarian, but it is noteworthy that he achieved respectful obedience through justice and force of character, rarely by means of the harsh punishments common in his day.

On taking command of the squadron based

at Basseterre, St. Kitts, Truxtun organized an efficient convoying system in cooperation with Commodore John Barry,[6] operating out of Dominica. His orders to his own squadron specified that all ships were to patrol independently when not engaged in convoy escort. It was while on independent patrol with the *Constellation* off Nevis in February 1799 that he made the contact that led to the most notable action of the war.

Sighting a sail 15 miles to leeward in a strong northeast wind, Truxtun took a converging course in order to close and investigate. He flew first British and then American recognition signals, neither of which was answered correctly by the other vessel—now seen to be a frigate of about the same size as the *Constellation*. Finally the stranger hoisted the French tricolor and hauled off to the northwest. She was the *Insurgente,* considered the fastest frigate in the French navy, and she might have made good her escape but for an untimely accident. The wind suddenly rising to gale force, both vessels were caught in the

[6] Both Truxtun and Barry were captains, the highest rank in the U.S. Navy until the Civil War, but as commanders of squadrons they held the honorary rank of commodore.

squall. The *Constellation* shortened sail in time to avoid damage, but the *Insurgente,* not so prompt, lost her main topmast. The American frigate now closed rapidly. With his vessel heeling far over under her spread of canvas and her too heavy armament, Truxtun chose the leeward position in order to have continuous use of his main battery of 24-pounders. Ignoring a hail, he brought the *Constellation* up on the lee quarter of the *Insurgente* and fired a double-shotted broadside into her hull, wrecking her quarter-deck.

The French frigate quickly returned the *Constellation's* fire, aiming high but doing only moderate damage to her rigging—and almost none to her hull. Early in the hour-and-a-quarter battle, the Frenchman wore in an attempt to board, but the *Constellation* forged ahead and across the *Insurgente's* bow, delivering a raking fire. After a running cannonade on parallel courses, the *Constellation* once more crossed her opponent's bow and raked again. Then, falling off, she crossed her stern, ready for a third rake. At that the French captain, observing his situation to be hopeless, his decks littered with dead and wounded, hauled down his colors.

The French had suffered 70 casualties, the Americans only six, including a seaman who deserted his gun and was killed by his superior officer. Though the *Insurgente* had 40 guns to the *Constellation's* 38, the heavy main battery of the American frigate gave her an almost 3-to-2 advantage in weight of broadside. But even when allowances are made for the superiority of the *Constellation* and the early loss of the *Insurgente's* main topmast, the fact remains that the Americans clearly outsailed, outmaneuvered, and outfought their enemy. The *Insurgente* carried nearly a hundred more men than the *Constellation*, but she could never make full use of them because Truxtun saw to it that they had no opportunity for boarding.

Putting into Basseterre with his prize, Truxtun was warmly congratulated by British officers and civil authorities. At Basseterre he was able to send the wounded of both ships to a hospital. Here also he found assistance in taking care of his prisoners and facilities for making repairs. The advantage to the U. S.

Navy of being able to base in British ports was never more clearly demonstrated.

Hiring a schooner to take his dispatches to the United States, Truxtun typically rejected the first skipper who volunteered to go, finding him "too extravagant in his terms." His no-nonsense attitude appears also in a postscript to his report to Stoddert: "The French captain tells me I have caused a war with France. If so, I am glad of it, for I detest things being done by halves." The news of Truxtun's victory lost nothing in the telling as it spread through the United States. That year no Fourth of July celebration was complete without a toast to Truxtun of the *Constellation* and a huzza for the U.S. Navy.

A year later Truxtun was again commodore of the St. Kitts-based squadron and in command of an improved *Constellation*. Her 24-pounder main battery had been replaced by 18-pounders, her long 12-pounders on the spar deck by 24-pounder carronades. The net result was a slight reduction in weight of broadside, but this was more than offset by a faster rate of fire and a stiffer, more weatherly vessel.

In February 1780, almost a year to the day after the defeat of the *Insurgente,* Truxtun was cruising in the *Constellation* off Guadeloupe when he sighted a large vessel and gave chase. She proved to be the 50-gun frigate *Vengeance* bound for France and anxious to avoid action. All day long and into the night the pursuit continued. The Frenchman's stern chasers did not discourage Truxtun from working the *Constellation* up to his enemy's windward quarter and commencing, as he described it, "as close and as sharp an action as ever was fought between two frigates," an action lasting nearly five hours.

As usual, the Frenchmen fired high, the Americans low—in the British style. In the prolonged cannonade, the hull of the *Vengeance* was penetrated by more than two hundred shot, a hundred of her crew were killed or wounded, and her hull began filling with water. Her captain twice struck his colors, but in the darkness, the smoke, and the roar of battle, his action was unobserved and his hail went unheard aboard the *Constellation*. When at length the French fire was completely silenced, the American frigate was almost stripped of rigging and 40 of her crew were casualties. Before she could move in to take her prize, her mainmast, all shrouds and stays cut, snapped off at the deck. Midshipman James Jarvis, commanding the main top, had been aware of his danger but refused to leave his post without orders, remarking to the topmen that if the mast went they must go with it—and so they did, only one man being saved. By the time the wreckage was cleared away, the *Vengeance* was nowhere to be seen, and Truxtun conjectured she had sunk. But she had merely drifted off in the darkness, her crew desperately pumping and bailing in order to stay afloat. With only the stumps of her mizzen and foremast standing, she arrived at the Dutch island of Curaçao five days later. Her captain reported that she had engaged a ship of the line.

Truxtun, concerned with saving the *Constellation*, made no attempt to beat back to St. Kitts under jury-rig but fell off for Jamaica, 600 miles to leeward. En route he encountered the *Enterprise,* by which he sent his report back to the United States. Soon the entire nation was rejoicing in his victory. No one could deny that the *Constellation* through expert gunnery and seamanship had roundly defeated a larger vessel with a 50 per cent advantage in weight of broadside.

Throughout the war, President Adams had disappointed his more hot-headed supporters by continuing to seek agreement with France. Schemes to conquer Louisiana or to join the British in aggressive actions against French possessions did not appeal to his sense of what was best for the United States. Talleyrand was equally anxious to come to terms. He had no desire to drive the United States into further concert with the British. Moreover, blockaded France desperately needed the cooperation of American shipping to maintain the economy of her West Indies possessions.

Opposition within the United States delayed the sending of a commission during the period when Bonaparte was stranded in Egypt and France was on the verge of collapse. When the commissioners finally reached Paris in March of 1800, Bonaparte was in power as First Consul, and shortly afterward he gave the death blow to the Second Coalition by defeating the Austrians at Marengo. In this atmosphere the terms that the commissioners were able to obtain in an eight-year Convention of Peace, signed in September 1800, were less than satisfactory to most Americans. As finally ratified in July 1801, it annulled the embarrassing Franco-American treaties of alliance of 1778, but the price was high—nothing less than cancellation of all claims against France for spoliations of American commerce.

Announcement of the terms of the Convention, coming on the eve of the 1800 national elections, cost Adams the Presidency. Thomas Jefferson and his Republican Party took over the administration and won a substantial majority in Congress. Nevertheless a great deal had been accomplished. Hostilities were ended. The obnoxious French decree of 1798 was canceled. American warships, by defeating their equals and capturing more than 80 French vessels, had given the world a convincing demonstration that the U.S. Navy was a force to be reckoned with. And the way was opened for the purchase of Louisiana by the United States in 1803. Part of the price to France was the assumption by the U. S. government of the $7,000,000 in French debts to American citizens acknowledged by the unpopular 1800 Convention.

A New Policy and a New War

Under President Jefferson and his vigorous Secretary of the Treasury Albert Gallatin, the new United States Navy faced liquidation. The Administration had come into office pledged to reduce the costs of government. The success of the Quasi-War and signs that Britain and France would soon be at peace made naval power seem less immediately necessary to the United States. Hence the Navy became a principal target of the Republican economizing. Ships were sold, work was stopped on the 74's, and naval officers were discharged with four months' pay. Jefferson himself designed covered docks for "mothballing" the few best frigates that were retained.

In a world whose wounds appeared to be healing, one sore continued to fester. By 1800 the United States had paid out more than

SCENE OF UNITED STATES NAVAL OPERATIONS IN THE BARBARY WARS

$1,000,000 in money and gifts to the Barbary states. In the same year Mediterranean trade carried in American ships reached a new high of almost $12,000,000—an increasing temptation to the corsairs and an excuse to the greedy North African rulers for demanding more tribute. To prime the flow, the Barbary states used threats and insults and tortured hostages. A particularly galling example of their strong-arm methods was the commandeering of a United States frigate by the Dey of Algiers.

The *George Washington,* 24, arrived at Algiers in September 1800 to deliver the annual tribute. While the frigate lay under the guns of the Algerian forts, the Dey ordered her captain, that hard-luck officer William Bainbridge, to transport passengers and cargo to the Sultan at Constantinople. "You pay me tribute, by which you become my slaves," said the Algerian ruler; "I have therefore a right to order you as I may think proper."[7] By threatening war on American commerce, the Dey finally induced Bainbridge to sail under Algerian colors, carrying 200 passengers, as many animals, and a million dollars' worth of gifts—the Dey's own tribute to his suzerain. At Constantinople the *George Washington* was kindly received, but with some hesitation because the government there had never heard of the United States.

The atrocious conduct of the Barbary states put President Jefferson in a quandary. A peace-loving man of high principles, he was particularly sensitive to such lawlessness. His Secretary of State, James Madison, pointed one way out of the dilemma by suggesting that it would

[7] Gardner W. Allen, *Our Navy and the Barbary Corsairs* (Boston, 1905), 77.

cost little more to use the U. S. Navy's active warships against the corsairs than to maintain the vessels in their home ports.

While Jefferson was reluctantly considering the use of force, the Dey of Tripoli settled the matter. Discontented because his treaty commitments with the United States bound him to less generous terms than those accorded his more powerful neighbors Tunis and Algiers, he demanded that the question of tribute be reopened. But the Dey's mounting demands soon made it clear that he was not to be satisfied. He had recently made a treaty with Sweden, and it was the policy of the Barbary states always to be at war with at least one seafaring nation in order to give employment to their corsairs. The expanding American carrying trade in the Mediterranean now made the United States a most profitable enemy. In May 1801 the Dey of Tripoli had the American consul's flag pole chopped down—the North African equivalent of a formal declaration of war. Forewarned, Jefferson was prepared to commit his fleet.

The War with Tripoli: Two Years of Stalemate, 1801–1803

Approaching the problem as obliquely as possible, Acting Secretary of the Navy Samuel Smith issued orders for Commodore Richard Dale to take to the Mediterranean a squadron consisting of the frigates *President, Philadelphia,* and *Essex* and the schooner *Enterprise,* on what was ostensibly a training cruise. Reflecting Republican fears of creating an international incident, the Secretary wrote Dale:

"In all cases of clashing with the vessels, officers, or subjects of other Powers, we enjoin on you the most rigorous moderation, conformity to right and reason, and suppression of all passions, which might lead to the commitment of our peace or our honor."[8]

At Gibraltar, where Dale made his base with the permission of the British governor, he discovered two Tripolitan corsairs about to sortie into the Atlantic. These he left under observation of Captain William Bainbridge of the *Philadelphia*, with orders to pounce on them should they put to sea. The Commodore then visited Algiers and Tunis for a display of force, and late in July he blockaded the port of Tripoli. After 18 days however he was obliged to lift his blockade and retire to Malta for water.

En route to Malta, the 12-gun *Enterprise* fell in with a Tripolitan corsair, the *Tripoli*, 14. In a close engagement, the *Enterprise* nimbly side-stepped attempts at boarding and raked her opponent several times. After three hours the *Tripoli* was helpless, her crew begging for mercy. Twenty of her crew were killed, 30 wounded. Not a man aboard the *Enterprise* was injured, and the little schooner had suffered no material damage to hull or rigging. Because his orders made no provision for taking prizes, Lieutenant Sterrett, captain of the *Enterprise*, ordered the Tripolitan stripped to a single spar and sail and cast loose. When she at last made her way back to home port, the wrathful Dey had her wounded commanding officer paraded around Tripoli astride an ass and then given 500 blows on the soles of his feet. The effect of the *Tripoli*'s bloody defeat and the barbarous treatment of her captain was to frighten Tripolitan seamen from serving in the corsairs. When the news reached Gibraltar, most of the men in the two corsairs under observation by the *Philadelphia* abandoned ship and slipped across to North Africa in boats.

While the squadron of 1801 succeeded in temporarily overawing the Barbary states and undoubtedly saved numerous American merchant vessels from capture, it achieved nothing permanent. There were, complained Dale,

[8] *Naval Documents Related to the United States Wars with the Barbary Powers*, I (Washington, 1939), 468 [SHORT TITLE: *Barbary Wars*].

too few men-of-war simultaneously to maintain a blockade, escort merchantmen, and attend to their own replenishment. The difficulties of the squadron were compounded by the refusal of supply vessels to venture beyond Gibraltar, by lack of a base within the Straits, and by one-year enlistments, which required the periodic return of individual warships to the United States. These difficulties arose partly through temporizing by the economy-minded government but, as events were to show, a really vigorous, able, and determined commodore could accomplish far more with the ships and resources available than was achieved by either Dale or his successor.

Congress, deciding at length to push the war against Tripoli with greater vigor, early in 1802 appropriated funds for fitting out a larger Mediterranean squadron. At the same time provision was made for two-year enlistments. Thomas Truxtun was offered the new squadron but refused it because he was not allowed the normal and sensible arrangement of having a captain to command his flagship. Secretary of the Navy Robert Smith chose to interpret Truxtun's refusal as a resignation from the service, thereby discarding an officer who had done far more than most to mold the U. S. Navy into a professional team. In Truxtun's place Smith appointed Commodore Richard Morris, who arrived at Gibraltar toward the end of May 1802. Morris's squadron, five frigates and some smaller vessels, while affording improved protection to American trade, failed to intimidate the Dey of Tripoli, who demanded as his price for peace $200,000 and reimbursement for all costs of the war. After the squadron had captured one Tripolitan corsair, destroyed another with gunfire, and burned eleven beached coasting vessels, Morris raised the blockade of Tripoli, believing the Tripolitans no longer had the means to capture merchantmen. Besides, his ships were needed to watch the other Barbary powers, who had begun making warlike threats. In any event, a really tight blockade of Tripoli was out of the question, for small craft could generally avoid capture by hugging the coastal shallows where the American men-of-war could not reach them. Apprised of this situation, Congress authorized construction of additional brigs and schooners for inshore work. Before any could arrive in the Mediterranean, Secretary Smith in the summer of 1803 curtly ordered Morris back to the United States where a court of inquiry found him "censurable for his inactive and dilatory conduct," and he was dismissed from the service.

Preble Takes Command

Truxtun now swallowed his pride and offered to take out the third squadron, but Smith, ignoring him, secured the appointment of Edward Preble, then 42 years old and one of the most junior captains in the Navy. Included in the new squadron were only two frigates, the *Constitution* and the *Philadelphia*, which were intended mainly to back up the work of five shallow-draft brigs and schooners. In his orders dated July 13, 1803, Smith enjoined Preble to maintain "an effectual blockade of Tripoli," adding, "No place is to be considered by you in a state of blockade which is not actually besieged." Of previous operations against Tripoli, Smith stated bluntly: "The conduct for some time past pursued by our squadrons in the Mediterranean has, unhappily, not been calculated to accomplish the object of [this] government or to make a just impression on the enemy of our national character. We have therefore transferred to you the command of our forces in that sea, in full confidence that you will maintain the dignity of your station and that the FLAG of your country will not be dishonored in your hands."[9]

A hot-tempered down-Mainer, Preble was as taut a disciplinarian as Truxtun. He was scarcely known to his officers, for they were mostly from the central and southern states and he had spent the Quasi-War cruising in the *Essex* to the Far East and back, a voyage that had impaired his health and done nothing to improve his temper. After experiencing the rough side of Preble's tongue, most of his officers took a strong dislike to their commodore. Preble, for his part, was dismayed to find that not one of his commanding officers was as much as 30 years of age. "They have given me nothing but a pack of boys!" he was reported as saying.

Preble, with fewer frigates than either of his predecessors, was expected to achieve results

[9] *Barbary Wars*, II, (1940), 475–6.

under increasingly difficult circumstances. During the Peace of Amiens, American commerce had declined, giving the Mediterranean squadron less to protect. But after war between Britain and France broke out again in May 1803, merchantmen from the United States began to arrive in steadily increasing numbers. In June, Lord Nelson arrived in the *Victory* to blockade Toulon, and ships of the Royal Navy began picking Mediterranean sources bare of provisions and naval stores. British commanding officers were on the lookout for deserters and seamen of English origin to employ in their undermanned warships.

In mid-August 1803 Preble sailed for the Mediterranean in the *Constitution*. The crossing was uneventful, but one night as the frigate was approaching the Straits of Gibraltar a display of spirit by the new commodore won him the respect of every officer in his squadron. Observing a strange vessel looming through the darkness, Preble had the crew silently brought to quarters and then gave the routine hail, "What ship is that?" A voice from the stranger replied with the same question and got his answer but refused to identify his ship. At length Preble lost patience.

"I am now going to hail you for the last time," he shouted through the trumpet. "If a proper answer is not returned, I will fire a shot into you."

"If you fire a shot," replied the stranger, "I will return a broadside."

Preble then hailed, "What ship is that?"

"This is His Britannic Majesty's ship *Donegal*, 84 guns, Sir Richard Strachan, an English commodore. Send your boat on board."

Replied Preble, leaping on the hammocks: "This is the United States ship *Constitution*, 44 guns, Edward Preble, an American commodore, who will be damned before he sends his boat on board of any vessel! Blow your matches, boys."[10]

The strange vessel, which turned out to be a 32-gun British frigate, now quickly sent a boat with an apology and the explanation that her captain had been stalling for time to bring his men to quarters. That settled the matter

[10] *The Autobiography of Commodore Charles Morris, U.S. Navy* (Annapolis, 1880), 21. Morris witnessed this incident as a midshipman aboard the *Constitution*.

amicably and the frigates soon drew apart, but the crew of the *Constitution* was deeply impressed that their commodore had been perfectly ready to try conclusions with a ship of the line. This incident marked a turning point in Preble's relations with his subordinates. They gradually realized that he was a sick man, driving himself to carry out his orders by almost superhuman will. Under his rough exterior he was warm-hearted and understanding. More important, he had the stature, the determination, and the drive to achieve results where others had failed. His young officers were soon proud to be known as "Preble's boys," a title they carried into the War of 1812, in which nearly every one of them made a distinguished name for himself.

On arriving at Gibraltar on September 12, Preble found the *Philadelphia*, Captain William Bainbridge, with a Moorish corsair that she had taken at sea together with a captured American merchantman. When Bainbridge had given the Moorish captain his choice of producing official orders for making the capture or being hanged as a pirate, the captain had reluctantly shown his authorization. Evidently Morocco, in violation of treaty commitments to the United States, was again preying on American vessels.

Commodore Preble at once took countermeasures. Sending the *Philadelphia* and the schooner *Vixen* on ahead to blockade Tripoli, he went with the *Constitution*, two frigates of the squadron he was relieving, and a schooner across the Straits to Tangier. Here he anchored ostentatiously and cleared his decks for action. The Sultan of Morocco, arriving the same day, was so impressed by this display of force that he at once disavowed the operations against American commerce and reaffirmed the Treaty of 1786 without further payment. Preble, having thus assured the safety of his supply ships from the United States, proceeded to cruise in the Mediterranean.

The *Philadelphia*

The *Philadelphia* and the *Vixen* in early October 1803 appeared before Tripoli, on which they clamped a blockade. Learning from a neutral brig coming out of the harbor that a pair of Tripolitan corsairs were out cruising,

Captain Bainbridge detached the *Vixen* westward to look for them. While the schooner was thus occupied, a westerly gale drove the *Philadelphia* temporarily off station. This evidently was the opportunity for which the corsairs had been waiting. Bainbridge on returning to resume his blockade observed one of them trying to slip into the harbor and immediately gave chase. He now had occasion to regret the absence of the *Vixen*, for the corsair hugged the shallows where the American frigate could not follow and made its way to safety. Turning back toward open water, the *Philadelphia* drove hard onto an uncharted reef at such an angle of heel that neither of her broadsides could be brought to bear on the Tripolitan gunboats that soon swarmed around her. Bainbridge now belatedly recognized Preble's wisdom in sending the *Vixen* along with the *Philadelphia* and his own poor judgment in detaching her, for without the schooner he was helpless. Four hours of arduous effort are well summarized in his official report:

. . . Immediately lowered down a boat from the stern, sounded, and found the greatest depth of water astern. Laid all sails aback, loosed topgallant sails and set a heavy press of canvas on the ship, blowing fresh, to get her off. Cast three anchors away from the bows, started water in the hold, hove overboard the guns except some abaft to defend the ship against the gunboats which were then firing on us; found all this ineffectual. Then made the last resort of lightening her forward by cutting away the foremast, which carried the maintopgallant mast with it. But labor and enterprise was in vain, for our fate was direfully fixed.[11]

Luckily for the *Philadelphia*'s crew, the Tripolitans restricted their fire mainly to the frigate's masts and rigging—both to prevent her escape and to secure the vessel undamaged and the men as hostages. Bainbridge however was unaware that his ship's company was in little danger of being killed. Observing reinforcements, including the ketch *Mastico*, coming out from Tripoli, he had his signal books and ammunition thrown overboard and then struck his colors. That evening he and his crew were carried triumphantly into the city to begin a long imprisonment. Two days later, high water during a gale enabled the Tripoli-

[11] *Barbary Wars*, III (1941), 172.

tans to free the *Philadelphia* from her reef. They also fished up and remounted all her guns.

Preble learned of the loss of the *Philadelphia* from a passing British frigate while he was cruising off Sardinia in late November. It was a staggering blow, costing him nearly half the strength of his squadron. He had left now only the *Constitution*, two brigs, and three schooners. His loss was Tripoli's gain. The Tripolitans had never before had in their hands nearly so powerful a warship. With the *Philadelphia* added to their fleet of small armed corsairs, including a brig and two schooners, they were, Preble supposed, in a position to bid him defiance. Their 306 prisoners from the captured frigate moreover would enable the Dey to set stiff terms at any peace parley. "Would to God that the officers and crew of the *Philadelphia* had, one and all, determined to prefer death to slavery," wrote the Commodore to Secretary Smith; "it is possible such a determination might save them from either."[12]

A lesser man than Preble might have fallen back in panic to Gibraltar to await advice and reinforcements from home. Preble however made best speed to Malta, the neutral anchorage nearest Tripoli, in search of further information. It was a good choice, for the Danish consul at Malta had letters for him from Bainbridge, forwarded through the good offices of the Danish consul at Tripoli. The *Philadelphia*, reported Bainbridge, now rode at anchor in Tripoli's inner harbor.

Despite the convenient location of Malta, Preble rejected it as a base of operations for his squadron. At Gibraltar he had learned the price of sharing a British base—his deserters had found ready sanctuary in the Royal Navy's men-of-war. Heading north, he established himself at Syracuse, Sicily, a central position from which he could both police the Mediterranean and maintain his blockade. At Syracuse the Americans were treated as allies, for the Kingdom of Naples also was at war with Tripoli.

Another letter from Bainbridge pointed out that most of his crew were Englishmen, many of whom had jumped ship from British vessels in American ports. Could not Lord Nelson be induced to reclaim them, thereby lessening the Dey's bargaining power? Preble was bitterly aware that his squadron was manned largely by foreigners. The Navy could not compete for American seamen with the United States merchant marine, which offered higher wages. But to acknowledge that British deserters were aboard American ships would be inviting more trouble from the Royal Navy.[13]

One suggestion from Bainbridge accorded with a plan Preble had already discussed with some of his officers. Why not destroy the *Philadelphia*? "By chartering a merchant vessel and sending her into the harbor with the men secreted and steering directly on board the frigate," wrote Bainbridge, "it might be effected without any or a trifling loss." Though the Commodore was not quite so sanguine, this line of action appealed to him, whereas any attempt to seize the deep-draft frigate and work her out of the shallow harbor under fire would almost certainly prove fatal. To the Secretary, Preble wrote, "I shall hazard much to destroy her—it will undoubtedly cost us many lives, but it must be done."[14]

In December Preble sailed with the *Constitution* and the *Enterprise* to reconnoiter. On making landfall off the African coast, his lookouts sighted the *Mastico* just out of Tripoli. The *Enterprise* at once gave chase and took possession. When it was learned that the ketch had participated in the capture and plundering of the *Philadelphia*, she was declared lawful prize and taken into the U. S. Navy as the *Intrepid*.

During his reconnaissance of Tripoli, which was soon cut short by bad weather, Preble observed that the *Philadelphia* lay under the guns of the Dey's castle and within easy range of shore batteries and nearby men-of-war. Getting at and destroying her apparently would not be nearly so easy as Bainbridge had suggested. Preble had suspected as much all along, but he now had the means. The officer on

[12] *Ibid.*, 256. Preble was unnecessarily alarmed about what use Tripoli might make of the *Philadelphia*. The Dey, finding the frigate too much for his seamen to handle, had opened private negotiations to sell her.

[13] Some of the British seamen had been put through a brief naturalizing process and thus were technically Americans.

[14] *Barbary Wars*, III, 253, 258.

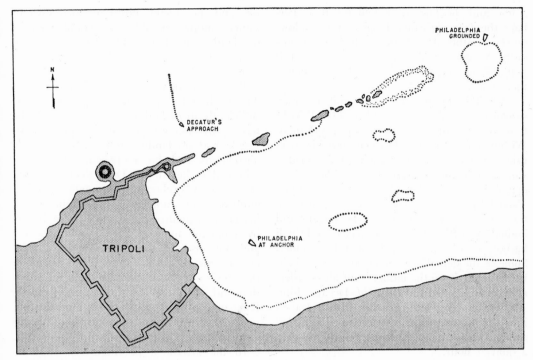

HARBOR OF TRIPOLI, 1804

whose skill and judgment he most relied had offered his services to lead the dangerous mission. This was the 25-year-old firebrand captain of the *Enterprise*, Lieutenant Stephen Decatur. Son of the officer who had made the first capture in the Quasi-War, Decatur had already earned a reputation in the Navy for ability and daring. Between him and his crusty commodore there had grown a sort of wry affection, not unlike that between Nelson and St. Vincent. Decatur asked for the ex-*Mastico*, pointing out that her Mediterranean rig would serve as a passport into Tripoli harbor. Preble agreed. The plunderer of the *Philadelphia* was thus to be the instrument for her destruction.

Plans for destroying the frigate matured at Syracuse during January 1804, while violent storms made cruising hazardous and blockading impossible. At length on February 3, the storms abating, Decatur called the crew of the *Enterprise* together and put the project before them. Every officer, man, and boy volunteered to go. When the crew of the *Constitution* clamored to be included, Decatur selected a few of these to add to his picked team from the *Enterprise*. He had already enlisted the

services of Salvadore Catalano, a Sicilian pilot who knew the harbor of Tripoli and could speak Arabic. That evening the *Intrepid* with the crew of volunteers slipped out of Syracuse accompanied by U. S. brig *Siren*, which was disguised as a merchantman. The *Siren* was to cover the retreat of the *Intrepid* or provide boats for bringing out survivors should she be destroyed. On the 7th the two vessels were off Tripoli but, the storms blowing up afresh, both were driven off to the east by a violent gale. After a harrowing week, they were again off the harbor on the 16th.

That night the *Intrepid*, to all outward appearance a native ketch, coasted into the harbor on a dying wind. Catalano had the helm and Decatur, in Maltese dress, stood at his side. All but a half dozen of the crew were concealed below decks. Presently the hull of the *Philadelphia* became visible in the dim light of a crescent moon. Hailed and warned to keep off, Catalano, at Decatur's dictation, stated that his vessel had lost her anchors in the storm and requested permission to tie up alongside for the night. The request being granted, both vessels in routine fashion sent over a boat with a line and the lines were tied together. Perhaps the *Intrepid*'s men lying in the shadows on the weather deck hauled a little too vigorously. At any rate, something aroused the Tripolitans' suspicion, and as the vessels touched there was a cry of "Americanos!"

"Board!" shouted Decatur, and 60 men swarmed onto the *Philadelphia*. The Tripolitans were too surprised to put up a real fight. Within a few minutes Decatur and his men, using sabers and iron "tomahawks," killed a score and drove the rest overboard. Meanwhile, demolition parties were bringing combustibles aboard from the *Intrepid*. According to plan these were distributed about the frigate and ignited. The *Philadelphia*, sunbaked in Tripoli harbor, caught fire and burned like tinder. Some of the demolition teams deep in the hold barely made it up the ladders, but all boarders at length regained the *Intrepid*. Decatur himself, last to get off the blazing frigate, leaped into the rigging of the ketch as she pulled away. The mission was completed in little over a quarter hour.

By towing with boats and using sweeps, the crew managed to extricate the *Intrepid*, her sails barely drawing in the light offshore breeze and her path lighted by the great torch of the burning *Philadelphia*. The Tripolitan batteries and warships opened a wild and erratic fire which was joined by the frigate's own double-shotted guns as the heat reached them, but the *Intrepid* slipped out the way she had come. Her only damage was a single shot through her topgallant sail. Not a man of Decatur's crew had been killed; only one was slightly wounded. The *Philadelphia* burned to the waterline, went adrift, and sank. Decatur's exploit won him a captain's commission and fame at home and abroad, including Lord Nelson's generous appraisal: "the most bold and daring act of the age."

Reaching Terms with Tripoli

The destruction of the *Philadelphia* removed a presumed threat to Preble's squadron but did little to improve his capability for offensive action. Blockade, though undoubtedly a nuisance to the Tripolitans, could never be really effective; the people's wants were simple, and they could subsist on their own resources, supplemented by what could be hauled overland from Tunis. The Dey, with more than 300 prisoners, knew his advantage and refused to abate his demands.

Preble's problem, then, was how to get at Tripoli—how to injure the interests of the Dey sufficiently to make him accede to reasonable terms. Invasion was out of the question, for Preble had no landing force. Moreover, the Tripolitans had far more guns afloat and ashore than he. In the Dey's fleet, consisting of a brig, two schooners, two galleys, and 19 gunboats, were more men than Preble had in his entire squadron, and these were backed by a defense force of 25,000 inside the city and the forts. In the circumstances, Preble's only means of attack was by naval assault on the Dey's city, forts, and fleet. As an aid to that end, the Commodore obtained from the King of Naples the loan of six gunboats and two mortar boats—and gunners, bombardiers, and seamen to help man them.

In the afternoon of August 3, 1804 the *Constitution*, three brigs, three schooners, and the two borrowed mortar boats stood off Tripoli's harbor fortifications at point-blank range. While the squadron took the forts, batteries, and fleet under fire, the mortar boats began hurling shells into the walled city. At the same time Preble's gunboats with Neapolitan crews and American boarding parties passed through the openings in the harbor reef and made for the Tripolitan gunboats. For various reasons only three of the attacking boats reached the enemy, but these under the command of Stephen Decatur took on nine opponents. The rest of the Dey's naval forces was kept at bay by the fire from Preble's squadron.

The Barbary pirates had for centuries been feared as the world's most ferocious and skillful hand-to-hand fighters. Hence their enemies at sea made every endeavor to hold them off with gunnery and seamanship. But on this occasion the Americans clearly outperformed the Tripolitans at their own specialty. Boarding and fighting superior numbers across decks with saber, pike, and tomahawk, they took three prizes and brought all their own boats out.

After this attack, the Dey signaled his willingness to negotiate. His terms now were $150,000 ransom for the *Philadelphia* captives and no further tribute or other payment from the United States. This was a far better offer than the first or second Mediterranean squadrons had been able to extract, but it was not good enough for Preble. He resolved if possible to destroy the Dey's ships and reduce his city and fortifications to rubble with American guns. During the next few weeks he made four more attacks, two at night, but the stubborn Dey refused to give in. As a last resort, before the season of bad weather drove the squadron from before Tripoli, Preble decided to employ a bomb vessel to blow up the remnant of Tripoli's naval and commercial shipping and possibly blast in the city wall. The *Intrepid*, again selected, was stuffed with 15,000 pounds of bulk powder and sent in on the evening of September 4 manned by 13 volunteers. As the ketch entered the harbor, the Tripolitans saw her and opened fire. Presently there was a flash and a roar. The American crews outside felt the concussion. The *Intrepid* had blown up prematurely, killing her crew and doing little damage to the enemy.

With Preble's vigorous prosecution of hostilities, the long-drawn-out war had gained stature in American opinion. Even the administration ceased to regard it as a mere inconclusive drain on funds. A final heavy thrust might now win a victory, restore peace, and end the payment of tribute—not only to Tripoli but to the other Barbary states, which presumably would be overawed. So Preble's squadron, which for nearly a year had been operating with only one frigate, was joined in August by another, the *John Adams*. A week after the explosion of the *Intrepid*, two more, the *President* and the *Constellation*, joined, with promise of more to follow. Aboard the *President* was Captain Samuel Barron, considerably Preble's senior. The Secretary of the Navy sent a letter to Preble praising his services but pointing out that seniority must prevail. Preble offered to remain with the squadron under Barron's command, but to avoid possible embarrassment he was ordered back to the United States, where President Jefferson received him with warmth and distinction. At Preble's urging, the government accelerated

the construction of gunboats for inshore work against Tripoli. This was his last service to his country. His health further declining, he died in August 1807 at the age of 46.

What Truxtun had begun Preble completed, and added a great deal of his own. Under Preble the officers of the Mediterranean squadron had evolved from an ardent but undisciplined set of individualists into a professional fighting team, with pride in the service and a desire to make it their life's work. This was the team that time and again faced superior odds before Tripoli and each time wrought far more injury than it took. In the entire campaign Preble's losses were only 30 killed and 34 wounded. The ideals of service Preble generated took time to spread through the fleet, but when the nation again took to arms in the War of 1812 his work was manifest. In the four years before Preble left the Mediterranean, 63 officers retained on the navy list had resigned, nearly a quarter of them from the two upper ranks; in the eight years following, only 26 resigned, and only two of these were from the upper ranks. By 1812 "Preble's boys" held most of the Navy's more important commands.

With Preble's departure, the spirit went out of the war against Tripoli. A light blockade was maintained, except during the period of severe storms in the late fall, but there were no more frontal attacks. The new squadron was the most powerful American naval force yet assembled, but it did little to complete Preble's promising beginning. Most of the ships remained at anchor at Malta or Syracuse. Part of the trouble was Barron's poor health, but illness had not kept Preble from performing his duty to the hilt.

In the absence of fleet activity, William Eaton, who had come out with Barron as Navy Agent for the Barbary States, devised a scheme for putting a more amenable tyrant on the throne of Tripoli. This was Hamet Caramanli, deposed elder brother of the Dey. After a considerable search, Eaton located Hamet and his followers in Egypt and readily induced them to invade Tripolitan territory. In early March 1805 a rag-tag army of 400 set out from Alexandria under "General" Eaton. Spearheading the force were a midshipman, a non-commissioned officer, and seven marines under Lieutenant Presley O'Bannon USMC—all from the brig *Argus*, which had brought Eaton to Egypt.

In a trouble-filled 600-mile march across the Libyan desert, Hamet's army was gradually swelled by the adherence of desert tribesmen to more than 700 fighting men and 500 camp-followers, including women and children. Toward the end of April this motley horde reached the Tripolitan coastal town of Derna, which they captured in joint operations with two brigs and a schooner from Barron's squadron. They held this position for several weeks and had beaten off a number of counterattacks when word came that the war was over. The Dey had agreed to a treaty requiring no further tribute or "gifts" and releasing the *Philadelphia*'s officers and men on payment of $60,000.

Opinion was divided in the United States regarding the Tripolitan treaty. Renewed attacks on Tripoli and exploitation of the position at Derna would certainly in time have brought the Dey to better terms and would have had a salutary effect on the other North African powers. On the other hand, by Barbary standards the ransom was light for so many prisoners, and the specification that there was to be no further tribute was unprecedented. Many felt that the price was not too high to pay for the release of the *Philadelphia* captives, who had already suffered 19 months of degrading imprisonment and maltreatment. As events were to prove, no amount of force could entirely cure the Barbary rulers of their insatiable greed.

Mr. Jefferson's Gunboat Navy

Early in the operations against Tripoli, American naval officers pointed out the need of gunboats to supplement the frigates, brigs, and schooners in shoal water. On their recommendation Congress during the war authorized the construction of 40. A typical gunboat was two-masted with schooner or sloop rig, carried a complement of 20, mounted two 32-pounders, and had a length of 71 feet, a beam of 18 feet, and a depth of hold of 4 feet, 8½ inches. Though these shallow-draft vessels were able to sail in blue water only by striking their guns below to improve stability, eight of them man-

aged to cross the Atlantic to join the Mediterranean squadron. These arrived after the departure of Preble, who, as we have seen, used borrowed Neapolitan and captured Tripolitan boats.

Preble had used his gunboats only against similar small craft. Tripolitan gunboats had of course captured the *Philadelphia*, but only after a freak accident had deprived her of the use of her guns. Nevertheless Jefferson and his Republican Congress were inspired by such small successes to embark upon a program so inimical to American interests that it still astonishes students of the period. This was the famous gunboat policy. To Jefferson the little vessels appeared a means of protecting the United States at a bargain price. On his recommendation naval appropriations and available materials were diverted for several years to the building of more and more gunboats. Even the fine, seasoned oak intended for Stoddert's 74's went into the program. By 1807 Congress had authorized construction of 278 gunboats, and 176 were ultimately built.

Hating war, Jefferson would have preferred to avoid the dangers inherent in trading with belligerents. Until 1807 he did not feel himself in a position actually to stop such trade, but he was unwilling to take the risk of giving it adequate protection. He believed that by conspicuously avoiding naval construction suitable for use on the high seas he could demonstrate America's peaceful intentions and thereby avoid further embroilment in the European conflict. On the other hand, should war come, he counted on the gunboats to protect America's coasts and harbors. In time of peace most of them would be laid up. At outbreak of hostilities they would be distributed along the coast from Maine to Louisiana. To repel an invasion they would cooperate with stationary land fortifications, artillery, and floating batteries.

History of course has shown that such passive defense is almost useless against a determined invader backed by naval firepower and able to pick his point of assault. Even supposing the scattered gunboats could be brought together quickly enough to oppose an invasion, they were defensively too weak to stand up against thick-sided frigates or ships of the line. Moreover the gunboat policy made no provision for carrying out such vital naval functions as backing up foreign policy, breaking a blockade, or protecting maritime commerce. It thus ignored the lessons of the Revolution and of subsequent American experience. Yet this fatuous policy reached its height just when the Americans had become virtually the only neutral traders on the high seas and when Britain and the French Empire, in their final struggle for survival, were each taking drastic steps to isolate the other from the rest of the world.

Summary

The United States Navy, established ten years after the American Revolution, came into being to protect an expanding maritime trade. Its early development was strongly influenced by the interplay of economic, political, and moral considerations, both national and international. At home it was frequently under attack by isolationist elements who opposed the new navy as prohibitively costly and as a means of involving the United States in foreign wars. Its continued existence was due in great part to its early victories and to the popular acclaim won by individual naval officers who became national heroes.

The Act of 1794 establishing the Navy was passed ostensibly to protect American merchantmen and their crews from capture by the North African corsairs. But the immediate reason for the act being passed at that time was the outbreak of war between Britain and France and the operations of each to curtail American trade with the other. Supporting the establishment of a navy was the Federalist Party, led by Hamilton and representing the commercial interests of the East; opposing it was the Republican Party, led by Jefferson and representing the agrarian interests of the South and West.

As difficulties with the North African states subsided, the Navy was on the point of extinction. It was saved by a personal appeal from Washington and in response to the mounting interference with American maritime commerce by Britain and France. Efforts to solve the problem of American neutrality fell into a pattern that was to be repeated, with variations, until the eve of America's entry into World War II. Either the United States would have to build a navy capable of protecting its merchantmen or abandon the seas and leave its carrying trade to foreign bottoms. The United States came to terms with Britain in Jay's Treaty, but this only served to inflame the French government, which insulted American representatives and began confiscating American ships carrying goods of British origin. As a result, Congress in 1798 resumed naval construction, established the Navy Department, and launched the Navy on an undeclared war against armed French vessels—the Quasi-War with France (1798-1801), fought mainly in the West Indies.

The victories of the Quasi-War, particularly those of Truxtun in the *Constellation*, aroused the pride of the American public in the new navy and assured the permanence of the Navy Department. But the pro-Navy and anti-Navy factions drew different conclusions from the war. The Federalists, aware that only Britain's ships of the line had made the Navy's moderate success possible, agreed with Secretary Stoddert that a bigger navy was needed. From the Republican point of view, the war proved the sufficiency of a small, cruiser navy. The Republicans, in office at the conclusion of peace, forthwith stripped the Navy down to minimum size.

The Dey of Tripoli's declaration of war forced President Jefferson reluctantly to send a series of naval squadrons to the Mediterranean. Here hostilities dragged out over four years (1801-05), partly because of temporizing and misplaced economizing by the Republican government and partly through lack of aggressiveness by the early squadron commanders. The war took on a new vigor when Preble arrived in the Mediterranean in 1803. The burning of the captured *Philadelphia* in the teeth of Tripolitan defenses aroused the enthusiasm of the American public. Assisted by ardent officers like Decatur, Preble established a base at Syracuse and in 1804 clapped a tight blockade on Tripoli and staged a series of naval assaults against city, fortifications, and shipping. The administration, stimulated at last into action, finally sent adequate naval forces to the Mediterranean. And though Preble was superseded, he had paved the way for a treaty requiring no further payment of tribute to Tripoli.

The Republicans, still in office at the conclusion of the Tripolitan War, drew from it the extraordinary conclusion that the United States and American interests could be adequately defended by gunboats operating in cooperation with artillery and fortifications ashore. For the next few years all appropriations for naval construction were diverted to the building of more and more gunboats. At the same time Napoleon was issuing new decrees and the British new Orders in Council so severely restrictive to neutral shipping that the United States Navy would soon be forced into a war for which it was materially unprepared.

Yet, despite the crippling Republican policies, the United States Navy preserved two advantages that were to make American naval operations in the War of 1812 among the most memorable in the nation's history. These were, first, the finest ships of their type in the world, notably the *Constitution*-class frigates, and, second, a corps of skilled officers, thoroughly imbued with the ideals and attitudes of a professional service.

11:

The War of 1812

In the post-Trafalgar period the intensifying commerce warfare between Britain and France left the United States the only major neutral trader on the high seas. American merchant shippers enjoyed unprecedented prosperity both in the general carrying trade and as exporters of American wheat, tobacco, and cotton. At the same time American merchantmen and even naval vessels, caught between Britain's Orders in Council and Napoleon's retaliatory Decrees, were subjected to increasing interference that eventually grew intolerable. Yet, despite continual restrictions and humiliations, the United States, for seven years after Trafalgar, maintained a technical neutrality. When at last in 1812 the Americans again took up arms in defense of their neutral rights, they chose Britain as their antagonist, for French ships had been virtually driven from the seas. The declaration of war was the result of no specific new incident. It was rather an explosive reaction to tensions built up through years of friction with the Royal Navy and of bitter feelings aggravated by British support of marauding Indian tribes in America.

The new pattern of interference with American shipping was set as early as 1806, when two British frigates virtually blockaded New York harbor, searching both deep-water and coastal merchantmen. On the slightest pretext they sent vessels to Halifax for condemnation. A shot fired by one of the frigates to force a sloop to heave to for inspection killed an American seaman.

Warships of the Royal Navy, constantly in and out of American harbors to victual and to gather intelligence on merchant ship movements or French privateers, flaunted their power. Most galling was their practice of pressing seamen from American ships. British naval officers, operating with undermanned crews that were further depleted by desertions, insisted on the right to search neutral vessels for British subjects. In their desperate need for men, they were likely to consider as an Englishman anybody who understood the English language. Possibly as many as 10,000 American sailors were forced to serve in the Royal Navy. There were other thousands of questionable cases, for it was not difficult for a British deserter to obtain false citizenship papers. Hence there was often justification for skepticism on the part of British captains, especially since they knew that no rebuke would be forthcoming from their professional superiors.

In the spring of 1807 the notorious *Chesapeake-Leopard* affair gave credence to the most extreme stories of British abuses. The British claimed that three of their deserters were enrolled in the crew of the newly commissioned American frigate *Chesapeake*, commanded by Commodore James Barron. Barron investigated, concluded that the British claims were false, and departed Hampton Roads in the *Chesapeake* with official dispatches for France. Waiting for him off the Capes on orders of the British admiral at Halifax was H.M. frigate *Leopard*. The British captain hailed the *Chesapeake*, demanding the three men. When they were denied him, he fired several broadsides into the American frigate, killing or wounding a score of her crew. Totally unprepared for action, Barron lowered his flag.

The American public reacted violently to this outrage. Impressment of merchant seamen was bad enough, but removing sailors by force from an American warship was an act of extreme provocation. The incidental slaughter of other Americans was indefensible under any circumstances short of war. President Jefferson's protests eventually brought a begrudging acknowledgment that the Royal Navy had gone too far. More than that the President could not expect, for he had neither the will nor the means for active defense of American rights. His pacifist sentiments were widely known. His navy consisted only of scores of useless gunboats and the two frigates and four smaller men-of-war then in commission.

The *Chesapeake-Leopard* affair confirmed Jefferson in his conviction that American warships should remain in their home ports. He believed moreover that an embargo prohibiting American merchantmen from trading with foreign nations might be the best answer to the extreme restrictions of the British Orders in Council of 1807. Toward the end of that year, Congress passed the Embargo Act that Jefferson wanted. The Act was designed as economic retaliation short of war, but during the 15 months it was in effect it created greater hardships at home than abroad. Because the crews of America's idle merchant ships could not be absorbed by the labor market, the only practical recourse for many an American sailor was to slip into Canada and sign on a British merchantman or warship. Jefferson through his Embargo thus inadvertently helped relieve the British manpower shortage. Illicit trade sprang up along the Canadian border, providing luxury imports but no revenue to the Federal government. Prices for American export produce plunged for want of a market. Only France profited by the disruption of Anglo-American trade. Napoleon, on the pretext of aiding the United States enforce the Embargo, seized 134 American ships and their cargoes, valued at $10,000,000, in ports under his control.

Jefferson was unprepared for the bitterness and lawlessness the Embargo aroused. Not only the British but the American government was denounced as the destroyer of American prosperity. In 1809, in response to popular protests, Congress repealed the Embargo, replacing it with a less stringent non-intercourse act. American commerce quickly revived, accompanied by a resumption of spoliations of American merchantmen by the warships of Britain, France, and their allies. By 1810 the British had seized nearly a thousand American ships; the French, some 500; the Danes, Neapolitans, Spaniards, and Dutch together, about 300.

British impressment of seamen however continued to be the focus of American indignation. When H.M. frigate *Guerrière*, 36, flagrantly seized a man from a merchant brig off New York harbor in May 1811, Captain John Rodgers was ordered to take U.S. frigate *President*, 44, out of the Chesapeake and run her down. Off the Virginia Capes Rodgers sighted a vessel hull down which he took to be the *Guerrière* and promptly gave chase. Not until after dark was he within hailing distance of the stranger, which was in fact H.M. sloop *Little Belt*, 22. After a confused exchange of hails, both vessels opened fire. The *Little Belt* was badly battered and had 31 casualties, but sailed away at dawn, refusing assistance. Because evidence was conflicting as to which vessel first opened fire, the governments took no official action, but many Americans felt that the *Chesapeake-Leopard* affair had been avenged.

The question of neutral rights on the high seas, though always in the background, did not itself actually bring on the War of 1812. The northeastern states, with the strongest maritime interests, were definitely against war. Prospering in spite of losses and humiliations, they demanded an enlarged navy to protect commerce. But they opposed retaliatory measures that could bring on armed conflict with Britain and thereby disrupt American seaborne commerce altogether. The impetus that eventually brought about war came not from the Eastern seaboard but from the agricultural and pioneer South and West.

James Madison succeeded Thomas Jefferson as President in 1809, thereby perpetuating Republican control. The Congressional election of the following year swept in a younger generation of Republican "War Hawks," led by Henry Clay of Kentucky and John C. Calhoun of South Carolina. These fiery young statesmen reflected the pioneers' insatiable land hunger. They were empire builders who would be happy to see the boundaries of the United States extended from the Atlantic to the Pacific and from the Isthmus of Panama to the North Pole. To them the national destiny required the seizure of Spanish Florida and British Canada. From the former, Creek and Seminole

Indians periodically raided into the Deep South. In the Northwest the Indians had been formed into a confederacy under Chief Tecumseh, partly to oppose the westward advance of American pioneers. The Indians in both areas were widely believed to have been armed and encouraged by the British. Tecumseh's repulse in the Battle of Tippecanoe in November 1811 merely convinced the War Hawks that the trans-Ohio pioneer could be safeguarded only through the conquest of Canada. Knowing little about maritime matters and caring less, the ultranationalist War Hawks nevertheless denounced impressment and loudly condemned trade restrictions, particularly when they hurt commerce originating in the Mississippi Valley. Yet they voted consistently against every measure designed to strengthen the U.S. Navy for a sea war against Britain. The way to get at Britain and her feeble ally Spain, they insisted, was to strike at their possessions in America. "On to Canada!" became their monotonous cry. Capture of Canada, wrote Jefferson, would be "a mere matter of marching." Clay insisted that if necessary the Kentucky militia could capture it all by themselves.

Britain's difficulties and Napoleon's continuing successes encouraged the War Hawks to spur President Madison into action. In April 1812, Congress, under their leadership, authorized the President to reimpose the Embargo and call up 100,000 militia. On June 1 Madison presented his war message, drawing particular attention to impressment, neutral rights, and Indian affairs. In Congress the War Hawks rode down the opposition of Congressmen from the Northeast. The House of Representatives decided for war by a vote of 79 to 49; the Senate, by a vote of 19 to 13. On June 18, 1812, the United States with defense forces consisting of a 6,700-man army, a total of 18 seagoing warships, and a scattering of gunboats, mostly out of commission, formally declared war on the Mistress of the Seas.

The Atlantic Front—1812

The last thing the British wanted in the summer of 1812 was war with the United States. Their contest with Napoleon was approaching a crisis. The cost of the Peninsular War and American restrictions on trade had seriously weakened Britain's financial structure. In England unemployment was widespread and inflation severe. British troops in Spain needed American grain. The prosperity of the British West Indies was dependent on American trade.

In the circumstances, the British attitude toward the United States had become increasingly conciliatory. In late June, before news of the American declaration reached London, the British government revoked the Orders in Council. When the declaration of war arrived, the Cabinet decided to await American reaction to the revocation of the Orders and to pursue a defensive policy, hoping that "the accustomed relations of peace and amity between the two countries may yet be restored."[1] Admiral Sir John Warren, placed in over-all command of the combined Halifax and West Indies stations, was instructed to propose restoration of peace. Failing that, he was to encourage peace sentiment in New England while avoiding offensive naval action along the American coast.

When peace efforts failed—over the issue of impressment, which the British considered a purely domestic matter—the Royal Navy began to build up Warren's squadrons. In December 1812 the news reached London of the virtual annihilation of Napoleon's armies in Russia. The need to come to terms with the United States now appeared less urgent. A few days later the British government announced a commercial blockade of Delaware and Chesapeake Bays, a measure intended to weaken the position of the United States government by sowing discontent, while sparing the merchants of New York and New England.

By contrast, the United States Navy plunged into the war with vigor, and early obtained striking success—even though the Navy Department had only one shipyard in commission and no plan of operations. The U. S. Navy's great assets were three outsize frigates and a corps of experienced young officers, mostly "Preble's boys," whose professional competence was soon to win universal respect. Within a few hours after learning of the declaration of war, John Rodgers departed New York with a squadron comprising three frigates, a sloop, and a brig. Fruitless search for a British con-

[1] In the King's speech from the throne on the opening of Parliament, July 30, 1812.

voy known to be at sea carried Rodgers almost to the English Channel, but the squadron returned home almost empty-handed. Ill luck rather than poor judgment was to blame, but the experience supported the view, soon officially adopted, that American men-of-war should operate not in squadrons but singly or in pairs, as commerce raiders.

The frigate *Constitution* could not join Rodgers' squadron when the war began, for she was fitting out at Annapolis under her new Preble-trained commander, Captain Isaac Hull. Aware of the danger of being blockaded in Chesapeake Bay, Hull sailed for New York in mid-July and nearly fell into the hands of a British squadron off the New Jersey coast, which he mistook for Rodgers'. During the persisting calms of the next two and a half days, the *Constitution*'s crew, by kedging and by towing with ship's boats, kept the frigate out of range of the pursuing British and finally made good their escape to sea during a summer squall. Thus cut off from New York, Hull steered for Boston. From here he departed

for a raiding cruise in the Gulf of St. Lawrence. After capturing several merchantmen, Hull learned that the British Halifax squadron was in the vicinity, whereupon he prudently headed south. On the afternoon of August 13, when about 700 miles due east of Boston, the *Constitution* sighted a sail and stood down to investigate. The stranger proved to be H.M. frigate *Guerrière*, Captain James D. Dacres commanding, which had been detached from the British squadron and ordered to Halifax for repairs.

What followed is a classic of frigate tactics in single ship combat between competent commanders. Dacres, determined not to flee from his heavier American opponent, took the defensive. By repeatedly wearing ship as he retired slowly down wind, he presented alternate broadsides which threatened to rake the *Constitution*. During the final closing, he relied on the firepower of his stern chasers while maintaining his downwind course and kept his frigate as steady a gun-platform as possible, ready to overwhelm the *Constitution* with the

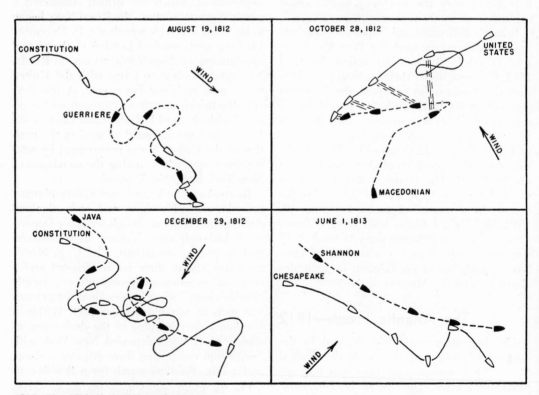

FRIGATE ACTIONS IN THE WAR OF 1812

rapidity of his broadsides. Hull, on the offensive, first reduced his canvas for battle, then bore down upon the *Guerrière,* avoiding her raking fire by yawing whenever his opponent wore. Setting the main topgallant sail to speed the *Constitution* in his final approach, Hull surged up on his opponent's port quarter. Within 20 minutes of close action, the *Guerrière's* mizzenmast went by the board, acting as a rudder that turned the ship's beam to the wind, slowed her down, and enabled the *Constitution* to cross her bows and rake her with several broadsides. As the *Constitution* wore to avoid being raked in turn, the *Guerrière's* bowsprit thrust into the American frigate's mizzen rigging. Each side prepared to repel boarders, and heavy casualties were inflicted by short-range musket fire in the brief interval before the *Guerrière's* fore- and mainmast went over the side, leaving her rolling helplessly in the heavy seas. The next day, after the prisoners had been removed, the shattered hulk was burned. American losses were 7 killed and 7 wounded; British, 15 killed and 63 wounded.

No flaw can be found in Hull's tactics, in which he made optimum use of his far superior ship and his larger and better trained crew. The *Constitution* had a 7-to-5 advantage in weight of broadside and carried 468 men, as compared to 263 aboard the *Guerrière.* The American frigate was more strongly built and hence withstood damage better. The British fired more rapidly, but their shot was poorly aimed, being generally high, whereas the American shot had repeatedly hulled the *Guerrière* as well as brought down her masts.

While the Americans were still celebrating Hull's victory and before the British had finished explaining it away, the U.S. Navy scored another triumph. Captain Stephen Decatur in the *United States,* 44, was off Africa plying the southern westbound transatlantic route in October 1812 when his course crossed that of the British frigate *Macedonian,* 38, fresh out of refit, bound for the West Indies. The *Macedonian* was a very fast ship, but her heaviest long guns were only 18-pounders. She could have escaped with ease from the notoriously slow *United States,* whose 24-pounder long guns and 42-pounder carronades held the advantage in range and almost a 2-to-1 advantage in weight of broadside. Her captain, John S. Carden, a very senior frigate commander, itching for a fight but grossly underestimating the quality of his opponent, believed he could close with and outfight the lumbering American frigate. Decatur, though only 33 years old and a notable fire-eater, fought with the utmost caution, restraint, and shrewdness. The battle was "no contest." Carden made a blundering approach, while Decatur fell off the wind before him and inflicted heavy damage long before Carden's 18-pounders had the range. During the engagement Carden never got within a hundred yards of the *United States.* At the end, Decatur mercifully declined an opportunity to rake the Briton. Carden surrendered, and the *Macedonian* was taken into the U.S. Navy. The British had suffered over a hundred casualties, the Americans only a dozen. Decatur had handled the situation so ably that the veteran Carden appeared downright incompetent by comparison.

In December the Americans won their third successive frigate victory. Off Bahia, Brazil, the *Constitution,* now commanded by Commodore William Bainbridge, met the *Java,* Captain Henry Lambert, in one of the hardest fought frigate actions of all time. The two ships were superficially well-matched, each nominally a 44. The American was heavier and had a somewhat heavier weight of broadside (654 lbs. to 576 lbs.) and slightly larger crew (475 to 426); the Briton was faster and handier. Engaging, the two frigates for almost two hours pounded hulls, shattered rigging, and bloodied the decks in "a succession of evolutions . . . accompanied by a continual play of the guns."[2] The *Constitution's* wheel was shot away fairly early in the action, but her crew handled her with great skill by means of the less efficient relieving tackles. About an hour later, the *Java* lost her bowsprit and foremast and was caught in stays and swept by at least two broadsides. Bainbridge was twice wounded; Lambert was killed by a shot from the tops. Inexorably, the heavier, better-aimed American broadside fire reduced the British frigate to a hulk. The inadequately trained British crew suffered 122

[2] Captain A. T. Mahan USN, *Sea Power in Its Relations to the War of 1812,* II (Boston, 1918), 4–5.

casualties; the well-trained Americans, 34. The wreck of the surrendered *Java* was burned next day, and the *Constitution* returned to Boston for repairs. Commodore Bainbridge, the unfortunate captain of the *Philadelphia* in the Tripolitan War, had completely justified the Navy's faith in him.

After piling honors on Hull, Decatur, and Bainbridge, the United States Congress enthusiastically voted funds for six additional frigates and four ships of the line, none of which could be completed in time to see action in the war. The British were surprised and exasperated; not in almost a decade had a captain of the Royal Navy struck his colors.

Of the nine naval engagements fought in 1812, five were American victories.[3] But the U.S. Navy could neither protect American commerce nor seriously disrupt British commerce, protected as it was by a well organized convoy system. Though the British losses in warships were numerically greater than the American losses, they amounted to less than one per cent of Britain's warships, while the small United States fleet had lost more than 20 per cent of its men-of-war. Even the victorious American frigate actions were costly, for after the engagement each of the frigates had to break off its commerce raiding cruise and return to port for repairs. Once in port, American warships were likely to be bottled up. The famous *Constellation,* for example, never throughout the war found an opportunity to escape from her Norfolk base to conduct operations against the enemy.

The Extension of the Blockade—1813–1814

"It is of the highest importance to the character and interests of the country," a nettled British Admiralty informed Admiral Warren,

[3] In addition to the three frigate battles described, the following engagements took place during the year between British and American warships. In July H.M.S. *Shannon,* 38, defeated U.S.S. *Nautilus,* 14. In August U.S.S. *Essex,* 32, defeated H.M.S. *Alert,* 16; and H.M.S. *Barbados,* 28, defeated U.S.S. *James Madison,* 14. In October U.S.S. *Wasp,* 18, defeated H.M.S. *Frolic,* 18, but along with her prize was captured the same day by H.M.S. *Poictiers,* 74. In November H.M.S. *Southampton,* 32, defeated U.S.S. *Vixen,* 14.

"that the naval force of the enemy should be quickly and completely disposed of." This was a large order, never literally achieved, but Warren set to attain the same effect with an ever-tightening blockade. Early in 1813 he extended the blockade from New York to New Orleans, and before the end of the year he added Long Island Sound. Commodore Decatur, trying to put to sea from New York with the frigates *United States* and *Macedonian* and a sloop, was chased by a superior force and had to seek refuge up the Thames River at New London. There the two frigates remained for the duration of the war. Off the southern New England coast the Royal Navy kept a large blockading force, including as many as three ships of the line in addition to frigates and smaller vessels. "Serious depredations have been committed even in our harbors," complained the Governor of Connecticut, "and to such an extent that the usual communication through the Sound is almost wholly interrupted."[4]

In early 1813 no officer in the U.S. Navy was more renowned than James Lawrence, then only 32 years old. Idolized by the public, he was a favorite of his fellow officers. He had early won fame as Decatur's second-in-command in the burning of the *Philadelphia.* In the first few weeks of 1813 he refurbished his reputation by gallant actions off the Brazilian coast, where he had remained in command of U.S. sloop *Hornet* after the departure of the *Constitution* following her victory over the *Java.* Eluding a British 74, Lawrence captured a brig with $20,000 aboard, and shortly afterward sank H.M. sloop *Peacock* in a brief, bloody battle. His reward was promotion to the command of U.S. frigate *Chesapeake,* 38, lying in Boston harbor under the surveillance of two British frigates. Captain Lawrence took command of the *Chesapeake* in May with orders to prepare her for a raid on shipping in the Gulf of St. Lawrence. His immediate problem was to obtain an adequate crew. Since American seamen signed on men-of-war for a cruise only, the best professional sailors in the Boston area, tempted by tales of riches to be had, were by this time at sea in privateers. Hence Lawrence had to man his ship largely with raw recruits.

[4] Quotations from Mahan, *War of 1812,* II, 151–2.

In the circumstances, Lawrence might well have awaited an opportunity to slip out to sea past the blockaders, as other American frigates had done, in order to exercise his green crew at gunnery and shiphandling before taking them into action. Certainly the Navy Department had not expected him to seek battle with another frigate. Even an American victory in such an engagement could easily damage the *Chesapeake* enough to prevent her from carrying out her strategically more important commerce-raiding assignment. But when Captain Philip B. V. Broke of H.M. frigate *Shannon*, 38, pointedly dismissed his other blockading frigate and paraded back and forth before Boston harbor, the ardent young Lawrence could not resist the implied challenge. On June 1, even before Broke's written challenge reached him, he put to sea. He was taking out the ill-manned *Chesapeake* against a formidable antagonist, for the *Shannon* was in several respects the crack frigate of the Royal Navy. Broke, a gunnery expert, had commanded her for seven years. Improving upon the reforms of Sir Charles Douglas, he had adopted novel devices for control and accuracy of fire. In a period when most British naval officers neglected gunnery practice, Broke drilled his men at the guns twice a day, five days a week.

Broke led the way seaward until at 5 PM the *Shannon* hove to, awaiting the *Chesapeake*. This was to be no battle of maneuver. About an hour later, with both ships under reduced sail and only 50 yards apart, the firing began. The *Chesapeake*, coming up on the *Shannon*'s windward quarter, had her headsails shot away and her helmsman shot down. Out of control, she turned into the wind, was taken aback, and, with sternway on, drifted down into Broke's raking broadsides. Led by their captain, the British swarmed aboard the American frigate. By this time, most of the American officers were casualties and Lawrence himself, mortally wounded by a musket shot from the tops, had been taken below decks. The British boarders quickly overwhelmed the leaderless American crew. The battle had lasted just 15 minutes. In that quarter hour 148 Americans and 83 British were wounded or lost their lives, more than in any of the earlier frigate actions. Reported Broke in laconic summary, "The enemy made a desperate but disorderly resistance." Lawrence died while being taken to Halifax, deliriously repeating, it is said, "Don't give up the ship."

Lawrence's defeat presaged the dark days ahead for Americans when the frigates of the U.S. Navy were rarely able to elude the blockade and get to sea. Napoleon's defeat at Leipzig in October 1813 and his abdication in April of the following year freed more and more British power for employment in the war against America. Finally at the end of May 1814 the blockade included "all the ports, harbors, bays, creeks, rivers, inlets, outlets, islands, and seacoasts of the United States. . . ." American commerce in 1812 was 65 per cent of that in 1811, with much of it under British license for delivery to Wellington in the Peninsula. In 1813, the lengthened blockade reduced it to 45 per cent, and in 1814 total blockade cut American merchant traffic to 11 per cent of the 1811 figure. The United States had exported almost 1,500,000 barrels of flour in 1812; this figure was cut to less than 200,000 in 1814. The practical cessation of coastal commerce seriously disrupted the internal economy. A host of wagoners, taking up this domestic carrying trade, was able to move only a fraction of the accumulated tonnage.[5] Hard money disappeared from the southern and central states into the Boston banks, until New England also was blockaded. Major crops found no local market, while the same kind of produce might bring grossly inflated prices only a few hundred miles away.

Under these conditions of growing commercial paralysis along the seaboard, America's skippers of close-winded schooners, who with intimate knowledge of local waters might skim out of shallow passages, gambled that they could outsail the British watchdogs. Of 526 privateers registered, 200 actually made one most popular, as well as most effective, means of maritime reprisal was privateering. The

[5] The magnitude of the problem is illustrated by the fact that wagons required 46 days in good weather to transport goods from Charleston, South Carolina to Philadelphia. Some newspapers in New England, where "Mr. Madison's War" was most unpopular, sarcastically listed the arrival of wagons, in columns formerly used to announce the arrival of ships.

or more cruises, taking 1,344 prizes. As early as 1812 Captain Joshua Barney set the pattern with the Baltimore schooner *Rossie,* which took 19 prizes. Captain Thomas Boyle, also of Baltimore, made 60 captures, including a schooner of the Royal Navy. Impudently scouring Britain's home waters for prizes, he sent by cartel to Lloyd's Coffee House a proclamation of blockade of the British Isles. And there was the notable fight of the privateer *General Armstrong.* Caught in the Azores by British forces en route for the Louisiana campaign, she inflicted heavy casualties and cost her opponents a three-week delay, vital time as it proved, before she herself was destroyed. Subject of many a romantic tale, the American privateers became symbols of daring retaliation against the British. Their pinpricks, by annoying Britain's politically powerful merchant class, at least contributed to the unpopularity of the war in England and, consequently, to the negotiated peace.

The principal naval weapon of the war however remained the blockade of the American coast by the Royal Navy. "The pressure brought to bear on America by the British blockade was exceedingly effective, but it was silent, and so historians have tended to forget it," wrote Theodore Roosevelt. "Its mere existence inflicted a direct material loss to the American people a hundred fold greater than the entire American navy was able to inflict on Great Britain from the beginning to the end of its gallant career in this war."[6]

Porter and the *Essex*

In late 1812, before the British blockade seriously restricted the United States Navy, Captain David Porter had put to sea in U.S. frigate *Essex,* 32, missed a South Atlantic rendezvous with Bainbridge and Lawrence, and proceeded independently around the Horn. For a full year the *Essex* cruised the Pacific. Her most successful venture was capturing a dozen ships of the British whaling fleet off the Galapagos Islands and driving the rest to cover. One prize was converted into a consort, the *Essex Junior,* carrying 20 light guns. Learning that Captain James Hillyar with

[6] In Sir William Laird Clowes, *The Royal Navy,* VI (London, 1901), 68.

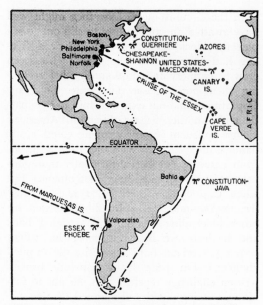

FRIGATE ACTIONS AND CRUISE OF THE *ESSEX*

H.M. frigate *Phoebe,* 38, and two sloops-of-war had arrived on the Chilian coast in pursuit of him, Porter sailed to the South Seas and completed a thorough refit in the Marquesas. Then instead of continuing around the world, he could not resist the challenge of Hillyar's presence off Chile. He returned to the South American coast, reaching Valparaiso on February 3, 1814. The *Phoebe* and the sloop *Cherub* arrived five days later.

Porter at once found himself and the *Essex* in a precarious position. His fire power was short range, concentrated in a main battery of forty 32-pounder carronades. The *Phoebe* and *Cherub* outranged him with their long guns, and their combined weight of broadside was greater than his. Porter hoped to get to sea, separate the British vessels, and defeat them one at a time, but Hillyar anchored to windward at the seaward end of the roadstead prepared to intercept any move the *Essex* might make.

Porter waited in vain for over six weeks to catch Hillyar nodding. Then, on March 28 under the strain of a gusty south wind, the *Essex* went adrift. One anchor cable parted; the crew cut the other when the second anchor failed to hold. Close hauled, the *Essex* tried to claw out to windward, and in fact reached the open sea. But Porter's good luck had run its course. With escape in sight, the *Essex* was hit by a violent squall. Losing her maintopmast, she put in toward the coast, anchoring again a few miles north of Valparaiso. The British, ignoring the question of neutral waters, closed in to attack. Hillyar's opening cannonade at 4 P.M. damaged the *Essex*'s rigging and cut the spring lines Porter had rigged to enable him to turn broadside to the enemy. Hillyar then stood off and prepared to anchor in long-gun range of the *Essex*'s seaward quarter, instructing the *Cherub* to keep underway. With the British to leeward, Porter elected to cut his cable and bring the *Essex* down on them within range of his carronades, rather than be shot to pieces at their leisure. In the furious gunfire that ensued, the *Phoebe* also maneuvered to leeward, keeping the *Essex* within range while suffering little damage herself. As a last resort, Porter tried to run his frigate ashore, but the dying wind failed him. Reluctantly he lowered his colors after giving any crew member who wished to swim ashore a chance to do so. The *Essex* lost 58 killed and 65 wounded, about half her crew, while the *Phoebe* and *Cherub* together had only 15 casualties. Porter had made the common error of a commerce raider in seeking battle instead of pursuing his strategic objective, the enemy's merchantmen.

The Burning of Washington, 1814

By the spring of 1813 the British had decided to supplement the blockade and to victual the blockading ships by making punitive raids along the coast. Rear Admiral Sir George Cockburn with four ships of the line and smaller vessels twice penetrated the Chesapeake Bay country that year. He reached the head of the Bay in April, destroyed supplies and armaments, and even disrupted traffic on the main highway between Philadelphia and Baltimore. In mid-summer he again swept the Bay. On the whole, Cockburn's activities were on the gentlemanly side. He licensed American grain ships for passage to Europe and, if there had been no resistance, paid private owners for the livestock and supplies the British had helped themselves to. The local American gunboats, designed to prevent just such an invasion, hastily retreated up into

shoal rivers beyond Cockburn's reach. That year the heaviest fighting in the Bay occurred when American forces successfully repulsed a British effort to capture Norfolk, and the *Constellation* blockaded there, but only three of the invaders were killed in the encounter.

In 1814, when 2,500 veterans of Wellington's army arrived from France under Major General Robert Ross, the British had a combined force of about 4,000 troops, 30 transports, and 20 warships with which to stage a more ambitious raid, both for its own effect and to prevent the United States from concentrating forces against a British offensive to be staged simultaneously in the Lake Champlain area. Their immediate objective was the capital of the United States.

Warned of the forthcoming attack, President Madison called his Cabinet together on July 1. The only defense force then available was a few hundred regulars, some marines, and Commodore Joshua Barney's flotilla of 13 barges and gunboats which the British had bottled up in the Patuxent River. The government authorized calling up 93,500 militiamen and assigned 15,000 to Brigadier General William H. Winder for the defense of Washington. But as usual in this war, it was easier for the government to summon than to obtain men. Seven weeks later, when the British raid began, Winder had a force of only 6,000.

The Royal Navy first established an advance base at Tangier Island, then landed the troops, unopposed, on the west bank of the Patuxent River. The British struck with the speed and precision of the crack professionals they were. General Ross marched his veterans briskly north on a road parallel to the river while, on the river itself, British warships drove the American gunboats ahead of them and stood ready to support the army's movements. They almost trapped Commodore Barney at Upper Marlboro, forcing him to burn his boats and retreat to join the defending army with his 400 men and their guns. In the final approach, Ross slipped north to Bladensburg, outflanking Winder's prepared positions, and with a single rocket-supported charge routed the hastily reformed militiamen who stood between him and the capital. Only Commodore Barney and his gunners courageously presented a core of resistance. Four hundred against 4,000, they were outflanked and captured. The British attackers lost 64 killed and 185 wounded; the American army disintegrated, losing only 12 killed and 40 wounded. With no further opposition, the British marched on to Washington and that night burned both the Capitol and White House. United States authorities meanwhile burned the Navy Yard, a frigate on the stocks there, and other public property to keep them from falling into the enemy's hands. The next day General Ross and his army withdrew without suffering a single additional casualty.

Simultaneously a British squadron of two frigates and three sloops had sailed up the Potomac for an attack coordinated with that of Ross's army. Delayed by Kettle Bottom Shoals and contrary winds, against which they kedged their way upstream for 50 miles, they arrived after Washington was burned. Nevertheless, they forced the capitulation of Alexandria and seized the American shipping there before retiring down the river. Against haphazard opposition, the squadron had lost only seven men killed, 45 wounded.

The British fleet then transported the army north to attack Baltimore, where for two weeks the citizens had been busily preparing defenses. Ross landed his troops between the Patapsco and Back rivers and drove through the first defense line at the cost of his own life. The death of Ross, the earthwork defenses of the city, and the British fleet's inability to force an entrance to the harbor obliged the attackers to cancel the raid. On the night of September 13-14, Francis Scott Key, an American civilian held aboard one of the British ships, witnessed the unsuccessful bombardment of Fort McHenry and wrote "The Star-Spangled Banner" to memorialize the event. A month later, except for the blockade ships, the British fleet had departed for its winter station in the West Indies.

The Great Lakes Campaigns

While world events and British sea power determined the course of history on the Atlantic seaboard, the war along the Canadian border developed in a manner entirely unforeseen by the United States. Instead of winning a quick, bloodless victory in Canada—Jefferson's "mere matter of marching"—the United States military forces made no headway at all. At the outbreak of war, the elderly American generals in command, in many instances veterans of the American Revolution, lacked ability to organize and energy to carry out an effective offensive. Under their indecisive leadership many American militiamen, exercising a legal prerogative, refused to cross the border into Canada at all.

The United States had not overestimated the weakness of Canada. There were only 4,500 British regulars to defend a thousand miles of frontier. Along that frontier ran their single line of logistic support, the St. Lawrence-Great Lakes waterway. Each of their bases—Malden on Lake Erie, the Niagara forts, York (Toronto) and Kingston on Lake Ontario, and Montreal and Quebec on the St. Lawrence—would be cut off if the Americans captured any of those downstream from it. Canada had no alternate supply route for traffic of wartime volume, for her waterways provided such efficient peacetime transportation as to make all-weather roads between towns a luxury the thinly populated country could not afford.

That the key to the northern front was control and use of the Great Lakes and St. Lawrence at first escaped the appreciation of the Americans, who attempted to launch separate thrusts across the narrow land bridges along the border. (See map page 217.) In the west, General William Hull, Captain Isaac Hull's irresolute and aging uncle, crossed into Canada from Detroit but was immediately thrown back by the vigorous action of General Isaac Brock. Without firing a shot, Hull ignominiously surrendered Detroit to the British on August 16, 1812. A small British raiding party had already captured the United States post on Mackinac Island at the head of Lake Michigan, and another had taken Fort Dearborn (Chicago). With Lake Erie and all the border country west of the Detroit River and beyond temporarily secure, General Brock doubled back to Niagara and repulsed an assault there, though at the cost of his life. When a desultory American advance toward Montreal also failed, winter brought an end to a year of complete frustration to American ambitions for conquest.

That September the Navy Department had

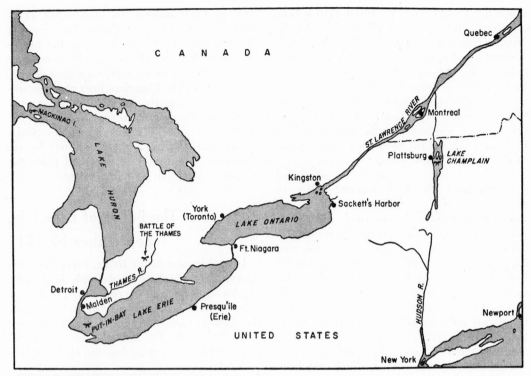

LAKE CAMPAIGNS OF THE WAR OF 1812

ordered Captain Isaac Chauncey to command on the Great Lakes. With the brig *Oneida*, 18, on Lake Ontario as his only man-of-war, his immediate task was to establish bases and build up fleets with which to control the waterways. Recognizing the strategic weakness of Canadian communications, he established his headquarters at Sackett's Harbor, New York, where the waters of Lake Ontario enter the St. Lawrence River, and selected Presqu'Isle (now Erie), Pennsylvania as the base for his subordinate Lake Erie command. By late spring, 1813, he was able to support the American army in a raid on York (Toronto). There a 30-gun ship was burned as well as much of the town itself, a fact used by some of the British to justify their burning of Washington the next year.

The British by this time were strengthening their Canadian defenses as rapidly as possible. Admiral Warren assigned one of his best captains, Sir James Lucas Yeo, to Lake Ontario and a veteran of Trafalgar, Commander Robert H. Barclay, to Lake Erie. Then Yeo at Kingston and Chauncey at Sackett's Harbor,

with only the width of the island-studded headwaters of the St. Lawrence between them, concentrated their energies on a ship-building race in which neither ever achieved what he considered enough superiority to launch an all-out attack. Since occasional skirmishes left the rivals' relative strength about the same as before, the Lake Ontario front degenerated into a battle of adze, hammer, and chisel that eventually produced great 100-gun ships destined never to fire a shot in battle. The Ontario campaign thus turned into a stalemate of wasted opportunities and wasted lumber. Without control of Lake Ontario a military decision in that general area proved impossible of attainment.

On Lake Erie however, 27-year-old Oliver Hazard Perry showed what brilliant naval leadership and intelligent cooperation with the army could accomplish for the United States. Volunteering for duty on fresh water to escape the boredom of the blockaded seagoing Navy, Master Commandant Perry arrived in the spring of 1813 at the new naval base at Presqu'Isle. His first task was to bring

THE WAR OF 1812　　217

down the *Caledonia,* a captured British brig, and four schooners from Black Rock on the Niagara River near Buffalo. His second was to complete the building of two brigs. These brigs, mounting eighteen 32-pounder carronades and two long 12-pounders, would be the most powerful men-of-war on the lake. One of them Perry named the *Niagara;* the other, which was to be his flagship, he named the *Lawrence,* for his good friend the captain of the ill-fated *Chesapeake.*

Despite shortage of materials and skilled personnel and the back-breaking labor of transporting guns, ammunition, cables, and stores from Pittsburgh via river and barely passable road, Perry had completed the two brigs in July, ready for transfer across the sand bar that separated the Presqu'Isle anchorage from Lake Erie. It had required all of his extraordinary drive to push the work through. At one point, exasperated beyond endurance by official lethargy and lack of cooperation, he asked to be relieved. But the Secretary of the Navy refused, concluding: "It is right that you should reap the harvest which you have sown."

Since the fall of Detroit in the previous year, Commander Barclay's squadron of five small vessels had maintained control of Lake Erie. Now, fearful of the consequences of Perry's activity, Barclay blockaded Presqu'Isle. But catching the blockaders off station, Perry floated the new, unarmed brigs across the bar and then quickly installed their guns. The anxious moment when the American squadron might have been totally destroyed by a resolute British attack had passed. With his augmented fleet, Perry immediately took control of the lake. The strategic situation was reversed. It was now Barclay who was threatened with calamity. With his line of communications cut and with 14,000 Indians as well as his own naval forces and troops at Malden to feed, he had either to regain control of the lake or evacuate overland what he could, leaving the Detroit area open to re-conquest.

While Perry patrolled the lake, Barclay fell back on his base at Malden, awaiting completion of the ship-rigged *Detroit,* armed with 17 long guns of various sizes and two carronades, a conglomeration of weapons from the ram-

parts of Fort Malden. In mid-August Perry moved his squadron to Put-in-Bay, opposite Malden, and cruised in that area, having intelligence that the *Detroit* would soon carry Barclay's flag in an attempt, regardless of cost, to re-establish the Canadian lines of communication. Early on the morning of September 10 the two fleets came in sight of each other. Perry's three major vessels *Lawrence, Caledonia,* and *Niagara* were supported by six schooners. The American fleet had twice the weight of broadside of its opponents.

The Battle of Lake Erie, September 10, 1813

In anticipation of the battle, Perry had consciously followed Nelson's example in describing his battle plan to his captains. The line of battle was to be adhered to so as to pair off the flagship *Lawrence* against the British flagship *Detroit,* the *Caledonia* against the *Hunter,* and the *Niagara* against the *Queen Char-*

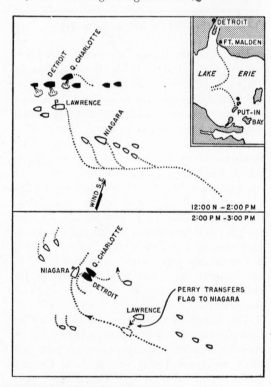

BATTLE OF LAKE ERIE, SEPTEMBER 10, 1813

lotte. The schooners, of slight value in such a battle, would fire at targets of opportunity. Perry's final instruction encouraged all captains to lay their ships close alongside the enemy.

Just before noon the two fleets were on parallel courses in light airs. Perry, having the wind, stood down in the *Lawrence* to bring his carronades to bear. But his second in line, the *Caledonia,* a sluggish ex-merchantman armed primarily with long guns, did not follow the flagship to close the range, and the *Niagara,* third in line, kept station behind the *Caledonia.* Consequently, the *Lawrence* for two hours became the sole target for the concentrated attack of three British men-of-war. While severely damaging her opponents, she herself was reduced to a wreck, suffering nearly 60 per cent casualties. A little after 1:30 PM the purser, the chaplain, and Perry himself fired her last serviceable gun. Leaving the national ensign still flying in the shattered *Lawrence,* Perry embarked in a small boat and was rowed to the *Niagara,* which, in the freshening breeze, had just passed to windward of the *Caledonia.* With him Perry took his commodore's pennant and his battle flag, a blue banner carrying in white letters Lawrence's dying words: "DONT GIVE UP THE SHIP."

In his fresh flagship Perry forged ahead and bore up as if to break through the British line just ahead of the *Detroit.* To avoid being raked and also in order to bring a fresh broadside to bear, the *Detroit* wore. In doing so she collided with the *Queen Charlotte,* which was ranging ahead to leeward. As the two British ships lay fouled, Perry sailed the *Niagara* athwart the bows of one and the stern of the other, his starboard guns sending double-shotted raking fire the length of their decks. Shortly afterward the *Detroit* and *Queen Charlotte,* reduced to helplessness, lowered their flags, and the smaller British vessels soon followed suit. American casualties numbered 123, two-thirds of them in the *Lawrence;* British casualties numbered 135. Taking an old letter from his pocket, Perry scribbled across the back his report to General William H. Harrison: "Dear Gen'l:—We have met the enemy and they are ours; two ships, two brigs, one schooner, and one sloop. Yours with great respect and esteem. O. H. Perry."

By the end of the month, sooner than the enemy believed possible, Perry had repaired his ships and transported General Harrison's army across the lake. The British, promptly evacuating Detroit and Malden, retreated up the Thames river valley with their Indian allies, but Harrison's forces overtook and dispersed them. In this encounter, known as the Battle of the Thames, the Indian leader Tecumseh was killed. With his death, Indian opposition to the Americans collapsed. The "northwest" rested securely in American hands, and British plans to create an Indian buffer state between the United States and Canada had to be abandoned.[7]

The Battle of Lake Champlain, September 11, 1814

In 1813, at about the time when the British government could foresee the possibility of a more vigorous land campaign in North America, the Czar of Russia as an ally of England and friend of the United States offered to mediate the Anglo-American struggle. Although England declined the Czar's offer, that November the British prime minister proposed that direct negotiations between British and American delegates be held at Ghent, in Flanders. President Madison accepted the proposal, and discussions finally began in August 1814. Mindful that victories in the field would strengthen their position at the conference table, the British increased activity on the northern front, abetted the Creeks in an Indian war along the Florida border, and even launched an expedition for the conquest of Louisiana.

[7] Today it is difficult to appreciate how serious a threat to the integrity of the United States had been contained in British occupation of Detroit. British statesmen abandoned the idea of an Indian state as a buffer between the United States and Canada with great reluctance even after Perry's victory in reality decided the question. Such a buffer state was again proposed during the peace negotiations in 1814, its southern boundary to run from Sandusky, Ohio, on Lake Erie to Kaskaskia, Illinois, on the Mississippi, south of St. Louis.

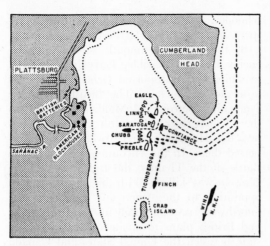

BATTLE OF LAKE CHAMPLAIN, SEPTEMBER 11, 1814

Up to this time both the Americans and the British had neglected the Champlain country, Burgoyne's invasion route in the American Revolution. Now in 1814 the British believed that a successful thrust deep into New York state with an available 15,000-man army, including four brigades of Wellington's veterans, could certainly force the United States to accept the British peace terms. Sir George Prevost, Governor General of Canada and commander in chief, would personally direct the campaign.

Despite an American squadron controlling the lake, collusion of private citizens with the enemy and official blundering made the American situation desperate. American farmers drove hundreds of beef cattle across the Vermont border to the British commissaries. Twice Americans had been intercepted on the lake towing large spars, obviously masts for the ship-rigged *Confiance* building at the British naval base just inside the Canadian border at the foot of the lake. When the British army under General Prevost began its unopposed march south into the United States, only 1,500 men under General Alexander Macomb at Plattsburg stood in its way. The British took their time however, for they wished to gain control of the lake and use it to support the advance of the army. As soon as the Royal Navy could complete the *Confiance*, armed with 27 long 24-pounders and 10 carronades, General Prevost expected the British squadron under Commander George Downie to be able

to sweep the waters clear of the American vessels. The new British flagship would be by far the most powerful single man-of-war on Lake Champlain.

Master Commandant Thomas Macdonough, another of "Preble's boys," commanded the American naval forces. Like Perry, he had succeeded in building a fleet practically from the keel up. By mid-summer 1814, his heterogeneous squadron consisted of the corvette *Saratoga*, mounting 18 heavy carronades and eight long 24-pounders, the brig *Eagle*, the schooner *Ticonderoga*, the sloop *Preble*, and ten gunboats.

The British regulars occupied Plattsburg on September 6. General Macomb withdrew across the Saranac River into a prepared defensive position on the peninsula between the river and the lake. This defense-work he strengthened with every means at hand, using the torn-up bridges for breastworks. Volunteers poured in from New York and Vermont, now that their country was threatened, and Macdonough brought his squadron into Plattsburg Bay to cover Macomb's flank from attack by Downie.

Macdonough's move was a gamble. If Prevost defeated Macomb, British artillery could force the American squadron out into the lake to almost certain defeat by Downie. On the other hand, if Downie first repulsed the Americans on the lake, he could then use his guns to support Prevost ashore. Macdonough therefore assumed the strongest defensive position he could devise. He anchored his four major vessels in a line between Plattsburg and Cumberland Head. (See diagram.) There would be no sail handling; each vessel would be a steady gun-platform with maximum gun crews. Shoal water would prevent the enemy from doubling his van. Spring lines would wind ship to present fresh broadsides. Only the encounter itself was left to chance.

The presence of Macdonough's squadron exerted the pressure needed to force Prevost into a fatal error of judgment. Seeing the American men-of-war, the British general goaded Downie into bringing his squadron out for an immediate joint attack, although workmen were still engaged aboard the *Confiance*. On September 11, with his squadron off Cumberland Head, Downie had himself rowed around the point in a small boat to size up the American disposition. He planned to sail close hauled up the American line and wear ship into the interval between the leading Americans so that he could rake them both with his broadsides. His bold plan might have won the victory had it been possible of execution.

American gunfire and the fickle breeze under Cumberland Head defeated Downie. The best the *Confiance* could do was anchor near the head of the American line, her consorts strung out astern. Murderous crossfire burst from both of the anchored squadrons. In the first 15 minutes Downie was killed. The American brig *Eagle,* badly shot up, extricated herself by cutting her cables and reanchoring astern of the *Saratoga.* When the engaged broadsides of both flagships were about smashed into silence, Macdonough wound ship, bringing his fresh broadside to bear. Attempting a like maneuver, the *Confiance* turned only half way and took the raking blasts of the *Saratoga.* With rising water below threatening to drown her wounded, the British flagship surrendered. The battle was over. Two hours and 20 minutes of close fighting had cost 200 American and 300 British casualties. Except for a pair of gunboats that made good their escape, the entire British squadron was captured.[8]

Macdonough's victory and Macomb's stubborn resistance to heavy British attacks persuaded Prevost to retire to Canada for the winter. As a consequence of his failure, the British government restudied its position, accepted Wellington's estimate that the cost of launching a successful offensive outweighed

[8] Neither Macdonough nor Downie can have failed to note the rough similarity of Macdonough's disposition on Lake Champlain to that of Brueys in Aboukir Bay in 1798, for all naval officers of the day made a special study of Nelson's battles. But Macdonough had taken all the precautions that Brueys had failed to take and expected to make the situation work to his advantage. He counted in fact on having the wind blowing down his line, from van to rear, during the engagement, for the prevailing winds in Champlain are either north or south, and the shallow-draft lake vessels could come up the lake only on a northerly wind. Because nearly every circumstance that worked to Nelson's advantage proved disadvantageous to Downie, the Battle of Lake Champlain is sometimes called the False Nile.

the probable gain, and modified instructions to its delegates at Ghent, paving the way for conclusion of peace before the end of the year.

The Negotiated Peace and After

"At the moment of the declaration of war, the President, regretting the necessity which produced it, looked to its termination," wrote the U.S. Secretary of State James Monroe in August, 1812 to the American chargé d'affaires in London. Negotiations of one sort or another for ending hostilities began with the declaration and continued until the delegates agreed upon the final terms two-and-a-half years later. In the early stages, the United States insisted that peace required British recognition of the illegality of impressing seamen from American ships. On this point however the British would not yield. Moreover in 1814, when their North American offensives were beginning, they seized Maine from Penobscot Bay north and insisted that the terms of the treaty must be based on the actual possession of territory. This demand had a portentous ring in the ears of American delegates, who were fully aware that in 1814 the British also expected to strike in the Champlain country and in the Louisiana-Florida area as well.

Eventually each opponent compromised. With the release of British seamen from duty in European waters, the question of impressment fast became a mere legalistic issue which the United States government was willing to drop rather than continue an increasingly ominous war. Across the Atlantic, the news of Macdonough's victory and the mounting complaints of merchants harassed by American privateers spurred the war-weary British government in instructing its negotiators to accept a return to the *status quo ante bellum.* And so the Treaty of Ghent was signed on December 24, 1814. Leaving the Maine-Canada boundary and questions concerning fishing rights to arbitration, the treaty opened the way to peaceful settlement of all disputes between Britain and America. Many Englishmen felt that the Americans had gotten off lightly, for the treaty certainly was not vindictive. The Americans rejoiced when the treaty arrived on February 11, 1815 and received prompt ratification.

In the interval between reaching agreement at Ghent and communicating cease-fire orders to the scattered naval and military units, several bloody battles were fought. On land, the most famous was Major General Andrew Jackson's repulse of the British attack on New Orleans. Vice Admiral Sir Alexander Cochrane RN, who had relieved Admiral Warren in command of the American station, had been directed to close the mouth of the Mississippi to American trade, to occupy "some important and valuable possession," and incidentally to relieve Spanish Florida, which American forces had penetrated.[9] Cochrane, concluding that capture of New Orleans would best carry out the intent of his orders, sent his forces inland from the Gulf of Mexico by the shortest route, via Lake Borgne. Lieutenant Thomas and Catesby Jones' five gunboats on the lake proved as helpless to defend New Orleans as Joshua Barney's had been to protect Washington. Some 40 armed ships' launches and gigs brushed them aside, permitting the advance column of British troops to reach the Mississippi, eight miles below the city, on December 23, 1814. Here they were harassed by Jackson's riflemen, and also by the guns of the naval schooner *Carolina* on the river. The British succeeded in burning the *Carolina* with hot shot, but in a series of skirmishes ashore the American riflemen, with their more accurate aim and their longer range, gained confidence and won a moral ascendancy over the in-

vaders. By the end of the first week in January, 9,000 veterans of the Peninsular War, under Major General Sir Edward Pakenham, were assembled on the left bank of the Mississippi, prepared to attack. Upstream meanwhile, also on the left bank, Jackson's force had been raised to about 4,000, mostly frontier sharpshooters, and he had fortified his men behind breastworks in a dry canal bed, with his left flank on a swamp and his right on the Mississippi. His right was further secured by guns across the river, taken from the naval schooner *Louisiana* and manned by seamen gunners under Master Commandant Daniel Patterson. On January 8 Pakenham foolishly marched his veterans in a frontal assault of Jackson's strong position. When the smoke of the rifles lifted, Pakenham and more than 2,000 of his troops lay dead, and the rest were in flight. American losses were 71. The American victory, won two weeks after peace had been signed, had of course no effect on the war, but it set Jackson on the road to the White House.

On the seas, the heavy frigate *President*, under command of Captain Stephen Decatur, was captured in mid-January 1815 while trying to elude the British blockading squadron off New York harbor.[10] The lucky *Constitution*, under Captain Charles Stewart, had meanwhile made good her escape from Boston, and late in February 1815 in a single action captured both the small frigate *Cyane* and the sloop *Levant*. The last shots of the war

[9] Spain finally ceded all of Florida (or more precisely the Floridas, East and West) to the United States in 1819 in exchange for a clear title to Texas, to which the Americans had some claim through the Louisiana cession treaty.

[10] U.S. frigate *President*, taken into the Royal Navy under her American name, was broken up in 1818. A new *President*, built on the exact lines of the old, was launched at Portsmouth, England in 1829. Later in the century, many Americans and Englishmen, seeing H.M. frigate *President* tied up at the West India Docks, London, where she served as a drill-ship for the Royal Navy Reserve, supposed that she was Decatur's *President*. In the late 1890's, Admiral Stephen B. Luce wrote Assistant Secretary of the Navy Theodore Roosevelt suggesting that steps be taken to secure the return of the frigate to the United States. To this proposition Roosevelt replied: "I confess I don't like the idea. There is nothing glorious in the history of the *President*. She is a fair trophy for the British and she ought to be kept by them. If I were an Englishman I would not want to have the *Macedonian, Guerrière*, or *Java* in my Navy; and as I am an American I don't want the *President*."
Subsequently Sir W. Laird Clowes, the eminent British naval historian, wrote Luce: "I know that many of your countrymen believe her [the ship at the West India Docks] to be the craft captured in 1815 . . . but there is no truth to this idea, and I am glad that we do not retain any prize made in that war, which I think is best forgotten."
The new *President* was sold in 1903. Since then three other ships have successively served as drill-ship at the West India Docks, each taking the name *President*.
Quotations from Rear Admiral Albert Gleaves USN, *Life and Letters of Rear Admiral Stephen B. Luce, U.S. Navy* (New York and London, 1925), 285.

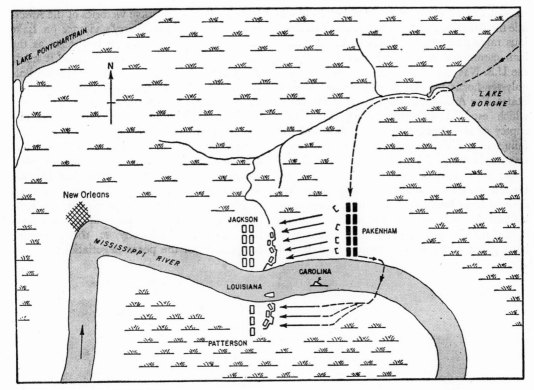

PAKENHAM'S ATTACK, BATTLE OF NEW ORLEANS

were fired by U.S. sloop *Peacock* when she fell in with the ex-American brig *Nautilus* while cruising the East Indies in April 1815.

Summary

From the British point of view the War of 1812 was a limited war, concluded by a negotiated peace, in which England became reluctantly involved while using her control of the seas to help bring about the defeat of Napoleon. From the American point of view, the War of 1812 was a struggle to end British-inspired Indian forays, to acquire Canada, and to defend the nation's rights as a neutral against British interference.

The war developed on the Atlantic along classical lines of blockade and reprisal, while on the northern front victory hinged on control of water-borne logistic transport and support. European events determined the tempo. The short-handed British were on the defensive in 1812, being unwilling to devote more than minor resources to the North American theater. In 1813 the British remained on the defensive in Canada, while extending the coastal blockade and indulging in raids on the Atlantic front. By 1814, with Wellington's veterans available, British political considerations rather than United States military power determined the amount of offensive effort Britain would devote to America.

On the seas there were during the war 25 engagements between British and American men-of-war; of these the Americans won 13, the British 12. In all instances but two, the side with the heavier firepower won. These exceptions were Captain Jacob Jones' victory in the American sloop-of-war *Wasp*, 18, over the British sloop-of-war *Frolic*, 18, and Broke's victory in the *Shannon* over the *Chesapeake*. These 25 engagements proved that the U.S. Navy produced sea-fighters at least as good as those in the Royal Navy, but they had no effect on the outcome of the war. Great Britain's overwhelming numerical superiority in men-of-war of all types enabled her to blockade the American coast and to conduct amphibious raids almost at will. Inconclusive American commerce raiding, whether by ships of the U.S. Navy or by privateers, constituted the only sea-borne reprisal possible to the United States. For Americans, the crowning indignity, which established beyond doubt the bankruptcy of the gunboat defense policy and the failure of a militia system for national defense, was the burning of Washington.

On the Canadian border, the failure of the United States to obtain its initial objectives derived from haphazard planning, inadequate leadership, and, once again, the weaknesses of the militia system. Frustration might well have given place to catastrophe had it not been for the two decisive victories of the American lake squadrons. Perry's victory on Lake Erie is considered by many historians as the most important of the war because it made possible another American victory in the Battle of the Thames that followed. Those two victories together removed the threat of the creation of an Indian buffer state. Other historians consider Macdonough's victory on Lake Champlain of equal or even greater significance. It is only conjecture as to what course the war might have taken had Downie won and Prevost continued south, but news of Macdonough's victory precipitated a British reconsideration of the war strategy and thus contributed directly to the successful compromise of the peace negotiations.

12:

Navies in Transition, 1815–1860

The period 1815–1860 was for the United States and Western Europe an epoch of rapid growth in population, wealth, and industrialization. Inventions destined to change the whole pattern of civilization came with bewildering rapidity: the sewing machine, improved farm machinery, chemical fertilizers, the telegraph, the railroad. More significant changes in the way men lived took place in this 45-year period than in the preceding 2,000 years.

This was also the time of transition for seaborne commerce. The tall-masted sailing vessel was being replaced by the ugly steamer. It is true that the far-ranging Nantucket Whalers and the exquisitely designed clippers of Donald Mackay still flourished as late as 1860, but this was the glorious Indian summer of sail. Improved engines and steam plants, the screw propeller, and iron construction made the demise of commercial sail a certainty.

Naval development too reflected the dynamic industrial and scientific revolution. The major navies of the world began the shift from sail to steam, from wood to iron, and from solid shot to shell. The first and most striking stage in this rapid evolution of naval weapons may be said to conclude with the launching in 1860 of Britain's steam-driven, screw propelled, armored, iron-hulled *Warrior*, the forerunner of the 20th century battleship and a very different fighting machine indeed from Nelson's *Victory*.

But 1815–60 was a period of comparative peace. Naval warfare was small scale and infrequent. There were no fleet battles at sea and hence little opportunity to devise appropriate tactics based on experience for the emerging steam navies. Naval operations were largely confined to an occasional bombard-

ment, supplying troops ashore, exploring and surveying, and, as always, protecting commerce.

United States Naval Operations After 1815

The War of 1812 fostered in the United States a spirit of nationalism and a renewed appreciation of the Navy. Though the Republicans remained in office, there was no return to narrow sectionalism, and no immediate slashing of the naval forces—as had occurred following each of the nation's preceding wars. On the contrary there was, for a while at least, widespread support for naval expansion. The war had clearly revealed that the Navy was both inadequately administered and too weak to protect American interests. Something would have to be done about both of these defects.

The principal weakness in the naval administration was that there was no clear distinction between logistic control and operational control. Both moreover were assigned to a harassed and inexperienced civilian Secretary, with no professional officers specifically appointed to advise or assist him in either. In 1815 Secretary Benjamin Crowninshield easily induced Congress to establish a Board of Naval Commissioners, composed of three senior captains, to handle logistics and to advise him on operational and policy problems.

To strengthen the Navy, Congress during the war had authorized the building of four ships of the line, six frigates, and six sloops-of-war. Following the Peace of Ghent nine more ships of the line were authorized. Though this ambitious building program was subsequently cut back, the United States in the postwar period acquired a respectable fleet. In line with the American policy of building outsize versions of each type, the standard armament for the heavy ships completed after 1820 was 86 guns. One, the gigantic *Pennsylvania*, carried 120 guns and was the largest warship afloat at the time of her launching in 1837.

The chief task of the U.S. Navy between 1815 and 1860 was promoting and protecting America's growing overseas commerce, which nearly quintupled in value during the period. American traders operated in all quarters of the globe, many in areas where political upheaval was normal and where piracy flourished. Hence the Navy early established semi-permanent squadrons in the Mediterranean, in the Pacific, off Brazil, in the West Indies, and in the East Indies. The African Squadron, organized during the same period, was established chiefly to control commerce in slaves.

The Mediterranean Squadron was revived shortly after the Peace of Ghent specifically to carry on the work of earlier squadrons sent to the area, i.e., to deal with the perennial nuisance of the Barbary corsairs. The treaty of 1796 with Algiers, providing an annual tribute payment in return for immunity of American ships from capture, had not been fully honored by either party since 1807. In 1812 the United States government had broken off diplomatic relations. In 1815, soon after the restoration of peace with England, Congress declared war on the Algerians.

In May 1815 Commodore Stephen Decatur shaped course for the Mediterranean with three frigates and several lesser sail. After capturing the Algerian flagship and a brig while at sea, Decatur put in at the port of Algiers. Here he opened negotiations that led to a treaty guaranteeing American vessels from Algerian molestation without further payment of tribute. Decatur next visited Tunis and Tripoli, where he demanded and received indemnity for unfriendly acts committed during the War of 1812. To underscore the warning, three separate American squadrons appeared off the Barbary coasts in the year following Decatur's cruise. Thereafter the U.S. Navy maintained its Mediterranean Squadron regularly until the American Civil War, using leased base facilities at Port Mahon, Minorca.

In the 1820's the squadron had its hands full in the eastern Mediterranean combating piracy growing out of the ten-year-long Greek War of Independence.

The revolt of the Central and South American states against Spanish rule provided the U.S. Navy with both opportunities and problems. On the one hand, the decision of the British government to back the Monroe Doctrine, closing the Americas to further colonizing, interposed the Royal Navy as a shield between the Americas and colony-hungry western Europe. On the other, the revolutions in Latin America led to wars among the victors and also released into the Caribbean and adjacent waters a swarm of privateers that readily resorted to piracy. This became a serious problem for the United States because, with heavy western migration, New Orleans, principal outlet for the Mississippi Valley, soon grew to be the second largest port in the United States, surpassed only by New York. To deal with the problem of piracy and yet to retain the friendship of the new Latin republics required a deft combination of firmness and diplomacy. The task fell mainly to the Navy, which here and elsewhere virtually took over the functions of the State Department. Commodore Oliver Hazard Perry in 1819 elicited from Venezuela a guarantee against attacks on American merchantmen, but the West Indies Squadron was obliged to use more direct methods. For several years it was fully occupied in running down pirate craft and in extirpating the hundreds of pirate nests infesting the Caribbean islands and even the Gulf coast of the United States.

Commodore James Biddle, first commander of the West Indies Squadron, found himself hampered by lack of small craft to get at the pirate hideaways. And even when he captured a gang of pirates, American courts were likely to release them for lack of evidence. Biddle's successor, Commodore David Porter, was more successful because he demanded and got enough light-draft vessels for the work at hand, and when he caught a pirate, he usually found legal reasons for turning him over to the British pirate hunters in the area, who promptly hanged him without resort to civilian courts. But the bellicose Porter overreached himself at Foxardo in Puerto Rico. One of his officers having been briefly imprisoned by the local Spanish authorities, he obtained an apology by sending a landing party ashore and threatening to destroy the town. The Spaniards complained, and a court-martial found that Porter had exceeded his authority. At that he resigned from the service and accepted a commission as Commander in Chief of Mexico's navy.[1] In 1841 the West Indies Squadron, having successfully completed its mission, was absorbed into a new Home Squadron.

By the 1830's expanding American trade with the Orient required more protection than could be afforded by the occasional visit of a man-of-war. The need was emphasized in 1831 when the inhabitants of Quallah Battoo on the coast of Sumatra plundered an American merchantman and slaughtered a number of her crew. The following year a United States frigate put ashore a landing party that stormed the fortifications and burned the town. The U.S. East India Squadron, established in 1835, not only protected American commercial interests from China to Arabia but also engaged in some of the most fruitful diplomacy of the century. At the conclusion of the First Sino-British Opium War in 1842, Commodore Lawrence Kearny set out to obtain for the United States commercial privileges similar to those acquired by the victorious Britons. By alternating courtesy and tact with a show of force, Kearny not only obtained from China the assurances he sought but was offered a treaty putting the United States on a "most favored nation" basis. Kearny refused to formalize the treaty, believing that beyond his authority, but he had laid the firm foundation for subsequent successful diplomatic negotiations. In the next decade, Commodore Matthew Calbraith Perry, employing means similar to those used by Kearny, opened the ports of Japan to American shipping.[2]

Closely related to the Navy's trade-protecting function were important contributions to exploration, survey, and research made by American naval personnel. No voyage of the

first half of the 19th century aroused wider interest than that of the United States Exploring Expedition of 1838–42, and none added more to man's knowledge of the Pacific Ocean area. Carrying scientists with elaborate equipment, the squadron of six vessels, commanded by Lieutenant Charles Wilkes USN, skirted Antarctica, touched at the Tuamotu, Society, and Fiji Islands, and surveyed what is now the west coast of the United States. Wilkes' book about the expedition became a best seller and brought the Navy much favorable publicity.

The contributions of Lieutenant Matthew Fontaine Maury USN to the science of oceanography were unique, justly earning him the title Pathfinder of the Seas. On duty in charge of the Depot of Charts and Instruments (the antecedent of the U.S. Naval Observatory and Hydrographic Office), Maury studied old log books. In these he found his first clues to the habits of wind, weather, current, temperature, and barometric pressure from season to season and from area to area in the world's oceans. Aided by information supplied by mariners of many nations, Maury prepared charts showing the best whaling grounds and the prevalent temperatures, winds, currents, and weather conditions at all seasons. His *Sailing Directions*, which appeared as a ten-page pamphlet in 1848 but rapidly expanded in succeeding editions to more than a thousand pages, indicated the best sea routes for maximum speed and optimum conditions. The *Sailing Directions* enabled mariners to cut the average sailing time from New York to California, for example, by 47 days, at a saving of $2,000,000 a year.

Despite these solid contributions, all was not well with the Navy during the period following the War of 1812. One basic trouble was the usual log jam in promotions that follows a war. The situation was aggravated in this instance by the fact that the young United States Navy had been led for the most part by young officers. These regulars, remaining in the naval service, monopolized the higher ranks through the long period of peace after 1815. The result was stagnation in the rank structure, which Congress intensified by refusing to establish any higher naval rank than captain, with "commodore" as a courtesy title for squadron commanders. Because there were

[1] As a result, his son, the future Admiral David Dixon Porter, began his naval career under the Mexican flag.

[2] The story of Perry's negotiations with Japan is told in chapter 19.

so many lieutenants, midshipmen of 30 became commonplace, and at least one reached the age of 50 without being promoted. The naval hierarchy became divided into a large body of very junior officers and a comparatively small body of lieutenants, commanders, and captains. The aging midshipmen were in fact scarcely officers at all. They messed with the crew and had little association with their seniors. Their education, carried out generally at sea, was entrusted to chaplains and to politically appointed schoolmasters.

At the other end of the scale, the elderly heroes of 1812–15 squatted on their rank. These veterans took turns on the Board of Navy Commissioners, which for 20 years was dominated by Commodore John Rodgers. Misreading the history of the American Revolution and the War of 1812, they accepted the view widely held in political and military circles that national security should be based on a strategy of coast defense and commerce raiding. Coast defense was to be a function of the Army, using elaborate fortifications. Few remembered that the Navy's *guerre de course* in the two wars against England, while producing some brilliant exploits, had no important effect on the outcome, or that commerce raiding had been wholly ineffective against strongly defended convoys.

But while the Navy languished strategically, it became increasingly receptive to new technological ideas. This was the result mainly of the energies of a few men with the intellectual flexibility to see that naval weapons had to keep pace with the new scientific revolution. Chief among these were Matthew Calbraith Perry[3] and the officer-politician Robert F. Stockton, both veterans of 1812; the ordnance expert John A. Dahlgren, who by sheer merit broke through the promotion deadlock; and John Ericsson, the Swedish inventive genius, whose services were procured by the U.S. Navy through the intercession of Stockton.

To men of this caliber it was apparent that the naval officers at last succeeding to positions of command were all too frequently unprepared for their responsibilities. Obviously the system of schoolmasters-at-sea was inadequate. Maury, Perry, and Perry's brother-in-law

[3] Younger brother of the victor of Lake Erie, who died in 1819.

Alexander Slidell Mackenzie, among others, advocated a school ashore to provide midshipmen with a complete, uninterrupted education —a school in every way the equal of the Army's Military Academy, which had been operating at West Point since 1802. Congress, unwilling to go so far, at first merely authorized schools at Norfolk and Philadelphia which midshipmen could attend between voyages. It remained for the historian George Bancroft, who became Secretary of the Navy in 1845, to initiate the necessary action. He obtained from the Naval Board of Examiners a report recommending the establishment of a naval academy at Annapolis, Maryland. The absence of the Secretary of War from Washington gave him his opportunity. Acting temporarily as Secretary for both armed services, Bancroft signed over to the Navy the Army's old Annapolis post, Fort Severn. By the time Congress returned from recess in the fall of 1845, the United States Naval Academy was in operation. Since war with both Britain and Mexico then seemed imminent, Congress was in no mood to haggle over military expenditures. It accepted Bancroft's actions and appropriated funds for the Academy.

European Naval Operations After 1815

Following the downfall of Napoleon, European powers also turned their attention to the lawless practices of the Barbary corsairs. An international commission of the Congress of Vienna concluded that the time had come to end this nuisance forever. Britain, which had profited most from Barbary raids against her commercial rivals, undertook to execute the decision and in 1816 demanded that Algeria abolish enslavement of Christians. Rebuffed, the British government dispatched Admiral Viscount Exmouth to the Mediterranean with a force including five of the line. Exmouth attacked the port of Algiers, concentrating his main force against the weakest point of the city's defenses. The Algerian Dey, after seeing his shipping burned, his capital bombarded, and his coastal fortifications battered out of action, accepted the British terms.

Exmouth's attack ended the formal system

of protection money, but the profits of piracy were too rich a temptation for the Barbary monarchs to resist for long. European and American squadrons were obliged to make periodic visits to the Barbary coast, until France in the 1830's conquered Algeria, citing as a justification the necessity of abolishing piracy. Actually it was not entirely ended until the 20th century, when the almost universal use of steam propulsion enabled merchantmen to outrun any raiding ships the technologically backward Barbary powers could send to sea.

Scarcely had Exmouth settled accounts with Algeria when clandestine resistance of the Greeks to their Turkish masters at length turned into open revolt. Numerous Greek privateers soon made the eastern Mediterranean a nest of piracy. When the Egyptian viceroy sent his army and fleet to Greece to aid his overlord the Sultan of Turkey, Britain, France, and Russia sent thither an international fleet, including ten of the line, under British Vice Admiral Sir Edward Codrington to suppress Greek piracy and to "prevent the spread of hostilities." On the mistaken assumption that the Turks would not dare attack his fleet, Codrington carried his ships into the Greek harbor of Navarino and anchored alongside the Turkish naval force, which now included a number of Egyptian men-of-war.

The British admiral had miscalculated. In the tense situation an exchange of small-arms fire quickly developed into a general engagement, in which the Turco-Egyptian fleet was practically annihilated by superior firepower and seamanship. As a result the Egyptians withdrew their army, and the Russian Czar was encouraged to intervene openly as a "defender of the faith." In 1830 the Sultan was forced to acknowledge Greek independence. Once more, land power unsupported by adequate sea power had proved insufficient to sustain a campaign in hostile country.

In the next quarter century Europe's navies engaged in no important campaigns. Operating on decreased budgets, uncertain whether the future of naval warfare lay with sail or steam propulsion, with solid shot or shell, the sea services nevertheless kept busy. They protected commerce, looked after imperial interests, conducted voyages of exploration and scientific research, and, in the language of the day, "showed the flag" and "chastised native insolence."

The scientific expedition of the greatest long-range influence was that undertaken by a tiny surveying vessel, H.M.S. *Beagle*, in the early 1830's. While the *Beagle* was exploring the coast of Patagonia, the Falkland Islands, the Galapagos Islands, and the west coast of South America, Charles Darwin, a civilian naturalist attached to the expedition, was collecting many of the specimens and data on which he later based his theory of biological evolution.

Around 1840, both the French and the British navies took part in military expeditions, all trifling so far as fleet operations were concerned. In reprisal for the riotous looting of a French bakery in Vera Cruz, Mexico, French warships turned their new shell guns on the harbor fortress, which soon surrendered. Units of the Royal Navy again bombarded St. Jean d'Acre—again, as in 1799, in support of the Turks and in opposition to the French and the Egyptians. In the Opium Wars with China, both Royal Navy and British East India Company warships participated. The main long-term effect of these operations was that they convinced a few naval officers of the value of shells, iron hulls, and steam propulsion.

The Mexican War, 1846–1848

As early as 1836 Texas had achieved *de facto* independence by defeating the Mexican army at San Jacinto and capturing the President-General, Antonio Lopez de Santa Anna. Although Mexico had repudiated Santa Anna's treaty and had never officially recognized Texan independence, the Mexican army had not managed to make any serious attempt at reconquest. Even the tiny Texas navy had held its own against the forces of Mexico. When Mexico City announced a blockade of the Texas coast, the Texan fleet blockaded Mexico instead, closing the port of Vera Cruz, capturing the town of Tabasco, and defeating Mexican naval squadrons.

California was almost equally free of Mexican control. Armed revolt here had driven out the central government's representatives. In 1845 the two chief officials were Californians, virtually self-appointed to office. The military commandant maintained his capital at Mon-

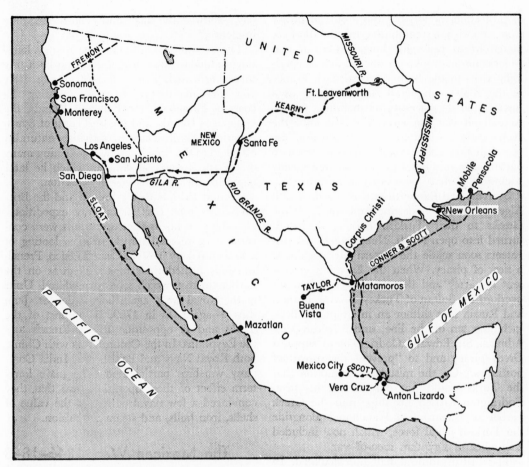

CAMPAIGNS OF THE MEXICAN WAR, 1846-1848

terey. The civil governor ruled southern California from Los Angeles. Antagonism between these two leaders, plus factional strife between the natives and American settlers, so complicated the governmental situation that intervention by the United States probably prevented civil war.

In the closing days of President Tyler's administration, March 1845, Congress, at the request of the Texans, voted the annexation of Texas. The first task of President Polk's incoming administration was to deploy the armed forces of the United States for maximum effectiveness in anticipation of war. George Bancroft issued most of the key orders. As Secretary of the Navy, he ordered Commodore John Sloat's Pacific Squadron to prepare to seize San Francisco and such other Californian ports as he could. As Acting Secretary of War, he

ordered General Zachary Taylor to advance into Texas and take position near the Rio Grande. As Secretary of the Navy, he ordered Commodore David Conner's Home Squadron to support Taylor by transporting troops, convoying supply ships, and protecting Taylor's bases. Informally he arranged for a small "exploring expedition" of frontiersmen and scouts under Brevet Captain John C. Frémont to cross the Rockies and advance into northern California. Later a column of soldiers under Brevet Brigadier General Stephen W. Kearny set out from Fort Leavenworth, Kansas for New Mexico.

Taylor's advance to the Rio Grande met resistance by Mexican troops, and in the spring of 1846 first Mexico and then the United States declared war. Commodore Sloat thereupon moved his squadron of four sailing vessels, including a frigate, from his temporary base at Mazatlan, Mexico to the California coast. In July he hoisted the American flag without opposition in both Monterey and San Francisco. Captain Frémont meanwhile had reached California, where he incited revolt among American settlers north of San Francisco. Under his leadership they seized the town of Sonoma, proclaimed California an independent republic, elected Frémont governor, and adopted a flag carrying the picture of a bear. Learning that Sloat had taken possession of Monterey, Frémont marched the Bear Flag army, 160 strong, to join him. Commodore Robert F. Stockton, who had succeeded the ailing Sloat in command of the Pacific Squadron, gladly accepted the cooperation of Frémont's men. Forming the crew of his flagship into a little army of his own, he joined Frémont in an unopposed march into Los Angeles.

General Kearny, having captured Santa Fe and annexed New Mexico, now headed for southern California, but receiving over-optimistic information that California was securely in American hands, he sent back all but a hundred of his men. By this time however the native Californians had risen in revolt, thrust the Americans out of Los Angeles, and surrounded Stockton's force at San Diego. Kearny on entering California came under attack, lost 18 men, and found himself besieged. Stockton, victorious at San Diego, was soon able to relieve Kearny, and their combined forces recaptured Los Angeles. The subsequent Treaty of Cahuenga, signed early in 1847, ended the war on the Pacific coast.

Though the conquest of California added to the United States some of its richest territory, it was militarily a small-scale affair involving only a few hundred combatants. The faintly comic-opera tone of the whole campaign was accentuated by the confusion that followed. Because the conquest had been achieved by three different forces in informal cooperation, no clear channels of command had been established. And because the Navy had no admirals, it was difficult to determine how a senior navy captain ranked with a junior army general, particularly when the navy captain held the courtesy title of commodore, and the general was actually a colonel with the courtesy brevet rank of brigadier general. As a result, Stockton and Kearny each regarded himself as senior officer in California. Stockton appointed Frémont governor, but Kearny disregarded the appointment and gave Frémont orders which Frémont refused to obey. When the confusion was compounded by the arrival of another commodore to relieve Stockton, Stockton went home in disgust. Kearny then managed to remove Frémont as governor and bring him to Washington under virtual arrest. Here a court-martial found Frémont guilty of insubordination, whereupon he resigned his commission.

Though General Taylor had meanwhile penetrated deeply into Mexico, he was still too far north to threaten the capital. To bring the war to a quick close therefore President Polk dispatched an army of some 12,000 troops under Lieutenant General Winfield Scott to land at Vera Cruz and march directly inland to Mexico City.

Such an ambitious undertaking would of course have been impossible but for the presence of Conner's Home Squadron in the Gulf of Mexico. Conner, operating out of Pensacola, was at first hampered by lack of a coaling base in Mexican waters, for his squadron included steamers as well as sailing vessels. He had early found an ingenious solution to this problem however by establishing a floating advanced base behind protecting reefs off Anton Lizardo 13 miles south of Vera Cruz. Here he kept a store-ship anchored, and here colliers could rendezvous periodically with his steamers. Conner thus anticipated by a century the mobile squadrons that serviced the U.S. Pacific Fleet in the lagoons of atolls during World War II. His attempts to close Mexican ports had been uniformly unsuccessful for lack of occupation forces to follow up and make good his captures. Nevertheless by the time General Scott's expedition got under way, his blockade of the Mexican coast was very nearly impenetrable, and the Home Squadron held undisputed command of the sea off Mexico's east coast.

Scott's planners at first thought of the Vera Cruz landing as primarily an army job. They expected a fleet of army transports to carry the landing force directly to the beachhead, whereupon the troops would enter specially constructed boats and row ashore. The Navy's role, in their opinion, should be limited to fire support. Luckily somebody, probably Conner, convinced Scott that the landing should be a carefully worked out joint operation, and that the ship-to-shore movement could best be planned and executed by navy personnel.

Reconnoitering the Mexican coastline in a small steamer, Scott, Conner, and their staffs decided to land on a strip of beach three miles south of Vera Cruz. At the Anton Lizardo anchorage the landing force, early on March 9, 1847, transferred from their transports to the vessels of the Home Squadron. The squadron then proceeded up the coast, towing the 65 surfboats that were to serve as landing craft.

Off the selected beachhead the troops of the first wave transferred to pre-assigned boats, a half-company of soldiers to each craft. The entire ship-to-shore operation was commanded by a navy captain, each division of boats was commanded by a navy lieutenant, and each boat was commanded by a navy junior or petty officer and manned by seamen rowers. When the landing craft were filled, they advanced in divisions to the line of departure, marked by a steamer anchored near the beach. Here they took station in double lines parallel to the coast, with each company of soldiers so boated as to be in prescribed order of battle for combat ashore. Between the lines and the beach were stationed seven light-draft gunboats armed mainly with 32-pounder shell guns. Like the LCI gunboats in the Pacific campaigns of World War II, these vessels were to provide close gunfire support to the landings.

On signal, the lines of boats headed toward the beach, and all guns of the fleet were trained to knock out resistance. As it turned out however the invasion was entirely unopposed. A rising against the government had drawn local military forces to Mexico City. The first wave of invaders made an almost simultaneous landing, not under fire but to the accompaniment of cheers and band music from the fleet. Promptly upon discharging their passengers, the landing boats hurried back to the ships to pick up the second wave. By 10 PM, 10,000 Americans were on the beach. The rest came ashore at leisure the next morning.

Conner and his staff had provided an excellent model, unfortunately overlooked or forgotten, for future American amphibious operations. It was, to be sure, in most respects not unlike the invasion carried out by Keith and Abercromby at Aboukir in 1801, but in one aspect it was unique. At Vera Cruz, for the first time in the history of amphibious warfare, the ship-to-shore movement was entirely navy planned and navy controlled, a practice not to become general until World War II.

In the subsequent assault on the city of Vera Cruz, the Navy assisted both afloat and ashore. A flotilla of two steamers and five gunboats battered at the sea wall and fort. At the same time navy gunners, under the general supervision of Captain Robert E. Lee USA, used a battery of six heavy naval guns to breach the land face of the city wall. When Vera Cruz surrendered, the conference of capitulation was attended by a representative of Commodore Matthew Calbraith Perry, Conner's successor in command of the Home Squadron. It had been a joint Army-Navy victory.

Scott now marched inland on Mexico City. Accompanying his army were 300 United States marines, who at Chapultepec fought the first inland battle in U.S. Marine Corps history. When Mexico City fell, Scott, desiring to impress the populace, selected the brightly uniformed marines to mount guard in the halls of Montezuma.

The Crimean War, 1854–1856

The causes of the Crimean War were both complex and obscure. A dispute over who should administer the Christian shrines in the Holy Land strained relations between Roman Catholic France and Eastern Orthodox Russia. Napoleon III needed a touch of military glory to consolidate his dynasty. Britain grew alarmed when Czar Nicholas I cast covetous glances at the Bosporus and the Dardanelles. In 1853 the Russians violated Turkish territory and brought on hostilities by marching an army into what is now Romania. To prevent any sudden Russian descent on Constantinople, Britain and France dispatched strong naval squadrons to the Sea of Marmora—in the belief that their mere presence would discourage any Russian naval operations in the Black Sea.

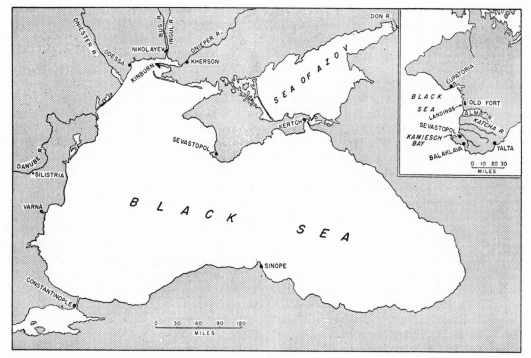

MAIN THEATER OF THE CRIMEAN WAR, 1854-1856

But Russia's Vice Admiral Nakhimov, far from being awed into inactivity, cruised freely in search of Turkish ships. In November 1853 he discovered Osman Pasha's winter squadron of seven frigates and several lesser sail off the ill-fortified Turkish port of Sinope, where it had taken refuge from a gale. Nakhimov had three ships of the line but, wishing to make a sure thing doubly sure, he sent to Sevastopol for three of Russia's most powerful men-of-war, 120-gun three-deckers with main batteries of 68-pounder shell guns. Then, stationing a line of auxiliaries from Sinope toward Constantinople to warn him if the British and French fleets came through the Bosporus, Nakhimov in the morning of November 20 took his six ships of the line through rain and fog into the roadstead of Sinope. In several hours of shelling, he sank all seven of the Turkish frigates, silenced the shore batteries, and set fire to the town. At a cost of fewer than 40 fatalities, he had killed nearly 3,000 Turks.

Western Europe was shocked by the ruthlessness of the Russians, who not only flouted tradition by attacking frigates with ships of the line but turned their guns indiscriminately on vessels trying to surrender, on boats, and on men struggling in the water. The British and French admiralties, which still preferred wooden construction to iron, were jarred into reappraising their naval weapons. Evidently wooden hulls had been rendered obsolete by the shell gun, which not only shattered them but set them afire.

Since Britain and France had informally undertaken to protect Turkey, the Battle of Sinope practically obliged them to declare war. Thus, in the same sense that the Japanese attack on Pearl Harbor in 1941 was a tactical triumph but a strategic blunder, Sinope won Russia a brief advantage but brought forces against her that made her defeat inevitable. Yet defeating the Russians was not nearly so easy as the British and French, in unaccustomed alliance, assumed it would be. Their armies and navies, like those of the United States, were dominated by veterans of the Napoleonic period, men hostile to change, wedded to bureaucracy and red tape, and made hesitant by age. The British army was further hampered by the system of buying and selling commissions. In the 1850's whole regiments had become the playthings of spoiled sons of the aristocracy.[4]

The title Crimean War obscures the fact that initially both Britain and France expected to make their main naval attack on Russia via the Baltic Sea. There in the summer of 1854 a major British fleet under Vice Admiral Sir Charles Napier joined a powerful French fleet under Vice Admiral Parseval Deschênes. In the face of such overwhelming force, the Russian Baltic fleet prudently remained in port. Napier and Deschênes, lacking specific orders covering such a situation, considered destroying shore installations at the principal Russian ports on the Gulf of Finland. When reconnaissance showed these to be impregnable, the combined fleet, in joint operations with 10,000 troops sent from France, seized the Åland Islands controlling the Gulf of Bothnia. With the approach of winter, and the possibility that the Russians might march over the ice and retake the islands, the allied fleet withdrew from the Baltic. Though these inconclusive operations aroused public outcries in both Britain and France, the expedition at least served to hold Russian troops away from the decisive theater in the Crimea. In 1855 an allied fleet of steamers went to the Baltic and won a propaganda victory of sorts by bombarding the fortifications of Helsingfors (Helsinki), but for want of a landing force the expedition could not exploit its success and so, like its predecessor, came home empty-handed.

Meanwhile in the late spring of 1854 another allied fleet, by landing 60,000 troops at Varna on the Black Sea, had taken the pressure off the Turkish army and induced the Russians to retreat across the Danube. The British and French commanders, casting about for something to do next, concluded that if they could transport their troops across to the Crimean Peninsula and seize the big Russian naval base of Sevastopol from its 45,000 defenders, they would avenge Sinope, humiliate Russia, and bring the war to a close before winter. The

summer passed however before the commanders could concert their plans and obtain agreement from London and Paris.

The passage from Varna to the Crimea was unopposed, the heavily outnumbered Russian Black Sea fleet choosing to remain at Sevastopol. The Russian reticence was fortunate for the allies because the French warships were so crowded with troops that they could hardly have fired a shot in self-defense. En route it became apparent that the allied commanders had not reached a meeting of minds after all. Vice Admiral Sir James Dundas RN, in command of the naval expedition, had recommended going ashore just north of Sevastopol. But by the time the French leaders reached the Crimea, they had decided that landing so near the enemy's base would be rash. Hence, while the fleets idled at anchor, the commanders cruised up and down the Crimean coast threshing out the matter afresh. At length, after much study of the shoreline and of maps of uncertain accuracy, they agreed on a stretch of beach 27 miles north of Sevastopol. Although the terrain surrounding the selected landing point was flat and hence favorable to advance, the beachhead proved a logistic nightmare. There was little or nothing to forage in the area, and except for a single spring all available water was salt or brackish. Because there was no harbor at or near the invasion beach, it could not possibly serve as a base of operations.

The actual landings, on the operational level, were smoothly carried out. To counter opposition, which never appeared, the French drew up a line of rocket-firing boats. To bring artillery ashore they used specially-constructed landing craft, and the British did almost as well with small steam paddle launches and decked-over pairs of boats. Yet the dilatoriness and indecision that had hampered the expedition from the beginning was nowhere so apparent as at the beachhead, where of all places movement should be well planned, swift, and decisive. Merely getting the men and their equipment ashore took from September 14 to September 18, and the British troops waited through rain and blazing sun for nearly three days before their tents were disembarked. Lacking adequate medical facilities, hundreds of men died of cholera and dysentery. The fault again was

---

[4] The system of commission by purchase grew out of the English Civil War (1642–60), to assure that the army would never again fall into the hands of men hostile to the wealthy aristocracy, which supported the Crown.

in planning rather than execution—materials moved back and forth between fleet and shore, while the commanders tried to make up their minds just what equipment the troops really needed.

When at last on the 19th the expedition got moving toward Sevastopol, the Russian defenders had interposed themselves on the Alma River. Here the allied infantry, displaying an *élan* and verve little merited by their incompetent leaders, stormed heights thought impregnable and hurled the Russians back into the city. Then, true to form, the high command paused overlong to decide what to do next. Taking advantage of their hesitation, Prince Menchikov, commanding the defenses of Sevastopol, scuttled a row of warships, including five of the line, across the mouth of the long, narrow harbor north of the city. Then, leaving Sevastopol garrisoned by the sailors from the sunken vessels, he withdrew his army to the northeast, hoping to take the invaders from the rear.

With Sevastopol harbor blocked against British and French warships, an allied attack from the north had become far too risky. Lord Raglan, commanding the British army, and General Canrobert, commanding the French, therefore marched their forces around to the south side of the city. This was a move long contemplated. Indeed, had not the beaches here been narrow and backed by steep hills, the Allies would have landed south of Sevastopol in the first place. In this area there were harbors, none really good, but capable in a pinch of serving as logistic bases. The British established their supply base on a narrow inlet at Balaklava; the French, on two open bays on the west coast.

While the allied leaders paused again, Menchikov brought his army back and locked the invaders in position by occupying the heights to their east, on the British right flank. Inside Sevastopol engineers, sailors, and civilians, including women, rapidly repaired neglected fortifications on the south side of the city.

In mid-October the Allies at length began offensive operations with a bombardment, in which both fleet guns and shore artillery participated. It was a waste of ammunition because though Sevastopol's southern defenses were wrecked, the cannonade was not followed by an assault. The operation however had a measurable influence on the history of naval warfare by convincingly demonstrating the advantages of steam propulsion. The sailing ships of the line, virtually becalmed, had to be pushed and towed into position off Sevastopol by small steamers. Even then they were too far out to be effective. Unable to maneuver, they were mere stationary targets for the Russian shore batteries, which inflicted great damage. By contrast, two screw-ships, moving in close to the shore, knocked out some of the batteries and then sped nimbly out of harm's way.

The failure of the Allies to assault when assault was relatively easy turned the operation against Sevastopol into a siege and doomed the British and French to spend the winter in the Crimea. Before cold weather set in, the Russians under Menchikov, heavily reinforced, struck first toward Balaklava, eliciting the magnificent but futile charge of the British Light Cavalry Brigade. They then attacked farther to the north, but were repulsed by the Allies in the Battle of Inkerman. A severe storm in November tremendously complicated the allied supply problem by wrecking 21 store-ships, including one laden with winter clothing. The results of this gale, plus defective logistic planning, made the winter of 1854-55 one of abject misery for the invaders.[5]

Sevastopol fell at last on September 9, 1855, a year almost to the day after the initial allied landings in the Crimea. While engineers set about demolishing Sevastopol's dockyards and fortifications, an expeditionary force including some 9,000 troops proceeded by sea to Kinburn. Here at the end of a long spit of land three forts guarded the entrance to an estuary into which flowed the Bug, the Ingul, and the Dnieper rivers. Capture of the Kinburn forts would permit the Allies to close all three rivers, thereby cutting off from the Black Sea the naval base and arsenal at Nikolayev and the rich commercial city of Kherson. In mid-Oc-

[5] Relieved somewhat by the arrival in Turkey of Florence Nightingale and her staff of nurses in time to care for the wounded of Balaklava and Inkerman. Within a few months of their arrival, the death rate in the hospitals had been reduced from 42 to 2 per cent. In the summer of 1855, Miss Nightingale took over the superintendence of the allied hospitals in the Crimea as well as in Turkey.

tober the expeditionary force isolated the forts by landing troops on the spit above them. Two days later the Russian garrisons surrendered after a bombardment from land and sea.

Chiefly responsible for this quick victory were three ungainly little armored floating batteries, the *Tonnante,* the *Dévastation,* and the *Lave.* Hurriedly built by the French in reaction to the Battle of Sinope, they were the world's first ironclads to go into action. With sufficient steam power for maneuvering, but not for cruising, they had 17-inch-thick wooden hulls covered above the water line with 4½-inch-thick iron plates. As they battered the forts from a range of less than a thousand yards, solid shot merely bounced off their plates, and shells burst on impact, doing no damage at all. The fall of Kinburn had little effect on the outcome of the war, but the bombardment of the forts, viewed by officers of several nations, ushered in the age of naval armor.

The story of the Crimean War is one of tragic frustration. The Russians, constrained at last to capitulate, were obliged to leave Sevastopol dismantled, yet they received deserved credit for an effective defense. The Allies won the war but lost their military reputations. Luckily for the Allies, the hesitation, poor planning, and lack of coordination that handicapped their armies in nearly every operation were less evident in the British and French fleets. For without naval command of the Black Sea, the allied armies could not have expelled the Russians from the Balkans, crossed to the Crimea, or maintained their siege of Sevastopol.

Undersea Warfare

We have already noted the appearance of some of the technological innovations that in the 19th century revolutionized the navies of the world. One area of development, undersea warfare, has thus far not been mentioned because it made little impact in the period 1815–60, now under consideration. Yet as early as the American Revolution, David Bushnell, a Connecticut Yankee, had invented a practical marine mine and a practical submarine.

Bushnell's mine, in which gunpowder was exploded by means of a clockwork-operated flintlock, so impressed the governor of Con-

necticut that he backed the young inventor in the construction of his submarine, the *Turtle*— so called because it resembled a turtle, moving sidewise, tail downward, with a brass conning tower for a head. Built of oak reinforced by iron bands, the *Turtle* was manned by a single very busy operator. He admitted water into ballast tanks to sink, pumped it out to rise, rotated screw propellers for horizontal and vertical motion, guided himself with a rudder, and was equipped to attach one of Bushnell's clockwork mines to the underwater hull of a ship by means of a gimlet fastener. The *Turtle* first went into action in September 1776, when the British had expelled General Washington's army from Long Island and were about to cross to Manhattan. The target was the flagship of no less a personage than Lord Howe. But the *Turtle* was defeated then and later by British copper sheathing, through which the gimlet fastener could not penetrate.

During the War of the French Revolution, the American marine engineer Robert Fulton obtained the backing of Napoleon Bonaparte, then First Consul of France. For Napoleon, Fulton in 1801 built the *Nautilus,* a fish-shaped, four-man submarine with horizontal diving rudders and a sail for surface cruising. The *Nautilus* towed her mine, or "torpedo," as Fulton called it, at the end of a long line, which passed through an eye in a spike and thence to the submarine. When the submariners had driven the spike into the underwater hull of a vessel, the submarine moved on, bringing the torpedo up against the spike, whereupon the tightening line pulled a trigger and set off the explosion. The *Nautilus* in a test attack blew up a hulk in Brest Roads, but when she proved incapable of overtaking any of the British blockading vessels off the port, the French lost interest.

For William Pitt's government, to which he now turned, Fulton devised a system of using small surface craft to attach clockwork mines to the anchor cables of moored ships. Five such craft attacked the French invasion flotilla at Boulogne in October 1805 and sank a pinnace, but the British naval victory of Trafalgar, coming a few days later, caused the Admiralty to abandon experiments in undersea warfare, which it never liked anyway. "Pitt was the greatest fool that ever existed," grumbled Lord St. Vincent, "to encourage a mode of war which they who command the sea do not want and which if successful would deprive them of it."[6]

After 1805 the British and French had little to do with undersea warfare, calling it barbarous and recognizing it as contrary to their interests. The Americans however in the War of 1812 made ingenious if not particularly successful experiments with mines. The Russians too used mines in the Crimean War, with indifferent success, to defend their Baltic harbors. But little real progress in mine warfare was made until the period of the American Civil War. The development of the seagoing submarine had to await the eve of World War I.

Steam Propulsion

Naval officers were generally receptive to the idea of steam propulsion for fleets. Lord Nelson was one among many who, after unhappy experiences with calms and contrary winds, advocated naval experiments along this line. Yet nearly 40 years elapsed between the appearance of Robert Fulton's commercially successful steamboat *Clermont* on the Hudson River in 1807 and the widespread adoption of steam by the major navies.[7]

The reasons for the long delay were many, and not the least was the huge investment in sailing ships that the navies had made during the Napoleonic Wars. Even more valid was the argument that steam in the early 19th century was even less efficient than sail propulsion. Early engines were liable to breakdowns that could be fatal in action. The use of steam drastically cut down a ship's cruising radius. Whereas a sailing vessel, once laden with stores, could go thousands of miles without touching port, an early steamer would burn up all her fuel in less than a hundred. Moreover the paddle wheels masked as much as a third of

[6] Quoted in Farnham Bishop, *The Story of the Submarine* (New York, 1916), 33.

[7] Fulton's main contribution to the development of the steamboat, besides demonstrating that it could be made to pay dividends to investors, was his adaptation of the side paddle wheel.

the broadside, and while the superior mobility of the steamer was certainly an advantage in battle, one lucky shot could disable her paddle wheel or engines and leave her outsailed and outgunned. Hence naval officers preferred to let commercial vessels make the first, costly trial-and-error experiments that would at length produce dependable, high-speed steam engines that were economical of fuel.

There was, to be sure, one early experiment in naval steam propulsion. The United States Navy, exasperated by the British blockade in the War of 1812, had Fulton design and build a steam propelled blockade breaker. This was the *Demologos* (later renamed *Fulton*), the world's first steam warship. Built with sides five feet thick, carrying her machinery low in twin hulls with the single paddle wheel in between, she was nearly invulnerable to shot. Before the *Demologos* was ready for action, the war ended, and she was soon immobilized as a receiving ship. Thereafter for more than two decades the major navies did not build a single steam-driven combat vessel, restricting themselves to small wooden-hulled paddle packets, usually converted from commercial vessels and used as auxiliaries.

Builders of commercial steamers meanwhile were developing more economical and more efficient engines using higher and higher steam pressures. This meant devising means of transferring heat efficiently from fuel to water, building boilers capable of containing high-pressure steam, and inventing means of condensing the steam outside the cylinder. Coupled with these problems was that of distilling adequate quantities of fresh water to avoid the constant incrustation and fouling that resulted from the use of untreated sea water. Ultimately solutions were found for all these problems, but they were made possible only through a fuel changeover from wood to coal and by major improvements in design, metallurgy, and machine tools.

At length, in 1837 the U.S. Navy launched its second steam-driven man-of-war, the *Fulton II*. She was a smaller and more conventional paddle-wheeler than the first *Fulton*, but she was speedy for her time. Her most important service, as it turned out, was interesting her captain, Matthew Calbraith Perry, in the possibilities of the steam warship. Partly through his influence, the U.S. Navy in 1842 took a strong, if temporary, lead over the rest of the world's navies by launching the 3,200-ton side-wheelers *Mississippi* and *Missouri*.

The Screw Propeller

The widespread reluctance to adopt steam for combat vessels was eventually overcome by the development of a really practical screw propeller. This was achieved independently in England by John Ericsson and by Francis Pettit Smith, a farmer with no engineering training. The screw had none of the objectionable features of the paddle wheel, but the British Admiralty could not at first be convinced that a screw-propelled vessel could be steered. Rebuffed in England, Ericsson was easily persuaded by Captain Robert F. Stockton USN to come to the United States. Here Stockton, through his insistence and political influence, got the Navy in 1842 to authorize the building of a screw steamer to Ericsson's specifications. This was the sloop-of-war *Princeton*, the first screw-propelled naval steamer. She was also the first warship to have all her machinery below the water line and thus out of reach of shot.

The Royal Navy, at length convinced of the merits of the screw, launched the screw-sloop *Rattler* shortly after the appearance of the *Princeton*. The *Rattler*, by triumphing over a paddle-wheeler of the same horsepower in a tug-of-war and in several speed trials, firmly established screw propulsion. In the next few years Britain converted a number of her old veterans of the Napoleonic wars to steam and screw. In 1850 France launched her first screw battleship, the *Napoléon*. Two years later Britain followed suit with the *Agamemnon*. In the mid-1850's the United States began launching the *Merrimack* class of fast steam frigates that were to play an important part in the coming American Civil War.

By 1860, largely because of the lessons of the Crimean War and the steady progress of steam engineering, the navies of Britain, France, and the United States had come to regard warships without steam power as already obsolescent. But while floating batteries, coast defense vessels, and river boats might be powered

by steam alone, steam continued for many years to be used as merely auxiliary to sail in seagoing ships. Not until the 20th century were sails everywhere entirely removed from warships.

The Iron Hull

In the first Opium War the British East India Company used a pair of iron-hulled steam gunboats built by the famous English ship building firm of William Laird and Sons. As relations became strained between the United States and Mexico in the early 1840's, the Mexican government ordered from the Lairds two iron-hulled frigates. At the same time the U.S. Navy contracted with the Stevens Brothers of Hoboken for a fast, ironclad, iron-hulled ship (the "Stevens Battery"), which however was never completed. By 1844 Britain and the United States each had a small iron-hulled naval steamer on the Great Lakes. By then the Royal Navy had begun ordering iron frigates. But just when it appeared that iron was about to be universally adopted for naval hulls, a series of tests convinced the British Admiralty that iron, in its current state of metallurgical development, was even more vulnerable than oak. The Royal Navy thereupon converted its new iron frigates into troop transports, and iron construction of naval vessels was virtually abandoned for several years. No iron ships fought in the Crimean War.

Britain was spurred into resumption of iron construction by the appearance in 1859 of the 5,600-ton French frigate *Gloire*, a wooden ship armored with 4¾ inches of iron plates. The Royal Navy countered by contracting for an armored battleship, H.M.S. *Warrior*. The *Warrior*, launched in 1860, was 380 feet long, displaced 9,000 tons, and had a 4½-inch armor belt backed with 18 inches of teak. No wooden hull could have stood the strain of such length or carried the weight of her armor, her necessarily powerful engines, and her 40 guns, all immensely heavier than any regularly used afloat in the age of sail. Recognizing this, her architects had made her hull completely of iron.

The launching of the *Warrior* ended the era of the wooden warships. There remained of course numerous veterans of earlier years that were to see some service. Wooden steam sloops and frigates, for example, were to play a major role in the impending American Civil War. But after 1860 Britain built warships only of iron or, later, steel. And though there was some backtracking in other navies, all eventually followed Britain's example.

Armor

The idea of so strengthening the decks or sides of a ship as to make her invulnerable to enemy shot is almost as old as the naval gun. In 1592 the Koreans under Admiral Yi Sun Sin defeated a Japanese fleet by using a galley with an ironplated turtleback deck. The French in their siege of Gibraltar in 1782 used floating batteries protected with sloping casemates of five-foot-thick timbers. Fulton's thicksided *Demologos* was in a sense the first steam armorclad.

The 19th century term *ironclad* referred to a warship whose hull, whether of wood or iron, was armored with thick plates of iron. The first vessel to fit this description was the U.S. Navy's Stevens Battery of 1843. In early tests her four to six inches of iron armor resisted the fire of the heaviest naval ordnance, but before she was completed the versatile Ericsson had invented a gun that could easily pierce plates of that thickness. Plans were made to install heavier armor, but before the plans could be carried out, still more powerful ordnance was available, and completion of the battery was indefinitely suspended.

The experience of the Stevens Battery foreshadowed a race of several decades between protection and penetration. Each improvement in armor was followed by the development of more powerful guns that could penetrate it. By mid-century, guns were in the ascendant, and both armor and iron hulls were in disfavor. Then came the shock of the Battle of Sinope. Evidently wooden hulls—or for that matter unarmored iron hulls—simply could not stand up to the newest shell guns. The French navy reacted by ordering five ironclads, the first ever to be completed. Britain built four more in time to participate in the concluding campaigns of the Crimean War. The operations of three of the new French ironclads, *Dévastation*, *Tonnante*, and *Lave*, against the Kinburn forts so impressed the British that they ordered four more armored batteries, three with iron hulls.

After the war the French built the *Gloire*, the first seagoing ironclad. Britain, as we have seen, replied with the *Warrior*, the first iron-hulled, ironclad, steam-driven battleship. For all their defensive strength, the *Gloire* and the *Warrior* were already vulnerable the day they were launched, for ordnance capable of penetrating their plates had been developed. This was but another stage in the long race between offense and defense. As guns became more and more powerful, iron armor increased in thickness to 8, 12, 14, and 24 inches. Then, when progress in the science of metallurgy permitted, these super-thick plates were replaced by steel of increasing hardness.

Heavy Ordnance

At the end of the Napoleonic Wars naval guns were little different in construction and performance from those used in the Spanish Armada campaign. There had been some improvements in loading and aiming, and better carriages had been devised, but the gun itself was still the cast-iron, smoothbore, solid-shot-firing muzzle-loader used of old. Ranges were about the same, averaging 300 yards point blank and 2,500 yards extreme. Attempts at improving accuracy were largely nullified by the fact that the solid shot was only roughly spherical; hence there had to be considerable "windage"—difference between diameter of shot and diameter of bore—to avoid wedging. As a result, the ball went bouncing along the sides of the barrel to emerge at unpredictable angles. The carronade, with even shorter ranges and less accuracy than the long gun, was widely used in the late 18th and early 19th centuries, but was discredited by the War of 1812, when both Englishmen and Americans learned to stand off beyond carronade range and batter enemy vessels with their long guns. Thus in 1815 warships found themselves armed much as they had been for the past two centuries.

The introduction of the paddle wheel, by cutting down on the number of guns a vessel could carry, stimulated experiments toward developing more effective gunfire with fewer guns. These experiments led to a number of closely related developments: (1) bigger and stronger guns, (2) better shells and shell guns, (3) rifled gun barrels, (4) breech loading, and (5) revolving gun turrets. Though navies had not adopted all of these improvements by 1860, all had been developed and were ready for use.

During the War of 1812 Major George Bomford of the U.S. Army had attacked the problem of providing bigger guns by inventing the Columbiad, a compromise in weight, length, and diameter of bore between the long gun and the carronade. Experiments after 1815 toward solving the same problem were directed chiefly to strengthening gun barrels to enable them to fire heavier projectiles with heavier charges without bursting.

In the early 1840's Ericsson developed a stronger gun barrel by shifting from brittle cast iron to wrought iron. His 12-inch gun Oregon, installed aboard U.S.S. *Princeton,* was apparently a complete success. But Captain Stockton put an end to this line of experiment when, without a tenth of Ericsson's knowledge of metals, he designed a deceptively similar gun, the Peacemaker, which he also installed in the *Princeton.* During demonstration firing the Peacemaker blew up, killing several congressmen, the Secretary of the Navy, and the Secretary of State. The U. S. Navy thereupon barred further use of wrought-iron guns, and ordnance experts everywhere viewed them with suspicion.

Captain Thomas Rodman of the U.S. Army tackled the problem from a different angle. Using Bomford's Columbiad as his basic gun type, he cast it hollow around a sand core and then cooled the interior first, so that the outer metal shrank gradually onto the hardened inner core. To take strain off the barrel, he developed a slow-burning powder. Compressed into solid cakes, with holes to regulate burning speed, it produced much lower gun pressures than the prevailing fine-grained, fast-burning powder.

In the early 1850's Commander John A. Dahlgren of the U.S. Navy improved upon Rodman's work by discarding the Columbiad as his basic gun and developing a smoothbore gun of a new shape, worked out after thorough study of the pressures generated in the barrel at firing. Built to offset his derived "curve of pressures," Dahlgren's guns were very thick at the breech with considerable taper toward the muzzle. An obvious improvement over ordnance then in use, the Dahlgren gun was quickly adopted by the U.S. Navy.

Ironically, the Dahlgren, though widely used for a quarter of a century, was outmoded at last by a principle of gun construction that had been recommended by Captain de Thiery of the French army back in the 1830's. De Thiery suggested making gun barrels of two concentric tubes, the inner of cast iron, the outer of wrought iron. The outer tube was to be slipped over the inner while glowing hot and left to shrink firmly into position. This shrinking of an outer band or sleeve onto an inner one (using cast iron, wrought iron, or steel) is the principle of the built-up gun, which proved the ultimate structural solution for strengthening gun barrels. The U. S. Navy ordered a few guns built on the de Thiery plan but refused to use them when the *Princeton* explosion made wrought-iron ordnance temporarily unacceptable. Thereafter for 15 years the built-up gun was neglected, until the Royal Navy, alarmed at the building of the *Gloire,* reappraised available ordnance and began ordering them in quantity. The Admiralty's choice was the British-designed Armstrong gun. Its inner barrel was a wrought iron bar, coiled and welded into tubular form. Thus the metal received the stresses of firing along its length instead of across its width. But even the Armstrong gun was on the way to obsolescence, for in Prussia the Krupp works had begun producing guns of steel.

Shells, Shell Guns, and Rifling

Explosive-filled projectiles, called *bombs, shells,* or *grenades,* are almost as old as the gun. For centuries they were used mainly in attacking fortifications, into which they were lobbed by mortars. Fleets operating against shore installations employed small mortar-boats or bomb-ketches for this work. Around 1700 armies began using howitzers to fire fused shells with a flatter trajectory directly at the target. Naval officers early recognized the advantage of shellfire, but they long considered shells too dangerous to carry in the main fleet, and those that could be fired by standard 24- and 32-pounder guns were too small to be very effective. The carronade with its light charge and large bore was well adapted to shell, but gunners found its heavy shot so useful for splintering wooden hulls that they neglected its possibilities as a shell gun.

After the Napoleonic Wars the problems of naval shellfire came under study by a visionary French artillery officer, Henri-Joseph Paixhans, who saw in the combination of shell gun and paddle-wheeler a means of wresting command of the sea from the Royal Navy. He designed a shell gun, shorter, lighter, using smaller charges than guns of the same caliber designed for solid shot, and in 1824 demonstrated its potentiality by splintering an old two-decker. Though both the French and the British navies adopted the Paixhans gun in the late 1830's, it was regarded as a special-purpose weapon, secondary to solid-shot ordnance. It required the annihilation of the Turkish fleet at Sinope in 1853 to convince everyone in naval circles that the shell for offense, as well as iron hulls and armor for defense, had come to stay.

Until the middle of the 19th century, shells as well as solid shot were spherical. The fuse was a hollow cylinder filled with hardened gunpowder. Cut to burn for a period of time roughly corresponding to the range of the target, the fuse was pounded or screwed into a hole in the shell until the after end was flush with the outer surface. The shell was then inserted through the muzzle into the barrel of the gun, where it was held in place, fuse pointed outward, by a collar called a sabot. When the gun was fired, the flames flashed around the shell and ignited the fuse as the projectile passed along the barrel.

Understandably, such time-fused shells tended to explode too soon or too late. The alternative was the percussion fuse, to set off the explosion on impact, but the projectile would have to strike fuse-first, and that was impossible to control with spherical shells. An elongated shell tended to tumble end-over-end—unless it were made to rotate on its long axis. Such rotation could be imparted by rifling the gun barrels, as makers of small arms had long since demonstrated. But for the rifling to be effective the shell would have to fit snugly in the barrel, thereby building up pressures that could burst contemporary ordnance.

Before the development of the sturdy built-up gun, British ordnance experts sought to achieve the effect of rifling while preserving windage. The result was the Lancaster gun, which fired an elliptical shell from a twisted elliptical bore; and the Whitworth gun, which fired a hexagonal shell from a twisted hexagonal bore. Such makeshifts proved not good enough. In the Crimean War rifled small arms demonstrated clear superiority in range and accuracy over smoothbore field pieces. To regain their ascendancy over the infantry, French artillerists threw caution to the winds and began using rifled guns with insufficient strength of barrel. The results were often disastrous.

The built-up Armstrong was the first gun in general use that could safely withstand the pressures produced by rifling. It fired elongated projectiles coated with lead that engaged the rifling on firing, its touchhole was in a replaceable vent-piece, and it was breech loading, with a non-interrupted screw closing the breech. Adopted by the British armed forces in 1859, the Armstrong gun revolutionized the science of gunnery.

The U. S. Navy long resisted the trend toward rifling. Throughout the Civil War and for 20 years thereafter, the smoothbore Dahlgren was standard on American naval vessels. There were good reasons. Dahlgrens, with their round shot and heavy charges, were better at penetrating armor than contemporary guns using smaller caliber elongated projectiles. The greater range conferred by rifling was considered a standing temptation to shoot off one's ammunition before closing with the enemy. American naval officers were confirmed in their prejudice by their experience with the Parrott gun. This was merely a rifled Rodman with a heavy wrought-iron band shrunk around the breech. Lacking reinforcement along the whole length of its barrel, the Parrott had a notorious tendency to blow off its own muzzle.

The Turret

The first-completed turret ship was Ericsson's *Monitor,* which fought the *Virginia* in the Battle of Hampton Roads in 1862. The idea of a revolving turret however was not new. It had long before been tried ashore and suggested for use at sea. It had even been anticipated by the pivot gun, which, mounted on the weather deck, could be swung round in any direction. In 1843 an American, Theodore R. Timby, filed a caveat at the United States Patent Office for a "Metallic Revolving Fort" for use afloat or ashore. And though Timby, so far as we know, had no influence on the design or adoption of turreted warships, Ericsson's firm was obliged to pay him royalties. In 1859 a British naval officer, Captain Cowper Coles, patented drawings and specifications for a turret with a revolving hemispherical shield, and interested the British Admiralty in his design. Experimental models were built and tested with such complete success that the Admiralty ordered the construction of a mastless ironclad, H.M.S. *Prince Albert,* mounting twelve guns in six of Coles's cupolas. Before construction got under way, news arrived in England of the Battle of Hampton Roads. Ericsson was thus recognized as the first to get an armored turret into operation, but Coles shares the distinction of introducing the invention into naval warfare. The *Prince Albert* was completed with Coles-designed turrets, and until his patent ran out Coles received royalty on every turret constructed for the British navy.

Tactical Theory

The advent of steam propulsion stimulated naval theorists into extensive and sometimes far-fetched speculation about its impact upon tactics. As seamen of the last days of sailing ship warfare had largely abandoned the conterminous line, certain early steam tacticians advocated abandoning the line altogether. The simple column had been imposed upon earlier navies by the difficulties of keeping station under sail, but with the advent of steam, so the theorists believed, there was no longer any limit to maneuver—any sort of formation had become possible. What was needed, said they, was a formation that provided defense in depth, that permitted massing of gunfire for close mutual support, that uncovered bows and sterns so as to permit fore-and-aft fire and the ready use of rams, and that avoided fouling of screws by lines, spars, and

sails shot away from ships ahead. An early solution, providing only a partial answer, was the indented line—a double column, with vessels staggered so as to cover the distances between ships in the adjacent column. More favored was the echelon formation. Most favored was the double echelon or inverted V formation, with ships in two lines of bearing led by the flagship at the apex. This last was to have a trial in battle before navies reverted to the single column as best after all.

Administrative Changes in Response to the New Technology

It was early evident that the naval organization of the age of sail was inadequate to deal with the problems posed by the new technology. To meet the challenge, the leading navies made major changes in administration and command. Because the period was one of comparative peace, the emphasis everywhere was on logistics; little was done to improve over-all operational command. Changes made in the navies of Britain and the United States illustrate the trend.

The British Admiralty was completely reorganized in 1832, when Sir James Graham, then First Lord, broke up and redistributed the top administrative commands. In the new set-up, five Sea Lords, all officers, reported to him directly in the Board of Admiralty. Each of the Sea Lords superintended the work of one of the five Civil Departments of the Admiralty. Each department was headed by an executive officer who reported to the cognizant Sea Lord. The executive officers bore the titles Surveyor of the Navy, in charge of materials and design; Accountant General, or treasurer; Storekeeper General; Controller of Victualling; and Physician General. Ten years later the U.S. Navy replaced the Board of Navy Commissioners with a similar departmental system, which was even more closely adapted to the navy of iron and steam. The organization set up in 1842 provided for five bureaus, each headed by an officer: Yards and Docks; Ordnance and Hydrography; Construction, Equipment, and Repair; Provisions and Clothing; and Medicine and Surgery.

The only means of coordinating the new departments or bureaus was, in the Royal Navy, through the First Lord of the Admiralty; in the U. S. Navy, through the Secretary of the Navy. Both were political appointees and members of the Cabinet. In the United States the Secretary has traditionally been a civilian. Since the incumbency of Lord Barham, of Trafalgar days, this has been true also of the First Lord, though a few retired officers have held the position. Neither navy had an officer in over-all command of operations, and the British Sea Lords and the American Bureau Chiefs were too involved in logistics to advise the civilian head of the navy on the conduct of war. Except for certain temporary, makeshift arrangements this was the situation until after the end of the century.

On the operational level, changes were equally necessary to meet the new challenge. Hence in 1837 the Engineer Officer appeared in both the Royal Navy and the U.S. Navy. But there was a difference. In the U.S. Navy the Engineer was from the beginning a commissioned officer. In the Royal Navy aristocratic tradition, which put the warrior on a higher plane than the ship handler, kept the Engineer in the status of warrant officer for ten years. When in 1847 senior British engineers received commissions, they assumed the curious title Inspector of Machinery Afloat.

Summary

The years 1815–60 were a period of minor military operations. The American and British navies, to be sure, humbled Algiers. British and French fleet units were involved in imperialistic wars against China. The United States Pacific and Home Squadrons participated in the Mexican War of 1846–48. The Royal Navy and the French *Marine* operated in both the Baltic and the Black seas during the Crimean War of 1854–56. None of these however were major wars, and none produced fleet battles at sea.

The period nonetheless was momentous in naval history. After 2,000 years of oar propulsion and 300 years of sail propulsion, the navies of the world now made their third great shift—to steam propulsion. At the same time they began adopting armor; the iron hull; rifled, built-up guns; and the percussion-fused shell. The world's armies, while not so completely revolutionized by the new technology, also found themselves with an arsenal of new weapons.

No one doubted that the technological changes would have a great impact upon the nature of warfare. Armchair tacticians filled the military journals with their theories. But in 1860, when H.M.S. *Warrior* was launched, few of the new weapons and few of the new theories had been put to the test of combat. Hence the outbreak of civil war in the United States the following year drew the prompt attention of military thinkers all over the world. As the war developed into a major conflict, various governments sent observers to report how the new weapons performed under fire. The American Civil War thus became, among other things, a testing ground for the new military technology.

13:

The American Civil War: the Blockade and the Cruisers

In the United States, the political compromises that had so long allowed the nation to exist half free and half slave-holding began to break apart in the decade of the 1850's. In February 1861, a month before Abraham Lincoln was inaugurated as President of the United States, the Confederate States of America proclaimed themselves a new nation. The stage was being set for armed conflict.

The root causes of the American Civil War include cultural antipathy, economic conflict, the slavery issue, the struggle for political dominance, and the right of secession, but guns began firing over a more immediate and practical question: Who has a right to Federal property in the territory of states that elect to secede from the Federal Union? In the seven states that had first seceded there were the Pensacola Navy Yard, 15 forts guarding harbors, and six Federal arsenals. In addition, there were in Texas 18 military posts, with substantial quantities of weapons. Though hoping to avoid war, the Southerners were aware of its possibility. Hence to secure these positions and their considerable armament became for them a pressing objective.

The position of the secessionists was that in seizing Federal property the states were merely exercising the sovereign prerogative of eminent domain. Recompense in money would be granted to the United States government after suitable negotiation. For the most part, the custodians surrendered the property without resistance—partly because those in charge were in many instances sympathetic to the secession movement; partly because they possessed inadequate strength for a fight; partly because President James Buchanan gave no clear, unequivocal orders demanding resistance. Fort Pickens at Pensacola, Fort Taylor at Key West,

and Fort Jefferson on the Tortugas, because of their remoteness and strength, remained in Federal hands. Also the forts at Charleston, under the command of Major Robert Anderson USA, were not immediately surrendered, though only one, Fort Moultrie, was garrisoned at the time of South Carolina's secession.

Because Charleston had been an early center of the secessionist movement, the forts in the harbor—Castle Pinckney, Fort Moultrie, and Fort Sumter—assumed a symbolic significance as soon as it became clear that they would not be peaceably surrendered. (See map page 312.) Toward the end of 1860, Buchanan let it be known that he would not order in reinforcements unless Fort Moultrie were attacked, but on December 26, Anderson on his own initiative moved his garrison force of 83 men to the much more defensible Fort Sumter. The South Carolina government thereupon seized and occupied Castle Pinckney and Fort Moultrie and ordered the emplacement of supplementary batteries to command the water approaches to the city more thoroughly.

General-in-chief of the United States Army Winfield Scott, with the President's approval, now ordered reinforcements and supplies sent to Anderson. On January 5, 1861, the chartered merchant steamer *Star of the West* left New York, with Charleston as her secret destination. But as almost invariably happened with secret missions in the early part of the war, intelligence of this effort reached the South before the ship did.

When the *Star of the West* entered Charleston harbor on the morning of January 9, new batteries on Morris Island opened fire on her. The ship received one or two hits but quickly passed out of effective range. The course of the channel however would have required her to pass under the ready guns of Fort Moultrie. The captain, having lost the advantage of surprise, thought better of making the attempt. He turned and steamed out through the fire of the Morris Island batteries, and Major Anderson got no reinforcements. Thus the first shots of the Civil War were fired in a bloodless naval encounter.

There now followed a drawn-out tacit truce in Charleston Harbor while a committee of Confederate senators carried on a dilatory correspondence with the President. Buchanan welcomed the opportunity to postpone unpalatable decisions but was indisposed to retreat any further. Meanwhile General Pierre Beauregard, wearing the brand-new stars of a general officer in the Confederate States Army, arrived in Charleston to prepare for the capture of Sumter, if it could not be won by negotiation.

The Surrender of Fort Sumter

Sumter, a powerful, newly constructed fort, situated on a man-made island in Charleston harbor, would have been almost impregnable had it been properly manned and armed. But when Anderson occupied it, only 48 of its 140 guns had been emplaced, and Anderson's small detachment numbered only about an eighth of full garrison strength. Beauregard, a skilled military engineer, therefore undertook assault preparations with confidence, mounting batteries to breach the walls and constructing defenses against expected reinforcements. On April 1 he telegraphed Confederate President Jefferson Davis in Montgomery, Alabama that all was ready. The next day all traffic to and from the fort was prohibited. On the 11th Beauregard demanded the surrender of Sumter, and Anderson refused. Proposals and counterproposals delayed the attack until early morning of April 12.

At dawn on the 12th, the Charlestonians, who were out in force to witness the spectacle, saw the first mortar shell curve through the air and fall into the parade of Fort Sumter. One after another the various Confederate batteries responded to this signal, and in a matter of minutes the fort was under general bombardment. Anderson chose to wait until daylight made his more difficult targets on

the shore visible. At about 7 AM Sumter began returning a spirited fire. The cannonade continued for two days and a part of a third, during which time Anderson, by keeping his men from the exposed barbette positions and the parade, avoided casualties to his force.

Meanwhile a pair of small screw sloops, a revenue cutter, and a transport carrying 200 soldiers stood off Charleston harbor impotent to intervene. This was part of a relief expedition organized for the U.S. Navy Department by Gustavus V. Fox, a former naval officer turned business man. Fox's plan, to send in the transport with supplies and reinforcements for Sumter, depended upon the presence of u.s.s. *Powhatan,* a big paddle-sloop, to provide fire support. Unknown to the Navy Department however, the big sloop had been sent elsewhere. Secretary of State William H. Seward and Lieutenant David Dixon Porter USN had obtained permission from Lincoln to use the *Powhatan* in a secret expedition for the relief of Fort Pickens. This piece of interdepartmental meddling proved salutary in that it enabled Secretary of the Navy Gideon Welles to demand a clearer definition of cabinet areas of authority, but it rendered the Sumter relief expedition futile.

On April 13 the administration buildings at Sumter were fired by hot shot. The magazines thereby threatened, it became necessary to jettison most of the powder. Major Anderson had been authorized by Lincoln to surrender when in his judgment no useful purpose would be served by prolonged resistance. Without prospect of relief, with limited supplies, and no longer with any effective power to fight back, he bowed to the inevitable and capitulated. The flag of the United States was hauled down on April 14, and Sumter was evacuated—the troops being carried away by Fox's otherwise fruitless relief force.

The events in Charleston harbor made war inevitable. Lincoln's response was prompt and firm. In a proclamation on April 15 he summoned 75,000 state militia.

The promise of coercive action by the Federal government led the other four Southern states to join the Confederacy. Seeing the middle position between Secession and Federalism melt away, Virginia, Arkansas, North Carolina, and Tennessee passed ordinances of

secession. There was strong secessionist sentiment in the slave-holding border states, Missouri, Kentucky, and Maryland, but a combination of geography and loyalist majorities
kept them in the Union.

Loss of the Norfolk Navy Yard

The surrender of Fort Sumter, except as a
blow to Northern pride, was a much less serious loss than the nearly contemporaneous
abandonment of the Norfolk Navy Yard. The
Norfolk Yard, biggest in the country, had one
of the two large naval drydocks and was a
storage arsenal for the Navy's reserve ordnance. Here were stored 300-odd modern
Dahlgren guns, 50 or more of which were 9-
inch weapons of the latest design. Here too
were a number of vessels under repair, including the 50-gun screw frigate *Merrimack*.

While matters were coming to a head in
Charleston harbor, the city of Norfolk seethed
with secessionist sentiment. Though Virginia
had not yet joined the Confederacy, recruitment for the Virginia militia was being actively pressed, many of the officers stationed
at the Yard were resigning, and desertion and
petty acts of mutiny were becoming common.
On April 10, Secretary Welles warned the
aging commandant, Commodore C. S. Mc-
Cauley, to exercise "great vigilance." On the
12th, Engineer in Chief Benjamin F. Isherwood was ordered to Norfolk to supervise the
reassembling of the *Merrimack's* machinery so
that she could be shifted to Philadelphia. Isherwood quickly complied, but McCauley, reduced
to a panicky irresoluteness by the distressing
march of events and fearing to provoke an
armed clash by any purposeful activity, finally
ordered Isherwood to draw the boiler fires. By
this time Virginia had passed her secession
ordinance. Secretary Welles lost no time in
dispatching Commodore Hiram Paulding to
relieve McCauley and to evacuate or destroy
all naval material and shipping at Norfolk.

Equipped with combustibles, Paulding took
U.S.S. *Pawnee* to Norfolk, arriving the evening
of April 20. Here he discovered the *Merrimack*
and three other ships, scuttled by McCauley's
order, gradually sinking in the anchorage.
Paulding would have to hurry to complete

his mission of destruction. Though reinforced
by a troop contingent from Fortress Monroe,
across the James River, he lacked an adequate
force to defend the sprawling Navy Yard if
the Virginia militia assembled outside were
to storm the gates.

Marines and bluejackets from the *Pawnee*,
dividing into small work parties, mined the
drydock, spread turpentine-soaked cotton waste
and gunpowder around the wooden buildings
and the top-hamper of the sinking ships, and
made unsuccessful efforts to sledge off the
trunnions of the big guns in storage. In a matter of hours preparations were as complete as
they could make them, and a little before
dawn the powder trains were lighted off. As
the firing parties rowed from the shore, the
whole yard turned into a sheet of flame.

The work of destruction proved far from
complete, for when the fires burned themselves
out, the Confederates found undamaged
among the ruins the largest cache of modern
ordnance in the Western Hemisphere. Since
at this time the South had no facilities for
producing such weapons, this was good fortune beyond price. These were the guns that
would arm the new forts defending Southern
harbors. Moreover, a reckless band of Virginia militia had rushed into the yard in the
nick of time to save the drydock by flooding.

Military Resources
of the Adversaries

The Union and the Confederacy were not,
except in area, at all well matched. The population of the Union exceeded that of the
seceded region by a five-to-two ratio.[1] The
disparity in material resources and particularly
in developed industry was much more marked.
Even in textile manufacture, the South was
far from self-sufficient. In heavy industry, the
basic component of economic war potential,
the superiority of the North was overwhelming.
The South lacked not only foundries and metal
works to make guns and supply her railroads
but also the skilled workmen and experienced

[1] The North had a population of 22,000,000 (1860
census); the South, 9,000,000, of whom approximately 3,500,000 were slaves.

engineers to run such plants. Her transportation system was hardly adequate to handle her peacetime needs; in relationship to her area, her railroads were relatively few, and these were not planned as a system. In the North, on the other hand, the 1850's had seen a boom in rail construction, and the great trunk line systems were already in operation.

In 1860 the exports of the South—mostly cotton and tobacco—were valued at $31,-000,000; those of the North, at $331,000,000. Furthermore Northern ship-owners monopolized the carrying trade; there was not in the entire Confederacy an adequate number of experienced merchant seamen to man a navy—even if there had been the industrial wherewithal to build one. The United States Navy began the Civil War woefully unprepared, but the Confederacy had no navy at all.

Though the South was an agricultural region, it was not well supplied even in basic foodstuffs because of the large areas devoted exclusively to raising cotton. The incursions of Northern armies, especially the splitting of Texas and Arkansas from the rest of the Confederate states, combined with the breakdown of transportation and inflation of the currency to produce near-starvation. Even if Lee had saved the Army of Virginia at Appomattox, the South would have been starved into submission within a year. In summary, the North had the economic wherewithal to fight a war, and the South had not.

In the face of these facts, how did the South dare to provoke a war? There is no single answer to this question. In the first place, nobody planned the Civil War: secession was planned, but very few even of the leaders of the Southern population believed that force would be necessary to accomplish it. Second, the educational level of the South was low: a great many ignorant and unreflecting people gave serious credence to the demagogic assurance that the "Yankees are cowards." Third, there was no understanding of the economic demands of modern war; even Jefferson Davis and his cabinet did not at first realize the problem they faced. Fourth, there was some reliance on the hope that Northern "politics" would make the successful prosecution of the war by the North impossible. The Democratic party in the North still had many adherents, and Southern sympathizers were in fact active (though ineffectual) in some Northern states.

Fifth, it was widely believed that to cut off "King Cotton" from British and French mills would ruin their industry and compel Britain and France to intervene in the war, or at least to breach the blockade. Sixth, the South counted on simple war weariness and the mounting cost of the war in casualties and treasure to prompt the people of the North to demand a peace. Seventh, in spite of all her handicaps, the South enjoyed certain real advantages: she had a proud and virile rural population, accustomed to the use of firearms and possessed of a tradition of violence;[2] she had a ready-made officer corps in the large number of officers of the United States Army who resigned their commissions to take new ones in the Confederacy; furthermore in Lee, Jackson, Joseph Johnston, Beauregard, and others, she had some of the ablest military men of the day.[3] The territory of the Confederacy was extensive and could be successfully invaded and held only by vast armies campaigning through years of fighting. Also, the bulk of the Southern population was passionately loyal to the cause. By concentrating on the few Southern strengths, and minimizing the many Southern weaknesses, even shrewd men in the South could bring themselves to believe in the prospect of ultimate victory.

War Preparations

Both the North and the South anticipated a short war. When the issue was joined after months of vacillation and negotiation, there was an almost pathological eagerness for battle. From the middle of April, war preparations went on rapidly on both sides.

The Confederate government, which already had some 11,000 men in arms at Charleston

[2] The duel, for example, which had disappeared in the North, was still an integral part of a Southern gentleman's "code of honor."

[3] In order to avoid asking too much financial sacrifice on the one hand and the imputation of "buying loyalties" on the other, the Confederate government wisely offered identical rank and pay to "transfers" from the United States regular forces.

and at Pensacola, had on April 8 called for a contingent of 20,000 from the seceded states; on April 16 there was a further call for 34,000 volunteers. In the seized arsenals the South found much military equipment, including over 100,000 stands of arms. Other weapons were secured by purchase from abroad. The forts, especially those of Charleston, furnished heavy guns. The occupation of the Norfolk Navy Yard, as previously noted, made available heavy artillery that the South could not herself have produced. Agents were dispatched to Europe, both to work for diplomatic recognition and a line of credit, and to procure military stores and naval shipping. Further fortification of the Southern coast was undertaken; plans were made to blockade the Mississippi River as far north as Columbus, Kentucky. (See map page 249.) At the special session of the Confederate Congress, President Davis announced that he "had in the field, at Charleston, Pensacola, Forts Morgan, Jackson, St. Philip, and Pulaski, 10,000 men, and 16,000 are now en route for Virginia." He also promised the immediate organization of an army of 100,000 men.

Corresponding preparations were made by the North. Lincoln's call for volunteers on April 15 brought an enthusiastic response from all the free states, and from nearly every prominent citizen in the North. The state governors immediately set about recruiting and exceeding their quotas. Nearly double the 75,000 volunteers sought presented themselves for induction.

It takes some time to enlist, assemble, equip, and transport recruits, but in three months both sides had taken these first steps in the creation of citizen armies. Such was popular demand, and such was the inexperience of the general officers (commanding comparatively large forces for the first time in American history), that these untrained innocents were thrown at each other at the first opportunity, a discreditable performance known as the first Battle of Bull Run (July 21, 1861). Since the Union disorganization was the greater, and many of the blue-clad troops panicked in retreat, the South hailed it as a great victory. The North was correspondingly cast down. Southern officers also lost control of their troops in the field however, and the pro-

fessionals on both sides were content to withdraw to train their forces into armies of soldiers. There were no further land engagements of consequence in 1861.

For the Union, the Battle of Bull Run was simply the culmination of a series of alarms and frustrations in the unlucky spring and summer of 1861—the loss of Fort Sumter, the abandonment of Norfolk, the quite reasonable fear that Maryland would secede and leave Washington a besieged city in a hostile land. Yet, though there were to be four long years of bloodshed and heartache before the Army of the Potomac could march in the victory parade down Pennsylvania Avenue, the foundations of a victorious grand strategy were already being laid.

Naval Secretary Gideon Welles

In a cabinet that included William H. Seward, Salmon P. Chase, and, later, Edwin M. Stanton, Gideon Welles, the new Secretary of the Navy, a Connecticut politician and newspaper editor, was far from being the most prominent member. Yet in many ways he was Lincoln's wisest selection. For one thing, he had had experience as a naval bureau chief. For another, he was completely loyal to Lincoln, whom he recognized from the first to be a great leader. Finally, he possessed most of the qualities of a great administrator, possibly all except the capacity to delegate authority. This failing he compensated by an enormous capacity for hard work. His extensive diaries reveal a man of first rate intelligence and great firmness of purpose—with an uncanny eye for character weakness in his peers.

Welles was ably assisted by Gustavus V. Fox. After the unhappy Sumter Relief Expedition, Fox had been appeased by his appointment as Chief Clerk in the Navy Department; shortly afterward he became the first Assistant Secretary of the Navy.

The "Anaconda Policy"

The history of the Federal Navy in the American Civil War is an account not of winning sea supremacy but of exercising it, of making potential control actual control. Ex-

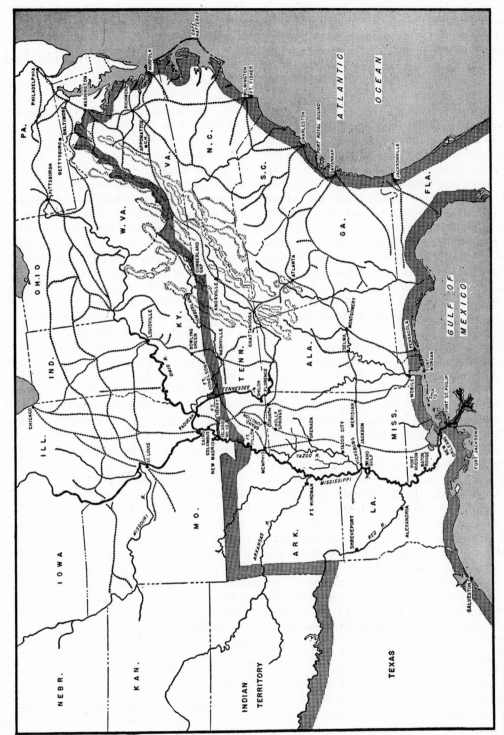

THE CONFEDERACY

cept locally and under atypical conditions, the South made no effective challenge to the superior Northern sea power. Nevertheless, it required arduous service by hundreds of ships and thousands of men to make this superiority a heavy weight in the balance of victory and defeat. Offensive operations of great diversity were undertaken by the Union Navy. Coastal forts were bombarded, joint amphibious assaults were effected, Confederate commerce raiders were hunted down. Above all, the ceaseless patrol off the Southern ports was maintained. It may be said that every Confederate naval effort was an attempt to breach the blockade, while nearly every operation undertaken by the Union Navy was related to the constant effort to strengthen it. The blockade of the South was aptly characterized by General Winfield Scott as the "Anaconda Policy." Just as a python's coils grasp its prey loosely at first, then grip tighter and tighter until the victim is squeezed to death, so the improvised navy of Gideon Welles gradually extinguished the commercial life of the Confederacy.

The South was peculiarly vulnerable to blockade because of the specialization of her economy. As the Anaconda tightened its coils, not only were there progressive shortages of munitions, uniform cloth, drugs, and surgical instruments, but even such commonplace materials as harness leather became unprocurable. In the months before Appomattox, shoes and even flour disappeared from the market. Having relied for nearly all of her manufactures on imports from the North and from Europe, the South lacked industrial economic strength in every major category—capital goods, financial institutions, technicians and engineers, and above all, manpower, in view of the demand for men in the armies. Cotton bales accumulated on docks and in warehouses. The blood stream of foreign exchange dried up. The credit of the Confederacy in Europe, never good, became progressively worse as the war wore on.

Shortages of consumer goods precipitated a rise in prices in the Confederacy, where the misguided government answered the popular outcry against high prices by simply issuing more currency. As prices spiraled steeply, "printing press" inflation caused the Confed-

erate dollar to decline to 1/225 of its worth in one year and by September 1864, one gold dollar exchanged for $2,000 in Confederate currency.

Proclamation of the Blockade

Yet it was the South that started economic warfare. On April 17, 1861, Jefferson Davis issued a proclamation offering letters of marque and reprisal to armed privateers of any nation. Two days later Lincoln replied with a counter-proclamation, instituting a blockade of Southern ports from South Carolina to Texas.[4] Secretary Welles in a heated Cabinet quarrel argued that it had been a mistake to proclaim a blockade as such, since this had the effect of conferring belligerent rights on the South and was a tacit recognition of the Confederacy's claim to being a separate nation with rights of sovereignty. Welles, with Congressional support, argued that the proper procedure would have been to "close" the ports of the South—a legalistic difference aimed at identifying the struggle as a domestic matter in which the rest of the world could have no proper interest. A law was finally passed requiring the President to proclaim a closure of the ports. He did so, remarking wryly that it would be "like the Pope's bull to the comet." Since the previously proclaimed blockade was not explicitly canceled, no real purpose was served by the second proclamation.

The immediate task facing the United States Navy was a formidable one. Under international law, neutrals are not bound by a "paper blockade." To secure foreign recognition of the blockade, it had to be made effective. And following the high water mark along shore from Alexandria, Virginia to Brownsville, Texas, the Confederacy had 3,550 miles of coast, much of the Atlantic portion of it a "double coastline." There were 189 harbors and navigable river mouths to watch. For this task, the Navy in early 1861 had 7,600 men and 90 warships, of which 42 were actually in commission; 21 of the remainder were reckoned as "unserviceable." Many of those in

[4] The limits of the blockade were extended to include Virginia and North Carolina as soon as they seceded.

commission were sailing vessels of a type that proved of little value. To cap this poor preparation, three of the vessels were in the East Indies, and 22 ships (236 guns total) were in the Pacific. On the other hand, eight of the ten navy yards were in the Union,[5] and Norfolk was regained in 1862. Extensive shipyards and machinery-fabricating facilities existed in the North. Besides, the golden age of the American merchant marine was just drawing to a close, and numerous merchant vessels and trained seamen were available.

Welles immediately ordered home all ships but the Anti-Slaver Patrol off West Africa. All seaworthy craft were put in commission. Presently there were 76 vessels rated at 1,783 guns available for naval orders. In the same initial burst of activity the Navy purchased and adapted over a hundred vessels, including grain barges and ferry boats—anything stable enough to be a satisfactory gun platform. Construction was pushed in private yards and navy yards. By December 1861, 264 vessels—in aggregate 218,000 tons—were in commission. This figure was added to at a somewhat less frantic pace as the war progressed. The North was also to build 74 ironclads during the war.

Recruiting for the wartime service was initiated promptly, and by December 1861 the Union Navy had a strength of over 20,000. There was no "boot camp" in 1861, and the new "naval volunteers" were often standing watches at sea within a few days of taking their oath. Though the veterans of the "spit-and-polish" traditions of Matthew Calbraith Perry's navy shuddered at the new men's lack of smartness and their occasional ignorance of ceremonial observances, they were nearly all trained seamen from the merchant marine, soon indistinguishable from the men of the "Old Navy."

Once the blockade was initiated, it became obvious that its full implementation would require logistic support of a scale and variety not previously contemplated. The inshore patrol would be steam-propelled; hence colliers and coaling stations, preferably near the blockading stations, would be required. As more ships joined the squadrons, more and larger

base facilities would be necessary. Though there were adequate bases in the North, there was an evident need for others close to the Southern ports the Navy was attempting to seal. Possession of a base near Charleston and Savannah, for example, would greatly increase the number of Federal ships on station by eliminating the need for individual blockade vessels to return periodically to Washington or Philadelphia. Furthermore, ships taking on coal or undergoing repairs at such an advanced base would always remain available as a ready reserve for speedy reinforcement of the ships on patrol. (See map page 249.)

So the Navy planned to capture strategic sites for advanced bases as soon as adequate amphibious forces could be assembled. With the ships and troops available in 1861, any attempt to seize fortified ports such as Charleston, Savannah, or Wilmington, N.C. was out of the question. Yet the sites to be occupied would have to provide good, deep anchorages and the possibility of developing docking facilities. Furthermore, they had to be near the Confederacy's major ports and at the same time be easily defensible from the landward side. Luckily, the length and convoluted nature of the Southern coastline, which made blockade so difficult, facilitated capture of the sort of bases the Navy required. With thousands of miles of coast and almost 200 harbors, the Confederacy could hardly manage to fortify in advance every place the Navy might strike.

Hatteras Inlet

The short-lived Strategy Board,[6] headed by Captain Samuel F. Du Pont, selected as the first coastal "key position" to be seized, Hatteras Inlet, a break in the offshore sand barrier between the Atlantic and Pamlico Sound, off the North Carolina coast. This inlet, and the low-lying sand dunes on both sides, was believed suited to the special needs of the blockade, for it was easily defended and yet reasonably close to Beaufort and Wilmington, which were good ports and railroad terminals. On August 26, 1861, Flag Officer S. H.

[5] Kittery, Portsmouth, Charlestown, Sackett's Harbor, Brooklyn, Philadelphia, Washington, Norfolk, Pensacola, Mare Island.

[6] This was one of three officer boards appointed by Welles that helped the Secretary in his most important decisions. The others were the Retirement Board and the Ironclad Board.

Stringham with seven ships, and Major General Benjamin F. Butler with 860 soldiers sailed from Fortress Monroe against Forts Clark and Hatteras, guarding Hatteras Inlet. These log and sandbank forts, armed largely with antique 32-pounders, were lightly manned and inadequately supplied. After a gunnery duel on August 28 between the ships and the outranged shore batteries, 300 of Butler's men landed behind Fort Clark, which was abandoned by her defenders. The next day the unequal contest concluded with the capitulation of Fort Hatteras. As a base for the blockaders, Hatteras Inlet proved a disappointment. The shoal waters and shifting channels made it unsatisfactory even as an anchorage, and subsequent operations in this general section had to be undertaken later. The action is notable only as the first amphibious assault of the war.

Port Royal

Of much greater strategic and tactical significance was the Port Royal operation, which was undertaken less than a month later. Besides Norfolk, Beaufort, and Wilmington, the only Atlantic ports in the South with rail connections to the rest of the Confederacy were Charleston and Savannah, both of which were stoutly defended by stone and masonry forts with numerous heavy guns. But Port Royal

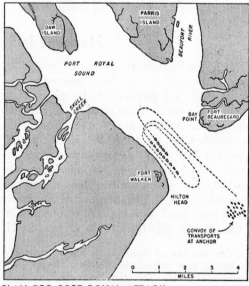

PLAN FOR PORT ROYAL ATTACK

Sound, which lay between them on the South Carolina coast, though far more formidably fortified than Hatteras Inlet, offered a suitable objective. In virtually all respects it would make an ideal blockade base, for there was ample deep water, it was close to major Southern ports, and counterattack from the interior would be difficult because the country back of Port Royal was so swampy as to be almost impassable. On the other hand, Forts Walker and Beauregard, at the entrance to the Sound, were strong enough to make the issue by no means the foregone conclusion the Hatteras Inlet action had been. In 1861 the Union Navy could not afford to lose many ships, and there had been till this time too little experience involving wooden steamers against forts for anyone to be able to say what the gun power afloat had to be to insure the overpowering of a given number of guns ashore.[7]

Under these circumstances, Captain Du Pont, designated "commodore" to lead this expedition, delayed sailing until he was joined by the first of the "90-day gunboats" Welles had ordered built, and until he had collected a truly formidable flotilla of warships, transports, and supply vessels. Not counting a collier and supply convoy of 25 ships that sailed separately under naval escort, Du Pont's force, when it weighed anchor in Hampton Roads, comprised eleven large warships, 36 transports carrying 13,000 men under Brigadier General Thomas W. Sherman, and a number of smaller gunboats.[8]

Heavy weather off the Carolina coast scattered this armada badly. Two supply vessels were driven ashore, and a transport was broken up at sea, though the 300 marines embarked were providentially saved. The expedition had been planned as a joint operation, but the loss of many of the landing boats in the storm

[7] Traditionally, one gun in a fort was reckoned "equal" to four or five guns of similar caliber afloat in a sailing vessel. The problem in its new form was essentially a question of the degree to which the greater vulnerability of steam vessels, which could be disabled by a single shot, was compensated by their superior maneuverability.

[8] The warships included several screw sloops of the "tribal" class (*Pawnee, Iroquois, Mohican*) carrying 11-inch Dahlgren smooth-bores. The transports were mostly chartered vessels, including big packets from the transatlantic run. The 90-day gunboats were vessels of 507 tons, carrying 4 to 7 guns.

compelled Du Pont to change the plan to a purely naval offensive. On November 4, 1861 the flagship with about half of the force crossed the bar that lies about ten miles off Hilton Head and anchored out of range of the forts to wait for the stragglers. Meanwhile boat parties took local soundings and reset channel markers, which the Confederates had everywhere moved or altered as a defense measure.

The entrance to Port Royal Sound lies between Hilton Head and Bay Point, which are 2½ miles apart. Because Fort Walker, on Hilton Head, was the stronger fort, Du Pont determined to concentrate his attack on it first. Reconnaissance indicated that Fort Walker was strong on its seaward (eastern) front. On its northern face, fronting the Sound, it was armed only with two obsolescent guns. The Commodore therefore elected to run up into the Sound and bombard the flank of the defenses.

In the morning of November 7, Du Pont led 14 of his strongest vessels in two columns up the middle of the channel, firing at both forts as they passed between them. Inside the channel a defense flotilla comprising a river steamboat and two small gunboats made a gesture of resistance and then fled to safety up a nearby creek as the Union ships turned their fire upon them.

Du Pont's plan was for his starboard division of five gunboats to remain inside the Sound, delivering a deliberate fire on the weak northern flank of Fort Walker, while he led his main force of nine vessels on an elliptical course in and out of the Sound, passing and re-passing the face of Fort Walker while delivering point-blank fire. But when the flagship, the 46-gun steam frigate *Wabash*, turned to port to lead back past the fort at close range, only two vessels followed her. The rest stayed well inside the Sound with the gunboat division, joining them in delivering enfilading fire.

The three ships with Du Pont completed two ellipses and began a third. Actually it did not seriously matter that these vessels operated alone, for among them they carried nearly half the guns of the Union attack force, which as a whole enjoyed a 5-to-1 superiority in volume of fire over both forts together. The forts replied as best they could, making hits and inflicting casualties, but they found themselves

gradually overwhelmed. At 1:00 P.M. the defenders of Fort Walker abandoned the works. Fort Beauregard was vacated later in the afternoon. General Sherman's troops then came ashore and took possession of both. The total success of the operation in spite of only partial compliance with orders prompted Du Pont to withhold censure of his awkward or insubordinate captains.[9]

In terms of casualties suffered, the Port Royal action was only a minor action, comparable to a skirmish of patrols in the land war. The fleet had eight killed, 28 wounded; the forts, 11 and 48. Ten of the 13 guns on the channel face of Fort Walker were dismounted, but the fort was abandoned only when powder was running low. In terms of strategic importance however, it was a notable victory, enormously raising Northern morale and demonstrating that wooden ships could stand up to forts. Port Royal became a major base and supply depot for the blockaders and was so used throughout the war.

The Port Royal expedition has been described in some detail because of its place in the history of naval tactics and also because it is the archetype of numerous other expeditions undertaken later in the war. Similar in purpose, these differ only in detail from Du Pont's operations. Some were uncontested; others were resisted with much spirit by the local defenders. Operations against Roanoke Island and Elizabeth City, and the capture of New Bern in early 1862 by amphibious forces under Flag Officer L. M. Goldsborough and General S. E. Burnside gave the Union control of Albemarle Sound. As a result North Carolina's military strength was largely diverted to local defense, and the transport of the abundant provisions of the Carolina country to the Army of Virginia was thrown upon the inadequate railroad system. Du Pont's concurrent occupation of Amelia Island and Jacksonville, Florida, and the Union recovery of St. Augustine and Norfolk, reduced Confederate control of the

[9] Du Pont's kindly impulse has led to confusion among historians. The account in *Official Records of the Union and Confederate Navies in the War of the Rebellion* [SHORT TITLE: *Official Records*], Series I, volume XII, describes the plan rather than the actual battle. The most authoritative detailed analysis of this action is the unpublished study by Rear Admiral John D. Hayes USN (Ret.).

Atlantic seaboard to the port of Savannah and the stretch of blockaded coastline between Wilmington and Charleston. The recapture of Pensacola (where Fort Pickens had never been surrendered) was an important preliminary to the seizure of New Orleans and Mobile and the closing of the Gulf coast to blockade runners.

European Intervention

From the first, informed public opinion in the South confidently looked forward to European intervention—perhaps initially with proffers of mediation, but then, if the United States rejected such offers, with naval assistance. A number of reasons were plausibly adduced why the British would intervene, the most generally accepted being that the cutting off of Southern cotton by the blockade would depress British industry to the point of bankruptcy. This would presumably compel British intervention at least to the extent of raising the blockade.

But "King Cotton" proved a grievous disappointment to those who enthroned him. The record cotton crop of 1860, coupled with the threat of trouble, had resulted in inflated inventories in both England and France. It took nearly two years of mill operation to work off this raw material backlog. After that, the effects of the blockade began to be felt. Throughout the war some cotton reached Europe from the South, both through blockade-running and through licensed shipments from ports in Union hands. But by 1864 American cotton received in England and France annually was only about one tenth that received in the pre-war years. Still, the British government did not feel compelled to intervene. The textile manufacturers compensated themselves for reduced volume of production by charging higher prices. The textile workers, who before the end of the war were hard hit by the shortage, were not yet enfranchised. Furthermore, actively and effectively propagandized by Northern abolitionists, the workers remained sympathetic to the people of the North.

Britain came closest to intervening, not to assure herself a supply of Southern cotton, but, ironically enough, over an infringement of her neutral rights by a warship of the United States. The Confederacy, disappointed at not receiving full-fledged recognition in Europe—

the right to maintain a ministry, to negotiate a state loan, and so forth—designated two of her most prominent statesmen, former United States Senators James M. Mason and John Slidell, as plenipotentiaries to advance her cause in Europe. No secret was made of this intention; it was widely advertised in the press, and, characteristically, the plan was as generally known in the North as in the South. The emissaries, with families and secretaries, successfully ran the blockade to Havana, where they embarked on the British mail-packet *Trent*, bound for England. Without orders, Captain Charles Wilkes USN, then commanding the screw sloop *San Jacinto*, took pains to intercept the British packet. On November 8, 1861, he compelled the *Trent* to heave to by firing twice across her bow, and sent a boarding party over. After a *pro forma* show of force, Mason and Slidell were taken off to the *San Jacinto*.

This simple and apparently effective thwarting of the will of the Confederacy made Wilkes a national hero all over again to a public surfeited with the frustrations and disappointments of that black year. The United States had fought Britain in the War of 1812 for the principle that the flag conveys its nationality to the ship that flies it, that the ship's deck is a floating piece of the country where it is registered. Now the shoes had changed feet! But the British public failed to see any glory in Wilkes' challenge to their flag. Viewing it as a rude and deliberate affront, they expected and desired war. The fondest hope of the Confederate leadership seemed about to be realized.

A variety of circumstances conspired to thwart this stroke of fortune—the common sense of Lincoln (who pointed out that the act had not been sanctioned by the government), the timely intervention of the British Prince Consort, and the slowness of transatlantic communications, which permitted a lapse of time to cool the hotheads on both sides of the ocean. After acrimonious debate in the United States Cabinet, Secretary of State Seward penned a conciliatory note to Lord Lyons, the British Minister in Washington, and Mason and Slidell were released from their dungeon in Boston harbor.

Despite her quick reaction to the "*Trent*

Affair," Britain did not enforce a very strict interpretation of neutral rights. She was adamant only in cases involving "the honor of the flag." She officially recognized the Union blockade, thereby setting the pattern that other European states followed. She acquiesced in some strained interpretations of international law, and allowed the U. S. Navy to set new precedents therein. This apparently paradoxical surrender of selfish interests resulted partly from Britain's tradition of defining belligerent rights broadly, and partly from a far-sighted realization that these precedents might be of value to her in future wars.

While British governmental leaders consistently opposed armed intervention in the American conflict, they generally favored mediation —but the time never seemed ripe for it. Napoleon III of France also favored mediation and finally tired of waiting for the British to lead the way. In January 1863, after the defeat of the Army of the Potomac at Fredericksburg, he actually offered himself as peacemaker. The Union firmly declined, and that was as far as European intervention ever got.

Blockade Running

Up to the time of the fall of New Orleans, blockade-running was not unduly hazardous. Vessels of all types were loaded with cotton bales to make the run to Havana, Nassau, Bermuda, or St. Thomas. As the blockaders became more efficient and more numerous, it became no longer feasible to run through in small sailing vessels. Only fast steamers were left in the business. Even so, the risks of capture became progressively greater as the war went on. By the summer of 1863, the Union Navy had captured 850-odd blockade-runners, and already specially-built craft were being employed.

The more efficient the blockade became, the greater were the rewards to those who could run goods through. Joint-stock companies were formed in Britain; Clyde-built ships especially adapted to blockade-running and commanded by British officers were sent out to Nassau and Bermuda.

These blockade-runners were fast, wooden-hulled, shoal-draft vessels of about 450 tons. For the most part they were paddle-wheelers,

burning anthracite to avoid smoking. They had fine lines, a length-beam ratio of eight or nine to one being common. They were, above everything, fast. Some could make 17 knots or better. Many of them had telescopic stacks; there was little top-hamper; the masts were mere sticks. Painted gray, low in freeboard, proceeding "blacked out" at night, they were nearly invisible.

In a typical run, the blockade-runner would load at St. George's, Bermuda, be piloted out the intricate channel at nightfall, and dodge the Union vessels lying in wait outside the reefs. Through the night she would steam at something less than her best speed, maintaining a sharp lookout for Union cruisers. Navigating carefully, she would try to make a precise landfall two days later in the early evening, at, for example, Savannah. She would make her approach after dark, hugging the shore, and exchanging light recognition signals with the coast stations and the forts. Then came the final dash at top speed, past the "inshore blockade." At the pier the crated munitions and such luxuries as liquors, Paris gowns, linens, laces, corsetry, tea, and coffee were quickly unloaded and the company's agent took charge of speedily moving them to a warehouse. Without delay, bales of cotton were stacked in the hold and tiered on deck, with a few extra bales on top on the captain's personal account. The ship would then be fumigated with sulfur to smoke out any stowaways. At nightfall, the ship's officers got a fix on any blockaders visible and plotted them on their chart. Since the blockaders usually anchored at night, it was sometimes not too difficult to steam silently between them in the dark. Strict silence on board the blockade-runner was of course the rule, and sometimes the outward dash was altogether undetected. If discovered, the blockade-runner could still rely on her superior speed.

Even after escaping the inshore blockade, there was still the chance of being sighted by one of the faster Union ships at sea. But on any one given voyage, the odds favored the blockade-runner as long as there was a port in Confederate hands to run to. Up to January 1865, 84 specially-built steamers had been regularly employed in blockade-running. Of this number, 37 were captured, 25 were lost by grounding, collision, and accident, and 22 survived the war.

In the period 1863-64, the profits of blockade-running were so large that two or three successful round trips, which might be accomplished in as many weeks, would more than pay off the cost of the ship. Coffee, for example, worth 12¢ a pound in Nassau, brought $2.75 (in gold) in Richmond. As early as December 1862, the accepted freight rate from Nassau to Savannah was $500 a ton. Owners of a single lucky ship could easily clear over a million dollars a year. As the risks multiplied, even the officers and crews came to enjoy what were then deemed fabulous returns. A merchant skipper who in 1860 earned perhaps $140 to $160 a month received $5,000 a month for commanding a blockade-runner—and this was supplemented by opportunity for private speculation. Ordinary seamen received base pay of $100 a month, a bonus of $50 for each successful round trip.

It must not be supposed that the blockade-runners in any significant sense defeated the strategy of blockade. Indeed by draining off the South's slender supply of trained seamen, by attracting capital that might otherwise have gone into further development of the South's war industries, by stimulating the gold flow out of the country and hence further debasing the currency, the blockade-runners weakened the South.[10] Their total carrying capacity was inadequate to move any but a small fraction of the cotton grown, and the higher profits in carrying expensive luxuries made a disproportionate share of the incoming cargoes frivolous items of no possible benefit to the war effort. The "blockade auctions" featured bolts of silk, jewelry, and French brandy while industry was in desperate need of chemicals and boiler iron, and while the hospitals utterly lacked opiates and other drugs. The resentment stirred by the speculative few who amassed fortunes while the Army of Northern Virginia fought in rags compelled the Confederate Congress to pass an act (March 1, 1864) that forbade the importation of luxuries. This law was ap-

[10] It is of interest that the Confederate government itself entered this field of unrestricted "private enterprise," being the secret owner of four blockade-runners, and having a part interest in a number of others.

parently not generally enforced however since editorial denunciations of the "speculators" were as frequent in the Southern press afterwards as before.

Southern Privateers

It was Davis' idea originally, as is evidenced by his Proclamation of April 1861, cited above, to broadcast letters of marque and reprisal. Recognizing that the South lacked the ingredients of a navy, Davis hoped that foreign adventurers would be attracted by the profits of privateering. By establishing legal sanction to freebooting, by extending the protection of the flag, the South hoped to strike at the sources of Northern economic strength, and, equally important, to destroy the blockade by compelling the Union Navy to scatter its ships in high-seas search for the privateers. Once Confederate sovereignty was fully recognized, consular prize courts could be established in foreign ports and prizes disposed of far from the harbors of the Confederacy.

In the light of the naval tradition of the United States, it was natural for the Southern leaders to think first of *guerre de course* as basic naval policy. In both the American Revolution and the War of 1812, privateering had been the principal American offensive strategy on the high seas. But the drift of the times was against this practice. It had in fact been outlawed by the Declaration of Paris of 1856, to which the United States was not a signatory. The Confederacy itself, and also certain of its member states as individual sovereignties, actually commissioned a number of privateers, mostly small, ill-armed vessels. But few ships were available, and there was no seafaring population to man ships. Furthermore, after the first few weeks of the war, it proved extremely difficult to get prizes in through the blockade. England refused to allow prize courts anywhere in her far-flung territories, and France felt constrained to follow the lead of her recent ally. Foreign capital and foreign adventurers hence found the slender prospects of reward incommensurate with the risks, and were not attracted.

All told, there were only about 30 privateers sent out by the Confederacy and the several states combined. In the first year of the war these were not wholly unsuccessful. For example, the brig *Jefferson Davis*, five guns, 74 men, 230 tons, in a seven-week cruise ranging from Cape Cod to Trinidad captured ten merchantmen. The Union Navy at one time had eight vessels assigned to running her down—suggesting that enough like her would have materially reduced the effectiveness of the blockade and other Union naval operations. Few as the privateers were, in the first five months of the war they captured between 50 and 60 merchantmen, with a loss of two of their own number. Marine insurance rates went up; transfers to foreign registry by United States vessels became common.

Yet as one by one the privateers were captured, no others came forward to take their places. Anyone with the necessary capital and a taste for this kind of speculation was drawn into the somewhat less hazardous and distinctly more profitable business of blockade-running. By mid-1862, privateering had virtually disappeared.

Confederate Cruisers

The most effective naval effort by the South remained commerce-raiding after all; but instead of privateers, national cruisers became the instrument. These Confederate Navy vessels—most often foreign-built and foreign-manned, though officered by Southerners—inflicted enormous injury on the Northern merchant marine. Some notion of the "direct damage" done is furnished by the fact that the Geneva Tribunal adjudicating the "*Alabama* Claims" later awarded the United States $15,500,000 for merchantmen destroyed by cruisers built in British yards.[11]

Moreover, the indirect costs occasioned by the raiders were vastly greater. Marine insurance costs were of course much raised. American shipping firms sold many of their vessels, some even abandoning the business altogether. One hundred twenty-six United States ships

[11] A modern reader has difficulty in appreciating the magnitude of this figure in terms of the 1865 monetary situation. To put these damages in historical perspective, consider that the average annual *total receipts* of the United States government for the period 1861–65 was $161,000,000. For a comparable economic effect today, these claims would have to run to hundreds of millions.

were transferred to foreign registry in 1861, 135 in 1862, and 348 in 1863, when the cruiser *Alabama* was at the height of her depredations.

Of greater importance to the Southern cause was the large number of Union naval vessels diverted from the blockade and scattered over the oceans in "needle in a haystack" searches for the elusive commerce-destroyers. The *Alabama*, for example, had a squadron of seven vessels looking for her in the Caribbean alone. Inasmuch as some ocean-going cruising by the United States Navy would have been necessary in any event, it is impossible to cite a precise figure for the number of ships pulled off the Southern coasts and away from inshore operations by the necessity of tracking down Confederate raiders. But it can be no exaggeration to say that the Confederate cruisers, few in number as they were, so diverted at least ten times their own tonnage. This, rather than mere destruction, was the principal objective of the Confederate government.

Considering the poverty of naval resources in the South, the strategic decision to send forth commerce-raiders was perfectly sound. They accomplished more than their most sanguine proponents could reasonably have anticipated. They certainly rendered the task of the Union Navy in strengthening the blockade tremendously more difficult. It is possible that if the blockading squadrons had had available the sloops and other units that were pursuing the raiders, the Union timetable of amphibious operations might have been advanced and the war concluded sooner.

The first of the regularly commissioned naval vessels to undertake commerce-raiding was the *Sumter*, a screw steamer of 500 tons converted from a peacetime packet. Bought by the Confederate government from a New Orleans shipping firm, she was refitted for war and armed with an 8-inch pivot and four short 24-pounders in broadside.

Captain Raphael Semmes took her down the lower Mississippi in June 1861 and played hide-and-seek with the blockading *Brooklyn*, whose draft was too deep to get over the bar. The favorable moment for escape finally came when the *Brooklyn* went off on a local chase. The *Sumter* made a dash for it and outdistanced the *Brooklyn* when the latter attempted to retrieve her lapse. Cruising in the Caribbean and off the coasts of Spain and Portugal, the *Sumter* took 17 prizes, of which six were burned, two recaptured, and two ransomed. Seven that had been sent to Cuban ports for disposition were seized by the Spanish authorities and later released to their Northern owners.

After the *Sumter*'s escape from the *Brooklyn*, the *Niagara* and the *Powhatan* were detached from the Gulf Squadron, and joined the *San Jacinto*, the *Iroquois*, the *Richmond*, and the *Keystone State* to scour the Caribbean in what proved a fruitless search. In January 1862 the *Sumter* was finally run to earth at Gibraltar by U.S.S. *Tuscarora,* which was presently joined by the *Kearsarge* and the *Ino.* Apart from the obvious danger of being blown out of the water if he ventured forth from his neutral sanctuary, Captain Semmes was bedeviled by a number of other problems. He could get no coal at Gibraltar, his boilers were rusted through, and his engines needed repairs. So Semmes had the *Sumter* surveyed and sold. But she continued to work for the Confederacy, for her British owners converted her into a blockade-runner.

The brief career of the *Sumter* as a raider is fairly typical of other cruisers. Its principal significance is that it was the apprenticeship of the master-raider of them all, the redoubtable Raphael Semmes. From the cruise of the *Sumter,* Semmes learned to avoid such frequented roadsteads as Gibraltar, to destroy his prizes rather than risk losing by diplomacy in neutral ports what his guns had captured. And he so perfected the timing of his cruises that he was apparently able to anticipate every move of his pursuers.

The *Sumter* was unusual in being a Southern-owned steamer converted to a war-vessel. Lacking facilities for building ships, the South was obliged to rely largely on the efforts of her agents abroad in purchasing vessels and in having them built. Shortly after the firing on Fort Sumter, the Confederate Congress authorized the purchase of, and made appropriations for, six sail-steam cruisers to cost $165,000 each, and two million-dollar ironclad rams. James D. Bulloch and James H. North, both former officers in the U.S. Navy, were sent to England to try to procure these vessels. This assignment was to involve a great deal of intrigue

and peculiarly British red tape, problems with which the able and persistent Bulloch proved quite capable of coping. The American Minister to Britain, Charles Francis Adams, and the American consuls in the British shipbuilding ports attempted by every possible expedient of diplomacy and British law to circumvent the Confederate agents' efforts.

The British neutrality laws, like those of all civilized nations in 1861, specifically forbade the "equipping, furnishing, fitting out, or arming" of a ship intended for making war on a friendly state. The manufacture and sale of arms or other contraband to either belligerent was permitted, though this could be done only at the subject's own risk. So far as the courts of England were concerned, proof of the vessel's warlike character had to be established to warrant seizure of the vessel. This provision opened the possibility that commerce-raiders could be constructed in British yards, then as unarmored vessels be cleared to a dummy foreign purchaser. The Confederacy had agents in many European and Caribbean ports. Some of these were foreign nationals. Meanwhile ordnance could be manufactured in England and transported to a previously agreed-on rendezvous. There the raider would be armed and commissioned. She need never have seen a Confederate port from first to last. Guided at every step by British legal counsel, Bulloch successfully followed this procedure to the end of the war, sending forth the *Florida,* the *Alabama,* and the *Shenandoah,* among others.

The purchase of British-built ironclads was another matter, since the warlike purpose of such vessels would be established by the details of their construction. Even the ingenuity of Bulloch proved unavailing. The firm of Lairds of Birkenhead contracted to build two "rams" carrying a battery of 9-inch rifles, ostensibly for the French government, later for the Pasha of Egypt, then for a French private firm. Lord Russell, British Foreign Secretary, ordered them seized in 1863 shortly before their completion. Had they actually been delivered to the Confederacy, they would have posed a severe problem for the Union Navy.

The *Florida* was completed in March 1862. She sailed to Nassau, where through the connivance of the colonial authorities she was armed with two 7-inch and six 6-inch rifles, and commissioned under the command of Commander John N. Maffitt CSN. She had an eventful and successful career, being finally captured in October 1864 by U.S.S. *Wachusett* in the harbor of Bahia, Brazil. This barefaced violation of Brazilian neutrality was later apologized for very handsomely by the United States. But the *Florida* herself was sunk in an "unforeseen accident" at Hampton Roads before she could be delivered back to Brazil.

The Alabama

The *Alabama* was justly the most famous of the Confederate raiders. Barkentine rigged, she was 230 by 32 feet; loaded she drew 15 feet. Her 300 horsepower engine gave her a trial speed of 13.5 knots. While cruising she normally depended on her sails to conserve coal.

To avoid possible seizure by the British authorities, the *Alabama*, once she was launched, simply never returned from her trial run, proceeding rather to a rendezvous in the Azores where arms, coal, and her prospective officers were sent by Bulloch to fit her out. While the Portuguese port officials in Porto Praya were encouraged to believe that the *"Enrica"* was merely coaling from the chartered *Agrippina*, a battery consisting of six long 32-pounders in broadside, a rifled 100-pounder, and an 8-inch shell gun were winched into place in the cruiser. Eighty-three of the sailors who had brought the ship from England, mostly English and Irish adventurers from the Liverpool waterfront, volunteered as a skeleton crew to be filled out with volunteer recruits from prizes. Raphael Semmes took his ship outside territorial waters to perform the commissioning ceremony: mustering the crew, reading his orders, and raising the Confederate ensign. The *Alabama* was past her period of masquerade. She was a ship-of-war, ready to fulfill her mission.

Semmes was a stern and able disciplinarian; no lesser man could have handled his crew of Liverpool toughs. He spent the first two months in the North Atlantic, making 20 captures. Profiting from his experience in the *Sumter*, he took what he wanted from the prizes, then put them to the torch. When the

accumulation of prisoners aboard the *Alabama* became too great a problem, Semmes stripped a captured vessel and made a cartel ship of her, on which the superfluous passengers could make their way to land.

After cruising as far as the Grand Banks, the *Alabama*, her coal nearly exhausted, made for Fort de France, Martinique, a previously arranged fueling rendezvous. The *Agrippina* awaited her, but before coaling could be accomplished U.S.S. *San Jacinto* appeared and began patrolling just outside the three-mile limit. Sending his tender ahead, Semmes slipped past the *San Jacinto* at night and completed coaling in an obscure little port of Venezuela.

Semmes now cruised in the Caribbean, hoping to intercept one of the "treasure steamers" on the run from Colon to New York with California gold in her cargo. The captured gold would enable him to pay the long-overdue wages of his crew, which had already attempted mutiny. He had no such luck. Of a number of captures in this area, the most valuable was a large passenger liner outbound from New York that yielded less than $10,000 in silver dollars and U. S. Treasury notes.

Semmes next moved into the Gulf of Mexico with the object of interfering with an expected amphibious operation against the Texas coast. Off Galveston, which a Union squadron was bombarding, the *Alabama* steamed slowly, inviting the attention of a Federal man-of-war. Presently the gunboat conversion U.S.S. *Hatteras* came out to investigate. Twenty miles away from the support of the rest of the squadron, the *Hatteras* hailed the *Alabama*, which first identified herself as a British ship. But when the Union vessel sent off a boarding party to inspect her papers, Semmes bellowed, "This is the Confederate States steamer *Alabama!*" and immediately ordered a broadside. The superior armament of the *Alabama* made short work of the Union gunboat. In a sinking condition, the *Hatteras* fired a gun to leeward to signify surrender. Semmes quickly transferred the surviving members of her crew to his own ship, and a few minutes later the *Hatteras* sank. The *Alabama* then made a quick run to Kingston, Jamaica, to put her prisoners ashore on parole before the alarm was spread.

For another 18 months Semmes played cat-

and-mouse with the Union cruisers scouring the sea lanes of the world in fruitless pursuit. Operating successively in the Caribbean, the South Atlantic, the Indian Ocean, Sunda Strait, the South China Sea, and the Bay of Bengal, the *Alabama* gradually became the victim of her own successes. As Semmes worked farther and farther afield, he found progressively fewer Northern merchantmen. Doubling back to the South Atlantic again, the *Alabama* made two final captures as she cruised north to Europe to refit. On June 11, 1864 Semmes took his ship in to the port of Cherbourg and requested docking facilities from the French government.

While operating earlier in the broad oceans, Semmes had been able to forestall pursuit by timing his moves to anticipate Union vessels sent out to intercept him. Because there were no transoceanic cables, he normally had several days or even weeks of leeway. But when the *Alabama* anchored in Cherbourg, the United States consul was able to telegraph Captain John A. Winslow of U.S. screw sloop *Kearsarge*, anchored off Flushing on the Dutch coast. Three days later the Union warship appeared off Cherbourg. Without anchoring, the *Kearsarge* took up a patrol station just outside the port.

It had been Semmes' plan to dock his vessel and send his crew off on a well-deserved leave. But it soon became apparent that he was unlikely to be granted the dock facilities he had requested, and the practical alternatives open to him were to accept internment in Cherbourg or to go out and fight. Because the *Alabama* and the *Kearsarge* appeared to be evenly matched, Semmes allowed his temperamental bias in favor of the bold course to have its way. Through the United States consul he challenged Winslow to a single-ship duel as soon as the *Alabama* had refueled.

On the morning of June 19 the *Alabama* headed out to sea. The *Kearsarge* steamed ahead to clear territorial waters. The new French ironclad *Couronne* followed and anchored at the three-mile limit. The private yacht *Deerhound*, of British registry, hovered about to witness the impending action. Thousands of spectators lined the shore.

When about seven miles from the coast, the *Kearsarge* reversed course and bore directly down on the *Alabama*, which sheered off to port in order to present her starboard battery. The *Alabama* fired the first broadside at 2,000 yards. Most of her shot fell short, but one or two cut into the *Kearsarge*'s top-hamper. Winslow held his fire as his ship bore down on his opponent. Quickly reloading, the Confederate got off another broadside at 1,000 yards. Only then did the *Kearsarge* in turn sheer off to port, present her starboard battery, and begin firing.

In the ensuing action, the two ships turned in a clockwise direction on opposite sides of a circle a half mile in diameter. This maneuver was the result of both ships keeping starboard batteries bearing while on opposite courses, and of each endeavoring to achieve a raking position on her adversary. A three-knot tidal current gradually set the rotating vessels down toward the coast west of Cherbourg.

It soon appeared that the antagonists were not evenly matched after all. The tired machinery of the *Alabama* could not keep up with her opponent's speed. To conserve ammunition, the Confederate gunners had neglected drill. The *Alabama*'s powder and shells had deteriorated. The *Kearsarge*, on the contrary, was freshly refitted and battle-ready. Moreover, Winslow had protected her engines and boiler spaces by hanging chains down her sides and sheathing them over with boards, both to conceal them and to hold them secure. After an hour of battle, and seven rotations, the *Alabama* was in a sinking condition while the *Kearsarge* was only slightly damaged. Semmes now attempted to beach the *Alabama* on the coast, but water rushing in through her riddled hull extinguished her furnace and left her helpless. The *Kearsarge* now cut across her bow and raked her, whereupon Semmes struck his colors.

As the stricken *Alabama* began to sink, both victor and vanquished quickly launched boats, and the *Deerhound* came up to help in the work of rescue. Semmes flung his sword into the sea and then plunged overboard. Twenty minutes after her surrender, the bow of the *Alabama* rose perpendicularly in the air as she sank stern first. Semmes, together with 40 of his ship's complement, was picked up by the *Deerhound* and taken to England. In Union eyes this avoidance of capture was the only flaw in the news of the victory. Winslow received the thanks of Congress and was promoted to commodore.

Between September 5, 1862 and April 27, 1864, the *Alabama* had captured 71 Union vessels, destroying most of them at sea. Semmes' epic cruise is by all odds the most successful in the history of commerce-raiding. Besides the direct damage inflicted, the *Alabama* caused enormous indirect losses to Union shipowners —higher marine insurance premiums, delays and cancellations of sailings, and spoilage of cargoes.

To take the place of the *Alabama*, Bulloch purchased the *Shenandoah*, which was armed in the Madeira Islands by a tender in October 1864. The *Shenandoah* sailed at once for the Pacific, where she began her depredations the following month. Operating chiefly around the Aleutian Islands, she captured a total of 36 vessels, mostly whalers, and gave the American whaling industry a blow from which it never recovered. Because news of the Confederate surrender did not reach Captain Waddell until August 2, 1865, two thirds of the *Shenandoah*'s captures were made after the end of the war. The destructiveness of the *Shenandoah*'s cruise was second only to that of the *Alabama*.

Summary

From a naval point of view, the American Civil War, like the American Revolution, the Napoleonic Wars, and the War of 1812, was primarily a war of blockade and counterblockade. From the beginning, Union naval strategy was based on cutting off the Confederacy from imported war materials and impoverishing the South by destroying her export trade. Nearly all Union naval operations along the American coasts were to implement the blockade or to support amphibious operations for securing bases (such as Port Royal) to facilitate the blockade.

The South, on the other hand, both by diplomacy and by naval operations, sought to loosen the coils of the Anaconda. Directly or indirectly, the strategy of the Confederate Navy was always designed to subserve this purpose. Such cruisers as the *Alabama* and the *Shenandoah*, by their raids on Union shipping in distant seas, were mainly useful to the South in compelling a major naval effort by her enemy in waters far away from the military theaters of conflict.

There is some question as to the importance of the commerce raiders in the total war picture. Certainly they were too few to constitute a counterblockade such as the German submarines were almost to achieve in the world wars of the 20th century, but their effect was far from negligible. It appears possible that a dozen *Alabamas* operating simultaneously could have destroyed Union sea commerce completely and thereby have disrupted the Northern war effort.

14:
The New Technology: Ironclads in Action

The year 1861 had been one of surprise and bitter disappointment for the Union. The outbreak of war had climaxed a disastrous policy of drift. The ignominy of Bull Run had made the faint-hearted wonder if perhaps the reconquest of the South might not be beyond the capacity of the Lincoln government. The Confederate States of America was seen to emerge with an apparently stable and efficient government, evidently well able to maintain armies and wage war.

Union Strategy

Yet the Union had made real progress. First and most important, Lincoln had demonstrated a determination to wage the war to a finish, and in spite of spotty political opposition, the people of the North rallied to his support with real patriotic intensity. Second, a workable master plan had been hammered out.

The grand strategy early decided on by Lincoln and his advisers entailed large scale efforts by both army and naval forces: (1) The Army of the Potomac would simultaneously cover Washington and threaten Richmond; (2) in the West, an effort would be made to secure the line of the Mississippi, thereby splitting off the Southwest from the rest of the Confederacy; (3) the border areas—Missouri, Kentucky, West Virginia, and Maryland—would, if necessary, be occupied and held in the Union; (4) the Navy, which had already occupied Port Royal, would continue amphibious operations along the coast in support of its major mission of blockading, and the strength of the blockade would be improved; (5) foreign intervention would be obviated by a judicious combination of show of force, diplomatic ingenuity, and willingness to compromise.

The economic preponderance of the North was gradually mobilized in support of the Union as it became increasingly obvious that a sustained war was going to be necessary. The Civil War was the first in history in which the steam engine, the railroad, and the industrial process generally were to have a decisive role. It was the good fortune of the North that in this vital area she was overwhelmingly superior.

In November 1861 the talented but unstable George B. McClellan succeeded elderly, ailing Winfield Scott in command of the Army of the Potomac. Supremely competent as a drillmaster, "Little Mac" trained his soldiers to a new excellence in the encampments around Washington. Urged by Lincoln to press directly south against the outnumbered Southern force around Manassas, McClellan favored a grand flanking operation against Richmond via the peninsula between the York and the James rivers.

This plan had the advantage of providing secure lines of water-borne communication defended by superior Union sea power. Since the Union already held the extreme lower peninsula—Newport News and the area around Fortress Monroe—the troop movement could be accomplished without enemy harassment. The success of the earliest stages of the operation would incidentally insure the evacuation of Confederate forces from Norfolk. McClellan of course hoped that the tempo of the advance would produce major results before General Joseph E. Johnston could realign his forces to meet this unanticipated threat.

A principal disadvantage of the plan was

that it involved uncovering Washington. This danger required splitting off a considerable force (McDowell's corps), to be held in northern Virginia. Second, McClellan was soon to reveal that he lacked the sturdy and decisive personality to command an "all or nothing" campaign. Third, the element of secrecy, which was highly desirable if not absolutely essential to the success of the operation, was apparently unobtainable in those days. Richmond knew of his plans about as quickly as McClellan's own division commanders. Finally, the absolute control of the Potomac, York, and lower James rivers, and of Chesapeake Bay—on which McClellan's lines of supply and reinforcement depended—was seriously threatened at the very time the first great adventure of the Army of the Potomac was to begin.

The Ironclad *Virginia*

At Norfolk the scuttled *Merrimack* had been raised by the Confederates and was being converted into an ironclad. Should she prove impervious to the fire of the wooden Union blockaders, the essential precondition of Northern naval supremacy in the lower Chesapeake and on the Virginia rivers would be destroyed. Equally disastrous, the blockade would be ruptured.

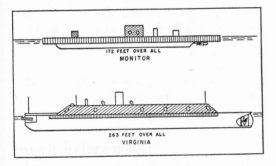

U.S.S. *MONITOR* and C.S.S. *VIRGINIA*

Stephen R. Mallory, Confederate Secretary of the Navy, had been chairman of the Naval Affairs Committee in the United States Senate. He brought to his job an intelligent awareness of the impending technological revolution in naval material. Two months before Secretary Welles had diffidently recommended an "Ironclad Board" to the U. S. Congress, Mallory had addressed the Chairman of the Confederate Naval Affairs Committee thus:

I regard the possession of an ironclad ship as a matter of the first necessity. Such a vessel at this time could traverse the entire coast of the United States, prevent all blockade, and encounter, with a fair prospect of success, their entire navy. If, to cope with them upon the sea, we follow their example, and build wooden ships, we shall have to construct several at one time, for one or two ships would fall an easy prey to their comparatively numerous steam frigates. But inequality of numbers may be compensated by invulnerability, and thus not only does economy, but naval success, dictate the wisdom and expediency of fighting iron against wood without regard to first cost.[1]

Plans were speedily drafted on the general style of the new British ironclads. In early July 1861, Mallory formally approved the project of raising the frigate *Merrimack*[2], repairing the hull and engines, clearing away the burnt-out superstructure, and replacing it with an armored casemate.

Work was started at once. Only the lack of metalworking industries prevented the South from securing thereby a prompt and possibly decisive advantage in the technological race. There was at that time only one rolling mill in the Confederacy capable of turning out the two-inch iron slabs for side armor. The only source of iron was used rails from the railroads.

In spite of the best efforts of the engineers in charge, the work progressed slowly. All through the summer, fall, and winter of 1861, Northern spies brought through the lines detailed accounts of its progress. These reports speeded the tardy countermeasures of the Union Navy.

In conversion, the *Merrimack* was cut down to the waterline, and provided with an ar-

[1] Dated May 8, 1861. Cited by William C. Church, *The Life of John Ericsson* (New York, 1891), I, 245.
[2] U.S.S. *Merrimack* had been commissioned in 1856—the first of a class of six steam frigates, then generally regarded as the finest of their type in the world. She was 300 feet over-all, 250 feet on the keel, had a beam of 51 feet, 4 inches, and drew 28 feet. Battle-loaded, she displaced 4500 tons. She had two 600-horse-power engines of new design, four tubular boilers, and a variable pitch screw. Like all such vessels in her day, she was ship-rigged. She carried a battery of 40 Dahlgren guns: two ten-inch pivots; 14 eight-inch, and 24 nine-inch in broadsides.

mored superstructure with sides sloping from the vertical about 35 degrees. The deck length of this casemate was 170 feet. The hull had only about two feet of freeboard forward, and rather less astern—under way at her plodding four knots, she carried her after deck virtually awash.

The casemate was framed with 20-inch pine beams overset with four-inch oak planks. The armor was two layers of iron plates, the first bolted on horizontally, the second vertically. The sloping sides of the casemate were to be smeared with tallow before the ship went into action, so that solid shot would tend to ricochet harmlessly. The top of the casemate was protected by a heavy iron grating, 120 feet by 20 feet, which would permit ventilation of the gun deck beneath.

The *Merrimack,* recommissioned as c.s.s. *Virginia,* mounted three 9-inch Dahlgrens and two 6-inch rifles in broadside, and had in addition two 7-inch rifled pivots. A heavy iron wedge was affixed to her bow as a ram. A crank, unseaworthy craft, of awkwardly deep draft for the shoal inland waters in which she was to operate, the *Virginia* was nevertheless an ingenious adaptation of the materials at hand and a tribute to her builders' skill at improvisation.

When the vessel was nearly completed, Commander Franklin Buchanan, an able former United States naval officer,[3] was designated to command her. Since the agrarian South had no merchant marine, finding a crew of trained seamen was more difficult. Eighty sailors were discovered in a New Orleans regiment at Yorktown. Seamen from Norfolk and inexperienced army volunteers made up the rest of the crew of about 350 men.

The Confederate authorities were actuated by a terrible sense of urgency, for espionage and ill-advised revelations in the Northern press kept them informed not only of McClellan's invasion plan but also of the construction of u.s.s. *Monitor,* a mysterious countermeasure to the *Virginia.* If the *Virginia* could be gotten underway in time, the five wooden ships

[3] Buchanan, the first superintendent of the United States Naval Academy (1845–1847), was one of a handful of outstanding naval leaders who resigned from the Union service in order to serve the Confederacy.

of the Union Navy blockading Norfolk and the lower Chesapeake could be smashed like matchwood, in spite of their 222 guns. Interrupted transatlantic traffic would once more flow to Norfolk. The position of the Union troops in Newport News and Fortress Monroe would become untenable. The threat of the flanking operation against Richmond would of course evaporate. Well might the patriotically inspired workmen, laboring nightly to rush the *Virginia* to completion, feel that on them depended the success of the Confederacy.

The temperate Mallory in his orders to Buchanan revealed the magnitude of his hopes from the *Virginia*:

The *Virginia* is a novelty in naval construction, is untried, and her powers unknown; and hence the department will not give specific orders as to her attack on the enemy. Her powers as a ram are regarded as very formidable, and it is hoped that you will be able to test them. Like the bayonet charge of the infantry, this mode of attack, while the most destructive, will commend itself to you in the present scarcity of ammunition. . . .

Could you pass Old Point [Comfort], and make a dashing cruise in the Potomac as far as Washington, its effect upon the public mind would be important to our cause.

The condition of our country, and the painful reverses we have just suffered, demand our utmost exertions; and convinced as I am that the opportunity and the means for striking a decisive blow for our navy are now, for the first time, presented, I congratulate you upon it, and know that your judgment and gallantry will meet all just expectations . . .[4]

Buchanan and his hastily assembled, untried crew were eager to fulfill the expectations of the Secretary.

The Ironclad Board

The United States Navy was not quick to realize the danger created by the early Confederate decision to build an ironclad or attempt to purchase one or more abroad. The subject of ironclad construction, discussed in the Navy Department in May 1861, was tabled in the face of the more pressing problem of finding more wooden vessels to implement the

[4] Cited in John T. Scharf, *History of the Confederate States Navy* (New York, 1887), 155.

blockade. In early July the Secretary in a message to the extra session of Congress requested authority to constitute an Ironclad Board and asked an appropriation. On August 3, Congress authorized the board and appropriated $1,500,000 for the "construction or completing"[5] of iron- or steelclad steamships or steam batteries.

The Ironclad Board selected by Welles and Fox was composed of three able and distinguished officers—Commodore Joseph Smith, Commodore Hiram Paulding, and Commander Charles H. Davis. None of them however possessed much background or experience in scientific innovation. The board itself was mindful of its technical limitations, and in its report officially deplored the fact that, though they had requested a qualified naval constructor as a consultant, "they [were] all so employed on important service that none could be assigned to this duty."

Nevertheless the board reviewed more than a hundred ironclad proposals submitted to the department and prepared a detailed and precise report, which was submitted in September 1861. In summary, this important document, which established ironclad policy in the U.S. Navy for the Civil War period and for some time thereafter, stated: (1) Armored ocean-going cruisers are, for the time being, impractical. (2) For coast defense and operation in sheltered water—harbors, bays, and rivers—armored gunboats of relatively shallow draft are feasible; such vessels should be constructed at once. (3) Armored vessels of this type cannot successfully cope with masonry forts. (4) Wooden vessels will always be faster than ironclads, of whatever description. (5) At the current stage of technological development, smooth-bore cannon firing spherical shot are superior to rifled ordnance and shell. (6) Though the United States could doubtless get armored vessels more cheaply and more expeditiously by purchase in England, it would be better policy to build them at home. (7) Three contracts for armored vessels are recommended —with the firms of Merrick and Sons and C. S. Bushnell and Co., and with John Ericsson.

These contracts were undertaken with comparatively little delay, and three vessels were

[5] An obvious reference to the unfinished Stevens battery.

duly produced. The *New Ironsides* (Merrick and Sons), a broadside type of ironclad, was to do good service at Charleston. The *Galena* (Bushnell) was a rather lightly armored gunboat that was mercilessly pounded at Drewry's Bluff and was regarded as a failure. By far the greatest historical interest centers in the *Monitor* (Ericsson). She was the Union ironclad first in naval action, by her arrival in Hampton Roads she frustrated the Confederate counterstrategy, she was the first of a succession of "Monitors" in the U.S. Navy, and she was the most influential American innovation in naval design in the 19th century.

The *Monitor*—A Study in Innovation

John Ericsson, Swedish-born builder of the *Monitor*, was by 1861 already an internationally famous inventor and engineer. Justly chagrined at the parsimony of the United States Congress after the building of the *Princeton*, Ericsson had left Washington with the resolve never to return.

But the Civil War touched both his patriotic enthusiasm and his professional instincts; it was easy for his friend Bushnell to persuade him to offer his original project for an armored battery, and to explain to the less agile minds in the Navy Department just why it would work.

In mid-September 1861 Welles promised him a contract, and Ericsson began work at once. In 101 working days the *Monitor* was afloat— perhaps the most original design in the history of naval architecture. The plan and supervision of the entire project were Ericsson's contribution. The hull, the turret, and the engines and other machinery were contracted to various firms in the New York area.

The building of the *Monitor* was a remarkable *tour de force*. There was never any comprehensive complete design or scale model. Yet Ericsson prepared well over a hundred detailed drawings to guide the workmen. Nearly everything about the ship was radically new and untried. The first engineer of the *Monitor* estimated that the ship contained at least 40 patentable innovations.

The major distinctive features of this new

instrument of warfare were these: she was designed to have very little reserve buoyancy, so that she offered only a foot or so of free-board—and consequently a very small target area; her battery was concentrated in two guns of largest size, mounted side-by-side in a heavily armored turret; all exposed vertical surfaces were heavily armored; the deck was plated also, and an overhang protected the screw and rudder; all nonessential top-hamper was dispensed with. Such a vessel, Ericsson reasoned, would offer a minimum and impregnable target to the enemy, while packing tremendous offensive strength on a moderate draft and displacement.

The finished *Monitor* was a hull 124 feet long, on which was riveted a raft-like deck 172 feet by 41½ feet, the vertical sides of which carried 4½-inch iron armor backed by oak. This deck was protected from plunging fire by one-inch armor on its horizontal surface. The 9-foot-high turret, 20 feet in diameter, was set on a brass ring laid into the deck. Eight layers of one-inch rolled iron plates made up the laminated sidewalls of the cylindrical turret. The turret cover was a grating of railroad rails. The 140-ton turret rested on a spindle which extended down to the keel. This spindle was cogged to a steam auxiliary engine that could turn the turret through a complete 360-degree revolution.

The battery consisted of two 11-inch Dahlgren smoothbores. When their muzzles were inboard of the ports (as for cleaning and loading), the ports were automatically shielded by heavy iron "port stoppers" that swung over like pendulums. It was Ericsson's opinion that the turret should be revolved to bring the enemy under fire only an instant before actual firing, so that the exposure of the gun crews in opening the ports would be kept to a minimum.

The engine was of the then conventional double-trunk type, with its 36-inch cylinders bored in a single casting. There were two return-tube box boilers. The *Monitor's* first commanding officer was Lieutenant John L. Worden USN—a brave man and a beloved leader, though rather lacking in the technical background this novel type of ship was to demand. The *Monitor* was commissioned on February 25, 1862 and after brief testing was ordered to Hampton Roads.

The Battle of Hampton Roads

In early March the fortunes of the North and the South appeared to be hanging in unstable balance. McClellan believed that in the Army of the Potomac he had at last the well-oiled fighting machine needed to win the war in a single crushing campaign. His carefully worked out plan for advance up the peninsula appeared almost foolproof. The inferior Confederate armies would be pinned to their positions by the necessity of defending Richmond to the last. Only the latent threat offered by the presence of the *Virginia* in the Elizabeth River clouded the rosy expectations of the Union commander. If in fact the Confederate ram could impair the absolute sea control of the Union Navy, the transports could not venture into Hampton Roads, and McClellan's whole strategy would have to be modified or abandoned.

The events of March 8 and 9 in Hampton Roads constitute one of those rare "set pieces" of history—not only in the dramatic reversal occasioned by the *Monitor,* but in that they occurred in a kind of natural naval amphitheater. The anchorage is essentially the lower James River, here broadened to six miles in width before its confluence with Chesapeake Bay. The north shore was held by Union forces: Fortress Monroe on Old Point Comfort, and Newport News Point to the west, where newly emplaced batteries covered the approach to the James River proper. The Confederates held the entire south bank: they had heavily fortified Sewell's Point, six miles almost due south of Fortress Monroe, and they had less formidable works at Pig Point to the west. So restricted were the dimensions of the battleground that thousands on both sides—Union troops, and a good part of the population of Norfolk—were able to witness the events related below.

Flag Officer Louis M. Goldsborough, commanding the North Atlantic Blockading Squadron, had concentrated in Hampton Roads what by earlier standards was a formidable blockading force—the 50-gun screw frigates *Minnesota* and *Roanoke* (sister ships of the original *Merrimack*), the sailing frigates *St. Lawrence* and *Congress,* both 44's, and the sailing sloop *Cumberland,* 24. Goldsborough correctly assumed that when the *Virginia* was

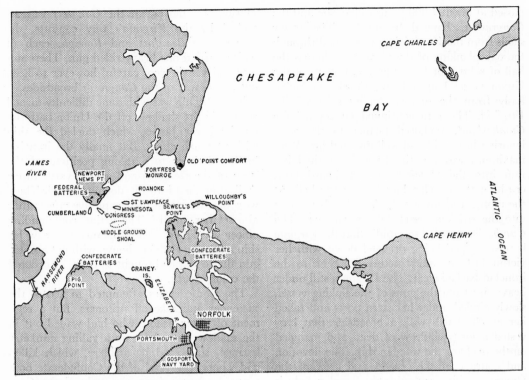

THE NORFOLK AREA, MARCH 8, 1862

first brought into action she would head for the *Congress* and the *Cumberland,* which were anchored farthest to the west, blockading the James. Goldsborough's plan was to run down the Confederate ram with the *Minnesota* (flagship) and any other large steam vessels that might happen to be in the anchorage. His aim was, above all, to prevent the *Virginia's* retreat back up the Elizabeth River. The plan involved an underestimation of the defensive strength of the *Virginia;* it also took too little account of the shoalness of the water, which seriously restricted rapid maneuver by any of his deep-draft vessels.

On March 8, 1862 Flag Officer Buchanan took his new command out from the Navy Yard into Hampton Roads. Her officers and crew were still strangers to each other. Workmen were still putting on the finishing touches as the *Virginia* was warped by armed tugs down the Elizabeth River. There were no engine run-ups and no gunnery drills. This, her trial cruise, was to be directly into action. Cheers went up from the crowds on the wharves and rooftops of Norfolk.

The deficiencies of the hybrid vessel became apparent as she steamed into deeper water by Sewell's Point. In calm water, her engines could manage at best a sluggish five knots. She answered her helm so reluctantly that it took more than a half hour to turn her completely around.

Some small converted gunboats constituting the Confederate "James River Squadron" were blockaded up the river at Newport News by the *Congress* and the *Cumberland,* which lay at anchor at the northwestern extremity of Hampton Roads. Buchanan therefore turned first on these latter ships, intending by his attack on them to enable the Confederate gunboats to enter the anchorage.

The *Virginia* chugged ponderously northwest toward her adversaries. The Union vessels had hardly expected action that day. The commanding officer of the *Cumberland* was absent at a board of inquiry in the *Roanoke,* and on both the *Congress* and the *Cumberland* boats were at the booms, and laundry was drying in the lower rigging. The ships were hastily cleared for action, and when the *Virginia* passed at about 1,500 yards range, she and the *Congress* exchanged broadsides. The heavy shells from the *Virginia's* guns crashed through the oak planking of the *Congress,* whereas the hail of solid shot from the port battery of the Union vessel bounced and ricocheted harmlessly from the greasy, sloping sides of the *Virginia.* The ram continued on toward the *Cumberland,* anchored farther to the west, ignoring her rapid and well-directed fire. With maximum way on, the *Virginia* crashed her ram into the *Cumberland's* starboard bow, crushing the wooden hull like an eggshell. At the moment of impact she fired her bow pivot into the stricken vessel, killing ten men. The *Cumberland* settled so rapidly that the *Virginia* barely escaped being dragged down with her victim, but the ram structure broke off as the ironclad backed clear. The *Virginia,* still under heavy fire from the guns of the sinking vessel, slowly circled under her stern ports and raked her at 200 yards with a broadside that harvested a long windrow of dead and mangled on the decks of the wooden ship. The devotion and courage of the officers and crew of the *Cumberland* in continuing the hopeless fight is a splendid example of what the Old Navy meant by "iron men in wooden ships." With a third of her crew dead or wounded, with water surging into a hole in her side big enough to drive a horse and cart through, the *Cumberland* kept firing with every gun that would bear. As she sank, deck by deck, the gun crews simply joined the depleted crews on the deck above, until at length the magazines were flooded out and the vessel careened crazily to port. The last remaining gun crew fired its final shot and leaped into the water. Coming to rest on the shallow bottom, the *Cumberland* still had her mastheads above the water, and the flag of the sunken vessel still fluttered at her peak.

Meanwhile the *Virginia,* which had suffered only superficial topside damage and two casualties, turned her attention to the *Congress.* That ship, her officers realizing the invulnerability of the *Virginia* to their guns, had gotten under way with jib and topsails, and with the aid of a tug was run in near Signal Point to get the support of the land batteries. The *Congress* grounded in the shallows where the *Virginia* with her great draft could not follow to ram.

During this movement the *Congress* was attacked by the *Virginia's* tiny consorts, the armed tugs *Beaufort* and *Raleigh,* each of which carried one heavy rifled gun. These unarmored vessels were careful however to keep out of the way of the *Congress's* broadsides.

The *Virginia* was with some difficulty turned around in the shallows off the Union batteries on the lower James, which dueled the ship without much effect. But finally the ironclad lumbered down to a raking position off the stern of the *Congress* and at 150 yards threw shell after shell into the doomed vessel. These were devastating in their explosive effect; they also set her on fire. The acting commanding officer was killed. When his successor saw his ship a flaming slaughterhouse, with not a single gun that could be brought to bear, he ordered the colors struck.

The Confederates attempted to accept the surrender and take off prisoners. But a regiment of troops ashore who had waded out in the shallow water kept up a galling musketry barrage, supported by artillery, which killed and wounded several of the Confederate boat party. Buchanan in a rage ordered the *Congress* bombarded with red hot shot. Climbing topside to observe this operation, he was drilled in the leg by a Minie ball from an infantryman's rifle. Lieutenant Catesby ap Roger Jones thereupon succeeded to the command of the *Virginia.*

During the two hours while the *Virginia* was destroying the *Cumberland* and the *Congress,* the James River squadron joined the *Virginia* and her diminutive escorts. The *Minnesota,* the *Roanoke,* and the *St. Lawrence* all had attempted to come to the aid of the stricken Union vessels. All had grounded before coming into effective range—the *Minnesota* so firmly that she was not successfully floated for four tides.

The *Virginia,* accompanied by the *Patrick Henry* and the *Jamestown* of the James River squadron, now turned her attention to the helpless *Minnesota.* The shoalness of the water however prevented a near approach by the *Virginia,* and her marksmanship at 2,000 yards was such that only one shell struck its target at this time. The rifled guns of the smaller Southern gunboats did much more damage, but the single gun that the *Minnesota* was able to bring to bear finally drove them off. After about three hours of trying to approach nearer the *Minnesota,* the *Virginia* and her consorts steamed triumphantly back in the gathering dusk to an anchorage under Sewell's Point.

In a single afternoon the Confederate ram had sunk a heavy frigate and a large sloop of war and had damaged another Northern vessel. Two hundred and fifty Union sailors had been killed or drowned. Including injuries to the boarding party, the *Virginia* and her consorts had 21 killed and wounded. The *Patrick Henry* had four men scalded to death when her boiler was struck by a ball from the Newport News batteries.

Except for the loss of her ram, which occasioned a bad leak forward, the *Virginia* had suffered only superficial damage. The muzzles of two of her guns were smashed, and the top-hamper was riddled and partly shot away. But her armor was not penetrated at any point, and she was ready for action on the following day.

Yet it was not so much in her accomplishments that the Confederates exulted. It was rather in the illimitable opportunities that seemed to be opening up. There appeared to be no reason why the *Minnesota,* the *Roanoke,* the *St. Lawrence,* and the host of little Union gunboats which remained in Hampton Roads could not be readily destroyed or driven away. The blockade would be broken. McClellan's planned flank attack on Richmond had become impossible. Foreign intervention was now, so it seemed, infinitely more likely. All the fondest hopes of Secretary Mallory appeared fully justified by the invulnerable *Virginia.* Bonfires of celebration were lighted all over the South as the telegraph spread word of the victory.

Arrival of the *Monitor*

Yet even while the *Virginia* was wreaking havoc in the Union squadron off Norfolk, Ericsson's strange-looking little *Monitor* was laboring down the coast to get to the scene of the battle. Towed by a tug, and convoyed by two wooden steamers, she had left New York after perfunctory trials on March 6. About noon on the 7th she ran into rough weather off the Delaware capes. Waves surging over the vessel flooded through the badly stoppered hawse-pipes into the hull and down the stack and blower pipe. With the blowers disabled, the furnaces had insufficient draft, and the engine spaces filled with gases. The engineering force narrowly escaped asphyxiation: they were dragged topside unconscious to revive on the turret top. With all machinery inoperative, the water in the bilges was a serious worry to Lieutenant Worden; an awkwardly long bucket brigade attempted to maintain the vessel's small positive buoyancy. Toward evening the weather and sea improved, making it possible to start the engines again. But in the early morning of the 8th, the blowers were again flooded out. To render the volunteer crew even more miserable, the wheel-ropes jammed, so that the safety of the ship depended entirely on the manila hawser connecting her to the tug. This nightmarish voyage concluded about 4 PM on March 8, when the *Monitor* rounded Cape Charles and started up the bay toward Hampton Roads, whence could be heard the sound of cannonading.

To a large extent the seagoing deficiencies of the *Monitor* stemmed from small, easily corrected defects of workmanship, and from the inexperience of her personnel. The voyage is an eloquent reminder of the need for careful and detailed trials, for which there was no time with the *Monitor.*

Worden cleared his ship for action as he conned her up to Old Point Comfort. About nine in the evening he reported to Captain John Marston, Senior Officer Present, in the *Roanoke.* Marston ordered the *Monitor* to protect the grounded *Minnesota.*[6]

Her way was lighted by the flaming *Congress,* whose magazines finally exploded a little after midnight. The *Monitor* anchored just west of the *Minnesota,* and her exhausted crew attempted to get some sleep. Efforts continued all night to get the *Minnesota* afloat, but in vain.

About 6:30 AM on March 9 the morning fog had thinned just enough for the seamen in the Union vessels to see the exhaust steam of the *Virginia* as she came out of her anchorage under Sewell's Point. An hour or so later the sun appeared. By now the huge black ram had

[6] Marston had received Navy Department orders to have the *Monitor* proceed to Washington. These he wisely disregarded.

come south of the Middle Ground, and fired a shell into the rigging of the *Minnesota*. It was evident that she intended to turn into the channel north of the Middle Ground shoal. The *Minnesota* fired ineffectually with her stern guns.

Worden upped anchor and steamed around the *Minnesota* to approach the ram directly and engage her as far as possible from the nearly helpless frigate. Although the Confederates at first took her to be a mere floating buoy, or a "cheese box on a raft," the *Monitor* was nevertheless soon recognized by Jones and his officers as the radically designed Union ironclad of which they had read in the Norfolk papers.

The *Virginia* opened fire with a rifled gun, and missed. Conserving her fire to point blank range, the *Monitor* swung her turret to bear at the moment she came alongside and rattled the frames of her adversary with two 11-inch shot, which struck the sloping casemate without penetrating. The *Virginia* turned to starboard sufficiently to bring her three-gun broadside to bear, and fired again, this time striking the *Monitor's* turret. The Confederate gunners were chagrined to see their heavy shell break up like ripe melons against the *Monitor's* plates, without discernibly denting them.

There ensued a two-hour gunnery duel at very close range. Like a terrier baiting a bull, the *Monitor* kept close to her larger adversary, so that the *Virginia* could sometimes hardly bring a gun to bear. The *Virginia* was working badly, and in any event her 23-foot draft made her awkward to maneuver in the shallow waters of the Roads. The *Monitor* was operating as Ericsson had dreamed, and her mere 12-foot draft gave her much more working room. It was Worden's hope by repeated hits at pistol shot range to batter the *Virginia's* plates loose if he could not penetrate her armor. Blinding clouds of steam and black powder smoke enveloped the vessels most of the time during this duel at 40 yards or less.

Realizing the futility of trying to penetrate the armor of the *Monitor,* Jones determined to ram his opponent or to board her. After an hour of discouraging maneuvering with this end in view, Jones thought he saw his opportunity and ordered, "Full speed ahead!" But as the *Virginia* lumbered down upon her, the *Monitor* turned nimbly so that the blow was a glancing one, damaging the *Monitor* not at all, and springing another leak in the *Virginia's* own bow. The far greater maneuverability of the *Monitor* made boarding similarly infeasible. The Union vessel was virtually able to pick and hold any position relative to the *Virginia* that her commanding officer wished.

Resolved at any rate to destroy the *Minnesota*, Jones turned suddenly away from the *Monitor* and attacked the wooden frigate with the rifled bow gun of the *Virginia*. The *Minnesota* sought to defend herself with her broadside and her 10-inch pivot. This exchange had the expected result. The *Virginia* was apparently undamaged, and the battered *Minnesota* was set on fire. A tug that had been futilely trying to pull the *Minnesota* off the bar was destroyed by a shell through her boiler.

As quickly as possible, Worden brought the *Monitor* between the *Minnesota* and the enemy. In maneuvering for position, the *Virginia* now grounded. Both the *Minnesota* and the *Monitor* pounded their immobile adversary, and at this moment it seemed safe to predict the ram's destruction. But now occurred one of those chance events that so often upset the odds in battle. While the *Monitor* was standing in at 10 or 15 yards to try to deliver a *coup de grâce,* the *Virginia's* officers shifted their point of aim from the invulnerable turret of the *Monitor* to the tiny pilot house on the foredeck. The pilot house, projecting only four feet above the deck, was made of 9-by-12-inch cast iron bars with a narrow eyeslit under the topmost bar. Inside were the stations of the conning officer, the pilot, and the helmsman.

About 11:30 a lucky shell from the *Virginia* exploded against the front of the pilot house, and drove powder fragments through the eyeslit into Lieutenant Worden's eyes—blinding him temporarily and wounding him seriously about the face. Worden sent for Lieutenant Samuel D. Greene, the executive officer, who was in the turret, but Greene did not assume the con of the ship for about 20 minutes. During this time the helmsman, lacking immediate direction, followed Worden's last order, which was to "sheer off." The effect was that the *Monitor* withdrew to the east toward Fortress Monroe.

The *Virginia* profited from this withdrawal

to put out boats with kedges, by means of which she was successfully warped off the bottom. Seeing his iron protector apparently in retreat, the commanding officer of the *Minnesota* grimly made preparations to blow up his vessel rather than to allow her capture by the *Virginia.*

But the position of the ram herself was far from comfortable. Her leak forward had been made worse by her grounding. Furthermore her bow was so lightened by the loss of her prow and anchors that the water inside her greatly increased her draft at the stern, whereas her bow tended to ride up so that her shield was almost out of water. When her pilots reminded Lieutenant Jones that the tide was falling, he decided that the risk of remaining on the scene was not justified by the slight advantage to be gained by destroying the battered *Minnesota.* The *Virginia,* leaking badly, her top-hamper utterly shot away, chugged slowly back to her Sewell's Point anchorage. The fight had lasted more than four hours.

Meanwhile Lieutenant Greene, having at last taken the con, wheeled the *Monitor* about and came back to the *Minnesota.* He threw two or three long-range shots at the departing *Virginia* but made no further attempt to pursue. Thus indecisively ended the most celebrated single-ship duel ever engaged in by American vessels.

Damage to the *Monitor* was slight, and entirely confined to the pilot house. The *Virginia,* though no shot penetrated her casemate, was struck by nearly all of the 41 solid shot that the *Monitor* fired at her; these cracked her plates, and in some instances fractured the wooden backing. Damage to her superstructure and hull required extensive repairs in drydock.

Aftermath of the Battle

The usual conclusion of historians is that the battle was a tactical draw but a strategic victory for the *Monitor.* Yet the thoughtful student is left with certain tantalizing questions that can be answered only with careful reservations: Why was the engagement so indecisive? Why did the *Monitor* fail to pursue her adversary toward Norfolk? Why was the duel never renewed? How could the evident structural superiority of the *Monitor* have been made the basis of the complete victory which Ericsson had a right to expect from his invention?

A partial answer to several of these questions can be summarized as inadequate testing of material, and inadequate training of personnel. This in turn stemmed not so much from oversight or carelessness as from the precipitate need of the *Monitor* in Hampton Roads as the single adequate weapon to cope with the *Virginia.*

The new 11-inch battery of the *Monitor* was restricted by Bureau of Ordnance order to 15-pound charges. Yet later experience was to make 25- and even 30-pound charges common. On seeing their shot fail to penetrate the *Virginia's* casemate, Worden and Greene must have been sorely tempted to increase their charges. Yet with the two guns mounted side by side, to burst a barrel would have been to destroy completely the offensive power of the ship. To disobey a categorical order and thereby to risk the destruction of an unfamiliar engine of war entrusted to them is surely too much to expect of junior officers.[7] There can however be no question that the *Monitor* would have destroyed her antagonist if she had used sufficient powder charges.

The officers and crew of the *Monitor,* as the above account indicates, began the fight nearly exhausted from the harrowing voyage down the coast. This may explain why Greene did not see fit to pursue the *Virginia* under the guns of the Confederate shore batteries. Assistant Secretary of the Navy Fox, who was at the scene of the engagement in a tug, apparently was not altogether satisfied with Greene's performance however: he immediately relieved him of his temporary command of the *Monitor.*

Washington was still jittery over the threat of the *Virginia,* and on March 10 Gideon Welles, either on his own initiative or on the advice of the President, issued peremptory orders that the *Monitor* was not to be taken under the fire of the shore batteries. Too much depended on her continuing to exercise control of the Roads to risk her injury or destruction. The grand strategic offensive of McClellan's

---

[7] The celebrated explosion of the Peacemaker aboard the *Princeton* was a fresh enough memory in the minds of naval officers to insure double respect for bureau restrictions against overcharging.

army could best be served by a tactically defensive objective on the part of the Navy.

The *Virginia* was badly enough damaged to require much repair work. In addition, her officers realized she was no real match for the *Monitor*. Nevertheless, Josiah Tatnall, her new commanding officer, took her out into the Roads on April 11, May 8, and May 9. The Confederate command had worked out a scheme by which the *Monitor* would be boarded by crews of the wooden gunboats while the *Virginia* kept her closely engaged. This desperate plan was frustrated by the arrival of substantial reinforcements to the Union blockading force, including the ironclads *Galena* and *Naugatuck*. Goldsborough had moreover acquired a large fast vessel, the *Vanderbilt*, which was to be used as a ram against the *Virginia*, if she could be enticed out into deep water. Both sides exercised caution in their use of their strongest naval weapons, since the risk of loss of either the *Virginia* or the *Monitor* seemed to outweigh the advantage of destroying her adversary. The arrival of the *Monitor* had made McClellan's Peninsula campaign possible after all; her loss would seriously hamper his operations. On the other hand, the Confederate government deemed Norfolk safe from assault as long as the *Virginia* stood at its water gates. The ram was a one-ship fleet-in-being.

By April 5 some 121,500 blue-coated soldiers of the Army of the Potomac, with all their equipment, had been landed on the Peninsula. In spite of overwhelming numerical superiority, McClellan dallied before the thinly held Confederate line anchored on Yorktown until Johnston quietly abandoned it on the night of May 3. Pursuit brought on a partial and indecisive engagement near Williamsburg on May 5, after which the Confederates continued their withdrawal unmolested. The effect however was to leave the whole lower peninsula from the York to the James River, up to the line of the Chickahominy, in Union hands, and to open the James River to Union gunboats. Norfolk and Portsmouth were now between two Union forces—the Army of the Potomac and Burnside's command, which was advancing north from North Carolina. Finding their position no longer tenable, the Confederate forces on May 10 reluctantly abandoned the Norfolk area with its invaluable Navy Yard. Almost at once Union troops from Fortress Monroe moved in.

An effort was made to lighten the *Virginia* enough to take her up the James River to Drewry's Bluff, but the scheme had to be given up as impracticable. On the other hand, her general lack of seaworthiness and her undependable engines made it impossible for her to try to fight her way out into the bay and to the open ocean. Regretfully, Commander Tatnall ordered her blown up.

The crew of the *Virginia*, together with those of the *Patrick Henry* and the smaller gunboats, manned the Confederate batteries at Drewry's Bluff, where they were to stop the Union gunboats in their efforts to fight their way up the James to Richmond. After a number of severe battles (Seven Pines, Seven Days', Gaines' Mill), McClellan's force, though its farthest advance reached almost to the suburbs of Richmond, was withdrawn. McClellan, the magnificent drillmaster, had created an unconquerable army. But he had demonstrated all too clearly that he lacked the perseverance and moral courage that his army deserved in its commander. The Federal occupation of Norfolk was the only permanent harvest of the campaign.

Later in the year the *Monitor* foundered in a gale off the Carolina capes, taking with her a part of her crew. In her brief life she had by stopping the *Virginia* not only averted a serious threat to the blockade; she had also by her presence in Hampton Roads made possible the carrying out of the Army's offensive in the Peninsula. And her design fathered a numerous class of improved models, which were to perform notable service in the war. She was an important influence in ship design for more than 40 years—both in the United States and abroad.

Other Ironclads

The Confederates built a number of other ironclads, but none achieved the early success of the *Virginia*, for the South never again had the initial advantage of surprise and novelty and, in any event, lacked the means to profit by the technological lessons of the *Virginia-Monitor* engagement.

Early in 1863 two small ironclads (roughly of the *Virginia* model) sortied against the wooden blockaders off Charleston and inflicted some injury. But these were contained by superior Union ironclads that were sent down for the purpose. Later the same year Savannah sent out the *Atlanta,* an ironclad in most respects more formidable than the *Virginia.* She was immediately engaged by the monitor *Weehawken,* which with just five shots compelled the Southern vessel to surrender. Two solid shot from the monitor's new 15-inch Dahlgren gun smashed through the four-inch armor belt of the *Atlanta* and devastated the interior of the ship.

Another Confederate ironclad, the *Albemarle,* was the occasion of a dashing exploit by a junior officer. This vessel was built in 1864 for service on the North Carolina sounds, with the object of interfering with the blockade and Union amphibious activity in the area of Plymouth. Since no Union ironclads could be spared immediately to cope with her, Lieutenant William B. Cushing USN volunteered to destroy her at anchor with a spar torpedo rigged to the bow of a launch. One night in late October 1864, he went in with a picked crew and succeeded in getting his boat under the counter of the ram just as he was discovered and fired upon. Cushing exploded his "torpedo" successfully, blowing the bottom out of the *Albemarle,* which immediately sank. The launch was also sunk by the explosion, but Cushing and one of his men, who plunged into the chilly water, swam downstream to safety. Two of Cushing's men were killed; 19 were captured.

The Union with its vastly superior industrial facilities maintained a considerable ironclad building program throughout the war. Not only were improved "monitors" built in quantity, but broadside-type armored vessels were improvised out of any hulls on hand. The fighting on the western rivers was to produce its own peculiar but efficient shoal-draft iron- and "tin"-clads.

Mines and Submarines

The idea of destroying an enemy vessel of war by underwater explosives was by no means wholly novel in the 1860's. Bushnell's and Fulton's experiments a half century and more earlier were remembered. Samuel Colt (of revolver fame) had conducted a series of successful and widely publicized tests with electrically fired mines between 1842 and 1845. Public opinion in both the North and the South however was at first revolted by what seemed a very unsporting kind of warfare. Yet the magnitude of the South's naval defense problem in protecting 3,000 miles of coastline made the Confederacy's reluctant acceptance of "torpedoes" (as stationary mines were then called) almost inevitable.

Matthew Fontaine Maury, who had resigned his U.S. Navy commission to join his native Virginia in the war, was the original moving spirit in this branch of naval innovation, and was the first chief of the Confederate States Naval Submarine Battery Service. The mines produced were of various sorts—all rather primitive in design but often highly effective. The most common was the moored "keg torpedo," a pitch-lined beer barrel filled with black powder and triggered by contact fuses studded around its body. Other types were "frame torpedoes," which lay on the bottom, floating multi-unit "barrel torpedoes," and "pronged torpedoes"—variously fired either by fulminate caps on contact or by shore-directed electrical impulse. For river and harbor defense, the electrical torpedoes proved most successful, and over ten per cent of the South's considerable mine production was of this type. Still more might profitably have been used, but it was typical of the poverty of the Confederacy's industrial base that insulated copper wire was almost unprocurable in the South at any price.

To explode a lethal charge against an enemy vessel, the only device available was the spar torpedo—the type used by Cushing in sinking the *Albemarle.* To counter the torpedo threat, the Union navy developed torpedo nets to shield anchorages, as at the siege of Charleston in 1863–65. A crude mine sweep made of a raft festooned with chains and grapnels was on occasion pushed ahead of a Union ironclad.

In spite of failures through seepage into the powder charges and breaks in the insulation of firing cables, the Confederacy's mine warfare was effective. Thirty-one Union vessels were lost to mines—more than to any other cause. A well-founded fear of torpedoes made Union commanders increasingly circumspect in approaching Confederate harbors and river mouths, and in many instances hampered the planning of Union operations.

In 1861 the idea of a submarine was certain to appeal to a negligible naval power opposed to a considerable naval power. And in fact in the Confederacy there were a number of efforts to devise a successful submersible or semi-submersible. The first of a curious hybrid-type torpedo boat known as "Davids" was built at New Orleans but never had an opportunity for combat trial. Others were built for use against the Union blockading forces in the siege of Charleston. The David was a steam-driven, cigar-shaped craft, 50 feet long and carrying a crew of four. She cruised wholly submerged except for her hatch and funnel. For offense she carried a spar torpedo, to be detonated by an impact fuse when rammed against the underwater hull of a vessel.

At sunset on October 5, 1863, a David left Charleston with the objective of sinking the U.S. Navy's powerful ironclad *New Ironsides*. After passing unobserved through the blockading fleet, the semi-submersible came alongside her intended victim about 9 PM. Here at last she was seen and hailed, whereupon her commanding officer replied with a shotgun blast that mortally wounded the *Ironsides'* officer of the deck, then drove his torpedo into the ship's starboard quarter six feet below the water line. The resulting blast threw up a column of water that extinguished the David's fires. Her crew, supposing she was sinking, jumped overboard. The captain and a seaman swam away and were captured, but the engineer and the pilot presently climbed back into the little torpedo boat, relighted her fires, and made good their escape. The 60-pound charge of the David's torpedo proved too light to sink the thick-sided *Ironsides,* but the concussion opened numerous leaks and did widespread internal damage, requiring docking and extensive repairs.

This moderate success moved the Confederacy to invest funds in a true submersible being developed by a civilian, Horace L. Hunley, and his associates at Mobile. The submarine, named c.s.s. *Hunley,* carried a crew of nine, eight of whom "manned the cranks" to operate her propeller. She was 25 feet long and had floodable compartments fore and aft for stability. Hauling her torpedo at the end of a line, she was expected to dive under an enemy vessel and surface on the other side just as the torpedo was exploded by striking her victim's underwater hull.

At Mobile during trials, the *Hunley* stuck in the mud and drowned her entire crew. Nevertheless, the need for a weapon to break the blockade of Charleston was so urgent that the submarine was brought thither by rail. Here she sank out of control three more times, drowning nearly every member of her crew each time. Finally General Beauregard, commanding the Confederate forces in the area, forbade her being operated submerged again.

In February 1864 the *Hunley,* operating as a David, semi-submerged with a spar torpedo projecting from her bow, made an attack on the new u.s. screw sloop *Housatonic.* She was observed, but before the sloop could open fire or get under way, the *Hunley* had rammed her torpedo into the ship's hull. The *Hunley* and the *Housatonic* sank together.

Three weeks later another of the Charleston Davids struck the u.s. screw steamer *Memphis,* a captured blockade runner, but the fuse had deteriorated and failed to detonate the charge. In April 1864, a David made repeated attempts to torpedo u.s. screw frigate *Wabash,* sister-ship of the *Merrimack,* but was defeated by heavy swells that almost flooded the tiny craft.

Most of the technological innovations attempted by the South were well conceived, but the lack of enough trained engineers and, above all, the lack of an adequate industrial base prevented much success. It was the misfortune of the South that it was compelled to fight in the first modern war—a war in which economic war potential was as important as personal bravery and skill in command.

15:
The Mississippi Valley Campaign, I: The Road to Vicksburg

"The Mississippi is the Backbone of the Rebellion," said Abraham Lincoln in 1861; "it is the key to the whole situation." Subsequent events proved Lincoln right, for the Federal victories that won control of the river and split the Confederacy made possible the ultimate preservation of the Union.

The significant steps of the first year of the war in the Mississippi Valley were: (1) political and military preparations for open warfare, (2) the series of engagements by means of which Union forces broke through the Confederacy's first line of defense—the "Northwest Barrier"—and withstood the Confederacy's desperate counterattack, (3) the Union navy's capture of New Orleans, and (4) the collapse of the Confederacy's second line of defense on the Memphis and Charleston Railroad. At the end of the first year, Union forces briefly controlled all the Mississippi.

The Mississippi Valley Prepares for War

In the spring of 1861 the Mississippi River and its tributaries drained a confused, disjointed land. The up-river states were as firmly loyal to the Union as the down-river states were to the Confederacy, and each area provided the greatest reservoir of manpower and foodstuffs available to its side. Between them lay the four border states—Missouri, Arkansas, Kentucky, and Tennessee—and those western counties of Virginia that were tied to the economy of the Ohio Valley. Divided loyalties and interests, and heavy political pressure by both North and South finally split this border country asunder. Arkansas and Tennessee seceded to join the Confederacy. Missouri was torn by civil strife that lasted for more than a year before the state was brought entirely under Union control. Kentucky's legislators declared their state "neutral." Virginia's 50 western counties formed the new state of West Virginia as part of the Union.

The down-river Confederate states had tried to reassure the Northwest that the Mississippi would be kept open to free navigation. But Confederate artillery had to control the heights at Vicksburg as a precaution against invasion. This led to rumors that river boats were being stopped for customs payment at each of the seceded states. Prophets of gloom predicted disaster for the up-river farmers, much of whose produce had usually been shipped to market via New Orleans.

The natural northern anchor of the Confederacy's river defense system was Columbus, important river and rail center. But Columbus was in neutral Kentucky. Both sides had been accepting volunteers from Kentucky; each was hopeful the state could be won over. Finally, in September 1861, the Confederacy risked sending General Leonidas Polk north with forces to occupy Columbus as a countermove to Federal activity on the Missouri shore across the river. This "breach of neutrality" prompted the Kentucky legislature at last to declare for the Union. Federal occupancy of Paducah soon followed. The struggle for the Mississippi was to be resolved by force of arms.

As in the East, neither side was prepared for war. Each government had to start from scratch to get a properly trained force in the field. Each government suffered from a plague of military amateurs and the mistaken belief that victory would be quick and cheap. Furthermore, transportation, communications, and the logistics of this first "modern" war presented entirely new problems, magnified by the complications of joint and amphibious operations.

The river system itself was of unique importance, for steamboats still provided the primary means of transportation in this region.[1] Besides "Ole Man River," winding 1,000 miles to cover the 500 miles between Cairo and New Orleans, there were its navigable tributaries—the Ohio, the Tennessee, the Cumberland, and the Red. Whoever controlled these rivers enjoyed four major advantages: (1) the most dependable line of logistic support, (2) control of the economy of the area drained by the river, (3) denial of these advantages to the enemy, and (4) a barrier obstructing normal use of the railroads and highways that crossed the river. Though such control could be exploited only with the aid of naval forces, when hostilities began there was not a single warship on the Mississippi.

The Confederacy lacked the wherewithal to build an adequate naval force on the inland waters. No Southern mill west of Richmond could roll iron plates thick enough to stop anything heavier than a rifle bullet. Only through great ingenuity did the Confederacy eventually produce three ironclads—the *Manassas,* the *Louisiana,* and the *Arkansas*—which saw ac-

[1] The railroad, available for the first time in a major war, provided the second most efficient means of transportation. A single line might easily replace the 2,000 wagons and 10,000 horses required to supply a Civil War army of 50,000 men at a distance of three days' march from their nearest base. There were disadvantages as well: rolling stock was in short supply; trackage became an obvious target for guerrillas and cavalry raids; in unfriendly territory, large numbers of troops had to be withdrawn from the combat forces for guard duty. The movement of men and materials on the inadequately developed Southern railroads proved more expensive and less reliable than transportation by means of the rivers. A third means of communication, the telegraph, likewise profoundly influenced the war. The mischief of interference with the commander in the field by telegrams from the higher level commander in the rear —all the way up to the President, whether Lincoln or Davis—has been better publicized than the greater efficiency and the possibility of centralized direction that it fostered.

tion on the Mississippi, and a small fleet of wooden gunboats converted from river steamers. By contrast, the industrial North was able to build a formidable array of ironclads, the nucleus of a steadily augmented fleet of river warships. These were supplemented at times by ships from the seagoing navy.

The first Union gunboats on the Mississippi were the *Tyler,* the *Lexington,* and the *Conestoga,* converted from wooden side-wheelers. They averaged 180 feet in length and 42 feet in beam, and like all vessels built for up-river work, they drew no more than six feet of water. Each was protected against musket fire by a five-inch oak bulwark, and each was armed with 32-pounders and 8-inch guns. These were soon followed by the seven Eads ironclads, four of which were built at Carondelet, near St. Louis, where 4,000 men worked day and night, seven days a week, under a contract awarded in August 1861 to James B. Eads. The *St. Louis, Carondelet, Cincinnati, Louisville, Mound City, Cairo,* and *Pittsburg* had casemates at a 35-degree angle, plated with 2½-inch sheet iron and pierced for three bow guns, four guns to each broadside, and two stern guns. Two single-cylinder engines turned a 22-foot sternwheel protected by the after casemate, driving these ponderous craft (175 feet in length, 51½ in beam) at about seven knots. Most powerful of all the river warships was the *Benton,* Eads' conversion of a twin-hulled "snagboat," which was to become the flagship of the fleet. She was 200 feet long, had a beam of 75 feet, carried 16 guns, and was somewhat more heavily armored than the other ironclads. Ninth and last of the original ironclads was the converted *Essex,* almost as big as the *Benton.*

The Western Flotilla, as these ships were officially called, was originally under army control. The ships were commanded by regular naval officers however, and the very existence of the flotilla as a fighting force must be credited to its flag officer, Captain Andrew Hull Foote USN. Secretary Welles had ordered Foote in September 1861 to report to the army and prepare an inland fleet. In the midst of the chaos of mobilization, Foote had a task to accomplish that demanded the utmost of his experience and perseverance. Overcoming every obstacle created by an ambiguous command relationship and by shortages of money, material, trained personnel, and supply, he created the naval forces with which he later spearheaded the first major Union offensive in the Mississippi Valley.

The First Line of Confederate Defense

In all the Confederacy there was no natural line of defense connecting the Mississippi and the Alleghenies. Without the Ohio River as a barrier, the best the South could do in preparation for the inevitable Union attack was to substitute a makeshift line of strong points anchored on the Mississippi at Columbus and in the Alleghenies at Cumberland Gap. Between the Confederate left flank, where General Polk's artillery denied the use of the river to the Northerners, and the right flank, where a Confederate army at Mill Springs guarded the approaches to the pass through the mountains, there were two possible invasion routes. One was via the Tennessee and Cumberland Rivers, each of which was navigable into the southern heartland. To plug this route the Confederates erected forts on the rivers where they flowed only 12 miles apart just south of the Kentucky border. The other invasion route was via the Louisville railroad, which branched at Bowling Green to provide connections with all the main rail lines in the South. To safeguard that route, a Confederate army occupied Bowling Green and proceeded to fortify its position.

There was a critical weakness in the Confederate line of defense. Taken together, the western extremes of Kentucky and Tennessee form a peninsula, bounded on the west, north, and east respectively by the Mississippi, Ohio, and Tennessee rivers. If the Tennessee were in Northern hands, the Confederate first line of defense on the Mississippi could be outflanked by water and made untenable. The Tennessee River is paralleled in part by the Cumberland. Using the Cumberland, Northern gunboats could sever both of the rail lines supplying the Confederates at Bowling Green. In short, against properly coordinated Union naval and military power, the so-called "Northwest Barrier" would be most difficult to defend.

Flag Officer Foote and the Union army commander in that area, Brigadier General Ulysses S. Grant, fully appreciated this. They believed that a rapid thrust, with water-borne logistic and gunfire support, could drive a salient through the Confederate line before the South was ready. Grant had already demonstrated initiative and strategic grasp. He had established a base at Cairo when General Polk occupied Columbus. It was he who had occupied Paducah—which commands the lower Ohio, Tennessee, and Cumberland rivers— before the Confederates could seize it. Furthermore, Grant and Foote knew how to cooperate. In early 1862 they secured permission to launch a joint operation with seven gunboats and 17,000 troops against the forts on the Tennessee and Cumberland.

The Gunboats Capture Fort Henry

Fort Henry, hastily constructed by the Confederates on low, partially flooded ground on the east bank of the Tennessee River about 60 miles upstream from the Federal base at Paducah, was the initial Union objective of this campaign. Its few guns and small garrison could offer only token resistance against Flag Officer Foote when he arrived with the seven gunboats on February 6, 1862, four days after his departure from the main Union river base at Cairo. The action that followed was short and decisive. Foote did not wait for the Federal army, delayed by muddy roads and high water, to make the simultaneous attack from the rear that the official plan had called for. As soon as the gunboats were within range, he opened fire, closed to 600 yards, and within two hours pounded Fort Henry into surrender. Most of the 3,000-man Confederate garrison had withdrawn to Fort Donelson, 12 miles away on the west bank of the Cumberland River, leaving General Tilghman and fewer than 100 men to delay the Union offensive. Of the eleven Confederate guns, seven had been rendered useless. Casualties were light on both sides, the greatest damage being suffered by the ironclad *Essex*, which lost 32 men, most of whom were scalded to death when a shot pierced her middle boiler. The brief action illustrated clearly the advantages that accrued to the Union from its gunboat flotilla.

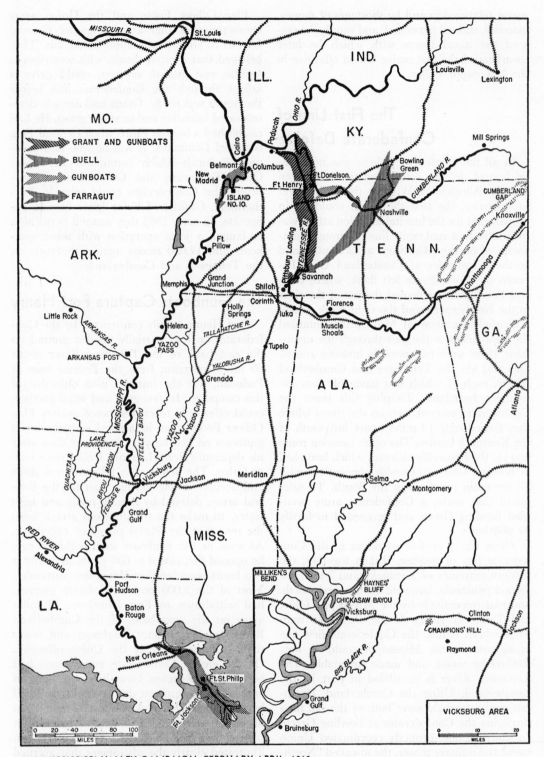

THE MISSISSIPPI VALLEY CAMPAIGN, FEBRUARY-APRIL, 1862

Naval power permitted the joint operation against Fort Henry to achieve surprise and gain tactical success. It demonstrated that in the Mississippi Valley heavy artillery—the gunboats' batteries—might be moved more rapidly by water than even infantry could move by land. It opened and controlled an avenue for adequate logistic support. Further, it allowed for a speedy exploitation of the victory, keeping the enemy off balance. Union gunboats immediately proceeded up river and penetrated into the Confederacy's heartland as far as Muscle Shoals at the head of navigation near Florence, Alabama. They compelled the Confederates to blow up several shiploads of military stores and captured the large steamer *Eastport*, which was being converted into a gunboat. Their landing parties ripped up the rails and destroyed the bridge of the only railroad connecting Columbus and Bowling Green. By disrupting enemy communications and by making an advance base at Fort Henry immediately available to Grant, they enabled the Union forces to turn promptly to their next major objective. The Union army's appreciation of its navy's activities is reflected in the renaming of Fort Henry as Fort Foote.

Unconditional Surrender at Fort Donelson

Fort Donelson had been constructed to guard the river route to Nashville. It stood above a great bend in the Cumberland on the high ground of the west bank. There Brigadier General Gideon J. Pillow csa with about 15,000 men elected to resist the Union attack. The Confederate army had its back to the river, its right flank made unassailable by flooded Hickman Creek, and its front established on a series of well-fortified ridges paralleling the river. On its left flank, a road leading south through Charlotte to Nashville was its only line of retreat.

While Foote's gunboats made the long passage down the Tennessee and then up the Cumberland, the Union troops marched across the barren winter countryside without interference. By February 13, 1862 Grant's lines formed an arc running south from Hickman Creek and then east toward the Cumberland.

When the first of the gunboats, the ironclad *Carondelet*, arrived, Grant ordered her to provide diversion by firing on the fort so that the Union troops could advance to cut the Charlotte road. The other Union gunboats, convoying 5,000 fresh troops and all necessary supplies, arrived on the morning of the 14th to strengthen the army, in which some soldiers had frozen to death the night before in a snow and sleet storm and 12-degree temperature. The ironclad gunboats then led the way upstream against Fort Donelson's water batteries. A heavy artillery duel followed. Only two of the fort's guns had a range equal to that of the gunboats' heavy armament, but instead of bombarding from an advantageous distance, Foote advanced to within 400 yards. He concentrated on the water battery, hoping to pass by it and then destroy the fort on the bluff by enfilade fire, but plunging shot from the fort soon disabled his two best ironclads, and a bursting gun forced the *Carondelet* out of the action. Wounded himself, Foote reluctantly ordered his ships to withdraw. The flotilla had suffered more than 50 casualties as well as serious material damage.

In spite of this Union reverse, the Confederate forces were trapped by Grant's army, and the mere presence of the Union gunboats helped to make a mass escape across the Cumberland impossible. At a staff meeting during the night of February 14-15, the Confederate leaders decided to open the next day's battle with a desperate attack in an effort to recapture the Charlotte road as a line of retreat. Early on the 15th, while Grant conferred with Foote aboard the *St. Louis*, 8,000 Confederate soldiers broke the Union hold on the Charlotte road so easily that General Pillow forgot about withdrawal and attempted to roll up the Union line. But Grant rallied his numerically superior forces and, with some aid from the *Carondelet*, inflicted 2,000 casualties and forced Pillow's army back into its original position. The Confederate general with a small force escaped up river during the night in the two steamers available, while Colonel Nathan B. Forrest's cavalry stole away through the frozen marshes. The next day Fort Donelson's 10,000 surviving defenders accepted Grant's demand for "unconditional surrender."

The North was jubilant. Grant became the popular hero—"Unconditional Surrender"

Grant. Union gunboats controlled the Cumberland and the lines of communication crossing it. The Confederate forces that had already withdrawn from Bowling Green to Nashville now withdrew from the Tennessee capital before Foote's gunboats could destroy the railroad bridge there. The state government officials hastened away from the undefended city, which was soon occupied by Union troops.

Repercussions of the victory immediately made themselves felt on the Mississippi. At Columbus, Confederate General Polk had to move fast to avoid being trapped. He sent much of his artillery to Island No. 10, the nearest Confederate strong point downstream, and retreated with most of his army all the way to Corinth, Mississippi, a junction where major east-west and north-south railroads crossed and which was to become the key position in the second line of Confederate defense.

With control of the Tennessee, and the Nashville flank secured, Grant and Foote with available reinforcements could have overwhelmed all Confederate defenses on the Mississippi above and including Memphis. By maintaining the initiative they might have prevented the regrouping of Confederate forces for a counterattack. Instead, Grant's victorious army was kept inactive for almost two months while Major General Henry W. Halleck, commander of the Department of Missouri and Grant's immediate superior in the chain of command, pursued various secondary objectives. During the opening year of the war neither the North nor the South could be made to realize that a military victory had to be fully exploited if a final decision was to be reached.

Action on the Mississippi— Island No. 10

Union victories in Missouri as well as at Fort Donelson necessitated a general Confederate withdrawal on both sides of the Mississippi to a strong defensive position 60 miles below evacuated Columbus. Here the river made two 180-degree turns, carving two thumb-shaped peninsulas out of the river-bottom country. The more easterly of these peninsulas extended south from the Missouri shore. It was heavily wooded and almost entirely flooded by

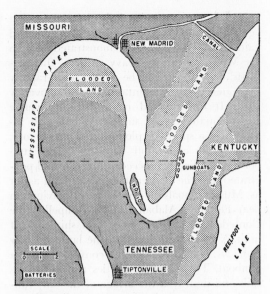

ISLAND NO. 10

the high water of early spring. Off its tip lay Island No. 10, the tenth island down river from Cairo. On that island and on the high ground of the westerly thumb, which extended north from the Tennessee shore, 7,000 Confederate soldiers and 130 guns withdrawn from Columbus were reinforced by a garrison that, after spiking its guns, had abandoned New Madrid on the Missouri shore. Six gunboats and several support ships augmented these forces. These wooden gunboats the Confederates considered practically irreplaceable; they were not to be used against Federal artillery, or ironclad gunboats, except in the gravest emergency.

Opposing this Confederate force in the spring of 1862 was Brigadier General John Pope in Missouri with a Federal army of 20,000 men, supported by part of the gunboat flotilla. Pope's problem was to get at the enemy. Reelfoot Lake, marshes, and spring floods made it impossible for the Federals to march along the east bank of the Mississippi in an encircling movement, and it was just as much out of the question to cross the river below Island No. 10, where the Confederate warships could make short work of the rafts and small boats to which the Union army would be limited.

Pope first occupied New Madrid and established his base there. Then, for direct water-borne logistic support, he had the Army Engineers cut a canal across the flooded Missouri peninsula on a line beyond the range of the Confederate guns. The canal was not dug; it had to be sawed out of the woods. The Engineers devised a special rig, operated from a flat boat, by means of which they cut through the tree trunks under water and cleared a channel four and a half feet deep for the transports. Pope's communications were thus improved but his basic situation was not altered, for the ironclad gunboats drew at least six feet and the canal could not be deepened until the river receded months later. Somehow Pope had to get an ironclad or two downstream where their heavy guns could cover a river crossing and enable him to cut the single road leading out of the Confederate position.

Even ironclads were not then expected to survive the hail of shot and shell in a daylight run past the Confederate defenses; nor was it thought that a cumbersome ironclad could possibly be navigated at night through the wayward currents of that tortuous gantlet without grounding—and grounding while trying to stay in the deep water on the Confederate side of the bend would mean capture. But among Foote's gunboat commanders Captain Henry Walke of the *Carondelet* was of a different opinion. He believed that his ship could make it under cover of darkness, with heavy chain faked down on deck for protection against plunging shot and a coal barge lashed alongside to protect the unarmored midships section. Since no one had a better alternative suggestion, he was given permission to try.

Walke made his departure on the night of April 4–5, 1862 while a furious thunderstorm was roaring down the river. Lightning flashes, he hoped, would aid his pilot and might blind the Confederate gunners. The *Carondelet's* crew, armed with cutlasses to repel boarders and reinforced by a contingent of volunteer army sharpshooters, was ready. The shielded ironclad steamed slowly out into the wild night. Running so close that the Confederate guns fired too high, she swept around Island No. 10 without a single casualty. Proof that it could be done encouraged the ironclad *Pittsburg* to navigate the gantlet two nights later, also in a timely thunderstorm. Together the two gunboats gave Pope all the fire support he needed.

The complete Union victory that followed was an anticlimax. The Confederate ships scurried out of harm's way down river, so that there was no serious opposition to Pope's crossing below the Confederate defenses or to his seizure of the single line of retreat. Once more a Southern force was hopelessly trapped. The Confederate troops surrendered the next day with their heavy guns and a great quantity of supplies and ammunition. Thanks to the *Carondelet*, the victory had not cost the life of a single Union soldier.

This victory had little influence on the course of the war beyond effecting an immediate reduction in Confederate strength. Within a few days a great battle was to be fought on the banks of the Tennessee and the ironclad gunboats would be left with the task of clearing the Mississippi all the way south to Vicksburg.

The Confederate Attack: The Battle of Shiloh

Although most of the details of the bloody Battle of Shiloh, April 13–15, 1862, belong in the realm of military rather than naval history, an understanding of the Union conquest of the Mississippi demands some appreciation of what happened at Shiloh and of the part played there by naval power. The surrender of Fort Donelson had deluded the North into the expectation of a quick, final victory in the west. Presumably the Union forces would continue on the offensive with their immediate objective the defeat of the Confederate army covering the railroad junction of Corinth, Mississippi. Halleck planned to lead the attack in person. He could supplement Grant's army with Buell's, brought from Nashville, and reinforce them both with newly recruited troops from the North. Supplies could be shipped up the Tennessee River to Pittsburg Landing, on the west bank, only 20 miles northeast of Corinth. But administrative work in St. Louis caused Halleck to delay leaving his headquarters.

Meanwhile divisions of the Union army gradually assembled. Grant established his headquarters nine miles downstream from Pittsburg Landing at Savannah, the point on the east bank of the river where Buell's forces were expected to arrive on their way from Nashville. The bulk of Grant's army advanced to

Pittsburg Landing and deployed almost exactly as General Pillow's Confederate forces had at Fort Donelson. The Union force was backed against the Tennessee. But the river was a source of Union strength—a broad highway for supplies, reinforcements, and, if necessary, withdrawal, not a barrier as the Cumberland had been for the Confederates at Fort Donelson. The Union army's flanks were covered by two creeks large enough to be of natural defensive value. Its front extended a short distance along both sides of the road leading to Corinth. There, just beyond the rough, wooded terrain near the river, stood the Shiloh meeting house, a simple log structure from which the battle takes its name.

The Confederate leaders, perfectly aware of what Halleck intended to do, had begun an energetic concentration of their own forces under the skilled leadership of General Albert Sydney Johnston, who held a command position in the South analogous to Halleck's in the North. In a little over a month's time he assembled 45,000 men at Corinth. By moving fast, he planned to strike the 33,000 Federals under Grant at Pittsburg Landing before Buell's army of 20,000 had time to join. He would strike as soon as possible, break the Union left flank in a surprise attack, capture Pittsburg Landing to prevent escape via the river, and pin the disorganized defenders in a bend of the creek that covered their original right flank. As events proved, Johnston was gambling his life and almost won.

Grant's division commanders, anticipating their own offensive, had taken only routine precautions against an attack on their troops. There was no plan for fire support from the gunboats. The troops were merely camped, not properly deployed. When the Confederate attack came on the morning of April 13, 1862 Grant was down river at Savannah. There, just the previous evening, he had informed the commanding general of the first of Buell's divisions to arrive that his troops would be taken to Pittsburg Landing by boat some time the following week. Although Grant later denied that he was tactically surprised, certainly he thought that Johnston was patiently waiting for him at Corinth.

During the first day's battle the Confederates crushed the Union left flank and almost reached Pittsburg Landing, as planned. That night the river boats brought up Buell's 20,000 troops and artillery from Savannah. During the second day Union counterattacks regained all lost ground. Early the third day the Confederate forces withdrew. Casualties exceeded 20,000 out of a total of nearly 100,000 combatants on both sides. Strategically Shiloh was a Union victory, for the South had failed in its effort to repulse the invaders. In other respects it was a draw which left the Union army in possession of the field, too stunned by slaughter and too battle-weary to pursue the retreating Confederate forces to their fortified positions at Corinth.

The turning point in the battle had occurred toward the end of the first day's fighting. After the Union left flank collapsed, victory was just beyond the Confederates' grasp. One immediate objective remained. Johnston's troops had to break through the Union rear, seize Pittsburg Landing, and thus sever Grant's riverborne line of communications. It was just at that point that two of the original wooden gunboats, the *Tyler* and the *Lexington*, made a crucial contribution to the battle. There is no evidence that they scored many hits, but their booming guns discouraged the weary Confederates and put heart into the retreating Union troops. The Union naval commanders concentrated on Confederate artillery batteries and sent shells screaming up the ravines that the attackers would have to cross. After the assault was repulsed, the gunboats fired fused shells at intervals all night long and caused the Southern troops to withdraw as far as the abandoned Federal camps where the action had been begun. "In this repulse," reads Grant's official report, "much is due to the presence of the gunboats."

The entire campaign and in particular the outcome of the battle of Shiloh hinged upon control of the rivers by naval power. Had the *Tyler* and *Lexington* been in Confederate hands or had there been even a single Confederate ironclad—a ship like the *Carondelet*, for instance—Shiloh might well have been a Confederate victory. As it was, only the rapid reinforcing of the Union army by Buell's riverborne divisions and artillery determined that it was the Confederate, and not the Union, forces that broke off the encounter.

After Shiloh most of western Tennessee was secure in Union hands. The Confederacy's northwest barrier was lost, the strongest counterattack that the South could launch was repulsed, and Halleck would himself assemble an overwhelming army with intent to crush the second line of Confederate defense. Shiloh was a defeat for which the Confederacy would continue to pay. Defenses elsewhere had been dangerously reduced in complying with Johnston's urgent request for forces to turn back Grant before it was too late. As an immediate result, Shiloh contributed to the outcome of the major campaign, essentially naval, that was about to wrest New Orleans, the "Queen City of the South," from the Confederacy.

New Orleans and its Defenses

Commercial enterprise and 170,000 inhabitants made New Orleans the Confederacy's richest and largest city. Trade was her life, guaranteed to her in abundance because of her unique geographical position. Lying in a bend of the Mississippi about 100 miles above the Head of the Passes, where the river divided to enter the Gulf of Mexico through three major channels, New Orleans controlled all the lower Mississippi Valley. From the decks of river steamers and ocean packets, passengers could look down into her bustling streets and prosperous business houses, secure behind the levee. It is true that railroads were changing transportation patterns and that the farmers of the Northwest were diverting more and more of their grain to New York for transshipment abroad, but New Orleans had fattened on almost 50 years of steamboat trade and still prospered.

The outbreak of actual hostilities and the appearance of the *Powhatan* and *Brooklyn* on blockade duty in the Gulf ended abruptly the hopes for a free Mississippi and a free port that New Orleans' citizens had held when Louisiana seceded. For a short time war seemed a glorious thing to them. The more optimistic assumed that the fate of the Northwest lay in their hands; the young men eagerly enlisted, delighting in exotic uniforms and marching to military bands. They viewed the Union blockade with contempt. The many-mouthed Mississippi and adjacent waters gave blockade runners an advantage over any blockading squadron the Union had ships to maintain. Their commerce-raiders would make the Yankee merchantmen pay dearly for the war. They hardly noticed the city's businesses closing one by one for the duration, as though for a holiday.

In September 1861 the Union navy seized Ship Island. This island, about midway on the coastal route between New Orleans and Mobile, had been partially fortified by the Confederates and then abandoned. In Union hands it increased the efficacy of the blockade by providing a sorely needed advance base. In October a Union squadron of four ships—*Richmond, Vincennes, Preble,* and *Water Witch*—occupied the Head of the Passes. They were intended to exert a strangle hold on all ocean shipping to and from New Orleans; instead, the Confederates made a laughingstock of them. Shortly before dawn on October 12 the Confederate ram *Manassas,* a football-shaped ironclad armed with one gun, led the attack, supported by some fire rafts and, at a safe distance, a little flotilla of wooden boats. Approaching unobserved, the *Manassas* rammed the *Richmond* and stove in three planks of the Union warship but lost her own smokestacks and the use of one engine. While she retreated up-stream, the panic-stricken Union fleet made a frantic effort to get out of the river. The *Richmond* grounded, and the *Vincennes* not only went aground but was abandoned with a slow fuse lighted to explode her magazines. Later, when it was apparent that the fuse must have sputtered out, the large ships were refloated; the Union squadron thereupon deserted the river for the more navigable waters of the Gulf. Reporting on these events, the British and French consuls in New Orleans questioned the ability of the Federal government to maintain the blockade.

Nevertheless by the beginning of 1862 the Confederate leaders felt serious concern for the safety and welfare of New Orleans. Cotton was piled high awaiting shipment. The rotting wharfs were falling into the river. Hard money had gone into hiding. Worst of all, the Con-

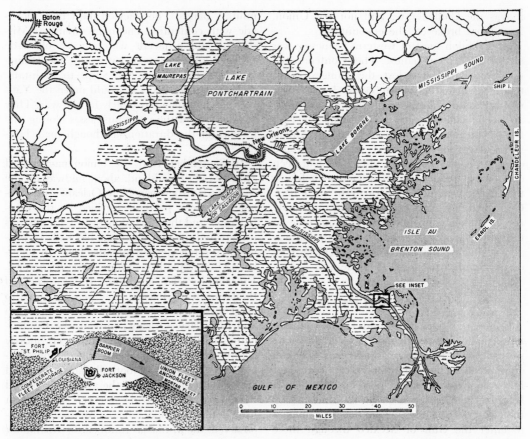

NEW ORLEANS CAMPAIGN, 1862

federate government's policy of giving priority to the defense of the Tennessee Valley kept drawing men, equipment, and supplies away from New Orleans. As a result, work progressed haphazardly on the city's defenses.

In theory, those defenses were excellent, comprising as they did an interior and an exterior line. The interior line consisted of fortifications thrown up around the city, extending from Lake Ponchartrain to the Chalmette Battery on the river, where Jackson had defeated the British in 1815. Such defenses would be unnecessary if the exterior line held. It was thought, and correctly, that the swamps around the city would discourage an overland approach. The weakest point was the river itself, and so the exterior defenses were concentrated on blocking the Mississippi about 90 miles below New Orleans at the Plaquemine Bend, where the river made one final turn before flowing into the Gulf. On that narrow

front two forts, supported by the Confederate naval forces, were expected to repel the heaviest attack that the Union Navy could bring to bear.

Fort Jackson, a star-shaped, brick structure, a hundred yards to a side and rising 22 feet above its moat, stood on the right bank of the river bend. It was armed with some 90 guns, 16 of them casemated. Slightly up-stream on the left bank stood Fort St. Philip, somewhat less formidable, mounting 52 guns, none casemated. The two forts together never had more than 39 guns of a caliber equal to the 165 guns of the Union ships that were to be opposed to them in battle.

Below the forts but close enough to be covered by the fire of their guns, a great boom spanned the 700-yard wide river. It was constructed of the trunks of cypress trees, 40 feet long and five feet thick, held a few feet apart and parallel to the stream by large crosswise beams and by heavy chains, the bitter ends of which were secured on the banks of the river. A score and more of 3,000-pound anchors were attached at intervals along the boom to hold it against the current. Only some cataclysmic force, it was supposed, could penetrate such a barrier. No enemy ships could ram their way through it against the 4-knot current, and all efforts to sever the boom would be subjected to the fire of the forts and of the Confederate naval patrols. But winter storms, floating down thousands of tons of debris in spite of all Confederate efforts to tow the drift ashore, finally accomplished what was thought to be impossible. The boom broke, leaving a gap that was plugged as well as possible with dismasted schooners chained together, bows upstream.

In addition to these fixed defenses there were a dozen unarmored gunboats and the ironclad *Manassas* with her single 32-pounder carronade. Six of the gunboats belonged to the River Defense Fleet, nominally under the command of the Confederate army but actually handled by an unreliable, undisciplined lot of river-men who would take orders from no one. Of the six others, two were of the Louisiana State Navy and four of the Confederate Navy. This jumbled command situation might not have been a fatally serious weakness if the ironclads upon which New Orleans' defenders really counted had been ready. These were the *Louisiana* and the *Mississippi*, of 16 guns each. It is conceivable that either of these ships, if completed and able to operate as originally planned, could by itself have saved New Orleans. Labor troubles (including strikes), shortage of materials, a slow start, and an interminable struggle with inadequate machinery left these vessels unready when the need for them came.

What vitiated this entire defense system was the inability of the Confederacy to comprehend the urgency of the situation and the might of the Union navy. With their spirits buoyed up by faith in the traditional invulnerability of New Orleans, Southerners generally believed that any real danger to the city was bound to come, if at all, from the north. Chains that might have repaired the shattered boom were being strung across the river north of the city as a protection against Foote's ironclad gunboats based at Cairo. The popular confidence

has been well summed up in two sentences: "Nothing afloat could pass the forts. Nothing that walked could get through our swamps."[2] But Major General Mansfield Lovell, Commander of Confederate Department Number 1, with his headquarters in New Orleans, had very little with which to back this feeling of confidence. When Pensacola was abandoned, its guns went to Mobile, not to New Orleans as Lovell requested. Even when a major Union naval expedition appeared in March 1862 and began working large warships over the bars and into the Mississippi, Confederate troops and guns were being ordered out of New Orleans to the Tennessee Valley. By early April, with attack imminent, all regular troops had departed for the fighting north of Corinth. Lovell's entire force consisted of the garrisons for the forts—fewer than 1,500 men—and in the city, 3,000 ninety-day militiamen, 1,800 of them armed only with shotguns, and a couple of companies of sharpshooters.

Union Preparations for the New Orleans Campaign

The Federal War Department originally estimated that the capture of New Orleans would require an army of at least 50,000 men with full naval support in a major campaign. Union army commanders assumed as a basic military truth that wooden ships, confined to a narrow channel and reduced by the current to a maximum speed of about four knots, could not survive an attempt to pass a heavy, casemated fortification such as Fort Jackson. That is why they turned a deaf ear to Assistant Secretary of the Navy Gustavus Fox when he insisted that a fleet alone could destroy Forts Jackson and St. Philip and compel the city to surrender. But Fox's opinions found ardent support from a naval officer who had become thoroughly familiar with the New Orleans area as a steamship captain in peacetime and who in November 1861 had just returned to Washington from duty with the Gulf Blockading Squadron. This officer was Fox's good friend Commander David Dixon Porter, the second son of Commodore David Porter of *Essex* fame in the War of

[2] *Battles and Leaders of the Civil War*, II (New York, 1887), 19.

1812. He espoused Fox's plan for a naval attack on New Orleans with enthusiasm, ingenuity, and a wealth of descriptive detail, as shown in conferences with Secretary of the Navy Welles, President Lincoln, and George B. McClellan, then General in Chief of the Union armies. The Army's objections were overcome by providing for a special mortar flotilla (Porter's idea) with which to silence the forts and by the Navy's willingness to undertake the expedition with only 13,000 troops, about to become available under Major General Benjamin Franklin Butler, as occupation forces.

Appropriately, the proposed mortar flotilla was commanded by Porter. Now 48 years old, he had the vigor and enterprise of a much younger man. He was considered by many of his juniors the Union navy's most capable officer—an opinion probably shared by himself. Ambitious and self-confident, he frequently irritated his seniors, especially by habitually by-passing them in his voluminous personal correspondence with Gustavus Fox. For overall command of the expedition however, Secretary of the Navy Welles had to find a senior officer, a man of action and of character, one who had the sound judgment of maturity, unflagging energy, and the respect of his officers and men. The success or failure of the expedition might well be determined by this choice.

In Welles' view, not one of the first 36 officers on the list of captains was both available and qualified. Number 37 was David Glasgow Farragut, a native of Tennessee and Porter's foster brother, 60 years old at this time. In Norfolk at the outbreak of the war, like Robert E. Lee at Arlington, Farragut had had to choose between his state and the Union. He and his wife considered themselves Virginians, but on the day that Virginia seceded, he embarked with his family for New York. Like Lincoln, he placed the Union first. Many in the South considered him a traitor; some in the North distrusted him, fearing that an underlying sympathy for the South might interfere with the rigorous execution of his duty in the war. But Farragut was Gideon Welles' choice for the command. The Secretary of the Navy recognized Farragut's loyalty, professional competence, and character; moreover, he sensed the rightness of having the expedition led by a man who had already felt the heartache of the struggle. As events proved, Welles could not have made a better choice. Later he was to refer to "the innate fearless moral courage of Farragut."

During the winter of 1861–62 the expedition was outfitted with unusual dispatch. In January Farragut received his orders naming him commander of the Western Gulf Blockading Squadron and designating the *Hartford* as his flagship. By the end of the month he sailed from the Chesapeake for the Gulf. He was to await the arrival of the "formidable mortars," collect all ships that could be spared from the blockade, "reduce the defenses which guard the approaches to New Orleans," take possession of the city, and "hoist the American flag thereon." His orders, dated January 20, 1862 and written before any of the successes in the Tennessee Valley, also ingenuously stated: "If the Mississippi expedition from Cairo shall not have descended the river, you will take advantage of the panic to push a strong force up the river to take all their defenses in the rear." For good measure, Secretary Welles added: "You will also reduce the fortifications which defend Mobile Bay and turn them over to the army to hold."[3]

The mortar flotilla departed right on Farragut's heels. Porter had employed his "restless energy" to good cause. He supervised the purchase of 21 schooners in the New York-Philadelphia area, had them reinforced with heavy timbers amidships for service as mortar boats, and managed to get the 13-inch mortars, one for each boat, manufactured in Pittsburgh along with 30,000 rounds of ammunition. By the end of February the entire flotilla was holding target practice at Key West under Porter's direction, and Farragut was establishing his operational base at Ship Island.

The Union assault fleet consisted of four first-class steam sloops, *Hartford, Richmond, Pensacola,* and *Brooklyn*; the veteran sidewheeler *Mississippi*; and 12 smaller steam sloops, usually referred to as gunboats. The flagship *Hartford* was almost new, 225 feet long, of 2,900 tons, and capable of a maximum speed of 13 knots under sail and power but only eight knots when driven by her propeller alone. Under Farragut she usually carried 22

[3] *Official Records of the Union and Confederate Navies in the War of the Rebellion,* Series I, XVIII, 8.

nine-inch Dahlgren shell guns and two rifled 30-pounders fore and aft. The other first-class sloops were similar in general dimensions and armament. Three of the smaller ships (*Oneida, Varuna,* and *Iroquois*) were 1,000-tonners with an average armament of nine guns and classified as screw corvettes; the nine others (*Cayuga, Itasca, Katahdin, Kennebec, Kineo, Pinola, Sciota, Winona,* and *Wissahickon*) were 500-tonners armed with two guns and classified as screw gunboats. Though built of wood and not armored, all 17 vessels were stanch, seagoing ships.

In early March 1862 Farragut had written Fox from Ship Island: "The moment Captain Porter arrives with his Mortar Fleet, I will collect my vessels, which are pretty close around me, and dash up the river, but I do not wish to make a display before I am ready, as I wish to keep up the delusion that Mobile is the first object of attack."[4] The Mississippi mud canceled this plan. Between the Confederate positions and the large ships of the assault fleet with their 16-foot draft the sand bars which had built up during the past year lay across the mouths of the river, so that the unused channels had in places only about 15 feet of water even during the early spring flood stage. Those obstructions held up the fleet for a full month. After repeated tries the *Brooklyn* plowed through mud into the deeper water at the Head of the Passes on March 12. The *Hartford* passed over the next day, but the *Richmond* took another ten days of trying. After two weeks of pulling and hauling, interrupted by a return to Ship Island for the removal of all possible weight, the *Pensacola* and the *Mississippi* finally worked their way through the mud on April 8. The *Colorado,* the largest of Farragut's ships, with a draft of 23 feet, never did get into the river and so cannot be numbered in the assault fleet. The smaller sloops and mortar boats were of sufficiently light draft to come and go as they pleased.

Farragut made good use of this month to collect intelligence and prepare his plans for the attack. He had been supplied with detailed descriptions of Forts Jackson and St. Philip. These were brought up to date by deserters who divulged the strength of the garrisons and reported that the Confederates were "sending

[4] *Ibid.,* 47.

every man they can to the northern army."[5] A Union raid on Biloxi brought him captured newspapers deploring the fall of Nashville. Secretary Welles warned him of the ironclads under construction in New Orleans, for c.s.s. *Virginia* had just demonstrated at Hampton Roads what an ironclad could do against wooden ships. The added burden of administrative details in connection with maintaining the blockade from Mobile to the Mexican border and problems of supply forced Farragut to spend long hours at his desk. He had to borrow coal from the Army, only one of his ships had solid shot for use against an ironclad, and his requests for extraordinary supplies brought loud protests from the bureaus in Washington, where estimates were still based on a half century of peacetime frugality.

The Battle of New Orleans

In 1862 the Confederacy's confidence in the strength of the defenses below New Orleans received the full support of orthodox military opinion, but the events of the week of April 18–24 were without modern precedent—Farragut's fleet accomplished the "impossible." Taken together, the actions of that week have long been referred to as "The Battle of New Orleans," although they occurred far from sight or sound of the city; severally, they include: (1) the bombardment of the forts by the mortar flotilla, (2) the opening of the boom, (3) the fleet's run past the forts on the night of April 24, and (4) the near annihilation of New Orleans' naval defense forces.

Most of Farragut's captains were so impressed by the vulnerability of wooden ships against forts that they too believed the success of the attack depended upon the mortar flotilla. And many were firmly convinced that to run by the forts, leaving them in Confederate hands, was to place the fleet in a trap. Flag Officer Farragut did not concur. He had always been mildly skeptical of the mortars, but was willing to see what they could do and to let them distract the enemy while he prepared for the main assault. He expected that the forts, if by-passed, would soon surrender, for they were dependent on river-borne logistic support.

[5] *Loc. cit.*

Porter's mortar boats moved into position on the night of April 17. Fourteen of them, their masts camouflaged with bushes, moored around the bend below Fort Jackson where they were screened from the fort by woods. The six others anchored out in the stream where they could fire on Fort St. Philip. When the bombardment opened on the 18th, fused shells were accurately lobbed into the forts at an easy two-mile range. That day the citadel and quarters in Fort Jackson were burned out and the magazines temporarily endangered, but the Confederates put up a well-aimed counterfire, scored hits on the mortar boats out in the stream, and forced that group to retire around the bend. On the second day, while the mortar flotilla threw a shell a minute into Fort Jackson, Farragut ordered his gunboats to take turns offering themselves as moving targets out in the stream in order to distribute the Confederate fire. One mortar boat was sunk by a direct hit; otherwise the bombardment was maintained day and night without the loss of a ship.

Thousands of mortar shells buried themselves deep in the mud before exploding. Physical impairment to the military value of the forts was slight, but that proved less important than the effect of the bombardment on the morale of the defenders. High water and breaks in the levee turned Fort Jackson into a swamp, and the day and night shelling forced the disheartened garrison to live in the casemates, more like muskrats than men. Farragut's sailors, over-estimating the effectiveness of the mortar fire, were confident of victory.

The night of April 20 marked important developments on both sides. While the mortars fired away, two of the gunboats, the *Itasca* and *Pinola*, attempted to open a breach in the Confederate barrier across the river. With masts removed, the ships made very difficult targets as they steamed up on the schooner hulks in the boom. After plans to blow up one schooner miscarried, it was found possible to cast off the chains holding another. In maneuvering, the *Itasca* went hard aground. Eventually pulled off by the *Pinola*, she found herself in a position to surge upstream through the gap, spin around, and steam down on the boom at full speed. She drove down between two of the hulks, rode high out of the water

before her weight snapped the chains holding them, and left behind her a hole amply wide for the large ships of the fleet. During the hours that the *Itasca* and *Pinola* worked against the boom, the Confederate ironclad *Louisiana* was being towed into place under the guns of Fort St. Philip. She had left New Orleans loaded with workmen, her machinery practically inoperable, an inefficient floating battery (for her gunports were too small) rather than a fighting ship. The Confederate Army commander wanted her moved down nearer the boom where she would attract some of the mortar fire away from the forts, but her captain insisted she should be protected by the forts until her guns and machinery were ready.

By this time Commander Porter hoped that 48 hours of additional bombardment would take care of Fort Jackson, leaving only Fort St. Philip, which was virtually undamaged, for the ships to contend with. These last hours were spent in perfecting preparations. Masts were removed from five gunboats. Most ships daubed mud for camouflage on topsides, faked anchor chains over the midships section, piled sand bags around machinery spaces, readied howitzers in guntubs in the fore and main tops, strung splinter nets, and in some instances painted decks white to assist in handling the guns in darkness. All ships were trimmed by the bow so that, if run aground, they could back off with the help of the four-knot current. The 48-hour bombardment had so little effect that Porter himself became somewhat discouraged. Farragut, unperturbed, made his last tour of the fleet "to know positively," as he said, "that each commander understood my orders for the attack and to see that all was in readiness."[6] At two in the morning of April 24, two red lanterns, the signal to get underway, were hoisted in the mizzen rigging of the *Hartford*.

Farragut had divided the assault fleet into three divisions, originally planning to have two heavy divisions of ships advance together on parallel courses, each concentrating its gunfire on the fort on its side of the river, and a third division of gunboats bring up the rear, presumably in a safe position because of the damage the lead divisions would inflict on the forts. The entire movement was to be sup-

[6] *Official Records*, XVIII, 156.

ported by the mortar boats and Porter's auxiliary craft, which were to close up within range of the forts. This plan was followed except that the narrowness of the opening in the boom required the fleet to proceed in one long column.

The Confederate defenders had noted the placing of certain markers and were expecting the attack. Piles of brush were ready for lighting on the banks of the river to silhouette the Union ships, and fire rafts were prepared to throw them into confusion when under the guns of the forts. That some of the defenders recognized the urgency of the situation is shown by the prophetic answer to the Confederate captain who said that he could not move the *Louisiana* to a position near the boom for another 24 hours, "Tell Captain Mitchell that there will be no tomorrow for New Orleans, unless he immediately takes up the position assigned to him with the *Louisiana*."[7]

The little gunboat *Cayuga* led the way, followed closely by the *Pensacola*, the *Mississippi*, and five more gunboats of the first division. The general battle began as soon as the *Pensacola* passed through the barrier. Porter's mortar shells arched like skyrockets against the dark sky. Both forts opened fire, and the ships replied with broadsides of grape and canister as soon as their guns bore on a target. Moving very deliberately, the *Pensacola* almost stopped opposite Fort St. Philip to deliver two broadsides at close range, close enough so that Union sailors and Confederate soldiers could swear back and forth at each other. The *Mississippi*, paddling leisurely through the smoke of battle so as to maintain her station astern of the *Pensacola*, was dealt a glancing blow by the ram *Manassas* while engaged with Fort St. Philip and was then swept across the river where she threw a broadside at Fort Jackson before drawing out of range upstream.

By this time the second division, *Hartford*, *Brooklyn*, and *Richmond*, was crowding through the boom. The *Hartford* had an exciting encounter with a fire raft off Fort St. Philip. "In trying to avoid it," Farragut wrote, "I ran the ship on shore," and then the Confederate tug *Mosher* "pushed the fire raft on to me and got the ship on fire all along one

side. I thought it was all up with us, but we put it out and got off again and proceeded up the river fighting our way."[8] Shells rolled from the deck of the flagship had destroyed the raft and a single broadside sank the unarmed tug. According to her log, the *Hartford* spent less than half an hour under fire.

Of the large ships, the *Brooklyn* received the greatest damage. She collided with the gunboat *Kineo* of the first division while trying to pass through the boom, but after a struggle both vessels got clear and back on course. Off Fort St. Philip she was rammed by the *Manassas*, which had waited concealed against the shore after the attack on the *Mississippi*. Several of the *Brooklyn's* planks were stove in. A survey after the battle revealed that the ramming came much closer to having fatal results than the ship's crew had realized in the heat of the encounter.

Most of the other ships passed through the gantlet without heavy damage. Most severely shot up was the gunboat *Iroquois*, which blundered into collision with the stationary ironclad *Louisiana* and lost eight killed and 24 wounded before she got on course again. She was the last of the Union ships to pass the forts. Three gunboats had to turn back —the *Itasca*, with a shot through a boiler, and the *Winona* and *Kennebec*, which were fouled in the obstruction at the boom. The entire action between fleet and forts lasted a little over an hour. All of Farragut's ships took hits, but none was sunk.

In the early dawn several sharp ship-to-ship encounters took place above the forts. The *Manassas*, like a submarine stalking a convoy, tried to get in a final blow. But she was discovered by the *Mississippi* and ran herself ashore in trying to avoid the charging old paddlewheeler. The leading Union gunboats, sprinting ahead, made short work of their Confederate opponents. Only the *Governor Moore* put up a real fight. Bearing down on the *Varuna*, she fired through her own bow to rake the Union ship, which was forced ashore and destroyed. Other Union gunboats soon accounted for the *Governor Moore*. All Confederate warships except two which found temporary refuge under the guns of the forts were captured or destroyed, as eventually

[7] Alfred T. Mahan, *The Gulf and Inland Waters* (New York, 1883), 70.

[8] *Official Records*, XVIII, 142.

were the Confederate auxiliary ships that fled to New Orleans.

By afternoon the Union fleet was anchored off Quarantine, preparing to continue up the river to New Orleans the next day. Farragut did not worry about the forts behind him. "I think if you send a flag of truce and demand their surrender, they will do it," he wrote Porter, "for their intercourse with the city is cut off."[9]

Total casualties had been light on both sides: Union, 39 killed and 179 wounded; Confederate, 84 killed and 110 wounded. The Confederacy could find little consolation in those figures; the defense had failed. Only the *Manassas* had made repeated efforts to stop the Union ships. The *Louisiana* could have been of more use anchored in midstream as a navigational hazard. Someone failed to light important beacon fires. The scurrying Confederate gunboats had allowed themselves to be picked off in detail upstream, whereas their only conceivably profitable employment would have been down at the boom as the Union ships were trying to find their way through. The gunners in the forts had generally fired high, for they were not experienced artillerists and no match for the naval gunners of the Union fleet.

The Capture of New Orleans

Only token resistance and the formalities of negotiating surrender intervened between the battle and the occupation of New Orleans by General Butler's troops on May 1, 1862. The Union fleet anchored off the city on the afternoon of April 25, having smothered the Chalmette Battery with a few broadsides from the large ships. Farragut was appalled by the sight before him. Fires raged through all property that might be of value to the Union, including 13,000 bales of cotton. The river was ablaze with the debris of burning ships and stores, and in the midst of it all floated the smoldering hulk of the unfinished ironclad *Mississippi*. Farragut's representatives went ashore through the hysterical mobs with a demand that the city surrender. As soon as General Lovell withdrew his handful of troops to save the city from bombardment by the guns of the fleet,

[9] *Ibid.*

negotiations were opened with the civilian government. These parleys were somewhat protracted by the mayor's insistence that as a civilian official he did not have the authority to make a military surrender. Consequently, Farragut had some difficulty showing the American flag on the city hall, as Gideon Welles had ordered. But with the help of 250 marines and a howitzer, even that was accomplished. Actual Union seizure of the city had to be postponed until the arrival of General Butler's occupation troops.

Down river, Commander Porter worried about the forts and the *Louisiana*. "You will find the forts harder to take now than before, unless their ammunition runs out," he wrote Farragut; adding, "I hope you will open your way down, no matter what it costs."[10] But rumors of the surrender of New Orleans and the fact that General Butler's troops were now entrenched across the levee roads leading from the forts to the city caused the demoralized troops in Fort Jackson to mutiny, leaving the Confederate army commander no choice in the matter. He surrendered on the 28th. When the Confederate naval commander learned of the army's capitulation, he set fire to the *Louisiana*, which drifted out into the stream and exploded, killing a man in Fort St. Philip and almost taking down Porter's ship with it.

Victory in the New Orleans campaign was the greatest triumph, both in its military and in its political consequences, that the Union had won in more than a year of war. Farragut had demonstrated, as so many commanders on both sides had not, what could be accomplished by prompt, vigorous action based on sound judgment. It was he who took advantage of the South's incapacity to meet the threats poised simultaneously, like a classical pincers movement, from north and south. If he had delayed as much as a month, low water and Confederate ironclads could probably have frustrated the best Union effort. Instead, the entire lower Mississippi River was open to Federal warships.

Perhaps the true significance of the fall of New Orleans can be most readily appreciated by its effect on the international situation. Under Napoleon III France had thinly veiled ambitions in the Caribbean area. The Em-

[10] *Official Records*, XVIII, 143.

peror's schemes might prosper if there were a Confederate States of America, friendly and indebted to him. England sat on the fence, but France would recognize the Confederacy as soon as the South gave clear indication that it could maintain its independence from the North. If the Union attack on New Orleans failed, that might be the time for France to act, but when New Orleans fell, French recognition of the Confederacy was indefinitely postponed.

The early Federal conquest of the entire Mississippi Valley and of Mobile, the one major Confederate port of the eastern Gulf Coast open to blockade runners, might well have followed on the heels of the New Orleans campaign. Instead, May and June 1862 saw numerically superior Union forces fritter away almost every opportunity for decisive action. From the point of view of the Blockading Squadron, Mobile was a plum ripe for plucking, its defenses ill-prepared and undermanned. The *Hartford*-class sloops, supported by a division of mortar boats and a small force from Butler's army, would have had little difficulty at that time in capturing the forts guarding the entrance to Mobile Bay and sealing off the blockade runners from the city of Mobile. From the point of view of Lincoln and his cabinet however, clearing the Mississippi had to come first. In truth, both objectives were then attainable. Everything that Farragut's large ships could accomplish on the river in the spring of 1862 could be achieved equally well by his gunboats, leaving the large vessels to operate against Mobile. Once again Union naval power was to be operationally limited to blockade and to those functions which it could perform in support of land power.

Summary

If Kentucky had joined the Southern cause, the Confederacy could have established its first line of defense in the West along the Ohio River. But when Polk occupied Columbus in September 1861, Kentucky declared for the Union and Federal forces crossed the Ohio. As a consequence, the Confederates were obliged to establish a makeshift defense line—the so-called "Northwest Barrier"—from Columbus on the Mississippi to the Cumberland Gap in the Alleghenies. Between these two flank positions the Confederates plugged the obvious invasion routes by occupying and fortifying Bowling Green on the Louisville railroad and building Fort Henry on the Tennessee River and Fort Donelson on the Cumberland River.

In February 1862 Grant's army and Foote's gunboats penetrated the "Northwest Barrier" by capturing the two river forts. These captures not only gave them access to the South via the Tennessee but permitted them to outflank the other Confederate positions on the Barrier. But Halleck refused to permit Grant to exploit his victory; hence the Confederate troops that evacuated Columbus had time to establish themselves strongly a few miles downstream at Island No. 10. However two Federal gunboats, by running past Island No. 10, were able to support a crossing of the Mississippi still farther downstream by Pope's army, which trapped the Confederate forces by cutting their line of communication.

Meanwhile the main Confederate army, under A. S. Johnston, had established a Second Line of Confederate Defense along the railroad from Memphis to Chattanooga, with headquarters at Corinth, Mississippi. The choice both of the defense line of the headquarters was dictated by the railroads, which could bring up supplies from the south, and also shift forces east and west to meet enemy concentrations. As Grant moved southward up the Tennessee toward Corinth, A. S. Johnston decided to advance and strike before Grant's army could be reinforced by Buell's coming from Nashville. The result was the Battle of Shiloh (April 13–15, 1862). Grant was saved when the river boats brought down Buell's troops and artillery, giving him an overwhelming preponderance of strength.

Farragut meanwhile was preparing to break through the Confederate defenses below New Orleans—Forts Jackson and St. Philip on the Mississippi. Early in April he had brought his fleet over the bar into the river. On the 18th, just three days after the Battle of Shiloh, Porter opened mortar fire on the forts. On the 24th, Farragut's fleet by-passed the forts and defeated the Confederate River Defense Fleet. On the 29th, the Federals occupied New Orleans. The Confederate forces that might have stopped Farragut had been sent north to stop Grant.

The Mississippi campaign of 1862 is a classic example of the strategy of the *exterior position* opposed to the strategy of the *interior position*. Federal forces undertook to penetrate Confederate defenses in the Mississippi Valley simultaneously from the north and from the south. Obviously the Confederate forces in between could shift reinforcements as needed directly north or south by river and railroad far faster than the Union forces could shift strength the long way around via the East

Coast. Had the Confederates possessed military power in the Valley anywhere near that possessed by the Union, their interior position would thus have been an immense advantage. But so great was the Federal predominance that the Union forces profited by their exterior position. The Confederates looked to their forts below New Orleans to *hold,* or *contain,* Farragut while their army *struck* Grant at Shiloh. In fact, however, Grant *held* the bulk of Confederate military strength while Farragut *struck* at New Orleans with minimum opposition.

16:

The Mississippi Valley Campaign, II: Vicksburg and After

The Confederate plan to hold a second line of defense between Memphis and Chattanooga along the Memphis and Charleston Railroad—the only direct rail connection in the Confederacy between the Mississippi River and the Atlantic coast—was born of necessity out of the Fort Donelson disaster. Neither the Battle of Shiloh nor the Union occupation of New Orleans had altered the basic strategic pattern. The Federal campaign against the rail junction of Corinth was renewed under the direct command of General Halleck who, dismayed by the fearful bloodletting at Shiloh, felt bound to use his armies with caution. Only after assembling 100,000 men did he resume the advance. Confederate General Beauregard had no more than 50,000 troops with which to delay the Union forces. He had to save his army while the Confederacy rallied its full strength—even at the cost of abandoning Corinth. Brilliantly impeding Halleck by every means short of a major battle, Beauregard capitalized on Halleck's caution to prolong the 20-mile advance for a whole month. When Federal soldiers finally entered Corinth on May 29, 1862, they found the fortifications empty. Beauregard's entire army had slipped south to Tupelo, 60 miles away. In the meantime, Union naval activity on the Mississippi largely depended upon the progress of Halleck's campaign.

After the capture of Island No. 10 in early April 1862, the Union gunboats steamed downriver to lead the Federal attack against the next Confederate strong point. That was Fort Pillow, on the east-bank bluffs of the Mississippi, the sole river fortification between the

Union forces and Memphis. General Pope's 20,000 men landed above the fort but had made little progress before they were ordered to join Halleck in the Corinth campaign. In the absence of strong army support, the Union ironclads took turns guarding mortar boats which were brought down to bombard the Confederate position, for only the high arching trajectory of mortar fire could reach the fort from the river. Such activity had become routine by May 9 when Flag Officer Foote, incapacitated by the wound he had received at Fort Donelson, turned over his command to Captain Charles H. Davis. The very next morning a surprise attack by the rams of the Confederate River Defense Fleet produced a spirited engagement at Plum Point Bend above Fort Pillow. After the Union ironclads *Cincinnati* and *Mound City* were sunk, the attackers withdrew with several of their ships damaged but able to drift downstream to the protection of the fort.

The action was humiliating to the North, even though both sunken gunboats were soon raised and repaired. The enemy had dashed in for a telling blow, taking advantage of Northern laxity, and had escaped from superior forces on which they had inflicted greater damage than they themselves had received. However this Confederate success did not save Fort Pillow. The Federal bombardment was resumed and continued for another three weeks until the Union victory at Corinth gave the Confederates in their outflanked position a dubious choice: either abandon the fort or remain to be captured in it. Explosions heard on the night of June 4 notified the gunboats that the fort was being evacuated. Burning their stores and destroying their precious artillery, the Confederate defenders withdrew.

Captain Davis, his force augmented by four maneuverable rams commanded by Colonel Charles Ellet of the Union Army Engineers, now had an opportunity to avenge the humiliation of Plum Point Bend. His fleet steamed down to Memphis, arriving early on June 6. The townspeople lined the heights along the river to see the show, confident in the eight rams of the Confederate River Defense Fleet, which were formed in a double line before the city. As Davis' five ironclads approached within range, two of Ellet's rams, *Queen of the West* and *Monarch,* darted ahead of the attackers to deliver the first blows. The surprised Confederate vessels, expecting to fight only sluggish gunboats, were thrown into disorder. The *Queen of the West* rammed and sank her first opponent, while the *Monarch,* slipping between two others, saw the Confederate rams crash into each other. Then the big Union gunboats closed in. In an hour's melee four of the River Defense Fleet were sunk and three captured. Only one escaped downstream. None of the Union ships was lost. Flag Officer Davis accepted the surrender of Memphis, reported four large river steamers seized as prizes, and, by 11 o'clock that morning, turned the city over to Colonel Fitch for occupation by a detachment of the Indiana brigade. The Mississippi was now open to Federal gunboats as far south as Vicksburg.

From New Orleans to Vicksburg

Neither Farragut nor the captains of his fleet were at all happy in their irregular advance up the Mississippi during the month following the occupation of New Orleans. If the *Hartford* had been a great sperm whale from the Pacific, she could not have been more out of her element—fighting the mud, snags, driftwood, current, and unending corkscrew bends of the river. "The elements of destruction to the Navy in this river are beyond anything I ever encountered, and if the same destruction continues the whole Navy will be destroyed in twelve months," Farragut lamented. "More anchors have been lost and vessels ruined than I have seen in a lifetime,

and those vessels which do not run into others are themselves run into and crushed in such a manner as to render them unseaworthy . . . their sides are smashed in, their cutwaters entirely broomed up and removed. . . . They all require more or less repairs to their machinery, but the hulls all require docking—ribs broken, plank sheer gone, stems torn off to the wood ends, etc."[1]

Baton Rouge, then a town of 7,000 people, was occupied on May 8, and the ships pressed on. Even with the large Federal sloops in danger of being trapped hundreds of miles above New Orleans when the spring flood waters subsided, Farragut had no choice but to carry out his original orders. He sent the gunboats ahead and followed after them. On May 12 the *Iroquois* accepted the nominal surrender of Natchez, and by May 18 the *Oneida* was off Vicksburg demanding its surrender. The Military Governor there boasted, "Mississippians don't know, and refuse to learn, how to surrender to an enemy."[2] Farragut transferred his flag to the *Kennebec* and was himself off Vicksburg four days later to determine the best course of action. "There is very little use in attacking Vicksburg," he wrote General Butler, "as the guns on the height are so elevated that our fire will not be felt by them." He decided to leave the gunboats to blockade Vicksburg "until the battle of Corinth shall decide its fate,"[3] and returned to New Orleans with the heavy ships.

Instead of waiting for Halleck's army to move, Farragut would willingly have taken prompt action against Mobile. Porter was all for it, but a message from his friend Fox showed how the wind blew in Washington. The Assistant Secretary wrote in a dispatch to Porter on May 17, while Farragut was in fact at Natchez, "Someone has made a most serious blunder in persuading the Flag Officer to go at Mobile instead of obeying his instructions to go up the Mississippi River." He added rather hysterically and on the strength of nothing more than the Plum Point Bend fracas, "Davis has repulsed the iron rams of the

[1] *Official Records of the Union and Confederate Navies in the War of the Rebellion,* Series I, XVIII, 521.
[2] *Ibid.,* 492.
[3] *Ibid.,* 507.

enemy, but they are going at him and if they should be successful, Halleck would have to fall back and we should lose St. Louis, Cairo and everything."[4] The Confederate rams were of wood, not iron, and they made no second try, but Fox's message serves to underscore the official recognition of control of the waterways as *sine qua non* for successful Federal military operations in the Mississippi Valley.

From New Orleans Farragut sent in a full-length report to Secretary Welles, beginning almost wistfully: "I have just arrived here from up the river as high as Vicksburg, at least 300 miles farther than I was ever from sea water before since the days of my childhood."[5] Clearly he considered it quixotic to ascend the river again. Nevertheless, after suggesting to Welles that a monitor would be a more appropriate ship, he obediently set the *Hartford* to shepherding a flock of Porter's mortar boats and a segment of Butler's army north toward Vicksburg.

Midway between Memphis and New Orleans, Vicksburg occupied the naturally strongest point on the river and the only one that was then fortified by the Confederacy. Halleck's 100,000 men were now idle victors at Corinth, 300 miles away, but only 80 miles by rail from Memphis whence steamers could easily transport a large army, its artillery and supplies, to Vicksburg. If 20,000 troops under Grant had been sent down at this time, they would certainly have captured the city. But Halleck was taking no chances—and winning no further victories.

When Farragut arrived for the second time off Vicksburg, the cooperating land forces were still far too weak to attempt a frontal assault. On June 28 he ran past the Vicksburg batteries with eight of his ships, three turning back in the confusion of battle. As Farragut had predicted, fleet fire had little effect on Confederate guns emplaced on the heights.

Davis had come down the river from Memphis without hindrance and at last the inland and the sea-going navies were joined. In vain Farragut wrote Halleck for army reinforcements. The Federal offensive had stalled in its tracks. A year and a week would pass after

[4] Richard S. West, Jr., *The Second Admiral* (New York, 1937), 149.
[5] *Official Records*, XVIII, 519.

Farragut's rendezvous with Davis before the Stars and Stripes flew over Vicksburg.

As President Lincoln with prophetic foresight had told Commander Porter in November, 1861, when they were discussing plans for the capture of New Orleans: ". . . we must have troops enough not only to hold New Orleans, but to proceed at once toward Vicksburg, which is the key to all that country watered by the Mississippi and its tributaries. If the Confederates once fortify the neighboring hills, they will be able to hold that point for an indefinite time, and it will require a large force to dislodge them."

Operations in the Vicksburg Area —Summer, 1862

When three of Farragut's ships failed to follow the *Hartford* around the horseshoe bend of the Mississippi past the guns at Vicksburg, the Admiral's troubles had just begun. Ostensibly of course July 1, 1862 was a day of Union triumph. That was the day when the fresh water and salt water navies joined forces and anchored together above the city. Only a narrow neck of land separated them from the warships and troop transports that remained below. Casualties inflicted during the run past had been very light. General Halleck now informed Farragut that he would be able to send down troops in a few weeks, even though none were available at the moment. The three Union commanders at Vicksburg—Farragut, Davis, and Brigadier General Thomas Williams, whose 3,000 soldiers from Butler's army had been escorted up the river by the navy—agreed that no assault should be attempted until reinforcements arrived from Corinth. In the meantime, to harass Major General Earl Van Dorn and his 15,000 men working on the city's fortifications, four of Davis's mortar boats above Vicksburg supplemented 16 of Porter's below in lobbing their shells into the Confederate positions. Lookouts in the rigging of the *Hartford* reported occasional hits. At the same time the Union Army turned to digging a canal across the narrow neck of land between the two segments of the fleet. A new channel which would by-pass Vicksburg beyond range of the city's guns might even make a direct assault on the Confederate position unnecessary. Neither undertaking progressed very far. The mortar bombardment was no more than started when orders arrived from Secretary Welles transferring Porter and 12 of the mortar boats 2,000 miles to the aid of McClellan in Virginia. The canal diggers, stricken by steaming heat and malaria, soon had over a third of their number on the sick list. The navy's binnacle lists were almost as long. By mid-July the Union position off Vicksburg was clearly becoming untenable. At last Halleck admitted that he could not send an army. Farragut was worried, for his large ships, needed on blockade duty in the Gulf, might be trapped in the river by low water. Action, when it came, was a result of the audacity of a single Confederate ironclad gunboat, the *Arkansas.*

During those critical weeks of June and early July, one of the many Confederate defense projects was completion of the *Arkansas,* which to escape capture at Memphis had been towed to an improvised navy yard at Yazoo City on the Yazoo River north of Vicksburg. The ship was much like the Union ironclads in size, appearance, and armament. In lieu of armor plate, railroad rails covered her casemate. Her engine drove two propellers, but her machinery was entirely inadequate and never dependable. When she was completed in mid-July, the Confederates set in motion a grandiose plan for her to run down the Yazoo and through the Union fleet to Vicksburg, help liberate New Orleans, and eventually join the Confederate defense of Mobile.

On July 15, the very day that the *Arkansas* steamed down the Yazoo, the ironclad *Carondelet,* the wooden gunboat *Tyler,* and the ram *Queen of the West* set out on a reconnaissance up the Yazoo. When the Union ships encountered the Confederate, they turned and ran. What followed, Secretary Welles described as "the most disreputable naval affair of the war."[6] After forcing the *Carondelet* aground and pursuing the others right into the midst of the Union fleet where she received numerous hits, the *Arkansas* steamed at a majestic two knots—her crippled engines could drive her no faster—through the completely sur-

prised Union ships and to temporary safety under the guns of Vicksburg. With "deep mortification," Farragut officially reported, "none of us had steam or could get it up in time to pursue her, but she took the broadside of the whole fleet."[7] Battered though she was, the *Arkansas* now threatened the mortar boats and transports below the city. That night Farragut took his fleet and the ram *Sumter* past Vicksburg in an unsuccessful attempt to sink her. A few days later the ironclad *Essex* and the ram *Queen of the West* participated in an equally unsuccessful daylight attempt. Just at that juncture Farragut received orders giving him permission to withdraw downstream. The ships of the salt water fleet, with the *Essex* and *Sumter* and General William's army (by this time 75 per cent incapacitated by illness), departed with alacrity. Shortly afterwards, Davis took the fresh water navy 300 miles upstream to base at Helena, Arkansas. Thus, by default, 500 miles of the Mississippi were reopened to the Confederacy.

Delighted by this turn of events, General Van Dorn immediately dispatched part of the Vicksburg garrison to join other Confederate troops under Major General John C. Breckenridge in an effort to recapture Baton Rouge. To make a simultaneous attack, as planned, the *Arkansas* cast off her lines at Vicksburg and had steamed within sight of Baton Rouge when her engines broke down. The Confederate army's assault was repulsed, thanks in good part to the *Essex* and two Union gunboats, which fired over the town and into the Confederate ranks as directed by a naval officer who had a clear view of the action from the top of the Louisiana State House. The *Arkansas*' crew worked all that day and night to get their ship back into operation. When the *Essex* led a reinforced Union fleet upstream against her the next day, the *Arkansas* steamed out, but her engines immediately broke down again and she drifted helplessly ashore. Her crew, at last forced to abandon ship, set her afire to prevent capture by the Union flotilla. The *Essex* threw in shells from a safe distance until the *Arkansas* was destroyed by the explosion of her own magazines.

General Williams had been killed in the battle, and the outnumbered Union troops were

---

[6] Charles Lee Lewis, *David Glasgow Farragut: Our First Admiral* (Annapolis, 1943), 123.

[7] *Official Records,* XIX, 4.

soon afterwards withdrawn from Baton Rouge. In the meantime the defeated Confederate forces began to fortify Port Hudson, on the east bank of the Mississippi a few miles upstream from Baton Rouge. Port Hudson's fortifications were intended to stop Union offensives from the south, as Vicksburg had so successfully stopped those from the north.

The Vicksburg— Port Hudson Bastion

As the geographical advantage had favored the North in breaking the first and second lines of Confederate defense, now the advantage shifted to the South. At one time in the geological history of the Mississippi Valley, a long arm of the sea had extended up from the Gulf of Mexico even beyond present-day Cairo, Illinois. The bay thus formed, filled with sediment from many rivers, finally became an alluvial plain, so flat that the Mississippi meandered along in numerous, shifting coils. Wherever the river ricocheted against the foot of the bluffs—the shoreline of the ancient sea— that bounded the plain to east and west, it created what became in the Civil War a natural strongpoint for the Confederate defenders. Columbus, Fort Pillow, Memphis, Vicksburg, Grand Gulf, and Port Hudson were all such natural strongpoints on the east bank. Of these Vicksburg was paramount. (See map page 300.)

Geography left Vicksburg vulnerable to attack only from the firm ground east of, or behind, the city. On the north the Yazoo basin, an elliptically shaped flood plain bounded on the east by the bluffs and on the west by the Mississippi, extended for 200 miles to Memphis. On the south another basin extended from Vicksburg west of the Mississippi all the way to the Gulf, and on the east bank the town of Grand Gulf and the Big Black River covered the city's southern flank. Where the Mississippi made almost a 180-degree turn in front of Vicksburg, the sloping east bank reached its greatest height of 264 feet, the high point of a 30-mile ridge extending north to Haynes' Bluff on the Yazoo and south to Grand Gulf on the Mississippi. During the second half of 1862 the Confederates made this entire ridge part of an integrated system of fortifications and the northern anchor of their defense bastion.

Port Hudson, 150 miles south of Vicksburg, commanded a similar bend of the river from similar heights. Because it was never threatened by forces as powerful as those the Union brought against Vicksburg, its defenses were less fully developed. Port Hudson's importance as a southern anchor for the Confederate defense was not so much in denying the Mississippi to the Federal government as in preserving for the Confederacy its last line of east-west communications via the Red River. The Red River flowed into the Mississippi just above Port Hudson from deep in the Confederacy's southwest. Down it came Confederate meat and grain in vast quantities and European products shipped via Mexico. So long as the Confederacy held this line of communications with the outside world, there persisted the hope that the war could be pursued until foreign intervention or Northern war-weariness brought hostilities to an end. But if either Vicksburg or Port Hudson fell, the Red River would be blocked, and the fall of the remaining strong points must shortly follow. With the Mississippi firmly in Union hands, the "backbone of the rebellion" would be broken.

Failure of the First Attack on Vicksburg

The successful Confederate counterattack under General Braxton Bragg which had penetrated almost as far as Louisville, Kentucky during the summer of 1862 had thoroughly alarmed the Federal government. There was a consequent reshuffling of armies and commanders. Grant's forces holding the Memphis-Corinth line were so reduced in numbers that they had all they could do to maintain their position while awaiting reinforcements through the summer and early fall of 1862. A clash at Iuka, southeast of Corinth, resulted in a concentrating of Confederate forces and gave General Van Dorn hope that he might be able to defeat Grant's divided army in detail and force the Union troops all the way back to Fort Donelson. Van Dorn's attack in October accomplished just the opposite result. The

Confederates lost 5,000 men—casualties and prisoners—and Van Dorn was replaced by the more cautious John C. Pemberton. Grant was at last free to resume the offensive.

Since retiring to Helena after the *Arkansas* fiasco, Flag Officer Davis' gunboats, on the defensive, trying to hold what had previously been gained, had been fighting guerrillas and convoying supplies on the Ohio, Cumberland, Tennessee, and Mississippi rivers. In October the 15 river gunboats were transferred from the Army to the Navy and, as the "Mississippi Squadron," were placed under the command of David Dixon Porter, now back from Virginia. Porter immediately reorganized his force along navy lines, had the older ships repaired and more heavily armed, and began adding new ironclads and "tinclad" patrol craft to the fleet until eventually he had more than 60 vessels of various sorts. Meanwhile he established himself on his flagship, the large river steamer *Black Hawk*, with adequate facilities for administering his command.

In November 1862 Grant at last received permission from Washington to launch an offensive. His main base of supply at this time was at Columbus; his operational base, at Grand Junction; and his advance supply base, at Holly Springs. His army depended for communications on a single rail line joining those points. (See map page 299.) His objective was the major Confederate base at Jackson, the capital of Mississippi, which flanked Vicksburg just as Corinth flanked Memphis. He knew that the Confederate Army, after withdrawing as far as Grenada, was preparing to contest his advance. Grant's plan was to trap the Confederate forces by making a double attack. A combined operation of some 32,000 men under Sherman, supported by Porter, would depart from Memphis by ship for a direct attack on Vicksburg. In the meantime Grant himself would attack Grenada, expecting to fight a holding action which would keep so many Confederate soldiers occupied that Sherman would have no trouble. If the Confederate forces at Grenada retreated to Vicksburg, Grant would pursue and trap them there. If they retreated only to Jackson, he would pursue and be joined by Sherman's troops from Vicksburg. Grant's plan, for all its ostensible

logic, was wrecked by its dependence on an inadequate line of communications.

The Confederate defense plan was perforce flexible and opportunistic. Likelihood of a Federal offensive had caused President Davis to visit both Jackson and Vicksburg in early December. He recognized their weakness and, in attempting to find a remedy, may have committed one of the great blunders of the war. Instead of ordering reinforcements from the secondary Arkansas theater of operations, as advised by General Joseph Johnston, who was now in command of all Confederate forces between the Mississippi and Alleghenies, the Confederate President had 10,000 men transferred to Pemberton from eastern Tennessee. This was just 11 days before the great battle of Stone's River that ended the East Tennessee campaign in Confederate defeat. Even with these reinforcements, Pemberton had strength only for a delaying action. But the winter rains favored the defense as roads turned to mud, and the railroad down which the Confederates retreated, tearing up rails and ties as they went, would require time-consuming repairs before it would be of much use to the Union invaders.

Making excellent use of their interior position and knowledge of the terrain, the Southern generals proceeded to teach Grant some lessons. First, a raid by Forrest's cavalry cut the telegraph and wrecked the rail line between Grant's advancing army and his main base at Columbus. For exactly those 12 days (December 19–30) during which Sherman took his army down-river and attacked Vicksburg, Grant had no communication with the outside world. The fatal blow was struck by Van Dorn with 2,500 men on a cavalry raid around Grant's flank. Catching the 1,500-man guard at Holly Springs completely by surprise, Van Dorn's men destroyed the entire $1,500,000 supply dump. With no logistic support, Grant's army ignominiously retreated 80 miles to Grand Junction, living off the land. Not only did Grant's holding action collapse, but the Confederate regiments that faced him at Grenada were shifted by rail to Vicksburg in time to parry the second Union blow.

Sherman and Porter meanwhile had reached the Vicksburg area via the Mississippi. Porter's

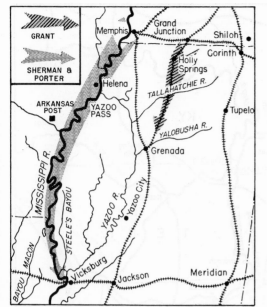

**FIRST UNION ATTACK ON VICKSBURG,
DECEMBER, 1862**

task now was to convoy the transports into the Yazoo and protect them during the debarkation. First however the gunboats had to clear the lower Yazoo of mines, one of which sank the ironclad *Cairo*. The river fleet continued minesweeping until the Yazoo was cleared from its mouth, eight miles above Vicksburg, to Haynes' Bluff, where Confederate batteries controlled the river. The day after Christmas Sherman's troops, virtually unopposed under cover of the gunboats, landed on the flats between the Mississippi and the high ground to the east. By this time Sherman had good reason to suspect that Grant was meeting resistance, but he had no way of learning what actually had happened. He could only proceed on the assumption that the "holding action" was not so unsuccessful as to expose his own Vicksburg attack to certain defeat.

In drenching December rain, the Union forces deployed for assault along the five paths that led through swamplands to the Confederate fortifications on the bluffs. Though Sherman's troops outnumbered the Confederates three to one, the defenders' strongly entrenched position on the heights gave them an immense advantage, for the Union columns, confined to narrow approaches, could not bring their numbers to bear on a broad front. In the Battle of Chickasaw Bluffs on the 29th, every Union attempt to storm the well-placed Confederate fortifications crumpled under massed artillery and rifle fire. At the end of the day Sherman had lost 2,000 men; the Confederates, only 187.

Sherman nevertheless planned a second attack for the new year. This time it was to be a night assault by 10,000 troops farther up the Yazoo, where the Confederate batteries were within range of the heavy guns of Porter's fleet. Dense fog delayed the troop-laden gunboats so long that only a suicidal daylight attack would have been possible. By this time it was clearly evident to both Sherman and Porter that Grant's plans had gone awry and that in view of the rising river waters and the continuous rain, the only sensible choice was to withdraw.

In their first attempt to capture Vicksburg, Grant, Sherman, and Porter thus tasted the humiliation of defeat by numerically inferior forces.

The Winter Campaign Against Vicksburg

Mud, politics, and common sense finally compelled Grant to transfer his base of operations to the Mississippi in the winter of 1862–63. The heavy rains of an unusually wet season turned all roads into quagmires. If the Union Army was to advance in strength with artillery support, it must be by ship. After the failure of the Chickasaw Bluffs attack, Admiral Porter and General Sherman had cooperated in a secondary, face-saving operation against Arkansas Post, where taking 5,000 Confederate prisoners had cost a thousand Federal casualties. This undertaking was commanded by General John A. McClernand, an Illinois politician who had talked President Lincoln into allowing him to raise troops in Illinois for an independent expedition against Vicksburg. To his everlasting credit, Halleck thwarted this threat to a unified command; the upshot was that McClernand took a position over Sherman but subordinate to Grant. The Arkansas Post victory removed a nuisance from the Union flank but did not justify a general diversion of about

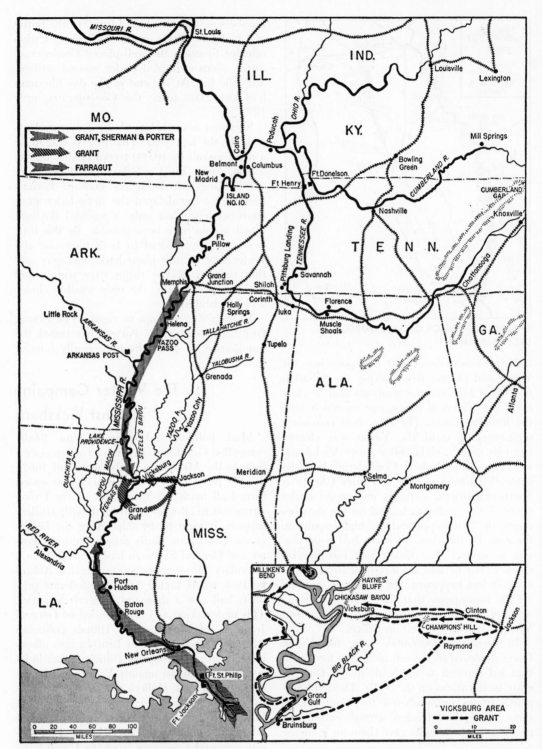

THE MISSISSIPPI VALLEY CAMPAIGN, 1863

30,000 men to a trans-Mississippi campaign. Grant ordered an end to that "wild goose chase," as he correctly called it, and by the end of January took command on the Mississippi himself as the only way of controlling both McClernand and the Vicksburg campaign. He established his combined army on the west bank at Milliken's Bend just above Vicksburg with his rear base at Memphis 400 miles upstream.

Too strong to be stormed, the Vicksburg defenses had to be flanked. The problem was: how? High water made it impossible to march an army past Vicksburg through the cypress swamps and flooded underbrush of the west shore, and even supposing the troops could get past, no line of communications could be maintained on the river under Vicksburg's guns. Grant seems to have believed that nothing decisive could be accomplished until the land again became dry enough for marching, but he was willing to try any likely alternatives that would keep his forces occupied and satisfy the impatience of his superiors. Actually, four ingenious schemes were undertaken during the winter of 1862–63, and these together constitute the second campaign against Vicksburg.

(1) *Grant's "Big Ditch."* While Farragut and Davis dallied above Vicksburg in July 1862, General Williams' troops had actually made a good beginning on their canal across the finger of land pointing towards the Confederate stronghold. The falling level of the Mississippi and the Federal government's opinion that the fate of Vicksburg was going to be settled by a great Union victory under Halleck in the vicinity of Corinth made completion of the canal less important than saving the lives of the malaria-infected soldiers. Now, in the winter of 1863, this project was revived, for it was remembered that a canal had succeeded at Island No. 10. The new ditch was to be a little over a mile long, 60 feet wide, and nine feet deep. The Northern press played up the progress the Army Engineers were making, trumpeting great expectations. By March 8 the goal was almost reached and flood waters were sweeping down the Mississippi to break through the last barrier. But instead of gouging out the last of the canal, the tumultuous waters flooded the peninsula, drowned horses and mules, swept away tents,

destroyed machinery, made men flee for their lives to high ground, and plugged with silt and debris what canal there had been. The opponents of the canal who from the first had considered it an unholy interference with nature felt that their opinion had been vindicated. The project was abandoned.

(2) *Lake Providence and the Tensas Basin.* There was another possible way around Vicksburg. By cutting through miles of cypress swamp a route 400 miles long could be constructed from Lake Providence, on the west bank of the Mississippi about 75 miles north of Vicksburg, via the Bayou Baxter cypress swamp to Bayou Macon, then down the Macon, Tensas, and Ouachita rivers to the Red, and finally down the Red River to the Mississippi. Presumably the route could be used for Grant's troops to coordinate with Banks' in the capture of Port Hudson, which would in turn become the base for an attack from the south against Vicksburg. Union troops hacked away for two months at this nightmarish project before Grant withdrew them to take part in his spring offensive.

(3) *The Yazoo Pass Expedition.* A more promising possibility for a joint expedition consisted of opening a route that would outflank Haynes' Bluff, the northern point of the Vicksburg outer defense line. Just south of Helena, Arkansas and convenient to the Memphis base lay Yazoo Pass running from the Mississippi to the tributaries of the Yazoo River. Some steamboats had regularly taken the route until it was plugged by a flood-control levee in 1853. Shortly after Grant established his headquarters at Milliken's Bend, Porter broached the subject of this 700-mile outflanking expedition and received the General's approval. The levee was blasted open and the waters of the Mississippi poured through. Two ironclads, six "tinclads," and two rams led the way. They were supported by 4,500 Union troops embarked in 13 transports. The alert Confederates had felled huge trees across the channel, some as much as four feet in diameter and reaching from bank to bank. In the two weeks it took the expedition to hack its way through the Pass, a combination of narrow channels, overhanging trees, cypress stumps, and debris, abetted by Confederate sharpshooters, was unable to stop the

slow progress of the Union fleet. At the end of a month's struggle the ships were approaching the final bend of the Tallahatchie where it joins the Yalobusha to form the Yazoo. There the desperate Confederate defenders were in the process of throwing up an earthwork and cotton-bale fortification, Fort Pemberton, armed with two heavy guns and supported by infantry. Occupying a flooded peninsula, the fort could not be attacked by anything short of amphibious infantry or ships painfully restricted by the narrow, tortuous channel. This was the "roadblock" that stopped the Union advance. During repeated attacks made over a period of several weeks, each ironclad gunboat was severely damaged. Since the Navy's gunboats failed to silence the fort and the Army was unable to stage an attack over the flooded countryside, each service found fault with the other. Reinforcements were brought up, but by then the Union leaders had become more interested in another alternative. On April 10 the entire expedition was back in the Mississippi with nothing to show for the two months' effort.

(4) *The Steele's Bayou Fiasco.* At the very time that the Union forces were attempting to batter down Fort Pemberton, Admiral Porter himself had launched a final expedition aimed at opening a route from the Mississippi to a point on the Yazoo between Yazoo City and Haynes' Bluff. If successful, this attack would place the navigable, upper stretches of the Yazoo in Federal hands, bring about the abandonment of Yazoo City (and, of course, of Fort Pemberton, which was in essence a northern outpost of the Yazoo City defenses), and secure a good advanced base in Yazoo City for outflanking Vicksburg from the north. The route was even narrower and more tortuous than that of the Yazoo Pass. Porter was able to push five of the old Eads ironclads through the forest of cypress and willows, but the lighter warships and transports did not have power and weight enough to fight their way through the willow-choked channel. Overhanging branches knocked off smokestacks, cypress trees had to be pulled up by their roots, and the willows had to be chopped down one by one. Finally the flotilla ground to a halt within sight of clear water but in a tangle of felled trees. Confederate sharpshooters kept

the Union crews behind the protection of the casemates, and the ironclads, walled in by the levee on either side, found their big guns useless. When Southern slaves were forced to fell trees behind the gunboats, the expedition stood on the brink of disaster. Only the prompt arrival of the Army saved the ships. General Sherman himself accompanied the major relieving force, its way lighted by candles in a fantastic night march. Porter's feelings of relief found expression in his official report: "I do not know when I felt more pleased to see that gallant officer. . . ."[8] As it was, it took 11 days for the ironclads to extricate themselves. The channel was so narrow that the ships could not be turned around. Rudders were unshipped and, "rebounding from tree to tree,"[9] the ironclads reached the Mississippi again on March 27.

Porter was thoroughly discouraged. "With the end of this expedition ends all my hopes of getting into Vicksburg in this direction. . . . There is but one thing now to be done, and that is to start an army of 150,000 men from Memphis, via Grenada, and let them go supplied with everything required to take Vicksburg."[10]

Grant, influenced by recent developments on the Mississippi and the political temperature in Washington, had other and more daring ideas. Advance through the Yazoo basin was hopeless, as Porter said, but returning to Memphis would look like defeat, and an attack via Grenada to be successful would require protecting a long line of communications and rebuilding a railroad line as the army advanced. Grant knew what that meant only too well from his bitter experience of the past December. Yet he had to get behind Vicksburg. If he could not do it from the north, he would have to do it from the south.

The Winter's Naval Activity
on the Mississippi

General Banks had replaced General Butler in New Orleans at the end of 1862. More

[8] *Official Records,* XXIV, 477.
[9] Alfred Thayer Mahan, *The Gulf and Inland Waters* (New York, 1883), 150.
[10] *Official Records,* XXIV, 479.

troops had arrived. The grand strategy now called for a joint expedition under Banks and Farragut to reduce Port Hudson, but neither the Army nor the Navy was ready. Banks' position was very complex and entirely thankless. He had earned the nickname of "Dancing Master" through his efforts to win over the influential citizens of the occupied city. He was plagued by speculators with political backing who demanded that the Army make it possible for them to get out the upland cotton. He was gravely concerned for the safety of New Orleans, threatened more than once by Confederate armies in the general vicinity. His strength was thus largely absorbed by a multitude of tasks that had little to do with getting on with the war.

For Farragut too the year began badly. On New Year's Day two Confederate cotton-armored steamers with a single gun apiece captured the gunboat *Harriet Lane* and either seized or drove away the other Union ships blockading Galveston, Texas. In reporting to Welles, the Admiral admitted that it would be difficult "to conceive a more pusillanimous surrender of a vessel to an enemy already in our power. . . ."[11] Three weeks later the Confederates also opened the blockade off Sabine Pass, when two of their cotton-clad gunboats took advantage of a calm day to capture the two Union sailing ships stationed there. All efforts to re-establish the blockade at those points failed.

On the Mississippi, the most important enterprise either Porter or Farragut could undertake was to dispute control of the river between Vicksburg and Port Hudson and raid the South's Red River source of supply. Porter tried it first.

On February 1, Colonel Charles Ellet received orders to run the ram *Queen of the West* past the Vicksburg batteries, sink the steamer *Vicksburg* moored there, and then raid the Red River commerce. The Union ram was hit repeatedly by solid shot and shell but got by the city in broad daylight on the morning of the 2nd without a single casualty. En route she damaged but did not sink the *Vicksburg*. Within the next few days the *Queen of the West* captured several valuable prizes, including a steamer with 110,000 pounds of

pork and 500 hogs and another with 20 barrels of molasses, 10 hogsheads of sugar, and 30,000 pounds of flour. Both vessels had been bound with their provisions for the Confederate Army at Port Hudson.

Porter sent the new ironclad *Indianola* past Vicksburg on the night of February 13–14 to join Ellet. That impetuous 19-year-old colonel had been raising havoc up the Red River, but the *Queen of the West* grounded and was captured on the very day that the *Indianola* steamed down to join her. Then the Confederates completely turned the tables. Using the *Queen of the West* to head a flotilla, they pursued the *Indianola* and caught up with her just below Vicksburg, where she was defeated, run aground, and captured. The last, if wry, laugh was Porter's. Because his other ironclads were bulldozing the willows and cypress of the Yazoo Basin or patrolling up river, the *Indianola* and *Queen of the West* in Confederate hands posed a real danger. So the Admiral had a coal barge equipped with barrel-pile smokestacks and log guns to look like a monitor and floated her past Vicksburg at night. She grounded below the city on the west bank but was pushed back into the stream by the Union troops stationed there. News of her coming caused the apprehensive captors of the *Indianola* to blow up their stranded prize, and the *Queen of the West* retreated to the Louisiana waterways where she was eventually sunk by Farragut's gunboats.

The goings-on around Vicksburg struck Farragut as so much tomfoolery. If Porter intended to hold his ironclads for such time-wasting operations as the abortive Steele's Bayou expedition, Farragut considered it was up to him to regain control of the Mississippi. When he learned of the capture of the *Queen of the West* and the *Indianola,* he lost all patience. "I am all ready to make an attack on or run the batteries at Port Hudson," he wrote Secretary Welles, "so as to form a junction with the army and navy above Vicksburg."[12] The fact that Banks was ready to stage no more than a diversionary attack did not stop him. "The time has come," said Farragut, "there can be no more delay. I must go—army or no army."[13]

[11] *Ibid.*, XIX, 440.

[12] *Ibid.*, 644.
[13] Lewis, *Farragut: Our First Admiral*, 168.

Once again Farragut directed the detailed preparations for taking a fleet past fortifications. This time he had the *Hartford, Richmond, Monongahela,* and *Mississippi,* with the gunboats *Albatross, Genessee,* and *Kineo.* The large ships were to proceed in that order past Port Hudson, each of the screw-sloops with a gunboat lashed to her port quarter and the side-wheeler *Mississippi* bringing up the rear. A flotilla of mortar boats and the ironclad *Essex* were assigned to shell the fortifications while the fleet steamed by. "I expect all to go by who are able," Farragut wrote in his general order to his fleet, "and I think the best protection against the enemy's fire is a well-directed fire from our own guns—shell and shrapnel at a distance and grape when within 400 or 500 yards."[14]

Leading the way in the *Hartford* on the dark, quiet night of March 14, Farragut was probably in the best command position to accomplish his difficult undertaking. Besides a score of heavy Confederate guns and half again as many field pieces, he had to contend with the five-knot current, a 150-degree bend in the river, and the ingenuity of the defenders, who spotted the ships with locomotive headlights from the east bank and silhouetted them against huge bonfires on the west bank.

While making the sharp turn under Port Hudson's batteries, the *Hartford* was thrown against the shore, but with the aid of the *Albatross* alongside, she returned to the channel and proceeded upstream. Not another ship got past. The *Richmond* lost power when her steam safety valves were opened by a freak hit, and the *Monongahela* went off course in the smoke and spent 25 minutes aground under fire. Both screw-sloops managed to escape downstream with the help of their escorts. The *Mississippi* however went aground on the west bank directly opposite the Confederate batteries. Here as she caught fire from enemy shells her crew abandoned ship. The next morning she floated free, blew up, and sank.

Although only two of his vessels had succeeded in running the gantlet, Farragut set about determinedly patrolling the river between Vicksburg and Port Hudson so as to deny Red River supplies to both Confederate

[14] *Official Records,* XIX, 669.

strong points. Meanwhile Grant was completing preparations for his spring offensive.

The Capture of Vicksburg and Port Hudson

In early April 1863, the falling level of the Mississippi finally made an overland route down the west bank available to the Union forces, and Grant began marching his army south. His plan was to cross the river, capture Grand Gulf, the southern outpost of the Vicksburg defenses, send 20,000 troops downstream to assist Banks in capturing Port Hudson, and then use the combined armies in the eventual overwhelming of Vicksburg. He expected Porter to run the ironclads past Vicksburg to support his crossing with their heavy guns.

On the night of April 16 the Union fleet got under way. Flares and roaring bonfires lighted up the Federal ships for the Confederate gunners, and the vagaries of the current threw each of the larger ships into at least one 360-degree turn while passing the city. Remarkably enough, not a single Union sailor was killed and not one ironclad was critically damaged. Of the three supply-laden transports, one was sunk. A few nights later additional supply ships ran past Vicksburg to join the Union forces.

When prolonged bombardment from the ironclads failed to knock out the batteries at Grand Gulf, Grant and Porter shifted army and ships south and staged a practically unopposed crossing at Bruinsberg, six miles farther downstream. At the same time, to divert Confederate attention, Sherman staged a mock landing near Haynes' Bluff at the opposite end of the Confederate defenses just above Vicksburg. Sherman put on such a realistic show that the Confederates thought that his was the main thrust and Grant's the diversionary move.

Thus were initiated the most brilliant operations of Grant's career. By his success in moving his army to the east bank of the Mississippi he acquired the initiative, and did not relinquish it until he had captured Vicksburg. Moving first on Port Gibson, where the Bruinsberg-Vicksburg and Grand Gulf-Jackson roads converged, the Union van on May 1 defeated a small Confederate force and thereby made Grand Gulf untenable. When the Union ships returned to Grand Gulf, they found it already evacuated, and Grant's army marched in from the east on May 3.

Grant had originally planned to move a part of his force south at this time, cooperating with Banks against Port Hudson. But Banks was not ready. Although Grant's army of 45,000 (including Sherman's men) was confronted with Confederate forces in Mississippi numbering more than 65,000, Grant elected to keep the offensive. The essence of his strategy was to concentrate all his force against segments of the enemy one at a time.

Pemberton with 45,000 men was in the Vicksburg perimeter. Johnston was assembling a force of 20,000 at Jackson. If Grant moved east against Johnston, Pemberton would sever his line of communications from Grand Gulf. On the other hand, if Grant moved north against Pemberton, Johnston could come in behind him. But the Union cavalry commander, Colonel Benjamin H. Grierson, had already been dispatched with a thousand men on a 600-mile raid through Mississippi: between April 17 and May 2 he had destroyed 60 miles of telegraph lines, cut three railroads, and disrupted Johnston's communications from the north, east, and south. Disregarding the cautious advice of his principal subordinates, Grant cut loose from his base on the river and marched on Jackson.

Grant brushed aside a small Confederate force at Raymond, and struck directly at Johnston's little army in the state capital, driving the Confederates out. In the meantime Pemberton was expending the energy of his troops in grim determination to cut the nonexistent line of communications between Grant and the Mississippi River. Johnston, vainly attempting to unite the divided Confederate forces, ordered Pemberton to join him at Clinton, northwest of Jackson. He was too late. Grant had already turned west toward Vicksburg, and on May 16 intercepted and routed 18,000 of Pemberton's troops at Champion's Hill. Continuing in hot pursuit, Grant on the following day brought to bay a 5,000-man Confederate force, smashing it and capturing a third of the men. Johnston was by now frantically ordering Pem-

berton to abandon Vicksburg. But Sherman's corps surged northwest to engulf Haynes' Bluff from the rear, and to compel the evacuation of all defenses along the Yazoo north of Vicksburg. Firing from the gunboats on the river, the Union sailors watched Sherman's cavalry chasing the enemy from Chickasaw Bluffs, where his men had suffered defeat five months earlier. Pemberton and his decimated army were surrounded in Vicksburg. Grant's hungry men could once more be supplied from the fleet.

With supporting fire from the gunboats, Grant tried to storm Vicksburg but was repulsed. The Union force entrenched for a protracted siege. Time was on Grant's side: a steady stream of reinforcements poured into his camp; the steady bombardment from land artillery and the gunboats in the river was reducing Vicksburg to rubble. Cut off from supplies, the garrison was ultimately bound to be starved out.

After six weeks of siege, the end came. On July 4, 1863 Pemberton surrendered; his 37,000 men marched out, stacked their arms, and departed on parole. Falling on the day following the defeat of Lee's army at Gettysburg, the capture of Vicksburg shares with it a climactic position in the history of the Civil War.

Grant gave generous credit to the Navy for its vital role in the campaign. For not only did the Union ships maintain the Army's single line of communications—the Mississippi River between Cairo and Vicksburg—at the end of which the army was suspended like a Federal bucket in a Confederate well, but the Navy by its control of the river cut Pemberton off from reinforcement from, or escape to, the west. Operating at once as mobile heavy artillery and troop ferries, the gunboats ranged over the whole navigable waterway system in the theater of operations, destroying Confederate supplies, supporting Union garrisons under attack, and cutting off all enemy water-borne traffic.

Meanwhile Farragut's squadron had been performing similar services downstream. Urged on and closely supported by the Admiral, General Banks began the long-postponed offensive against Port Hudson in mid-May of 1863. An assault on May 27 failed, and the pattern of bombardment and siege began. The Confederate garrison was still holding out when news of the fall of Vicksburg reached them, convincing them that protracting the struggle no longer conferred a military advantage. On July 8 they surrendered.

The river was clear at last to merchant shipping from the Northwest and Ohio Valley. The Confederacy was split, in effect extending the "Anaconda" from the Gulf to Cairo. The Union's right flank was secured from any major enfilading threat from the west. The sweeping right wing offensive that was to carry Sherman's troops through Atlanta to the sea to cut off the retreat of Lee's army in 1865 was now a strategic possibility.

The Red River Campaign

After the fall of Vicksburg and Port Hudson, the next logical objective for joint army-navy operations was certainly Mobile. Both Grant and Farragut favored an expedition whereby the armies of Banks and Grant, with the support of Farragut's squadron, would invest the last remaining Confederate port on the Gulf. The Gulf blockade would thus be completed, and the Union forces could then advance north to trap the Confederate army being driven down from central Tennessee. But instead Grant was obliged to give his personal direction to the fighting at Chattanooga, and Banks became involved in strategically eccentric operations in Texas.

Although from a purely military point of view campaigning west of the Mississippi was a needless dissipation of Union forces, there were reasons for it. The war was being fought to restore the authority of the Federal government; hence it was going to be necessary ultimately to occupy all Confederate territory. Furthermore, military successes in Texas could cut off the traffic in foreign goods that reached the Confederacy via Mexico. The Union government was also aroused by the implications of French activity south of the border. Napoleon III had permitted the use of French troops to support the Austrian Archduke Maximilian's intervention in Mexican affairs. It was believed that the French emperor favored an independent buffer state between Mexico and the United States. If the Confederacy could

not maintain its independence, then perhaps Texas could be reconstituted an independent republic. Successful Union occupation of positions in Texas might forestall serious postwar difficulties. Halleck accordingly ordered Banks to try.

Banks' first effort was a badly executed amphibious attempt against Sabine on the Louisiana-Texas boundary. This was an ignominious failure. Next, Banks with naval support occupied Brazos Island at the mouth of the Rio Grande and moved inland to capture Brownsville. The expedition then leapfrogged back up the coast with various minor triumphs until it reached Galveston. When Banks requested additional forces to reduce the Confederate defenses there, Halleck demurred.

For some time Northern cotton manufacturers had been exerting heavy pressure on the Union government to make it possible to obtain a greater supply of Southern cotton. Thousands of bales might be procured in the valley of the Red River, which was navigable from the Mississippi northwest across Louisiana to Shreveport—in an area where there were reputedly many Northern sympathizers. Halleck suggested that Banks abandon the Galveston operation and make Shreveport the primary military objective of a campaign up the Red River. If Banks cared to enter Texas via Shreveport, he could have the support of Major General Frederick Steele's Arkansas army and the loan of a detachment from Sherman's force to assist him. So the new year found Banks back in New Orleans, where he was as much occupied by making arrangements for the inauguration of civil government in Louisiana in March as by planning the Red River campaign.

Banks' army was to march overland to rendezvous at Alexandria, Louisiana on March 17, 1864 with Sherman's 10,000 men under Brigadier General A. J. Smith, who would come up the Red River with Porter and the gunboats. The combined force would then advance 350 miles on Shreveport from the south via the river while Steele's army would leave Little Rock to descend on Shreveport from the north. Since Smith's corps was on loan for only the 30-day period when the water in the river would be high enough for the gunboats, the expedition had to be executed swiftly.

The campaign got off to an uneven start. Only Admiral Porter and General Smith carried out their assignments on schedule. With 18 gunboats, including the *Essex*, the *Benton*, and the four remaining Eads ironclads, Porter had waited off the mouth of the Red River until Smith's transports arrived on March 11; then the joint expedition ascended the river to Alexandria in five days. Smith's corps quickly captured Fort de Russy, the only prepared Confederate position between the mouth of the river and Alexandria; the Union Navy swept aside obstructions in the river and made raids up the navigable tributaries. By contrast, Banks' army started late, marched slowly, and did not reach Alexandria until the end of the month.

The progress of the combined force was greatly retarded by unseasonably low water in the river, which necessitated dragging the larger ships over the rapids at Alexandria, transshipping supplies from heavier transports below the "falls" to lighter transports above, and leaving behind a sizable garrison to safeguard the supply line.

Marching overland from Alexandria, the Union army was deprived of the heavy artillery support of the gunboats when Banks selected a road well back from the river as his route of advance. Encumbered by an extensive baggage train and poorly deployed in a long column that wound along the road through dense woods, the Federal forces had covered half the distance to Shreveport before running into heavy Confederate resistance in the vicinity of Pleasant Hill on April 8. At that time Porter was working up the river with some of the lighter gunboats and part of Smith's corps. By April 10 he had reached Springfield Landing, two-thirds of the way to Shreveport, where the river was so narrow that the Confederates had succeeded in blocking it by sinking a ship athwart the channel from one shore to the other. News then reached Porter that Banks' army was in retreat. The troops with him were ordered to return down river at once.

Blame for the Union rout that ensued rests unequivocally on Banks. Although the Confederate attack at Pleasant Hill had thrown the poorly organized Union column into confusion, a second Confederate attack the next day failed completely. For reasons best known to himself, Banks decided to retreat. Skilfully harassed by

the Confederates under Major General Richard Taylor, the Union forces made an ignominious withdrawal to Alexandria, burning and pillaging as they went. Porter was in a particularly precarious position. The water was falling, transports and gunboats were repeatedly grounding, and Confederate troops were severely harassing the ships. The *Eastport* and several smaller vessels were lost with heavy casualties.

By the end of April the entire expedition was back in Alexandria, where the Union Navy was faced with disaster. Instead of the normal 12 feet of water over the rapids at that time of year, there was little more than three feet. Ten gunboats (including the Eads ironclads drawing seven feet of water) and two tugs were trapped. Porter wrote despondently to Secretary Welles, urging a major relief expedition and recommending that command of the army be turned over to General Smith. He had neither hope nor expectation of getting his vessels out and no prospect except the destruction of the best part of the Mississippi Squadron. But later he was able to write: "There seems to have been an especial Providence looking out for us, in providing a man equal to the emergency. Lieutenant Colonel Joseph Bailey, acting engineer of the Nineteenth Army Corps, proposed a plan of building a series of dams across the rocks at the falls and raising the water high enough to let the vessels pass over. This proposition looked like madness, and the best engineers ridiculed it, but Colonel Bailey was so sanguine of success that I requested General Banks to have it done, and he entered heartily in the work."[15]

Bailey, who had had experience with log dams in his native Wisconsin, knew what he was doing. Valiantly assisted by a regiment of "down Maine" lumbermen who happened to be among the troops, he constructed his dam of trees, their trunks parallel to the current, and large log cribs. He weighted and filled in this skeletal structure with any material available, even the machinery of a nearby sugar mill. Under his direction 3,000 men in eight days built a structure that raised the water level high enough for ships to get through. Then the dam gave way in one section. Several of the lighter craft managed to run down

[15] *Official Records*, XXVI, 130.

in the rush of water. Next, Bailey constructed wing dams at the upper falls within three days, thus creating a total rise in the river level of over six feet and finally making it possible for the entire lightened fleet to pass through the gap. Backwater from the Mississippi had filled the lower Red River sufficiently to enable the ironclads to make good their escape.

That dramatic episode marked both the end of the Red River expedition and the last major campaign of the Mississippi River Squadron. By midsummer Porter was transferred to more important duty on the East Coast. The Mississippi Squadron went on patrolling the rivers and keeping them open for the support of the armies. The many spirited minor engagements fought between gunboats and Confederate troops or guerrillas have little historic significance. The war was obviously entering its final stages, and any threat from the outside, French or otherwise, could be best answered after termination of the war between the North and the South.

Summary

The drama of the army campaigns in the East has fostered an underestimation of the total significance of the fighting in the West. Whereas the operations of the Federal Army of the Potomac were largely restricted to north-ern Virginia, the armies of Halleck and Grant maneuvered over many thousands of square miles, the fleets of Porter and Farragut over hundreds of miles of rivers. Whereas the strategy of the Federal campaigns in Virginia was essentially "on to Richmond" and nothing more, the strategy of the Union armies and amphibious forces in the West involved a number of sub-strategies, each successively appropriate to the evolving military situation.

The ultimate aim of the Federal campaigns in the West was of course to win control of the Mississippi River and its navigable tributaries—thereby at the same time securing water communications to and from the north central states and also splitting off Texas, Arkansas, and Louisiana from the rest of the Confederacy. By sweeping the rivers of Confederate vessels, and by holding the dominating shore positions—Port Hudson, Vicksburg, Memphis, Columbus, and other, less strategic, points—the Union could project thousands of miles inland the constrictions of the blockade that was choking the life out of the Confederacy.

Federal operations to capture the Mississippi Valley, begun early in 1862, concluded in mid-1863 with the capture of Vicksburg and Port Hudson. The following table shows concurrent operations of Union forces coming down from the north and up from the south and also major military events in the Virginia area.

1862	MISSISSIPPI VALLEY		EAST
	NORTH	SOUTH	
February	6—Ft. Henry captured 15—Ft. Donelson captured		
March			8-9—Battle of Hampton Roads
April	4—Island No. 10 bypassed 13-15—Battle of Shiloh	24—Farragut bypasses Fts. Jackson and St. Philip 29—New Orleans occupied	
May	29—Federal forces take Corinth		31—Battle of Seven Pines (Peninsular Campaign)

1862	MISSISSIPPI VALLEY		EAST
	NORTH	SOUTH	
June	4—Ft. Pillow captured 6—Memphis occupied 28—Farragut runs past Vicksburg		
July	1—Farragut and Davis meet above Vicksburg 15—*Arkansas* runs through the Union river fleets		
August			30—Second Battle of Bull Run
Sept.			17—Battle of Antietam
Dec.			12—Battle of Fredericksburg
	29—Battle of Chickasaw Bluffs		
1863			
January	11—Capture of Arkansas Post		
March	Failure of Yazoo Pass and Steele's Bayou expeditions. Destruction of Grant's "Big Ditch."	14—Farragut runs past Port Hudson	
April	30—Grant's army crosses Mississippi at Bruinsberg		
May			1-3—Battle of Chancellorsville
	14—Battle of Champion's Hill		
July			1-3—Battle of Gettysburg
	4—Fall of Vicksburg		
		8—Port Hudson captured	

When the heavily reinforced Army of the Tennessee obliged Beauregard to abandon Corinth in late May 1862, the Federal gunboats under Davis moved down the Mississippi, capturing Fort Pillow and defeating the Confederate River Defense Fleet at Memphis. There now remained only one fortified Confederate position on the Mississippi—the city of Vicksburg, which Lincoln called "the key to all that country watered by the Mississippi and its tributaries."

In late June, Farragut, coming up from New Orleans, bombarded the Vicksburg batteries while running his fleet past the city. This fruitless attack merely demonstrated that a position so elevated and so strongly fortified as Vicksburg could not be captured by fleet action alone. On July 1, Farragut temporarily joined forces with Davis's gunboat squadron above Vicksburg, but by now it was generally accepted that an attack on Vicksburg, to be successful, would have to be a major joint army-navy operation. In 1862 and again in 1863 Grant, who had replaced Halleck in command of the Army of the Tennessee, attacked the Confederate river stronghold. In both operations he had the cooperation of the Federal river gunboats, now under the command of Porter.

The first joint operation against Vicksburg (December 1862) was planned to achieve concentration through a *double envelopment* or *pincers movement*. Grant, with 40,000 troops, would initially be the *holding* element. He would march down the high ground east of the Yazoo River and attack the Confederate army at Grenada. While the main Confederate force was thus contained, Sherman with 32,000 troops, escorted down the Mississippi by Porter's gunboats, would attack Vicksburg from the river with naval support.

Grant's plan, ostensibly sound, depended upon the closest coordination between the two arms of his pincers. But the Confederates, making excellent use of their interior position and their knowledge of the terrain, rendered coordination impossible by destroying Grant's communications—*of both sorts*. Striking in his rear, they cut off his supplies by destroying his supply dump and wrecking the railroad line along which he was advancing. They disrupted his means of communicating by cutting the telegraph line behind him. Without logistic support, Grant's army was obliged to retreat, living off the land. Without telegraph, Grant could not warn Sherman. The Confederates thus removed one potential Union menace and set up the other for defeat. With one arm of the Federal pincers turned back, the Confederate army at Grenada shifted by rail to reinforce Vicksburg in time to turn back the other arm at Chickasaw Bluffs.

The humiliation of his defeat taught Grant that (1) he had better limit his attack to a single main line of advance, (2) that he could not depend upon maintaining overland communications, and (3) that Vicksburg was too strong to be taken from the river front—somehow he would have to get his army onto the high ground behind the city.

During the winter of 1862–63, Grant and Porter undertook four schemes for getting behind Vicksburg. Two of these were designed to carry the army to the *south* of the city—by digging a canal across the peninsula opposite Vicksburg, or by cutting through the swamps to the rivers that flowed into the southern Mississippi from the west. The other two schemes were designed to carry the army across the Yazoo basin to the high ground *north* of Vicksburg. All failed.

In April 1863, the receding waters of the Mississippi permitted Grant to march his army down the west bank of the river to a point south of Vicksburg. Porter ran his squadron and some army transports past the Vicksburg batteries and ferried the troops across, while Sherman held Confederate forces at Vicksburg with a realistic mock landing north of the city. Grant now cut loose from his communications and, living off the land, advanced rapidly eastward into the state of Mississippi. At the same time, he sent his cavalry in a 600-mile circuit, cutting telegraph lines and railroads used by the Confederates. Grant meanwhile, making use of his superior mobility, placed his army between those of Johnston and Pemberton. Using the interior position thus attained, he defeated Johnston at Jackson and then Pemberton at Champion's Hill. Next, using the exterior position, he and Sherman closed in on Pemberton as he retreated into Vicksburg. After a six weeks' siege, during which Porter's river fleet supplied and reinforced the Union army and bombarded the city, Vicksburg surrendered on July 4, 1863. Four days later, Port Hudson, recently fortified by the Confederacy, surrendered to General Banks, who had been supported and supplied by Farragut's fleet. The heart of the Confederacy was now surrounded—cut off from Europe by the Federal blockade and from the resources of the Southwest by the capture of the Mississippi.

The Red River expedition of 1864, to capture cotton and to place the Union flag on Texas soil as a counter to the ambitions of Napoleon III, proved a fiasco—notable chiefly for the extraordinary efforts to extricate Porter's river fleet from the receding waters of the Red River. It was in any event unnecessary, for Federal forces had already captured Brownsville on the Mexican border.

In the East a precarious military balance had been maintained up to the time of Lee's defeat at Gettysburg. The fall of Vicksburg and Port Hudson, occurring at the same time as Gettysburg, signaled the end of the Western campaign as a major operation. It was now possible for the Union to throw the great weight of its forces released from the West into the scales in the East. Drafts from the western states would be available to fill the decimated ranks of the Army of the Potomac. Sherman's vision of destruction in the vitals of the Southern economy could become a reality. The Federal warships could turn to sealing the last of the Confederacy's deep water ports. Winning the Mississippi campaign had set the stage for the Union victory.

From the war in the West emerged two of the great commanders of the war, Grant and Farragut—so different in appearance and superficial character attributes, so alike in fundamental leadership qualities. Both were unsparing of themselves and their subordinates in preparation and execution. Both manifested bulldog tenacity in the face of adversity, cut-

ting their losses when they had to, but never accepting the ultimate possibility of anything but complete victory. Like good commanders of all times they recognized the destruction or neutralization of the enemy's armed forces confronting them as the immediate end of battle. But neither lost sight of the fact that battle is not an end in itself but only a step toward victory in the war. Battles are fought not solely to destroy the enemy, but to win control over communications and territory. It requires exceptional breadth of vision and strategic insight for the commander in the field, beset by detail and a multitude of command decisions to keep this guiding principle in mind. Both Grant and Farragut had this rare strategic insight, and the good judgment in big issues that flows from it.

17:
Closing the Confederate Ports

From the very beginning of the war, the North looked forward to the time when Fort Sumter would be recaptured and Charleston, hotbed of secession, occupied by Union troops. After the capture of Port Royal (November 1861) blockaders based on Hilton Head had made blockade-running from Charleston hazardous, but a trickle of traffic from Nassau and Havana continued to leak through. It was part of the Anaconda strategy to set about the capture of the important port cities of the South as soon as an adequate force could be mustered. Though possessing far less strategic value than New Orleans or Wilmington, Charleston had such symbolic value to both sides that it was inevitable that the North should attempt to occupy it at the first opportunity.

The Defenses
of Charleston Harbor

The Navy believed this opportunity had arrived when it could send the first considerable number of improved monitors to Rear Admiral Samuel F. Du Pont, commanding the South Atlantic Blockading Squadron. Drawing a false comparison between the problem of passing the Charleston harbor forts and the hazards offered earlier at Port Royal and in the lower Mississippi below New Orleans, Secretary Welles encouraged Du Pont to try a purely naval bombardment. The powers of the Navy Department were well aware that the obstacles were far more formidable than in the earlier campaigns, but reasoned that the advantage of heavy armor should largely compensate for the greater exposure to enemy fire. Thus, as at Port Royal, it fell to the lot of Admiral Du Pont to be an innovator. At Port

Royal he had successfully made the experiment of pitting wooden steamships against land fortifications. At Charleston he commanded the first considerable force of ironclads to duel heavy masonry forts.

As the map indicates, the sea approaches to Charleston gave little room for an attacking force to maneuver. Distances between the various Confederate forts and batteries were measured in hundreds of yards rather than in miles. A column of naval vessels could approach only via the main ship channel, which would bring them successively under the fire of Fort Wagner (on Morris Island) and Battery Gregg; then between the formidable fire

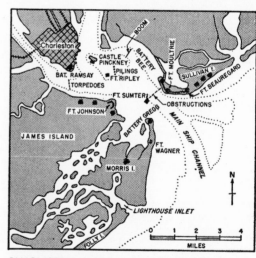

CHARLESTON HARBOR FORTIFICATIONS, 1863

of Fort Sumter to port, and the various defenses on Sullivan's Island to starboard—Fort Beauregard, Battery Rudledge, Fort Moultrie, Battery Marion, and Battery Bee. If an attacking fleet succeeded in passing the barrier booms between Fort Sumter and Battery Bee, it still would face Fort Johnson, Fort Ripley, and Castle Pinckney, as well as numerous improvised batteries all along shore around the harbor. Furthermore, the harbor was so small that after passing into the anchorage area, attacking ships would still remain in effective range of the outer forts. Charleston Harbor was, in effect, a cul-de-sac. Merely passing the outer forts would not be enough. These forts would have to be substantially silenced.

In addition to the masonry forts (Sumter, Moultrie, and Castle Pinckney), the wartime extensions of the defensive system (such as Fort Wagner) were triumphs of military engineering. Indeed the demonstrated value of the sandbag- and earthwork-protected battery in the Civil War spelled an end to the much more expensive and less efficient masonry fort. General Beauregard, who had designed the system and who was in command of the military district, and Brigadier General Roswell S. Ripley, who in 1863 was in tactical command of the defenses, were both military engineers of great skill. Assuming from the beginning that ultimately they would be attacked, they followed a policy of constantly strengthening their works. The forts mounted a total of 149 heavy guns (9-inch minimum), besides a much larger number of smaller weapons. Most of the ordnance was of latest design; much of it was rifled—firing cored conical shot of great penetrating power.

Underwater and surface obstacles in the channel were of several varieties: heavy piles driven into the bottom, a log and chain boom, rope barriers designed to foul propellers, and frame, cask, and electrically-fired torpedoes. Considering the strong currents and narrow channels of the harbor approaches, and the poor maneuvering qualities of ironclads generally, it is not surprising to learn that these obstacles were entirely successful against the Union vessels. Ceaseless Confederate vigilance guarded against reconnaissance by Union boat parties. The principal line of obstructions, between Fort Sumter and Battery Bee, was designed to arrest an attacking formation at the point at which the defense batteries had maximum fire potential. General Ripley had planned interlocking zones or cycles of fire: range stakes were set out, range and deflection errors were predetermined by test-firing each piece of ord-

nance. All things considered, the path of an attacking column of ships would lead directly through the most devastating heavy artillery fire that could then be concentrated anywhere on earth. Every defensive arrangement available to an intelligent and well supplied adversary was developed, tested, and ready. In addition to the shore batteries and forts, the Confederates also had two formidable ironclads inside the harbor, the *Palmetto State* and the *Chicora,* which had—in January prior to the arrival of the United States monitors—sallied out and damaged the gunboat *Mercedita* and the steamer *Keystone State.*

Apart from the maintenance of an effective blockade, Northern efforts against Charleston for the first two years of the war were neither concerted nor particularly effective. At first an attempt was made to close the port by a "stone blockade," that is, by sinking schooners laden with granite across the ship channels outside the harbor. This precipitated a flurry of diplomatic exchanges, the South indignantly protesting to England the illegality, under international law, of "permanently" destroying a port. Presently however the tides swept open new channels, and the scheme was abandoned as impractical. Only in early 1863, as the *New Ironsides,* the monitors *Passaic* and *Nahant,* and later other ironclads were added to Du Pont's fleet, did it become possible to consider direct attack on the shore fortifications.

Du Pont first tried out his new ships against Fort McAllister, a Confederate earthwork guarding the upper reaches of the Ogeechee River, digested the technical lessons of this test attack, and readied his flotilla for a grand attack on the Charleston forts on April 7, 1863.

The First Major Attack on Charleston Harbor

Admiral Du Pont's plan of attack was a simple one. His nine ironclads, with the monitor *Weehawken* (Captain John Rodgers) in the van, would proceed in column a cable's length up the main ship channel, holding fire until at a point 600 to 800 yards north and east of Fort Sumter, which was to be the primary gunnery objective, to be reduced by deliberate, aimed fire. Once Sumter was silenced, the next objective would be the Morris Island batteries. The flag was to be in the casemated ironclad *New Ironsides*, fifth ship in the line. Of the other eight ironclads, seven were monitors. Bringing up the rear was the *Keokuk*, a queer, experimental type with two stationary round casemates.

The problem of the mines and obstructions was to be met by an invention of Ericsson, a minesweeper in the form of a V-shaped raft, with trailing grapnels to foul the anchor lines of the torpedoes. Designed to fit around the bows of a monitor, the sweeper was to be pushed into the barriers by the *Weehawken*. It is evident however that Du Pont's battle plan did not contemplate going beyond the outer barrier in the first day's fighting.

The planned approach was delayed a half hour by the *Weehawken*'s getting the grapnels of her minesweeper fouled in her anchor chain. Another hour was consumed by the other ironclads in getting under way. The cumbersome *New Ironsides* proved so awkward to handle in these narrow waters that she twice had to anchor to avoid running aground. The head of the Union column reached the outer barrier about mid-afternoon, at which time the pre-aimed Confederate guns opened up with all their fury. For about 50 minutes the entire Union force was subjected to a blanket of fire till then unparalleled in weight of metal and accuracy. After the battle Captain Rodgers counted 53 shot marks on the *Weehawken* alone, 47 projectiles struck the *Patapsco,* and the other vessels reported numerous damaging hits. Hundreds of rounds of heavy and well-directed shot were fired at the Union ironclads, while the fleet, firing slowly, got off a total of only 139 shots, nearly all of which were directed against Fort Sumter. Fifty-five of these struck the walls and parapet, others falling inside the works. Considerable damage was done to the masonry, and the officers' quarters in the parade were demolished, but Sumter's fighting efficiency was not materially impaired.

In order to get back over the bar before dark, Du Pont at 4:30 signaled recall and shepherded his battered line out into deep water. He planned to renew the engagement the next day, until the damage reports from his captains caused him to change his mind.

The ironclad *Keokuk* was injured worst, having been struck more than 90 times. Nineteen shot pierced through her at and just below the waterline. She successfully withdrew from action, but sank the following morning. The damage done to the monitors and to the *New Ironsides* was not severe. Armor plates had been jarred loose, turrets had jammed, and bolt heads, sheared off by concussion, had hurtled lethally about inside the turrets. Yet, despite the fury of the battle, only one man had been killed and few were wounded in the nine vessels. Clearly, the new ship armor was more than adequate defense against the artillery of the times. Among the monitors, only the *Passaic* required immediate yard overhaul.

On the other hand, it was evident that the forts could not be silenced in a duel of this sort: the captains in their reports unanimously recommended against a renewal of an attack fraught with risks and without prospect of commensurate gain. The Navy Department and the President reluctantly concurred with the judgment of the Admiral and his subordinates. The capture of Charleston was acknowledged to be beyond the means of a fleet unsupported by amphibious troops.

Admiral Du Pont was presently relieved of command of the South Atlantic Blockading Squadron after nearly two years of arduous duty skillfully performed. Though he failed, it was in attempting the impossible. He deserves to rank with the best of his contemporaries—both for his services to the Navy and for his contributions to naval science.

The Siege of Charleston

With the arrival of Rear Admiral John A. Dahlgren as Du Pont's relief came a change in plans. Charleston would be invested by a regular siege. Brigadier General Quincy A. Gillmore of the Army Engineers would conduct the land phase, and the function of the fleet would be to support the operation.

Troops were moved to Folly Island in July 1863. Here Gillmore constructed batteries to command the Confederate works on the south end of nearby Morris Island. On July 10 he attacked across Lighthouse Inlet, strongly supported by the fire of four ironclads. These vessels paralleled the advance of the troops on the beach, laying down a barrage immediately ahead of them as they progressed to the outer defenses of Fort Wagner, which they reached after 14 hours. The *Catskill*, coming under severe fire during this support operation, was struck some 60 times by fire from Fort Wagner and considerably damaged. The other vessels were less severely treated.

The next day Gillmore's division tried to storm Fort Wagner, but was repulsed with considerable losses. Again on July 18 a more deliberate and carefully planned infantry assault was repulsed. The Navy served as mobile heavy artillery; joined by guns ashore it took Wagner under a ferocious crossfire that drove the Confederate gunners to their underground bombproofs. But as the attacking columns moved up, the Southerners rushed to the parapets once more and poured grapeshot and canister into the assault parties. This murderous action cost more than 1,500 Union soldiers killed and wounded. The 600 yards of sandy beach between the Union rifle pits and the walls of Wagner were so carpeted with blue-clad bodies that the fleet withheld fire on the fort until the wounded were removed.

After this, General Gillmore contented himself with establishing siege parallels[1] and erecting heavy batteries on Morris Island—both to take Fort Wagner under fire and also to deliver fire on Fort Sumter and on the city of Charleston itself, five miles away. By mid-August the army had 60 heavy guns mounted, and periodically thereafter the fleet joined in the incessant barrage kept up on Forts Wagner and Sumter and Battery Gregg. As the bombardment reached a crescendo preparatory to an assault on Wagner planned for September 7, the defenders evacuated both Wagner and Gregg and slipped away to the mainland by night. Gillmore then had the satisfaction of being able to turn a score of the Confederates' own guns on Charleston's remaining harbor defenses.

The pounding of army and fleet guns had by this time reduced Fort Sumter to ruins, with most of its guns dismounted. Dahlgren, hoping to exploit the defenders' new position to retreat, sent in a flag of truce with the demand that the fort be surrendered. To this demand General Beauregard replied: "Admiral Dahlgren must take it and hold it if he can."[2] Sumter was in fact nearly defenseless, but the Confederates had come to regard it as a symbol and a post of honor—not to be abandoned. Anticipating an early assault following the surrender demand, the commander of the fort, Major Stephen Elliot, made every possible preparation to repel it.

Elliot's estimate was more than correct. The Union army and navy were each independently planning to storm the fort on the night of September 8–9. In the afternoon of the 8th, Dahlgren surprised Gillmore with the laconic signal: "I will assault Sumter tonight." Gillmore then requested that the naval attack force be added to his own, but Dahlgren declined. The only concert of operations was the use of the word "Detroit" for recognition, and an agreement that the first force to take the fort would display a red light.

The naval attack got under way first. A little after 10 PM, a tug steamed off from the fleet toward Sumter, with a long tandem tow of ships' boats loaded with 500 navy and marine corps "boarders." The monitors *Lehigh* and *Montauk* moved up in close support. The hastily developed plan was to send in a small diversionary force which would attack first near the northwest angle of the fort. Commander Thomas Holdup Stevens, in tactical command, intended to withhold the bulk of his force until the defenders' attention had been distracted from his chosen attack point—the southeastern corner. So imperfectly was this plan understood by the boat officers and coxwains that, as the diversionary party swept forward, many of the main attack force did likewise. Since surprise was essential, Stevens refrained from shouting orders over the water within easy earshot of the fort. Instead, he quietly passed the word to the remaining boats to advance at best speed.

Though Sumter lacked heavy guns, there was no lack of garrison and no lack of small arms. The defenders, on the alert for an attempted assault, withheld their fire until they could see the dark shapes of the boats on the

[1] Parallels: a series of interconnected trenches dug one after another parallel to and ever closer to the enemy front—a means of advancing on the enemy's position with minimum exposure to his fire.

[2] *Official Records of the Union and Confederate Navies in the War of the Rebellion*, Series I, XIV, 548.

water beneath them. They then let go with a fusillade of rifle fire, grenades, fire bombs, and even bricks. Within a few minutes all the surrounding Confederate forts and the c.s. ironclad *Chicora,* inside the harbor, opened up with heavy guns zeroed in at the base of Sumter. Instead of the easy victory Dahlgren had anticipated, the attacking force had run into an ambush.

Most of the navy boats that had not touched down hauled off with or without orders and fled back to the fleet. General Gillmore's storming party of some 700 infantrymen, already afloat, turned back to Morris Island. More than a hundred sailors and marines however made landings. Most of these found only a vertical brick wall with no means of scaling. Some reached breaches in the wall, visible by day from the fleet, but found them blocked with loose sand. Recognizing their situation as hopeless, the landing party quickly surrendered and were brought inside the fort as prisoners of war.

The lessons of this small-scale defeat are too obvious to require much elaboration: the possible strategic advantages to be gained were not worth the risks; there was a needless lack of coordinated action between army and navy; there was inadequate advance briefing of the assault parties; there is good evidence that the Confederate garrison had advance word of the attempt. Dahlgren was a generally capable, even brilliant, officer, whose work both as Chief of the Bureau of Ordnance and as commander of a combat fleet are a source of pride to the Navy. But the episode of the night of September 8, 1863 adds nothing to his reputation.

After this fiasco, there were not for some time any substantial offensive operations in the vicinity of Charleston. Gillmore banged away with his heavy batteries ashore, and the ironclads occasionally cooperated. Over Fort Sumter the Confederate flag continued to flutter on the stump of the flagstaff.

A joint effort in October 1863 to force evacuation of Sumter through sheer weight of bombardment also failed. Through the next 12 months there were a variety of minor episodes: bombardments, Confederate attacks with their "Davids," landing party reconnaissances up and down the coasts, and "cutting out" expeditions in the rivers, but no major efforts were made to breach the harbor defenses. "Brave Charleston" came to be a Southern watchword: news of the unyielding garrison was telegraphed daily all over the Confederacy.

Atlanta Threatened

After the simultaneous Union victories of Gettysburg and Vicksburg in July 1863, military activities came virtually to a standstill in the Virginia area and along the Mississippi; central Tennessee became for a time the principal theater of the Civil War. When General William S. Rosecrans USA forced General Braxton Bragg CSA below Chattanooga on the Georgia border, Lee detached Longstreet's corps and sent it by railroad to reinforce Bragg. At the same time Hooker entrained two Federal corps to reinforce Rosecrans. Longstreet arrived first, and at the Battle of Chickamauga (September 1863) the Confederates won a partial victory, forcing the northern army back into Chattanooga. Grant, now given supreme command in the West, relieved Rosecrans and came in person to take charge. He succeeded in restoring the Federal line of communications, and in the Battle of Chattanooga (November 1863) chased Bragg from his entrenchments and into Georgia. Grant now left Sherman in command of the western army and proceeded to Washington to assume supreme command of the Union forces and to exercise direction in the field of the Army of the Potomac.

Now at last a unified land strategy was to be carried out. Grant would strike hard at Lee in Virginia, destroying or at least containing the Army of Northern Virginia, while Sherman headed into Georgia in a great flanking movement, the first major stage of which would be the investing and capture of Atlanta.

The advance on Atlanta gave a new sense of urgency to Farragut's long-cherished scheme to close the port of Mobile. For Sherman reasoned that if a demonstration were made against the Confederacy's only remaining Gulf port, the garrison of Mobile might be reinforced by detachments from the army of General Joseph E. Johnston (who had now replaced Bragg). In any event no assistance from Mobile would be available to the defenders of Atlanta. So in July 1864, the monitors Farragut had previously requested in vain were made available, and a troop contingent was provided to besiege and capture the forts.

Confederate Defenses at Mobile—1864

Mobile, Alabama, which had been the leading cotton-shipping port of the United States before the war, lies at the head of a shallow bay in delta country some 25 miles from the open waters of the Gulf of Mexico. To reach the city, large ships were forced to use the single deep-water channel that entered the southwest corner of the bay between Mobile Point and Dauphin Island, while vessels of six-foot draft or less might also employ a secondary channel, north of Dauphin Island, which connected the bay with Mississippi Sound. Thus geography determined that the Confederate defense of Mobile, as of New Orleans, was to consist of forts distant from the city guarding the water approaches and supported insofar as possible by naval vessels.

The fixed defenses at the time of the Union attack consisted of Fort Powell controlling the lesser entrance and Forts Gaines and Morgan flanking the main channel on either side. Extending from Fort Gaines on Dauphin Island were submerged pilings to form an obstruction almost two miles long between the island and the edge of the ship channel. A triple line of moored torpedoes extended the barrier to within a quarter of a mile of Fort Morgan on Mobile Point. About a fifth of the total were powerful and durable cask torpedoes; the rest were powder-filled metal cones, easily corroded by salt water. The eastern end of the minefield was marked by a buoy, between which and Fort Morgan the Confederates had left open a 150-yard wide channel for blockade runners. As a consequence Fort Morgan—a casemated, pentagonal structure with a water battery and a total of 45 heavy guns—was the key defense work for Mobile Bay.

Again, as at New Orleans, the hope of the defense rested to a great extent on completing an ironclad powerful enough to sink any Union ships able to fight their way past Fort Morgan. This ship, the *Tennessee*, had been

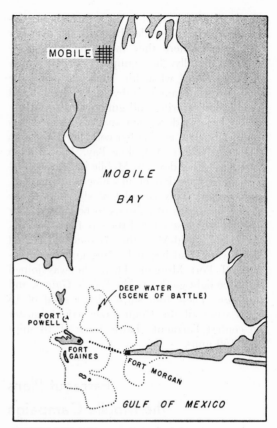

MOBILE BAY, 1864

building for more than a year at Selma, 150 miles up the Alabama River from Mobile, under the supervision of Admiral Franklin Buchanan, first commander of the *Virginia*. Not so long as the *Virginia*, which she closely resembled, the *Tennessee* was a new ship from the keel up. Her slanting casemate extended below the waterline and then back to the hull to form a "knuckle," making her impervious to the ramming of any likely opponent. Around the bows the knuckle became a ram of unusual strength, a marked improvement over the beak carried by the *Virginia*. Her armament was two pivoted 7-inch rifles fore and aft, firing 110-pound solid shot, and two 6.4-inch rifles firing 90-pound solid shot on each broadside.

Events were to demonstrate that the *Tennessee's* strength in armor and armament was offset by defects of construction. Equipped with engines that had previously driven a river steamboat, she could make no better than six knots when loaded for battle. As the result of an oversight her steering chains, instead of being concealed beneath, led over her stern deck where they might be severed by gunfire. Finally, her gunport shutters easily jammed closed when hit. Thus she could use her powerful ram only by lucky chance and readily lost steering and gunpower in battle.

To her builders such matters seemed less important than getting her completed and into the deep waters of Mobile Bay. The wooden hull was towed down to Mobile in March 1864 for the installation of machinery, armament, and armor. This completed, she had to be raised by means of caissons to be shifted over the bar which separated the city from the bay. At last in mid-May the *Tennessee* reached deep water and began holding gunnery practice off Fort Morgan. There she was joined by three light gunboats, the *Selma, Gaines,* and *Morgan.* These four ships with a total of 16 guns were all the Confederacy could muster to contest Farragut's battle force of 18 ships and 159 guns.

Farragut Plans the Mobile Campaign

As soon as Admiral Farragut returned from leave to the West Gulf Squadron in January 1864, he made a reconnaissance at the entrance to Mobile Bay and found that the Confederates had made little progress with their defenses in the 20 months since the fall of New Orleans. "I am satisfied that if I had one ironclad at this time," he reported to Secretary Welles, "I could destroy their whole force in the bay and reduce the forts at my leisure by cooperation of our land forces, say, 5,000 men."[3] His estimate of the situation was accurate enough, but so many Union ships were assigned to the expedition against Charleston or earmarked for the spring campaign in the Red River that he was obliged to wait until the defenses of Mobile Bay had achieved their greatest strength before he could lead an assault against them.

All during the seven months' wait Farragut kept himself informed of every Confederate move through captured Southern newspapers or the reports of deserters. Meanwhile his

[3] *Official Records,* XXI, 52.

blockading squadron had its hands full, for the entire Gulf coast from Brownsville to Pensacola still abounded with blockade runners, many of them old foxes who had shifted their operations from the Atlantic coast. To one of Farragut's nature, routine success in blockading could not relieve his chagrin at his inability to get troops or monitors before the *Tennessee* reached Mobile Bay.

On July 8 the first of the Federal monitors, the *Manhattan,* was reported at Pensacola; three more were to follow: the *Tecumseh* from the Atlantic, and the *Winnebago* and *Chickasaw* from the Mississippi. Then the Admiral also learned that he could count on obtaining the required number of troops under Major General Gordon Granger by the end of the month. Within a few days he developed his basic plan for the attack. He decided on an early morning assault when he could count on a flood tide to help carry the ships past Fort Morgan into Mobile Bay and on a southwest wind to carry the smoke of battle away from the ships and into the fort. The wooden ships would be lashed together in pairs as at Port Hudson. The flagship *Hartford,* with the *Metacomet* on her port side, would lead the way through the open channel between the mine field and Fort Morgan. The *Brooklyn* and the *Octorara,* the *Richmond* and the *Port Royal,* the *Lackawanna* and the *Seminole,* the *Monongahela* and the *Kennebec,* the *Ossipee* and the *Itasca,* and the *Oneida* and the *Galena* would pair up and follow in that order.

The battle plan was later modified to include the four monitors, which were to proceed in a parallel column between the wooden ships and the fort. "The service that I look for from the ironclads," said Farragut, "is, first, to neutralize as much as possible the fire of the guns which rake our approach; next to look out for the [Confederate] ironclads when we are abreast of the forts; and, lastly, to occupy the attention of those batteries which would rake us while running up the bay."[4] A second modification, which Farragut made with great reluctance, placed the *Brooklyn* and her consort in the lead, the *Hartford* in second place. This change, urged upon him because of the *Brooklyn's* greater forward firepower and a tor-

[4] *Ibid.,* 404.

pedo-cowcatcher arrangement on her bows, he was to regret. The late arrival of the monitor *Tecumseh* caused a 24-hour postponement which prevented the fleet from making its attack simultaneously with the army's landing on Dauphin Island to lay siege to Fort Gaines; otherwise the Union attack was launched according to plan.

The four monitors were well equipped for the role assigned them. The single-turreted *Tecumseh* and *Manhattan* were 1,000-ton craft armed with two 15-inch guns which could throw a 440-pound steel-headed bolt as an armor-piercing projectile. The rotating turret was protected by 10-inch armor; superimposed on it was the pilot house, which could be entered only through the turret. The *Winnebago* and *Chickasaw* were shallow-draft, double-turreted river craft protected by 8½-inch armor and armed with four 11-inch guns apiece. No faster than the *Tennessee*, they had heavier armor and larger guns.

Passing Fort Morgan

At 5:30 on the morning of August 5, 1864 the Federal fleet got underway for the entrance to the channel. Every protective device that had proved valuable at New Orleans or Port Hudson was employed and, if possible, improved upon. The *Tecumseh* steamed slowly along the Fort Morgan side of the channel, somewhat in advance of the *Brooklyn* pair on a parallel course. The first shots were exchanged just after seven o'clock, the *Tecumseh* firing twice at the fort; she then reserved her fire for the *Tennessee*, which was discovered moving slowly into the bend in the channel beyond the Confederate mine field. While a general cannonading was joined behind him, Captain Craven of the *Tecumseh* devoted his attention exclusively to the Confederate ram. Her position and the narrowness of the channel between the mine field buoy and Fort Morgan made him doubt his orders from Farragut: "The vessels will take care to pass to the eastward of the easternmost buoy, which is clear of all obstruction."[5] Craven turned his monitor to head for the *Tennessee* on a collision course, and passed about 300 yards ahead of the *Brooklyn*. His 15-inch guns loaded with

[5] *Ibid.*, 398.

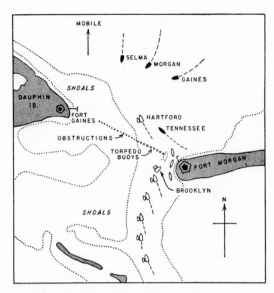

BATTLE OF MOBILE BAY, AUGUST 5, 1864

60-pound charges and steel bolts, he bore down on his opponent. On the Confederate ship the officers and crew braced themselves for the shock, for Admiral Buchanan ordered them to hold fire until the two ships actually came together. At this tense moment when they were little more than 100 yards apart, the *Tecumseh* ran upon a mine which exploded and ripped out her bottom. The monitor sank bow first almost instantly, her stern rising out of the water so that her propeller was seen turning in the air as she plunged to the bottom. Of her complement of over 100, only 21 survived.

Fortunately for the Union attack, this catastrophe did not prevent the other monitors from maintaining their proper stations and carrying out their assigned duties, but a disastrous situation was rapidly developing among the wooden ships. The *Brooklyn's* captain, hearing a confused report of objects in the water ahead, stopped his ship and then backed her down against the current. Within a matter of minutes the *Brooklyn* and her consort lay across the channel, bows on and abreast the fort, while the other wooden ships bore down on them.

Farragut had sent his pilot into the maintop for a clear view above the smoke of the guns; he himself had taken a station in the port main rigging, climbing higher as the smoke rose and maintaining a position of easy communication with the pilot, with the captain of the *Metacomet* on the paddlebox of his ship alongside, and with the captain of the *Hartford*. When the *Tecumseh* sank, the Admiral had ordered a boat from the *Metacomet* to rescue survivors in the water. Now, with the *Brooklyn* barring his way and threatening to congest his entire fleet where the channel passed close to Fort Morgan's guns, Farragut ordered the *Hartford* to pass to port around the stern of the *Brooklyn*, through the mine field, and into the channel again. It was on this occasion according to certain postwar accounts that Farragut shouted "Damn the torpedoes! Full steam ahead!"[6] Although her crew reported hearing the primers of the torpedoes snapping, the flagship passed through. As the Admiral had suspected all along, most of the torpedoes were harmless through long immersion.

The *Hartford* proved too nimble for the clumsy *Tennessee*, which finally turned back to attack the other Union ships. The flagship meanwhile suffered casualties from the enfilading fire of the Confederate gunboats until she had room to maneuver and bring her guns to bear on them. Her broadsides then quickly repulsed the gunboats, and the *Metacomet* cut loose and went after them.

After blocking the rest of the Federal ships under the guns of Fort Morgan, the *Brooklyn* had at length got back on course and led the column through the mine field a mile behind the *Hartford*. Several vessels were hit by the fort's guns but only the *Oneida*, at the end of the line, was disabled. Even she got past with the help of her escort and the flood tide. As the wooden vessels trailed into the bay, they were met by the *Tennessee*, which lumbered along and through the line, exchanging broadsides with ship after ship but seriously damaging none and in return receiving no injury worse than a perforated smokestack.

The *Metacomet*, fastest ship in the Union fleet, had no difficulty overtaking the Confed-

erate gunboat *Selma,* which she forced to surrender. The other two gunboats meanwhile had come under fire by Farragut's battle line. The *Gaines,* in a sinking condition, was beached by her crew. Only the *Morgan* escaped; slightly damaged, she sought refuge under the guns of Fort Morgan, and eventually made her way to Mobile.

Four miles up the bay the *Hartford* anchored, and Farragut sent his crew to breakfast. The other Union ships soon anchored nearby. The captain of the flagship summed up the battle at that point by remarking to the Admiral: "What we have done has been well done, sir; but it all counts for nothing so long as the *Tennessee* is there under the guns of Fort Morgan."[7]

The End of the *Tennessee*

The Confederate admiral had decided to use his remaining six hours' fuel supply in an unexpected attack on Farragut's ships. After doing all the damage she could, the *Tennessee* might in his opinion serve as a floating battery in the defense of Fort Morgan. Characteristically Buchanan wanted above all else to have another chance at the *Hartford*.

When Farragut was told that the *Tennessee* was returning, he could scarcely believe it. He had feared that the ram might attack the light ships he had left outside the bay, or wait to make a night attack on the fleet. Instead, Buchanan was playing directly into his hands —bringing his slow, awkward ram in broad daylight against 17 Federal warships, most of which could outmaneuver, outrun, and outgun him. "I did not think old Buck was such a fool," exclaimed Farragut.[8]

What followed was a wild melee. First the *Monongahela* and then the *Lackawanna* rammed the Confederate, each attacker taking far greater damage than she inflicted. At last the two flagships came together obliquely, collided at the bow, and ground past each other port side to port side. The *Hartford's* shot, fired at a ten-foot range, bounded off the *Tennessee's* casemate, while the Confederate, plagued throughout the battle by bad

---

[6] Farragut himself records that he sought Divine guidance through prayer and heard an inner voice tell him to go forward. Eye-witnesses agree that the Admiral did signal for full speed ahead. For a discussion of this point, see Charles Lee Lewis, *David Glasgow Farragut: Our First Admiral* (Annapolis, 1943), 469.

[7] Lewis, *op cit.*, 274.

[8] *Battles and Leaders of the Civil War* (New York, 1884–88), IV, 407.

primers, was able to fire only one shot, her last, into her opponent. Then the *Lackawanna* steaming at full speed for the *Tennessee* crashed instead into the circling *Hartford* near where Farragut was standing.

The monitors now moved in on the *Tennessee*. The *Chickasaw* followed behind the ram as though being towed, her shot jamming port shutters, cutting the steering chains, and wounding Admiral Buchanan. The only shot that penetrated the ram's armor however was a steel bolt from a 15-inch gun of the *Manhattan*. One of the Confederate officers reported that it "admitted daylight through our side, where, before it struck us, there had been two feet of solid wood, covered with five inches of solid iron."[9]

Almost dead in the water, three port shutters jammed, her steering gone, stack shot away so that her gun-deck was filled with suffocating heat and fumes, the *Tennessee* was in a hopeless position. As the entire Union fleet was moving in for the kill and the Confederates could bring no guns to bear, Captain Johnston, with Admiral Buchanan's consent, climbed out onto the casemate top to show the white flag. It was then 10 AM.

The Confederate naval forces had lost a total of 12 killed and 20 wounded in the entire battle, and only two were killed and nine wounded in the *Tennessee*. Union casualties for the battle were 52 killed and 170 wounded, not counting those lost when the *Tecumseh* sank. The *Hartford* alone had 25 killed and 28 wounded.

Final Stages of the Mobile Campaign

Fort Powell was evacuated and destroyed by its garrison on the night following the naval battle. The next day Fort Gaines surrendered. General Granger's troops were then transferred to Mobile Point, and Fort Morgan capitulated before the end of the month.

These victories brought to an end Mobile's traffic with the outside world. The city's military importance to the Union had already passed, for Mobile was no longer needed as a Union base for a land campaign. No serious

[9] Lewis, *Farragut*, 277.

attempt was directed against the city itself until the spring of 1865, when six Union ships and a launch were sunk by mines while the Navy was cooperating in siege operations undertaken by the Army. With the fall of outlying fortifications, Mobile was finally occupied by Union troops on April 12, three days after the surrender of Lee at Appomattox.

Sherman's March

In the meantime, Sherman had forced Johnston back on Atlanta. Using Fabian tactics, the weaker army of Johnston obliged Sherman to take 74 days to achieve a 100-mile advance. But President Davis, demanding action, replaced Johnston with Hood, who went on the offensive and was beaten three times in succession. Sherman now cut loose from his line of communications and circled Atlanta, severing rail lines and obliging Hood to evacuate the city to avoid being bottled up and captured. The near coincidence of the Battle of Mobile Bay and the fall of Atlanta (September 2, 1864) marked the beginning of the end for the Confederacy.

Leaving General George H. Thomas in command of a force adequate to defeat Hood, Sherman himself set out with 60,000 men on his celebrated march to the sea. Living off the country, his army laid waste to a strip 60 miles wide through the one remaining major granary of the South. He emerged at Savannah in late December, 1864, captured the city, and headed north into the Carolinas, where a small Confederate army under Johnston was unable to make effective resistance.

As word of Sherman's advance reached Dahlgren off Charleston harbor, the admiral formed a naval brigade equipped with two field howitzers, which was to do good service in General John G. Foster's command, campaigning between Savannah and Charleston. In addition, the Navy's shallow-draft gunboats were employed to good advantage in providing logistic and gunfire support to Sherman's army as it marched north from Savannah. The doom of Charleston was sealed as Sherman's victorious Westerners closed in behind the city, which the Confederate garrison had to evacuate on February 18, 1865 in order to avoid capture.

And so at long last the officers of the fleet walked the nearly deserted streets of the city that had so long defied their guns.

The last act in the tragic drama of the Civil War was about to begin. Discounting Johnston's small force operating independently, Grant envisioned the final strategy as a pincers movement on Lee's army, tied to Richmond by the determination of the Confederate government to hold the capital at all costs. As Sherman's legions pushed inexorably north, Grant suddenly shifted the bulk of his forces to reinforce the Army of the James operating to the south and east of Richmond. Petersburg came under siege; the Petersburg-Richmond area became a gigantic fortress, covered by over 40 miles of entrenchments and dependent on rail connections to the south and west for supplies and reinforcements. The Weldon railroad line, connecting Richmond with Wilmington, North Carolina, 225 miles to the south, was of special importance to the Confederacy, for Wilmington was by now the principal port of entry for foreign supplies brought through the blockade. Through the summer and fall of 1864, various Federal operations against the Weldon line and the other railroads leading into Richmond and Petersburg achieved partial success. But by breaking bulk below Petersburg and transshipping by wagon, the defenders of the last Confederate bastion continued to bring in a trickle of war supplies from overseas.

The Fort Fisher Campaign

As early as the winter of 1862, Secretary Welles had unsuccessfully petitioned the War Department to provide troops for a joint Army-Navy attack on the Confederate defenses at the mouth of the Cape Fear River in North Carolina. Wilmington, at the fall line of the river, was already a principal port for the blockade runners. The dual approaches to the river mouth, the notoriously dangerous Frying Pan Shoals off Smith's Island, and the comparative remoteness from Union bases made the maintenance of a close blockade here especially difficult. The excellent rail connections between Wilmington and Richmond and other points in the interior of the Confederacy gave Wilmington a vital strategic

importance—far greater than that of Mobile, second only to that of New Orleans. But with the multitude of demands for troops Secretary of War Stanton for nearly three years could never seem to spare even the modest contingent required. Meanwhile the principal fortification at the mouth of the river, Fort Fisher, was gradually developed by the Southern command from a scantily manned "sand battery" to a very formidable complex of well protected ordnance.

In September 1864 Secretary Welles renewed his proposal for an amphibious operation. Grant was interested in the operation as a step in isolating Lee from all outside supplies, and promised an adequate force by the first of October. Because of failing health and near exhaustion, Farragut declined the proffered naval command. Admiral Porter, eager to regild his somewhat tarnished laurels after the fiasco of the Red River, embraced this new opportunity with his characteristic enthusiasm.

The First Fort Fisher Expedition

The plan of campaign as originally conceived was simple. A fleet mounting 150 guns would bombard Fort Fisher, which was known to be defended by some 1,800 men with about 75 pieces of ordnance. An army force to consist of not fewer than 8,000 troops would be landed under covering fire on the open beach north of the fort. This force would throw a trench line across to the Cape Fear River, thereby cutting off the fort from reinforcement and supply from the city. Capture of the fort by assault or siege could then be hazarded.

By mid-October a heterogeneous fleet of nearly a hundred vessels was mustered at Hampton Roads; it included everything from the latest screw frigates and ironclads down to makeshift gunboats converted from harbor ferries. It was the largest fleet to be assembled under the United States flag in the 19th century. Drilling of this awkwardly large and varied force in simple maneuver and gunnery presented an unusual command problem, which Porter cheerfully faced. The naval commander adopted an improved and more precise set of blockade instructions to govern interim operations off the mouths of the Cape Fear River, set about getting to know his captains better, and had lithographed for general distribution a chart of the projected bombardment showing the position of each of the 55 gunnery vessels.

There ensued a period of tiresome waiting: the bombardment force had been concentrated by dangerously stripping the blockading force all up and down the coast. Both Porter and Welles feared that any protracted delay might jeopardize the operation. Yet with Army and Navy serving only as cooperating entities without an over-all commander, a coordinated plan required a high measure of compatibility between Army and Navy seniors. This was notoriously lacking between Porter and General Benjamin Butler, who was to furnish the troops from his force at Bermuda Hundred. Moreover Butler was disposed to be dilatory.

After what appeared to Porter to be maddening procrastination, General Butler appeared on board his flagship at Hampton Roads in late November. Instead of simply sending the agreed-on assault force, Butler further exasperated the impatient Porter by propounding a pet project he had conceived to make the job easy. This was to mine Fort Fisher by exploding a powder-laden ship near its walls immediately prior to the landing. Though dubious of the probable effects of this giant "torpedo," Porter, a born innovator, listened to the tepidly favorable opinion of certain civilian scientists and decided it was worth a try. In any event it would get the expedition under way, and that was the big thing.

Into the steamer *Louisiana*, weakened by dry rot and eligible for survey, was stuffed 215 tons of black powder. Fuse trains were laid about, and a clockwork device was improvised to set off the explosion after the volunteer crew had placed their strange weapon in position. Gathering the powder from various army and navy magazines, embarking the troops, and a spell of severe gales caused further delay, so that it was mid-December before the Union armada left Hampton Roads. By this time of course the South knew almost as much of the Union plan, including the powder-ship, as did the Union commanders. Any possible advantage of surprise had long since been frittered away.

As the transports were making rendezvous with the fleet, another gale blew up, causing the attempt to be postponed again. The naval vessels simply cast anchor and rode it out, but the transports scurried back to Beaufort. The bold venture was finally arranged for the night of December 23-24.

The *Wilderness* towed in the doomed *Louisiana*, which was finally anchored with some difficulty 300 yards from the beach. A party of volunteers then set the clockwork mechanisms and candles that were to ignite the fuses. To insure the destruction of the powder, which might be captured by the Confederates if the exploding devices failed, they also started a pine-knot fire in a cabin aft. During the approach and afterwards—though the night was dark—there was a constant danger of a premature explosion from accident or from a ranging shot from the Confederate stronghold. At length the volunteers began to appear at the rail of the *Louisiana*, to be checked off by the boatswain as they slipped into the waiting boats. Presently Commander A. C. Rhind, in charge of the operations, gave the order to pull away to the *Wilderness*, waiting at a discreet distance.

There was an unexplained delay in the explosion. The clocks were set for 1½ hours, but apparently it was the fire that finally set off the power—20 minutes past the scheduled time. After the painful suspense of the risky preparations, the enterprise proved a disappointing failure. A tall pillar of flame shot up from the powder-ship, and four separate explosions were heard. But the shock was scarcely felt in the fleet, and bothered the well-protected Confederates not at all.[10]

At daylight on the 24th, the fleet stood in to their scheduled bombardment positions and opened a terrific cannonade. About 115 shots a minute registered on or within the walls of the fort. Two Confederate magazines were blown up by the Union shells, and wooden structures were set on fire. So quickly were the defenders harried to the shelter of bombproofs

[10] It is probable that most of the powder simply burned, rather than exploded. In view of the Halifax (N.S.) disaster during World War I and other unscheduled explosions of munitions ships, it is possible that Butler's plan—in theory—was better than generally credited.

that they inflicted no casualties whatever in the fleet. In a little over an hour the fort was completely silenced. Though the bombardment was continued throughout the day, no transports appeared. At sundown the bombardment ships withdrew from range, having at least established that they could at will overpower the guns ashore.

The next morning, Christmas Day, the transports finally arrived. Porter dispatched 17 gunboats to cover the landing and provided 100 ship's boats for putting troops ashore. At long last the assault was to be made.

Once more the fleet stood in and took the fort under slow, deliberate fire, while the soldiers were landed five miles to the north. Porter was delighted to see the blue-clad skirmish line reconnoitering and sharpshooting near the outer works of the fort. One bold infantry officer coolly clambered up the parapet and seized a Confederate flag that had been shot away by naval gunfire.

Then came the incredible news that only 2,200 of the 6,500 available troops had been landed and that these were being re-embarked. Not knowing the circumstances of this decision, Porter assumed the attack would be made the next day, and detailed the ironclads to keep the fort under fire through the night. But he presently received word from Butler that the assault was impracticable—"as it [Fort Fisher] was left substantially uninjured as a defensive work by the navy fire."[11] Contented with 300 prisoners captured in some outposts, Butler firmly announced his decision to return to Hampton Roads at once.

Porter's exasperation at this turn of events was matched only by Grant's. Butler was put on waiting orders at home, and Brigadier General Godfrey Weitzel succeeded him in command of the Army of the James. Porter pressed for a renewal of the attack under a bolder army command. Meanwhile, he returned the fleet to Beaufort to replenish ammunition.

The Second Fort Fisher Expedition

If the North had learned a lesson in the first expedition, so had the South. Fort Fisher had been entirely repaired and considerably strengthened. Reinforcements enlarged the gar-

[11] *Official Records*, II, 251.

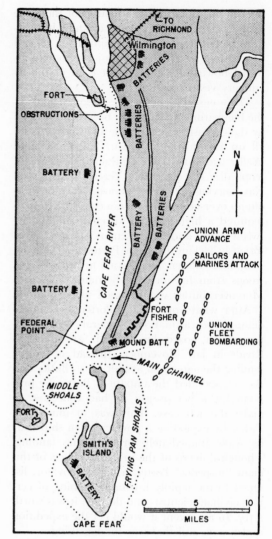

SECOND ATTACK ON FORT FISHER
JANUARY 13-15, 1865

rison. General Braxton Bragg was placed in command.

Meanwhile Brigadier General Alfred H. Terry USA had arrived in command of the original landing force, which had now been augmented to 8,000—the number the Navy had requested in the first place. On January 13, 1865 the Second Fort Fisher Expedition got under way. Terry well knew Grant's determination that there should be no further delay. As soon as the transports anchored, he prepared to land the troops.

With close inshore support from shoal draft gunboats, Terry's men poured ashore as fast as a shuttle service of 120 boats could transport them. Within an hour after they had landed, they had "dug in" all the way across the peninsula, cutting the fort off from support from the mainland. The fleet meanwhile kept up an avalanche of fire on the fort.

General Terry kept his men busy entrenching through most of the night, and on the morning of January 14 his position was reckoned by General Bragg as too strong for attack. Rapidly extending their trench system, the Union infantry pushed their outposts to within 500 yards of the fort. The 2,500 defenders were cut off completely, closely beleaguered, and hammered mercilessly by the massed floating artillery of Porter's ships. Porter had his divisions carefully organized and positioned for maximum bombardment effectiveness. A firm believer in the efficacy of mass and volume of fire, he never neglected precise planning and accuracy. The monitors and the *New Ironsides* kept up a night bombardment as well.

The entire fleet renewed its barrage at daybreak on the 15th, and maintained it up to the scheduled time of assault, which was 3 PM. The Navy was to be represented in the storming of the fort by a force of 1,600 bluejackets and 400 marines, who would attempt to "board" the naked sea face of the works. Simultaneously, the Army infantry would attack from their trench line, and take the enemy in the flank and rear.

The initial phase of the operation went as scheduled. The "Mound Battery" returned the ships' fire with some effect at first, but the defenders were soon driven from their guns to the bombproofs, and the ships' boats with their landing parties were scarcely fired on. The sailors and marines "dug in" just above the beach, and ditched their way forward to within 200 yards of the sea face of Fort Fisher.

The signal for the final rush was given at 3 o'clock. The ships raised the curtain of fire to the upper batteries. Every steam whistle in the fleet was blown. The race for the parapets began. Led by division officers, the sailors, armed with revolvers and cutlasses, dashed gallantly forward. The plan had been for the marines, lying in the advanced rifle pits, to deliver covering small arms fire, and keep the enemy from the parapet. In the inevitable confusion of this unrehearsed operation, the marine party was not properly stationed, and enemy troops stood up on the parapets and poured a withering musketry fire into the advancing blue line. Three times the surviving officers rallied their men to try the assault again. A very few of the sailors reached the parapet, only to be clubbed and bayoneted by the defenders. In a matter of minutes the brave effort was over, an evident failure. Leaving nearly 300 of their number on the bloody sand, the survivors streamed back to their rifle pits.

Meanwhile the Army was having better luck. Profiting from the distraction offered by the sailors' assault, Terry's men stormed and captured two traverses. As the Confederate defenders on the parapets saw the sailors' attack break off, they paused to give three cheers—only to receive a volley of rifle fire in their backs as the Union infantry wave swept in behind them. Each of the traverses was a separate little fort in itself. The infantry methodically set about storming them one by one, while the fleet kept its support fire just ahead of their advance. Finally the Mound Battery was reached and successfully assaulted. The surviving Confederates fled down the beach toward the end of Federal Point. Realizing the hopelessness of their position, they finally threw down their arms and surrendered—1,800 men. More than 700 Confederates had been killed or wounded.

Union Army losses were 691. The Navy lost 309. In terms of the numbers involved, this was one of the bloodiest battles of the war.

Tactically, the Second Fort Fisher Expedition has a special interest as being the only successful large-scale amphibious attack against a strongly fortified position made by the Army and the Navy in the whole course of the war. It demonstrated the value of heavy, aimed support fire by ships. It showed the feasibility of bold, well coordinated assaults on even the strongest and best engineered defenses.

Strategically, the capture of Fort Fisher and the consequent sealing of the port of Wilmington completed the "Anaconda," and may be said to have finished the Navy's primary role in the war.

The Finale

With his seemingly inexhaustible reinforcements and supplies, Grant was in a position ultimately to outflank the defenses of the Richmond-Petersburg bastion to the north and to the south. Striking in first one sector, then in the other, he went on applying pressure to the depleted Confederate forces. Lee was finally forced to evacuate Richmond (April 2, 1865) to avoid encirclement. As the Army of Northern Virginia headed west with the object of joining forces with Johnston in the mountains, Grant made his final, checkmating move. Shifting his main force parallel and to the south of Lee, Grant placed himself in an intercepting position. With Sheridan's cavalry directly athwart his line of retreat, Lee surrendered at Appomattox (April 9). A week later Johnston surrendered to Sherman. The war was over. At the cost of nearly a million casualties, the Union was preserved and the institution of slavery destroyed.

Summary

The significance of the American Civil War in the development of military strategy and tactics has been enormous. Coming as it did in a comparatively peaceful period of history and in a time of rapid industrialization and technological advance, the war immediately became a principal study of war colleges and general staffs all over the world. In many respects it was a "modern war": railroads were first utilized to move large bodies of troops; armored naval vessels were first employed on a substantial scale; the telegraph, submarine mines, rifled ordnance, and breech-loading small arms were first used extensively. Above all, it was the first war in which industrial capacity itself became a major (if not in fact the decisive) weapon.

The Union's five-to-two manpower advantage and its overwhelming superiority in material resources and developed industry made the defeat of the Confederacy nearly inevitable. Nothing short of foreign intervention could have saved the South—intervention on which the South counted but which never came. In the circumstances, it is nothing short of remarkable that the Confederacy held out through four years of bitter fighting despite everything the Union could send against it.

The strategies of both the Union and the Confederacy were to a great extent dictated by the peculiar fact that the capitals of the opposing powers were on the periphery of their territories—and only a hundred miles apart. Had the Confederacy retained its capital at Montgomery, Alabama, it is conceivable that the South might have held out still longer. For then the Union forces, driving long distances overland to seize the seat of the Confederate government, would have been ever lengthening their lines of communication and leaving them vulnerable to guerrilla warfare—as England's overland communications were subject to harassment in the American Revolution. But in shifting its capital to Richmond, the Confederacy was obliged to tie up a mass army, the bulk of its military power, in Virginia. The Union placed a larger mass army in Virginia, to defend Washington and attack Richmond, but the superior military skill of the Southern generals quickly turned the situation there into a stalemate.

Evidently the Confederate army commander in chief, General Robert E. Lee, could not be defeated by frontal attack. The Union had sufficient surplus military power however to engage also in peripheral campaigns. These gradually cut off Lee's sources of supply until his Army of Virginia was starved into submission. The campaigns in Virginia were thus merely part of a holding operation. The decisive campaigns were fought elsewhere.

Between McClellan's Peninsular campaign of 1862 and Grant's campaign against Richmond in 1864, the Union navy played little direct part in the war in Virginia. It is notable however that Lee invariably struck at the Union right (west) flank rather than risk striking on the Union left and thereby bringing his army in contact with tidewater, where naval power might be brought to bear against him or his communications.

Mainly as a result of the situation described above, the over-all Union strategy developed as follows: to contain Lee in Virginia and progressively isolate him by shrinking his logistic base through (1) blockade of the Confederate coasts, (2) capture of the Mississippi to cut off from the Confederacy the resources of the Southwest, (3) a drive across the Confederacy from west to east (Sherman) to cut off the Deep South, (4) a drive from the south (Sherman) to coincide with a drive from the north (Grant), squeezing the Confederate military forces into an ever more restricted area. Confederate strategy was purely defensive, with no capacity to launch a sustained offensive.

It was in the Union's peripheral operations that the U. S. Navy performed its main role. Lacking substantial naval opposition, the Federal navy did not need to *achieve* sea control; it could at once begin to *exercise* it. By blockade it cut the South off from imported supplies and foreign assistance. By shore bombardment and support to amphibious operations, it enormously aided the Union armies. Patrolling the rivers, it carried the blockade inland, maintained the Army's communications, and even captured forts and cities.

In due course the Union surrounded the Confederacy with military force. The South thus held the interior position, which is more often than not an advantage, because a military power operating from an interior position can usually move forces across the interior faster than the exterior power can move forces around the periphery. But in the American Civil War, the exterior forces held the advantage because they were operating on the Ocean, the Gulf, and the rivers and thus had far greater mobility than Confederate forces operating overland, where roads and railroads were in poor condition.

While the surrender of Lee and Johnston in April 1865 marked the effective military termination of the war, the surrenders were made inevitable by the army-navy capture of Fort Fisher the preceding January. This operation blocked Wilmington, the last port of ingress for materials to support the Confederate armies. Fort Fisher was thus the last major step in the long process of shrinking Lee's logistic base.

18:
Naval Developments in the Late 19th Century

The success of U.S.S. *Monitor* in the Battle of Hampton Roads led the United States Navy to construct many small single-turreted monitors and some big, seagoing monitors for coastal service in the Civil War. Immediately after the war two of the large monitors made remarkable ocean voyages for ships of their type, the *Monadnock* cruising from Hampton Roads to San Francisco, and the *Miantonomah* from New York to England and Russia. Until 1866 however, ironclads had fought only in coastal and inland waters. In that year a British shipyard completed the 4,000-ton turret ship *Affondatore* for the Italian navy just in time to take part in the first battle of ironclads on the high seas.

The Battle of Lissa, July 20, 1866

If the ships of the Italian navy in 1866 had been soundly built, properly equipped, and effectively manned and commanded, Italy would have had the most powerful navy in the world. Her fleet included twelve seagoing armored ships, of which seven were steam-and-sail frigates. The newest of these, the *Re d'Italia* and the *Re di Portogallo*, were protected by 7-inch armor and mounted 36 and 28 guns respectively, most of them large Armstrong rifles up to 10 inches in caliber. The turret-ram *Affondatore*, expected momentarily from England, was armed with two 10-inch Armstrong rifles in individual turrets and a 26-foot iron ram. The principal wooden ships of the Italian navy were seven frigates of from 32 to 54 guns and four corvettes of from 6 to 20 guns rang-

ing in caliber up to 7 inches. All the Italian ships were steam propelled, most were screw-driven, and none of the ironclads was more than five years old.

Nevertheless this navy had serious weaknesses. The new ironclads were hastily built and inadequately fitted out. The Italian sailors who manned them were enthusiastic but untrained. The flag officers who commanded the fleet and its subdivisions lacked aggressive spirit. In particular the commander in chief, Admiral Count Carlo di Persano, had little enthusiasm for the war or the naval campaign in which he was ordered to engage.

The war began on June 14, 1866, when Prussia attacked Austria as a part of Bismarck's plans for winning control over the rising nation of Germany. Bound by an agreement with Prussia, Italy declared war on June 20 with hopes of recovering Venice from Austria. The Prussian army was quickly successful on land and by July 3 had won a decisive victory at Sadowa. Meanwhile the Austrians had badly beaten an Italian army at Custozza on June 24. To counterbalance their defeat on land and increase their bargaining power at the peace conference, the Italian government desired some success at sea.

The Austrian opposition to the Italian navy was a much inferior fleet under the command of Rear Admiral Wilhelm von Tegetthoff, who had only seven ironclad ships to oppose the twelve of Admiral Persano. All of them were frigates, protected by armor five inches or less in thickness. They mounted from 18 to 30 guns, but most of these were of smaller caliber than the Italian guns; about half were muzzle-loading smoothbores. Tegetthoff's principal

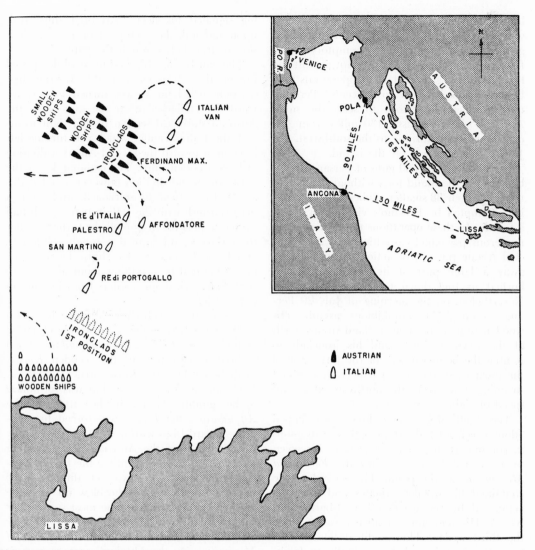

BATTLE OF LISSA, JULY 20, 1866

wooden ships were the *Kaiser,* a 92-gun line-of-battle ship, five frigates of 31 to 51 guns, and one 22-gun corvette. Only a few guns on each of the wooden ships were rifles.

On the day Italy declared war, the Ministry of Marine ordered Admiral Persano to move his fleet from Taranto at the heel of the Italian boot to Ancona about halfway up the Italian Adriatic coast, where it would occupy a more central position for offensive operations against the Austrian fleet at Pola, some 90 miles across the Adriatic to the northward. Twelve days before, Persano had been ordered to "sweep the enemy from the Adri-atic and to attack and blockade them wherever he should find them." Since the Austrian fleet was inferior to the Italian, Tegetthoff's orders were properly less aggressive. When Tegetthoff requested permission of the Archduke to take the offensive, he was directed not to extend his operations beyond Lissa, to the south, and to keep the mouth of the River Po and the coast of Venice covered.

During the first few weeks of the war, Persano, instead of carrying out his aggressive orders, avoided an opportunity for action off his own fleet base against an inferior squadron under Tegetthoff. Instead, he engaged in useless maneuvers in the central Adriatic, during which he did not even exercise his untrained gun crews. At length came peremptory orders from the King himself to "attempt against the hostile fortresses or fleet what operations may be thought likely to obtain a success." Persano, thus prodded, undertook to seize the small Austrian island of Lissa, 130 miles from Ancona across the Adriatic to the southwest. On July 17 his fleet was off the island.

For two days the 600 guns of Persano's ships bombarded the island forts without being able to silence their 88 smaller-caliber guns. A landing attempted by Persano's vice admiral was a failure. In these operations the fleet suffered numerous personnel casualties, had one ironclad frigate put out of action, fruitlessly shot away a large part of its ammunition, and burned its fuel down to a two-day supply. Nevertheless, on the morning of July 20 Persano resumed his amphibious assault. His wooden ships were about to land troops north of the town of Lissa, and his ironclads to resume the bombardment of the forts around the town when the Austrian fleet was sighted steaming down from the northwest at its full speed of eight to ten knots.

Tegetthoff's ships were in three wedge-shaped (double echelon) divisions with the divisions in column. In the first wedge were his seven ironclads led by his flagship the *Ferdinand Maximilian* at the point. The second wedge contained his wooden frigates and one corvette, led by the wooden line-of-battle ship *Kaiser*. His remaining smaller vessels formed the third wedge. This modified line abreast formation was intended principally to facilitate ramming.

Persano first ordered his ships to form line abreast, evidently also planning to make use of his ships' rams. As the Austrian fleet approached however, he formed his immediately available ironclads in column and steered across the head of the enemy formation, probably with the intention of attacking its left flank. At this critical moment he shifted his flag from the *Re d'Italia* to the *Affondatore* in the belief that the fleet commander should be free of the line of battle to supervise the movements of his other ships. As a result a wide gap opened between the first three Italian ships and the rest of the force. Tegetthoff, having signaled his fleet, "Armored ships rush upon and sink the enemy," took his van division of ironclads through the gap.

The van Italian ship had meanwhile opened fire on the port section of the Austrian first division, which in answer turned to port toward the Italian van. At the same time the Austrian starboard section turned right to attack the Italian center, which was turning left in column toward the second Austrian division of large wooden ships. The commander of the Austrian second division however avoided this attack by a turn to starboard, and after a brief skirmish with the Italian rear, which had turned to port to cut him off, he turned farther to starboard and formed a rough column to attack the Italian wooden ships. These in the meantime had been milling about aimlessly to the southward, despite orders from Persano to join battle.

The battle now became a melee in which the movements of ships were mostly obscured by fog and smoke. Twice the *Affondatore* tried without success to ram the wooden *Kaiser*. With better luck the *Kaiser* struck the *Re di Portogallo* a glancing blow but was set ablaze by her gunfire. After a further attack by the *Affondatore*, the *Kaiser* was forced to withdraw toward Lissa with most of the other large wooden ships of the Austrian fleet following in her wake. In the meantime the Italian ironclad gunboat *Palestro* was set afire by shell; shortly after the battle she blew up with the loss of nearly all hands. The most spectacular action of all was the ramming of the *Re d'Italia* by Tegetthoff's flagship, the *Ferdinand Maximilian*. As the *Maximilian* groped about in the murk of battle, she came upon the *Re d'Italia* broadside to. The Italian ship had lost rudder control and was barred from going ahead by another Austrian ship. Backing down, the *Re d'Italia* was dead in the water when the *Maximilian* at full speed plunged her ram into her side, heeling her heavily to starboard. While the *Maximilian* backed slowly away, the *Re d'Italia* righted herself and then heeled on over from the force of her own momentum and the weight of tons of water rushing into a great hole in her side. As she capsized and sank, her ill-trained but spirited crew shouted a cheer for their king.

Shortly after noon Tegetthoff ordered his

fleet to re-form in the vicinity of Lissa, and Persano, after several abortive efforts to renew the battle, retired to the west. Since the Austrian fleet had had several vessels damaged and was still inferior to the enemy, Tegetthoff did not pursue. In any event, his mission was accomplished, for he had driven off the Italian fleet and prevented its seizure of Lissa. Despite their damages, all his ships except the *Kaiser* were still fit for action, and even she was sufficiently refitted in 24 hours. His casualties amounted to only 38 killed and 138 wounded. On the Italian side, in addition to the losses in the amphibious operation, 667 men had been killed and 39 wounded, the new *Re d'Italia* and the *Palestro* had been sunk, and the *San Martino* had been badly damaged. Low on fuel, Persano withdrew to his base at Ancona, where the *Affondatore* later sank in a storm, probably as a result of battle damage.

The strategic lesson of the battle is apparent. Persano might best have sought out and destroyed the Austrian fleet in order to gain control of the Adriatic Sea before involving himself in an amphibious operation in those waters. Or at least, if he felt that the disadvantages of engaging Tegetthoff at or near the Austrian base would offset his own superiority of force, he should have been prepared at all times to cover his operation against interference by the enemy. Instead he was forced to rush into battle with no tactical plan and with his forces scattered and disorganized. On the Austrian side, Tegetthoff demonstrated how much can be done even with an inferior force by an aggressive leader who understands his objective and pursues it wholeheartedly with the means at his disposal.

The tactical lessons were not quite so clear and were much debated by contemporaries. Since gunfire had not sunk any large armored ship, whereas the big *Re d'Italia* had been suddenly destroyed by ramming, the ram seemed to be the decisive weapon. If so, the line abreast formation seemed superior to the line ahead, because it was better suited for ramming tactics. However, it was noted that although repeated attempts at ramming were made by both sides, only the *Re d'Italia* had been sunk in that manner, and she had no way on at the time. So far as the effectiveness of armor was concerned, the ironclads had shown

little more invulnerability than the wooden *Kaiser*, which survived a terrible shelling. Furthermore, the battle was no real test of the gun. Although Persano's apparent attempt to form column and cross ahead of the enemy formation to attack its left flank suggested that he understood how to take advantage of his superior gunpower, the delay caused by his shifting his flag had spoiled his maneuver and brought on a melee, in which accurate gunnery counted very little. Anyway, the Italian gunnery throughout the action was wretched. Thus, none of the problems of weapons and tactics posed by the battle had been really solved—and no generally accepted solutions would be found until the end of the century.

The Contest Between Guns and Armor

In 1865 the British navy had abandoned breech-loading guns for muzzle-loaders because of numerous accidents with breech mechanisms. But even muzzle-loading rifles like those of the ironclad *Bellerophon*, launched in that year, could penetrate 11.4 inches of wrought iron—5.4 inches more than her own heaviest armor. The largest muzzle-loader ever used in the Royal Navy, an 80-ton monster of 16-inch caliber installed aboard the *Inflexible* in 1881, could penetrate 24.3 inches of wrought iron. About this time however the Royal Navy returned to breech-loading. Because the big muzzle-loaders had barrels that were too long to be withdrawn into their turrets, they had to be loaded by depressing and aligning the barrels with deck handling rooms that housed hydraulic loaders. Furthermore, the development of the interrupted screw for breech-closing mechanisms by the French navy had largely overcome the tendency of breech-loaders to burst. A terrible explosion of a muzzle-loader on the *Thunderer* in 1879 finally convinced the British Admiralty that such guns were not inherently safer and led to the gradual adoption of breech-loading in the Royal Navy. The heaviest gun of the century, a breech-loading rifle of 16.25-inch caliber weighing 110 tons, first mounted in the *Victoria* of 1889, could penetrate 37.5 inches of wrought iron. Even the power of this gun was exceeded by that of the 12-inch, 46-ton wire-wound guns of the *Majestic,* completed in 1896, which could penetrate 38.5 inches.

These great increases in gunpower were made possible by developments in metallurgy, chemistry, and mechanics. Wrought iron replaced cast iron in gun barrels, and steel replaced wrought iron for strengthening sleeves that were shrunk on the liners of built-up guns. By 1881 naval rifles were being made entirely of steel. At the same time slow-burning "brown" powder, in which slightly charred straw was used as charcoal and the sulfur content was reduced, permitted the lengthening of gun barrels to secure higher muzzle velocity and greater range. In 1887 the French government adopted smokeless powder, or guncotton, made by nitrating cellulose—an improvement that was quickly copied by the rest of the world. The penetrating power of armor-piercing shells was increased by improvements in design of the point. But the great guns would have wrought destruction only upon their own crews had it not been for the concurrent development of hydraulic mechanisms that could absorb the force of their recoil—amounting to as much as 100,000,000 foot-pounds—and return them to battery without a jar. As a result of all these technological improvements, toward the end of the century naval guns could shoot many times the range at which they could be accurately aimed and it was a rough rule of thumb that at battle ranges a naval gun could penetrate as many inches of the finest armor as its own caliber.

Even this degree of resistance in armor was achieved only by a long and complicated process of improvement in metallurgy. The term "ironclad" correctly indicated the material with which early armored ships were protected. It began to be a misnomer when compound armor, made of iron plates covered with a steel face, was used on the turrets of the *Inflexible,* designed in 1874. Her waterline belt of 24-inch wrought iron, the ultimate in thickness, could just be penetrated at close range by 16-inch muzzle-loading guns like her own. The complete use of compound armor in H.M.S. *Colossus,* designed in 1879, permitted the reduction of the waterline belt to 18 inches. Thereafter the introduction of nickel-steel armor made possible further gradual reductions in armor thickness, until the Harvey process for face-hardening steel by heat and water treatment, and the even better Krupp process of 1895, reduced capital-ship belt armor to its minimum thickness of six inches in the Royal Navy's *Canopus* authorized in 1897.

Developments in Hull Design

Along with the improvement of armor ran a parallel evolution of the hulls built to carry it. In the early race with the French to build ironclads, the British had converted some wooden-hulled ships to carry armor, but their policy for new construction was to use iron for the hull, as they had in their first ironclad, the *Warrior.* The French, whose timber reserves were larger but whose iron industry was weaker than England's, continued to build wooden-hulled ironclads until 1872, when they took a long step ahead of the British by using steel combined with iron in the hull structure of the *Redoubtable.* The British answer to this challenge was Sir William Siemen's open-hearth process, which permitted such precise control of the alloy content of steel that the British were able to launch all-steel-hulled warships in 1886. The French were unable to match this development until 1891.

Nevertheless, as gunpower outpaced armor resistance, no hull could carry sufficient armor to give a ship complete protection throughout its length. From the earliest days of the ironclad, designers had been obliged to compromise between inadequate protection everywhere and absolute protection in the most vital areas. The earliest ironclads, following the design of the sailing ship of the line, carried guns along nearly their entire broadsides. Since a primary function of the armor was to protect the guns and their crews, the armor had to extend along the entire broadside too. As guns grew in size and power, and as ramming tactics, advocated by some naval theorists, seemed to increase the value of bow fire, fewer broadside guns were deemed necessary. Instead, designers began to concentrate the guns in a box-like structure about the central portion of the ship, around which the armor could be concentrated also. Since there was less area

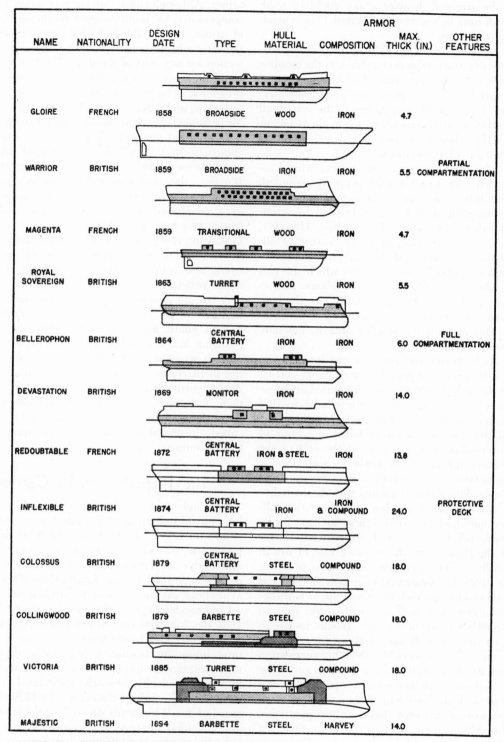

NAME	NATIONALITY	DESIGN DATE	TYPE	HULL MATERIAL	ARMOR COMPOSITION	MAX. THICK (IN.)	OTHER FEATURES
GLOIRE	FRENCH	1858	BROADSIDE	WOOD	IRON	4.7	
WARRIOR	BRITISH	1859	BROADSIDE	IRON	IRON	5.5	PARTIAL COMPARTMENTATION
MAGENTA	FRENCH	1859	TRANSITIONAL	WOOD	IRON	4.7	
ROYAL SOVEREIGN	BRITISH	1863	TURRET	WOOD	IRON	5.5	
BELLEROPHON	BRITISH	1864	CENTRAL BATTERY	IRON	IRON	6.0	FULL COMPARTMENTATION
DEVASTATION	BRITISH	1869	MONITOR	IRON	IRON	14.0	
REDOUBTABLE	FRENCH	1872	CENTRAL BATTERY	IRON & STEEL	IRON	13.8	
INFLEXIBLE	BRITISH	1874	CENTRAL BATTERY	IRON	IRON & COMPOUND	24.0	PROTECTIVE DECK
COLOSSUS	BRITISH	1879	CENTRAL BATTERY	STEEL	COMPOUND	18.0	
COLLINGWOOD	BRITISH	1879	BARBETTE	STEEL	COMPOUND	18.0	
VICTORIA	BRITISH	1885	TURRET	STEEL	COMPOUND	18.0	
MAJESTIC	BRITISH	1894	BARBETTE	STEEL	HARVEY	14.0	

NINETEENTH CENTURY DEVELOPMENTS IN BATTLESHIP DESIGN

to be armored, heavier armor could be used. Such ironclads were called "citadel" or central-battery ships.

Another means of reducing the armor surface necessary to protect a ship was the monitor design. Since the monitor had little freeboard, it required heavy armor only along its waterline and on its turrets. Although the very small freeboard of the monitors made them unseaworthy, they were still considered useful at the turn of the century.

The advantages of the turret, which afforded all-around fire if properly mounted, and full protection for guns and crew, were so manifest that it was early used in vessels of other types than the monitor. However, many designers who liked the feature of all-around fire preferred the barbette, an uncovered low circular tower within which the gun revolved. The barbette provided some protection and much better visibility for the gun crew, thereby promoting accuracy of fire, and it also presented a smaller area to detonate enemy shells.

As barbettes and turrets came into general use, they were mounted on the citadel portion of the ship. Often two were mounted at diagonally opposite corners of the citadel so that both could fire ahead or astern together. The citadel was now used to house the guns of intermediate caliber. Toward the end of the century the turrets or barbettes were usually spread out along the centerline of the ship, and the heavily armored citadel was eliminated.

After the increased power of the major caliber gun had forced designers to concentrate the heaviest armor in only the most vital areas of the ship, a greatly increased rate of fire in smaller caliber guns presented a new problem. By 1889 the Armstrong Company in England had produced quick-fire guns up to 6 inches in caliber, and their 4.72-inch could fire ten aimed shots in 48 seconds. It was useless to keep the big shells out of the vitals of a ship if the quick firers could reduce her superstructure to scrap metal in a few minutes and make it impossible for her crew to operate her. To cope with this problem, designers were forced to provide at least light armor protection throughout most of the ship. To save the weight of the additional armor surface, they had to reduce the thickness of belt and turret armor. Although this reduction was somewhat compensated by improvements in the quality of armor, toward the end of the century designers could no longer provide absolute protection for any part of the ship. The best that could be achieved was a reasonable degree of protection at battle ranges for guns, magazines, waterline, and machinery, and some protection for personnel elsewhere against quick-fire guns.

A final safeguard against enemy fire was compartmentation, which could at least keep a ship from sinking after it was hit. Even the *Warrior*, the first iron-hulled ironclad, was partially compartmented, and the system was early recognized as an important safety feature in merchant ships. A further improvement in warship design was the location of bunkers in outboard compartments, where the coal would absorb the explosive force of shells that might penetrate them.

A feature closely related to compartmentation was the protective deck. Its main function was to guard the vitals of the ship against plunging fire. Located at the waterline, a full deck of armor sufficiently strong to stop plunging shells enclosed a space below of sufficient displacement to float the ship, no matter how many holes were shot through the sides above. Such decks were the only protection of so-called "protected cruisers" in the last quarter of the century.

The Torpedo and its Carriers

Although compartmentation was introduced into warship design as an adjunct to or substitute for armor, a strong impetus to its improvement was given by the development of automotive torpedoes. The first of these was designed in 1860 by the Englishman Robert Whitehead on the basis of research done by a Commander Lupis of the Austrian Navy. In 1867 the Austrians carried out official experiments with Whitehead's torpedo, to which its most important feature, a hydrostatic depth regulator, had meantime been added. Powered by compressed air, the early Whitehead was feeble and erratic in performance. In 1870 the speed of the Whiteheads was only eight knots, and the total distance they could travel was only 400 yards. The effective range was only a fraction of that distance. But the power of the Whitehead increased steadily throughout the remainder of the century, and after gyroscopic rudder control, an American invention, was introduced about 1885, its accuracy improved also. By 1898 its speed had increased to 30 knots and its effective range was about 500 yards. It was apparent moreover that it had by no means reached its technological limits.

Concurrently, with the development of the torpedo, special boats were designed to carry the new weapon. The earliest models carried spar torpedoes, which had to be brought by the boat into contact with the target, and Harvey towing torpedoes, which were so rigged that they could be swung out from the wake of the towing boat to strike the target ship. Experiments were made also with dirigible torpedoes that could be controlled by mechanical or electric cables, but these were used mostly on larger ships or for harbor defense and were generally unsuccessful.

The torpedo saw extensive battle service in the Russo-Turkish War of 1877–78. The Russians used squadrons of torpedo launches, supported by fast steamers as tenders, against a Turkish fleet of ironclads based on the Black Sea and another Turkish force of monitors in the Danube River. The first certain success of the torpedo launches was achieved by spar torpedoes, which sank a small armor-clad in the Danube. Later a force of two tenders carrying six torpedo boats operated on the Black Sea with dubious results. In June 1877 the squadron made an attack with spar torpedoes upon four Turkish ironclads off the mouth of the Danube. The attack failed because the ships were protected by anti-torpedo nets. Six months later the squadron attacked some Turkish ships near Batum and fired two Whiteheads, one of which probably dived and struck a rock, while the other failed to explode and was captured by the Turks. The following month at the same place, according to Russian accounts, two Whiteheads fired at 80 yards sank a 2,000-ton Turkish warship. All the torpedo actions of the war cost the Russians not a single man, but on the other hand the Turks suffered no admitted loss from Whitehead torpedoes, despite their ships' lack of any quick-fire guns for close defense.

The Whitehead torpedo was not used again in warfare until the Chilean Civil War of 1891, in which the Chilean fleet of ironclads supported the Congress against the Presidential forces. On January 27 a steam launch from the Congressional ironclad *Blanco Encalada* fired a Whitehead torpedo at the Presidential armed steamer *Imperial* but missed. Three months later the *Blanco* herself was hit by one of two or three Whiteheads fired by a Presidential torpedo-gunboat squadron. In two minutes the *Blanco* became the first admitted loss of an ironclad to a torpedo. It should be noted however that the *Blanco* was at anchor and unprotected by nets, that although searchlights had been developed for use against torpedo boats, the *Blanco* made no use of hers, and that she made only late and ineffective use of her quick-fire guns. Consequently the torpedo-boat was able to fire its torpedoes at a range of only 50 yards, and even so only one of two or three fired struck home. The action proved merely that an unwary ship can often be sunk by surprise attack. In like manner, during the Brazilian revolution of 1893–4, the insurgent turret ship *Aquidaban* was sunk by one of several torpedoes fired from less than 400-foot range by a loyalist torpedo boat.

Meanwhile the British navy had developed craft called *torpedo-gunboats* or *torpedo catchers* to combat the smaller torpedo boats. They turned out to be too large, unmaneuverable, and slow for their task. What was needed was a ship large enough to keep the sea in heavy weather and carry a substantial armament but at the same time small enough to have great speed and maneuverability. Such a vessel could be used for both torpedo and anti-torpedo work. The successful compromise was the torpedo-boat destroyer. The first of these, the *Havoc*, launched in 1893, displaced 240 tons and had a speed of 26.7 knots. Before the turn of the century larger and faster destroyers were being built and their usefulness and versatility were becoming generally recognized.

Improvements in Propulsion

The surprisingly high speed of the first destroyer was made possible by developments in boilers and engines following the American Civil War. Early boilers were simply iron boxes reinforced internally by iron stay rods. As progress in metallurgy made it possible to build stronger box boilers, steam pressures rose from 20 to 40 pounds. At the same time the development of the cylindrical boiler, in which numerous tubes carried the hot gases of combustion through the water, increased efficiency by providing greater surface for heat absorption, thereby achieving increase of steam pressures up to 60 pounds. The water-tube boiler, invented by Julien Belleville in 1855 and developed principally in France, further increased thermal efficiency. This type provided much greater heating surface than the fire-tube boiler by containing the water in steel tubes around which the gases of combustion pass. In the early 1880's the British developed a water-tube boiler for use in destroyers. A little later the French installed water-tube boilers in battleships and armored cruisers. By the end of the century the newest ships of both the British and American navies were using water-tube boilers capable of working pressures up to 250 pounds. To make full use of these higher steam pressures, compound or double-expansion engines and, later, triple-expansion engines had meanwhile been developed. In these the steam expanded in successively larger cylinders, instead of in only one cylinder, thus yielding more power to be applied through the piston-rods to the crankshaft.

As a result of all these improvements in engines and boilers, the horsepower of British battleships climbed from 5,200 in 1861 to 14,000 in 1892, with a resulting increase in speed from 14 to 18 knots, despite an increase in displacement from 9,000 to 14,000 tons. However, the type of ship that profited most from these mechanical developments was the cruiser. Often having nearly as great displacement as its battleship contemporaries but carrying smaller guns and lighter armor, the cruiser could accommodate sufficient machinery and fuel for both high speed and great range. The speed of British cruisers rose from 16.2 knots in 1868 to 24.0 knots in 1895, while at the same time their endurance increased from 2,800 miles to 25,000.

By the late 1890's the basic warship types of the next half-century had evolved, and their capabilities were nearly equal to those of similar types in World War I—in which, as a matter of fact, many late 19th-century ships fought.

Battleships displaced up to 15,000 tons; they carried armor of face-hardened nickel-steel up to 14 inches in thickness, mounted breech-loading rifles up to 16.25 inches caliber in heavily armored turrets, and could make speeds up to 18.5 knots. Armored cruisers were often nearly as large as battleships; they carried armor up to 6 inches, mounted guns up to 9.2 inches, and could steam as fast as 24 knots. Protected cruisers displaced up to 5,600 tons, had armored decks up to 2.5 inches in thickness, mounted quick-firing guns as large as 6 inches, and could make as much as 20 knots. Destroyers were small—the largest not much over 400 tons—but they had made trial speeds up to 35.5 knots.

Tactical Theory and Practice

The swift and radical changes in naval weapons during the second half of the 19th century simply compounded the tactical confusion introduced by the advent of steam propulsion. Students of naval tactics, like their forebears of the Spanish Armada period, had to make up their minds as to what was now the decisive weapon for naval warfare, which the best type of ship to carry that weapon, and which the most effective formation of ships for using it in battle. The expected complexity of battle formations and the loss of visibility due to funnel and gun smoke raised the further problem of the best position for the commander in chief to take in order to direct his forces most effectively.

The choice of weapons lay first between the gun and the ram. Later the torpedo arose as a challenger to both, and the gun alternative became complicated by a choice between the slow-firing heavy gun and the lighter quick-firer. Even if the big gun was to be the decisive weapon, there was still the problem of the best type of ship to carry it. Should big guns be mounted in large numbers on the largest and most heavily armored ships that could be constructed? Or, if armor was ineffective against gunfire, should the guns be mounted singly in small, fast, highly maneuverable gunboats? If, as some claimed, the big guns could rarely hit anything, why not rely on gunless rams? As the torpedo began to show promise, its proponents advocated the torpedo boat as the nemesis of all so-called "capital" ships. Since the choice of weapons determines the specific tactics to be used, it is little wonder that a leading British naval officer remarked toward the end of the century that naval tactics were "in a state of chaos."

The selection of weapon and ship type would of course determine the formation to be used. The ram would be most effective, it appeared, in a line abreast formation, or some modification of line abreast such as the indented (sawtooth) line or the double echelon (wedge) — both of which, as we have seen, were advocated by tactical theorists soon after the advent of steam propulsion. In either of the suggested variations on line abreast, ships to the rear would be in a position to ram an enemy trying to ram friendly ships ahead. Some ram enthusiasts, especially in France, advocated the use of "pelotons," groups of from two to four ships in various triangular and echelon arrangements. The gun however could not be entirely disregarded. Even the most ardent proponents of the ram and of ram formations had to take into consideration the fact that big ships carrying centerline turrets or guns in broadside could achieve maximum firepower only by use of the traditional column. A compromise solution was found in so arranging the turrets, usually on a diagonal, as to permit maximum fire ahead as well as abeam. This would permit ships to fire all major caliber guns in a bows-on approach until the final, decisive moment of ramming. Though the gun gradually regained its position as the decisive naval weapon in the judgment of most naval theorists, the divided opinion of the late 19th century is reflected in the fact that for many years—until the early 1900's—all capital ships were provided with rams as well as guns.

Whatever weapon, ship, and formation was finally to be chosen, there was general agreement that fleet maneuvers under steam would not only be more swift but immensely more complex than anything seen in the days of sail. To meet this new problem, continual exercise at sea was considered essential. Hence "squadrons of evolution" were organized so that commanders could frequently practice the tactical maneuvers that might be required in battle—the so-called "applied tactics." Moreover, to perfect officers in the handling of both

squadrons and single ships, "evolutionary" maneuvers of the greatest complexity, having no conceivable use in battle, were also practiced. It was an exercise in such "pure tactics" as these that resulted in the sinking in 1893 of the H.M.S. *Victoria* by H.M.S. *Camperdown* by accidental ramming. Vice Admiral Sir George Tryon, commander in chief of the British Mediterranean fleet, signaled the parallel columns these two battleships were leading to countermarch (reverse course) by turning inward in succession toward each other. Unfortunately the columns were only 1,200 yards apart, while the tactical diameter[1] of the battleships was 800 yards.

Many naval officers recommended that the commander in chief take station outside the line of battle in some swift, highly-maneuverable, well-protected ship, from which he could better observe the movements of his force. Such a position, they argued, would give him the advantage of being able to signal corrective instructions after the battle was joined. Other officers contended that the advantages to be gained by such a departure from sailing ship tradition would be more than offset by the loss of the commander's inspiriting presence in the line. Again, if the line of battle was to be a column, the question arose whether the commander in chief should lead it for maximum morale, or take the sailing ship position in the center of the line in order to facilitate communication.

The chaos in tactical thinking was compounded by the fact that the middle and late 19th century provided little opportunity for putting tactical theory to the test of battle. The sinking of the *Cumberland* and the *Congress* by the *Virginia* in the Battle of Hampton Roads and the sinking of the *Re d'Italia* by the *Ferdinand Maximilian* in the Battle of Lissa seemed to support the proponents of the ram. But the victims in each instance had been stationary at the time of ramming. The *Tennessee* did no serious damage to Farragut's maneuvering wooden ships in the Battle of Mobile Bay, and Tegetthoff's rams achieved only the one lone, if spectacular, sinking. In the Battle of Lissa, a bows-on attack had de-

[1] Tactical diameter: Diameter of the half-circle a ship describes in reversing course with constant rudder angle.

feated a column, but in the next fleet action, the Battle of the Yalu of 1894, a column defeated a line abreast. Obviously there was ample evidence to support a variety of points of view.

While theorists were groping toward a suitable doctrine for fleet battles under steam, a group of naval officers in France were attracting adherents to their so-called *Jeune Ecole*. The *Jeune Ecole* put forward the theory that naval weapons of offense and defense had canceled each other out and hence that there would be no more great fleet battles. The proponents of this view advocated a naval strategy of commerce warfare and coast defense analogous to that of the United States throughout most of the century, and motivated in part by similar reasons of economy. Both the offensive and defensive phases of this strategy would be carried out by light forces—the commerce warfare by fast cruisers or even torpedo boats, which were thought by some to be capable of operations on the high seas; the coast defense, by gunboats, rams, and torpedo boats. The *Jeune Ecole* and other proponents of light forces, though highly vocal, did not win ascendancy on the Continent and found very few supporters indeed among Royal Navy officers. France and Italy, as well as Britain, continued to concentrate their building efforts on big ships armed with heavy guns.

Developments in techniques and weapons finally settled the major issues with regard to naval tactics. Improvements in the torpedo, making it an effective short-range weapon, defeated both the ram and the line abreast. Any would-be rammer would surely be sunk by torpedoes before he could get close enough to make his attack. Although the torpedo had won great respect by the end of the century, it was relegated to a subordinate position by its continuing ineffectiveness at long range and by the vulnerability of torpedo boats to the new quick-firers. Thus the demonstrable shortcomings of other weapons restored to the gun its unchallenged position as the dominant naval weapon, and the victory of the gun over its competitors re-established the column as the basic formation for fleet battles. This was the view held all along by the majority of naval officers, and the one advocated by the most reputable British authorities on naval warfare.[2]

The subordinate question of the big gun versus the quick-firer was not resolved until early in the 20th century, when improvements in fire control forced columns in combat farther and farther apart until the quick-firer was utterly outranged. Big guns in big ships in line ahead thus became the established pattern of the battle line before the outbreak of World War I. At the same time there was general recognition of the need for light forces, cruisers and destroyers, to screen the battleships against attack by similar forces.

Improvement in visual communications and fleet control through the use of smokeless powder nullified arguments that the commander in chief should be stationed anywhere but in the line. In smaller fleets and in segments of larger fleets, the flagship took the leading position at the head of the column. But in extended battle lines, such as those of the British and German fleets in the Battle of Jutland, the commander in chief continued to command from a position at the center.

The main problems concerning naval tactics under steam had thus been solved or were on the way to solution by the end of the 19th century. However, steam surface navies never had sufficient experience under fire to enable them to reach the mature doctrines that marked the closing years of the Age of Sail. Before steam doctrines were fully developed, the aircraft and the aircraft carrier arrived to present a new set of problems requiring solution.

The Decline of the United States Navy

At the end of the American Civil War the U.S. Navy had in service 700 ships displacing 500,000 tons and mounting 5,000 guns. By December 1870 this fleet had dwindled to 200

---

[2] Among these were Rear Admiral P. H. Colomb, the most prolific and one of the most respected writers on tactics among British naval officers of the period, the historian Sir W. Laird Clowes, and Commander F. C. D. Sturdee, who was to lead big-gun British battle cruisers to victory at the Falkland Islands in World War I.

ships displacing 200,000 tons and mounting only 1,300 guns. Of these only 52 ships mounting 500 guns were in full commission. All of them were obsolete in comparison with the ships of European navies.

Perhaps the main reason for this deterioration was the concentration of American thought and energy on internal problems—reconstruction after the Civil War and the development of the West. Reinforcing this absorption in domestic affairs was a widespread feeling that American security was sufficiently guaranteed against European aggression by the 3,000-mile breadth of the Atlantic, which would greatly handicap the coal-burning ships of European navies operating in American waters without adequate supporting bases. With this safety factor in mind, American political leaders, and most naval officers as well, expected the Navy to use the traditional American naval strategy in the event of war: passive defense of seaports combined with offensive warfare against an enemy's commerce.

To implement the strategy of harbor defense, the Navy had left over from the war against the Confederacy many small monitors and a few large seagoing ones. For warfare against an enemy's commerce a new class of fast steam-and-sail vessels, originally designed to cope with Confederate raiders like the *Alabama,* were completed. Their advanced engineering plants were the product of competition between the designs of private contractors and those of Chief Engineer Benjamin Franklin Isherwood of the Navy's Bureau of Steam Engineering. Regarding sail as only an auxiliary means of propulsion, Isherwood designed both ship and power plant to produce the maximum possible speed under steam. In 1868 the first of the class completed, u.s.s. *Wampanoag,* achieved a maximum speed of 17.75 knots and a sustained speed of 16.6 knots on her trials.[3] Isherwood designed his ships in the best possible manner for their assigned task; like the American frigates of the War of 1812,

they could outrun anything they could not outfight.

Yet the Navy Department rejected Isherwood's principles of design. In the year following the *Wampanoag* trials a board headed by Rear Admiral L. M. Goldsborough recommended that the ship be redesigned to carry more sail power at the expense of her steam power, and the Secretary of the Navy issued a general order requiring that all vessels of the Navy except tugs and dispatch vessels be fitted with full sail power. The *Wampanoag* and her sister-ship the *Ammonoosuc* were condemned as unfit for naval service and laid up. The Goldsborough board also recommended that four-bladed screws on naval vessels be replaced with less efficient two-bladed screws, which could be lined up vertically with the keel to increase speed when the ship was under sail. Many ships were so altered, and this policy was defended by Admiral of the Navy David D. Porter as late as 1871.

There were two related reasons for the Navy's emphasis upon sail power at the expense of steam. In the first place, the traditional American wartime strategy of commerce raiding would require ships to cruise individually at great distances from their home ports. Coal would be difficult to get and could therefore be used only sparingly.[4] Furthermore, the Navy's peacetime mission was considered to be the showing of the flag in distant quarters of the world to protect American merchant ships and their crews against injury and interference by the "uncivilized" peoples of Asia and Africa. This mission, too, required ships that could operate independently over great distances for long periods without recoaling.[5] But the underlying reason for the sail-power preference was economy, which indeed was the basis for general American naval strategy. By denying the necessity of maintaining a strong navy of capital ships able to take the offensive

[3] An English authority claims that her actual speed did not exceed 15 knots and that she was excelled by H.M.S. *Inconstant* before she was completed. See H. W. Wilson, *Ironclads in Action* (Boston, 1896), II, 254.

[4] The danger of a vessel that depended principally upon sail power and could make only moderate speed under steam being run down and destroyed by a locally-based fast steam vessel does not seem to have entered into the calculations of the proponents of sail.

[5] It should be noted that for similar reasons European navies also continued to fit major combatant types with sails as late as the 1880's.

against an enemy fleet, the defensive naval policy saved money. So strong was the economy motive in naval operations that commanding officers were ordered to enter in the log in red ink their reasons for getting up steam, and at one time the Secretary of the Navy even contemplated making them pay for the coal they burned if the reason seemed inadequate.

As the ships of the Navy aged, the expense of maintaining them became greater. Consequently a continually larger share of the annual naval appropriation found its way into the hands of contractors and suppliers for the repair of ships which should long ago have been surveyed and scrapped. Navy yards flourished, while the forces afloat languished and their equipment became more obsolete. As late as 1884 the United States Navy was still using 9-inch Dahlgren smoothbores and Parrott rifles —both muzzle-loading relics of the Civil War. In 1883 a French admiral who made a call on Captain Alfred Thayer Mahan USN aboard the screw sloop *Wachusett* on the Pacific station was struck by the outmoded armament of the ship. Noticing one of the ancient pivot guns, he murmured nostalgically, *"Ah! Capitaine, les vieux canons!"*[6] At a time when the British navy, though not at war, was active in every quarter of the globe, extending and protecting the Empire and supporting the rights and ambitions of its citizens, American naval officers were ashamed to meet even the officers of those small South American republics whose navies were more modern than their own.

Naval Activity in the Years of Decline

Even with its obsolete ships and weapons the U.S. Navy performed its task of protecting American lives and property in distant parts of the world. At the very moment when the French admiral was reminiscing over Captain Mahan's old pivot gun, the mission of the *Wachusett* was to safeguard American lives and property in Chile during the long war between Chile and Peru. In 1881 a similar screw sloop, the *Marion,* rescued the crew of the American whaler *Trinity* from Heard

[6] Capt. A. T. Mahan USN (Ret.), *From Sail to Steam* (New York, 1907), 197.

Island in the South Indian Ocean. That same year Commander R. W. Shufeldt USN negotiated a treaty with Korea that gave Americans trading privileges and provided for the protection of American seamen. Ten years earlier, when the American trading bark *General Sherman* disappeared in the vicinity of Korea, Rear Admiral John Rodgers USN, commanding the Asiatic Squadron, investigated and took punitive action.

Throughout this period of material decay, the Navy was active also in Arctic exploration, though with more loss than gain. U.S.S. *Polaris* was crushed in Arctic ice in 1871, happily without loss of life. The *Jeannette* Expedition eight years later was less fortunate. The steamer *Jeannette* had been purchased by the newspaper publisher James Gordon Bennett to explore the Arctic by a new route through Bering Strait, and Congress had authorized the United States Navy to refit and man the vessel. The expedition ended in disaster for ship and all but one boat party under command of Passed Assistant Engineer George Melville. His long and arduous search of the Lena Delta in northern Siberia for his commander proved him a man of many parts besides engineering genius. Along with Commander Winfield Scott Schley, later commodore of the Flying Squadron in the Spanish-American War, Melville also participated in the Navy-commanded Greely Relief Expedition, which rescued Lieutenant A. W. Greely USA and the pitiful remnant of his exploring party from Ellesmere Island, where they had been marooned for nearly three years.

Much more important than Arctic exploration for the future of the United States Navy was the growing interest of naval officers in acquiring positions for advanced naval bases. Without coaling and repair bases, steam-propelled warships simply could not operate in distant waters. In the Caribbean area, a treaty to acquire the Virgin Islands was negotiated with Denmark as early as 1867 but was not ratified by the United States Senate. Later negotiations with the Dominican Republic were abandoned because of the political difficulties involved in the annexation of a territory inhabited by a large Negro population. In the Pacific Ocean area efforts were more fruitful. Commander William Reynolds USN acquired

Midway Island for the United States in 1867. A reciprocity treaty with Hawaii in 1875, which recognized the islands as "an American sphere of influence," was renewed in 1884 with the additional right to construct and maintain a naval base at Pearl Harbor. A treaty with Samoa for a naval station at Pago Pago, Tutuila, which Commander R. W. Meade USN made in 1872, was not ratified at that time, but a similar treaty was ratified six years later. Thus a start had been made in the direction of American naval control of the Pacific even before the Spanish-American War.

Intellectual Progress

In the last 15 years of the 19th century the most important developments for the future of the United States as a great naval power came in the realm of ideas. The richest source of these revitalizing ideas was the Naval War College, established in 1884 at Newport, Rhode Island on the recommendation of a board headed by Rear Admiral Stephen Bleecker Luce USN, commander of the Training Squadron for apprentice seamen. Luce had long advocated better education for both enlisted men and officers. His concept of a naval war college curriculum included post graduate courses in such subjects as ordnance, international law, higher mathematics, languages, astronomy, and hydrography, but its main feature was to be a study of the science of war.[7] This in turn would require a "philosophic study of naval history." From its beginning the function of the War College was, as Luce intended, "the systematic study of military operations, by land or sea, applying the experiences of history to contemporary conditions, and to the particular theaters of possible war in which the nation may be interested." The definer and principal teacher and developer of this study was Captain Alfred Thayer Mahan, who at Luce's request was assigned as an instructor in October 1885.

Mahan had earlier published *The Gulf and Inland Waters,* a book about the operations of the Federal Navy in the Civil War, but little

in it gave promise of the line of thought that he was to develop in the lectures he prepared for delivery at the War College. In fact, at the time Rear Admiral Luce asked him to come to the War College, Mahan believed the United States should avoid acquiring territorial possessions overseas, not only to save the expense of the large navy that would be necessary to protect them, but also to avoid the dominance of a powerful military caste over the democratic processes of the government. In line with these feelings he accepted the naval maxims of his time and country that commerce destruction and coast defense were the only tasks the U.S. Navy needed to perform in time of war.

But as Mahan began to study history in preparation for his duties at the War College, he discovered that "control of the sea was an historic factor which had never been systematically appreciated and expounded."[8] From this time on he had his vocation. Examining the situation and characteristics of nations that had been great sea powers, especially England, he perceived certain factors he thought made the development of sea power possible: (1) geographic position, (2) physical conformation, (3) extent of territory, (4) number of population, (5) character of the people, and (6) character of the government.[9]

The most important of these factors in the rise of English sea power had been the insular position of Britain off the coast of Western Europe. As an island nation England had enjoyed easy defense against rival land powers. Consequently she had been able to get along with only a small army and devote the bulk of her military expenditures to the maintenance of a large and powerful navy. Even more important, England's position flanking the North Atlantic sea lanes had enabled her to dominate the lines of sea communication between the countries of Western Europe and the resource areas of America, Africa, and Asia that were opened up by the explorers of the

[8] *From Sail to Steam,* 276.

[9] Developed in Mahan, *The Influence of Sea Power upon History* (Boston, 1890), 25–89. Summarized on page 44, above. Chapters 2–9 of this book generally develop Mahan's sea power thesis. All other chapters reflect it.

[7] The technical subjects recommended by Luce have since been absorbed into the curriculum of the U.S. Naval Post Graduate School, established early in the 20th century.

15th and 16th centuries. In time of war England had therefore been able to interrupt her enemies' trade with these overseas regions and at the same time acquire colonies and trade for herself. The final result of this advantageous position, skillfully exploited, was the British Empire of the 19th century, and the dominion of the seas then enjoyed by the Royal Navy.

All the sea power factors that had made Great Britain mistress of the seas Mahan saw potentially present in the situation of the United States. The breadth of the Atlantic and Pacific Oceans and the absence of strong rival powers to north and south made the country strategically an island from the point of view of defense. With an Isthmian canal dug and the vast Pacific area developed, the United States would enjoy a dominant position on important trade routes. The country had many good harbors, and the vast extent of its territory was no handicap to defense because it also had a large and rapidly growing population, a considerable part of which came from seafaring stock and followed the sea for a living. The people of the country were inclined toward commercial pursuits and had a consequent tendency to trade upon the sea. Although the foreign commerce of the United States had diminished since the first half of the 19th century, when American clipper ships were supreme upon the trade routes of the world, the country could develop the steel shipbuilding capacity to win back from Great Britain the position it had lost to her in the second half of the century. All that was needed to bring these factors into harmonious coordination and develop a great American sea power to rival or surpass that of England was a government that understood the value of sea power and the importance of control of the sea to the security and prosperity of the nation. This last essential factor could be developed by persuasion.

However it would not suffice merely to convince the people and their government of the advantages of sea power and show them how it could be developed; it was equally important to show them how it should be used. According to Mahan the principal mission of a navy in warfare was to control the areas of sea communication in order to secure their use to one's own cargo vessels and transports while denying their use to an enemy's. In a conflict with another sea power that possessed a strong fleet of capital ships, such control could be achieved only by destroying or neutralizing the enemy's fleet with a more powerful fleet of one's own. Commerce warfare by fast cruisers might in part deny the use of the sea to the enemy's merchant marine, but it could not secure its use to one's own; it was merely an adjunct to the main objective of destroying the enemy's most powerful organized fighting force wherever it might be.

But modern warships could not carry sufficient coal to cross an ocean and fight an enemy fleet on equal terms. Hence the need for overseas bases to extend the range of the fleet into any area where one's sea communications might be threatened. Since a base exists to support the fleet, and not the fleet to support the base, ideally a base should be self-sufficient. Hence bases are most favorably located in colonies, which can provide resources and are under one's own control. Colonies in turn make trade more profitable, and thus nourish the merchant marine which is the *raison d'être* of sea power in the first place. Thus Mahan's line of reasoning led him from his original isolationist politics and defensive naval strategy to a position that was politically imperialistic and strategically offensive in concept.

The concrete result of Mahan's study and reflection was *The Influence of Sea Power upon History, 1660–1783,* published in 1890, in which he showed how the fortunes of the British Empire rose when her statesmen understood and used sea power correctly while France's ambitions failed from misunderstanding and neglect. Two years later *The Influence of Sea Power upon the French Revolution and Empire* continued the story to the end of the Napoleonic Wars. In 1905, he published a sea power analysis of the War of 1812. Meantime he had been writing numerous magazine articles in which he called to the attention of the American public the importance to their security of such measures as American ownership of an Isthmian canal and the acquisition of naval bases in Cuba and Hawaii.

Although Mahan's lectures at the War College had interested a number of naval officers in his ideas, his *Influence of Sea Power* did not immediately receive the acclaim in the United States that it was accorded in Europe, where his reasoned exposition of principles that many British statesmen had followed instinctively was flattering to the English. The German Kaiser also was so impressed that he ordered a copy placed in the wardroom of every ship of his new navy. Moreover it was perhaps significant for the future course of history that more of Mahan's works were translated into Japanese than into any other language. In the United States however an adverse school of opinion was represented by the incumbent Chief of the Bureau of Navigation (who directed the assignment of officers) when he said, "It is not the business of a naval officer to write books." However, Mahan's ideas were already winning him influential friends; on this occasion he was saved from sea duty to complete his second book on sea power by the intervention of Secretary of the Navy Benjamin F. Tracy. Even more important for the future influence of his ideas was the interest of Theodore Roosevelt, who became Assistant Secretary of the Navy in 1897, and Henry Cabot Lodge, Chairman of the Senate Naval Affairs Committee. By the time Flag Captain Mahan returned from a European cruise with honorary degrees from Oxford and Cambridge, nearly everyone would admit that there was something to be said after all for naval officers writing books.

The New Navy
of the United States

Influential as Mahan's ideas became in the 1890's, it cannot be said that they brought about the rebirth of the United States Navy. That process had begun much earlier. Some tentative efforts at improvement were made 15 years before Mahan had even begun to think about sea power, when Secretary of the Navy George M. Robeson took it upon himself to use appropriations for maintenance and repairs to reconstruct old ships and build new ones. His bold misappropriations became the subject of a Congressional investigation that publicized the disgraceful condition of the Navy and spurred Congress in 1873 to authorize the construction of eight "steam vessels of war, with auxiliary sail power" totaling 8,000 tons. Under this authorization the Navy built three iron gunboats, four wooden corvettes, and the frigate *Trenton*.

Several international incidents involving Americans helped the rebuilding program by demonstrating the weakness of the Navy. In 1873 a Spanish cruiser captured the American merchant ship *Virginius* in the act of running arms and volunteers to Cuban insurgents and took her to Havana, where the Spanish authorities executed several dozen of the passengers, many of them Americans. An attempt to mobilize the fleet to support United States protests brought together a force that was fairly numerous but entirely obsolete. Continuing troubles with Spain over Cuba during the next decade helped to keep alive the country's concern about its naval weakness. In 1889 the rumor of a clash between American and German ships over Samoa prompted another stock-taking. Two years later a sailors' brawl that started in the True Blue Saloon at Valparaiso during a Chilean insurrection resulted in the killing of some American sailors on liberty from U.S.S. *Baltimore*. When hostilities with Chile threatened, the American public was surprised to find that its navy still had no armored cruiser or battleship in service.

Yet the reconstruction of the American navy had then been in progress since James A. Garfield became President in 1881. Conditions at that time had been peculiarly favorable to Congressional appropriations for a naval building program. The War of the Pacific (1879–84), in which Chile defeated Bolivia and Peru, showed that some small South American countries had navies stronger and more modern than that of the United States. Operations of the French de Lesseps Company in Panama threatened to put an Isthmian canal under European control. The United States had already acquired some territorial interests in the Pacific. Most important of all, the strong financial condition of the country made payment for a naval building program seem relatively painless. Determined to improve the condition of the Navy, William H. Hunt, Secretary under Garfield, appointed a board of officers to advise him what types and numbers of ships should be recommended to Congress.

The recommendations of the board were conservative. To use the large supply of ship timber on hand and provide employment in Eastern building yards for wooden ships, the board recommended construction principally of a large number of small wooden cruisers with steam engines and full sail power. A minority however, including Benjamin Isherwood, recommended construction of armored cruisers and seagoing armored warships. The following year the board went along in part with Isherwood's proposal by recommending the construction of several steel ships. As authorized by Congress in 1883, this program produced the steam-and-sail protected cruisers *Atlanta, Boston,* and *Chicago,* and the dispatch vessel *Dolphin*—popularly known as the "ABCD's." At the same time Congress encouraged the retirement of outmoded wooden ships by limiting the amount of money which could be spent on their repair to 30 per cent of the cost of a similar new vessel. A commission was appointed also to recommend elimination and consolidation of navy yards, which had mushroomed along the coasts with more regard for the constituencies of Congressmen than the requirements of the Navy. Some years later, to promote efficiency in procurement, all navy purchases were consolidated in the Bureau of Provisions and Clothing (afterwards renamed Supplies and Accounts), and the General Storekeeping system and property accounts for capital items were established.

As the shore establishment readied itself to support a new fleet, the forces afloat grew slowly in numbers and modernity. The work was handicapped however by American inexperience in warship design and lack of steel ship-building capacity. Construction plans for the cruiser *Charleston,* authorized in 1885, the Navy's first battleship, the *Texas,*[10] and the protected cruiser *Baltimore* of the following year had to be purchased in England. And

[10] With the construction of the new fleet, the U.S. Navy began the practice of naming ships according to type—battleships taking the names of states, and cruisers the names of cities.

though Congress directed that these ships be built in American yards, the shafting had to be supplied from abroad for lack of facilities to produce it in the United States. Two years later however an authorization for seven cruisers required that all parts without exception be manufactured in the United States.

Meanwhile a better understanding of the strategic and tactical use of a modern navy had begun to develop slowly in the government. While the Congress was authorizing cruisers, the House Naval Affairs Committee was recommending seagoing battleships which could operate in defense of the entire coast. In 1886 Senator Matthew C. Butler of South Carolina derided commerce warfare and advocated a strong fleet of first-class battleships. Three years later the Navy Department established a "squadron of evolution" which organized all the new ships then in service into a single tactical unit. The following year Chairman Charles A. Boutelle of the House Naval Affairs Committee finally succeeded against strong opposition in getting authorization for three "seagoing, coast-line battleships," the *Indiana, Massachusetts,* and *Oregon.*

Although these ships and the later *Iowa* were designated "coast-line" by Congress to indicate that they were intended for the defense of American waters and not for offensive action in foreign waters, some naval officers and politicians, following Mahan, had more aggressive ideas about the strategic function of a battle fleet. Secretary of the Navy Tracy in his Annual Report for 1889 wrote of the necessity to "beat off the enemy and threaten his coast," and in 1890 his Policy Board recommended in addition to a coast-defense fleet of battleships with limited coal capacity, a fleet of long-range battleships for offensive operations against an enemy. Finally in 1897 the organization of three first- and two second-class battleships and two armored cruisers into a powerful North Atlantic Squadron gave at least partial implementation to Mahan's concept of an offensive fleet.

Thus by the eve of the Spanish-American War the United States had acquired a navy which, though far from being the most powerful in the world, still had a respectable number of modern ships. The three battleships of the *Indiana* class each displaced more than

10,000 tons, carried armor up to 18 inches in thickness, mounted 13-inch guns in their main battery, and could make almost 17 knots. The larger *Iowa*, last battleship completed in time to fight the Spaniards, carried improved 15-inch armor and was somewhat faster. These ships compared favorably with the contemporary British *Majestic* class, which, though several thousand tons larger and therefore longer-range and slightly faster, carried lighter armor and smaller main and intermediate caliber guns. In all, the Navy had in service four

first-class battleships, two second-class battleships, two armored cruisers, ten protected cruisers, and a considerable number of gunboats, monitors, and torpedo boats. The United States had acquired this largely modern fleet without the tremendous expense of experimentation and obsolescence to which England and France had been put. In addition, through the teachings of Mahan, the American navy had at its disposal a body of strategic and tactical doctrine that explained how its new power could be effectively used.

19:

The Rise of Japanese Naval Power

We have seen how the voyages of discovery originating in Western Europe at the end of the medieval period established a sea power link between East and West. The Portuguese, followed by the Dutch, the English, and the French, rounded Africa to found an immense trade empire in India and the East Indies. The Spaniards, operating out of their bases in the New World, captured the Philippines. The Europeans were successful in part because they came mainly as traders, not as home-seekers, in part from lack of organized opposition. India they found divided into a hundred separate principalities, often mutually hostile. Japan was suffering from centuries-long clan wars. China, in some respects highly civilized, could scarcely muster strength to police her own vast realms.

Yet navies and naval warfare were not unknown to the Far East when Europeans first arrived. Like insular England, insular Japan was early the target of expanding continental powers across the narrow seas. In 1273 and again in 1279 Kublai Khan had attempted to invade Japan from Korea and China. These were large-scale operations involving armies of 50,000 and 150,000 men respectively. The second expedition required the levy of virtually all the shipping in the Chinese Empire to lift the troops. Under the Mongol threat the Japanese temporarily abandoned their internal strife and united to contain the enemy beachheads. In this they were successful, thanks in part to providential typhoons that on both occasions scattered and sank much of the invasion fleet. Thus the *kamikaze* ("divine wind") became a part of the Japanese patriotic tradition.

Once more united, this time under the strong rule of the Shogun Hideyoshi, the Japanese in 1592 and again in 1597 undertook to invade the continent. As before and later, the path of intended conquest was via Korea, which has been called the Flanders of Asia. In both attacks, the Japanese invaders overran part of the Korean peninsula but were eventually thrown back by a combination of Chinese armies and the Korean navy. The Far Eastern fleets, like the Christian-Moslem fleets in the contemporary Battle of Lepanto, were made up mostly of galleys armed with light cannon. Naval victory in the Far East, as in the Mediterranean, was achieved in most instances by grappling and boarding. But in 1592 the Koreans, led by Yi Sun Sin, "the Eastern Nelson," rammed their way through the Japanese line with the aid of a special galley fitted with an iron-plated turtleback having gunports forward. The confusion caused by this novel weapon enabled the conventional Korean galleys to keep clear of Japanese boarding parties while pouring in cannon and musket fire and flaming arrows.

Even more inglorious for the Japanese was the end of their 1597 invasion. Yi Sun Sin, in an Asiatic Trafalgar that cost him his life, furiously attacked the numerically superior invaders at sea and destroyed their navy as an effective fighting organization. Three centuries were to elapse before a Japanese fleet again ventured into Korean waters.

After the death of Hideyoshi, the intense nationalism of the unified Japanese archipelago turned inward upon itself. Japan, as a great trading nation with geographical advantages similar to those of England, might have become the Great Britain of the East. Instead the Shogunate chose to discourage trade and exclude foreign influence of all sorts. A "bamboo curtain" was to surround Japan for 250 years. It was the Western powers that finally broke through Japan's "bamboo curtain" and launched the Japanese again upon the path of conquest, this time far better equipped for the role of conqueror.

Western Powers in the Far East

Before the end of the 18th century, Europe's Far Eastern empires had reached a relatively peaceful equilibrium among themselves and with the Asian powers. First the Portuguese and later the French had virtually been forced out of the East, but the English were well established in India, the Dutch held unchallengeable sway in the East Indies, and the Spaniards ruled undisturbed in the Philippines.

In the first half of the 19th century, this equilibrium was upset by new military advantages accruing to the West as a result of the technological advances of the Industrial Revolution, notably steam-powered ships and improved ordnance. Furthermore, increased productivity in the West greatly unsettled the balance of trade with the Far East. Soaring demand by the new European middle classes for tea and silks was not accompanied by a corresponding increase in Oriental markets for Western manufactures. The self-sufficient Chinese generally demanded silver in payment until foreign traders hit on the expedient of bringing in Indian opium and raw cotton. By 1830 opium came to account for more than half of all Chinese imports and threatened to drain specie from the country. In banning the drug to avert monetary stringency, the Chinese brought on the first crisis in their relations with modern industrial sea power nations.

What the Western powers had been unable to attain through diplomacy, they proceeded to take by force. Britain waged war in China from 1839 to 1842; and Britain and France jointly, from 1856 to 1858. These campaigns, successfully conducted, obliged the Chinese to open their major ports to trade, permit free navigation of the Yangtse River, receive diplomatic missions in Peking, accept extraterritoriality, and cede Hong Kong outright to Great Britain. The United States, following up the European military successes with diplomatic missions, received trade concessions similar to those Britain and France had obtained through

open warfare. The treaties embodying China's concessions largely defined Chinese relationships with Western nationals until 1945. At the same time they seriously weakened Chinese sovereignty, and by advertising China's weakness constituted an open invitation to further encroachments, particularly by Russia and Japan.

Though Japan maintained her deliberate isolation from the West, the lesson of China was not altogether lost on the Shogunate. The harshest features of the exclusion edicts were modified in 1842 to permit succor to survivors of shipwreck and aid to vessels in distress. For the United States this concession was not enough. After 1830 the American whaling fleet had gradually shifted its center of operations from below the equator to the North Pacific grounds off Hokkaido; hence the attitude of the Japanese became increasingly a matter of concern to the American Department of State. The acquisition of California and the development of the Oregon territory made the United States a Pacific power. The prospect of a scheduled transpacific steamship service forecast a special need for docking privileges in Japan, since the Island Kingdom lay directly athwart the great circle route to Shanghai. Unsuccessful American attempts to establish diplomatic relations with the Japanese at length persuaded President Fillmore that a show of force was required.

To Commodore Matthew Calbraith Perry, commanding the United States East India Squadron, the President gave a personal letter from himself to be delivered to the Emperor of Japan. Perry was instructed to negotiate a treaty guaranteeing protection for American persons and property in Japan and free access to one or more ports for supplies and trade. He was to use force if necessary, but only as a last resort. After carefully studying all available information about Japan, the Commodore concluded that his best approach would be to demand all courtesies due from one nation to another and to treat with only the highest officials. He was aware, he reported to the Secretary of the Navy, that a haughty, exclusive demeanor would secure most respect from "these people of forms and ceremonies." For such a mission, so conducted, Perry was eminently fitted. Impressive, able, somewhat pompous, he was just the man to match dignified behavior with the Oriental specialists in dignity.

After a protracted fitting-out period during which the Commodore accumulated a large assortment of gifts—typical American machinery and other industrial products—the expedition got underway in early 1853. The squadron which Perry took into Tokyo Bay consisted of the paddle frigates *Susquehanna* and *Mississippi* and the sailing sloops-of-war *Plymouth* and *Saratoga*. From the moment the squadron anchored in Tokyo Bay on July 8, Perry maintained his attitude of impressive dignity and firmness, mingling a formally correct manner with an insistence on freedom of movement about the bay. As "Lord of the Forbidden Interior," he refused even to meet any dignitary below the rank of prince of the realm. On the arrival of the Emperor's representative, the Prince of Idzu, Perry went ashore in a state procession and ceremoniously delivered the President's letter. He announced that he would come back for the imperial reply the following spring. Returning to his flagship, he disregarded the protests of the authorities and took his squadron to within six miles of Tokyo. After the city's two million inhabitants had obtained a good view of the ships, the Commodore left for China. Perry's gifts as a negotiator nowhere showed to better advantage than in the timing of his departure. He knew better than to press the Japanese for a decision when they had a valid reason to reject his demands for lack of discussion.

While the squadron wintered in China, its strength now increased by a paddle frigate and two sailing sloops, the appearance of a Russian squadron at Shanghai prodded Perry into expediting his second visit to Tokyo. To prevent the Russians from reaping where he had sowed, he hastened back to Tokyo in midwinter. In negotiation Perry matched the Japanese representatives in obstinacy. The Council of State had hoped to put him off while preserving friendly relations. Perry finally convinced them that these were separate and irreconcilable policies. The Council must choose between a treaty and open war. The Council reluctantly accepted the inevitable, for they well knew Japan's military weakness. The Treaty of Kanagawa, completed March 31,

1854, guaranteed protection to Americans and provided for the opening of the ports of Shimoda and Hakodate to American shipping, but there were no concessions on trade.

Perry's firm but judicious pressure had yielded the most that could have been obtained under the circumstances. Townsend Harris obtained more generous terms two years later, but that was after the Shogun had come to recognize foreign trade as a means of promoting the technical and industrial revolution that Japan had to undergo to insure her security and independence.

Neither treaty was popular with the nobles of Japan. The great clans, ancient enemies of the Shogun, stirred ominously. Mori, lord of the clan of Chosu, took matters into his own hands by firing on foreign vessels using the strait of Shimonoseki separating the islands of Honshu and Kyushu. Opening this passage required the naval efforts of three nations in four expeditions of increasing power during 1863 and 1864. First, the American screw sloop *Wyoming*, then two French warships, then six British men-of-war, and finally, an international force of 17 vessels attacked Mori's ships and fortifications before the stubborn chieftain could be brought to terms.

These operations opened the eyes of the clan chiefs, who developed a great respect for naval power. They abandoned their xenophobia and welcomed intercourse with other nations, at least to the extent of acquiring western military techniques. They now turned their warlike energies against the Shogun, whom they overthrew in the course of a two-year civil war, and "restored" the Emperor. Under the "Meiji Restoration," the nation became westernized with a rapidity that amazed foreigners. In the forefront of institutions that underwent reform were the army and the navy.

The modernization of the navy had been taken in hand even before the downfall of the Shogunate, the first dockyards and slipways of the Yokosuka navy yard having been laid out in 1865. Officers and officer-candidates were sent abroad to naval schools of all levels, principally in Great Britain and the United States.[1]

[1] Beginning with two students admitted in 1870, the United States Naval Academy graduated Japanese in most of its classes for the next quarter century.

Beginning in 1874, the Japanese commissioned foreign yards to construct warships of the latest design, at the same time making every effort to construct improved imitations at home. By the last decade of the 19th century, they were launching cruisers as good as any built in Europe.

The strategic problem confronting Japan after 1870 was in many respects analogous to that faced by Great Britain. Both nations occupied insular positions off continents that were liable to domination by one or a combination of dynamic land powers. Little strategic insight was required to recognize that Japan was in a dangerous position vis-à-vis Russia and China, and that what Japan had to fear most was the emergence of China as a naval power and the march of Russia toward ice-free ports. Strategically Japan was in a stronger position than either of her rivals, for her strength was concentrated by her geographic situation. While she was weaker numerically than either of her presumptive antagonists, neither of them could employ full strength against her as long as she remained undefeated at sea.

But the Japanese Pitts soon yearned for Napoleonic roles. They revived the imperialistic ambitions of the era of Hideyoshi and steadily pursued a policy that aimed first to establish a defensive barrier off the east coast of Asia and then to exercise political control of the enclave formed by it. The new road to empire witnessed the annexation of the Bonin Islands in 1876 and the Ryukyus three years later. Formosa and the Pescadores belonged to China, and the central corridor, Korea, was nominally her vassal. Sakhalin, the northern flank, was Russian. To complete her proposed barrier, Japan would have to seize all these territories. Acquiring them meant warfare with both China and Russia. The Japanese leaders accepted the necessity. In 1894 they attacked China, the weaker of the two.

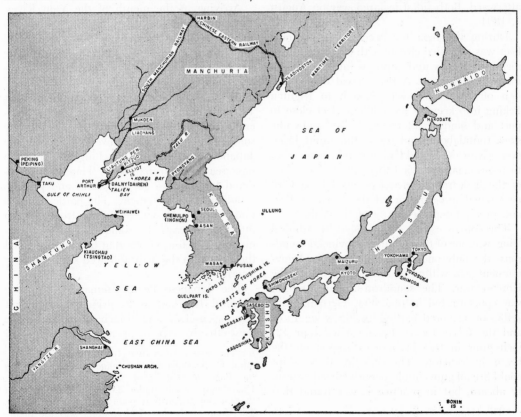

NORTHEAST ASIA, 1894-1905

The Sino-Japanese War, 1894–1895

The pretext for war was provided by a Japanese-fomented rebellion in Seoul, the Korean capital. China moved in forces to restore order, whereupon Japan seized upon a treaty technicality to land troops at Inchon (then called Chemulpo). Advancing to Seoul, the Japanese replaced the Korean king with a puppet "regent" and demanded that the Chinese withdraw from the peninsula. When China, instead of submitting to this demand, began rushing troops to Korea by sea, four cruisers sortied from the Japanese naval base at Sasebo and without formal declaration of war attacked the Chinese troop convoy, battering a cruiser, destroying one gunboat and capturing another, and sinking a loaded transport. Japan had inaugurated the practice she was to employ in subsequent wars—strike first and declare war afterward. Both sides declared war on August 1, 1894.

During the next few weeks, the Japanese fleet was occupied chiefly with covering movements of troops and supplies into Korea via Pusan and Inchon. A brief naval demonstration off Weihaiwei was enough to frighten Peking into keeping the Chinese fleet close to port and sending all troops to Korea by the slow, roundabout land route. But rapid Japanese advances obliged China in mid-September to resort again to sea transport. The crossing of the first troop convoy, escorted by a Chinese naval force, attracted the Japanese fleet and precipitated the Battle of the Yalu.

The convoy escort, commanded by Admiral Ting, was one of four Chinese provincial squadrons—the only one China's decentralized government was willing at first to commit to the Korean war. The squadron's main strength was concentrated in two slow, German-built, 7,400-ton armored battleships, the *Ting Yuen* and the *Chen Yuen*.[2] Each carried four 12-inch guns in two barbettes disposed on the beam in echelon. Theoretically these ships could fire all guns simultaneously ahead, astern, or abeam, but in practice it was found that

[2] The Captain of the *Chen Yuen* was an American, Philo McGiffen, a graduate of the United States Naval Academy.

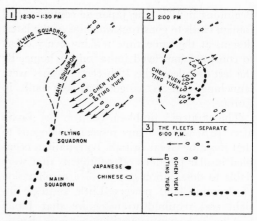

BATTLE OF THE YALU, SEPTEMBER 17, 1894

they could fire together only ahead without causing blast damage to the superstructure. In addition to these big guns, the Chinese force mounted a bewildering variety of smaller calibers, including only three quick-firers, all 4.7 inch.

Arriving at the mouth of the Yalu River, Ting detached a cruiser, a sloop,[3] and two torpedo boats to accompany the transports up the Yalu and cover the disembarkation. The ten ships of his battle line stood guard at anchor off the river's mouth.

At ten o'clock the next morning, September 17, the Chinese crews were exercising at general quarters when lookouts reported heavy smoke at sea to the southwest. Evidently the Japanese fleet was approaching. In order to have sea room to maneuver, Ting at once ordered his ships to get up steam and prepare to advance on the enemy. The battle line was underway by 11 AM, deploying from column into line abreast, the standard approach formation. The four vessels that had accompanied the troops up the Yalu followed some distance astern.

The Japanese fleet, commanded by Vice Admiral Ito, had as its principal armament sixty-seven 4.7- and 6-inch quick-firers, the most effective type of naval gun in the period

[3] The nomenclature here follows that in Vice Admiral G. A. Ballard, *The Influence of the Sea on the Political History of Japan* (London, 1921). Unarmored vessels under 2,000 tons displacement that are not primarily torpedo craft are called *sloops*. The sloop of the late 19th century was the predecessor of the modern destroyer, that is, the type next after the cruiser in size and armament.

before improved techniques of aiming gave the advantage to long-range fire by heavier guns. The fleet was divided into two semi-independent squadrons. The Flying Squadron, commanded by Rear Admiral Tsuboi, comprised four cruisers capable of 17 knots. The Main Squadron, under Ito's direct command, was composed of four more fast cruisers, followed by a pair of obsolescent ironclads that managed to keep up only by cutting corners during evolutions. The Japanese were further hampered by a train consisting of an armed merchant steamer and a dispatch boat that were ordered to trail on the disengaged side. None of Ito's ships were heavily armored.

The opposing battle lines, ten ships in each, made visual contact at 11:40. The Japanese warships were in single column. The Chinese were still in line abreast, now very ragged with flanks trailing. At the Chinese center were the two battleships *Ting Yuen* and *Chen Yuen*, flanked by five cruisers and three sloops.

If Ting intended to fight in line-abreast formation, he was probably influenced by the ahead-fighting characteristics of his ram-bowed battleships and by a strong segment of tactical opinion that still favored a bows-on attack—as carried out by Tegetthoff at Lissa. But Ting had left his flanks fatally weak, with two sloops on his extreme right and a sloop and a light cruiser on his extreme left. For this reason it has been suggested that what he actually intended to do was to order ships right on contact so as to form column headed toward his nearest base, Port Arthur. If so, the ragged state of his line made the maneuver impossible, and the swift-moving Japanese allowed him no time to bring order out of disorder.

Approaching from Ting's left at double his speed, Ito headed diagonally across the Chinese front. His intention was to strike first at Ting's weak right flank—even at the risk of leaving stragglers in the path of their oncoming opponents. To conceal his intention, he signaled Tsuboi's Flying Squadron, in the lead, to head first for the enemy center. When this unorthodox approach had fixed the puzzled Chinese in position, Tsuboi wheeled slightly to port and led the Japanese fleet toward Ting's right wing. Disregarding futile Chinese fire, which opened at 6,000 yards, Tsuboi held his own fire until he was close enough to make

effective use of his quick-firers. These at length he turned with deadly effect on the two sloops on Ting's right as he steamed across their bows and doubled around the Chinese flank.

It had been Ito's intention, after rounding the flank, to steam across the Chinese rear. This his Main Squadron did, coming up on the Chinese left. But Tsuboi's Flying Squadron turned first to the north to chase away Ting's four reinforcements coming from the Yalu and then south to support the weak Japanese rear, which had come under heavy Chinese fire. As a result, Ting's formation was caught between two fires and quickly disintegrated. Already ablaze, one of the sloops of the Chinese right went down; the other grounded on a nearby island. The two ships on the Chinese left, heavily damaged, ran for Port Arthur. Two Chinese cruisers became separated from the battleships and were sunk by Tsuboi's squadron, which steamed widely through the battle area seeking out stragglers and disabled.

Ito meanwhile concentrated upon the *Ting Yuen*, the *Chen Yuen*, and two cruisers—all of Ting's fleet that had not sunk or fled. Circling at 2,500 yards, he kept up a rapid and steady fire, taking the two battleships as his special targets. His heavy shells riddled their superstructures. His quick-firers repeatedly swept their decks, killing gun crews in exposed stations. Yet the vitals of the big ships, protected by 14 inches of armor, remained unimpaired. Keeping their bows turned toward their attackers, they continued to fire slowly. Though a corrupt government had provided them with faulty ammunition—including shells filled with sawdust or sand—they gave a good account of themselves. Toward 3:30 one of their 12-inch projectiles detonated ready ammunition in Ito's flagship, causing a hundred casualties and putting the ship out of action.

Ito at length concluded that the battleships were indestructible with the armament he carried. At 5:30, fearful of a night attack by torpedo boats out of Port Arthur, he broke off action. At that time the *Chen Yuen* had only three 12-inch shells left; these were loaded in the guns for a final salvo. The *Ting Yuen* was in almost as bad a situation.

The antagonists kept each in sight until dark and then lost contact. Ito, misestimating Ting's destination, shaped course for Weihaiwei. Early next morning the four surviving ships of the Chinese battle line reached Port Arthur. Ito's lack of aggressiveness in the final stage of the battle had cost the Japanese a decisive victory. Though the Chinese had lost several ships, and their morale was disastrously impaired, their strongest units returned safely to their Port Arthur base.

Because the Japanese had nevertheless won a victory of sorts and had clearly outfought the Chinese, naval theorists examined their tactics for useful lessons. This proved something of a puzzle. The Battle of the Yalu provided a situation similar to that at the Battle of Lissa—a broadside attack in column opposed to a bows-on attack. This time however the column had defeated the bows-on attack. Thus the tactical lessons of the two battles seemed to cancel each other out, except for one fact—at Lissa and again at the Yalu, as at Trafalgar long before, the victorious fleet had fought in separated divisions. The tactical flexibility and the possibilities for achieving winning combinations through dividing one's force were keenly studied by naval officers everywhere. The United States Navy employed a Flying Squadron of its own four years later in the Spanish-American War. The Japanese again used divided force, as we shall see, in their climactic battle with the Russians in 1905, and in World War II their naval forces almost invariably operated in divisions.

From the standpoint of naval technology the results of the Battle of the Yalu River were rather indecisive. The controversy then raging over the rival claims of the big gun and armor was stimulated rather than settled. Armor appeared to have met a crucial test with complete success. Yet it was also true that the heavier Japanese guns did not actually hit Chinese armor. Damage to several heavy guns in barbette mounts indicated a need for turrets despite the increased weights involved. The deciding factor however was firepower. The Japanese had twice as many heavy guns as the Chinese and an overwhelming superiority in quick-firers. With such an advantage, the Japanese could hardly have come away from the engagement without a large measure of victory.

Following the sea battle, the Japanese army and navy worked together closely. As the Japanese troops, victorious in Korea, crossed the Yalu and invaded Manchuria, Ito's fleet escorted a large infantry force from Japan to the Liaotung Peninsula with the aim of isolating and laying siege to Port Arthur. Ito devoted himself rather too exclusively to his mission of protecting the transports, for while he was so employed, Ting's force slipped out of Port Arthur and escaped to Weihaiwei, where it was belatedly reinforced by ships from the other Chinese provincial squadrons. In mid-November, Ito covered the landing of siege guns at Talien Bay, to which the newly-landed Japanese army had advanced. Three days later the army assaulted the Port Arthur defenses; to the astonishment of the world, the forts were overrun in six hours. The Japanese fleet was now provided with ample base facilities in the operations area.

The Chinese squadron at Weihaiwei had to be destroyed, for it threatened the flank of a scheduled Japanese advance on Peking. Cutting out the ships required more joint operations, this time in the depths of a particularly severe winter. Since a large Chinese army occupied much of the Shantung Peninsula, there was no opportunity for repeating the strategy of Port Arthur. Weihaiwei, at the tip of the peninsula, could not be isolated. It had to be assaulted frontally, and by surprise. This required a swift, closely coordinated campaign.

In mid-January 1895, Tsuboi landed a diversionary force 70 miles west of Weihaiwei. Two days later, the main Japanese invasion force of 32,000 men and 6,000 horses began landings 24 miles east of the objective. In five days the whole army was ashore with six weeks' supplies and was rapidly advancing on the Chinese base. In five more days, before the Shantung army could intervene, the Japanese had marched across frozen rivers to Weihaiwei, captured the eastern forts and the firing station for the channel mines, and removed the boom closing the eastern entrance to the harbor. In two days more of fighting, the invaders had secured the entire harbor shore. Ito's naval force, blockading outside, now took over the weight of the offensive. In such extreme cold that men at exposed watch stations froze to death, he launched a series of night torpedo boat attacks that sank the battleship *Ting Yuen* and a cruiser. Admiral Ting ordered the surviving ships to make a dash for freedom. Only two managed to reach safety; the other 13 were captured or driven on the rocks.

His situation hopeless, Ting on February 12 arranged for surrender and for the personal safety of his crews and then drank a lethal dose of opium. Two weeks later, the Chinese Manchurian army was decisively defeated at Liaoyang, whereupon Viceroy Li Hung Chang opened negotiations for peace. The Treaty of Shimonoseki (April 17, 1895) was dictated by the victors. In addition to paying the full costs of the war, China ceded Formosa, the Pescadores (between Formosa and the mainland), and Port Arthur.

Events Leading to the Russo-Japanese War

The results of the Sino-Japanese War brought Japan into immediate diplomatic conflict with Russia, though actual warfare did not break out until nine years later. Checked by the Crimean War in her quest for a warm water port to the south, Russia had expanded into East Asia and in 1860 had acquired the Pacific naval base of Vladivostok. Because the new port was closed by ice three months each year, Manchuria and its warm water outlet, Port Arthur, became the most attractive area for renewed Russian expansion. But the Treaty of Shimonoseki, as we have seen, ceded Port Arthur to Japan. Russian reaction was immediate and effective; St. Petersburg secured the cooperation of the French and German governments in making a friendly *démarche* to Japan, warning that Japanese acquisition of any part of the Chinese mainland would create a "permanent obstacle to peace in the Far East." The Japanese yielded to "the dictates of humanity" and forthwith proceeded to double their army and triple their navy.

While Japan was obliged to withdraw her army from Korea and abandon possession of Port Arthur, Russia was pushing her Trans-Siberian Railway across North Asia. In 1896, in return for a treaty of alliance and loans to pay her war indemnity to Japan, China granted Russia the right to extend her railroad line to Vladivostok by the most direct route, through Manchuria. The next year the Russians secured a lease on Port Arthur and the right to connect it with the Manchurian segment of their railroad. Two years later Russia coolly appropriated Port Arthur outright and extended her control over all Manchuria. She then began intrigues to acquire a dominant position in Korea.

Japan, forced to stand by while Russia took over the fruits of her conquests, grimly prepared for war. While six battleships and six heavy cruisers were building for her in Europe, her diplomats worked to insure that when war came the ring should be clear in the Far East. In 1902 they negotiated the Anglo-Japanese Alliance guaranteeing mutual support should either nation become involved with more than one enemy over China or Korea. The Japanese government then demanded withdrawal of Russian troops from Manchuria. Evacuation was postponed and negotiations dragged on until February 1904. On February 6, Japan broke off diplomatic relations with Russia.

The Japanese went to war in the face of apparent disadvantages. They had to capture enemy-occupied territory by amphibious assault. They had less than half as many troops as Russia had. Their fleet was numerically weaker—six modern battleships to Russia's 15, 21 destroyers to Russia's 38, though the Japanese also had 39 seagoing torpedo boats, and 25 cruisers to Russia's 19. Russia was economically the more self-sufficient and was allied with France, the leading creditor nation of continental Europe. But Russia's advantages in numbers and finance were more than offset by Japan's military concentration at the strategic center. Most of Russia's troops were at the far end of the Trans-Siberian Railroad. Her naval forces were divided into three fleets of nearly equal strength in the Baltic, the Black Sea, and East Asia. The uncertain attitude of Great Britain contained the first of these in Europe until after the outbreak of war. The second was confined to the Black Sea by the London Treaty of 1870, that closed the Dardanelles to foreign warships. Most of Russia's Far Eastern Squadron was at Port Arthur, but four heavy cruisers were at Vladivostok, and a cruiser and a gunboat were at Inchon, Korea. The Russians had no first-class naval base in the Far East, and the best of what repair facilities they had were at the undefended commercial port of Dalny, 20 miles from Port Arthur. The Japanese, on the other hand, had four major naval bases and eleven large commercial docking and repair establishments in their home islands. In the circumstances, Japan's obvious strategy was to hit first and hit hard; Russia's, to delay—to avert a decision on land and sea and gain time to reinforce her military strength in the Far East.

Opening Operations

As in her war with China, Japan opened hostilities with an attack on the enemy fleet before war was formally declared. In the evening of February 8, Vice Admiral Heihichiro Togo arrived off Port Arthur with the main body of the Japanese Combined Fleet and sent in his destroyers for a night torpedo attack on the unsuspecting, brilliantly lit-up battleship-cruiser force anchored in the outer roadstead. Two battleships and a cruiser were hit. Though flooding was controlled and the damaged vessels got underway, the battleships grounded at the harbor entrance, blocking the channel to the rest of the squadron. At noon the next day, Togo's heavy ships stood in and opened fire on the Russian ships outside the harbor, but shore batteries forced the Japanese again out to sea before they could do any serious damage. Meanwhile, a Japanese cruiser-destroyer force had attacked and crippled the Russian cruiser at Inchon, obliging both it and the accompanying gunboat to scuttle themselves to avoid capture. A week later, after war had been declared, the Japanese First Army went ashore at Inchon under cover of Togo's battleships. Bogged down by spring thaws, the invaders did not reach the Yalu until the end of April. They then stormed the river crossings and forced the Russians back toward Liaoyang.

In the meantime Admiral Togo on three occasions took his ships under the shelter of the unfortified tip of the Liaotung Peninsula and bombarded the Port Arthur base with his 12-inch guns. Both sides laid mine fields, the

Russians attempting to interdict approach to ports and beachheads on the peninsula, the Japanese aiming to seal the base. For two months the Port Arthur squadron remained strictly on the defensive, a mere anchored "fortress fleet," sacrificing mobility to perform the function of a stationary fort. During this period, the squadron had two cruisers, a minelayer, and a gunboat sunk, and two battleships and a cruiser put out of action without damaging the Japanese or hampering their movements on the seas. Early in March however, all such passivism was temporarily swept away with the arrival at Port Arthur of dynamic Vice Admiral Stepan Osipovich Makarov, newly-appointed commander of Russia's East Asia naval forces.

Makarov was the ablest officer in the Russian navy. He was an accomplished seaman and an expert on naval tactics and hydrography, but it was his strong personal leadership that brought to Port Arthur the quality most needed. He set about at once to restore morale, develop an aggressive spirit, and establish high standards of material and performance. The day after his arrival, his destroyers engaged the Japanese patrols and inflicted considerable damage. Japanese Commander in Chief Togo quickly realized that his opponents had at last discarded their no-risks policy.

Unhappily for the Russians, the new broom did not last long enough to sweep away all the defeatism and inefficiency that lay like a pall upon Port Arthur. A month after his arrival, while chasing a Japanese mining force, Makarov's flagship, the battleship *Petropavlovsk*, struck a mine and went down, carrying the new commander and more than 600 of the crew. Makarov's death was an irreparable loss for Russia. "With him," wrote a destroyer commander, "all hope of rendering the squadron efficient was buried."

Rear Admiral Vilgelm Karlovitch Vitgeft, Makarov's successor, promptly resumed the defensive. The Grand Duke Alexis, head of the navy, announced soon afterward that the Port Arthur force would thenceforth be known as the First Pacific Squadron and that a Second Pacific Squadron would leave the Baltic at the end of July and arrive in the Yellow Sea four or five months later. This announcement however merely confirmed Vitgeft in his decision to wait, conserving his force until the squadron from the Baltic could arrive with reinforcements.

The Liquidation of Russian Sea Power in the Far East

The Japanese now began to move with quickened determination. By early May, their First Army was across the Yalu and extending its left toward Port Arthur. Their Second Army, covered by Togo's fleet, landed at Pitzuo on the Liaotung Peninsula and stormed the narrow neck leading down to the Russian base. Vitgeft meanwhile lay at anchor, disregarding his opportunity to make a surprise appearance and sweep the flanks of the assaulting columns with naval gunfire. In mid-May fate presented him with yet another opportunity. Within a few hours Russian mines sank two of Togo's battleships. Though Vitgeft now had six battleships to Togo's four, he still did not move.

So long as Port Arthur held out, Vitgeft's inactivity was not entirely illogical. Now that the Baltic squadron was on the way, the Japanese faced a convergence of naval power that would outnumber them two to one. But in early August 1904, when Port Arthur came under fire by Japanese artillery and the fall of the base was imminent, Russian fleet action of some sort was clearly called for. Vitgeft should doubtless have launched his squadron at Togo to do as much damage as possible. Even if he were beaten, he had a chance of so weakening the Japanese fleet that it could easily be defeated by the approaching Baltic fleet. Instead, orders from above forced him into flight. From Czar Nicholas II came a personal message: "Put out with full strength for Vladivostok."

Seventy-two hours later, at dawn on August 10, the Port Arthur squadron—six battleships, four cruisers, and eight destroyers—made its dash for freedom. Alert Japanese scouts soon picked up the fugitives and maintained contact until Togo's arrival. The Japanese commander in chief summoned every combat ship in the area by radio. When he sighted the Russians to the northwest at noon, he had with him or nearby four battleships, three heavy and three light cruisers, and some obsolescent armored craft, including the *Chen Yuen* and other relics of the China war.

Despite a nearly two-to-one superiority in large-caliber guns and the advantage of a knot in speed, Togo held off at long range. Opening fire, he crossed and re-crossed the head of the Russian column in an effort to turn it from its line of advance. On his third crossing, Togo swung too far and then lost time turning in succession so that his flagship would remain at the head of his column. Vitgeft, seizing his opportunity, slipped past and headed at top speed for the Straits of Korea.

Outmaneuvered, Togo refused to steam in Vitgeft's wake. That would have brought his battleships under fire from the cruisers at the rear of the Russian column, while the Russian battleships, in the van, were beyond the reach of Japanese guns. Instead, he made a detour to the south, intending to close and resume fire only when his speed advantage had brought him abreast of the Russians. There ensued an afternoon-long battle of the boilers that was also a race with the sun. Toward sunset the Japanese at length pulled abeam of Vitgeft's fleeing column and opened fire. Here if ever was the time for Togo to close to decisive ranges but, ever mindful of the need to conserve his ships, he could not bring himself to do so. By 6:30 long-range gunfire had knocked out two Russian turrets; it had also disabled five Japanese 12-inch guns. It appeared that Vitgeft might yet escape in the approaching darkness.

A few minutes later the whole situation was dramatically altered. Two 12-inch shells hit the Russian flagship *Czarevitch* almost simultaneously. The first swept the bridge with fragments. Every officer of the staff went down; among those killed was Admiral Vitgeft. The second hit the conning tower, killing or stunning everyone inside and jamming the helm. Out of control, the flagship made a sharp left turn, away from the enemy, and continued on around as if to ram her own column. The Russian fleet, leaderless, baffled by the strange antics of the *Czarevitch*, fell into confusion.

To Togo it was apparent that something had suddenly gone very wrong in the enemy fleet. Seizing his opportunity, he closed to 4,000 yards for the kill, his cruisers circling to close a ring around their milling opponents. Presently however Togo sighted Russian destroyers approaching and, fearing a torpedo attack in the gathering darkness, he broke off action.

During the night the Russians scattered. Five battleships, a cruiser, and three destroyers fled back to Port Arthur. A lone destroyer was driven ashore near Weihaiwei by Japanese destroyers. A cruiser and a destroyer reached Shanghai, where they were interned. Another cruiser was interned at Saigon, Indo-China. A third cruiser and three destroyers reached Kiauchau, where they were joined by the damaged *Czarevitch*. At Kiauchau the German authorities disarmed all except the cruiser, which coaled and departed within 24 hours. This ship, the speedy *Novik*, ran up the east coast of Japan and passed through the strait between Hokkaido and Sakhalin. But she had been sighted from a lookout station, and two Japanese cruisers intercepted her on the last lap to Vladivostok. After putting up a game but hopeless fight, she was scuttled by her crew to prevent her capture.

Togo's excessive caution, especially manifest at the decisive moment of action when he failed to follow up and destroy the confused mass of Russians, lost the Japanese an important strategic advantage. Because the siege of Port Arthur had been undertaken mainly to eliminate Vitgeft's fleet, annihilation of the fleet by Togo would have made capture of the base less urgent, perhaps unnecessary. The troops thereby released might well have made good the lack of strength that denied the Japanese a decisive victory at Liaoyang a month later.

Only three of the four Russian cruisers at Vladivostok were ready for sea, but these set out belatedly to facilitate the escape of the Port Arthur squadron. Still ignorant of Vitgeft's defeat, they arrived off the island of Tsushima on August 14. Here they ran into a force of four Japanese cruisers under Vice Admiral Kamimura, who instantly gave chase. Superior Japanese gunnery soon forced the slowest of the Russian cruisers out of line, so wrecked and helpless that she was scuttled by her crew. The other two rather remarkably made it back to Vladivostok. Here, with the cruiser that did not sortie, they constituted a still-formidable squadron. But news of the fate of the Port Arthur squadron so shattered mo-rale at Vladivostok that they were of little further use in the war.

Failure of the Japanese land forces to trap the main Russian army at Liaoyang and knowledge of the approaching naval reinforcements from the Baltic spurred Japan into a supreme effort against Port Arthur. Abandoning orthodox siege tactics, the Japanese troops made a general assault, introducing the "banzai charge" and the use of human torpedoes to blast paths through barbed wire entanglements. But the Russian resistance was equally desperate. The advance of the Japanese in December to the high ground overlooking the base cost them 60,000 men.

By this time the Port Arthur squadron had long since ceased to be even a fleet-in-being. Its secondary batteries and a large proportion of its crews had been incorporated in the land defenses. Now the squadron suffered the ultimate humiliation for a naval force as artillery ashore began to batter it to pieces. Port Arthur surrendered on January 2, 1905, though not before the last of the Russian ships there had been sunk or scuttled. Russia now had to attempt with her squadron from the Baltic what she should have undertaken earlier in the war with her whole fleet.

The Voyage of the Baltic Squadron

The defeatism that early dampened the ardor of Russia's forces in the Far East did not at first extend to St. Petersburg. Here, throughout the opening months of the war, high officials, as well as the public, regarded Japan's armed forces with contempt. Russian defeats were explained away as temporary setbacks. Even Togo's scattering of the Port Arthur squadron failed to jar the Admiralty into a sense of urgency in fitting out the naval reinforcements then being gathered in the Baltic.

Appointed to command this Second Pacific Squadron, was Vice Admiral Zinovi Petrovich Rozhdestvenski. Given a free hand, Rozhdestvenski drew to the squadron some of the ablest officers in the Russian navy. But despite his indefatigable zeal, his genius at cutting through red tape, and his fiery temper, he could not hurry the fleet into readiness. He knew that

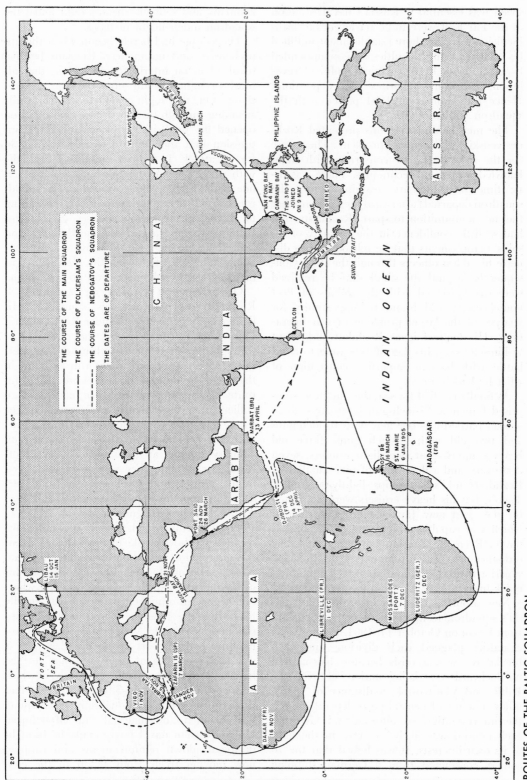

ROUTES OF THE BALTIC SQUADRON

speed was essential if Russia's naval situation in the Far East were to be retrieved, but gross inefficiency in the shore establishment nullified his efforts. Local difficulties were compounded by graft, news leaks, incipient political revolution, and court favorites in key positions. Hence the summer of 1904 passed with the squadron still unready.

The men behind the guns presented Rozhdestvenski a still graver problem. They were for the most part new conscripts with slight knowledge of naval techniques. There was little time for systematic training before the squadron departed; afterward there was neither fuel nor ammunition to spare. Rozhdestvenski had so little confidence in the capacity of his ships' complements that he felt obliged to disperse his ablest officers through the fleet. Consequently he and the small staff he retained were overburdened with the details of fleet housekeeping and found no opportunity for analysis of the larger problems of war operations. His tactical ideas Rozhdestvenski kept to himself; even his flag officers were to enter battle with but an imperfect conception of what he had in mind.

As finally readied for sea, the squadron comprised four new 12-inch-gun battleships, three weaker battleships—one new with 10-inch guns and two old with 12-inch guns, three old heavy cruisers, four new light cruisers, seven destroyers, and a fleet train of nine auxiliaries. Rozhdestvenski's battleships slightly outgunned Togo's, but his heavy cruisers were no match for the eight new Japanese cruisers, each of which was capable of standing in the line of battle. Even the Russian advantage in heavy ordnance was more than offset by Japanese superiority in speed and in 8-inch guns and quick-firers.

New problems crowded in on Rozhdestvenski's squadron from the hour of its departure from Libau on October 14, 1904. Engine room casualties plagued each division, and each breakdown was a crisis because Russia had no dockyards or coaling stations between the Baltic and Vladivostok, a distance of 18,000 miles. The use of neutral ports depended upon the interpretation of international law that each neutral was likely to make in the light of its own interests. It was hoped that the 70 colliers contracted from a German shipping company and sent on ahead would make the squadron independent of bases.

The voyage had barely begun when the apprehensive and unpracticed Russians became involved in an international incident that almost brought Britain into the war against them. On the night of October 21, while steaming through the North Sea, the squadron opened fire on British trawlers under the impression that they were destroyers coming in for an attack. In a brief but heavy fusillade, with some Russian ships firing at each other, one of the fishing vessels was sunk. The squadron continued on its way without attempting to rescue survivors, but cruiser divisions of Britain's Royal Navy closed the Russians and kept them in sight all the way to Gibraltar, being called off only when the Czar's government agreed to submit the case to arbitration.

On arriving at Tangier on November 4, Rozhdestvenski divided his squadron. His lighter craft he detached under Rear Admiral Folkersam to proceed by the short route through the Suez Canal. With his deeper draft ships, which he feared might run aground in the canal, he pushed south around Africa. En route the main Russian force met German colliers in several French and German ports, where local officials made a liberal time allowance for coaling. The divisions rejoined on January 9, 1905, at the island of Nosy Bé off Madagascar. Here they were soon reinforced by five cruisers and two destroyers, from Russia. Here too the squadron learned that Port Arthur had just surrendered.

The government might now properly have recalled Rozhdestvenski to the Baltic to await the completion of a really formidable fleet, already approved. With the forces under his command at Nosy Bé, he had no edge whatever over his opponent, and it was hardly likely that the Japanese would permit him to slip unopposed into Vladivostok, the only remaining Russian port in the Far East. Yet it was now more urgent than ever that he take his squadron to Vladivostok, promptly, at whatever cost, for the Trans-Siberian Railway had proved utterly unable to maintain an adequate flow of men and material into Manchuria. Unless Russian naval forces could be brought in to cut down reinforcements and supplies now moving freely from Japan to the continent, the Russian army faced disaster. So the Admiralty ordered Rozhdestvenski to press on, informing him that he would be joined by Rear Admiral Nebogatov with an old battleship, the *Nicholas I,* a cruiser, and three coast defense ironclads, "superfluous encumbrances" that Rozhdestvenski would willingly have done without.

Commander Second Pacific Squadron would gladly have departed the vicinity of Madagascar at once. He well understood that only by a rigorous routine of training and steaming at sea could the fighting spirit of his men be maintained against the corrosive combination of tropical heat, bad food, and bad news. He realized too that the success of his mission depended upon the speed with which he reached the Far East and hit the Japanese before they could dock or refit. Plans for an early start were frustrated however when the Germans abruptly terminated their coaling contract, claiming danger to their colliers should they go north of Madagascar. Two months of negotiation in Europe were necessary to obtain a contract renewal. During this time the ships and men of the Baltic squadron deteriorated in the steaming heat of the tropics. Spent in health and spirit, Rozhdestvenski at last weighed anchor for the China Sea on March 16, accompanied by four German colliers.

The next stage of the voyage, extending over 5,300 miles, ranks as one of the great endurance feats achieved in the era of coal-burning warships. For three weeks the Indian Ocean swallowed up Rozhdestvenski and he was neither observed nor heard from. Fuel was taken from the colliers at sea by means of specially constructed lighters. Entering the China Sea through the tortuous and comparatively little used Malacca Straits, the Baltic squadron anchored in Camranh Bay, Indo-China on April 14, 1905.

Protests from Tokyo impelled the French government to request the Russians to leave, but Rozhdestvenski merely moved north 60 miles to Van Fong, where he stood in and out of the bay until May 9, when Nebogatov joined. The next four days were spent at anchor while inflammables were jettisoned and the fleet was made ready for action. On May 14, the combined Russian forces, 53 ships in all, steamed out of Van Fong Bay for the final run to Vladivostok.

Rozhdestvenski had the choice of three routes from the China Sea: through the Korean, the Tsugaru, or the Soya Straits. The first was Togo's most likely point of concentration, and here too was Sasebo, the Japanese navy's principal operating base. The Tsugaru and the more remote Soya passages would afford more sea room for the approach but would involve at least a thousand additional miles of steaming. The Japanese fleet meanwhile would enjoy the advantage of an interior position in the Sea of Japan. In addition to the known difficulties of fog and rocks, the northern straits were suspected of being mined —and so they were. Weighing all factors, Rozhdestvenski decided to take the shortest route, the Tsushima passage on the eastern side of the Korean Straits.

The Russian fleet rounded the eastern side of Formosa, out of the frequented routes, and escaped detection. On May 23, near the Ryukyus, colliers came alongside for the last time, and each ship was ordered to take aboard only enough coal to insure good battle trim on the 27th, the day they expected to meet the Japanese fleet. Soon afterward Rozhdestvenski turned northeastward and shaped course for Tsushima Island. To lessen the threat of torpedo attack, he reduced speed to eight knots so that the fleet would pass the island at noon on the 27th and cross the area of maximum Japanese concentration in daylight. During the approach to the strait, Admiral Folkersam died of a heart attack, but his death was not disclosed to the fleet—or to Nebogatov, who thereby automatically became second in command. Folkersam's flag was kept flying on the *Osliabya,* and her captain was directed to exercise command of the division.

Here it should be pointed out that Rozhdestvenski was faced with an almost insoluble problem. One of the oldest principles of warfare requires that a commander undertake to attain only one major objective at a time. Rozhdestvenski was confronted with three: 1) he had to meet the opposition of the Japanese fleet; 2) he had to take his own fleet to Vladivostok; and 3) because the breakdown of the Trans-Siberian Railway had created shortages at Vladivostok, he had to take his service force with him. He had thus at the same time to solve the problems of combat, flight, and convoy protection. His opponent, on the contrary, would have to concern himself exclusively with defeating the Russian fleet.

Rozhdestvenski's preoccupation with maintaining his unreliable weapons had left him little time to work out a tactical plan suitable for his intricate task. His battleships were to fight in column. His cruisers, also in column, would support the battle line or cover the convoy as directed. A purely defensive role was assigned to the destroyers in daytime action and to the heavier ships at night.

The Battle of Tsushima, May 27–28, 1905

Correctly estimating that the Russians would attempt to transit the Korean Straits, Togo had based his battle line of four battleships and eight heavy cruisers at a secret anchorage near Masan, Korea. His light cruisers and older vessels operated from the Island of Tsushima, maintaining a constant patrol. Fifty miles to the southwest, a line of converted merchantmen covered the outer approaches. One of these at 4:45 AM on May 27 made contact with Rozhdestvenski's fleet and flashed the word by radio. Shortly after dawn the Japanese light cruiser divisions were shadowing the Russians.

At 6:30 the Japanese battle line steamed out of Masan anchorage. Togo, leading the First Division in the *Mikasa*, closely followed by Kamimura, leading the Second Division, headed east to intercept the Baltic squadron abreast of Tsushima. As in the Battle of August 10, Togo's battle line would move like an articulated barrier back and forth across the Russians' line of advance in order to turn them back. Light cruiser divisions were to engage the Russian cruisers and auxiliaries. At nightfall all gunnery ships would hand over the enemy to the destroyer flotillas and withdraw to the north to give them a clear field. At dawn the next day, the main units would sweep south to re-engage. The pattern would be repeated until the Russian fleet was annihilated.

During the approach to Tsushima, Rozhdestvenski's battle line, three divisions of four ships each, including eight battleships, was in single column ahead and to port of his service ships and their cruiser-destroyer escort. The whole squadron was held down to ten knots by the auxiliaries and by Nebogatov's obsolescent warships in the rear division of the battle line. At 1 PM Rozhdestvenski, desiring to change to a line-abreast approach formation, led the way—column right and then ships left—with his First Division, battleships *Suvorov* (fleet flag), *Borodino, Alexander III,* and *Orel.* But noting that his maneuver was observed by Japanese cruisers, which appeared to the northwest, he canceled the order for line abreast and signaled the *Borodino,* the *Alexander III,* and the *Orel* to fall in behind the *Suvorov,* thus re-forming his First Division in column, but off to starboard of the others.

Meanwhile, Togo had led his twelve-ship battle line from west to east, across the Russians' line of advance and then headed southwest in order to attack them from the east. On this course he at length made out his own cruisers shadowing the Russian columns, which soon came into view eight miles away. Having rounded Tsushima, they were now on a more northerly heading, course 023 for Vladivostok, than that last reported to Togo. This new course called for an attack on the Russian left flank in order to turn them away. Rozhdestvenski himself made this feasible by hastening to return his First Division to the head of his battle line. Taking all this in, Togo a little after 1:30 PM changed to course northwest and led his line back across the head of the oncoming enemy divisions, then still out of range at 15,000 yards. He then turned his line left in succession and came down on the port bow of the Russians and on an opposite course. At this moment signal flags started up from the *Mikasa's* bridge, reading: "The fate of the Empire depends on the issue of this battle; let every man do his utmost."

A passing exchange of broadsides would have been indecisive. For Togo to continue on course southwest moreover would risk letting Rozhdestvenski get past him—as Vitgeft had got past the preceding August—and turn the battle into another chase. Togo, determined that nothing of the sort should happen again,

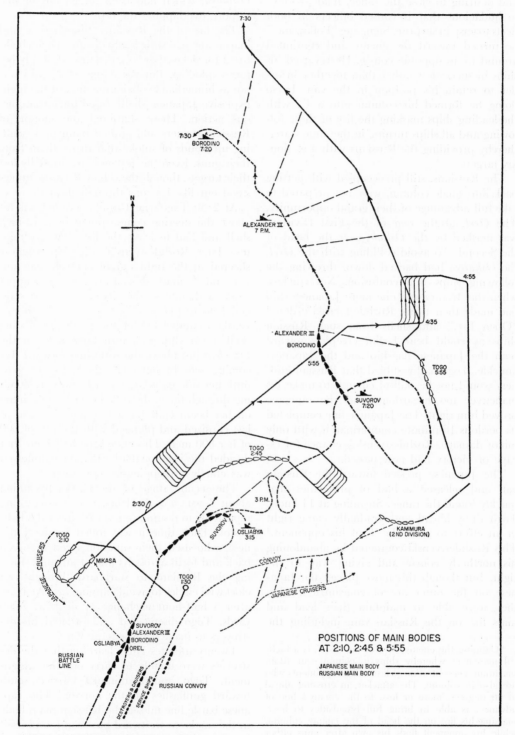

BATTLE OF TSUSHIMA, MAY 27, 1905

Labels within figure:

7:30

7:30
BORODINO
7:20

N

ALEXANDER III
7 P.M.

4:55

7:30
BORODINO
7:20

ALEXANDER III
BORODINO

4:35

5:55

TOGO
5:55

SUVOROV
7:20

TOGO
2:45

2:30

3 P.M.

KAMIMURA
(2ND DIVISION)

TOGO
2:10

SUVOROV

OSLIABYA
3:15

CONVOY

JAPANESE CRUISERS

JAPANESE CRUISERS

MIKASA

TOGO
1:30

SUVOROV
ALEXANDER III
BORODINO
OREL

OSLIABYA

RUSSIAN
BATTLE
LINE

DESTROYERS & CRUISERS

SERVICE SHIPS

RUSSIAN CONVOY

POSITIONS OF MAIN BODIES
AT 2:10, 2:45 & 5:55

JAPANESE MAIN BODY
RUSSIAN MAIN BODY

and desiring to close the range, made a move so audacious that it caused officers in both fleets to gasp in surprise. Signaling "Follow me," he turned toward the enemy and continued around to an opposite course. He reversed his ships in succession rather than together in order to retain his position in the van. In so doing he formed his column into a U, with the leading ships masking the fire of those following and all ships turning in the same water, thereby providing the Russians with a stationary target.

The Russians, still preoccupied with getting back into single column, were not prepared to take full advantage of their grand opportunity. The *Orel*, at the rear of the First Division, was masked by the *Osliabya*, at the head of the Second. To avoid colliding with the *Orel*, the *Osliabya* had backed down, throwing the following ships into confusion. Nevertheless, when the *Mikasa* and one more Japanese ship had made their turns, Rozhdestvenski ordered "Open fire," and shells from such Russian ships as could bear began creeping toward both the Japanese flagship and the Japanese knuckle. Togo had gambled that Russian gunners would not be skillful enough to make his maneuver too hazardous, and the outcome proved him right. The Japanese line completed its perilous 16-minute countermarch with only minor damage. Rozhdestvenski's chance for escape or victory had now passed.

The Japanese pressed toward the Russian van and released a hail of projectiles that quickly found the range. Steaming at 14 knots, Togo drew ahead and gradually came right in an effort to cross the T of his opponent.[4] This Rozhdestvenski countered by abandoning his northerly course and giving way to the right. But though this move placed the Japanese on the outer arc of concentric circles, they were able to maintain their lead and mass fire on the Russian van, including the

[4] Capping the enemy, or crossing his T, is a tactical maneuver whereby ships in column can attain maximum concentration of fire against opponents who are also in column. The attacker, in crossing ahead at 90 degrees, more or less, to the enemy's line of advance, is able to bring full broadsides to bear, massing his fire on the head of the enemy column, while his opponent finds his own after guns either "closed out" or able to bear only on the extremities of the attacker's column at relative long range.

Osliabya, which had been forced out of line to port, overlapping the *Orel*.

The fire of the Russians, though slow and inaccurate, was sufficiently deadly. Their shells, fused for delayed action, penetrated deeply before exploding. But the damage they did was not as immediately obvious as that of the high-explosive Japanese shells, fused for instantaneous action. These shattered the morale of Russian gunners and ignited paint fires, sending up clouds of smoke that drove them from their guns. Even the Japanese occasionally lost their targets, though the yellow Russian funnels stood out like beacons through the pall.

At 2:30 Togo's next-to-rear cruiser was hit above the steering compartment by a 12-inch shell and had to leave the line. Twenty minutes later Rozhdestvenski's flagship *Suvorov* sheered to the right out of control, one funnel and a mast shot away and her upper works a shambles. She circled once and staggered off to the northeast, carrying Rozhdestvenski wounded out of the battle. Exploding shells meanwhile had torn huge holes in the *Osliabya* just above the waterline forward. Incoming seas brought her down by the bow until her side guns were awash. Rapidly flooding through these, she rolled over to port, hung on her beam ends for a few minutes, and at last capsized and plunged with the loss of 600 of her 800 men. This ended the half hour that decided the issue of the battle. What followed was chiefly a mopping-up operation.

The second stage of the battle, beginning about 3 PM, saw the Russian line attempting repeatedly to resume course 023, toward Vladivostok. Each time it was foiled by the Japanese, who used their superior speed to sweep back and forth across its line of advance, forcing the Russians to starboard through two clockwise circles to avoid capping fire. At 4:35, after a half-hour exchange of shells at 7,000 yards, Togo disengaged and ordered his destroyers to make a torpedo attack.

Twenty minutes later, learning that the destroyers were unable to carry out this assignment, Togo and Kamimura hurried south toward gunflashes on the horizon. The Japanese battle line missed the Russian main body in the smoke to westward but soon found itself heading into the battle of the light cruisers, which had been going on indecisively since noon. Kamimura stayed to lend support in this area, while Togo headed northwest after bigger game.

The third phase of the battle began at 5:55 as the north-steaming Japanese First Division again sighted Russian battleships bearing northwest on their port bows. Togo turned in four points to close the range quickly before dark. But the Russians were still full of fight, and he now found himself running into heavy fire with all the advantages on the other side, since the sun was setting directly in the eyes of his pointers and his six ships were engaging ten. A quick turn to the right opened the range another 2,000 yards, and Togo came to a parallel course. As the light gradually shifted in the Japanese favor, silhouetting the Russians against the afterglow, Togo's vessels massed a deadly, accurate fire on the *Alexander III*, at

the head of the line. Fifteen minutes later, burning fiercely, her bows nearly blown off, she turned left out of line, capsized, and went down. The Japanese had already shifted fire to the new van ship *Borodino*. As darkness came on she caught fire, thus presenting an easy target to the Japanese range finders. At 7:20 two of her magazines exploded, whereupon she capsized, floated bottom upward a few minutes, and then sank.

The loss of the *Borodino* broke up the Russian column. Signaling "Follow me," Nebogatov in the *Nicholas I*, led a disorganized mass of ships to the southwest. The Japanese battleships and cruisers now left the area according to plan and steamed north at 14 knots toward the morning rendezvous near Ullung Island. With their departure the battle entered a fourth phase: a series of scattered and fiercely contested night torpedo actions.

The Japanese destroyers had already sunk the heavily damaged *Suvorov*, but not before a Russian destroyer had come alongside and removed Rozhdestvenski, who was insensible from head wounds. In the darkness the Japanese torpedo craft, 21 destroyers and 37 torpedo boats, now closed in on the bewildered Russian fleet from all directions, sinking two battleships and so damaging two cruisers that they were scuttled to avoid capture.

At dawn on May 28, 140 miles north of the previous day's battle area, Togo's staff were sweeping their glasses over an empty horizon when a light cruiser division 60 miles to the south reported Russian ships. The Japanese battle divisions steered toward the contact and at 9:30 sighted battleships *Orel* and *Nicholas I*, two coast defense ironclads, and a cruiser. Shots fired from beyond the Russian range brought no response save the hoist of a table cloth in lieu of a white flag on the *Nicholas*. The Russian cruiser made off at high speed and escaped.

The surrender had been made on the order of Admiral Nebogatov, on whom the Russian command had devolved. As he left the deck of his flagship to hand his sword to Togo, he turned to the crew and said, "I am an old man, over 60, and I do not care whether I live or die. I shall be shot for this, but that does not matter. You however are young, and you will be called upon some day to restore

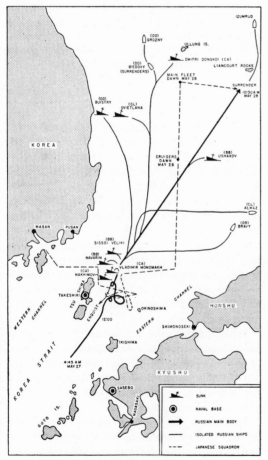

FLEET TRACKS, BATTLE OF TSUSHIMA

the glory and the lost honor of the Russian navy. On these ships are 2,400 men whose lives are more important than mine."[5]

Of the separated Russian units, a coast defense ironclad of the battle line was heavily hit and scuttled; two cruisers were driven ashore; four destroyers and four auxiliaries were sunk; two destroyers, including the *Bedovyi* with Rozhdestvenski aboard, were captured; and three cruisers, three auxiliaries, and a destroyer reached neutral ports, where they were interned. In the course of the battle, eight of the twelve Russian armored vessels, including five battleships, had been sunk. Of the 53 ships that had left the Baltic, a cruiser and two destroyers reached Vladivostok.

The Battle of Tsushima was decisive in every sense. Russia could no longer hope for victory on land because internal revolt prevented her from further reinforcing her Far Eastern armies. When the defeat at sea dashed her final hopes, she welcomed the mediation of United States President Theodore Roosevelt. At the Portsmouth, New Hampshire, peace conference, her delegates did not do badly. They obtained a much-needed treaty of peace at the cost of Port Arthur and southern Sakhalin, both ceded to Japan. The mediators rejected a Japanese demand for cash indemnity on the ground that the Russian army, though defeated, withdrew intact and was still in the field.

Had Togo lost the battle, his nation would have experienced one of the greatest disasters in history. The Japanese army would have been isolated in Manchuria and its supply lines severed. Russia would undoubtedly have imposed heavy terms that would have made her the paramount power in the Far East, if not potentially the world's greatest power.

From the naval point of view the battle was highly significant. The value of heavy armor and the need for heavy guns were strikingly demonstrated. The Japanese enjoyed a great advantage through having in their battle line only swift, homogeneous ships with uniform tactical characteristics. The torpedo performed disappointingly. Togo's tactics, generally skillful, appeared brilliant because the Russians fought for the most part without leadership, and

[5] Frank Thiess, *The Voyage of Forgotten Men* (Indianapolis, 1937), 367.

the Japanese retained the initiative throughought. Kamimura, like Collingwood at Trafalgar, was given a large measure of initiative, which he used effectively. This further confirmed many officers, particularly in the Japanese navy, in their opinion that much was to be gained by operating in semi-independent divisions.

As for strategy, the lessons of the war have nowhere been more trenchantly summarized than in a letter of March 3, 1909 that President Roosevelt wrote to his successor, William Howard Taft, at the urgent request of Mahan:

Dear Will: One closing legacy. Under no circumstances divide the battleship fleet between the Atlantic and the Pacific Oceans prior to the finishing of the Panama Canal. . . . It is nearly four years since the close of the Russian-Japanese War. There were various factors that brought about Russia's defeat; but the most important by all odds was her having divided her fleet between the Baltic and the Pacific, and, furthermore, splitting up her Pacific fleet into three utterly unequal divisions. The entire Japanese force was always used to smash some fraction of the Russian force.

Summary

Among the established and rising sea powers of the early 20th century, Japan was an anomaly in that she completely skipped the Age of Sail. The defeated fleets of Hideyoshi in the late 16th century were composed mostly of galleys. The victorious fleets of Ito in the Battle of the Yalu in 1894 and of Togo in the Battle of Tsushima in 1905 were composed of steam ships of the most advanced design. Between these two periods the Japanese, deliberately isolating themselves, did without a national navy until resurgent Western imperialism, forced them again to look to their seaward defenses.

With remarkable astuteness Japan's new naval leaders not only assimilated the lessons of three centuries of sea warfare in the West, but actually outstripped many Western thinkers in developing naval weapons and strategic and tactical concepts.

In strategy, the Japanese showed themselves masters of concentration, particularly with regard to defeating the enemy in fractions. In the Sino-Japanese War, they brought their main force against one of the Chinese provincial squadrons and defeated it before the others were committed. In the Russo-Japanese War, they used their interior position to neutralize successively the three segments of Russia's Far East fleet—at Port Arthur, at Inchon, and at Vladivostok. Then, conserving their ships and practicing continually at gunfire and maneuver, they were prepared with the same naval forces to defeat the Russian Baltic squadron when it arrived.

In tactics, the Japanese early perceived the paramount value of the column and of broadside fire. Using speed and maneuver, they generally succeeded in breaking up enemy formations and bringing a preponderance of fire against successive fractions of the enemy fleet.

In accordance with the principle triumphantly demonstrated by Nelson at Trafalgar, they operated in semi-independent divisions in order to attain great flexibility in battle and to permit part of the fleet to proceed at any time by the shortest line to the point where it was most needed.

As a result of her victories over China and Russia, Japan in the early 20th century emerged as a first-class naval power—a power with which the acknowledged Mistress of the Seas did not disdain to conclude an alliance. But Japan, regarding herself as robbed by the West of the fruits of her victories, continued to strengthen her fleet against the day when opportunity would enable her to assert her supremacy in the Far East.

20:

The Spanish-American War

If any single event be selected to mark the emergence of the United States as a major power, perhaps no better choice could be made than the Spanish-American War of 1898. Lasting a little over a hundred days and costing some 3,000 American lives, this brief, one-sided conflict involved the United States in the complex problems of the Far East and served notice on the European powers that henceforth American military strength would have to be reckoned with. For the Americans themselves it marked a turning point toward greater participation in world affairs.

Although the first major sea battle of the Spanish-American War was fought half a world away in the Philippines, the conflict arose out of the anarchy in Cuba. Here a chronic state of revolution against Spanish misrule finally erupted into fiery rebellion in 1895. The *insurrectos*, vying in cruelty with their Spanish masters, set about a policy of deliberate devastation in which the property of American citizens was not spared unless protection money was paid, and this in turn was expended to finance the revolt or to spread propaganda. Indeed, a major reason for United States intervention was to protect the largely American-owned cane plantations and sugar mills. These interests were not inconsiderable, amounting to $50,000,000 in investments and $100,000,000 in annual volume of trade. Determined to put an end to the intolerable conditions in Cuba, the Spanish government early in 1896 sent General Valeriano Weyler to Havana, with orders to apply stern measures. Weyler's solution was to herd civilians into reconcentration areas, where they could not support the rebels. Here unhygienic conditions brought death to thousands, mainly women and children. The American public, already stirred by the skillful efforts

of the Cuban junta in New York, reacted violently against the inhuman methods of "Butcher Weyler," and many urged that the rebel "government" be accorded recognition forthwith. Responding to the clamor, Congress passed a resolution demanding recognition of Cuban belligerency. Anti-imperialist President Cleveland ignored the resolution as an intrusion upon his executive powers, declaring that he would refuse to call out the army rather than go to war with Spain, but to the Spanish government he intimated that American respect for Spanish rule in Cuba might be "superseded by higher obligations, which we can hardly hesitate to recognize and discharge."

When a new, liberal Spanish ministry in 1897 recalled Weyler, modified the reconcentration system, and granted the Cubans a certain degree of autonomy, Americans began to lose interest in the Cuban cause. Then in February 1898 there occurred two events which aroused a storm of public indignation in the United States. One was the publication in the New York *Journal* of an indiscreet private letter written by Dupuy de Lôme, Spanish minister in Washington, and somehow obtained by the Cuban junta. In his letter the minister hinted at Spanish duplicity in discussions on pending trade agreements and referred to President McKinley as a "small-time politician." A week later, the battleship *Maine*, which had been ordered to Cuba to protect American lives and property, was torn apart by an explosion that killed 260 of her crew. The American public believed that the explosion was external, caused by a mine planted and set off by the Spaniards. The New York *Journal* offered a $50,000 reward, never claimed, for the apprehension and conviction of the perpetrators. Though subsequent studies have shown that the explosion might well have been internal and accidental, the United States was brought to the brink of war.

Because, in event of armed conflict with Spain, Cuba would be the primary military objective and Puerto Rico a secondary one, the bulk of the United States Fleet was concentrated in the Atlantic. To strengthen forces already there, the battleship *Oregon* made her celebrated voyage from Puget Sound around South America to the Caribbean, a 15,000-mile passage completed in 66 days at an average speed at sea of nearly 12 knots. Her arrival raised the strength of the North Atlantic Squadron to five battleships and two armored cruisers, plus smaller types. Meanwhile, the Navy Department maintained only a small Asiatic Squadron of light cruiser types in the Pacific, which was generally regarded as an area of lesser naval significance.

The effect of the *Maine* disaster was not lost upon the Spaniards, who tried to appease American wrath, but at the same time prepared for war. Upon learning of the explosion, the Spanish Minister of Marine alerted the fleet and advised Admiral Pasquale Cervera, commanding the main home force, to be ready to destroy the American base at Key West and then to blockade the American coast.

To Cervera, constitutionally pessimistic, such an assignment appeared fantastic in the extreme, for his operational strength consisted only of four cruisers and two destroyers, all in poor shape. He pointed out his naval inferiority in comparison to the Americans, the absence of powerful Spanish bases beyond the Atlantic, and the probable lack of adequate logistic support for his fleet in Cuba and Puerto Rico. He expressed the opinion that the most practical naval strategy for his country in event of war would be to retain forces for defense of the homeland and asserted that his fleet could make the American coast a profitable military objective only if Spain could enlist a powerful naval ally capable of furnishing assistance. The Ministry thereupon modified its directive but insisted that the naval forces should at least defend Puerto Rico. On April 8, 1898 Cervera, still regarding his mission as hopeless, steamed from Cadiz and advanced to the Cape Verde Islands to await further political developments.

Word of the sortie of the Spanish home fleet caused a tremendous war scare along the American East Coast. Badly informed citizenry everywhere had visions of coastal bombardment and invasion by the enemy. Both Army and Navy received frantic calls for coast defense. Secretary of War Russell Alger afterwards remembered that "the calls made upon the department for immediate rescue from the advancing Spanish fleet were pathetic in their urgency. Telegrams, letters, and statesmen representing the imperiled localities poured into the War Department. They wanted guns everywhere; mines in all the rivers and harbors on the map."[1] Theodore Roosevelt later recalled that nervous Boston financiers, fearful for the safety of their investment securities, removed them 50 miles inland to Worcester for safer keeping.

No harm was done, and some nerves were calmed, by a general trundling out of obsolete Civil War guns to points along the coast, whence they were aimed futilely at the empty Atlantic. But demands for fleet protection simultaneously of all parts of the East Coast were something else again, for a fleet is by reason of its mobility a weapon of attack. Even when its mission is defensive in purpose, its units should never degenerate into static platforms for guns.

The Navy Department was well aware that the North Atlantic Squadron ought in the circumstances to operate as a unit. Even if Cervera should strike elsewhere than in the Caribbean, where he was expected, a fleet with its integrity preserved could still strike a retaliatory blow. Spreading the fleet thin along the coast could prove military suicide; yet the clamor of the coastal cities for naval protection had to be satisfied in some manner. The solution was a compromise—the North Atlantic Squadron was divided into two main parts. One, under Acting Rear Admiral William T. Sampson, was based at Key West, poised and ready for offensive operations against Cuba and Puerto Rico. The other, the so-called Flying Squadron, was organized at Norfolk under the command of Commodore Winfield Scott Schley, as a mobile fortress fleet for the roving protection of the Atlantic seaboard. A smaller

[1] Russell A. Alger, *The Spanish-American War* (New York, Harper and Brothers, 1901), 38.

Northern Patrol Squadron of obsolete and generally useless vessels guarded the coast from the Delaware Capes northward.

Meanwhile, the Spanish Ministry was vacillating over American demands that Spain grant an armistice to the *insurrectos* and put an end to reconcentration—fearful of revolution at home if they capitulated and of war with the United States if they did not. By April 9, the Ministry had given in on both points. It was already too late however, for President McKinley had now come to realize that the Democrats with their cry of "Free Cuba!" would defeat him in the next elections unless he put a definitive end to the wretched conditions in the Spanish colony. So he sent a war message to Congress on the 11th, requesting authority to use the Army and Navy. A week later Congress passed a joint resolution declaring Cuba free and independent, demanding the withdrawal of Spanish forces, and directing the President to use armed force to put the resolution into effect. A final clause, the so-called Teller Amendment, pledged that whatever the outcome the United States would not annex Cuba.

On April 22, 1898 the Navy Department directed Sampson to establish a blockade of Cuban waters from Havana around the western tip of the island to Cienfuegos on the south coast. On April 25 Congress declared a state of war to have existed since April 21. On the 29th Cervera's fleet left the Cape Verdes and steamed to the defense of Puerto Rico. Cervera was given "entire freedom of action as to route, port, and cases and circumstances in which battle should be sought or eluded."[2]

The Philippine Campaign

No cries for coastal protection split the small American naval force in the Pacific. Indeed, many Americans were scarcely aware that Spain had possessions in that area. One man in Washington however knew very well that the Spaniards owned the Philippines and had a fleet of sorts there. That was Theodore Roosevelt, Assistant Secretary of the Navy. When trouble with Spain loomed, Roosevelt decided

that the United States must be prepared to strike in the Pacific as well as in the Atlantic.[3] Casting about for a man capable of striking a quick and effective blow against naval forces in the Philippines, he selected Commodore George Dewey and had him appointed Commander in Chief of the U.S. Asiatic Squadron.

Dewey at the time of his appointment was holding the routine administrative post of President of the Board of Inspection and Survey, but he had experienced extensive combat duty in the Civil War and had a reputation for aggressiveness. Dewey was much more than merely aggressive, however. Like his old commanding officer, David Glasgow Farragut, he combined a keen eye for tactical situations with a capacity for meticulous attention to detail. Before leaving Washington he read everything he could find on the Philippines and studied all available charts of the surrounding waters. Urgently requesting the Navy Department to forward ammunition as soon as possible, he left for Japan in early December 1897. A month later he boarded the flagship *Olympia* at Nagasaki and assumed his new command.

Dewey soon moved his squadron to Hong Kong in order to be nearer Manila. Here he received a cablegram from Roosevelt, then Acting Secretary: "Keep full of coal. In the event . . . of war your duty will be to see that the Spanish squadron does not leave the Asiatic coast, and then offensive operations in Philippine Islands." Dewey needed no such prompting, for he was already furiously at work in preparation for his coming task. He purchased a collier and a supply steamer to serve as fleet train. He had his warships docked, the machinery overhauled, the underwater hulls scraped, and the white sides painted battle gray. The Commodore personally inspected all details, seeing to it that crews underwent daily drill and that all machinery was ready for sustained operation at a moment's notice. Lacking information on the Spanish fleet and fortifications in the Philippines, he sent a spy to Manila and disguised his own aide as a tourist to pick up data from travelers arriving in Hong Kong. To by-pass British neutrality

[2] Office of Naval Intelligence, *Notes on the Spanish-American War*, 10 v. (Washington, 1899), VII, 65.

[3] Note that Roosevelt made this decision eleven years before he wrote the letter to Taft quoted on page 364.

rules once war was declared, he arranged for a temporary anchorage at Mirs Bay in Chinese waters some distance up the coast.

On April 25 came a cable from the Secretary of the Navy: "War has commenced between the United States and Spain. Proceed at once to Philippine Islands. Commence operations at once, particularly against the Spanish fleet. You must capture vessels or destroy. Use utmost endeavors." Dewey waited 36 hours until the American consul arrived from Manila with the latest word concerning Spanish preparations. On the 27th Dewey sailed for the conquest of the Philippines.

The American squadron comprised four cruisers, including the flagship *Olympia* (5,870 tons), the *Baltimore*, the *Raleigh*, and the *Boston;* two gunboats, the *Petrel* and the *Concord;* and the revenue cutter *McCulloch*. These vessels totaled about 20,000 tons and carried some 100 guns, only half of them larger than 4-inch. Six hundred miles away in the Philippines waited the fleet of Rear Admiral Don Patricio Montojo. Montojo's only modern vessel of any real consequence was the *Reina Christina* of about 3,500 tons, mounting six 6.2-inch guns. Another of his cruisers, the old wooden *Castilla,* was unable to move under her own power. In addition, he had five ships of 500 to 1,100 tons. Estimating that he would have no chance of defeating the American squadron in a battle of maneuver, Montojo planned to fight at anchor, using his ships as a fortress fleet to supplement shore batteries.

En route to the Philippines, the American squadron made final preparations for action, including battle drills in daylight and darkness, practice in fire fighting and damage control, and removal of practically all woodwork to lessen fire hazards. In the afternoon of April 30, after reconnoitering Subic Bay and finding the Spanish fleet not there, Dewey remarked, "Now we have them," and headed for the passage south of Corregidor leading into landlocked Manila Bay.

Despite his outward assurance, the Commodore had inward qualms. Manila was regarded throughout the Far East as impregnable. The passages into the bay had been mined. Thirty years before, his old commander Farragut had damned the torpedoes, in deed if not in word, and steamed into Mobile Bay. Since then of

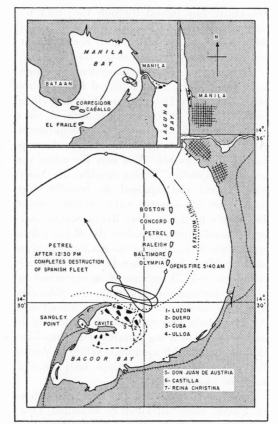

BATTLE OF MANILA BAY, MAY 1, 1898

course mines had greatly improved, but Dewey, judging that there were no engineers in Manila skillful enough to place mines properly in the deep waters off Corregidor, determined to take his fleet in under cover of darkness. "Whenever I have been in a difficult situation, or in the midst of such a confusion of details that the simple and right thing to do seemed hazy," he wrote afterward, "I have often asked myself, 'What would Farragut do?' In the course of preparations for Manila Bay I often asked myself this question, and I confess I was thinking of him that night when we entered the bay, and with the conviction that I was doing precisely what he would have done."[4]

On May 1, 1898, a little after midnight, when the American squadron had almost completed its passage into the bay without encountering any live mines, a few of the batteries on shore opened fire. But shells from the American ships quickly silenced the guns and

[4] *Autobiography* (New York, 1916), 50.

the entire line passed through the strait unscathed. At dawn, Dewey's squadron was off Manila looking for the Spanish fleet. The city batteries opened fire but made no hits.

To spare the city bombardment by American guns, Montojo had placed his squadron off Cavite. Here Dewey found him and closed to 5,000 yards to conserve ammunition, since there was no nearby source of replenishment. At 5:40 AM the Commodore said to the captain of the *Olympia*, "You may fire when you are ready, Gridley." Firing steadily, the Americans passed and repassed the Spanish ships in a series of countermarches reminiscent of Du Pont's tactics in Port Royal Sound. Several Spanish ships, including the *Reina Christina*, made futile attempts to advance but were sunk or driven back. When Dewey temporarily withdrew at 7:35 because of an erroneous report of ammunition shortage, the *Christina* and the *Castilla* had already been abandoned. At 11 o'clock Dewey resumed battle and in another hour of firing completed the annihilation of the Spanish squadron. When he ceased fire all of Montojo's warships were burned, sunk, or abandoned.

Spanish casualties, in the fleet and ashore on Cavite, were 381 killed or wounded. Dewey's squadron had suffered no fatalities and only seven wounded. The Americans, who had drilled regularly at gunnery, had made at least 170 hits; the Spaniards, who had had no practice at all, made only 15. The American victory was as much a result of superior preparation as of superior power. "The battle of Manila," said Dewey, "was won in Hong Kong harbor." He might have added that it was a timely victory, for had he not promptly located and defeated Montojo's force, his supply situation would have become precarious.

With no Spanish naval power left in the area, Dewey anchored off Manila to hold the Philippines against outside interference. His problem was complicated by the arrival of five German warships on the lookout for a chance to pick up the Philippines for colony-hungry Germany, should the United States not be interested. The United States however was very much interested. Some 11,000 Army troops were soon on the way from San Francisco to seize Manila and occupy the islands. En route to the Philippines the cruiser *Charleston*, escorting the troop convoy, made a bloodless capture of Spanish Guam, where the governor had not even heard of the war. Less than a month later, the United States, with visions of growing empire, at long last annexed the independent Hawaiian Islands.

On August 13, 1898, under combined army and navy bombardment, Manila capitulated after a token resistance. Thereafter the Army and the Navy faced the three-year task of putting down an insurrection among the Filipinos, who had hoped for independence and not merely an exchange of imperial masters. Nearly half a century would pass before the United States would deem the Filipinos ready to govern themselves. Meanwhile, with the cession of the Philippines by the treaty of peace, the United States became permanently involved in the affairs of the Far East.

The Caribbean Campaign

Admiral Sampson, intellectual, somewhat remote, but by no means lacking in aggressiveness, proposed opening hostilities against Spain with an amphibious assault upon Havana. By capturing the capital and military stronghold, he hoped to bring the conflict to an early end. Navy Secretary Long disapproved Sampson's proposal because the Army was far from ready and also because he considered it unwise to risk the American fleet against the guns of Havana while an enemy fleet was still at large. The accumulated experience of warfare suggested that before exposing one's ships to the perils of attack against a fortified coast one must either have gained command of the sea by destroying any enemy forces which might interfere, or else one must have the equivalent of two fleets, a Support Force to attack the coast and protect the invasion troops and a Covering Force to act as a shield to the beachhead and Support Force, fending off any approaching enemy fleet.

With the North Atlantic Squadron divided between Norfolk and the Caribbean, Long simply did not feel that Sampson had sufficient strength for amphibious operations while Cervera's fleet remained intact. In this opinion he was seconded by the new Naval War Board. This board, composed of Admiral Sicard, retired commander of the North Atlantic

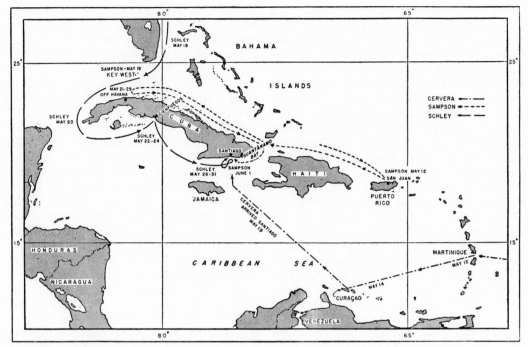

CARIBBEAN CAMPAIGN

Squadron, Admiral Crowninshield, Chief of the Bureau of Navigation, and Captain Mahan, the naval historian and philosopher, was intended originally as a mere intelligence agency but came in time to act as a central strategy board. As such, it served to unify the efforts of the Navy, though it sometimes embarrassed local commands when it ventured into tactical directives. The Board was a great step forward from the somewhat hit-or-miss central direction in earlier wars, but no machinery had yet been developed which, like the Joint Chiefs of Staff in World War II, could coordinate army and naval operations.

When Cervera, on orders from Madrid, cleared the Cape Verde Islands on April 29, he was as gloomy as ever. He knew he was hopelessly outmatched. Moreover, his best cruiser, the *Cristóbal Colón,* lacked her two 10-inch guns, and another, the *Vizcaya,* was slowed by a badly fouled underwater hull.

Sampson soon learned of Cervera's sortie and at once conceived the plan of going out to meet him at San Juan, Puerto Rico, where he believed the Spanish fleet would have to put in for coal. Mahan also had estimated that the Spaniards would touch first at San Juan

and had suggested placing scout cruisers in that area to detect Cervera and notify Sampson. The American fleet could then advance to San Juan and seek a decisive naval action. However, Sampson partially lifted his blockade of Cuba on May 3 and headed for Puerto Rico with battleships *Iowa* and *Indiana,* armored cruiser *New York,* two monitors, and a torpedo boat. Slowed down by the monitors, which had to be towed, he did not reach San Juan until the 12th. Finding no signs of Cervera, he bombarded the port for an hour, taking eight personnel casualties from shore guns and doing only minor damage.

Mahan condemned Sampson's advance to Puerto Rico. The main objective of American operations in the Caribbean was capture of Cuba by invasion, following defeat or blockade of the Spanish fleet. Until Cervera was located, therefore, Cuba was the strategic center of the campaign. In the circumstances Sampson in abandoning Cuba was, in Mahan's terms, sacrificing his position at the strategic center for an eccentric operation of dubious advantage.

As a matter of fact, Cervera had outguessed Sampson by estimating that Sampson would do exactly what he did. While the North Atlantic Squadron was widely scattered, with Schley at Norfolk, Sampson at San Juan, some vessels at Key West, others on blockade off Cuba, and the *Oregon* en route from the Pacific, the Spaniards successfully eluded them all and slipped into Cuba's back door. After crossing the Atlantic at less than seven knots, Cervera had applied for coal at Martinique. Refused assistance there by the French, he had proceeded to Curaçao, where the Dutch authorities proved more hospitable. Thence he proceeded straight for Cuba.

Sampson was already returning from his fruitless advance to San Juan when he learned of Cervera's arrival in the Caribbean. He thereupon dropped his monitors and made full speed for Key West, arriving on May 18, a few hours after Schley's Flying Squadron had arrived from Norfolk. Believing that the Spanish fleet was bringing ammunition for defense of the capital, Sampson strengthened his blockade of Havana and sent the Flying Squadron, reinforced by the *Iowa,* around to the south coast of Cuba to blockade Cienfuegos, which was connected to Havana by rail. In the meantime, once more outguessing Sampson, Cervera had made directly for the isolated port of Santiago, far to the southeast. Here on the morning of the 19th he was received with congratulations when he steamed through the narrow channel into the harbor. Merely reaching Santiago safely was a real achievement. But now he could think of nothing better to do than remain anchored in the harbor until the American blockade closed on him nine days later.

Meanwhile Schley was taking his time getting to Cienfuegos. Once there he found he could not see inside the harbor, but he did see smoke and from that assumed that the Spaniards might be present. With evidence piling up that Cervera was elsewhere, Sampson sent Schley word by fast dispatch boat: "Spanish squadron probably at Santiago. . . . *If you are satisfied they are not at Cienfuegos,* proceed with all despatch, but cautiously, to Santiago de Cuba, and if enemy is there blockade him in port."[5] On the 24th Schley made contact with Cuban insurgents ashore and, determining at last that Cervera was not at Cienfuegos,

headed for Santiago. Keeping down for a while to the 6-knot speed of one of his gunboats, which was having trouble in the mounting seas, he did not complete the 315-mile run until May 26. While still 20 miles from Santiago he made contact with three American scout cruisers, none of which had sighted Cervera.

Schley now began to worry about the state of his coal supply, and though he had a collier with him, the rough seas made coaling at sea impossible. So that night he ordered his squadron to head back toward Key West for recoaling. Delayed by engine trouble in his collier, he was overtaken by a scout cruiser next morning with a terse message from Washington: "All Department's information indicates Spanish division is still at Santiago. The Department looks to you to ascertain facts, and that the enemy, if therein, does not leave without decisive action." To which Schley replied: "Much to be regretted, cannot obey orders of the Department; forced to proceed for coal to Key West, by way of Yucatan passage; cannot ascertain anything respecting enemy."[6] Luckily, the seas soon calmed so that the Flying Squadron was able after all to take on coal. Schley therefore returned to Santiago and took station off the harbor in the evening of May 28. The following morning the *Cristóbal Colón* was clearly visible anchored at the entrance, where she had been for the past four days. On June 1 Sampson arrived off Santiago, his squadron strengthened by the newly-arrived *Oregon,* and assumed over-all command. At last the various parts of the North Atlantic Squadron had been brought together.

The American vessels now took blockading stations, with the five battleships in a semicircle four to six miles off the entrance and smaller craft patrolling closer inshore. At night the ships closed in somewhat and a searchlight from one of the battleships played upon the harbor mouth. During the month-long blockade the fleet frequently bombarded the Morro and other shore batteries guarding Santiago harbor, and at night the experimental cruiser *Vesuvius* participated spectacularly but not

[5] Winfield Scott Schley. *Forty-Five Years under the Flag* (New York, 1904), 270.

[6] Schley communicated with the Department via dispatch cruiser to nearby Haiti, which had cable-telegraph connections with Washington. The dispatches are quoted from Schley, *op. cit.,* 278–9.

very effectively, firing 1,500-pound dynamite shells by compressed air from three fixed 15-inch tubes. In order to secure an advanced base near Santiago for coaling, supply, and general maintenance of the blockading vessels, some 650 marines seized Guantanamo, Cuba on June 10 and in a week of fighting made good their position. These were the first Americans to fight on Spanish soil.

Cervera in the landlocked harbor of Santiago was harmless enough, yet his squadron still constituted a fleet-in-being that exerted a restraining influence upon American operations elsewhere because there always existed the possibility that he might escape. The United States could not exercise unchallenged command of the seas around Cuba so long as there was any likelihood that Spanish warships might interfere with landing or other operations. Sampson's fleet could not however penetrate the narrow, winding channel into the harbor because of mine fields planted there, and the mine fields could not be cleared because of the nearby shore batteries. Any attempt to run through the mines might result in a vessel in the middle of the attacking column being sunk and so splitting the fleet by blocking the ships already inside from those still outside. The alternative to going in and destroying Cervera's squadron was to close the harbor entrance with a sunken hull that could not be by-passed at night or blown away by storms. For such a stopper Sampson chose a small collier and sent her in with a picked crew of seven under Naval Constructor Richmond P. Hobson to blow her up and sink her across the narrowest part of the channel. But the collier was detected by the Spaniards, whereupon shore batteries opened fire and so smashed her steering gear that she drifted past the narrows and sank in a position where she was only a minor obstacle.

With the failure of the harbor-blocking experiment, it became clear that if the danger was to be removed, the Spanish squadron would have to be induced to come out and fight or Sampson's fleet would have to go into the harbor after it. Sampson therefore called on Washington for sufficient army troops to capture the shore batteries so that he could send in boats to clear the mines.

Meanwhile the Army, eager to take part in the war which up to then had involved only the Navy and a few Marines, quickly assembled 16,000 soldiers at Tampa, under command of Major General William R. Shafter USV. On May 31 the War Department sent Shafter his orders, which read in part:

> Proceed under convoy of the Navy to the vicinity of Santiago de Cuba, land your force at such place east or west of that point as your judgment may dictate, under the protection of the Navy, and move it onto the high ground and bluffs overlooking the harbor or into the interior, as shall best enable you to capture or destroy the garrison there, and cover the Navy as it sends its men in small boats to remove torpedoes, or, with the aid of the Navy, capture or destroy the Spanish fleet now reported to be in Santiago harbor.[7]

Shafter thus had been given considerable latitude, including the right to exercise his own judgment and, if he saw fit to do so, initiate a campaign against the city of Santiago and the main Spanish army. The fact that he was given a choice of operations, when the Navy had asked for one specific task to be done, reveals serious lack of liaison between the War and Navy Departments. Moreover, Shafter and Sampson, who would have to work together closely in mutual support, had no common superior below the level of the President of the United States.

Sailing from Tampa in mid-June in commercial transports escorted by naval vessels, the expeditionary force reached Santiago on the 20th. Present were General Leonard Wood's Rough Riders, including Theodore Roosevelt, who could not bear to remain behind his desk at the Navy Department when fighting was in prospect. Four days were consumed in leisurely, laborious landing operations at Daiquiri, 18 miles east of Santiago, with the Navy standing by to lend support and providing boats to ferry the troops to the beach.

On June 20 Admiral Sampson, together with General García and other Cuban officers, held his only conference with General Shafter. There appears to have been no firm decision reached, but Sampson left the conference satisfied that Shafter had accepted the harbor batteries as his objective. Shafter left equally convinced that the Admiral had agreed to the city of Santiago as the Army's proper objec-

[7] *Annual Report, Secretary of War, 1898,* I, 87.

tive. The General afterward asserted that his decision to attack Santiago was included in a memorandum he dictated to a member of Sampson's staff. In any event, when Shafter directly afterward plunged into the interior with his troops, Sampson seems to have regarded the move as a feint, to be followed by an early attack on the batteries. He was astounded a few days later when the General informed him by message that the city was the true objective of his march.

Meanwhile, hampered by rough bridle paths and barbed wire, the soldiers had advanced slowly under the blazing tropical sun, many dropping out with heatstroke or typhoid fever. At San Juan Hill and El Caney the Spaniards took a stand and inflicted on the invaders casualties amounting to nearly ten per cent. Alarmed, on the verge of retreating, Shafter, who was 63, weighed more than 300 pounds, and was confined to his tent with fever, sent Sampson an urgent message: "Terrible fight yesterday, but my line is strongly entrenched three-quarters of a mile from town. I urge that you make effort immediately to force the entrance to avoid future losses among my men." Thus the Army, halted by a variety of causes at the city's outskirts, was now requesting the Navy to enter over live mine fields in order to assist the land forces in a campaign the Admiral regarded as a misconception of the Army's proper mission. Exasperated by his inability to reach an agreement with Shafter by messenger regarding the respective roles the Army and Navy should play, Sampson on July 3 steamed eastward along the coast in his flagship *New York* for a personal interview with the General. Sampson's departure from the Santiago blockade set the stage for a subsequent dispute involving Schley.

Before Sampson could set foot ashore, his differences with Shafter were resolved by Cervera himself. Though the situation looked grave enough to the Americans, it looked graver still to the Spaniards, who were convinced that Santiago was about to be captured and the fleet with it. Rather than see that happen, Governor General Blanco, at Havana, telegraphed Cervera to get out of port at any cost, and Cervera seized the opportunity of making his sortie while Sampson was off station in the *New York*, and the *Massachusetts*

was coaling at Guantanamo. The Spanish flagship *Maria Teresa* led the way at 9:35 A.M, followed by the cruisers *Vizcaya, Cristóbal Colón*, and *Oquendo* and two destroyers. Sighting the smoke of the *Teresa* as she approached the entrance, the *New York* promptly came about, hoisted the signal for action, and sped westward trying to catch up with the running battle being fought by Schley, whom Sampson had left in tactical command during his absence.

Off Santiago harbor, the blockaders closed in, firing at the *Teresa* as she emerged. The *Brooklyn*, Schley's flagship, with the *Teresa* approaching as if to ram, swung to starboard across the bow of the nearby *Texas*, which had to back all engines to prevent a collision. Making almost a complete circle the *Brooklyn* finally headed west with the rest of the ships. These were already pursuing the Spaniards, who had broken through the blockade. Why the *Brooklyn* at first turned east instead of west, whether to avoid being rammed, to unmask the batteries of other American ships, or to open the range, was never satisfactorily explained, even by Schley, who stated merely that "it was the proper military maneuver under the circumstances" and that "it saved the day beyond any doubt."[8]

Soon the swift *Brooklyn* made good her loss in range and took the lead among the pursuers, with the *Oregon, Iowa, Texas,* and *Indiana* following. At the same time the little converted yacht *Gloucester* closed on the two Spanish destroyers. Coming under concentrated fire from the American battle line, the *Teresa,* hit about 30 times, her steam lines severed, her wooden decks on fire, turned toward shore and beached six miles west of the harbor mouth.

The *Oquendo* and the *Vizcaya* next came under heavy fire, began to blaze, and likewise grounded. Only the *Colón,* last and swiftest of Cervera's cruisers, outran the range of American shells and made a gallant bid to escape. Her stokers spurred to extraordinary exertion by libations of cognac, she steamed westward at 14 knots. After a 55-mile chase, when the alcoholic stimulation of her black gang had turned to drowsiness, the *Brooklyn* and the *Oregon* finally caught up with her and began

[8] Schley, *Forty-Five Years,* 302.

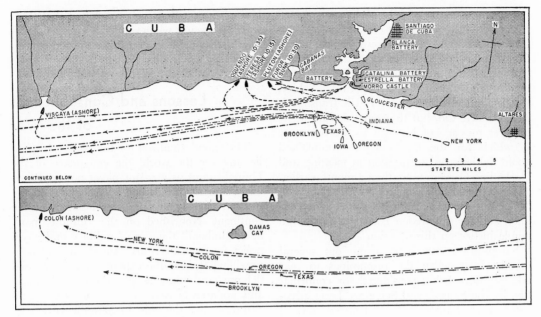

BATTLE OF SANTIAGO, JULY 3, 1898

making hits. At that, the *Colón,* only slightly damaged, struck her colors, steered for the beach, and surrendered. Meanwhile, the two Spanish destroyers, hotly engaged by the little *Gloucester,* had come under fire of the *Indiana* as she sped by. One destroyer was almost cut in two by a 13-inch shell; the other, heavily damaged by a smaller shell, sank after lowering her colors to the *Gloucester.*

As in the Battle of Manila Bay an inferior fleet had been annihilated by a superior, better-managed fleet. Spanish losses in the Battle of Santiago were 160 men killed and 1,800 captured, including Cervera himself. American losses were one man killed and one wounded.

The defeat of Cervera had far-reaching effects. Within a fortnight, Santiago, under naval bombardment and running short of food, became untenable, whereupon General Toral formally surrendered the city and his 22,000 troops to General Shafter. Spain's few remaining warships, en route to attack Dewey in Manila Bay, turned around in the Red Sea and headed back home to defend Spanish shores from a possible attack by the victorious North Atlantic Squadron. Now that the United States was in undisputed command of Caribbean waters, American expeditionary forces, with naval support, landed in Puerto Rico and headed

for the capital. By the end of July, with United States forces victorious everywhere, the Navy laid plans for a cruise against the Spanish mainland, whereupon the Spaniards promptly sued for peace. In the final treaty, signed on December 10, 1898 in Paris, Spain relinquished all claim to Cuba and ceded Puerto Rico, Guam, and the Philippines to the United States.

The Sampson-Schley Controversy

For their services in the Spanish-American War, Dewey, Sampson, and Schley were made permanent rear admirals. It would appear that there was glory enough for each, but bitter recriminations arising between the adherents of Sampson and Schley served in some measure to dim the renown of both.

In the first newspaper stories of the Battle of Santiago, genial, obliging Schley, a favorite of the press, received almost unanimous credit for the victory, though the preliminary planning had been done by Sampson, who, unluckily, was off station when the enemy fleet emerged. As newspapers began to reach the fleet off Santiago a week after the battle, Schley went to Sampson with a message which he asked him to transmit to the Secretary of the Navy: "Feel some mortification that the newspaper accounts of July 6th have attributed victory on July 3rd almost entirely to me. Victory was secured by the force under command Commander-in-Chief, North Atlantic Station [Sampson], and to him the honor is due." After reading the message, Sampson said, "Schley, this is kind and generous; I will transmit it at once." He did, but that same day he wrote a secret message of his own to the Secretary in which for the first time he complained about Schley's procrastination in locating and blockading Cervera more than a month earlier. "This reprehensible conduct," wrote Sampson, "I cannot separate from his subsequent conduct, and for this reason I ask you to do him ample justice on this occasion."

Sampson's secret letter came out several months later when the promotions to rear admiral were being considered for confirmation by the Senate, and Secretary Long advocated that Sampson be advanced several numbers over Schley. Schley defended his conduct so well in a letter to the Senate Naval Affairs Committee that the inequity was canceled. Two years later however Schley's indignation was again aroused by the appearance of a third volume of Edgar Maclay's *History of the United States Navy,* the first two volumes of which were in use as textbooks at the United States Naval Academy. Maclay not only put the severest interpretation upon Schley's actions preceding the blockade but implied that Schley's turnaway to starboard in the *Brooklyn* was an act of cowardice. At this Schley requested a Court of Inquiry to determine what his war record had been.

For 40 days the Court held session under the chairmanship of Admiral Dewey. After 2,000 pages of testimony and findings had been assembled, the Court issued a majority and a minority report. The majority found that Schley's conduct prior to June 1, 1898 "was characterized by vacillation, dilatoriness, and lack of enterprise" and concluded that "the turn of the *Brooklyn* to the eastward was made to avoid getting her into dangerous proximity to the Spanish vessels." The brief minority report just as vigorously praised and defended Schley's conduct.

Schley protested the majority findings to Theodore Roosevelt, then President of the United States. Roosevelt concluded that there was "no excuse whatever from either side for any further agitation on this unhappy controversy." So the matter rested.

Lessons and Consequences of the War

The war dramatized for the American public and for the world the emergence of the United States as a major naval power. Previously, American eyes had been focused on the western frontier and the development of the continent. Nourished on the "minute man" and "gunboat" theories of military and naval policy for over a century, Americans had been unwilling to bear the expense of a substantial defense establishment. But the overwhelming and apparently easy victories of Dewey and Sampson and the epic 15,000-mile voyage of the *Oregon* furnished a popular emotional point of departure for acceptance of a "big navy" policy.

Meanwhile American officers with characteristic pragmatism combed the experiences of their first naval war in a long generation for lessons—technical, tactical, and strategic. Among their more fruitful findings were the following:

(1) American fire control techniques needed improvement. At Santiago, for example, the North Atlantic Squadron had made only 42 major-caliber hits out of 1,300 rounds fired at point-blank range.

(2) In warships, wood and other inflammables should be reduced to an absolute minimum in exposed positions. Under fire the pitch-seamed decks of the Spanish vessels had turned into sheets of flame.

(3) Especially needed by the United States armed forces was a sound amphibious doctrine. The amateurish Daiquiri landings would have failed against a properly defended beach.

(4) Outlying coaling and repair bases were needed to extend the radius of American fleet action.

(5) The first use in war of refrigerator ships, a hospital ship, and a hull repair vessel demonstrated the value of such auxiliaries, and suggested the desirability of further developing logistic fleet support afloat.

(6) The need of more effective liaison between Army and Navy was clearly demonstrated.

(7) The political pressures put on the Navy to divert mobile forces to static harbor defense illustrated the need of a better public understanding of the Navy's role. The division of force resulting from such demands was compounded by the Navy's tendency to scatter its fleet units in strategically eccentric operations. Clearly the time had come for both statesmen and officers in the United States to acquire a clearer understanding of the principles of naval warfare. Luckily, Mahan's *Influence of Sea Power upon History* and subsequent works were already at hand to fill the need.

The thoughtful student of the Spanish-American War was forced to the conclusion that the United States Navy, though performing creditably, still showed much room for improvement. It was not likely to repeat the sweeping victories of Manila and Santiago without better material, better techniques, and better understanding of principles. "We cannot," warned Mahan, "expect ever again to have an enemy so entirely inapt as Spain showed herself to be."[9]

The most important long-term consequence

[9] *Lessons of the War with Spain* (Boston, 1899), 157.

of the war was that the United States had acquired an overseas empire. The occupation of Puerto Rico and Guantanamo would actually aid the Navy in its mission of defense of the continental United States. But the new Pacific possessions posed far more problems than they solved.

Attempts to find solutions to these problems, as we shall see, dominated much of the Navy's thinking and planning for the next 40 years. Most perplexing was the question of how to defend the great Philippine archipelago—7,000 miles from the United States but only 1,000 miles from Japan and less than 300 miles from Japanese-held Formosa. Against a militaristic, expansionist Japan, the Philippines could be defended only by maintaining effective fleet superiority in Far Eastern waters. Once lost to Japan, or any other strong Oriental power, they could be recovered only by securing effective control over most of the Pacific. Either alternative would require fortified base facilities far beyond anything the United States possessed in 1898. In the chain of events leading to America's involvement in World War II, her acquisition of the Philippines forms an indispensable link.

21:

The United States
Becomes a Naval Power

In the light of subsequent world events, it is apparent that the most significant naval development of the early 20th century was the coming of age of the United States Navy. The American people, acting through their elected representatives in Congress, finally determined to maintain a fleet consonant with America's wealth and commercial importance. Under the influence of Alfred Thayer Mahan and Theodore Roosevelt, the Navy finally achieved a long-term policy. The ambition and brilliance of officers like Bradley Fiske and William Sowden Sims stimulated the service to become pre-eminent in gunnery, in tactical procedures, and in material. It was in this period that the modern American navy was born—the navy that in World War II was to defeat Japan and to make possible the invasions of Europe.

Yet in the perspective of 1900 or of 1914 the rise of the United States as a naval power to the first rank did not appear of great importance outside the Western Hemisphere. Though America's naval budget was generally larger than Germany's, the Kaiser's fleet was definitely the stronger in 1914. The United States Navy in fact had the prospect of sinking to fourth place as the French building program progressed. Throughout the pre-World War I period, Britain successfully maintained her "two power policy," never letting her fleet fall in tonnage and number of capital ships below the combined total of the second and third strongest powers.

The Anglo-German Naval Race

Yet Britain was experiencing progressively greater difficulty and expense in perpetuating her absolute naval superiority in European waters. In the rise of German sea power she perceived the greatest threat to her security since the days of the first Napoleon. British naval estimates were composed with one eye on the German construction program. British diplomatic relations with France, Italy, Japan, and the United States were largely guided by the dictates of naval policy. The signing of the Anglo-Japanese Alliance (1902), the creation of the Triple Entente with France and Russia (1907), and the gradual concentration of the British fleet in home waters all stemmed from the presence of a formidable and growing naval rival across the narrow waters of the North Sea. From the British point of view, nothing was more important than maintaining her "margin of safety"[1] and by favorable alliances creating a balance of power.

Ostensibly the German aim was not to grow stronger than Britain, but rather to build a fleet able to "challenge" Britain, to induce Britain to hesitate before involving herself in a continental war. For Germany suffered the fatal naval weakness of having strong potential enemies on her land frontiers. The German army was of necessity her "first line of defense," and consequently had first call on her defense budgets. But such was the proud dynamism of the young German nation, and such was the inventive genius and engineering talents of her people that her naval threat to England was substantial and real.

The guiding genius of German naval policy at this time was Alfred von Tirpitz, successively Chief of Staff of the Supreme Naval Command (1892), Secretary of State for Naval Affairs (1897), and Admiral of the

[1] Germany's naval expenditures between 1905 and 1914 increased steadily from £11,301,370 to £23,444,129 a year. In the same period, Britain's increased from £33,151,841 to £51,550,000.

Fleet (1911–16). Politically astute, administratively able, he made sure that ship for ship the High Seas Fleet would match or outmatch any in the world. His long-range aim was to forge a fleet that could be a trump card in dealings with Britain. Ultimately he thought it would make Germany "worthy of a British alliance." He insisted on emphasizing the battleship line even at the expense of cruiser construction, and was an exponent of extensive compartmentation and extra-heavy armor.

In the German naval estimates of 1900, which, by doubling the German capital ship line, is usually taken as initiating the Anglo-German naval race, Tirpitz reluctantly accepted the "idea of risk." Well aware of how the news of the German plans would be received in England, he established a steady replacement and expansion program in the fleet. The 1904, 1906, and 1908 programs, which progressively reduced the retirement age of combatant vessels, further increased new construction, to which he succeeded in devoting a very large percentage of total naval expenditures.

In the Royal Navy the opposite number to Tirpitz was the brilliant, cantankerous First Sea Lord, Sir John Fisher. Like Tirpitz a determined believer in material improvements, Fisher made his period of control one of those rare times during which the Royal Navy was pre-eminent in invention and innovation. Remarkable in his imaginative insights, Fisher could perceive the merits of radical untried designs and see better than most of his contemporaries the potentialities of weapons still in their pioneering stages. He encouraged and secured appropriations for radical ship designs, and for seaplanes, airships, and a submarine fleet while most admiralties still regarded these weapons as scarcely more than toys. With the aid of naval budgets seldom less than equal to those of Germany and the United States together, Fisher was able to build the most powerful instrument of sea power the world had ever seen.

The United States Adopts a New Naval Policy

Yet an ultimately greater sea power was already in an active stage of early growth.

Since 1881, as we have seen, there had been something of a naval renaissance in the United States. But in 1898 this was still in an early, experimental stage. The fleet had not yet reached the standard of excellence of the best of the European navies. Naval policy in the United States was haphazard, short-term, and at the mercy of the accidents of political expediency. Though Mahan had attained a world-wide reputation, it was still largely the fame of a scholar among scholars. In the years preceding the Spanish-American War, it would appear that few members of Congress, not to speak of the voting public at large, really read Mahan's works. His ideas, which were fundamental to United States naval policy in the 20th century, had to be relayed secondhand by the eloquence of such men as Theodore Roosevelt and Henry Cabot Lodge to become politically effective.

Though the naval debates in Congress from 1898 to 1914 were often protracted and acrimonious, through this period there came to be a widely accepted goal of building policy—a Navy second only to that of Great Britain. Increasingly there was an awareness of the close relationship between naval policy and effective foreign policy. Congressmen as a group, though disagreeing often as to the implications of overseas political alignment, at least were generally in agreement on basic naval strategy—the United States Navy must be prepared to defeat the main force of any enemy rather than merely to raid commerce and aid in passive coast defense. United States building policy would be increasingly related to those of foreign navies—especially to those of Germany and Japan. After 1898, America had a genuine naval policy. The United States had become a naval power.

The Influence of Theodore Roosevelt

The personal influence of Theodore Roosevelt, both as vigorous Assistant Secretary of the Navy (1897–98) and as President (1901–09) was enormously important in giving definition and direction to America's naval policy. In an age when erudition was an uncommon attribute for a political figure, Roosevelt was a phenomenon. He was an omnivorous reader, with a keen appetite for history and monographs on international relations. He was at once a nationalist, an imperialist, and something of a militarist. For the Navy what was most important was that he had a good understanding of strategy and an abiding ambition to develop a fleet.[2]

In 1897 Roosevelt, as Assistant Secretary, burst into the placid bureaucratic routines of the Navy Department with all the enthusiastic vigor of a man with a mission. He scorned to dissemble his views, which were at this time at variance with the pacific attitudes of his superiors. He championed a big navy, to be maintained constantly on a near-war footing, and developed an uncompromising, expansionist foreign policy. He took pains to try to educate anyone who would listen—including Secretary Long and President McKinley.

In the fall of 1901 an assassin's bullet made Roosevelt the youngest President in American history. The brash young Assistant Secretary of the Navy of four years ago was Chief Executive of the United States. Whereas he had formerly been obliged to plead and cajole, he could now, in a measure, dictate. Through his own terms of office and that of his handpicked successor Taft, such was Roosevelt's prestige and personal force that his concept of correct foreign and naval policy was to a large degree the country's.

The Imperial Legacy

Among the effects of the Spanish-American War was America's acquisition of a Caribbean and Pacific island empire. Cuba was temporarily under a protectorate, though the Platt Amendment had guaranteed it independence as soon as feasible. Puerto Rico became a permanent possession. The problem of what to do with the Philippines was finally resolved by occupying and taking possession of the whole archipelago. Guam in the Marianas was annexed. Indirectly the Spanish-American War was responsible for the annexation of Hawaii (1898) and American Samoa (1899).

The new Amercan Empire enormously increased the Navy's responsibilities. Its potential area of operation was expanded to include the entire Pacific Ocean. Overseas coaling stations and bases, and a canal across the Isthmus of Panama or Nicaragua became immediate necessities. The defense of the empire became a principal argument for the advocates of a big navy.

Directly following the war, there was no immediate restatement of naval policy in terms of these new problems. Occupation of Cuba and Puerto Rico, the Philippine Insurrection, and the Boxer Rebellion gave a coloring of "continuing emergency" to military and naval needs. But the improvised auxiliary cruisers recruited from the merchant marine were sold or returned to their owners. The peacetime "cruising stations" were instituted once more, and the wartime fleet organization was abandoned.[3] The General Board of the Navy was established in 1900 to provide a high level professional body to advise the Secretary. The impetus the war had given to shipbuilding had persisted until 1900,[4] but in 1901 Congress refused to authorize any ships at all. The reelection of McKinley and the continued secretaryship of Long gave every prospect of a continued policy of drift and compromise. But the unexpected elevation of Roosevelt to the Presidency changed the character and direction of American naval development.

Roosevelt regarded foreign policy and naval policy as the warp and the woof of a seamless garment. It is evident from his writings and published speeches that from the first he had in mind clearcut diplomatic ends, and that he endeavored to fashion his weapons with these foreign policy objectives in mind. He believed in a continuum of policy and did not hesitate to extrapolate existing relationships and trends into the future. He conceived of the President's role as that of dynamic leadership and policy-making, and that of Congress as a critic and ratifier of Presidential policy.

[2] In 1882, at the age of 24, Roosevelt had published his *The Naval War of 1812*, precocious monument to its author's interests and to his firm grasp of naval first principles.

[3] As the Sprouts point out, this was ". . . a surprising failure to profit from one of the most obvious lessons of the war." (H. and M. Sprout, *The Rise of American Sea Power*, 246.) The Bureau of Navigation apparently had no fleet policy, as such.

[4] 1898: three battleships, sixteen destroyers; 1899: three battleships, three armored cruisers; 1900: two battleships, three armored cruisers.

Roosevelt was typical of the American tradition up to that time in retaining the diplomatic ideal of "isolation from entangling alliances." But he had a better awareness than most that as a recognized first-class power, the United States could not ignore the affairs of other major powers.

Anglo-American Relations

As an imperialist and an admirer of England, Roosevelt welcomed the developing confidence and mutual trust between Great Britain and the United States. Traditional "enemy" in Fourth of July orations through the 19th century, England had evidenced a new friendliness in the last quarter of the century. After the strained relations prevailing before the settlement of the *"Alabama* claims" (1872), there had been no major quarrel between the two nations. During the Spanish-American War, Britain alone of the major powers had shown positive sympathy. She had undertaken to guard American interests in Spain during hostilities. She had put no bar in the way of American acquisition of two warships building in English yards, originally on Brazilian order. She encouraged Canada to permit the transfer of revenue cutters from the Great Lakes to the Atlantic via the St. Lawrence River. The commander of the British squadron in Manila Bay, during the trying period between the naval battle and the occupation, gave moral support and tacit encouragement to Dewey.[5]

The Alaskan boundary dispute dragged on into Roosevelt's administration. A joint commission settled this problem in 1903 in an award wholly favorable to the United States. The British concession of exclusive United States control of the projected canal in Panama was also an American diplomatic victory, widely and correctly judged to be evidence that Britain meant to meet the United States

[5] The popular account current at the time had it that Captain Sir Edward Chichester RN placed his cruisers between Dewey's force and that of von Diederichs' German squadron. The Germans, who hoped to acquire part of the archipelago, had already aroused Dewey's wrath by failing to observe his blockade regulations. However, there is in fact no evidence that either Dewey or von Diederichs ever seriously considered starting a private war.

more than half-way in any clash of interest. The permanent withdrawal of the British West Indies squadron from Jamaica (1904–05), though part of the long-term policy of fleet concentration in home waters to overbalance the growing German strength in the North Sea, amounted also to an unspoken acknowledgment of American supremacy in the Caribbean. Responsible Britons and Americans were beginning to refer to the chance of any further war between the two countries as an "impossibility."

The implications for naval building policy of this relationship with Great Britain were important. Since Britain alone by virtue of her American bases (Halifax, Bermuda, Kingston) and the size of her fleet was in a physical sense able to wage a naval war in the Western Hemisphere, the certainty of her continued friendliness made America's continental security nearly absolute.

German-American Relations

It was Germany whose navy came to be the yardstick of American needs in congressional debate during the first decade of the 20th century. Germany, as last of the major nations of Europe to adopt an avowed imperialist policy, had aroused American suspicions and hostility on a number of specific occasions (Samoa, 1889; Manila Bay, 1898; Second Venezuela Crisis, 1902). The brutal efficiency of German development of their new colonies in Africa and at Tsingtao and the arrogant public utterances of the Kaiser made the American public distinctly unfriendly to the Hohenzollern Empire.

Furthermore, either Germany or the United States would be the possessor of the "navy second only to Britain's." In numbers of battleships and armored cruisers, the United States rose from fifth position in 1904 to second in 1907. But as a balanced fleet, Germany's seagoing navy was superior to that of the United States during most if not all of the pre-World War I period. In any event both the United States Congress and the American public regarded the relative rank of the United States Navy as a matter of great importance.

Relations of Japan and America

Relations of the United States with Japan were generally good up to the 20th century. It was an American naval force that had "opened up" Japan in the mid-19th century. Many of the ranking officers of the Japanese navy who fought in the Sino-Japanese War (1894) and the Russo-Japanese War (1904–05) had graduated from the U.S. Naval Academy. What Americans knew, or thought they knew, about the Japanese people came for the most part from Gilbert and Sullivan's *Mikado,* Puccini's *Madame Butterfly,* and the romantic writings of Lafcadio Hearn. The Japanese were judged to be a childlike, art-loving people, much given to artistic flower arrangement and water-color painting—deserving of American sympathy because they were in a measure protégés of the United States. Furthermore, as government officials and naval officers came to respect the professional efficiency of the Japanese services as shown in the Chinese War, Japan came to be regarded as a useful makeweight against Russian designs on North China and Korea.

The Russo-Japanese War in Japanese history corresponds in a way to the Spanish-American War in United States history: it made the world realize that a new major power had emerged. At the beginning of this war, Japan was viewed as the underdog. The American administration and the American public wished Japan well, but with little confidence in her success. The sweeping Japanese victories culminating in the fall of Port Arthur and the Battle of Tsushima compelled a new and soberer assessment of Japanese strength. For the first time in modern history an Oriental nation had decisively defeated a major western power in war. And this nation, highly disciplined, intensely nationalist, compulsively imperialistic, was very close to the new American possessions in the Philippines. The time might come when Japan would be an active threat to American interests in the Orient.

Furthermore, though Roosevelt's good offices had helped the Japanese to secure favorable peace terms in the Treaty of Portsmouth (1905), the Japanese demand for an indemnity was not met. The Japanese press and the Japanese public were inclined to feel that Roosevelt had helped to cheat them of the just deserts of their victory. In 1906 and the years following, the naval debates in the American Congress came to include frequent reference to Japanese as well as German naval building programs.

On the other hand, the Anglo-Japanese Alliance (1902) was not viewed by the United States government as being in any way directed against the United States. Even in the light of the cordiality of American relations with Britain this may seem strange. There is good evidence however that Roosevelt in 1905 entered into a secret agreement with the Japanese prime minister, by the terms of which the United States virtually became a secret third party to this treaty. This agreement involved a formal recognition by Japan of American sovereignty in the Philippines and an acknowledgment by America of Japan's sovereignty in Korea. It provided for "conjunct" action in the event of vaguely defined contingencies, presumably if British, Japanese, or American possessions were attacked by more than one power.[6] This agreement was never submitted to the Senate, where it would unquestionably have received short shrift. On the other hand it was morally binding, at least so long as Roosevelt was President.

The United States Navy Expands

In the period immediately preceding World War I, the growing naval power of Germany, the United States, and Japan competed with Britain, each in its own respective geographic area. It is not surprising that to some extent they should compete with each other as well. Certainly the growth of German and Japanese naval strength stimulated American fleet expansion.

Various private industrial interests now had a stake in continued expansion. Shippers and exporters, and especially shipbuilders and steel companies not unnaturally favored a large navy. In 1903, these groups joined retired officers and disinterested citizens in founding the Navy League of the United States. As a prosperous organization with a limited and definite aim, it was immediately effective. As

[6] T. Dennett, "Roosevelt's Secret Pact with Japan," *Current History* (October 1924), 15.

a lobbying organization, some of whose members had a pecuniary interest in achieving a bigger navy, the League was subject to attack by the Congressional minority of anti-naval partisans. But in its unwavering insistence on a consistent long-term policy, the League's influence was salutary.

Beginning with 1903, the Navy Department began laying down two capital ships a year. Though there were exceptions in the ensuing decade, this came to be the norm of naval construction. Generally speaking, the building policy of Taft's Administration (1909–13) continued the aims of Roosevelt's.

Some idea of the increased emphasis on the Navy can be gained from the following table:

FISCAL YEAR:	TOTAL FEDERAL EXPENDITURES:	NAVAL EXPENDITURES:	PER CENT OF TOTAL BUDGET*
1890	$318,040,711	$22,006,206	7.0
1900	520,860,847	55,953,078	10.8
1901	524,616,925	60,506,978	11.3
1905	567,278,914	117,550,308	20.7
1909	693,743,885	115,546,011	16.7
1914	735,081,431	139,682,186	19.0

* These budgetary percentages do not necessarily reflect the ratios of columns one and two, which are *ex post* figures.

Most of the increase in the costs of the naval establishment was due to the increase in the size and complexity of war vessels. In 1903, a first-line battleship cost $5,382,000. The *Delaware* and *North Dakota* of the 1907 program, with standard displacement of 20,000 tons, cost $8,225,000 each. By the time of World War I, costs had soared (in the United States) to $15–20,000,000. The typical first-line battleship at the turn of the century was less than 400 feet long, and displaced perhaps 10,000 or 11,000 tons. By 1914 ships of over 30,000 tons were being built.

An obvious weakness of the United States building policy was its dominant emphasis on capital ships. The Roosevelt and Taft Administrations and their professional advisers were well aware of this. Their reasoning was that battleships took up to four years to build, and that smaller craft could be constructed in case of need in a much shorter time. Often Congressional opposition to increased expenditure could be mollified by canceling plans for smaller vessels as a compromise proposal. On the other hand, the resultant fleet was unbalanced and not immediately prepared to develop its maximum potential. And, in the sort of war it was called on to fight in 1917–18, this emphasis in building policy proved to have been especially unfortunate.

The Panama Canal

In the period 1898-1914, the U.S. Navy was called on from time to time to implement or to aid in promoting four major foreign policies of the United States: (1) the acquisition of the Canal Zone, (2) maintaining the Monroe Doctrine and extending its scope, especially in the Caribbean area, (3) maintaining the "Open Door" in China and promoting United States Far Eastern interests, and (4) helping to maintain the balance of power in Europe. On the whole, the Navy acquitted itself well in each of these missions.

The idea of an Isthmian Canal to connect the Caribbean and the Pacific is at least as old as Balboa, who first crossed the isthmus in the early 16th century. In the last quarter of the 19th century the de Lesseps company, which had already successfully completed the Suez Canal, undertook the mammoth engineering task of constructing a waterway across the narrow neck of the Isthmus of Panama. The tangled story of the French failure and the ensuing intrigues over the sovereignty of the canal right-of-way are too involved for retelling here. It is enough to observe that for a decade before the Spanish-American War expert opinion had come to support Mahan's view that such a canal was essential to enable the U.S. Navy to accomplish its mission. And obviously such a canal unequivocally under American sovereignty was preferable. There were two hurdles barring this: Colombian possession of the Isthmus of Panama and the Clayton-Bulwer Treaty (1850) with Great Britain, whereby England and the United States agreed to cooperate in building a canal and engaged not to fortify it.[7]

The *Oregon's* voyage through the Straits of Magellan during the Spanish-American War

[7] The discovery of gold in California had given topical interest to the subject at that time. An American company completed the railroad across the Isthmus in 1855.

gave the American public an object lesson in the need for a canal. The acquisition of the Philippines and Hawaii, it was argued, meant that the United States must maintain a large Pacific fleet, or else have the canal to facilitate transit from one ocean to the other.

Secretary of State John Hay in 1900 concluded with the British ambassador the First Hay-Pauncefote Treaty, permitting American construction and ownership of the canal. When this was rejected by the U.S. Senate, a second Hay-Pauncefote Treaty was negotiated in 1901. This agreement, which permitted exclusive American control of the Canal—including fortification and defense—was quickly approved by the Senate.

The remaining obstacle was the problem of securing treaty rights from Colombia. Hay signed a preliminary treaty with the Colombian chargé d'affaires in Washington (Hay-Herran Treaty, 1903), whereby the United States was to secure a six-mile-wide transitway for $10,000,000 and a $250,000 annuity, but the Colombian senate refused to approve the treaty.

Colombia's motivation was apparently a desire for more money. The French New Panama Canal Company was to receive $40,000,000 from the United States for its work and equipment. Its concession however ran out in October 1904, at which time all physical assets reverted to Colombia. From the Colombian point of view, the simple exercise of a year's patience appeared likely to be very profitable.

This was a mistake, for it neglected the entrepreneurial talents of Philippe Bunau-Varilla, chief agent of the New Panama Company, who engineered a revolution in Panama from his headquarters in the old Waldorf-Astoria Hotel in New York. It also neglected the impatience of President Roosevelt, who was eager to "make the dirt fly."

Revolution in Panama was no novelty. According to Roosevelt's count, there had been 53 revolutions in 53 years. But this particular revolution had a synthetic look, for the patriot army of 500 men had cost $200 a head and was supplemented only by a reserve of 441 members of the Panama fire departments. But Bunau-Varilla was fairly confident that American support would sustain his patriotic efforts.

Under the terms of the Treaty of 1846 with New Granada (Colombia), the United States was pledged to maintain "perfect neutrality" and "free transit" in the Isthmus. On November 2, 1903 U.S.S. *Nashville* arrived at Colon. On November 3 the standard of revolution was raised ashore, and on November 4 the Republic of Panama was born officially. There was no overland route from Bogota. Colombian troops sent by water were politely told they could not land, since America had treaty obligations to uphold, and for them to proceed would obviously create an unneutral disturbance. The guns of the *Nashville* were an eloquent unspoken argument. Presently the *Dixie* arrived with a force of marines for any necessary policing ashore. The United States recognized the fledgling member of the family of sovereign nations on November 6.

Bunau-Varilla, who never relinquished his French citizenship, now appeared in Washington as agent plenipotentiary for the Republic of Panama. On November 18, some 15 days after the revolution, the Hay-Bunau-Varilla Treaty conveyed to the United States a zone ten miles wide in perpetuity for $10,000,000 and a $250,000 annuity; the treaty was ratified by the Senate on November 23. In 1921, the United States government paid $25,000,000 "conscience money" to Colombia as a belated apology.

Whether this episode constituted "international piracy," as some liberal journals claimed, or simply an indirect exercise of a kind of "right of eminent domain," it was not calculated to increase the popularity of the United States in Latin America, particularly in Colombia. But in any event the organizing ability and technical skill of the U.S. Army Corps of Engineers and a decade of labor by an army of workers produced the desired result. The canal was opened in August 1914 as the world was going to war. The U.S. Navy had its priceless transitway between the country's widely separated coasts.

Intervention in Latin America

The prospect of the Canal's completion gave a new importance to the Caribbean. With the decay of the 18th century sugar trade, the area had become a cul-de-sac far removed from the important trade routes. Now it would become part of a vital sea artery in peace and war. In terms of strategic value, all Caribbean real estate went up. The Canal was a priceless asset, but only insofar as it was defensible—which entailed not only coast artillery but naval bases. Furthermore there must be bases far from the Canal itself to protect the approaches to the Caribbean. Equally important, no new footholds by foreign powers could be permitted, since these might become threats to the Canal. The destruction of the locks of the Canal could be the strategic equivalent of sinking half the United States fleet.

Happily, intervention by foreign powers was contrary to the Monroe Doctrine, and any administration could count on overwhelming popular support in invoking it. But considering, as Roosevelt was inclined to do, that the western European powers and the United States had a mandate from "civilization" to impose moral rectitude on the "backward nations," he was unwilling that the Monroe Doctrine should become a shield behind which less progressive Latin nations could allow anarchic disregard of the rights granted foreigners under international law. This dilemma Roosevelt resolved in 1904 by what has come to be called the "Roosevelt Corollary" to the Monroe Doctrine. The Roosevelt Corollary provided that the United States might feel obligated ". . . in flagrant cases of . . . wrong-doing or impotence [in Latin America] to the exercise of an international police power." In other words, if any situation appeared to demand intervention to protect lives or enforce treaty rights, the United States Navy and a force of marines would do the intervening. This policy was followed until 1930, when it was repudiated by the United States government. European nations were glad enough to have their chestnuts pulled out of the fire on occasion, and the Caribbean countries, to which the Roosevelt Corollary in practice was held to apply, were too weak to make any effective protest.

In addition to the unilateral Roosevelt Corollary, treaty right permitted United States intervention in Cuba. Although the United States was morally and legally bound to speed Cuban independence, the geographic proximity of the island to continental North America and to the Canal Zone gave the United States more than a casual interest in its political stability. Private American interests had a large stake in Cuba, particularly in the sugar industry. Furthermore the Cubans, though a gifted and vigorous people, had no experience with the institutions of democracy. Rather, they had a bitter tradition of revolution. It was reasonable to expect occasional violence and discord in the island.

The problem in prospect was provided for by the Platt Amendment, which was at once an amendment to the Cuban constitution and the substance of a permanent treaty between Cuba and the United States. Among many other provisions, it provided for the right of intervention by the United States ". . . for the preservation of Cuban independence, the maintenance of a government adequate for the protection of life, property, and individual liberty. . . ." It also provided that the United States should have the right to lease or buy naval reservations for coaling and repair.[8]

During a period of anarchy in 1906, Roosevelt intervened on the recommendation of the United States consul-general, and sent marines to Havana. This occupation lasted from 1906 to 1909, during which time an American civilian governor acted as chief executive. Again in 1912, President Taft sent in the marines. In 1917 Wilson refused to sanction revolution in Cuba, whereupon American marines formally occupied Santiago, and marine officers found themselves in the novel role of supervising a "free" Cuban election. Cuba's joint belligerency on the side of the Allies in World War I was a justification for maintaining a marine force on the island until 1922.

In the first quarter of the 20th century, small-scale intervention in various revolution-torn countries of the Caribbean area was common. Naval and marine forces were involved in both campaigning and governmental administration in Nicaragua, Haiti, and the Dominican Republic. Usually United States military occupation promptly brought law and order. Where the occupation was of long duration there were normally also spectacular improvements in public health measures and road

---

[8] The United States secured naval stations at Bahia Honda and Guantanamo for $2,000 a year. In 1913 the former was abandoned. The Guantanamo grant has since been extended and enlarged.

building. Generally speaking, administration of civilian government functions by professional military men has tended to be fair but paternalistic—often resented more by neighboring countries than the ones occupied. To the stronger, stable countries of Latin America, this casual exercise of sea power by the United States was simply another evidence of "Yankee imperialism."

The most serious Latin-American imbroglio involving the United States during the 20th century occurred early in Wilson's administration. In Mexico, the idealist Madero had upset the Diaz dictatorship in 1911 but had been unable to establish a stable government. After two years of continued and confused revolution, Madero was murdered, apparently at the behest of Victoriano Huerta, who proclaimed himself provisional President. Wilson refused to recognize this government, discouraged recognition by other American nations, and lifted the embargo against shipments of munitions to private persons in Mexico. Considerable United States naval forces were stationed on both Mexican coasts.

On April 9, 1914 Mexican authorities arrested for no apparent reason a United States naval boat-party loading gasoline at the pier in Tampico. The prisoners were promptly released, but Rear Admiral H. T. Mayo, commanding the U.S. squadron, demanded a formal apology and a 21-gun flag salute, which the Mexicans refused. President Wilson thereupon ordered a blockade of Mexican harbors and shortly afterward directed the customs house at Vera Cruz to be seized. It looked as though the Second Mexican War was under way.

Supported by naval gunfire from the *Prairie*, *Chester*, and *San Francisco*, a mixed force of marines and bluejackets on April 22 fought their way into the city, occupying the customs house, cable office, and other waterfront buildings. By this time Rear Admiral Charles J. Badger, Commander in Chief of the United States Fleet, had arrived with five battleships. The force ashore was powerfully reinforced, and the occupation of the entire city was accomplished by noon of the 22nd. Presently an army detachment came to take over the occupation.

Before hostilities could spread, a joint arbitration proposal by Argintina, Brazil, and Chile was accepted, and all-out war was averted. Huerta went into voluntary exile in July. American warships remained on station close off the Mexican coasts until November.

The United States Navy in the Far East

In the Philippines, a part of the native population under the leadership of Emilio Aguinaldo had risen in rebellion against the Spanish garrisons after the Battle of Manila Bay but before the arrival of the American forces of occupation. Without treaty relations or indeed formal recognition by the United States, they regarded themselves as allies of the Americans. They were successful in gaining control of most of Luzon before General Merritt arrived to occupy the archipelago formally. Comparing their position to that of the Cubans, who had been promised independence, Aguinaldo and his lieutenants at first hailed the Americans as liberators. Their confidence was shaken when Merritt refused to permit the Filipino forces to share fully in the occupation of Manila. When the Filipinos realized that—at least for the time being—they had simply exchanged masters, they prepared for war anew. Hostilities broke out in February 1899, and for the next three years the United States Army (ultimately with a force of about 60,000 men) was obliged to fight a colonial jungle war. The Asiatic Squadron, considerably reinforced since Dewey's victory, took an active part in suppressing the Philippine Insurrection, providing gunfire support to American forces ashore, ferrying troops and supplies, furnishing landing parties, and establishing blockades.

The long-term prospects of the ill-equipped and badly supplied Filipino insurrectionists were of course hopeless. But defeated in pitched battles, they broke into small units and conducted a guerrilla campaign with the secret support of much of the population. Not until March 23, 1901 was Aguinaldo captured. Even then desultory bush fighting took place for over a year longer. In order to complete the pacification of the islands, the exasperated army commanders were driven to a partial adoption of the "reconcentration" tactics of the despised Spanish General Weyler (in Cuba). The Philippine Insurrection cost the United States over $175,000,000 and the lives of 4,300 men. It tied up a substantial part of the regular army and a fair portion of the fleet.

The United States Asiatic Squadron, preoccupied with its support mission in the Philippines, was abruptly called on in 1900 to participate in the defense of American lives and property in China. Chinese nationalism, deeply stirred by Russian, Japanese, and German aggression in North China, had given rise to a fanatical patriotic movement called the "Boxers"—pledged to the expulsion of all "foreign devils" from Chinese soil. The weak and corrupt government of the Dowager Empress gave tacit support to the Boxers. In late spring of 1900, the foreign legations in Peking began requesting military and naval support from their home governments. The United States sent armored cruiser *Newark* to Tientsin and a 56-man reinforcement to the legation guard in the walled European compound of the city. Soon afterward, the Boxers began attacks on the legation area. An improvised international relief column of some 2,000 men under British naval command tried unsuccessfully in June to fight its way inland to Peking. About a hundred United States bluejackets under Captain B. H. McCalla of the *Newark* participated gallantly in this effort.

A second "international army" of 18,600 men, including 2,500 American soldiers and marines, succeeded after hard fighting in raising the siege of the legations on August 4, 1900. In September 1901 the Chinese government acceded to a joint allied protocol which engaged her to pay an indemnity of $333,000,000 in 39 annuities. The American share was later partly returned to the Chinese to provide for scholarships for study in the United States.

The Boxer Rebellion might well have been the excuse for a final partitioning of China into European dependencies and spheres of influence. American participation in the fighting however gave the United States a voice in the councils of the nations concerned. Secretary of State Hay made this the occasion of a new affirmation of his "Open Door" policy, calling on the powers to preserve China's territorial integrity, and to "safeguard for the world the principle of equal and impartial trade with all parts of the Chinese empire."

The Boxer Rebellion, in which Japanese troops had fought with bravery and skill beside the soldiers of western nations, probably helped to encourage Japan to make the challenge to expansionist Russia in 1904. The Japanese victory in the Russo-Japanese War gave further confidence to this proud people. Hence the action of the San Francisco School Board in 1906 in instituting segregation of Oriental school children was deeply resented by the Japanese as an arrogant and undeserved imputation of inferiority. Magnified by yellow journalism both in Japan and in the United States, this became the occasion of a full-blown diplomatic crisis. Earlier in 1906, when there had been a near-crisis over the issue of Japanese seal-poaching in American territorial waters in the Aleutians, Roosevelt had ordered all capital ships of the Asiatic Squadron to stand by to leave for United States ports on order. He now ordered the armored cruiser squadron then on duty in the Far East to be replaced by lighter units, and to concentrate in home waters. These initial operational preparations for war happily proved needless. In the so-called "Gentlemen's Agreement," Japan engaged to restrict emigration to the United States, in return for which the city of San Francisco was persuaded to rescind its objectionable policy.

The Round-The-World Cruise of the U.S. Fleet, 1907–1908

Roosevelt, equally enraged at Japanese truculence and at the state of California, wanted by a dramatic gesture to show Japan the power that lay behind the soft words of American diplomacy. This gesture he made with his order for a round-the-world cruise to be undertaken by the 16 first-line battleships of the United States fleet. On invitation, Yokohama was included as a port of call. In the light of present-day technical knowledge and operating procedures, it is difficult to see this cruise in the perspective it offered to the world in 1908.

To begin with, such a thing had never before been done. "Experts" freely predicted that breakdowns and fuel difficulties would make a fiasco of the attempt. Others suggested that for the battleship fleet to enter Far Eastern waters would be an unprovoked challenge to Japan. Congress at first demurred because of the extraordinary expense. Roosevelt's political instinct however was never more right. He brushed aside the difficulties and in December 1907 the battle line under Rear Admiral Robley D. Evans steamed south from Hampton Roads on the first leg of its 46,000-mile, 14-month voyage.

In every way the cruise was an unqualified, spectacular success. The Japanese populace, as if to atone for their bitterness four years earlier, welcomed the American warships with delirious enthusiasm. In the Antipodes and in Middle Eastern and European ports of call, the fleet was hailed as exciting and tangible evidence not only of the might but of the good will of the United States. Material performed well; the predictions of the pessimists proved unfounded. The sustained steaming provided exceptional training and suggested improved operating procedures. And the performance of the fleet was a proud dramatization to the American people of their collective might.

From a technical and professional point of view, the cruise was an eloquent reminder of the need of an improved collier and supply service. For in war, the friendly offices of foreign powers might not be available. Further, the need of developed bases and coaling stations in the Pacific was made more apparent. The mere possession of islands was not enough. Expensive facilities were needed if any of these was to be regarded as a useful base in a strategic sense.

The problem of yards and bases, properly a purely strategic one, was during this period in fact still somewhat political. Tens of millions of dollars of appropriations were poured into needless and redundant shore facilities at home, and the really necessary installations overseas (where American "nationals" had no votes) were allowed to languish. In spite of vigorous efforts by Roosevelt and responsible naval officers, not until 1911 was an appropriation voted for Guantanamo; only the impending opening of the Panama Canal was a

sufficiently eloquent argument. The problem of an offshore Pacific base was also postponed from year to year, and only in 1909 was work begun on Pearl Harbor. Minor installations at Olongapo and Cavite (on Luzon) never were developed into major facilities.

Technical Developments in the Navies of the World

Technical progress in guns, armor, engines, and hull design had been so rapid through the second half of the 19th century that it was not unusual for a ship to be obsolescent by the time she was commissioned. This breakneck rate of material improvement continued almost unabated through the first two decades of the 20th century.

The heavy gunnery vessel, the battleship, was the backbone of the fleet. In 1906 a design revolution relegated all previous battleships to a "second-class" or reserve status. The British Admiralty commissioned the secretly constructed *Dreadnought*, which proved to be the archetype of all subsequent battleships. Her predecessors had carried a main battery of four big guns in twin centerline turrets fore and aft, an intermediate battery of 6- to 8-inch rifles, and a secondary battery of smaller quick-firing, cartridge-loaded guns, which might include weapons of several different calibers. For example, the United States *Rhode Island*-class of battleships (1904) carried six different calibers. The *Dreadnought* was described as an "all-big-gun" ship. She carried ten 12-inch guns in five turrets (three centerline, one on each beam), and an anti-torpedo-boat quick-firing battery of twenty-four 12-pounders. She thus had an effective main battery firepower 2½ times that of any other existing battleship. This simplification of her ordnance also made for a less cluttered topside, and enormously simplified the problems of munitions stowage and fire control. The *Dreadnought* was somewhat larger than most earlier battleships, with a designed displacement of 17,900 tons. She was 490 by 82 feet, with a loaded draft of 26½ feet. She carried eleven inches of armor on her belt and over the turrets and barbettes —more than any earlier British vessel. Her turbines had an indicated horsepower of 27,500;

she clocked an impressive 21.5 knots in her speed trials. At £1,813,100 she cost more than any other war vessel constructed in Britain up to that time.

At once the admiralties of all the naval powers recognized the *Dreadnought's* superiority. All major navies scrapped or modified existing building plans, and turned to designing "dreadnoughts."[9] United States battleships increased in tonnage between 1898 and 1914 from 12,000 to 31,400 (e.g., the *Pennsylvania*, still an effective fighting ship in World War II). The cost of a first-line vessel nearly tripled.

In foreign navies, the battle cruiser type had by 1914 rendered the older "armored cruiser" obsolescent. This too was a British innovation. Like the *Dreadnought*, it had been fostered by Sir John Fisher. The first battle cruisers were the *Indomitable*, the *Inflexible*, and the *Invincible*, all launched in 1907, and commissioned in 1908 and 1909. These vessels were gunned like battleships, carrying eight 12-inch guns in double turrets on a 17,250-ton displacement; their hull dimensions were 530 by 78½ by 26; their test speed was 26 knots. They were designed as "cruiser-killers." They could outrun battleships and could outgun cruisers of the conventional type. Britain had built ten of them by the outbreak of World War I. Germany launched her first battle cruiser, the *Von der Tann*, in 1909 (commissioned 1911), and had a total of eight built or building in 1914. Japan copied the type also. The United States and the other principal naval powers preferred to put their appropriations for major vessels into the slower but more heavily armored battleships.

The destroyer as a ship type may be said to have evolved rather than to have come into being as a sudden surprise unveiled by a single navy. Through the late 1880's and 1890's torpedo boats were simply built larger, faster, and more heavily armed so that they could outfight enemy torpedo boats as well as serve their primary function of torpedo attack. The Germans, who have a claim to pioneering the type, were

building the first of their "D" boats as early as 1887—vessels just under 200 feet in length with designed speeds over 20 knots. These vessels were of course unarmored and lightly armed except for their torpedo tubes. Britain launched its first class of very fast (27-30 knot) vessels of this type in 1894-95. In the United States Navy, the first destroyers were already highly evolved, displacing 420 tons and making over 28 knots.[10] In the first decade of the 20th century, the tactical use of destroyers as a "screen" for capital ships became doctrine in all navies. The destroyer flotilla also became a necessary adjunct to the scouting line. World War I was to demonstrate their value also in antisubmarine warfare.

Armor-making processes had improved enormously since the days when wrought iron plates backed with oak were the best protection available. The American "Harveyizing" process, involving heavily "carbonizing" the face of steel plates, had been refined and improved by Krupp (of Germany), whose secret processes included using a gaseous hydrocarbon as the carbonizing agent and introducing nickel or chromium in the alloy for the body of the plate. Germany, Britain, and the United States were in the van of progress in improving armor. In the United States, the Bethlehem Steel Company, the Midvale Steel Company, and the Carnegie, Phipps Company all produced naval armor of top quality.

Capped projectiles, increased gun calibers,[11] and improved propellants gave new advantages to the gun as opposed to armor. But the torpedo, as a means of "defeating" armor by striking below the armor belt, also received much technical improvement. Gyroscopic stabilization, introduction of alcohol heaters, and increased size made it a formidable and accurate weapon. Its range was also extended.

However, no light surface vessel could survive in daylight the hail of shells an enemy capital ship could rain on it long before it could close to effective torpedo range. Hence all navies were interested in the American

---

[9] United States naval experts still dispute whether the *South Carolina* (1908), mounting eight 12-inch guns, or the *North Dakota* (1908), mounting ten 12-inch guns, was the first American "dreadnought." The *South Carolina* was entirely designed before the British vessel was launched.

[10] *Dale, Decatur, Lawrence, Paul Jones, Perry*—all launched in 1900.

[11] In 1900, the heaviest weapon installed in capital ships was the 12-inch gun. In 1914 the *Queen Elizabeth*, under construction in the British navy, carried 15-inch guns.

innovation, the submersible or "submarine," which could launch its deadly underwater missiles at ranges up to 2,000 yards. John P. Holland and Simon Lake independently devised workable submarines, the former as early as 1875. The French *Gymnote,* laid down in 1886 and launched in 1888, was the first commissioned submersible. The Italians and the Germans also built small experimental submarines in the 1890's. In 1888 the United States Navy solicited submarine designs, but not until 1895 was the contract let for Holland's *Plunger.* Holland learned so much in the course of her construction that he proposed that the Navy take back the money so far advanced and not yet paid out and order an improved model instead. Hence the first commissioned American submarine was the *Holland* (1900), a tiny craft by modern standards, but even so a real weapon of war.

The *Holland* was only 54 feet long; submerged she displaced 74 tons. Her single screw was driven on the surface by a gasoline engine and she had batteries and an electric motor for underwater propulsion. She had a single, fixed torpedo tube and carried a "dynamite gun." She incorporated many of the hull design and stability features of modern submarines, including a cigar-shaped hull, with ballast tanks emptied by compressed air, and hydroplanes. She had no periscope; a small hump on her back with eye slits served as a conning tower.[12]

Her test speed surfaced was seven knots; her range, 1,500 miles. She could make nearly seven knots submerged for short distances at full power; at low speed she could cruise submerged about 30 miles. She could dive to 28 feet in eight seconds. Naval authorities were enough impressed at her trials to order five similar, slightly larger vessels from the builder. The English Vickers Company purchased rights to the *Holland* design; from Vickers in late 1900 the British Admiralty ordered five boats of the type.

In the ensuing decade all navies adopted the submarine. Bigger and bigger submarines were built, so that by 1914 the newer types were of 500 to 800 tons, capable of long voyages at sea. The problem of accurate underwater navigation with a magnetic compass had at first been nearly insoluble because of the unpredictable and erratic deviation caused by changes in the magnetic field of the electric cables. The perfection of the gyrocompass (1908) made relatively sustained submerged cruising possible. The German diesel engine (1909) was promptly and universally adopted for submarine surface propulsion, adding enormously to safety and cruising range.

The submarine had been conceived as a device primarily for attack on armored vessels. Ocean-going types were to be fleet vessels. Smaller submarines were for harbor and coast defense—inhibitors of close blockade. The potentiality of the submarine against merchant shipping was apparently entirely unrecognized. Certainly it was not appreciated by the Germans, who were slow to adopt the new weapon (1906), and who built relatively few of them before 1914. When World War I began, there was no weapon that could reach a submarine submerged below ramming depth, and no admiralty had been much concerned with finding one.

It is instructive to compare the submarine strength of the naval powers in 1914. Built and building, Britain had 97 boats with a total tonnage of nearly 50,000, Germany had 45 submarines with a total tonnage of 28,540, France had 86 submarines, and the United States, 49. Even Russia had more submarines than Germany.

Improvements in forging techniques and metallurgy had made possible the building of large-caliber rifled naval ordnance as early as the late 1880's. But fire control optical instruments, range clocks, and deflection calculators were not perfected until much later. Even in the World War I period only capital ships were equipped with adequate fire control. Furthermore as late as 1900 gunnery training and operating procedures were, at least in the United States Navy, inadequate to develop the potentiality of the weapons carried.

[12] The submerged *Holland* approached the surface until only the conning tower showed above the water. Inside, the captain, with his head in the tower, conned the vessel.

In the latter part of 1904 the *Holland* based at the U.S. Naval Academy. Here midshipmen of the first and second classes were taken aboard in pairs for training runs in the mouth of the Severn River. Chester W. Nimitz was among the midshipmen who made their first submergence during these runs.

As in so many aspects of naval progress, the British were in the van of gunnery improvement. Admiral Sir Percy Scott RN, inventor of the "master sight" or director, devised an elaborate training routine based on a sort of "time and motion study" of a typical gun crew. He showed it was possible with the improved elevating gear then used to keep the gun "on target" throughout the roll of the firing ship. Earlier it had been the practice for the guns to be stationary, and hence on target at only one instant in the ship's motion. Scott devised a training aid called a "dotter,"[13] which enabled gunners to practice continuous-aim fire under simulated sea conditions even when moored at a pier. Rapidity of fire, as well as accuracy, was also stressed.

In the U.S. Navy, William S. Sims, who came to know Scott and his methods while on the China Station, became a single-minded zealot for improved gunnery. By the vigor and force of his personality, Sims, though still a junior officer, imposed his variant of Scott's system on his own navy. Roosevelt made him Inspector of Target Practice. The fact that his innovations worked converted even those officers who were personally resentful of Sims' methods. In 1898, optimum battle range for the big guns was thought to be about 6,000 yards. In World War I, effective director-controlled salvo fire at ranges over 20,000 yards was commonplace.

Of all weapons of war, none is so characteristically American as the airplane. The first successful heavier-than-air flight was made by Wilbur and Orville Wright at Kitty Hawk on Nag's Head in 1903. Military potentialities of aircraft were at once recognized by certain officials of the Army and the Navy. The destructive employment of planes was too remote to be anticipated at this time, but as a means of scouting and fire control at long ranges the invention was considered very promising. In 1910 and early 1911, Eugene Ely made successful takeoffs from a ship and landings on an improvised flight deck, thus demonstrating the feasibility of the aircraft carrier. Glenn H. Curtiss developed and built the first seaplane in 1911. The same year the U.S. Navy purchased two planes from Curtiss, and one from the Wright Brothers. In 1912, Lieutenant T. G. Ellyson (Naval Aviator Number One) flew a plane from a compressed air catapult mounted on a barge in the Potomac River. Rear Admiral Bradley Fiske, one of the most inventive and progressive officers in the service, proclaimed the practicability of the torpedo plane, and designed a workable torpedo release gear.

The first naval aviation unit was established at Annapolis, Maryland. The Pensacola Naval Air Station was organized in 1913. Lieutenant John H. Towers made the first scouting flight in fleet exercises during that year. Scouting and spotting flights were made in combat during the Vera Cruz operation in 1914.

In invention and in trial-and-error pioneering, the U.S. Navy was well advanced. But for all that, neither Congress nor the Navy Department was prepared to take naval aviation seriously until World War I demonstrated dramatically the usefulness of aircraft in antisubmarine warfare. Up to 1917, appropriations for naval aircraft were inadequate even for a worthwhile research program.

In contrast, the British accepted the plane as an adjunct to operations as soon as flyable aircraft were available. Before World War I, Britain already had over 100 aircraft, mostly seaplanes, and had a fleet tactical doctrine for their employment in connection with patrol flotillas. She had six seaplane stations in commission. The Royal Flying Corps[14] stood prepared to test any aircraft brought to it, and stimulated manufacturing efforts in all possible ways. By January 1914, aircraft of the Naval Wing alone had logged 131,081 miles, with only two fatalities.

In 1914 Germany was most advanced in military aircraft of all types. She had four seaplane stations along her short coastline, and had over 500 airplanes. In 1913 a German pilot established an air endurance record of 16 hours, 20 minutes.

Other principal European powers had made some progress in military and naval aviation. The United States and Japan in 1914 were classified in *Brassey's Naval Annual* as "minor

[13] This device is described in some detail in Elting E. Morison, *Admiral Sims and the Modern American Navy* (Boston, 1942), 84–85.

[14] The British at this time allocated all aeronautical matters to the R.F.C., which had two branches, a Naval and a Military Wing.

air powers" whose current development was not worth mention.[15]

On the eve of World War I the attention of the experts was strongly drawn to airships—including the new "rigid" type perfected by Count von Zeppelin for Germany. The loss of the L-1 and the L-2 in successive disasters in 1913, far from discouraging the German admiralty, simply stimulated research into new protective devices. The Germans were apparently determined to hold their design lead in building "battle airships," as their big dirigibles were coming to be called.

Great Britain and the other European powers were fostering the development of local blimp and dirigible industries. In 1914, Winston Churchill, as First Lord of the Admiralty, announced in the House of Commons the order from the Vickers Company of Britain's first zeppelin-type rigid airship. The United States, in spite of her priceless monopoly of noninflammable helium gas, showed no official interest in this type of aircraft.

Space considerations preclude a detailed description of all the technical improvements that enhanced the efficiency of navies between 1898 and 1914. It was a period of rapid development in the industrial arts; innovations and discoveries in chemistry, metallurgy, hydraulics, and electrical science helped to solve problems peculiar to the naval service. The obvious advantage of instantaneous communications made Marconi's "wireless" an object of early interest and experiment by most of the world's admiralties. By 1900, it was operational equipment in the British and the United States fleets. A host of developments in subsequent years enormously extended the range, selectivity, and dependability of this primitive radio apparatus. The first operational use of wireless appears to have occurred in the Boer War. The device proved itself in the Russo-Japanese War. Oil-burning capital ships were laid down.[16] Electrical and hydraulic gear on shipboard became more important as more

and more heavy manual jobs were eased by the application of power. Improved ventilation of ships' spaces and increased utilization of refrigerated foods made shipboard life far more comfortable for the crews.

Many changes were to ensue after 1914: the development of the depth charge, underwater "listening" devices, the antenna mine. The carrier was to emerge as a type in the next decade. And of course the World War II period was to see a hothouse forcing of radical applications of science to new problems. But even so by 1914 the newest ships in the world's navies were beginning to acquire a "modern" look. And indeed some of them were to show real combat value 30 years later.

Other Aspects of Naval Growth

In the early 20th century the shore establishment of all the world's navies grew in size, variety, and relative importance. Permanent ordnance proving grounds, air stations, offshore bases, and vastly expanded "fleet schools" were added to the naval establishments of every country.

In the United States the lead offered by Stephen Luce a generation earlier was followed out. Whereas in the earlier 19th century it had been customary to recruit naval seamen from the merchant marine, it had increasingly become the practice to get landsmen, the younger the better, and to train them in the Navy's own schools. The increased complexity and variety of equipment on shipboard required more intelligent and better educated men. When Wilson's Secretary of Navy, Josephus Daniels, in 1913 held up the ideal of the Navy's being "a great university with college extensions ashore and afloat," he was giving recognition to what was already becoming an actuality. In the wooden ship days, illiterates could be taught to "hand, reef, and steer." But it requires a background of reading ability and mathematical skills to learn to man fire-control apparatus, to run an engine room, to keep complicated electrical equipment in repair.

Simultaneously there was a gradual change in the basic problems of leadership by officers. The example of conspicuous personal gallantry

[15] *Brassey's Naval Annual* has a quasi-official authority, and may be taken as embodying British expert opinion.

[16] *Oklahoma* and *Nevada* (1914) in the United States Navy, and the *Queen Elizabeths* (1914–15) in the British service.

never lost its value, but superior intelligence and general administrative ability became even more important than formerly.

The growth of naval tonnage necessarily demanded increased personnel. The U.S. Navy was at this time notoriously undermanned however, especially in the commissioned officer category. According to President Roosevelt, in 1902 the United States had fewer than half enough officers to fill the complements of ships in commission and building. Gradual increases in the numbers of Naval Academy graduates and of enlisted men were effected, but at the end of 1908 the United States not only had less than a third as many line officers as Great Britain; she had only about half as many as Germany, France, or Japan.[17] This was in spite of the fact that United States tonnage was only slightly less than Germany's and very much greater than Japan's.

Strategic Doctrine

From the Spanish-American War to the outbreak of World War I, the only important fleet operations were in the Russo-Japanese War. However, both the Tripolitan War (Italy *vs.* Turkey, 1911–12) and the First Balkan War (Turkey *vs.* Greece, Bulgaria, and Serbia, 1912–13) were object lessons in the value of sea power. Italy and Greece, respectively, made effective use of their fleets in the Aegean area. Naval superiority conferred superior mobility to their forces and insured victory in both wars.

British naval doctrine through this period, as already sufficiently indicated, was one of increased concentration in home waters. New bases on the Humber, at Rosyth on the Firth

[17] Navy Department *Annual Report,* 1908, 12.

of Forth, and at Scapa Flow in the Orkneys were activated, thereby shifting the main naval front from the English Channel to the North Sea. As the military and naval planning of England and France tended to merge on the eve of world war, Britain even came to reckon on France's ability to keep naval dominance in the Mediterranean.

The growth of the world's navies in the years preceding the first world war was a costly tribute to the teaching of Admiral Mahan. He had shown how political potency and wealth had come to Great Britain through her superior sea power. Britannia's secret weapon was the trident. And in 1914, Britain, by her tremendous expenditures, the technical excellence of her material, and her shrewd diplomacy, still appeared to grasp firmly her naval ascendancy.

But Britain had rivals whose ultimate potential could predictably upset this superiority; Japan and the United States could be conciliated by diplomatic means and made into allies, tacit or actual. Germany, already the strongest military power in the world, was in a different category. Her mighty dreadnoughts were too close to home. Should Germany occupy Holland and Belgium, a strong German navy operating from the mouths of the Rhine and the Scheldt would be a new pistol pointed at the heart of England. Then only the armored walls of her Grand Fleet battleships could save her from invasion and defeat.

Because of this threat, Britain could no longer maintain her "splendid isolation." Again, as in the Napoleonic period, she had to bind herself into the complexities of continental power politics. Paradoxically, the new German fleet made England's safety depend in part on the French army.

22:

World War I: Opening Operations

In the late summer of 1914, Europe plunged into a war that impoverished England, bled France white, destroyed imperial Germany, dismembered the Austro-Hungarian Empire, and brought revolution and civil war to Russia. World War I undermined the social, political, and moral order of continental Europe, making possible the triumph of Communism in Russia and of Fascism in Italy and Germany. Thus World War I set the stage for World War II.

Of crucial importance among the causes of the war were the elaborate alliance systems that had grown up—each secured by a network of secret treaties, financial arrangements, and military "understandings." In 1914 power appeared to be about equally balanced between the major groupings—the Triple Alliance (Germany, Austria-Hungary, and Italy) and the Triple Entente (France, Russia, and Britain).

The immediate cause for the outbreak of war was the assassination at Sarajevo of the heir apparent to the Austrian throne by a Serbian patriot. The Austrian foreign minister, emboldened by Germany's unqualified support (the so-called "blank check"), fired off an ultimatum to Serbia demanding compensation and punishment of the guilty. These Serbia could promise. But Austria also demanded the right to police Serbian territory, a demand that the Serbs rejected.

Russia, whose foreign office for a generation had been preaching "pan-Slavism" in the Balkans, had a mutual defense pact with Serbia. When Austria and Serbia mobilized, so did Russia. The Germans, whose strategy for a two-front war was to overwhelm the French first in a lightning thrust before Russia could fully mobilize (the "Schlieffen Plan"), felt compelled to move at once. Austria declared

war against Serbia on July 28, 1914. Germany declared war against Russia on August 1, against France on August 3, and against Belgium on August 4. The British government, bound by honor and interest to support France and defend Belgium, at midnight on August 4 declared war against Germany.

The Opposing Admiralties

At the outbreak of World War I, neither the British nor the German admiralty was organized to direct the naval war with maximum efficiency. In common with other naval establishments around the world, they were well set up to handle logistics but unprepared to devise naval strategy or to control large-scale fleet operations. This was the consequence of a long period in which technological change was constant while combat was small-scale. Both nations entered the war with materially excellent navies but without the established policies, the developed doctrines, or the top-level organizations needed to wield them properly.

The British government had been feeling its way toward a solution of the naval command problem since early in the century. A British Order-in-Council of 1904 took some of the burden of decision off the civilian First Lord of the Admiralty by elevating the First Sea Lord, at that time Admiral Sir John Fisher, to a position of supremacy over the other Sea Lords. This change clarified the command and advisory situation, but Fisher's duties were too much concerned with material to leave him much time for directing or advising on operations, which in fact were not his principal concern. In 1910 Fisher, raised to the peerage, retired. The following year Prime Minister

Herbert Asquith brought the brilliant, dynamic Winston Churchill to the Admiralty as First Lord. Churchill took office with the understanding that he was expected to organize a naval war staff comparable to the Army's General Staff. Churchill did so over the protests of many naval officers. The War Staff was not an immediate success. British naval officers were not trained for general staff work. They lacked the military education and the breadth of understanding to think in grand strategic terms. " 'The Silent Service' was not mute because it was absorbed in thought and study," said Churchill, "but because it was weighted down by its daily routine and by its ever complicating and diversifying technique. We had competent administrators, brilliant experts of every description, unequalled navigators, good disciplinarians, fine sea-officers, brave and devoted hearts: but at the outset of the conflict we had more captains of ships than captains of war."[1]

With the onset of hostilities, England turned to the aging giants of the preceding generation for advice and guidance. Immediately after the outbreak, Asquith called upon Field Marshal Lord Kitchener to join the Cabinet and head the War Office as Secretary of State for War (war minister). In October 1914 Churchill obtained the recall of Lord Fisher as First Sea Lord. The British armed forces thus secured the services, at the highest military level, of their foremost soldier and foremost sailor. But the British government still had no adequate machinery for making rapid wartime policy decisions, and none at all for converting decisions into prompt military action. In November 1914 Prime Minister Asquith took steps to remedy this defect by establishing a super-cabinet called the War Council, responsible for the high-level conduct of the war. The Prime Minister presided at War Council meetings. Kitchener and Churchill represented the armed services. Other Cabinet officers sat regularly with the Council, with the occasional addition of men responsible for the production or transport of munitions. Though this small super-cabinet held immense responsibility and great authority, it lacked a military staff. This lack it partly filled by bringing in a senior general and a senior admiral for consultation.

[1] *The World Crisis* (New York, 1931), 62–3.

The Council was thus enabled to reach quick decisions on simple military problems. More complex problems were referred to Kitchener or Churchill, who consulted their staffs and later reported their decisions or recommendations. The execution of decisions reached in the Council was the responsibility of the War Office and the Admiralty.

Lord Kitchener, refusing to delegate authority and acting as both war minister and army chief of staff, was, in effect, the War Office. His monolithic control backed by his great prestige gave his utterances weight before the War Council. Churchill's words carried no such weight. His colleagues on the Council frequently consulted Lord Fisher, who sat as the Admiralty staffer at their meetings. Moreover, they expected Churchill to win Fisher's approval of whatever Admiralty plan he presented to the Council. Lord Kitchener, on the contrary, so overshadowed his adviser from the War Office that he spoke alone for the Army. It thus developed that three strong-minded men, the 65-year-old Kitchener, the 40-year-old Churchill, and the 72-year-old Fisher, dominated military advice to the Council. But in this threesome Kitchener held the balance of power, for he could support either Churchill, his colleague in the Cabinet, or Fisher, his opposite number in the armed services. In rare instances Asquith resolved a particularly thorny question by indicating his preference. Hence each important military problem confronting the Council produced a contest of wills among Kitchener, Churchill, Fisher, and Asquith—thereby encouraging policy-making characterized by negative decision or compromise.

The German Admiralty at the outbreak of World War I was organized even less effectively than the British. By the naval reorganization of 1899, Kaiser William II had become the navy's supreme commander. Immediately under him and exercising the right of direct approach were the Admiralty Staff and the Naval Cabinet, responsible for command functions, and the Imperial Navy Office and Naval Secretary of State, responsible for administration. This fragmentation of the naval high command, with each chief authorized to confer with a Kaiser who was hesitant to make critical decisions, inevitably led to personality clashes and conflicting strategic recommendations.

At the outbreak of hostilities, Admiral Tirpitz, who was both Chief of the Imperial Navy Office and Naval Secretary of State, offered to centralize the German naval effort by assuming the entire control of the Navy. His offer was rejected and Tirpitz eventually was maneuvered out of office. Because there was no German super-cabinet like Britain's War Council and because too many naval officers came directly under the Kaiser, German naval policy was haphazard, and strongly influenced by the Army and by political groups.

Meanwhile, the German Army was headed by the most tightly organized General Staff in Europe, a staff with a philosophy of "total war" based, many contend, upon a misreading of the works of the military philosopher Karl von Clausewitz. The influence of the General Staff on the minds of the Kaiser and other government leaders established the concept of a strictly continental war strategy. Germany had in some respects the finest surface navy in the world, second in strength and numbers only to that of Britain, but nobody could decide quite what to do with it. The German navy did not develop any really coherent policy until the Kaiser in 1917 ordered unrestricted submarine warfare.

Geography and Strategy

The grand strategy of World War I derived to a large degree from the relative location of the opposed coalitions. The Central Powers, Germany and Austria-Hungary, occupied the interior position—a band of territory across Europe almost completely separating Russia from her western allies, Britain, France, and Belgium. The German high command, by using the splendid system of railroads that had been developed in Germany with military requirements in mind, could quickly shift forces as needed from one front to the other. Theoretically the Allies, making use of their exterior position, should have been able to counter the German advantage by applying simultaneous pressures on both the French and Russian fronts in a gigantic pincers operation. Actually, with insufficient strength, no unified command, and inadequate communications between east and west, the Allies were never to achieve this strategic ideal.

Naval grand strategy in the war was largely dictated by the geographic configuration of the British Isles and the north coast of Europe. Germany, which enjoyed the strategic advantage in the land struggle, was in a disadvantageous position in the sea war. Her ships could reach the ocean only via the North Sea, which the Royal Navy dominated.

But Germany had the advantage of the interior position in the close proximity of the Baltic and North seas, joined by the Kiel Canal across the base of the Danish peninsula (Jutland). The Canal had recently been widened to enable the Germans to shift even the largest units of their fleet from one sea to the other. Throughout the war the Baltic remained a German lake, a valuable training area for the High Seas Fleet, and a priceless transitway for steel, timber, and other resources from the northern neutrals.

Britain, unlike Germany, was absolutely dependent on imported foodstuffs. Controlling almost half the existing merchant shipping, she could draw on the economic resources of the world—but only as long as she had control of the oceans. Hence the paramount task of the Royal Navy was *defensive*—to keep open the sea approaches to Britain's home ports. The main offensive tasks initially assigned the Royal Navy were the blockade of Germany, containment or attrition of the High Seas Fleet, and the destruction of enemy cruisers in nearby or distant waters. The blockade of Germany, though not decisive, was to prove a major contribution. Mines, aircraft, and submarines had made the close blockade of earlier times impossible, but Britain's geographic advantages made it easy for her navy to bar Germany from the North Atlantic.

Whereas the role of the British navy was to exercise control of the sea, that of Germany was to dispute it. The Kaiser's hope was to win the war on land within a few weeks by defeating France while holding Russia. German fleet policy therefore initially was to be a careful husbanding of ships. Though the German fleet was statistically inferior, undamaged it could be a strong bargaining counter at the peace conference. At first, the German navy also pinned some limited hopes on a *guerre de course* conducted by its far-ranging cruisers. The main offensive strategy of the High Seas Fleet however was to attempt by hit-and-run raids, partial actions, and ambush to whittle down the British margin of superiority in the North Sea. Perhaps ultimately, if the war continued longer than anticipated, the High Seas Fleet could challenge the Grand Fleet on more nearly even terms in a fight to the finish. The great naval battle, if it ever occurred, would necessarily take place in the North Sea —both because the Royal Navy would obviously never permit the German fleet to enter the Atlantic, and because the High Seas Fleet was essentially a defensive force, not built for long-range operations.

In the long run, the most serious operational naval effort the Germans were able to make was a counter-blockade by submarine offensives against the British, Allied, and neutral merchant marines. This new and deadly version of commerce warfare was not anticipated however by either belligerent before 1914 and was not important in the early months of the war.

In the period in which the outbreak of warfare was foreseen and more and more regarded as inevitable, there occurred in British military circles a debate over how Britain could best employ her armed forces against the enemy. All parties accepted the blockade of Germany and the protection of Allied shipping as appropriate tasks for the Royal Navy. But Britain at the beginning of the war had more naval power in certain categories of ships than was needed to carry out these functions. The debate concerned how best to use this excess and how best to employ Britain's efficient and growing army.

One school of military thought, which Lord Fisher espoused, looked for its inspiration to Britain's strategy in the Seven Years' War and in the first three coalitions of the Napoleonic Wars. This school preferred a peripheral strategy and opposed, for British arms at least, the continental strategy of driving straight at the enemy. It was argued that Britain should use the mobility conferred by her geographical position and her sea supremacy to strike around the periphery of the enemy's position, probing for weak spots where amphibious attacks could weaken his military strength,

draw his forces from the main theaters, and break up his potential alliances. The war in the main continental theaters, said this school, should be left to the armies of Belgium, France, Russia, and any other powers that could be attracted to the Allied cause. These Britain would support by subsidy, partly financed by capture of German trade, and by any other means short of actually providing large numbers of troops at the main fronts. The peripheral school, in short, called for a return to the main features of Pitt's Plan, the strategy on which the British Empire was founded.

The opposing school saw no alternative to putting a major British army in the main western theater of the continental war. It drew its inspiration from the War of the Fourth Coalition, which had finally defeated Napoleon. A British army, supported by the armies of Spain and Portugal, had driven up from the south; while the army of Russia, combined with those of Austria and Prussia, advanced from the east. Between them, these combined forces had crushed the Napoleonic empire. The diplomatic and geographical situation in 1914 provided, it was argued, a close counterpart to this decisive combination. The Kaiser, like Napoleon, was surrounded. He had no choice but to fight a two-front war. Britain's best contribution, said the continental strategists, was to place her main army at once on the Continent.

The British continental school had of course the full support of French military leaders. Their arguments were persuasive. General Ferdinand Foch, commandant of the French Staff College, convinced General Sir Henry Wilson, British Director of Military Operations, who pledged 150,000 soldiers to fight on the Allied left flank in Western Europe under French strategic direction. Kitchener, on becoming minister of war, prepared not only to honor Wilson's pledge but in time to place on the Continent an army far stronger than either Foch or Wilson had envisioned.

Kitchener did not entirely rule out peripheral operations but insisted that they must be secondary to the main effort on the Western Front. The British Admiralty, in considering such operations and also the protection of trade, early focused its attention on the Mediterranean, where British shipping had reached an annual value of £125,000,000. As the summer of 1914 advanced, the Royal Navy was alerted to be prepared for trouble in the Mediterranean—trouble involving Germany, Austria, Italy, or all three. Turkey might well have been added to the list of potential enemies.

The Goeben and the *Breslau*

Germany had been shrewdly cultivating her influence with Constantinople for a dozen years, and had high hopes of a successful economic thrust—a *"Drang nach Osten"*—into the undeveloped but potentially valuable Middle East. The convention of 1907 between Britain and Turkey's ancient enemy Russia made the Turks the more willing to strengthen their rapprochement with the Germans.

The Turks had expansion plans of their own, mainly at Russian expense. To carry out their expansion, they would have to control the Black Sea; hence in 1912 Turkey placed an order with British shipyards for the construction of two battleships to stiffen her own small fleet. Germany was invited to furnish a military mission to train the Turkish army. Accordingly, German General Liman von Sanders arrived at Constantinople in December 1913 to assume the office of Inspector General of Turkey's land forces.

In late July 1914 Turkey, expecting Britain to remain out of the war, offered Germany a secret alliance which the Germans eagerly accepted. Then Britain issued an ultimatum to Germany, and Churchill requisitioned the two Turkish battleships for use by the Royal Navy. The result was rage and dismay in Turkish governing circles. In panic, the head of the leading Turkish faction even considered canceling the alliance with Germany and signing one with Russia. To steady the wavering Turks, Germany proposed furnishing substitutes for their lost battleships. At the Austrian base at Pola in the Adriatic were the powerful German battle cruiser *Goeben* and her consort, the light cruiser *Breslau*. With war imminent, it would be impossible for these ships to reach the North Sea in safety. Germany had at first planned to combine them with the small Austrian fleet. But on the very eve of war she ordered them to proceed to Constantinople.

Turkey's relationship to the war now depended upon whether or not these vessels could elude the French and British warships in the Mediterranean.

Though the British were aware of Germany's influence in Turkish affairs, they had no knowledge of the Turko-German alliance and no inkling of the proposed destination of the *Goeben* and the *Breslau*. They had in the Mediterranean, under the command of Admiral Sir Berkeley Milne, three battle cruisers, four armored cruisers, four light cruisers, and 14 destroyers. An Admiralty dispatch to Milne on July 30 ordered him to support the French in transporting their Algerian army across the Mediterranean to France. On August 3 Milne received further orders to watch the mouth of the Adriatic and to locate and shadow the *Goeben*. The same day the French Toulon fleet under Admiral de Lapeyrère left port with orders "to watch the German cruiser *Goeben* and protect the transport of the French African troops." The two admirals were thus given independent and overlapping objectives with no means of coordination or even of communication with each other. While Milne was organizing his forces in order to carry out his various tasks, he was given still another objective—to cover Gibraltar to prevent the German cruisers from escaping into the Atlantic to attack Allied trade. In the meantime, unknown to Milne, the passage of the French troops had been postponed because of the presence of the German ships.

The confusion resulting from the welter of Allied orders permitted German Admiral Souchon to slip out of the Adriatic with the *Goeben* and the *Breslau* just as Germany and France were going to war. On August 4 he bombarded the Algerian staging ports of Bône and Philippeville and then turned back to Messina, Sicily to take on coal for the dash to Constantinople. En route to Messina he encountered two of Milne's battle cruisers headed for Gibraltar. The British ships could not open fire because the British declaration against Germany was still several hours away. Their attempts to shadow were frustrated by the high speed of the German ships, fresh from overhaul at Pola.

Italy had now declared her neutrality; hence Souchon would have to leave Messina within

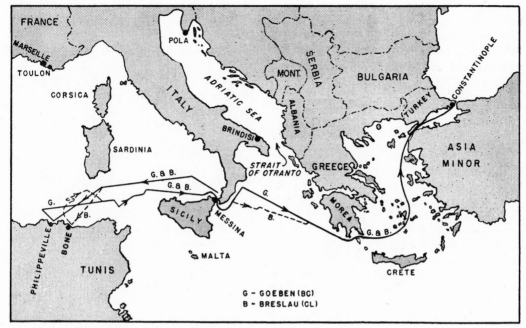

ESCAPE OF THE *GOEBEN* AND THE *BRESLAU*, 1914

24 hours. Milne, with his multiple objectives in mind, disposed the bulk of his forces northwest of Sicily, to be between the Germans and the supposed French transports, and at the mouth of the Adriatic. Only the light cruiser *Gloucester* watched the southern exit from the Strait of Messina. From here in the late afternoon of August 6 she saw the Germans emerge and kept them under observation as they headed northeast as if to enter the Adriatic. Toward midnight the German cruisers turned southeast and shaped course for the Aegean, still shadowed by the *Gloucester,* which continued to radio information of the German movements until ordered back off Cape Matapan, the southernmost point of Greece.

In the meantime, Rear Admiral Troubridge, who had been covering the entrance to the Adriatic with four armored cruisers, had taken an intercepting course. He hoped to close the *Goeben* and *Breslau* at dawn, when his cruisers would be at minimum gunnery disadvantage. But in the early hours of August 7 he gave up the chase, for it appeared that he could not reach the Germans till full daylight, when the *Goeben's* longer-ranged guns might well send his ships to the bottom, one after another.

On receiving the *Gloucester's* warning, Milne proceeded to Malta to fill his bunkers with coal in preparation for a long chase. But on August 7, as he set out on an easterly course with three battle cruisers to overtake Souchon, he received an Admiralty dispatch erroneously announcing war with Austria. In compliance with standing orders in such a contingency, Milne turned away to support Troubridge in the Adriatic. On the 8th the Admiralty corrected its premature announcement and ordered Milne to resume his pursuit of the Germans. It was too late. Souchon arrived unmolested at the Dardanelles on August 10, and then steamed slowly to Constantinople.

The inadequate diplomatic intelligence, the poor liaison between navies, the lack of command initiative, and the general bungling that permitted Souchon to escape were a sobering reminder that the Allies were ill-prepared to conduct far-flung operations. This was the result of extended preoccupation with material matters at the expense of plans and training for allied operational control.

On August 13 the Turks announced the "purchase" of the *Goeben* and the *Breslau,* but the original crews remained on board and

Souchon remained their commander. Late in October Souchon led a Turko-German squadron against the Russian Black Sea ports of Odessa and Novorossysk, laid mines off Sevastopol, and sank a Russian gunboat. These provocative acts resulted in war between Turkey and Russia.

The Fleets and the Armies

When hostilities appeared imminent, the British Home Fleets and the German High Seas Fleet had gone to war stations. The principal combat strength of the British Home Fleets was concentrated in the Grand Fleet, commanded by Admiral Sir John Jellicoe, with a main base at Scapa Flow in the Orkneys and subsidiary bases in the Scottish firths. The Grand Fleet included 24 first-line battleships and battle cruisers. Its principal functions were to prevent the escape of German ships into the Atlantic, to guard the North Sea, and to watch the High Seas Fleet, bringing it to battle and destroying it if a favorable opportunity occurred. Cruiser-destroyer patrols operated out of Dover, Harwich, and the Humber to guard the British coast. After the outbreak of war, a Channel Fleet, including 17 second-line (pre-dreadnought) battleships, was organized to assure the safe passage of British troops and supplies to France. The German High Seas Fleet, commanded by Admiral Ingenohl, included 16 first-line battleships and battle cruisers and 8 second-line battleships. It was based in the estuaries of the Weser and Elbe rivers and in Jade Bay ("the Jade"). Its assigned functions were to guard the German coast from British attack and to seek opportunities to weaken the British fleet.

The British Home Fleets were first put to the test as the movement of British troops began, chiefly from Southampton to Le Havre. It was a risky business, one that the Germans might well have made an all-out effort to interrupt. But in contrast to the failures in the Mediterranean, this carefully planned operation was executed with flawless precision. The Grand Fleet moved out into the North Sea, ready to pounce upon the High Seas Fleet should it venture from base. The Channel Fleet with the assistance of British and French coastal patrols closed both ends of the English Channel, maintaining ceaseless watch against raids by enemy ships and submarines. The troops meanwhile crossed in independently sailing transports, which shuttled back and forth as fast as loading, unloading, and fuel endurance would permit. Between August 9 and 22, 1914, a British Expeditionary Force of five divisions crossed to France in complete safety and, what is more remarkable, in almost complete secrecy.

The Germans were already initiating the western phase of their modified Schlieffen Plan: to sweep through Belgium, capture Paris in a great wheeling movement, and thus put France out of the war. But in the First Battle of the Marne, fought in early September on Paris's doorstep, a hundred thousand British regulars held the Allied left flank and helped drive a wedge between two separated German armies. The invaders were pressed back to the line of the Aisne River, and Paris was saved.

Allied sea power, which had made possible the presence of the British troops, indirectly provided the thin margin of successful resistance to the initial German surge. By the end of September a quarter of a million troops, virtually all of Britain's professional army, had landed in France. Through the entire war, the "sea bridge" across the Channel was never to be successfully attacked by the German navy.

The Heligoland Bight Action, August 28, 1914

The first surface action in the North Sea set the pattern of ambush and counter-ambush that characterized later operations in this area. British submarines of Commodore Roger Keyes' command reported German scouting operations in the Heligoland Bight, the triangular body of water off the Elbe and Weser Rivers. (See map page 413.) Late each afternoon German light cruisers escorted destroyers to sea for a night patrol. At dawn the cruisers met the destroyers 20 miles northwest of Heligoland Island and shepherded them back home. Keyes saw in this regularity an opportunity for the British fleet, and worked out a plan for taking the enemy by surprise. Using his submarines as bait, and holding strong surface support just over the horizon, he would lure

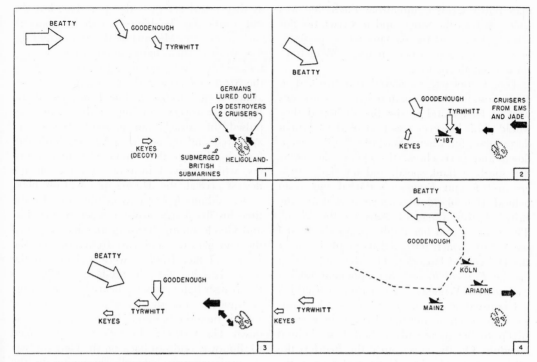

HELIGOLAND BIGHT ACTION, AUGUST 28, 1914

the Germans into the waters west of Heligoland, whereupon the British surface vessels would sweep down from the north and then turn west, cutting out any enemy vessels they encountered. Keyes believed that the British could thus smash the night destroyer patrol and with a little luck get the cruisers as well.

Going in person to London, Keyes submitted his plan to the Lords of the Admiralty. The Admiralty accepted the plan but at first limited the surface support to the two Harwich flotillas, comprising 33 destroyers and two light cruisers under Commodore Reginald Tyrwhitt. On further consideration, after Keyes had departed, the Admiralty decided to send additional support forces from the Grand Fleet. These were a squadron of six light cruisers under Commodore William R. Goodenough and a squadron of five battle cruisers, including the *Lion, Queen Mary,* and *Princess Royal,* largest and newest of their type, under Vice Admiral Sir David Beatty. Through an administrative mixup, neither Keyes nor Tyrwhitt got word of the Admiralty's change of plan. They put to sea prepared to make do with what they had, never suspecting that such formidable support was on the way. The situation was further complicated by the fact that the Germans had got wind of Keyes' scheme and were planning to spring a counter-ambush. Like Keyes and Tyrwhitt however, they had no information that Goodenough's and Beatty's squadrons had been added to the British support.

Before daylight on August 28, 1914, three British submarines took surface stations some 40 miles west of Heligoland, trying to attract attention. At the same time, to spring the trap, Tyrwhitt's destroyers and his light cruisers *Arethusa* and *Fearless* were coming down from the northwest. Behind Tyrwhitt, at a distance of eight miles, came Goodenough's six light cruisers, and 30 miles farther off and to the west were Beatty's five battle cruisers. At dawn Tyrwhitt sighted Goodenough's cruisers and, taking them for an enemy force, prepared to attack. But Goodenough identified himself in time and a battle between friends was averted.

The Germans had 19 destroyers and two light cruisers near Heligoland. To the east and south they had four more light cruisers, and inside Jade Roads 60 miles away was the German Battle Cruiser Squadron. Each side was trying to trap the other, and if Tyrwhitt's flotillas had not had the backing whose presence he did not at first suspect, matters might have turned out ill for him.

To all appearances Keyes' trap worked to perfection, for the German destroyers came out west of Heligoland as the British hoped they would. This however was part of the German decoy plan, for when Tyrwhitt's flotillas swept down and gave chase, the enemy destroyers fled south at flank speed, and the light cruisers *Stettin* and *Frauenlob* darted out from behind Heligoland to engage and draw the British within range of guns on the island. The *Fearless* and her flotilla promptly chased the *Stettin*, which retreated temporarily under the Heligoland batteries. The *Arethusa*, firing on the *Frauenlob*, sent her opponent reeling back toward Wilhelmshaven with 50 casualties.

Disgusted at his meager success, Tyrwhitt gave up the chase and signaled for the western sweep to begin, already a half hour behind schedule. On the new course the *Fearless* flotilla encountered a lone German destroyer, the *V-187*, and quickly reduced her to flaming wreckage.

Goodenough's light cruisers meanwhile had arrived in the Bight west of Tyrwhitt's position without meeting any enemy. Observing the attack on the *V-187* in the distance, Goodenough detached two of his cruisers and sent them toward the scene of action. Keyes, also steering toward the action, presently saw Goodenough's two detached cruisers through the mist. Mistaking them for enemy, he reported by radio that he was shadowing a pair of German cruisers. Goodenough, intercepting this message, headed with his four remaining ships to Keyes' assistance, but as he came into view Keyes thought four more enemy cruisers had arrived and called all the louder for help. In the confusion Goodenough tried to ram one of Keyes' submarines, and Tyrwhitt came dashing up to provide support against the nonexistent enemy. An hour was lost before Keyes correctly identified the cruisers he was following and learned that not only Goodenough's light cruisers but Beatty's battle cruisers were in the area.

Admiral Ingenohl had ordered the German battle cruisers to proceed to Heligoland as soon as they could get over the Jade bar, but the tide would not be high enough for that till early afternoon. Meanwhile the *Stettin* and the four fresh German light cruisers were speeding toward Tyrwhitt's flotillas. Just before 11 AM the *Stralsund* appeared out of the mists and attacked the *Arethusa*. The *Fearless* and the British destroyers, coming to the rescue, repulsed this attack, but presently the *Stettin* appeared and opened fire. At Tyrwhitt's call for help, Beatty ordered in Goodenough's cruisers, which arrived in time to drive off the newest arrival, the *Mainz*, in a hail of shells.

Beatty himself was now on the way. By the time his five battle cruisers reached Tyrwhitt and Goodenough, the *Stralsund* had rejoined the engagement, and two fresh cruisers, the *Köln* and the *Ariadne*, were arriving on the scene. Leaving the already-beaten *Mainz* to the British light cruisers, Beatty's battle cruisers quickly sank the *Köln* and the *Ariadne*. By this time the battered *Mainz* also had gone down. The *Stettin* and the *Stralsund* managed to slip away and fall back on the German battle cruisers, now belatedly hastening to the scene of action. When these at last arrived, all the British ships had departed the area.

The British had drawn first blood in a surface action. The Germans had lost three light cruisers and a destroyer, with more than 700 men killed and 400 taken prisoner. The British experienced only slight damage and lost 35 men. Coming at a time when the German armies were rolling across Belgium and northern France, the news of the British victory was a welcome tonic to the Allied peoples. But the officers of the British Admiralty were aware that they had served the fleet ill. The last-minute change of plans and the failure to warn the sea commanders almost resulted in British ships sinking other British ships.

The German Admiralty was no less aware that it had mishandled operations. Despite advance warning of the British ambush, German forces powerful enough to destroy the attackers on Germany's own doorstep were caught unready or unable to put to sea. The Kaiser, shocked at the loss of his ships and men, determined henceforth to take control of fleet movements into his own hands. He advised Ingenohl that no sortie should be made without his personal approval. The Heligoland area was mined. A battleship division was held in readiness and battle cruisers with steam up were stationed in Shillig Roads, prepared for counterattack should the British make a second venture.

Within a few weeks after the Heligoland Bight Action, German submarines operating in the North Sea had a series of successes that had a profound effect upon subsequent British naval operations. The first victim was H.M. cruiser *Pathfinder,* sunk by the *U-21* in the Firth of Forth on September 5, 1914. On September 22, the *U-9* in a matter of minutes sank the elderly British cruisers *Aboukir, Hogue,* and *Cressy.* These ships, patrolling together off the Dutch coast, were following a geometric pattern at constant speed—an ideal set-up for the attacker. When the *Aboukir* was hit, the other cruisers slowed down to rescue survivors and in turn were picked off in quick succession. Their 1901 and 1902 hulls and compartmentation were defenseless against the improved and efficient German torpedo. They sank quickly with great loss of life. This triple tragedy so dramatized and underscored the new threat that the British Admiralty greatly extended its submarine research and development program. Later in the year, Britain lost four more warships to submarine torpedo attack.

The submarine threat forced a temporary withdrawal of the Grand Fleet, first to western Scotland, later to North Ireland, while the net and boom defenses at the Scapa Flow anchorage were improved. This temporary diversion of Britain's powerful surface force was less important however than the effect of the sinkings upon British naval policy. Through the rest of the war, British fleet operations in the North Sea were hampered by somewhat excessive caution—particularly in chase situations, in which the enemy might lead Royal Navy units over mine fields or into submarine ambush.

The Battle of Coronel, November 1, 1914

In the 1890's Germany had acquired a naval base at Tsingtao, China. Subsequently she developed a number of her Pacific island colonies in the Caroline and Marshall Islands as coaling stations. In the summer of 1914, a half

dozen German cruisers were operating in the Pacific under the command of Admiral Graf von Spee. Shortly after the outbreak of the war, Japan sent an ultimatum to Germany demanding the withdrawal of her warships from China and Japan and the surrender of Tsingtao.

Spee was then at Ponape in the Carolines with his 11,600-ton armored cruisers *Scharnhorst* and *Gneisenau* and his light cruisers *Emden* and *Nürnberg.* At Ponape, 2,700 miles from both the British China Squadron at Hong Kong and the considerable Australian force at Sydney, the Germans were for the time being relatively safe. But Spee knew that if he ventured into the western Pacific or remained in the central Pacific he would eventually be hunted down. So he decided to cruise to the South American west coast. Here friendly Chile would supply him with coal to continue operations. He dismissed commerce warfare as a primary objective for his squadron as a whole, but detached the *Emden* with a collier to proceed westward across the Pacific in order to raid British shipping in the Indian Ocean.

En route to South America by easy stages, Spee picked up the protected cruiser *Leipzig* and the light cruiser *Dresden* at Easter Island. Then, receiving intelligence that British cruisers were already operating off the west coast of South America, he proceeded thither at once. By the end of October the German squadron was cruising off Chile, with only the *Leipzig* breaking radio silence in an effort to deceive the British into supposing that only one German ship was in the area.

In early September Rear Admiral Sir Christopher Cradock had been appointed commander of a force of British cruisers operating off the coast of Brazil, in an area where two German cruisers had been raiding merchantmen. The appearance of Cradock's cruisers patrolling the South American coast buoyed the confidence of shippers in the ability of the Royal Navy to keep merchant ship losses at a minimum. In mid-September the Admiralty advised Cradock that when he had superior force he should search the Straits of Magellan and either cruise to Valparaiso to destroy German cruisers thought to be there or return to the Atlantic and cover the estuary of the River Plate.

On October 21 Cradock left Port Stanley in

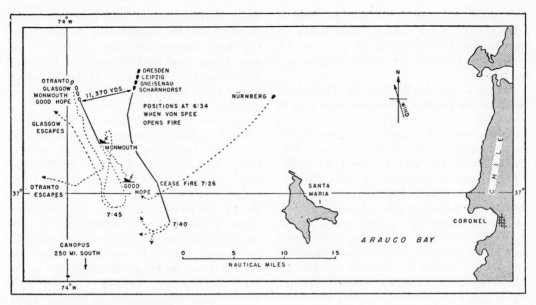

BATTLE OF CORONEL, NOVEMBER 1, 1914

the Falklands with the 12-knot pre-dreadnought battleship *Canopus,* the armored cruisers *Good Hope* and *Monmouth,* the light cruiser *Glasgow,* and the auxiliary cruiser *Otranto.* Passing into the Pacific via the Straits, he took a northerly course, ordering the slow *Canopus* to join him at Juan Fernandez Island, west of Valparaiso. The fast *Glasgow,* forging on ahead, arrived off Coronel and heard German naval radio signals which she correctly identified as coming from the *Leipzig.* Spee's ruse was working.

Early on November 1, a German merchant steamer signaled Spee that the *Glasgow* had anchored off Coronel, to the south. The German commander quickly headed for that area. At the same time, Cradock's main body, hearing strong German radio signals, was sweeping north seeking the *Leipzig.* Picking up the *Glasgow,* Cradock did not consider it necessary to wait for the plodding *Canopus* to join.

Shortly after 4 PM the two forces came within visual range, and each commander was surprised to find that he was encountering more than one opposing cruiser. The *Scharnhorst* and the *Gneisenau* cleared for action with significant advantages over their main antagonists, the *Good Hope* and the *Monmouth.* Only the two 9.2-inch guns of the *Good Hope* were in a class with the sixteen 8.2-inch guns of the

two German armored cruisers. The German crews, who had served together for three years, were famous for their excellent gunnery, the *Scharnhorst* having won the Battle Practice Cup in 1913 and placed second in 1914 to the victorious *Gneisenau.* Of great importance also was the German possession of a director system, not yet introduced in British cruisers.

A little after 6 PM Cradock attempted to cross the German T. Failing, he shifted to a southerly course, parallel to and westward of the Germans. Spee, with the setting sun in his eyes, held his fire and kept the range open. But as soon as the sun had gone down, silhouetting the British cruisers in the afterglow, he moved in and opened fire at 11,370 yards. Within five minutes superior German gunnery had obtained decisive hits, destroying the forward turret of the *Monmouth* and the forward turret and conning tower of the *Good Hope.* The strong southeasterly winds drove heavy seas against the port bows of all the warships, thereby interfering more with British than with German gunnery. By 6:50 the *Monmouth* was limping south out of the battle line, fires raging within her hull; shortly afterward her guns went silent. At 7:26 the two German van cruisers ceased fire. A series of gusty rain squalls so limited their vision that they did not learn the fate of Cradock's flagship *Good Hope,* which, after taking some 30 hits from the *Scharnhorst,* was destroyed by an exploding magazine.

Spee, eager for the kill, directed his force to locate and finish off the British vessels. In the gathering darkness, the *Leipzig* actually charged at flank speed right through the *Good Hope* wreckage without realizing it. The *Nürnberg* chased and destroyed the crippled *Monmouth* at 8:58. Meanwhile the *Otranto* and the speedy *Glasgow* had escaped to westward.

Strategically, the Germans had gained little. For a short time the nitrate, copper, and tin shipments from Peru and Chile were held up, but the Plate trade continued in undiminished volume. On the other hand, the Germans had clearly won a tactical victory. Two British cruisers and their crews had been wiped out, whereas Spee's force had received only six inconsequential hits and had two men wounded. The German admiral had used shrewd tactics with superior force, and had taken skillful advantage of position, light, wind, and sea. Yet even in defeat, Cradock had lessened the chances of continued German success, for Spee's squadron had expended 42 per cent of its 8.2-inch ammunition in an area where there was no replenishment to be had.

The Battle of the Falkland Islands, December 8, 1914

As soon as the British Admiralty heard the grim news of Coronel, battle cruiser support suddenly was no longer reserved for waters nearer home. Lord Fisher, who had returned to the Admiralty just two days before the Coronel action, ordered Admiral Sir Doveton Sturdee to proceed with the fast battle cruisers *Invincible* and *Inflexible* at best possible speed to the Falkland Islands, where British intelligence estimated Spee might next appear. Meanwhile, to bolster defenses in the Falklands, the old *Canopus* was lightly grounded in Port Stanley harbor for protection of the anchorage. Sturdee's force arrived on December 7, joining six British cruisers already there.

Spee had inched his way around the tip of South America, spending three days coaling from a captured Canadian sailing ship. This lost time he could never recover. On the morn-

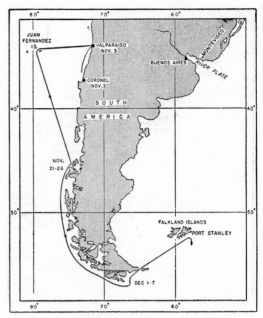

SPEE'S MOVEMENTS FOLLOWING THE BATTLE OF CORONEL

ing of December 6, he held a conference with his captains, who recommended attacking Port Stanley in order to destroy the radio station, capture the British governor, and seize the coal stored there. The Admiral accepted this objective.

Off the Falklands on the morning of December 8, Spee ordered the *Gneisenau* and the *Nürnberg* to advance on Port Stanley harbor to reconnoiter and to take the radio station under fire. At this time the British were coaling inside the harbor in preparation for a sweep south. When the two German cruisers were sighted from the signal tower at 7:50 AM, Sturdee's force was taken completely by surprise and could not immediately sortie. At 9:20, however, the *Canopus* opened indirect fire, which fell short. Soon afterward the *Gneisenau,* moving toward the harbor entrance, caught sight of the tripod masts of the British battle cruisers and flashed the alarm. As the British piped "action stations" and their engineers hastened to get up full steam, the Germans beat a hasty retreat and gained a head start of 15 miles. The sea was calm, the sky clear, and visibility good—all factors favorable to British engineering and gunnery.

By 12:50 PM the British were within range

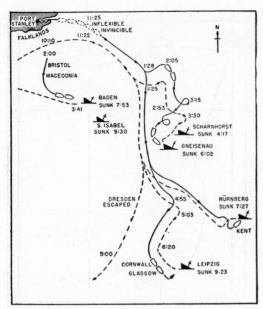

BATTLE OF THE FALKLAND ISLANDS,
DECEMBER 8, 1914

of the rearmost German ship, the *Leipzig*. Spee, realizing that the battle cruisers would quickly exploit their superior 12-inch guns, decided that his situation was hopeless if he kept his force concentrated. He therefore elected to sacrifice his main units in order to facilitate the escape of his three smaller cruisers. These dispersed to the southwest, pursued by cruisers *Glasgow, Cornwall,* and *Kent.*

The main action between the British battle cruisers and the *Scharnhorst* and *Gneisenau* began at 1:20 at 14,000 yards, some 1,000 yards outside the extreme range of the German guns. The British at 3 PM obtained damaging hits on both German vessels. At 4:17 the *Scharnhorst* listed heavily to starboard, burning furiously forward and amidships, and then plunged to the bottom with her entire crew. The *Gneisenau* lasted longer, but by 5:30 her speed had been reduced to five knots. After receiving concentrated fire from both the battle cruisers and from the armored cruiser *Carnarvon,* her captain ordered her sea cocks opened, whereupon she quickly heeled over and sank.

To the southwest the secondary action was scarcely less decisive. The *Kent* overhauled the *Nürnberg* and destroyed her. The *Glasgow* and the *Cornwall* sank the *Leipzig,* while the *Bris-*

tol and the *Macedonia* were destroying two of the three German colliers.

The British squadron returned to Port Stanley triumphant, having sustained only slight battle damage and few casualties. Only two of the German ships escaped, and they soon would be out of the war. The surviving collier was interned in Argentina, and the *Dresden* was tracked down by the *Glasgow* and destroyed at Juan Fernandez Island in March 1915.

German Surface Raiders

Judging from the success of his detached cruiser *Emden,* Spee would have been well advised to disperse all his cruisers for commerce raiding. During the last five months of 1914, some 80 British merchant ships passed from the Pacific to the Atlantic through the newly opened Panama Canal. These were only a fraction of the Allied shipping then plying the Pacific. A half dozen raiding cruisers at large in this area would undoubtedly have created havoc before effective counter-measures could be taken.

Threading through the Netherlands East Indies, Captain Müller brought the *Emden* into the Indian Ocean at the end of August 1914 and on September 5 began raider operations against important Allied trade routes. Disguised with a dummy extra stack to make her look like a British county-class cruiser, the *Emden* within a week had destroyed four British merchant vessels and captured two others for use as a supply train. The Australian government, thoroughly alarmed, held up the sailing of the Australian and New Zealand troop convoys.

Müller quickly shifted area. Off Madras, India, he used shellfire to ignite oil storage tanks ashore. Then, heading into the waters south of India, he captured seven and sank six British merchantmen. After overhaul and coaling at the lonely island of Diego Garcia, where the British subjects were unaware of the state of war, the *Emden* moved east to the Malay Peninsula. Here in Penang harbor, in a surprise early morning attack, Müller sank a Russian light cruiser and a French destroyer.

In the course of a two-month, 30,000-mile cruise, the *Emden* captured or destroyed 21 ships, which together with their cargoes were valued at $10,000,000. Her activities diverted scores of Allied warships from other important assignments to try to track her down. She was finally intercepted on November 9 as Müller was about to cut the cable connections of the Cocos-Keeling Islands, south of Sumatra. A radio call for help brought the Australian cruiser *Sydney*, only 50 miles away. With superior speed and guns that outranged those of the *Emden*, the *Sydney* stood off and shot the raider's hull full of holes, leaving her beached on a reef.

The second most successful German surface raider was the new, fast light cruiser *Karlsruhe*. Between August 31 and October 24, 1914, operating off the Brazilian coast on the main meat and grain route from South America to Europe, she sank or captured 14 British merchantmen. In early November, while descending on the Bahamas for a surprise attack, she was blown apart by an accidental explosion. The Germans concealed this loss for many months, while Allied cruisers continued to search and to arrange sailings with regard for her possible presence.

Five other German vessels employed as raiders early in the war deserve mention, although their combined sinkings amounted to less than those of either the *Emden* or the *Karlsruhe*. The converted passenger liner *Kaiser Wilhelm der Grosse* was destroyed off Spanish Morocco after having sunk 10,000 tons of merchant shipping. The *Dresden* sank 11,000 tons and the *Leipzig* 10,000 before they joined von Spee's squadron. The light cruiser *Königsberg* sank a British light cruiser and captured one merchantman in the western Indian Ocean before she was chased up an African river and blockaded by British monitors. Months later, in the summer of 1915, she was scuttled by her crew after being heavily damaged by indirect monitor fire spotted by aircraft. The converted passenger ship *Kronprinz Wilhelm* accounted for about 30,000 tons of British shipping. But lack of logistic and base support, the great problem of all the raiders, at length obliged her to seek sanctuary in the neutral port of Norfolk, Virginia, where she was interned in April 1915.

Despite the success of some of the raiders, their effect on the conduct of the war was not great. Radio telegraphy made such extended cruises as that of the *Alabama* impossible. It was simply a question of time, rarely more than a few weeks, before a raider was run down or driven from the seas. By early 1915 the surface raider threat was virtually ended. Allied overseas communications were safe. This however was only a temporary situation. In February the German Admiralty unleashed its U-boats against Allied shipping. Later, when all restrictions had been removed from U-boat attack, several submarines each sank more than twice as much tonnage as the *Emden* sank.

The Dogger Bank Action, January 24, 1915

In December 1914, German battle cruisers bombarded the Yorkshire coast. In January 1915 Beatty's battle cruisers, seeking to retaliate, made a fruitless sweep west of Heligoland Bight. As a result of Beatty's sortie and of British operations in the Dogger Bank area, Admiral Ingenohl ordered Vice Admiral Franz von Hipper to sea on January 23.

Hipper's force comprised three battle cruisers and an armored cruiser, supported by a half dozen light cruisers and more than a score of destroyers. His orders were to reconnoiter Dogger Bank in the early hours of the 24th in order to intercept and destroy any British scouts in the area. (See map page 433.) The German plan was thus a simplified version of the British plan that led to the Heligoland Bight action: to bring a superior concentration by surprise against enemy light units.

Unknown to the Germans however, the British had gained a secret advantage that almost precluded the possibility of their being surprised. The Russians had captured the hulk of a German light cruiser that grounded in the Baltic, and in the shallows alongside, one of their divers recovered a jettisoned code book, waterlogged but still legible, including the German military grid of the North Sea. This priceless find the Russians turned over to the British Admiralty. Because the Germans never radically changed their code, the British navy thereafter usually had advance information of High Seas Fleet operations. Radio direction finder stations, spaced along the British east coast from Scotland to Kent, picked up most

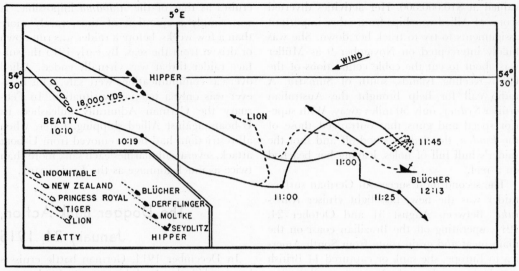

DOGGER BANK ACTION, JANUARY 24, 1915

German surface and submarine dispatches, pinpointed their origin, and forwarded them to the Admiralty for decoding and possible action. In this manner British radio intelligence intercepted and decoded the message to Hipper ordering a sortie.

Fifteen minutes after Hipper cleared the Jade in the late afternoon of January 23, Beatty was leaving the Firth of Forth with five battle cruisers and Commodore Goodenough's First Light Cruiser Squadron. Beatty's three newest battle cruisers had a slight speed advantage over the German battle cruisers, and mounted 13.5-inch main batteries in contrast to Hipper's 11- and 12-inch guns. The Germans however had slightly heavier armor protection, and they had better shells, gun mounts permitting greater elevation, and superior fire control apparatus.

Beatty and Goodenough were directed to rendezvous with Commodore Tyrwhitt's force of light cruisers and destroyers at 7 AM the next morning about 30 miles north of Dogger Bank and 180 miles west of Heligoland—the position where Hipper was expected to be at that time, calculated with remarkable accuracy. Slightly ahead of time on the morning of January 24, on a calm sea with a light breeze from the northeast and good visibility, Beatty, Goodenough, and Tyrwhitt reached the intercepting position. A few minutes later Hipper's force, promptly on schedule, came steaming up from the southeast.

The Germans, recognizing the tripod masts of the British battle cruisers when about 25,000 yards distant, quickly reversed course and sped back toward base. Hipper's flagship *Seydlitz* took the lead on the retirement course, followed in order by the other battle cruisers, *Moltke* and *Derfflinger,* with the older and slower armored cruiser *Blücher* in the rear.

The three new British battle cruisers, *Lion* (Beatty's flagship), *Tiger,* and *Princess Royal,* soon increased speed to 29 knots, and the slower *New Zealand* and *Indomitable* began to fall behind. A little before 9 AM the *Lion* opened with slow and deliberate ranging fire and soon made her first hit—on the *Blücher.* Presently the swift British battle cruisers had sufficiently closed the distance between themselves and the Germans for the *Lion* to shift fire to the *Derfflinger,* while the newly commissioned *Tiger*[2] took the *Blücher* under fire. Beatty continued to gain on Hipper until the guns of the *Lion* reached the head of the enemy column. He then signaled, in accordance with current British naval gunfire doctrine, "Engage your opposite number." Since there were five British vessels to four German, this command produced some confusion. The captain of the *Tiger,* incorrectly assuming that the rearmost British vessel could reach the

[2] The *Tiger* was the only British battle cruiser in this action equipped with the director system of central fire control.

rearmost German, counted from the rear forward and joined the *Lion* in massing fire on the *Seydlitz*. The other captains, counting from van to rear, left the *Moltke* to the *Tiger*. The *Princess Royal* took the *Derfflinger* as target, and the *New Zealand* took the *Blücher*. Thus for several vital minutes the *Moltke* did not come under fire, and the rearmost British ship, the *Indomitable,* could not reach a target.

Meanwhile the retiring German battle cruisers all massed fire on the *Lion,* endeavoring to put her out of action.[3] Before they suceeded, a 13.5-inch British shell struck the *Seydlitz,* penetrating an after turret and setting fire to charges in the reloading room below. Flames flashed down through the ammunition chamber, the adjacent ammunition space, and up into the other after turret. In an instant 159 men died in these seared spaces. Only the prompt action of a petty officer in flooding the after magazines saved the *Seydlitz* from destruction.

The Germans now obtained their first damaging hit on the *Lion,* as a shell ripped through the top of her forward turret. During the next hour she received several more hits. Shortly before eleven Beatty signaled the *Indomitable* to attack the *Blücher,* by this time a flaming hulk, listing and turning out of line to the north, well astern of the German battle cruisers. Then the *Lion* was struck by several shells in quick succession. Her speed dropped to 15 knots, and she took on a 10-degree list to port. At the same time her lookouts reported, "Submarines off the starboard bow." This informa-

tion, later proved false, caused Beatty to order his entire squadron to turn eight points to port.

As the *Lion* was obliged to fall out of the battle line, Beatty made three final flag signals: "Course northeast," "Attack the enemy rear," and "Keep closer to the enemy." With the line steaming almost directly into the wind, the flags were very hard to make out from positions astern of the flagship. Only the first two signals were seen and read by the other battle cruisers. Rear Admiral Archibald Moore, who now assumed command, was well back in the line in the *New Zealand.* He completely misundestood Beatty's intentions, which were to leave the already wrecked *Blücher* to the *Indomitable* and the light cruisers, and to press on with the *Tiger, Princess Royal,* and *New Zealand* after the three German battle cruisers, one of which was known to be severely damaged. Moore did not know that an imagined submarine contact had caused Beatty's port turn and supposed it was to make certain that the *Blücher* did not get away. Moreover the *Blücher* bore northeast, the course Beatty had last signaled. Obeying what he believed to be unequivocal commands, Moore led the entire line to join the light cruisers and overwhelm the old armored cruiser in a tornado of shells. The chance for a major British victory was thereby lost. The *Blücher* went down after a gallant, hopeless fight,[4] but the rest of Hipper's force made good its escape.

Although victorious, the British had missed the opportunity for a much greater victory because of faulty communications, confused initial target distribution, and the selection of the slow *New Zealand* for the second-in-command. The Germans had massed their fire on the leading British pursuer, whereas the British initially had tried to distribute their fire evenly along the German column. Through Moore's misunderstanding of Beatty's intentions, the British finally massed against the already beaten *Blücher.* Intentional massing of German fire thus led to an unintentional massing of British fire that permitted the German battle cruisers to escape.

The near-loss of the *Lion* should have taught

---

[3] When major warships attained accurate, long-range fire in the early years of the 20th century, some naval theorists advocated massing the *fire* of one's entire line against one ship at a time in the enemy line. This was of course equivalent to the massing of *ships* against a part of the enemy line in sailing ship days, and a similar objection was raised against it: it invited the enemy ships not under fire to mass fire on a portion of one's own column. It was generally agreed however that massing of fire was good tactics in certain circumstances—notably on the head of the enemy column when crossing his T, or on the head of a pursuing column when the enemy flagship was in the van. In the latter situation, the ships in the column being pursued could more readily reach the head of the pursuing column than the ships in the pursuing column could reach the head of the column being pursued. Putting the flagship out of action could be counted on to produce confusion among the pursuers.

[4] Before she plunged, a British photographer obtained one of the war's most vivid action shots, later widely publicized, showing her listing over on her port side, survivors clinging to her side, underwater hull exposed, and guns pointing crazily skyward.

the British the lesson that turret tops should carry at least as much protective armor as the vertical sides of the turrets and the barbettes, if not more; also that flameproof scuttles between handling rooms and magazines are essential safety features. The Germans learned; the British did not. The Germans strengthened their battle cruisers' side plating and turret tops, and improved their magazine systems and techniques to reduce the chance of flash-back. The British did however hasten to install directors and central fire control in their battle cruisers.

The Germans had good reason to be proud of the stoutness of construction of their battle cruisers. Despite severe punishment, the *Seydlitz* made it back to her anchorage under her own power at only slightly reduced speed. Her captain reported however that his ammunition allowance had been insufficient, only 200 rounds remaining. His recommendation for more magazine space and more ammunition for the German battle cruisers was approved and acted on.

The Germans were at fault in sending the obsolescent *Blücher* with the faster battle cruisers. Hipper, in his action report strongly recommended that in the future only fast vessels be included in the battle cruiser line. Although the loss of the *Blücher* had contributed to Hipper's escape, the sending along of a sacrificial victim to draw the enemy's fire scarcely commended itself as tactical doctrine.

The Dogger Bank action cost Admiral Ingenohl his job. Incorrectly anticipating that the German battle cruisers would be engaging inferior British forces, he made no arrangements to support Hipper. Earlier he had failed to have battle cruisers available for the action at Heligoland Bight. Admiral Pohl, who succeeded him in command of the German fleet, was advised by the Kaiser to be more cautious than his predecessor.

Summary

The outbreak of World War I found Britain in the strategic situation common to all her wars with France except the War of the American Revolution: (1) she had the most powerful navy in the world; (2) she had powerful allies on the Continent; (3) she was able to blockade the enemy's coast while she herself had free access to the sea; (4) her enemy was an aggressive, centrally located West European power, committed to continental strategy and without a realistic fleet doctrine. Instead however of reverting to her pre-Trafalgar peripheral strategy, Britain chose to resume the strategy of the Fourth Coalition by placing an army on the Continent to support her allies on the Western Front. This decision proved fortunate, for in the first campaign of the war Britain's army provided the thin margin of military power that saved France from prompt defeat. Germany, instead of using her interior position to hold an unready Russia with light forces while smashing the Western Front, was now obliged to balance her available strength between two fronts.

The unreadiness of the British Admiralty for controlling operations was demonstrated by the escape of the German cruisers *Goeben* and *Breslau* to Constantinople, where they were instrumental in bring Turkey into the war on the side of the Central Powers. It was further demonstrated by the failure of planning and communications that nearly produced a clash of British forces in the Heligoland Bight Action (August 28, 1914). Nevertheless the Royal Navy early revealed its efficiency by covering the transport of British troops to France without a single loss. The shortcomings of the German naval high command were revealed in both the Heligoland Bight and Dogger Bank (January 24, 1915) actions, in which strong German forces were unready to support weaker German forces in contact with the British.

In the early stages of World War I, neither cruiser warfare nor blockade played a vital part. Except for local and small-scale successes, Germany's cruiser war proved a disappointment to her hopes—not only in failing to disrupt Britain's commerce but also in failing to cause Britain to weaken her Home Fleets in order to protect trade and the distant outposts of her Empire. The Royal Navy, early taxed by the threat of German warships at sea and humiliated in the Battle of Coronel (November 1, 1914), avenged itself in the Battle of the Falklands (December 8, 1914), and ruthlessly hunted down the individual German raiders. Britain's tight blockade however at first proved less effective than in earlier wars.

It soon appeared that the railroad, which had revolutionized land transportation, and the achievements of scientists in creating substitute materials, had lessened the effect of naval blockade against continental powers. The Central Powers could be reduced to want but not to quick defeat by loss of access to the sea. Nevertheless the Allied Powers possessed an immense advantage in their ability to use the oceans while denying their use to their foes.

The mine and the submarine early influenced naval operations. The British fleet could not approach close enough to force the Germans out of their anchorage. British naval officers became cautious in pursuit lest they be led over mine fields or into submarine ambush. The German fleet, recognizing its statistical inferiority, avoided contact with the full strength of the British fleet. As a result the surface naval war, soon confined to the narrow waters of the North Sea, was reduced to attempts to ambush segments of the enemy fleet. The situation here became a stalemate, with the British Grand Fleet and the German High Seas Fleet serving merely as fleets-in-being to restrain the operations of the other.

On land too the war soon reached a stalemate. Outflanking attempts by both sides on both fronts merely extended the fronts. At this particular moment in the development of weapons, the defensive had a slight advantage over the offensive. Men dug into the earth and could not be dug out. By November 1914, the Western Front had become an entrenched line meandering 450 miles from Belgium's North Sea coast across northern France to the Swiss border. The Eastern Front was almost as stabilized. Allied forces on the two fronts could not coordinate, taking advantage of their exterior position, for want of sufficient strength, for want of unified command, and for want of adequate communications.

23:
The Campaign for Constantinople

The stabilization of the Western Front in the fall of 1914 turned the war of movement into a war of grinding attrition. Millions of men and vast quantities of munitions were fed fruitlessly from both sides into a line that did not shift significantly in four years.

With a view to breaking the stalemate, the Allied High Command early began examining the possibilities of outflanking the Western Front by means of peripheral operations. French military leaders generally opposed such operations because peripheral attacks might withdraw or withhold troops from France. Here, said they, the Allies were barely holding their own. Any weakening of the Allied position in France would surely open the way for a German advance. With this point Lord Kitchener was in agreement, but he continued nevertheless to look for some way around the impasse. Since both geography and the manpower situation required that any outflanking attempt be mainly or exclusively a naval operation, the problem was referred to the British Admiralty.

The main objective of the peripheralists was to join hands with Russia. Such a juncture could mean more effective employment of Russian military manpower. It would enable the western Allies to provide Russia with munitions, of which she was in short supply, and to draw from Russia vast quantities of grain and other foodstuffs, which she had in excess since Turkey had closed the Dardanelles to her exports. A successful Russian offensive would take the pressure off the Western Front, it would incline the wavering Balkan States and Greece toward the Allied side, and it would offset the influence of Turkey.

The state of Russian railroads in 1914 did not commend use of the Arctic Ocean-Archangel route—to be employed later in World War II. Neutral Persia and belligerent Turkey blocked the Persian Gulf route, even if there had been adequate railway connections in this area. The inadequacy of the Trans-Siberian Railroad from Vladivostok had been demonstrated in the Russo-Japanese War. Clearly if a waterway was to be opened between the western Allies and Russia, it would have to be via the Baltic Sea or via the Black Sea.

The German High Seas Fleet controlled the Baltic; it could not be assailed directly without endangering the vital Allied control of the English Channel. Yet Lord Fisher preferred the Baltic route. He proposed defeating the High Seas Fleet by mounting a series of amphibious raids into Germany, beginning on the North Sea and working around into the Baltic. Fisher argued that repeated assaults, each by an army division and pre-dreadnoughts, would provoke several battles on terms favorable to the Grand Fleet. Eventually, he insisted, attrition would eliminate the High Seas Fleet and give Britain a Baltic beachhead where Russian troops could land for the decisive campaign—directed at Berlin. Kitchener opposed Fisher's Northern Project because it would divert troops from France. Churchill at first espoused the Project, but in the face of Kitchener's prestige he could win no support in the British War Council.

So long as Turkey remained neutral, treaty agreements closed the Black Sea by denying the Turkish Straits to belligerent shipping. But when Turkey joined Germany in late October 1914, the treaty neutralizing the Straits no longer applied. Britain could now open a waterway to Russia by capturing Con-

EUROPE, FALL OF 1914

stantinople. Gradually Churchill's interest shifted from hard fighting in the Baltic to a less costly assault up the Dardanelles and across the Sea of Marmora. In December he wrote Fisher, "I am shy of landing under fire—unless there is no other way." By Christmas 1914 he was ready to advocate purely naval action against Constantinople. Kitchener also wanted to strengthen Russia till she could open a decisive second front. He too preferred a naval effort toward Constantinople because it would divert few Allied troops from France. By early January 1915 agreement in principle between Churchill and Kitchener opened the way for a decision in the War Council. It also sub-

jected the Admiralty to a costly contest of wills between Fisher and Churchill.

Events in the Middle East brought the issue to a head. Turkey, in line with her expansion plan, invaded the Russian Caucasus. The Russian Army chief thereupon asked Kitchener if Britain could manage a diversion in the Aegean that would draw Turkish infantry from the Russian border. Kitchener gave prompt assurance that Britain would act. He then talked to Churchill about the possibility of a naval assault to be launched without delay up the Dardanelles. This talk crystallized Churchill's growing preference for action in the Middle East and assured him strong support in the

War Council. The Turkish invasion of Russia quickly collapsed, but it had already served as a powerful catalyst to British military thinking.

The Decision Where to Act

Churchill fought hard for War Council approval of his new project. To get around the Council's lack of a general staff, he directed Admiralty planners to produce a staff study that would force the Councillors to act. Fisher was chairman of the Admiralty officers who studied the Turkish project. His staff paper began by asserting that Constantinople must be the strategic objective of any campaign to open a waterway from the Aegean into Russia. Fisher then listed the following conditions as essential for converting Constantinople into an Allied base: (1) the operation must begin promptly to forestall Turkish counteraction; (2) an army division must support a strong pre-dreadnought squadron supplemented by minesweepers as well as by troop transports and supply ships; (3) no ship should enter the Sea of Marmora before the Dardanelles was safe for unarmored merchantmen; (4) troops and their gear must be combat-unit loaded in England or Egypt to permit prompt landing at the Straits; (5) one man must command all Allied forces in the campaign; (6) at the outset, regimental units must seize each headland flanking the Dardanelles mouth; (7) with troops covering each flank, and as fast as sweepers cleared the mine fields, gunnery ships must move up the Dardanelles supporting the troops ashore until the latter controlled all dominating heights; (8) with the Dardanelles secure for unarmored merchantmen, pre-dreadnoughts must convoy troops to Constantinople and cover their prompt landing. Other senior officers at the Admiralty supplemented Fisher's basic staff paper by stressing the paramount need for secure passage of unarmored supply and transport vessels through the Dardanelles as a prerequisite for attacking Constantinople.

This unanimous judgment of his senior planners confronted Churchill with a dilemma. Kitchener had promised Russia that Britain would move against Constantinople, and Churchill had promised Kitchener that the navy would do the job with very little help from the army. But senior Admiralty officers, documenting their analysis by specific reference to previous failures in the Sea of Marmora, insisted that no squadron of ships then available could menace Constantinople without at least a division of infantry. Churchill knew that Kitchener would refuse to divert so many troops from France.

Churchill lacked the prestige to override Kitchener or to overrule a solid phalanx of senior officers in the Navy. He resolved the dilemma by outflanking his Admiralty staff. First he branded Fisher's staff paper as hopelessly out of date because it relied on experience from the past. Twentieth-century weapons, particularly large-caliber naval guns, Churchill asserted, were so revolutionary that they wiped out lessons learned in earlier wars. Then the First Lord by-passed Fisher and appealed directly to Vice Admiral Sackville H. Carden, commanding in the Aegean. Could Carden's squadron, Churchill asked, force the Dardanelles by using naval gunfire alone and without infantry support.

Carden answered by telegraph with a prompt affirmative. If the Admiralty sent out several minesweepers and unlimited ammunition, Carden added, his squadron would attack by February 15 and reach Constantinople in mid-March. Carden also produced an operational outline prepared by his staff, which divided the proposed assault into four distinct steps:

STEP 1. Destroy all forts at the Dardanelles mouth.

STEP 2. Sweep mine fields as far upstream as the Narrows.

STEP 3. Reduce forts within the Narrows.

STEP 4. Sweep mines from the Narrows, eliminate forts and mines above the Narrows, and enter the Sea of Marmora.

Armed with the telegram from his admiral nearest the proposed objective, Churchill went before the War Council on January 15. In presenting the case there, he simply ignored Fisher's staff paper with its heavy emphasis on the need for infantry to support ships. Churchill also ignored the fact that Carden's staff had offered no plan for dealing with mobile field artillery.

The War Council supported the Kitchener-Churchill-Carden project for using sea power in the Eastern Theater, but it did not authorize the Navy to begin operations. Instead, the Councillors directed the Admiralty to draw up plans "for a naval expedition in February to bombard and take the Gallipoli Peninsula with Constantinople as its objective." When completed, the new staff paper was to be submitted to the War Council for final approval before active operations began. Complicating the work of the Admiralty planners was a basic conflict between the language of the War Council directive and the Kitchener-Churchill-Carden concept. Technically *naval expedition* implied the use of marines or seamen-infantry, and *take the Gallipoli Peninsula* implied the landing of men armed to hold positions ashore. Thus the War Council directive fell much closer to Fisher's first staff paper than it did to the Churchill-Carden plan for combat by naval gunfire alone.

Again guided by Fisher, the Admiralty planners drafted a second staff study for the War Council. It was a sharply modified version of their first paper, differing from the Churchill-Carden plan in only one significant respect. Convinced that the Turks would mine the lower Dardanelles and then defend their mine fields with mobile field artillery as well as with fortress guns, they insisted on a modest infantry force to capture or destroy the guns.

Churchill however still backed Carden's assertion that naval gunfire alone could breach the outer defenses of Constantinople. Instead of settling this significant professional disagreement behind Admiralty doors, Churchill arranged for the Prime Minister to hear and settle his differences with Fisher. On January 28 Asquith ruled for Churchill, thereby forcing Fisher to acquiesce or resign. Later the same day Churchill urged the War Council to accept the plan Carden had telegraphed two weeks earlier. The Councillors approved half of it, formally directing the Admiralty to carry out steps 1 and 2. But the fleet was to proceed beyond the Narrows only if results justified pressing on to Constantinople. The Council thus authorized no more than a naval reconnaissance-in-force one third of the way up the Dardanelles.

Intelligence Estimates

The difference of opinion dividing Churchill and Fisher was based not only on their differing concepts of what naval guns could do but in the degree of confidence each placed in British intelligence reports. The question here was whether British military intelligence was complete enough to form the basis for strategic planning. Churchill thought it was; Fisher thought not.

As early as December 1914 Turkish intelligence agencies had learned that a British effort against Constantinople was imminent. As a result, according to British intelligence, the Turkish government was on the brink of collapse. The frightened bureaucrats had entrusted the defense of Constantinople to the German ambassador, who had placed German Admiral Guido von Usedom in military command. Usedom, believing that his only hope lay in keeping Allied warships out of the Sea of Marmora, massed all his resources along twelve miles of water below the Dardanelles Narrows. There, according to foreign diplomats in Turkey, Usedom had sent workmen to repair forts and to mount heavy cannon. Thither also he had sent all his gunners and every mine and heavy shell he could muster. So meager were Usedom's resources, the reports stated, that he had left the landward faces of the forts undefended.

When Churchill studied the reports, he was not disturbed by their silence regarding the location of Turkish infantry and field artillery. He assumed that British intelligence had complete knowledge of all steps the defenders could take, and that the attackers might therefore draft military plans without any concern for alternative action by the enemy. Thus, it was with Usedom's weak defenses in mind that he backed the Carden plan for attack with ships alone. He assumed that a vigorous admiral could push through to Constantinople without using either army or naval infantry. Backed by Kitchener in the conviction that Constantinople would fall of her own weight, Churchill won the assent of the War Council and then forced the Carden plan on the Admiralty.

Fisher and other competent officers in the

Admiralty refused to accept Churchill's version of conditions in Turkey. Knowing from professional experience that intelligence reports rarely contain the whole truth, they followed the prudent rule of basing war plans upon what the enemy might be capable of doing rather than on an informed guess of what he would probably do. Hence the Admiralty officers insisted on infantry support for the ships fighting their way up the Dardanelles because the Turks might muster enough mobile field artillery to prevent wooden minesweepers from opening the Strait. They insisted moreover on army support as soon as the ships reached Constantinople because rioting street mobs could prevent small naval detachments from organizing an advanced base in the city.

The Admiralty officers were entirely correct in distrusting the British intelligence reports. The reports, based largely on diplomatic sources, were correct as far as they went, but they completely overlooked a vital part of the military picture. More specifically, they did not take into account the activities of General Liman von Sanders, head of the German military mission to Turkey. At odds with his own ambassador, Sanders had been forced out of Constantinople. Thereafter the foreign diplomats in the Turkish capital seem to have forgotten that he was still in Turkey.

In fact Sanders had made close contact with a faction of "Young Turk" officers who despised their central government. Toward the end of 1914 they arranged for Sanders to command "their" army stationed along the Bosporus. Significantly this army did not rely on the government in Constantinople but drew its logistic support from local officials in Asia Minor.

Aware of the impending British attack, Sanders traveled through portions of Asia Minor to study the prospects of defending Constantinople. His estimate of the situation emphasized the following points: (1) no enemy could convert Constantinople into an advanced base until he landed enough troops to police the entire city; (2) the Allies could not move essential troops into Constantinople without first winning an amphibious beachhead along the Bosporus or on the Gallipoli peninsula; (3) Russia lacked the ships to establish an amphibious base on the Bosporus; (4) the British could not win a Gallipoli beachhead until they assembled amphibious infantry at some yet-undeveloped advanced base in the upper Aegean; (5) Usedom's mine fields would check warships below the Narrows until British amphibious infantry assembled, but only if reinforced by at least one regiment of mobile field artillery. Acting promptly, Sanders sent engineers from his own army to repair bridges in Asia Minor so that an artillery regiment could march from the Bosporus to the lower Dardanelles without passing through Constainople. By keeping steps for this reinforcement secret, even from Usedom, Sanders also kept it from filtering into British intelligence reports.

At the end of January, strategists in both Britain and Turkey were gambling heavily on the accuracy of their respective intelligence reports. The War Council decision to send Carden up the Dardanelles without army support was in effect a gamble that no one could reinforce Usedom at the Straits or in Constantinople. Kitchener, Churchill, Carden, Usedom, and the diplomats in Constantinople were all in agreement with the War Council assumption. Fisher and Sanders rejected it. When Fisher argued that Carden must be prepared to drive field artillery from the Strait and then fight for Constantinople, he had no inkling that Sanders was taking steps to make his prediction come true. Sanders, acting on his own initiative, trained the Bosporus army for last-ditch defense of Constantinople. Much preferring to fight in Asia Minor or on Gallipoli, he gambled that no British infantry would land along the Strait before March 1, when his bridges in Asia Minor would support reinforcements for Usedom. The arrival of Sanders' reinforcements would then oblige the British to land troops.

Every decisive incident in the campaign for Constantinople, as well as its bitter outcome, derived ultimately from the fact that the British based their strategy on an assumption about Turkish intentions, while Sanders acted on his professional knowledge of British capabilities. Churchill gambled everything on his estimate that ships would force the Dardanelles

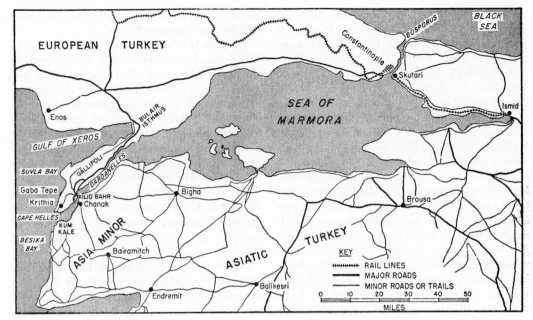

THE TURKISH ROAD NET

without the risk of landing infantry under fire. Sanders bet heavily on making the British fight his army in Asia Minor or on Gallipoli instead of in the streets of Constantinople.

The Dardanelles Attack: Preliminaries

The War Council's decision to launch Carden's squadron up the Dardanelles no later than February 15, 1915 gave the Admiralty a mere 18 days for preparation. The decision also meant that Usedom would have to withstand 14 days of attack before his unexpected artillery reinforcements from Sanders could arrive. Inside the Strait, the defenders waited uneasily. In London, Churchill by-passed Fisher and handled personally all Admiralty preparation for Carden's attack.

Though Churchill arranged to send Carden additional firepower, he failed to provide him with an advanced base in the Aegean. At Tenedos, an island 20 miles south of the Dardanelles mouth, the Aegean squadron used an anchorage lacking facilities for even emergency repairs. In Mudros harbor at the island of Lemnos, 40 miles southwest of the Darda-

nelles, Churchill planned in due course to set up an amphibious base. But in early February there was at Mudros only a fishing village with one rickety pier to serve a large and windy anchorage. The nearest place suitable for combat-loading of troops was Alexandria, 700 miles from Gallipoli. The nearest fleet base was equally distant at Malta. Here Carden's pre-dreadnoughts were reinforced by four obsolete French battleships, two new British battle cruisers, a new British battleship, some wooden minesweepers manned by civilian fishermen, and, in some concession to Fisher's opinion, two battalions of marines. Not altogether confident of Carden's resoluteness, Churchill also sent Rear Admiral John de Robeck as second-in-command and Commodore Roger Keyes as chief of staff in order to provide vigorous leadership.

By mid-February Usedom had manned heavy guns in strong forts at both the Narrows and the Dardanelles mouth. Rows of mines lay cross-channel from the Narrows almost to the entrance headlands. Fixed guns on Gallipoli and a few mobile field guns in the Asiatic ravines stood ready to catch hostile minesweepers in a crossfire laid down at close range. Entirely without riflemen to protect his ordnance, Usedom hoped fervently that the British would not land infantry. He made a final, desperate appeal to Germany for more mines and heavy shells.

As Carden's force steamed from Malta to Tenedos, de Robeck and Keyes reviewed Steps 1 and 2 of the Carden plan. They knew that the Dardanelles resembled a river flowing into the Aegean. At its mouth Cape Helles on Gallipoli and Kum Kale on the Asiatic shore formed entrance headlands 2,000 yards apart where the outgoing current flowed at four knots. To complete Step 1, Carden's force had to destroy all guns in the forts on the two headlands. To take Step 2, the Aegean squadron had to move upstream twelve miles to the Narrows, a short dog-leg 1,400 yards wide where the current ran at five knots. Overlooking the Narrows from Gallipoli lay Kilid Bahr plateau, the decisive point en route to Constantinople. Fortress guns on Kilid Bahr, supplemented by others in Fortress Chanak directly across the Strait, could fire heavy projectiles 12,000 yards downstream. To complete Step 2, Carden's gunnery ships had to prevent Turkish guns on both sides of the Strait from damaging the wooden minesweepers as they cleared mines from a broad channel right up to the Narrows and then use flat-trajectory, point-blank fire to dismount all guns at Chanak and Kilid Bahr.

Most experts agreed that, if Carden completed Step 2 quickly, he could push on to the outskirts of Constantinople without serious difficulty. But there was serious doubt about Carden's ability to maintain his squadron in the Sea of Marmora if any Turkish guns remained along the Strait to sink unarmored colliers and supply ships.

Step One

Carden reached Tenedos late on February 18. The next day, after waiting for the winter sun to rise high enough to disperse the morning shadows, he sent six of his heavy ships for deliberate fire against the forts at the Dardanelles mouth. Several hours of leisurely bombardment drove the Turkish gunners to cover, but they quickly manned their guns again when an Allied ship moved in close. Carden withdrew all his ships at dusk. He then waited

five days at Tenedos for weather he considered suitable for renewing his attack.

In their bombardment of February 25, the British used different tactics. While some of the heavy ships stood off at medium range and drove the Turkish gunners to shelter, the others closed rapidly to point-blank range. These, using flat-trajectory fire, reduced each of the entrance forts to rubble and dismounted a number of guns. Satisfied with the day's work, Carden again withdrew his heavy ships to Tenedos. He left de Robeck at the entrance to the Dardanelles to clear a channel upstream with the wooden minesweepers covered by destroyers. Instead of sweeping under cover of darkness, de Robeck waited until first light the next morning.

On the 26th accurate fire that destroyers could not suppress turned back de Robeck's sweepers before they had advanced four miles. De Robeck thereupon recalled his destroyers to support demolition parties he had improvised to complete Step 1 by blowing up the Turkish guns still mounted on the headlands. After hours of futile effort to persuade Carden that the time had come for using the marines, de Robeck sent in his demolition parties without infantry support. They were quickly repulsed by Turks already sifting back into the headland forts.

Carden now waited five more days for enough wind to lift reconnaissance seaplanes from the water. In the interval Sanders' field artillery regiment from the Bosporus by-passed Constantinople and marched over the newly repaired roads and bridges in Asia Minor to Chanak. Between March 1 and 4, batteries of this regiment took position on both shores of the Strait. On the 4th they threw back the marine battalions Carden finally sent onto each headland to dismount the fortress guns. Thus, after 16 days of sporadic Allied effort, a powerful Franco-British naval squadron had not completed Step 1 toward Constantinople, and Sanders' secret artillery reinforcement had arrived. From March 4 onward, conditions inside the Strait conformed to the estimates prepared by Fisher and Sanders instead of to assumptions by Kitchener, Churchill, Carden, Usedom, and the diplomats in Constantinople.

Carden began to sense that the situation had changed. At the end of February, he was bombarding the Admiralty with urgent calls for troops to land on Gallipoli in order to take Kilid Bahr from the rear. The increasing delay merely hardened Churchill's determination to follow the original plan. He did not push the lagging work at Mudros, press Kitchener to send troops from Egypt to Gallipoli, or relieve Carden. Instead he goaded his hesitant admiral with a whole flight of angry telegrams. Stung into action, Carden undertook to carry out the intent of Step 1 by posting his ships to neutralize the Turkish guns on the headlands whenever Allied vessels entered the Strait.

Step Two

Carden's staff began Step 2 during the first week in March while their admiral continued to call fruitlessly for army support. Minesweepers operating at night, escorted by destroyers that failed to suppress artillery fire, cleared a channel to within 9,000 yards of Kilid Bahr. On March 7 two old battleships entered the Dardanelles in daylight and closed to within 12,000 yards of the Narrows, hurling salvos as they steamed back and forth across the channel until the fortress gunners upstream ceased fire. Carden did not seize this opportunity to send sweepers forward to clear a path for the battleships to close and employ the point-blank, flat-trajectory fire that alone could dismount the fortress guns. Instead he withdrew all Allied vessels from the Strait. The following night a single Turkish vessel laid a long string of mines perpendicular to the cross-channel tracks of the bombarding battleships.

Still goaded by Churchill, Carden tried to make his minesweepers more efficient. With volunteers from the fleet to stiffen their crews, the sweepers made a determined effort each night from the 10th through the 16th to move above the mine field and sweep downstream with the current. But the gunners in the battleships and destroyers supporting the nightly sorties could not adapt their blue-water fire control methods to the firefly targets offered by the mobile field guns. The sweepers and their gear suffered so heavily that most of the mines laid on the 8th remained unswept at dawn on the 18th. The failure to improvise a

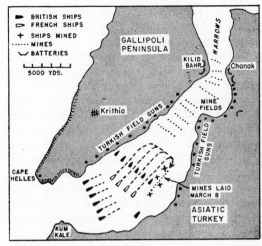

NAVAL ACTION OF MARCH 18, 1915

sure technique for sweeping mines at night produced the climax of Step 2.

Since early March Churchill had been pressing for daylight assault of Kilid Bahr and Chanak, insisting however that no ship should pass the Narrows while Turkish mine fields lay unswept. Convinced that any daylight attack would fail, Carden was sleeping little and eating scarcely at all. Nevertheless, on the 16th he wired Churchill that the climactic effort would begin as soon as weather permitted. Then, at the insistence of physicians who feared his nervous collapse, he resigned his command. De Robeck, promoted to vice admiral, then set the all-out effort for March 18. Churchill promptly approved.

Day broke warm and clear on the 18th. As soon as shadows masking the enemy had dissolved, de Robeck deployed six heavy British ships in a support line 14,000 yards below the Narrows. Holding bows-on to the current and beyond range of the fortress guns, they battered Kilid Bahr and Chanak for a full hour. Then the four old French battleships moved through the support line and closed gradually to within 9,000 yards. For two more hours the French vessels, backed by the British support line, fired steadily at the Narrows forts while Turkish shells made a shambles of their topsides and holed two French hulls at the waterline. According to plan, de Robeck recalled the Frenchmen and moved up six British replacements. As the French column wheeled right onto a prearranged retirement course, it ran down the line of unswept and unsuspected mines laid on March 8. One battleship struck a mine and sank like a stone.

Firing deliberately from 9,000 yards, the six British ships in the new advance line gradually silenced all the guns at the Narrows. De Robeck then ordered his sweepers, now largely manned by officers and seamen from the fleet, to lead the gunnery ships forward. As the wooden craft advanced, field guns on each shore caught them in a devastating cross fire that the armored ships could not suppress. A hail of shell carried away sweeping kites, smashed rudders, and knocked out engines. Such craft as were still operational gathered in survivors as they retired behind the support line.

De Robeck had explicit orders from Churchill to sweep a channel before any ship entered the Narrows. Hence, when the minesweepers withdrew, he was obliged to recall the forward bombardment line. Taking the retirement course used by the French, two British battle cruisers struck mines. One made it heavily damaged out of the Strait, but the other began to sink. A British battleship, attempting to take the sinking battle cruiser in tow, also struck a mine and both ships went down. Heroic work brought off many survivors, but the climactic attack had failed. De Robeck had no recourse but to order a general retirement.

The Assessment

Through the night de Robeck and his staff held council and faced the facts. Four heavy Allied ships were lost and all vessels afloat required repair available no closer than Malta. Refit would require at least a month. Keyes sensed an enemy on the brink of defeat if some of the Allied destroyers could be converted into minesweepers. But even the sanguine Keyes admitted that the conversion would take at least two weeks, and even with destroyer-minesweepers available there remained the problem of moving unarmored colliers through the Narrows to support a squadron in the Marmora. Each of these factors weighed heavily with de Robeck; but Churchill's standing order against passing an unswept mine field proved decisive. The Aegean Squadron could

not enter the Narrows as long as Sanders' artillery remained on both shores of the lower Dardanelles.

Belatedly there was an alternative to attacking Constantinople with naval gunfire alone. On March 18, General Sir Ian Hamilton had reached Mudros with forward echelons of an army strong enough to move across Gallipoli onto Kilid Bahr. On the 20th de Robeck admitted that an amphibious landing on Gallipoli held the best hope for opening a way to Constantinople. Hamilton agreed. Together they recommended to London that fleet action inside the Strait be postponed until the army seized Kilid Bahr.

When Kitchener and Churchill insisted that the Constantinople campaign continue, the War Council acquiesced without formal meeting. No one in London liked the idea of postponing fleet action till Hamilton opened the Strait, but no one pressed hard for the only alternative—a coordinated army-navy assault against Kilid Bahr. Finally on the 28th Kitchener and Churchill formally canceled Step 2 of Carden's plan and directed Hamilton to open the gate to Constantinople. By using "impossible" roads in Asia Minor, Sanders had demonstrated that even modern ships must have either armored auxiliaries or infantry support when they fight in narrow waters against respectable artillery.

The Amphibious Assault: Preliminaries

The decision to land British troops on Gallipoli altered drastically the campaign for Constantinople. A desperate Turkish government gave Sanders command at the Dardanelles, thereby recognizing his army as the real defender of Constantinople. If Hamilton managed to take Kilid Bahr during March he could force Sanders to fight in European Turkey, away from his Asiatic supply base. If the Bosporus army reached Gallipoli before the British landed there, Hamilton could win Constantinople by defeating Sanders in battle or by pushing his army eastward into Asia Minor. Thus for the first time since mid-February, British arms held the initiative.

Liman von Sanders moved fast. As soon as he reached Gallipoli on March 26, he set all available men digging trenches. Working only at night, they threw up ragged lines of raw earth that implied the presence of at least a division of infantry supported by engineer battalions. Then Sanders started his Bosporus army toward Gallipoli, gambling that empty trenches would forestall a British landing while his own regiments were scattered along 200 miles of road and waterway.

Unaware of the crucial necessity for speed, the high command in London allowed Sanders a full month to organize his defenses. On March 12 Kitchener had given Hamilton command of four divisions earmarked to occupy Constantinople in April. The next day Hamilton was hustled off to the Aegean with neither staff nor plan. At the same time, the troops assigned to him began converging on Mudros —the 29th Army Division and a naval infantry division, from England; a French brigade, from Africa; Australians and New Zealanders, from Egypt. Kitchener made it clear that the 29th Division was Hamilton's mainstay. He insisted moreover that Hamilton was not to land a single man until the entire assigned force had arrived at Mudros ready for combat.

On March 19, just a week after Hamilton's notice to be ready in April, the new situation demanded an immediate landing on Gallipoli. But few of Hamilton's troops had yet arrived, and those that had were not ready for combat. The random battalions reaching Mudros were without field packs. Guns arrived without limbers, shells without primers. Key units of the 29th Division were still two weeks away. The medical staff had not left England. Converting Hamilton's scattered army into combat teams would require complete unloading, sorting, and reloading—an operation impossible at Mudros, with its few boats, single pier, and feeble shore establishment.

The illusion Sanders had created of Turkish strength on Gallipoli, Kitchener's explicit order against landing before the whole force was ready to fight, the lagging 29th Division— all these fell into a pattern that gave Hamilton no choice. With full agreement from responsible officers at Mudros, he rerouted all transports to Alexandria. Here combat-unit loading over cluttered wharfs occupied everybody for nearly a month—leaving no time for staff organization, thorough planning, tactical rehearsal, or organization of beachhead logistics.

Liman von Sanders made good use of the month of grace bestowed by the Admiralty's neglect of Mudros and the War Office's failure to ship out combat-ready units. Lacking water transport, Sanders' Bosporus regiments marched to the Sea of Marmora, ferried across to Asia Minor, and then marched to a ferry station at Chanak. To supplement his own army and its independent logistics, Sanders drew from Constantinople whatever infantry or supply a demoralized government would ship down the waterway or send over one narrow pack trail linking Gallipoli to a railroad in Europe. Engineers improved the poor roads on Gallipoli, with particular attention to the few wells on a notoriously dry peninsula. The Dardanelles provided an interior line for tactical maneuver, but an acute shortage of shipping held Sanders' margin of supply to the absolute minimum even for infantrymen who could (as one Englishman put it) "live off the smell of an oily rag."

The beaches in the Dardanelles area dictated Sanders' defensive disposition. He posted two divisions (15,000 men) at Kum Kale within easy march of several Asiatic beaches. At Bulair, 50 miles to the north, he ordered two more divisions to dig in behind a broad beach linked to the isthmus by a single long causeway across marsh land. His other two divisions (7,500 men in each) he placed on Gallipoli proper, basing one at Krithia village, the other near Kilid Bahr. Two companies of the Krithia division and all the divisional machine guns he stationed on the heights of Cape Helles, above the most suitable Gallipoli beach. He also scattered small outposts 15 miles along the Aegean shore above Helles to watch lesser beaches and sandy coves. The Kilid Bahr Division was his infantry reserve. The artillery attached to this division, he emplaced at Gaba Tepe on the Aegean shore opposite, where the guns could dominate the beach in this area. With his other field guns, Sanders lined the Strait below the Narrows— both to keep naval gunfire away from Kilid

Bahr, his strategic center, and to assure his own use of the Dardanelles for reinforcement and supply.

The six divisions of Turkish infantry thus lay like a scimitar along the Dardanelles, with strong units at the hilt and tip, a relatively thin center, the smallest possible outpost screen along the Aegean, and field guns along the inner edge of the blade. Sanders hoped Hamilton would entrap himself at Bulair, where coastal mountains blocked any march either toward Constantinople or toward Kilid Bahr. If Hamilton sidestepped from Bulair into Europe, the shallows of the inner Gulf of Xeros would cause him to lose touch with the fleet. If British artillery on the isthmus cut Sanders' lines to Constantinople, supply from Asia Minor could still sustain the Turkish left and center. Should Hamilton land in force near Kum Kale, Sanders expected the Turkish left flank to thrust the British inland, away from Kilid Bahr. Finally, if Hamilton should evade both flanks and land on Gallipoli, Sanders expected his field guns on the Strait to forestall any joint army-navy assault, and he trusted the hostile Gallipoli terrain to check the British for 72 hours. Shrewd as were his dispositions, Sanders had to gamble heavily that the British would not overrun Kilid Bahr before his inadequate pool of boats could ferry in reinforcements from his flanks.

While Sanders baited his traps and British divisions loaded their combat units, Hamilton laid plans of his own. A warning from Kitchener against entrapment in Asia ruled out any landing in force at Kum Kale. His own prudent estimate that Sanders could supply Kilid Bahr from Asia ruled out Bulair. Hamilton decided to feint realistically at both Turkish flanks, sending the French division of 16,000 men against Kum Kale and the Royal Naval Division of 10,000 against Bulair, while army units sprang a trap of their own on Gallipoli. He proposed to land the Australian and New Zealand Corps (Anzac) of 30,000 men at Gaba Tepe, where he expected the infantrymen to seize high ground in mid-peninsula and attract whatever troops Sanders had posted near Kilid Bahr. Simultaneously the 29th Division (17,000 men) would cross the only suitable beach on Cape Helles and

drive to Kilid Bahr after the Anzac forces had drawn off the defenders. A brigade in Egypt, which Hamilton had sought persistently as his reserve, was not released to him when the troops returned to Mudros, but he hoped to improvise a reserve by ordering the Naval Division to feint at Bulair without actually landing.

The curious coincidence of plans made by the opposing generals thus pitted 47,000 British soldiers against 15,000 Turks on Gallipoli, and gave the British 72 hours for reaching Kilid Bahr before Sanders could reinforce his thinly held center. Hamilton's obsessive secrecy however offset his clear advantage. A completely unpracticed army-navy team, commanded by a two-man committee (Hamilton and de Robeck), was about to undertake an amphibious assault upon brutal terrain. Yet, though he had ample time en route to Mudros, Hamilton did not explain his plan to his brigadiers and battalion commanders.

At nightfall on April 24, the French division and the Royal Naval Division were en route for their feints at Kum Kale and Bulair. Later, General Sir William R. Birdwood got under way with his Anzac force for a pre-dawn landing at Gaba Tepe. Major General Sir Aylmer Hunter-Weston waited off Mudros for sunrise, when his 29th Division would assail Cape Helles. Hamilton and his staff boarded ship to spend the next day afloat visiting both assault areas so that Hamilton could keep in touch with the generals to whom he had delegated tactical control. Hamilton's secrecy had prevented close reconnaissance of the hostile shore. Birdwood had no inkling that artillery from one Turkish division commanded Gaba Tepe. Hunter-Weston had no way of knowing that all the machine guns from another division covered Beach V, where his combat supply would go ashore. Nevertheless Hamilton's chance for success was good. Skillful feints at Kum Kale and Bulair would isolate the Turks on Gallipoli, where accurate naval gunfire could shatter beachhead defenses. But the fate of Constantinople hung on the answer to a single question: Was either of Hamilton's assault forces strong enough to by-pass prepared defenses and win a 72-hour race for Kilid Bahr?

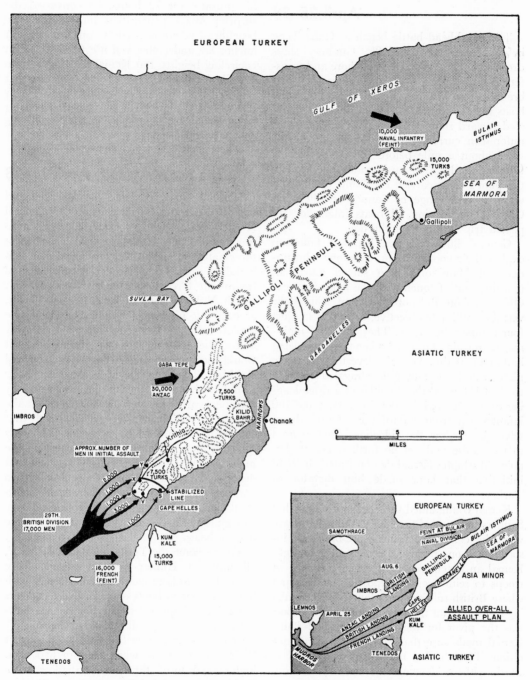

EUROPEAN TURKEY

GULF OF XEROS

10,000
NAVAL INFANTRY
(FEINT)

BULAIR
ISTHMUS

15,000
TURKS

*SEA OF
MARMORA*

Gallipoli

GALLIPOLI PENINSULA

SUVLA BAY

DARDANELLES

ASIATIC TURKEY

GABA TEPE

30,000
ANZAC

7,500
TURKS

KILID
BAHR

Krithia

NARROWS

Chanak

0   5   10
MILES

APPROX. NUMBER OF
MEN IN INITIAL ASSAULT

2,000

Y

1,000

X

7,500
TURKS

1,000

W

1,000

3,000

S

STABILIZED
LINE

CAPE HELLES

29TH.
BRITISH DIVISION.
17,000 MEN

1,000

KUM
KALE

15,000
TURKS

16,000
FRENCH
(FEINT)

IMBROS

TENEDOS

Allied Over-all Assault Plan inset:

EUROPEAN TURKEY

SAMOTHRACE

FEINT AT BULAIR
NAVAL DIVISION

BULAIR ISTHMUS

SEA OF
MARMORA

GALLIPOLI PENINSULA

DARDANELLES

AUG. 6

BRITISH
LANDING

ASIA MINOR

IMBROS

CAPE
HELLES

ALLIED OVER-ALL
ASSAULT PLAN

LEMNOS

APRIL 25

ANZAC LANDING

BRITISH LANDING

KUM
KALE

BRITISH LANDING

FRENCH LANDING

MUDROS
HARBOR

TENEDOS

ASIATIC TURKEY

GALLIPOLI: LANDINGS AND DISPOSITION OF FORCES, APRIL 25, 1915

The Anzac Beachhead, April 25–28

The beachhead battle began at Gaba Tepe before dawn on April 25. Gunnery ships dropped anchor 3,000 yards offshore and transferred into pulling boats the troops they had brought from Mudros. Steam trawlers took the boats in tow, formed a ragged line and struggled toward shore. In pre-dawn darkness, an unforeseen current pushed the flotilla northward about a mile before the boats cast off to cover the last 300 yards under oar. Luckily the pilot's error carried each unit of the first wave beyond range of Sanders' artillery on Gaba Tepe, leaving all boats intact for repeated trips throughout the day.

General Birdwood and his staff failed to exploit their good fortune. Everyone who understood Hamilton's plan stayed afloat all morning, out of touch with the landed troops. Officers ashore did not know that Kilid Bahr was their ultimate objective, or that it lay just four airline miles away. They saw only nightmarish terrain, far too broken for organizing battalions as they landed. Nevertheless, a few platoon and company units straggled up from the beach toward the shoulder of a ridge leading directly to Kilid Bahr. By 8 AM some 100 infantrymen from several units found themselves just below the ridgeline. They paused to reorganize and got no farther, for at that point Mustapha Kemal demonstrated the bold initiative that later made him dictator of Turkey.

Kemal commanded the reserve division that Sanders had posted near Kilid Bahr. At dawn, while he conducted routine pre-breakfast inspection of one regiment, a messenger brought Kemal an urgent request for one company of troops to reinforce an outpost above the spot where British soldiers were landing. Recognizing instantly that the ridge behind that outpost was the pivot for the defense of Kilid Bahr, Kemal made sure that his troops had ammunition. Then he led the entire regiment forward without feeding his men or asking permission to commit Sanders' general reserve. Sending back word for the rest of his division to follow, Kemal reached the top of the ridge barely in time to check the British advance.

Feeding in reinforcements as they arrived, he hung on throughout the day. Then, sustaining his pressure for 72 hours, he converted the surprise Anzac penetration into a defensive beachhead where not only troops but ships at anchor lay under observed fire from Turks on encircling heights. But Kemal had played into Hamilton's hands. The absolute urgency that required Kemal to move against Birdwell with the entire Gallipoli reserve left fewer than 8,000 Turks south of Kilid Bahr to face the assault of Cape Helles.

The Main Assault, April 25–28

Hamilton had delegated the planning and tactical control of his main assault to General Hunter-Weston, who expected to put his division onto Cape Helles in two echelons—a three-battalion assault force followed by a ten-battalion main body. Hunter-Weston wanted his assault force to win a divisional base at Beach V by 8 AM on April 25. By 10 AM, according to his plan, the main body would be deployed into a line stretching all the way across the tip of Gallipoli. By nightfall it would occupy a dominating ridge beyond Krithia village. On the 26th the main body would push on to Kilid Bahr, supported by divisional artillery and by survivors of the assault force. Hunter-Weston assumed that the ships' fire would be accurate. The only difficulty he anticipated lay in deploying the main body by 10 AM on the 25th. To meet that deadline, he tried to plan his way around two major obstacles: the strong defenses at Beach V, the only clear stretch of Helles shore large enough for a divisional base, and an inadequate pool of boats.

To overcome the Turks defending Beach V, all units of Hunter-Weston's assault force would have to land nearly simultaneously with few casualties to boats or men. Swift currents around the Cape ruled out landing in darkness. A dawn assault would bring heavy casualties. An attack in full daylight could not begin before 10 AM, when the sun had risen high enough to lift the morning shadows from Beach V. On advice from the navy, Hunter-Weston set his beach assault for sunrise. Between first light and the time when the rising sun would cast long, black shadows to conceal the defenders from the naval gunners, the fleet could give the assault troops a full hour of presumably accurate gunfire support. To give the assault force momentum, the General arranged to send in all three battalions together—one, in the conventional pulling boats; the other two, aboard the collier *River Clyde,* which had been hurriedly converted into a landing ship. This three-battalion landing force, if it got safely ashore, would have ample strength to overrun the defending infantry and man a perimeter above Beach V by 8 AM.

Stretching the navy boat pool to land a full division, followed by supply for 48 hours of combat, required even greater ingenuity. Hunter-Weston decided to land his main body in two echelons, with five battalions going ashore at sunrise over four small beaches (S, W, X, and Y) that flanked Beach V. Naval gunfire from first light till sunrise would, the General hoped, enable these to go ashore intact and leave boats available to push the five remaining battalions of the main body over Beach V as soon as it was secured. They would then deploy into line and pick up the flank battalions as they pushed on to Krithia. After all the infantry had landed, boats already used twice would bring artillery, ammunition, and water onto Beach V.

When the time came to convert this intricate plan into action, Hunter-Weston expected to control the entire movement personally—just as he would if his division were fighting conventionally on land. To forestall independent action, he ordered each flank battalion to wait above its own beach until the main body moved up Gallipoli, and then join the advancing line. Hunter-Weston assigned no general officer to land with the early echelon of his main body, made no plan for using the main body to exploit a hard fight at Beach V, and gave no battalion commander a briefing about D-day objectives. Hence when April 25 dawned, the 29th Division was tied to a rigid plan, in which everything depended on accurate naval gunfire during the hour before sunrise.

The navy opened fire according to plan soon after dawn on the 25th. Two battleships and a cruiser, lying 2,000 yards offshore, raised a luminous cloud over Beach V. Firing without forward observers to spot the fall of shot, ships'

gunners made no direct hit on any machine gun or barbed wire entanglement. When the harassing fire moved inland, the dazed Turks had a full ten minutes to crawl back into their semicircle of tumbled rock as the rising sun lit up their natural shooting gallery.

The assault force was now moving toward Beach V, a cove rimmed with a narrow strip of sand from which the ground sloped upward, forming a sort of ampitheater. Silence fell as the distant naval guns ceased fire. Into the Turkish ambush rowed a thousand men. The *River Clyde* followed close behind with nearly two thousand more concealed below. Astern she towed lighters that her commanding officer hoped to rig into a floating gangway. There were no gunboats nearby to provide close support—such as the British had used in the Aboukir assault of 1801, and the British and Americans were to use in the amphibious assaults of World War II. The only offensive weapons carried by the assault force were the rifles of the infantrymen and two sandbag-protected machine guns mounted topside in the *River Clyde*. The assumption was that the hour of area fire from the three ships a mile offshore would wipe out all effective opposition at the beachhead. Had not Churchill insisted that the modern naval gun rendered the lessons of history invalid?

The lead boats touched bottom, yards from dry land. At that instant, the silence was broken by a volley from the slopes and crest of the ampitheater, slaughtering most of the advance batallion and destroying all but a half dozen of their irreplaceable boats. The *Clyde* then grounded, her machine guns silencing fire from the enemy center. Seamen leaped overboard and manhandled the lighters forward. Waist deep in chilly water, hanging on to lines, they shouted for the infantrymen to hit the beach. Few made it. Crossfire from both flanks filled the lighters with dead, and killed or wounded the seamen holding the lighters in place. By the time a battalion had left the *Clyde*, 700 casualties blocked the drifting gangway. Raw courage was not enough without accurate fire to support it. After more than an hour of desperate struggle, the invaders abandoned their effort to land. All day a handful of British hugged the lowest rocks ashore, and a thousand infantrymen lay below decks in the *Clyde,* while the two sandbagged machine guns held the Turks at bay.

At Beach W, a few hundred yards west around Cape Helles, the British had somewhat better luck. There, as at V, naval guns fired for an hour from 2,000 yards—with the same negative result. As the sun rose, Turkish infantrymen returned to their rifle pits on a pockmarked cliff. At the same time, three companies from one battalion of the British main body rowed up to a narrow shelf of gravel, while their reserve company waited offshore. As at Beach V, touchdown by the first boats triggered a rifle volley that wiped out the first British wave and tore up most of the boats. The reserve company thereupon veered left behind an outcropping that masked Turkish fire and, scaling the cliff, got above the defenders. A spontaneous effort by this company to drive along the cliff top toward Beach V produced a day-long struggle.

Though Sanders had been lured north by reports of the feint at Bulair, his subordinates in southern Gallipoli acted with nearly the same quick efficiency that Kemal had shown at Gaba Tepe. All day Turkish reserves marched from Krithia faster than the few remaining boats could land British reinforcements. By mid-morning Hunter-Weston had lost all of his brigadiers, leaving him in personal command of a firefight to win the base ashore. Finally, when dusk hid them from Turkish snipers, boated British infantrymen broke through to Beach V. The *Clyde* survivors landed under cover of darkness and joined them in a thin perimeter. Here weary men stood to arms all night, firing sporadically at Turks who clung to rubble at the British right.

Completely absorbed in the struggle for his critical beachhead, Hunter-Weston ignored good news from Beaches S, X, and Y. Naval gunfire from 500 yards, instead of from 2,000, had enabled four of the flank battalions to establish beachheads with slight loss. Then Hunter-Weston's failure to brief his battalion commanders cost him heavily. The commanders had not been told that the immediate British objective was the ridge beyond Krithia. The ridge was plainly visible from the beachheads, an hour's march away. It was undefended after 10 AM, when heavy fighting about Beach W stripped Krithia of Turks. Uninformed, four fresh battalions waited all day for word from their general.

General Hamilton, in his battleship, remained off Gaba Tepe on the 25th until vague messages about trouble at Beach V sent him steaming toward Helles. En route, about 10 AM, he saw British troops idling above Beach Y with no sign of any enemy. He thereupon advised Hunter-Weston by radio to shift his main landing over to Beach Y. When Hunter-Weston replied that the navy lacked boats to land men anywhere but at Beach V, Hamilton was tempted to take personal command of the battalions already landed at Beaches S, X, and Y. He decided however to wait until he had talked with Hunter-Weston. At about the same time one of his staff officers, studying charts, perceived the totally unexpected opportunity to march up a 12-mile ravine leading from Beach Y directly to Kilid Bahr. He urged Hamilton to bring the Naval Division down from off Bulair and send it up this natural corridor. Hamilton refused. It was far too early, said he, for him to commit his only strategic reserve.

After Hamilton visited Hunter-Weston and observed the critical boat situation for himself, he said no more about exploiting Beach Y. At dusk on the 25th, the Turks began night-long harassment at each of the beachheads. The next morning the two battalions at Beach Y, having disintegrated during the night, withdrew without orders, but the battalions at the other beaches held fast. Before noon on the 26th, the beachhead at V was handling supplies. By nightfall the Division held a secure line from Beach X across Gallipoli to Beach S. Though it had taken Hunter-Weston two full days, he had succeeded in carving out an adequate beachhead 24 hours before Turkish reinforcements from Kum Kale or Bulair could block the way to Kilid Bahr.

There were however no troops available to exploit the British opportunity. The 29th Division, virtually without sleep for three nights and burdened by the need to manhandle supplies up from the waterfront, could not move on April 27. Hamilton still refused to commit his corps reserve. The reserve brigade he had been begging for since March still idled in Egypt. When at last Hunter-Weston's division pressed forward on April 28, it was too late. Fresh Turkish units, rushed in from the flanks, quickly halted the British advance. Sanders had won his gamble.

At the time no one recognized that Hamilton's best opportunity had passed. Failure to rehearse for major amphibious assault had deprived both de Robeck and Hamilton of the chance to correct in advance a myriad of small technical errors that cost the infantry dearly. Inadequate staff work in London, poor naval gunfire support, a shortage of boats, and Kemal's inspired initiative all played their part in the British failure. Nevertheless, Hamilton could have unlocked the gates to Constantinople at mid-morning on April 25 by exploiting his priceless opportunity to seize Kilid Bahr with the four fresh battalions ashore backed up by his Naval Division.

Stalemate

From May through December of 1915, neither the Turks nor the British were able to advance. Logistic weaknesses on both sides reduced the campaign to a long-drawn-out artillery duel. Turkish field guns, moved away from the Strait into strong redoubts at Helles, held their own against naval ordnance and stopped each British charge by firing into the flanks of the advancing infantry. At the Anzac beachhead, continual harassing fire kept the Australians and New Zealanders from assembling an assault force. Allied naval gunners improved with experience, but they never learned to deliver on call the pinpoint fire required to support an infantry breakthrough. And when some ship registered her guns on an enemy trench, the Turks, under cover of darkness, simply dug forward so close to British lines that the naval shells struck friend as well as foe. When the Turks left their trenches, a combination of fire from small arms and naval guns always stopped them. Throughout the long stalemate, trench systems expanded, logistic demands increased in geometric progression, and casualties mounted.

Even though naval gunfire could not pave the way for an advance to Kilid Bahr, the navy did provide the logistic margin that kept the Allied troops on Gallipoli. At Anzac and Helles, ammunition, drinking water, medicine, and food—delivered daily in all weathers—sustained infantry clinging to the inhospitable terrain. Artificial harbors that the navy built

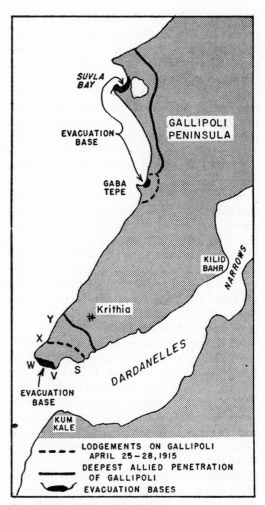

GALLIPOLI: FINAL SITUATION

at Helles anticipated by 30 years the larger structures constructed off Normandy in 1944. Armored boats with bow ramps foreshadowed the LST of World War II. So busy was the Navy with logistics and support fire that only its submarines made any independent contribution to the campaign during the entire stalemate.

From late April through December a heroic handful of British and French submariners showed how really determined men can make the "impossible" look easy. Small submarines, designed for brief missions in shallow water, repeatedly penetrated the Dardanelles for patrols in the Sea of Marmora. Such operations entailed endurance beyond anything anticipated by the boats' designers or builders. The tiny craft were too slow on the surface to breast the Dardanelles current, and had too little endurance submerged to take full advantage of counter-currents beneath the surface. Nevertheless most of them managed to navigate the 35-mile Strait, patrol the Marmora, and return. When the Turks laid a submerged net across the Narrows, the submariners broke through by ramming into the net and then surging ahead or astern till something gave way. In the Sea of Marmora one- or two-boat patrols harassed Turkish shipping for seven months. They destroyed supply vessels, sank two ships moored in Constantinople, shot up trains, and raided briefly ashore. If Sanders had been forced to rely solely on supply transported by ship down from Constantinople, these submarines would have provided the margin for Allied victory. But a steady trickle of supply from Asia Minor found its way across the Dardanelles in small ferries and satisfied the minimum needs of the Turks holding Gallipoli.

All through the long stalemate a few bulldog wills persisted in seeking some way to put British guns onto decisive Kilid Bahr. On August 6 Hamilton, by then commanding 120,000 men, set ashore two green divisions at Suvla Bay on the Anzac left. The new invaders were to coordinate with the Anzacs in a move to cut across Gallipoli and swing down upon Kilid Bahr. But neither the quality of British divisional command nor the efficiency of British tactical communications had improved since April. The effort was neutralized by disjointed effort, knife-sharp ridges, dead-end ravines, and generally confusing terrain in which whole battalions became lost. A mixed battalion of English and Gurkhas after heroic effort reached the heights and at last looked down upon the Dardanelles, only to be struck by a salvo of 12-inch shells, probably from the fleet. Nevertheless they held on until Mustapha Kemal, on orders from Sanders, arrived to command their opponents. Kemal, three days and three nights without sleep, drove his exhausted men harder than the British were driven. Under Kemal's dynamic leadership, the Turks thrust the scattered invaders off the key ridges and back into an entrenched beachhead line that neither antagonist was able to break before the British withdrew in December.

From late March until fall Roger Keyes retained his conviction that armored minesweepers could convoy heavy ships through the Narrows. As both armies dug in deeper, Sanders gradually withdrew artillery from the waterway to bolster his hard-pressed lines. Keyes saw in this decrease of enemy firepower inside the Dardanelles the opportunity for the truly coordinated infantry-fleet action that he insisted could capture the Strait. His plan called for gunnery ships, led up the Dardanelles by armored sweepers, to box in the Turks at each beachhead with shellfire and intercept their supplies. When the Turkish forces at Anzac and Helles had thus been fixed in position, fresh British infantry should land at Beach Y, cut through the lightly held area between, and put artillery on Kilid Bahr. The artillery emplaced here could then take over the task of keeping Sanders' army pinned down and at the same time secure the Strait for merchantmen. These, escorted by the Aegean squadron, could transport troops to undefended Constantinople. But not even Keyes' persistence could overcome the handicap of divided amphibious command. Senior officers of neither service could be convinced that an infantry-fleet effort could be coordinated successfully.

By November it had become obvious that Allied forces would not move from Gallipoli to Constantinople. Nearly half a million soldiers, British and French, had been employed in the attempt. Nearly a quarter of a million were casualties, but the Allies were no nearer Constantinople than they had been in April. The Turks had used about the same number of men and suffered similar casualties, but they still held Kilid Bahr, the key to the Dardanelles and to Constantinople. Reluctantly, Kitchener ordered Gallipoli evacuated.

During December and early January, staff officers of both services demonstrated how well they had learned the lessons of amphibious logistics. Rebuilding artificial harbors destroyed in winter storms and making full use of ramped boats, they pulled out 115,000 men in a series of night withdrawals. Meticulous planning, rigid discipline, and strict adherence to a realistic timetable highlighted the most remarkable amphibious evacuation in the history of warfare up till that time.

The Anzac troops were particularly ingenious in devising tricks to simulate the usual pattern of rifle and artillery fire, even after their trenches were empty. For five nights, units withdrew on a carefully worked-out timetable, and during four days men ashore skillfully counterfeited the normal appearance of a crowded beachhead. British sharpshooting had set the stage for this piece of illusion. So wary had the Turks become of snipers that they did not dare risk the daylight reconnaissance and observation that would have unmasked the British deception.

When the Turks at Anzac found the British beachhead empty, they marched down to reinforce their troops at Helles. Nevertheless the British in this area also successfully withdrew, pulling out all infantry and artillery in a little over a week, despite one heavy Turkish attack. The success of this evacuation, like that at Anzac, was due partly to Turkish respect for British small arms fire. It was facilitated also by the fact that the Turks had no real desire to hinder the British departure. But mainly it was the result of careful planning and excellent logistic support. Had the invading British troops enjoyed the benefits of such planning and such support, Hamilton's April assault would undoubtedly have succeeded. Where in April there had been too few rowboats, in December there was a generous supply of ramped, engine-driven, armored landing craft. Where in April there was a rigid plan known only to a few, there now was a realistic, flexible plan thoroughly understood by all who were concerned with putting it into effect. Adversity had again proved a hard but effective teacher.

The Aftermath

From nearly every point of view the Campaign for Constantinople ended in failure and defeat for Allied hopes. For the Allies its only value was that it tied up the whole Turkish army for nine months. Even this was a mixed blessing, for when the Allies finally evacuated Gallipoli, they left behind a hardened, well-trained army that the British were obliged to fight again in defense of the Suez Canal.

None of the Allied forces released by the evacuation could be brought to the Western Front, as had been hoped. Those that were not retained to defend Suez were sent, too late as it turned out, via Salonika to relieve Serbia, under attack by Bulgaria. For Bulgaria, emboldened by the impending Allied defeat on Gallipoli, had joined the Central Powers. The following year, German and Bulgarian armies joined to defeat Romania, thereby bringing all the Balkan States under Central Power Control.

The Gallipoli fiasco, besides immensely worsening the Allied strategic situation, was a great spoiler of reputations. Few of the highly-placed persons who made the decisions for the campaign entirely escaped its stigma. Lord Fisher ended his career in May 1915 by resigning in protest against sending more ships to the Aegean. Soon thereafter Churchill was forced out of the Admiralty with a tarnished reputation that he did not fully retrieve until World War II. Hamilton was never again entrusted with a field command. Kitchener, his prestige undermined, was forced to restore authority to the General Staff and ceased to dominate the War Council. The further decline of his prestige, and doubtless his expulsion from office, was averted only by his untimely death when the cruiser *Hampshire,* conveying him on an official visit to Russia, struck a mine and went down off the Orkneys. Asquith outlasted the others in office, but he never overcame the blot on his name left by his participation in the Dardanelles decision. The loss of the Balkans aggravated the popular discontent with his manner of conducting the war. At the end of 1916, Asquith was succeeded as Prime Minister by David Lloyd George, who had previously succeeded Kitchener as Secretary of State for War.

Yet the campaign for Constantinople, viewed in retrospect, was one of the most brilliant strategic conceptions of World War I. Had it succeeded, as it nearly did, Russia with her massive manpower might have been provided with the munitions to drive into Germany from the East as her allies struck hard from the West. The two drives, between them, could have crushed the Central Powers. This of course is not mere speculation, for that is precisely what happened in World War II. Not only might a dual drive have brought World War I to an earlier end, but the tonic of victory might well have averted the Russian Revolution, or at least altered its form—with less likelihood that the mid-century would see a world hostilely divided between Communist and non-Communist powers.

But the campaign failed. The British War Council, when time was still on the Allied side, had willed the end without willing the means.

Summary

When the land warfare reached stalemate with the stabilization of the Western Front in the fall of 1914, the British Admiralty studied means of using Britain's sea power supremacy to outflank the Front and join hands militarily with Russia. The feasible routes were two—via the Baltic Sea and via the Black Sea. Opening either waterway would permit the western Allies to supply Russia with the arms needed to make optimum use of her vast manpower reserves.

Opening the Baltic Sea would require the prior destruction of the German High Seas Fleet. Opening the Black Sea would require the capture of Constantinople. The British War Council, concluding from inadequate intelligence that the capture of Constantinople would be relatively easy, chose to open the Black Sea, using ships supported by a minimum of infantry for an attack on the Dardanelles. The failure of this attempt and of the succeeding Gallipoli campaign revealed serious weaknesses in British military organization, planning, and doctrine.

At the very top of their command structure, the British lacked machinery for prompt decision in matters of grand strategy. In the early months of World War I, the War Council was a mere committee of cabinet officers, each busy gearing his own department for war. The lack of a staff to serve the Council required Churchill to assign War Council work to his busy Admiralty staff planners throughout the crucial month of January 1915. As a result of this additional work, and of the contest of wills when Churchill forced through the only plan acceptable to Kitchener, the Admiralty's adjustment to the war was delayed by several irretrievable months. The effect of this delay, compounded by errors in estimates of the enemy's strength, appeared in the failure to provide base facilities in the area of operations, in the failure to provide armored minesweepers manned by navy crews, in the failure to have munitions combat-unit loaded, and in generally poor strategic and logistic planning.

The War Office shares with the Admiralty and the War Council the blame for mismanagement. Key men in all three organizations based their decisions upon invalid assumptions about Turkish weakness. None made allowance for Turkish strength not reported by diplomats or intelligence agents. Missing from their calculations were the field artillery and infantry serving under Sanders, whose reinforcements and initiative kept the Turks one step ahead of the Allies throughout the campaign.

Carden failed at the Dardanelles because he refused to employ ships and marine infantry as integral arms of a single force during the two weeks before Sanders' artillery regiment reached the Strait. De Robeck failed because no one acted soon enough to provide the Aegean squadron with armored minesweepers, colliers, and supply ships. The warships of World War I did not have the means to defeat respectable shore defenses without infantry support or armored auxiliaries.

Hamilton's amphibious assault of Gallipoli failed because the British forgot certain lessons learned in the struggle against Napoleon. Hamilton and de Robeck tried to re-enact the 1801 victory of Aboukir Bay without employing the means worked out by Abercromby and Keith.

The naval support at Gallipoli was inadequate for assault on a defended coast. There was no extended *preparatory fire* delivered against the beaches. On the morning of the assault most of the gunnery vessels stood off delivering *area fire,* which is demonstrably ineffective against an enemy with prepared defenses. What was needed was close-range *point fire,*[1] that is, fire aimed at the enemy's positions, which must be located by prior reconnaissance and continuous observation. Gunboats were not provided to accompany the assault forces to the beach in order to neutralize the enemy's fire during the actual landing. Once the troops were ashore, no means was provided for aiming indirect fire support from the ships. What was needed was front-line observation by men who understood naval guns and could communicate directly with the gunners afloat.

[1] Formerly called *pinpoint fire.*

The boat pool for the Gallipoli landings was totally inadequate. Each boat was earmarked for numerous ship-to-shore movements, carrying first personnel and then munitions and supplies. Such multiple use would have been possible only if few or none of the boats had been damaged. The heavy attrition of boats off Beach V however disrupted the landing schedule and made it impossible for Hunter-Weston to shift troops from beach to beach as emergencies or opportunities dictated.

The officers and men of the assault forces were neither rehearsed nor properly indoctrinated. Hamilton and the generals to whom he delegated tactical control generally remained afloat but acted as if they were campaigning ashore in close contact with all their subordinate commanders. Most significantly, conforming to Hamilton's desire for secrecy, they did not brief battalion commanders concerning objectives. As a result, both the Anzac force and the 29th Division lost momentum.

Hamilton himself violated a basic axiom of amphibious warfare when, at mid-morning on April 25, he failed to exploit his first opportunity to break through a gap between the Turkish units. He did not take control of the four idle battalions on Beaches S, X, and Y to seize the ridge beyond Krithia. He refused to commit his general reserve to race up the natural corridor across Gallipoli to seize Kilid Bahr. The only reserve he was willing to commit was a brigade held in Egypt despite his repeated requests that it be made avaliable to him. In land campaigns a general may often withhold his reserve forces until the enemy has committed his. The commander of an amphibious assault has no such freedom of action. Once the assault is launched, time tends to favor the defender. The attacker must be prepared to commit all his forces in order to exploit opportunities as soon as they appear.

Sanders' enforced removal of his artillery from the Dardanelles opened up a final possibility for Allied capture of Kilid Bahr. Keyes, recognizing the opportunity, proposed spearheading the attack with a coordinated infantry-fleet assault up the Dardanelles. But by this time senior officers of both services recognized that no adequate machinery had been evolved for combined operations. They preferred to avoid risks involved in divided command.

Some military analysts, taking into account only the defeat of the invaders, concluded from the failure of the Constantinople campaign that daylight assault had become impractical against a beach defended with modern weapons. But the campaign was more than a laboratory test of modern defense against amphibious assault. The attempt nearly succeeded, and its failure is attributable to errors that could have been corrected. In fact, as we shall see, careful analysis of the errors of Dardanelles-Gallipoli became the foundation upon which the overwhelmingly successful Allied amphibious doctrines of World War II were erected.

24:
The Battle of Jutland

The entry of Italy into the war on the side of the Allies in May 1915 served to divert Austrian forces from the Eastern Front. But the failure of the Allies at Gallipoli far more than offset this Allied advantage. The Gallipoli failure denied Russia the arms she needed to stage an offensive, it made the manpower of the Balkans unavailable to the Allies, it gave the Central Powers direct contact with Turkey via Bulgaria, and it released the Turkish army for operations elsewhere. The Turks, supplied and prodded by Germany, had already threatened not only Suez but the oil wells of Persia that provided fuel for the British fleet. To protect these vital interests, the Allies at length dispatched more than a million men for campaigns in the Middle East.

In the circumstances, with Russia weakening and the possibility of winning adherents in the Balkans gone, the idea of outflanking the Western Front ceased to commend itself to the western Allies. Evidently the decision would have to be attained in the West. By the end of 1915, the British and French high commands had concluded that their best strategy lay in maintaining all possible pressure on the German armies in France while ever tightening the maritime blockade of Germany. German military power was already stretched nearly to the utmost. If Britain and France could only hold on till the full reserve power of the world-wide British Empire could be brought into play, the German line must at length be cracked.

The German High Command likewise concluded that the decision would have to be sought in the West. But there was a greater urgency in German planning, for the strangle-hold of Allied sea power was beginning to produce shortages of strategic raw materials in Germany. Evidently time was fighting on the side of the Allies. Britain, rendered secure by her naval strength, could deny seaborne supplies to the Central Powers and at the same time import the materials of war needed to keep her continental allies in the field. The only effective answer to this modern-day version of Pitt's Plan, said General von Falkenhayn, Chief of the German General Staff, was to weaken British sea power and to strip Britain of friends on the Continent. The German navy had failed to interdict British supplies; hence, said Falkenhayn, it was up to the German army to achieve not merely a decision but a victory of annihilation over Britain's allies. Of these, Russia appeared exhausted, and Italy was immobilized behind the Alpine barrier. Only France, "the sword of England," remained. On February 21, 1916 at Verdun, Falkenhayn launched the offensive aimed at breaking France.

German naval leaders, stung by the implications of Falkenhayn's appraisal, undertook a reorganization of their high command. Admiral Reinhardt von Scheer, an aggressive nominee of Tirpitz, succeeded to command of the High Seas Fleet. Three weeks later, as the assault on Verdun gathered force, the Kaiser sanctioned offensive operations by the German surface fleet.

Scheer's opposite number was Admiral Sir John Jellicoe, unexcelled administrator, gunnery expert, master of fleet maneuvers, and the most widely-experienced officer in the Royal Navy. Early recognized for his ability by Fisher, he had been groomed since 1911 to take command of the Grand Fleet in event of war. This he did, to the gratification of the British fleet and public, the day before Britain declared war on Germany. His handling of the fleet since then had only served to increase general confidence in his abilities.

Scheer's plans aimed at bringing the strength of the Grand Fleet down to parity with his own. U-boats were to mine the vicinity of British bases and patrol the areas off the entrance channels. German surface forces would skillfully bait traps to entice Admiral Jellicoe to divide his fleet and thus provide a chance for a portion to be cut off and destroyed. Scheer could afford to gamble. With boldness he might gain much from his opponents' mistakes—perhaps command of the North Sea. On the other hand, defeat could not greatly worsen the strategic situation of the High Seas Fleet.

Britain, on the contrary, had everything to lose from defeat or severe attrition at sea. She was not only the chief entrepôt for Allied war supplies, but she was obliged also to import her own foodstuffs and basic war materials. Hence, despite the superiority of the Grand Fleet, Jellicoe felt obliged to avoid risks. Churchill called him "the only man on either side who could lose the war in an afternoon." To dig the High Seas Fleet out of its fortified and mined bases was out of the question. Like Scheer, therefore, Jellicoe resorted to ambush, but with a difference: his objective was to bring on a decisive fleet engagement. To encourage that end he made periodic sweeps of the North Sea.

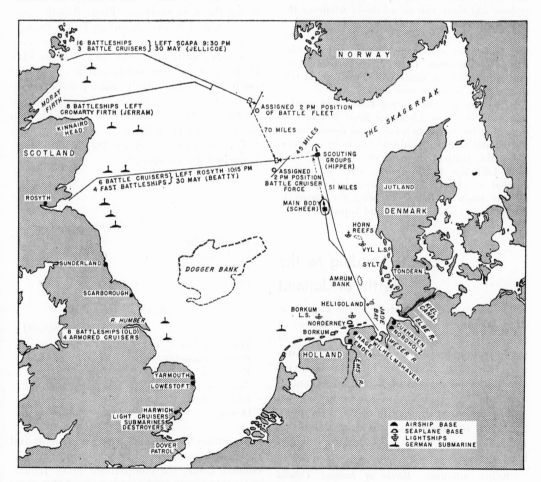

THE APPROACH OF THE FLEETS, MIDNIGHT–2:15 PM, MAY 31, 1916

In 1916 no accumulated battle experience could serve as a tactical guide for handling dreadnought fleets. The last major fleet action had been fought at Trafalgar, 111 years before. The one-sided engagement at Tsushima offered little of doctrinal value. But Jellicoe, believing that with his numerical superiority he could annihilate the enemy in a day gunnery duel, was determined to fight under conditions of his own choosing. At whatever cost to his reputation, the Grand Fleet must come out of an engagement preponderantly superior to the High Seas Fleet. In summarizing his tactical views for the Admiralty on October 19, 1914, Jellicoe had stated:

> The Germans have shown that they rely to a very great extent on submarines, mines, and torpedoes, and there can be no doubt whatever that they will endeavour to make the fullest use of these weapons in a fleet action, especially since they possess an actual superiority over us in these particular directions. It therefore becomes necessary to consider our own tactical methods in relation to these forms of attack. . . .
>
> If, for instance, the enemy battle fleet were to turn away from an advancing fleet, I should assume that the intention was to lead us over mines and submarines, and should decline to be so drawn.
>
> I desire particularly to draw the attention of their Lordships to this point, since it may be deemed a refusal of battle, and, indeed, might possibly result in failure to bring the enemy to action as soon as is expected and hoped.[1]

Events Leading to the Battle of Jutland

The new offensive strategy of the High Seas Fleet got under way with a bombardment of Lowestoft late in April 1916 by a force of battle cruisers and light cruisers. Jellicoe countered with an attempt to lure the Germans into battle, but to no avail. Scheer next planned to bombard the important shipbuilding town of Sunderland at the mouth of the Tyne in an endeavor to draw out naval detachments, which he would attack with submarines, zeppelins, and surface forces. Ship repairs and bad

[1] British Admiralty, *Battle of Jutland, Official Despatches* (London, 1920), 601-3.

weather however delayed operations until the ambushing U-boats had to leave station. Hence Scheer planned instead a raid on Allied shipping off southern Norway, hoping thereby to attract British fleet units. Here the Skagerrak provided a ready avenue of escape to Kiel should he be cut off from his North Sea bases. To carry out the raid off Norway, the High Seas Fleet sortied from Jade Bay in the early hours of May 31, 1916.

On May 30 the British Admiralty, still reading encoded German radio dispatches, had notified Jellicoe that a German force intended the next day to enter the North Sea by the eastern swept channel off Horn Reefs. On Admiralty orders, the main body of the Grand Fleet sailed from Scapa Flow and Cromarty Firth on the evening of the 30th, rendezvousing at sea the next morning. From Rosyth came Vice Admiral Beatty's Scouting Force. Beatty's instructions were to sweep eastward. If he made no contact with the enemy by 2 PM on May 31, he was to turn north and get in visual touch with the main body under Jellicoe, which at that time would be about 70 miles to the northwest. The combined force would then sweep toward Horn Reefs.

The line of battle of the two British forces comprised the following:

	BRITISH	GERMAN
Scouting Forces		
	(Beatty)	(Hipper)
Dreadnoughts	4	0
Battle cruisers	6	5
Light cruisers	14	5
Destroyers	27	30
Battle Fleets		
	(Jellicoe)	(Scheer)
Dreadnoughts	24	16
Pre-dreadnoughts	0	6
Battle cruisers	3	0
Armored cruisers	8	0
Light cruisers	12	6
Destroyers	52	31

Discounting the German pre-dreadnoughts and the British armored cruisers as being of slight combat value, the comparison shows Jellicoe able to bring 37 capital ships (battleships and

BRITISH GRAND FLEET

Battle Fleet................Adm. Jellicoe

Flagship *Iron Duke*...	1 battleship
1st Battle Squadron...............V. Adm. Burney.............	7 battleships
2nd Battle Squadron...............V. Adm. Jerram..........	8 battleships
4th Battle Squadron...............V. Adm. Sturdee...........	8 battleships
3rd Battle Cruiser Squadron...R. Adm. Hood...............	3 battle cruisers
1st Cruiser Squadron...............R. Adm. Arbuthnot.......	4 armored cruisers
2nd Cruiser Squadron...............R. Adm. Heath............	4 armored cruisers
4th Light Cruiser Squadron...Commo. LeMesurier......	6 light cruisers
4th Destroyer Flotilla..	19 destroyers
11th Destroyer Flotilla.............1 light cruiser, 15 destroyers
12th Destroyer Flotilla..	16 destroyers
Attached Vessels............4 light cruisers, 1 destroyer, 1 destroyer-minelayer

Battle Cruiser Fleet
(Scouting Force)................V. Adm. Beatty

Flagship *Lion*...	1 battle cruiser
1st Battle Cruiser Squadron...R. Adm. Brock............	3 battle cruisers
2nd Battle Cruiser Squadron...R. Adm. Pakenham.......	2 battle cruisers
5th Battle Squadron...............R. Adm. Evan-Thomas.........	4 battleships
1st Light Cruiser Squadron....Commo. Alexander-Sinclair..	4 light cruisers
2nd Light Cruiser Squadron...Commo. Goodenough.........	4 light cruisers
3rd Light Cruiser Squadron...R. Adm. Napier...........	5 light cruisers
1st Destroyer Flotilla.............1 light cruiser, 9 destroyers
9th Destroyer Flotilla..	4 destroyers
10th Destroyer Flotilla...	4 destroyers
13th Destroyer Flotilla.............1 light cruiser, 10 destroyers
Attached vessel..	1 seaplane carrier

GERMAN HIGH SEAS FLEET

Battle Fleet................V. Adm. Scheer

Flagship *Friedrich der Grosse*................................	1 battleship
Battle Squadron I............V. Adm. Schmidt......	8 battleships
Battle Squadron II............R. Adm. Mauve.........	6 battleships
Battle Squadron III............R. Adm. Behncke......	7 battleships
Scouting Group IV........Commo. Reuter.......	6 light cruisers
Destroyers..	31 destroyers

Battle Cruiser Fleet
(Scouting Force).............V. Adm. Hipper

Scouting Group I.............V. Adm. Hipper.........	5 battle cruisers
Scouting Group II.............R. Adm. Boedicker...	5 light cruisers
Destroyers..	30 destroyers

ORGANIZATION OF THE OPPOSING FLEETS AT JUTLAND

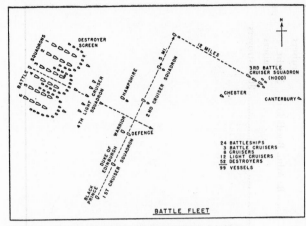

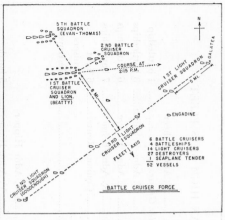

GRAND FLEET CRUISING FORMATIONS, MAY 31

battle cruisers) against 21 German. The Grand Fleet also enjoyed a corresponding superiority in lighter units. And against 244 German guns of 11 and 12 inches, Jellicoe could bring 344 of 12 and 15 inches.

Neither the British nor the German commander knew that the other was at sea. Before leaving port Jellicoe had enjoined radio silence on the Grand Fleet. His information from the Admiralty indicated only that a German sortie of some sort was intended. It stated incorrectly that Scheer's flagship *Friedrich der Grosse* was still at Wilhelmshaven, for the German admiral had taken the precaution of having a radio guardship acknowledge all messages addressed to him, using the call sign of his flagship. Neither side had the advantage of air scouting, for weather grounded Scheer's zeppelins, and Beatty conserved the seaplane tender *Engadine*'s seaplanes for use when contact was imminent. Two German submarines off Rosyth sighted Beatty but their reports were misleading, indicating that only small detachments were at sea.

Beatty, zigzagging at 19 knots on an easterly course, had his three light cruiser squadrons disposed eight miles ahead of his flagship *Lion* on a NW-SE scouting line 25 miles in width.[2] At 1:30 PM on the 31st he changed formation preparatory to joining Jellicoe, ro-

[2] All courses and bearings in this chapter are magnetic to conform with official reports. Local variation was 13° 15' W, which should be subtracted to obtain true directions.

tating the scouting line right to ENE-WSW and ordering Rear Admiral Evan-Thomas's 5th Battle Squadron of four dreadnoughts to take station five miles on his port beam. The scouting line would then be disposed for maximum coverage on the sweep to Horn Reefs, and the 5th Battle Squadron would be in a position to take its assigned place in the van of Jellicoe's force.

As Beatty was turning northward, the cruiser *Galatea* made out a column of smoke to the eastward. Closing to investigate, she sighted a Danish merchant vessel stopped by two German destroyers. Immediately the *Galatea* flashed a warning by radio. This contact brought on the Battle of Jutland and probably cost the British a decisive victory, for otherwise it is likely the opposing forces would have met much farther north, with the Grand Fleet concentrated and with Scheer's escape to the Jade cut off.

On receiving the *Galatea*'s report "Enemy in sight" at 2:20, Beatty brought his six battle cruisers to course SSE and increased speed to get between the enemy and his base. His four battleships continued to the north for several minutes because heavy funnel smoke had obscured Beatty's turning signal from Evan-Thomas. When the battleships finally turned, the distance between Evan-Thomas and Beatty had opened to nearly ten miles. Nevertheless Beatty pushed on. He suspected that German battle cruisers were in the area and knew that there could be no more than five. Convinced that ill luck had cheated him of an overwhelming victory in the Dogger Bank action, he was determined that the enemy should not elude him again. Receiving no reports of enemy capital ships from his scouting vessels, Beatty ordered the *Engadine* to send up a seaplane reconnaissance. The aircraft, hampered by a 1000-foot ceiling, reported only German light cruisers and destroyers and then was forced down by a broken fuel line.

Beatty's light cruisers had in fact made contact with Hipper's Scouting Group II. Scouting Group I, Hipper's battle cruisers, was steering NW to support these light units, and Beatty was working around to course NE to cut them off. Beatty's changes of course enabled Evan-Thomas to cut corners and reduce his distance. At the same time the British 1st and 3rd Light Cruiser Squadrons, under fire by Scouting Group II, had drawn off far to

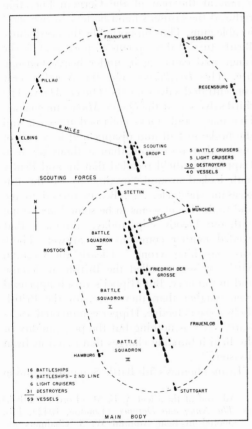

HIGH SEAS FLEET CRUISING FORMATIONS, 2:15 PM, MAY 31

the NW, where they had no chance of sighting Hipper's battle cruisers. The British and German capital ships, on converging courses, thus had no vessels at all between them. At 3:25 the opposing battle cruiser squadrons sighted each other. Neither had received a single report of the presence of the other. While the British light cruisers had successfully lured the Germans to the NW, the light units on both sides had singularly failed to carry out their scouting mission.

Beatty promptly changed course from NE to E to cut off the German battle cruisers. Hipper, in the *Lützow,* ordered Scouting Group I to countermarch to the right and at the same time recalled Scouting Group II. At 3:45 the opposing battle cruiser squadrons were on parallel courses heading ESE, disposed temporarily on lines of bearing—Germans on the port quarter, British on the starboard—to keep each ship clear of its neighbor's smoke. Hipper now prepared to lead the British toward Scheer's guns. His destroyers were on his disengaged side, his light cruisers astern.

The British 1st and 3rd Light Cruiser Squadrons had by this time maneuvered themselves quite out of the battle. But Commodore Goodenough, who had refused to be drawn to the NW after the other light cruisers, took his 2nd Light Cruiser Squadron five miles ahead of Beatty, watching the southern horizon—in the direction of the German bases.

Phase 1: The Battle Cruiser Action

At 3:48 when the range between the battle cruiser forces was down to 16,500 yards, Hipper signaled to open fire, and salvos rippled down the German line. Atmospheric conditions at this time favored the Germans: the western horizon was clear, and the British vessels were silhouetted against a blue sky. Low-lying mists rendered visibility to the northeast extremely patchy, so that the British range finders were giving readings in excess of actual ranges. This caused Beatty to hold his fire so long that he lost the advantage of the greater range of his guns. Captain Chatfield of the flagship *Lion* finally opened fire on his own responsibility. In the opening phase the Germans shot splendidly. They used their superior optical instru-

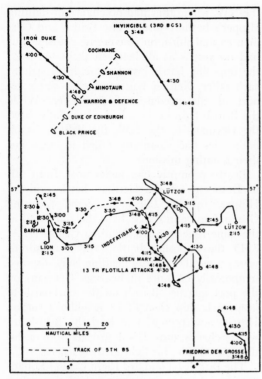

**APPROACH OF THE FLEETS
AND BATTLE CRUISER ACTION**

undoubtedly saved the flagship, for somewhat later burning debris in the turret set off a powder charge that sent flames flaring down into the handling room and up through the open turret roof higher than the mastheads.

A few minutes after the near-fatal hit on the *Lion,* two salvos landed in quick succession on the *Indefatigable,* at the rear of the British battle cruiser line. Apparently the second penetrated her forward turret and ignited powder charges. Flames reached the magazines, which had not been flooded. Two cordite fire balls leaped upward, accompanied by a rending explosion. The *Indefatigable* rolled over and sank at once, leaving only three survivors.

Soon afterward Evan-Thomas's 5th Battle Squadron, having closed to within 19,000 yards of Hipper's rear battle cruisers, opened fire. The leading battleship, the *Barham,* made a series of 15-inch shell hits on the *Von der Tann,* at the rear of the German line, that reduced the cruiser's main battery to two serviceable guns. Thus supported by the battleships, Beatty turned three points to port to close the range and came again under heavy German fire. The *Derfflinger* and the *Seydlitz* now concentrated salvos on the *Queen Mary.* The third salvo set off the *Queen Mary*'s magazines. Her masts and stacks collapsed inboard, and she broke in half and disappeared in a pall of smoke that rose more than a thousand feet. Captain Chatfield recalled that he and Beatty both looked around "in time to see the unpleasant spectacle. . . . Beatty turned to me and said, 'There seems to be something wrong with our bloody ships today,' a remark that needed neither comment nor answer. There *was* something wrong."[3] Clearly the German battle cruisers excelled the British in defense and in gunnery. But Hipper's vessels appeared even tougher than they were, for the British shells were defective. Hipper commented afterward, "It was nothing but the poor quality of the British bursting charges that saved us from disaster."[4]

Evan-Thomas's 5th Battle Squadron, coming

ments to advantage and were early on their targets. Their closely-grouped half-salvos fell at 20-second intervals.

By 3:55, when the converging squadrons had closed to 13,000 yards, shells began to find their targets. Within a couple of minutes the *Seydlitz* and the *Lion* were lightly damaged, and the *Tiger* and the *Princess Royal* had received turret damages that temporarily cut down their fire power. Beatty now turned slightly away to open the range. A minute later shells from the *Queen Mary* made the second British hit of the battle, piercing the midships turret of the *Seydlitz,* where igniting powder charges killed the turret crew. Prompt flooding of magazines, routine practice in the High Seas Fleet, saved the ship.

At 4 PM the *Lion* received a penetrating 12-inch hit on her midships turret that blew off a roof plate. Most of the loading crew were killed, but the turret officer, a major of marines, lived long enough to order the handling-room crew to flood the magazine. He thereby

[3] Admiral of the Fleet A. E. M. (Lord) Chatfield RN, *The Navy and Defence* (London, 1942), 143.
[4] Quoted in Rear Admiral W. S. Chalmers RN, *The Life and Letters of David Beatty, Admiral of the Fleet* (London, 1951), 234.

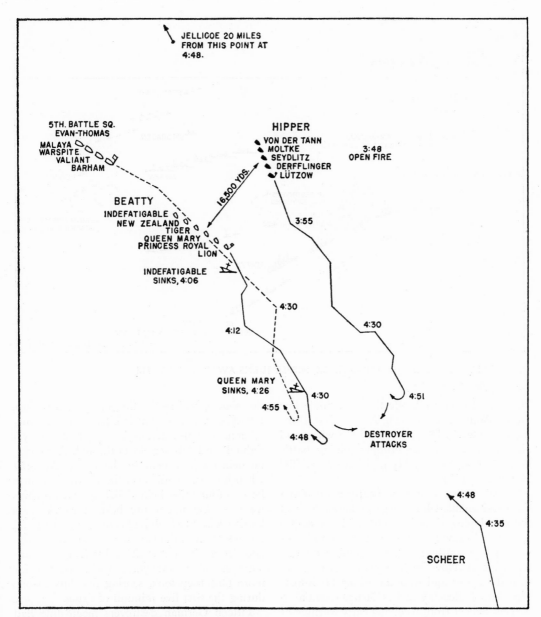

PHASE I: BATTLE CRUISER ACTION, 3:48–4:48 PM

into full action, deterred Hipper from closing to exploit his advantage after the destruction of the *Queen Mary*. British destroyers meanwhile on Beatty's orders had forged ahead and were approaching the German line of advance in perfect position for a torpedo attack. Hipper, thus menaced at the same time by battleships, battle cruisers, and destroyers, considered that he had pressed his luck far enough and turned away to disengage. By 4:30 he was steering east, nearly at right angles to Beatty's line.

Beatty's attention was now attracted elsewhere by electrifying news: "Battleships SE." Goodenough's cruisers had sighted Scheer's battle fleet and flashed the word by searchlight. Goodenough promptly radioed Jellicoe:

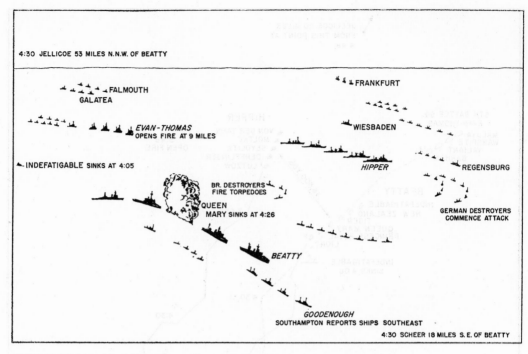

FALMOUTH
GALATEA

FRANKFURT

EVAN-THOMAS
OPENS FIRE AT 9 MILES

WIESBADEN

INDEFATIGABLE SINKS AT 4:05

HIPPER

REGENSBURG

BR. DESTROYERS
FIRE TORPEDOES

QUEEN
MARY SINKS AT 4:26

GERMAN DESTROYERS
COMMENCE ATTACK

BEATTY

GOODENOUGH
SOUTHAMPTON REPORTS SHIPS SOUTHEAST

4:30 SCHEER 18 MILES S.E. OF BEATTY

QUEEN MARY SINKS, DESTROYERS ATTACK, HIPPER TURNS AWAY, 4:20–4:30 PM

"Course of enemy's battle fleet, N, single line ahead. Composition of van, *Kaiser* class. Bearing of center E. Destroyers on both wings and ahead. Enemy's battle cruisers joining battle fleet from northward. My position lat. 56° 29′ N, long. 6° 14′ E."[5]

Hipper's turnaway gave Beatty a breathing spell and enabled him to get a better look at the developing situation. He held his course and at 4:40 saw a long line of masts and funnels on the southern horizon coming directly toward him. Now he had an opportunity to turn the tables and lead the whole High Seas Fleet into Jellicoe's clutches. It was essential to prevent Scheer from receiving early warning of the Grand Fleet's approach; Hipper's scouting forces must be kept close to their battle fleet or headed away if they should approach Jellicoe too far in advance of their main body.

The *Lion* signaled a 16-point turn in succession and the battle cruisers at 4:43 headed at full speed to close Jellicoe by the most direct course. This well-timed maneuver kept the ships out of range of Scheer's guns. The 5th Battle Squadron now bore down on the oppo-

[5] *Jutland Despatches*, 453.

site course, and as the *Barham* passed abeam, Beatty signaled the battleships to turn in succession. Because Evan-Thomas had not yet sighted the High Seas Fleet through the smoke, he delayed in executing the order. At 4:57 when he had steadied on the northerly course he was four miles behind Beatty and his ships were coming under fire both from Hipper's battle cruisers, which had countermarched and taken station in the van of Scheer's battle fleet, and from the battle fleet itself. But Evan-Thomas's fine new battleships gave out far more that they took, scoring five hits to one during the first five minutes of firing.

Fifteen German destroyers meanwhile had advanced to attack the dozen British destroyers that had helped force Hipper temporarily out of action. Between the battle lines they engaged in a furious melee, in which two of the German destroyers were sunk, one by gunfire, the other by torpedo. Though Beatty at 4:50 ordered his destroyers to close him, several in the Nelsonian tradition disregarded the signal and pressed in under heavy fire to attack Hipper's battle cruisers as they countermarched. Of ten torpedoes fired from less than 5,000

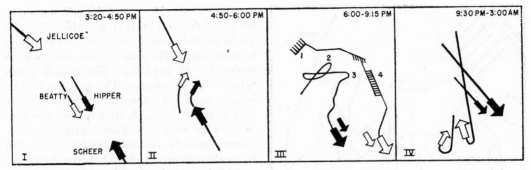

THE PHASES OF THE BATTLE OF JUTLAND

Phase I: The Battle Cruiser Action–the Run to the South.

Phase II: The Run to the North.

Phase III: The Main Fleet Action:
  1. Jellicoe's battle line deploys into column.
  2. Jellicoe caps Scheer's "T."
  3. The Crisis. Jellicoe again caps Scheer's "T."
  4. Jellicoe turns away.

Phase IV: The Night Action.

yards, one hit the *Seydlitz*, flooding a compartment. The battle cruiser took a list but maintained her position in the line. So close was the action at this point that the destroyers blazed away with their 4-inch guns, causing casualties among bridge personnel and damaging searchlights and radio antennae of the battle cruisers. Some of the destroyers launched torpedoes at the German battleships, now coming up fast. These avoided damage by quick maneuvering, but the attacks helped ease the pressure on Beatty's withdrawing squadrons. Two of the British destroyers, heavily damaged, lay dead in the water and were sunk by the concentrated fire of Scheer's van battleships, but not before they had launched their last torpedoes.

Phase II: The Run to the North

From 4:50 to 6 PM the German fleet pursued Beatty's forces. Scheer's 16 battleships and 7 pre-dreadnoughts cruised in a single column. His six cruisers formed an oval screen. Astern of the retiring British scouting force, Goodenough's cruisers maintained contact under fire at 16,000 yards, reporting German movements to Jellicoe. During the next hour Goodenough's flagship *Southampton* avoided between 50 and

60 heavy shells, most of which burst on impact with the water and showered the decks with fragments. Her own guns, ranged for a maximum of 14,500 yards, were silent. Goodenough when later asked how he escaped being sunk replied: "Simply by steering for the splashes of the last enemy salvo."[6]

The gun duel between the 5th Battle Squadron and the High Seas Fleet continued steadily. Evan-Thomas was steaming at 25 knots but Scheer's dreadnoughts at 22 knots converged on his course and kept him within range. The Germans with many more ships made 17 hits; the British made 12, most of them on the battle cruisers. That the British battleships received no serious damage clearly demonstrated the value of their heavy armor. Toward the end of the hour the German fire became sporadic as the sun came out from clouds near the horizon and blinded the spotters.

When Jellicoe received Beatty's 3:45 dispatch informing him that his battle cruisers were about to engage Hipper, he changed to

[6] Quoted in Chalmers, *Earl Beatty*, 243. Actually his navigator carefully calculated the distance between the successive "walking salvos," steering from them when they moved away, and through them when they approached.

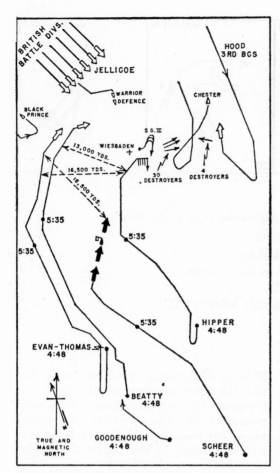

PHASE II: THE RUN TO THE NORTH, 4:48–6 PM

a SSE course to close and increased speed to 20 knots. His 24 battleships steamed in six parallel columns, or in "division line abreast," a cruising formation that would enable them to deploy into a line of battle on either flank in minimum time. A destroyer flotilla screened each battle squadron. Eight miles ahead of the main body eight armored cruisers formed a 25-mile scouting line with light cruisers linking them and the battleships. Rear Admiral Hood's 3rd Battle Cruiser Squadron steamed in column 15 miles ahead of the cruiser line. At 4:05 Jellicoe ordered Hood's three battle cruisers and four destroyers to support Beatty. Hood reported his position, course (SSE), and speed (25 knots) to show that he was already converging on the British Scouting Force.

Goodenough's 4:38 contact report gave Jellicoe his first intimation that the German battle fleet was at sea. He passed the information to his squadrons and at 4:51 sent the Admiralty the brief and stirring message: "Fleet action is imminent." His primary task now was to deploy his 24 battleships like a wall across Scheer's line of advance. The wall would then be advanced and rotated to fend the German fleet from its bases. A stern chase, the contingency he so greatly feared, would in these circumstances be avoided. Should darkness fall he would maneuver to keep between the enemy and his base, eschewing the risks of night action, and be ready to use his gun superiority at dawn.

Such was Jellicoe's tactical doctrine, but many of his officers advocated a more flexible system in the Nelsonian tradition.[7] Concentration could be most easily achieved, they argued, by independent squadron action, a method that possessed the additional virtues of requiring the exercise of initiative by subordinates and of bringing the Grand Fleet's numerical superiority to bear most fully The principal difficulty confronting the "decentralizers" was communication. Operating procedures had not yet been devised to enable a commander in chief to retain over-all tactical control when squadrons moved independently at high speeds in smoke-filled battle areas or beyond visual range. Under modern conditions it seemed that Nelsonian indoctrination of subordinates in the principle of the objective, no matter how thorough, was an inadequate substitute for firm central direction. There were also important subsidiary problems of target distribution and fire control that seemed to find their most satisfactory solution in terms of the fleet line of battle. While it was generally agreed in 1916 that concentration by squadrons was desirable in theory, no one had produced a reliable scheme for giving it effect under conditions prevailing in the North Sea.

Beatty, on turning north, dispatched by radio a detailed account of his contact. The message reached Jellicoe considerably garbled. This was the first of many misleading reports that were to go to the flagship *Iron Duke*. Beatty's given position varied as much as 20 miles from those reported by Goodenough, and none of those could be reconciled with radio fixes of the

[7] See Vice Admiral K. G. B. Dewar RN, *The Navy from Within* (London, 1939), 265-81.

German fleet positions sent by the Admiralty. The Grand Fleet had been at sea for 17 hours, and separated components had been subject to differences of current and wind that magnified errors of dead reckoning. Astronomical fixes of positions had not been possible.

Hood in steering for Beatty's force was considerably to the eastward and would have missed it altogether had not light cruiser *Chester* stumbled on Hipper's Scouting Group II and lured it through the low-lying mist under the guns of Hood's battle cruisers. These opened a rapid and accurate fire with their 12-inch guns and quickly put light cruiser *Wiesbaden* out of action in a position where she was to come under attack by practically every segment of the Grand Fleet. Scouting Group II quickly countermarched under a smoke screen and Hipper switched his 30 destroyers to its support. This proved a serious error. Hood's four destroyers absorbed the attack 7,500 yards from his battle cruisers. Hipper's destroyers sank one of Hood's, but in doing so they missed an opportunity to make torpedo attacks against Jellicoe's deploying battleships and Beatty's battle cruisers.

At 5:30 Beatty, still leading the German scouting and battle forces northward, changed course 45 degrees to starboard and opened fire at 15,000 yards in order to turn them away from the approaching British battle fleet. With visibility now in his favor and no German destroyers to interfere, he inflicted heavy punishment. His attack forced Hipper to give way to the right. Scheer's battleships, six miles astern, followed in Hipper's wake.

At 5:32 Beatty's van screening units sighted the *Black Prince*, Jellicoe's southernmost cruiser, thereby establishing visual contact with the British battle fleet. Judging that Jellicoe would deploy to the left, Beatty turned closer to Hipper, forcing the enemy scouting forces still farther away from Jellicoe's advancing battle divisions. Hipper, with no destroyers immediately available for counterattack, temporarily reversed course and fell back on Scheer. Exaggerated reports of the encounter between Scouting Group II and Hood's battle cruisers led Scheer to conclude that the British main body was much farther to the east than it actually was.

Hood, heading NW after engaging Scouting Group II, observed Beatty approaching directly ahead. Under cover of the destroyer battle, he countermarched into line at 6:17, three miles in advance of the *Lion*. Beatty had steamed across the heads of Jellicoe's deploying columns and had come around a full 90 degrees to course SE. He was now leading the 1st Division of British battleships and was working across the path of the German advance.

Phase III: The Main Fleet Action

Jellicoe, advancing to intercept the High Seas Fleet, which Beatty was leading north, attempted to reconcile the discrepancies in the information available to him. He desperately needed to know Scheer's location before deciding on the direction of his deployment. It would take four minutes to bring his battleships into a single line, and another 15 to 20 minutes to turn the long line to any fighting course. If he deployed the wrong way, he risked missing Scheer altogether or engaging in a passing situation, which could not force a decision. If he waited for actual contact in the misty weather of the North Sea, where gun range exceeded visibility, he risked engagement with his line incompletely formed and some of his batteries masked. Successful deployment before contact required a preliminary flow of accurate information, and this information Jellicoe did not have.

It was a shock to the staff on the bridge of the *Iron Duke* when the *Black Prince* at the western end of the cruiser line at 5:42 reported enemy battle cruisers five miles ahead—only 11 miles from the Grand Fleet battleships. Jellicoe concluded correctly that the battle cruisers must be his own, and received confirmation a minute later from the battleship *Marlborough* on the right flank. But the contact placed Beatty—and therefore the enemy—at least eleven miles farther west than had been anticipated. At 6:00 Beatty's ships were sighted five miles from Jellicoe's flagship on the starboard bow, heading east across the heads of the battleship divisions. Jellicoe signaled: "Where is the enemy's battle fleet?" Beatty, heavily engaged with Hipper and unable to see Scheer's column, replied, "Enemy battle cruisers bear to SE." To gain more ground to the westward, Jellicoe

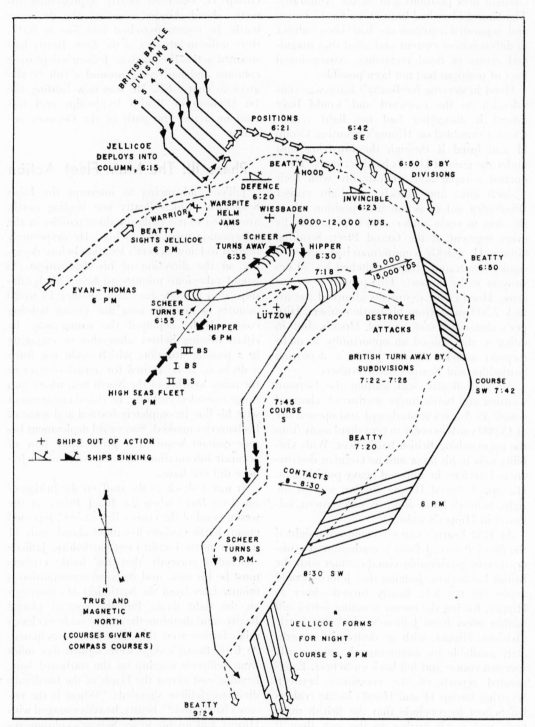

BRITISH BATTLE DIVISIONS
6 5 4 3 2 1

JELLICOE DEPLOYS INTO COLUMN, 6:15

POSITIONS 6:21

6:42 SE

6:50 S BY DIVISIONS

BEATTY
HOOD

DEFENCE 6:20

INVINCIBLE 6:23

WARRIOR

WARSPITE HELM JAMS

WIESBADEN

9000-12,000 YDS.

BEATTY 6:50

BEATTY SIGHTS JELLICOE 6 PM

SCHEER TURNS AWAY 6:35

HIPPER 6:30

7:18

8,000 15,000 YDS

EVAN-THOMAS 6 PM

SCHEER TURNS E 6:55

LÜTZOW

DESTROYER ATTACKS

BRITISH TURN AWAY BY SUBDIVISIONS 7:22-7:25

HIPPER 6 PM

III BS
I BS
II BS

HIGH SEAS FLEET 6 PM

COURSE SW 7:42

7:45 COURSE S

BEATTY 7:20

+ SHIPS OUT OF ACTION

SHIPS SINKING

CONTACTS 8 - 8:30

8 PM

N

TRUE AND MAGNETIC NORTH

(COURSES GIVEN ARE COMPASS COURSES)

SCHEER TURNS S 9 P.M.

8:30 SW

JELLICOE FORMS FOR NIGHT

COURSE S, 9 PM

BEATTY 9:24

PHASE III: MAIN FLEET ACTION, 6-9 PM

turned his divisions somewhat to starboard. But since he expected to sight the enemy momentarily, he quickly headed back to SE, directly for the point of expected contact.

Jellicoe first intended to deploy to the right in the direction of the firing, but he realized that this would put his oldest battleships in the van, and immediate contact would put him at a tactical disadvantage. He accordingly decided to deploy to port and work around between the German fleet and the coast. He waited until the last moment however, hoping for a report from some ship that had both fleets in sight. The information came at 6:14 when Beatty, having crowded Hipper's scouting forces back on Scheer's battle divisions, sighted the main body and signaled, "Enemy battle fleet bearing SSW." Evan-Thomas confirmed the information at the same time. Jellicoe then ordered the British battleship divisions to deploy into single column with the port wing division leading on course SE by E.

At that moment Beatty's battle cruisers were steaming at high speed across the van of the British battleship divisions, making smoke which concealed the opposing battleship forces from each other. In advance of Jellicoe's dreadnoughts his armored cruiser screen was converging rapidly on Beatty and at the same time coming under enemy fire. Between the British and German forces lay the helpless *Wiesbaden* under attack by Beatty's destroyers. Here at "Windy Corner," as this general meeting point came to be called, "there was handling of ships . . . such as had never been dreamt of by seamen before."[8]

As the British battleships deployed, the armored cruisers cleared the range and passed over to the disengaged side of the battle line. The *Defence,* flagship of the 1st Cruiser Squadron, followed by the *Warrior,* made a wide turn to right, passing so close to Beatty's oncoming ships that the *Lion* swung sharply left to avoid collision. The squadron commander wanted to finish off the *Wiesbaden* and get in a final contact report on the German fleet. As the two armored cruisers passed down between the battle lines, they came under such concentrated fire that the *Warrior* staggered

[8] Quoted by Commander Holloway H. Frost USN, *The Battle of Jutland* (Annapolis, 1936), 305.

out of action and the *Defence* blew up with all hands.

Evan-Thomas, coming up four miles astern of Beatty, turned his ships sharply left in succession at 6:18 to fall in behind the 6th Battleship Division in the rear. While excuting this maneuver the *Warspite* jammed her helm and swung toward the German dreadnoughts, drawing enemy fire away from the shattered *Warrior.* But both the battleship and the cruiser were too badly crippled to continue. The *Warspite,* saved by her thick armor decks, made it back to port under her own steam; the *Warrior* sank the next day while under tow. Meanwhile the luckless *Wiesbaden,* taken under fire by each British battleship and battle cruiser division, was reduced to a wrecked hulk without a gun in action. That night she went over on her beam ends and sank.

By deploying his 24 battleships from six columns of four each into a single column with the battle cruisers in the van and Evan-Thomas's three remaining battleships in the rear, Jellicoe brought the Grand Fleet into it's long-practiced battle formation. Notwithstanding the dead reckoning errors in the positions of Beatty and Jellicoe, and in spite of Jellicoe's lack of accurate scouting information, the Grand Fleet could hardly have been deployed more advantageously if Jellicoe had controlled the movements of both contending fleets. Though the distances and low visibility concealed the situation from all commanders, the relative movements were such that the Grand Fleet was heading, first, to cap the German T, and then, by a turn to the south, to block the German retreat back to base.

At 6:21 Hood's 3rd Battle Cruiser Squadron, then somewhat in advance of the main British line, opened heavy fire on the head of Hipper's Scouting Group I, leading the German battle fleet. Hipper thereupon turned right to course SE to avoid being capped. In a brief, fierce engagement, Hipper's flagship *Lützow,* after receiving her 20th hit of the battle, fell out of action. For the next three hours command of the German battle cruisers was assumed by Captain Hartog of the *Derfflinger.* Meanwhile Hood's flagship *Invincible* took a hit in her midships turret, and the flash from ignited powder charges penetrated to the magazine. Flames and two gigantic fireballs burst from her hull. Her midship structure collapsed, and she broke in two and sank, taking down a thousand men, including Admiral Hood.

When the van of Scheer's battleship column reached the waters where Hood and Hipper had engaged, Jellicoe's leading battleships began crossing Scheer's T delivering heavy fire. In reply the Germans could do very little, for all they could see to the north was a line of flashes from British gunfire. Conditions were not much better for the Grand Fleet. "Only three or four ships [were] in sight at a time from the van and center," wrote Jellicoe in his report. "Ships fired at what they could see when they could see it."

When Scheer learned that his van ships were taking hits, he knew that he was in a situation from which he had to extricate himself quickly. Luckily for the Germans, they were well trained in just the maneuver to back out of such a spot. At 6:35 Scheer ordered a *Gefechtskehrtwendung* (battle turn)—a ripple movement beginning at the rear—180 degrees to the right. After completing this intricate reversal of direction without collision, he steadied on a southwesterly course.

Both the lateness of the hour and the poor visibility made it imperative that Jellicoe lose neither time nor contact. But, though several British battleships had observed Scheer's turnaway, they failed to report it. Jellicoe knew only that some German ships had appeared and then as suddenly disappeared into the smoke and mist. Instead of turning to follow the Germans, Jellicoe maintained course for four minutes after his battleships had lost contact. Then he changed fleet course only one point to the right, to SE. Fortunately for the British, the vigilant Goodenough left the rear of the line and headed for the German ships to keep them under observation.

As the Grand Fleet continued to SE without finding targets, Jellicoe concluded that the range was opening. So at 6:50 he ordered the 24 battleships of his main body to turn south by divisions. At that moment Scheer in the *Friedrich der Grosse,* after 15 minutes on the reverse course, was twelve miles SW of the British fleet. The German commander in chief now ordered his squadrons into another battle turn and headed east in a single column for the enemy. The battered German battle cruisers resumed their places at the head of the line, less than 10,000 yards from the British battleships and closing them at right angles. It is not clear why Scheer put the battle cruisers in his van when undamaged battleships were available to lend power to his fighting front. He appears at this time to have been groping by instinct. His reasons for turning again toward a concentrated enemy after he had barely completed disengagement he afterward set forth in his memoirs in very general terms: "The maneuver would be bound to surprise the enemy, to upset his plans for the rest of the day, and if the blow fell heavily it would facilitate our breaking loose at night. The sight of the *Wiesbaden* helped also to strengthen my resolve to make an effort to render assistance to her and at least save her crew."[9]

From this explanation it appears that Scheer hoped by an offensive maneuver to extricate his fleet in order to clear the way for a return to base. His move was bold, not to say rash, for without any dependable information regarding Grand Fleet movements, he was charging blindly into the unknown. Meanwhile Jellicoe, in turning south, had again placed himself athwart the German line of advance.

At 6:55, when Scheer issued orders for the battle turn against Jellicoe, the German destroyer commodores ordered an attack; but the blow was deprived of full force by a further decision to detach eight destroyers—four to succor the *Wiesbaden* and the others to cover the *Lützow.* At 7:04 Goodenough sent the vital information that the German fleet was heading east. One minute later Jellicoe turned all his battleships 34 degrees toward the enemy, to course SSW.

The Battle of Jutland now moved to its crisis. The *Derfflinger* came into view of the British and was straddled by battleships capping the German line. Light cruiser *Regensburg* and the massed destroyers were also seen approaching from the west, nearly ahead. Jellicoe promptly, at 7:09, pulled his battleships back to course S to put them into

[9] Reinhardt von Scheer, *Germany's High Seas Fleet in the World War* (London, 1920), 155. Some students of Jutland believe that Scheer, placing Jellicoe farther south than he actually was, hoped to escape across the British rear.

division columns. Scheer's battleships now appeared out of the mist, and the German van ships came under a deluge of British projectiles without being able to make more than a feeble response from their own turrets. Forty-five minutes after his first escape, Scheer had cast aside all advantage and was marching his fleet into the maws of an unassailable antagonist. Total disaster for the Germans was now within measurable distance.

Scheer from his position in the center of the line did not realize that his battle cruisers were already in the van and ordered them at 7:13 to turn and attack the enemy. One minute later he modified his order, directing the battle cruisers to "operate against the enemy van." Then at 7:15 he began to dispatch the order for a third battle turn by the fleet. Hartog, in temporary command of the Scouting Force, realized that it was impossible to go on even before he received Scheer's orders. His ships were under the most devastat-

ing fire yet experienced in the action and suffering heavy hits in rapid succession. At 7:14 the message to attack came in, and Hartog ordered course SE. But the German battle cruisers, under fire since 7:05 from the westernmost British battleship division, had meanwhile emerged from the smoke and mist into plain view of the next division ahead. The concentration of 36 additional heavy guns only 7,500 yards away caused Hartog to increase speed to 23 knots and continue his swing southward until he was on a course roughly parallel to the British. With visibility now heavily favoring the latter, the unequal contest continued for another five minutes.

The German van ship *Derfflinger* staggered under crippling hits. A 15-inch shell came through the roof of her after turret and exploded, igniting two powder charges. The resulting turret fire swept down the hoists and burned out the handling rooms. Though all but one of the 75-man turret crew perished,

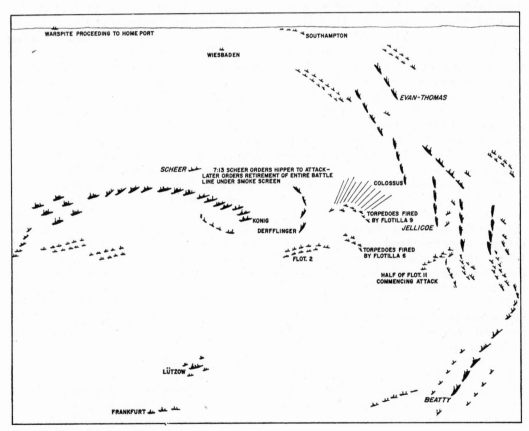

THE CRISIS, 7:15–7:20

magazine doors and scuttles remained intact. Another fire flared up topsides as a heavy hit demolished part of the main deck and the nearby bridge structure. Fire fighting parties, and secondary battery gun crews who swarmed out to assist them, were cut down in large numbers by projectiles that passed through the stacks and burst overhead like gigantic shrapnel. Still another large caliber hit penetrated the "C" turret barbette and wrecked the guns. Here nearly a dozen ready charges caught fire, but again the anti-flame baffles and rapid flooding saved the *Derfflinger*'s magazines. Though communications to fire control and spotting stations aloft were lost, and the main battery plotting room was untenable from gases of high explosives, the gunnery officer ordered rapid salvos from the two remaining turrets—as much to maintain the spirits of the ship's company as with expectation of scoring hits. While the *Derfflinger* was thus taking punishment, the other three battle cruisers in the line were also receiving heavy damage. At 7:23 Hartog turned away two points to SW, and shortly afterward the battered battle cruisers became disengaged as attacking destroyer flotillas advanced and covered them with smoke.

In the meantime the German battle fleet, despite damages in the van from British shells, was successfully turning away. Scheer kept on around to course W. The High Seas Fleet was now withdrawing at right angles to the course of the Grand Fleet.

Jellicoe had already begun maneuvers to rotate his fleet axis to the right in order to bring the powerful ships of his van battle squadron closer to the enemy. As the divisions turned to form a single line ahead on the new bearing, Jellicoe discerned the first groups of German destroyers approaching in V-formation to attack. Four destroyers headed in to 7,500 yards at 7:21, fired 11 torpedoes and withdrew behind smoke. Nine more attacked three minutes later and got off 20 torpedoes. The British battleships opened with their secondary batteries, putting six destroyers out of action and sinking a seventh with a single heavy shell. A third wave, intercepted by the 4th Light Cruiser Squadron, was broken up before it could get within effective torpedo range.

At the first torpedo splash, Jellicoe ordered the orthodox countermeasure, to turn *away* from the advancing torpedoes. He changed the course of the battle fleet by 45 degrees from S to SE, each sub-division of two ships twice turning two points. This maneuver probably cost Jellicoe the decisive victory almost in his grasp. With only 115 minutes of daylight remaining, it was imperative for him to maintain contact with the enemy. If he had turned *toward* the torpedoes he would have incurred little more risk than by turning away, and he would have had the overwhelming advantage of closing the enemy. His turnaway would make it difficult for him again to reach a decisive range during the remaining minutes of daylight.

At 7:35, fourteen minutes after Jellicoe's turnaway, the torpedoes were crossing the British battle line. Because their tracks were visible from the tops a mile away, the British ships easily avoided them. Jellicoe now swung back 56 degrees (five points) toward the German smoke screens and at 7:42 another 34 degrees (three points), coming eventually to course SW. Since Scheer was also steering SW, Jellicoe believed himself again to be in position to fend his opponent from his base.

As Jellicoe steadied on course SW in single line ahead at 7:45, Beatty's battle cruisers were six miles on the starboard bow of the van battle division and on a parallel course, with an armored cruiser midway between as a communicating ship. The Grand Fleet was extended in a gradually curving formation 16 miles long. Beatty had not conformed to the British battle fleet's turnaway and was keeping the German battle cruisers in sight. They were still heading SW at 7:45 when he lost them behind the smoke of the van destroyers. "Enemy bearing NW," Beatty reported, and then: "Urgent. Submit van of battleships follow battle cruisers. We can then cut off whole of enemy's battle fleet." A hitch in transmission held up delivery, but Jellicoe, on receiving Beatty's first report at 7:59, immediately turned the battle fleet by divisions to course W.

Meanwhile at 7:45 Scheer had brought the High Seas Fleet to course S. His battle cruisers now came abeam of the German pre-dreadnoughts, which had been in the van position since the 7:18 turnaway. Again Scheer's weakest units led his battle line, and the two fleets with their flagships 16 miles apart were rapidly converging.

A little after 8 PM Beatty's light cruisers made contact with Hartog's and opened fire. Beatty, turning west to lend support, encountered Scouting Group I and with a series of salvos disabled the *Derfflinger*'s last effective turret and wiped out the forebridge crew of the *Seydlitz*. As Hartog's battle cruisers disappeared to the west behind smoke, Beatty made out the German pre-dreadnoughts. After another rapid exchange of fire, the pre-dreadnoughts also swung away to west. Jellicoe had already turned his battleship divisions four points away, again forming column on course SW. Once more with the advantage all on his side, he declined to develop the contact and was preparing to take night dispositions. Beatty's battle cruisers, which had fired the first British salvos five hours before, had fired the last of the day.

In his report Jellicoe explained his refusal to seize his last opportunity to reach a decision:

Darkness was now rapidly setting in; the mist was increasing and it became necessary to decide on the future course of action. The British fleet was between the enemy and his base. . . . I rejected at once the idea of a night action between heavy ships, as leading to possible disaster owing, first, to the presence of torpedo craft in such large numbers, and secondly, to the impossibility of distinguishing between our own and enemy vessels. Further, the result of a night action under modern conditions must always be largely a matter of pure chance. I was loath to forego the advantage of position which would have resulted from an easterly or westerly course, and I therefore decided to steer to the southward, where I should be in a position to renew the engagement at daylight.

Jellicoe changed course to S at 9 PM. Twenty-four minutes later Beatty also headed south.

Scheer had ordered course SW at about the same time that Jellicoe did. Unaware that he had again nearly run into the British battle fleet, he ordered course S at 8:36. Had this order been promptly carried out, it would have brought the fleets once more into contact. But such was the confusion among the German squadrons that the change of course was not executed until after 9 PM. Thus, without realizing it, Scheer was conforming exactly to Jellicoe's movements. By 9:30 Scheer, steaming southward, was in Beatty's wake, trailing him by eight miles. Jellicoe was on his beam, nine miles to the east.

Phase IV: The Night Action

Beginning at 9:17 the British battle fleet maneuvered into night cruising formation. The four battle squadrons took station one mile apart with the cruisers ahead and on the starboard quarter. Beatty's force was 13 miles on the starboard bow of the battle fleet. Jellicoe stationed his seven destroyer flotillas five miles astern "in a position in which they could afford protection to the fleet from destroyer attack and at the same time be favorably situated for attacking the enemy's heavy ships." But the destroyers had no attack orders and no instructions other than the stationing signal.

Jellicoe's task now was to bar passage of the High Seas Fleet until dawn, which would come before 3 AM. Correctly estimating that Scheer would attempt to reach the nearest swept channel, close to Horn Reefs, he sent the fast destroyer-minelayer *Abdiel* to mine the entrances.

Scheer at 9 o'clock had only five hours in which to break through the enemy interposed between him and his base. Determined to avoid another daylight battle, he characteristically chose the simple solution. Even though he was fairly sure that the Grand Fleet lay in his path, he took the risk of the shortest route home. At 9:30 he headed for the breakthrough. Shifting his crippled battle cruisers to the rear, he ordered the fleet to turn in succession to SSE ¼ E and hold the course regardless of cost—"*durchhalten*." A series of short and deadly encounters at point blank range flared up at intervals between 10:15 PM and 2 AM as the German battleships and cruisers forced their way through the screening light forces, passing a scant half dozen miles astern of the British battle fleet.

The confused night encounters began when the German light cruisers opened fire on a flotilla of British destroyers and then on Goodenough's light cruisers. Two British cruisers suffered heavy damage and the German light cruiser *Frauenlob* was sunk by a torpedo. The German van reached the center of the British

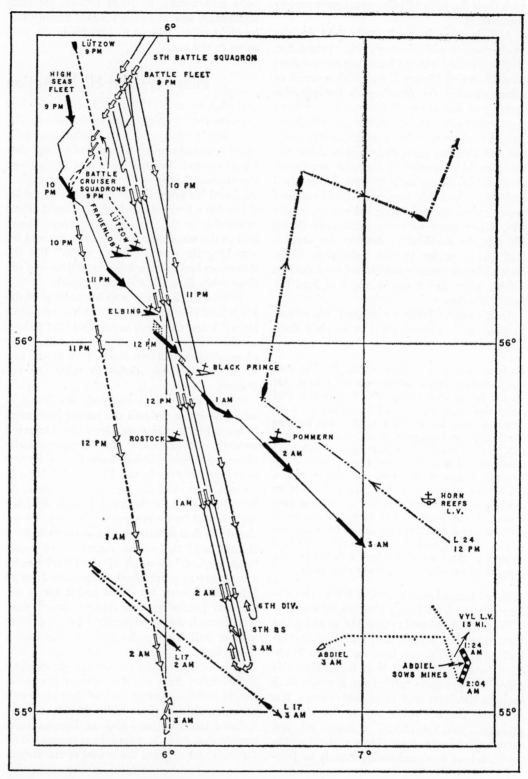

PHASE IV: THE NIGHT ACTION, 9 PM, MAY 31–3 AM, JUNE I

rear at 11:45. A scene of wild confusion followed, collisions, torpedo attacks, and gunfire all playing their parts. The action was seen by the *Malaya* and the *Valiant*, but they failed to report it because, in the words of a senior officer, "as it took place in full view of their own [squadron] flagship, it would have been most improper to have done so."[10] Instead the German penetration continued, the Germans suffering the loss of a pre-dreadnought and two light cruisers; the British, of an armored cruiser and five destroyers. By 3.30 it was over. Scheer was through with a clear path to Germany.

The night action resulted in large part from the fact that Jellicoe had correctly estimated the German fleet's position but not its course. Jellicoe's major error lay in his failing to put a correct interpretation upon the gunfire astern passing progressively from west to east. He decided that it was confined to scattered light units, and no information reached him to disabuse him of this impression. Incomplete intelligence from the Admiralty also confused the situation. Jellicoe preferred to accept the reports of men on the spot. That he lacked adequate information from his subordinates was the result of inadequate emphasis in training. That he failed to foresee the route of the German fleet from other evidence is the measure of his own responsibility as a commander. His failure was Scheer's salvation.

At 2:30 AM, Jellicoe, realizing at last that he no longer stood between the Germans and their base, turned the British fleet north. He had intended to close Horn Reefs at dawn, but the night action had so scattered his light forces that none were in sight. One Admiralty intercept now weighed heavily with him—a High Seas Fleet request for submarines. He concluded that it was "undesirable for the Battle Fleet to close the Horn Reef at daylight, as had been my intention when deciding to steer to the southward during the night. It was obviously necessary to concentrate the Battle Fleet and the destroyers before renewing action." Before this concentration had been effected, he received another Admiralty intelligence report announcing that the High Seas

[10] *The Naval Memoirs of Admiral of the Fleet Sir Roger Keyes, Scapa Flow to the Dover Straits, 1916-1918* (New York, 1935), 62n.

Fleet at 2:30 had been only 17 miles from Horn Reefs. Scheer had passed safely through the *Abdiel*'s mine field, though one of his battleships struck a mine farther south and proceeded to port with difficulty.

The Grand Fleet looked on an empty sea on this "glorious first of June" and cruised over the battle area until noon, when it headed for its bases. At that time Scheer heard the cables of the *Friedrich der Grosse* rattling through the hawse in Jade Bay.

The Aftermath

In sheer magnitude the Battle of Jutland, involving 254 ships displacing 1,600,000 tons, was the greatest battle in naval history up till its time. It was the culminating surface action of the Age of Steam—as Lepanto was the culmination of the Age of the Galley; and Trafalgar, of the Age of Sail. For the next quarter century all naval establishments the world around gave it the most intensive study. Yet, for all its sound and fury, Jutland had but few lessons of abiding value to teach.

Strategically the battle was of minor importance. Scheer had successfully escaped annihilation by flight. The blockade of Germany and the reinforcement of the Allied armies continued unimpaired. The Grand Fleet and the High Seas Fleet became what they had been before, fleets-in-being, watching each other, seeking opportunities for advantageous contacts that never came.

Tactically the battle demonstrated what British naval leaders had already concluded: that technological developments had undermined the flexibility on which concentration tactics are based. Long-range guns, high speeds of operation, and diversity of ship types had not been accompanied by a corresponding extension of the commander's "eyesight." At Trafalgar, Nelson had the whole enemy fleet in view for several hours during the slow approach. At Jutland, the opposing fleets sometimes approached each other at express train speeds, and the commanders had only minutes to make decisions based upon little or no dependable information. In the circumstances, both Jellicoe and Scheer felt it necessary to maintain a single line of battle and to hold independent squadron action to a minimum. The fleets at Jutland have aptly been compared to bodies without arms. Neverthelss, Jutland taught useful tactical lessons. When Admiral Beatty assumed command of the Grand Fleet in November 1916, he directed attention to the importance of the offensive in destroyer tactics, and promulgated the doctrine of immediate attack and maximum torpedo fire. Direction of the light cruiser forces was unified under a single commander, who was made responsible for the orderly development and reporting of contacts. Revision of the Battle Orders was taken in hand, and among other changes, divisions were directed to turn *toward* torpedoes. The name Battle Orders was changed as being too restrictive to initiative. The Battle Instructions which replaced them merely defined the intentions and objectives of the commander in chief in battle.

The material results of the Jutland battle were of considerable significance in that they taught the Royal Navy the lessons in damage control and protection that the Germans had absorbed and utilized after the Dogger Bank action. After Jutland, the British worked additional armor onto turret tops and protective decks. They installed additional fire screens, baffles, and flameproof scuttles to prevent downward flashes from cordite in turrets from setting off magazines. They improved fire control instruments and redesigned their armor-piercing shell, adopting a less sensitive bursting charge so that the shells would penetrate before exploding.

The greatest effect of the Battle of Jutland was psychological. While the retreat of the

	British	Germans
Personnel killed, wounded, and prisoners of war	6,784	3,039
Tonnage lost by sinking	111,980	62,233
Ships sunk:		
battleships	0	1
battle cruisers	3	1
armored cruisers	3	0
light cruisers	0	4
destroyers	8	5
Ships damaged:		
battleships	4	12
battle cruisers	3	5
light cruisers	3	5
destroyers and flotilla leaders	10	5

High Seas Fleet could not be called a victory, the Germans were elated in that they had more than held their own against a superior force. The ratio of fleet strength in the battle was 8 to 5 in favor of the British. The ratio of losses was approximately the same, but in favor of the Germans, as the accompanying table indicates.

The blunt communiqué released by the British Admiralty immediately after the battle made no attempt to conceal the losses. It was received by the British public and the Royal Navy with bitter disappointment, the more so because both had been schooled in the Nelsonian tradition of annihilation.

For the moment the new German navy was left with a sense of achievement, but the moral effects of its excellent showing against the world's most powerful fleet were gradually dissipated by continued inactivity in port. For after Jutland, as before, the High Seas Fleet dared not risk battle with the British main body. Save for an occasional timid training sweep and two abortive hit-run attempts on convoys to Norway, it was bottled up in port for the remainer of the war.

Offsetting the indecisive action at Jutland was the failure of Falkenhayn's offensive against Verdun. Aided by a Russian drive in Galicia and a chiefly-British offensive on the Somme, the French at Verdun held out, despite fearful attrition, through eleven months of almost continuous fighting. France was saved; the stalemate was unbroken. But at the end of 1916 several new developments foreshadowed a change one way or the other in the static war on the Western Front. Answers to the machine gun had been found in improved infantry tactics, in the invention of the military tank, and in the development of the "creeping barrage," a moving curtain of artillery fire behind which troops advanced. Russia tottered on the brink of revolution. The United States appeared about to intervene on the side of the Allies. Germany, unable to achieve decisive gains on land or on the sea, was about to launch all-out submarine warfare. "If we are not finally to be bled to death," wrote Admiral Scheer, "we must make full use of the U-boat as a means of war, so as to grip England's vital nerve."

Summary

The Battle of Jutland, the only major fleet action of World War I, came about as a result of the German decision to use surface forces more aggressively than previously. The new commander of the High Seas Fleet, Reinhardt von Scheer, attempted to lure the British into U-boat traps or to snare detachments of the Grand Fleet into one-sided action with his battleships. In the course of setting such a trap on May 31, 1916, the High Seas Fleet sortied from Jade Bay in two sections, the Scouting Force consisting of five battle cruisers and their escorts, under Vice Admiral Hipper, and the Battle Force consisting of 16 battleships and six pre-dreadnoughts with escorts, under Admiral Scheer.

A few hours earlier, on receipt of news that a portion of the High Seas Fleet was about to sortie, the British Grand Fleet had put to sea for a sweep toward the Skagerrak. Like the German force, the British Grand Fleet was divided into a Scouting Force and a Battle Force. Vice Admiral Sir David Beatty, commanding the Scouting Force, had six battle cruisers and Evan-Thomas's 5th Battle Squadron of four fast battleships, as well as three light cruiser squadrons and accompanying destroyers. Admiral Sir John Jellicoe, commanding the Battle Force, had 24 battleships, eight armored cruisers, twelve light cruisers, and three battle cruisers. Neither Scheer nor Jellicoe knew that the other was at sea. Hipper's Scouting Force took station some 40 miles to the northwest of Scheer, while Beatty's steamed some 70 miles southeast of Jellicoe. The first contact came about as a result of the chance interception of a neutral merchant ship, which enabled Beatty's force to engage Hipper's.

The Battle of Jutland divides into four phases. The first of these, the battle cruiser action between the two scouting forces, lasted from 3:20 to 4:50 PM on May 31. Hipper, outnumbered by Beatty, raced to the southeast in an attempt to lure Beatty's force under the guns of Scheer. Beatty's main strength, the four fast battleships, got separated in the preliminary maneuvering and took no effective part in the early stages of this phase. During the running battle between the opposing battle cruisers, the British took far more damage than they inflicted. Two of Hipper's ships were heavily hit, but the British lost both the *Indefatigable* and the *Queen Mary*. As Evan-Thomas's squadron came within range, Commodore Goodenough's cruiser scouts spotted Scheer's battleships approaching. Beatty now had the opportunity of luring Scheer under Jellicoe's guns. Accordingly he turned away, covering his maneuver by destroyer attacks and by the enterprising actions of Evan-Thomas's battleships.

In the second phase of the battle, lasting from 4:50 to 6 PM, Beatty and Evan-Thomas steamed to the north, pursued by the combined forces of Hipper and Scheer. Beatty led the Germans to an unsuspected rendezvous with Jellicoe. On joining the British Battle Force, Beatty led his battle cruisers across the front of the formation, while Evan-Thomas added his battleships to the rear of Jellicoe's battle line.

The third phase, the main fleet action, lasted from 6:00 PM until darkness at approximately 9:15. Jellicoe, as he waited for Beatty to rejoin, urgently needed reliable information on the location of the German fleet. Here he was ill-served by his subordinates, especially Beatty, who sent few and inadequate reports. Rather than risk missing the Germans altogether or permitting them a free run back to Germany, Jellicoe delayed his deployment into battle line until the last possible moment. Finally, at 6:15 PM, he deployed to the left, eastward. As he completed his line, turning to course SE by E, he successfully capped the T on Scheer coming up in column from the southwest. A more effective deployment could hardly have been arranged, even if Jellicoe had controlled the movements of both opposing fleets. Under the misty conditions of the North Sea however, Jellicoe did not realize his opportunity, and did not open decisive fire. At 6:35 Scheer, seeing nothing ahead but gun flashes, executed a "battle turn" to disengage. Jellicoe, losing contact, turned south by divisions, while Scheer at 6:55 turned back east to re-engage. Scheer's move carried his column head-on through smoke and mists once more into the center of the British Battle Force, which thus again capped his T. Scheer now realized that he could not penetrate and repeated his "turnaway," covering his turn with a battle cruiser sortie to draw fire and with a destroyer attack. At this moment, the crisis of the battle, Jellicoe lost sight of his objective of destroying the German fleet and turned away by sub-divisions to avoid torpedoes fired by the German destroyers. This evolution again broke off the engagement. Almost by chance the fleets drew together once more a little after 8 PM. There was an exchange of fire by the vans, but Jellicoe declined to develop the contact because of the approach of nightfall. When darkness came, the fleets were steaming on parallel southerly courses. Jellicoe, planning to renew the action at daybreak, was between Scheer and his base.

The fourth phase, the night action, lasted from 9:30 PM, May 31, until 3 AM, June 1. Scheer, determined to regain his base, shifted to course SSE ¼ E, ordering his fleet to hold the course regardless of cost. Having dropped behind the British main body, he forced his way through the British rear with the loss of an old battleship and two light cruisers, while sinking a British armored cruiser and five destroyers. He had completed his breakthrough before Jellicoe could get a clear picture of the situation in his rear. At 2:30 Jellicoe, realizing that his quarry had escaped, and not daring to venture closer to the German mine fields, turned north. Scheer reached Jade Bay that afternoon.

Jutland was the last surface action fought between lines of battleships in daylight. It revealed the off-balance development of naval technology, in which speed and long-range fire had outstripped the commander's means of observation or controlling his own forces. In the circumstances, tactical doctrine for steam surface navies never reached maturity.

25:

The War against Shipping

The continuing war at sea was conducted mainly for the protection, interdiction, or destruction of shipping—military and mercantile. From the first to the last day of fighting, each side carried on this unceasing battle, for on its outcome depended all else, on land, sea, or in the air. Britain, following her tradition of centuries, imposed a blockade on Germany, expecting it to be even more effective than in the past because of the increased need for imports imposed on Germany by industrialization. Yet by judicious stockpiling, development of substitute materials, and by imports through neutrals, Germany blunted the edge of the blockade and endured four years of relative isolation from the markets of the world. She struck back at sea, weakly at first, but with gradually increasing effectiveness. Her most telling instrument in this counterblockade, the U-boat, was at the beginning discounted by nearly everyone as an inefficient means of commerce raiding, as indeed it was if used in accordance with the then generally recognized rules of visit and search. Used unrestrictedly however the U-boat brought Germany to the brink of victory.

Conceived as a scouting auxiliary to the fleet and as a means of making underwater attacks on warships, the submarine appeared at first to present no vital danger to merchant shipping. In fact commerce raiding occupied a low position in Germany's initial strategy, for the continental-minded General Staff expected to win the decision quickly on land. Even in the German navy this view of commerce raiding prevailed, for as students of Mahan's writings they believed that *guerre de course* could not result in the destruction of enough shipping to force Britain from the war, and would have even less effect against France.

Both the British and the German navies viewed the naval war largely in terms of conventional naval battle. Each side recognized the North Sea as the area of decision. Specifically designed for North Sea operations, the German High Seas Fleet had a combat radius of only 575 miles. Hence most of its ships were useless as raiders. With no possibility of the German main fleet's breaking out into the Atlantic to interdict supplies to Britain, all Britain had to fear were small squadrons such as Spee's in the Pacific, occasional surface raiders such as the *Emden,* and armed, disguised merchant ships. The possibility that the submarine might prove a new and deadly peril to Britain's Merchant Navy, outside as well as inside the North Sea, was foreseen by few and generally dismissed from serious consideration. Only Lord Fisher anticipated the submarine menace, but Churchill and Admiral Prince Louis of Battenburg, the First Sea Lord at the outbreak of war, discounted his warnings.

The British Blockade

Britain's establishment of the blockade against Germany was not as simple as it had been against France in the Napoleonic wars. In the first place, Germany had control of the Baltic and could import freely from northern neutrals. Second, changes in ships and guns, the invention of the submarine and the mine, and the threat of the still untested airplanes made close blockade impossible, and distant blockade could not be fully effective. Yet under International Law, a blockade to be legal must be effective. In an effort to resolve this dilemma, an international commission had met in London in 1909. The resulting Declaration of London defined new distinctions in contraband: *absolute contraband,* such as munitions and other obvious war materials, and *conditional contraband,* including food, clothing, and railroad equipment, which could be used for peaceful as well as wartime employment. Finally there remained *free goods,* presumably of no war value. The Declaration applied the doctrine of continuous voyage only to absolute contraband, so that in perfect conformity with the doctrine, Germany during the war would presumably be able to import any item on the conditional contraband list through neutral countries.

Britain had refused to ratify the Declaration of London, which would have struck at the heart of her sea strategy. When war broke out she adhered to its provisions only for a few months, and even then only as she chose to interpret them. By frequent Orders in Council she arbitrarily transferred items from the conditional to the absolute contraband list. She enforced her contraband-control measures primarily by the Tenth Cruiser Squadron, based at Liverpool and in the Shetland Islands. This squadron, consisting of 18 and later 24 cruisers and armed merchant cruisers, intercepted and sent to British ports many German vessels making for home. But they could not intercept them all in the characteristic conditions of low visibility in the North Sea.

In order to control neutral shipping, the British on October 2, 1914 proclaimed a mine field across the southern end of the North Sea from the Thames to Belgium. Neutrals had to call at English ports for contraband-control search before receiving sailing instructions through the mine field. A month later the British Admiralty proclaimed the entire North Sea and the waters between Iceland and the Norwegian coast a war zone and prescribed one swept route through the Channel and into the Baltic. The effect of these two proclamations was to give Britain control of all shipping to Northern Europe, for, with negligible exceptions, merchant ship captains were glad to put into British ports, even though it meant inspection of cargo, in order to get clearance and safe passage on to their destinations. Germany not unnaturally proclaimed the blockade to be uncivilized warfare waged against helpless women and children and strove with all possible means to break it. Her first U-boat operations struck at the blockading warships, with the sinking in September 1914 of cruisers *Pathfinder, Aboukir, Hogue,* and *Cressy,* all engaged in blockade patrol. Such operations however could have little effect on Germany's situation. Since her own merchant marine was largely swept from the sea, she turned more and more to using neutral bottoms to import the necessities of life. British inspections of neutral ships resulted in the confiscation of any contraband consigned to Germany. Further, the British also rationed neutral imports of certain strategic commodities to the average of pre-war levels in order to cut down on transshipment to Germany. These measures caused keen resentment in neutral countries, but the British had to ignore such reactions in order to keep the blockade effective. To encourage the maximum amount of shipping, the British inaugurated a State War Risks Insurance scheme which was effective for all ships carrying British goods, provided their masters conformed to Admiralty routing instructions.

The First U-Boat Campaign, February 22 to September 20, 1915

In response to the British declaration of November 2, 1914 of the entire North Sea as a War Zone, Tirpitz submitted to his govern-

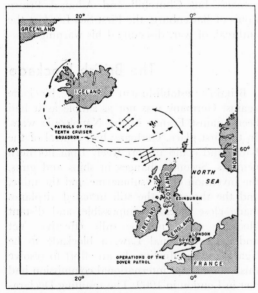

THE BLOCKADE OF GERMANY

ment an appreciation urging the use of U-boats against Britain's trade. Since it took considerable time to weigh the political implications, including the possibility of American entry into the war against Germany, U-boat warfare against merchant ships was delayed until February 1915. On February 4, Admiral Pohl published in the Imperial Gazette the following warning:

(1) The waters around Great Britain and Ireland including the whole of the English Channel are hereby declared to be a War Zone. From February 18 onwards every enemy merchant vessel encountered in this zone will be destroyed, nor will it always be possible to avert the danger thereby threatened to the crew and passengers.

(2) Also neutral ships will run a risk in the War Zone, because in view of the British authorization of January 31 of the misuse of neutral flags and hazards of sea warfare, it may not always be possible to prevent attacks on enemy ships from harming neutral ships.[1]

To implement this first U-boat campaign, the German navy had 24 U-boats ready for operations, a gain of six since the opening of the war. U-boats employed in World War I fell into four main classes, as follows: (1) U-cruisers: with great range and maximum surface speed of 16 to 17 knots, but carrying comparatively few torpedoes; (2) U-boats: generally 600 to 900 tons surface displacement, having a surface speed of 15 to 16 knots and an underwater speed of 7.5, and carrying from 10 to 16 torpedoes or from 34 to 36 mines; (3) UB-boats: approximately 125 tons, later enlarged up to 500 tons, with a surface speed of 12 to 13 knots and a submerged speed of 7.5 knots, and carrying four torpedoes; and (4) UC-boats: principally designed for minelaying, at first 150-ton boats of 6-knot surfaced and 5-knot submerged speed; later versions displaced 400 tons.

The principal U-boat bases were in the German Bight of the North Sea, with additional training establishments at Kiel and Danzig. In the Mediterranean the operating bases were Pola and Cattaro on the eastern shore of the Adriatic. In March 1915 the Flanders U-Flotilla was established, operating chiefly UB- and UC-boats from Zeebrugge and

Ostend with repair yards at Bruges. Boats proceeding from Germany usually took station in the North Sea or followed the long route around Scotland to reach the Western Approaches area, the focal waters to the west of the British Isles through which all ships bound for British ports had to pass. Flanders-based boats operated generally in the English Channel and up to the mouth of the Thames and also employed the Channel as a short route to the Western Approaches. Not until the summer of 1918 were the British able effectively to close the Dover Strait to U-boats.

In response to orders based on the declaration of February 4, 1915, some 20 U-boats took station in the North Sea, the English Channel, and the Western Approaches area. In spite of neutral, especially American, protests against a "paper blockade," the U-boats struck, sinking an average of 1.3 ships daily for the remainder of the year, or nearly 100,000 Gross Register Tons per month.[2]

The first campaign soon fell foul of stronger American diplomatic pressure. On May 7, 1915 the unarmed, unescorted British liner *Lusitania,* steaming slowly off the coast of southern Ireland, was torpedoed and sunk by *U-20.* Among the dead were 128 Americans. The United States dispatched a stiff diplomatic protest to Germany, characterizing the attack as murder on the high seas. The note demanded guarantees for the safety of Americans on the seas, and immunity of passenger steamers to attack. Germany merely dismissed the note with the reply that the *Lusitania* had been carrying war materials and was therefore a legitimate target of war. Great was American indignation, yet, as Germany had foreseen, the United States was not prepared to go to war.

A few months later, in August, the British steamer *Arabic,* off Kinsale, Ireland, crossed the path of *U-24,* which promptly sent her to the bottom. The loss of three American lives in this sinking brought American protests to the point of threatening war. Germany now wavered. Chancellor Theobald von Bethmann-

[1] Arno Spindler, *Der Handelskrieg mit U-booten* (Berlin, 1932), III, 87.

[2] Gross Register Ton, abbreviated G.R.T., is an internationally accepted measure of the carrying capacity of a cargo ship, computed on the basis of 100 cubic feet of cargo space per ton. Warship tonnage is measured in displacement tons. A freighter of 3,000 G.R.T. would have about 5,000 tons displacement.

Hollweg and Admiral Georg Müller of the Emperor's Naval Staff both urged a conciliatory approach to the United States. As a result, all U-boats not in the operational area were held at dockside until a decision could be made. On September 20, the first phase of the U-boat campaign came to an end with the order that passenger liners would be immune from attack. In view of the tense diplomatic situation in the North Atlantic, Germany shifted the focus of her operations to the Mediterranean, where she sank over 100 Allied merchantmen during the remainder of the year.

The year 1915 ended without either side gaining a decisive advantage in the commercial war. Britain's new construction replaced all but a few thousand tons of her merchant ship losses. German U-boat losses remained well within acceptable limits. Germany had lost 23 boats from all causes since the beginning of the war, but she now had 68 in commission. Her construction-to-loss ratio was almost five to one. In spite of the limitations imposed on the U-boats, they had done a remarkable job, and senior naval officers such as Tirpitz and Scheer longed to release them for unrestricted submarine warfare.

Germany's Second U-Boat Campaign, 1916

Early in 1916 Germany reconsidered her U-boat policy. General Ludendorff and Admiral Tirpitz mistakenly believed that the United States had become somewhat more sympathetic toward U-boat warfare. But the Kaiser, after considerable wavering, brushed aside the protests of General von Falkenhayn and, ignoring Tirpitz altogether, postponed the campaign and prescribed that attacks without warning be made only within the war zone and on merchant ships carrying guns for protection from submarines. Deeply offended, Tirpitz resigned.

Within two weeks a new German-American crisis arose. On March 24 *UB-29* sank the unarmed, unescorted French steamer *Sussex*. Three Americans were injured. The United States immediately threatened to break diplomatic relations with Germany unless she conducted submarine warfare in strict conformity with International Law. The German government replied with the "*Sussex* pledge," promising that submarine attacks on commerce would be conducted in the future in strict conformity to Prize Law, which required visit and search and provisions for the safety of passengers and crew before sinking. Admiral Scheer, believing that war conducted by U-boats in accordance with Prize Law could not possibly succeed, recalled his submarines from Western waters and announced that the U-boat campaign against British commerce had ceased. The Kaiser approved of Scheer's abandonment of the war against merchant shipping and ordered a vigorous U-boat campaign against warships.

From May to September 1916 the Germans attempted several U-boat ambushes of the type Jellicoe had foreseen when he wrote his famous letter to the Admiralty in October 1914.[3] Scheer planned raids against unfortified British east coast cities, using surface units as bait and submarines to ambush any British forces lured out. A dozen U-boats were so employed at the time the British Grand Fleet sortied for the sweep that led to the Battle of Jutland. In August U-boats sank the British cruisers *Nottingham* and *Falmouth*.

In the Mediterranean the war against commerce continued unabated. In mid-March 1916, Britain began to direct Australian and Far Eastern shipping from the Suez Canal-Mediterranean Sea route to the longer but safer passage around the Cape of Good Hope. This measure proved a prudent anticipation of the German threat, for losses in the Mediterranean were second only to those in the North Sea.

Germany's Decision to Adopt Unrestricted U-Boat Warfare

As 1916 drew to a close, increasing pessimism in the German army brought recognition that if Germany was to win the war, her chief hope lay in the U-boat arm. General Field Marshal Paul von Hindenburg, now Chief of the German General Staff, realized that Germany was losing the war simply because she

[3] See page 434, above.

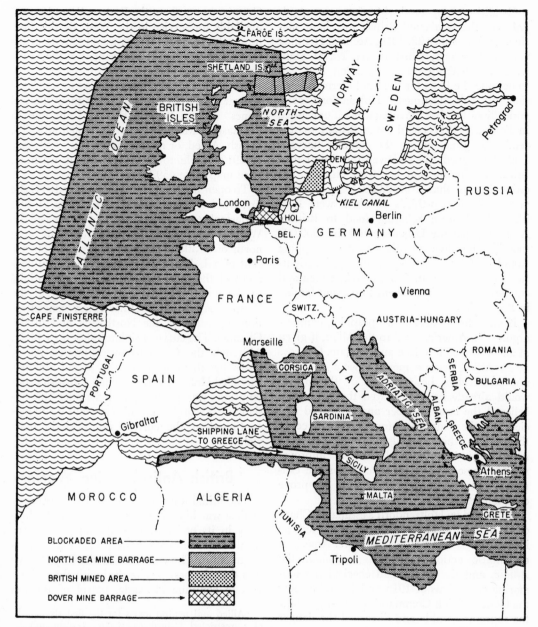

ALLIED MINED AREAS AND GERMAN BARRED ZONES

was not winning. No longer could she afford a military stalemate. The great Verdun offensive had drained German manpower, and the inexorable crush of the British blockade had caused suffering in the Fatherland itself. All weapons had been tested and exploited to the full except one—the U-boat. In the first campaign of 1915 the Germans believed they had destroyed a monthly average of 120,000 G.R.T. of Allied shipping and in the second of 1916, 216,000 G.R.T.[4]

[4] These figures are German wartime estimates which formed the basis for their decision. Actual sinkings averaged 113,000 G.R.T. per month for the 1915 campaign and 192,000 G.R.T. for that of 1916.

Conditions appeared ripe for a *coup de grâce* to the weakened British merchant marine. On December 22, 1916, Admiral Henning von Holtzendorff, Chief of the Naval Staff, wrote Hindenburg an appreciation that was to become the basis for the final German decision. In this document, Holtzendorff categorically stated that the submarines if unleashed in February 1917 could force Britain to surrender by June, before the summer harvests could be reaped. He reviewed the situation of Britain's shipping and her food imports. His estimate was that 10,750,000 tons of cargo vessels, about two-thirds of which were British registry, were bringing food to Britain. Assuming that the U-boats could sink 600,000 monthly for five months, neutral shipping would be driven from the traffic by the frightful losses, and the surviving merchantmen and cargoes would be insufficient to prevent famine in England.

Holtzendorff dismissed possible counterarguments. American aid to the Allies, if given at all, would be too little and too late. Convoys as an Allied defense measure were obviously not practicable, he assumed, or the British would already have employed them. He also believed the large number and improved efficiency of the underwater force Germany could throw into the campaign would outweigh Allied antisubmarine technological improvements. These predictions, except for the estimated tonnage to be sunk, were to prove completely wrong.

Impressed by Holtzendorff's estimates, Chancellor Bethmann-Hollweg finally supported the idea of unrestricted U-boat warfare. American diplomatic action over the *Lusitania,* the *Arabic,* and the *Sussex* had checked the submarine campaigns of 1915 and 1916, but now the German High Command was ready to take the supreme gamble and disregard the danger of an American declaration of war.

On January 9, 1917 the Kaiser ordered his 82 North Sea and Flanders boats to begin unrestricted submarine warfare on February 1. "The U-boat war is the last card," commented Bethmann-Hollweg ominously. For better or for worse Germany had set her fate upon a cast and now waited the hazard of the die. Ironically enough, a month after the campaign began revolution broke out in Russia, and soon German troops from the Eastern Front became available for service in the West. By this time however, American troops were ready to counterbalance German reinforcement of the Western Front.

As the first step in implementing unrestricted U-boat warfare, Germany proclaimed "Barred Zones" around Britain, France, Italy, and in the Eastern Mediterranean, in which all ships, British, Allied, or neutral, were, after February 1, 1917, liable to be sunk without warning. (See map page 459.)

To open the campaign in February 1917, the first wave of boats from the North Sea Flotilla undertook to run the Straits of Dover to the Western Approaches, for the roundabout route north of Scotland normally consumed 50 per cent of a U-boat's patrol time. Thus, employment of the short passage added substantially to the number of U-boats on station in the Western Approaches. Other heavy concentrations operated in the North Sea and in the Channel. The curve of sinkings shot up rapidly. Although the Germans overestimated Allied losses by about a third, the actual sinkings exceeded Holtzendorff's estimate.[5] British economy and war potential reeled under the onslaught. It soon became obvious that if sinkings continued at the current rate, Britain must yield.

British Antisubmarine Warfare

The initial use of U-boats in 1914 primarily against warships encouraged the British Admiralty in its belief that no special precautions would be necessary for the protection of merchant ships. The consensus in the Royal Navy was that the best way to deal with the U-boat was to continue blockade, patrol of the sea

[5] Allied and neutral losses for the first six months of unrestricted U-boat campaign as estimated by the Germans and actual figures:

Month of 1917	German estimate (G.R.T.)	Admiralty record (G.R.T.)
February	781,500	536,334
March	885,000	603,440
April	1,091,000	875,023
May	869,000	594,654
June	1,016,000	684,667
July	811,000	549,047
Monthly average	908,917	680,628

routes, and knocking out the bases from which the boats operated. Hence the British made bombing raids on the U-boat bases and sent increasing numbers of submarines, airships, and surface ships to patrol waters traversed by the U-boats.

At the outset the Admiralty and the War Council decided that the convoy system that had safeguarded British shipping in the wars against France would not be reinstituted during the war against the Central Powers. A spirit of *laissez faire* had come upon British shippers and on their government during the century of peace following the defeat of Napoleon. British ships carried the Red Ensign to all parts of the world, following well recognized routes and bringing to Britain 80 per cent of her foodstuffs and most of the raw materials essential for war. Since the coming of steam propulsion made predictable schedules possible, British shipping had come to an increasing extent to run on a timetable that war restrictions and the frustrations of convoy would upset completely. Also, it was argued, should the British government impose war restrictions on British shipping, neutral carriers would be quick to take over large portions of the intensely competitive carrying trade. To sum up: economic considerations argued that government control of shipping, even in time of war, was undesirable.

Another reason for the decision to allow shipping to proceed on a peacetime basis was the overwhelming professional opinion that convoys, economically feasible or not, merely served to bunch targets, to add to the dangers of collision, to delay sailings, and to cut the efficiency of shipping to an unacceptable extent. While these assumptions could not be statistically proved, neither could the contrary, for Marine Insurance Underwriters such as Lloyds no longer had valid actuarial documents. During the Napoleonic wars Lloyds had offered insurance at substantially lower premiums to ships sailing in convoy than to those undertaking an independent voyage. The reason was obvious. Their statistics showed that ships in convoy were four to five times safer than "runners," as independents and those that broke convoy were called. But with the Industrial Revolution, the vast increase in size and cargo capacity of ships, and the regularity

of routes and schedules made the lessons of the past appear to be no longer applicable. Proponents of the *status quo* argued that if the ships were well spread out in their customary routes the enemy could not hope to destroy more than single units, while with expert gunnery he might wipe out an entire convoy. The Admiralty, they maintained, should make the sea routes safer by patrol.

Behind this expression "sea routes" lies a major revolution in naval thought headed by Mahan, whose books had affected professional thinking in the admiralties of the world. Unfortunately Mahan, having to invent a terminology to carry his meaning, had borrowed from land warfare such phrases as "lines of communication," "communication routes," and "sea lanes." These expressions quickly became catch phrases to naval strategists. Since it is easier to quote Mahan than it is to read him, his disciples employed his terminology without noting the careful qualifications he had employed. As long as great circle lines connecting ports could be drawn on a chart, they became "sea lines of communication" and by 1914 navies conceived it their duty to protect these "lines." Actually their business was and is to protect *ships*. Sea lines of communication carry nothing; ships carry the trade of the world. No major naval power has ever failed to protect a reasonable number of its ships when it did not divert its efforts in the attempt to protect sea routes.[6]

When the Germans launched their first campaign against merchant shipping in the spring of 1915, the British Admiralty continued the same methods of patrolling and minesweeping. Since it was physically impossible to patrol and to sweep the entire area customarily used in peacetime, and since the British had themselves by means of mine fields closed large areas of the waters around the British Isles to shipping, the plan was to force merchant ships into well-defined channels, which in theory would be easy to protect. The end result however was to make it easier for the U-boats to find their victims. The mere presence of patrolling vessels usually indicated that ships would follow, for

[6] The best study of routes *vs.* ships is to be found in David W. Waters, "The Philosophy and Conduct of Maritime War," *Journal of The Royal Naval Scientific Service*, May and July, 1958.

it was British practice to hold shipping until a "safe route" had been prepared. Many an enterprising U-boat commander merely kept out of the way until the patrols were past and then waited, confident that a freighter would blunder his way. Under this system of "offensive patrolling," U-boats by the end of 1916 had sent to the bottom 1,660 ships, a few by submarine-laid mines, but most by torpedo and gunfire. In addition, delays in waiting for "safe routes" caused a 30 per cent loss in shipping capacity.

The British meanwhile desperately sought any and every measure to carry the war to the U-boat. Almost from the first, large merchant ships were provided with guns and gun crews so that they could fight it out with a surfaced U-boat. These vessels were at a considerable disadvantage. The silhouette of a U-boat offered a small target for their generally poorly trained gun crews. To make matters worse, many armed merchant ships never had a chance to use their guns at all, for the Germans regarded them as warships, not entitled to any of the conventions protecting merchant ships under International Law. Hence many were sunk by torpedo without warning.

The problem of locating a submerged U-boat remained the crux of the antisubmarine effort. The hydrophone, invented in 1915, had very limited use until late in 1917. This was a device that could pick up underwater noises and indicate their bearing but not their range, although a skilled operator could make an estimate of the range by the volume of noise made by a propeller. If two hydrophones could be employed from widely differing bearings, the cross bearings would then give a reasonable approximation of the location of a U-boat. Unless the U-boat was moving, the hydrophone was useless. U-boat commanders quickly learned that by lying quietly on the bottom, they could escape detection.

The next major problem was to destroy the U-boat. Early experiments with howitzers proving of little success, the British turned to the depth charge, a canister of TNT fitted with a hydrostatically operated pistol to function at a pre-set depth. There were two types of depth charge, one containing 300 pounds of TNT, the other, 120 pounds. The limited supply of depth charges restricted the allowance per patrolling ship to two of each type. In practice not even all destroyers obtained their complete allowance and other ASW vessels received none at all. Not until 1917 were production details ironed out. The small model was then abolished. Early in 1918 destroyers carried 30 to 40 of the larger model.

One of the most enthusiastically attempted countermeasures was the submarine decoy known as the "Q-ship." First employed in 1915, Q-ships operated with considerable success from Queenstown, Scapa Flow, and elsewhere until the adoption of unrestricted U-boat attacks rendered their tactics useless. Nearly every type of vessel was employed in this service—cargo carriers, drifters, trawlers, sailing ships, ketches, and "convoy sloops," so called to distinguish them from standard sloops. At first the method was for the Q-ship to allow herself to be stopped by the surfaced U-boat, whereupon she would drop screens concealing guns and open fire. Picked gun crews proved so effective that U-boats became wary and began to rely more and more on submerged torpedo attack. Q-ships then countered with some small success by means of hydrophones and torpedo tubes which could fire torpedoes set to hit a submerged U-boat.

Underwater traps for the U-boats were also attempted in narrow straits and off important headlands. Submarine nets were occasionally effective, although most U-boats managed to wriggle free. Best results were achieved by a combination of nets and mines, with patrolling aircraft and surface vessels to force the U-boats to submerge. It was this combination which in June 1918 caused the general abandonment of the Dover Strait route for boats of the North Sea U-flotilla.

In spite of all these measures, in spite of the employment of thousands of surface craft and hundreds of aircraft, in spite of the laying of more than 22,000 mines by the end of 1916, the sinkings continued. In September 1916 three U-boats operated in the small area of the Channel between Beachy Head and Eddystone. In that same area were patrolling 572 antisubmarine vessels—49 destroyers, 48 torpedo boats, 7 Q-ships, and 468 armed auxiliaries. The presence of the U-boats was known, shipping was delayed, and every effort was made to track down and sink the three U-boats. At the end of a week they escaped unscathed, having sunk 30 ships.[7]

By late 1916, the Germans were sinking an average of over 150 ships per month, and several prominent officers, including Admiral Jellicoe, predicted Britain's collapse unless some means could be devised to counter the U-boat and to offset losses.

Reorganization of the Admiralty

From his flagship at Scapa Flow, Jellicoe had bombarded the Admiralty with memoranda on the U-boat peril. Partly as a result of these notes, Lloyd George, on taking office as Prime Minister in December 1916, appointed Jellicoe First Sea Lord. The continuing loss of merchant shipping Jellicoe made his chief concern. He realized that he faced a revolution in naval warfare. The U-boat, by its grim efficiency in destroying ships, had given a secondary naval power the capacity to defeat a major sea power dependent for survival on imports by sea.

To enable him to grapple with this new realization, Jellicoe obtained approval of a reorganization of the Admiralty which brought about two outstandingly important reforms. Before this reorganization, the First Sea Lord, as we have seen, had no effective control over operations, which in practice were carried out by the Chief of Staff, often on instructions coming directly from the civilian First Lord. The primary responsibility of the First Sea Lord lay in logistics and material for the naval establishment, and he was too burdened with petty administrative decisions to deal adequately with major strategic problems. After the reorganization, the First Sea Lord took on the title also of Chief of the Naval Staff and became in fact head of plans and operations. He thus had a role equivalent in function to the United States Chief of Naval Operations, an office established two years earlier.

Under the First Sea Lord were a Deputy Chief of Naval Staff, to conduct fleet opera-

[7] Example taken from D. W. Waters, "Historical Survey of Trade Defence Since 1914," *Royal United Services Institute Journal*, August, 1954.

tions, and an Assistant Chief of Naval Staff, to direct the defense of merchant shipping and the war against the U-boat. The effect was to give increased emphasis to antisubmarine measures and the protection of shipping.

The United States Navy in 1914–1915

When Europe went to war in 1914, the United States was fully occupied with its domestic problems and had little thought to spare for the conflict beyond the seas. Economic depression had gripped the country since 1909, and voter dissatisfaction in 1912 had resulted in the election of a Democratic President, Woodrow Wilson. Although Wilson favored the Allied cause, he was determined on a policy of strict neutrality. Yet in face of British sea power, actual neutrality was impossible. If the United States sold goods to all customers, she would aid France and Britain, whose navies cut off all shipments to Germany. If the United States embargoed war shipments, she would not only be cutting her own economic throat; she would aid the Germans by weakening the Allies. Because most American government leaders were pro-Ally in sentiment, and because no one in or out of office dreamed of crippling American economy by means of an embargo, the United States elected to sell goods to all comers. The primary concern was for American enterprise, rapidly recovering under the war boom. Aid to the Allies was a more or less acceptable by-product.

The same sea power that preserved Britain brought her trouble with the United States. As one of the largest participants in the world's carrying trade, the United States demanded of the belligerents neutral rights, freedom to trade where she pleased, and guarantees for the safety of ships and crews. This policy collided head-on with Britain's blockade. Since inspections of ships for contraband on the high seas in submarine waters was a risky business for the inspecting warship, the British, arguing "exceptional conditions," ordered neutral ships into British ports where complete inspections —sometimes requiring months—could be made. Infuriated ship owners, whose demurrage costs rose spectacularly, denounced the British and demanded protection from these seizures. American protests went regularly to Britain, but the British, with the acquiescence of the pro-British American Ambassador, Walter Hines Page, played a waiting game. Their strategy was sound. With every passing week, American economy, emerging from depression, became more bound to Allied war purchases. Soon many of those who had most loudly clamored for American men-of-war on Britain's doorstep happily accepted Allied contracts and sent their ships regularly to Britain and France. Nonetheless, incidents involving stoppages and delays of American ships remained to some degree a cause of Anglo-American friction until the United States entered the war.

The U.S. Navy in 1914 looked on the war in Europe as remote and undertook no program of preparedness specifically envisioning American participation. Still thinking in terms of a navy "second only to Britain's," American naval leaders concerned themselves with the fleet as an instrument of international force, without concern over where that force might best be applied. The 1914 program of the General Board increased its previous year's recommendations only slightly, and, in the name of economy, Secretary Josephus Daniels cut these proposals drastically.

In the interests of efficient planning and operations, the Navy had for some years sought to create an Office of Naval Operations. This plan, drafted anew in 1915, fell foul of opposition on the part of those in Congress who feared military influence high in government and of those representatives from inland states who saw little value in the navy. Eventually a much weakened version was passed, providing for a Chief, "who shall, under the direction of the Secretary of the Navy, be charged with the operations of the fleet, and with preparation and readiness of plans for its use in war." In March 1915 Rear Admiral William S. Benson became the first Chief of Naval Operations. He brought his broad experience to bear on problems of readiness. He required the Bureaus to report on their war readiness, and provided for naval inspection of merchant vessels to determine their fitness for service in time of war. He gave full support to improvements in radio communications and communication security

and arranged for the procurement of additional ordnance and ammunition. In 1915 the U.S. Navy established a Consulting Board, including such prominent scientists as Thomas A. Edison, Elmer Sperry, and Dr. William Coolidge, to study problems in technological research and development, particularly in antisubmarine warfare. This move marked the beginning of the navy's close alliance with science and industry which made possible some of the greatest advances of the 20th century.

"A Navy Second to None"

In 1916 American public opinion came increasingly to favor the Allies. The change was partly a result of skillful British propaganda; partly, the result of increasing numbers of sinkings by U-boats of ships carrying Americans. The *Lusitania* case and the legalistic excuses of the German Foreign Office cut the ground from under many German sympathizers and stiffened Wilson in his determination to insist on American rights. Germany had strengthened Wilson's pro-Ally position. The President saw a great difference between the British blockade which merely cost money and the counter-blockade by Germany which cost the lives of women and children. In vain might Germany protest that the British blockade would starve many more women and children than would ever be lost at sea. So strong was Wilson's second note to Germany on the *Lusitania* sinking that the pacifistic Secretary of State, William Jennings Bryan, resigned in protest, averring that it would bring war.

Wilson, too wise to repeat the error of 1812 by going to war with a divided country, frankly joined the ranks of those who counseled preparedness and swung his weight behind the naval building program pending before Congress. Entrenched opposition appeared so strong that Wilson took his case to the country, speaking of the need for America to have the "greatest navy in the world." After much maneuvering, the Naval Act of 1916 became law on August 29. Behind it lay America's new desire to possess a navy equal to any afloat—"a navy second to none," as the slogan became. During the debates, the Battle of Jutland had strengthened the hand of those favoring big ships. If Germany could defy the

Grand Fleet, America must look to her own navy, for the British might not be there the next time to block the Germans. Then, so the propaganda went, America would be vulnerable to forays by a successful expansionist Germany. As a result, the Act proposed to add to the American navy in the short space of three years 10 battleships, 6 battle cruisers, 10 scout cruisers, 50 destroyers, 9 fleet submarines, 58 coast submarines, and 14 miscellaneous vessels. Other important features of the Naval Act of 1916 were the enlargement of the Office of Naval Operations and the statutory requirement that its chief hold the rank of admiral. It provided for a Naval Flying Corps and a Naval Reserve Force, thus providing a way for the navy to correct some of its glaring personnel deficiencies.

The passage of the Naval Act did not mean that the United States Navy was getting ready for participation in the war. The act was long range in its aims, being interpreted by the Administration as a plan to insure "normal growth," envisioning a postwar situation when America would take her rightful place as a world leader. Meanwhile, despite protests from administrative officers and from the Chief of Naval Operations, Secretary Daniels resisted all pressure to prepare for war. He refused to allow the navy to build suitable antisubmarine vessels, to equip and man the ships they had in commission, or to put the ships themselves in top condition. President Wilson was running for re-election on the slogan "He kept us out of war." The Secretary regarded effective war preparations as politically inexpedient.

America's Road to War

Before Wilson had taken the oath of office for his second term, Germany announced her policy of unrestricted U-boat warfare. The note proclaiming this decision as delivered to the United States contained the mocking provision that one American vessel a week would be allowed to proceed to and from Britain, provided the vessel conformed strictly to German instructions and carried no contraband. In the face of this calculated effrontery, Wilson, as he was bound to do by his stand on the "Sussex pledge," severed diplomatic relations with Germany on February 3, 1917. Shortly afterward followed the notorious Zimmerman note of March 1, an attempt to bribe Mexico to join Germany in the event of war with the United States in return for Texas, Arizona, and New Mexico. This sensational proposal had been intercepted by the British and turned over to the American government. It roused even those Americans still urging neutrality.

Meanwhile, on February 26, Wilson had requested authority from Congress to arm American merchant ships. Passed overwhelmingly in the House of Representatives, the legislation was killed in the Senate by a filibuster. "A little group of willful men," Wilson declared, ". . . have rendered the great Government of the United States helpless and contemptible." Wilson's legal advisers then assured him that he already had, as a part of his executive powers, the authority he desired. Accordingly Wilson issued orders for American ships bound for the war zone to be armed. In March the first merchantmen so armed put to sea.

Wilson still hoped that Germany would not go to the length of sinking American ships. Lacking "overt acts," Wilson was prepared to go no further. On March 12, the American steamer *Algonquin* was sunk without warning near the British Isles by gunfire from a German U-boat. A week later three more American ships went down before U-boat attack with the loss of 15 lives. Now there was no more hesitation. On April 2, Wilson grimly told Congress, "The world must be made safe for Democracy. . . . The right is more precious than peace, and we shall fight for the things which we have always carried nearest our hearts." Four days later the United States declared war.

The Crisis of the War

In early 1917 the Allies fared badly in the war at sea. Ships were going to the bottom faster than shipyards could replace them. In the four months following the declaration of unrestricted U-boat warfare, sinkings from all causes rose to 1,175 ships, totaling over two and a half million tons. Yet these figures do not tell the whole story. The British Admiralty had not kept differential statistics indicating the losses in short voyage as opposed to long voyage ships or between coastal and cross-

Channel as opposed to ocean shipping. From the beginning of the war the Admiralty had released weekly statements of the numbers of arrivals and departures from British ports and the number of ships sunk. Since the arrival and departure figure averaged about 5,000 and the weekly losses, even as late as March 1917, amounted to only 60 ships a week, the impression was given that only 1.17 per cent of shipping was going down. But actual ocean entrances and clearances averaged only 140 a week, and the loss among ships engaged in ocean trade was in the neighborhood of 20 per cent.

This method of announcing shipping losses was of course intended to keep the Germans from accurately estimating the success of their U-boat campaign. Nonetheless, it concealed even from those in high positions the gravity of the situation. It also wedded the Admiralty to the defense-of-routes theory, for it was obviously impossible to provide escorts for 5,000 ships a week.

In early April, Rear Admiral William S. Sims USN was sent to England to study the shipping situation and make recommendations for the employment of the American navy in the event of war with Germany. By the time he reported to Admiral Jellicoe on April 9, 1917, the United States had entered the war. When Sims learned of the desperate condition of British shipping, he was appalled. In February German U-boats had sunk nearly half a million tons. They had increased this figure in March. April promised to be even worse. The Royal Navy frankly predicted defeat by November unless the U-boat could be conquered. Jellicoe could see no solution except additional patrolling, mining, and evasive routing—intensification of methods already proved unsuccessful.

The Adoption of Convoy

A group of younger officers in the Admiralty headed by Commander Reginald Henderson RN had been quietly studying shipping operations and losses. They found that cross-Channel coal convoys, instituted in February at the demand of the French, were getting through almost unscathed. Out of 2,600 sailings in that service by the end of April, U-boats had sunk

five ships, a loss rate of 0.19 per cent. During this period losses had mounted not only in the North Sea and Western Approaches but in the very waters being traversed by the successful convoys. In the trade with Norway in the spring of 1917 the loss rate was in the neighborhood of 25 per cent for the round trip. In April, on his own responsibility, the officer in charge of this shipping began convoys on that route. A month later the loss rate had dropped to 0.24 per cent, a 120-fold reduction.

Armed with such figures as these, Henderson's group recommended that the Admiralty adopt convoy generally, especially ocean convoy. The Admiralty refused even to consider the recommendation. The Sea Lords deemed convoy essentially defensive; only offensive measures, patrolling and mining, said they, could defeat the U-boat. They had four principal objections to convoy as such: (1) valuable time would be lost by reducing the speed of convoys to that of the slowest ship; (2) simultaneous arrival of a large convoy would jam port loading and unloading facilities; (3) merchant masters could not sail in the tightly packed formation required in convoys without undue losses from collision; and (4) vessels could not be spared from offensive duties to undertake the defensive escort of convoys.

Each of these arguments proved specious in the event. The reduction of a convoy's speed to that of the slowest member could be minimized by separating slow and fast ships into separate convoys over the same route. The dependability of arrival of a convoy at a certain port on a certain date made it possible to plan unloading and transport from the harbors more efficiently than had been possible with independently sailed ships, maintaining radio silence and therefore likely to appear with no notice. Merchant masters proved to be generally quite capable of maintaining station in convoy. Supplying convoy escorts required never more than 15 per cent of the naval ships in commission and more generally no more than five per cent. For the most part the ships engaged in escort duties came from the ineffective patrols and were not suited for fleet operations.

After studying the recommendations of Henderson's group, Sims enthusiastically supported their arguments. Having the opportunity for discussions with Prime Minister Lloyd George, Sims forcefully argued for the convoy system. Lloyd George, once convinced, became one of the strongest supporters of convoys. His pressure upon the Admiralty led Jellicoe to order Henderson to prepare an even more systematic study. As a result the Admiralty at length decided that convoys were "entirely practicable." Reluctantly, on April 30, the Sea Lords assented to an experimental ocean convoy.

Sims meanwhile had kept the United States informed of developments. He told the grave news of Britain's desperate situation, urging that every possible antisubmarine vessel be sent. In spite of his urgent requests, the ships were slow in coming and came in smaller numbers than Sims had requested. Like the British Admiralty, the U.S. Navy Department was not convinced of the efficiency of convoys and had in addition a fear of American interests being subordinated to those of the British. The reasons were not difficult to find. In the first place, American strategic planning had been preoccupied with the Caribbean, scene of the United States' most recent war, and now doubly important because of the newly completed Panama Canal. Professional thinking of American naval officers had been much conditioned by the War Games of 1915, called War Plan Black, which assumed engagement with an enemy battle fleet in the Caribbean. It was no easy matter for the Navy Department to shift its strategic vision to war in European waters and to accept the prospect of moving substantial numbers of its ships to the other side of the Atlantic.

On June 2 Sims received a cable from the Secretary of the Navy: "In regard to convoy, I consider that American vessels having armed guard are safer when sailing independently." In the previous six weeks 30 armed merchantmen had been sunk near Britain. Sims turned to his friend Ambassador Page, who supported him in every particular, for aid in convincing the Navy Department that American ships were needed in European waters and that convoy was the only way of defeating the U-boat.

On July 2 the Navy Department accepted convoys but sent Sims a list of six principles for Anglo-American naval cooperation, a list which indicated that the U.S. Navy was still wedded to the "defense-of-routes" theory. Among the points included was an offer of "most hearty cooperation" on the submarine problem, modified by a statement that the main role of the Navy lay in "safeguarding the lines of communication" of the Allies. The Navy Department did however promise to send all antisubmarine vessels that could be spared from home needs. Although the Navy Department's list rejected the idea of strictly defensive operations—and American naval officers as well as British considered escort of convoy as defensive—it did pave the way for substantial aid in escorts for convoying shipping. It enabled Benson to take action as he saw fit in using American forces to combat the U-boat menace. Sims, in his new capacity as Commander United States Naval Forces Operating in European Waters, immediately threw himself and his gradually growing forces into the battle against Germany's U-boat offensive. The first six American destroyers, Destroyer Division Eight, under command of Commander Joseph Taussig, arrived at Queenstown on May 4, 1917. The story of their arrival has become something of a naval legend. Commander Taussig, reporting to the Commander Western Approaches, was asked when he would be ready for duty. "I will be ready when fueled, sir," he replied. In the ensuing three months, 31 additional destroyers and two tenders arrived. All of these forces were assigned to antisubmarine work, mostly escorting under British command.

Meanwhile the convoy system was getting started. Regular Homeward Ocean Convoys of ships bound for the British Isles began in mid-July. The U-boats thereupon promptly concentrated their attacks on outward-bound ships. A month later Outward Ocean Convoys came into being. As the number of ships convoyed increased, the sinkings steadily decreased, despite increasing numbers of U-boats at sea in the proclaimed War Zone. The number of ships sunk per boat per month fell dramatically from 10.6 in April 1917, to 4.9 in July, to 2.0 by the end of the year. The diagram on page 468 shows the story graphically.

In November 1917 the convoy system was

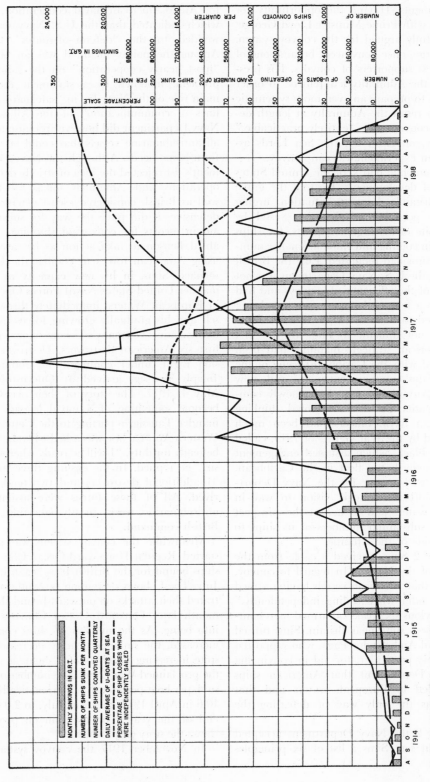

U-BOAT WARFARE, 1914–1918

MONTHLY SINKINGS IN G.R.T.
NUMBER OF SHIPS SUNK PER MONTH
NUMBER OF SHIPS CONVOYED QUARTERLY
DAILY AVERAGE OF U-BOATS AT SEA
PERCENTAGE OF SHIP LOSSES WHICH
WERE INDEPENDENTLY SAILED

PERCENTAGE SCALE

SINKINGS IN G.R.T.

SHIPS SUNK PER MONTH

AND NUMBER OF U-BOATS OPERATING

SHIPS CONVOYED PER QUARTER

NUMBER OF

NUMBER OF U-BOATS OPERATING

extended to the Mediterranean. There, despite minimal convoy escorts because of the commander in chief's belief that patrol was much better, the convoy loss rate was one per cent and convoy escorts accounted for two thirds of all U-boats sunk in that area during the year of convoy operations.

In the Atlantic the convoy system forced the U-boats to resort to submerged torpedo attacks, though against independent ships they still freely employed their guns unless it appeared that the victim was armed. Finding the ships too well protected in the Western Approaches area, the U-boats moved into the Irish Sea and the English Channel. Except for the cross-Channel coal convoys, shipping in these areas still sailed independently and here the U-boats reaped a rich harvest. As the convoy system expanded, the sinkings by U-boats fell almost in proportion. It was primarily with vessels sailing independently that U-boats found their victims. The loss rate of independent ships to those sailing in convoy averaged 12 to 1 throughout the period of extensive convoy operations, from May 1917 to November 1918. The graph on page 468 shows the relative losses of independents to convoyed ships.

To implement Germany's political decision for unrestricted U-boat warfare, the German navy had committed all available boats. Because of the estimate that Britain could be brought to her knees in five months, the Germans had scheduled their U-boat operations on a basis of maximum effort for the estimated time, cutting down maintenance and repairs necessary for extended operations. In this manner they were able to maintain a daily average of some 45 boats at sea, rising to a peak of 52 in July 1917. The results of the injudicious German policy on submarine maintenance soon made themselves felt. With increasing losses of U-boats, and the cut-back in U-boat building, another result of the wishful estimate of early Allied collapse, the number of U-boats at sea steadily declined.

To offset losses, the Germans undertook large U-boat construction programs in the fall of 1917, not only in Germany but also at Pola and Cattaro. By September 1918 the delivery rate of new boats approached 30 a month, and Scheer had obtained the Kaiser's approval to increase it to 40 a month. By this time however the increased production was too late to have any decisive effect in the war.

Convoy Operations

In May 1917 the Admiralty formed a Convoy Section under the Assistant Chief of Naval Staff. This organization had the duty of assembling, routing, and protecting convoys, while the office of the Ministry of Shipping, acting in close liaison with the Convoy Section, controlled wharfage, loading and unloading, and procurement and allocation of ships and coordinated shipping requirements with convoy needs. Each port of assembly both in Britain and overseas had an officer charged with organization of convoys, with providing sailing orders and other instructions to the masters of the ships, and with reporting movements to the Admiralty.

The merchant ships of the convoy were controlled by a convoy commodore who was usually a retired captain or admiral or, occasionally, a very experienced merchant master. He came under the over-all command of the escort commander, who bore responsibility for the entire convoy. At sea the escort commander received frequent reports from the Admiralty on estimated U-boat positions. The Admiralty also issued changes in routing instructions to keep the convoy clear of U-boat concentrations.

The word *convoy* has two meanings. In discussing naval operations it is customary to use the word to mean the entire collection of vessels, both warships and merchant ships, sailing in company. In describing convoy operations, the practice is to limit the word *convoy* to mean only the merchant ships, while the warships are termed the *escort* or *screen*. An escort may be formed of any type of accompanying warships, while strictly speaking a screen is an anti-submarine escort.

Outward ocean convoys from the United Kingdom had a screen as far as 15° W. Here the convoy dispersed, the ships continuing their voyages independently, while the ships of the screen met a homeward-bound convoy that had crossed the Atlantic under the control of a single escort, either a cruiser or an armed merchant cruiser.

The ocean convoy of World War I tended to be small, with 20 to 30 ships, formed in four, five, or six columns, while the escorts generally patrolled the flanks. Slow convoys, those sailing at eight to ten knots, had escorts ahead as well as on the flanks. The Gibraltar convoys, slowest of all, were routed at seven knots. Fast convoys included ships up to 16 knots. Ships able to make greater speeds customarily sailed independently. Cooperation on the part of the merchant masters and naval officers, and between the British and American navies, made the convoy system work.[8]

Antisubmarine Air Operations

Since 1915 the Royal Naval Air Service had undertaken air operations against U-boats. Increasing numbers of aircraft enabled more extensive patrols to be flown over coastal and transit waters. Until the institution of the convoy system in 1917, aircraft had little success, but with careful coordination of air operations and shipping schedules, the increased effectiveness of the air branch became apparent. During the last six months of the war, 565 aircraft of all types, land planes, sea planes, and lighter-than-air ships, were assigned to antisubmarine operations in support of convoy. With 312 available daily for operations, they flew a monthly average of 14,000 hours,[9] sighted 28 U-boats, and attacked 19. Although they achieved no kills themselves, having no lethal attack weapons, their presence effectively discouraged U-boat attacks. Of the hundreds of convoys with air as well as surface escort, only six were attacked and only five ships were sunk. With improved weapons and improved methods of detection, the airplane in World War II was destined to become an important U-boat killer.

[8] The principal inbound convoy routes were: (1) Gibraltar to England, every four days; (2) Sierra Leone, Africa to England, every eight days; (3) Dakar to England, every eight days; (4) Hampton Roads to England, every eight days; (5) New York to England, every eight days; (6) Halifax to England, every eight days; (7) Sydney to England, every eight days. The outward ocean convoy routes were similar but the frequency of sailing was slightly different.

[9] A record unequaled in World War II until mid-1943.

Mining Operations

In an attempt to prevent U-boats from getting to the operating area, the Allies decided on three more mine barrages. The most famous, the vast North Sea Mine Barrage extending from the Orkneys to Norway, received Allied approval at the end of November 1917 in spite of Sims's active opposition. Concurrently a British-laid Dover Strait Barrage during the winter months of 1917-18 blocked the Flanders U-Flotilla from working the Channel. Because this was a relatively small area, easy to patrol against German minesweeping operations and offering easy opportunities for replacing lost mines, the Dover Barrage proved highly effective, destroying some twelve U-boats by August 1918, completely closing the Strait, and forcing abandonment of the Flanders U-boat base.

The story was quite the reverse with the North Sea Mine Barrage. Encouraged by the unqualified success of the Dover Barrage, both the British and the American navies enthusiastically supported this most extensive mining operation in history. The field was 230 miles long and 15 to 25 miles wide, with the mines at random depths from the surface down to 240 feet. The development of the American antenna mine, designed to explode when a ship or U-boat touched the antenna, brought the required number down to a quarter of the original estimate. Nevertheless over 70,000 mines were laid, 80 per cent by American forces. Possibly one U-boat was lost as a result of this vast undertaking. The conditions of visibility and the great distances involved in the North Sea made effective antisweeper patrol impossible, and U-boats continued to use the waters at will, occasionally escorted by German minesweepers.

With the third barrage the British attempted to close the Strait of Otranto and bottle the Mediterranean U-boats up the Adriatic. The barrage sank one U-boat, but the Germans continued to use the route freely until the end of the war.

The submarine also proved an effective killer of U-boats, sinking 19. The psychological effect on the Germans was even greater than the actual losses, for the threat of an unexpected torpedo in a submerged U-boat greatly reduced morale in the U-boat service.

Anti-U-Boat Raids

To strike at "the hornet's nest" instead of "hunting hornets all over the farm," as President Wilson put it, the British planned to block the two exits of the Flanders U-Flotilla at Ostend and Zeebrugge. Command of the expedition fell to Vice Admiral Roger Keyes. He planned a simultaneous assault on the two ports, to sink blockships in the channel entrances, and then to evacuate under the cover of darkness and smoke. The problem at Ostend can be simply stated, although its solution was far from easy. Since gun defenses here could not be neutralized, the blockships would simply have to force their way in unsupported by diversionary activity.

At Zeebrugge a long curving mole mounting heavy gun emplacements had to be neutralized, or the blockships would be sunk before they

could get into position. Keyes planned to seize the mole by amphibious assault, blowing up a viaduct leading to the shore in order to prevent reinforcement.

After two false starts, canceled because of wind shifts, Keyes got under way on April 22, 1918. An old armored cruiser, H.M.S. *Vindictive,* had been especially modified for the raid, mounting extra topside guns and a series of ramps by which the assaulting marines and sailors could climb up to the mole. As the *Vindictive* entered the harbor just before midnight, she came under heavy fire and missed her assigned position by some 340 yards. This error brought her troops under heavy fire and prevented them from seizing their assigned guns. Meanwhile an old British submarine loaded with explosives ran in under the viaduct, her crew setting fuses and then escaping in a skiff. The submarine blew up, wrecking the viaduct. The blockships, all this time under heavy fire, valiantly strove to reach their assigned positions. When at last they had been

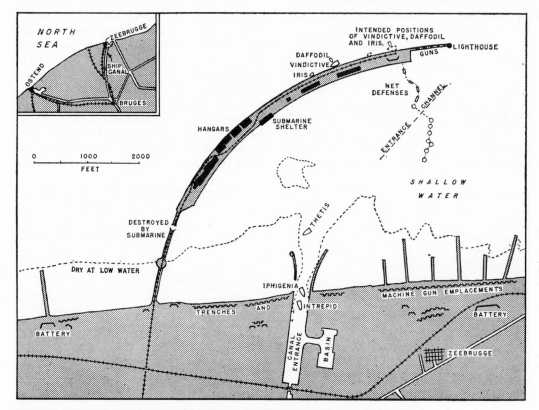

HARBOR OF ZEEBRUGGE, SHOWING GERMAN DEFENSES AND BRITISH BLOCKSHIPS

scuttled one by one in approximately the correct locations, the *Vindictive* signaled the recall, and all forces retired.

The attack on Ostend resulted in complete failure. Neither of the two assigned blockships was able to reach its position. The entire operation cost the British over 1,200 casualties in killed, wounded, and missing.

The results of the raid are difficult to assess. The primary aim, hindrance of the Flanders U-Flotilla, failed, for U-boats could use the Ostend exit at once, and after a few hours the Germans managed to dredge a passage around the scuttled ships at Zeebrugge. By mid-May no impediment to navigation remained. However the Ostend-Zeebrugge raid was officially proclaimed as a highly successful operation. Hence it acted as a valuable tonic for public morale, depressed by the great German spring offensive in France. Most important, it showed that Gallipoli had not killed amphibious operations, although the British now tended to think of raids rather than massive assaults. From the raid on Zeebrugge was born the idea of especially trained raiding troops, the famous Commandos of World War II.

American Contributions

America's role in the war at sea was undramatic. Setting up three main bases at Queenstown, Gibraltar, and Brest, as well as numerous smaller ones in Britain and France, the U.S. Navy participated extensively in patrol and convoy escort operations. One of America's particular contributions was the 110-foot wooden-hulled submarine chaser. Manned almost entirely by reserves, these SC's were armed with 3-inch guns and depth charges. Eventually nearly 400 SC's operated from such diverse places as Murmansk, Queenstown, Plymouth, Brest, the Azores, Gibraltar, and Corfu. They were particularly effective in the English Channel in protection of convoys after the ocean escort had left.

Reversing its earlier policy on piecemeal commitment of the American fleet, the U.S. Navy sent five battleships to Scapa Flow to reinforce the Grand Fleet and help to insure against forays by the German High Seas Fleet. Battleship Division Nine, the *New York, Wyoming, Florida, Delaware,* and *Texas,* commanded by Rear Admiral Hugh Rodman, operated as Battle Squadron Six of the Grand Fleet, employing British tactical doctrine and British methods of signaling. The Allies thus had an overwhelming preponderance of strength in the vital North Sea.

The United States Navy bore primary responsibility for the safe transport of American troops and supplies to France. General Ludendorff had estimated that the U-boats would prevent passage of significant American forces to Europe. Here again convoy proved its worth. Strongly escorted troop convoys regularly made the transatlantic passage with no losses on the eastbound run. The more lightly escorted westbound troopship convoys lost only three ships. By mid-summer 1917, 50,000 troops a month made the crossing to France in convoys of four

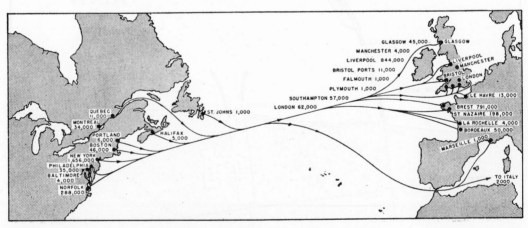

PORTS OF EMBARKATION AND DEBARKATION FOR UNITED STATES TROOPS

to twelve heavily escorted transports. A year later the monthly average reached 200,000. In all, over two million American troops crossed the Atlantic, 46 per cent in American ships and 48 per cent in British. Americans provided almost all the escort forces and in addition stationed three battleships, the *Nevada, Oklahoma,* and *Utah,* in Bantry Bay as insurance against German surface attack on the vital troop convoys.

Because the United States had only 1,000,000 tons of shipping available at the outset of war, the United States Shipping Board organized an immense program for building up the American merchant marine. The Board's first move was to seize and recondition all interned enemy ships, including the huge German passenger liner *Vaterland,* renamed the *Leviathan.* The newly designed, mass-produced Liberty ships appeared in large numbers, while experimental ships of wood and even of concrete carried vital supplies.

Much of the American material and the majority of American troops entered France through the port of Brest. At first almost unusable because of shortage of fuel storage space and lack of shop and repair facilities, Brest became of increasing importance as the United States supplied the material to build it up as a fully equipped naval base. Its geographic position made it possible to avoid exposing troop convoys to U-boat concentrations in the narrow waters of the English Channel.

The 1918 Crisis and Allied Victory

The transfer of German troops from the Eastern Front as a result of the Russian collapse gave Germany a numerical superiority on the Western Front for the first time since 1914. Germany hoped to exploit this advantage to force a decision before the United States could make its weight felt. The new, improved infantry tactics, supported by tanks and creeping barrages, had restored the advantage to the offensive. Evidently a war of movement had again become possible. Ludendorff, with an army retrained in the new tactics, planned to drive a wedge between the British and the French and roll the former back into the Channel and the latter to Paris. On March 21, 1918 he hurled a massive offensive against the

British but failed to take Amiens. In this military crisis, the Allies agreed on the appointment of a supreme commander in France and designated French Field Marshal Ferdinand Foch for the post. As casualties mounted, the Allies urgently appealed for troops from the United States. There followed a race against time as the Americans and British attempted to transport enough troops to Europe to alter the balance before Germany could win the war.

On the Western Front the crisis came on July 18, 1918, when Paris was threatened in the Second Battle of the Marne. American troops aided the weary French in checking the German drive and saving Paris. Then Foch struck decisively. The British and Belgians in the northwest, the French at the center, and the Americans in the southeast rolled back the Germans so swiftly that by November most of occupied Belgium and three quarters of German-held France were liberated.

Part of the American navy went ashore during the campaign of 1918. Some of the heaviest fighting fell to the lot of 25,000 U.S. Marines at Château-Thierry, Aisne-Marne, St. Mihiel, and Meuse-Argonne, where they suffered some 2,500 casualties. Meanwhile large caliber naval guns mounted on railway flat cars struck at German railroads, bridges, and ammunition dumps. The effectiveness and accuracy of this fire played no small part in the Allied offensive.

Germany's offensive of 1918 had been a last desperate gamble. She could not make another. The slow strangling blockade had done its work. By 1916 Germany was already suffering terrible privation. Only the conquest of Romania and the occupation of the Ukraine had enabled her to secure the crops needed to prevent widespread starvation. Shortages developed in oil, fertilizers, meat, and fats. Austria-Hungary suffered even more than Germany. The Central Powers never managed to recover from the shortages of 1916. In spite of being able to draw on the resources of a continent, Germany and Austria suffered from the lack of critical materials to such an extent that the efficiency of the fighting forces went downhill. The war had already cost Germany more than twice her entire pre-war annual national income.

By October 1918, her submarines defeated at sea by the effectiveness of Allied convoys, her armies reeling back to German soil, her High Seas Fleet in mutiny, her population reduced to near starvation level, and with revolution imminent, Germany could see no solution but surrender. On November 9, the Kaiser abdicated, and two days later German representatives affixed their signatures to the Armistice document.

Summary

In World War I the Central Powers occupied the interior position relative to the Allied Powers. Anticipating the alignment of belligerents, the German General Staff planned to overwhelm France first, driving in through Belgium, and then use the same forces to defeat the Russian army, which presumably would be slow to mobilize. But British and French military leaders also foresaw the alignment of powers, and anticipated the German strategy. After the outbreak of war in the summer of 1914, Britain promptly placed an army in France, which together with the French army blunted the German drive and gave Russia time to mobilize, so that the Central Powers were obliged to fight a two-front war.

When the land warfare in France reached stalemate in the fall of 1914, Britain sought means of outflanking the Western Front to join hands militarily with Russia in order to strengthen the Eastern Front. This meant a return to Britain's traditional peripheral strategy, using the mobility conferred by her sea power supremacy to strike at weak points around the edges of the enemy's position. The plan finally adopted, largely through Winston Churchill's strong support, was to advance up the Dardanelles and capture Constantinople, thereby establishing communications between the two Allied fronts via the Black Sea. The operation, though strategically sound, failed through inadequate intelligence, poor planning, and a series of tactical errors. The Allies were repulsed both in their attempt to drive up the Dardanelles with naval forces and in their subsequent campaign to seize the Gallipoli Peninsula. As a result of their failure, large-scale amphibious assault fell into disfavor in most military services.

The strategic center of the purely naval war was the North Sea. Here also operations were stalemated, largely because the statistically inferior German High Seas Fleet refrained from offering battle. The Germans preferred to whittle away at British naval strength until they could meet the Grand Fleet on something like equal terms. The result was a series of decoy operations and attempted ambushes. These brought about the Heligoland Bight Action (August 1914), the Dogger Bank Action (January 1915), and finally the Battle of Jutland (May-June 1916), in which the German battle line, attempting to ambush British battle cruisers, was lured into contact with the British battle line. In the main fleet action at Jutland, the Grand Fleet twice capped the German T and succeeded in getting between the High Seas Fleet and its base. The Germans however escaped back into port after inflicting more damage than they took. The stalemate in the North Sea continued, the Grand Fleet and the High Seas Fleet serving merely as fleets-in-being to restrain the operations of the other.

In the war against shipping, Britain did not attempt to clamp down her traditional close blockade because of the danger of mines, submarines, and aircraft. Nevertheless her position athwart the sea approaches to Germany enabled her to cut off German commerce on the oceans completely. The surprise was that this distant blockade took so long to be effective. Although barred from overseas resources while fighting a mechanized war, Germany and her allies managed to operate with stockpiled and substitute materials and with imports through neutrals.

The second surprise of the commerce war was the extraordinary success of the German counterblockade. Germany's early attempts at commerce raiding by use of cruisers produced only limited results. Some cruisers, notably the *Emden*, wreaked havoc for a while on Allied shipping, but in due course the Royal Navy ran all the cruisers down. The submarine however proved the perfect commerce raider, catching the Allies by surprise with no immediate countermeasures. The German U-boat in fact very nearly won the war for the Central Powers. While losing 187 of their number, the U-boats sent to the bottom, either through direct attack or through mine-laying, 5,234 ships amounting to 12,185,832 G.R.T. In addition they sank five battleships, eight cruisers, and seven destroyers.

Until mid-1917 no Allied commander in a position of high responsibility could see a means of averting defeat through submarine attacks on Allied commerce. Then with the institution of convoy, losses to U-boats fell steadily while sinkings of U-boats mounted rapidly. More than two thirds of all U-boats lost were sunk during the period of extensive convoy operations. By mid-1918 the U-boat had ceased to be a serious menace except to the vessels that continued to sail independently.

Germany's unrestricted submarine warfare, while threatening the Allies with defeat, brought the United States in on their side. The defeat of the U-boat by the convoy system helped make possible the transportation of two million American soldiers to France, more than enough to offset the collapse of the Russian army, enough in fact to assure Allied victory.

26:
Disarmament and Rearmament

World War I utterly destroyed the polity of Europe, so carefully nurtured through a hundred years of painstaking statesmanship. What survived was no brave new world but the wreckage of a social and economic order. Nor could anyone hope to restore that serenity and confidence in inevitable progress which had characterized the preceding century.

In the Allied states demobilization and rebuilding began at once. Munitions and shipbuilding programs were shelved. Obnoxious controls could be abolished. Dangerously inflated national budgets could be balanced. In the United States particularly, the tradition of isolationism made the people impatient to get back to what President Harding a little later was to call "normalcy."

Postwar Operations of the United States Navy

The immediate task of the Navy was to bring home from France the American Expeditionary Force—more than 2,000,000 men. All available ships—cruisers, battleships, cargo vessels, German steamers turned over to the Allies under the terms of the Armistice—were diverted to ferrying troops. Though as many as 340,000 men were transported in the single month of June 1919 at the peak of the program, it was nearly a year after the Armistice before all of America's citizen army was back on American soil. Another major chore was the lifting of the North Sea Mine Barrage, now simply a hazard to peaceful shipping. A fleet of 89 sweepers accomplished this difficult and dangerous task by September 1919.

In the Adriatic and in the Eastern Mediterranean the Allied navies had important quasi-diplomatic missions. The commander of the American Adriatic Squadron administered 300 miles of the Dalmatian coast until the Treaty of Versailles finally awarded the territory to the new state of Yugoslavia. Rear Admiral Mark Bristol, appointed American High Commissioner in Constantinople in 1919, for eight years skillfully mixed diplomacy and naval power. Bristol sent cruisers and destroyers to evacuate refugees in the Black Sea ports of Russia after the final Red victories, and cooperated in the evacuation of 262,000 Greeks from Asia Minor after the Turkish victory in the Greco-Turkish War.

Combined Allied expeditionary forces with strong naval support were sent to Archangel and Vladivostok to guard or destroy war materials that had been shipped there before the collapse of the Russian armies. In Siberia the well-founded fear that the large Japanese force intended to use the occupation as an excuse for permanent territorial aggrandizement kept the American army contingent and most of the United States Asiatic Fleet at Vladivostok until April 1920.

After accomplishing those missions which grew directly out of the war, the U.S. Navy found itself faced with the public apathy characteristic of post-war periods. With little more than housekeeping appropriations throughout the 1920's, the fleet assumed its classic role of "showing the flag." A Yangtze Patrol was established as a symbol of continuing American interest in the China trade. The bulk of the fleet was based on the West Coast. A new emphasis on technical research and development, and on improved operating procedures was characteristic of the whole interwar period.

The New Alignment of Powers

The prewar balance of power in Europe was destroyed. Germany was prostrate, presumptively disarmed for the indefinite future. The Hapsburg Empire and Turkey were dismembered. Russia was in the throes of a bloody civil war. Nor did the victors fare much better. France and Italy were on the verge of bankruptcy. Even mighty England, whose world-wide investments had earlier allowed her to levy tribute on the economic activities of the rest of the world, now found herself relatively poor. All the principal European combatants had suffered casualties so severe that they would experience a dearth of able leadership for a generation to come.

The effect of the war on Japan and the United States was quite otherwise. Japan, except for token forces, had limited her contributions to the Pacific area. The United States, which made a tremendous, all-out effort in the final months of the war, had nevertheless not experienced severe casualties. Even her colossal expenditures had been well within the capacities of the country. America, which in 1914 had been a "debtor nation," now found herself the world's foremost creditor. The industrialization of her economy had been accelerated and diversified by the necessities of the war. Perhaps most important, the war had taught America and the world the miracles American industry could accomplish.

Great Britain had emerged from World War I still the world's strongest sea power. Her war losses in capital ships had been much more than made up by new construction. The United States Navy, which had shelved its ambitious 1916 building program in favor of the destroyers and patrol craft that the Allies needed to defeat the submarine threat, had increased in tonnage, but remained for the moment statistically inferior. And immediately after the Armistice there seemed to be a good expectation that the British would receive a powerful reinforcement in the form of ships from the defeated Germans.

However, the impoverishment of Great Britain and the conviction of her leaders that there was no immediate prospect of a major war led to the Cabinet's adoption in 1919 of the curious "Ten Year Rule,"[1] which posited peace for a decade to come and which thus excused cutting all defense appropriations to the bone. This projection was renewed every year until 1932, and helps to account for Britain's general unpreparedness at the outbreak of World War II in 1939. Even in the 1930's, in spite of substantial naval programs in 1934 and 1936, the air arm received the bulk of defense appropriations—somewhat at the expense of the navy and the army. The naval wing of the wartime Royal Flying Service was absorbed into the new Royal Air Force, and naval aircraft development was given such a low priority that the British carriers were flying planes completely obsolete by the standards of other navies. Not until 1937 were the operations of the Fleet Air Arm transferred back to the Navy, while procurement remained an R.A.F. function.

The End of the German Fleet

The Armistice had specified among other things that Germany must immediately subject to internment 10 battleships, 6 battle cruisers, 6 light cruisers, 50 destroyers (of recent design), and surrender all of her submarines. The larger units demanded were specified by name, and included the newest and finest vessels in the German navy. On November 21, 1918, with the Grand Fleet under Admiral Sir David Beatty lined up in parade ground regularity on either side of the huge anchorage, the German dreadnought line steamed slowly into Scapa Flow—a navy undefeated, but the navy of a defeated nation. These were the ships that had fought at Jutland—the *Friedrich der Grosse*, the *Koenig Albert*, the *Kaiser*, and the rest. There too were the battle cruisers—the *Seydlitz*, the *Moltke*, the *Derfflinger*, the *Von der Tann*. Tears streamed down the cheeks of the German officers and veteran ratings alike at this moment of humiliation. For them it not only signaled the end of a career; it seemed the end also of a tradition they had devoted their lives to building. The German submarines were ordered to Harwich.

[1] Not made official policy until 1923, after the Washington Disarmament Conference. (See pages 480 ff.)

They came in batches of 20 or so and sur-rendered to Rear Admiral Sir Reginald Tyrwhitt's force. By January 1, 1919, 114 of the 160 submarines demanded had been delivered.

The Germans regarded their disarmed vessels at Scapa Flow as simply interned as hostages for their good behavior until the peace treaty could be arranged. Officers and skeleton crews remained aboard without restriction. But the British and French, who disagreed about so much in writing the treaty, had no trouble in agreeing that Germany should never have the ships back. Indeed the question of division of naval spoils was informally canvassed almost at once.

The Versailles Treaty particularized the naval disarmament of Germany. In addition to the vessels already in British hands, the German Admiralty was to deliver its remaining 8 dreadnoughts, 8 more light cruisers, 42 more destroyers, and 50 torpedo boats. All these vessels would become the property of the Allies for such disposition as they might agree on. Furthermore, the future German navy was to possess no more than 6 pre-dreadnoughts, 6 light cruisers, 12 destroyers, and 12 torpedo boats. It was to have no submarines. All construction under way was to be broken up.

As soon as the news of the treaty provisions reached the interned German vessels at Scapa Flow, and their officers and higher ratings came to realize that their compatriots were actually going to sign the treaty, they determined on the one course open to them to strike back. At 11:15 AM, June 21, 1919, on signal from the *Emden,* every captain in the German fleet ordered the sea cocks opened. Almost before the British realized what was happening, the scuttled German vessels were sunk at their moorings. For all practical purposes, the German navy had ceased to exist.

This gesture, which in retrospect has a certain magnificence, had a peculiarly infuriating effect on British and French public opinion at the time. It was as though a hated criminal had forestalled the executioner by a secreted dose of cyanide. As condign punishment, Germany was compelled to deliver five of her remaining light cruisers, 300,000 tons of float-ing docks, and 42,000 tons of floating cranes, dredges, and tugs—in a word, practically everything still afloat in her silent harbors.

Ultimately nearly half of the 50 sunken German vessels were salvaged, but this figure includes only four of the major units. The remnants of the German navy were scrapped, or distributed to other navies. France and Italy received light cruisers, destroyers, and submarines. Poland, Finland, and even the neutral Netherlands secured small craft from the breakup of the German naval establishment.

Every German submarine afloat or on the ways was destroyed or carried off.[2] All navies were particularly interested in the large cruiser submarines (US-V boats), which Germany had built during the latter part of the war. These were to have a significant influence on submersible design in all navies, and were the exact prototype of the Japanese I-boats.

Postwar Building Programs

All through the war, the Japanese had pursued an active naval building program in their new yards, and immediately afterwards were pushing to completion several capital ships on the ways. On the other hand, French and Italian construction had been largely suspended during hostilities, and the empty national treasuries of those countries gave little prospect of a spirited renewal of large-scale building.

Of all the naval powers, only Britain's recent ally, the United States, seemed in any position to challenge Britain's naval ascendancy. Since the English at this time had been bred to regard mastery of the world's oceans as a natural prerogative, it did not immediately occur to them that their well-meaning American cousins would dream of a bigger fleet than theirs. Britain had had a long, tough war, and felt entitled to a period of relaxation. Certainly it would be less than friendly for the United States at such a time to bring on a naval armaments race.

This pardonable British prejudice however failed to take into account the stubborn, complex personality of the American President. A man of peace dedicated to the spirit of reform,

[2] Eventually 187 were surrendered to the British. Another 160 were scrapped in Germany.

he had nevertheless been the Commander in Chief of a great nation in time of war. To the common man the world over, Wilson emerged from the war period as the one compelling, truly great figure. What the cynical leadership in Europe's capitals could never quite realize about Wilson was the incredible fact that he always meant what he said. It might be naive to say, "The world must be made safe for democracy," but Wilson, saying it, dignified the phrase by his passionate sincerity. When at the peace conference he came to realize that Clemenceau and Lloyd George had always assumed he was merely spouting a good propaganda slogan, he withdrew his full confidence in them.

This aside on Wilson's character is germane to American naval policy in the immediate postwar period. For the United States had actually intervened in the war over maritime issues—to preserve neutral rights America had fought for a hundred years earlier. The second of Wilson's celebrated "Fourteen Points" had spelled it out:

Absolute freedom of navigation upon the seas, outside territorial waters, alike in peace and in war, except as the seas may be closed in whole or in part by international action for the enforcement of international covenants.

Literally interpreted, this seemed to deny the legality of blockade itself, to say nothing of the long-sanctioned belligerent right of search and seizure of contraband. The British, not unnaturally, had little enthusiasm for such a proposition. At their instance, the Allies did not even consider it at the peace conference. Wilson's reaction was to request Congress for a new building program that would *double* the heavy 1916 schedule.

At the end of the war the United States had 16 dreadnought battleships, none more than eight years old. Though the British could count 42 capital ships in their navy, 13 of these were already obsolescent. Besides, after the experiences of Jutland, the nine battle cruisers in the total could be questioned as vessels worthy of a place in the line. For the United States merely to complete its original 1916 program, incorporating the lessons of the war in the new ships, would have provided 35 modern units,

and a fleet qualitatively much superior to the battle-worn British Grand Fleet.[3] The entire proposed 1919 program would mean a fleet of over 50 first-line vessels, utterly eclipsing the British navy unless Parliament strained every resource of money and yard capacity to try to match the American schedule.

British popular and official reaction to the President's proposal was first one of incredulity, then of outrage. With the German fleet gone, it seemed to the English that such a naval building policy was pointed squarely at themselves. With much talk in government circles of their not having fought the war to relinquish their traditional sea supremacy to even the most trusted of allies, the British began to plan what would be needed to match or excel the American program.

President Wilson's exact motivation is not easy to fathom. It is unlikely however that he expected the entire 1919 program, even when authorized, ever to receive the necessary appropriations. Even for the rich United States, the cost would have been a serious burden, requiring a budget of wartime dimensions. And there was no compelling reason for such an increase.

Most probably, Wilson, irritated at the British attitude on the "freedom of the seas" issue and concerned over Japanese saber-rattling in the Far East, simply desired a much larger navy. He may well have assumed that Congress would automatically whittle down any administration request and hence asked for much more than he felt really essential. On the other hand, it has also been suggested that he intended to use the threat of completion of the 1919 program as a club over the head of the British, who did not then appear enthusiastic about Wilson's dream—the League of Nations. Since Wilson had made clear that he felt that any limitation of armaments should take place through the mechanisms of such a permanent organization, presumably an astronomical competitive building program would appear to

---

[3] Besides the 16 battleships in commission, the *Idaho, Tennessee,* and *California* were nearing completion at the time of the Armistice. Of the 16 capital ships in the 1916 program, only the *Maryland, West Virginia, Colorado,* and *Washington* had been laid down.

England as an unattractive alternative to supporting the League of Nations.

The Background of the Washington Conference

Whatever Wilson intended, his vision of a new world order flickered out in the last year of his Presidency. The rejection of the League by his own country, his party's repudiation in the 1920 election, and his own serious illness all combined to embitter his departure from the White House. He excoriated America's "sullen and selfish isolation."[4]

With popular support, Harding and the Republican Party had disowned the League, but the notion of disarmament appeared to have great public appeal. In early 1921 Senator Borah of Idaho introduced what was to become a joint congressional resolution favoring a tripartite disarmament conference; it passed the Senate unanimously, and the House by a vote of 332 to 4. Almost immediately the British Foreign Office intimated that it would be happy to follow America's lead in calling such a conference. Accordingly Charles Evans Hughes, Harding's able Secretary of State, made informal overtures to the governments of Britain, Japan, France, and Italy.

All but Japan promptly replied with polite enthusiasm. The Japanese appeared reluctant. Diplomatic friction between Japan and the United States had been frequent and acute. During and immediately after the war, Japanese territorial aims on continental Asia had become more obvious. With good reason the Japanese suspected that the conference was in part a device to abrogate the Anglo-Japanese Alliance, which they wished to preserve. On the other hand, they were persuaded that the projected American naval building program was directed at them. And they could afford an armaments race with the United States even less than the British. Besides, it would be incompatible with the dignity of Imperial Japan to stay home from a major conference attended by all the other first-class powers. So, after a two-and-a-half-week delay, Tokyo announced that Japan too would discuss naval disarmament and Far Eastern affairs in Washington.

The Washington Conference

The conference met in Washington on November 12, 1921 with all the fanfare appropriate to the first international congress of this kind ever to be held in the Western Hemisphere. At the first plenary session, Secretary Hughes astonished his listeners and delighted the newspaper-reading public of the whole world by dismissing polite generalities, and laying specific American proposals on the table at once.

Briefly summarized, these were: an agenda based on the existing strength of navies;[5] a ten-year "holiday" in capital ship construction; a scrapping program (with specific ships named) which would result in a 5:5:3 ratio as among the United States, Great Britain, and Japan. Moreover the scrapping schedule Hughes proposed went far beyond anything the foreign delegates had contemplated. Of America's postwar fleet, including vessels on the ways, the Secretary calmly proposed to scrap 30 ships, aggregating 845,750 tons.[6]

The British and the Japanese applauded Hughes with some sincerity at this point in his address. He had disposed of their countries' fears of a naval armaments race. But they were a bit premature. They listened in silence as the American Secretary went on to tell them what the United States would regard as a commensurate sacrifice. He enumerated 36 British and Japanese vessels with a total tonnage of 1,032,303, which must also be junked.

Hughes has been criticized for putting his cards face up on the table before the game began. But it was a calculated move, tremendously effective because totally unexpected. There is a real question whether the American aims in the conference were wise ones, but

[5] Defined to mean "ships built and ships building." To have admitted only ships built would have rendered permanent a British superiority that was no part of the American aim.

[6] This figure invites comparison with the 500,000 tons which became the legal limit to U. S. and British capital ship tonnage under terms of the Treaty.

[4] Speech of November 11, 1923.

granting for the moment that they were, there is little doubt that this dramatic beginning to the conference vastly shortened the time of negotiation, and helped assure the acceptance of most of the American proposals. The reactions of the press and pulpit all over the world were tremendously enthusiastic. If Hughes' address was intended as an oblique bid for worldwide popular support, it was outstandingly successful.

The details of drafting the naval treaty of course fell to the technical committees, who by concession and compromise hammered out an acceptable text. France and Italy were included in the treaty. The aim was ultimate stabilization of the world's capital ships at 500,000 tons each for the United States and Britain; 300,000 for Japan; 175,000 each for Italy and France.

Other provisions of the treaty were: (1) Japan might retain the new *Mutsu*, which Hughes had named for scrapping. In return for this concession, the United States and Britain each were privileged to finish two more ships of up to 35,000 tons. (2) The proposed 10-year capital ship building holiday would otherwise be respected. (3) Aircraft carrier allowances should be 135,000 tons for Britain and the United States, 81,000 for Japan, 60,000 each for France and Italy. (4) No capital ship would be completed with tonnage greater than 35,000,[7] no battleship gun exceed 16 inches in bore, no carrier exceed 27,000 tons,[8] no cruiser carry heavier ordnance than the 8-inch gun. In addition there were procedural rules for scrapping, replacement building, and subsidized construction of merchant marine auxiliaries. At Britain's behest, the treaty draft included a limitation on the use of submarines as commerce-raiders, as well as an agreement prohibiting the use of poison gas. These clauses were never binding however, for France refused to ratify them. An Ameri-

can effort to extend the ratios to cruisers and lesser naval types also came to nothing because of the reluctance of both Britain and Japan. The American delegation could not afford to be insistent because in existing strength of cruisers the United States was not only far behind Great Britain, but also considerably weaker than Japan.

The Non-Fortification Clause

An integral part of the treaty was the controversial non-fortification clause, bitterly denounced by the professional representatives of the American navy. This provided that the Pacific powers were not to arm or fortify bases in their island possessions, except that the Japanese might do as they chose in their home islands, and the Americans in the Hawaiian group. This provision did not apply to Australia or New Zealand. It did mean however that Britain was barred from fortifying Hong Kong, Borneo, the Solomons, and the Gilberts; Japan was barred from further fortifying Formosa or the former German possessions in the Pacific north of the equator, which had been mandated to her—notably the Marianas (less Guam), and the Carolines; the United States was barred from fortifying Samoa, Wake, Guam, and, most important, the Philippines.

American naval authorities were shocked at the agreement to forego the development of adequately defended naval bases in Guam and the Philippines. To them it appeared that the United States was automatically forswearing the possibility of successful fleet operations in Asiatic waters and in effect underwriting Japanese naval supremacy in the Far East. Subsequent history has of course largely substantiated this view.

Yet in the context of the times, the willingness of the American delegation to surrender on this point is understandable. The Japanese were displeased at the imputation of inferiority implied in the 5:5:3 ratio. It is likely that the non-fortification clause was an essential part of their price of acceptance of the treaty. Second, there was a well-founded conviction on the part of the American delegation that it was bargaining away an empty right, one that Congress would probably either never exercise

[7] The British secured an exception for the battle cruiser *Hood*, which was nearing completion. With a designed tonnage of 41,000, she was for two decades the biggest warship afloat.

[8] An exception was allowed the United States, to permit completing the 33,000-ton *Lexington* and *Saratoga*. Providing they did not exceed their tonnage allowances, the other powers could exercise a similar privilege.

at all or else implement on too modest a scale to make any difference in event of war. After all, both Guam and the Philippines had already been American possessions for 23 years without anything much being done toward military and naval development. What real prospect was there of a change of American policy? On the other hand, there was good reason to think Japan would fortify her island possessions, in the absence of a treaty prohibition.[9]

The Nine-Power Treaty and the Four-Power Pact

Finally, although the Disarmament Treaty was the most important product of the Washington Conference, it was of course related to the simultaneously negotiated Nine-Power Treaty and the Four-Power Pact.[10] The Nine-Power Treaty was essentially a multilateral endorsement of the "Open Door" policy: it reaffirmed the territorial integrity of China. The Four-Power Pact was designed to save face for Japan in the abrogation of the Anglo-Japanese Alliance. It provided that the signatory powers would "respect" each other's Far Eastern possessions.

Both of these treaties represented considerable triumphs for American diplomacy. In them Japan, the only nation at all likely to be harboring aggressive territorial designs in the Far East, agreed formally to policies inconsistent with aggression. Historic American aims were subserved by the joint action of many powers.

It is true that, under the pressure of Canada, Great Britain was more than willing to abandon the Japanese alliance. On the other hand the Japanese recognized that it was a cardinal American aim that they give up the specific guarantees of their alliance with England. The conference was a matter of compromise, and the Japanese in giving up a major security

guarantee expected a security guarantee of another sort—the nonfortification clause in the disarmament treaty.

The Results of the Washington Conference

At the time, world opinion hailed the Washington treaties as a triumph of diplomacy, a milestone in the world's progress to a millennium of peace. The treaties were ratified by the legislatures of the powers, and the world's navies settled down to a period of comparative stagnation in new construction.

The American State Department could count the conference a success in achieving its main goals: (1) Great Britain gave official recognition to naval parity; (2) the Anglo-Japanese Alliance had ceased to exist; (3) Japan had accepted a statistical naval inferiority; (4) United States China policy was advanced; and (5) a naval armaments race had been averted.

On the other hand, the disarmament treaty had, in failing to limit cruiser tonnage, to some extent simply diverted British and Japanese appropriations to lesser naval types, in which the United States was to become progressively more and more inferior. Furthermore, bemused by the prestige values involved, the American and the British delegations in seeking to weaken the comparative position of each other were being needlessly blind to the political realities of their time. Quite apart from considerations of blood, language, traditions, and recent wartime alliance, the two powers had a substantial identity of interest that made the possibility of war between them too remote to be worth serious consideration. Both had hostages to fortune in the Far East. The possibility of Japanese aggression against British and American possessions was already real enough to have been the subject of a number of widely read books.[11] Even in the light of contemporary developments, it did not make sense for the United States and Britain to bargain themselves into a position that would

[9] In fact, of course, the Japanese broke their word on this provision, but not until several years after the treaty.

[10] Nine-Power Treaty: United States, Great Britain, Japan, France, Italy, Netherlands, Belgium, Portugal, China.

Four-Power Pact: Great Britain, United States, Japan, France.

[11] Of which Walter B. Pitkin's *Must We Fight Japan?* (1921) and Frederick McCormick's *The Menace of Japan* (1917) will serve as examples. See E. E. Tupper and G. E. McReynolds, *Japan in American Public Opinion* (New York, 1937), 156.

allow Japan a free hand in the Far East even in the face of their joint power. Finally, and perhaps most damning, there is the criticism made particularly by the American naval service itself: the most obvious lesson of history is that treaties are more often honored in the breach than in the observance. The simple fact is that aggression has seldom been arrested by a "scrap of paper." The United States, dynamic and powerful, could easily have eclipsed Japan and even Britain in any armaments race. It may reasonably be argued that the naval limitations of the Washington Disarmament Conference were in fact a step along the path leading to the Pearl Harbor attack. Certain it is, in any event, that the naval treaty made no such contribution to world peace as its sponsors hoped.

Later Naval Disarmament Conferences

After the Washington Conference, the heavy vessels of the U.S. Navy were decimated in accordance with the provisions of the Washington treaty. Moreover, ten 7,500-ton, 6-inch gun, four-stack cruisers of the *Omaha* class were the only American vessels in the cruiser category fit to operate in a modern navy. Partly as a result of the currently strained relations with Japan,[12] President Coolidge countenanced the Naval Act of 1924, which provided for the eight 8-inch gun, 10,000-ton "treaty cruisers" —the *Northampton* class. This measure however was far from adequate to restore America's comparative strength in cruisers. At the time of the Geneva Naval Conference (1927), Japan had in commission or under construction 213,955 tons of modern cruisers, whereas the United States had but 155,000.[13]

The Geneva Conference, called by Coolidge specifically to impose the 5:5:3 ratio on cruiser tonnage, was a total failure. France and Italy refused to participate at all. The British delegation, agreeing in principle to the theory of parity with the United States, insisted on a tonnage figure much higher than the American delegation deemed necessary. The British and American delegates also wrangled without reaching agreement over the size and gun calibers allowable to a cruiser, the British preferring more but smaller ships armed with 6-inch guns, and the Americans demanding the 10,000-ton allowance continued and the 8-inch caliber permitted.

Another fatal liability to the success of the conference has already been foreshadowed. In 1921-22 at Washington, Hughes had based the capital ship ratio on "existing strength." For the American delegation at Geneva to have accepted a similar basis for a cruiser ratio would have meant acceptance of permanent inferiority not only to Britain, whose worldwide empire at least gave an excuse for a very large cruiser force, but also to Japan. The conference broke up without even a pretense at agreement.

The next attempt at naval disarmament came at the London Conference of 1930. Britain and the United States reached a compromise on the troublesome cruiser issue, each to be allowed 339,000 tons (more than the United States had afloat or authorized), and each to be allowed more of the cruiser type it preferred. Japan acceded to the London agreements conditional to an altered 10:10:7 ratio in cruisers, and parity in submarines. Submarine tonnage for all three powers was fixed at 52,700 each. The ban on capital ship construction was extended to the end of 1936. Since France and Italy had refused participation, it was felt necessary to include certain "escape clauses" permitting further construction in the event a nonsignatory power engaged in competitive building. Even in 1930 the auguries for navies regulated by the precise scales of diplomacy had ceased to be favorable.

Throughout the decade of the 1930's, the post-Versailles international political system was on greased skids sloping off to war. A General Disarmament Conference in 1932-33 at Geneva failed abjectly. The Second London Naval Disarmament Conference (1935-36) was a final effort at perpetuating the principle of treaty limitation of navies. The aggressions of Japan, Italy, and Germany, and their manifest

---

[12] The 1924 Immigration Act had revived the touchy racial issue so unsettling to the Japanese in 1906.

[13] The U.S. figure includes the unfinished *Northamptons*, of which only two had been laid down at the time of the Geneva Conference. Strictly speaking, the designation of all of these cruisers as being of one class is not quite accurate. There were a number of differences of design among the vessels.

contempt for existing treaties foredoomed the London Conference. Britain had already surrendered a principle to Germany in a bilateral naval treaty in 1935, by the terms of which Germany was "allowed" 35 per cent of Britain's naval tonnage, and parity in submarines.[14] Both France and Italy were engaged in substantial building programs. Italy refused participation at the start. The Japanese then demanded full parity in all categories. The American delegation demurring, the Japanese withdrew from the conference. The United States, Great Britain, and France finally signed a treaty so watered down with "escalator clauses" as to be virtually meaningless. For practical purposes, all treaty limitations of navies expired December 31, 1936.

American Building Policy in the 1930's

American building policy entered a new phase beginning roughly with the inauguration of Franklin D. Roosevelt as President in 1933. Like Theodore Roosevelt earlier, Franklin Roosevelt showed a perception of the intimate relation between diplomatic and military strength. He recognized the true seriousness of the deteriorating world situation, and knew that navies cannot be improvised in the face of an emergency. Furthermore, again like the earlier Roosevelt, he had gained professional knowledge of the service as Assistant Secretary of the Navy and had a hobbyist's enthusiasm for the sea service.

The first substantial naval authorization of Roosevelt's first term came as a relief measure to assist the depressed steel and shipbuilding industries; section 202 of the National Industrial Recovery Act of June 16, 1933 authorized new construction in cruisers and lesser types to full treaty strength. On March 27, 1934, the Vinson-Trammel Bill passed, providing for an eight-year replacement building program amounting to 102 ships. From 1934 to 1940, the American naval appropriations implementing the Vinson-Trammel program grew year by year, finally approaching a billion dollars annually. The Second Vinson Act of 1938 au-

[14] This was of course a tacit admission by Britain that the Versailles Treaty was dead.

thorized an additional 20 per cent over-all tonnage increase. In addition to new construction, modernization of older vessels was undertaken; a new emphasis on naval aircraft and on carriers became apparent; new naval bases and air stations were established.

After the fall of France, in June 1940, the limiting factor in American defense expenditures ceased to be Congressional reluctance to underwrite the services' maximum programs: it was from then on simply the physical limitations of America's industrial capacity. By the time of the Pearl Harbor attack (December 7, 1941), the United States Navy had the following combat vessels in commission or on the ways:

	IN COMMISSION	BUILDING
Battleships	17	15
Carriers	7	11
Cruisers	37	54
Destroyers	171	191
Submarines	111	73

The United States Merchant Marine

Virtually since the American Civil War, the American merchant marine has been at a competitive disadvantage in comparison with the shipping of other countries. In the 20th century, this has stemmed both from high construction costs and high costs of operation, which in turn have largely stemmed from high American labor costs. In those enterprises to which assembly-line techniques can be adapted, American industry can pay high wages and still undersell foreign competition in world markets. But neither the building nor the operation of ships lend themselves to the assembly line. In spite of high tariff protection, American ship building and operation could never compete effectively with that of other countries except with the additional crutch of federal subsidy. Up to 1936, this subsidy took the disguised form of a liberal government loan policy and of excessive payments for carrying the mails. In addition, American shippers after World War I had been able to purchase surplus vessels from the government at bargain rates.

In 1936, Congress passed an important Shipping Act, which established a five-man Maritime Commission under Rear Admiral Emory S. Land USN (Ret.), and initiated a new program of direct subsidy, both for construction and operation. The design of subsidized construction had to meet the approval of the commission, which examined it with the criterion of auxiliary use in wartime in mind. To qualify for subsidy, an operator had to carry crews two thirds of whom were United States citizens, and submit to certain investigatory and regulatory powers exercised by the commission.

Beginning in 1938, the Maritime Commission fostered a replacement program in the merchant marine which aimed to retire slow, obsolete craft at the rate of 50 ships per year. The following year this rate was stepped up. Under the forced draft of wartime, new construction was enormously increased. Yard capacity and the availability of shipyard workers were the only effective limiting factors after the Pearl Harbor attack. By September 1942, 300 tankers and 2,000 standard-design Liberty and Victory ships had been contracted for. Even after allowing for large losses to submarines, the American merchant marine had a net growth by the time of the German surrender to over 30,000,000 tons.

Technological Progress in the United States Navy

It is probable that the 15-year building holiday somewhat retarded advance in capital ship design. On the other hand, the *North Carolina* and the other battleships of the "new" battle line, launched shortly before and during World War II, represented an enormous advance over the *West Virginia* (1923), last of the treaty ships. The *North Carolina* was seven knots faster and possessed superior armor and much improved fire control. She also of course had a very much bigger and more effective antiaircraft battery. Other naval types made a more than commensurate advance.

In 1919-21 the collier *Jupiter* was converted into the *Langley* (19,360 tons), the first United States Navy aircraft carrier. Two battle cruiser hulls, which otherwise would have been scrapped under the Washington Treaty, were

converted to the 33,000-ton *Lexington* and *Saratoga,* commissioned in 1928. It was on the flight decks of these three vessels that the operational techniques were worked out that were to make the United States Navy's air arm the world's finest. By December 7, 1941, as we have seen, America had seven carriers in commission, and eleven more on the ways.

The United States submarine service was expanded between the wars. The new and larger "fleet boats" were in the late 1930's already rendering obsolete the dependable old S-boats. Improved submarine rescue devices and methods were perfected. Antisubmarine methods were the subject of a continuing research and development program.

Other scientific advances changed standard tactics in important ways. Complete conversion of the United States fleet to oil fuel shortly after World War I led to the building of high speed naval tankers and an effective technique for fueling at sea. This in turn expanded the possible radius of action of the fleet, no longer dependent on closely spaced coal depots. Carrier aircraft and long-range naval reconnaissance planes effectively took over the traditional scouting role of cruisers. Much improved radio communication promised to increase effective operational control by the higher echelons of command.

The Breakdown of Collective Security

Throughout the between-wars period, the diplomacy of the western democracies aimed at providing a collective security system. The original cornerstone of this system was conceived to be the enforcement of the Versailles Treaty, which undertook to insure the permanent disarmament of Germany, and the strengthening of the League of Nations. The Bolshevik threat was "solved" by the *"Cordon Sanitaire,"* a row of small buffer states along Soviet Russia's western border. France also by loans and diplomacy promoted a "Little Entente" (1924) of friendly states in Middle Europe. These were Yugoslavia, Czechoslovakia, and Romania, all of which had received territory from the dismembered Austrian Empire.

Joint international action was the order of the day. Besides the disarmament conferences described above, there were conferences on war debts and reparations, treaties of conciliation and of commerce.[15] Germany entered the League of Nations after the Locarno Treaties (1925). Even Communist Russia, outcast among nations, was at the behest of France admitted to the League in 1933. Through the decade of the 1920's, there seemed no good reason to think a new war inevitable. Probably most statesmen, and certainly most ordinary men, felt that diplomacy had displaced large-scale war for their lifetime at least.

But the apparent stability was extremely temporary. To Britain, France, and the United States, the *status quo* was satisfactory. For that very reason, their diplomacy was passive, and as the following decade was to show, comparatively impotent. They failed to take effective joint action, and as war loomed nearer and nearer, their inadequate armaments and pacifistic populations emboldened the dictator-states to make more and more brazen demands. Russia too, which existed altogether outside the collective security system until 1933 and then was received grudgingly and suspiciously in the councils of the democracies, was preoccupied by a gigantic effort to build a modern state. Her influence in determining events was not important until after Munich (1938).

Japan, Germany, and Italy, the self-styled "have-not" nations, nationalistic, imperialistic, and opportunistic, came to assume the dynamic roles in the history of the 1930's. They were not satisfied with the *status quo,* and were prepared to risk war to remold their corners of the world.

The proximate causes of the aggressions of the Fascist countries in the 1930's may well be the alleged "injustices" of the Versailles Treaty (in the case of Germany), and the Great Depression that by destroying the means of livelihood of millions of men made them ready to follow any demagogue. But the deep-rooted underlying causes were the grandiose national objectives of Germany, Italy, and Japan—un-

[15] Viz., Dawes and Young Plans, the Rapallo Treaty (Germany and Russia), and the Locarno Treaties.

challengeable dominance in Middle Europe, in the Mediterranean, and in the Far East. For Adolf Hitler's Germany the immediate objective was the absorption of all German-speaking areas—Austria, Sudetenland, Polish Silesia, and Danzig; the ultimate objective was to subjugate the Balkans and the Ukraine. For Mussolini's Italy the short-term goal was an African empire comparable to France's—Ethiopia supplementing Libya, Eritrea, and Italian Somaliland; and a foothold on the east shore of the Adriatic—Albania, perhaps later a part of Greece. For Japan, the irreducible minimum was Manchuria; the more distant objective, hegemony over China, Malaya, and the East Indies.

In a sense World War II may be said to have begun on September 18, 1931, when a bomb explosion on the track of the South Manchurian Railway near Mukden signaled the beginning of the first "Chinese Incident," the invasion of Manchuria by the Japanese. The failure of the democracies to cope with this treaty-breaking threat to the general peace was a lesson not lost on Mussolini and Hitler.

Italy next broke the peace by the invasion and conquest of Ethiopia in 1935. It was not so much the intrinsic importance of Manchuria and Ethiopia to the democratic world that counted. Rather it was that these naked aggressions proved at once the impotence of the League of Nations at its designed function and the bankruptcy of the collective security system. With the advance connivance of the conservative governments of France and Britain, Mussolini manufactured a border incident and made it an excuse for aggressive war. After a brave but futile fight the tribesmen of Haile Selassie were defeated. Meanwhile, popular support for the League proved surprisingly strong in Britain and France. The League did act to the extent of applying financial sanctions —i.e., forbidding loans or financial assistance to Italy. It also embargoed munitions for the Italians. As could have been predicted, such measures were entirely ineffective in arresting a small-scale colonial war. Oil sanctions, which might have been effective, were not applied. Britain ostentatiously moved a fleet into the Mediterranean, apparently for the purpose of allowing its personnel to watch Italian transports carry an army through the Suez Canal to Eritrea. About the only solace that friends of the League could distill from the sorry story was that the double-dealing foreign ministers of Britain and France—Sir Samuel Hoare and Pierre Laval—were forced by popular indignation to resign.

The mere threat of oil sanctions, and the disturbing reports he received of public hostility to Italy in the democracies, caused Mussolini to reassess his relations with Nazi Germany—with which Italy had recently been distinctly unfriendly. Up to 1935 Germany had been largely unarmed. But in that year, after some domestic massacres to consolidate his power at home, Hitler felt secure enough to denounce the Versailles Treaty and to announce to the world the rearmament of Germany. A rearmed Germany would be worth Italy's sympathetic attention, reasoned Mussolini. The Rome-Berlin "Axis" dates from 1936.[16]

Adolf Hitler, an ill-educated demagogue, brilliant but with paranoiac tendencies, had come into power in Germany in 1933, pledged to cure unemployment and to destroy the Versailles settlement. By rearming Germany he did both. In 1936, in the face of French threats, he marched his new armies into the "permanently demilitarized" Rhineland—a necessary preliminary to defense of the industrial Ruhr should a major war develop later.

In the Spanish Civil War (1936-39) both Hitler and Mussolini intervened on the side of the rebels with men and material—perhaps decisively. Though in the beginning popular sympathy in the democracies was 2 to 1 in favor of the Loyalist government, it was not the democracies but Russia that provided material assistance to the Loyalists, and that too little and too late. As the Spanish War dragged on to its miserable conclusion, the small Spanish Communist Party, by virtue of its determined and ruthless leadership, became the dominant group in the Loyalist government. This of course made effective intervention by the democracies even less a political possibility.

In early 1938 German rearmament had

[16] The German-Japanese "Anti-Comintern" Pact later in the year made Germany the kingpin in a Rome-Berlin-Tokyo Axis. The term "Axis" was in common use from 1937 on.

made Hitler bold enough to undertake his first really big gamble. With the cooperation of the Nazi party in Austria, he simply marched to Vienna and announced an *Anschluss*—a union of Austria with Germany. Not being challenged, later in the year he demanded of Czechoslovakia that she cede to Germany the German-speaking Sudetenland, a fringe of parishes along Czechoslovakia's borders.

Unlike the Austrians, the Czechs are primarily a Slavic, not a Germanic, people. They had military alliances with France and Russia. With mountainous frontiers, a good army, and a substantial armaments industry, they were prepared to fight. Nearly everyone in Europe expected war. Instead, the prime ministers of France and Britain flew to Munich for a personal conference with Hitler. The upshot was that France dishonored her commitment. In exchange for empty and false promises from Hitler, Daladier and Chamberlain bargained away the Czechs' freedom. Moreover Russia was able to claim later that because the western democracies had proved they could not be trusted, Russia herself had to look elsewhere for her security. But in the West such was the passionate hope for peace that cheering multitudes surrounded Chamberlain's homecoming plane at Croydon Airfield. The peace that he had so dearly bought was in fact to last a little less than a year.

American Public Opinion in the 1930's

During the period 1930-38, though the United States occasionally showed signs of a positive Asiatic policy, it shunned collective action in Europe. The American people unquestionably disapproved very strongly of Hitler, especially of his merciless persecution of the Jews, but they even more strongly rejected the idea of American commitments that might lead to war. Indeed in the United States the self-evident failure of diplomacy to promote collective security in the 1930's stimulated a popular revulsion against the very practice of diplomacy. In 1934 headlines were made by the investigations of the Nye Committee in the Senate, which rehearsed in detail the well-known fact that American steel companies and munitions manufacturers had made handsome profits during World War I. World Peaceways and similar pacifist pressure groups promoted the erroneous conclusion that the war industries had been "responsible" for America's entrance into the war. The "merchants of death" propaganda thereby engendered helped make possible the neutrality legislation of the late 1930's, which amounted to a deliberate surrender of the neutral rights the United States had twice gone to war to preserve.[17] As in Great Britain and France, in the United States there was a widespread feeling that no war was worth fighting. Contemporary literature reflected a profound cynicism about the motives and competence of World War I leadership.[18] A great many American students gave vociferous approval to the "Oxford Pledge," by which British undergraduates were swearing "under no circumstances" to serve King and country.

Popular Thinking on Grand Strategy

Along with a pacifistic and isolationist public opinion went a popular misconception of grand strategy that made many persons feel that in any event American participation was

[17] The 1935 Neutrality Act forbade the sale or transport of munitions to a belligerent; the President might also prohibit Americans from travel on belligerents' ships.

The 1936 amendment prohibited loans to belligerents.

The 1937 Neutrality Act applied the earlier provisions to "civil strife" as well as war between nations. It permitted sales to belligerents of goods other than munitions on a "cash and carry" basis.

The 1939 Neutrality Act extended the "cash and carry" provision of the 1937 Act by lifting the embargo on munitions, and gave authority to the President to forbid American ships' entering designated "danger zones." The Neutrality Act of 1939 was repealed on November 13, 1941, a little over two weeks before Japan attacked the United States.

[18] Dozens of titles might be cited. Ernest Hemingway's A Farewell to Arms, C. S. Forester's The General, Erich Maria Remarque's All Quiet on the Western Front are examples from the novels. Plays and movies with a strong pacifist overtone reached nearly all of the population in the Western democracies.

not necessary. Captain B. H. Liddell Hart and other military writers of reputation had severely criticized Allied generalship in World War I for useless sacrifice of men in trying to break the trench line. It was freely predicted that, if World War II came, the pattern of the Western Front would be the same except that this time the Allies, snug in the impregnable Maginot Line, would remain on the defensive. The Germans, finally driven to action by the relentless pressure of naval blockade, would break themselves on the Maginot barrier. The French and British land offensive, when it came, would be a matter of sweeping up the exhausted fragments of the Wehrmacht. In brief, the war would be won by a combination of the Maginot Line and superior British sea power. America could afford to keep hands off. In view of the fact that apparently the French general staff accepted this concept, it is perhaps pardonable for a large part of the American public to have done so.

As everyone knows, the Maginot Line was to prove anything but impregnable. For that matter the role assigned to sea power in the prospective Allied strategy was not a realistic one. Sea power is a prerequisite to world power. It facilitates rapid shifting of forces among widely separated theaters of operations. Sea blockade can be decisive against an island nation dependent on imports for food and raw materials. But World War I had demonstrated that blockade cannot be decisive against a continental power with adequate internal communications. Hence naval supremacy alone was not enough to defeat Germany, even though German naval supremacy would have promptly defeated England. By the speedy development of synthetic oil and rubber industries, German scientists supplied at home the two bulky strategic materials their nation had previously lacked for waging war.

As the prewar German building program showed, Hitler and his generals tended to discount the relevance of sea power to Germany's situation and to place naval construction in a third priority behind that for the army and that for the Luftwaffe. Not until 1938 did Hitler begin a substantial buildup of his fleet.

Rather than stemming from Mahan, the theoretical foundations of Nazi world strategy largely derived from Karl Haushofer's "geopolitical" writings,[19] which in turn were based on the ideas of the distinguished British geographer, Halford J. Mackinder.

"Democratic Ideals and Reality"

When in 1919 Mackinder published *Democratic Ideals and Reality,* he meant it as a warning to his countrymen. The book came nearer to being a blueprint for Nazi Germany. Briefly summarized, Mackinder's argument runs: (1) Contrary to the implications of Mahan's writings, sea power and land power have been alternately decisive in the long periods of history. (2) When land power has been ascendant, it has often been able to defeat sea power by taking its bases in land campaigns. (3) England's effective control of the seas gave her world hegemony until the 20th century, but now the steam and gasoline engines, and rail and highway networks are depriving the sea of its monopoly of bulk transportation; therefore England's inherent relative power has declined as compared to continental power. (4) Once it has achieved adequate communications and a high level of economic development, the center of the greatest land mass will be in a position to exert the greatest power. This "Heartland" comprises western Siberia and European Russia. (5) A vigorous people, armed with modern technology, may through control of the Heartland come to control the entire "World Island," i.e., Eurasia and Africa. (6) The superior resources and population of the World Island may well ultimately make possible domination of the Fringe Lands, i.e., Great Britain, Japan, Australia, and North and South America.

Writing shortly after the end of World War I, Mackinder expressed the view that the victorious powers had very narrowly escaped catastrophe. Had Germany confined her military effort to the Eastern Front, it is conceivable that, operating out of her strategic position in East Europe, she might have conquered the Heartland. Then after employing her advanced technical means to develop this area into a vast base for further military operations, she could have advanced in all directions to the oceans, taking the bases of sea power from the landward side. With the whole World Island as her base, she might have launched a new cycle of sea power to conquer the rest of the world. Mackinder warned that the defeat of Germany in 1918 did not permanently remove the danger. If Germany and Russia should combine by agreement, or by conquest of one by the other, they would be in a position to rule the world. He put his warning into a simple formula:

Who rules East Europe commands the Heartland:
Who rules the Heartland commands the World-Island:
Who rules the World-Island commands the World.[20]

Accepting the validity of Mackinder's views, Haushofer attempted to orient German territorial aspirations to the East. In the opinion of the Nazi geopoliticians, with a conquered Russia as a German base, Hitler could afford at last to defy the superior British fleet.

Herein lies the ultimate rationale of Germany's attack on Russia in 1941, perhaps also of the adventures of Rommel's *Afrika Korps* in Germany's North African campaign. Haushofer himself, through whom Mackinder's ideas reached Hitler, cannot be deemed responsible for the poor timing of the Russian campaign, since it was also part of his program that Germany should at all costs avoid another two-front war. But the idea of conquering Russia sooner or later, of making a large part of it a German colony, was at least thoroughly consistent with his program.

It is easy to criticize Mackinder.[21] The Heartland, the limits of which are vaguely defined, includes vast tracts of tundra and arid pasturage. Except insofar as its immensity furnishes space for defensive maneuvering, its size is more a liability than an asset. Control of such an area would not necessarily advance a

---

[19] Professor General Karl Haushofer was the founder and head of the *Institut für Geopolitik* in Munich. In addition to his writings, his personal influence with the Nazi hierarchy was important.

[20] *Democratic Ideals and Reality* (New York, 1919, 1942), 150.

[21] See, for example, *America's Strategy in World Politics* (New York, 1942) and other writings by Nicholas J. Spykman.

program of world domination. Control of the centers of industry, wherever located, would still appear to be vastly more important. And over-all technological and industrial superiority seem more important still.

In any event, Mackinder never pretended to "prove Mahan wrong." He simply warned against a naive acceptance of an oversimplified version of Mahan's ideas. And as a matter of interest, Mackinder himself was to acknowledge shortly before his death, in 1947, that a power combination centering in the North Atlantic and including Western Europe and North America might more than offset the rising power of the Eurasian Heartland. For in spite of the vast population and great resources of the Soviet Union and Red China, the manpower- and developed resource-base of the non-Communist world remains greater still. The Communist threat of world domination is bound to stimulate a new political cohesiveness among the Western nations and render effective alliance systems that otherwise would hardly have existed.

At this writing, the struggle between the Communist-dominated "Heartland" and the "Fringe Lands" of the West remains unresolved. Certainly improved internal communications and the increase of economic self-sufficiency through the development of synthetics have strengthened the Soviet Union in this long-term conflict. On the other hand, the extended radius of naval firepower contributed by carrier aircraft and submarine-based missiles, the long head start of the West in technology, engineering, and over-all economic development, and American acceptance of responsibility for Free World leadership may more than compensate for the new-won advantages of the Iron Curtain countries. It is, in any event, probably safe to say that no oversimplified theory of the historical process can be a trustworthy basis for predicting the unpredictable.

27:
World War II:
Atlantic Surface Operations, I

"It is peace in our time," said Britain's Prime Minister, Neville Chamberlain, when he returned from the Munich conference with Hitler. Less than a year later, at 0445[1] on September 1, 1939, Nazi armies hurled themselves against Poland, and the holocaust of World War II began. The danger signs had been unmistakable from the latter part of August, when Hitler signed with Russia a non-aggression pact that freed him from the danger of Soviet intervention. England and France had mutual aid treaties with Poland, but Hitler had no reason to suspect that they would honor them any more than they had fulfilled their Munich-repudiated moral obligations to Czechoslovakia. The German *Führer* planned a swift campaign that would smash Poland while Britain and France vacillated. He thus would present them with a *fait accompli*. But he failed to consider the change in temper of both leaders and people in the two western countries. This time he would be opposed with force to the utmost, on land, on sea, and in the air. The British presented the Germans an ultimatum during the evening of September 1 and issued a final warning at 0900 on the 3rd. At 1115 on September 3, 1939, in a broadcast to the nation, Prime Minister Chamberlain announced that His Majesty's Government was at war with Germany. France followed suit that afternoon. The same day a round-faced, chubby man of dynamic fighting spirit returned as First Lord of the British Admiralty, an office he had relinquished 24 years earlier. A signal was flashed to the fleet: "Winston is back."

There was little that Britain or France could do to aid Poland. Germany unleashed a new kind of warfare on the Polish plains, a war of rapid movement, heavily mechanized, in which tanks were used to spearhead long lines of advance and to encircle whole armies. Overhead, the *Luftwaffe* swept the ineffectual Polish Air Force from the skies, and then roared in with Stukas and Messerschmitts to wipe out Polish infantry strong points in the way of the onrushing German divisions. In a few weeks all was over on the Polish front. Here the *Blitzkrieg*, or lightning war, tactics had done their work. But all was not over in the West. Though British and French mobilization had come too late to help Poland, Britain and France laid plans to meet any westward thrusts of the German *Wehrmacht*—Britain primarily through the use of her sea power; France by means of her armies sheltered behind the Maginot Line.

Hitler had no wish to face a real war with Britain and France—at that time. He accepted the Russian occupation of half of Poland in an effort to keep the war localized. He hoped that he could persuade Britain and France to accept the situation and agree to peace, thus affording him time to build up his navy for a war in the West in 1944 or 1945. Hence, after the Polish operation had been completed, Hitler refrained from any offensive action on the Western Front, a measure of restraint that brought about what has been called the "Phony War." Through the winter of 1939-40

---

[1] This and the following chapters use 24-hour time, which came into almost universal use for military purposes in World War II. Unless otherwise indicated, all times and dates in the remainder of this book are local.

German troops in the Siegfried Line faced French troops in the Maginot Line with only small skirmishes relieving the monotony.

The War Begins at Sea

Near the end of 1938, Grand Admiral Erich Raeder, *Oberkommando der Kriegsmarine*,[2] presented Hitler with a choice of plans. One, based on the assumption that war was imminent, called for most of Germany's naval resources to be devoted to weapons of commerce warfare—U-boats, raiders, minelayers, and coast defense forces. The other, known as PLAN Z, was a long-range program, based on the assumption that war was not to be expected for ten years. Under this plan, Germany would build a surface fleet of ships so superior to those of the Royal Navy that she could wrest mastery of the oceans from Britain.

Hitler informed Raeder that he should proceed on the basis of PLAN Z. The reason for this decision, sorely mistaken in the light of subsequent events, is difficult to fathom. Hitler valued the big ships for their political influence. He also appears to have been seized with a desire to emulate and perhaps outstrip Great Britain, little anticipating that his projects on the Continent would involve him in war with her. When he overreached himself in Poland, he was stunned by the British ultimatum. Not until 1940 did he give up hope of Britain's agreeing to peace.

Whatever the reason for Hitler's decision, it left his navy in no condition for war. By the end of 1939 PLAN Z was well launched, but the fleet would not be combat-ready before 1945. Experiments had yet to be evaluated. Only interim ship types had been completed. Having begun by laying down conventional vessels, the Germans were gradually introducing bolder experiments. To ensure long radius of action they depended heavily on diesel propulsion, but in 1939 some German ships had

[2] Usually abbreviated OKM. The German high command structure was pyramidal, with Hitler as Commander in Chief, or *Oberkommando der Wehrmacht* (OKW). He had a small staff (also known as OKW) headed by General Keitel. The three fighting services were the *Kriegsmarine* (navy), the *Luftwaffe* (air force), and the *Heer* (army). The term *Wehrmacht* is properly used only to apply to all three services together.

mixed power plants, using both diesel and steam.

At the outbreak of war, the German navy comprised the following units: two battleships, *Scharnhorst* and *Gneisenau*,[3] completed; two battleships, *Bismarck* and *Tirpitz*, nearing completion; three pocket battleships,[4] *Deutschland*, *Scheer*, and *Graf Spee;* three heavy cruisers, *Hipper, Prinz Eugen,* and *Blücher;* and five light cruisers, *Karlsruhe, Köln, Leipzig, Nürnberg, Emden* and *Königsberg.* Twenty-six merchant ships had been converted into armed merchant cruisers. A respectable number of destroyers, torpedo boats, mine sweepers, and auxiliaries completed the surface fleet. German submarine warfare, which was directed by Commodore Karl Dönitz, began operations with only 56 U-boats.[5] Twenty-one submarines, the *Graf Spee,* and the *Deutschland* were at sea in waiting areas even before the outbreak of the war.

The Germans at sea struck hard from the first. The day England entered the war, the British passenger liner *Athenia* was sunk by *U-30,* whose commander could not resist the temptation when he found her in his periscope sights. Dönitz, Raeder, and Hitler all issued denials of German responsibility—in good faith because they could not believe a U-boat commander had disobeyed their orders to spare passenger ships. In less good faith was Propaganda Minister Goebbels' declaration that Churchill had engineered the whole thing himself in the hope of involving the United States in the war.

British naval strategy was necessarily almost the converse of Germany's. The Royal Navy promptly blockaded the German North Sea

[3] In British histories these vessels are often referred to as battle cruisers, but the Germans always called them battleships. They mounted 11-inch guns.

[4] The pocket battleship was an experimental vessel mounting 11-inch guns on a nominal 10,000-ton hull. It was supposed to be able to outrun a battleship and outgun everything else.

[5] If Raeder had been allowed his way, under Plan Z the German navy of 1948 would have comprised 10 battleships up to 54,000 tons, 12 small battleships of 20,000 tons, 3 pocket battleships of 10,000 tons, 5 heavy cruisers, 22 light cruisers, 22 scouting cruisers, 4 aircraft carriers, 68 destroyers, and 249 U-boats, plus adequate minecraft, escort vessels, and auxiliaries.

coast and the exits from the Baltic by means of the Home Fleet based on Scapa Flow. Britain's most vital task however was to ensure that ships bringing more than 40 million tons of cargo a year entered British ports and discharged their cargoes. Oddly enough, pre-war British planning to attain that goal overlooked the lessons of World War I. Reviving the old misconception that convoys are less efficient in delivering goods than independently routed ships, the Admiralty planned to continue independent sailings. The sinking of the *Athenia* however changed Admiralty minds, and convoys were quickly instituted.

The first convoy sailed for Halifax on September 8. Its escort accompanied it for 300 miles, then picked up an inbound convoy and brought it safely to United Kingdom ports. This was the early pattern of convoy operations, because shortage of escorts did not permit protection far beyond the British coast. During the first two years of the war moreover, the Admiralty considered it necessary, because of the activity of German surface raiders, to provide each convoy with a heavy escort, a battleship or cruiser if possible, otherwise a converted, armed passenger liner.

That the threat from German surface raiders was real was soon made apparent by the activities of the *Deutschland* and the *Graf Spee*. By the middle of October the *Deutschland* had sunk two merchant ships and committed a first class diplomatic blunder by seizing the American freighter *City of Flint*. Under a prize crew, the *City of Flint* sailed to Murmansk in North Russia. Later, en route to Germany via Norwegian territorial waters, she was intercepted by the Norwegians and returned to her master. The incident caused much anti-German sentiment in the United States. It was also the first incident to attract Hitler's attention, militarily, to Norway. On her return to Germany, the *Deutschland* was renamed *Lützow* lest home morale suffer should a ship named *Deutschland* be lost.

The Battle of the River Plate, Decembr 13, 1939

The *Graf Spee* operated in the area between Pernambuco and Cape Town, although in November she slipped over into the Indian Ocean south of Madagascar for a brief period. On the way back, she met her supply ship *Altmark*, refueled, transferred prisoners, and then resumed her search for victims. The effectiveness of her cruise, completely apart from the 50,000 tons she sank, is shown in the number of Allied ships assigned to chase her. Out of Freetown, the British naval base on the western bulge of Africa, operated the carrier *Ark Royal* and the battle cruiser *Renown;* from Dakar two French heavy cruisers and the British carrier *Hermes* joined the search. The heavy cruisers *Sussex* and *Shropshire* were poised at the Cape of Good Hope, and up and down the east coast of South America ranged Commodore Sir Henry Harwood's force consisting of the two heavy cruisers *Cumberland* and *Exeter* and the light cruisers *Ajax* and H.M.N.Z.S. *Achilles.*

Commodore Harwood's group, less the *Cumberland* which was refitting in the Falklands, on December 13 succeeded in intercepting the *Graf Spee* in the approaches to the River Plate. The contact presented Harwood a ticklish tactical problem. The *Graf Spee*'s six 11-inch guns outranged the cruiser guns by about 8,000 yards. None of the cruisers could long withstand her fire. Their only opportunity would be to come in from widely diverging angles in order to force the *Graf Spee* to divide her fire. The cruisers would not be able to reply until they had passed through the danger zone from about 30,000 yards, the range of the *Graf Spee*'s guns, to about 22,000 yards, the extreme limit of the cruisers' main batteries. If the *Graf Spee* had been properly handled, she would have turned directly away from the cruisers, forcing them to a stern chase. Even with their speed advantage of about five knots, it would have taken the cruisers nearly half an hour to pass through the danger zone. Probably they would never have made it. But Captain Hans Langsdorff thought he had a cruiser and two destroyers to deal with. Since they stood between him and the open sea, he ran down to meet them and to break his way through to freedom. The three British cruisers were in column, the *Ajax* leading and the *Exeter* in the rear. At 0617 the *Graf Spee* opened fire, whereupon the *Exeter* made a turn to port to engage from the south, while the two light

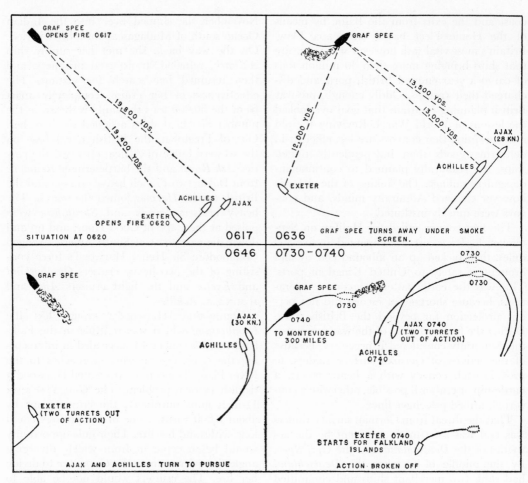

BATTLE OF THE RIVER PLATE, DECEMBER 13, 1939

cruisers held their northerly course to engage the enemy's opposite bow. On the completion of her turn, at 0620, the *Exeter* opened fire at a range of 19,400 yards. The *Ajax* and *Achilles* commenced fire a few minutes later, and the 6- and 8-inch shells from all three ships began to hit effectively. The *Graf Spee*'s shells also took their toll. Soon the *Exeter* received a hit that knocked out her "B" turret, destroyed bridge communications, and killed or wounded nearly everyone on the bridge. The German then shifted fire to the two light cruisers and turned away under a smoke screen, apparently to make for the River Plate. As the *Ajax* turned in pursuit, the *Graf Spee* once more shifted fire to the *Exeter,* again under control. By 0725, both the *Exeter*'s forward turrets were out of action, and at 0730 power was lost to the after turret. Meanwhile the *Ajax* had two turrets put out of action, and Commodore Harwood decided to break off until night, when he would have a chance to make a torpedo attack. The *Exeter* started on the long voyage to the Falklands, while the wounded *Graf Spee* set her course for Montevideo, dogged by the *Ajax* and *Achilles*. Occasional exchanges of fire occurred all day, but neither side attempted to renew the battle. A little after midnight, the *Graf Spee* entered Montevideo. There Langsdorff hoped to effect repairs and force his way clear at a later date. He had chosen Montevideo on the advice of his navigator and was not aware of the political situation whereby he would have received a much more sympathetic welcome in Buenos Aires, farther up the river.

Frenzied diplomatic activities on the part of the German consular representatives were unsuccessful in getting permission for the *Graf Spee* to remain in port longer than 72 hours. British propaganda was more successful in giving the impression of a large British fleet just offshore. Actually only the *Cumberland* had joined the battered *Ajax* and *Achilles*. From Berlin Langsdorff received the option of fighting his way out or scuttling his ship. Shortage of ammunition decided him to take the latter course. Having landed wounded, prisoners, and most of his crew, he got underway on the afternoon of December 17. The British cruisers went to action stations, but before they could engage her, the *Graf Spee*'s skeleton crew abandoned her just before she blew up. Langsdorff shot himself shortly afterward. Thereafter for several months the Germans abandoned the use of surface raiders.

Other Operations at Sea

While the *Graf Spee* was still finding victims, other units of the German navy had been active. Most striking was the penetration of Scapa Flow on the night of October 14 by *U-47* under the command of Lieutenant Günther Prien, who was to become one of Germany's U-boat aces. Prien successfully navigated the tortuous channel and sank the battleship *Royal Oak* with the loss of 786 of her officers and men. In late November the two German battleships *Scharnhorst* and *Gneisenau* passed out into the Atlantic through the North Sea, primarily to cover the return of the *Deutschland* from her mid-Atlantic raiding, and incidentally to see what they could pick up in the way of British merchant shipping. They came upon H.M.S. *Rawalpindi*, a converted passenger liner armed with four old 6-inch guns and carried on the Admiralty List as an armed merchant cruiser. Her commander, thinking he had found the *Deutschland*, was under no illusions about the outcome of such an encounter, but he accepted the odds against him. The *Scharnhorst* opened fire and the *Rawalpindi* replied as best she could. In a few minutes, the British ship was reduced to a helpless wreck. Before she sank, the two cruisers *Newcastle* and *Delhi* arrived on the scene, but only to lose contact with the Germans in the darkness and heavy rain. The British Home Fleet sortied from Scapa Flow, but the two Germans, their presence revealed and hence their usefulness lost, headed for home, slipping through the British cordon. The hopeless fight of the *Rawalpindi* had not been in vain, since the two powerful raiders were driven from the sea before they could get into the commerce areas.

The *Altmark* Affair

The German supply ship *Altmark,* which had replenished the *Graf Spee* shortly before her final action off Montevideo, was serving as a floating prison for some 300 British seamen taken by the pocket battleship. The British were anxious to capture the *Altmark,* but she successfully hid in the South Atlantic for nearly two months. Gambling that the search had died down, she attempted to make her way back to Germany. She was favored by the weather and was not sighted until February 14, in Norwegian territorial waters. A flotilla of destroyers under Captain Philip Vian in H.M.S. *Cossack* intercepted her at Jossing Fiord but took no further action pending a directive from the Admiralty. When Vian received his instructions, he sent two destroyers with orders for a boarding party to examine the vessel. Two Norwegian gunboats met the small force and told Vian that the *Altmark* was unarmed, had been examined, and had received permission to proceed to Germany, making use of Norwegian territorial waters. Accordingly the destroyers withdrew for further instructions.

Churchill now sent orders for Vian to board the *Altmark,* using force if necessary in self-defense. While the Norwegian authorities continued their protests, the *Altmark* made the first belligerent move by getting under way and attempting to ram the *Cossack,* which evaded the clumsy attempt and then ran alongside the German ship and sent over a boarding party. After a sharp hand-to-hand fight, the German crew surrendered. Examination revealed that the British prisoners were battened down in storerooms and that the ship had two pom-poms and four machine guns.

Although the British action was a violation of Norway's neutrality, Norway's position was by no means clear. The *Altmark* had not, in fact, been searched, claiming immunity by reason of the special service flag which made her a naval auxiliary. The British claimed that she was not on "innocent passage," since she was returning from war operations and had prisoners on board, and that it was up to Norway to enforce her own neutral rights. Yet Norway was in the unhappy position of not daring to enforce her rights against her two powerful belligerent neighbors. Although most of her people were sympathetic with the Allied cause, they feared Germany and her ever-present threat of action. Hence Norway made strong protests to Britain over the *Altmark* affair, hoping, no doubt, thereby to stave off German counter-action.

The Invasion of Norway

Norwegian hopes of being allowed to remain on the sidelines of the war were vain. A glance at the map gives a partial reason; from the Norwegian coast the British naval base at Scapa Flow can be outflanked. If Germany intended to operate either U-boats or surface units in the open Atlantic, she could get them out more easily from Norwegian than from German bases. But another feature, not so readily apparent, made use of Norwegian waters even more vital to Germany. Norway's coast, extending from Egersund to North Cape, offers a 1,000-mile-long sheltered passage between the offshore islands and the mainland. This passage, known as the Leads, has served Norway as a means of communication since Viking times; it also served the Germans in the two world wars. Ignoring Norwegian neutrality, German ships could take advantage of their own air cover in traversing the Skagerrak or Kattegat, make a dash across the narrow seas between the Skaw and Kristiansand or Egersund, and then follow the Leads until they chose to make a break through to the Atlantic.

Yet the use of the Leads by warships was only a small part of the story. The principal reason for the German invasion of Norway can be given in the single word, *iron*. Annually Germany imported 15 million tons of iron ore, and of this total, nearly 75 per cent came from Scandinavia. In summer this ore was carried through the Baltic Sea from the Swedish port of Lulea to Germany, safe from the Royal

Navy, which could not penetrate the Skagerrak. But the Baltic freezes in winter, and then the iron ore had to be transported overland to the Norwegian town of Narvik. Forty-one per cent of Scandinavian iron came by this route. Thus Norway was vital to Germany.

Admiral Raeder early brought the Norwegian situation to Hitler's attention, but argued that Norway's neutrality was to the advantage of Germany, provided it was respected by the British. Yet, realizing that Britain would not allow such a gaping hole in her blockade to go unplugged, Raeder ordered his naval staff, the *Seekriegsleitung*,[6] to prepare plans for the invasion of Norway, should it be necessary. In an attempt to win his goal by peaceable means, he arranged for a meeting between Hitler and the strongly pro-German Vidkun Quisling, who he mistakenly believed could win control of the Storting, the Norwegian parliament. The winter proved that events would not take the course that Raeder hoped. Quisling, instead of offering help to the Germans, began to ask for aid himself. The *City of Flint* and the *Altmark* affairs indicated that the Leads were not as safe as they had seemed. Then intelligence reports reached Berlin indicating that the British were planning to mine the Leads. The Germans believed that the Norwegians would acquiesce. Hence on March 1, 1940, Hitler issued the order for Operation WESERÜBUNG, the invasion of Norway and Denmark.

The operation violated every principle of naval strategy except one—surprise. The invasion force would make its way across the sea in the face of the power of the foremost navy in the world and would land at several widely separated points, some nearly a thousand miles from German bases. It would have to establish and maintain itself and fend off the inevitable British counterattack. Yet these things had to be done if Norway was to be captured. One feature gave the key to success—the geography of the area. (See map page 497.) After the initial assault, German supply lines could be maintained through the Kattegat with only a short dash through the Skagerrak from the Skaw to Oslo Fiord. In this area, close to German air bases in the north, the Royal Navy could not operate. To protect this route the

[6] Usually referred to as the SKL.

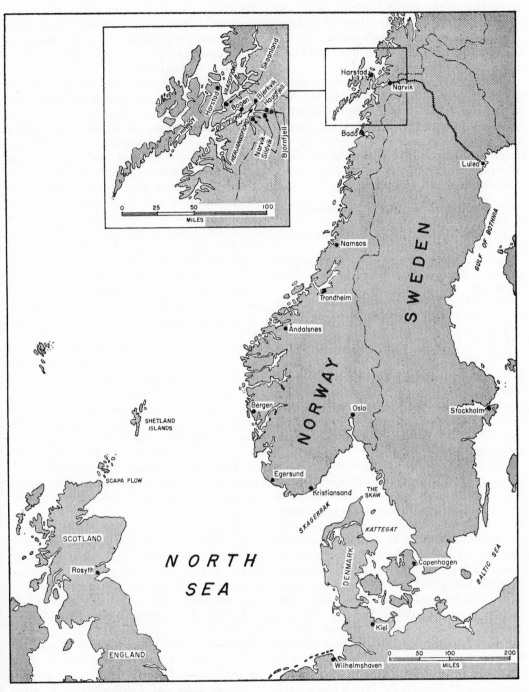

NORWEGIAN CAMPAIGN, APRIL–JUNE 1940

Germans decided to occupy Denmark as well as Norway. Thus Raeder and the SKL estimated that if the initial landings could take place without excessive loss, then the positions could be maintained through sea transport to Oslo and by overland transport from Oslo to the various occupied positions.

The Germans committed their entire surface navy and most of their U-boats to the Norwegian operation. Raeder fully expected to lose half. Dönitz, to his intense annoyance, was ordered to provide 25 U-boats to be stationed off Norway. He had to strip the North Atlantic hunting grounds to comply. Surface ships were assigned as follows:

Group I: Narvik: *Gneisenau, Scharnhorst,* and ten destroyers with 2,000 troops.

Group II: Trondheim: *Hipper,* four destroyers, and 1,700 troops.

Group III: Bergen: *Königsberg,* the old training cruiser *Bremse,* small vessels (E-boats), and 900 troops.

Group IV: Kristiansand and Arendal: *Karlsruhe,* a depot ship, a torpedo boat flotilla, and 1,400 troops.

Group V: Oslo: *Blücher, Lützow, Emden,* a few small vessels, and 2,000 troops.

In addition, two naval groups were assigned to Denmark. One with the old battleship *Schleswig-Holstein* had the responsibility for the Great Belt area, while a smaller group of light craft with 1,000 men undertook the capture of Copenhagen.

All landings were to be carried out simultaneously in the early morning of April 9, 1940. While the German preparations were going forward, the British, in one of the major coincidences of the war, were themselves planning operations in Norway. To attempt to stop the German use of the Leads, the Admiralty planned to lay mine fields off Narvik, announcing their intention to the Norwegian government simultaneously with the act. This operation was scheduled for the night of April 6, and had it been carried out then, it might well have balked the German scheme. Anticipating that the Germans might react vigorously to the mining, even to the extent of an invasion of Norway, the British had a small expeditionary force embarked in ships to proceed with the minelaying forces. However, because of last minute difficulties, the under-

taking was postponed for 48 hours, and as intelligence of German activity reached London, the Cabinet decided to disembark the troops until the situation was "clarified." Thus, when the German expedition sailed, the troops so sorely needed for prompt counteraction in Norway were in England.

The opening event of the Norwegian drama took place at sea on April 8 with a chance encounter between a German destroyer and the British destroyer *Glowworm.* Before either ship was seriously damaged, the German heavy cruiser *Hipper* from the Trondheim group appeared on the scene. Gallantly the *Glowworm* attacked the newcomer, making effective use of smoke. At length, in a sinking condition, she rammed her adversary, tearing a hole in the cruiser's side. As the *Glowworm* fell away, she blew up and sank. The Germans rescued some 40 survivors. Her captain was posthumously awarded the Victoria Cross.

The next act took place about 0330 on the morning of April 9, when the battle cruiser *Renown* encountered the *Gneisenau* and *Scharnhorst* in a brief, inconclusive engagement. To the British, the circumstances did not seem to indicate a major German assault on Norway, although the Admiralty believed that these forces might be bound for Narvik. The Norwegians also did not consider the events ominous, nor had they taken warning from the sinking of the German transport *Rio de Janeiro* by a submarine a few hours earlier off Kristiansand. When these warnings were misinterpreted, the situation passed its critical moment. The German gamble was beginning to succeed.

Denmark offered little resistance. A thousand soldiers landed in Copenhagen, and a smaller detachment on the western side of the island quickly seized key positions and communications. Before the Danes realized what was happening, they were under the Nazi heel.

In Oslo the Germans received one of their most serious setbacks. They had to traverse the 70-mile-long Oslo Fiord, where they could not expect to escape observation, even at night. Near the naval base at Horton, some 25 miles south of Oslo, the Fiord narrows to about 200 yards, and here the naval guns were alert. Opening a prompt and effective fire, the Norwegians sank the cruiser *Blücher* at 0623.

While the German naval attaché waited anxiously on the pier at Oslo, the German assault forces landed south of Horton and seized it from the rear. This accomplished, they pressed on. In the meantime Fornebo Airfield at Oslo had been seized by airborne troops, and the city was soon under control of the Germans. The King however had removed the government to Hammar, 100 miles to the north.

At most other points the landings were unopposed or met little serious resistance, except that the guns at Bergen heavily damaged and immobilized the light cruiser *Königsberg*, allowing British naval aircraft to sink her the next day. At Narvik, far to the north, the German invasion force was opposed only by the Norwegian coastal defense ships *Eidsvold* and *Norge*, which were sunk after a gallant but futile resistance. Then the ten destroyers proceeded up the Fiord to land their troops, while the two battleships carried out their mission of general support.

It seemed that Operation WESERÜBUNG had succeeded beyond the most optimistic expectations of its planners. The losses had been very light and all objectives were in German hands by the end of April 9. It was now up to the Army to exploit the opportunities won for them by the Navy. The Navy still had the tasks of getting its warships out of Norwegian waters and of maintaining the supply lines to Norway.

The first counterattack came at Narvik. The British Admiralty, recognizing the supreme importance of this port, prepared to act as swiftly as possible. Believing that only one destroyer had entered Narvik, they ordered Captain B. A. W. Warburton-Lee, commanding a destroyer flotilla: "Proceed to Narvik and sink or capture enemy ship. It is at your discretion to land forces, if you think you can recapture Narvik from the number of enemy present." Later, learning that the Germans were stronger than had been anticipated, they gave Warburton-Lee the option of canceling the operation if he believed German defenses made it impracticable. His reply was characteristic of the traditions of the Royal Navy: "Going into action."

Accompanied by the destroyers *Hunter*, *Havock*, *Hotspur*, and *Hostile*, Captain Warburton-Lee in the *Hardy* entered West Fiord before dawn. In the approach phase, the *Hotspur* and *Hostile* engaged the shore batteries while the other three ships pressed into the port. There they found not one, but five German destroyers and several merchant ships. In the first attack, the *Hardy* torpedoed the German destroyer *Wilhelm Heidkamp*, killing the German commodore. Another German destroyer was sunk by gunfire and a third was beached. Recovering from their surprise, the Germans opened fire and straddled but failed to hit the *Havock*. The British ships then retired under a smoke screen. Shortly they returned for a second attack, augmented by the *Hostile* and *Hotspur*, the latter sinking two merchant ships. The British pressed home a third attack, but this time the fortunes changed. Warburton-Lee discovered three fresh German destroyers coming down on him from Herjangs Fiord. At a range of 10,000 yards he opened fire and turned away. The British ships then commenced a retirement, keeping up a running fire, but ran into an ambush at Ballangen Fiord, where two more destroyers were awaiting them. The *Georg Thiel* engaged the *Hardy*, which shortly afterward took a hit on the bridge that killed Warburton-Lee. The *Hardy* sank a few minutes later. Making a swing to the left, the *Georg Thiel* launched a spread of torpedoes at the *Hunter*, which also sank. The *Hotspur* and *Hostile* were both damaged, but, together with the *Havock*, made their way to the open sea. The damage the Germans had sustained made them helpless to follow or to carry out their planned retirement to Germany. On the way out, the three surviving British destroyers encountered the German ammunition ship *Rauenfels*. After a few salvos from their guns, the German blew up in a tremendous explosion.

A few days later, on April 13, a heavy British naval force including the battleship *Warspite* and the carrier *Furious* finished off the work begun by Warburton-Lee, sinking all eight destroyers that had survived his attack. The lesson of these two battles was plain. Warburton-Lee, much outnumbered, had accepted action in an area where the speed and maneuverability of his ships were restricted and in an area that afforded many chances for ambush. Effecting tactical surprise on his arrival, he did considerable damage, but was surprised himself by being caught between two forces, one of which blocked his way to the open sea. In the second battle, the British properly used overwhelming force to ensure completion of the job.

In general, British reaction to the German operations in Norway was marked by indecision and improvisation. Keenly conscious that the Germans had flouted Britain's sea power, the British eagerly sought a way to hit back at the invaders. The times called for rapid, decisive countermeasures, for the German forces were the most vulnerable immediately following the landings. Until road and rail communications were opened from Oslo to the several points of German occupation, troops had to live on the materials already provided them. The sea could not serve for supply in face of an alerted British Home Fleet. While the Germans worked feverishly to build internal communications in Norway, the British Cabinet lost critical days in trying to decide where to counterattack. With most of their troops already committed to the French front, there were very few available for operations in Norway, although the French were willing to supplement the British contingent with a brigade of Chasseurs Alpins and two brigades of the Foreign Legion. Where the Allied troops could best be placed was the big strategic problem facing the Cabinet. Two main possibilities offered themselves, Narvik and Trondheim. As has already been noted, Narvik was of supreme importance, since it controlled the export of iron ore from Norway and Sweden, and also it appealed to several officials, including Churchill, in view of the success already won there by the naval forces. On the other hand, Trondheim had its adherents because here Norway narrows to only a few miles and all land communications to the north can be controlled from that city. The Cabinet started to follow up the naval successes in the Narvik area, but when this operation was barely under way, the government shifted the point of the main attack to the Trondheim area.

Narvik

The first detachment of troops sailed for Narvik on April 12, 1940, with troops under the command of Major General Mackesy,

while the naval forces in support were under Admiral of the Fleet Lord Cork and Orrery. General Mackesy's instructions contained the following points:

It is clearly illegal to bombard a populated area in the hope of hitting a legitimate target which is known to be in the area, but which cannot be precisely located and identified.

* * *

The object of the force will be to eject the Germans from the Narvik area and establish control of Narvik itself. . . . Your initial task will be to establish your force at Harstad, ensure the cooperation of Norwegian forces that may be there, and obtain the information necessary to enable you to plan further operations. It is not intended that you should land in the face of opposition. . . . The decision whether to land or not will be taken by the senior naval officer in consultation with you If landing is impossible at Harstad, some other suitable locality should be tried. A landing must be carried out when you have sufficient troops.

The cautious tone of these instructions seems to have impressed itself so deeply upon General Mackesy's mind that he took little account of a more aggressive suggestion in a personal letter from General Ironside, Chief of the Imperial General Staff: "You may have a chance of taking advantage of naval action and should do so if you can. Boldness is required."

The manner in which the Narvik attack was planned clearly reveals British unpreparedness for conducting amphibious operations. Mackesy's instructions emphasized caution, when boldness was needed. Mackesy and Cork were made equal commanders, with no clear-cut definition of their individual or joint responsibilities. Most curious of all was the choice of Harstad for the initial landing. Forces at Harstad could not interdict German supplies to Narvik, the main objective, and to attack Narvik from Harstad would require further amphibious operations.

While the expedition was en route to Harstad, Cork received a dispatch from the Commander in Chief of the Home Fleet suggesting that, in view of the success of the attack by the *Warspite* and *Furious,* a direct assault on Narvik could be carried out. Cork urged Mackesy to make the attempt, but the General refused, pointing to his instructions with regard to bombing civilian areas. Further pressed,

Mackesy insisted that the German defenses at Narvik were too strong to be forced by means of naval bombardment. Finally, he admitted that his transports were not combat loaded. In the face of Mackesy's opposition and unpreparedness, Cork had no alternative but to proceed with the original plan.

Next came a dispatch from the Cabinet urging the bolder course on Mackesy:

> Your proposals involve damaging deadlock at Narvik and the neutralisation of one of our best brigades. We cannot send you the Chasseurs Alpins. The *Warspite* will be needed elsewhere in two or three days. Full consideration should, therefore, be given by you to an assault upon Narvik covered by the *Warspite* and the destroyers, which might also operate at Rombaks Fiord. The capture of the port and town would be an important success. We should like to receive from you the reasons why this is not possible, and your estimate of the degree of resistance to be expected on the waterfront. Matter most urgent.

Mackesy remained adamant, and the landing at Harstad proceeded. Once ashore, he announced that he was unable to advance on Narvik until the snow melted and until he had built up his supplies. Thus while the Germans strengthened Narvik, British troops at Harstad suffered attrition from the cold and from *Luftwaffe* attacks that seriously imperiled attempts at supply and reinforcement.

Trondheim

Meanwhile the British cabinet had turned its attention to Trondheim. The plan called for a main assault at Trondheim itself, with subsidiary landings at Namsos, a hundred miles to the north, and at Åndalsnes, a hundred miles to the south. The landing at Namsos took place under heavy German air attack on April 15, and that at Åndalsnes three days later. The main landing at Trondheim was to follow April 22. But on the 18th, the Chiefs of Staff began to have reservations about the Trondheim landing, emphasizing the tremendous risks of the long approach up the Fiord. They recommended instead that the landings at Namsos and Åndalsnes be developed into main drives, to capture Trondheim by a double envelopment. At length this view prevailed in spite of the opposition of Churchill and of Admiral of the Fleet Sir Roger Keyes, who offered to take some older ships into Trondheim himself. The counsel of caution once more carried the day.

The Allied Evacuation From Norway

It soon became evident that the Allies could not maintain their beachheads at Namsos and Åndalsnes in the face of growing German air power operating from captured Norwegian airfields. British and French cruisers and destroyers could bring in supplies and reinforcements by night, but during the day the *Luftwaffe* ruled the air, bombing the Allied bases into rubble and interdicting Allied communications. British carriers attempted to provide fighter support, but there were not enough carriers to operate aircraft continuously and not enough fighters to provide simultaneous protection for the carriers, other naval forces in the area, and the troops ashore. An attempt by a squadron of fighters from H.M.S. *Glorious* to operate from a frozen lake while the carrier pulled out of German bomber range resulted in the prompt destruction of the fighters. The Allies had no alternative to evacuating their forces in late April and early May, leaving the Germans in possession of all of southern and central Norway.

There remained however the British toehold at Harstad, in the north. On April 20, the Cabinet, exasperated by General Mackesy's repeated delays, appointed Lord Cook to overall command of the operations against Narvik. Finally, in mid-May, the British made their assault, not directly against Narvik, but against Bjerkvik, to the north, with the intention of building up a force there and then attacking Narvik across Rombaks Fiord. The Bjerkvik operation, supported by planes from the *Ark Royal,* was a complete success. By now airfields had been prepared ashore for use by the R.A.F., and carriers *Glorious* and *Furious* ferried in enough fighters to offset the growing German air power in the area through the next stage in the campaign.

By this time however Germany had invaded the Low Countries and France, and total Allied defeat was imminent on the Western

Front. Accordingly fresh instructions went to British forces in the Narvik area: capture the city, destroy the installations, and prepare for evacuation. Narvik fell to the British on May 28, following a successful crossing of Rombaks Fiord the preceding day. The evacuation took place soon afterward, being completed by June 8, in three convoys transporting 24,000 men and quantities of equipment and supplies.

To oppose this evacuation Raeder sent the *Scharnhorst* and the *Gneisenau* to the northern area. Known as Operation JUNO, this sweep had the further purpose of covering the movement of other elements of the German fleet to Trondheim. With the British Home Fleet committed to support of the Narvik evacuation, the German ships reached Trondheim safely. The *Scharnhorst* and *Gneisenau* surprised and sank the *Glorious* before she had a chance to get her planes into the air, together with her two escorting destroyers, which made gallant efforts to save their charge. In addition the Germans sank two merchant ships and an antisubmarine trawler. The remainder of the Allied Expeditionary Force reached England safely.

Thus ended the Norwegian campaign. Brilliantly conceived and executed by the Germans, it showed what could be accomplished by a ruthless nation, willing to take any advantage of friendship and neutrality. Germany's use of the sea routes across areas theoretically commanded by British sea power showed what an inferior naval force can accomplish through surprise. Once the Germans had made good their beachheads they no longer had to rely on surprise, for they could supply and reinforce their forces via the Kattegat, immune to Allied attack, and then overland in Norway.

The British operations in Norway had to be undertaken, if only for political reasons, but they cost Britain more prestige than they gained. The Belgians, the French, and, later, the Greeks remembered Norway when their own days of crisis arrived.

28:
Atlantic Surface Operations, II

The disastrous Allied expedition into Norway brought about the fall of the British government. On May 10, the day that Hitler struck at the Low Countries, Neville Chamberlain yielded the office of Prime Minister to Winston Churchill, who set out to form a National Government with ministers representing all parties, in contrast to the Conservative Government of his predecessor. Under Churchill's leadership the war was pursued with vigor and courage through the darkest hours, when Britain stood alone.

Neither Holland nor Belgium was able to make a significant resistance to the *Blitzkrieg* of the Nazi forces pouring across the Rhine. Hitler, finally abandoning all hopes of a compromise peace with the West, had hurled his armies through the Low Countries, as the Kaiser had done a quarter of a century before. The Allies were forced back at point after point, overwhelmed as the Poles had been by a combination of air power and panzer (armored) divisions. Although the French and British air forces occasionally achieved local superiority, they were never able to stop the onrushing Germans. Despite French protests, the British retained 25 air squadrons for home defense, refusing to commit everything to what was rapidly becoming a lost cause.

By again advancing through Belgium, as in World War I, the Germans simply passed around the left flank of the Maginot Line. Then, in a new modification of the Schlieffen Plan, the panzer divisions, followed up by motorized infantry, drove westward from Sedan to the English Channel, trapping the British Expeditionary Force in Belgium and Northern France. As early as May 20, the Admiralty, recognizing that a supreme effort was now needed to save the army, began to organize shipping for an evacuation from Dunkirk, on the French coast near the Belgian border. Private British boat owners spontaneously aided naval efforts, volunteering themselves and their craft for service. The Lords of Admiralty accepted these gladly, but there was hard naval planning as well. They hoped to rescue about 45,000 men in two days.

Hitler, believing that the *Luftwaffe* would render escape impossible, ordered his panzer forces to stop short of Dunkirk—partly in fear that he was over-extended and partly to give Air Marshal Hermann Goering's planes the glory of wiping out the would-be evacuees. Goering intended to paralyze the troops on the beach by repeated bombing and to sink the rescue ships as fast as they appeared. He reckoned however without three factors. First, bombing of the troops was ineffective, the soft sand absorbing much of the force of the explosions. Second, the Royal Air Force was fully committed to protecting the Dunkirk beachhead; even the British Metropolitan Air Force, the last reserve that had been withheld from the defense of France, entered the battle. Third, the presence of evacuation ships and craft in such large numbers provided simply too many targets. Pleasure boats, fishing craft, destroyers, minesweepers, trawlers—ships and boats of all types—shuttled from Dunkirk beach to English ports and then back to reload. When the operation was completed, 338,226 men had been safely delivered to England by 861 vessels, with a total loss of 243 vessels sunk and many damaged. Less spectacularly, nearly half a million British and French, soldiers and civilians, were lifted from other French ports during the last hours of France's freedom.

On June 11, in order to participate in the German victory, Italy declared war on France and Britain, and Italian troops crossed the French border. Paris fell to the Germans on June 14, and the next day Premier Reynaud requested the British government to release France from her pledge not to make separate terms with Germany. The British agreed on the condition that the French fleet would not fall into the hands of the common enemy. Determined to fight on, Britain urged France to continue the battle from her colonies in North Africa and from overseas. Churchill even went the length of offering France union with England, the two peoples to share common citizenship. The French Assembly rejected this appeal and could see no way to comply with Britain's requests for continuation of the war. Churchill and Reynaud advised General Weygand to surrender in the field, as this would not tie the hands of the French government. Weygand refused. He would not surrender, said he, unless an armistice were negotiated by the national government. Such a national armistice would of course be binding on all French armed forces, not simply on the army as Churchill and Reynaud desired. For the French navy to continue the war from overseas would be a violation of the armistice terms, and Germany would be able to undertake whatever measures she saw fit in retaliation. Weygand of course was imposing his desires on the political level, but Premier Reynaud did not relieve him. Reynaud was in fact in no position to take any action, for the next day, June 16, he was forced to resign, being succeeded by Marshal Phillipe Pétain, who immediately appealed for an armistice. The Germans put the capstone on French humiliation by conducting the armistice proceedings in the same railroad car that had been used for the German Armistice in 1918. France was divided into two zones: occupied France, the Atlantic front and all of the northern part including Paris; and unoccupied France, with a government under Pétain but dominated by the Nazi sympathizer Pierre Laval and his associates.

Meanwhile Admiral Darlan, Commander in Chief of the French navy, who had pledged his word of honor that the French fleet would not fall intact into the hands of the Germans, sent all ships the following message in code:

I refer to the clauses of the armistice now being telegraphed in plain language by other channels. I am taking advantage of the last coded messages I can send in order to make known my views on this matter.

First—The demobilized warships are to stay French, under the French flag, with reduced French crews, remaining in French metropolitan or colonial ports.

Second—Secret preparations for auto-sabotage are to be made in order that an enemy or foreigner seizing a vessel by force shall not be able to make use of it.

Third—Should the Armistice Commission charged with interpreting the text come to a decision different from that in paragraph one, warships are without further orders to be dispatched to the United States or, alternatively, scuttled, provided that no other action is possible to preserve them from the enemy. Under no circumstances are they to fall into enemy hands intact.

Fourth—Ships that seek refuge abroad are not to be used in operations against Germany or Italy without prior orders from the Commander in Chief.[1]

The armistice terms as finally announced provided that French ships were to be assembled in ports to be specified, either in France or in French colonies under German or Italian control. Germany solemnly declared it her intention not to make use of the French ships herself or to claim them at the conclusion of peace. On the other hand, the armistice provided that French Atlantic bases must be placed completely at the disposal of the Germans for U-boat operations. Italian terms were almost identical with the German. The armistice with both Germany and Italy became effective at 0035 on June 25, 1940.

Despite French assurances and despite their knowledge of the general provisions concerning the French fleet, the British felt far from satisfied that the French navy would in fact be kept from Axis hands. Some French ships were already in British ports—two battleships, four light cruisers, a few submarines, eight destroyers, and about 200 minesweepers and antisubmarine vessels. But a large number of vessels were in French national or colonial ports, where the Germans might gain control of them.

[1] Admiral Paul Auphin and Jacques Mordal, *La Marine Française Pendant la Seconde Guerre Mondiale* (Paris, 1958), 143-4.

The situation confronted the British with a dilemma. Hourly expecting invasion, hard put to fulfill existing naval commitments, they were in no shape to cope with a fleet the size of that remaining to France. Having no knowledge of Darlan's orders of June 24, the British felt that they could not stake their national security on the word of their enemies. Noting that the ships would be under Axis control and that the armistice could be voided at any time by Germany on grounds of "non-compliance," the British War Cabinet reluctantly decided to take whatever measures were necessary to see that the French fleet did not fall into Axis hands, accepting the risk that their action might bring France into the war against them. On June 3, 1940, all French ships at Plymouth and Portsmouth were seized. Some of the French sailors volunteered to man their former vessels and serve under the Free French flag, taking as their commander General Charles de Gaulle, who had established himself as head of the Free French Government in Exile in opposition to the German-dominated Vichy government of Marshal Pétain.

The resolution of the problem of the French fleet in the Mediterranean brought tragedy, as will be recounted in the next chapter. To immobilize the French battleship *Richelieu* at Dakar, on the western bulge of Africa, the British carrier *Hermes* approached and sent in six torpedo-bombers which attacked the battleship, doing enough damage to keep her off the seas for a year. Two French cruisers and a carrier in the West Indies were neutralized through the diplomatic efforts of President Roosevelt. Thus, while attaining only partial success, the British were able to preserve their tenuous command of the sea, but at a cost of embittering their former French allies. This unfortunate by-product of their operations was to exact its toll at the time of Operation TORCH, the invasion of North Africa in late 1942.

German Plans for the Invasion of England: Operation Sea Lion

Jubilant over his swift conquest of France and confident that Britain would capitulate in a few weeks, Hitler at first paid scant attention to any idea of invading England. In this belief he was encouraged by *Luftwaffe* commander Hermann Goering. Admiral Raeder however feared the situation was such that Hitler might suddenly order a cross-Channel attack. Raeder regarded Britain as the chief foe, but had little confidence in the success of an invasion since he felt that he had inadequate time and resources to stage it. Although his exploratory soundings got no response, Raeder went ahead with preliminary planning in order not to be caught off guard when it became obvious even to Hitler and Goering that Britain had no intention of surrendering. Raeder understood the difficulties far better than the army commanders, who commenced to show an interest in invading England, for they had millions of victorious troops on hand and no place to go with them. They eyed the English Channel and thought that crossing it would present no more problems than crossing a very wide river. Encouraged by the army, Hitler on July 16, 1940, issued a directive for the invasion of England, Operation SEA LION.

This directive, drawn up by the army, showed little grasp of the naval problems involved. It ordered that the landing be made on a broad front extending from Ramsgate to a point near the Isle of Wight, a front of approximately 200 miles, and that it be ready to jump off by August 13. Patiently Raeder explained that landing on such a scale would require many harbors for preparation of the invasion fleet, that the French ones were too damaged for use, that the concentration of shipping in these harbors would infallibly reveal the plan to the British, and that in any event Germany did not have anything like the number of ships the operation would require. Raeder emphasized that the assault must be on a narrow front where there could be a reasonable hope of maintaining a supply line across the Channel. From his point of view the only possible landing sites lay between Dover and Beachy Head. On hearing this proposal, the Chief of the Army General Staff retorted, "I might just as well put the troops that have landed straight through a sausage machine." The Naval Chief of Staff replied that he wanted to put the troops ashore and not at the bottom of the sea.

Hitler finally had to intervene personally to

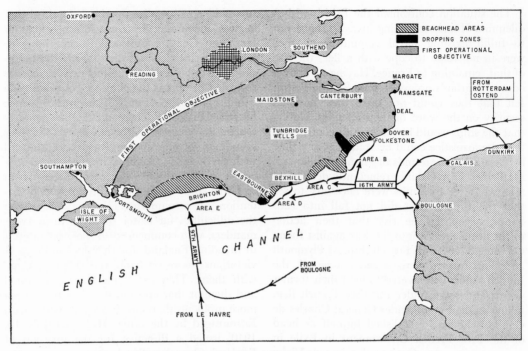

GERMAN PLANS FOR INVADING ENGLAND, SUMMMER 1940

resolve the conflict. The plan, as finally worked out, was for landings in four main areas: Folkstone-Dungeness, Dungeness-Cliff's End, Bexhill-Beachy Head, and Brighton-Selsey Bill. This compromise pleased no one, but both the army and the navy proceeded to draw up their plans in accordance with it.

In the meantime, everything depended on the *Luftwaffe*. All agreed that command of the air was an absolute prerequisite to an invasion attempt. The *Luftwaffe* unleashed heavy attacks against air installations in the south of England and other points to gain superiority over the R.A.F. The air effort was also intended to force Britain to sue for peace. The hope of sweeping the R.A.F. from the skies was vain. The British refusal to commit the 25 home defense squadrons to the Battle of France now paid off in the air "Battle of Britain." The British pilots shot down nearly two planes to each loss of their own. During the early critical period of the air war, the month of August 1940, the *Luftwaffe* was never able to whittle the R.A.F. strength down to an acceptable level for risking Operation SEA LION.

The day of decision for SEA LION was September 14, 1940. At a meeting of the Grand Council, after hearing reports from his commanders in chief, Hitler decided against giving the order to launch the invasion, scheduled for September 28. This decision meant that there was little prospect that SEA LION could be staged that year, since suitable tide and moon conditions could not be expected until October 24. Then bad weather could be expected to interfere.

On October 12, 1940 Hitler postponed the cross-Channel attack indefinitely, but continued preparations for invasion in order to maintain pressure on the British. On December 18 he in effect canceled Operation SEA LION altogether by issuing an alert for Operation BARBAROSSA: "The *Wehrmacht* must be prepared, even before the end of the war against England, to overthrow Russia in a quick campaign."

Before Hitler could launch his attack on the Soviet Union, he was obliged to divert forces to North Africa and to Greece. He planned the campaign against Russia in order to remove a potential enemy and to capture a new source of materials and manpower. He moved forces to the Mediterranean theater in order to rescue defeated Italian troops and to shore up the Axis position there. But he also saw both operations as means toward ultimately bringing Britain to terms. In this context, his attack on Russia was intended to eliminate a possible British ally. His North African campaign grew into a drive against the Suez Canal via Egypt, to be followed by a drive against India via Iran. As Hitler thus strategically faced east, an undefeated and defiant Britain behind his back obliged him to retain 49 divisions in western Europe to guard the Atlantic coast.

The point especially to be noted is that Hitler was attempting *simultaneously* to duplicate Napoleon's campaigns of 1798 and 1812, and for much the same reasons. Both of Napoleon's campaigns, it will be recalled, ended in failure. An additional factor in the strategic picture of 1941 was that Great Britain could look to the United States for support. Hitler's armies marched into Russia on June 2. The United States immediately extended Lend-Lease aid to the Soviet Union. Six months later, as the Russian winter stalled the German drive, the United States was in the war on the side of Britain and Russia. What Churchill called "the Grand Alliance" was complete.

We must now backtrack to consider the continuing war at sea and on the Atlantic front.

Dakar

Despite the immobilization of battleship *Richelieu,* the British Cabinet remained uneasy with Dakar in the hands of the Vichy French government. For Dakar, on the westernmost point of Africa, commands the narrows of the Atlantic. Should it be taken over by the Germans for use as a base for submarines and surface raiders, Dakar could pose a real threat to British commerce and to British military transport around Africa to Egypt. Accordingly the Cabinet ordered an offensive operation to "liberate" Dakar into the hands of the Free French. The landing, which presumably would not be seriously resisted, was to be carried out by 4,200 British and 2,700 Free French troops, the latter under the direct command of General de Gaulle. The landing operation was to be supported by a naval force of two battleships, a carrier, and several cruisers and destroyers under Vice Admiral J. H. D. Cunningham.[2] Transports and support in early September 1940 proceeded toward the British port of Freetown, southeast of Dakar, which was to be the advanced base of operations.

Through coincidence and mismanagement the Dakar operation came to naught. The coincidence was that just at this time a Vichy force of three cruisers and three destroyers set out from Toulon for Libreville, French Equatorial Africa. Through diplomatic sources the British Admiralty learned of this departure, and a British destroyer sighted and briefly shadowed the Vichy force in the Straits of Gibraltar. Yet nothing immediately was done to prevent the arrival of these reinforcements in the vicinity of Dakar. The significance of the movement was not immediately perceived at the Admiralty. Admiral Sir John Somerville, commanding naval Force H, and Sir Dudley North, Commander North Atlantic Station, both at Gibraltar, each assumed that the other had orders from the Admiralty to intercept the Vichy ships. When at last the Admiralty awakened to the situation, the ships were far down the African coast. Cunningham, belatedly alerted, succeeded only in chasing two of the cruisers into the port of Dakar, where they added to the defense force, though Dakar had not been their destination.

On September 23, 1940, Cunningham at last stood off Dakar. Instead of finding a ready welcome for de Gaulle and his troops, he was met by determined resistance. A landing attempt was repulsed. British bombardment of the harbor on the 24th and 25th achieved little. On the contrary, the immobilized *Richelieu* and the two Vichy cruisers, firing through a smoke screen laid by a destroyer, made most of the hits. On the 25th, the British battleship *Resolution,* already battered by four shells, was heavily damaged by a torpedo fired from a Vichy submarine. On receiving news of this, the Admiralty ordered the action broken off. The operation seemed to the world to be a prime example of confusion, delay, and muddle.

Although the Dakar attack failed, the flexibility of the War Cabinet enabled Britain to

[2] Not to be confused with Admiral Sir Andrew B. Cunningham, Commander of the Mediterranean Fleet.

retrieve something from the operation. By landing de Gaulle and his Free French forces at Douala in Cameroons, the British barred the Vichy French from a proposed penetration into French Equatorial Africa—thus removing a threat to Freetown and providing the British with an important air base in Central Africa.

German Surface Raiders in 1940

The pocket battleship *Scheer* made her debut into Atlantic waters in October 1940, followed a month later by the heavy cruiser *Hipper*. Both cruised the North Atlantic in an effort to break up the convoys from Halifax to the British Isles.

On November 5 the *Scheer* encountered the independently-routed British merchantman *Mopan*, which she sank after taking off the crew. As the *Mopan* was going down, the masts of Convoy HX-84, consisting of 37 ships, loomed over the horizon. The requirements of the Mediterranean theater at that time were such that Convoy HX-84 was being escorted by only one vessel, the armed merchant cruiser *Jervis Bay*.

Here was a situation made to order for the *Scheer*. With her speed and firepower she was apparently in a position to sink the greater part of the convoy. Two things balked her: the lateness of the hour and the fight put up by the *Jervis Bay*. While the convoy scattered, making smoke, the escort radioed an alarm and closed the pocket battleship at flank speed. The 6-inch guns of the *Jervis Bay* were of course no match for the 11-inch guns of her opponent, but the hour it took the *Scheer* to finish her off saved most of the convoy. The pocket battleship was able to overtake and sink only five of the 37 vessels before nightfall ended the chase. After dark the *Scheer* fled the area to elude the British forces which the Germans knew would be converging from all directions in response to the *Jervis Bay*'s radio warning. Evidently ships in convoy, even when poorly escorted, were safer than ships sailing out of convoy. The *Scheer* steamed rapidly south, refueled from a supply ship, made a brief appearance in the West Indies, and then disappeared into the South Atlantic and Indian Oceans, returning to Kiel in April 1941, having sunk 16 ships totaling 99,000 tons.

The *Hipper* achieved little. She attacked a convoy near the Azores, only to find it escorted by four British cruisers. After a brief action, the *Hipper* managed to shake off pursuit and make her way back home.

The *Bismarck* Breaks Out

In the spring of 1941, the *Hipper, Scharnhorst,* and *Gneisenau* again made brief sweeps into the Atlantic, sinking more than 20,000 tons in two months of operation. The *Hipper* returned to Germany, but in late March the two battleships were at Brest, a strategically located port from which to launch further raiding operations.

Admiral Raeder had now conceived the most ambitious raider operation of the Atlantic war. In the Baltic lay the great battleship *Bismarck,* newly completed, and the heavy cruiser *Prinz Eugen.* Raeder planned to send these vessels out into the Atlantic, where they would be joined by the *Scharnhorst* and *Gneisenau.* The powerful squadron thus formed, supplemented with a stepped-up U-boat campaign, could be counted on to paralyze British shipping. In preparation for this operation, supply ships and tankers were dispatched ahead to pre-arranged rendezvous areas far from shipping lanes, and German merchantmen disguised as neutrals combed the convoy routes in search of information.

But damage suffered by the *Scharnhorst* on her last cruise could not be repaired in time, and in April the *Gneisenau* was put out of action by a torpedo from a British aircraft. Yet, not to delay the operation, for which extensive preparations had been made, Raeder ordered the *Bismarck* and the *Prinz Eugen* to Bergen, Norway. Here they were to await thick weather and then break out into the Atlantic, the long way around north of Iceland. The *Scharnhorst* was to join them as soon as her damages were repaired.

The *Bismarck* and the *Prinz Eugen,* while passing through the Kattegat, were sighted by a Swedish cruiser. Sweden passed the word to England, and British reconnaissance aircraft got a look at the two raiders as they neared Bergen. The British Admiralty correctly estimated the German intention and made plans to forestall it. Eleven convoys, including one troop convoy, were in the Atlantic or about to sail. A concentration of German naval strength against them would have been calamitous.

The Admiralty was particularly concerned about the *Bismarck.* In the spring of 1941 she was the most powerful battleship in commission. Mounting eight 15-inch guns in her main battery, she had a secondary battery of twelve 5.9's and an antiaircraft battery of sixteen 4.1's. Her armor was the most advanced on any capital ship, amounting to 16,000 tons dead weight. She had skillfully designed compartmentation to prevent flooding. All the available resources of the Royal Navy were required to track her down and sink her.

The weather closed down on the Norwegian coast as the *Bismarck* and the *Prinz Eugen* reached Bergen. On May 22 a British aircraft in a daring reconnaissance ascertained that the raiders had departed. Admiral Sir John Tovey, Commander in Chief of the British Home Fleet, who was anxiously awaiting news of their movements, immediately took steps to intercept. The Admiralty placed at his disposal all the heavy ships that could be spared. Tovey had with him at Scapa Flow the battleships *King George V,* flagship, and *Prince of Wales* and the battle cruiser *Hood* in addition to destroyers and cruisers. In England were the carrier *Victorious,* which had not yet had her working-up cruise, and the battle cruiser *Repulse.* At Gibraltar, under the command of Admiral Sir James Somerville, were the battle cruiser *Renown* and the carrier *Ark Royal.* The battleships *Rodney* and *Ramillies* were on duty escorting convoys in the Atlantic, and the battleship *Revenge* was at Halifax. All these ships played some part in tracking down and sinking the *Bismarck.*

In order to keep the various routes available to the *Bismarck* under observation and to have a force capable of striking at any of them, Tovey had to divide his force to cover all possible contingencies. Bad weather hampered his efforts. Because he had to keep the least likely passages under the lightest observation, he covered the passage between the Orkneys and the Faroes only by air search. He stationed a cruiser force in the passage between the Faroes and Iceland and headed thither himself in the *King George V* with the *Victorious* and *Repulse.* The heavy cruisers *Suffolk* and *Nor-folk* patrolled the Denmark Strait, between Iceland and Greenland, supported by the *Prince of Wales* and *Hood,* en route at high speed from Scapa Flow, under the command of Vice Admiral L. E. Holland in the *Hood.*

First contact with the raiders was made in the early evening of May 23 in the Denmark Strait by the *Norfolk* and *Suffolk* under the command of Rear Admiral Wake-Walker. The *Suffolk,* which made the sighting, immediately took refuge in a fog bank and began tracking the Germans by radar. All night the two cruisers hung on to the German warships, broadcasting information that would enable the big ships to bring them into action.

On board battle cruiser *Hood,* Admiral Holland calculated his intercept course and prepared for action at any time after 0140, May 24. Contact was not made until 0535, whereupon the *Hood* and the new battleship *Prince of Wales* advanced into action. Admiral Holland, maneuvering both his ships together, ordered a head-on approach which denied him the use of their after guns. The Germans opened fire, concentrating on the *Hood.* To confuse their aim and to bring his after turrets to bear, Holland ordered a 20-degree turn to port, but scarcely had the ships begun to swing in response to the signal when the *Hood* disintegrated, hit in the magazine by a shell from the *Bismarck.* The *Prince of Wales* had to swing hard a-starboard to avoid the floating wreckage of the *Hood.* The situation had dramatically reversed. Tactical superiority had passed to the Germans. To make matters worse, the *Prince of Wales,* too new to have the mechanical difficulties worked out of her, was able to fire only about three guns a salvo.

Rear Admiral Wake-Walker, who had been enjoying a ringside seat from the bridge of the *Norfolk,* now found himself senior officer present with the full responsibility for the *Bismarck* on his shoulders. In view of the loss of the *Hood,* the inefficiency of and battle damage to the *Prince of Wales,* and the comparative weakness of his cruisers, he decided to resume shadowing tactics in hopes of enabling Tovey's force to arrive on the scene.

The loss of the *Hood* can be blamed in large measure on British lack of readiness to spend money on conversion of older ships during the lean years of peacetime budgets. She was known

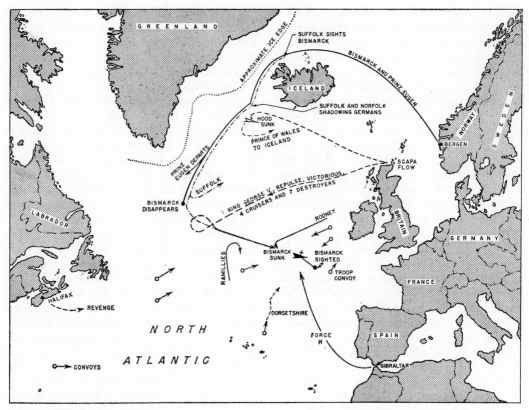

THE CHASE OF THE *BISMARCK*

to be vulnerable to plunging fire, but during the pre-war years nothing had been done to strengthen her. When war came it was too late; as long as she could operate, she could not be spared.

The *Bismarck* Disappears

"*Hood* has blown up."

The signal stunned the Admiralty. Nearly every officer on duty in the War Room had served in the *Hood* and remembered her as the pride of the British Fleet, the backbone of Britain's sea defenses. Now she was gone. With saddened hearts but redoubled determination they plotted the *Bismarck*'s death. Already they had ordered Admiral Somerville's Force H to sea from Gibraltar to participate in running the Germans down. Now they summoned battleships *Rodney* and *Ramillies* to break off from convoys and join in the chase. Battleship *Revenge* raised steam and proceeded with all possible speed from Halifax.

After being dogged all day by the *Norfolk, Suffolk,* and *Prince of Wales,* the *Bismarck* suddenly turned on the *Suffolk,* which opened range rapidly. This move was made to cover the departure of the *Prinz Eugen,* which escaped to the south and entered Brest ten days later. Once again the game of shadowing went on. Since the ships were by this time entering known U-boat waters, all British vessels were zigzagging. On the outward leg of one of these zigzags, the *Suffolk* lost radar contact and failed to regain it. Once more the *Bismarck* was loose. Three courses of action seemed to be open to her. She was known to be trailing oil from the encounter with the *Hood* and *Prince of Wales.* She might be in need of repairs. If so, she would head for Germany or for one of two French ports, Brest or St. Nazaire. Alternately, she might be heading for a rendezvous with a supply ship and then on to operations in whatever quarter of the globe she chose. When radio direction finder signals led Tovey to believe that she was heading for the North Sea and Germany, he steamed north for several hours to attempt an interception. Both he and the Admiralty had begun to have misgivings about this course of action, when a recomputation of the direction finder bearings aboard the *King George V* revealed a strong probability that the *Bismarck* was heading for a French port. A new dispatch from the Admiralty plotted the German battleship as being within a 50-mile radius of the position lat. 55° 15′ N, long. 32° 00′ W, about 600 miles southeast of Cape Farewell on the southern tip of Greenland. Tovey accordingly turned to attempt to intercept the *Bismarck*'s probable course toward Brest, but his cruisers and the carrier *Victorious* held for home, being too short of fuel to continue. Tovey also ordered the damaged *Prince of Wales* to proceed to England. Convoys were diverted to get them out of the probable danger area. The *Rodney*'s course toward the North Sea was not immediately corrected, and she crossed ahead of the *Bismarck* on the afternoon of May 25. If she had been alerted, she could easily have made an interception. As it was, Somerville's Force H, consisting of the carrier *Ark Royal*, the battle cruiser *Renown*, and escorting ships, was now the only British force in position to do so.

Realizing that the shortage of fuel for the smaller ships would soon leave the larger vessels exposed to submarine attack, the Admiralty decided that five destroyers could be spared from the Convoy WS-8B and one from the Irish Sea Patrol and sent them under Captain Vian of the *Altmark* affair to rendezvous with Tovey. During the night all forces raced toward the *Bismarck*'s most probable position.

Bismarckdämmerung

By the morning of May 26, the pursuers began to lose hope. The wind had increased during the night, forcing Somerville's ships to slow from 25 to 17 knots. The flight deck of the *Ark Royal* was pitching between 53 and 55 feet, but in spite of the difficulties and dangers of air operations, a search patrol set out from the carrier at 0835. Still no word of the *Bismarck*. Suddenly at 1030, a Catalina flying patrol from the Coastal Air Command broadcast a sighting of a battleship in position lat.

49° 33′ N, long. 21° 50′ W, approximately 750 miles west of Brest, steering course 150 at 20 knots. On all ships, plotting officers hurried with their work. It was no British battleship. The *Bismarck* was found.

On receipt of the news, Captain Vian in the destroyer *Cossack* decided to disregard his instructions to rendezvous with Admiral Tovey and turned with his five destroyers to intercept the *Bismarck*. Swordfish aircraft from the *Ark Royal* took over shadowing the German, but her position was too far ahead of any of the forces to make interception likely. Only an air strike from the *Ark Royal* could hope to slow her down until the heavy ships could come up. The strike preparations began immediately, while the cruiser *Sheffield* darted away at high speed to take up a station shadowing the Nazi battleship. Then came near-tragedy. The pilots, improperly briefed, attacked the *Sheffield,* which had accompanied them from Gibraltar, under the impression that she was the *Bismarck*. Only highly skilled shiphandling and a belated radio warning averted a calamity. The next two strikes found the *Bismarck,* for the *Sheffield* had gone ahead and already located her. The pilots of these strikes had been briefed to fly to the *Sheffield* and take their departure from her. She would coach them on the target, which she did with alacrity. The results of this strike were at first confused, and early reports led Tovey to believe that no significant damage had been done. However, he eventually learned that the *Bismarck* was heading in a northerly direction. Since this course was directly into the teeth of her enemies, the conclusion could only be that either the ship was having rudder difficulties or that damage was forcing her to take the heavy seas on her bow. In fact, both conjectures were true. The *Bismarck* had been hit in her steering engine compartment, and her rudders were jammed full over. Only by maneuvering with her engines could she avoid circling. Also a following sea would threaten further flooding because of the weakened bulkheads of the steering engine compartment. There was no choice. The *Bismarck* had to head into the sea. She was obliged at last to face her gathering enemies.

Darkness fell, and with it came Captain Vian and his destroyers to assist the *Sheffield* in shadowing. Vian saw no objection to attempting to put a few torpedoes into her as well. His first concerted attack the *Bismarck* drove off without damage either to herself or the destroyers. Captain Vian then stationed one destroyer on each bow and one on each quarter and himself took position astern. During the night each destroyer made several torpedo attacks on the *Bismarck* but made no hits because each time fire from the battleship forced the attacking destroyer to break off the action before it could get to effective torpedo launching position.

Raeder had been making every effort to save the *Bismarck*. He summoned all available submarines to the area, but those closest had already expended all their torpedoes and could only watch impotently. By an odd chance, one U-boat passed within 400 yards of the *Ark Royal,* but having fired her last torpedo the previous day, was powerless to harm the British carrier.

By morning the heavy British ships reached the scene of action. At 0847 battleships *Rodney* and *King George V* exchanged the first salvos with the *Bismarck* at a range of 25,000 yards. The *Bismarck,* although badly crippled, still had magnificent endurance and splendid fire control. Her third salvo straddled the *Rodney,* but soon the weight of British firepower began to tell, hitting the *Bismarck*'s main battery director early in the action so that the accuracy of her fire diminished appreciably. Soon the *Bismarck* was a helpless wreck, rolling sluggishly in the trough of the sea. But she refused to sink. At length Admiral Tovey, with barely enough fuel to get home, had to break off. Cruiser *Dorsetshire* requested permission to expend her last three torpedoes on the *Bismarck* before leaving, and as her third torpedo hit, the *Bismarck* slowly rolled over and disappeared beneath the waves. The *Hood* had been avenged.[3]

The loss of the *Bismarck* put an end to German use of major combat ships for attack on transoceanic commerce. Raeder's standing with Hitler took a decided drop. German commerce

[3] The damage control officer of the *Bismarck* has stated that the *Dorsetshire*'s torpedoes did not sink the *Bismarck,* but that she was scuttled by her own crew. German naval records fail to support this claim.

warfare on the high seas thereafter was left to Dönitz' U-boats and a few disguised merchant raiders.

The Channel Dash

British pride in the efficiency with which the Royal Navy had hunted down and destroyed the *Bismarck* was somewhat quenched early the following year when the Germans brought home the last of their big surface raiders under the very noses of the Admiralty. After the *Bismarck* episode, the *Scharnhorst, Gneisenau,* and *Prinz Eugen* had remained at Brest. Despite damaging air attacks staged from Britain, all three were repaired and ready for operations by February 1942. Noting this, the British Admiralty anticipated that they would soon put to sea in an effort to regain home ports.

Hitler, convinced that the Allies were about to attack Norway, desired to concentrate all his naval strength there. Hence he ordered the three ships at Brest to make a break for home. They were not to proceed by way of the open Atlantic, which had proved a grave for the *Bismarck,* but use the shortest route, through the English Channel. Coming this way they would at least have strong land-based fighter support.

The Germans estimated that if they could maintain complete secrecy and leave Brest after dark, they would be through the most dangerous waters before the British could organize their defenses. With the Home Fleet far away at Scapa Flow, the German ships could expect opposition only from light surface forces, air attacks, and mine fields. Carefully sweeping the Channel route, the Germans prepared to give maximum air cover and provided the big ships with an escort of six destroyers and three torpedo boats. Eighteen more torpedo boats would join the escort as the force swept past Le Havre.

The *Scharnhorst, Gneisenau,* and *Prinz Eugen,* under command of Vice Admiral Ciliax, left Brest after dark on February 11, 1942. The night departure ran contrary to British estimates, for the Admiralty had assumed that the Germans would leave Brest during the day in order to pass through the Straits of Dover in darkness. The Royal Air Force had night reconnaissance planes over the Brest area, but

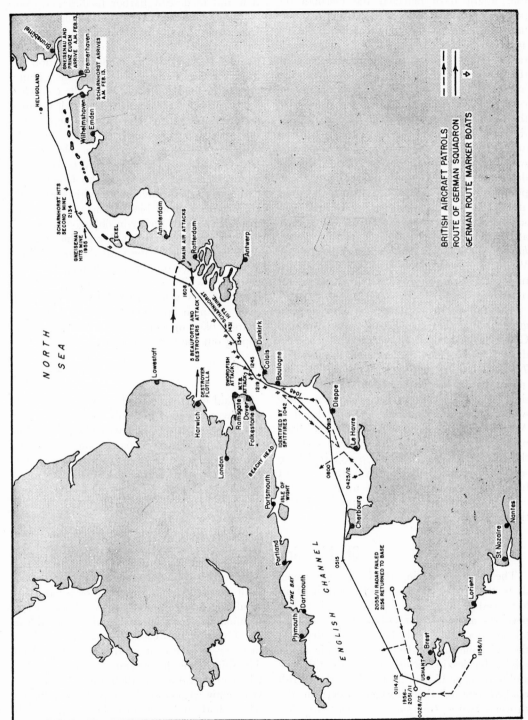

THE CHANNEL DASH

radar failed to function in the only two planes that might have detected the German departure. Worse, R.A.F. headquarters failed to notify the Admiralty of the breakdown. Finally, at 1100 on the 12th, an R.A.F. plane made radar contact through thickening weather with the German force, but even this contact was incorrectly evaluated. By the time a corrected report of the contact reached the Admiralty, the German ships had already passed through the Straits into the North Sea. The British attacked with coastal guns, torpedo boats, and with hundreds of aircraft without slowing down the fleeing Germans in the least. Tempestuous weather defeated a British destroyer attack. Unscathed, the three big German vessels reached waters off the Dutch coast. Here at last they ran into trouble: both the *Scharnhorst* and the *Gneisenau* hit British-laid mines. While the damage to the *Gneisenau* was minor, the *Scharnhorst* was out of action for months.

The failure to stop the Germans aroused great indignation in Britain. "Vice-Admiral Ciliax has succeeded where the Duke of Medina Sidonia failed," thundered the London *Times*. "Nothing more mortifying to the pride of sea power has happened in Home waters since the 17th century." Nevertheless there were compensating advantages. The threat to Atlantic convoys from Brest had been eliminated. More important, the ineffectiveness of the Royal Navy's air striking power had been so clearly revealed that the Navy at long last began to receive its share of up-to-date aircraft, formerly exclusively the prerogative of the R.A.F.

St. Nazaire

The month following the German Channel dash, the Royal Navy recovered much of its lost prestige by a raid on St. Nazaire. The port was an important U-boat base and contained a lock that could be used as a drydock, the only one outside Germany capable of receiving battleship *Tirpitz*. To destroy this lock and to damage U-boat installations, the British readied one of their former American destroyers, H.M.S. *Campbeltown* (ex-U.S.S. *Buchanan*), as an explosive blockship to ram and destroy the lock gates. To support the operation and to destroy harbor facilities, a group of motor launches carried a raiding force of Commandos. Entering the Loire late at night on March 27, 1942, the group under Commander R. E. D. Ryder made recognition signals, thereby gaining four valuable minutes during the final approach. When the *Campbeltown* had only 1,000 yards to go, all German batteries opened fire. Her captain increased to full speed and rammed the lock squarely, bringing her time-set explosive charge into perfect position. The crew was taken off in motor launches. Meanwhile the Commandos had fought their way ashore with great difficulty and set about blowing up port and lock machinery. With the main objective achieved, Ryder gave the recall signal, and the survivors made good their escape with the loss of three motor launches on the way home. The next morning, while a group of senior German naval officers were inspecting the *Campbeltown* to plan her removal, the demolition charges blew up, wrecking the lock gate and wiping out the inspection party.

Dieppe

A raid on Dieppe conducted on August 19, 1942 was intended not only to inflict damage but also to test amphibious techniques. Some 5,000 Canadian troops participated. Counting heavily on surprise, the army refused naval gunfire support; hence only eight destroyers with 4-inch guns accompanied the troops. Through a chance encounter with a small German coastal convoy, the raiders on one flank lost surprise and were repulsed with heavy losses, the few men who got ashore being quickly killed or captured. The other flank met with success, but the main assault on Dieppe itself also failed. The presence of a battleship would, in the opinion of the Naval Force Commander, have "probably turned the tide in our favour." The Canadians lost some 3,350 men, or 67 per cent of the troops involved. The raid, while discouraging to ideas of cross-Channel operations in 1942 and 1943, did reveal many weaknesses in amphibious planning which had to be rectified before the forthcoming major landings in Africa and Europe.

Reorganization of the German Navy

The German surface ships were gradually transferred to bases in Norway, where they could repel the invasion Hitler feared and where they would be in a position to strike at Arctic convoys to North Russia. In the early morning hours of December 31, 1942, a German raiding force composed of pocket battleship *Lützow,* heavy cruiser *Hipper,* and six destroyers made contact with a convoy meagerly protected by five destroyers, two corvettes, and one trawler. The Germans split up, the *Hipper* with two destroyers attacking the escort, the *Lützow* and four destroyers making for the helpless convoy. Then ensued one of the most amazing actions of the war. Captain R. S. V. Sherbrooke managed his tiny escort force so brilliantly and so aggressively that the entire German force had to turn to deal with him. For more than an hour he held the attention of the Germans, losing only one destroyer, while the convoy escaped into the fog. On the arrival of the British cruisers *Sheffield* and *Jamaica,* the Germans obeyed their standing order to avoid engaging major forces and retired. The convoy reached Russia without the loss of a ship. The Germans lost a destroyer and sustained heavy damage to the *Hipper.* The most important damage however was not to the ships but to the German navy, for this action caused a major reorganization in the German naval high command.

When word of the action reached Hitler, he stormed and raged. He would have all the heavy ships scrapped, he declared, so that their steel could be used by the army and the *Luftwaffe* and their personnel could be sent to man the submarines, which were the only naval forces carrying on a useful fight. He ordered Admiral Raeder to report to him to receive the scrapping order in person, but Raeder managed to get the meeting postponed until January 6. As he waited for Hitler to cool off, he prepared for him a kind of child's guide to sea power, pointing out the importance of the German heavy ships in tying down the British navy. But in the meantime, Goering had got Hitler's ear. Goering had always been intensely jealous of Raeder and sought any method of encompassing his ruin. A braggart, a schemer, and an unscrupulous liar, Goering proposed to win the war with his *Luftwaffe* alone. He had promised to reduce Britain by air attack, and he had failed. He had promised to reduce Russia by air attack, and he had failed. He had promised to keep the German forces in Russia supplied, and he had failed. He had promised to keep German forces in North Africa supplied, and he had failed. He had promised to destroy Allied shipping to Britain, and he had failed. He had promised to himself that he would scuttle Raeder, and he succeeded. Goering promised that his *Luftwaffe* could do, and do better, all that the surface ships could do, and Raeder was out. He resigned on January 30, 1943 and was succeeded by Dönitz. The contrast between the two men was great. Dönitz was an ardent Nazi; Raeder a professional naval officer, generally aloof from politics. Dönitz was a man of action; Raeder, something of a naval philosopher and historian.

When Dönitz took command of the German navy, he was convinced that Hitler's position was sound. This conviction lasted only a few months. When he began to see the war as a whole in contrast to the limited view he had had as U-boat admiral, he realized that Raeder was right; there was more to sea power than submarines. He succeeded in persuading Hitler to reverse the order, so that no ships were scrapped. The rescued ships however were not immediately used significantly. Nearly a year passed before the next major use of a surface ship occurred, once more against the North Russian convoys. Meanwhile the British in September 1943 had immobilized the *Tirpitz* by a midget submarine attack.

The *Scharnhorst's* Last Cruise

On Christmas Eve of 1943, the *Scharnhorst* set out from Norway to intercept a convoy bound for North Russia. But the convoy had been diverted to the northward, and the battleship met instead a cruiser scouting force of the British Home Fleet. In the morning of December 26, H.M.S. *Belfast* made radar contact with the German and opened fire, joined by the

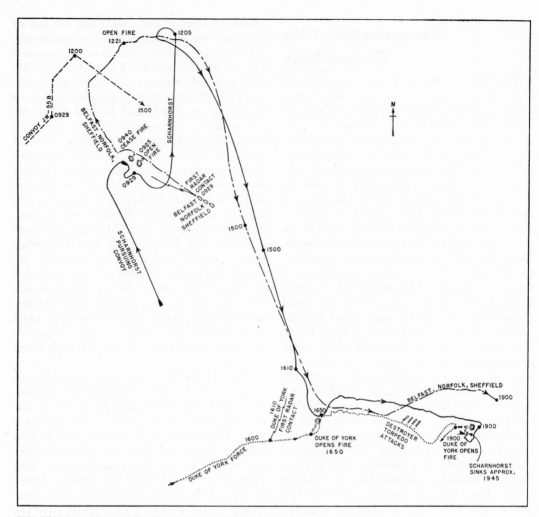

THE SINKING OF THE SCHARNHORST, DECEMBER 26, 1943

Sheffield and the *Norfolk,* but foul weather so reduced the speed of the British cruisers that they soon lost contact. Vice Admiral Robert Burnett, judging that the *Scharnhorst* would make for the convoy, headed to intercept and again made radar contact a little after noon. Destroyers which Burnett now sent in to attack with torpedoes were defeated by high seas, but the threat was enough to make the battleship head for Norway. This suited Barnett exactly, for the German line of retirement provided a perfect intercept course for the battleship *Duke of York* and the cruiser *Jamaica,* under command of Admiral Sir Bruce Fraser, who had relieved Sir John Tovey as Commander in Chief of the British Home Fleet. The *Belfast, Sheffield,* and *Norfolk* made no further attempt to engage, contenting themselves with shadowing the German. By late afternoon the two British forces were both in the area of expected contact. Because in those latitudes it was already pitch dark, Burnett illuminated with starshell, whereupon the *Duke of York* and the *Jamaica* sighted the *Scharnhorst* and immediately engaged at 12,000 yards. A high-speed eastward chase developed until the 14-inch shells of the British battleship began to take effect, and the *Scharnhorst* lost speed. British destroyers then further slowed her with torpedo attacks. Ordered to sink her with torpedoes, the *Belfast* and the *Jamaica* attacked in concert with destroyers and sent the *Scharnhorst* down off North Cape a little before 2000.

That the *Scharnhorst* was mishandled is evident. She was superior to the three British cruisers which first engaged her and stood a good chance of fighting it out with them to a successful conclusion. If she had done so and then continued toward the convoy, interception by the *Duke of York* would have been impossible, at least until after the *Scharnhorst* had wreaked havoc among the freighters. Her running to the south to regain the Norwegian ports meant that she was running toward the most likely route for the approach of British reinforcements. In running for safety, the *Scharnhorst* adopted the course that offered the least probability of inflicting damage to the British and offered the greatest risk to herself. She had been sent out with a specific task, that of inflicting the maximum damage to the convoy. Her abandonment of her task meant that she was expended uselessly, with no gain to compensate for her loss.

The End of the *Tirpitz*

The chief remaining German surface ship was the huge battleship *Tirpitz* at anchor in Kaa Fiord, an inlet of Altenfiord far in the north of Norway. Here she was a particular threat to the North Russian convoys. On the night of September 19–20, 1943, three months before the *Scharnhorst* was sunk, the *Tirpitz* had been attacked by British midget submarines. Four midgets, known as X-craft, survivors of six that had been towed across the North Sea by fleet submarines, penetrated the outer fiord. There the *X-10,* beset with misfortunes, turned back. The other three pressed on. One was never heard from again. The other two, *X-6,* commanded by Lieutenant D. Cameron RNR, and *X-7,* Lieutenant B. C. G. Place RN, placed time charges beneath the keel of the *Tirpitz.* Although the Germans discovered and captured the crews of these two midgets, they were unable to move the *Tirpitz* sufficiently to avoid the consequences of the explosion, which unseated her main engines and did heavy damage to her rudders and steering engine.

Following the sinking of the *Scharnhorst,* and when Allied intelligence reports revealed that the Germans had nearly completed repairs to the *Tirpitz,* the British determined to hit her again lest she attack North Russian convoys or make a break for the open Atlantic as the *Bismarck* had done. This time the Admiralty decided to employ carriers. After receiving special training, flyers from H.M. carriers *Victorious, Furious, Pursuer, Searcher,* and *Emperor* prepared to launch their attack. Sailing from England on March 30, 1944, in order to coordinate with a convoy bound for Russia, they attacked in the early morning of April 3. The *Victorious* and the *Furious* carried bombers, while the other three carriers provided the fighter escort. Attacking in two waves, the planes scored 15 hits, doing extensive damage without however impairing the ability of the *Tirpitz* to steam, for the bombs could not penetrate the eight inches of steel that formed her armor deck.

After the worst of the damage had been repaired, the ship was still not completely seaworthy, and as the dockyards in Germany were too battered to repair her, the Germans decided to move her to Tromsö, north of Narvik, where she might be employed as a floating battery. Tromsö was within range of the R.A.F. long-range bombers. On November 12, 1944, Lancasters capsized her by direct hits with six-ton bombs. This time there was no question of repair. The *Tirpitz* was gone.

Summary

The use of surface forces by the British and Germans during World War II shows a major strategic difference between a nation that *must* use the seas at all times and one that *may* use the seas at times of its own choosing. When the German heavy ships went to sea, they could briefly achieve local equality or even superiority, since the British naval forces had to be spread thin to have strength available in any area where the Germans might attack. Given time, as with the end of the hunt for the *Bismarck,* the British could assemble sufficient force to deal with any German threat on the high seas. The prime requirement of the Germans was not to allow this time, while doing maximum damage to the convoys which supplied the necessities of Britain's very existence.

The campaign in Norway proved to the British that the Royal Navy with its shortage of aircraft carriers could not operate successfully in areas dominated by land-based aircraft. The unscrupulous German assault on Denmark and Norway showed how an inferior navy with a limited objective, a limited time in the operating area, and a secure supply line could place a force on a strategic flank and maintain it in face of British sea power. However important Norway was to the strategic and political aims of the Western Allies, Britain was helpless to oust the Germans when the British themselves could not develop a secure line of supply and could not significantly interfere with that of the Germans.

The navy of the Third Reich played no important part in the operations against the Low Countries and France, which were overcome by the army and the *Luftwaffe*. Yet once again, as was traditional in British military operations, a defeated British army fought its way to the sea, and once again the Royal Navy successfully evacuated it to form a core of trained men for future operations. With the fall of France and the entry of Italy into the war, Britain's sea superiority was so threatened that she was forced to act drastically, albeit reluctantly, against the French fleet to ensure that she would not have to face two hostile navies in the Mediterranean or the Atlantic.

When Hitler reached the Channel, he found the British still defying him, still prepared to fight to the end—without allies if necessary. The worst the *Luftwaffe* could do merely hardened their will to resist. Unable to bring the stubborn British to terms, Hitler, like Napoleon, turned his back on the Channel and struck eastward, at Egypt and Russia. But unlike Napoleon, he undertook both campaigns simultaneously. Just as his armies were bogging down in both areas, American forces entered the war against him in decisive strength.

The German surface fleet proved as ineffective as the army and the *Luftwaffe* in forcing Britain to capitulate. After the loss of the *Bismarck,* the Germans made offensive use of their warships only for attacks on convoys to North Russia. Little was accomplished, and the *Scharnhorst* was lost at sea, while the *Tirpitz* died ignominiously as she lay at anchor. Only one arm of the *Wehrmacht* proved really effective against Britain. That was Dönitz' U-boats, which in the Battle of the Atlantic brought the British to the verge of defeat.

29:

The Struggle for the Mediterranean

As war approached in 1939 Britain and France, recognizing the vital importance of the Mediterranean theater, laid joint plans to exploit its strategic opportunities and to deny them to the Axis. Britain traditionally considered the Mediterranean her lifeline to the Suez Canal and the Far East, while France considered it her main high road to her colonies in Algeria, Tunisia, and French Morocco. To a great extent the safety of British and French commerce and installations depended on the role Italy would assume in the war. On the assumption that Italy would be an active participant, the Anglo-French allies agreed that British naval forces would assume responsibility for the eastern half and French naval forces the western half of the Mediterranean. At the outbreak of war, the British had a strong Mediterranean Fleet. In addition to their major base at Alexandria, they had secondary establishments at Malta and Gibraltar. The French had three battleships, eleven cruisers, 33 destroyers, and 45 submarines disposed at Toulon, Oran, Mers-el-Kebir, Bizerte, Morocco, and Dakar.

Ever since the Italian invasion of Ethiopia in 1935, the Italian navy had been operating on a quasi-war footing. When the Italians went into Albania in April 1939, the British, not having anticipated the move, hurriedly concentrated their Mediterranean Fleet at Alexandria. In May Hitler and Mussolini proclaimed a Pact of Steel, promising to aid each other in any military action. This dramatic public announcement was secretly modified by the Cavallero Memorandum in which Mussolini informed Hitler that he would not be ready for war for three years and asked him to postpone military action until 1942. Although Hitler agreed in principle, on August 11 the German foreign minister informed his Italian opposite number that Germany was about to attack Poland. Mussolini, mindful of his obligations under the Pact of Steel, sent a lengthy request for raw materials for Germany to supply to Italy. Hitler refused the requested items and informed Mussolini that he would not be expected to enter the war. Consequently, when Germany invaded Poland on September 1, 1939, Mussolini proclaimed Italy's non-belligerence.

In the face of this unexpected development, the British, urgently requiring ships in other theaters, left the Mediterranean largely on a caretaker basis. Withdrawing most of their ships for service elsewhere, they depended on the French to keep order and to assist the few remaining British ships in enforcing Allied Shipping Control measures. Meanwhile the British bent every effort toward strengthening their positions in the Middle East. In Egypt they had, in addition to the naval base at Alexandria, a body of troops and a Royal Air Force command, stationed there in accordance with the Anglo-Egyptian Treaty of 1936. Because the Egyptian government had done little to build up its armed forces and facilities, the British made great efforts during the winter of 1939–40 to make good the deficiencies.

By spring of 1940 Mussolini was chafing under Allied shipping restrictions and was anxious to extend Italian influence and territory. For years he had dreamed of restoring a Roman Empire in the Mediterranean; his conquests of Ethiopia and of Albania had been moves in this direction. Now he dreamed of an Empire which would challenge in splendor that of the Caesars. He sought means of expelling the two great powers he saw as standing in his way—Britain and France. Meeting

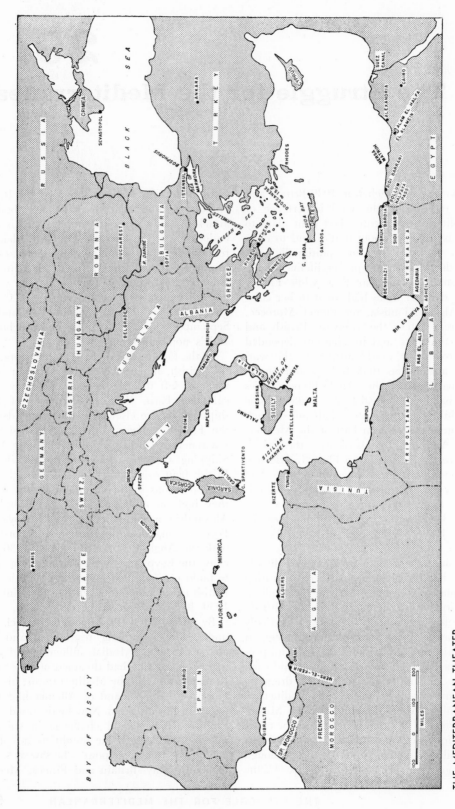

THE MEDITERRANEAN THEATER

Hitler at the Brenner Pass in March 1940, he promised to intervene on the German side at the appropriate time. Soon thereafter he announced to the King and to his military leaders his concept of a "parallel war," which would assist Germany indirectly but which would be designed primarily to further Italian interests. As he watched the rapid success of the Germans in Norway and France, Mussolini made hurried plans to join the war before it should be too late. "To participate in the peace," he proclaimed, "one must participate in the war."

As the British began to see signs that Italy's non-belligerency might soon shift to outright war, they reviewed their earlier policy of non-provocation of Italy, proposing to substitute a show of force. But Mussolini had already made up his mind. On April 17 he was restrained from a declaration of war only by the strong protests of Marshal Badoglio, chief of the Italian armed forces, on the grounds of unreadiness. Unobtrusively the British began to return strength to the Mediterranean. They resumed responsibility for the eastern Mediterranean, and on April 29, 1940 issued an order that Allied merchant ships bound to or from India or elsewhere in the East would be routed around the Cape of Good Hope. Simultaneously reinforcements for all three services began to appear at British bases in and around the Mediterranean. On the arrival at the end of May of four battleships and the aircraft carrier *Eagle,* Sir Andrew B. Cunningham, Commander in Chief Mediterranean Fleet, shifted his flag from Malta to the *Warspite* and his base of operations to Alexandria. In June seven cruisers and a force of destroyers arrived. Also under Admiral Cunningham at Alexandria was a French force commanded by Vice Admiral René Godfroy, consisting of the battleship *Lorraine,* three heavy cruisers, one light cruiser, three destroyers, and six submarines.

Italy Enters the War

Marshal Badoglio had been right when he told Mussolini that the Italian armed forces were not ready for war. The army was not fully mobilized and was in a poor state of training, while the Italian air force, although strong on paper, had little operational experience. The navy was feeling the consequences of insufficient maintenance and insufficient replacement of ships. The Italian armed forces were inefficiently organized for naval war in the Mediterranean. The three service commands, *Superesercito* (army), *Superareo* (air force), and *Supermarina* (navy), were co-equal but subordinated to the supreme headquarters, *Comando Supremo.* The officers in *Comando Supremo* tended to hold the continental viewpoint of the army and the strategic bombing concepts of the air force; hence they had little sympathy for naval problems and little appreciation of naval opportunities. When the Italian air force was organized in 1923, the navy had been directed to give up all of its aviation to the new service. The navy thus had no control over the aircraft it needed to carry out its missions. Nor did it have any aircraft carriers, for both *Comando Supremo* and Mussolini considered Italy itself to be a gigantic aircraft carrier. Since planes operating from Italian air bases would be able to cover the central Mediterranean, *Comando Supremo* argued that the air force could perfectly well perform all the tasks usually allotted to naval aviation. Air force pilots however were not trained for naval tasks, and the air force, like the *Luftwaffe* and all other major air forces in the war, wished to conduct the fighting in accordance with its own strategic concepts. Thus, when the navy requested aircraft for support of naval operations, the planes were all too frequently allocated elsewhere. The navy controlled only units for naval reconnaissance, and even these planes were flown by air force pilots.

The Italian navy at the outbreak of war consisted of six battleships (of which only two, the *Cavour* and the *Giulio Cesare,* were actually in service), seven heavy and twelve light cruisers, and some 50 destroyers. In addition Italy had 108 submarines, nearly double Germany's total. Two older battleships, the *Duilio* and *Doria,* were being modernized and would join the fleet shortly, while four fast new battleships, the *Littorio, Vittorio Veneto, Roma,* and *Impero,* were in various stages of construction. The first two of these were nearly ready for service, but the others would require several years to complete. In the Red Sea at Massawa the Italians had a small force of seven destroyers and eight submarines which would be able to pose a threat to Britain's shipping to and from the Suez Canal. Class for class, the Italian ships were more lightly armored but faster than their Allied counterparts. These high-speed characteristics and comparatively small fuel capacity gave them a severely restricted combat radius.

The chief Italian naval base was at Taranto, with subordinate bases at Naples, Spezia, Brindisi, Augusta, and Palermo on Sicily, Cagliari on Sardinia, and Tripoli and Benghazi in Libya. Generally the Italian navy envisioned its strategy in war as defensive in the eastern and western Mediterranean, while in the central Mediterranean it must at all costs protect shipping between Italy and her armies in Libya. Italian naval doctrine prescribed weakening the Allied fleets by raids and by submarine and frogman attack while avoiding encounters with superior forces.

As May wore on, the British recognized that France might be forced from the war and anticipated that Mussolini would wish to join the attack on France so that he might have a place at the victors' feast. In addition to building up the Mediterranean Fleet, the War Cabinet understood that Britain might have to assume responsibility for the western Mediterranean as well as the eastern and took steps to provide a naval force to be based on Gibraltar. Also abandoning the non-provocation policy, the British on May 23 ordered that all Italian merchant ships should be stopped for contraband-control searches. On June 6, Mussolini announced that all waters within twelve miles of Italian territory were dangerous to navigation. Forewarned by this announcement, Admiral Cunningham had most of the Mediterranean Fleet at sea when Italy's declaration of war against Britain and France became effective at one minute after midnight on June 11, 1940.

Cunningham's initial sweep, by which he hoped to surprise units of the Italian navy, met with no success, while an Italian submarine sank the British cruiser *Calypso*. The first two days of the war however cost Italy 130,000 tons of merchant shipping through capture, scuttling, or internment. On June 14 a force of French cruisers bombarded Genoa, the French cooperating in the war against Italy

for 15 days until their own surrender to Germany took place.

With France's surrender, as told in the preceding chapter, Britain's concern over the French fleet became acute. The British situation in the Mediterranean in a short month had gone from overwhelming superiority to nearly hopeless inferiority. Instead of having two powerful forces watching a non-belligerent, the British now had the care of the entire Inland Sea with a hostile Italy and the strong possibility that the powerful French ships would be used against them. The War Cabinet therefore ordered its commanders in the Mediterranean to take action.

In anticipation of having to assume responsibility for the eastern Mediterranean, the Admiralty had already assembled a force at Gibraltar designated as Force H, including the battleships *Valiant* and *Resolution,* the battle cruiser *Hood,* the aircraft carrier *Ark Royal,* two cruisers, and eleven destroyers. Vice Admiral Sir James F. Somerville, its commander, received orders from the War Cabinet to present to the commander of the French detachment at Mers-el-Kebir, the naval anchorage of Oran, the following proposals:

A. Sail with us and continue to fight for victory against the Germans and Italians.

B. Sail with reduced crews under our control to a British port. . . .

C. Alternatively, if you feel bound to stipulate that your ships should not be used against Germans or Italians, since this would break the Armistice, then sail them with us with reduced crews to some French port in the West Indies—Martinique, for instance—where they can be demilitarised to our satisfaction, or perhaps be entrusted to the United States of America, and remain safely until the end of the war, the crews being repatriated.

If you refuse these fair offers, I must with profound regret require you to sink your ships within six hours. Finally, failing the above, I have the orders of His Majesty's Government to use whatever force may be necessary to prevent your ships from falling into German or Italian hands.[1]

On Admiralty orders, Somerville took his entire force to Mers-el-Kebir, arriving early on the morning of July 3, 1940. Sending Captain

[1] J. R. M. Butler, *Grand Strategy*, II (London, 1957), 223-24.

C. S. Holland, former British naval attaché in Paris, and a personal friend of the French commander, Admiral Marcel Gensoul, to deliver his note, Somerville waited off shore. Sensing an ultimatum, Gensoul refused to receive Holland, but sent his flag lieutenant to represent him. In reply to the British note, Gensoul wrote that previous French assurances still held good, that under no circumstances would French ships be allowed to fall into Axis hands, and that French ships would defend themselves by force. Gensoul felt that he could accept none of the alternatives offered him without breaking the armistice; accordingly he informed his government only that he had been offered an ultimatum. As Admiral Darlan was not available, his chief of staff ordered forces at Toulon and Algiers to Mers-el-Kebir. Meanwhile all participants attempted to find a solution. In the afternoon Gensoul received Holland, proposing a gentleman's agreement, but Somerville, alerted to the coming of French reinforcements, set a final deadline. Unable to accept any of the French counterproposals, Holland withdrew and at 1756 Somerville opened fire, the first shots fired by the British against the French since Waterloo.

The French fleet at Mers-el-Kebir had, during the negotiations, seized the opportunity to prepare for battle. It included four battleships and six super destroyers, as well as a seaplane tender. During the brief action, which included a carrier air strike, three French battleships were either sunk or beached, while the *Strasbourg* made good her escape and reached Toulon undamaged.

At Alexandria the personal friendship between Admirals Cunningham and Godfroy averted tragedy. Cunningham had an advantage over Somerville in that he did not have to fear the arrival of reinforcements, and he was in a position to demand more latitude from his government than Somerville had had. On July 5, the two commanders worked out a gentleman's agreement by which Godfroy would discharge fuel, remove firing mechanisms from his guns, and make no attempt to break out to sea. Cunningham, for his part, agreed to undertake no measures to seize the French ships by force as had been done in England. Thus there remained under Vichy control in the Mediterranean one battleship, one aircraft carrier, four heavy and eight light cruisers, 30 destroyers, and 70 submarines.

Enraged by this attack by their former allies, the French-Vichy government ordered reprisal measures against the British. On July 5 French planes attacked Gibraltar, but the bombs all fell harmlessly in the harbor. On July 8 the Vichy government severed diplomatic relations with Britain but failed to declare war.

Thus at terrific cost the British had ensured themselves against a significant part of the French fleet. The risk had been great; the full cost would not be known for years.

Britain against Italy in the Mediterranean

The entry of Italy into the war created serious doubt in the minds of the British on whether they could hold Malta. Its defenses were pitifully weak, promised guns and aircraft having been sent elsewhere to meet desperate needs of the moment. Its proximity to Italy made it of negligible value as a naval base. It could however prove of inestimable value as an air base from which to attack Italian shipping to Libya. Italy lost no time in attempting to knock Malta out altogether, sending 36 raids against the island during June. As a result the submarines which had been based there were forced to leave, and women and children were evacuated. During the next two and a half years, Malta remained under siege, but always a menace to Axis shipping in the Mediterranean.

While covering the evacuation convoys, the British Mediterranean Fleet had its first action with the Italian fleet off Calabria, the toe of the Italian boot. Disposed in three groups, the British had a scouting unit of five light cruisers in the van, followed by the battleship *Warspite*, Cunningham's flagship, screened by five destroyers. Some miles astern were the two older battleships *Malaya* and *Royal Sovereign* with the carrier *Eagle*, carrying 19 planes, and escorted by ten more destroyers. As a diversion Force H made a sweep of the western Mediterranean.

The Italian force, heading northward toward Italy after escorting a convoy to Benghazi, consisted of the battleships *Giulio Cesare* and the *Cavour,* six heavy cruisers, twelve light cruisers, and destroyers—under command of Admiral Angelo Campioni, Commander in Chief of the Italian Fleet. This force had been especially strengthened in expectation of battle on the return trip.

A strike launched from the *Eagle* failed to find the battleships and expended its torpedoes fruitlessly against the cruisers. The course of the Italians suggested to Cunningham that they were covering movements to Libya; accordingly he maneuvered to get between the Italian force and its base at Taranto. In the afternoon the British light cruisers came upon the Italian cruisers. Heavily out-numbered and out-ranged, the British fought on until the *Warspite* came to the rescue. Soon thereafter the *Warspite* sighted the two Italian battleships and engaged them at 26,000 yards. After a few rounds, the Italian flagship *Giulio Cesare* received a hit at the base of the forward funnel. Campioni then sent his destroyers in for a torpedo attack and retired behind a smoke screen, to head for Messina. Firing now became general and the battle more confused as the British attempted to cut off the Italian retreat. By 1700 superiority in speed enabled the Italians to make good their escape, and Cunningham, unwilling to risk running into a submarine ambush within 25 miles of the Italian coast, broke off pursuit. Meanwhile two convoys to Alexandria had sailed, taking advantage of the diversion caused by the battle. Cunningham's force covered their passage, absorbing air attacks which otherwise would have been directed against the merchant ships.

The action off Calabria seemed to prove the soundness of Cunningham's aggressive policy. Although the Italian battleships mounted lighter main battery guns than the British battleships, they had more of them, and the two Italian battleships could have engaged the British flagship closely before the two slower British battleships could have got into action. The Italian force was greatly superior in cruisers. Yet Campioni did not press his advantage. Although the British had a carrier within striking range, it had played an in-

effective role. Italian land-based air, on the other hand, had been poorly coordinated, arriving after the battle and then attacking the Italian instead of the British fleet. Happily for the Italians, their airmen's bombing was as inaccurate as their recognition, and no ship was hit.

Italian reluctance to engage approximately equal forces was displayed again on July 19 in the Battle of Cape Spada, when three British destroyers on an antisubmarine sweep northwest of Crete ran into two Italian light cruisers. The destroyers fell back upon the support of the Australian light cruiser *Sydney* and another destroyer, which were to the northward of them. When the Italians sighted the *Sydney* they retired to the southwest, although they had superiority in 6-inch guns and only a slight inferiority in smaller calibers. In the pursuit the *Sydney* sank the *Bartolomeo Colleoni;* her damaged consort, the *Bande Neri,* managed to reach Tobruk.

After these actions the Admiralty and Cunningham effected a redefinition of the responsibilities for the Mediterranean. Since the Italians had many interests in the eastern half of the area and since the British forces in Egypt and the Middle East required constant support, the eastern fleet was made stronger, while Force H at Gibraltar would be a raiding force, available for operations in the Mediterranean and, under Admiralty control, in the Atlantic. The Flag Officer Commanding North Atlantic, Admiral Sir Dudley North at Gibraltar, could also call upon Force H for assistance in preventing enemy ships from passing the Straits. Cunningham desired to rid himself of his two *Royal Sovereigns* and wanted instead a total force of three or if possible four *Queen Elizabeths,* including the *Valiant,* which had radar. He also requested an increased number of heavy cruisers to enable him to cope with the Italian preponderance in that type of ship. He particularly desired the carrier *Illustrious* to supplement the inadequate *Eagle.* The redistribution of strength, called Operation HATS, took place in late August and early September unopposed except by moderate air attacks. Cunningham took advantage of the operation to send a small convoy into Malta.

The Italian Offensive in Libya

On September 7, 1940, Mussolini ordered Marshal Graziani, commander of the Italian army in Libya, to begin a land offensive against Egypt. On September 14 the Italians captured the important port city of Sidi Barrani but were unable to go farther because the British navy began to harass their sea-borne supply routes by attacks on Benghazi, Sollum, Bardia, and Sidi Barrani itself. British submarines had met with little success because Italian ships clung as far as possible to shallow coastal waters, where it was difficult for British submarines to operate successfully. Nor was there adequate air strength on Malta. Until December the Italians lost no ships on the Italy-Libya run either from submarine or air attack while they delivered 692,403 tons to Libya during the year. Until Malta could be built up, the British were helpless to interdict this traffic.

Italy Invades Greece

Against the advice of his naval officers, Mussolini on October 15, 1940, at a meeting with army and political leaders, issued orders for the invasion of Greece. He kept his intention to attack a secret from Hitler, who he knew would not approve.

The Greeks had long feared an Italian invasion of their country, but were determined to avoid giving a pretext. Hence they refused to allow the British to send aid ahead of time, to send military advisers, or even to be informed of the Greek strategy of defense. Thus on October 28, when Italian troops crossed the Greek frontier, the British, with slender resources, were faced with a difficult decision. To maintain their position with neutrals in the Middle East, they were obliged to support Greece in her struggle. Any troops that might be sent to Greece would have to be drawn from General Archibald Wavell's forces in Egypt. The problem of air support was equally difficult. The entire British position in the Middle East might be lost if the defenses of Egypt were weakened.

In view of these considerations, the British War Cabinet agreed to send munitions and money and an R.A.F. contingent. Also by arrangement with the Greek government, the British established a naval fueling base on Crete. The Greeks as it turned out did not at the time need troop assistance, for the Italian offensive stalled on November 8, and a few days later a Greek counteroffensive pushed the invaders back to the Albanian border. Thus in both his North African venture and in his Greek invasion, Mussolini, because of inadequate planning and inadequate support, failed in his attempt to make political expediency promote military success. Instead of winning glory, Mussolini became a laughingstock.

The Carrier Raid on Taranto

In view of the reluctance of the Italian navy to accept decisive action at sea, Cunningham sought to attack their ships at their Taranto base. Originally scheduled for October 21, Trafalgar Day, the operation was twice postponed because of other urgent commitments and because of damage to the *Illustrious*. The delays proved to be fortunate for the British, for when the raid finally took place late at night on November 11, all six of the Italian battleships were in port.

At the last moment the *Eagle* developed defects and had to be left behind. Five of her Swordfish planes were transferred to the *Illustrious*, which arrived at the launching point with 21 aircraft. The latest reconnaissance photographs, flown aboard the carrier on the afternoon of November 11, revealed the position of every Italian unit. As the first wave of twelve planes neared its target, four bombers split off to make a diversion in the inner harbor, and two other planes broke away to drop flares to the east in order to silhouette the battleships for the six torpedo planes. The first attack worked perfectly, the flares showing the targets clearly to the torpedo-plane pilots, who scored hits on the *Cavour* and *Littorio*, at the cost of one plane. A second wave of eight planes an hour later used identical tactics. This wave scored a hit on the *Duilio* and two more on the *Littorio*. This wave also lost one aircraft.

The attack reduced the Italian fleet to three available battleships, the *Giulio Cesare, Vit-*

torio Veneto, and *Doria.* The *Cavour* never went to sea again, while the *Littorio* and *Duilio* were out of action for some months. The surviving Italian major ships abandoned Taranto as a fleet base, moving to Naples immediately after the attack. Italian air reconnaissance had completely failed to spot the British forces moving up for the attack or the Malta convoy which took advantage of the diversion caused by fleet movements for the Taranto raid. The British gained an additional dividend from the operation, for a light force wiped out a small convoy of four ships bound for Brindisi.

Germany to the Rescue

As a result of the Greek success in repelling the Italian invaders and of their own success in the Taranto operation, the British found their Mediterranean situation much improved. On December 9, General Wavell opened an offensive out of Egypt, capturing Sollum on the 16th, Bardia and Tobruk in January, and reaching Benghazi on February 1. By February 9 the entire bulge of Cyrenaica was in British hands, and Wavell's forces stood before El Agheila at the threshold of Tripolitania.

Throughout the winter of 1940–41, the Mediterranean Fleet had assumed the task of moving supplies from Egypt to Wavell's advancing army. An Inshore Squadron carried the brunt of this labor, its small ships suffering heavy losses to aircraft based in Sicily. Its operations were a brilliant example of the flexibility of sea power in bringing essential materials to an army advancing along a seacoast. The supplies needed were difficult if not impossible of transport along the sand trails and inadequate roads of the Western Desert.

In the face of repeated Italian setbacks, in Greece, in North Africa, and at sea, the OKW[2] held a series of meetings to consider what could be done to retrieve the situation. As early as November 12, 1940, Hitler had decided that it would be necessary to extricate Italy from the consequences of her "regrettable blunder" in Greece. But at the same time, Germany was busy with other commitments, including ex-

[2] The German High Command. See note, page 492.

ploratory staff discussions for Operation BARBAROSSA, the invasion of Russia. Once the officers of the OKW turned their attention to the Mediterranean, they proposed to do what was necessary to make the Inland Sea an Axis lake. First, they planned to give direct troop support to Italy in Greece and Albania, coming down through Romania and Bulgaria in order to insure that the output of the Romanian oil fields would come to Germany. The second part of the plan, Operation FELIX, envisioned having Spain enter the war against Britain. If Spain would not take this step, diplomatic arrangements would be made to allow German troops free passage of Spanish soil in order to capture Gibraltar. A part of this operation was the capture of the Canary and Cape Verde Islands in order to control the entrances to the Mediterranean. If France objected to the passage of German troops for this purpose, all France was to be occupied. Third, Germany planned to send a *Luftwaffe* corps to Italy to cooperate with the Italian air force. Finally, they would send mechanized infantry to Africa, to be designated the *Afrika Korps,* under command of General Erwin Rommel.

During December and January the German *X Flieger Korps* (Tenth Air Fleet) of some 500 planes, specially trained in attack on ships, moved from Norway to airfields in Calabria and Sicily. Its tasks were to protect Axis shipping with North Africa, prevent the passage of British convoys through the central Mediterranean, and neutralize Malta by air attack.

After a part of the German air reinforcements had already arrived, a British convoy of four cargo ships escorted by two battleships, one aircraft carrier, four cruisers, and destroyers of Force H passed Gibraltar January 6 en route to Malta and Greece. About the same time the battleships *Warspite* and *Valiant,* the carrier *Illustrious,* and seven destroyers of the Mediterranean Fleet sailed from Alexandria to meet the convoy and cover other convoy movements between Malta and Alexandria. In support of the operation Malta-based aircraft attacked the Italian fleet at Naples on the 8th, damaging the battleship *Giulio Cesare* and forcing her and the *Vittorio Veneto* to move to the small base at Spezia well away from the strategic area. This attack left the *Vittorio Veneto* the only serviceable Italian battleship. On the evening of the 9th after daylight attacks by Italian aircraft from Sardinia, the Gibraltar force turned back undamaged, leaving the convoy with three cruisers and several destroyers to proceed to Malta. That night the cruisers drove off an attack by Italian destroyers, sinking one of them, but a British destroyer struck a mine and had to be towed to Malta. The next day an Italian force from Spezia searched the western Mediterranean for Force H, which had long since passed out of reach.

Around noon on January 10 the Alexandria force, which had joined the convoy from Gibraltar during the night, was attacked west of Malta by about 50 Stuka dive bombers from Sicily. Unlike the Italian pilots, who attacked from high level, the Germans pressed home their attacks with great skill through very heavy antiaircraft fire. Concentrating on the *Illustrious,* they hit the carrier several times. Steering with her engines, the *Illustrious* headed for Malta, and despite an afternoon attack which started large fires, managed to make port that evening. Next day, en route to Alexandria, the cruisers *Gloucester* and *Southampton* were damaged by air attack, the latter so badly that she had to be sunk by her own force.

At Malta the *Illustrious* became the target of numerous air attacks. Nevertheless, the naval constructors succeeded in making temporary repairs to her, and on the night of January 23 she slipped out of the harbor and reached Alexandria without further damage. Since the *Illustrious* had to go to the United States for permanent repairs and the *Eagle* was unserviceable, the Mediterranean Fleet would be without a carrier until the arrival of the *Formidable,* which the Admiralty had immediately ordered transferred from the South Atlantic.

While maintaining air attacks on Malta at the rate of three or four a day, the *Luftwaffe* did not neglect the eastern end of the Mediterranean. At the end of January German aircraft from the Dodecanese Islands began dropping magnetic mines in the Suez Canal in such numbers that it had to be closed intermittently throughout the month of February. Thus in the brief space of one month the intervention of the German air force had dramatically reversed the situation in the Mediterranean.

To send ships through the Mediterranean was to subject them to extreme peril. The only feasible route to maintain supply for Britain's Middle Eastern army was the long one around the Cape of Good Hope, through the Red Sea and the Suez Canal. Regular Cape convoys designated WS,[3] brought men, stores, tanks, and ammunition to the Middle East Command. Yet this route was by no means secure. In addition to the obvious threat from the Germans in the Atlantic, the Italians had substantial forces east of Suez, with seven destroyers, two motor torpedo boats, and eight submarines based at Kismayu on the Indian Ocean and at Massawa on the Red Sea. In January 1941 British forces from Kenya and the Sudan began a campaign with fleet support to drive the Italians out of East Africa. In February the Italians abandoned the port of Kismayu, and in early April British forces took Massawa while torpedo planes from the *Eagle* sank two Italian destroyers and drove one ashore. The remaining Italian naval forces in East Africa scuttled themselves or fled the area. As a result, the President of the United States was able under the Neutrality Act to proclaim the Red Sea open to American shipping, and British convoys had security from attack near their destinations.

In the next few months the British Mediterranean Fleet endured its most severe trial. When the Germans intervened in Greece, the Greek government accepted the active participation of British troops and air forces in the mainland fighting. Although reinforcement of Greece meant that General Wavell's drive had to be stopped short of the Tripolitan border, the War Cabinet felt that the political reasons for aiding Greece outweighed all other considerations. The Mediterranean Fleet, shouldering the responsibilities for transport and protection of three divisions and an armored brigade with their supplies, had to commit so much of its strength to the Aegean that it could spare little attention for Italian convoys to Libya. The result was nearly fatal to the

[3] For Winston's Specials.

British position in North Africa, for during the month of March, Italian ships carried General Rommel's *Afrika Korps* across the Mediterranean.

The first British convoy sailed for Piraeus March 5, others following every three days. Italian explosive motor boats sank a British cruiser in Suda Bay on the night of March 26, and a few days later an Italian submarine sank another. During a period of about six weeks however the fleet carried 58,000 troops with their equipment and supplies to Greece without loss.

The Battle of Cape Matapan, March 28–29, 1941

Pressed by the Germans, the Italian navy planned to employ their last operational battleship, the *Vittorio Veneto*, with eight cruisers and a number of destroyers to strike at British convoys to Greece. Commanded by Admiral Angelo Iachino, the force sailed under the misapprehension that the British could oppose them with only one battleship, for *Fliegerkorps X* claimed to have put the *Warspite* and *Barham* out of action.

During the morning of March 27 air search and cover by the German and Italian land-based air forces proved ineffective, and about

noon the Italian naval force was shadowed by a British flying boat about 80 miles east of Sicily. Worried by these developments, the Italian naval command ordered the northern cruiser group to rejoin the main body before it could make its assigned sweep. On the morning of March 28 the *Vittorio Veneto,* screened by destroyers, was south of the west end of Crete steering southeast with a division of three cruisers and destroyers seven miles in the van and a northern group of five cruisers and destroyers 25 miles to eastward.

Warned by the British intelligence service in Italy, Admiral Cunningham had taken measures to counter the Italian thrust. Clearing convoys from the way, he ordered Vice Admiral H. S. Pridham-Wippell to leave Greece with his cruiser-destroyer force and rendezvous with him south of Crete on the morning of March 28. Cunningham himself sortied from Alexandria in the *Warspite* with the *Valiant*, the *Barham*, the recently arrived carrier *Formidable,* and nine destroyers after dark on the 27th.

At dawn on the 28th search planes from the *Formidable* sighted the Italian cruiser group and almost simultaneously a scout plane from the *Vittorio Veneto* spotted Pridham-Wippell's light forces. A few moments later, Pridham-Wippell sighted another Italian light force. As at the Battle of Jutland neither commander

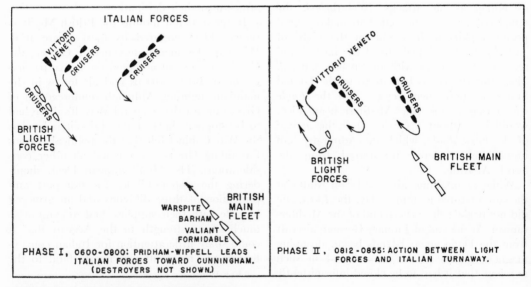

BATTLE OF CAPE MATAPAN, MARCH 28, 1941

knew of the presence of heavy forces nearby. Also, as Beatty had done at Jutland, Pridham-Wippell turned to lead the group he had just sighted toward Cunningham's battleships, a running fight continuing for nearly an hour, with no hits on either side. At 0900 Iachino directed his light forces to break off the action, as they were nearing the range of British shore-based air. Pridham-Wippell followed their retirement in order to keep in touch. To prevent his light forces from running into a trap, Cunningham ordered the *Formidable* to make a torpedo strike on the unengaged group of Italian cruisers. The planes however had so far to go that before they arrived on the scene the next dramatic development occurred. At 1100 a lookout on the *Orion,* Pridham-Wippell's flagship, spotted the *Vittorio Veneto,* which immediately opened accurate fire with her 15-inch guns. Caught between the *Vittorio Veneto* and the cruisers, Pridham-Wippell turned south behind a smoke screen. At this point the *Formidable*'s torpedo planes arrived and attacked the Italian battleship. Although they scored no hits, they caused Iachino to break off the chase and set a course for home at 25 knots, with the British in pursuit.

For the next few hours the *Formidable* made repeated strikes in an effort to slow the Italian force so that the British battleships could come up. At 1520 a torpedo hit stopped the *Vittorio Veneto* temporarily, but an hour and a half later she was making 19 knots. Cunningham meanwhile had ordered Pridham-Wippell to press on at 30 knots with his cruisers and attempt to make visual contact with the fleeing Italian force. The battle fleet followed at its top speed of 24 knots. Because the British underestimated the speed of the *Vittorio Veneto* by four knots, their intercept courses were wide of the mark. Against just such a contingency Cunningham ordered another strike by the *Formidable*'s planes, which stopped the cruiser *Pola,* the Italian main body continuing its run for home.

After these events the battle lost form. Misjudging the course and speed of the enemy, Pridham-Wippell failed to maintain contact after passing the crippled *Pola.* The battleships coming up later first mistook as British an Italian cruiser force returning to the aid of her helpless sister. Quickly rectifying that error, the battle fleet engaged the Italian group, sinking three cruisers, including the *Pola,* and two destroyers. The remainder of the Italian force made its way safely to port.

The British had achieved a considerable tactical victory at almost no cost to themselves. Although the *Vittorio Veneto* escaped them, they had sunk three Italian cruisers and two destroyers. One British cruiser had been slightly damaged, and one plane and pilot were lost. Belated air attacks by the *Luftwaffe* failed to do any additional damage to the British force.

The disproportionate victory provided a much needed lift to the morale of the Alexandria fleet and the British public at a time when the Mediterranean situation seemed dark. It had the important strategic consequence that the Italian fleet did not venture from the safety of its ports to interfere with British naval operations in the waters around Greece and Crete.

The Loss of Greece and Crete

British troops did not remain long in Greece. From Bulgaria the German army had invaded southern Yugoslavia and Greece on April 6. To the 800 supporting aircraft of *Fliegerkorps IV,* the Royal Air Force could oppose only 80 operational planes plus two long-ranged bomber squadrons flying night missions from Egypt. Outflanked and outnumbered, the Greek and Yugoslav armies retreated. Yugoslavia capitulated on April 17. The Greeks had already decided that their cause was lost. The Greek King informally suggested that, to spare

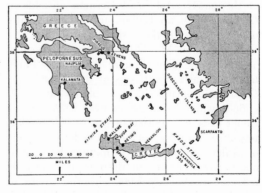

SOUTHERN GREECE AND CRETE

the country the ravages of further fighting, the British send no more troops and evacuate those already there. The War Cabinet immediately agreed to evacuate the mainland, and all British troops began to fall back on embarkation ports. On April 24 the Greeks surrendered. On the same night the British evacuation began.

For this task, even more difficult than Dunkirk, the Mediterranean Fleet had available seven cruisers, 20 destroyers, 21 transports, and a number of small craft. The port of Piraeus having been destroyed by the explosion of an ammunition ship early in April, the evacuation had to be managed from three beaches in the Athens area and three in the Peloponnesus. To avoid air attack, the evacuating ships were ordered not to approach the beaches until one hour after dark and to leave by 0300. For six days the operation continued, with no air cover, with embarkation ports widely separated, and with less effective organization than at Dunkirk. Ship losses were heavy. Yet at the end over 50,000 British troops were saved. In addition, one cruiser, six destroyers, and four submarines of the Greek navy escaped to Alexandria.

Although the British had been forced out of Greece, they determined to save Crete. Its strategic position for controlling shipping in the eastern Mediterranean made the War Cabinet take the decision to hold it at all costs. A large number of troops evacuated from Greece served to stiffen the island's defenses, although loss of replacement parts caused the evacuation of all planes except for those the fleet might be able to provide. On the other hand, Crete lay within easy reach, 60 miles, of the newly established German airfields in Greece and of an Italian strip on Scarpanto, only 45 miles to the east.

At dawn on May 20 the expected German assault came. The primary attack was made by 16,000 airborne troops of the *XI Fliegerkorps* transported in 530 planes and 100 gliders, while following up were 7,000 reserve troops to be transported by sea. At 0800 gliders towed by transport planes landed troops west of Maleme airfield, and 15 minutes later parachute troops began to drop to the east. By the end of the day 5,000 airborne troops of the Seventh Airborne Division had landed,

and Maleme field, though still under British artillery fire, was partly in German hands. Retimo and Heraklion fields had also been attacked, but less strongly, and the British forces there had held. Next day the Germans used Maleme airfield to build up their forces, even though many of their aircraft had to crash-land on the shell-pocked field.

For the sea defense of Crete Admiral Cunningham divided his forces into three groups. To the east and west of Crete two cruiser-destroyer forces were stationed during daylight hours with orders to carry out sweeps north of the island at night or when enemy forces were known to be at sea. The main body, including the *Valiant,* the *Warspite,* a cruiser, and eight destroyers, provided general support. On the night of May 21, a cruiser force which swept around the west end of the island met a German invasion flotilla of small craft 20 miles to the northward and sank about 15 of them, drowning some 4,000 troops. Low on ammunition, the cruisers withdrew to the westward to join the battleship force. Meanwhile another British cruiser force sweeping to the northwest sank several small vessels of another German convoy and drove it off.

Since it was now daylight and the British ships were low on ammunition and already under heavy air attack, their commander, satisfied that the convoy was retiring, did not pursue it but instead retired to the southwest and asked for support from the battleship force. Before the forces could join, two cruisers were damaged, and at 1330 the battleship *Warspite* was hit and a destroyer was sunk by Axis planes. Of two cruisers sent to help the stricken destroyer, one was sunk by air attack in Kithira Strait at 1550. About an hour later another British battleship was damaged, and in the next two and one half hours another cruiser was hit twice and finally sunk. During this night and day of wild activity, no German soldier reached Crete. Yet, although the Mediterranean Fleet had prevented the seaborne invasion of the island, on May 22 German airborne forces made Maleme airfield operational and began landing 20 troop-carrying planes and towed gliders an hour.

During the next few days the British forces fared badly on sea and land. On May 23 two destroyers en route to Alexandria were sunk by air attack. On the 26th while making an air strike against Scarpanto airfield the carrier *Formidable* and a destroyer were badly damaged. Ashore German troops broke through to Suda Bay, and the British troops there began to retire across the mountains to Sphakia on the south coast. Late that night the British decided to evacuate their forces from Crete. Next morning the *Barham* was damaged while covering the retirement of lighter forces from Suda Bay.

Like the withdrawal from Greece, the evacuation of Crete had to be carried out during darkness. On May 28 three cruisers and six destroyers manned by exhausted crews sailed from Alexandria for the Heraklion area in response to Cunningham's signal "Stick it out, we must never let the Army down." Although one cruiser was hit and forced to retire during the approach, the rest of the force embarked 4,000 troops that night. Homeward bound a damaged destroyer lost steering control and had to be abandoned, and air attacks sank a destroyer and damaged another and two cruisers. A bomb that exploded on the crowded mess deck of the cruiser *Orion* killed or wounded 540 troops. In the whole force a total of 800 troops were killed, wounded, or captured.

Evacuation from Sphakia on the south coast was naturally less costly. During the night of May 29 four cruisers, a fast transport, and three destroyers picked up 7,000 troops and got away with damage to only one cruiser. Meanwhile the British forces in the Retimo area had surrendered. The next night 4,000 more troops were evacuated from Sphakia with the loss of still another cruiser.

In all the Royal Navy saved about 17,000 troops from Crete, at a cost to itself of three cruisers and six destroyers sunk; one aircraft carrier, three battleships, six cruisers, and seven destroyers damaged, and just over 2,000 casualties. Although the British had suffered about 13,000 casualties, their stubborn defense had cost the Germans 400 planes and 15,000 to 20,000 troops, including 5,000 men of their only airborne division. The British defense of Crete actually saved Malta, for after their Cretan experience the Germans had no airborne force available for further operations.

But the post-Crete situation of the Mediterranean Fleet was not a happy one. Despite the arrival of reinforcements consisting of a battleship, two cruisers, and six new destroyers in early May, at the beginning of June only two battleships, three cruisers, and 17 destroyers were operational. The British supply line from Alexandria to Malta was now flanked to the northward by German air forces based on Crete. As Malta grew weaker from lack of supplies, the Axis supply line to North Africa would become more secure.

Another threat to the eastern flank of the British army in Egypt and the fuel supply of the Royal Navy had developed meanwhile in the Middle East. In early April the pro-Axis Rashid Ali seized control of the government of Iraq. On the 18th, British naval forces under the Commander in Chief India supported a landing at Basra which quickly forced Rashid Ali to flee to Iran. By mutual agreement British and Russian forces moved into Iran in August to prevent its seizure by the Germans.

In Syria German agents, encouraged by the anti-British feelings of the Vichy-minded French colonial government, had been active. Here the French had a small naval force of two super destroyers armed with five 5.5-inch guns and capable of 40 knots, three submarines, a sloop, and a patrol vessel. To oppose these the British Mediterranean Fleet sent two cruisers and four destroyers to Haifa, Palestine. In early June a fast attack transport supported by another cruiser and two more destroyers landed British troops in Syria while other British and Free French forces advanced from Palestine. Three days later an armistice was signed. Before the fighting ended at sea however, one of the French super destroyers heavily damaged a British destroyer, and French aircraft severely damaged two others. Reinforced by two more cruisers, British ships and naval aircraft sank a super destroyer en route to Syria with arms for the French and damaged the two that were already there. They also sank a submarine and two merchant ships.

Rommel Takes the Offensive

While the British vainly attempted to save Greece and Crete, disaster loomed on the Egyptian border. Although the *Afrika Korps* had arrived during March, at first Rommel was concerned only with halting Wavell's drive toward Tripoli. Rommel himself had arrived in February and had devoted himself to stiffening the Italian defenses. Establishing a base at Tripoli, Rommel organized a group of small coasting ships to transport supplies from Tripoli to the port of Sirte, and later Ras el Ali some 250 miles to the east, a move necessitated by the fact that the Italians had never built a railway along the coast. Field Marshal Walther von Brauchitsch, Commander in Chief of the German army, had informed Rommel that there was to be no question of a major German offensive in North Africa and that he could expect no reinforcements. Rommel realized however that limited objectives could not be held in the desert, and that if he were to carry out his instructions to take Benghazi, he could not hold it, but must take all of Cyrenaica in order to obtain a position where he could secure his flanks.

Although Rommel's orders were not to begin even a limited offensive until the end of May, he feared that the delay would enable the British to strengthen the El Agheila-Bir es Sueva position, so he launched his attack on April 2. Wavell, who had sent part of his forces to Greece, and who had been forced to relieve his most experienced troops in Libya with inexperienced units fresh from home, could not withstand the precision of Rommel's advance and gave permission to fall back to Benghazi, or further if necessary.

Agedabia fell to the Germans on the first day of their offensive, and reports came to Rommel that Benghazi had been evacuated. At this point, the Italian Commander in Chief, General Graziani, attempted to assert his authority and stop Rommel's advance as exceeding instructions from Rome and as impossible of support in the precarious supply situation. Rommel refused to consider wasting his opportunity. While the two men argued, Rommel received a dispatch from the OKW giving him complete freedom of action. After this, the *Afrika Korps* moved rapidly, seizing Benghazi the following day. Cutting across the bulge of Cyrenaica, Rommel reached Derna on April 8, capturing the city and some 800 men.

Immediately Rommel drove on toward To-bruk, which the British were busily reinforcing by sea through the efforts of the Inshore Squadron. After several unsuccessful attacks on Tobruk, thwarted by stubborn British resistance, the necessity for using inexperienced Italian troops, and the preoccupation of the *Luftwaffe* with strategic bombing rather than tactical support, Rommel decided to by-pass Tobruk and drive for Sollum, just over the Egyptian border where he expected to stabilize his front. By the end of May the *Afrika Korps* had established a strong position in the Sollum-Halfaya-Sidi Omar triangle, where it sought to build supplies for an offensive into Egypt.

The arrival in May of a special convoy, code-named Tiger, laden with 238 tanks, the first successful passage in several months of merchant ships from Gibraltar to Alexandria, made it possible for General Wavell to mount a counteroffensive against Rommel's position. Covered by maximum tactical air support, the drive, Operation BATTLEAXE, opened June 15. After heavy fighting, the attack failed, and General Wavell was replaced as Commander in Chief of the British Armies in the Middle East by General Sir Claude Auchinleck. The North African front thereupon stabilized for some months, neither the British nor the Germans having sufficient strength to mount an offensive. Further, while Tobruk remained in British hands Rommel could not advance to the important outpost of Mersa Matruh, whose airstrip would have enabled him to strike at Alexandria, Cairo, and the Suez Canal.

Off North Africa the Inshore Squadron kept up the supply of beleaguered Tobruk throughout the spring and summer. In August the overworked ships of the Tobruk Run were further burdened by the task of removing from Tobruk and replacing with others 19,000 Australian troops which the Dominion Government desired at home for defense against the Japanese threat. By the end of October the Inshore Squadron had completed the exchange and at the same time had delivered about 8,000 tons of stores for the garrison. Finally in November Auchinleck launched an offensive that raised the siege of Tobruk on December 10 and reached Benghazi two weeks later. In the 242 days of the Tobruk siege, the Inshore Squadron had brought in some 33,000 troops,

92 guns, 72 tanks, and 34,000 tons of supplies. During the same period its ships had removed 34,000 troops, 7,500 wounded, and 7,000 prisoners. The entire support operation had cost two destroyers, one minelayer, 24 small naval vessels, and six merchant ships sunk, with damage to seven destroyers, one attack transport, 19 smaller naval vessels, and seven merchant ships.

The Battle of Supplies

During the summer, both sides in North Africa undertook to build up strength. The Germans, consolidating their gains in Greece, Crete, and Cyrenaica, used the maximum of Axis shipping capacity to send troops and supplies to North Africa. To oppose this flow of goods to Rommel, the British had to depend on Malta.

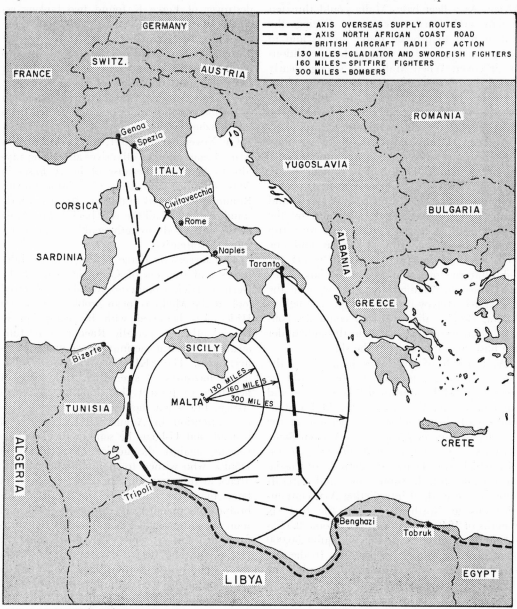

THE IMPORTANCE OF MALTA

Situated almost at the mid-point of the Mediterranean, Malta not only served as a way station for ships passing between Gibraltar and Alexandria; it also sat squarely athwart the normal sea routes between Italy and Libya. Fighter planes and bombers based on Malta forced Axis shipping to make wide detours beyond the range of air strikes, effectively cutting down the efficiency of transport to North Africa. As a fleet base, Malta could threaten Italian and German convoys, forcing the Italian fleet to provide heavy escorts and to accept action under unfavorable conditions of air cover. When Malta was strong, nearly two fifths of Axis shipping for North Africa went to the bottom; when the island was weak, over 95 per cent arrived safely. The chart on page 535 shows this story graphically.

To keep Malta supplied, the British decided to send strongly escorted convoys approximately once a month. They had to provide heavy cover in view of heavy attacks to be expected from the Italian and German air forces and because of the danger of opposition by the Italian fleet. As a rule two convoys were run simultaneously, one from Gibraltar and one from Alexandria. Force H would escort the Gibraltar convoy as far as the Sicilian Channel, while the Mediterranean Fleet gave the Alexandria convoy protection right through to Malta. Despite all the British could do, convoys often were unable to win through under the blistering attacks from the skies.

As a result of the losses incurred in the Greek campaign, no surface ships could be spared for Malta during the late spring and summer, but in other respects the Malta situation greatly improved, largely because of the transfer in June of *Fliegerkorps X* from Sicily to Greece to replace half of *Fliegerkorps IV*, which was being transferred to Russia. Meanwhile British submarines and aircraft kept up the work of interdicting Axis communications to North Africa. In the first six months of 1940, the Axis shipped some 2,372,-000 tons of material, losing not quite 80,000 tons for a loss rate of 3.4 per cent. In the second half of the year, while shipping only some 1,750,000 tons, they lost nearly 400,000 for a loss rate of 22.7 per cent.

To strengthen Malta's offensive capacity, in October 1940 two cruisers and two destroyers dispatched from England were based on the island and designated Force K. On the night of November 8 they intercepted a Tripoli-bound convoy of seven German supply ships protected by two Italian cruisers and six destroyers, sinking all seven supply ships and one of the escorting destroyers. A British submarine sank another of the Italian destroyers the next day. About two weeks later a cruiser and a destroyer of Force K found two tankers escorted by two destroyers and sank both tankers while the escort escaped. At the end of November Force K was reinforced by two more cruisers and destroyers. In the middle of December four destroyers of Force K caught the Italian cruisers in the desperate expedient of rushing gasoline to Tripoli and turned them into blazing torches.

On November 18, 1941, the British Eighth Army began another offensive, advancing rapidly to Benghazi. Because of heavy losses in Axis shipping and lack of reinforcements, Rommel was forced to retreat after a masterly stand. He pulled all the way back to Agedabia before increased strength enabled him to resume the offensive.

The success of Force K and other Malta forces and the loss of Cyrenaica caused the German High Command to take a renewed look at the Mediterranean problem. Although Hitler was bemused with his campaign in Russia, others, especially Raeder, were fully aware of the strategic importance of the Mediterranean. The SKL (German naval staff) urged measures to strengthen Italy's use of her fleet to protect the shipping to North Africa. But when these matters came to Hitler's attention in August 1941, he ordered instead that U-boats be sent to the Mediterranean, against the advice of Raeder and Dönitz, who wished to maintain the Atlantic attack at full strength. The first two waves of boats made the passage of the Straits of Gibraltar in September and November 1941, and soon thereafter made their presence felt dramatically. On November 11, *U-81* sank the *Ark Royal,* and twelve days later *U-331* sent the *Barham* to the bottom. In maneuvering to escape after the attack, the U-boat lost control and went to a depth of 820 feet safely, 490 feet deeper than her designed depth.

Other German efforts to stiffen the Medi-

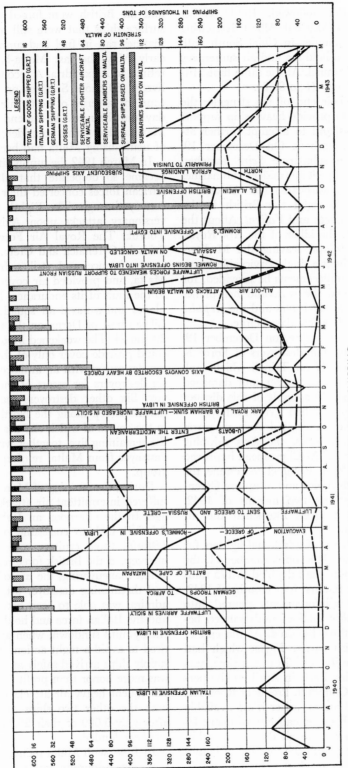

EFFECT OF THE STRENGTH OF MALTA ON AXIS TRANS-MEDITERRANEAN SHIPPING

terranean Theater followed. In December Hitler sent Field Marshal Albert Kesselring to Italy as Commander in Chief South with orders to gain and hold sea and air supremacy in the Sicilian Channel. At the same time Hitler sent *Fliegerkorps II* to Sicily.

To hold up their end of the struggle, the Italians agreed to provide heavy ship support for vital convoys and to attempt further attacks on British harbors. On December 19, 1941, the Italian submarine *Scire* launched three two-man torpedoes (midget submarines with detachable warheads) in Alexandria which severely damaged the British battleships *Queen Elizabeth* and *Valiant*. About the same time *U-81*, the killer of the *Ark Royal*, damaged the *Malaya*, leaving the Mediterranean Fleet without a single serviceable heavy ship. Nor could replacements be provided, for Japan had entered the war, and her planes had sent the *Prince of Wales* and the *Repulse* to the bottom only a few days before.

To make matters worse, on December 19, three cruisers and four destroyers of Force K ran into a mine field off Tripoli which sank one destroyer and one cruiser and damaged two other cruisers. As a result of this disaster a big Axis convoy reached Tripoli safely.

Because of these increased Axis measures and severe British losses, the Axis shipping picture in the central Mediterranean improved enormously, enabling Rommel to resume the offensive in North Africa and recapture Cyrenaica during the first two months of 1942. Simultaneously the Axis intensified the air assault on Malta.

Despite the arrival of additional fighters for the defense of the island on November 11, the scale of attack more than doubled to 175 raids in December. In the first four months of 1942, as German air reinforcements poured into Sicily, the monthly total of raids ranged between two and three hundred. At the end of March the British carrier *Eagle*, which had been flying in twelve Spitfires at a time, was laid up for repairs. Early in April, at the personal request of Churchill, President Roosevelt made the United States carrier *Wasp* available to fly in its much larger capacity of about 60 Spitfires, but these were all destroyed within a few days. That month the tonnage of bombs dropped on Malta reached a high of 6,700,

and the British were forced to withdraw the surface ships that were still operational. Submarines ran in fuel and ammunition, but in early May the last Malta-based submarines retired to Alexandria. A second *Wasp* trip delivered 60 more Spitfires on May 9, just in time for a series of costly air battles on that day and the next. At the end of these battles, Marshal Kesselring considered that his task of neutralizing Malta had been accomplished.

In March 1942 the supply situation at Malta became so desperate that all British North African forces concerted their efforts to get a convoy through. The Eighth Army made diversionary attacks upon Axis airfields near Tobruk. The Royal Air Force attacked airfields in Cyrenaica and Crete, carried out air reconnaissance and strikes from Libya and Malta, and provided air cover for the convoy to the limit of its endurance. Royal Air Force planes and a naval air squadron bombed the Libyan port of Derna on the nights of March 20 and 21. The weakened Mediterranean Fleet could provide cover only of three cruisers and ten destroyers with an antiaircraft cruiser and six destroyers for escort of the four-ship convoy. Six other destroyers made an antisubmarine sweep along the North African coast, in the course of which one destroyer was sunk; the remaining five, together with a cruiser and destroyer from Malta, reinforced the covering group.

During the morning of March 22 the convoy suffered intermittent air attacks without damage. In the afternoon an Italian force under Admiral Iachino consisting of the battleship *Littorio,* three cruisers, and four destroyers intercepted the British force north of Sirte. By adroit maneuvering, the use of smoke screens, and threatening destroyer attacks, the British admiral was able to keep between his convoy and the Italian force and hold off the superior enemy until sundown, when again Iachino retired to avoid a night action. Two of the four supply ships arrived safely at Malta. Yet there was more honor than profit in the victory, for subsequent heavy air attacks upon the harbor sank the other two ships at their moorings after only 5,000 of their 26,000 tons of cargo had been landed.

In June, with Malta reduced to near starvation, the Admiralty made another desperate effort to send in two convoys, one each from Alexandria and Gibraltar. The first of eleven ships was escorted by seven cruisers and 26 destroyers with several smaller warships and the ancient, unarmed battleship *Centurion* pretending to be a capital ship. Nine submarines took station to the north of the convoy track to intercept the Italian fleet if it should leave port. Maximum air support covered the convoy as it advanced.

In spite of aircraft and submarines, the Italian fleet came on, losing one cruiser to a submarine, and suffering damage to the *Littorio* from an aircraft torpedo. Although the Italian fleet never made contact, Admiral Sir Philip Vian had to order the convoy to return to Alexandria since his ships had exhausted their ammunition fighting off air attacks.

The eastbound convoy had better luck. Once it reached the Sardinian Narrows it came under heavy air attack, and then in the Sicilian Narrows it encountered a force of Italian destroyers. But, after heavy fighting, two of the six merchant ships won through, bringing temporary respite to Malta.

Operation Hercules— The Axis Plan to Seize Malta

In the spring of 1942 German and Italian leaders agreed that for their North African ventures to succeed in winning through to Suez and making possible the acquisition of Iranian oil fields, they must first neutralize or capture Malta. Forces based there still exacted a toll of Axis shipping. Accordingly Hitler and Mussolini, meeting at Berchtesgaden late in April, agreed to launch an assault on Malta in July, after Rommel's forthcoming offensive. Rommel was to stop at the Egyptian border so that the *Luftwaffe* planes could be employed for the Malta operation. The plan provided for newly trained German airborne troops to be supported by Italian naval forces and seaborne troops. Hitler, never wholly supporting this operation, constantly sought an excuse to avoid it. He hoped that Rommel would be able to capture Tobruk, which the Axis might then use as a supply port for ships routed via Crete, beyond attack radius of aircraft based on Malta.

On May 26, Rommel resumed his offensive. His forces reached Tobruk on June 19 and broke through the defense perimeter the next day. On June 21, Tobruk fell. For this accomplishment Hitler promoted Rommel to field marshal. Rommel remarked, "I would rather he had given me one more division." The Germans in seizing Tobruk captured vast quantities of stores. In view of this unexpected windfall and with the port of Tobruk now available, Rommel requested permission to take advantage of his momentum and drive into Egypt. Hitler, seeing a chance to avoid the assault on Malta, wrote Mussolini a letter in which he described the Egyptian opportunities in glowing terms and urged him to agree to allow Rommel to attempt to capture Suez. Mussolini acquiesced. Shortly thereafter Operation HERCULES was postponed until September and then canceled.

Rommel drove hard, seizing Mersa Matruh and its important air base. Then an incredible thing happened. Hitler diverted reinforcements scheduled for Africa to the Russian front. Of the 60,000 tons of supply Rommel had requested for June, only 3,000 were sent. He was able to keep going only by seizing British materials. At one point 85 per cent of his transport consisted of captured British vehicles. Thus Rommel had to call a halt at El Alamein, only 60 miles from Alexandria.

The Turn of the Tide

Once again the supply race was on. While the Axis had to undertake only a three-day voyage to send material to North Africa, the British had to depend on the three-month voyage around the Cape of Good Hope. Rommel chiefly required food, fuel, and light vehicles, while the British desperately needed tanks. When Tobruk fell, the United States sent 300 brand-new Sherman tanks and 100 self-propelled 105 mm. guns.

Ever since Japan had entered the war and begun operations in the Indian Ocean, the British had been haunted by fears of an Axis base being established at Diego Suarez on Madagascar. From this base German or Japanese naval or air forces could not only threaten India but could operate against the vital WS convoys to Egypt. Madagascar belonged to France, but

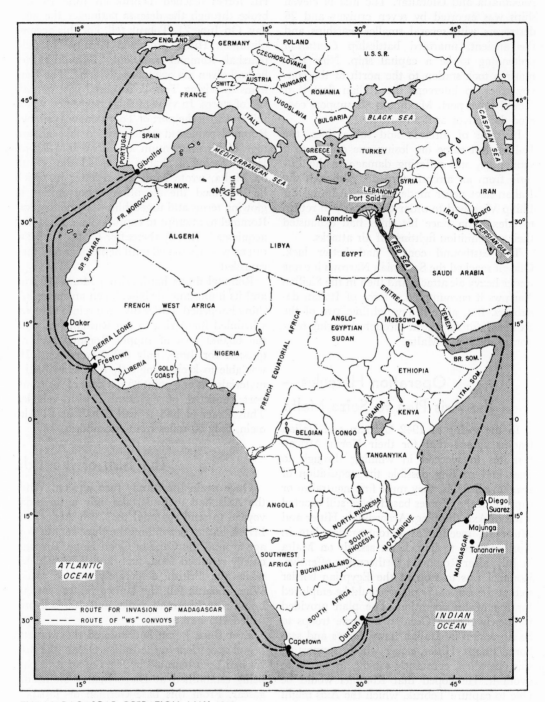

THE MADAGASCAR OPERATION, MAY 1942

the British had little faith in the Vichy Government, especially after reports of Admiral Darlan's visit to Germany at the beginning of the year and after Vichy's virtual cession of French Indo-China to Japan. Vichy clearly wished to be aligned with the winning side and still believed in an ultimate Axis triumph.

Heavy ships for Operation IRONCLAD, the capture of Madagascar, came from Force H, and included two aircraft carriers, the *Illustrious* and *Indomitable,* as well as the battleship *Ramillies,* two cruisers, eleven destroyers, with smaller craft, and 15 transports and assault vessels. Force H was replaced at Gibraltar by ships from the Home Fleet, which was in turn reinforced by American heavy ships temporarily transferred to Scapa Flow.

The assault on Diego Suarez took place at 0430 on May 5, 1942. After an uncertain start, a flanking attack by 50 marines turned the edge of the defenses, and within a few hours Diego Suarez was in British hands. A few weeks later the British also took Majunga and Tananarive. Once the Vichy officials had been supplanted, the people of the island generally supported the Allied cause.

With the danger to the Cape route cleared up, reinforcement of the British Middle Eastern position proceeded rapidly. In Egypt the British had approximately 630,000 men, and Churchill became impatient for a desert offensive. Shortly after the fall of Tobruk, he made up his mind to go to Cairo to see for himself why General Auchinleck delayed his scheduled attack on Rommel. He found Auchinleck so concerned with his responsibilities for the entire Middle Eastern area that he had not recognized the full importance of North Africa. After many discussions, Churchill decided to split the Middle East command in two, to relieve Auchinleck, and to give the new Near East Command to General Sir Harold Alexander and the Eighth Army to General Sir Bernard L. Montgomery. The latter, immediately on taking over on August 13, began to reorganize and retrain his forces to meet the expected German attack on the El Alamein position and for an eventual offensive. Montgomery planned not merely to roll the Germans back on their supply lines as previous British offensives had done but to destroy them as a fighting force so that they could not be turned against the forthcoming Anglo-American landings in North Africa.

Meanwhile the air reinforcement of Malta continued. Serviceable aircraft on hand rose from a low of 23 in May to 169 in September. Even more important than the increase in numbers was the greatly extended range of the new torpedo planes being delivered. In 1939 the effective attack radius of Malta-based torpedo planes had been only 100 miles; in 1942 it had increased to 400 miles. Now it was impossible for Axis shipping to avoid attacks, even by the most circuitous routing. Even in the harbors of Bardia, Tobruk, and Mersa Matruh, ships suffered heavy attack. Axis coastal shipping also met heavy losses. Thus while Rommel attempted to build up stores for resuming his offensive before September, the supplies he received barely covered his daily requirements for his infantry forces, and not half of what he needed for the Panzer Army. Only captured British supplies alleviated the situation.

Rommel knew that if he was to win a breakthrough at El Alamein, he would have to attack before the expected British heavy reinforcements could arrive in September. The Italian *Comando Supremo* promised heavy shipments of oil and gasoline, and Kesselring agreed to fly in 500 gallons of gasoline a day during the offensive. Accepting these promises, Rommel took the risk and on the night of August 30–31, 1942, hurled an attack at the ridge of Alam el Halfa, hoping to outflank the El Alamein defenses. Montgomery refused to be drawn out and contented himself with allowing Rommel's drive to spend itself against his strong defensive positions while the R.A.F. made punishing attacks on the German armor. None of Rommel's promised fuel oil or gasoline arrived, and on September 2, Rommel called off the attack.

"With the failure of this offensive," wrote Rommel, "our last chance of gaining the Suez Canal had gone. We could now expect that the full production of British industry and, more important, the enormous industrial potential of America . . . would finally turn the tide against us."[4]

When Rommel withdrew on September 3,

[4] B. H. Liddell Hart, editor, *The Rommel Papers* (New York, 1953), 283.

Montgomery did not pursue him. With his own supply line to the eastward secure, Montgomery continued to build up his forces for a massive offensive which began at El Alamein on October 23. After eleven days of furious fighting, the Eighth Army finally broke through and rolled on to the westward. Tobruk was in British hands again on November 13 and Benghazi on the 24th. On December 15 the Eighth Army reached El Agheila, and Rommel was in retreat toward Tunisia. Far to the westward British and American forces that had landed in Morocco and Algeria were advancing upon his rear. The tide of war in the Mediterranean had turned for the last time.

Summary

Although Italy remained a non-belligerent until June 1940, both Britain and France had prepared to protect their vital interests in the Mediterranean. After Italy entered the war and France fell, the British had to take drastic action to maintain their position in the Middle East. By a reluctant attack on the French fleet at Mers-el-Kebir, and by means of a gentleman's agreement at Alexandria, the British assured themselves that the Axis could not turn French ships against them. Establishing the main Mediterranean Fleet at Alexandria and a *force de raid* at Gibraltar, the British prepared themselves for war against the Italians. Because early actions showed the Italian navy reluctant to engage approximately equal forces, the British were generally able to carry out scheduled operations. In a carrier raid on Taranto in November 1940, the British knocked out one Italian battleship and forced the others to retire to Naples. A later raid drove them farther from the strategic center to Spezia.

In September 1940, the Italian army in Libya began an offensive against Egypt, and late in October Italy invaded Greece. Both drives stalled, and the following spring Germany intervened. British forces sent to Greece had to be evacuated, and when they retired to Crete were unable to hold the island in the face of the Axis assault, which cost Germany her only airborne division.

In North Africa the ebb and flow of fortune was a direct result of supplies received by the opposing commanders. The key to Axis strength was Malta, for when the island was strong, delivery of Axis supplies dropped to a trickle. When Malta was weak, Axis forces were soon able to undertake offensives. The British had the vital task of maintaining supplies to Malta in the face of terrific losses. Meanwhile their own supplies went around the Cape of Good Hope, through the Red Sea and the Suez Canal to Egypt. Threats to this route were eliminated by the destruction of Italian forces in the Red Sea and Persian Gulf and by the capture of Madagascar.

The Axis had plans to seize Malta and thus eliminate the threat to their shipping across the Mediterranean. When Rommel's offensive in July 1942 proved successful however, both Hitler and Mussolini agreed to postpone the invasion of Malta to allow Rommel to drive for Suez. Then Hitler diverted Rommel's reinforcements to Russia, and the *Afrika Korps* came to a halt at El Alamein. On the last day of August Rommel made a final, desperate, unsuccessful thrust at Alam el Halfa. Seven weeks later General Montgomery hurled a massive British attack at the Axis forces and drove them hundreds of miles to the west. Meanwhile British and American troops had landed in Northwest Africa, and the Axis position there was doomed. The attack on Europe soon followed.

30:

The Battle of the Atlantic

"The only thing that ever really frightened me during the war was the U-boat peril."[1] So wrote Winston Churchill after the victory. From the Allied point of view, the Battle of the Atlantic was being won when nothing was happening. Every time a convoy arrived in port, the battle was that much nearer victory. When a dramatic action took place at sea, the Allied cause came that much nearer defeat. Victory was won by many people, by merchant seamen who sailed in the freighters and tankers, by stevedores who loaded and unloaded them, by seamen, ratings, and officers who manned the escorting vessels and aircraft, by shipyard workers who built both merchant ships and escorts, and by thousands of people on both sides of the Atlantic who plotted U-boat positions, routed convoys, organized sailing lists, experimented with new devices, and analyzed the results of previous actions.

The most curious thing about the Battle of the Atlantic is that neither side really prepared for it. Although the Anglo-German Naval Treaty of 1935 allowed Germany under certain conditions to build her U-boat arm up to parity with that of Great Britain, the Germans constructed few boats because their building yards were fully occupied in preparing surface ships under PLAN Z. Thus Germany began the war with only 56 operational U-boats, of which only 22 were suitable for Atlantic service; of the remainder, ten had not completed operational readiness tests, and 24 were 250-ton boats of short radius, suitable only for North Sea operations.

Britain had allowed preparations for antisubmarine warfare to lapse into the status of a minor activity. Emphasis on big ships in the disarmament treaties had gone hand in hand with economies imposed by the "Ten Year Rule." In the name of economy, the Admiralty had abolished its Mine Sweeping, Antisubmarine, and Trade Divisions. Britain built few small ships for antisubmarine work, for she expected in the event of another war that "the convoy system will only be introduced when the balance of advantage is in its favour and when sinkings are so great that the country no longer feels justified in allowing ships to sail by themselves but feels that, for the protection of their crews, the convoy system is necessary. . . . It is simply a matter of expediency . . . [that] as convoy will not be needed immediately on the outbreak of war it will give us time to improvise protection, while orders are given to build the sloops which we shall eventually require."[2] Because efficient convoy escorts could not be improvised, most of the escorts early in the war were hurriedly adapted from fishing trawlers and other small craft, ill-suited for the rigorous duties they had to undertake. Fortunately with asdic, and the parallel development of sonar in the United States, both the British and the Americans had a reliable underwater detector which, in the hands of an experienced operator, showed the direction and also the range of a submerged submarine out to approximately 1,500 yards. However the U-boats were later to adopt night surfaced attacks, thereby largely nullifying the advantage of asdic. In 1937 the Admiralty had regained full control of the Fleet Air Arm. Although this move had been made for the sake of fleet carrier operations, the Royal Navy

[1] Winston S. Churchill, *The Second World War*, II (Boston, 1949), 598.

[2] Quoted in D. W. Waters, "The Philosophy and Conduct of Maritime War," *Journal of the Royal Naval Scientific Service* (July, 1958), 184.

could now integrate the Fleet Air Arm efforts into its antisubmarine warfare operations. At the same time the navy also attained close cooperation with the R.A.F. Coastal Command in matters pertaining to the protection of shipping. This harmonious partnership proved a decisive factor in the Atlantic struggle.

Phase I: U-Boat Operations Until the Fall of France

When hostilities began Commodore Karl Dönitz was obliged to operate with only a handful of boats rather than the 300 he considered a minimum. Yet one of this handful, *U-30,* by torpedoing the *Athenia* on the opening day of the war, provided an apparent indication of German intentions regarding the resumption of unrestricted U-boat warfare and abruptly dispelled the British Admiralty's hesitation in adopting the convoy system. On August 26, the Admiralty had assumed control of all British merchant shipping, and immediately after the *Athenia* sinking ordered convoys to be established over the principal routes for ships of speeds between nine and 14.9 knots. Ships outside these limits sailed independently. Later in the war, slower ships were included in slow convoys of about six to seven knots. Escort endurance precluded close support beyond 15° W or beyond 47° N for Gibraltar and Sierra Leone convoys. East Coast convoys operated successfully throughout the war with a loss rate of one tenth of one per cent. In October convoys between Britain and Norway began and continued with no losses until the invasion of Norway. Meanwhile a Dover mine barrage closed the Strait to German U-boats.

The success of these measures contrasts sharply with so-called "offensive" operations against U-boats. H.M. carrier *Ark Royal* on antisubmarine patrol narrowly avoided torpedoes on September 14; three days later *U-29* sank the 22,500-ton carrier *Courageous* patrolling with an inadequate screen off the Irish coast. Remembering the mythical success of the North Sea Mine Barrage of World War I, the British planned a similar barrage in World War II. After the fall of Norway, it was laid between Iceland and Scotland. It destroyed one U-boat, but otherwise did not affect U-boat movements at all.

The Germans too resorted to mine laying on a large scale, employing the *Luftwaffe,* surface vessels, and U-boats to sow their offensive mine fields in harbor entrances, estuaries, and shallows of the English Channel and the North Sea. These mines were of a magnetic impulse type, impossible to sweep by normal methods. On November 23, 1939, the British recovered a German magnetic mine which a plane had dropped in the mud flats in the Thames Estuary. Examination disclosed the operating principle, and the British were able partly to counter the magnetic impulse feature by means of an electrically charged cable running horizontally around each ship. This device, known as a "degaussing cable," cut to some extent into the effectiveness of the German mine laying campaign. Nonetheless, in the first four months of the war, German mines caused serious dislocations to coastal shipping and sank 79 merchant ships totaling 262,697 Gross Register Tons, almost all sailing independently.

Meanwhile the convoys came through. U-boats sank 153,879 tons of Allied and neutral shipping in September, yet not one of their 41 victims was sailing under escort. By the end of 1939 the Royal Navy had escorted 5,756 vessels with the loss of only twelve ships, four being claimed by U-boats; during the same period 102 independently routed merchant vessels had been lost. Dönitz had lost nine U-boats, nearly a sixth of his strength. As he later revealed, "U-boats at sea in operational areas during the winter 1939–40 never exceeded ten in number and at times fell as low as two."[3]

Because of wide fluctuations in escort availability, screening dispositions changed frequently. Theoretically the best defense against U-boat assault was a formation that completely enclosed the merchant ships. These were disposed on a broad front with short flanks, a formation which reduced the U-boat's opportunities for beam attacks. To protect a convoy with a perimeter of seven miles (e.g. ten columns of four ships, columns 600 yards

[3] Karl Dönitz, *Essay on the Conduct of the War at Sea* (Washington, 1946), 4-5.

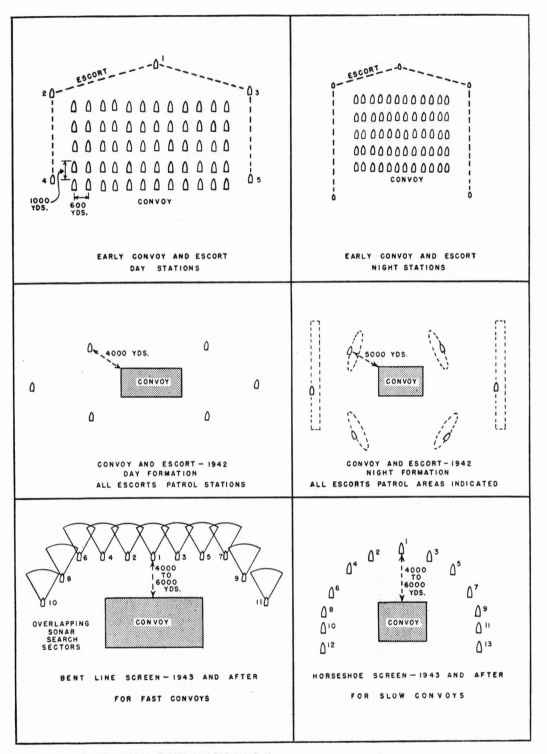

PRINCIPAL CONVOY FORMATIONS, WORLD WAR II

apart, ships in column 400 yards apart, as was the practice in 1939–40) escort commanders initially adopted the box screen of World War I, stationing an escort on each corner of the merchant formation and ordering any additional units into the arc directly ahead. Early in World War II it was customary to employ cruisers or battleships in the escort, but when the threat of surface raiders diminished, the practice was abandoned as too dangerous to the large ships.

A typical early transatlantic convoy was made up of 30 to 40 merchant ships steaming in from nine to twelve columns.[4] The customary rectangular formation with a broad front was adopted for several reasons. First it reduced a U-boat's opportunities to attack from the advantageous beam positions; second, it was the most convenient one for inter-ship visual communication; third, it reduced the tendency of ships in the rear of a long column to surge up on the ships ahead; and fourth, it was the best compromise formation for controlling, with few escorts, the largest number of ships with the least risk of collision. Furthermore, it gave the escorts the most favorable opportunities both to deter U-boats from attacking and for attacking the threatening U-boats. Grouping of ships does, obviously, bunch targets, but a "browning shot," one fired in the general direction of a convoy, is unlikely to find a target if the ships are adequately spaced. Also the risk that a U-boat might slip through the defenses submerged by day or surfaced by night and sink a number of ships with a single salvo can likewise be reduced by appropriate inter-ship spacing.

Early British doctrine called for a prompt "hold-down" on an attacking U-boat. Such tactics, though successful in limiting convoy losses before the advent of wolf pack opera-

[4] Allied convoys were designated by a combination of letters and numbers indicating the port of origin, destination, and the particular convoy number. Principal ocean convoy routes and their destinations were: Halifax-United Kingdom, HX; United Kingdom-Halifax, ON; Sydney, Nova Scotia-United Kingdom, SC; United Kingdom-Sydney, ONS; Boston-Halifax, BX; United Kingdom-Gibraltar, OG; Gibraltar-United Kingdom, HG; United Kingdom-North Russia, PQ (later JW); United States-Gibraltar, UGS; Gibraltar-United States, GUS.

tions, seldom produced a kill because there were so few escorts with each convoy, and most of these were of such relatively low speed, that they were obliged to rejoin their convoy before they could gain the opportunity of delivering a *coup de grâce*. Thus a U-boat that had evaded its attackers could often resume stalking the same convoy. Dönitz' submariners favored night surfaced attacks from 45 degrees on either bow of the convoy, ensuring a short torpedo run that afforded the merchantmen little time for evasive action. Evolving British escort doctrine called for heavier bow defenses, ultimately producing in 1942 the "bent-line" screen, which provided strong protection on the bows while deploying additional warships directly ahead to intercept "down-the-throat" approaches. The problem of how to frustrate browning shots bedeviled escort commanders until 1942, when, using shipboard radar and H/F D/F (high frequency radio direction finder), they were able to extend their screens to ranges of 4,000 to 6,000 yards from the main body. At the same time the interval between columns was increased from 600 to 1,000 yards, a measure which reduced by about 50 per cent the probability of a browning shot hitting a ship, while increasing the perimeter of the convoy by less than 8 per cent.

U-boat mining operations in British waters during the first quarter of 1940 offered little indication of the intensified campaign that Admiral Dönitz was soon to unleash. Continuing their concentration in the Southwestern Approaches, German U-boats sank 85 ships aggregating 280,829 tons during January and February; only seven of their victims were in convoy and these sinkings from convoy were achieved only at the cost of three U-boats. In the next three months, merchant ship losses declined as a result of a major redeployment of Dönitz' flotillas for the invasion of Norway, to which some 25 boats were committed.

In the ultimate success of the Norwegian invasion the U-boats played no part, being frustrated by widespread torpedo failures. Off Narvik, Günther Prien launched repeated attacks on anchored transports and cruisers, only to have all his magnetic torpedoes run deep. An exhaustive analysis of such unsuccessful attacks convinced the SKL that torpedo failures had prevented U-boats from claiming one or more battleships, seven cruisers, and a number of destroyers and transports.[5]

Humiliating as these northern operations proved for BdU,[6] the spring of 1940 laid substantial foundations for Dönitz' subsequent months of triumph in the Atlantic. The acquisition of Norway's entire coastline and the subsequent conquest of the Low Countries and France gave to Hitler the means of turning Britain's maritime flanks. While secondary U-boat havens were being established in Norway, Dönitz personally supervised the creation of heavily fortified bases on the French Atlantic coast at Brest, Lorient, St. Nazaire, La Rochelle, and Bordeaux. Possession of these French bases meant a reduction of over 50 per cent in the transit time of U-boats to their Atlantic hunting grounds. Unfortunately for Britain, the R.A.F. was so heavily engaged over the Channel that it was unable to disrupt the construction of massive concrete "pens" in these Biscay ports, with the result that they were strengthened to the point of invulnerability. Late in July *Luftwaffe* support added to the strategic effectiveness of these French bases.

Phase II: The Mid-Atlantic Offensive Based on French Ports

In July 1940 U-boats began operating from French bases. The reduction in cruising time to patrol stations had the effect of increasing the number of U-boats available in the operating areas. Thus Dönitz was able to make an attack on convoys by the tactical innovation of *Rudeltaktik,* or wolf pack operations. Still preferring to attack independent shipping, the U-boats nevertheless now had a means of forcing their way through the escorts to the body of the convoy. The toll of Allied shipping mounted ominously, exceeding 500,000 tons in June; U-boats accounted for 58 merchantmen of 284,113 tons, largely in the vulnerable Southwestern Approaches. These June sinkings were but a prelude to the French-based "Golden Age," of the *U-Waffe,* a four-month campaign in which Dönitz' wolf packs, abetted by the *Luftwaffe,* unleashed their first crippling assaults on North Atlantic convoys. Midway in July BdU concentrated his strength in the waters off Rockall Bank, 260 miles west of Scotland, and for the first time employed wolf pack tactics. When a U-boat made contact with a convoy it would not attack immediately, but would trail, decks awash, well behind the target, while it reported the convoy's course, speed, and composition to BdU headquarters in France. BdU would then assume tactical command, ordering the other boats of the pack to make contact with the shadower. On the scene, the senior commander would then take over, attempting to coordinate a night surfaced attack that would swamp the escort and then annihilate the convoy.[7]

In order to assist in the new campaign, Italy dispatched some 27 submarines to the Atlantic to cooperate with the Germans against merchant shipping. With German assistance, the Italians established a submarine base at Bordeaux, from which the Italian boats operated under German strategic command. At first the Germans attempted to integrate the Italians into pack warfare, but because the Mediterranean boats were slow and unhandy, the results were less than ideal. At length the Italians were allocated the waters south of 45° N as their operating area. Because most Allied traffic operated north of this parallel, the Italians found few targets.

The British were hard pressed to meet the new threats. Casualties to destroyers and other escorts during the Norwegian campaign and

[5] Subsequent investigations, which resulted in a shakeup of the German Torpedo Inspectorate, revealed that the magnetic torpedo had an unreliable detonator as well as a tendency to run well below the selected depth settings. These were virtually the same by-products of inadequate testing that were soon to plague American submariners in the Pacific. Unfortunately for the Allies, the Germans rectified their deficiencies much more promptly than the Americans did.

[6] *Befehlshaber der U-Boote*: Properly this term means Commander of Submarines, while the name for the command was *Befehlshaber der U-Boote Bereich.* In practice the Germans used BdU to refer to the command as well as the commander.

[7] Dönitz, soon concluding that effective control of pack attacks was impossible on the scene, began directing the operations by radio from U-boat command headquarters.

the Dunkirk evacuation had been heavy. Since at that time there was a daily average of 2,000 British merchant ships at sea, the need for escorts was desperate. Additional destroyers were ordered and two new types were authorized—corvettes and frigates. The former were vessels of less than 1,000 tons, mounting one or two 4-inch guns, equipped with depth charges and asdic. Corvettes were unsuited for operations in the North Atlantic, yet they had to be used there because nothing else could be provided in time. The new frigates, appearing considerably later, were much larger and had better sea-keeping qualities than the corvettes. These two types, assisted by trawlers, luggers, and other small vessels, bore the brunt of escort work in the North Atlantic for half the war. To tide them over the difficult times ahead, Churchill as early as May 1940 requested the loan of some 50 American destroyers for convoy work.

In July 1940 the British extended the limits of close escort of convoy from 15° W to 17° W for transatlantic convoys, a move that served to nullify a part of the gain of the U-boats' time on station. On the other hand, escorts of ocean convoys were severely weakened by withdrawal of larger escort ships to be used in anti-invasion patrol during the summer of 1940. Some convoys sailed protected by a single escort. Sinkings naturally mounted as summer wore on. The following table for seven months in 1940 shows the results of pack operations and of weakening convoy escorts. The sinking figures are losses in tons from all causes.

March	April	May	June
107,009	158,218	288,461	585,496

July	August	September
386,913	397,229	448,621

In October, to try to cut down the slaughter, the Admiralty again extended the westward limits of ocean convoy escort, this time to 19° W. The benefit of this move however was largely lost by the reduction in the upper speed limit of convoys in order to permit more ships to sail independently. In spite of Admiralty arguments to the contrary, an economic committee, worried about decreasing amounts of cargo reaching Britain, in November persuaded the

War Cabinet to permit faster ships to sail independently in order to make swifter passages. The Admiralty clearly realized that some ships might make individual voyages more quickly, but they also realized that the ships had to remain afloat if they were to deliver cargoes, and knowing that individual ships got sunk more quickly than convoyed vessels, predicted that these ships would soon be delivering fewer cargoes. In the event, the Admiralty was proved right by differential statistics of losses. Though the economic experts insisted on counting stragglers from convoys as sailing in convoy, independent losses by their count were still twice those of ships under escort. Not until June 1941 was the upper speed limit of 15 knots restored.[8]

U-boats preferred to enjoy the easy kills of independent ships rather than employ wolf pack tactics to tangle with convoys, however inadequately they might be escorted. For a five-week period in late 1940, not a single ocean convoy was molested, yet independent losses soared. In the mid-Atlantic, not only were ships unescorted, but the U-boats had immunity from air attack. In spite of long-range air patrols from Britain and from Canada, there remained a broad stretch of the central North Atlantic which land-based aircraft simply could not reach. In this "Black Pit" the U-boats reaped a rich harvest among ships sailing independently. As convoy escort was extended westward, the U-boats perforce had to make pack attacks on escorted convoys. Most heavily hit was eastbound SC-7, a slow 34-ship convoy intercepted some 250 miles northwest of Bloody Foreland, north Ireland. Attacking at dusk, Lieutenant Commander Otto Kretschmer in U-99 with six other experienced boats penetrated the four-ship screen, sinking 17 merchantmen in a midnight melee. Scarcely had this "Night of the Long Knives"[9] ended, when weakly escorted HX-79, a fast 49-ship convoy, ran afoul of Günther Prien's U-47 and five others which again swamped the defense and claimed an additional 14 vic-

[8] Waters, "Philosophy of Maritime War," 187.
[9] So called from the Nazi "Night of the Long Knives," June 30, 1934, the Blood Purge in which Hitler and his associates massacred members of the Nazi Party whom they suspected of disloyalty to themselves. "Long Knives" was a name given white settlers by the American Indians.

tims. Several boats had already exhausted their torpedoes and had begun homeward passage when eastbound HX-79A entered these same waters, at the cost of seven more merchantmen.

These one-sided encounters climaxed Dönitz' first determined foray into the Northwestern Approaches, the "Happy Time" in which his U-boats sank 217 merchant vessels, totaling over 1,100,000 tons, at the cost of only six boats. Such success firmly convinced BdU of the bright prospects of wolf pack operations, yet, because of the limited number of boats available and their need for replenishment, they could not maintain this attrition rate. Less than half a dozen U-boats patrolled off Rockall during the last two months of 1940, and heavy weather frustrated efforts to locate the increasingly evasive British convoys. Allied merchant tonnage losses from U-boat attack declined to an average of some 180,000 tons during November and December. By Christmas 1940 only one U-boat lurked in the Northwestern Approaches, and when Dönitz reckoned accounts at the end of the year, he discovered that construction had barely made good the loss of 31 boats since the war's outbreak.

In the spring of 1941, the *U-Waffe* achieved increased success. Late in February, Dönitz dispatched several of his most experienced commanders to conduct an all-out blitz in the Northwestern Approaches where, on the evening of March 6, four boats located westbound OB-293, which they attacked for 24 hours. At dusk on the 7th, Prien in *U-47*, seeking to increase his tonnage bag of some 160,000 tons, attempted to penetrate the screen under the cover of a rain squall. H.M.S. *Wolverine* spotted Prien's submarine through the gloom and dispatched the killer of the *Royal Oak* with a barrage of depth charges. Eight days later the remainder of the group located HX-112. Although Schepke in *U-100* promptly sank a 10,000-ton tanker, the U-boats achieved no further sinkings until the night of the 16th when *U-99*'s commander, Otto Kretschmer, slipped through the screen and, racing up and down the columns, torpedoed four tankers and two freighters before disappearing astern of the main body. At midnight the escort commander, Commander Donald Macintyre in

H.M.S. *Walker,* detected *U-100* approaching on the surface. Crash diving, Schepke escaped, but a determined joint attack by two destroyers forced him to the surface where he was fatally rammed by H.M.S. *Vanoc*. Minutes later the *Walker* blasted *U-99* to the surface with an accurate pattern of depth charges. Most of the crew, including Kretschmer, were subsequently rescued by Macintyre. Thus the British captured the *U-Waffe's* most brilliant tactician, whose score of 266,629 tons sunk was unequalled during the war.

The loss of their three outstanding aces within little more than a week produced profound depression at BdU headquarters at Lorient. With other losses, the Germans were suddenly confronted with an attrition rate of nearly 20 per cent in the Northwestern Approaches. As foul weather continued to frustrate *Luftwaffe* reconnaissance over the North Channel, between Ireland and Scotland, Dönitz reluctantly shifted his wolf pack operations some 200 miles to the west, beyond the range of Coastal Command bombers based on Northern Ireland. This move provided the first indication of his "tonnage warfare," the strategic corollary of wolf-pack tactics. Tonnage warfare was founded on the concept of concentrating U-boat activity in areas where the most Allied merchant tonnage might be sunk at least cost to the *U-Waffe*. Thus, when defenses became strong in one area, Dönitz would shift his boats to another in order to capitalize on remaining "soft spots," even though vital Allied cargoes might meanwhile be delivered to crucial areas. As a result, during several critical periods in the war the North Atlantic was almost completely uncontested.

On April 1, 1941, the British Admiralty received operational control of Coastal Command aircraft and hence was able to integrate air activities directly with convoy movements. Beginning in April, long-range aircraft were based on Iceland, whence they were able to cut drastically the size of the Black Pit, which now came to be known as the Greenland Air Gap. With these changes came increased fuel capacity in the newer escorts, which enabled escort to be provided as far as 35° W. The increasing strength of the Royal Canadian Navy permitted the Canadians to undertake escort in the western Atlantic and to establish a link with the British. On May 27, 1941, there sailed from Halifax Convoy HX-129, the first North Atlantic convoy to be escorted all the way across the ocean.

This sailing marked the end of the second phase of the Battle of the Atlantic. Since the beginning of the war, the U-boats had sunk some 650 ships, yet only ten per cent of these had been lost from escorted convoys, and none had been sunk when air escort supplemented surface escorts. On the other hand, 60 per cent of all U-boats lost had been sunk while attacking convoys. Now, the Germans would be obliged to attack convoys, accepting an increased loss rate of U-boats if they were to maintain their rate of sinkings.

Phase III: "All Aid to Britain Short of War"

From the earliest days of the war the United States had watched the events in Europe apprehensively, and most Americans desired to remain on the sidelines. The U.S. Navy had studied the Battle of the Atlantic, but America's primary naval efforts were directed at keeping the belligerents out of the Western Hemisphere. On September 5, 1939, in an effort to avoid involvement, President Roosevelt had established a Neutrality Patrol. Early in October, the Pan-American republics had announced a neutrality zone extending some 300 miles out into the Atlantic. Both of these measures were designed to keep the war localized. As we have seen, strong anti-war sentiment had resulted in the American Neutrality Act of 1937, which abandoned many of the neutral rights the United States had fought for in World War I and established the "cash-and-carry" principle that belligerents could trade with the United States only if they bought goods with cash and carried them in their own ships. The Act prohibited trade in munitions, but rising pro-Allied sentiment in November 1939 brought about a change to permit munitions to be sold on the same basis. Although by language the cash-and-carry policy was strictly neutral, actually it favored the British, for their blockade allowed no German shipping in the North Atlantic.

The end of the period of "Phony War" awakened the American Congress to the threat from abroad. Swiftly it passed legislation providing for a two-ocean navy and for the first peacetime draft in United States history. Events however were moving faster than legislation. Great Britain's desperate need for destroyers grew more evident every day. On the other hand, considerable doubt existed, in Washington as elsewhere, that Britain could survive the German onslaught. The prospect that the Royal Navy might be turned over to Germany made it necessary for the United States to conserve ships and to build new ones as rapidly as possible. Accordingly, President Roosevelt sought assurance from Churchill that the British fleet would never be surrendered to Germany. Churchill refused to make an unequivocal promise. The most he would say was that *he* would never do it; in the event of a British defeat, his government might be turned out of office and another group might use the fleet as bargaining chips at the surrender table.

Although this assurance was somewhat less than satisfactory, Roosevelt decided to take a calculated risk and transfer 50 American destroyers to the British flag. There was of course a danger that Germany would declare war on the United States, but Hitler had no desire to involve himself with America until the situation in Europe was settled.

Lord Lothian, British Ambassador to the United States, concluded arrangements in late July 1940 for a deal whereby the United States would give 50 "obsolete" destroyers to Great Britain in return for 99-year leases on a series of bases running from Newfoundland to Trinidad. Final agreement was signed in September. By mid-April of the following year, the 50 destroyers had been delivered, as well as ten *Lake*-class Coast Guard cutters well equipped for antisubmarine duty.

The American destroyers alone were not enough to solve Britain's problems of supply. In response to the destroyers-bases deal, Hitler on September 6, 1940 removed the last restrictions on U-boat warfare against British ships and accepted the possibility that some American ships might accidentally be sunk. He even toyed with the idea of seizing some of the Atlantic islands, but Raeder warned him that the German navy was in no position to mount such operations.

In an effort to give further assistance to Great Britain in her struggle against Nazi Germany, President Roosevelt in December 1940 proposed the idea of Lend-Lease. British ships would still have to pick up the goods; only the "cash" part of the "cash-and-carry" policy was to be changed. This proposal, unlike the destroyers-bases deal, required Congressional approval, which took place in March 1941 after extended hearings. Once again Hitler did not declare war.

The change from the Neutrality Act to Lend-Lease was another step in the President's "all aid short of war" policy. In order to see how America's efforts could best be directed to the common cause, Roosevelt sent military representatives to England in August 1940 for "exploratory talks." These discussions led to plans for cooperation in the Atlantic war in the event of American participation. This conference was followed by another in Washington in late January 1941, which resulted in the "ABC-1 Staff Agreement," which spelled out, first, America's "short of war" contribution and, second, the action to be taken by the United States in the event she was forced into the war. Fundamental to this doctrine was the basic concept that in event of war with Japan, Britain and the United States would devote their primary effort to defeating Germany first. Germany was considered the more dangerous, because of her industrial development, the achievements of her scientists, her proximity to Britain and Russia, and her military achievements thus far. This strategic decision was never changed during the war, even though it later became possible to take the offensive in both oceans at the same time. The United States agreed that in the near future the U.S. Navy would assist in escorting convoys in the North Atlantic.

To prepare for these new responsibilities, the Navy Department reorganized the Neutrality Patrol and gave it the more appropriate title of United States Atlantic Fleet. On February 1, 1941 Admiral Ernest J. King hoisted his flag as its commander. By mid-June plans for American escort of transatlantic convoys were made whereby the U.S. Navy was to con-

centrate on the segment from Argentia, Newfoundland to Iceland, where British escorts would take over.[10] The acquisition of terminal bases for these operations posed a difficult problem, one whose solution was suggested early in March when Hitler publicly extended his U-boats' war zone right up to Greenland's three-mile limit. Under strong British persuasion, the government of Iceland on July 7 permitted an American naval force to land the First Marine Brigade at Reykjavik as an advance element in the relief of Britain's garrison already there. Within two months, United States naval patrol squadrons were flying convoy coverage from Reykjavik, while surface escorts refueled at nearby Hvalfjordur.

While the Atlantic Fleet's short-of-war operations provided badly needed protection for Allied and neutral shipping that joined American-escorted convoys, these operations were, for political reasons, initially declared to be independent of the North Atlantic convoy pattern that Britain had developed between Nova Scotia and the British Isles. By July the Anglo-Canadian system had achieved at least minimum antisubmarine surface escort for both slow (6½-knot) and fast (9-knot) convoys all the way across the North Atlantic. Canadian escorts normally shepherded these "Halifax" convoys as far east as a Mid-Ocean Meeting Point (MOMP) at the 35th meridian, where British warships based in Iceland took change, proceeding with little air cover to the EASTOMP, about the 18th meridian, before turning the convoy over to Western Approaches forces for the final run to the North Channel. A heavy attack on Convoy HX-126, which lost nine ships off Cape Farewell, Greenland, during May, underscored the pressing need for continuous air escort for North Atlantic convoys, but two grim years lay ahead before such coverage could be extended to the Greenland Air Gap.

Three events of May 1941 brought about a further bold American step despite dangers of involvement in the war. First was the sinking by a U-boat of the neutral Egyptian ship *Zamzam* carrying about 150 American passengers. The second was the sinking in late May of the South Africa-bound American

[10] American forces operated as far east as the 26th meridian.

freighter *Robin Moor* by a U-boat which left without making any provisions for the safety of the crew. The third was the appearance of the *Bismarck,* which shocked American as well as British public opinion by her sinking of the *Hood.* On May 27, the very day the *Bismarck* was sunk, President Roosevelt declared an Unlimited National Emergency and announced to the country that more vigorous steps would be taken to keep the Germans from American waters.

The United States Navy found itself as ill-prepared for antisubmarine war as the British had been in 1939. The obvious need was for an escort vessel smaller than a destroyer and especially designed for convoy work, a vessel which could be built more rapidly than a destroyer and at lower cost. While in many ways a destroyer is an ideal escort ship, her high speed and versatile offensive power are largely wasted in escort-of-convoy work. The answer was found in the destroyer escort, a smaller version of the destroyer, slower, and especially designed for antisubmarine operations. The British and Canadian navies began building steam versions of these vessels at the rate of about eight a month, and in July 1941 American shipyards started construction of them for the British at the rate of ten a month. American models included both steam and diesel-electric types.

The German invasion of Russia in June 1941 added considerably to the problems of supply, for the Russians were also afforded Lend-Lease aid and had few ships in which to transport the goods. To discuss this problem and others, Churchill and Roosevelt met at Argentia, Newfoundland in August. This meeting enabled the Chiefs of Staff of the two countries to discuss plans for American escort of convoys, and it produced the Atlantic Charter, a statement of the war aims of England and the United States.

For a considerable period American warships on Atlantic patrol had broadcast to the British the location of U-boats detected, although the Americans had refrained from attacking. After Admiral King had described such U-boats as "potentially hostile," there was some doubt as to what action an American naval vessel should take if it should encounter a U-boat in the American zone of responsibility. That question was answered by the affair of the *Greer.* U.S. destroyer *Greer* was about 200 miles southwest of Iceland when on September 4, 1941 she received a signal from a British plane that a U-boat was about ten miles ahead of her. The *Greer* made sound contact with *U-652,* keeping the contact for over three hours, but not attacking. At length, the U-boat fired a torpedo at the *Greer,* which evaded, and then counterattacked with depth charges. Thus the first shots were exchanged in the undeclared war between German and American naval forces. President Roosevelt issued a statement declaring, "From now on, if German or Italian vessels of war enter the waters, the protection of which is necessary for American defense, they do so at their own risk."

By this time Dönitz had an increased and rapidly growing number of U-boats and was responding to Allied end-to-end convoys by strong wolf pack attacks. The *U-Waffe* however had been frustrated by fog and inadequate air reconnaissance, claiming only 377,339 tons of shipping during the third quarter of 1941. In mid-October BdU succeeded in staging a major attack against North Atlantic convoys. On that occasion, American escorts dispatched to the relief of convoy SC-48 learned a number of hard lessons, including the futility of indiscriminate depth charging and the need for aggressive night patrolling. Assaulted some 400 miles south of Iceland, this 50-ship convoy had already lost three vessels when five U.S. destroyers and two British escorts reached the scene. Their close screening tactics failed to prevent the U-boats from sinking six more ships with relative impunity, and shortly thereafter they torpedoed but failed to sink the American destroyer *Kearny* as she was silhouetted by one of the burning freighters. The Atlantic Fleet had scarcely digested the lessons of this encounter when it sustained its first loss, U.S.S. *Reuben James,* on October 31 as she and four other American destroyers were escorting HX-156 some 600 miles west of Ireland.

Notwithstanding these early disasters, British naval officials keenly appreciated the growing United States commitment in the North Atlantic, and by mid-October 1941, following American agreement to extend convoy coverage east to within 400 miles of Ireland, the Commander in Chief, Western Approaches (Cincwa) found it possible to shift three escort groups from the Northwestern Approaches to supplement the escorts of hard-pressed convoys bound for Gibraltar and West African ports. This strategic redeployment proved highly opportune for the Admiralty, now confronted with reports of U-boat activity in several new maritime theaters. Heavy weather weakened Dönitz' North Atlantic campaign during the last quarter of 1941, a period in which U-boats sank only 342,820 tons of Allied shipping, yet these same months saw increasing concentrations of U-boats all the way from North Cape to the African Gold Coast. Long-range 1,100-ton (Type IX-B) U-boats had launched operations off Freetown, West Africa in May 1941, highlighted by the record success of *U-107*, which sank some 87,000 tons of shipping in a single patrol and obliged the Admiralty to divert convoys well west of the Canaries. German plans for a mid-winter blitz off Capetown were temporarily frustrated by British success in sinking two German supply ships, but it was evident that South African antisubmarine defenses would soon be strained to the utmost.

In spite of Allied air bases in Iceland, there still remained the Greenland Air Gap, where U-boats ranged freely in the continued absence of aircraft and where convoys still sailed with inadequate numbers of surface escorts. To assign fleet carriers to the convoys for air protection was out of the question, for the fleet had too few for its other needs. Yet something had to be done not only to afford protection in the Greenland Air Gap but also to protect ships from *Luftwaffe* attacks, which had accounted for 44 ships of 94,551 tons in the months of June, July, and August. Early experiments with catapult-equipped merchant ships flying off expendable aircraft had been obviously makeshift, and the Admiralty had been experimenting with inexpensive, easily constructed carriers especially designed for operating with convoys. At first the British converted merchant ships or naval auxiliaries; later they designed escort carriers from the keel up. The first to see action, H.M.S. *Audacity*, a converted German prize, proved herself in her short career. The *Audacity* accompanied Convoy HG-76 of 32 ships, whose escort of 12 corvettes, sloops, and destroyers, was under command of Captain Frederick John Walker, one of the Royal Navy's ablest antisubmarine tacticians.

The initial U-boat onslaught on December 17 was disrupted by several of the *Audacity*'s planes, which sighted *U-131* some 20 miles ahead, homed in five escorts, and assisted them in sinking the contact keeper. Another stalker, *U-434*, was sunk by destroyers on the 18th, and although *U-574* managed to blow up H.M. destroyer *Stanley* during a midnight melee that also claimed a merchantman, H.M. sloop *Stork* finished off the U-boat by ramming. On December 21, after the *Audacity*'s airmen had destroyed four German Kondor aircraft, several U-boats finally succeeded in pentrating the screen at night, sinking one ship. The *Audacity*, steaming alone, ten miles from the convoy screen, fell a victim to *U-751* some 500 miles west of Cape Finisterre. Counterattacking with disciplined coordination, Walker's escorts flushed *U-567*, sending her veteran crew to the bottom. Concurrently the convoy came within range of United Kingdom-based air escorts. The combined effect broke the back of the pack's running assault and induced BdU to break off this costly attack. Upon reviewing this nine-day operation, Dönitz recognized that the aggressive British escort tactics and particularly the use of the escort carrier, which had cost him five boats, raised serious doubts about the future of wolf pack operations in the eastern Atlantic. Renewed opportunity for successful tonnage warfare now beckoned from the west however, and by the close of 1941 the BdU was eagerly planning his first campaign in North American waters.

Phase IV: The U-Boat Offensive in American Waters

After the Japanese attack on Pearl Harbor on December 7, 1941 had brought the United States officially into the war against the Axis powers, Churchill and his Chiefs of Staff visited Washington to work out with Roosevelt and the American Chiefs of Staff the strategic direction of the war. Churchill recognized that American aid to Britain would necessarily be cut back for the time being as the United

States began to grapple with her new responsibilities in the war. He recognized however the potential power of the New World and was confident of victory.

Top military direction of the war was organized at the Washington meeting. The British representatives—Admiral Sir Dudley Pound, the First Sea Lord; Air Chief Marshal Sir Charles Portal, the Chief of the Air Staff; and Field Marshal Sir John Dill, the former Chief of the Imperial General Staff[11]—sat down with General George C. Marshall, U.S. Army Chief of Staff; General Henry H. Arnold, Chief of Staff of the U.S. Army Air Corps; and the newly appointed Chief of Naval Operations, Admiral Ernest J. King. These men, or their successors on the British side, and with the addition of Admiral William D. Leahy, Chief of Staff to the President, constituted the Combined Chiefs of Staff. On their shoulders rested the burden of the responsibility for global war.

Direction of the American effort in the war fell to the Joint Chiefs of Staff—the four top American military men, Leahy, Marshall, Arnold, and King. To King in particular the earliest burden fell, since it was at sea that America could first challenge the Axis and first was challenged.

To meet these new threats, the United States Navy was extensively reorganized in the early months of the war. King had relieved Admiral Harold R. Stark as Chief of Naval Operations (CNO) in December 1941. Admiral Chester W. Nimitz relieved Admiral Husband E. Kimmel as Commander in Chief of the Pacific Fleet (Cincpac) in the same month. King's old job as Commander in Chief of the Atlantic Fleet (Cinclant) was taken over by Admiral Royal E. Ingersoll. In March 1942, because of confusion as to the division of function of the offices of the Chief of Naval Operations and that of the Commander in Chief, U.S. Fleet (Cominch), the two offices were vested in Admiral King, who became the first and only man ever to hold both titles. Also, because the Naval District organizations were primarily administrative commands, King found it advisable to set up operational commands known as Sea Frontiers which would conduct operations in the waters they included. These commands were the Eastern Sea Frontier in the Atlantic, the Caribbean Sea Frontier, the Gulf Sea Frontier, the Panama Sea Frontier at the approaches to the Canal, and the Western, Northwestern, and Hawaiian Sea Frontiers in the Pacific.

Japan's attack on Pearl Harbor had proved a complete surprise to Germany. Thus, although Germany and Italy declared war on the United States on December 11, over a month elapsed before the U-boats could launch an attack on vulnerable American shipping. To the chagrin of Dönitz, eager for a spectacular blow, the SKL insisted on retaining a large proportion of some 64 Atlantic boats in the Mediterranean and in the heavily patrolled approaches to Gibraltar. As a result, BdU was initially able to allocate only five 1,100-ton U-boats for the impending attack on shipping between Cape Hatteras and the Gulf of the St. Lawrence. This opening thrust, designated Operation PAUKENSCHLAG, was designed to paralyze offshore traffic, thus reducing the flow of oil and other raw materials to the East Coast industrial areas. By a gradual extension into the Gulf of Mexico and the Caribbean, BdU hoped to stretch Allied escort strength to the breaking point. Broadly speaking, Dönitz calculated that seaborne trade in the Western Atlantic, weakly protected by inexperienced forces, might yet provide a key to tonnage victory. According to BdU estimates at this time, a sustained monthly merchant ship attrition of 700,000 tons was necessary to achieve this objective. Even if Britain could not be completely strangled, she might yet be driven to accept a negotiated peace.

The U-boat assault in North American waters temporarily stunned both United States and Canadian defense forces. Hard-hitting Group *Paukenschlag* of five boats had been closely followed across the Atlantic by six 740-ton boats which unleashed a concurrent attack in the waters off Newfoundland. Group *Paukenschlag* swiftly ambushed a score of independents between Hatteras and Cape Breton Island. From the outset, these U-boats found particularly happy hunting off the Carolina Capes, discovering many merchantmen un-

[11] The Chief of the Imperial General Staff, General Sir Alan Brooke, had assumed his duties only a month before, and was left behind under the Deputy Prime Minister in charge of British military operations.

armed and some still burning their running lights. In the absence of convoys *Rudeltaktik* was unnecessary. Operating individually, the Germans lay submerged offshore until dusk, then moved in with decks awash and dispatched their victims with gunfire or torpedoes. Worldwide merchant tonnage losses were greatly inflated by this mounting slaughter. From December's toll of 124,070 tons lost to U-boats, the totals climbed in January to 327,357 tons, 467,451 tons in February, and 537,980 tons in March. During March, 28 vessels aggregating 159,340 tons were sunk in the Eastern Sea Frontier alone, over half of these ships being tankers.

Against this onslaught, American shipping defense measures proved inadequate, notwithstanding the remarkable fact that Dönitz never had more than a dozen boats in the Western Atlantic. Because of demands from the Pacific and a continuing commitment of other available destroyers to North Atlantic convoys, Commander Eastern Sea Frontier, Vice Admiral Adolphus Andrews, possessed negligible surface forces and only nine patrol aircraft at the close of 1941. Although 170 army and navy aircraft were committed to offshore patrol by late March 1942,[12] Andrews regarded his hundred-odd destroyers, Coast Guard cutters, converted yachts, and armed trawlers as insufficient for coastal convoys. Convinced that a "convoy without adequate protection is worse than none," a dictum contrary to British wartime experience, the Eastern Sea Frontier resorted to a series of emergency measures, including hunter groups, "offensive" patrols, and Q-ships. The slight value of these measures can be seen not only in the destruction of 23 ships in the Eastern Sea Frontier during April, but also in the fact that not a single U-boat had been sunk in this area during the first three months of the East Coast blitz. It is small wonder that the U-boat crews referred to this period as the "Second Happy Time."

Drastic measures were required to avert a shipping catastrophe, for in March total Allied merchant ship losses had soared to over 800,000 tons for the first time in World War II. In February the British had given the United States 24 trawlers and ten corvettes, all provided with the latest asdic equipment. The first step toward providing coastal convoys was taken by the establishment of "Bucket Brigades," small convoys that ran escorted during daylight hours and put into protected anchorages at night. Midway in April the Admiralty decreased the frequency of its convoy sailings from Halifax from five to seven days, enlarging the convoys and releasing two desperately needed escort groups for service in American waters.[13] It took another month to establish a convoy system on the East Coast of the United States. "Escort is not just one way of handling the submarine menace," wrote Admiral King, "it is the only way that gives any promise of success. The so-called hunting and patrol operations have time and again proved futile." That King was right can be seen from the results. U-boats had sunk 87 ships of 514,366 tons during their first four months off the East Coast, yet Dönitz promptly began shifting his boats southward on the appearance of convoys, making no effort to contest them by wolf pack tactics. The Germans found profitable hunting in the Gulf of Mexico and Caribbean where no convoy system existed, and sank 41 vessels of 219,867 tons during May, nearly half being tankers torpedoed off the Passes of the Mississippi. This onslaught was checked by the establishment of an Interlocking Convoy System which enabled ships to transfer at sea from one convoy to another. This system required extremely careful planning of convoy movements and rendezvous, but it offered the necessary flexibility for the complicated pattern of Caribbean and Gulf shipping.

Moving once again in search of unprotected ships, U-boats fell upon independent traffic off Trinidad, Rio de Janeiro, and Capetown,

[13] Increasing the size of convoys cut the ratio of escorts to the ships protected, for the number of ships which can be protected depends on the *area* of the circle enclosing them, while the number of escorts depends on the *circumference* of a larger concentric circle. Thus a 45-ship convoy might be covered by seven escorts; the same degree of protection could be afforded a 90-ship convoy with only nine escorts. As this fact became officially recognized in March 1943, the size of convoys increased, so that, later in the war, convoys of well over a hundred ships were not uncommon.

[12] After extended discussions with Marshall, King succeeded in mid-1942 in having land-based planes assigned to antisubmarine missions transferred to navy control.

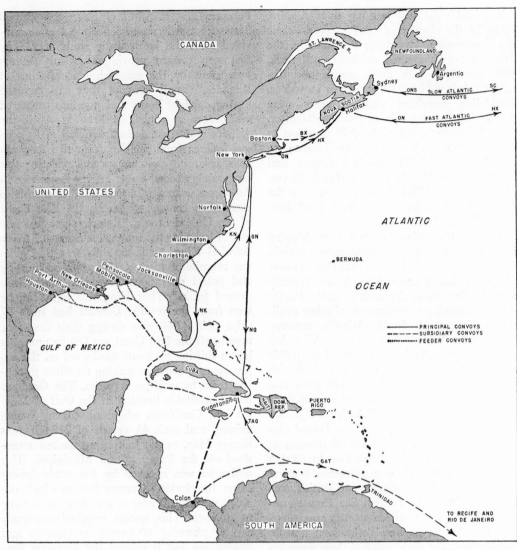

THE WESTERN ATLANTIC, SHOWING THE INTERLOCKING CONVOY SYSTEM AS DEVELOPED IN 1942

exploiting the logistic versatility of a handful of new 1,700-ton supply U-boats or "milch cows." Thus supported, U-boat commanders managed to double the length of their patrols off the Panama Canal and along the Guianas coast, with devastating results. In the Western Atlantic, U-boats claimed 26 merchant ships in May and averaged over 20 victims in the four ensuing months, notwithstanding the extension of convoys to Port of Spain in July. Round-the-clock air cover, as distinct from air escort, failed to deter these U-boats because they evaded radar detection by conforming to

convoy course and speed during their furtive assaults. Allied escort forces succeeded in destroying three U-boats in these waters in the fall of 1942, yet the Germans continued to exploit the Trinidad approaches with profit to the end of the year since many independent ships continued to use these waters.

Caribbean operations accounted for but a fraction of the 1,505,888 tons of Allied shipping lost to U-boats in the third quarter of 1942. Midway in August ten U-boats moved into Brazilian waters for a blitz against coastal and transatlantic shipping. Five Brazilian freighters were torpedoed by *U-507* off Bahia, provoking Brazil to declare war on Germany and emphasizing the urgency of extending the coastal convoy system southeast of Trinidad. Escort shortages delayed creation of this final link, but Vice Admiral Jonas H. Ingram, commanding the U.S. South Atlantic Fleet, scraped together sufficient forces to frustrate German hopes of reaping yet another windfall of shipping. Although dissatisfied with the meager results of this attack, Dönitz dispatched a second wave of U-boats to the Cape San Roque area during November and December. His U-boats claimed over 20 ships before the establishment of regular convoy between Trinidad and Bahia, and the destruction of *U-164* and *U-507* by Catalinas broke the back of this distant offensive.

Phase V: Return to the Mid-Atlantic

Following the adoption of convoys with air as well as surface escort in American waters, Dönitz decided to shift the burden of his attack back to the mid-Atlantic, where the U-boats would be free to attack convoys without air escort. Yet immediately he was called upon to divert a significant portion of his strength to attacking Allied convoys on the "Murmansk Run" to North Russia.

British convoys to North Russia, begun in August 1941, had suffered negligible losses to U-boat and air attack during the first three months of 1942, but with a northward shift of German surface strength, the situation changed rapidly. The new battleship *Tirpitz*, sister of the *Bismarck*, now in service, moved to Norwegian bases, as did the *Scheer*, *Lützow*, and *Hipper*. The next few convoys met increasingly severe air and U-boat attack. At this time, because of the Madagascar operation,[14] American units reinforced the Home Fleet at Scapa Flow and were available for operations to protect the convoys bound for North Russia.

These convoys both Roosevelt and Churchill held to be political necessities for keeping Russia in the war. Yet increasingly severe attacks on ships making this passage led professional opinion to consider these convoys little better than suicide. Convoy PQ-16 in May lost seven out of 34 ships, and casualties to the accompanying warships had been heavy. The SKL planned an all-out attempt, Operation RÖSSELSPRUNG, to annihilate the next convoy to Russia, employing the *Luftwaffe,* U-boats, and heavy and light surface forces.

Fully aware of the grave risks, the Admiralty provided PQ-17 with 21 escorts and a covering force of three destroyers and four cruisers, while dispatching a distant support force of two battleships, H.M.S. *Duke of York* and U.S.S. *Washington,* three cruisers, 13 destroyers, and H.M. aircraft carrier *Victorious.* The convoy left Hvalfjordur, Iceland on June 27, 1942 with 33 merchant ships, three rescue vessels, and a fleet oiler. Routed well north of Bear Island, where the midnight sun provided continuous daylight for air attack, the convoy was subjected to three days of intensive onslaught reaching a climax on July 4. Throughout, the convoy maintained taut discipline, thereby minimizing casualties and destroying several German planes. After thwarting these attacks with the loss of only four ships, one a cripple that eventually reached port, the convoy's confidence was high. Then came a stunning series of messages from the Admiralty:

9:11 P.M. Most Immediate. Cruiser Force withdraw to westward at high speed.
9:23 P.M. Immediate. Owing to threat of surface ships, convoy is to disperse and proceed to Russian ports.
9:36 P.M. Most Immediate. Convoy is to scatter.

Behind this extraordinary series of messages lay the Admiralty's conviction that the *Tirpitz* would be able to engage the convoy and the cruiser force. Reconnaissance planes had lost contact with her, but the British knew that she might be in position to intercept any time after 0200 July 5. The support force of battleships and the *Victorious* was too far west to interfere, for it was protecting westbound QP-13, which was beyond Jan Mayen and thus out of serious danger. The First Sea Lord had based his decision on negative intelligence and interfered with operations 1,500 miles away where he could not know the situation. In view of the urgent tone of the Admiralty messages, Rear Admiral L. H. K. Hamilton, command-

[14] See above, pp. 537-9.

ing the cruiser force, expected to see the *Tirpitz* at any moment and felt he had no alternative but to comply. The destroyers with the escort also detached themselves to support the cruisers in their anticipated desperate battle with the *Tirpitz*.

Ironically, though the *Tirpitz, Scheer,* and *Hipper* did begin to carry out Operation RÖSSELSPRUNG, as a result of confused aerial reconnaissance and of Hitler's no-risk policy, they returned to port after ten hours at sea. The British Admiralty had no way of knowing that the Germans would not attack, but they did know from past experience that German surface ships were reluctant to engage strongly escorted convoys and consistently refused action with escorts of even cruiser strength.

As a result of the order to scatter, PQ-17 lost 21 more ships. Of the 13 that reached port, 11 had joined rump convoys. Two ships were lost from the rump convoys, but 19 independents were sunk. Thus, the subsequent fate of PQ-17 indicates that even under the most difficult circumstances, convoy integrity provides the greatest chance of survival of merchant ships.

Significant consequences flowed from this operation, most notably the British decision to suspend convoy sailings to North Russia until the fall of 1942. American disappointment over the futile employment of the *Washington* and her consorts led to Admiral King's rapid transfer of these ships to the Pacific. Henceforth King viewed combined U.S.-British naval operations with disfavor. German forces in Norway had meanwhile been thoroughly roused by the success of RÖSSELSPRUNG, making a resumption of Allied convoys to North Russia additionally perilous.

When powerfully protected PQ-18 of 40 merchant ships sailed in September, it included in its escort the British escort carrier *Avenger,* whose planes, together with the convoy's antiaircraft guns, destroyed some 40 German planes. The surface escort sank three U-boats. Although the convoy lost 13 ships, only three were sunk by U-boats. Instead of scattering, the convoy remained together, vindicating once again the wisdom of convoy integrity. For the next few months, because of the impending landings in North Africa, the British were unable to send convoys to Russia. By means of

Operation TRICKLE, the dispatch of small "flights" of unescorted merchant ships in company, they managed to "pray through" only five of the 13 ships they sent, losing over 60 per cent.

In the south too U-boats became active. In mid-October, Group *Eisbaer* passed through the Atlantic narrows, and after waylaying isolated shipping, including the ill-fated British transport *Laconia,*[15] prepared to unleash an offensive off Capetown. One of these raiders, *U-179,* was promptly sunk, but the remaining boats proceeded to devastate shipping east of the Cape, claiming in October and November 31 ships off Capetown and in Mozambique Channel before beginning the long return passage.

Dönitz recognized that a decisive victory could be obtained only in the mid-Atlantic. U-boat production had by July 1942 reached the rate of 30 boats a month, and this increase in strength enabled him to accept increased risks in making attacks on convoys. The risks were constantly mounting, for most Allied air and surface escorts were now equipped with radar. In addition the availability of larger numbers of escorts permitted Admiral Sir Max Horton, Commander in Chief Western Approaches, to form Antisubmarine Support Groups of six to eight destroyers, frigates, and corvettes. These Support Groups, manned by highly experienced personnel, had no regular escort duties, but were available to come to the aid of convoys undergoing heavy U-boat attack.

Keenly conscious of the added danger of air escorts, Dönitz concentrated his attack in

[15] The *Laconia* was sunk on September 12 northeast of Ascension Island by *U-156,* which discovered that the transport carried 1,800 Italian prisoners of war as well as 811 British servicemen. On orders from BdU, other *Eisbaer* boats moved to the rescue, while *U-156* broadcast a plain language appeal for assistance. The U-boats had several hundred survivors under tow on the afternoon of the 16th when an American B-24, flying from Ascension, circled and finally attacked *U-156,* even though she displayed a Red Cross flag on her bow. On receiving a report on these proceedings, Dönitz forbade all attempts to rescue merchant ship survivors. During the Nuremberg Trial, Allied prosecutors attempted to prove that this "*Laconia* order" had actually constituted a veiled attempt to encourage deliberate slaughter of survivors. A full examination of relevant facts, including known cases of atrocities, destroyed this contention.

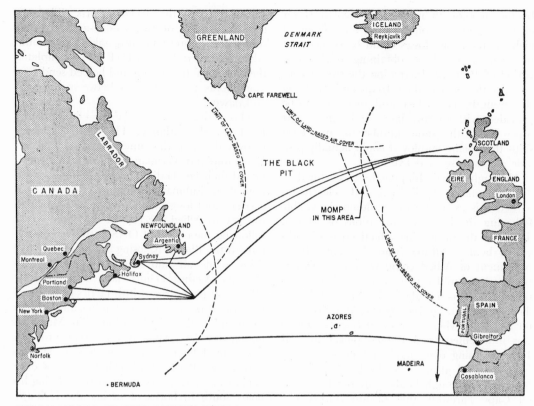

TYPICAL NORTH ATLANTIC CONVOY SYSTEM, 1942

the Black Pit area. He stationed picket lines on both sides so that convoys moving in either direction could be attacked throughout its entire width while the U-boats enjoyed virtual immunity from air attack. The loss figures mounted, reaching a peak of 807,754 G.R.T. in November 1942, at which time Dönitz was forced to weaken the attack in a belated effort to disrupt the North African landings. Nonetheless, U-boats continued their efforts in the Black Pit area, rising to a crescendo in March 1943.

By Christmas 1942 the Allies recognized that they must devise some methods of countering the flexibility of strategic deployment enjoyed by the highly centralized U-boat command. Hence when the Allied heads of state met with the Combined Chiefs of Staff at Casablanca in January 1942, they agreed that "the defeat of the U-boat must remain a first charge on the resources of the United Nations" and ordered a staff conference to reorganize Atlantic convoy control. The consequent Washington Convoy Conference rejected politically explosive proposals for a unified Allied antisubmarine command and on March 1 adopted Admiral King's formula whereby the British and Canadians retained control of North Atlantic convoys, while the United States assumed responsibility for Central Atlantic convoys (to the Mediterranean and to the south from ports south of Halifax) as well as for the Interlocking Convoy System.

In Britain, Admiralty Operations Research scientists in analytical studies of the convoy battles of 1941–42 discovered that the number of ships sunk from convoys was completely independent of convoy size. Instead sinkings depended only on numbers of attacking U-boats and, when no air escort was present, on the number of surface escorts. Thus if the average size of convoys could be increased from 32 to 54 ships, the number of escorts would increase from six to nine, while convoy losses would be reduced 56 per cent by the enlargement of the convoy and 25 per cent by the increase in number of escorts. If air escort was present only during an average of eight hours a day, losses could be reduced 64 per cent from those obtaining during the period of 1941–42. Increasing the size of convoys would reduce their frequency, enabling the strengthened surface and air escorts to be provided without any increase in the escort forces. Also the same number of merchant ships then being employed could actually provide an increase in deliveries.[16]

Although Allied shipping losses declined to 344,680 tons in April 1943, BdU clearly regarded this as a temporary slump, inevitably following the intensive operations of March. To offset the decreasing effectiveness of individual boats resulting from the marked improvement of Allied countermeasures, Dönitz prepared to build a new concentration of unprecedented magnitude in the North Atlantic. The showdown in the North Atlantic came on April 28, when westbound convoy ONS-5 was intercepted by a U-boat picket line off Iceland, losing one merchantman and escaping a general attack only by heading into a fog bank. Although badly scattered by a gale off Cape Farewell, this 42-ship convoy was brilliantly rounded up by its escort commander, Commander Philip W. Gretton RN, and headed south into what proved to be a concentration of 51 U-boats. Newfoundland-based Catalina aircraft claimed *U-630* on May 4, but by nightfall U-boat Group *Fink* was moving in from all quarters, catching the freighters sharply etched against the northern lights. Eleven U-boats nearly swamped ONS-5's escort and sent seven ships to the bottom before dawn, adding four more victims the next morning from among the stragglers. The corvette *Pink* succeeded in depth charging *U-192* fatally, but by dusk, as some 15 U-boats moved in, the battered convoy faced annihilation. Then the tactical situation changed completely. Nosing into another fog bank late on the evening of May 5, ONS-5 sustained no fewer than 25 separate attacks without losing a single ship. Lacking radar, Dönitz' boats were repeatedly

driven off by the seven escorts. The aggressive attacks of two freshly-arrived Antisubmarine Support Groups, taking maximum advantage of radar and H/F D/F, completed the Germans' frustration and helped send four more boats to the bottom between midnight and dawn.

This action proved to be the climax of the Battle of the Atlantic. The *U-Waffe* never recovered from this unexpected reverse off Newfoundland. German wolf packs had decimated their last Halifax convoy. The intervention of Antisubmarine Support Groups, escort carriers, and long-range aircraft had provided the key to Allied success. In the three weeks following the ordeal of ONS-5, twelve convoys crossed the Black Pit, losing a total of only five ships, while air and surface escorts sank 13 U-boats. Against Dönitz' large and relatively blind wolf packs, the British tactics of bait and kill now came to fruition, forcing the U-boats to abandon the North Atlantic in May and search for less dangerous hunting grounds. Confronted by the enormous loss of 41 submarines in "Black May," Dönitz resorted once again to tonnage warfare strategy, ordering his boats south in hopes of saving the *U-Waffe* from annihilation until technological developments permitted a return to the North Atlantic. This decision permitted relatively unimpeded passage of Allied convoys in the twelve months before the invasion of Normandy. Thus, under combined pressure of vastly improved Allied antisubmarine measures and a great increase in American shipbuilding, the strategy of tonnage warfare collapsed. In July monthly Allied ship production at last exceeded world-wide shipping losses from Axis action, and by the end of the year the Atlantic Allies achieved an annual production rate of 14.4 million tons of merchant shipping, exceeding German estimates by 40 per cent.

The devastating antisubmarine offensive undertaken by Anglo-American forces late in the spring of 1943 was the product not simply of mounting warship and aircraft production but also of extensive reorganization, systematic indoctrination of personnel, and decisive advances in the science of undersea warfare. The creation of the U.S. Tenth Fleet, invested with broad supervisory control of American anti-

[16] The authors are obliged to Commander F. Barley RN and Lieutenant Commander D. W. Waters RN, F.R.H.S., of the Historical Section of the Admiralty, for these figures.

submarine development, proved of fundamental importance in stimulating effective training, supplying scientific methods to the perfection of weapons and tactics, and coordinating operational intelligence. Established on May 1, under the personal command of Admiral King,[17] this secret administrative organization provided comprehensive support for operations of the Atlantic Fleet, whose newly-activated Hunter-Killer Groups of escort carriers and destroyers were soon to distinguish themselves in the Central Atlantic.

Phase VI: The Central Atlantic and Biscay Offensives

Dönitz' decision late in May 1943 to shift pack operations southwest of the Azores presented Commander U.S. Atlantic Fleet, Admiral Ingersoll, with a long-awaited opportunity to employ his new Hunter-Killer Groups. For rapidity of tactical innovation, operations during the next three months by groups centered on escort carriers *Bogue, Card, Core,* and *Santee* in support of Central Atlantic convoys are virtually unsurpassed in naval history. Airmen from the *Bogue,* pioneering Wildcat-Avenger team tactics, located Group *Trutz* on June 3 while escorting Convoy GUS-7A, sinking *U-217* and milch cow *U-118* and damaging several other boats. Subsequent efforts by this 17-boat pack to locate Central Atlantic convoys were frustrated south of the Azores in mid-July by the widely-roving *Core* and *Santee* groups, which destroyed four more boats, including two supply submarines, while introducing "Fido," the U.S. Navy's new antisubmarine homing torpedo.

Driven to desperation by these aerial tactics, remaining German submariners fought back on the surface, enabling the *Bogue, Santee,* and *Core* groups in mid-summer to claim five more victims. Meanwhile the *Card*'s air group, commanded by Captain Arnold J. Isbell, had sent four more submarines, includ-

[17] Because of his heavy responsibilities as Cominch and CNO, King relied on Rear Admiral Francis S. Low, Chief of Staff, Tenth Fleet, for close supervision of antisubmarine operations in the Atlantic.

ing two milch cows, to the bottom. In less than three months, Ingersoll's Hunter-Killer Groups had sunk 15 U-boats, eight operating as supply boats, with the loss of only three aircraft. This attrition of U-tankers, sharply contrasting with the sinking of one convoyed merchantman, effectively disrupted German efforts to concentrate on Central Atlantic convoys and greatly reduced the impact of U-boat operations in the Caribbean and in the South Atlantic and Indian Oceans.

Severe as were the *U-Waffe*'s losses in mid-Atlantic, they were of less concern to BdU than the concurrent slaughter of U-boats in the Bay of Biscay, where since the spring of 1942 the R.A.F. Coastal Command had been attempting a sustained offensive. Employing radar, the British aircraft had enjoyed a limited success in detecting U-boats in this transit area. This advantage disappeared when Dönitz began fitting his U-boats with a radar receiver called *Metox,* which could pick up the radar search signal at a far greater range than the reflected signal could be detected by the search receiver. Early in 1943 however planes suddenly resumed attacking surfaced U-boats while *Metox* was giving no indications. BdU interpreted this phenomenon to mean that *Metox* was emitting a signal detectable on passive radar and accordingly ordered commanders to discontinue its use. Actually the British had developed a new ultra-high-frequency radar of ten centimeter wavelength, which *Metox* could not detect. The attacks continued, aided by the aircraft Leigh Light, an 80-million candlepower attack searchlight, employed in conjunction with radar in sudden blinding night attacks from the air. Throughout March and April many of these attacks were limited in success because of the U-boats' regular practice of crash diving when attacked. While German scientists worked desperately and fruitlessly to improve *Metox,* Dönitz added antiaircraft armament to his U-boats and, reversing his previous instructions, ordered all Biscay transients to proceed submerged at night and surface to charge batteries only in daylight. Most significantly of all, BdU advised all commanders to fight back on the surface whenever their aerial attackers were too close to permit crash diving.

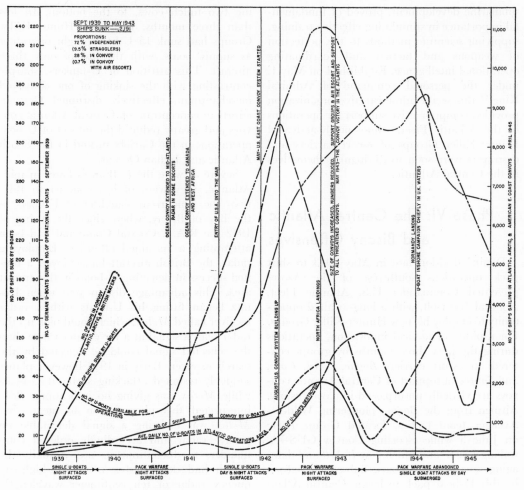

THE EFFECT OF THE CONVOY SYSTEM

Although British bombers destroyed six submarines in the Bay of Biscay during the first three weeks of July, the "Big Bay Slaughter" did not get underway until the 28th. In the next week, American and British aircraft and the British Second Support Group sank nine U-boats. Under such relentless pressure BdU not only discontinued its group transit policy but early in August suspended all departures from Biscay bases. Thus the Bay offensive culminated in a virtual blockade of Dönitz' West France flotillas. Later BdU managed to resume sailings, routing its U-boats along the northern coast of Spain, where they enjoyed virtual immunity from radar detection. Altogether during the campaign 28 U-boats were sunk in attempting passage of the Bay of Biscay.

Phase VII: The Final Struggle for the North Atlantic

After some three months of comparatively fruitless exploitation of tonnage warfare, Dönitz on September 19, 1943 gave orders to strike once again at the main Allied North Atlantic convoy routes. He was now prepared to employ a new weapon, the *Zaunkönig,* or acoustic torpedo, which would "home" on a ship's screws. Designed to be employed against the escorts, it was supposed to blast a hole in the screen to permit attacks on the merchant ships with conventional torpedoes. In September Group *Leuthen* struck at westbound convoys ON-202 and ONS-18, sinking three escorts, damaging one, and sending six merchant ships to the bottom. To counter the *Zaunkönig,* British and American warships began using a noisemaking countermeasure called "Foxer," which when trailed astern drew the acoustic torpedoes harmlessly into it.

Ultimately however the German offensive in the North Atlantic was smothered by systematic day-and-night close air escort of all threatened convoys—in the old Black Pit as well as elsewhere. In this escort work land-based planes coordinated with aircraft flying from escort carriers, which operated either with the convoys or with British Antisubmarine Surface Support Groups. The Surface Support Groups were now also able to join the land-based planes in providing night as well as day escort of convoys. These Allied countermeasures proved so effective that Dönitz withdrew his boats from the Black Pit and in October attempted a concentration south of Iceland, only to lose three U-boats to land-based aircraft. Although Dönitz recognized the extreme peril of attacking convoys in the North Atlantic, he persisted in doing so until February 1944, enduring heavy losses while inflicting only slight damage to Allied shipping. The combination of close surface escort, land-based air escort, and Antisubmarine Support Groups with escort carriers for local air support had made the North Atlantic convoys virtually immune to attack.

In mid-October the Portuguese granted the British permission to operate Coastal Command aircraft from the Azores. This acquisition of a mid-Atlantic base, combined with night air escort of threatened convoys, proved the final blow to Dönitz' hopes of organizing a renewed campaign against convoys in the North and Central Atlantic. Renewed Allied successes in the Bay of Biscay, regular air patrols from the Azores, and the relentless probing of British and American Hunter-Killer Groups in the Outer Bay effectively broke the back of this last wolf pack effort. Pending the activation of the high-speed Type XXI U-boat, whose production was beginning to suffer under Allied bombing raids, Dönitz candidly stated, "In the present phase of the campaign it is not victory but the survival of boats and their crews that must take priority."

Phase VIII: The Final Campaign

For several significant reasons, including the Anglo-American invasion of France, U-boat losses, which had totaled 237 during 1943, increased during the following year, while the production of the much-vaunted hydrogen-peroxide Walther U-boat continued to be delayed. Dönitz, now commander in chief of the German navy, was obliged to expend his *U-Waffe* in operations far from the vital North Atlantic.

The Royal Navy's escort carrier groups came fully into their own with the Murmansk convoys, which became the sole focus of wolf pack activity during 1944. The Admiralty had resumed North Russian convoys again late in 1943.[18] The northbound convoy JW-58 provided an example of an antisubmarine task force convoy, being escorted by two escort carriers, two antiaircraft cruisers, and a close screen of nine warships, and enjoying the close cover of two Antisubmarine Support Groups. Captain F. J. Walker RN, who had commanded the *Audacity* group in December 1942, was in command of the escort. His group claimed the first shadower, *U-961,* on March 29, after which aircraft from H.M.S. *Tracker* and *Activity* teamed up with the close escort to dispose of three more boats, while the convoy proceeded without loss to Murmansk. Operating continuously within sight of the convoy, British escort carriers imposed an intolerable rate of exchange on the U-boats. Altogether British escort carriers destroyed 13 U-boats in northern waters during 1944, a period in which Murmansk convoys suffered the loss of only six ships. Increasingly heavy *Luftwaffe* attacks on subsequent convoys proved futile. Thus ended the grimly dramatic history of the North Russian convoys.

During 1944 American Hunter-Killer Groups, assigned the task of affording distant protection to North Africa- and Mediterranean-bound convoys, fulfilled their purpose chiefly by attacking U-boats refueling near the Cape

---

[18] The British had resumed convoys to Murmansk in mid-December 1942 and continued operations with relative success until the following March, when they again suspended sailings in order to transfer escorts to the North Atlantic, currently at the peak of its U-boat crisis.

Verde Islands en route to major offensives off Capetown and in the Indian Ocean. Late in February *U-709* blundered into a Hunter-Killer Group built around the escort carrier *Block Island* and was promptly finished off by two destroyer escorts, the *Bronstein* and *Thomas*. Shortly after midnight on the 29th the *Bronstein*'s captain, Lieutenant Sheldon H. Kinney, detected *U-603* moving toward the *Block Island,* drove the German down, and shortly thereafter applied the *coup de grâce*. After a brief respite the group headed southwest toward an apparent concentration of U-boats off the Cape Verdes, being rewarded on March 17 when the *Corry* and *Bronstein,* following up a series of aerial attacks, sent the *U-801* to the bottom. Two days later the *Block Island*'s aircraft spotted and destroyed *U-1059,* thus concluding a highly successful cruise for this new Hunter-Killer Group.

Disturbed by growing evidence of Hunter-Killer activity, Dönitz moved his main fueling rendezvous some 700 miles farther west in mid-April, only to discover that these waters too were infested with carrier aircraft. The impossibility of continuing U-tanker operations was grimly revealed to Dönitz by the report of *U-66,* which radioed on May 5, "Mid-Atlantic worse than Bay of Biscay." Scarcely had the German completed this transmission when he was located by a plane from the *Block Island*. Lacking bombs or depth charges, the pilot homed in the destroyer escort *Buckley,* which at 0320, May 6 succeeded in closing the range to 2,100 yards before scoring a hit forward of the submarine's conning tower. During the ensuing quarter-hour engagement, the *Buckley* evaded a torpedo and then rammed the German directly across her foredeck. As the Germans hastily abandoned ship, several boarded the *Buckley* to escape drowning. The Americans, misinterpreting their intention, at first beat them off with everything from machine guns to coffee cups. Later, in a search that lasted till after sunrise, the *Buckley* rescued 36 German survivors.

German transients henceforth exercised extreme caution in surfacing off the Cape Verdes, keeping a sharp lookout for escort carriers. Late in May, *U-549* escaped several attacks by aircraft from the *Block Island* and, penetrating the screen, on the night of the 29th, sent two torpedoes into her. Amid the confusion of rescue operations and depth charge barrages, the U-boat succeeded in blowing the stern off the destroyer escort *Barr* with a *Zaunkönig,* only to be destroyed by three patterns of hedgehogs, ahead-thrown antisubmarine weapons. The *Block Island*'s loss was avenged early in June when a group built around escort carrier *Guadalcanal,* Captain Daniel V. Gallery, achieved one of the most spectacular successes in the entire Atlantic struggle. On June 4, 1944 the destroyer escort *Chatelain* blasted *U-505* to the surface with assistance from the carrier's Avengers. As the Germans hurriedly abandoned ship, a boarding party from the destroyer escort *Pillsbury* plunged down the conning tower hatch, disconnected the scuttling charges, and checked the flooding. Skillfully brought in under tow by the *Guadalcanal,* the *U-505* proved an exceptionally valuable capture, for with her code books and cipher machine, naval authorities were henceforth able to decipher operational orders from BdU.[19]

The Indian Ocean venture, though providing the *U-Waffe* with its single area of feasible operations during 1944, tended, like patrols in the Mediterranean, to be a one-way proposition. Of the some 45 U-boats dispatched to those waters, 34 were sunk, many en route.

Belated German adoption of *schnorkel,* an air intake and exhaust trunk that permits a submarine to recharge batteries without fully surfacing, provided Germany with a slender hope of preserving the remnants of its *U-Waffe* long enough for the Walther boat to become operational. During the summer and fall of 1944, following the failure of his sizable anti-invasion flotilla to disrupt the Normandy landings, Dönitz dispatched several schnorkel boats to the waters east of the Grand Banks with

[19] *U-505* was by no means the only submarine captured during the war. The Germans took two British boats; the British seized three Italian and two German submarines. *U-570* surrendered to Coastal Command aircraft and was later commissioned in the Royal Navy. In capturing *U-110* on May 9, 1941, the British avenged the *Athenia,* for the *U-110*'s commanding officer, Kapitänleutnant Fritz-Julius Lemp, who did not survive, had commanded the boat that sank the liner. See S. W. Roskill, *The Secret Capture* (London, 1959).

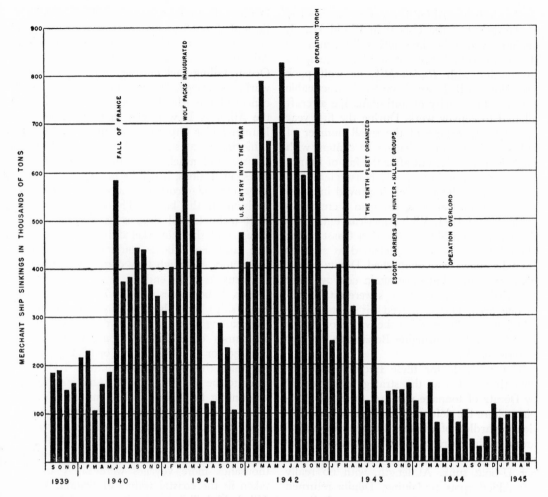

Chart labels (vertical axis): MERCHANT SHIP SINKINGS IN THOUSANDS OF TONS

Annotations on chart: FALL OF FRANCE · WOLF PACKS INAUGURATED · U.S. ENTRY INTO THE WAR · OPERATION TORCH · THE TENTH FLEET ORGANIZED · ESCORT CARRIERS AND HUNTER - KILLER GROUPS · OPERATION OVERLORD

Horizontal axis: S O N D (1939) | J F M A M J J A S O N D (1940) | J F M A M J J A S O N D (1941) | J F M A M J J A S O N D (1942) | J F M A M J J A S O N D (1943) | J F M A M J J A S O N D (1944) | J F M A M (1945)

BATTLE OF THE ATLANTIC: MERCHANT VESSEL LOSSES TO U-BOATS

orders to operate as weather reporters. Hunter-Killer operations against these furtive boats proved relatively unrewarding, partly because the boats made no serious attempt to molest North Atlantic convoys. Amazingly enough, German submariners had sunk only half a dozen merchant ships en route from North America to the British Isles during the twelve months before Operation OVERLORD, and their performance during the last year of the war was no more impressive. Nevertheless they managed to achieve minor success in British and American coastal waters, often lying on the bottom for hours to evade sonar detection and then cautiously launching torpedoes at their victims by means of sound bearings. These tactics were briefly effective in the Irish Sea

early in 1945, but for the most part schnorkel boats were as ineffective offensively as they were difficult to locate. Allied shipping losses to submarine action in the Atlantic rose from a monthly average of 30,580 tons in 1944 to some 63,270 tons during the first four months of 1945, but the pattern revealed by these sinkings indicated inshore nuisance activity rather than a threat to transatlantic convoys.

Summary

Entering the war with only 56 U-boats, the German *U-Waffe*, as in World War I, brought Britain to the brink of defeat before counter-measures were adopted similar in principle to those used in World War I. These turned the battle in the Allies' favor. Convoy, the key to the defeat of the U-boat in World War I, again proved to be the solution. This measure the Germans had foreseen and had attempted to counter with *Rudeltaktik,* or wolf pack operations, which were rendered practicable only by the paucity of antisubmarine aircraft allotted to convoy work. During the first year of the war, because of the small number of U-boats, the Germans had to be content with single boat attacks, but after the fall of France and the establishment of Norwegian and French bases, the situation improved immeasurably for the Germans, rising to a crescendo in the fall of 1941. With American entry into the war came a blitz on the East Coast of the United States, promptly defeated as soon as coastal convoys were established. Dönitz moved his boats south, but once again convoys were extended. Each time convoys were established in one area, Dönitz moved his boats to another, eventually reaching the waters off South America, thereby bringing Brazil into the war against the Axis.

The rationale for these frequent shifts in operating area was the strategy propounded by Dönitz of tonnage warfare, to attack shipping where the defenses promised little retaliation, regardless of whether shipping in critical areas might thereby be left uncontested, his measure of effectiveness being tonnage sunk per U-boat sunk. At length, with no really soft Allied spots remaining, Dönitz returned his boats to the North Atlantic to challenge convoys by means of overwhelmingly strong wolf packs. This effort was defeated by radar, H/F D/F, the escort carrier, British Antisubmarine Support Groups, and the extension of land-based air escorts. The attack on ONS-5 in late April and early May 1943 proved the decisive battle of the war, for shortly thereafter

Dönitz called off his attack on the mid-Atlantic and dispatched his boats to widely divergent areas—the Barents Sea, the Central Atlantic, the Capetown region, and the Indian Ocean, falling back once again on his tonnage warfare strategy. By this move he virtually conceded the Allied victory in the Battle of the Atlantic. It was then that the American Hunter-Killer Groups came into prominence, achieving great success in sinking U-boats at the scene of milch cow refueling rendezvous. These operations, it will be noted, came about after convoy escort had already forced the decision in the battle. The development of such technological devices as *Metox, Zaunkönig,* and the schnorkel did not reverse the tide, and the U-boats could no longer hope for victory, although they doggedly continued the struggle to the end.

Axis U-boats destroyed 2,775 Allied merchant ships, but only some 28 per cent of these were sailing in convoy. Of over-all losses from all causes of 23,351,000 tons, U-boats accounted for 14,573,000 tons, or 62.4 per cent. All told, the Germans committed 1,175 U-boats to the war and lost 781, American forces accounting for 191. The Italians lost 85 submarines, 21 in the Atlantic. Against these figures, it can be noted that Allied merchant ships successfully completed over 300,000 voyages across the Atlantic, while hundreds of thousands more voyages were safely undertaken in the coastal waters of Britain. When Allied shipbuilding capacity reached its peak, the U-boats had no hope of winning. They lost because they dared not maintain the attack on the North Atlantic convoys which brought the material of victory to Britain. Convoy escorts proved to be a decisive task force for offensive action against attacking U-boats.

31:

The Allied Offensive
against North Africa

In World War I, at the First Battle of the Marne, the British and French armies only by the narrowest margin had stopped the initial German drive. Shortly afterward the Western Front settled down into a four-year stalemate. Continental strategy eventually won the war for the Allies, but only at a terrible cost in lives and treasure. The British Empire alone lost nearly a million men. To outflank the static Western Front, Winston Churchill had advocated peripheral strategy in the form of a campaign to seize Constantinople. The outflanking attempt failed both within the Dardanelles and among the rugged crags of Gallipoli, but in the years following World War I military analysts had concluded that Churchill's plan was strategically sound—that it failed through poor Allied planning, through a series of avoidable Allied errors, and as a result of the foresight and initiative of Liman von Sanders.

In World War II also, the war in the West had begun with a German drive aimed at the quick defeat of France. This time the Germans succeeded. France was knocked out of the war, and the British Expeditionary Force was thrust off the Continent. Churchill, the advocate of peripheral strategy in World War I, returned to the same concept as Prime Minister and Minister of Defense in World War II. After the fall of France and the evacuation of the British army, he had no stomach for a return to western Europe—at least until Germany was greatly weakened. And in fact Britain had insufficient troops to man a new Western Front without allies. On the other hand, Britain possessed ample naval power. In the circumstances, Churchill and the British

Chiefs of Staff limited their offensive against the Axis powers to air attacks on German industries and communications, to attacks on German and Italian naval forces, to operations aimed at restoring British communications in the Mediterranean, to the Egyptian campaign, to distant attacks at Dakar and Madagascar, and to operations in Greece and Crete and probes at St. Nazaire and Dieppe. When Hitler invaded the Soviet Union, Churchill announced: "We shall give whatever help we can to Russia and the Russian people." Thus Britain was reviving two of the main features of Pitt's Plan: lending all possible material support to allies on the Continent, while using her naval power to support operations around the enemy's continental position and beyond the seas. In other words, the British were reverting to their strategy of the Seven Years' War and the first three coalitions against revolutionary and Napoleonic France.

Soviet leaders, from the moment they found themselves in the war on the side of the British, opposed the concept of peripheral strategy, demanding a "Second Front Now." When the United States entered the war at the end of 1941, the American Joint Chiefs of Staff, General Marshall in particular, also insisted on an early return of Allied forces to France. What Marshall proposed was to seize a beachhead in France in the late summer of 1942, Operation SLEDGEHAMMER. This was to be followed in 1943 by a major invasion, Operation ROUNDUP, and a drive into Germany, involving a double envelopment of the Ruhr—as was actually carried out in 1944–45. In preparation for SLEDGEHAMMER and ROUNDUP, the Joint Chiefs gave top priority to the production of landing and beaching craft and began sending troops to Britain. But the British Chiefs, after tentatively accepting the American plan, turned it down.[1]

Yet something had to be done in 1942. The Germans on the Russian front reconquered the territory lost during the winter and thrust toward Stalingrad on the Volga. There they could disrupt the flow of oil from the Caucasus and block American and British supplies to Russia via the Persian Gulf route. In North Africa, Rommel's tanks, forging ahead toward the Egyptian delta, appeared to have the momentum that would carry them through to Cairo and the Suez Canal.

Churchill proposed an invasion of western North Africa. There was much to commend in the proposal. Tunisia, Algeria, Morocco, and French West Africa, though loyal to the Vichy French government, were not occupied by the Germans. If the area were brought over to the Allies, Rommel could be trapped between the invading forces and the British Eighth Army, Malta could be relieved, and the Mediterranean could be reopened to Allied shipping, with a consequent saving of crucially short merchant tonnage. Moreover, bases would be secured for attacks on Italy and elsewhere in Southern Europe, a French army might be mustered for action against the Axis,

and phosphates and other resources would be denied the enemy.

President Roosevelt at first opposed the move into North Africa. He wished to see American forces in Europe as soon as possible— to boost the morale of the American public, to fulfill promises to Russia, and to end the war quickly. The Joint Chiefs of Staff opposed the African invasion because they saw it as a strategically eccentric move that would draw more and more Allied forces away from the strategic center in western Europe and delay the invasion of France at least two years. Prime Minister Churchill insisted however that the invasion of North Africa was the best possible preparation for the invasion of France, since threatening the periphery of the Axis empire would draw German forces away from the invasion areas on the French coast.

Churchill at length convinced Roosevelt that if the Anglo-American forces were to see action against the Axis that year, there was really no alternative to his African plan. For once Roosevelt overruled his military advisers in a matter of strategy. On July 25, 1942, the Combined Chiefs of Staff committed themselves to the North African invasion, which was given the code name Operation TORCH.

Strategic and Political Plans and Preparations

The immediate objectives of the landings were three major North African ports outside the operational radius of the *Luftwaffe:* Algiers and Oran on the Mediterranean shore and Casablanca on the Atlantic. Bizerte and Tunis, in Tunisia, and Bone, in Algeria, were rejected as too close to enemy airfields in Sicily; while Dakar, in West Africa, was too far south to be useful. The choice also reflected a compromise between American Army planners, who wished to forestall possible German counteraction through Spain, and British planners, who expected the major enemy opposition to come through Tunisia. Once the immediate target cities were secured, part of the Allied forces would have to race the Germans for occupation of the ports in Tunisia while others rushed from Casablanca to the frontier of Spanish Morocco to guard the vital com-

[1] SLEDGEHAMMER, according to the initial Anglo-American agreement, was to be carried out only as an "emergency" or an "opportunity" operation—in the event either the Russians or the Germans appeared on the verge of defeat. But President Roosevelt later urged that SLEDGEHAMMER "be pushed with the utmost vigor" and without qualification, insisting that "it is of the highest importance that U.S. ground troops be brought into action against the enemy in 1942." The British War Cabinet and the British Chiefs of Staff flatly refused to agree to any invasion of the Continent on the President's terms in 1942.

For a brief analysis of the conflicting strategies, see Samuel Eliot Morison, *Strategy and Compromise* (Boston, 1958). For a more extensive study, see Trumbull Higgins, *Winston Churchill and the Second Front, 1940–1943* (New York, 1957). Higgins suggests that the difference might be considered basically theological. Says he in his preface (p. ix): "The strategic disagreement between Churchill and the Americans in the Second World War can be considered as a continuation of the basic split in English Protestantism, manifested in the British and American Civil Wars, between its Anglican Right and Puritan Left."

munications through the Straits of Gibraltar.

Best utilization of available ships and manpower determined the various assault force assignments. American Task Force 34, called the Western Naval Task Force, was to transport 35,000 troops directly from the United States to seize the Casablanca area. A Center Naval Task Force carrying 39,000 American troops with British naval support, all staging in Britain, would invade Oran. A third contingent, the Eastern Naval Task Force, would embark from Britain 23,000 British and 10,000 American troops assigned to seize Algiers. After the ports were taken, follow-up convoys would pour in reinforcements and supplies until the conquest was complete. Because intelligence reports indicated that defending Vichy forces would resist American troops less

vigorously than British, all ground commanders in the initial assaults were American. Lieutenant General Dwight D. Eisenhower USA was named Commander in Chief Allied Force, while Admiral of the Fleet Sir Andrew B. Cunningham RN assumed over-all naval command. D-day was set for November 8, 1942, the last date that year on which landings were deemed feasible across beaches exposed to the heavy ground swell usually prevalent on the Atlantic coast of North Africa during the winter season.

The venture was risky enough to satisfy the boldest. Much necessarily depended on the unpredictable reaction of the North African French. Because of the British attacks on French naval forces at Mers-el-Kebir and Dakar in 1940, the Germans had permitted

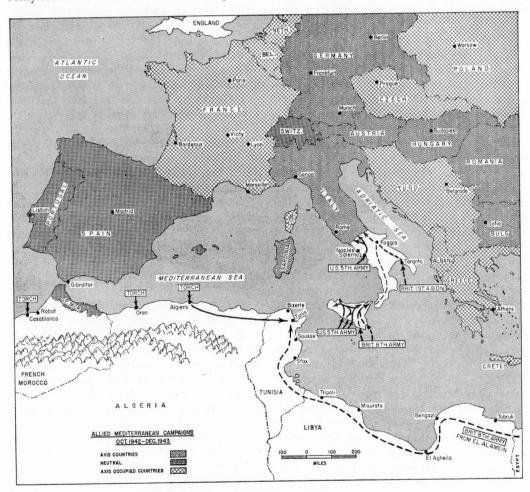

ALLIED CAMPAIGNS IN THE MEDITERRANEAN THEATER, 1942–1943

the French to assemble and equip a defense force of 120,000 men, 350 planes of fair quality, more than 200 tanks, a sizable amount of light artillery and mortars, and naval units which included the modern battleship *Richelieu* and a cruiser-destroyer force at Dakar. Another cruiser, the unfinished battleship *Jean Bart,* and numerous destroyers and submarines were in ports elsewhere along the coastline. If all these forces fought with determination, and if the Germans moved into Spanish and French bases to assist them, cutting the Allied supply route at Gibraltar, it appeared to many Allied staff officers that the invasion might be defeated. But it seemed more probable that the Franco government would resist a German entry into Spain and that many of the defending French units, if they fought at all, would put up only a token resistance. Success however hinged as much on political as on military and naval factors.

Within the limits imposed by the need for secrecy concerning the operation, everything possible was done to insure a favorable French reaction to the landings. Despite strong public pressure, the Roosevelt administration had refused to break diplomatic relations with the Vichy government. In the fall of 1940, Admiral William D. Leahy had been appointed Ambassador to Vichy with his main mission to stiffen French resistance to any German domination of French Africa. Since 1941 a corps of American consular officials, led by Consul-General Robert D. Murphy, had been assiduously cultivating the good will and cooperation of leading French political and military figures in North Africa while administering U.S. economic aid. They also had been collecting intelligence concerning beach defenses, surf conditions, roads, bridges, and other information essential to the success of the landings. Two weeks before the invasion was scheduled to begin, Major General Mark W. Clark usa landed from a British submarine to meet with Murphy and pro-Allied French commanders in a secret conference near Algiers. Without being given the exact date, the French were told that the assault was coming and were urged to disrupt anti-invasion plans when the operation began. At French urging, General Henri Giraud, a widely known French senior officer who had escaped from a German

prison, was spirited away from the Riviera by a submarine to Gibraltar in the hope that he could further rally Frenchmen to the Allied cause. On the eve of the attack therefore there were grounds for hope that many French army and air force units were "fixed."

There was no success in winning over the French navy beforehand however, and that was especially serious because the coastal defense batteries were manned by naval personnel. With few exceptions the Navy was tenaciously loyal to Admiral of the Fleet François Darlan, now Commander in Chief of the Armed Forces of Vichy France. As a dynamic leader who had brought the *Marine* to the peak of efficiency between wars, Darlan could both legally and morally command the allegiance of all French forces in North Africa with an authority second only to that of Pétain himself. A few weeks before the landings, Darlan sent feelers to American officials in North Africa suggesting negotiations. Murphy favored negotiating with the Admiral, but the U.S. State Department, deeply distrusting the Vichy government, feared that such contacts would lead to leaks concerning the forthcoming operation that would impel the Germans to rush troops and planes into Africa and thereby frustrate the entire scheme. Only three days before D-day however, Darlan flew to Algiers to be at the bedside of his sick son. Thus purely by chance he was well placed to exercise an immediate influence on the course of events. This totally unexpected development was to prove fortunate for the Allies.

Tactical Plans and Preparations

Because the war against the European Axis was primarily an army responsibility, it was from beginning to end commanded on the highest military level by an army officer, and naval forces were assigned to the Army as needed. As a result the Army dominated joint operations,[2] and the Navy deferred to the Army's desires, even in amphibious assaults.

[2] In American terminology a *joint operation* is one carried out by elements of more than one armed service of the same nationality; a *combined operation* is one carried out by forces of two or more nations. The British use the term *combined* for both sorts of operations.

This situation contrasted with that in the Pacific Ocean Areas, where the top command was naval, and army units were assigned to the Navy as needed. As a result amphibious operations developed along somewhat different lines in the two theaters.

Planning and preparation for Operation Torch were complicated by division of command and shortage of time. From his London headquarters General Eisenhower and his British-American staff directed the detailed planning for the assaults on Algiers and Oran. But because the forces for Morocco were to stage from the United States, plans and preparations for this phase of Torch were left to the Joint Chiefs of Staff. General Marshall delegated the planning for the landing force to the War Department, which delegated the detailed planning to Major General George S. Patton Jr., Commander Western Task Force. Admiral King delegated the fleet-level planning for the participating naval forces to Admiral Royal E. Ingersoll, Commander in Chief Atlantic Fleet, who delegated the detailed planning to Rear Admiral Kent Hewitt, the prospective commander of the Western Naval Task Force (Task Force 34). In the preparatory phase the army and navy commanders were independent, with no common superior below the President. The command structure was thus in the tradition of joint operations from Quebec in the Seven Years' War to Norway in World War II.

In practice, planning and preparation for the Moroccan attack were closely integrated, as indeed they had to be for so organic an operation as an amphibious assault. General Patton and Admiral Hewitt conferred frequently. To coordinate naval plans with those for the landing force, Hewitt's war plans officer spent several weeks in Patton's office in Washington. Then, to achieve final coordination, Patton's planning staff moved to Hewitt's headquarters at Ocean View, near Norfolk, Virginia. Because Hewitt, prior to assuming command of the Western Naval Task Force, was Commander Amphibious Force Atlantic Fleet (Comphiblant), the amphibious training for the Moroccan landing force was directed from his headquarters.

On October 13, 1942 the Joint Chiefs issued to all commands concerned with the Moroccan

operation their own high-level plan, titled "Joint Army-Navy Plan for Participation in Operation Torch." It provided that, once the expedition got under way, there should in each phase be a single commander at both the theater and the local level. For the first time in modern history a large-scale joint operation was to be under unified command throughout.[3] Command relations were set forth as follows:

(a) The Commander in Chief, Allied Force [Eisenhower], will command all forces assigned to Operation TORCH, under the principal of unity of command.

(b) The Western Naval Task Force will pass to the command of the Commander in Chief, Allied Force, upon crossing the meridian of 40° West Longitude. This command may be exercised either directly by the Commander in Chief [Eisenhower] or through the Naval Commander, Allied Force [Cunningham]. (Prior to that time these forces will remain under the command of the Commander in Chief, United States Atlantic Fleet [Ingersoll], who will arrange their movements so that they will meet the schedule of the Commander in Chief, Allied Force.)

(c) Command relations of the Subordinate Task Forces are initially set up as given in subparagraphs (d), (e), (f), and (g). They are subject to change as found necessary by the Commander in Chief, Allied Force.

(d) The command of units of the Western Task Force which are embarked in the Western Naval Task Force, will vest in the Commander, Western Naval Task Force [Hewitt], until such time as the Commanding General, Western Task Force [Patton], has established his headquarters on shore and states he is ready to assume command.

(e) When the Commanding General, Western Task Force, assumes command on shore, the naval forces designated to give further support to the occupation of FRENCH MOROCCO will pass to his control, acting through the Commander, Western Naval Task Force.

(f) Following the assault operations and when and as released by Commander in Chief, Allied

[3] The American invasion of Guadalcanal the preceding August had been under unified command, but that was not a joint operation because the landing force was composed of marines. The admiral commanding the amphibious force was and remained senior to the general commanding the landing force. This chain of command was retained in the U.S. Pacific Fleet even after army units were attached.

Force, the United States naval forces assigned thereto will revert to the command of Commander in Chief, United States Atlantic Fleet.

(g) The United States naval forces assigned for the operation of ports and for naval local and sea frontier defenses—Sea Frontier Forces, Western Task Force, and the Naval Operating Base, Center Task Force—will be under the command of the respective commanding generals of those task forces, under the principle of unity of command.

(h) The Commander in Chief, United States Atlantic Fleet, will exercise command over all forces employed for the cover and ocean escort in the ATLANTIC of follow-up convoys between the UNITED STATES and NORTH AFRICA.[4]

The point particularly to be noted is that in place of the traditional system in amphibious operations, whereby the general commanding the landing force and the admiral commanding the naval support force remained independent and coequal throughout the operation, first Admiral Hewitt and then General Patton would be in over-all command. And there would be at any given time only a single chain of command, via Admiral Ingersoll until the expedition reached mid-ocean, via General Eisenhower thereafter. Though the provision for unified local command was written only into the directive for the Western Task Force, it became the model for subsequent directives in the European theater of operations.

Plans for the three main landings, at Algiers, at Oran, and in the Casablanca area, while differing in such details as command relations, were otherwise similar in purpose and outline. The objective of the attacks was to enable the Allies to hurl a large army and air force into a prolonged campaign against a well equipped foe, for even if the French put up no resistance, German and Italian reinforcements were sure to be rushed to Africa. Since nothing like the huge volume of supplies required to sustain the invasion forces, 600–700 tons daily per division, could be handled across beaches, it was essential to seize well-developed ports with ample berthing, unloading, and stowage facilities. But because direct assault inside harbors in the teeth of harbor defenses was infeasible without prohibitive losses, plans called

for units to be landed on open beaches near the coastal cities so that their harbors could be taken from the flanks and rear. The troops would be carried to positions off the beaches in combat-loaded assault transports, and then transferred with their equipment to landing craft to be put ashore in surprise night landings. Gunnery ships and naval aircraft would support the flanking drives of the troops while landing craft shuttled in reinforcements and supplies until the ports were secured and readied for use. Since the best chance for the enemy to defeat the onslaught was to deny the ports, and consequently the supplies, needed to build up large forces, it was vital to take the harbors as quickly and with as little damage as possible. Preventing the defenders from scuttling blockships or demolishing quays was considered so important that special units were assigned to dash in at the start of the attacks and seize port facilities at all three objectives. Simple in concept, complex in detail, the hastily drawn plans served as a model for organizing further assaults in the European theater.

The training of the assault forces was beset by myriad difficulties. Few of the land, sea, or air forces assigned to the operation were completely ready when the attack was ordered, nor did it seem likely in the scant five months until D-day that they could be properly trained. Responsible officers realized this, but they also knew that to delay until all participants were fully trained might permit the Germans to move in first, thereby making an Allied landing in Northwest Africa out of the question.

Fortunately for the Allies, the U.S. Marine Corps and U.S. Navy entered the war with a developed amphibious doctrine and training program. And though the amphibiously trained U.S. marines were committed to the Pacific, the U.S. Army had commenced training based in part on their doctrine. During 1941 and early 1942 three American infantry divisions trained with the marines in the United States. Other infantry divisions, dispatched to Great Britain, trained amphibiously with British forces in Scotland and Northern Ireland. In the time available however, it was not possible to train sufficient U.S. Army units

---

[4] Quoted in George F. Howe, *Northwest Africa: Seizing the Initiative in the West* (Washington, D.C.: Dept. of the Army, 1957), 38.

to undertake all three North African landings. In view of the French attitude it would have been desirable to make the invasion an all-American show, but British troops had to make up the major part of the easternmost force, operating against Algiers.

By later standards the training both for the initial landings and for subsequent combat fell far short of what was desirable, but it had to suffice. Amphibious training of crews for transports and landing craft was especially deficient. Again, there was simply not enough time. Only half its assigned transports had reached the Western Naval Task Force by August 1, 1942, fourteen weeks before D-day. There was not enough time left even for adequate indoctrination. Moreover nearly all the ships required a good deal of work on communications equipment, and they needed alterations to their interior arrangements before they could participate in exercises. Landing craft were crucial items, for until the Army could seize and ready the ports, these little vessels would comprise the sole means of bringing in ammunition and supplies. Because of a failure to enlist small craft sailors, as such, when the war began, the Navy hastily assembled some 3,000 recruits, who commenced small craft training in June 1942. While the men worked hard and enthusiastically, for all practical purposes they had only two months to train specifically for the North African venture. It was soon apparent that the techniques of amphibious assault could not be learned in so brief a time.

German U-boat activity worsened matters by forcing the landing exercises for the Western Task Force into the sheltered waters of Chesapeake Bay at Solomons Island. As a result the landing craft crews were unable to gain needed experience in handling their craft in a heavy surf. Crews who trained in Great Britain, the majority Royal Navy, were able to practice under more realistic but still far from satisfactory conditions. The Army's historian of the North African campaign concludes: "Training for the amphibious operations in French North Africa . . . fell short of what was desired and perhaps below the requirements for victory over a well-armed and determined foe."[5] The massive assault forces

[5] Howe, *Northwest Africa*, 63.

that got under way from Britain and the United States knew that the French were not particularly well armed. They had yet to find out if they were determined.

Morocco: The Approach

The Western Naval Task Force, commanded by Admiral Hewitt in heavy cruiser *Augusta,* comprised 102 warships, transports, and auxiliaries which, when united at sea, covered more than 500 square miles of ocean. To mislead the enemy, the Northern and Southern Attack Groups sortied from Hampton Roads on October 23 and took a southerly course. The next day the Center Attack Group left Hampton Roads and took a northeasterly course as if headed for Britain. These groups later united and were joined on the 27th by a Covering Group sailing from Casco Bay, Maine; this group included the new fast battleship *Massachusetts* and two heavy cruisers. An Air Group dispatched ahead to Bermuda, comprising the aircraft carrier *Ranger,* four escort carriers newly converted from tankers, and a screen of a light cruiser and nine destroyers, joined the force on the 28th in mid-ocean.

After steering evasive courses to avoid or deceive known enemy submarine concentrations, the Western Naval Task Force neared the African coast in a strong northwest wind that raised heavy seas. Predictions from Washington were that surf on the Moroccan beaches would be too high for the landings on D-day, November 8, but Admiral Hewitt trusted the verdict of his aerological officer that the landings would be possible on the 8th but not for many days thereafter. He therefore proceeded according to plan. If impossible conditions developed, he could postpone the landings by radio and, if absolutely necessary, execute an alternate plan for landing inside the Mediterranean. As the task force approached Morocco, the men were cheered by the news that the British Eighth Army was pressing back Rommel's forces in Egypt after the great British victory at El Alamein on November 5.

On November 7 the Western Naval Task Force split apart. The Southern Attack Group turned south toward the small phosphate port

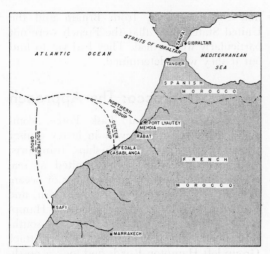

AMERICAN LANDINGS IN FRENCH MOROCCO,
NOVEMBER 8, 1942

of Safi, where it was to land 6,500 troops and 90 medium and light tanks to march on Casablanca from the south. The Center Attack Group headed for the small port of Fedala to land 19,500 troops and 79 light tanks to advance on Casablanca from the north. The Northern Attack Group shaped course for the coastal village of Mehdia to land 9,000 troops and 65 light tanks to capture the airfield at nearby Port Lyautey. The landings at Safi and Mehdia were expected also to tie down French units that might otherwise close in on the main landing at Fedala. The Covering Group moved toward Casablanca itself to take under fire any naval forces that tried to leave the harbor. The Air Group divided in order to support all three landings: one escort carrier to Safi, two escort carriers to Mehdia, the *Ranger* and one escort carrier to Fedala and Casablanca, only 15 miles apart.

The Army had insisted upon night landings —both to achieve surprise and because army officers were not yet convinced that naval gunfire could provide adequate support for a daylight landing. But surprise would be lost if the attack groups were sighted from the Moroccan coast in the evening of November 7. To allow time for the approach, for loading of landing craft, and for the ship-to-shore movement, all in total darkness, H-hour was set at 0400, two hours before dawn.

The Army also required what the Navy regarded as an excessive amount of equipment

to be carried in with the assault waves. This requirement put a strain on the supply of landing craft, which for this operation ranged from 36-foot plywood, gasoline-powered "Higgins boats" to 50-foot steel, diesel-powered LCM's (Landing Craft, Mechanized) capable of transporting a light tank. In subsequent assaults enough landing craft for army requirements would be brought to the beachhead area by LST's (Landing Ships, Tank), but for the North African invasion they were limited to the number that could be brought in by the transports.

Major General Jonathan Anderson, commanding the troops that were to land at Fedala, further complicated the landing craft situation for the Center Attack Group by a last-minute decision to increase the strength of the initial landing force by about 50 per cent. As a result, to provide enough landing craft for the assault waves, the Navy had to work out a complicated boat plan that would have been difficult for experienced coxswains to carry out on schedule even in daylight.

Morocco: The Main Assault

The assault plan for Fedala required the 15 transports of the Center Attack Group to anchor at midnight in four columns six to eight miles north of the landing beaches. The four transports of the inshore line each carried a battalion landing team.[6] These four landing teams, comprising altogether 6,000 men, were to make the initial, pre-dawn assault. Because no transport carried enough landing craft to boat a whole team, the transports of the second, third, and fourth lines were directed to send forward additional craft to specific transports of the first line. As the craft were loaded with men and tanks, they were to advance to one of four control destroyers positioned in the rendezvous area a thousand yards nearer shore. Here they were to form "waves" of six to eight boats. When each of the loaded landing craft, numbering more than 200, had reported to its designated control destroyer, the destroyers would conduct them forward to the line of departure 4,000 yards from shore. Meanwhile four beach-marking scout boats

[6] For an explanation of *battalion landing team* see Chapter 38, footnote 10, page 730.

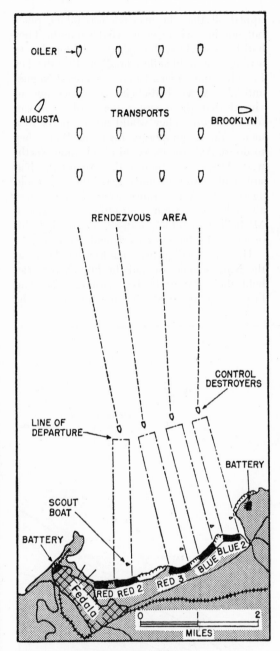

INITIAL LANDING PLAN FOR FEDALA

landing craft, on signal from the control destroyers, would head for their assigned beaches, accompanied by support boats armed with machine guns and guided by the flares in the scout boats. After putting the troops ashore, the landing craft were to retract and hurry back to the transport area for the follow-up troops. As we have seen, this elaborate and tightly scheduled plan had to be carried out in almost complete darkness.

As the Center Group transports, accompanied by cruisers *Augusta* and *Brooklyn* and ten destroyers, headed in toward their anchorage, the Fedala assault plan began to come apart. An unexpected current carried the Center Group off course, necessitating a series of emergency turns. The first line of transports, those carrying the initial assault forces, reached the anchorage shortly before midnight, but by then the rest of the transports were straggling badly and out of position. As a result the landing craft from these vessels were late in reaching their assigned transports or never found them at all. The schedule was further retarded by the troops, who, overloaded with 60-pound packs, debarked very slowly down the landing nets into the pitching boats. As a result of these delays, only about half the scheduled waves of boats had reached the rendezvous area by 0400. The control destroyers however could wait no longer and began conducting their waves to the line of departure, which they reached in about 50 minutes. The beach-marking scout boats, uninformed of the delays, had for some time been showing their lights, but this only caused confusion, for two of the scout boats were out of position, one by more than two miles. At 0500, an hour late, the first waves of boats headed for the beach, followed at five to ten minute intervals by the second and third waves. The noise of the landing craft, now operating at full throttle, finally attracted the attention of shore batteries, which turned on searchlights, at first upward to look for aircraft, and then down on the water. When the support boats opened fire with machine guns, the lights went out abruptly. Meanwhile the inexperience of the coxswains was taking its toll as landing craft collided, crashed into rocks and reefs adjoining the designated beaches, or were caught in the surf, spun about, and broached on the

would have advanced and anchored, each off one of the four segments of beach—designated Beaches Red 2, Red 3, Blue, and Blue 2—assigned to one of the four battalion landing teams. At 0335, the scout boats were to begin flashing flashlights seaward. At 0350, they were to ignite colored flares. At H-hour, 0400, the beach. Some troops were spilled into the sea where they were pulled down by their heavy packs and drowned. Of the landing craft that safely made shore, many were left stranded by the receding tide and could not retract. Yet the naval crews who lost their craft were the exceptions. Most, despite their brief training, the darkness, and the difficult sea conditions, brought their troops safely ashore with their equipment and quickly returned to the transports. By dawn 3,500 troops had been landed, and the first echelons advanced and seized control of the town of Fedala. The batteries flanking the beach however were still in French hands.

Would the French fight, or would they welcome the invaders? As first light grayed the morning sky, the eyes of the fleet were on the French batteries, which would provide the answer. Friendly officers in Morocco had been tipped off that the invasion was taking place but not just where or in what strength. They had been working through the night trying to arrange for a bloodless landing. But the key French commanders, Resident General Noguès and Vice Admiral Michelier, remained unconvinced that there was a powerful American force offshore. They would not be party to a mere raid or temporary invasion. Were they to do so, Axis forces would also invade Northwest Africa, and unless the Americans had sufficient power to make good their foothold against the Axis, France would suffer reprisals without gaining offsetting advantages. Michelier therefore refused to rescind his order to the batteries to defend the coast.

Had the landing been made after dawn, as the Navy wished, or had the French batteries held their fire until the morning mists had lifted and revealed the magnitude of the

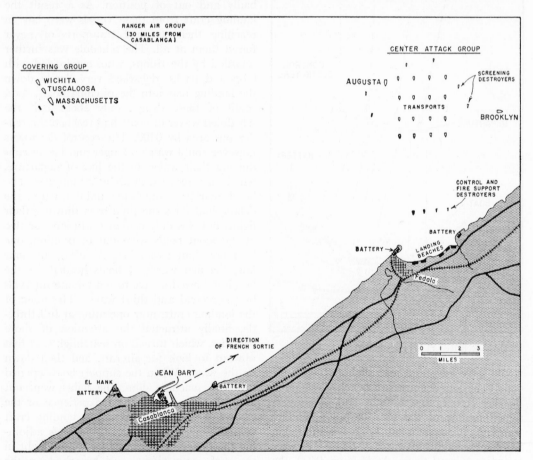

THE ASSAULT ON THE CASABLANCA AREA

American force, it is possible that General Noguès would have agreed to parley. But just as day began to break, shortly after 0600, the batteries flanking the Fedala roadstead opened fire on the landing forces and on the control destroyers. The destroyers quickly returned the fire, and were soon joined by the guns of the *Brooklyn* and the *Augusta*. The *Ranger*'s aircraft, over Casablanca, now came under attack by French fighters; in a brief dogfight seven French and four American planes were shot down. Spotting planes from the Covering Group were soon being attacked by antiaircraft fire and fighter planes. At 0700 the *Massachusetts* and her consorts, the *Tuscaloosa* and the *Wichita*, turned their 5-inch batteries on the French aircraft, shooting one down. Immediately afterward the battleship *Jean Bart* in Casablanca harbor and the powerful battery at nearby Pointe El Hank opened fire on the Covering Group, which replied at once. The battle was on. To Admiral Michelier, putting up a fight was no longer just a matter of policy or of carrying out orders from above; it had become a requirement of honor. When later in the day a deputation from General Patton drove to Casablanca with an American flag and a flag of truce to arrange a cease-fire, they were let in through the lines and cheered in the streets, but Michelier refused even to receive them. As one of the American officers began to argue with the Admiral's aide, he was interrupted by a salvo from the El Hank battery that shook the windows of the Admiralty. Said the aide, *"Voilà votre réponse!"*

The *Jean Bart*, though uncompleted and temporarily immobilized, had an operational turret of four 15-inch guns that made her a formidable floating battery. In Casablanca harbor also were eleven submarines, eight sloops, eleven minesweepers, two super-destroyers, seven smaller destroyers, and the light cruiser *Primauguet*. The principal task of the American Covering Group was to prevent a sortie of these vessels against the Center Attack Group and the landing forces 15 miles away at Fedala. The carrying out of this task was hampered by the guns of the *Jean Bart* and by steady and accurate fire from El Hank's eight well-protected 5.3-inch and 7.6-inch guns, which had straddled the *Massachu-*

setts at 20,000 yards with their first salvo. The *Massachusetts* concentrated the fire of her nine 16-inch guns on the *Jean Bart*. Her fifth salvo struck the barbette of the functional turret, jamming it in train. For 45 minutes more the ships shot it out with the El Hank battery, driving the gunners temporarily to cover but not demolishing the guns. Not a ship in the Covering Group had yet been hit.

The second phase of the Naval Battle of Casablanca was initiated by Admiral Michelier, who, observing that the Covering Group had maneuvered westward, away from the transports off Fedala, seized the opportunity to send seven of his destroyers to attack the Center Group. Eight submarines also sortied. This was Michelier's best chance to break up the landing. Steaming close inshore and making expert use of smoke, the French destroyers approached the American transports and had hit one landing craft when they were intercepted and driven back by the *Augusta*, the *Brooklyn*, and two of the Center Group destroyers, which had been deployed to screen the transports against just such an attack. The cruiser *Primauguet* now sortied and led the French destroyers in a new advance. Hewitt had already summoned the Covering Group to return to the area. For two and a half hours the French ships dodged in and out of their smoke screen, exchanging salvos with the vessels of the Center and Covering Groups. Planes from the *Ranger* meanwhile made several strafing and bombing runs on the enemy force. Three of the French submarines had already been sunk in Casablanca harbor, but the remaining eight sortied and entered the confused battle. Their torpedo spreads narrowly missed several American vessels.

In the face of the immense American superiority of force, the gallant French attack, however skillfully conducted, could hardly have ended other than in disaster for the attackers. When the engagement ended just before noon, none of the American vessels had received damage of consequence. Of the French ships however, all but one had been severely damaged. Two had sunk, two others were in a sinking condition, one was dead in the water, and one had been beached to avoid sinking. Only one of the submarines returned to Casablanca harbor, and two made Dakar.

Of the rest, attacked by American planes or destroyers, one was beached, one was scuttled at Cadiz, and the rest sank.

Early in the afternoon of November 8, the undamaged French destroyer and two sloops emerged from Casablanca to pick up survivors. Admiral Hewitt, taking this sortie for another attempt to attack his transports, ordered action resumed. The three French vessels made it back to the harbor under a smoke screen, but aircraft from the *Ranger* wrecked the *Primauguet*. At the end of the day the El Hank battery was still active, and workmen had completed repairs on the *Jean Bart*'s damaged turret.

At Fedala the defending troops, chiefly Senegalese, quickly surrendered, and even the navy-manned shore batteries were in American hands before noon. French fighter aircraft made a few strafing runs over the beach, but bombers were chased off by aircraft from the *Ranger*. General Anderson organized his troops to meet counterattacks and prepared for the advance on Casablanca. He was severely hampered however by the increasingly behind-schedule landings of troops and supplies. There were not enough landing craft left to do the job properly, and the performance of the boat crews, exhausted after having worked all night, did not improve with the coming of daylight. Collisions and broachings continued. The numerous boats stranded and abandoned on the beach were banged together and shattered by the incoming tide and rising surf. By nightfall on D-day nearly half the 347 landing craft of the Center Attack Group had been destroyed, and only 40 per cent of the 19,500 troops embarked in the transports had been brought ashore. Unloading of supplies was even further behind schedule. It was apparent that the transports would have to remain off Fedala for several days. As they were brought in closer to the shore, a minelayer sowed a protective mine field to eastward, and the destroyers patrolled in screening areas north and west of the transport area.

Morocco: The Southern Assault

Meanwhile, 150 miles by sea southwest of Casablanca, the Southern Attack Group had scored a spectacular success at Safi. In the blackness before H-hour, despite debarking troubles caused by a heavy ground swell and the inevitable errors of inexperienced personnel, the crucial phase of the assault was conducted according to plan. First, a scout boat located the turning buoy marking the entrance to Safi's small, breakwater-protected harbor. Next, guided by a light blinking seaward from the scout boat, came two old four-stack destroyers of World War I vintage, razeed to reduce silhouette. These, carrying about 200 assault troops each, led landing craft directly into the harbor. The French had been alerted and there was a lively exchange of fire as the first "fourpiper," the *Bernadou*, slowly steamed in and drove the French gunners to cover with her guns. Her consort, the *Cole*, was able to come directly alongside the quay without a single casualty. While the old battleship *New York* and the light cruiser *Philadelphia* were silencing the coastal batteries, American troops took over key positions in the town. That afternoon, after the ex-train ferry u.s.s. *Lakehurst* had brought in her load of medium tanks, all objectives of the assault were attained. Aircraft from the escort carrier supporting the Southern Group destroyed most French planes in the area on the ground. Naval gunfire stopped a half-hearted French attempt at counterattack. The entire operation had been carried out with dispatch. Though supporting landings were made on beaches flanking the harbor, only one landing craft was lost. All ships were completely unloaded in three days. By the time resistance officially ceased, an American tank force was on its way by road from Safi to Casablanca accompanied along the coast by the *Philadelphia*, several destroyers, and six gasoline-carrying landing craft.

Morocco: The Northern Assault

The primary objective of the Northern Attack Group was the Port Lyautey airfield, the only airport in Morocco with concrete, all-weather runways. Troops were to be landed on both sides of the Sebou, a narrow and winding but navigable river that connects Port Lyautey with the Atlantic. The initial attack was intended to overwhelm the seaside village of Mehdia and its ancient fortress, the Kasba, which guarded the mouth of the river. The invaders would then thrust inland to seize the airfield by double envelopment and to occupy Port Lyautey. u.s.s. *Dallas,* another razeed fourpiper, was to proceed upriver after a boom blocking access had been cut, and land a force to assist in the capture of the airfield. After the airfield was secured, an army fighter group catapulted from one of the escort carriers was to operate from the field, providing fighter cover for further operations by bombers flown in from Gibraltar.

The Northern Attack Group's assault plan was a smaller version of the one used at Fedala, except that the five landing beaches were much farther apart. Hence to the delays of debarking was added mounting confusion. Few of the troops reached the right beach. Badly scattered, they missed an early opportunity to seize the Kasba and the shore batteries near it, and were soon obliged to meet counterattacks by French colonial troops closing in from Port Lyautey. Efforts of a boat party to cut the boom blocking the river, and later efforts by the *Dallas* to ram it, failed completely under a hail of fire from the Kasba. The initial loss of landing craft was not great, but deteriorating weather and a rapidly rising surf made the build-up of supplies perilously slow. By the end of the second day only half the troops had been landed. Brigadier General Lucian K. Truscott, Jr., who commanded the landing force in this assault, did not at first make much use of naval gunfire. Light cruiser *Savannah* kept down the fire from the Kasba with her 6-inch shells, but the 14-inch shells of the old battleship *Texas,* which could have smashed the fort, were considered too dangerous to be fired at targets near where American troops were operating. Scout planes from both the cruiser and battleship however made a potent contribution in breaking up enemy tank columns by means of a novel but effective technique—dropping antisubmarine depth charges equipped with impact fuses.

On November 10, the situation took a turn for the better. In an early morning attack, the invaders broke through to the airfield against French defending troops who, expecting an early armistice, no longer offered strenuous resistance. By that time a boat party had at last cut the main cable of the river boom, enabling the *Dallas* to crash through and scrape her way up the shallow Sebou to land her troops near the airdrome. Shortly afterward the army planes from one of the escort carriers were flown in and began operating from the field. Bombers from the other escort carrier attacked the Kasba, which promptly surrendered to an American infantry team. French armored forces coming up the coast road from Rabat, the Moroccan capital, were turned back by destroyer and cruiser fire. When a column of troop-laden trucks was spotted advancing on Port Lyautey from the interior, the *Texas* reached more than eight miles inland and cratered the road with her big shells, whereupon the column quickly dispersed. That afternoon the French general in command of the area called for a cease-fire, which was granted at once. The attack had attained its main object, capturing the airfield—but too late to support the battle for Casablanca.

Morocco Secured

General Anderson's troops and armor meanwhile had advanced from Fedala to the outskirts of Casablanca. Two French corvettes, advancing at 1000 on November 10 to fire on the American troops, were chased back into Casablanca harbor by the *Augusta.* Then the *Augusta* took to her heels as shells from the repaired turret of the *Jean Bart* began to fall around her. Hewitt called for air support, and the *Ranger* sent in dive bombers that scored two hits with 1,000-pound bombs and left the French battleship settling in the harbor mud with her decks awash.

At the end of the 10th, the Americans had Casablanca surrounded. They planned an all-out attack from land, sea, and air for the next morning. Fortunately, before the attack could be launched, Admiral Michelier received orders to cease resistance, and a conference later on the 11th ended the fighting. At the conference Admiral Hewitt held out his hand to Admiral Michelier and expressed regret at having had to fire on French ships. "I had my orders and did my duty," said Michelier, taking the proffered hand, "you had yours and did your duty; now that is over, we are ready to cooperate."[7] Soon the French and the Americans were working together to restore the port as a major rear base for supplying the prospective campaign into Tunisia.

The Axis got into the Moroccan campaign after all, causing the Americans far greater material losses than the French did. U-boats that the American task force had evaded in the Atlantic were now converging on the Casablanca area. The transports of the Center Attack Group, with no troops aboard but still unloading cargo, were obliged to remain off Fedala because a new convoy approaching from the United States would occupy all available space in Casablanca's protected harbor. In the early evening of November 11, *U-173* slipped into the unloading area and sank a transport and damaged a destroyer and an oiler with torpedoes. The following afternoon, *U-130* got into the area and sank three more transports. *U-130* got away safely, but *U-173*, after heavily damaging an American cargo ship off Fedala on the 15th, was sunk the next day by three American destroyers.

Algeria: Algiers

When the Allied forces staging from England steamed through the Straits of Gibraltar into the Mediterranean, the fact that some major move was under way could no longer be concealed from the Axis powers. The Italian naval command correctly guessed that Algeria must be the Allied target, but they were overruled by the Germans, who first estimated that the convoys were going to southern France, and then that they were headed for Crete, for Tripoli, or possibly for the relief of Malta. Axis forces, submarine, surface, and air, concentrated in the straits of Sicily, leaving the Allied transports largely unmolested. One American transport was torpedoed by a German aircraft off the African coast, but most of its personnel arrived safely, if tardily, at their destination after a long voyage in landing craft and an escort vessel. Otherwise

[7] Samuel Eliot Morison, *History of United States Naval Operations in World War II*, II (Boston, 1954), 164.

the Eastern Naval Task Force arrived off Algiers without incident.

A massive array of naval strength supported the Mediterranean landings. The Royal Navy's Force H, based at Gibraltar, acted as a covering force. Consisting at this time of three battleships, a battle cruiser, two fleet aircraft carriers, and lighter vessels, Force H was to guard the amphibious forces from intervention by the Italian navy or by the Vichy French fleet based at Toulon. The Support Force of the Eastern Naval Attack Force consisted of three light cruisers, two escort carriers, three antiaircraft cruisers, a monitor, 13 destroyers, and 17 smaller warships. Directed from a British "headquarters ship," prototype of the later American amphibious command ship (AGC), the Support Force had the tasks of protecting the amphibious forces from air and submarine attack and from shore bombardment, and of providing tactical support for Allied troops while landing and ashore. Only 10,000 troops of the 33,000-man landing force were American, but because of the known French bias against the British, the major ground units were placed under American commanders so that the invasion would appear to be primarily American.

The plan for the capture of Algiers, capital of Algeria and best port on the Barbary Coast, called for simultaneous landings on three flanking beach areas and, as at Safi, a raid by two destroyers to seize port facilities and shipping in the harbor. In a relatively quiet and almost tideless sea, troops began to transfer to landing craft scheduled to hit the beaches at about 0100, November 8. Luckily for the invaders, there was no immediate opposition, for the troops and naval personnel assigned to this assault had had little opportunity for training in amphibious techniques. Hence the ship-to-shore movement to some of the Algerian beaches was even more confused and behind schedule than at any of the Moroccan landings. In one sector battalions were intermingled and scattered for miles along the coast. Nevertheless the landing forces managed to form up and push rapidly inland toward their objectives. Thanks to the activities of pro-Allied officers, many French troops, including the garrisons of two important airfields, surrendered without resistance. The swift Allied advance soon turned the operation into more of an occupation than a campaign, for only the coastal forts east of Algiers offered serious opposition.

Meanwhile two British destroyers had failed in their attempt to seize the port to prevent sabotage of facilities. Confused by darkness and strange waters in the early hours of November 8, the *Broke* and *Malcolm* missed the narrow harbor entrance on their first try. In their second, the *Malcolm* was so severely holed by shore batteries that she was forced to retire. The *Broke* however crashed through the boom, reached a quay, and landed her troops, who were quickly pinned down by small arms fire and captured. The *Broke* managed to escape, but she was so badly damaged that she later sank under tow.

Luckily for the Allies an early cease-fire at Algiers yielded them the port intact. Radio orders to stop resisting issued in the name of General Giraud had produced no effect. During the day however Robert Murphy succeeded in persuading Admiral Darlan to authorize the French commanding general to negotiate a truce. An oral armistice was reached at 1840, November 8, and an hour and 20 minutes later the Americans formally took over control of Algiers. Two days later Darlan, with Marshal Pétain's secret concurrence, ordered a cease-fire for all French units in Africa.[8]

It was well for the Anglo-Americans that the French were ready to quit. As D-day progressed, the weather worsened so rapidly that by 1800 all further support landings had to be canceled. By that time also, poor boat handling had cost the Eastern Naval Task Force 90 per cent of its landing craft. So few reinforcements and so little material had been unloaded that the situation ashore might have become desperate had French resistance continued. But Murphy's diplomatic triumph permitted the completion of the unloading of troops and supplies in the port of Algiers itself and paved the way for the launching of the Allied drive into Tunisia.

[8] The Marshal sent his approval by secret code. Officially and publicly however he was obliged to order French forces in Africa to continue resistance.

Algeria: Oran

The most powerful of the Allied attacks was that made at Oran by the Center Task Force. Because French feeling had been inflamed there by the British attack on the French fleet at nearby Mers-el-Kebir in July 1940, the planners allotted to this assault the best-trained American units available, the 1st Infantry Division and half of the 1st Armored Division, the latter including two armored combat teams with light and medium tanks and tank destroyers. For the same reason no British ground troops were assigned to the operation, although units of the Royal Navy screened and escorted the transports. The Center Naval Task Force included a battleship, a large carrier, two escort carriers, an anti-aircraft cruiser, 13 destroyers, more than a score of smaller warships, and transports carrying a landing force of 39,000 troops, nearly all American. The plan was almost identical to that for Algiers. Simultaneous landings were to be made at two beaches west of the city, and—the major effort—on a stretch of coast east of the city adjoining and including the small port of Arzew. Two converted United States coastguard cutters, given to Great Britain earlier in the war, would carry raiders into the port of Oran to seize harbor facilities and prevent sabotage. Airfields behind the city were to be quickly seized so that planes could be flown in from the airstrip at Gibraltar.

At Oran the transports debarked the troops smoothly and with little confusion into their landing craft shortly before midnight of November 7–8. Coming ashore between 0100 and 0130, the troops were much less scattered than in the other landings. They moved out quickly toward their assigned objectives. Sporadic and ineffective resistance was offered at Arzew, where infantry and a naval raiding party were able to seize intact four small ships and 13 French seaplanes fueled and loaded with torpedoes. The landings west of Oran were unopposed. Three shallow-draft tankers fitted to discharge tanks on the beach, prototypes of the LST, performed brilliantly, setting ashore armored units that rushed ahead of the main attack to seize an important airfield and vital road junctions on the plateau behind the city.

Satisfaction over the success of the Oran landings was tempered by the disaster that had overtaken the ex-United States Coast Guard cutters filled with raiders attempting to enter Oran harbor. At higher command levels there had been a serious dispute over the feasibility and timing of this strike scheduled for H-hour plus two. Objectors had pointed out that the defenses were very strong and that the long, narrow harbor was a trap. The only possible hope for success was either to effect complete surprise simultaneously with the landings on the beaches, or to wait until army troops had already entered the city before closing in on the docks. By entering the harbor two hours after the first attack on the beaches, the raiders had encountered alert defenses and forfeited support from other Allied units. The *Walney*, in the lead, bulled her way through a boom blocking the harbor entrance, only to be raked by point-blank fire from two French destroyers and a torpedo boat. Staggering to the head of the harbor, she blew up and sank with 75 per cent casualties among her sailors and troops. The *Hartland* gallantly followed her sister craft with no better luck. As she attempted to round a quay, she was taken under fire at 100-foot range by a French destroyer. Losing power, the cutter drifted away, shattered and burning. Half her personnel were mowed down when, forced topside by fires raging in every deck, they were exposed to machine gun fire from all quarters. The ship was abandoned and all survivors were captured. When the city was seized by advancing army troops, they found the harbor clogged with sunken merchant shipping and small warships, the result of French demolitions. Again the French navy had offered strong resistance, upholding its honor with a tragic loss of lives and ships. The ill-fated raiding force, as at Algiers, had gallantly but totally failed in its mission. Valor could not overcome the disadvantages of a faulty plan.

Although cut off from all support, the French garrison in Oran hung on for another day. But it was unable to check the American infantry and armored units from crashing into the heart of the city on the morning of November 10. When Admiral Darlan gave orders during the afternoon for all French troops to cease fighting, organized resistance at Oran had already ended. In marked contrast to the other landings, the landing craft here had been better handled with lower losses. With the help of the port of Arzew, the supply build-up was ample to sustain the fighting. Reflecting their better training, the soldiers had shown more skill and dash than in the other African attacks.

Tunisia

With Morocco and Algeria secure, the Allies had valuable rear base areas, but Tunisia, separated from Europe by the 90-mile-wide Sicilian Channel, was their real strategic goal. The Germans moved swiftly to keep Tunisia out of Allied hands. By 1130 on D-day, November 8, the Nazis had forced the Vichy cabinet to accept their offer of air support from Sicily and Sardinia. "This caitiff decision," as Churchill branded it, "enabled the Germans to take the quick decisive action of occupying airfields in Tunisia, with all its costly consequences on our campaign."[9] Then the Germans took over unoccupied France and attempted to gain possession of the Toulon fleet. Meanwhile Admiral Darlan, now fully committed to the Allies, was doing all he could to bring French forces and territory over from Vichy allegiance. He ordered the Toulon fleet to sortie to North Africa with the aid of British warships that stood by to offer help, but Admiral Laborde, the Vichy commander at Toulon, preferred neutrality, trusting a Hitler promise that Germany would never try to seize the ships. When the Nazis violated their word and broke into Toulon, Admiral Laborde settled the issue by scuttling his fleet.

Darlan sent orders to Admiral Estéva, senior French officer in Tunisia, for his forces to rally to the Allies, but German planes were already landing on Tunisian airfields. Except for an army contingent under General Barré that withdrew into the hills, French Tunisian forces that might have joined the Allies were quickly rounded up and disarmed. British troops joined the pro-Allied French troops on the Algeria-Tunisia border on November 12, but several thousand German paratroops landing

[9] Winston Churchill, *The Second World War*, IV (Boston, 1950), 623.

in Tunisia the following day made it apparent that the Allies could look forward to no easy victory. There was consolation however in the information that Dakar and French West Africa had joined the Allied cause on November 23 and that Rommel was fleeing westward with the British Eighth Army in close pursuit.

Hitler's decision to hold what he could of North Africa proved foolish in the long run, for the six-month campaign that followed was far more costly to the Germans than to the Allies. But at the end of the year, heavy rains in Tunisia had mired the Allies so badly that they pulled their forces back to better defensive positions, while out in the desert the advance of Montgomery's Eighth Army was delayed until supplies could catch up with him. Despite temporary setbacks, caused largely by inexperienced personnel—the Army's counterpart of the Navy's landing craft troubles—General Eisenhower was able to get the offensive rolling again in the spring, even though by then nearly 200,000 German and Italian reinforcements and great quantities of Axis supplies had reached Africa. While the Allied forces out of Algeria drove east, with General Patton's armored divisions distinguishing themselves, the British Eighth Army fought its way north through the fortified Mareth Line. Rommel, broken in health, was ordered home by Hitler. On April 7, 1943 Eighth Army and American patrols met, having crossed 2,000 miles of Africa between them, and by May 13 the Tunisian campaign was over. Some 275,000 Axis prisoners of war were taken. Allied air, surface, and submarine forces had sunk 433,000 tons of Axis shipping. Only a few Axis troops escaped across the straits to Sicily. The first British trans-Mediterranean convoy since 1941 left Gibraltar on May 17 and reached Alexandria on May 26 without loss. Reeling back from the Russian offensive at Stalingrad and driven out of Africa, the Nazis had an early foretaste of ultimate disaster.

The Casablanca Conference

Though at the end of 1942 it was not clear that the Axis had lost its capability of retrieving the initiative, strategic planning could not wait for the military situation to clarify. It was imperative that the Allied leaders get together and coordinate plans. Stalin could not leave Russia just as the Stalingrad campaign was reaching a climax, but Roosevelt and Churchill with their chiefs of staff met at Casablanca from January 14 to 23, 1943 to review the entire strategy of the war.

The main question before the Casablanca Conference was: What next? Since there had been no firm combined planning beyond the decision to seize the North African coastline, the British and Americans had to decide what further moves, if any, should be made in the Mediterranean theater once Tunis was secured.

General Marshall and the other United States Chiefs of Staff still hoped soon to direct all resources into a single, all-out cross-Channel attack somewhere in France, preferably in Normandy. If logistic difficulties made this impossible in 1943, as many American staff planners had at length concluded, then Marshall hoped that the Allies might pin down German troops by seizing the Brittany peninsula in western France. Against this view the British planners, armed with a host of statistics, were able to put up a convincing argument. They pointed out that the Germans could have 44 divisions in France by mid-1943 to oppose an Anglo-American landing, which by that time could muster no more than 25 divisions. Until the odds could be significantly bettered in favor of the Allies, the British believed that an assault on the coast of France could lead only to defeat in that area, and another costly, humiliating ejection from the Continent.

The British had every intention of invading France—but only after the German forces there had been considerably weakened. For the time being, the British planners insisted, the best way of achieving that goal, and also of assisting the Russians, was through a continuation of peripheral strategy. Diversionary attacks from the Mediterranean into Southern Europe, said they, would draw so many German units from France and from the Eastern Front that in those areas Hitler would be 55 divisions short of the total needed to defend his empire.

Continued peripheral operations in the Mediterranean theater, the planners continued, could knock Italy out of the war and possibly bring in the Turks. If all this occurred, Hitler would face defeat—even without a cross-Channel attack. But assuming that such an attack was to be carried out, the landing in France would have a far greater chance for success if the Germans were first weakened in the West by attacks elsewhere.

Though the American Joint Chiefs were not entirely convinced by the British logic, they could find no valid counter argument. They disliked seeing more Allied forces sucked into the Mediterranean, which they considered strategically eccentric to the main objective. However, one fact stood out—the British were unwilling to risk returning to France in 1943, and without full British concurrence and cooperation there could be no cross-Channel attack. After much discussion, during which Admiral King was able to present the case for stepping up the war with Japan by a series of limited offensives, the two Allies struck a bargain.[10] The British desired to see the war in the Pacific limited to a holding operation until Germany was defeated; then all available Allied force would be turned against Japan. They abandoned that position and consented to allocate more men and materials to the Pacific, thereby enabling the Americans to retain the initiative they had won in that theater. The Americans, for their part, consented to postpone the cross-Channel attack till 1944. Meanwhile enemy strength in Europe would be diverted and pressure maintained by means of a Mediterranean offensive in the summer of 1943. Air attacks against the heart of Germany and the *Luftwaffe* would be stepped up. Everyone agreed that the Allies must give top priority to the antisubmarine war. Otherwise no offensives anywhere could succeed.

The remainder of the conference was devoted to finding an appropriate place to strike in the Mediterranean. In the end the planners considered two possibilities, the islands of Sicily and Sardinia. Sardinia was the more weakly defended of the two and would provide bomber bases for raids on the industrial centers of northern Italy, but the island lacked a harbor adequate to mount a major amphibious assault. On the other hand, capture of

---

[10] King estimated that only 15 per cent of total Allied military resources was being used against Japan.

Sicily, although much more difficult, would more directly threaten Italy, possibly forcing her out of the war, would definitely secure the Sicilian Channel, and would offer the prospect of destroying more enemy forces. Sicily was therefore named the target, D-day being fixed for an appropriate time in July 1943. On this note of resolve and harmony the Casablanca Conference ended.

The day following the close of the Casablanca Conference, President Roosevelt startled statesmen and military leaders around the world by announcing to the press a policy that he himself had formulated, with the concurrence of Prime Minister Churchill. This was the decision that the United States and Britain would accept nothing short of "unconditional surrender" of Germany, Italy, and Japan. Terms would neither be offered nor considered. Not even Napoleon at the height of his conquests ever so completely closed the door to negotiation. To adopt such an inflexible policy was bad enough; to announce it publicly was worse.

The policy of unconditional surrender ran counter to the earlier insistence of British and American leaders that they were fighting not the people but the leaders who had misled them. The policy was the sort of mistake that statesmen of the 17th and 18th centuries never made. They understood better than some of their successors that today's enemy might be needed as tomorrow's ally. And a war pushed to the point of complete victory might ruin victor as well as vanquished.

Summary

Early conferences of the Combined Chiefs of Staff, generally dominated by the dynamic personalities of Roosevelt and Churchill, revealed a fundamental difference of opinion on how to defeat the European Axis. The Americans favored a massive thrust to be directed against the heart of Germany, with overwhelming force and as soon as possible. The British, while not ruling out an eventual return to western Europe, preferred attacks around the fringes, combined with air raids on German industries and communications, and material assistance to Russia. By such means they hoped so to weaken the enemy and draw his forces out of western Europe that an eventual Anglo-American cross-Channel attack would have a greater chance of success. When the British flatly rejected the Joint Chiefs' plan for a landing in France in 1942, to be followed up by a major invasion in 1943, the Americans reluctantly agreed to invade French North Africa as a means of alleviating Axis pressure in Russia and in Egypt.

D-day for North Africa was set for November 8, 1942. The initial objectives were three major ports, Casablanca in French Morocco and Algiers and Oran in Algeria. The assault on Casablanca, staged from the United States, was all-American. That on Algiers, staged from Britain, was Anglo-American. That on Oran, also staged from Britain, was chiefly American, with British naval support. Because the target cities were strongly defended against frontal attack, the Allies landed to right and left of the ports in order to seize them from the flanks.

Negotiations with the French for a bloodless invasion proved only partly successful, for many French units offered strenuous resistance. Only the unexpected presence of Admiral Darlan and his willingness to negotiate a truce, first for Algiers, at the end of a day's fighting, and then for all North Africa, two days later, relieved a supply situation that was becoming critical. Once peace was restored, all French elements cooperated readily with the invaders.

The North African landings were very ragged compared with later Allied amphibious operations, partly through lack of experience but mostly because there had been insufficient time to train. Both the Army and the Navy learned that there can be no substitute for adequate, careful planning and training. Skillful handling of landing craft was found vital on two counts, first, to get the troops ashore when and where they were supposed to land and, second, to avoid losses of boats so as not to disrupt build-up of supplies and reinforcements on shore. Admiral Hewitt's experience with the *Augusta,* doubling as flagship and support vessel, revealed the need for special command ships (AGC's). The British prototype LST's demonstrated the need for beaching craft, not only for landing tanks but to transport additional landing craft to the rendezvous area since transports cannot carry enough craft to boat all the troops embarked. The operations of the *Ranger* and the escort carriers off Morocco showed the effectiveness of carrier air in supporting invasions.

Because the assaults, despite the confusion and delays, seemed to have gone well enough, the Army continued to favor night landings as a means of attaining surprise. The naval commanders however advocated dawn landings after a night approach, pointing out that tactical surprise of an alerted enemy was unlikely and that the often chaotic North African landings must surely have failed against determined resistance. The naval commanders also advocated pre-landing bombardment to pave the way for the troops, and greater use of naval gunfire to support the troops ashore. But the army commanders continued to prefer the advantages of surprise to pre-invasion bombardment, which would alert the defense. Not realizing the accuracy of naval guns with modern fire control equipment, they distrusted naval fire support, fearing that their own troops might be hit.

With the Allied occupation of Casablanca, Algiers, and Oran, heavily reinforced Allied armies attempted to outrace the Germans and Italians to the Tunisian ports of Bizerte and Tunis. In this they were unsuccessful but in the end the failure proved an advantage, for the British Eighth Army pushing westward out of Egypt and the Allied forces advancing out of Algeria succeeded in joining hands in Tunisia and trapping not only the German *Afrika Korps* but Axis forces sent to Tunisia from Europe. With the occupation of North Africa, the Allies reopened the Mediterranean to their cargo convoys, relieved Malta, toughened their troops for further campaigns, and obtained bases for attacking Italy and other Axis territories on the Mediterranean.

Meanwhile at the Casablanca Conference of January 1943, the Allied leaders had agreed that when Tunisia fell the island of Sicily should next be attacked. If this invasion succeeded, Italy could be forced out of the war and the "end of the beginning," as Churchill expressed it, would have arrived. But at the close of the conference, Roosevelt announced the Unconditional Surrender Policy that canceled hopes of shortening the war through setting the German people against their leaders.

32:
Operations against Sicily and Italy

Following the successful landings in French Morocco and Algeria, United States warships withdrew from the Mediterranean, leaving Allied operations in those waters to the Royal Navy. Vice Admiral Hewitt returned to the United States to resume his regular duty as Commander Amphibious Force Atlantic Fleet (Comphiblant). The U.S. Navy remained responsible in North Africa only for the Moroccan Sea Frontier, including the port of Casablanca and the air base at Port Lyautey, and the port of Oran, including Mers-el-Kebir.

With the Allied decision to invade Sicily it became necessary for United States naval forces, personnel, and material to return to the North African theater of operations. In February 1943 Admiral Hewitt was relieved as Comphiblant by Rear Admiral Alan G. Kirk and proceeded to North Africa to assume command of all U.S. naval forces and operations in that area as Commander United States Naval Forces Northwest African Waters. In mid-March Hewitt's command was designated U.S. Eighth Fleet. For the rest of the war the Eighth Fleet included all United States naval forces in the Mediterranean. Operationally it was subordinate to Lieutenant General Dwight D. Eisenhower, the Supreme Allied Commander, through Admiral of the Fleet Sir Andrew B. Cunningham, Commander in Chief Mediterranean. Administratively, it was directly under Admiral King as Commander in Chief U.S. Fleet. In other words, Hewitt received his military orders from Eisenhower but drew his ships, men, and material from King. It was the immediate responsibility of Hewitt and his staff to carry out the naval planning for the American phase of the invasion of Sicily.

Code-named Operation HUSKY, the Sicilian invasion was planned and executed as an operation in itself, a limited objective. The Allied chiefs proposed to invade Sicily and then see what happened before assigning further Mediterranean targets. Several benefits were expected to result, stated by Churchill as: (1) making Mediterranean communications more secure, (2) diverting German pressure from the Russian front, and (3) intensifying the pressure on Italy.[1]

Churchill and the British Chiefs of Staff hoped that the fall of Sicily would lead to the collapse of the Mussolini government and the withdrawal of Italy from the war, thus opening the way to the Allies for further Mediterranean ventures. They also anticipated that the ensuing disaster to Axis arms might cause the Turks to abandon neutrality and enter the conflict against the Axis. Though the American Joint Chiefs of Staff were less enthusiastic, they admitted that Allied forces assigned to the European theater could not be kept idle until an invasion of France became possible in 1944, and that Sicily was the obvious target. All Allied leaders agreed that seizing a foothold on national territory of the Axis would bring a tremendous morale boost to the western Allies.

The military leaders who successfully concluded the Tunisian campaign continued in command of the Sicilian expedition. Eisenhower received four-star rank to assume overall command of Operation HUSKY. His deputy, General Sir Harold R. Alexander, controlled all ground troops; naval forces again served under Fleet Admiral Cunningham; and Air Chief Marshal Sir Arthur W. Tedder com-

[1] Winston S. Churchill, *The Second World War*, IV (Boston, 1950), 692.

manded the Allied air forces. Ground forces assigned to the assault included the American Seventh Army (Lieutenant General Patton) and the British Eighth Army (Lieutenant General Montgomery). The naval assault forces were the Western Naval Task Force (Vice Admiral Hewitt) and the Eastern Naval Task Force (Vice Admiral Sir Bertram Ramsay). Under Vice Admiral Sir Algernon V. Willis, an all-British Covering Force of 6 battleships, 2 fleet carriers, 6 light cruisers, and 24 destroyers would protect both landing forces against possible incursions of the Italian fleet.

Sicily: Planning and Preparations

Planning the Sicilian landings proved a long and complicated process. There was little opportunity for Eisenhower's top commanders to confer in order to iron out snarls. Headquarters of the commands were scattered across North Africa, far distant from each other. Moreover Alexander, Patton, Montgomery, and other senior officers were preoccupied with concluding the Tunisian campaign and could at first give Sicily scant attention.

Reconciling the strategic and tactical requirements of the various service arms vexed planning even worse. Everybody agreed that the ultimate tactical object was to seize the Straits of Messina as soon as possible. The main enemy supply artery would then be cut and Italo-German forces trapped before they could withdraw to the Italian mainland. But simply sailing in to land within the Straits was not considered feasible, because beaches therein lay beyond the range of effective Allied fighter cover. The only landing sites where adequate land-based air support could be provided lay in the southeast corner of Sicily between the cities of Licata and Syracuse. In this area Allied fighters from Malta, Gozo, Pantelleria, and the Cape Bon peninsula could effectively break up Axis air attacks. Yet this conclusion far from settled the matter. In the Licata-Syracuse region there were but three ports, of which only Syracuse had any considerable tonnage capacity. Both army and navy planners feared that the quantity of supplies that might be handled through these ports and across the beaches could not sustain the number of divisions necessary to defeat the enemy's

garrison in Sicily. The best compromise appeared to be to seize beachheads in the part of Sicily that could be covered by fighters, developing airfields to extend fighter cover, and then to land a few days later on beaches near the major ports of Palermo and Catania.

No one really liked this complicated plan of successive assaults. Generals Alexander and Montgomery flatly rejected it on the ground that enemy reinforcements might penetrate between the widely dispersed Allied armies. Army commanders demanded a single, massed assault in the region of Sicily that could be covered by Allied fighters, a requirement that naval commanders considered impossible to fulfill logistically.

In the nick of time two developments in amphibious technology broke the deadlock in planning. With the arrival of numerous newly built LST's and hundreds of DUKW's,[2] naval staff planners concluded that the army attack could just barely be supplied across the southeast Sicilian beaches with the help of the few available ports. Early in May General Eisenhower approved the new plan for a massed assault.

D-day was set for July 10, 1943, H-hour at 0245. The date and hour were selected to provide moonlight for paratroop drops, with the moon setting in time for the assault waves to close the beaches in total darkness. Because the selected H-hour exposed the fleet to a moonlight approach, navy planners suggested a later approach with landings after dawn, preceded by naval gunfire to neutralize beach defenses. The army planners discarded the suggestion, holding that ship-to-shore movement in darkness was necessary for surprise and insisting that naval gunfire would be ineffective because it was "not designed for land bombardment."

Admiral Hewitt's Western Naval Task Force, organized into three components codenamed *Joss, Dime,* and *Cent,* was to seize a beachhead incorporating the small ports of Licata and Gela and the fishing village of Scoglitti, along a 37-mile front on the Gulf of Gela. Subdividing into four groups, Admiral Ramsay's Eastern Naval Task Force was to seize the Pachino peninsula and an area along

[2] Amphibious cargo-carrying trucks, known also as ducks or amtrucks.

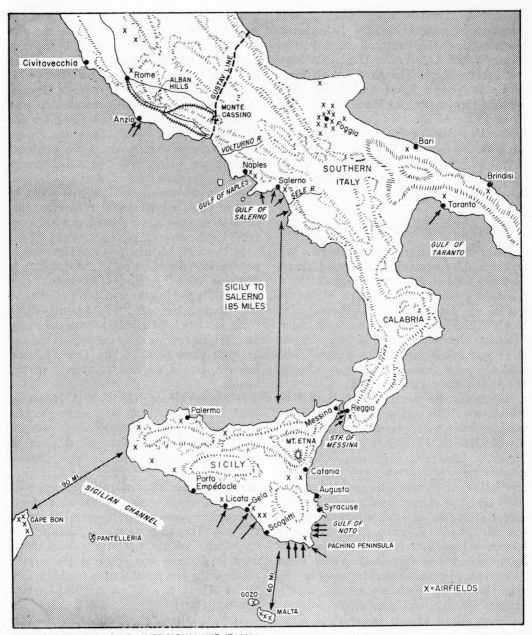

ALLIED OPERATIONS AGAINST SICILY AND ITALY

the Gulf of Noto just outside the coastal de-fenses of Syracuse. The landing front was tremendously wide, nearly 100 miles—the most extensive landing of any in World War II. In numbers also the actual assault phase was the most powerful of the war, not equaled even by the assault on Normandy a year later.

More than 470,000 troops, about half Ameri-can and half British, were assigned to the initial landings. Staging through every avail-able North African port from Bizerte west-ward, American forces embarked in a vast armada of 580 ships and beaching craft, carry-ing 1,124 landing craft. Staging from the Eastern Mediterranean and Tunisia, the British used 818 ships and beaching craft, including the vessels of the Covering Force, and 715 landing craft.

A serious defect in the preparations resulted from lack of cooperation of the Allied Air Forces because of a then irreconcilable difference of opinion regarding the employment of tactical air power. The Air Forces were addicted to their doctrine of "sealing off the beachhead" by blasting enemy communications so that there could be little or no movement into or out of the beachhead areas. Meanwhile attacks would be made on enemy airfields to ensure that air interference with the landings would be slight. The Air Forces believed that their technique would obviate the necessity of close tactical support available on call from ground observers on ships or shore. Hence they did not participate in the joint planning and forbade pilots to answer calls for support from ship-based or ground stations other than those approved by Air Force Headquarters in North Africa.

The Allied armies and navies mistrusted the effectiveness of this air doctrine. They wanted the kind of support that had been furnished off Casablanca by U.S. aircraft carrier *Ranger* and that was to become routine in Pacific operations. But Air Marshal Tedder had his way. Although a tactical air force was assigned to support the landings, it was to be controlled from North Africa with no assurance of priority to army-navy requests for aid. To fill the gap General Patton wanted aircraft carriers assigned to the assault forces to fly immediate strikes on call. But Admiral Hewitt felt that this could not really be justified in view of the great demand for carriers elsewhere and the presence of abundant land-based Allied air power from bases within easy range of the beachheads. The attack therefore proceeded without a firm air plan known to all the commanders. At best, air support would be slow; at worst, nonexistent.

Since no one wished to risk repeating the disasters that followed the attacks within the ports of Oran and Algiers, no forces were earmarked to land directly within enemy harbors. But British Commandos and American Rangers were to neutralize key enemy installations, and elements of two divisions of paratroops were to land before H-hour to seize vital airfields and bridges.

Because Sicily was such an obvious Allied objective, extensive efforts were made to convince the enemy that the main attack would come in Greece, with a secondary assault on Sardinia. The most dramatic was the dropping of a carefully prepared corpse into the sea off the Spanish coast to wash ashore near Cadiz. "Major William Martin," as the corpse was called, had a briefcase filled with choice misinformation that quickly fell into the hands of German agents. Local German and Italian commanders were not fooled, but Hitler and the German High Command were, with the result that German armored divisions and Axis mine and torpedo craft were moved to both Sardinia and Greece, where they contributed nothing to the defenses of Sicily. Slow Italian minelayers, left to mine Sicilian waters, did not lay enough mines to prove any serious obstacle.

Training for the Sicilian campaign was much more thorough than had been possible for the North African operation. As the new LST's, LCT's, and LCI's arrived in the theater, they were rushed into training maneuvers in virtually all ports, large and small, on the North African coastline.[3] While troops exercised with the crews of the new LCVP's in landing through the surf, shore parties practiced forwarding supplies, evacuating wounded, directing gunfire, and the myriad other tasks that are part of an amphibious assault. Most of the assault divisions managed to stage reasonably realistic rehearsals with their task forces on a divisional or near-divisional scale. While possibly no commander thought his particular unit had received enough training, by prior standards Hewitt's and Ramsay's task forces were well prepared.

A combination of beach gradient and surf

[3] The LST (Landing Ship, Tank), the LCT (Landing Craft, Tank), and the LCI (Landing Craft, Infantry) were *beaching craft*, permitting a shore-to-shore expedition by transporting men, vehicles, and supplies from one beach to another. The LCVP (Landing Craft, Vehicle and Personnel) and the LCM (Landing Craft, Mechanized) were smaller *landing craft*, generally carried aboard transports to make ship-to-shore landings.

in the tideless Mediterranean had caused the formation along the coasts of Sicily and elsewhere of "false beaches," sand bars a hundred yards or so offshore over which water shoaled too much to permit the passage of such large beaching craft as LST's.

The landing craft and bases command, under Rear Admiral Richard L. Conolly USN, resolved this problem during training in Africa by developing pontoon causeways, standard pontoon units shackled together to form a bridge to shore. It also proved feasible to "marry" LCT's to the larger LST's so that a sort of ferry service could be run between the LST's anchored offshore and the beach. Both methods worked; both were vital to the successful supplying of the Seventh and Eighth armies after the initial landings.

While the Allied forces prepared, so did the Axis. The Italian fleet remained the best weapon against the landings, for if it could evade the powerful British Covering Force it might play havoc with the assault convoys. But since Axis commanders could not know where or when the Allied blow would fall, their chance of achieving the necessary surprise for a successful naval counterattack was slight. Moreover the Italian *Supermarina,* citing lack of adequate fighter cover, forbade fleet operations within easy Allied air attack range in the waters around Sicily. The defending Axis commanders accordingly pinned their hopes on a successful ground and air defense. Air attacks and resistance by seven Italian coastal divisions were expected to pin the Allies to the beaches, while counterattacks by four Italian and two German mobile divisions were supposed to fling the attackers into the sea. Unwisely Mussolini refused Hitler's offer of three more German divisions. While coastal defenses around all the major ports were strengthened, anti-invasion exercises were held at Gela, for here both the Germans and the Italians expected an Allied landing. Mobile forces were billeted in strategic locations, and some 350,000 troops, including more than 50,000 Germans, awaited attack by the 470,000 Allied invaders.

To participants in the concurrent Pacific war, the odds, considering numbers only, would have appeared to favor the defenders overwhelmingly. In the New Georgia campaign, which roughly coincided with the Sicilian campaign, nearly 34,000 Americans spent six weeks wresting a small corner of New Georgia Island from about 8,000 Japanese defenders. In the Pacific, the Allies rarely undertook an assault without at least a 3-to-1 numerical superiority, and often the odds were far in excess of that. Yet, though air and surface support for Allied assaults against defended positions in the Pacific theater became increasingly powerful, the invaders could generally expect stout resistance. The Japanese would retreat only from an utterly hopeless situation. Few would surrender. If their retreat were cut off, they usually fought to the last man. To military men acquainted with that sort of war, the Allied plan to invade Sicily with only a slight numerical advantage over the defenders would have seemed an invitation to disaster.

But Sicily was a hollow shell. Poor deployment of defense forces, with little provision for defense in depth, was one reason. The main reason however lay in the attitude of the Italians. The Sicilian reservists, to whom Mussolini had entrusted the defense of their homeland, detested the Germans and were far from being ardent Fascists. The Sicilians, together with most of their compatriots on the Italian mainland, saw clearly that the war into which their government had led them was not likely to serve Italian interests. They regarded their military situation as hopeless and rather welcomed an Allied invasion that would take them out of the war and the hated Germans out of Italy.

As D-day approached, Air Chief Marshal Tedder's Mediterranean Allied Air Forces launched a series of raids that put all but a few airfields in Sicily out of operation and forced the Germans and Italians to base their remaining planes on the Italian mainland. And, though Tedder's planes failed to win complete control of the air over the target area, they badly disrupted the Sicilian transport system, and further reduced the already low morale of the Italian forces.

To the last, Mussolini and Field Marshal Albert Kesselring, the German army commander in Italy, remained confident that the invaders would be destroyed "at the water's edge," but General Guzzoni, the Italian commander in Sicily, knew his men and was less optimistic.

Sicily: Assault and Follow-Up

On July 8, 1943, the jam-packed North African harbors emptied as the huge Allied invasion fleet stood out to sea. Routed so as to make it appear that Greece and Sardinia rather than Sicily were the targets, the convoys passed safely through the extensive Allied mine fields, and in due course turned toward their departure points off Malta.

The weather was calm, and there had been no enemy air attacks. By the morning of July 9 however, the confidence that reigned in the Malta headquarters of General Eisenhower and Admiral Cunningham changed to anxiety as the seas made up steeply in a howling wind. Soon the beaching craft were plunging heavily through rough seas, and even the large transports were taking green water over their bows. Trusting to the aerologist's reports that the wind would die down by the morning of D-day, Admirals Hewitt and Ramsay decided to let their task forces continue. After painful reflection, the commanders at Malta decided not to interfere. Navigation became intensely difficult as lighter craft, especially the LCT's, were slowed by the storm. Nevertheless the general pattern of the approach was maintained. Remarkably close to schedule the assault ships closed their assigned beaches, marked by British beacon submarines that blinked signals seaward.

Admiral Hewitt's Western Task Force concentrated its attacks on three groups of beaches in the Gulf of Gela. The western flank at Licata was assigned to the *Joss* force, the center at Gela to the *Dime* force, and the eastern flank at Scoglitti to the *Cent* force. All was quiet as the transports and the troop-carrying LST's anchored in position. Ashore, fires blazed here and there from Allied bombings, and occasional distant gunfire marked areas where paratroops, dropped earlier in the night, were harassing the enemy. Scout boats stealthily closed the shore, some putting men on the beach to determine exact landing points for the infantry. This proved no easy matter, for

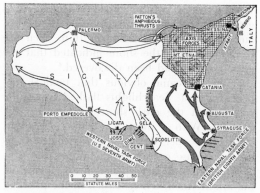

ALLIED INVASION AND AXIS EVACUATION OF SICILY

the smoke-shrouded hills looming in the darkness offered poor landmarks. Yet it was crucially important to place the troops on the right beaches lest the entire pattern of the attack be disrupted.

On the transports, organized confusion reigned as the ships rolled heavily in the aftermath of the storm. Rail loading the LCVP's that were to carry in the first assault waves was difficult, even impossible for some transports, so that for the most part the troops were obliged to clamber down the spray-drenched nets into the pitching small craft. Rocket-firing support boats suffered heavily; many were too damaged in launching to be able to participate. At Scoglitti, to which *Cent* force was lifted entirely in large transports that had steamed from Chesapeake Bay, the rolling of the ships so delayed launching that H-hour had to be postponed an hour. But from the *Joss* and *Dime* forces, waves of LCVP's circled until all their numbers had joined up and then, guided by minesweepers and submarine chasers, moved to the line of departure about 2,000 yards offshore.

Quiet still reigned as the first waves, on signal and guided by blinking lights from the scout boats, began the run from the line of departure to the shore. Admiral Hewitt, supporting the suggestion of the navy planners, had pleaded with the army to be allowed to deliver a dawn pre-invasion bombardment before the infantry hit the beach. But the army commanders, hoping to slip the men ashore in darkness before the enemy realized what was happening, refused. The best Hewitt could get was permission for supporting destroyers, gunboats, and rocket-firing craft to open fire if reaction from the shore indicated that the assault waves had been discovered.[4]

It soon became obvious that tactical surprise was lost. Searchlights flashed across the water from the dark shore, picking up the LCVP's. With a distant crackle enemy machine guns opened up. When artillery shells began to raise geysers in the water, the supporting craft at last opened fire. Meanwhile the infantrymen, tense, seasick in the pitching assault boats, awaited the end of their seagoing ordeal. As the boats touched down and the bow ramps fell, they hesitated momentarily, then rushed ashore, forgetting nausea, scurrying inland to locate and consolidate their assigned positions.

Enemy fire was heaviest at Licata. Here a group of LCI's, scheduled to land behind a first wave of LCVP's that were to clear the beach defenses ahead of them, instead found themselves the lead wave. In the darkness, the smaller craft had headed for another part of the beach. The LCI's, pressing in despite fierce enemy fire from automatic weapons, established fire ascendancy with their own guns and landed their troops.

Enemy fire gradually lessened on all beaches as the invaders rapidly overran enemy pill boxes and gun emplacements, or as supporting destroyers and gunboats blasted hostile positions one by one. For several hours enemy shells fell spasmodically on the various American landing areas, but by 0800 most enemy artillery was silent. The Americans climbed

[4] In the Pacific theater, where amphibious assaults were navy-controlled, assault forces from the beginning sacrificed some tactical surprise for the advantages of pre-invasion bombardment. Here the usual pattern was an approach in darkness, with preliminary naval bombardment and air attacks beginning at first light, followed by landings after sunrise. The duration of the preparatory fire depended on the degree that the beachhead could be isolated. For some of the Central Pacific islands and atolls, which could be absolutely isolated, it lasted for days. Guam received 13 days of preparatory fire. Against beachheads in Europe, where communications were highly developed, preparatory fire of long duration was out of the question. Opening of fire would pinpoint the beachhead and draw enemy reserves to the area. The beachhead had to be secured before the reserves arrived.

the hills toward their D-day initial lines well ahead of schedule. United States Rangers rushed into Licata and Gela—too late at the latter to prevent the dynamiting of an important pier earmarked for unloading. Except for some delays and scattering of troops on the wrong beaches as a result of difficulties of night navigation in landing craft, the landing had proceeded smoothly and more or less according to plan. Ground resistance was light, the Italian defenders happily surrendering at every opportunity.

With the initial beachhead secured, air attacks and unloading problems became Admiral Hewitt's principal worries. Of these, the air attacks proved the easier to deal with. A heavy volume of antiaircraft fire greeted the numerous flights that the Axis air forces placed over the ships, forcing the aviators to bomb inaccurately and indiscriminately. Use for the first time in the theater of proximity fused (VT) antiaircraft shells greatly increased the effectiveness of defensive fire. Hewitt's ship losses were a destroyer, an LST loaded with badly needed anti-tank artillery, and an ammunition ship in a follow-up convoy.

The false beaches badly hampered off-loading supplies on D-day, preventing LST's from landing vehicles directly on shore. Pontoon causeways proved hard to rig in the heavy weather, and the number of available components was scanty. Clearing of supplies from smaller craft, LCT's, LCVP's, and LCM's, while more efficiently done than in North Africa, remained a troublesome bottleneck at Gela and Scoglitti. Poor beach exits through soft sand and the inefficiency of the army shore engineers caused material to pile up at the water's edge. Loaded landing craft frequently had to return to their ships.

Fortunately for the invaders, the use of DUKW's mitigated D-day supply difficulties. Launched from LST's or transports, these ingenious vehicles could carry ashore the army's standard 105 mm. artillery piece or three tons of other supplies. Several hundred DUKW's expedited unloading and rushed supplies inland to army dumps. But the DUKW could not carry a tank or heavy truck. Getting these ashore continued to plague landing officers until sufficient causeways and LCT's were available to clear transports and LST's of heavy equipment. After D-day, matters vastly improved as Hewitt's forces shifted unloading to better beaches—those at Scoglitti were abandoned altogether—and the ports of Gela and Licata finally became available for the use of LST's.

The temporary shortage of tanks, anti-tank guns, and tank destroyers on D-day and the morning following enabled the navy to make its most spectacular contribution to the success of the Sicilian operations—and incidentally to convince some skeptical army commanders of the value of naval gunfire against shore targets. General Guzzoni, as soon as he received news of the Allied landings, ordered counterattacks on Gela by armored forces. These attacks proved the most serious threat the Seventh Army encountered in Sicily. Patton, and the army in general, now learned in dramatic fashion the value of coordinated, carefully directed naval gunfire. At about 0900 on D-day U.S. cruiser *Boise* and two destroyers, aided by seaplane spotting, checked and turned back a group of Italian tanks closing in on Gela. The next day the *Boise* gave a front-row repeat performance for General Patton. Going ashore that morning, Patton found the beachhead menaced by an advance of about 60 tanks spearheading the German section of Guzzoni's attack. From the top of a building in Gela, Patton could clearly see the 30-ton Panther tanks advancing across the flat plain, with no anti-tank artillery between them and the beaches. A young naval ensign nearby with a walkie-talkie radio inquired of Patton if he could help, and received an emphatic "Sure!" whereupon the ensign radioed *Boise* the location of the enemy. The resulting shower of 38 six-inch shells, together with fire from newly-arrived divisional artillery, halted the German advance. Throughout the rest of the day, Hewitt's ships continued to batter retreating enemy tanks, infantry, and targets of opportunity.

Naval gunfire might have been even more effective had it been possible to have better air spotting. As the fighting progressed, ground observers were sometimes blinded by smoke from burning wheatfields and buildings and were always limited in their fields of observation. SOC float planes from the cruisers, sitting ducks for Messerschmitt fighters that the Nazis

sent over the beachhead, were all too quickly shot down, though while they lasted they performed well in spotting targets. Fast fighters of the type used by Tedder's air forces, though clearly needed, were not available in Sicily.

The failure of the Air Forces to participate in joint planning now resulted in the most publicized disaster of the campaign. American paratroops had dropped behind Gela before the landings. Another drop from 144 transport planes was scheduled for the night of July 11–12. No one in the Western Task Force learned of this in time to get the flight routed away from the ships or to notify all antiaircraft crews. When the planes came over, their arrival coincided with the tail end of an enemy air raid. Through faulty identification, 23 of the Allied transports were shot down by antiaircraft guns on shore and in the task force. Two nights later another flight of transports was similarly handled over the British task force when eleven planes were downed by friendly fire.

Admiral Ramsay's Eastern Task Force, landing British troops on the Pachino Peninsula and in the Gulf of Noto in order to capture Syracuse, experienced conditions similar to those at the American landings. Rough seas hampered the swinging out and launching of assault boats. And although the British were somewhat more protected from the gale than the Americans, the problems of boat handling at the eastern beaches were formidable, and the waves of landing craft were mostly behind schedule. Fortunately for the invaders, enemy fire here was light, and in one area surprise, on which the Allied armies placed such high value, was so complete that Montgomery's troops caught the crew of an Italian fieldpiece fast asleep. Such batteries as opened fire were quickly silenced by Allied warships or by the rapidly advancing assault forces. Large numbers of Italian coastal troops actually stampeded in their eagerness to surrender. By the end of D-day the Eighth Army had not only made up lost time but was well ahead of schedule.

The British, because they were closer to enemy airfields in southern Italy than the Americans, suffered more severely from air attack. But the relatively new technique of ground-based fighter-director control of covering aircraft proved itself in this area, helping break up numerous raids. Admiral Cunningham, vividly recalling the savage bombing of his fleet at Crete two years earlier, found it little short of incredible that Allied naval forces could now remain off the enemy coast with near impunity.

The most spectacular success of the Eighth Army attack was the speedy capture of Syracuse. A company of Montgomery's paratroopers jumped to seize a key bridge by which the port is approached from the south, and held it against everything the defenders could send against them during D-day. That evening the 19 survivors of the heroic 73 who held the bridge were relieved by the vanguard of Montgomery's army coming up from the south. That night the British occupied Syracuse without a struggle. When nearby Augusta fell a few days later, the Allies possessed two of Sicily's best ports. Though many beaching craft were still employed in running supply shuttles from Africa, they of course found it much easier to discharge in captured ports. In Sicily, more than in most places, the worst port proved better for bringing in supplies than the best beach.

Sicily: The Axis Evacuation

The Allies hoped to capture most of the Axis forces in Sicily by entrapping them somewhere west of Mt. Etna in a great pincers movement. While Patton's Seventh Army swept northward across the interior of the island and then advanced eastward along the north coast, Montgomery's Eighth Army was to drive north along the east coast to capture Messina and cut the escape route to Italy across the Straits of Messina.

The Seventh Army carried out its part of the double envelopment with breathtaking speed. Two regiments advanced west along the southern coast and on July 16 captured Porto Empédocle, thereby acquiring a good port for supplying an advance to the north. In the Empédocle area the Americans at last found Italians who would fight, but nevertheless captured 6,000 of them. Advancing north across Sicily, elements of the Seventh Army in four days marched more than a hundred miles by road to enter Palermo on the north coast on July 22. Here they were greeted by crowds

shouting "Down with Mussolini!" and "Long live America!" By the 24th all western Sicily was in American hands, and Patton was advancing along the north coast toward Messina, accompanied by U.S. light cruisers *Savannah, Philadelphia,* and *Boise* and several destroyers to provide gunfire support and by beaching and landing craft to bring forward supplies.

Meanwhile the other arm of the pincers, Montgomery's Eighth Army, was stalled short of Catania on the east coast. To avoid having to make a costly frontal assault on this enemy strong point, Montgomery decided to leave the coast and strike inland, around west of Mt. Etna. Redeploying his forces for this change of front took until August 1. When the Eighth Army again began moving, it made slow progress in the rugged terrain at the base of the mountain, where minor defense forces could harass and delay much stronger attacking columns. Patton's Seventh Army, advancing in the interior and along the north coast, had by this time also lost momentum. The Allied armies were now in fact in line abreast on a front stretching from the north coast across the northeast tip of Sicily to Catania on the east coast. Patton three times employed his accompanying naval forces to land troops behind the enemy lines. No enemy troops were entrapped by these amphibious thrusts, but the first two, each in battalion strength, expedited the Axis withdrawal. The third, in regimental strength, fell short of the now rapidly retreating enemy. Admiral Cunningham, in a complimentary message to Admiral Hewitt, characterized the naval support that Patton had received as "a model of the effective application of sea power in the support of land operations."

On the other hand, Cunningham complained that "No use was made by the Eighth Army of amphibious opportunities."[5] Certainly Montgomery failed in his assigned task of cutting off the Axis at Messina. Patton actually got there ahead of him, but not in time. On July 17 the Axis forces in Sicily had received orders

[5] First Cunningham quotation from CinC Mediterranean dispatch 181751B, August 1943, quoted in Admiral H. Kent Hewitt USN (Ret.), "Naval Aspects of the Sicilian Campaign," *United States Naval Institute Proceedings,* July 1953, 723; second, from *London Gazette,* April 25, 1950, quoted in Morison, IX, 206.

to fight a delaying action and then to evacuate the island. Because the Eighth Army was nearer Messina than the Seventh, elite Axis units, mostly German, had been sent to the Etna area to hold Montgomery, while the rest of the Axis forces in Sicily headed north and east for the Straits of Messina, rotating clockwise like a swinging door with its hinge on Mt. Etna. The Seventh Army's early advance, for all its speed, was not so swift as the Axis withdrawal. By August 3 the German and Italian forces were in the northeast tip of Sicily holding back the Allied attack, and the Axis evacuation across the Straits of Messina had begun.

High level bombing by the Allied Air Force did little damage to the ferries, motor rafts, motor barges, and other Axis craft crossing and re-crossing the three-mile-wide Straits loaded with troops and equipment. Dive bombing was suicidal in the face of massed Axis antiaircraft fire. A few British motor torpedo boats penetrated the Straits but achieved little. The Allies were unwilling to risk larger naval craft against the formidable shore batteries that the enemy had assembled. By August 17 about 45,000 German and more than 60,000 Italian troops had made good their escape with most of their equipment.

Sicily: Conclusions

Some post-war military commentators, particularly among the Germans, have expressed the opinion that an initial assault in or near the Straits of Messina would have been feasible. A successful landing here, while the defenders were deployed to contest a landing elsewhere, would have bottled up Axis forces in Sicily as they had been bottled up in Tunisia. But after the landings in Northwest Africa, Allied commanders in the European theater made it a set policy never to stage an amphibious assault beyond the radius of land-based fighter support—a wise decision, as experience proved. Carrier air, which in the Pacific proved fully able to fill the gap, was not in sufficient quantity in the Mediterranean. American fleet carriers were all in the Pacific. Escort carriers, still in short supply, were busy in the Atlantic combating the U-boat. There were never enough British fleet carriers, and

these carried so few planes and of such inferior quality that they could do little more than provide air cover for the naval forces to which they were attached.

Despite the successful Axis evacuation, the Sicilian campaign was a major triumph for the Allies. Even before the campaign was over, the Axis coalition had begun to fall apart. In Italy the discouraging news from Sicily, climaxed by a 560-plane raid on Rome itself, finally prompted the King to make the popular move of deposing Mussolini and taking him into "protective custody." Marshal Pietro Badoglio, the new head of government announced that he would continue the war against the Allies, a pronouncement that nobody took very seriously. Hitler considered rushing in enough German troops from Russia to seize Italy with an immediate *coup d'état*, but conditions on the Russian front forbade it. The most he could do for the time being was to accept the change of government, while moving additional German divisions into Italy from France and Germany.

With less than five per cent Allied casualties (7,800 killed, 14,000 wounded), Operation Husky in just over a month's time had achieved most of the objectives set forth at the Casablanca Conference. Allied Mediterranean communications were now completely secure. Italy seemed certain to collapse. Italian troops, no longer reliable, would have to be replaced in Italy, France, Yugoslavia, Greece, and elsewhere by German troops. On the Russian front, German pressure, especially from the *Luftwaffe,* was somewhat relieved. The way was laid open for further Allied attacks against which the Nazis had to prepare by further deploying their forces. British hopes that Turkey would enter the conflict were not realized, for the Turks insisted that they were not yet ready. But the Sicilian success greatly reinforced the Allied position in the eyes of neutral nations. Soon Germany would be fighting alone against heavy odds.

Italy: Planning and Preparations

In May 1943, just as the Tunisian campaign was ending, Roosevelt and Churchill and the Combined Chiefs of Staff had met again, this time in Washington. Here they once more threshed over differences of opinion regarding the proper strategy for defeating Germany. The British advocated the invasion of Italy as the inevitable next step after Sicily. Their planners estimated that an Allied cross-Channel attack could succeed only if German forces in France were reduced to no more than 12 divisions. The surest way of attaining such a reduction, they argued, was to eliminate Italy from the war, for then the Nazis would have to send their own troops to replace 24 Italian divisions in the Balkans. An invasion of Italy moreover would enable the Allies to seize the complex of airfields about Foggia to strengthen the coming bombing offensive against Germany.

The Americans acknowledged the cogency of the British argument but reaffirmed their opinion that Germany could be defeated only by an invasion of Western Europe. A campaign in Italy, they pointed out, would tie up Allied as well as German forces and thus might further delay the cross-Channel attack. General Sir Alan Brooke, Chief of the Imperial General Staff, then expressed the opinion that the invasion of France in any event would not be feasible before 1945 or 1946. If so, replied General Marshall, the Allies ought to stop planning for an operation that was continually being postponed, and the Americans should shift their main force to the Pacific, where it could be used at once.

Evidently, if the Allies were to adhere to their plan of putting the primary emphasis upon defeating Germany, they would have to reach another compromise. Being reasonable men, they succeeded—though the details were not all spelled out until some time after the actual conference had ended. The Americans agreed to the invasion of Italy, with the important proviso that only the forces already in the Mediterranean should be used—less seven divisions that were to be withdrawn to the United Kingdom as a nucleus for building up the cross-Channel attack force, and a portion of the assault shipping for operations against Burma. The British, for their part, committed themselves definitely to an invasion of France, with May 1, 1944 as the target date. They agreed that the general conduct of the war in the Pacific should be left to the American Joint Chiefs of Staff. They also accepted in

principle the Joint Chiefs' "Strategic Plan for the Defeat of Japan," a remarkable document that we shall consider in a later chapter.[6] They insisted however that the "Strategic Plan" be carried out with forces already assigned to the Pacific theater. Thus Allied operations against both Italy and Japan were to be limited in order to build up forces in the United Kingdom to 29 divisions for operations against Western Europe.

Since the team of Eisenhower, Alexander, Cunningham, and Tedder was to be retained, it fell upon their staffs to begin planning the invasion of Italy on the eve of the Sicilian assault. Despite pressure from Churchill, Eisenhower refused to make a firm commitment regarding the Italian operation until he had tasted the strength of the enemy in Sicily. However, within a week after the launching of Operation HUSKY, Allied prospects were sufficiently bright for Eisenhower's planners to begin considering when and where Italy should be invaded.

The success of HUSKY shocked Kesselring and other German continental strategists out of their conviction that the Mediterranean was a moat to their fortress. Viewing it now as a highway open to Allied exploitation by the use of sea power, they fully anticipated an early Allied invasion of Italy. Some German planners estimated that the Anglo-American forces might land as far north as Rome, possibly even at Leghorn or Spezia.[7] In anticipation of a northern landing, the Germans made provisions to withdraw their forces rapidly beyond the Apennines to avoid having them trapped in the Italian boot.

But the Allied military leaders had no intention of invading beyond the range of their land-based fighter support. Original plans called only for an invasion via the toe of the boot. The final plan, authorized July 26, was for Montgomery's Eighth Army to cross the Messina Strait to Reggio as soon as feasible after the end of the Sicilian campaign. The invasion of the Italian toe was however to be now considered chiefly a diversionary attack, to draw the Germans away from the main

[6] See page 711.
[7] Vice Admiral Friedrich Ruge, Navy of the German Federal Republic, *Der Seekrieg* (Annapolis, 1957), 336.

assault. This was to be in the Gulf of Salerno, at the extreme attack radius of Sicily-based Spitfire fighters equipped with extra, droppable fuel tanks. Landing at Salerno on September 9, 1943, the newly formed Fifth Army under Lieutenant General Mark W. Clark USA was to drive for Naples 35 miles away.

What the Badoglio government wanted was merely to shift sides, to join Britain and the United States in an alliance against Germany without the humiliation of a formal surrender. But Roosevelt and Churchill, recalling the disapproving public reaction in their countries to the "Darlan deal" in North Africa, did not care to treat the Italians like returning prodigals. Besides, the President and the Prime Minister were inhibited by their own formula of "unconditional surrender." After lengthy and melodramatic secret negotiations reminiscent of spy fiction, a bargain was struck. Italy would surrender and get out of the war, the effective date to coincide with the landing at Salerno. From that date Italian troops who followed the Badoglio government would fight the Germans rather than the Allies. The Italian Fleet and Air Force were to proceed to designated points and place themselves under Allied control. Thus a major purpose of the Salerno and Reggio landings was fulfilled before the attacks began.

Because German troops continued to pour into Italy, Badoglio requested that the main Allied landing be made north of Rome, with an airborne division to be dropped on Rome itself. He promised to have Italian troops in place to join the Allied forces both near the beachhead and near Rome. Eisenhower favored the Badoglio plan, but uncertainty, shortage of forces, and lack of trust between the negotiating parties brought the project to nought. The Allies continued with their plan to land at Salerno, and did not risk informing an erstwhile enemy where the landing was to be. Hence the Italians were unable to assist the invaders in any way.

Meanwhile preparations for the Salerno operation were proceeding under circumstances even more trying than those for Sicily. For this assault Admiral Hewitt was to command all the Allied amphibious forces. These were divided into a primarily British Northern Attack Force carrying two divisions, and an

American Southern Attack Force of equal strength. Two more divisions in floating reserve would follow up. Twenty-six transports, 120 LST's, and 90 LCT's prepared to land troops on two groups of beaches about eight miles apart in the Gulf of Salerno. The landings were to be supported by seven cruisers (including three American), two monitors, and 35 destroyers and a Support Carrier Force of five escort carriers and ten destroyers.[8] The Royal Navy provided a Covering Force of four battleships, fleet carriers *Illustrious* and *Formidable*, and 20 destroyers. The Covering Force, in addition to fending off surface attack, was assigned the task of providing combat air patrol for the Support Carrier Force.

The immediate targets were the port and town of Salerno, the Montecorvino airfield, and the passes through the hills leading to Naples. These objectives were assigned to British forces and to United States Rangers. American forces, to the south, would cover their flank, add depth and body to the beachhead, and link up with Montgomery's Eighth Army coming up from Reggio. The chances of the Eighth Army's being able to join hands with the Salerno beachhead were considerably lessened however by Montgomery's demands for massive artillery support to cover his crossing of the Straits of Messina. Fulfilling his demands took until September 3, and then the Eighth Army finally crossed virtually unopposed.

As a landing site, Salerno had both good and bad features. Readily identifiable mountain peaks behind the beaches offered excellent guides to the assault forces, but the mountains also provided superb sites for observation, defensive gun emplacements, and staging areas for counterattacks. The beaches, with better gradients and fewer offshore bars than those at Sicily, were suitable in some places for LST's to beach directly at the shore. On the other hand, the Gulf of Salerno was readily mined, and Allied intelligence learned belatedly that mines were sown there in abundance. Hence extensive minesweeping would have to precede the ship-to-shore movement. That meant that the transports were obliged

[8] The British rated one of the escort carriers as a light carrier, but she lacked the speed to operate at sea with the fleet.

initially to put their troops into landing craft nine to twelve miles from the beaches, and required a complete rescheduling of the intricate landing plan.

Arrangements for air support over Salerno were superior to those for Sicily. The presence of the escort carriers in direct support would prove an immense advantage. Moreover Eisenhower demanded that the air forces cooperate more closely with the army and the navy. Admiral Hewitt now had his flag in the *Ancon*, an amphibious command ship (AGC), converted from a passenger-cargo vessel and equipped with elaborate radio and radar gear. Aboard the *Ancon* an air force general headed a fighter-director team, and there were two standby fighter-director ships. Air spotting for naval gunfire support was improved by the use of high performance army P-51's flown by pilots trained by naval aviators.

In other respects the planning for Salerno was less efficient than that for Sicily. Because the planners had great difficulty getting from the high command firm commitments for men and material, changes were being made on the landing plan even after the departure for the beachhead. Such apparent indecision was exasperating to the force commanders, who could not know that an important reason was the highly-secret peace negotiations, of which no more than a dozen men were informed. There were other reasons for last-minute changes. Priority for certain equipment had to be given to the Eighth Army, slowly working its way up the toe of the Italian boot. And while the Salerno task force was en route, several gunfire support cruisers, including U.S.S. *Boise*, were detached to join a force under Admiral Cunningham that would occupy the great naval base at Taranto when the Italian fleet steamed out to surrender under the terms of the armistice.

Again, as before HUSKY, the Army insisted that the landing be made in darkness and without pre-landing naval bombardment. Admiral Hewitt once more argued in vain against this plan. Complete surprise, he contended, was impossible, and in darkness confusion was inevitable. The *Luftwaffe* had already twice raided Bizerte, and these were no mere blind stabs, for Bizerte was the chief assembly point

for beaching craft. Enemy reconnaissance planes would undoubtedly detect the assault forces en route to the beachhead. In any event, the Axis high command must have noted Salerno as a likely invasion point, for it was the key to Naples, Italy's finest port, and it was just within extreme operational radius of fighter planes based on Sicily. The army commanders remained unmoved, arguing that though the enemy might suspect Salerno, a little surprise was better than no surprise at all. A bombardment, they said, would be a dead giveaway, attracting additional German forces to the beachhead without achieving important destruction of enemy defenses. As a result of the Army's decision, there was no gunfire preparation at Salerno, and, in the American sector, not even any supporting fire as the assault waves closed the beach.

The Germans were in fact already at Salerno in division strength. As we have seen, when the German high command suspected that the Badoglio government was negotiating with the Allies, they lost no time dispatching divisions to take over Italy. By the time of the Salerno assault there were eight German divisions in northern Italy under Field Marshal Erwin Rommel, and eight in central and southern Italy under Field Marshal Albert Kesselring. Kesselring had organized southern Italy for defense against Allied landings. Lacking the strength to check Montgomery's advance from Reggio, he settled for a delaying action by two of his divisions, distributing the rest to protect Rome and the Naples area. Suspecting that the Allies would land at Salerno, for the reasons adduced by Hewitt, he ordered thither the bulk of the 16th Panzer Division and a regiment of paratroops to dig in at and behind the landing areas. The Germans arrived at Salerno in time to mine and wire the beaches, to mine the Gulf, to emplace guns in positions from the hills right down to the water, and to deploy tanks for counterattack. Kesselring also drew up plans for moving other German divisions rapidly to Salerno. Everything possible was done to make the region a hornet's nest for the Allied invaders. There was a real possibility that the Germans might be able to throw the Allied forces into the sea at the outset, or at least that they might reinforce their troops more rapidly than the Allies and thus be able to counterattack effectively a few days later.

Only one serious flaw marred Kesselring's preparations. His superiors declined to commit additional forces near Naples. Influenced by Rommel, Hitler originally intended to withdraw German forces north of Rome. It was only through Kesselring's persuasion that he agreed to make any stand at all in the south. Rommel, who understood sea warfare better than most of Hitler's generals, saw clearly enough that the Mediterranean was no barrier to naval power. The Italian coasts were standing invitations to the Allies to outflank and cut off any German forces in the Italian boot. The Apennines, on the contrary, as they swing across northern Italy from the Adriatic Sea to the Gulf of Genoa, form a barrier where relatively few defenders can hold the line against strong attacking forces. Hitler, taking the advice of both Rommel and Kesselring, but the full advice of neither, straddled the issue. He ordered Kesselring to make a stand in southern Italy but gave him insufficient troops to defend Salerno and Naples.

Various elements of the Salerno assault forces departed Oran, Algiers, Bizerte, and Tripoli between September 3 and 6. These joined other elements from Palermo and Termini north of Sicily, and on September 8 (D minus 1) shaped course for the Gulf of Salerno. During the approach, the task force came under attack by German aircraft that sank an LCT and damaged several other vessels.

At 1830 on September 8, as the Allied attack forces were approaching the Gulf, General Eisenhower broadcast a radio announcement of the Italian armistice. Badoglio confirmed the news in a broadcast from Rome. Then he and the King fled to Brindisi, leaving no one in authority in the capital. To the Germans the announcement was the signal to execute their carefully planned Operation Achse for disarming the Italians and taking over control of all Italian administration and communications. This they speedily accomplished against weak resistance. Only the Italian fleet and some of the air force units were able to escape. Most of the disarmed

Italian troops simply vanished, blending into the civilian population. Mussolini, rescued by the Germans, was put at the head of a puppet government in northern Italy.

The Salerno-bound Fifth Army greeted Eisenhower's announcement with jubilation— and the conviction that the war was over. Senior officers found it difficult to convince the troops that, although the Italians had quit fighting, there were plenty of Germans to offer resistance.

Salerno: Assault and Follow-Up

For once the approaching Allied assault forces were enjoying perfect weather. There would be no problems of heavy surf at Salerno. Aboard the transports and beaching craft the troops stirred restlessly in the heat, but lulled by the erroneous belief that only surrendering Italians would greet them, they displayed little of the anxiety that had been prevalent at Sicily.

At midnight the transports carrying American forces were in position off the southern sector of the Gulf of Salerno, and minesweepers advanced to clear channels to the shore. Scout boats, using radar fixes from extinct volcanoes looming dimly in the distance, closed the shore, located their assigned beaches, and blinked signals seaward. Rail-loaded LCVP's splashed into the water, then cast off to begin seemingly interminable circling until their waves had joined. That completed, they opened throttles and raced through darkness to the line of departure 6,000 yards off-

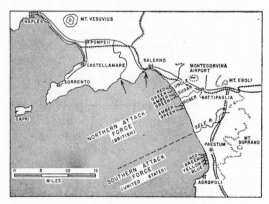

INVASION OF ITALY (SALERNO), SEPTEMBER 9, 1943

shore. From here, on signal, they headed for the beach. Tension grew as seasickness overcame many of the troops. Crews in the scout boats heard clanking and clattering and saw headlights ashore as German motorized troops moved to the water's edge to contest the landing. In this sector however the defenders chose to withhold their fire. Suddenly at H-hour, 0330, as the first wave of landing craft neared the beach, a loudspeaker ashore blared in English, "Come on in and give up! We have you covered!"

Despite the shock of realizing that they had a fight on their hands, the assault troops rushed resolutely ashore as, just at first light, the ramps of the landing craft slammed down. At that moment the quiet was succeeded by pandemonium. The German defenders at last opened up with rifle, machine gun, mortar, cannon, and tank fire, and German aircraft came sweeping over the beaches bombing and strafing. The troops of the first assault waves by-passed enemy strong points to gather in prearranged assembly areas. Then came DUKW's bringing ashore howitzers and ammunition. Thus armed, the invaders dueled German tanks and infantry at point-blank ranges. Landing and beaching craft pressed through heavy fire to land reinforcements. Sailors, struggling with pontoons, managed to rig causeways for landing tanks while shells slapped the water around them. By afternoon, though some individual beaches were completely interdicted by enemy fire, the Americans had seized a precarious hold on their sector of the beachhead.

In the British sector, to the north, the Germans inadvertently did the invaders a favor by opening fire on LST's before they could anchor in position to launch their LCVP's. That automatically canceled the Army's restriction against pre-landing naval fire support. Rear Admiral Conolly, commanding an amphibious group in this sector, had forehandedly prepared for such an opportunity by ordering three destroyers into position a mile off the beach. These now opened fire against shore installations. Rocket-firing beaching craft supported the first assault wave as it headed for the beach. Despite this support, the first wave, landing precisely at 0330, met strong resistance, and beaching craft advancing to land

ammunition and equipment suffered heavy damage from shell hits. Except on the extreme left flank, where American Rangers and British Commandos landed against little or no opposition and quickly pushed to the defiles in the hills, the pattern of combat was much the same in the northern sector as in the southern. Though by the end of D-day the Fifth Army had occupied all the designated beaches, the beachhead area in both sectors was still dangerously thin.

The beachhead, such as it was, had been saved by supporting warships. On call from shore fire control parties or using spotting aircraft, light cruisers *Philadelphia* and *Savannah*, a British monitor, and four destroyers off the American beaches repeatedly silenced mobile enemy batteries, knocked out machine gun positions, and dispersed concentrations of enemy infantry and tanks. Three British cruisers and a monitor off the northern beaches, unable to establish dependable communication with their shore fire control parties, achieved little on D-day; but six destroyers and three beaching craft successfully took over the whole support role in this area, at times approaching so close to the shore as to come under enemy rifle fire. By the end of the day, Hewitt's ships had expended many hundreds of rounds on dozens of call-fire missions, and not a few rounds without benefit of ground or air spot.

As soon as the Germans realized the crucial role played by the supporting warships, they shifted the weight of their air attack to these vessels. Although their sorties were fewer than at Sicily, they were more effective. High altitude bombers introduced a radio-controlled glide bomb, released from great heights when German fighter-bombers had drawn down the Allied air cover. On September 11 one of the glide bombs ripped through the *Savannah*, blowing out a section of her bottom and forcing her to retire for repairs. Two days later the British cruiser *Uganda* suffered a similar fate. But U.S.S. *Boise*, having completed her part in the Taranto operation, was en route to Salerno, and Admiral Cunningham ordered two more British light cruisers up from Malta. Meanwhile the *Philadelphia* was proving not only the most effective but the luckiest gunnery ship in Hewitt's force. Repeatedly near-missed by both conventional and glide bombs, sometimes by a matter of feet, she escaped severe damage and expended almost all of her ammunition on shore targets. The best defense against the glide bomb proved to be smoke. Even a fairly light smoke haze over the roadstead served to confuse the German radio operators who controlled the bombs.

By September 12 Clark's Fifth Army had somewhat enlarged its beachhead, but at the center it had not yet reached its assigned D-day line. On the 12th the supporting escort carriers were forced to retire to Palermo for refueling, first sending their aircraft ashore—not to the Montecorvino airport, which though in Allied hands was still under enemy fire, but to emergency airstrips hastily constructed within the beachhead. By now elements of five German divisions had reached the Salerno area and had massed 600 tanks and mobile guns for an all-out attack down the Sele River, the dividing line between the Allied sectors. The German strategy was to split the Fifth Army, concentrating first on one sector and then on the other.

This crisis came on September 13–14. As the German attack gained momentum, the Allied situation became so critical that General Clark asked Admiral Hewitt to prepare plans for evacuating either the northern or the southern Allied force and relanding it with the other. At Clark's request a division of paratroops was flown up from Sicily and dropped at Salerno at night. To avoid a repetition of the tragedy over Sicily, when paratroops were shot down by friendly fire, all antiaircraft guns in the Allied fleet and army were silenced. Meanwhile General Eisenhower ordered Marshal Tedder to support the Fifth Army with every available plane.

The German attempt to break through to the beach was defeated primarily by naval gunfire support, but also by the Fifth Army's hard fighting, by improved Allied air support, and by two faulty German decisions—one tactical, the other strategic. In the afternoon of the 13th, the local German commander ordered his main body of tanks to drive down the Sele toward a fork in the river and gain access to the beach across a bridge shown on German maps. But the bridge had already been destroyed, and the road that led to it was flanked by drainage ditches that prevented the tanks

from deploying. When the absence of the bridge stopped the German tank column, the Americans, having noted the German movement, were ready with infantry and two battalions of well-sited artillery. The tank force, trapped in the narrow road, was destroyed. This setback ended the most promising attack the Germans were able to make. The fact was that Kesselring lacked the means to match the Allied rate of reinforcement. Two more German divisions during the first week of the invasion might well have thrown the Allies into the sea. But Rommel, regarding the southern campaign as useless, refused to release any troops from northern Italy.

As Kesselring's forces renewed their attack on the 14th, the Allied cruisers and destroyers closed in to hammer tank columns and assembly points. The *Philadelphia* and *Boise* each expended several hundred rounds of 6-inch shell on all types of targets. As other ships, including the British battleships *Valiant* and *Warspite,* rushed to the Salerno area to assist, it became apparent that the tide had turned—though the venerable *Warspite* soon became the third victim of German glide bombs and had to be towed away.

On September 16, advance elements of the Eighth Army at last made contact with the Fifth Army. That same day Kesselring, concluding that his attempt to recapture the beachhead was proving too costly, decided to abandon Salerno and Naples and withdraw to a prepared defense line behind the Volturno River. "On 16 September," he afterward wrote, "in order to evade the effective shelling from warships I authorized a disengagement from the coastal front. . . ."[9]

As the Nazis withdrew, they demolished the harbor of Naples and did what they could to wreck the city—not only to delay the Allies and add to their logistic problems but also to wreak vengeance on the turncoat Italians. But the Allied navies, by opening the port of Salerno and performing near-miracles in supplying the army across the Salerno beaches, enabled Clark's Fifth Army to enter Naples on October 1, 1943. That concluded the Salerno operation, which had cost the Allies 2,100 killed, 4,100 missing, and 7,400 wounded.

[9] Albert Kesselring, *Kesselring: A Soldier's Record* (New York, 1954), 226.

Montgomery's Eighth Army meanwhile had occupied the Foggia airdrome near the Adriatic coast and pushed on to the northwest. On October 6 the two Allied armies abreast reached the Volturno. There the new battle line formed while both sides brought up reinforcements for the next round. The Navy's salvage experts, who had cleared the wreckage from harbors in North Africa and Sicily, had already set to work to restore Naples as the principal Allied port in Italy. Despite the German demolitions, Naples was soon receiving tonnage in excess of its peacetime capacity.

Most of the Italian fleet was now in Allied hands. On September 9 three new battleships, six cruisers, and ten destroyers had fled from Genoa and Spezia to give themselves up, as required by the terms of the armistice. Pounced upon off Sardinia by German bombers, battleship *Roma,* the fleet flagship, was sunk by a glide bomb with the loss of 1,400 lives. The rest of the force, and the older battleships from Taranto, proceeded to their destinations without being further molested. On September 11 Admiral Cunningham signaled the British Admiralty, "Be pleased to inform Their Lordships that the Italian Battle Fleet now lies under the guns of the fortress of Malta."[10]

Stalemate at Anzio

The invasion of the Italian mainland yielded disappointingly small dividends to the British and Americans. A few extra German divisions were tied down, and the Allies had gained additional combat experience, but even the value of the bomber base at Foggia proved to be largely negated by the barrier of the Alps. The Allies found themselves engaged in a major land campaign of minor strategic importance in a secondary theater of operations. Further advances would have to be conducted through terrain and weather that heavily favored the defense.

For the Germans the Volturno line was only a temporary stand, to be held while they prepared still stronger defenses farther up the Italian boot. Through October and the first

10 Admiral of the Fleet Viscount Andrew B. Cunningham RN, *A Sailor's Odyssey* (New York, 1951), 565.

two weeks of November, they fought rearguard actions as they backed off to their Winter Line, 40 miles northwest of Naples. This line, a system of carefully prepared defense positions on the mountain slopes, they intended to hold as long as possible. Northern and central Italy were now securely under Nazi domination, and Marshal Kesselring, left in command of all German forces in Italy by Rommel's departure for France, could count on 19 German divisions to hold the 14 that the Allied Fifth and Eighth Armies assembled for an all-out attack on the Winter Line.

In seeking a means of breaking the Nazi defense barrier, Generals Eisenhower, Alexander, and Clark had already initiated planning for an end-run landing behind the Winter Line in the vicinity of Rome. Their purpose was to cut the enemy's main lines of communication and to threaten his rear. Much the best beaches for attaining the first of these objectives were at Anzio. Anzio was 37 miles southeast of Rome and 20 miles south of the Alban Hills (*Colli Laziali*), which dominated roads and railroads leading from Rome down to the German defense line.

But beaching craft and landing craft were now leaving the Mediterranean for Britain in such numbers that only a single-division assault on the Italian coast could be mounted. Hence the Anzio assault was planned to follow the opening of the drive against the main German defenses. Only if this drive were sufficiently successful for the Fifth Army and the landing force to be mutually supporting would the landing be undertaken. Eisenhower in fact stipulated that the Allied armies advancing up the boot must have reached a position where they could expect to join the Anzio amphibious force within 48 hours after the landing, for with the shipping now at his disposal he could not be certain of supplying the beachhead much beyond that length of time.

Montgomery's Eighth Army began its advance against the Winter Line on November 28, 1943. Clark's Fifth Army started two days later. Both quickly bogged down in the face of stiff German resistance and almost continual rain that sapped the strength of the invaders and turned dirt roads into quagmires. Three weeks after the opening of the drive, the Allied armies had not advanced ten miles, and the right flank of the new German Gustav Line was firmly anchored on Monte Cassino, nearly 75 miles from Anzio. The end-run project was clearly infeasible. On December 22, Alexander, on Clark's recommendation and with Eisenhower's concurrence, canceled the Anzio operation.

At this point Churchill intervened personally. Meeting with the leading Allied commanders at Tunis on Christmas Day 1943, the Prime Minister insisted that the Anzio project be revived. The end-run must be made moreover without waiting to see if a renewed attack on the German line would succeed. Whether or not the Anzio attack was successful in cutting the German supply lines, it could not fail, said Churchill, to divert strength from the Gustav Line. He conceded however that in the circumstances a one-division assault would be too risky. But cancellation of a planned operation against the Andaman Islands in the Bay of Bengal had released 15 LSI's for use in the Mediterranean.[11] And at Churchill's request President Roosevelt permitted 56 LST's to remain a little longer in the Mediterranean, with two important provisos: that the cross-Channel attack remain the paramount operation, and that Churchill drop his insistence upon further peripheral operations to be directed against Rhodes and the Aegean islands.[12] Enough beaching craft and their

[11] The LSI (Landing Ship, Infantry) was a larger, British version of the LCI. The cancellation of the Andaman attack was part of the curtailment of the Joint Chief's "Strategic Plan for the Defeat of Japan" resulting from British and Chinese inability to carry out their part of the project.

[12] At the Teheran Conference the preceding November Churchill had stated that a major purpose of the operations he proposed against the German-held islands in the Aegean area was to open up a shorter, more easily defensible supply line to Russia —the main objective, be it noted, of his Dardanelles-Gallipoli campaign of World War I. Another purpose, said he, was to provide Turkey with air support as a further inducement to enter the war on the Allied side. Churchill hoped that the Turks might be influenced to attack German forces in the Balkans. If not, the Allies would at least be able to operate from airfields in Turkey, whence, among other targets, they could strike at the Ploesti oil fields in Romania, on which the Germans were heavily dependent.

associated landing craft were thus made available for a two-division assault on Anzio. That was enough for Churchill. He brushed aside objections by Eisenhower and others that even two divisions were insufficient for what would amount to an independent attack. Eisenhower in any event was about to leave the theater to prepare for the cross-Channel assault, which he was to command. His successor as Supreme Allied Commander Mediterranean, Sir Henry Maitland Wilson, accepted the risk of a two-division landing at Anzio. So did General Alexander. D-day was set at January 20, 1944. Drawn from the Fifth Army and earmarked for the assault were the United States 3rd Division, the British 1st Infantry Division, three battalions of Rangers, two battalions of Commandos, and a regiment of paratroops.

Ground forces for the Anzio attack were to be commanded by Major General John P. Lucas USA, naval forces by Rear Admiral Frank J. Lowry USN, Commander VIII Amphibious Force, U.S. Eighth Fleet. To meet the early invasion date, army and naval staffs immediately went to work and by all-out effort had plans completed and approved by January 12, ten days before D-day, which at General Lucas's request had been postponed to January 22. Meanwhile the Eighth Army prepared to apply pressure on its sector of the Gustav Line in order to keep the Germans from transferring any of the defending troops elsewhere, and on January 17 the Fifth Army renewed its attack on Cassino both in order to attract German reserves that might be used against Anzio and in the hope of breaking the Gustav Line loose from its anchor. The Allied Air Forces began "sealing off the beachhead" by means of intensive raids on roads, railroads, bridges, and enemy airfields, and on January 19 reported that they had succeeded in their mission.

With misgivings about the strength of the coming assault heightened by a dismayingly poor landing rehearsal in the Gulf of Salerno, the Anzio forces left Naples on January 21, advancing by a roundabout 110-mile route to deceive the enemy. LST's, LCI's and LCT's formed the bulk of the troop lift, with numerous LCVP's aboard to boat the first assault waves. Careful reconnaissance revealed that only weak enemy forces manned the beach defenses. Rocket-firing beaching craft were to lay down a barrage a few minutes before the LCVP's touched down, primarily to detonate the mines on the beaches.

In contrast to the disorderly rehearsal, there followed one of the smoothest landings of the entire war. Lowry's forces hit the beaches exactly at H-hour, 0200, and quickly solved the problems caused by enemy mines and the confusion inevitable in night landings. Enemy resistance at the beach was slight. For once Allied assault forces had attained real surprise, and a night landing without preparatory naval fire had paid off. For three nights before the assault, Kesselring, vaguely aware that something was afoot, had ordered an alert against enemy landings at any of several points, including Anzio. But on the night of January 21–22 he had let his staff persuade him to discontinue the alert in order to rest the men. Once aware of his error, he rushed mobile guns and numerous battalions of troops toward Anzio over roads, railroads, and bridges that had been quickly repaired following the Allied air attack. The beachhead had not been "sealed off" after all. Nor had the Fifth Army attack on Cassino succeeded; there the Germans still held. Nevertheless the end of D-day saw 36,000 Allied troops ashore at Anzio, with fewer than 150 casualties. Despite a severe storm on D-day plus 4, nearly 70,000 men, more than 25,000 tons of supplies, 500 guns, and 237 tanks crossed the beaches in the first week of the attack. Lucas and Lowry's task was to keep them there; Kesselring's was to contain them and push them out.

General Lucas faced a dilemma. He had two choices: to advance before consolidating, or to consolidate before advancing. If he advanced at once to the Alban Hills, his guns could block traffic to the Gustav Line before the Germans could bring up their forces in strength. Such a move would carry out the main intent of the original Anzio plan, but it would invite a German counterthrust that might cut Lucas's communications with the coast. General Clark, recognizing this danger, had ordered General Lucas only to seize and secure a beachhead and to "advance on" the Alban Hills, deliberately ambiguous phrasing that left Lucas considerable freedom of action.

Interpreting his orders conservatively, Lucas chose to pause and consolidate his beachhead, throwing up strong defenses before pressing inland.

The Anzio landings had thrown the Germans into panic, causing them temporarily to evacuate Rome. But Lucas's cautious course enabled them to re-estimate the situation, and allowed Kesselring time to augment the German defenses. The delayed Allied attack failed to break through to the Alban Hills, but the German counterattack stalled in the face of Allied defenses, reinforcements, and naval gunfire. The end result was a stalemate. "I had hoped," said Churchill, "that we were hurling a wildcat onto the shore, but all we got was a stranded whale."[13] The initial assault, as Eisenhower and other officers had foreseen, was too weak to carry out its mission, and the reinforcements came too late to do anything but save the beachhead. Lucas cannot be blamed for making the choice he did. The basic cause of failure was shortage of beaching and landing craft.

The saving of the beachhead was in itself something of a miracle. With naval forces and shipping at first considered barely adequate to lift, supply, and support the original two divisions, Admiral Lowry managed to evacuate most of the civilian population and ultimately to keep seven divisions supplied. The solution to the supply problem was the introduction of a system first worked out by the U.S. Seventh Fleet in the Pacific. Trucks and DUKW's were preloaded in Naples, driven aboard LST's, carried overnight to Anzio, and there driven directly to supply dumps. Through this means an LST that usually required a full day to unload could be emptied in an hour. By early February a regular ferry service had been established. Each day a convoy of six LST's left Naples carrying 1,500 tons of supplies preloaded in 300 trucks. Each week 15 LCT's made the run from Naples to Anzio. Every ten days four Liberty ships arrived at the beachhead with supplies from Naples or North Africa. Meanwhile the fleet, despite bad weather, fire from heavy German guns that rimmed the beachhead, enemy dive and glide bombs, and U-boat attacks, continued to sup-

[13] Winston S. Churchill, *The Second World War*, V (Boston, 1951), 488.

port the forces ashore and to maintain their overwater line of supply. In the process it suffered its roughest handling up to that time in the Mediterranean. The British lost two cruisers, three destroyers, four beaching craft, and a hospital ship; the Americans, a minesweeper, a minecraft, six beaching craft, and two Liberty ships. Damage to vessels, particularly from aircraft, was widespead.

The miserable Italian stalemate lasted until mid-May 1944. Nothing much was accomplished by either opponent on either front. It soon became clear that the Fifth Army, instead of achieving a double envelopment of the enemy, had merely split into two segments, while the Germans, enjoying the advantages of the interior position, were able to shift forces rapidly as needed between the Anzio beachhead and the Gustav Line. In March 90,200 Americans and 35,500 British were packed into a beachhead surrounded by 135,000 Germans with well-sited guns up to 280 mm. that were able to reach every part of the beachhead and the roadstead. German shelling, sporadic by day, was stepped up after dark. During the night the invaders could also expect from one to half a dozen air raids. Allied headquarters at Anzio were established in an underground wine cellar. Wherever possible the troops also sought underground shelter, but the continual rains so raised the ground water level that most foxholes and dugouts soon filled. Hundreds of thousands of sandbags were used to build crude shelters on the surface. In such conditions the men passed week after week, constant targets for enemy fire. It is not surprising that of the 59,000 casualties suffered by the Allied forces at Anzio, nearly a third were from disease, exhaustion, and neuroses. Of the rest, 5,000 were killed in action and 17,000 wounded.

As the rains ceased and the roads hardened with the advance of spring, the Allies prepared to infuse new vigor into their attacks on the Gustav Line. By May they had 27 divisions in action in Italy—7 at Anzio, the rest opposite the main German line. To oppose these, Kesselring now had 25 divisions. On May 11, the Allies began an all-out offensive against the German defense barrier. On the 19th, a French corps of the Fifth Army at last broke the German hold on Monte Cassino and

Allied troops surged up the Italian peninsula. On the 25th, an advance patrol coming up from the south made contact with a patrol out of Anzio. On the night of June 2–3, the Germans broke off contact all along the front and hastily withdrew to the north. On June 4, the triumphant Allies made an unopposed entry into Rome, where they were joyfully received by the inhabitants. On June 6, Allied forces in England crossed the Channel and invaded Normandy, thereby reducing the Italian front to a mere backwater of the European war.

Summary

By the Casablanca Compromise of January 1943 the British agreed to allocate more men and materials to the war against Japan, and the Americans agreed to invade Sicily in 1943, postponing the cross-Channel attack until 1944. The Sicilian campaign was planned and executed as an operation in itself, with the objectives of (1) making Allied communications in the Mediterranean more secure, (2) diverting pressure from the Russian front, (3) forcing Italy out of the war, and (4) encouraging the Turks to abandon neutrality and come in on the Allied side.

The Allied assault on Sicily, July 10, 1943, was highly successful, showing considerable improvement, especially in ship-to-shore movement, over the North African invasions. The value of naval gunfire support was demonstrated to the army, especially when naval guns played a major part in turning back tank attacks on General Patton's Seventh Army. The Allied air forces succeeded in putting the Axis airfields in Sicily out of operation and in disrupting the Sicilian transportation system, but poor liaison with the assault forces denied the invaders close fighter support and resulted in the shooting down of paratroop transports by friendly fire.

The Allies lost an opportunity to trap Axis forces in Sicily when elite units stalled Montgomery's Eighth Army at Catania, forcing it into the mountainous terrain west of Mt. Etna. The rapid, dispersed advance of Patton's Seventh Army could never overtake the fleeing Axis forces, most of which escaped across the Straits of Messina. Nevertheless the Allies attained the most important of their objectives.

Mussolini was deposed, the new Italian government under Badoglio shifted sides, Allied Mediterranean communications were made completely secure, and the German pressure on the Russian front was somewhat relieved.

The Allies meanwhile had reached another compromise whereby the Americans agreed to an invasion of Italy, provided only limited forces were used, provided the British committed themselves definitely to an invasion of France in May 1944, and provided the general conduct of the war in the Pacific was left to the American Joint Chiefs of Staff. Montgomery's Eighth Army crossed the Straits of Messina on September 3, 1943 and advanced up the toe of Italy to support the assault of Clark's Fifth Army directed against the Salerno area on September 9, a few hours after Eisenhower's radio announcement of the Italian surrender.

The Salerno invasion, like the Sicilian, was not preceded by naval bombardment of shore installations. But the army did not achieve the surprise on which it counted, for Kesselring had anticipated that the assault would come at Salerno and had strong German defense forces waiting behind the beach and nearby. Hence the Salerno assault was for a while in considerable danger of being thrown back. It was saved by hard fighting, by improved air support, by naval gunfire support, by German tactical errors, and by Hitler's refusal to send German reinforcements from northern Italy. In the face of steady and accurate shelling from the Allied naval task force, Kesselring was obliged to withdraw his forces from the beachhead area to a line northwest of Naples.

When the drive of the Fifth and Eighth Armies against the German Winter Line failed to achieve momentum, Alexander canceled a Fifth Army project for invading Anzio behind the German line. But at Churchill's insistence the Anzio project was revived, and Churchill obtained from Roosevelt the use of adequate numbers of beaching craft for a two-division landing. The price was another compromise: Churchill abandoned his plans for operations in the Aegean area.

The two divisions, smoothly landed at Anzio on January 22, 1944, failed to achieve their objectives of cutting German communications or threatening the German rear. The Anzio beachhead, which proved to be an independent operation and a mere nuisance to the Germans, was rescued in May 1944 when the Fifth and Eighth Armies at last succeeded in breaking the German Gustav Line. On June 4 the Allies entered Rome, just two days before the Allied cross-Channel assault on northern France.

33:

The Defeat of Germany

Following the Casablanca Conference in January 1943, Lieutenant General Sir Frederick Morgan of the British Army had been directed to set up a Combined Planning Staff to prepare for the coming Allied invasion of western Europe. Shortening his title Chief of Staff to the Supreme Allied Commander (designate) to Cossac, General Morgan built up a large and efficient organization that surveyed possible landing beaches from Norway to Portugal, with special attention to those on the English Channel, for the Channel beaches offered the shortest routes across water and hence the quickest turnabout of Allied shipping in the assault. The Cossac staff considered and dealt with problems as diverse as the tactical control of the Strategic Air Command in Britain and the availability of landing craft. On the solid foundation of General Morgan's work rested a great deal of the success of Operation OVERLORD, as the cross-Channel invasion came ultimately to be called.

By the time of the Teheran Conference in November 1943, Cossac had done all he could pending the appointment of the actual commander. At Teheran, Roosevelt, Churchill, and Stalin all agreed to the target date for OVERLORD of May 1, 1944, yet the supreme commander had still not been selected. When the cross-Channel attack was tentatively being planned for 1942 or 1943, the Combined Chiefs of Staff had reached an understanding that the commander of any large operation would be of the same nationality as the majority of the troops. Since at the earlier date British forces would necessarily predominate, Churchill had promised the command to Field Marshal Sir Alan Brooke; but as it became obvious that by May 1944 American troops

would outnumber the British, Roosevelt and Churchill agreed that the supreme commander should be an American. At first the President planned to give the command to General Marshall, but Admiral King and others protested this selection, insisting that Marshall could not be spared from the Joint and Combined Chiefs of Staff. In early December 1943 Roosevelt at last made his decision, appointing General Eisenhower to command Operation OVERLORD. The officers appointed to head the naval, ground, and air forces under Eisenhower were all British: Admiral Sir Bertram H. Ramsay, General Sir Bernard Montgomery, and Air Chief Marshal Sir Trafford Leigh-Mallory.

For his task Eisenhower was given the broadest of directives:

You will enter the Continent of Europe, and, in conjunction with the other United Nations, undertake operations aimed at the heart of Germany and the destruction of her armed forces. The date for entering the Continent is the month of May, 1944. After adequate channel ports have been secured, exploitation will be directed towards securing an area that will facilitate both ground and air operations against the enemy.

The significant thing about this directive is that it provided for nothing less than ending the war. All previous British and American operations in Europe had had more limited objectives, for Allied commanders realized that decisive results could be attained only by means of a drive on Germany from the West. Operation OVERLORD however was conceived on a scale that would permit attaining the ultimate objective. Unlike the landings in Sicily, where the assault forces included most of the combat troops available, the divisions that were to seize a beachhead in western

Europe were merely an advance force. Plans called for pouring in more than 50 divisions before the coming of winter.

Planning for OVERLORD was perhaps the most complex problem in the history of warfare. The problem had to be attacked from both ends at once, from the standpoint of strategic desirability and from the standpoint of logistic feasibility. Under the first consideration the planners of Supreme Headquarters, Allied Expeditionary Force (called Shaef for short) had to consider when and where to invade; under the latter, whether supplies, equipment, and personnel could be provided and transported to attain specific aims.

The choice of the landing area was a basic consideration. General Morgan had recommended a stretch of Normandy coast between the mouth of the Orne River and the Cotentin (Cherbourg) Peninsula, a selection accepted by Shaef and the Combined Chiefs. As Shaef planners recognized from the beginning, the chosen landing area was not ideal. An assault directly across the Strait of Dover to the Pas-de-Calais area offered the shortest sea route and hence the quickest turnabout of assault shipping. The Pas-de-Calais also offered the best natural beach conditions and was closest to the Dutch and Belgian ports and to the Ruhr, the industrial center of Germany. But it was obvious to Allied intelligence officers that the Germans expected the landing to come in that area and had made elaborate preparations to throw it back into the sea. Moreover the Pas-de-Calais beach area that could be quickly exploited was too narrow to support operations on the scale planned after the initial assault phase.

The Normandy coast had good beach conditions for part of its length, was somewhat sheltered by the natural breakwater of the Cotentin Peninsula, and was within operational radius of fighter planes based on England. And though the terrain behind the beaches offered special difficulties, it provided good possibilities for a breakout on both flanks. A thrust to the sea on the right flank would isolate German forces in the Brittany (Brest) Peninsula; a wheeling movement on the left flank would provide opportunity for capture of important French ports, notably Le Havre. (See map page 619.) Recognizing that cap-

turing ports from the rear would take time and that the Germans would destroy the port facilities before abandoning them, the Allies decided to construct artificial harbors off the beachhead to expedite unloading of the deluge of supplies that would be required.

General Morgan had recommended a diversionary attack on the southern coast of France, to be carried out simultaneously with the Normandy landings. This proposal the Combined Chiefs of Staff at first accepted, seeing in an invasion of France from the Mediterranean not only a diversion but a means of cutting off German troops in Southwestern France and of securing the port of Marseille for supplying and reinforcing the southern flank of the Allied advance into Germany. The southern project was initially given the code name ANVIL.

General Morgan also recommended that if the necessary landing and beaching craft could be made available the Normandy assault should be broadened to include landings on the east coast of the Cotentin Peninsula. Landings here would permit the early isolation and capture of the port of Cherbourg at the tip of the Peninsula. One of Eisenhower's earliest official acts in assuming command of OVERLORD was to accept Morgan's concept of a broadened front in Normandy and to send Montgomery ahead to London to demand that the strength of the intial cross-Channel assault be increased from three to five divisions. Since the only place the landing and beaching craft for a broadened OVERLORD could come from was ANVIL, Operation ANVIL had to be postponed until the middle of August so that craft assigned to it could first be used in OVERLORD. This expedient together with the reallocation of one month's production intended for the Pacific brought the number of beaching craft for OVERLORD to the just-acceptable minimum. So short was the supply that the loss of three LST's to German motor torpedo boats during an invasion rehearsal brought the reserve force of LST's down to zero. Landing and beaching craft, given top priority by the American Joint Chiefs in anticipation of a 1942 or 1943 cross-Channel attack, had been cut back both to step up construction of antisubmarine craft for the Battle of the Atlantic and as a consequence of uncertainty as to when if ever the Americans would overcome British reluctance to go ahead

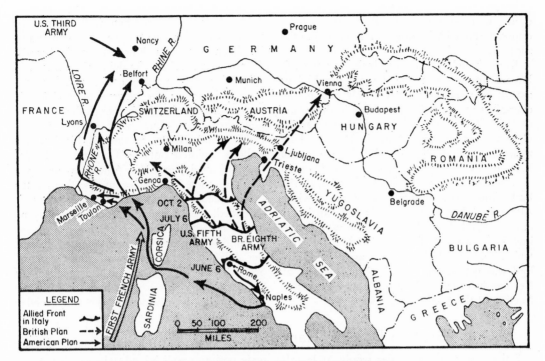

AMERICAN AND BRITISH STRATEGIES IN THE MEDITERRANEAN, SUMMER 1944

with the invasion of western Europe. The postponement of ANVIL meant of course that it could not serve as a diversion for OVERLORD, but to Eisenhower the advantage of securing a major Mediterranean port on his right flank made the southern invasion nevertheless eminently desirable.

Because troops for southern France would have to come from Italy, Operation ANVIL was nearly canceled when the Allied drive stalled at Anzio and before the German Gustav Line. Even after the Fifth and Eighth Armies broke the German line in the spring of 1944 and then went surging up the Italian boot, Churchill and the British generals insisted that ANVIL should be canceled. They wanted to exploit the momentum of the advance in Italy with a landing at Trieste on the Adriatic, followed by a drive through the Ljubljana Gap to Austria. The Ljubljana project was aimed as much at political as at military objectives, but it is questionable whether Allied forces attempting to penetrate the rugged Gap with its narrow, winding road could have overcome resistance by the 25 German divisions in the area in time to reach the Danube ahead of the

Russians. Eisenhower kept insisting on ANVIL, which for security reasons was renamed Operation DRAGOON. Backed by Roosevelt, who regarded the Ljubljana project as militarily eccentric, Eisenhower finally had his way.[1]

As plans for Operation OVERLORD finally crystallized, they called for three paratroop divisions to be dropped the night before D-day. Then after sunrise on D-day, two American and three British divisions would make nearly simultaneous assaults from the sea. Five beach areas were selected: Utah and Omaha for the American assault; Gold, Juno, and Sword for the British. Preceding the landings, the beaches and their defenses would be subjected to heavy aerial and naval bombardment. By now not

[1] For arguments supporting the Ljubljana project, see Winston S. Churchill, *The Second World War*, VI (Boston, 1953), 61–71; Chester Wilmot, *The Struggle for Europe* (New York, 1952), 446–57; and J. F. C. Fuller, *A Military History of the Western World*, III (New York, 1956), 576–7. For opposing arguments see Dwight D. Eisenhower, *Crusade in Europe* (New York, 1948), 281–4; and Samuel Eliot Morison, *History of United States Naval Operations in World War II*, XI (Boston, 1957), 227–32.

even the most skeptical Allied army officer opposed daylight landings and naval gunfire support.

Even though OVERLORD, including the follow-up forces, was the largest amphibious assault ever mounted, it was only part of the over-all strategy against Germany in the spring of 1944. The Fifth and Eighth Army had 25 German divisions tied down in Italy, making them unavailable for use elsewhere. On the Eastern Front, where the beaten German armies were being driven back toward the Fatherland, 212 divisions faced the Soviets. Although Allied forces in Italy and Russia far outnumbered those that would be used in the invasion of western France, they had the strategic effect of a holding force as far as Overlord was concerned, enabling the invaders at Normandy to exert their full power against a fraction of the total German strength.

German Defense Plans

Estimating that the Allies would at length attempt to re-enter the Continent from the west, Hitler ordered his western armies to prepare to throw the invaders into the sea. He also directed their commander in chief, Marshal Gerd von Rundstedt, to build an "Atlantic Wall" of casemated artillery to sweep every possible landing beach from Spain to Norway. But Hitler, his attention focused on Russia, could give only sporadic thought to the situation in the west. The Atlantic front remained the stepchild of the *Wehrmacht*.

Though the Germans agreed that the Allied assault on western Europe would come not later than the spring of 1944, they were not at all agreed as to *where* it would come. The army identified the Pas-de-Calais as the most probable target, both because it was nearest England and because here installations were being built for launching Hitler's V-weapons, pilotless aircraft and long-range rockets. As soon as the Allies detected these installations and recognized the peril they posed for England, they would doubtless drive at all costs for the launching sites. German army intelligence argued further that the Allies would avoid the Normandy beaches because these were backed by terrain that favored the defense—the difficult *bocage* country of small

fields separated by earthen walls topped by trees and thick hedgerows. German naval intelligence officers however reached quite different conclusions. Studying the pattern of Allied bombing, minesweeping, and minelaying, and noting the degree of activity in various British ports, they concluded that the landings would come west of the Pas-de-Calais. And Hitler, in one of his intuitive insights, pointed out the Cotentin and Brittany peninsulas as likely Allied targets. As a result of these varying estimates, though the Pas-de-Calais beaches were the most strongly defended, the Normandy beaches were by no means neglected.

Rundstedt meanwhile had come to distrust the Atlantic Wall concept of static defense. Studying the Salerno assault, he reached the conclusion that his armies had little chance of defeating the invaders at the water's edge in the face of naval gunfire support. Hence he came more and more to rely on mobile infantry and armored divisions placed in strategic positions well inland, whence they could be rushed to the coast to prevent the Allies from exploiting any beachhead they might succeed in seizing.[2]

In early 1944 Hitler placed Field Marshal Rommel under Rundstedt's command with the specific responsibility of defending the Atlantic coast from the Scheldt to the Loire, using the German Seventh and Fifteenth Armies. This appointment led to confusion and divided objectives, for Rommel, basing his estimate on his experiences in North Africa, concluded that Allied air power would prevent Rundstedt's mobile reserves from reaching the coast in time to achieve decisive results. He insisted that the armored defense forces must be placed within five miles of the coast. The decision, he argued, would have to be reached on the beach, and unless the invaders were thrown back into the sea within 24 hours, Germany faced defeat. Hitler, called upon to resolve the conflict between the theories of Rommel and Rundstedt, straddled the issue.

[2] By 1944, as a result of growing manpower shortage, the Germans had reduced their infantry divisions to 12,800 officers and men each. American and British infantry divisions retained a strength of 14,000, a figure considerably augmented for amphibious operations by the addition of artillery, tank, special weapons, transport, and medical troops.

DISTRIBUTION OF GERMAN DIVISIONS, JUNE 6, 1944

He placed some of the armored forces under the former, but not enough to carry out Rommel's plan. The bulk of the reserves Rundstedt retained in the hinterland.

Denied the forces he believed he needed, Rommel concentrated upon static defense. He even neglected training, using his troops as laborers. He energetically set about strengthening the Atlantic Wall, with emphasis upon concrete casemates. He set great store by mines, both sea and land, and planned to sow them thickly on all the beaches and in the beach approaches, but German factories could supply only four per cent of the hundred million mines he wanted. He planned several rows of beach obstacles on which landing craft would impale themselves. Fortunately for the Allies, the two rows that would have been effective at low tide were not installed in time. All the obstacles were intended to be mined, but the mining was far from complete at D-day. As a second line of defense, behind the coastal gun sites, Rommel had the lowlands flooded wherever possible. For obstacles against paratroop and glider landings, he had stakes set close together into the ground ("Rommel's asparagus") in likely stretches of open country. For lack of mines, he planned to install specially rigged artillery shells atop the stakes and join the detonators together with barbed wire that would set off explosions on contact. This plan was largely foiled because the shells arrived too late to be installed.

Rommel, the master of mobility and maneuver, did not rely entirely on static defense. He did what he could to provide for the swift movement of his infantry forces and of the panzer divisions that Rundstedt retained in the rear area. But he lacked sufficient motorized vehicles and, as a result of Allied air supremacy and of previous bombing and sabotage of railroads and bridges, what he had were all but useless for transporting troops at the time of the landings. It is ironic that the inventors of the Blitzkrieg were obliged to proceed to the battle area largely on foot and on bicycles.

Selecting D-Day and H-Hour

The target date for the invasion of France had been set for May 1, 1944, with the understanding that the actual date would be determined by the physical conditions of tide, visibility, weather, and availability of equipment. In order to get an additional month's production of landing and beaching craft, General Eisenhower, with the concurrence of the Combined Chiefs of Staff, postponed the target date to June 1. This was about as late as the invasion could well take place, for the Allies needed all the summer campaigning weather they could get to consolidate their conquest of France. With the June 1 target date in mind, the Shaef staff began to look for the combination of natural conditions most favorable for the landing. They desired a moonlit night preceding D-day so that the airborne divisions would be able to organize and reach their assigned objectives before sunrise. They wanted the naval forces and convoys to cross the English Channel during the hours of darkness

and to have 30 to 90 minutes of daylight before the landings so that preparatory bombing and naval bombardment of defenses would be effective. The crucial requirement, to which the others would have to be geared, was the tide. It must be rising at the time of the initial landings so that the landing craft could unload and retract without danger of stranding. Reefs and foul ground off the British beaches made a landing at low tide infeasible. Yet the tide had to be low enough that underwater obstacles could be exposed for demolition parties. The final choice was one hour after low tide for the initial landings. Follow-up waves would then have less and less beach to cross as the tide came in. All the required conditions could be met over a three-day period once each month. A fortnight after the three-day period they would be met again except for the moon, which would then be in its new phase. The earliest date after June 1 when the conditions would be fulfilled was June 5, with June 6 and June 7 also suitable. Eisenhower accordingly selected June 5 for D-day, with H-hours ranging from 0630 to 0755 to meet the varying tidal conditions at the five assault beaches.

The Naval Plan

The naval forces, predominantly British, bore large responsibilities for the Normandy invasion. They had to transport the assault troops to the beaches and land them with their equipment. They had to provide shipping to handle the enormous flow of supplies across the Channel—600 to 700 tons a day per division, in addition to mechanized equipment. They had to act as floating artillery until the guns could be put ashore. They had to provide for the orderly and timely arrival of reinforcement troops and their supplies and equipment, and they had to make provision for the evacuation of casualties. They had to keep German naval forces out of the Channel. They had to sweep lanes through the mine fields and clear the beaches of obstacles that would impede the landing and deployment of troops ashore.

Under Admiral Ramsay's over-all command, the 2,700 vessels (including beaching craft) of the Normandy attack force were divided into the mainly American Western Naval Task Force under the command of Rear Admiral

Alan G. Kirk USN and the mainly British Eastern Naval Task Force under Rear Admiral Sir Philip Vian. The Western Naval Attack Force was further subdivided into Task Forces U and O to support Utah and Omaha Beaches respectively, and the Eastern Naval Task Force comprised Task Forces G, J, and S, which held the responsibility for Gold, Juno, and Sword Beaches. The navy participated in training activities beginning in December 1943 and culminating in April and May, 1944 with full-scale rehearsals by each of the lettered task forces, including realistic landings on the south coast of England. These exercises simulated Operation NEPTUNE, as the naval phase of OVERLORD was called, in every respect except actually crossing the Channel. Even so, when the real NEPTUNE got under way, the meshing of the various task forces had to be extemporized from operational plans which until then existed only on paper. This was no small achievement, for the vessels came from points as widely separated as the Thames Estuary and Northern Ireland. Intricate timing was required to bring all the component parts of the invasion to the beaches on schedule; any disruption could prove disastrous.

Bombing the Railroads

The Combined Chiefs of Staff at the Casablanca Conference of January 1943 had ordered American and British strategic air forces based on Britain to join in a combined bomber offensive for the "progressive disruption of the German military, industrial and economic systems, and the undermining of the morale of the German people to the point where their capacity for armed resistance is fatally weakened."[3] The Allied air forces in short were to make an all-out attempt to defeat Germany by air attack alone. The combined air forces selected as their primary targets submarine construction yards, followed by the aircraft industry, transportation, oil plants, and other war industry, in descending order of priority. The Americans attacked by day in order to attain precision bombing; the British, regarding daylight bombing as too hazardous, pre-

[3] Quoted in Gordon A. Harrison, *Cross-Channel Attack* (Washington, D.C.: Dept. of the Army, 1951), 207-8.

ferred night area bombing that laid waste to industrial and military centers.

Whether this "strategic bombing" could actually force a determined foe to surrender was never really put to the test. The requirements of the Mediterranean theater delayed the offensive until the late spring of 1943. By then the *Luftwaffe* had acquired enough fighter aircraft to make the strategic bombing plan too costly. The drive to burn out German industry quickly shifted into a battle for air supremacy as the Allies concentrated their attacks on enemy planes, aircraft storage parks, and aircraft repair depots and on German aircraft and associated industries. Meanwhile the Germans were busily shifting their key manufacturing facilities to the southeast, beyond effective attack from the Britain-based bombers. At the end of 1943, when Allied victory in the air appeared to be in sight, photographic reconnaissance detected the V-weapon launching sites in the Pas-de-Calais area and elsewhere—all pointed ominously at England. Destruction of these was then given overriding priority.

General Eisenhower, on assuming command of the Allied Expeditionary Force, was determined to avert the lack of cooperation that had marked Allied air force operations in the Mediterranean theater. Hence he demanded and obtained control of the U.S. Army Strategic Air Force and the British Bomber Command, both based on the United Kingdom. On attaining control, he shocked the strategic air command by adopting Air Chief Marshal Leigh-Mallory's plan for diverting a portion of the Allied air power to the destruction of railroads in France and Belgium. No one denied the necessity of disrupting and delaying German ground movements by any means whatever, because for OVERLORD to succeed, the Allies would have to follow up their relatively light assault with reinforcements at a much faster rate than the enemy could move defense forces to the invasion area. But the strategic air command believed that bombing the railroads would have little lasting effect, that the attempt would be a waste of bombs and bombers that could be used more profitably on other missions. The air command's objections were backed by Churchill and the British War Cabinet, who feared that too many French and

Belgian civilians would be killed; having burned their fingers at Mers-el-Kebir and at Dakar, they had no desire again to risk turning potential allies into potential foes.

Despite resistance and counter-arguments, Eisenhower put Leigh-Mallory's "transportation plan" into effect in mid-April 1944. The Allied bombers first systematically worked over the railroad marshaling yards. Early in May they also began hitting bridges, with such success that before the end of the month not a single bridge spanned the Seine between Paris and the English Channel. On May 21, which the air forces called "Chattanooga Day," fighter-bombers began bombing and strafing tracks, rail facilities, and trains, putting more than a hundred locomotives out of commission the first day. The French and Belgians, far from resenting these Allied attacks on their own soil, recognized their value and gleefully entered into the spirit of the thing with wholesale sabotage. Many a piece of rolling equipment was found useless because some essential part had vanished or a wheel had been mysteriously cracked. Missing railroad spikes caused numerous wrecks.

The Leigh-Mallory plan proved more effective than its stanchest adherents had anticipated. By D-day rail traffic that could have served the German defenses in the invasion zone had declined by about 50 per cent. German attempts to make good the shortage by greater use of road transportation were largely defeated by lack of sufficient trucks or enough gasoline. The preponderance of the Allied build-up in their Normandy bridgehead was assured, particularly since the Allied air forces, despite the diversion of many of their planes, had by D-day won nearly complete command of the air.

On the Brink

Weeks before D-day the entire southern part of England became an armed camp, sealed off from the rest of the country. No one was allowed to cross the line in either direction without a special pass. Stores of all kinds crowded the depots, offering tempting targets to German bombers that never came. As early as May 30, troops began to embark in the transports and beaching craft that would carry them across the Channel. The next day the movement toward France began as 54 block-ships, to be sunk as breakwaters off the beaches, left western Scotland. A hundred and fifty minesweepers next advanced into the Channel to begin sweeping a clear passage for the convoys. By Saturday, June 3, all troops were embarked, the fire support ships had put to sea from Scapa Flow, Belfast, and the Clyde, and the convoys were beginning to form off the ports of southern England. NEPTUNE-OVERLORD, the most complex and most minutely planned military operation in history, was under way. Nothing that could be anticipated had been left to chance. There was nevertheless one element of uncertainty—the weather, and on that everything else depended.

Beginning on June 1, at Admiral Ramsay's headquarters in a country mansion near Portsmouth, General Eisenhower met twice daily with the top army and navy commanders of NEPTUNE-OVERLORD to hear the weather forecasts. On the morning of the 3rd the forecasts began to be discouraging, and grew more alarming through the day. At a special meeting at 0400 on Sunday, June 4, the meteorologists reported hopeless prospects for the 5th. High winds, low clouds, and high waves would combine in the target area. Air support would be impossible, landing of troops most hazardous, and naval gunfire undependable as a result of the storm conditions. When Eisenhower had considered all factors, he made the decision to postpone the invasion 24 hours.

A mighty coiled spring already unwinding had to be stopped, wound up again, and readied for release the next day. That this was done without serious consequence is a tribute to the skill and adaptability of everyone who played a part in the operation. Sunday evening, as the wind howled outside and the rain came down in squalls, the commanders met again at Ramsay's headquarters. Faces were gloomy. It seemed inconceivable that the weather could clear by the morning of Tuesday, June 6, the new D-day. If there had to be another postponement, it would have to be for at least two weeks. June 7 was out, for some of the warships and convoys that had been marking time at sea were running low in fuel. In two weeks security would be lost, morale would suffer severely, the whole world would know that something had gone wrong.

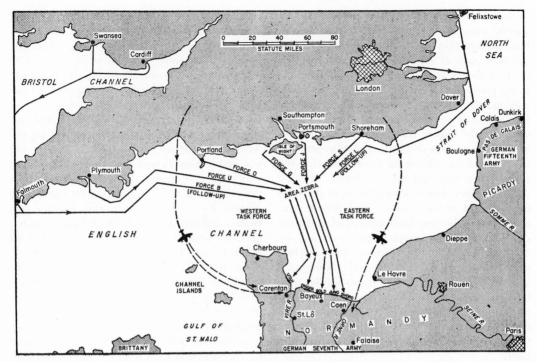

ROUTES OF THE INVASION CONVOYS, OPERATION OVERLORD, JUNE 6, 1944

To the relief of the commanders, the weather experts now reported prospects for a break in the weather. On this slender hope, Eisenhower set the invasion forces again into operation, but at Leigh-Mallory's request he called another meeting to be held a few hours later for the final decision. When Eisenhower left his mobile trailer camp headquarters to attend the last weather conference, it was still blowing and raining, but by the time the commanders had again assembled, the night sky had begun to clear. The meteorologists now brought in the word that the clearing weather would last at least until the afternoon of the 6th. On the basis of this report Eisenhower at 0415 made his irrevocable decision: "O.K. We'll go."[4]

Across the Channel later that morning, Marshal Rommel left his headquarters in his command car and headed for his home in Germany, where he planned to spend June 6, his wife's birthday. He and the other top German commanders in the West had been warned by their intelligence organization that

[4] Chester Wilmot, The Struggle for Europe (New York, 1952), 226.

the Allied invasion was about to be launched, but the commanders had received so many false alarms that they failed to take the accurate warning seriously.[5] At any rate, they considered a landing unlikely under the weather conditions then prevailing. For lack of meteorological stations west of Europe they had no intimation of the clearing weather on the way.

Once Eisenhower had made his decision, Operation NEPTUNE gathered momentum. From all ports along the south coast of England, from ports on the east and west coasts, from Northern Ireland, from Scotland, and from the Orkneys elements of the armada put

[5] German agents had penetrated Resistance groups on the Continent and learned the signal by which the underground would be alerted by BBC from London. It consisted of the first two lines of Verlaine's *Chanson d'Automne*. The first line, "*Les sanglots longs des violons de l'automne*," was broadcast on June 1; the second, "*Blessent mon coeur d'une langueur monotone*," was broadcast in the evening of June 5. German radio monitors heard and recorded both signals, but the practical-minded German commanders scoffed at the notion that the Allies would alert the underground by means of lines of romantic poetry inserted into a public broadcast.

to sea. Most headed for Area Zebra, the assembly area southeast of the Isle of Wight. Remarkably enough, despite blowing weather, the thousands of ships involved came together at Area Zebra and moved across the Channel in darkness on almost perfect schedule. Halfway across, each of the swept lanes divided into two—one for fast, the other for slow convoys. While fighter aircraft provided a protective umbrella overhead, minesweepers led the way for the advancing forces, marking the swept lanes with lighted dan buoys. Because Allied bombers had destroyed most of the German coastal radar stations, and Allied jamming made the rest ineffective, the Germans did not detect the assault convoys during the crossing. The Allied fire support ships reached their assigned anchorages off Normandy around 0200, June 6. Attack transport *Bayfield,* headquarters ship for Task Force U, dropped anchor off Utah Beach at 0230. Amphibious command ship *Ancon,* flagship of Task Force O, anchored off Omaha Beach 20 minutes later.

The Normandy Landings

The first troops to land in Normandy were the three airborne divisions, which were dropped about 0130 in the morning of June 6. The British 6th Airborne Division landed between Caen and Cabourg with the mission of seizing bridges over the Orne River and the adjacent Caen canal in order to prevent German reinforcements from moving in from the northeast. The American 82nd and 101st Airborne Divisions landed behind Utah Beach. Their assignment was to seize control of the causeways leading inland from the beaches over meadows that the Germans had flooded, and to capture bridges in the vicinity of Sainte Mère-Eglise and Carenten. The paratroops at first met only limited resistance because the Germans, convinced that the main assault would be directed against the Pas-de-Calais area, regarded the Normandy drops as a mere diversion. By dawn, the 6th and 101st Airborne Divisions were approaching their objectives, and the 81st was containing a German infantry division near Sainte Mère-Eglise.

Off the Normandy beaches, the Allied transports had begun lowering landing craft promptly after dropping anchor, and at 0400 they began debarking the assault troops. These were to advance in a series of waves along boat lanes to the line of departure, where the landing craft were to circle until signaled to advance to the beach. Between the transport area and the beach the fire support vessels were at anchor flanking the boat lanes—the battleships and cruisers 11,000 yards offshore, the destroyers 5,000 yards. Fire support for the American beaches was furnished by the old U.S. battleships *Texas, Nevada,* and *Arkansas,* which were to engage the heavy defenses with their 12- and 14-inch guns, while U.S. heavy cruisers *Tuscaloosa, Quincy,* and *Augusta,* five British and two French light cruisers, a Dutch gunboat, and 22 destroyers took on the lighter beach targets. In the British sector H.M. battleships *Warspite, Nelson,* and *Ramillies* provided the big guns, and were assisted by five British cruisers and numerous destroyers to blast smaller targets. As the leading boat waves headed in from the line of departure, they were to be accompanied by gunboats and rocket-equipped LCT's, which were to blanket the beaches with fire just before the troops stepped ashore.

A little after 0300 a German search radar station had at long last detected and reported "large craft" off the Normandy coast. The shore batteries thereupon were manned in full strength and readied for action. A little past 0500, when first light dimly outlined the silhouettes of the nearer fire support vessels, the batteries opened fire. A few of the vessels replied at once, and by 0600 the pre-landing naval bombardment of the beaches was under way in full fury.

At Utah Beach the support ships checked fire as 276 B-26 medium bombers from England swept over the beaches and dropped 4,400 bombs. Bombing visually through an overcast, many of the B-26's dropped their bombs harmlessly into the water. Nevertheless the American 4th Infantry Division went ashore at Utah in 26 waves against little opposition, the first wave hitting the beach right on schedule at 0630. Here lack of reference points ashore and a southerly tidal set caused the landing to be made three quarters of a mile south of the intended beaches. As it turned out, this accident proved fortunate for the Americans, because the beach obstacles were lighter in the actual landing area than in that designated in the NEPTUNE plan. Beaches in the Utah sector moreover were not protected by formidable obstacles, and here the coastal defense troops were from a "static" division of green reservists and foreign conscripts who were not inclined to fight past hope. By the end of D-day 21,300 troops, 1,700 vehicles, and 1,700 tons of supplies had been landed at Utah beach, and the invaders had suffered fewer than 200 casualties. The 4th Division had established a beachhead six miles deep and six miles wide, had made contact with the 101st Airborne Division, and was ready to press across the base of the peninsula and to link up with the V Corps in the vicinity of the Vire Estuary. As it turned out, the Americans took their heaviest material losses of the day in the waters off the beach, where undetected mines sank a destroyer, two LCI's, and three LCT's.

In sharp contrast to Utah, Omaha proved the most heavily armed and fortified beach that the Americans or their allies were to assault during the entire war.[6] Rommel had given this area special attention, and the defenders had armed the coast here to a strength approaching that of the Pas-de-Calais beaches. The Omaha defenses began 300 feet inshore of the low-water line with a row of 7-by-10-foot steel frames planted upright like gates. Behind these were sharpened, half-buried stakes pointed seaward. Next came a row of "hedgehogs," each composed of three six-foot iron bars crossed at right angles. Many of these obstacles were connected by wires and mined. Just inshore of the high-water line was a sea wall, partly concrete and partly piling, backed by a heavy coil of barbed wire. Behind this was a level shelf from 100 to 300 yards wide, thickly mined and crisscrossed by antitank ditches. On the far side of the shelf rose a line of bluffs, too steep even for tracked vehicles. Four deep ravines, breaks in the bluffs through each of which ran a narrow road, gave access to the interior. Guns were everywhere, some mobile, some casemated. Abandoned stone and brick villas at the foot of the

[6] This does not mean that Omaha Beach was necessarily the most formidably defended, for not even the hard-fighting Germans ever fought virtually to the last man, as the Japanese did on many an island in the Pacific.

bluffs had been converted into strong points. Trenches for riflemen ran along the top of the bluffs, and here also were machine-gun emplacements, artillery up to 88-mm. caliber, and mortars up to 90-mm. Other gun emplacements were dug into the bluffs so as to enfilade the beach and dominate the four exit ravines. Some of the defenses were manned by soldiers from a static division, such as guarded Utah Beach, but most of the defenders were first-line German troops of the 352nd Division. These had been moved from the interior to the coast at Rommel's insistence the preceding March.

At Omaha Beach shore batteries opened fire on the *Arkansas* at 0530. Some gunnery vessels replied at once, and at 0550 all began the scheduled bombardment of assigned targets. This beach was supposed to be bombed from high altitude by 480 B-24 heavy bombers. But the B-24's, obliged to bomb by instrument because of cloud cover, delayed releasing several seconds to avoid hitting ships or boats. As a result they scattered their 1,285 tons of bombs as much as three miles inland. At Omaha not a single bomb hit the beach or coastal defenses, and indeed the invasion forces did not know that the B-24's had passed overhead. But though bombers contributed little in breaching the Atlantic Wall, Allied fighter planes were entirely successful in keeping the *Luftwaffe* away from the American beaches throughout D-day.

The preparatory naval bombardment of Omaha Beach lasted only 35 minutes. Then all ships lifted fire as the first wave of landing craft headed in from the line of departure. The time allowed was obviously too brief, particularly since numerous targets had not been spotted in advance by aerial reconnaissance, and a good many of the known targets were invisible to spotter planes circling over the beaches. Despite the handicaps however, the ships had knocked out about half the enemy's guns.

The first infantry assault wave was preceded by LCT's carrying standard tanks and by amphibious tanks, some boated, some going in under their own power. Most of the non-boated amphibious tanks were swamped by the choppy sea and went down. The tanks that reached the beach came under heavy shelling, and several were stopped and set afire. LCVP's, coming in next, began taking hits while still 500 yards off shore. By the time they dropped ramps, at 0630 or thereabouts, the fire from the bluffs was intense. Through a hail of bullets and shells, the troops had to wade some 75 yards to the beach and then work their way 250 yards more through the obstacles to the dubious protection of the sea wall. A great many failed to make it.

While the first wave of assault troops huddled against the sea wall, 16 underwater demolition teams landed and proceeded to blast channels through the beach obstacles so that later waves could be brought in ever closer to the sea wall on the rising tide. The teams succeeded in blasting five broad channels, at the cost of more than half their number killed or wounded. Waves of infantry, coming in at ten-minute intervals after 0700, at first merely fed men into the growing mass of prone figures carpeting the beach behind the sea wall. A little after 0800 LCI's, LCM's, and DUKW's headed for the beach with artillery. Nearly all of the DUKW's were swamped or turned back by the choppy seas, and three of the LCI's were hit by shells, set afire, and sunk. Little artillery in fact reached Omaha Beach on D-day. But Army engineers managed to blow gaps in the barbed wire behind the sea wall, machine guns were set up, and under the leadership of surviving officers, small groups of men began rushing across the shelf and scaling the bluffs. By noon the Americans had begun to penetrate inland.

What enabled the invaders, with almost no artillery, to advance against the fearsome defenses of Omaha Beach? Sheer courage played its part and tanks helped, but the principal answer is naval gunfire. The *Texas,* the *Arkansas,* and two British and two French cruisers, using air spot by Spitfires based on England, sealed off the beachhead with a ring of fire, preventing the Germans from either reinforcing or shifting their defense forces. But the direct support that cleared the way for the asault forces was provided by nine American and three British destroyers. Closing the shore to within 1,000 yards, actually scraping bottom, these delivered call fire as requested by shore fire control parties or fired at targets of opportunity. The bluffs, which proved an ob-

stacle to vehicles, were a shooting gallery for the destroyers, which could supplement call fire by means of visual observation of enemy positions in the rising ground. During D-day U.S.S. *Carmick* alone expended 1,127 rounds of 5-inch shell, and other destroyers fired almost as many. Thus supported, by nightfall on June 6 some 34,000 troops, nearly five regiments of the 1st and 29th U.S. Divisions, had gone ashore at Omaha. Here they had overrun the bluffs, seized the exit ravines, and established a line more than a mile inland. The price had been high: casualties among the invaders amounted to about 2,000 killed, wounded, and missing.

The landings on the British beaches were easy compared to those at Omaha. In the British sector obstructions were less formidable and less thickly sown, and here the coast defenses were manned by troops of a static division including numerous Poles and Ukrainians. Here too the beaches got a far more extended preparatory naval bombardment than at either Utah or Omaha, for the British landings had to be delayed from an hour to an hour and a half to allow the rising tide to cover the reefs and foul ground in this area. By the end of D-day the 50th British, the 3rd Canadian, and the 3rd British Division, which had landed respectively at Gold, Juno, and Sword Beaches, had penetrated four miles inland, and the 3rd British Division had made contact with the 6th Airborne Division. Though the British D-day penetration was much deeper than that attained by the Americans at Omaha, it fell short of plans, which included the occupation of Caen. The British were in fact to enter Caen only after weeks of hard fighting.

The Allied invasion could hardly have caught the Germans more off guard. Because of the bad weather preceding D-day, the German Seventh Army, defending Normandy and Brittany, had been taken off alert. Rommel, muttering, "How stupid of me! How stupid of me!" hastened back to France, reaching his headquarters on the 6th a little before midnight. After he had heard the reports of the day's fighting, he said to his aide, "If I were commander of the Allied forces right now, I could finish off the war in 14 days." Still convinced that the Normandy landings

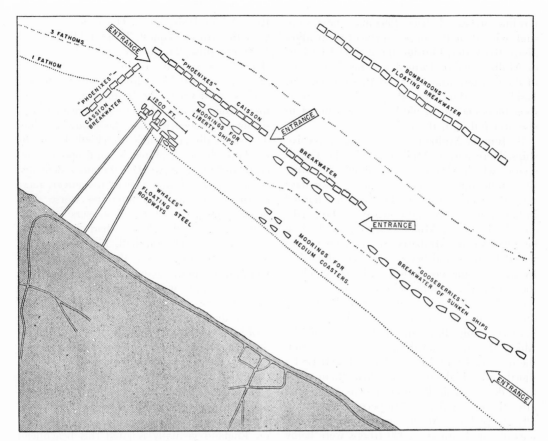

"MULBERRY A," OMAHA BEACH

were a diversion and that the main Allied attack would come against the Pas-de-Calais, Hitler's headquarters retained the bulk of the German Fifteenth Army in Flanders, holding back two panzer divisions that might have been rushed to the beachhead early on June 6. It was one of these divisions, belatedly committed, that initially kept the British out of Caen. Hitler now saw that an Allied drive south from Caen could isolate his Seventh Army from his Fifteenth, which continued to guard the Pas-de-Calais. He therefore ordered Rommel and Rundstedt to pour their available reserve strength into the Caen area, making it their focal point for the defense of the Continent. Hitler thus played neatly into Marshal Montgomery's hands. For it was Montgomery's plan to contain as many Germans as possible at Caen, while the Americans first captured the port of Cherbourg in order to assure an adequate inflow of supplies and then

thrust south and east in the vicinity of St. Lô. The Allied forces would thus pivot on their left, using Caen as the hinge, and face east on a strong front—both to defend the lodgment area and for an advance toward Germany.

In the evening of June 6 perhaps the strangest fleet ever to sail from any harbor anywhere had got under way from British ports. Included were tired old merchant ships (code name: Gooseberries) on their last voyage, huge concrete caissons (Phoenixes), enormous cruciform steel floats (Bombardons) with their heads visible above the surface, and quantities of tugs and other auxiliaries. This was Operation MULBERRY, which was to provide harbors where none existed—one off Omaha Beach, the other off Gold Beach.

Mulberry A arrived off Omaha Beach at dawn on the 7th after a 5-knot crossing. Construction began that afternoon with the sinking of a line of Gooseberries off shore. To extend the line of Gooseberries, Phoenixes next were sunk with their flat upper surfaces protruding above the water. Outside the artificial harbor, or Mulberry, thus formed was moored a row of Bombardons to act as a floating breakwater. Inside, extending from the beach, were pontoon piers ending in pierheads constructed to rise and fall with the tide.

By June 17 Mulberry A was ready to receive ships. Here and at Mulberry B in the British sector, which was ready at about the same time, unloading proceeded rapidly. Two days later the worst storm in the English Channel in half a century roared down from the northeast, so battering Mulberry A that it had to be abandoned. Mulberry B, somewhat protected by reefs and better sheltered under the lee of the cape north of Le Havre, survived the storm with comparatively minor damage. Before the invasion, many would have predicted that the loss of one of the artificial harbors would have meant disaster for the Allies. But while awaiting their construction the navy had found it possible to beach LST's shortly after high tide and unload them when the tide receded. By such means unloading after the destruction of Mulberry A was actually stepped up. At the end of June, 15,000 tons of supplies and 15,000 troops were being landed daily over Omaha Beach alone.

The Battle of Normandy

By June 18 a corps of the U.S. First Army had driven across to the Gulf of St. Malo, thereby sealing off the Cotentin Peninsula. The Americans then wheeled to the right and by the 24th had pushed the 40,000 German defenders to the northern tip of the peninsula and had surrounded Cherbourg. The army now called upon the navy to knock out the heavy coastal batteries guarding the waterfront and flanking the city. These batteries, up to 280-mm. (11-inch) caliber, and with a range up to 40,000 yards, were for the most part heavily casemated. Some were in revolving steel turrets capable of being trained inland as well as to sea. For naval vessels to attack such ordnance was contrary to established doctrine that warships should not expose themselves to coastal guns of caliber approaching their own. Nevertheless a naval force under

Rear Admiral Morton L. Deyo USN complied with the army's request. From 1200 till after 1500 on June 25, the *Nevada, Texas,* and *Arkansas,* U.S. heavy cruisers *Tuscaloosa* and *Quincy,* two British cruisers, and eleven destroyers stood up to the shore guns, pounding them from the sea while the American troops stormed Cherbourg from the landward side. The ships, directing their fire chiefly by means of shore fire control parties and spotter aircraft, did much to weaken the city's defenses. By use of smoke and violent maneuver, most of the vessels avoided anything worse than near misses. Two of the destroyers were hit however, and the *Texas* had her bridge wrecked by a 280-mm. shell. The next day the attacking troops received the surrender of the German defending general, and by July 1 the entire peninsula was in American hands. The Germans as usual had done their best to render the port unusable, but the destruction had been carried out so inexpertly that British and American salvage engineers had the harbor in partial use within two weeks.

During the drive for Cherbourg, the Allied forces in Normandy had established a continuous front and had attained an 18-mile southward penetration at the center. Aircraft based on England virtually isolated this beachhead area from the rest of France. German troops advancing from the interior had to move by night and in small formations. Highways leading to the Allied lodgment, under repeated attack from the air, became choked with dead men, dead horses, and shattered equipment. Meanwhile in the first 30 days 929,000 men, 586,000 tons of supplies, 177,000 vehicles, and vast quantities of armament poured into the beachhead from the Channel. The invaders thus attained over the enemy a two-to-one local superiority in manpower and a three-to-one superiority in tanks and guns. The time had come for the long-planned breakout on the western flank.

The British, continuing their pressure on Caen, opposite the eastern flank, entered the city on July 8, after it had been pulverized by artillery and 2,500 tons of aerial bombs. German-held St. Lô, after receiving a similar treatment, was occupied by the U.S. First Army on the 18th. The First Army then pressed southward, flanked on the left by elements of

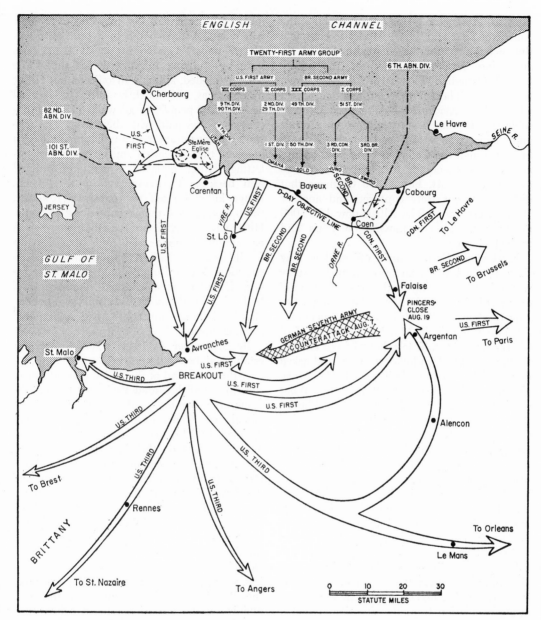

INVASION AND BATTLE OF NORMANDY

the British Second Army, and worked its way around the western flank of the German Seventh Army. This pressure on the Germans enabled the newly formed U.S. Third Army under General Patton to break through at Avranches and fan out south, east, and west. The effect was to seal off the Brittany Peninsula and to establish a broad front for an eastward advance in the direction of the Rhine, toward which Patton with his usual dash now directed the bulk of his army. Patton's drive to the east left the German Seventh Army surrounded on three sides. Common sense now dictated that the Germans retire eastward with all possible speed to avoid being entrapped, but Hitler decreed that they should drive to the west in a futile attempt to penetrate the U.S. First Army and cut Patton's communications at Avranches. This move enabled the American First and Third Armies to complete the encirclement of the enemy on August 19, advancing northward to meet the newly formed Canadian First Army driving down from Caen. Though the Germans entrapped within this "Avranches-Falaise pocket" were subjected to merciless pounding by aircraft and artillery, they managed on the 20th to break through the Canadians and hold open a corridor long enough for 40,000 troops to escape to the east. But 50,000 Germans that did not get out were captured and another 10,000 were killed. The Allies, now 1,500,000 strong, were already moving on Paris and toward Germany.

Most senior German army officers had long since reached the conclusion that Germany was defeated and that further resistance could only result in the ruin of the Fatherland. On July 1, when the British began their successful drive on Caen, Field Marshal Keitel, chief of the *Wehrmacht* staff, telephoned from Hitler's headquarters to Headquarters West and asked despairingly, "What shall we do?" "Make peace, you fools!" replied Rundstedt, "What else can you do?"[7] Hitler thereupon relieved Rundstedt, replacing him with Field Marshal Gunther von Kluge. On arriving in France, Kluge soon agreed with Rommel that further resistance was hopeless, and that if Hitler could not be brought to reason, they should seek a local armistice with Eisenhower and thus force the Führer's hand. On July 15, while directing operations in the vicinity of Caen, Rommel made a final attempt to convince Hitler before taking independent action. "The armies are fighting heroically everywhere," he reported, "but the unequal combat is nearing its end. It is in my opinion necessary to draw the appropriate conclusion from the situation. I feel it is my duty as Commander-in-Chief of the Army Group to express this clearly." Two days later Rommel was severely injured when a strafing fighter plane killed his driver, and his car crashed into a tree.

Meanwhile, officers nearer German headquarters, noting that Hitler seemed determined to pull Germany down in the ashes of his own funeral pyre, had decided that the Führer

must be assassinated. On July 20 the attempt was made. A time bomb in a brief case was placed under a table at which Hitler was standing studying maps with his staff. The bomb exploded, killing four officers, but Hitler himself was only slightly hurt. In reprisal nearly 5,000 people, in all walks of life, innocent or guilty, paid with their lives. The network of conspiracy and retaliation at length involved the "defeatists" in the general bloodletting. Hitler replaced Kluge and ordered him back to Germany. Fearing the worst, Kluge killed himself en route. To Rommel, the national hero, then recuperating at home, Hitler gave the choice of secretly taking poison or standing public trial and involving his family and his staff in his disgrace and destruction. When Rommel had poisoned himself, Hitler decreed national mourning and had him buried with full military honors. Rundstedt was required to read a prepared funeral oration.

By September 1, 1944, when Eisenhower established headquarters in France and took over the command of the Allied ground forces, the Allies had liberated Paris and crossed the Seine, the Somme, and the Meuse. Under Eisenhower, General Omar Bradley now commanded the 12th Army Group (U.S. First and Third Armies) on the right flank, and Marshal Montgomery commanded the 21st Army Group (Canadian First and British Second Armies) on the left flank. The need for a speedy advance by Montgomery through Northern France and Belgium had now become acute, for from these areas in mid-June the first of the German V-weapons had begun streaking toward London. This was the pilotless, winged, jet-propelled V-1. No sooner had the British learned to cope with the V-1, mainly by the use of VT-fused shells, than the Germans shifted to the more deadly V-2. Because these rockets sped faster than sound, the explosion was usually the first indication that the V-2 had been on the way. Against it there was next to no defense. The V-2's were in fact capable of destroying London, particularly if, as the Allies feared, the Germans were on the verge of producing an atomic warhead for them. Capture of the coastal V-2 launching bases was therefore given top priority.

[7] Wilmot, *The Struggle for Europe*, 347.

Operation Dragoon— The Invasion of Southern France

Not long after the Allied occupation of Rome, which, it will be recalled, nearly coincided with the invasion of Normandy, three American and two French divisions were withdrawn from the Italian front to provide a landing force for Operation DRAGOON, the invasion of southern France. Following the Normandy landings, beaching craft in large numbers left the English Channel for the Mediterranean. With the fall of Cherbourg at the end of June 1944, fire support ships headed south, until the Eighth Fleet had at its disposal to support the new invasion five battleships, U.S.S. *Arkansas, Nevada,* and *Texas,* H.M.S. *Ramillies,* and French *Lorraine,* and more than a score of cruisers, besides numerous destroyers. These were incorporated into Vice Admiral Kent Hewitt's Western Naval Task Force, which was to carry out the assault. The initial landing force, commanded by Major General Lucian K. Truscott USA, comprised two regimental combat teams of each of the three American divisions, with the third team of each serving as reserve. The two French divisions would provide early follow-up. D-day was set at August 15.

The selected landing area was a 30-mile stretch of coast between Toulon and Cannes. The immediate objective was to establish a bridgehead for invasion and to capture the neighboring ports, with special emphasis upon the capacious harbor of Marseille. Then, as the landing force was reinforced, ultimately to 21 divisions, it was to drive up the Rhone Valley to make contact with General Patton's U.S. Third Army in the vicinity of Dijon and take over the right flank of the Allied invasion of Germany.

DRAGOON was a far easier invasion than OVERLORD. For one thing the beach situation in

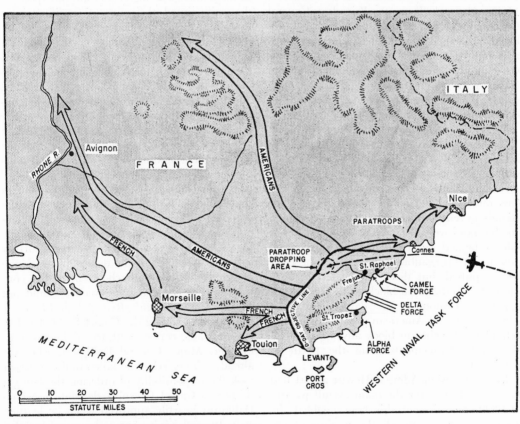

INVASION OF SOUTHERN FRANCE, AUGUST 15, 1944

southern France was much more favorable for the invaders than at Normandy. A comparatively steep gradient and small tidal range made placement of underwater obstacles difficult, the beach areas were more sheltered from the action of the sea than in the north, and the time of year augured for good weather in the Mediterranean. Though the beaches were thickly mined and backed by powerful batteries, manpower requirements elsewhere had left the defenses lightly manned, partly by Czech conscripts and Polish prisoners of war who readily surrendered. Nevertheless DRAGOON stands out as one of the best executed assaults of the war, partly because the commanding officers, with accumulated amphibious experience behind them, worked in close harmony and anticipated nearly every difficulty. Planning began in Algiers in early spring of 1944. During the final planning, training, and rehearsal phase, Vice Admiral Hewitt, Lieutenant General Alexander Patch, whose U.S. Seventh Army included the assault force, Major General Truscott, Brigadier General Gordon P. Saville, who commanded the land-based air support, and their staffs occupied adjacent headquarters in Naples, where they were in constant consultation. The Western Naval Task Force trained the landing force, which thereby attained perfect timing and close coordination with the fleet.

When in mid-August the Western Naval Task Force approached its objective, it was heading for a coast that had been pounded with 12,500 tons of aerial bombs since the preceding April. During the night before D-day, raiders landed on Levant and Port Cros Islands to seize batteries that could be trained on the more westerly invasion beaches. Other raiders landed on the flanks of the invasion area to set up roadblocks. Those on the right were repulsed, but those on the left made a successful landing and blocked the roads leading from Toulon. Before dawn more than 5,000 British and American paratroops landed behind the beaches to block any approach of German reinforcements from the north or northwest.

In this invasion Admiral Hewitt at last had his way: H-hour for the main assault was set at 0800. Selection of this hour enabled the Task Force to approach the beachhead entirely in darkness, it avoided the inevitable confusion of a night assault, it provided more than two hours of daylight for pre-invasion bombing and bombardment, and it allowed ample time for the troops to secure a lodgment before nightfall. At dawn on August 15, the Western Naval Task Force stood off the invasion beaches. It was divided into three attack forces, named from left to right *Alpha*, *Delta*, and *Camel*. Each attack force carried one American division, the assault forces in LST's together with their landing craft, the reserves in transports.

The main assault began shortly before 0600 as the first squadrons of 1,300 bombers, flying from Italy, Sardinia, and Corsica, swept over the beaches escorted by fighters. The aerial bombing was almost continuous till 0730, when it stopped to allow full play to the naval bombardment. The ships had already been pounding the shore for more than half an hour, whenever they could fire without danger to the bombers. Using cruiser aircraft spotting, they pinpointed their fire at specific targets that had already been detected by aerial reconnaissance. As the landing craft headed for shore, the battleships and cruisers ceased fire, the destroyers advanced their fire inland, giving the area behind the beaches a drenching, and LCI's leading in the first wave fired rockets into the beaches themselves to explode land mines. The assault troops stepped ashore at seven selected beaches on the 30-mile front. All the landings were on time, and none met any serious resistance.

The one difficult beach was Camel Red in the Golfe de Fréjus. But difficulty had been anticipated here; hence the landing at this point had been deferred till 1400 to allow the forces landed at Camel Beach Green, farther eastward, to take out the defenses. But as the deferred H-hour approached, enemy fire continued so heavy that minesweepers could not operate inside the gulf. Rear Admiral Spencer Lewis, commanding the Camel Force, tried to get into radio contact with the divisional commander, Major General Dahlquist, who was already ashore. When he failed to do so, Lewis took the responsibility of ordering the landing shifted to Camel Green, a decision of which Dahlquist heartily approved when he learned of it. In earlier invasions such an unscheduled shift would have produced a first-class logistic headache. That it could be carried out across a beach over which supplies were flowing to forces already ashore demonstrates the remarkable efficiency with which Operation DRAGOON was planned and executed.

Throughout the operation a force including seven British and two American escort carriers stood off the coast sending in planes to spot for the gunfire support vessels and to range inland to disrupt enemy communications and to break up enemy troop concentrations. Though the *Luftwaffe* succeeded in making one effective raid on the invasion forces and actually sank an LST off Camel Beach Green, the Allied carrier pilots neither on D-day nor for three days thereafter saw a single enemy plane. The few they encountered thereafter they promptly shot down.

The French divisions, landing after the initial assault, promptly advanced westward toward Toulon and Marseille, while the paratroops moved in the opposite direction toward the lesser ports of Cannes and Nice. At the same time the main body of the Seventh Army began its drive to the Rhone. The capture of both Toulon and Marseille required several days of combined land and air assault supported by naval guns. The harbors of both cities were defended by powerful batteries that proved difficult to silence. The hardest to deal with was a 340-mm. battery which the French had installed before the war as a result of Mussolini's sword rattling and the building of the Italian navy up to parity with the French *Marine*. At last on August 28 the Germans in both major ports capitulated. Meanwhile, also with naval support, the paratroops were achieving their objectives; on August 24 they entered Cannes and on the 30th they occupied Nice.

By this time the main body of the invasion forces had advanced far to the north, pursuing rapidly retiring Germans. Seven French divisions formed the nucleus of a newly-formed French First Army, commanded by Générale de l'Armée Jean de Lattre de Tassigny. Follow-up American forces were incorporated with the assault troops in Lieutenant General Patch's U.S. Seventh Army. The French and the American army together comprised the Sixth Army Group under Lieutenant General Jacob L. Devers. On September 11 Devers' Army Group made contact near Dijon with elements of Patton's Third Army from Normandy. Thus the two great thrusts combined, sealing off all German forces in southwestern France. The Sixth Army Group next wheeled to the east and drew up in a line along the German frontier from the Swiss border for a distance of about 80 miles where their left flank was in contact with the right flank of the U.S. Third Army.

The German Collapse

In the fall of 1944, after a breathtaking sweep across France and Belgium, the Allied armies under General Eisenhower reached the German frontier, stood on the Rhine near Strasbourg, and penetrated into Germany at Aachen. Then stiffening German resistance, worsening weather, and mounting problems of supply brought the advance in the West almost to a standstill. In Italy, the Allied Fifth and Eighth Armies, after pushing north of Florence, came virtually to a halt against the German Gothic Line. On the Eastern Front, the Russians continued to press forward in the north and south but came to a stop at the center just short of Warsaw.

In mid-December, Rundstedt, restored as Commander in Chief West, launched his last offensive. Taking advantage of bad weather that hampered Allied air operations, he committed Germany's last strategic reserves in a massive drive at the Allied center in the Ardennes. In what is popularly called the Battle of the Bulge, Rundstedt penetrated 50 miles westward, but there was never any real danger of his achieving his objective of splitting the Anglo-American armies apart. In fact, Eisenhower, who was aware of the existence of the German reserves, was glad of the opportunity of dealing with them early in the open rather than later behind their own fortifications. Improving flying weather and prompt Allied counterattacks soon obliged Rundstedt to pull back under threat of having his entire salient pinched off and surrounded. He had suffered greater losses than he had inflicted.

The Russians, resuming their offensive in mid-January 1945, advanced 250 miles to the Oder River in 30 days and directly threatened

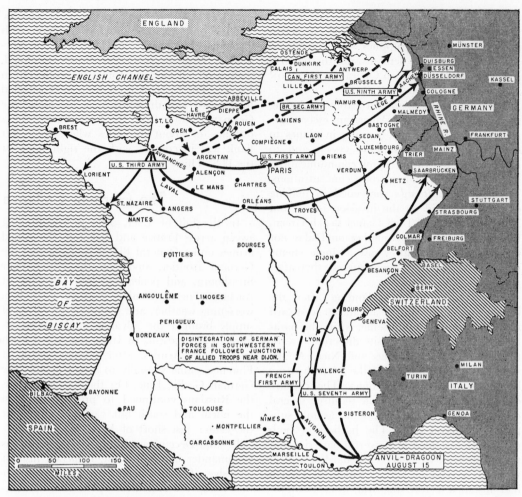

THE DRIVE INTO GERMANY, 1944

Berlin, which Hitler refused to leave. In the south, the Russian advance past Budapest obliged the Germans to withdraw hastily from Greece and the Balkans to avoid being cut off from Germany.

By March 1945 Eisenhower's armies were lined up along the Rhine, which because of its swift current and steep banks was a formidable barrier. General Bradley, correctly assuming that the retreating Germans would try to destroy every bridge over the river, had months before turned to the navy for help in getting across. Admiral Stark had readily provided Bradley's Army Group with landing craft, 96 LCVP's and 45 LCM's, together with crews, and the boats had been hauled to the front by Army trucks and trailers. As luck

would have it, the Germans failed to destroy the bridge at Remagen ahead of the fast-moving U.S. First Army, and on March 7 Bradley rushed five divisions across the Rhine to establish a shallow beachhead on the east bank. When the Remagen bridge collapsed under German bombardment ten days later, the naval landing craft were already at work on the river. Before the end of March they had ferried 14,000 troops and 400 vehicles of the First Army across the Rhine and assisted Army Engineers in constructing pontoon and Treadway bridges. As General Patton's U.S. Third Army had been the most spectacular in its sweep across France and into Germany, its use of landing craft for crossing the Rhine was also the most striking. Using the boats for a quick build-up at four points on the east bank between Mainz and Koblenz while bridges were being constructed, Patton was able to strike into the heart of Germany with scarcely a pause.

By the end of March all the Anglo-American armies in the West had crossed the Rhine. The Canadian First and the British Second Armies on the left flank raced for the German North Sea Ports. The U.S. Ninth and First Armies carried out Eisenhower's long-planned double envelopment of the Ruhr, cutting off this industrial region from the rest of Germany and entrapping 325,000 troops, including 30 general officers. The Third Army kept on right across Germany, entering Czechoslovakia and advancing down the Danube to meet the Russians, who had just captured Vienna. While the French First Army covered its flank, General Patch's U.S. Seventh Army swept through southern Germany, capturing Munich and advancing through the Brenner Pass back into Italy.

In April 1945 the Allied Fifth and Eighth Armies in Italy at length pierced the Gothic Line. Fanning out, they shattered the German Army Group in Northern Italy and joined hands on the Riviera with French troops advancing eastward from Nice and in the Alps with their erstwhile comrades-in-arms of the Italian campaign advancing southward through the Brenner Pass.

As the war in Europe drew to its thundering conclusion, three of the major national leaders died within a few days of each other. On April 12 President Roosevelt died at Warm Springs, Georgia of a cerebral hemorrhage. On April 28, Benito Mussolini was overtaken and killed by anti-Fascists while fleeing toward the Swiss border. His body, brought back to Milan, was exposed to public execration by the Italians whom he had led into a disastrous war. On May 1, with the Russians surrounding Berlin and fighting in the streets, Adolf Hitler, hiding in a bunker at his Chancellery, put a pistol into his mouth and shot himself.

The German armies, reduced to mobs of terrified fugitives, now began to surrender to the British and the Americans. In the early hours of May 7, Marshall Alfred Jodl at General Eisenhower's headquarters at Reims placed his signature on the general surrender document: "We, the undersigned, acting by authority of the German High Command, hereby surrender unconditionally to the Supreme Commander, Allied Expeditionary Force, and simultaneously to the Soviet High Command, all forces on land, sea, and in the air who are at this date under German control."

At 2301 May 8, 1945, World War II officially ended in Europe.

Summary

Germany's invasion of Poland on September 1, 1939 brought prompt declarations of war from Britain and France. The German *Wehrmacht* quickly crushed Poland, whereupon both sides settled down on the Western Front to several months of military inactivity known as the "Phony War." At sea however Germany struck without delay at Allied shipping, and Britain replied at once with a naval blockade. Because Germany's navy was unprepared for war, its first campaign at sea was relatively ineffectual, made by a handful of U-boats and a few surface raiders. On the other hand, German use of Norway's coastal waters somewhat vitiated the effect of the British blockade. The Germans, anticipating British plans to mine Norwegian waters, in April 1940 daringly invaded Denmark and Norway, achieving success through surprise. The British counterattacked with naval forces, captured the Norwegian iron ore port of Narvik, and attempted to capture Trondheim in order to cut German communications through central Norway. The naval attack was ineffective, the Trondheim expedition failed through lack of sufficient carrier air power, and the British were obliged to evacuate Narvik in order to mass all available strength against the Germans now advancing through the Low Countries into France. Germany, left in undisputed control of Norway, now had sites for naval bases outflanking Scapa Flow.

As in World War I the British initially adopted continental strategy against Germany by placing an army in France. In 1914 the Franco-British forces succeeded in stopping but not repulsing the advancing Germans. In 1940 however the combination of German air power and panzer divisions proved irresistible. Within a few days panzer divisions had swung in a great arc to the sea, surrounding the British Expeditionary Force and cutting it off from its French allies. In a remarkable evacuation, the British withdrew the bulk of their forces from the Continent by way of Dunkirk. As France succumbed to the German onslaught, Italy declared war on France and Britain, and Italian troops crossed the French border in order to participate in the German victory. Occupation of the French coast now gave the Germans sites for naval bases outflanking the British Channel forces.

Luckily for Britain she had refused to commit all her air force to the Battle of France. She was thus able to retain control of the air over England, thereby foiling German plans for a cross-Channel invasion. On the other hand, to ensure that France's navy could not be used against England, the British risked turning erstwhile allies into foes by seizing, disarming, and attacking French warships.

Decisions made in late 1940 and carried out in 1941 changed the whole focus of the war. Repulsed from the Continent, Britain reverted to her traditional peripheral strategy, using her sea-conferred mobility to probe for soft spots. Relieved of the threat of invasion and successful in her continuing struggle against the U-boat, she prepared to assume the offensive in the Mediterranean theater, where Italian troops had invaded Greece and Egypt. At the same time Hitler prepared to invade the Soviet Union, but before he could do so he was obliged to divert forces to the Mediterranean to rescue the Italians, who had begun to meet reverses. He was also obliged to leave powerful forces to guard Western Europe.

Hitler's overextending of his military strength was at length to prove fatal to Germany. At first however his armies were successful everywhere, threatening Moscow, conquering Greece and Crete, from which they drove the British, and invading Egypt, from which the British had recently expelled the Italians. Though German air power denied Britain the use of the Mediterranean for shipping, the British were able to strengthen their position in Egypt with supplies and reinforcements brought around the Cape of Good Hope. At the same time they cut deeply into Axis shipping to North Africa by means of

air attacks from Malta, which the Axis powers were never able to subdue.

In the Atlantic meanwhile, the British largely drove surface raiders from the sea. But as U-boats, using wolf pack operations, intensified their attacks, Britain again, as in World War I, faced defeat. Once more however the convoy system proved itself. The entry of the Soviet Union and the United States into the war at first offered new opportunities to the U-boats, which struck at shipping along the east coast of the United States and at the convoys to North Russia. The Allies succeeded in overcoming these threats, though at terrible cost, also by proper convoy measures. Convoy escort, supplemented by antisubmarine naval support groups, escort carriers, and improved land-based air cover, at length made U-boat attack on convoys so dangerous to the attackers that Dönitz reverted to his relatively ineffective tonnage warfare strategy.

Though the British and the Americans worked together closely and effectively as Allies, they frequently disagreed regarding strategy. The main difference arose over the American desire for an early invasion of western France followed by a drive into the heart of Germany. The British, thrice ejected from the Continent, preferred to continue peripheral strategy, at least until the Allies could be sure of a sufficient preponderance of strength to assure victory in Europe. The Russians also clamored for a "Second Front now," but it became increasingly clear that Britain and the United States lacked strength for immediate operations on the Continent. Yet something had to be done both to employ available Anglo-American forces and to take the pressure off Russia. The Anglo-American landings in French North Africa in November 1942 marked tentative American acceptance of peripheral strategy. A major purpose of this and ensuing Allied campaigns in the Mediterranean theater was to divert German strength from Western Europe in order to make the eventual Anglo-American cross-Channel attack less costly. In this respect the British plan, though it may have lengthened the war, apparently succeeded, for the British Empire in World War II lost only a little over half as many lives as in the shorter World War I.

The Allied landings in Northwest Africa

coincided with, and were a part of, the turning point of the war. The German advance had been halted in Russia and in Egypt. For the Germans, hitherto victorious on land, the rest of World War II consisted of a long retreat back to the Fatherland. In North Africa the Allied drive from the west coincided with a British offensive out of Egypt. The two offensives came together in Tunisia, where they succeeded in trapping 275,000 Axis troops.

The Anglo-Americans now invaded Sicily, in July 1943, thereby securing the Mediterranean communications and driving Italy out of the war. The following September they invaded Italy, now German-held, by way of Reggio and Taranto in the south and Salerno farther up the Italian boot. The assault at Salerno proved difficult, but lessons learned at the easier landings in North Africa and Sicily, particularly in the use of naval gunfire support, enabled the Allies to secure their beachhead and advance up the Italian peninsula. An Allied landing at Anzio near Rome in January 1944 was carried out in insufficient strength to attain its objective—cutting German communications to the principal front farther south—but the main drive at length regained momentum, relieved the Anzio beachhead, and forced the Germans back into northern Italy.

As their price for consenting to invade Italy, the Americans had exacted from the British an agreement to invade France in the spring of 1944. All during the campaigns in Sicily and Italy therefore the Allies had been building up strength for the forthcoming cross-Channel attack, while Allied air forces based on England were winning supremacy of the air over Western Europe and isolating the beachhead area in western France. Again American and British strategy diverged. Britain wished to exploit the position won in Italy to drive through the Balkans, while the Americans wanted to withdraw forces from Italy for an invasion of southern France in order to secure the port of Marseille, seal off the Germans in southwestern France, and supplement the cross-Channel forces in their drive into Germany. This time American ideas of continental strategy carried the day. The cross-Channel invasion of Normandy, made possible by overwhelming Allied strength and by defeat of the U-boat, took place on June 6, 1944. The landings in southern France followed on August 15, and the two drives pushed the Germans in France and the Low Countries back into Germany.

In the spring of 1945, as the British, Americans, and French drove from the west, and the Russians closed in from the east, Germany was beaten, although stubborn die-hards prevented the surrender until May. As in the war against Napoleon, peripheral strategy had given Britain her first opportunity to return to the offensive, and it had sapped enemy strength until overwhelming power could be exerted at the strategic center. But Hitler's empire, like Napoleon's, was finally defeated by concurrent continental drives thrusting in from opposite directions.

The final defeat of the European Axis was largely achieved by armies and air forces. Yet sea power provided the indispensable foundation for victory. The United States Navy and the Royal Navy escorted overseas the supplies and equipment that kept Britain from defeat and that provided the margin of victory for the Soviet Union. They transported to Africa and to Europe the Allied armies that were at length to occupy Italy and drive into Germany. With assistance from other navies, they carried invasion forces to beachhead after beachhead, put them ashore in the face of enemy resistance, and maintained them there with their guns until they had built up sufficient strength ashore to advance on their own. Through it all they waged unrelenting war against the U-boat and so kept open the flow of military strength from the New World to the Old. The navies thus carried out their major function of projecting and supporting decisive military power beyond the seas.

34:
Problems of the Pacific

The sea power situation of the 19th century is accurately reflected by a Mercator projection of the earth with the prime meridian running down the middle. At the center sits England, a position won for her largely by her Royal Navy. In 1885 the nations of the world tacitly acknowledged Britain's pre-eminence by adopting Britain's prime meridian, that running through the Greenwich observatory in London. Until then, major countries had their individual national meridians, to the confusion of chart makers and chart readers.[1]

From the point of view of England, the land on the left edge of the England-centered Mercator projection is the Far West; that on the right edge, the Far East—and so they are called. On this projection the Pacific Ocean is split in two, along the 180th meridian. Such division correctly represents the naval view of the 19th century, for no navy had yet been obliged to solve the problem of projecting its power across the Pacific. The primary military

[1] In 1884 there were no fewer than 14 prime meridians. The United States only narrowly avoided adding to the confusion, for in the early part of the century prominent Americans urged the U.S. Congress to follow the practice of other nations and adopt a national meridian, one running through Washington. The matter came to a head with the Congressional act of 1849 providing for an American Nautical Almanac. Preparation of the new Almanac was to be directed by Lieutenant Charles H. Davis USN, later famed as commander of the Federal gunboats on the Mississippi during the Civil War. Backed by the American Association for the Advancement of Science, Davis argued for adherence to the British meridian, because this was the one American seamen were accustomed to through long use of the British almanac and charts. Congress settled the matter in 1850 by adopting the Greenwich meridian.

communications between European nations and their Pacific interests and possessions had always been via the Atlantic and Indian Oceans. The Pacific Ocean was, and remained till the end of the 19th century, a military *aqua incognita*.

When at the end of the century the United States acquired the Philippines on the far side of the Pacific, it had to face the military problem of protecting its new possession or of re-capturing it should it be lost. The problem was intensified by deteriorating Japanese-American relations following the Russo-Japanese War of 1904–5. It became urgent when, by the Peace of Versailles ending World War I, Germany's Pacific islands north of the equator were mandated to Japan. Japan's new island empire comprised the Marshalls; all the Carolines, including the Palaus; and all the Marianas, excluding Guam, which the United States had annexed in 1898. Japan, in short, now controlled most of Micronesia, with numerous islands flanking any transpacific communications between the United States and the Philippines. As a result of this shift in the strategic balance and of the growing tension between the United States and Japan, the U.S. Navy and Marine Corps gave increasing thought after 1920 to the military problems posed by a war in the Pacific area.

American planners at the Naval War College and elsewhere realistically equated the problem of defending or recapturing the Philippines with that of defeating Japan. To them it was apparent that Japan, like Britain, was peculiarly vulnerable to blockade, and that even if conquering the Japanese should require actual invasion of their home islands, they would have first to be weakened by a

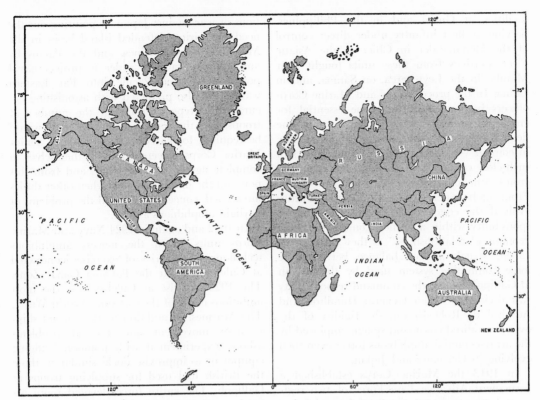

THE 19th CENTURY WORLD FROM THE SEA POWER POINT OF VIEW (COMPARE MAP PAGE 884.)

tight blockade that would cut them off not only from distant resources but from the continent of Asia as well. This last required introducing submarines into the Sea of Japan through mined straits, a problem that was under study at the Naval War College as early as 1923 and which was at last solved in 1945.

But before the Americans could operate against Japan, they would have to deal with certain difficulties posed by geographic features unique to the Pacific Ocean—its huge size, for example, and the fact that it contained an immense number of islands and atolls, most of them easily defensible and many having sites suitable for the construction of airfields. To fight its way across the Pacific the U.S. Navy would have to operate for extended periods far from established bases, and it would have to seize enemy island bases and convert them to its own use. Waging a successful war against Japan thus would require solutions to three major problems: (1) how to free the fleet from dependence upon rearward

bases, (2) how to isolate enemy island bases in the face of land-based air power, and (3) how to assault strongly defended island bases. Solutions were found to all these problems but in reverse order, and in that order they will be considered.

Amphibious Assault Doctrine

In 1894 Congress assigned to the U.S. Marine Corps the mission of providing units of fleet infantrymen that could establish and defend outlying bases.[2] Hard work then produced the battalion of fleet marines that in 1898 seized an advanced base at Guantanamo Bay, Cuba, stood off a more numerous enemy, and made of Admiral Sampson's blockaders a "fleet that came to stay."

Between 1900 and 1910 Marine Corps units constructed advanced base defenses and other

[2] For detailed treatment of this problem, see W. H. Russell, "The Genesis of FMF Doctrine: 1879–1899," *Marine Corps Gazette*, April–July 1951.

facilities at Guam and in the Philippines. Serving as fleet infantry under direct control of the Commander in Chief of the Asiatic Fleet, marines from these units fought near Manila, in the Leyte area, on Samoa, and in China. In the process Navy and Marine Corps officers hammered out doctrine essential for employing infantry as an integral arm of the fleet. At the same time, regular tours of duty in combat vessels kept marine commanders in such close contact with naval officers that each group came to understand the other's problems. From such experiences early in the century evolved the concept of complete tactical responsibility within a unified command. These "command relationships," as they came to be called, struck a nice balance between the loose committee system used by the British at Gallipoli, where the command responsibility was divided between General Hamilton and Admiral de Robeck, and the rigidity of the over-centralized command system employed by the army-centered amphibious forces even then evolving in Germany and Japan.

In 1913 the Marine Corps established a permanent Advance Base Force of two regiments, one equipped for fixed base defense, the other for mobile defense. Early in 1914 it was reinforced by a small aviation detachment and participated in fleet maneuvers at the island of Culebra off Puerto Rico. During the next two years this type-force of reinforced infantry gained valuable experience in a series of Caribbean police missions that required prompt naval action.

During World War I the U.S. Marine Corps expanded to 73,000 men. Most of these fought on the battlefields of France, but the Advance Base Force remained in full strength and at the end of the war numbered more than 6,000. In 1920 the force was based at Quantico, and the following year it was redesignated the Marine Corps Expeditionary Force. As before the war, its primary function was to defend bases against enemy attack. No one had yet contemplated the problems of landing large assault forces on heavily-defended shores.

But the year 1921 also saw the appearance of an epochal and prophetic operation plan, "Advanced Base Operations in Micronesia," by Lieutenant Colonel Earl H. Ellis USMC. In this plan Ellis correctly anticipated the opera-

tions of war against Japan by pointing out the need for seizing defended island bases in the Marshalls, the Carolines, and the Palaus by amphibious assault in order to project naval power across the Pacific into Far Eastern waters. He also predicted with astonishing accuracy the type of training, the number of troops, and the sort of techniques that would be required for carrying out his plan.[3] Senior Marine Corps officers expressed themselves in complete agreement with Ellis, and from this point on the marines, except when other duties intervened, concentrated upon the problems of daylight amphibious assault.

In 1922 and again in 1924 Navy and Marine Corps units tested the newest amphibious techniques in a series of exercises conducted at Culebra and at the Panama Canal Zone. The 1924 exercise at Culebra was the most ambitious effort of the sort since World War I. The Marines, in addition to their usual ship-to-shore movement and tactical problems ashore, experimented with pontoon bridging equipment to improvise docks similar to those the British had used for supplying troops at Gallipoli. The entire force devoted more attention to logistics than in any earlier amphibious maneuver. Brief as they were, even these limited "laboratory" efforts toward improved techniques ended in 1924 because the Marine Corps Expeditionary Force shifted its entire strength to China as part of a marine division called there by threatening developments.

Amphibious experiment by American forces did not end completely however, for in 1925 army and navy units in the Hawaiian Islands conducted an exercise to test the British-type amphibious doctrine advocated by the Joint Board of the Army and Navy. This maneuver was a "combined operation" in which army and naval officers shared the top command as British officers had at Gallipoli. Though it presented a realistic problem and marked the first significant test of army and naval air units, the Hawaiian exercise proved disappointing. Yet if it did nothing else, the maneuver convinced key officers from all the American services that the British doctrine would not produce an amphibious force capa-

[3] Ellis died mysteriously in 1923 in the Japanese-held Palau Islands. See "The Mystery of Pete Ellis," *Marine Corps Gazette*, July 1954.

ble of carrying out the United States' Pacific war plan.

Decisions flowing from the Hawaiian maneuvers, and the temporary emergence of logistics as a major study at the U.S. Naval War College, made 1925 the pivotal year in American amphibious development. By supplementing the techniques learned in the amphibious exercises with studies in logistic support and staff planning, American officers carried the evolution of modern amphibious doctrine into its final phase. After 1925 the new ideas enjoyed steadily increasing official support, whereas before they represented merely the thinking of a few individuals. In 1927 the Joint Board established the landing force role of the Marine Corps as national military policy. That same year however trouble broke out in Nicaragua that absorbed virtually all of the Corps' energy for several years.

Even this interruption contributed to amphibious development, for the anti-guerrilla operations in Nicaragua focused attention on small-unit infantry tactics. It provided an opportunity for bringing up to date the fire-and-movement techniques evolved in 1918. Nicaraguan experience with small patrols convinced the Marine Corps that small, efficient combat teams were needed for successful infantry assault. From teams such as those used in Nicaragua, the Corps built its battalion landing teams of World War II.

Nicaraguan experience also taught marines the value of close cooperation between air and ground elements of the same force. Because wiping out the elusive guerrillas required the ground force to operate in widely scattered units, small marine patrols faced severe handicaps. Reconnaissance planes repeatedly discovered guerrillas lying in ambush and warned ground patrols. Frequently aerial bombing and strafing helped ground units to drive off numerically superior guerrilla forces. Time and again pilots demonstrated the value of air supply and air evacuation of wounded. Though none of these efforts was part of pre-planned cooperative effort, they demonstrated in dramatic fashion the kinds of assistance integrated air support could provide combat infantry. The growing conviction that close-support airmen were merely "infantrymen bearing other arms" opened a whole new field for aircraft in time of war.

By 1930, as relaxation of tension in China and Nicaragua gradually released marines in substantial numbers, the various threads of amphibious development began to assume a recognizable pattern. Work at the Marine Corps Schools at Quantico in developing doctrine, the approach at Marine Corps Headquarters to the concept of a permanent type-force of fleet infantry, and concern at the Naval War College for a chain of island bases and for a Service Force to support the combat fleet, all began to complement each other.

In the academic year 1930–31 the Commandant of the Marine Corps Schools released marine Majors Charles D. Barrett, L. H. Miller, and Pedro del Valle and Lieutenant Walter C. Ansel USN from teaching duties so that under Barrett's chairmanship they might prepare a "Text for Landing Operations." The following year the schools devoted their entire time to amphibious studies. Divided into committees that functioned like the sections of an operational staff, they analyzed in detail the Dardanelles-Gallipoli campaign. Next they studied jointly with the Naval War College an advanced base problem following the current plan for a possible Pacific war. On December 8, 1933, the Secretary of the Navy implemented the Joint Board's 1927 policy decision by replacing the old Expeditionary Force with a Fleet Marine Force to operate as an integral part of the United States Fleet.

Though the FMF provided the tactical structure needed to carry out the Marine Corps' primary assigned mission, the marines still lacked a textbook for carrying out the necessary training. Hence the Marine Corps Schools suspended all classes, and faculty and student officers devoted nearly a year to completing the work of the Barrett Committee. They made full use of published works and of the most recent amphibious directive issued by the Joint Board, but when it came to fitting all the material into a coherent system, the Quantico officers drew heavily upon 40 years of amphibious experiment of the naval services. Late in 1934 the Marine Corps Schools completed the first United States manual to present a mature amphibious doctrine. Published as the *Tentative Manual for Landing*

Operations, this work separated the doctrine into six elements: (1) command relationships, (2) naval gunfire support, (3) aerial support, (4) ship-to-shore movement, (5) securing the beachhead, and (6) logistics. We shall now consider the six elements in this order, as they were treated in the *Tentative Manual.*

As used in the 1934 manual, the term "command relationships" covered organization of the amphibious force as well as command doctrine. The manual provided that United States overseas expeditions should be conducted as part of a naval campaign, with the expeditionary force organized as a naval Attack Force commanded by a naval flag officer. This task force was to have two main components: the Landing Force, comprising elements of the Fleet Marine Force, and the naval Support Force, including the Fire Support Group, the Air Group, the Transport Group, and the Screening Group. The Landing Force commander and the commander of each naval group was responsible directly to the Attack Force Commander, who had authority to make decisions affecting any of these subordinate units. The principal shortcoming of the manual on this subject was that it did not define when the assault phase of the invasion ended or provide for any change in the command structure at that point—nor did it envisage the possibility that the Landing Force might be army or mixed army and marine, situations that arose more often than not in World War II. The first American landing of the war, that on Guadalcanal in August 1942, followed the manual precisely. In the following October the Landing Force commander was still subordinate to the Attack Force commander,

though the latter was usually far away. To correct this situation the command relationships were altered.[4] In subsequent landings, as soon as the Landing Force commander established headquarters and indicated his readiness to control the forces ashore, he ceased to be subordinate to the Attack Force commander. Thereafter he had entire tactical control of his troops and reported to the next higher echelon, which in the Mediterranean-European theater and in the Southwest Pacific area was army, and in the Pacific Ocean Areas was naval.

Though amphibious assault follows exactly the same pattern as offensive action in conventional ground warfare, the fact that so much of the troop movement takes place on water seriously complicates the pattern of fire support for assault riflemen. Adapting naval guns to missions performed by ground artillery was a formidable task. Though naval fire control equipment was far more effective during the prewar years than that which forward artillery batteries could afford, the naval gun and its ammunition did not lend themselves readily to troop support. High muzzle velocity, flat trajectory, ammunition designed for sea battle, limited magazine capacity, and the problem of spotting targets invisible from the ship all served to complicate the situation. The *Tentative Manual* analyzed these problems brilliantly and laid a solid foundation for effective naval gunfire support. Not the least valuable contribution was the emphasis placed upon observation—aerial, shipboard, and ashore—to assist in fire control. Nevertheless the doctrine set forth in the manual required substantial development before naval guns were able to protect boated troops or infantry ashore against

[4] The Marine Corps historians provide a tongue-in-cheek acount of how marine General Thomas Holcomb initiated this change: "Shortly after this conference the Marine Commandant, General Holcomb, who had concluded his observations of the Marine units on Guadalcanal, sought to clear up the command controversy between General Vandegrift and Admiral Turner. Holcomb prepared for Admiral King, the Chief of Naval Operations, a dispatch in which he set forth the principle that the landing force commander should be on the same level as the naval task force commander and should have unrestricted authority over operations ashore. Holcomb then used his good offices to get Admiral Halsey to sign this dispatch. The Marine Commandant then started back to the States, and at Nimitz' office in Pearl Harbor he again crossed the path of the dispatch he had prepared for Halsey's signature. Holcomb assured Nimitz that he concurred with this message, and the admiral endorsed it on its way to King. It was waiting when Holcomb returned to Washington, and King asked the Commandant whether he agreed with this suggestion for clearing up the question of how a landing operation should be commanded. Holcomb said he did agree with it, and this led eventually to the establishment of firm lines of command for future operations in the Pacific." Lieutenant Colonel Frank O. Hough usmcr, Major Verle E. Ludwig usmc, and Henry I. Shaw, Jr., *History of U.S. Marine Corps Operations in World War II,* I (Washington, 1959), 341.

machine guns, mortars, or concealed artillery. For one thing, naval officers of the prewar period tended to place what proved to be excessive emphasis upon the danger to the fleet of enemy air and submarine attack. Many officers entered World War II with the conviction that naval gunfire support should be delivered at maximum range by ships moving at high speed and maneuvering radically, and that the ships should depart as soon as possible. With these limiting factors, the best that could be hoped for was area neutralization during the critical stages of the approach and landing, gunfire that would drive the defenders temporarily to cover. That this was not enough was first tragically demonstrated in the Pacific at Tarawa. Thereafter, to the credit of the Navy, fire was delivered at closer ranges over a greater period of time and with constantly improving accuracy.

The *Tentative Manual* did pioneer work in spelling out for the first time the role of aircraft in support of assaulting infantry. It provided for preliminary visual or photographic reconnaissance, air cover over transports and boats from disembarkation through the ship-to-shore movement, and for airborne fire support of boat waves during the final 1,000 yards of their trip to the beach. The manual also provided for aerial fire support once the troops stepped ashore until artillery could be landed in sufficient strength to assume its conventional role. The plan laid down by the manual was an outgrowth of Marine Corps experiences in Nicaragua and elsewhere in the Caribbean area, but there the planes had been slow, open-cockpit craft piloted by ex-infantrymen. To adapt to close support the new, swifter, closed-cockpit planes, flown by aviators with no experience in ground tactics, presented complex problems, not the least of which was maintenance of fast and dependable communications between ground and air. Really close support of infantry did not materialize until 1944.

In dealing with ship-to-shore movement, the *Tentative Manual* provided for precise preliminary planning and rigid control of boat movements during the attack. When possible each transport should carry one battalion of infantry reinforced with artillery and other arms to make it self-sufficient. Each transport should carry the landing boats assigned to the troops it had aboard. The manual specified the organization of boat groups and boat waves, with special formations adapted to the various situations a landing force might encounter. It prescribed control boats to lead the boat groups from the rendezvous area to the line of departure, buoys or picket boats to mark the line of departure, and guide boats and guide planes to lead the boats to the beach.

For securing the beachhead, the manual emphasized the techniques that permit infantry to survive the twilight period between full reliance on seaborne fire support and the landing of its own artillery. It gave special attention to establishing prompt communications between echelons ashore and afloat, as well as to the complex problem of organizing supply and medical services in the shallow area behind the front line. The 1934 manual prescribed both a Beach Party and a Shore Party. The former, commanded by a naval officer called a beachmaster, was to control not only boat movements but the unloading of supplies and equipment. The latter, besides other functions, would control the movement of supplies from the beach to supply dumps and to the front line. In exercises carried out in the summer of 1941 however, the Landing Force commander, Major General Holland M. Smith usmc, found this system unworkable. He recommended consolidating the two parties into a Shore Party under Landing Force control, with a naval beachmaster as assistant and adviser to the Shore Party commander. He further recommended use of special labor troops for unloading. Smith's recommendations were adopted, but by then war had been declared and they could not be tested in large-scale exercises. This lack of experience was to lead to serious confusion on the beach at Guadalcanal.

In the field of logistics the manual laid heavy stress upon tailoring all cargo loading to the requirements of the Landing Force. The 1934 planners asserted that each transport should not only carry one assault battalion and its landing boats, but that it should also carry the battalion's equipment—stowed in the order in which the various items would be needed. This concept of "combat unit loading" ran counter to the usual doctrine for loading cargo vessels because it implied stowing heavy equipment on deck, with lighter equipment in the hold. Yet inconvenient as this practice was from the point of view of seamen, it was essential to the success of the entire operation. The manual's emphasis on this point gradually forced navy men to develop attack transports suited especially to amphibious needs. As transports improved, the original combat unit loading doctrine underwent steady improvement until by 1944 it had become an essential element in the successful drive across the Pacific.

The basic doctrine set down in the *Tentative Manual for Landing Operations* in 1934 withstood prolonged trial by fire without fundamental change. Beginning in 1935 the Naval War College, the Marine Corps Schools, and units of the fleet took up the task of refining the techniques that were to convert a doctrinal theory into the kind of practiced teamwork required for military success. Annual fleet training exercises from 1935 through 1941 provided continuing "laboratory" tests of the basic doctrine. Conducted at Culebra, San Clemente Island near San Diego, and in 1941 at New River, North Carolina, these exercises refined amphibious staff work, stimulated the evolution of amphibious craft and radio equipment, underscored the need for improved gunfire and air support doctrine, and gave practical experience to thousands of soldiers, sailors, and marines. Though none of these exercises was sufficiently realistic to satisfy interested participants, they improved in direct proportion to the quality of the material available. Meanwhile the *Tentative Manual,* thus tested, underwent modification until 1938, when the Navy adopted it as *Fleet Training Publication 167.* In 1941 the Army issued virtually the same text as a field manual. These two publications were refined steadily throughout World War II, but remained the basic guides for amphibious planning and training.

The vital link between fleet and shore in any amphibious assault is sturdy and dependable landing craft for troops and equipment, but as late as 1936 no really suitable craft had been designed or built. That year, Andrew Higgins, a New Orleans boat builder, offered a shallow draft boat originally designed for use by trappers and oil drillers. For want of funds the Navy delayed a year before purchasing Higgins boats converted for amphibious operations. These boats, tested in the maneuvers of 1939 and 1940, won the enthusiastic approbation of the marines. The addition of a ramp for easy unloading at the beach provided the Navy and the Marine Corps with very nearly what they wanted. The ramped Higgins boat, first tested in the 1941 New River exercise, was in fact the prototype of the LCVP (Landing Craft, Vehicle and Personnel), which, according to General Holland Smith "did more to win the war in the Pacific than any other single piece of equipment."[5] Larger Higgins boats, also ramped, proved efficient tank lighters in the 1941 exercise; these were the precursors of the LCM (Landing Craft, Mechanized). A swamp vehicle called the "Alligator," built by Donald Roebling, attracted Marine Corps attention in 1937. Tested in 1939, the "Alligator" developed into the LVT (Landing Vehicle, Tracked) or amtrac, which could crawl ashore across coral reefs. In 1940 an armored amphibian designed by the Marine Corps went into production as the LVT(A).

Beginning in 1936 a trickle of old destroyers converted into transports afforded a stop-gap solution to an unsolved problem. Not until 1941 however did responsible naval officers perceive the need for the specialized attack transports developed during the war.

The lack of an adequate naval gunfire range, and Navy reluctance to rotate its modern ships through amphibious exercises, hampered the development of naval gunfire techniques. But by 1941 the services began to train both naval and marine officers for duty with fire-control parties that would accompany the assault waves, and Marine Corps specialists began to supervise the fire support training of several heavy ships. Establishment of a naval gunfire range in Chesapeake Bay during 1942 and combat experience early in the war contributed heavily to the evolution of sound naval gunfire techniques by 1944. Limited material and unrealistic conditions delayed, until after war began, the achievement of sound techniques

[5] General H. M. Smith, *Coral and Brass* (New York, 1948), 72.

for close air support and the funneling of supplies over a beach.[6]

Despite failure to implement the 1934 doctrine with adequate material and techniques before 1942, officers assigned to amphibious work brought about a near-miracle. For the first time in United States history, a military group proceeded logically from doctrinal theory through "laboratory" tests to the techniques which finally made possible what Major General J. F. C. Fuller has called "the most far-reaching tactical development of the war." By laying down first their sound doctrinal theory, these students of amphibious warfare saved time and money that would have been required had they been content to wait for normal evolution to produce amphibious craft and related equipment in quantity, after which they would have had to test the preliminary models in maneuvers, and then adapt their doctrine to whatever material the nation could afford.

Carrier Doctrine

When Admiral Beatty in the North Sea on May 31, 1916 ordered seaplane carrier *Engadine* to send up a plane for observation, he was making the first use of aircraft in connection with a naval battle. The *Engadine*'s plane rose a few hundred feet and then was forced down by a broken fuel line, having seen no enemy ships larger than a light cruiser. Half an hour later the British and German battle cruiser lines sighted each other with mutual surprise, and the Battle of Jutland was under way. Three hours after the battle cruiser contact, the British battleship line capped the T of the German battleship line without either fleet realizing what was happening. The light cruisers, "eyes of the fleet," had twice failed in their reconnaissance function. It was to provide better, more far-seeing eyes that the British Admiralty later in 1916 ordered several

[6] For more extensive accounts of amphibious maneuvers and the development of amphibious craft prior to World War II, see Jeter A. Iseley and Philip A. Crowl, *The U.S. Marines and Amphibious War* (Princeton, 1951), 14–71; E. B. Potter (ed.), *The United States and World Sea Power* (Englewood Cliffs, N.J., 1955), 575–87; and Hough, Ludwig, and Shaw, *U.S. Marine Corps Operations,* I, 8–24.

ships converted into carriers for land planes. Two of these, the *Furious,* built on a cruiser hull, and the *Argus,* converted from an unfinished liner, were completed before the end of the war. There were no more sea battles in World War I, but planes from the new carriers proved useful for general reconnaissance, for destroying Zeppelins, and for antisubmarine work.

Following the British lead, the U.S. Navy by 1922 had converted a collier into the first American aircraft carrier, the *Langley.* Providing a floating airstrip however was only a beginning. Fleet aviators and the *Langley*'s crew spent six years mastering the complex techniques for handling seaborne aircraft. The program stressed taking off, landing, air navigation, gunfire spotting, and aerial gunnery. Though carrier planes of the period were designed only as fighters, scouts, and gunfire observers, individual pilots also experimented with aerial bombs and torpedoes. The six years of training and experiment with the *Langley* had far-reaching effects. Immediately they provided a nucleus of aviators for the *Saratoga* and *Lexington* when these carriers, built on battle cruiser hulls, joined the fleet in 1928.

Meanwhile the Navy, to the accompaniment of much heated public discussion had already passed through the first stages of the long controversy over how to divide funds between heavy ships and aircraft carriers. In the public mind this controversy soon came to transcend mere naval policy, and embraced the national policy toward all civil and military aviation. It focused the first serious attention upon the question of whether there should be a United States air force independent of control by either the Army or the Navy—an air force that alone would control all military flying. Most vocal of proponents for a separate air force was Brigadier General William ("Billy") Mitchell of the Army Air Service. Mitchell went so far as to insist that air power was capable by itself of providing for the national defense. Armies he saw as useful only for occupying space conquered by planes. Surface warships he regarded as utterly obsolete. "If a naval war were attempted against Japan, for instance," he once wrote, "the Japanese submarines and aircraft would sink the enemy fleet long before it came anywhere near their coast."[7] When newspaper controversy over the alleged obsolescence of the Navy reached white heat, the services in 1921 attempted a series of objective tests wherein planes bombed ships slated for scrapping.

As events were to prove, devising a realistic mock combat between ship and plane was virtually impossible. The services selected as targets the captured German battleship *Ostfriesland* and several other over-age vessels. None of these ships afforded the kind of armored decks required to resist even the aerial bombs available in 1921, and none had anti-aircraft armament. Even if they had been designed to resist aircraft, few Americans would have approved a sham-battle in which combat crews and damage-control parties manned the vessels while they were under attack. The inconclusiveness of the tests was heightened by the fact that the main attack, against the *Ostfriesland,* was made while the battleship was at anchor off the Virginia Capes without any sort of defense and that it was not carried out according to plan. The Navy had assigned officers to go aboard after each bombing run to assess damages and to estimate the effect of proper damage control. But General Mitchell ignored the rules and ordered continuous bombing. Nevertheless at the end of the first attack the old battleship was still afloat. On the second day the army planes, again bombing continuously, climaxed their attack by dropping from low altitude seven 2,000-pound bombs, some of which hit the *Ostfriesland* squarely and at last sent her down. She thus was sunk without affording any objective evidence of what steps alert defenders might have taken to save her.

Most naval observers of the tests considered General Mitchell's violation of the rules a tacit admission that bombers could not sink a well-defended battleship. But for Mitchell the tests were a springboard for intensifying his campaign, which included a verbal attack on carriers as worthless in war because of what he considered their extreme vulnerability. The Navy's air devotees now entered the fray in force, headed by their chief spokesman, Rear Admiral William A. Moffett, chief of the new

Bureau of Aeronautics. The strident emotionalism of the "Billy Mitchell Controversy" at length moved President Coolidge in 1925 to appoint a board headed by his friend, the widely respected Dwight W. Morrow, to recommend basic aviation policy for the United States. The Morrow Board's findings, reached after extensive hearings, established the pattern that produced effective working relationships among the armed services, civilian aviation, and the aircraft industry. The Board went on record as opposing an independent air force at that time. It recommended that army aviators be organized as a separate air corps, in keeping with basic army organization, but proposed that naval aviators be integrated with the corps of naval line officers. Congress accepted the Board's findings and enacted them into law in the Air Commerce Act and the Air Corps Act of 1926.

Some naval aviators, who had argued for a separate naval air corps, were disappointed, but for Moffett the new legislation was a victory all the way. "Hell, we won't secede from the Navy," said he. "If we are half as good as we think we are, we'll take it over!"[8]

As for General Mitchell, he at length overreached himself by accusing his army seniors of "criminal negligence." He was tried by an army general court-martial, found guilty of indiscipline, and allowed to resign from the service. As a civilian he continued to crusade for air power. Though in some respects a man of great vision, Mitchell lacked the objectivity to formulate military policy—and certainly he was much too far ahead of his time.

The Morrow Board's findings and the subsequent legislation served somewhat to clear the air, but they left unresolved the original controversy over the relative emphasis to be placed on carriers and heavy ships. The difficulty arose over a cleavage of opinion within the Navy. Many officers regarded the carrier strictly as an auxiliary, of little use beyond reconnaissance and gunfire spotting. Others, including Admiral Moffett, saw the carrier as nothing less than the capital ship of the future.

In Fleet Problem X of January 1929 the naval air enthusiasts found an opportunity to demonstrate that the carrier could not only be

[7] General William Mitchell, "Building a Futile Navy," *The Atlantic Monthly,* September 1928, 412.

[8] Eugene E. Wilson, *Slipstream* (New York, 1950), 63.

used offensively but that it could operate successfully against shore targets. An attacking fleet from San Diego, commanded by Admiral William V. Pratt and including the *Saratoga*, was to strike the Panama Canal, which would be defended by 48 aircraft based on the Canal Zone and by a defending fleet including the *Lexington*. Rear Admiral Joseph M. Reeves, Commander Aircraft Squadrons, Battle Fleet, persuaded Admiral Pratt to approve a significant change in the plan for employing the *Saratoga*. Instead of advancing from San Diego directly toward the Gulf of Panama in a safe position behind the battle line, for which she was expected to scout, the big carrier made a wide sweep southward past the Galapagos Islands and then up the coast of South America, approaching the Canal from the southwest. En route the *Saratoga* was sighted by a defending scout cruiser which tracked her through the night, broadcasting her position by radio. The *Lexington,* advancing through thick weather to attack, came under "fire" from Pratt's battle line and had her speed, by decision of the umpires, reduced to 18 knots. As a result, the *Saratoga* was able, on the morning of January 25 while still 200 miles at sea, to take the Canal defenders by surprise with 17 dive bombers, 17 torpedo bombers, and 32 fighters. These quickly overwhelmed the defending land-based planes, struck at assigned targets, and returned to their carrier with only one technical loss. Theoretically, according to the umpires, two sets of canal locks had been blown up and two airfields damaged. This performance demonstrated that a carrier could assault targets far beyond the range of fleet guns.

The lessons of the Panama Canal attack were confirmed and emphasized by subsequent fleet problems. Of these, none was more convincing than Fleet Problem XIX, held in the spring of 1938. As part of this exercise, the *Saratoga* and *Lexington,* commanded by Vice Admiral Ernest J. King, were to strike first Pearl Harbor Naval Base and then Mare Island Navy Yard near San Francisco. A sudden epidemic among her crew kept the *Lexington* out of the Pearl Harbor attack, but King proceeded with the other carrier. Steaming far to northwestward of Oahu, the *Saratoga* entered an eastward-moving bad weather front and

under its cover ran a thousand miles back toward the Hawaiian Islands. Oahu-based Army Air Corps flyers, insufficiently trained to navigate over water in foul weather, completely missed the carrier; but the *Saratoga*'s aircraft struck out of the clouds and theoretically destroyed ships and numerous installations at the Pearl Harbor base without losing a plane. King thus foreshadowed the Japanese attack nearly four years later. The *Saratoga,* accompanied by the *Lexington* and several cruisers, now headed for the United States. En route King was annoyed to find his force being observed by a fast Japanese oiler. Defending American air and naval forces were not so successful, for again King achieved complete surprise. His aircraft approached the Mare Island yard at 15,000 feet, dived, made their attack, and returned to their decks, again without a single loss.

The success of the carrier planes was in large part the result of improving techniques, not the least of which was dive bombing. As early as World War I, naval aviators had recognized the difficulty of bombing moving objects from level flight. Individual flyers of several nations perceived the advantages of aiming the nose of the plane at the target, going into a shallow dive, and then releasing the bomb. After the war many pilots experimented with this technique. During the Nicaraguan campaign, United States marines adopted dive bombing as standard procedure in squadron operations, particularly against guerrilla bands. After returning from Nicaragua, marine flyers did much to popularize dive bombing by conducting exhibitions at air shows. During the 1930's, as stronger planes were made available, it became possible for aviators to dive steeply from 1,000 feet to 300 feet, drop bombs as they pulled out, and then use tail guns to strafe the enemy as they withdrew. But such techniques, the subject of experiment in all the armed services, could not be perfected until planes specially designed for dive bombing were provided in quantity. The same sort of restriction hobbled the development of doctrine for using carrier-based fighters and torpedo planes.

The United States possessed the capital, the engineering skills, and the industrial capacity to foster the development of the needed aircraft, but several practical factors impeded progress. First among these was the extremely high rate of obsolescence to which expensive aircraft are subject. Even a wealthy nation could not afford to mass-produce a particular model when designers promised far superior ones within a short time. Yet there could be no sound evaluation of either flight technique or carrier doctrine until the fleet acquired enough suitable planes to support realistic, full-scale maneuvers. On the other hand, a decision to provide the fleet with enough planes might well have alienated public opinion if even a single experimental foreign model had surpassed aircraft operating with the United States fleet.

American naval policy planners wisely resisted the temptation to standardize too soon. Not until 1937 did Chance Vought begin producing a single-wing scout bomber (SB2U) suitable for carrier operations, and only in 1941 did the Grumman Wildcat fighter (F4F) and the Douglas Dauntless dive bomber (SBD) join the fleet. The Douglas Devastator torpedo plane (TBD) was available as early as 1938, but the Grumman Avenger torpedo plane (TBF) did not reach the fleet until after the Battle of Midway in June 1942. By waiting till industry produced true carrier aircraft susceptible of rapid refinement, the policy makers enabled American naval aviators to fight World War II with steadily improving planes that performed exacting missions. A more conservative decision would have held the American naval pilots in the positon of their German or Japanese contemporaries, who were obliged to adapt planes designed in the mid-1930's for missions conceived during the 1940's.

Problems inherent in producing assault aircraft were no more complex than those facing designers of carriers capable of serving as capital ships. When u.s.s. *Ranger,* the first American vessel conceived as a carrier from the keel up, joined the fleet in 1934, carrier concepts had developed beyond her. Designed to carry fleet reconnaissance aircraft, she was never modified for assault missions. The *Langley,* long obsolete as a carrier, was converted in 1936 into a tender. Not until the *Yorktown* was commissioned in 1937 did the fleet acquire a third assault carrier. By then flight techniques and aircraft design had progressed

far enough to justify steady building. Carriers *Enterprise, Wasp,* and *Hornet* were all commissioned before the outbreak of the Pacific war in 1941. Nineteen more were then on order, but on Pearl Harbor day the U.S. Navy had only six assault carriers.

If American carrier doctrine had not fully matured by the time the United States entered World War II, it was largely because a substantial number of naval officers in positions of power and influence had not accepted the carrier as a capital ship. Many of these believed that the next war would be fought in much the same manner as the last, that fleet battles would again consist of gunnery duels between columns of heavy ships, and that the gun and not the plane was still the decisive weapon. Through most of the 1930's, in accordance with doctrine, carriers normally cruised to the rear of the battle line, which was in columns abreast. The carriers were attended only by a pair of guard destroyers to rescue crews of aircraft that landed in the water. On contact with the "enemy," the battleships deployed into single column, as in the Battle of Jutland, and the carriers took station on the disengaged side. For flight operations the carriers left the fleet in order to turn into the wind and moved freely about, keeping only within signal distance. As late as 1939 doctrine assigned to carriers only the following missions: (1) reconnaissance and shadowing, (2) spotting of fleet gunfire in surface actions and shore bombardments, (3) assisting to protect the fleet (particularly the carriers themselves) from attacks by enemy submarines and aircraft, and (4) attacking a faster enemy attempting to escape, in order to reduce his speed so as to enable the pursuing surface ships to take him under attack.

As early as 1930 Lieutenant Commander Forrest B. Sherman, who was to become U.S. Chief of Naval Operations 20 years later, advocated a fleet formation that anticipated the carrier-centered task force of World War II. The Navy was not then ready to experiment along such lines, but during the next few years development of the task force principle made Sherman's suggestion feasible. For centuries ships of similar type had operated together. Hence there was no conflict between fleet logistic and fleet operational organizations; one served for both. But in the 1930's the U.S. Navy went further than ever before in mixing types to attain flexibility for special missions. As a result, the fleet had to be organized in two different ways. While types—battleships, carriers, cruisers, and destroyers—might be intermingled in task forces for certain sorts of operations, they usually had to be serviced according to type, because a destroyer, for example, has quite different needs from a battleship. Hence for administrative purposes ships continued to be grouped according to type in squadrons and divisions, but for operational purposes they could be, and frequently were, intermingled freely in task forces.

In 1939, when Rear Admiral William F. Halsey's Carrier Division 2, the new *Yorktown* and *Enterprise,* joined Vice Admiral King's Carrier Division 1, the *Saratoga* and *Lexington,* King began experimenting with carriers operating together and turning into the wind simultaneously to launch or receive planes. He then went on to experiment with carrier task groups, including cruisers and destroyers, to escort and protect the carriers when they left the fleet formation to carry out flight operations. King strongly urged that cruiser-destroyer screens be permanently assigned to the carriers so that the carriers and their escorts could learn to operate efficiently together. But the "line" admirals, who always held the senior billets, consistently refused—on the ground that the cruisers and destroyers could not be spared from the "main" formation. As a result, whenever the carriers operated with a screen, there was much confusion and excessive signaling. When war came to the United States, the carrier commanders had not yet found answers to such elementary questions as whether one or more than one carrier should operate within a single screen, or whether carrier forces should rely more upon maneuver or upon antiaircraft fire when under air attack. And of course there were never enough planes or flyers available in the pre-war years to develop the system of relief carrier air groups that later in World War II enabled the carriers to operate almost continuously.

The Japanese, by disabling the American battle line, settled the battleship-carrier question for the United States on the first day of the Pacific war. The American carriers of necessity became capital ships at last, and at once acquired permanent escorts. As new fast battleships reached the Pacific, they were promptly integrated into the carrier screens. A similar battleship-carrier controversy in the Japanese navy was not so quickly settled. If it had been, the Battle of Midway might not have proved the turning point it was. At least, the four carriers in the Japanese striking force would not have been exposed to sinking by American carrier attack while the heavy Japanese ships with their powerful antiaircraft batteries were 400 miles away.

In view of the widespread undervaluing of the carrier in the U.S. Navy, it is remarkable that the United States had enough carriers at the outbreak of war to stop the Japanese advance and still more remarkable that enough were already under construction to enable the United States to go on the all-out offensive in late 1943. It was the carrier force that spearheaded the American drive across the Central Pacific, isolating enemy island bases in the face of land- and fleet-based air power and providing support and cover for a whole series of amphibious assaults.

Logistic Doctrine

The problem of freeing the fleet from rearward bases to operate at great distances across the Pacific is essentially one of logistics, the science of supplying, transporting, and maintaining forces. Yet the U.S. Navy, during its years of planning for possible war with Japan, while emphasizing strategy, tended to neglect the logistic base on which its strategy would have to be erected. As a result, most of the logistic problems of America's war in the Pacific had to be solved shortly before the outbreak and during the war. The Navy's logistic structure had largely to be improvised all the way from the Navy Department to the fleet and forward bases. It is remarkable that the problem was solved so quickly and so well.

No fleet can operate for long independent of the shore, and every improvement in naval ships during the industrial revolution increased the need for ships to return to base for replenishment and repair. As navies shifted from sail to steam and could no longer rely on wind for propulsion, they had to sacrifice storage space for fuel. Improvements in gunnery led to more rapid expenditure of ammunition, necessitating frequent replenishment. Increasingly complex machinery to be repaired, the need to carry large numbers of spare parts, enlightened personnel policies that required more space per man—all these cut down on space available and heightened the dependence of ships on bases.

When Admiral Dewey received orders to attack the Spanish fleet at Manila Bay in 1898, he had only to proceed to Hong Kong and purchase a coaling steamer and coal from the British. But if he had not won a quick and complete victory, his logistic problem would have been serious, because the British had decided to deny him further coal. His nearest source of supply for fuel and for replacement ammunition was the west coast of the United States.

To solve the problem of keeping ships in operating areas and freeing them from dependence on home bases except for major repairs, all navies began adding to the fleet groups of auxiliary vessels which came to be known as the Fleet Train. When the American Great White Fleet set out on its round-the-world cruise in December 1907, it was accompanied by two stores ships, a torpedo flotilla parent ship, a tender, and a repair ship, and was joined by several chartered colliers. In spite of all these auxiliaries, the Great White Fleet obtained about three fourths of its fuel from foreign purchases. Thus the famous cruise exposed a greater logistic weakness than anyone had anticipated during the planning stages.

Though President Theodore Roosevelt understood sea power and its uses, American strategic thinking continued to be conditioned by the concept of the Navy as America's first line of defense—with the mission of driving an attacker from American shores. Accordingly the Joint Board in 1909 advised against significant strengthening of establishments in the Philippines, but it did make the very important recommendation that the chief American naval base in the Pacific be established at Pearl Harbor. Locating a naval base more than 2,000 miles from the continent forced the Navy to expand its auxiliary branches in order to transport the necessary equipment and stores to the Hawaiian Islands. The next three decades marked a constant growth in the strength and importance of the Pearl Harbor base.

World War I was the first extended, large-scale war that the United States fought far from its continental base, but because the U.S. Navy was able to use British bases, it did not have to face fully the problem of overseas maintenance. Tenders could provide parts and equipment not available from the British, while major repairs and overhauls were carried out in the United States. Building bases in France took more of a toll of American energy, but even here much of the material and most of the labor came from French sources. The chief American naval problem in World War I was shipping. Yet in dealing with this problem, the Navy had to serve principally as carrier, for the Army handled the assembling and loading of cargoes. The U.S. Navy moreover did not have to face the complete burden of transporting troops to Europe for, as we have seen, American vessels carried less than half the total. World War I did however spur the Navy into conversion to oil fuel and the development of swift, alongside refueling at sea, which were to prove of major importance in America's later conquest of the Pacific.

With the end of the war, the U.S. Navy at last began seriously to look westward. Many of America's fine new ships transited the Panama Canal, and in 1920 the U.S. Pacific Fleet was organized. Not long afterward it received a most significant addition in the form of the Base Force Pacific Fleet. The Base Force was conceived as a Fleet Train plus—nothing less than a floating naval base, able to replenish the fleet at sea and to service it in any suitable anchorage in all respects except major repairs. The concept however never materialized. The Washington Treaties, limiting the fleet and providing for non-fortification of the Pacific islands, removed the possibility that the U.S. Navy would in the foreseeable future dominate the Pacific Ocean. Actually the treaties merely gave legal sanction to decisions already made by Congress and by the American people. Fleet exercises had to be undertaken under the limitations of meager budgets, regardless of whether such exercises were strategically relevant to geography and to probable wartime missions. In the temper of the times, treaties or not, nothing could have been done to strengthen naval bases in the Philippines and Guam, while the two Pacific bases already marked out for first priority, the Canal Zone and Pearl Harbor, under budgetary starvation, grew only slowly.

Many American naval officers of the Old School looked upon "shoveling coal and combat loading" as unworthy of serious consideration of an officer. As a result of this kind of thinking, the Logistics Section of the Naval War College was abolished in the late 1920's, and Fleet Problems were conducted on logistic assumptions that were wide of the mark. Not until 1940 were these trends reversed, particularly with regard to Pearl Harbor, where by the summer of 1941 it was at last barely possible to base the entire Pacific Fleet.

The cure however for logistic weakness was not to be found at Pearl Harbor but rather in Washington, where the leaders at the end of 1941 found themselves directing war on two oceans and with little logistic support available to implement strategic decisions. Fortunately for the Allies, American economy and American industry had already begun to shift to war production to fill orders from the British.

When a highly industrialized nation shifts from a peacetime to a wartime economy, it must make severe adjustments in its economic patterns. The military forces require equipment on an unprecedented scale, and these demands must be met by diverting civilian requirements. Minimum civilian necessities must be met as well, and sooner or later military and civilian desires conflict. Then allocations have to be made to each. These alloca-

tions in the United States are controlled by high-level civilians in the government. This realm of activity is known as *producer logistics*. The military departments present their requirements to civilian officials who make allocations in accordance with their views of the over-all situation. Military personnel are little involved in this phase of logistics, except for design and production supervision of the items allocated to them by an allocation board.

The other chief aspect of logistics is called *consumer logistics*, a preponderantly military function. From the military point of view there are four major steps in the logistic process: (1) determination of requirements, (2) procurement, (3) transportation, and (4) distribution. The first two of these are closely connected with producer logistics and require careful liaison with the various boards charged with the responsibility of balancing civilian and military requirements. The last two phases, transportation and distribution, are also connected with the civilian economy, but to a less extent than the first two.

In preparing to deal with supply and maintenance of its forces afloat, the U.S. Navy in World War II had to grapple with the problem of establishing two kinds of activities—overseas bases and mobile squadrons to bring materials to these bases and to forces afloat and ashore. Although it was clear that sound strategic planning could rest only on a firm logistic base, the Office of the Chief of Naval Operations had little control over logistic planning and logistic activities, for most of these were vested in the Bureaus, which came under

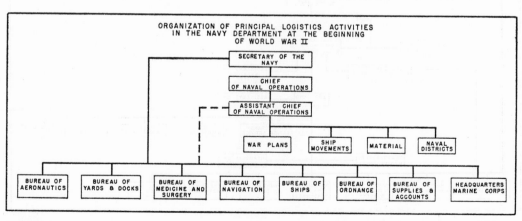

CHART A

the Secretary of the Navy. (See Chart A.) Hence those charged with logistic planning often had little knowledge of forthcoming operations which would affect allocations and procurement of material, while officers in the Office of the Chief of Naval Operations had to make strategic plans on the basis of logistic assumptions that often could not be fulfilled. That these assumptions worked at all was a tribute not to the logistics organization but to the productive capacity of American industry.

Admiral King, when he became Chief of Naval Operations, sought to institute reforms that would bring control of naval logistics into his own office. President Roosevelt however refused to permit this arrangement, on the ground that such a change would allow the military to exercise too much control over the civilian economy and would tend to undermine the principle of civilian control at the top level of the armed forces. Hence the ultimate reorganization took the form of parallel control whereby the Bureaus were still under the Secretary, but also reported to the Chief of Naval Operations through the newly created Office of the Vice Chief of Naval Operations, who became the principal logistics officer on the Navy Department level. (See Chart B.) Liaison between strategic planners and logistic activities nevertheless remained weak throughout the war.

Before strategic planning could be advanced very far, plans for bases had to be made and their requirements determined so that they could function in support of the fleet and forward area naval activities. In the Pacific, bases often had to be wrested from the enemy, and their sites usually had to be developed by bringing in all the necessities for operations, from wharfs to accounting machines. The first attempt to establish a base in the Pacific theater of operations was on the island of Bora Bora in the Society Islands. The difficulties, delays, and frustrations encountered in this undertaking during the early months of 1942 led to a recognition that more systematic planning of such endeavors was essential. Improved methods paid off in subsequent bases established at Tongatabu, Efate, Samoa, Noumea, and Auckland. To operate these bases Service Squadron Six was set up with broad logistic responsibilities in the forward areas.

Recognizing that as American offensives began to seize enemy positions in the Pacific it would be necessary to establish bases on islands recently captured from Japan, naval logistic planners concluded that it was essential to have standardized base components ready to move in quickly. These package components were supposed to include all material and personnel necessary for setting up the bases, maintaining them, and developing supply functions with respect to the fleet and shore-based activities. The advanced base units were desig-

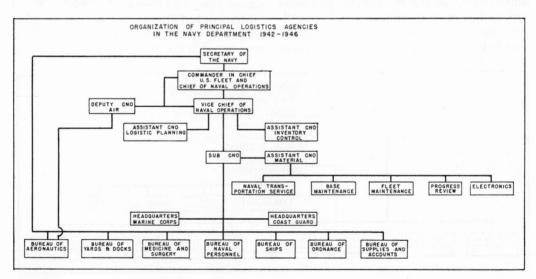

CHART B

nated Lions and Cubs, for major and secondary bases respectively. In addition, Acorns were similar units for naval air bases. In theory these units were ideal, but local conditions varied so greatly that commanders had to request many modifications in the components of Lions, Cubs, and Acorns. Thus the original idea proved in practice to be of limited usefulness. The basic components were eventually made flexible by a *Catalogue of Advance Base Functional Components,* a kind of mail order catalogue in concept, with the difference that items stocked were not listed individually but in terms of major or minor components of a base. Even so, this catalogue grew so fast and came to contain so many items that before the end of the war it consisted of 479 volumes weighing 250 pounds. Similarly established was an organization to recruit and train the men to build and service bases. At first these Construction Battalions, or Seabees, were comparatively standardized; later they were formed into more specialized units such as Base Aircraft Service Units (Basu's) and Carrier Aircraft Service Units (Casu's). Thus came the flexibility in base construction and servicing that was to prove essential to Allied victory in the Pacific war.

To move men and material to the advanced bases and to the forces afloat required a complete reorganization of American mercantile shipping. The problems of shipping involved far more than merely continuing ship movements under control of shipping lines but with the Navy assuming responsibility for their safety. The demands for military cargoes are far greater in war than in peacetime, while the demands for goods needed for non-military aspects of the economy do not lessen to the extent of the increase in military requirements. Overseas shipping activities during wartime show most clearly the intricate interrelationships between the civilian economy and military operations. Both military and the non-military activities must draw on the same pool of shipping, for the navy and the army never have enough of their own cargo-carriers to meet the needs of war. Thus a constant close liaison is required between civilian and military activities to assure the efficient procurement, repair, allocation, loading, unloading,

routing, and protection of ships. Except for ships built exclusively for the military services, the first three of these operations are exclusively civilian functions while the last is exclusively a military function. Loading, unloading, and routing are customarily performed by the user of the vessel, although when a convoy system is in effect, routing becomes a function of the military.

Since the national policy determines both military and economic policy, the decisions on the number and kinds of ships to be built under any sort of wartime emergency program must be based on decisions reached on a very high level. Limiting factors are the capacity of building yards, the port facilities, the availability of labor for construction and repair, stevedoring facilities, and the availability of trained crews to take ships to sea. (See chart below.) Once allocation has been made for materials for ships, and the vessels have been completed, then a predominantly civilian authority makes allocations of ships themselves to the military forces and to civilian shippers. In this way a relatively satisfactory arrange-

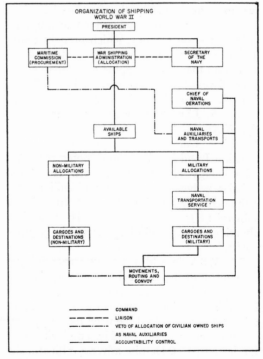

ORGANIZATION OF UNITED STATES SHIPPING IN WORLD WAR II

ment of ships can be worked out, assuring that both economic and military needs receive their fair share of essential shipping space. The problem is complicated however by the fact that many civilian carriers transport military cargoes under charter or contract, while all movements of ships come under naval control for purposes of protection.

Responsibility for military cargoes during World War II rested with the Naval Transportation Service, operating under the authority of the Chief of Naval Operations. The Naval Transportation Service included in wartime the Army Transport Service, and thus had to assume the burden for delivery of goods and personnel not only to naval but to army bases and operational areas as well.

In the early days of the war the Maritime Commission, which was charged with the procurement and allocation of cargo ships, tended to operate with little reference to military conditions. On occasions the Commission refused to transfer requested ships to the Naval Transportation Service on the ground of presumed greater need elsewhere. It quickly became clear that shipping had to be coordinated if chaos was to be avoided. Shortly after Pearl Harbor, President Roosevelt appointed a War Shipping Administration (WSA), which brought under a single head operation and control of all American merchant shipping other than coasters and vessels assigned to the military forces. The chairman of the WSA was Vice Admiral Emory S. Land USN, who had retired from the Navy in 1937 to become head of the Maritime Commission, a post he retained. Admiral Land handled the shipping problems with energy and resourcefulness. He struck a balance between civilian and military requirements by keeping the WSA from being subservient to the Navy but at the same time charging it with fulfilling "strategic requirements."

The WSA, in addition to its responsibilities for control of merchant shipping, was charged with provision of new construction to meet increasing wartime demands for shipping. Admiral Land recognized the need for a ship that could be constructed quickly, employing prefabricated parts. Despite adverse criticism, the WSA adopted the already existing design for the EC2 Liberty Ship, a vessel 442 feet long with a capacity of 10,800 deadweight tons.[9] The Liberty Ship had a speed of eleven knots and a cruising radius of 17,000 miles. Its chief advantages were simplicity of operation and ease of construction. The first Liberty Ship to be completed, s.s. *Patrick Henry,* delivered on the last day of 1941, took 244 days to build. Mass production techniques had by 1944 reduced the average construction time to 42 days. As a stunt, Henry J. Kaiser launched one in five days. Altogether 2,710 of these admittedly homely ships were built. Lesser numbers of other ships also came down the ways, but because all the other types were designed for greater speeds, they could not be completed as rapidly as the Liberty Ships, which, serving throughout the war, carried 75 per cent of America's cargoes.

As the Pacific war developed, it became important to be able to move bases rapidly to keep up with the westward advance of the offensive against Japan. Instead of employing fixed base facilities for each move, Service Force Pacific, the logistic arm of the U.S. Pacific Fleet, at length carried out the intent of the Base Force by developing Service Squadron Four, comprising repair vessels, tenders, barges, station tankers, and other units for service and supply. The squadron was in fact a floating base that could move with the fleet. Originally established at Funafuti in the Ellice Islands in October 1943, Service Squadron Four moved to Kwajalein in the Marshalls in March 1944. Here it became a part of the newly developed but much larger Service Squadron Ten. Parts of Service Squadron Ten moved as the fleet did. By the end of 1944 it was established in the lagoons of several Pacific atolls, and most importantly at Manus in the Admiralty Islands. At the same time Service Squadron Ten sent units to rendezvous with forces at sea for underway replenishment. At the end of 1944 it became possible to develop an organization especially for underway replenishment. The resulting Service Squadron Six comprised not only oilers, ammunition

---

[9] *Deadweight* tons measure the carrying capacity of a ship, which is computed by subtracting the loaded weight from that of an empty ship. *Deadweight tonnage* is approximately twice the *Gross Register Tonnage* for cargo ships and even more for tankers.

ships, and supply ships, but brought mail and provided replacement aircraft, personnel, and even the latest motion pictures. The versatility of Service Squadron Six was vital to the success of the Okinawa campaign in the spring of 1945.

The logistic problems of the U.S. Navy were solved in World War II largely because production was so plentiful that weaknesses of distribution and planning were canceled out by abundance. Nevertheless, without the planning that provided advanced bases, ashore and afloat, bases that moved forward with the fleet, bases backed by ample shipping, the Navy could not have projected its power across the Pacific nor kept it in Far Eastern waters month after month. By virtue of such planning, the U.S. Pacific Fleet of World War II regained much of the reach and endurance of fleets in the age of sail.

35:

The Period of Japanese Expansion

Japan started down the road to World War II with her conquest of Manchuria in the last four months of 1931. Although the United States refused to recognize changes brought about by force and sternly reminded Japan of her treaty obligations, the failure of the European powers to support the American position made it evident that Japan might pursue her course of aggression with impunity. The only danger was that of interference by Russia, which also had ambitions in Asia, and against that the Japanese provided by signing an anti-Comintern pact with Germany in November 1936. By this time military extremists were gaining control of Japan, removing by assassination those moderate statesmen who opposed their policy. When in the summer of 1937 the Army was ready, Japan embarked on the conquest of China proper.

Oil and Appeasement

In order not to deprive China of war supplies, President Roosevelt refused to invoke the 1937 Neutrality Act in this undeclared war. But the Japanese also benefited, for they were dependent on American steel scrap and Western Hemisphere oil.

In July 1939 Secretary of State Cordell Hull gave the Japanese the required six months notice for the abrogation of the commercial treaty of 1911, thereby clearing the way for an embargo on munitions. This move and the announcement the next month of the Russo-German non-aggression pact had a temporarily sobering effect upon the Japanese. Moreover, Japan was rapidly "bogging down" in the Chinese hinterland, and her resources were under severe strain.

But the outbreak of the European war eased Japan's difficulties and presented new opportunities. The fall of France and of the Netherlands in the spring of 1940 left Indo-China and the Netherlands East Indies "orphaned" colonies and so weakened Britain's position that she acceded to Japanese demands to close the Burma Road, China's last connection with the sea. The Imperial Japanese Navy, which had never favored the army's mainland adventure, now saw an opportunity for expansion into the East Indies to obtain oil, tin, rubber, and quinine. Japan had already worked her way south along the China coast and early in 1939 had occupied Hainan. Shortly after the fall of France the Vichy-controlled government of Indo-China permitted Japanese occupation of the northern part of the country. In September 1940 Japan concluded with the Axis powers an alliance that was an obvious warning to the United States not to interfere in either Europe or Asia.

With the termination in January 1940 of the treaty of commerce, the United States was free to embargo shipment of strategic materials to Japan. But the Roosevelt administration, warned by Ambassador Grew in Japan that an abrupt cessation of trade with the United States might cause the Japanese to invade the East Indies, delayed action in the vain hope that supplying the materials for aggression would somehow prevent aggression. In July 1940 Congress passed an act which provided for the licensing of exports. This stopped the sale of aircraft and aviation gasoline to Japan, but the export of iron and steel was not cut off till autumn, and the State Department continued to license the export of oil until July 1941.

Planning for War

As it became apparent that Japan was preparing to move south, the United States attempted to concert plans with potential allies. The ABC-1 Conference held in Washington early in 1941, besides establishing the European theater as primary, designated the Pacific theater as the responsibility of the United States in event of war with Japan. A conference at Singapore in April proved ineffectual, producing only a recommendation for mutual support against aggression.

The Japanese advance in Indo-China was, in American eyes, the crucial issue. When in July 1941 the Japanese announced that the Vichy government had agreed to a "joint protectorate" of Indo-China, the United States countered by freezing all Japanese assets in the United States, thus at long last shutting off the supply of oil. This move precipitated the final crisis. Japan had to have oil or see her military machine grind to a halt. In October the Konoye government fell, and a military government headed by General Tojo took over. In November a special Japanese envoy arrived in the United States to assist Ambassador Nomura in negotiations looking toward a resumption of the flow of oil. The failure of these negotiations led directly to Pearl Harbor.

United States Preparations

The approach of war in the Pacific found the United States preparing but still unprepared. In 1938, in accordance with a directive of Congress, the Hepburn Board had recommended an extensive program for development of Pacific bases. Except for the fortification of Guam, most of the board's recommendations were adopted, and work was under way when war broke out.

The greater part of the United States Pacific Fleet had long been based on the West Coast, but in the spring of 1940 President Roosevelt, in the hope of deterring Japan from further aggression, directed that it be based at Pearl Harbor. Here it lay somewhat exposed while, after the outbreak of war in Europe, much of the new construction went to the

Atlantic. In the spring of 1941, because of the necessity for convoying Lend-Lease goods, Admiral Harold R. Stark, Chief of Naval Operations, transferred from the Pacific to the Atlantic three battleships, the carrier *Yorktown,* four light cruisers, and two squadrons of destroyers. American plane production went chiefly to the Atlantic theater.

At the beginning of February 1941 the Atlantic Squadron, as we have seen, was made the Atlantic Fleet, while the fleet at Pearl Harbor became the Pacific Fleet. The small American force in the Far East, commanded by Admiral Thomas C. Hart, was for prestige purposes designated the United States Asiatic Fleet. It was provided that one of these three fleet commanders should also act as Commander in Chief United States Fleet. At the time of the attack on Pearl Harbor, Admiral Husband E. Kimmel was Commander in Chief both of the Pacific Fleet and of the United States Fleet.

In the Atlantic the Axis powers had not a single operational carrier, and the greater part of the British fleet was concentrated against the comparatively small German navy. In the Pacific the United States faced the formidable Japanese navy practically alone. Yet at the time of the Pearl Harbor attack the United States Fleet was fairly evenly divided between the two oceans, with nine battleships in the Pacific and eight in the Atlantic, three carriers in the Pacific and four in the Atlantic. True, the Atlantic Fleet lacked sufficient patrol craft and convoy escorts, but in the Pacific, even before the losses of Pearl Harbor, the fleet was inferior to the Japanese in every category. Most ominous, the three American carriers faced ten Japanese.[1]

The British had undertaken to reinforce Singapore, but the crisis in the Far East coincided with a desperate situation in the Mediterranean, where they had suffered severe losses. After considerable hesitation the Admiralty consented to send the new battleship

[1] At the outbreak of the war the Japanese had six heavy carriers, *Akagi, Kaga, Soryu, Hiryu, Shokaku,* and *Zuikaku,* two light carriers, *Hosho* and *Ryujo;* and two conversions, the light carrier *Zuiho* and the escort carrier *Taiyo.* The converted light carrier *Shoho* was commissioned in late January 1942.

Prince of Wales to join the battle cruiser *Repulse* at Singapore with the hope that the presence of two capital ships would have an additional deterrent effect upon the Japanese. The new aircraft carrier *Indomitable* was to have joined these two vessels, but during her shakedown cruise in the West Indies she was damaged by grounding. The Admiralty felt that no other carrier could be spared from the European theater. The Dutch had nothing heavier than light cruisers in the East. America's allies, it was clear, could do little to redress the unfavorable balance of power in the Pacific.

American naval forces in the Pacific seriously lacked fleet auxiliaries. Planes were few and largely obsolete. Antiaircraft armament was short in quantity and quality. The American 1.1-inch gun proved so unsatisfactory that the Navy had to turn to the foreign-designed Bofors and Oerlikon guns.

In the Far East the situation was even more grave. With Japanese on Formosa less than 300 miles to the north, on Hainan and in Indo-China to the west, and in the Marianas and the Carolines to the east, the Philippines were almost surrounded. In July 1941 Douglas MacArthur, then Field Marshal of the Philippine Army, was made Commanding General of the United States Army Forces Far East. Thereafter there was a rapid build-up in the Philippines both of air and of ground forces, designed to enable the islands to defend themselves by the spring of 1942.

In event of war with Japan, it had long been planned for the tiny U.S. Asiatic Fleet to fall back to the Malay Barrier, for it could hardly be expected to offer any significant opposition. But the increase of U.S. Army air strength in the Philippines gave hope that before long Luzon might be sufficiently secure to permit the fleet to continue operations from Manila.

Final Negotiations

The negotiations between the United States and Japan were foredoomed, for neither government would retreat an inch. They bargained only for time. The United States had the advantage of being able to read the Japanese diplomatic correspondence, for American cryptanalysts had succeeded in constructing machines for deciphering the Japanese diplomatic code. Hence Washington knew that the Japanese Foreign Office had set the latter part of November as a deadline for the conclusion of the talks, after which "things are automatically going to happen." Washington knew also that the Japanese were receiving information regarding the movements of the vessels of the Pacific Fleet and their berthing in Pearl Harbor, and that Japan was calling for more specific and more frequent reports.

On November 26th the United States handed the Japanese a note which demanded that Japan evacuate China and support the regime of Chiang Kai-shek. There was no expectation that Japan would accept such demands, and deciphered Japanese messages at once indicated that the Japanese regarded the note as ending the conversations. The ambassadors however were to continue the pretense of negotiating "to prevent the United States from becoming unduly suspicious." On November 27 the U.S. Navy Department sent to Pearl Harbor a "war warning" indicating that the Department expected a Japanese move against the Philippines, Malaya, or Borneo. Apparently American officials were so hypnotized by Japan's obvious preparations to move southward that they overlooked or rejected her capability of striking in another direction as well.

By December 6 it was known in Washington that the Japanese were sending to their Washington embassy a message for the U.S. State Department breaking off diplomatic relations, the sort of message that in times past had been followed up with a surprise attack on the opposing fleet. It was known too that Japanese diplomats in London, Hong Kong, Singapore, Batavia, Manila, and Washington were burning their secret documents and codes—usually done only when war is imminent.

Thus by Saturday afternoon there was every reason to believe that war with Japan was only hours away. Then between 0400 and 0600 on Sunday, December 7, the Navy Department deciphered instructions to the Japanese ambassadors to deliver their message at 1 PM. One o'clock in the afternoon in Washington would be 7:30 AM at Pearl Harbor.

The Attack on Pearl Harbor

Admiral Isoroku Yamamoto, Commander in Chief of the Japanese Combined Fleet, had early in 1941 proposed an attack on Pearl Harbor to make it impossible for the United States to attack Japan's flank while she was engaged in the conquest of the "Southern Resources Area." Details had been worked out in the early fall, and the final decision to go to war was made at an Imperial Conference on December 1.

Essentially the decision was a gamble on an Axis victory in Europe. In the fall of 1941 Rommel was threatening Egypt and the German armies were near Moscow. It seemed likely that the United States would be forced to let the Pacific go more or less by default while it faced the greater danger of an Axis triumph in Europe. In the meantime the Japa-

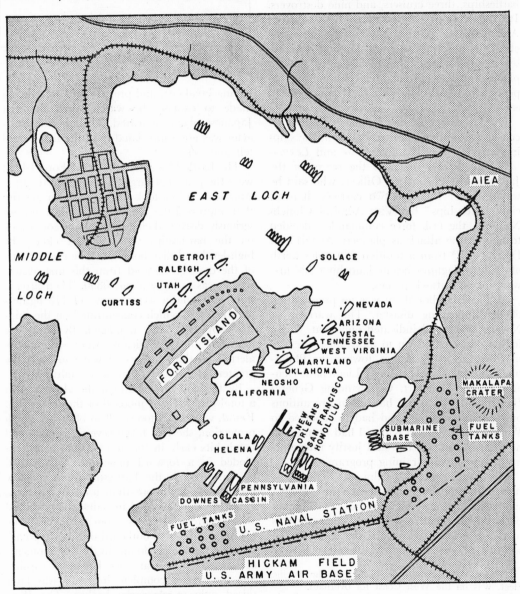

PEARL HARBOR, 0755, DECEMBER 7, 1941

nese would overrun Southeast Asia and the Southern Resources Area, and would protect them and Japan by a defensive perimeter of island air and submarine bases so strong that the United States would have to accept the *fait accompli.*

The attacking force, already at sea when the Imperial Council made its decision, consisted of six carriers—the *Akagi, Kaga, Soryu, Hiryu, Shokaku,* and *Zuikaku*—escorted by two battleships, three cruisers, and nine destroyers. Its course lay well to the north, both to avoid American air patrols and to decrease the chance of meeting merchant shipping. Twenty-seven submarines, of which eleven carried planes and five carried midget submarines to penetrate Pearl Harbor, had gone ahead earlier.

On December 6, the Japanese carriers received last minute information about the ships in Pearl Harbor. The *Enterprise* and *Lexington* were at sea, much to the regret of the Japanese Air Operations Officer, who said he would rather sink the two carriers than all eight battleships,[2] but Vice Admiral Chuichi Nagumo, the task force commander, decided to launch the attack as planned. At 0615 on December 7[3] from a position 230 miles north of Oahu, Nagumo began launching his first wave of 183 attack planes.

At Pearl Harbor there was no premonition of the impending disaster. The warning of November 27 had indicated only that Washington expected Japan to make an aggressive move to the south, that is, toward the Philippines or Malaya. Accordingly Lieutenant General Walter C. Short, Commanding General Hawaiian Department, had taken precautions only against sabotage and had so reported to Washington. Admiral Kimmel had been given no information which would justify interrupting a very urgent training program.

The Sunday morning calm was slightly disturbed at 0645 when a destroyer sank a midget submarine outside Pearl Harbor, but the report did not lead to a general alert. It was hardly a matter to concern the ships in the security of the harbor. Many officers were

[2] The *Colorado,* ninth battleship of the Pacific Fleet, was on the West Coast for overhaul.
[3] Hawaii time (zone plus 10½), West Longitude date.

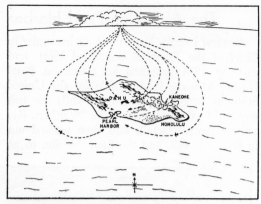

JAPANESE AIR RAID ON PEARL HARBOR, DECEMBER 7, 1941

having breakfast, and preparations were being made to change the watch when the first Japanese planes appeared. Their hostile character was not appreciated until the first bombs fell at 0755.

The battleships moored east of Ford Island were the principal target. Despite the surprise, American sailors took station with an alacrity that impressed the Japanese pilots but did not seriously disrupt their plans. A torpedo attack on the battleships was followed closely by high-level and dive bombing. The greater part of the damage resulted from this first attack, which was over by about 0830. Then after a brief lull came a second wave of 170 fighters and bombers, which concentrated on the ships that appeared least damaged. By this time however the Americans were thoroughly alerted, so that the second wave suffered the greater part of the Japanese casualties.

By the end of the attack the *Arizona* was a total loss. Moored inboard of the repair ship *Vestal,* which was too small to offer her much protection, she had taken several torpedo and bomb hits early in the action. One bomb exploded in a forward magazine. Surrounded by burning oil, the battleship sank quickly, taking with her more than a thousand men.

Of the ships moored in pairs, the outboard vessels suffered severely from torpedoes. The *Oklahoma,* moored outboard of the *Maryland,* received three torpedo hits in the first moments of the attack and at once began to capsize. She too was a complete loss and was later raised only to clear the harbor. The *West Virginia,* outboard of the *Tennessee,* was also torpedoed early in the action, but prompt counterflooding prevented her from capsizing, and her crew continued to fight as she settled to the bottom with only a moderate list. Their inboard partners fared much better. The *Tennessee* took two bomb hits and was threatened by burning oil from the *Arizona,* but suffered only moderate damage. The *Maryland* escaped with only a couple of bomb hits.

The *California* was moored singly. Hit by two torpedoes and a bomb, she later settled into the Pearl Harbor mud in an upright position. The *Nevada,* moored alone at the opposite end of "Battleship Row," was the only vessel to get under way. Although hit by a torpedo forward, she was able to sortie under a rain of bombs and finally beached herself to avoid the danger of being sunk in the channel. The *Pennsylvania,* flagship of the Pacific Fleet, was in drydock, where she was safe from torpedoes, and she put up such an effective fire that she suffered only a single bomb hit.

While the fleet had been the primary objective of the Japanese, they had also attacked the airfields in the area. There the Americans hastily improvised defenses, but they nevertheless took heavy losses in aircraft, which had been parked in compact rows as a precaution against sabotage. The Navy lost 80 planes; and of the Army's 231, only 79 were usable after the attack. The Japanese lost only 29 aircraft over the target, but several others crashed in landing on their carriers.

American personnel casualties totaled 3,681, the Navy and Marine Corps losing 2,112 killed and 981 wounded; the Army, 222 killed and 360 wounded. These losses in particular had the effect of uniting the people of the United States in a vigorous prosecution of the war that had been forced upon them.

From the American point of view, the disaster was less severe than it first appeared, and considerably less than it might have been. The old battleships sunk at Pearl Harbor were too slow either to fight Japan's newer battleships or to accompany the fast American carriers. Their chief use came for shore bombardment in the last two years of the war, after all but the *Arizona* and the *Oklahoma* had been raised and renovated. Their temporary loss freed trained personnel, of which there was a

great shortage, for use in carrier and amphibious forces, and it compelled the United States to adopt the carrier tactics that in the long run proved decisive.

In concentrating on ships, the Japanese had neglected the machine shops, leaving repair facilities substantially intact. They had overlooked the 4,500,000 barrels of oil exposed in tank farms near the harbor. This slowly accumulated fuel reserve was almost irreplaceable in view of America's European commitments. Without it, fleets could not have operated from Pearl Harbor for months. The greatest good fortune for the Americans was that their carriers had escaped. The *Saratoga* was on the West Coast, the *Lexington* was delivering planes to Midway, and the *Enterprise* was returning from having delivered planes to Wake. Moreover, very few cruisers or destroyers had been hit. Thus the ships for fast carrier striking forces, the most effective naval weapon of World War II, were left intact.

Guam and Wake

Before the end of the day on December 7, Admiral Kimmel received word that both Guam and Wake had been attacked by Japanese planes. Guam, in the southern Marianas, well over 3,000 miles from Hawaii and 1,500 from Manila, was flanked by Japanese bases and practically defenseless. Five thousand Japanese put ashore on December 10 easily overwhelmed it. Wake however was a different matter. Although it was within bomber range of the Japanese Marshalls to the south, only about 2,000 miles of open sea lay between it and Pearl Harbor. More than a thousand construction workers were engaged in building an air and submarine base on the little atoll. About 450 marines equipped with a dozen 3-inch antiaircraft guns and a half-dozen old 5-inch guns constituted the defense. On December 4, twelve F4F Wildcat fighter planes had been flown in from the *Enterprise.*

After the island had been "softened up" by bombers from Kwajalein in the Marshalls, a Japanese force of three light cruisers and six destroyers escorting several transports appeared at dawn on December 11. Commander Winfield S. Cunningham, the island commander, ordered the marines to hold their fire until the bombers were well within range. Then they opened up with their 5-inch guns, and the Wildcats took to the air. After the marines had succeeded in sinking two destroyers and damaging two cruisers and two more destroyers, the Japanese limped away without having put a man ashore.

Meanwhile Admiral Kimmel had made plans and issued orders for the relief of Wake. The *Saratoga* under Rear Admiral Frank Jack Fletcher was to cover the relief force directly while the other two carriers gave indirect support. But there were too many delays. The *Saratoga,* just arriving at Pearl Harbor from the West Coast, could not complete fueling and get under way till noon on the 16th. By the 21st she was only 600 miles from Wake, but she then paused for two days to refuel the destroyers of her group. There was hesitation at Pearl Harbor, where Admiral Kimmel's relief had not yet arrived.

The Japanese, quickly recovering from their initial repulse, sent against Wake on December 23 a new and stronger force covered by three heavy cruisers. Meanwhile Nagumo, returning from his attack on Pearl Harbor, had detached two of his carriers, the *Hiryu* and *Soryu,* to give air support to the landing. Planes from these carriers on the mornings of the 21st and 22nd destroyed the last planes on the island. Before light on the 23rd the Japanese landing craft came ashore, chiefly at points where the marines' artillery could not be brought to bear, while the bombarding cruisers remained outside the range of the 5-inch guns. After a struggle against hopeless odds, the defenders were forced to surrender.

On Wake and at other American bases civilian construction workers had been exposed to enemy attack without having either the training or the legal right to defend themselves. To remedy this situation, the Navy early authorized the creation of Construction Battalions—the famous "Seabees." Men of various construction trades were enlisted with appropriate ratings and were given military training. Often going ashore with the assault waves, these men performed vital functions in the Pacific war, from building bases and airfields to repairing equipment. In their hands the bulldozer became one of the instruments of victory.

Command and Strategy

The United States replied to the Japanese attack by declaring war on December 8, whereupon Japan's allies, Germany and Italy, declared war upon the United States. The new situation led to several command and administrative changes in the Navy. In mid-December Admiral Chester W. Nimitz was appointed Commander in Chief Pacific Fleet (Cincpac). The following April he was also made Commander in Chief Pacific Ocean Areas (Cincpoa), which gave him authority over the entire Pacific theater except for General MacArthur's Southwest Pacific Area and the inactive Southeast Pacific. Nimitz was a tow-haired, blue-eyed Texan, of the Naval Academy class of 1905. Tactful and modest, sound in his judgment of men and events, he was to prove a thoroughly fortunate choice.

Admiral King's first instructions to Nimitz, on December 30, defined his tasks as:

(1) Covering and holding the Hawaii-Midway line and maintaining communications with the west coast.

(2) Maintaining communications between the west coast and Australia, chiefly by covering, securing, and holding the Hawaii-Samoa line, which should be extended to include Fiji at the earliest practicable date.[4]

In broader terms, American strategy was to hold against any further Japanese encroachment a line running from Dutch Harbor through Midway to Samoa; thence to New Caledonia and to Port Moresby, New Guinea. To gain time for establishing this line Admiral Hart's Asiatic Fleet was to be sacrificed in a delaying action in the Netherlands East Indies.

Beginning the Allied Retreat

The U.S. Asiatic Fleet was in fact only a modest task force. Its flagship and most powerful vessel was the heavy cruiser *Houston.* She was seconded by the 17-year-old light cruiser *Marblehead.* When the light cruiser *Boise* arrived at Manila with a convoy early in December she also was "impressed" into the fleet. These cruisers were supported by 13 flush-

[4] Ernest J. King and Walter M. Whitehill, *Fleet Admiral King, a Naval Record* (New York, 1952), 353–4.

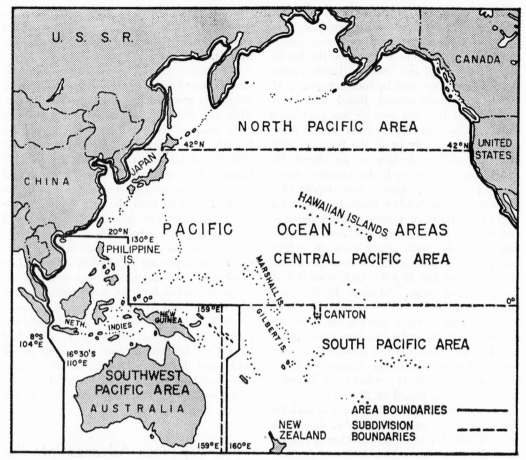

THE PACIFIC AREAS
Broken Vertical Line Shows South Pacific-Southwest Pacific Boundary as Altered August 1, 1942

deck, four-stack destroyers of the 1917–18 class. Twenty-nine submarines contributed a strong defensive element. It had been fully expected that the Japanese would attack the Philippines, and Admiral Hart had dispersed his fleet accordingly. The *Marblehead* with eight destroyers and a tender had been sent south to Borneo in November. The *Houston* and the *Boise* were in the relatively safe waters of the central Philippines.

News of the attack on Pearl Harbor reached Manila at 0300 on December 8, east longitude date. On orders from Admiral Hart, Rear Admiral William A. Glassford at once gathered several ships around the *Houston* and *Boise* and started south. Lacking dependable intelligence of enemy targets, the Army's 33 B-17's, of which only half had been transferred from Luzon to the comparative safety of Mindanao, were not sent to attack Formosa, as the Japanese feared they might. The Army fully expected a dawn air raid, and American planes took to the air on an early alert. But bad weather over Formosa delayed the Japanese take-off, and when the pilots finally arrived over Luzon about noon they found the American planes on their fields in neat rows. As in Hawaii, the aircraft were largely destroyed on the ground. With this loss there vanished any real hope of repelling a Japanese invasion.

The attack on the Philippines was only one of several simultaneous Japanese moves in the Far East. Imperial Army troops that had been poised in Indo-China at once overran Thailand, where there was little resistance. On December 8 and 9 forces from Hainan landed at Kota Bharu on the Malay Peninsula and began a rapid advance toward Singapore. The report of the landing at Kota Bharu caused Admiral Tom Phillips RN to take the battleship *Prince of Wales* and the battle cruiser *Repulse* north, escorted by four destroyers. Although the hard-pressed Royal Air Force warned that it could provide no land-based cover, Phillips, feeling that the Royal Navy could not stand idly by in the hour of crisis, made the gallant decision to go ahead. He arrived too late to catch the Japanese transports. Then acting upon a false report of a Japanese landing further south, he stayed too long within range of Japanese planes based in Indo-China. He had been shadowed for some time when the main attack came in a little before noon on December 10. Both the *Prince of Wales* and the *Repulse* took several hits, capsized, and sank. Admiral Phillips was among those lost.

The sinking of these two capital ships—the first ever sunk by aerial bombing while under way at sea—eliminated the possibility of serious naval opposition to the Japanese advancing on Singapore. By December 19 the invaders had reached the Straits of Malacca.

On the same day that the Japanese sank the *Prince of Wales* and the *Repulse,* they made on the Cavite Naval Yard near Manila a heavy air attack that substantially destroyed the base. This attack also coincided with the first Japanese landings on Luzon, designed to secure airfields to support an advance on Manila. At Aparri on the north coast the Japanese, harassed by bad weather and by the remnants of the U.S. Army air force, put their men ashore hastily and departed without unloading their heavy equipment. A similar combination of bad weather, air opposition, and local resistance delayed for a day an attempt to land on the northwest coast near Vigan.

As General MacArthur expected, the main Japanese landing came at Lingayen Gulf, on the west side of Luzon above Manila. Japanese transports from Formosa entered the Gulf on December 21. American submarines, hampered by shoal water, had little success in intercepting. A few army planes and navy PBY's annoyed the convoy, but despite bad management the Japanese got their men ashore and with the help of the Vigan detachment, which

had marched south to help, overcame resistance. On Christmas Eve the Japanese put another force ashore on the east coast opposite Manila.

MacArthur, already withdrawing from Manila, declared it an open city and moved his forces in a wheeling movement toward Bataan, while the Navy hastily moved from the city such material as it could. Rear Admiral Francis W. Rockwell, Commandant of the 16th Naval District, moved into the fortified island of Corregidor, and on the 26th Admiral Hart left by submarine to join his fleet in the south. Five days later the last of the American submarines left Manila. On January 2 the Japanese entered the city unopposed.

The stubborn defense of Bataan and Corregidor was important morally at a time when quick and easy enemy successes were all too frequent, and it had the important practical effect of denying Manila Bay to the Japanese, but it did not delay their advance toward the Indies. As early as December 17 they had landed on Borneo to begin seizure of its oil fields, and three days later in the Philippines they had landed at Davao Gulf, Mindanao, which became an important base for further thrusts to the south.

The Japanese Advance into the Netherlands East Indies

Thus in little more than two weeks from the outbreak of war the Japanese had moved into and past the Philippines. The pattern of their multi-pronged advance was becoming clear. One line followed the Asiatic coast from Indo-China to Malaya and Singapore. A second thrust followed the west coast of Borneo south toward Sumatra. From Davao the Japanese advanced through both Makassar and Molucca Straits, taking important points along the way. Their ultimate objective was Java, richest and most highly developed of the Indies, with a population as great as that of England.

The Japanese moved by a series of amphibious landings on islands that had almost no interior communications, so that control of the sea and air was decisive. Their method was to seize a key point where they could take

THE NETHERLANDS EAST INDIES AREA, 1942

1. Action off Balikpapan, January 24.
2. Madoera Strait, February 4.
3. Banka Island, February 13-14.
4. Badoeng Strait, February 19-20.
5. Java Sea, February 27-28.

over or develop an airfield that would provide air support for the next move. Allied defenses were spread so thin that the Japanese had little difficulty in building up local superiority. For the most part they employed only modest forces and seldom required carrier support.

By early January 1942 the U.S. Asiatic Fleet had fallen back to the Netherlands East Indies. On the 10th British General Sir Archibald P. Wavell arrived in Java to take supreme command of the American, British, Dutch, and Australian (ABDA) forces in the area. Admiral Hart was given the naval command, while the air and army commands went to the British and Dutch respectively. But the ABDA command, facing insuperable difficulties, was never able to function effectively, nor was it able to work out a unified strategy.

As the Japanese advanced in a vast pincers movement on Java via the waters east and west of Borneo, it appeared that the ABDA forces might be able to exploit their interior position by striking first at one and then the other of the divided Japanese forces. But throughout January Allied naval vessels were so much in demand for convoying that it was impossible to form a striking force. Consequently Admiral Hart had available only a few United States vessels when in late January reconnaissance reported a Japanese convoy approaching the Borneo oil port of Balikpapan. On the night of the 23rd these ships steamed up Makassar Strait. En route the *Boise* struck an uncharted pinnacle rock, which put her out of the campaign, while the *Marblehead* developed turbine trouble. Proceeding without cruiser support, the four destroyers in a surprise attack sank a patrol craft and four of the dozen transports present, besides damaging several others. This daring night raid was the only successful surface action fought by Allied forces during the entire Netherlands East Indies campaign.

After this, Japanese control of the air prevented adequate Allied reconnaissance while it assured the Japanese complete knowledge of all ABDA movements. As a result, ABDA forces were swung between the two arms of the Japanese advance without being able to strike effectively at either, and were often turned back short of their objective by Japanese planes. While Dutch ships were drawn

to the west by a mistaken report, a Japanese force supported by carriers *Soryu* and *Hiryu* and two battleships took Amboina, anchor of the Dutch east flank. Soon afterward the Japanese occupied Kendari, in southeastern Celebes, and planes from the two carriers for a time based there. These planes on February 3 bombed Surabaya, the principal Allied naval base in Java, and destroyed most of the Dutch fighter aircraft in the vicinity.

By this time the task of reinforcing Singapore had been completed and an ABDA striking force had been formed of vessels released from convoy duty. In it initially were the United States cruisers *Houston* and *Marblehead* and four American destroyers, the Dutch light cruisers *De Ruyter* and *Tromp,* and three Dutch destroyers. Command was given to Dutch Rear Admiral Karel Doorman. These vessels escaped damage in the attack on Surabaya, but next morning as Doorman led them forth to attack a Japanese force reported reassembling at Balikpapan, they were discovered by Japanese planes. In a prolonged attack in Madoera Strait, the *Houston* received a hit that put her after turret out of commission for the rest of the campaign, while the *Marblehead* was so badly battered that she had to return to the United States.

Doorman next had to turn his attention to the Japanese western force. With five cruisers and ten destroyers he rushed to the relief of the great oil port of Palembang in eastern Sumatra, but when he arrived off nearby Banka Island on the night of February 13 he was met with repeated air attacks. Although no ship of his force was hit, several were shaken by near misses, and he retired without accomplishing anything.

In mid-February Admiral Hart surrendered command of the ABDA naval forces to Dutch Vice Admiral Conrad Helfrich and returned to the United States, leaving Admiral Glassford senior United States naval officer in the area. Singapore surrendered on February 15. After that, the Japanese were ready to close the pincers on Java, which they had started softening up by daily bombings.

Doorman had just returned from Banka Island when word came that the Japanese were landing on the island of Bali at the opposite end of Java. Doorman determined at least to hit the Japanese transports before they could withdraw, but because his ships were now divided between Surabaya and Tjilatjap he decided to attack in three successive waves. For once the ABDA vessels outnumbered the Japanese warships, but the lack of concentration nullified this advantage. In the attack on the night of February 19, a Dutch destroyer was sunk and the cruiser *Tromp* badly damaged without inflicting damage on the Japanese.

By now Java was nearly isolated, and the Japanese set about cutting her last links with Australia. They first seized Timor, through which the Allies had been staging fighter planes from Australia to Java. Then on February 19 Admiral Nagumo's carriers raided Darwin, principal port of northern Australia. The Japanese planes sank a dozen ships in the harbor, including the United States destroyer *Peary*, and virtually destroyed the docks and warehouses. The battered city was evacuated before nightfall, and the port of Darwin was abandoned as a naval base.

The Battle of the Java Sea

General Wavell, convinced of the futility of attempting any further defense of Java, left on the 25th, thus dissolving the ABDA command and leaving the Dutch to coordinate the continuing defense as best they could. By this time the Japanese were poised for the final attack. To the northwest Rear Admiral Jisaburo Ozawa was waiting near the Anambas Islands with 56 transports and cargo vessels and their escorts. To the northeast Rear Admiral Shoji Nishimurā was waiting in Makassar Strait with 41 transports and a cruiser-destroyer covering force.

Doorman, after two days of patrolling along the north coast of Java to intercept any landing attempt, on the morning of February 27 was returning to Surabaya with his striking force for rest and refueling when a report came of Japanese transports west of Bawean Island. Although his crews were near exhaustion, there was nothing to do but put about for the ultimate battle.

Doorman's cruisers were in column, the flagship *De Ruyter* in the lead, followed by the British *Exeter*, the American *Houston*, the Australian *Perth,* and the Dutch *Java*. Three British destroyers screened the van, two Dutch destroyers were on the port flank, and four American destroyers brought up the rear. Half an hour after leaving Surabaya, Doorman sighted the enemy in two groups on his starboard bow, moving SW as if to cross his course. One group consisted of a light cruiser leading ten destroyers, the other of two heavy cruisers and one light, with a squadron of destroyers. Fire was opened at 28,000 yards, beyond the range of the light cruisers. Although the Japanese enjoyed the advantage of air spotting, for some time they scored no hits. Then an 8-inch shell struck the *Exeter*, slowing her and forcing her to turn out of column. The following vessels, assuming that Doorman had ordered a turn, also swung to port, throwing the Allied formation into confusion and presenting their broadsides to Japanese torpedoes. By good luck or maneuvering all escaped except one of the Dutch destroyers, which took a torpedo, broke in two, and sank. When the Japanese closed in for the kill, a British destroyer was sunk by gunfire as she covered the damaged *Exeter*. The other cruisers withdrew and re-formed under cover of a torpedo attack by the American destroyers.

After a futile thrust toward the Japanese transports in the growing darkness, the striking force again approached Surabaya about 2100. At that point the American destroyers, their torpedoes expended and low in fuel, returned to port. There they found the *Exeter*, accompanied by the surviving Dutch destroyer.

As the remainder of the striking force steamed west along the Java coast, one of the British destroyers blew up and sank—probably the victim of a Dutch mine field laid that afternoon without Doorman's knowledge. Turning north, Doorman passed through the area where the Dutch destroyer had been sunk and detached his last destroyer to pick up survivors. Then with his four remaining cruisers he continued his thrust to the north and at 2300 again encountered the Japanese covering force. After 20 minutes of firing, the Japanese launched torpedoes that caught both the *De Ruyter* and the *Java*. As his flagship sank, Doorman signaled the *Houston* and the *Perth*, all that remained of his striking force, to retire

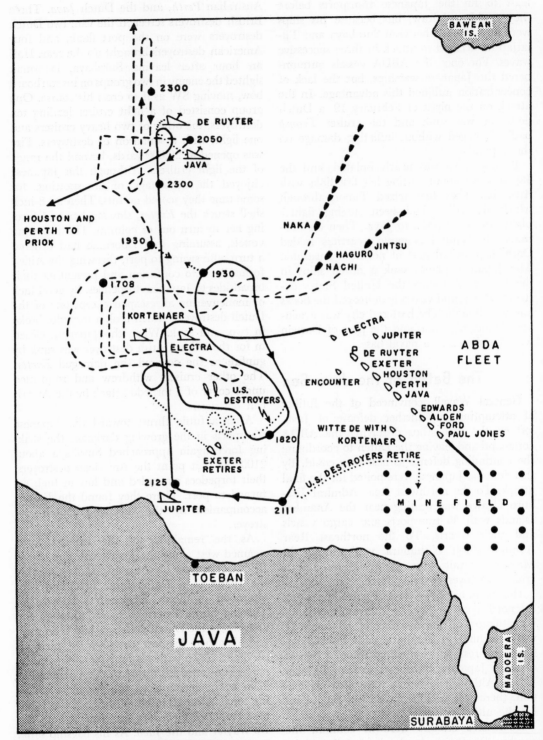

BATTLE OF THE JAVA SEA, FEBRUARY 27–28, 1942

to Tandjong Priok (the harbor of Batavia), which they reached safely a little after noon the next day.

The Retreat from Java

The Allied vessels surviving the battle were now divided between Surabaya and Tandjong Priok, with strong Japanese forces between. The problem was how to withdraw from the Java Sea, for the enemy now controlled all the exits. Only the four American destroyers escaped. Leaving Surabaya on the night of the 28th, they slipped through Bali Strait and after a brief skirmish with Japanese destroyers made their way to Australia. Because the *Exeter*'s draft was too great to permit her to follow the same route, she was sent west to Sunda Strait, but on the way she and two escorting destroyers were intercepted and sunk. The *Houston,* the *Perth,* and a Dutch destroyer left Priok on the evening of the 28th. They had almost reached Sunda Strait when, an hour before midnight, they encountered a Japanese landing force. The Allied cruisers sank or forced the beaching of four transports before the enemy covering force closed in and overwhelmed them.

The few Allied vessels based at Tjilatjap, on the south coast of Java, were authorized by Admiral Helfrich to withdraw on March 1. Nagumo's carrier-battleship force operating south of Java intercepted a few, including two United States destroyers and a gunboat, but most reached Australia.

The Japanese had begun landing on Java on the night of February 28. Batavia and Surabaya fell quickly, and by March 9 the Japanese were in possession of the entire island. The ABDA forces had been expended to gain time, and they had bought little enough of that. But it is adversity that brings out the true quality of men and of navies. There is nothing finer in United States naval history than the performance of the Asiatic Fleet in the face of overwhelming odds.

Holding the Line in the Pacific

While the ABDA fleet was buying time at the price of its own extinction, Allied forces elsewhere were stiffening the line that the United States was determined if possible to hold. This required reinforcing the essential bases on the route between the United States and Australia and then a build-up of forces in Australia itself. Vice Admiral Herbert F. Leary USN had arrived in Australia early in February to take command of an Anzac (Australian-New Zealand) Force, created on the recommendation of the Combined Chiefs of Staff after it became apparent that the ABDA forces were doomed. On March 17 MacArthur arrived at Darwin, designated at the request of the Australian government to take command of the Southwest Pacific Area, for which the United States had assumed responsibility. Already he was planning on a return to the Philippines, but for the moment he was a general without an army.

Although the United States was on the defensive, American strategy was far from passive. As Admiral King put it, American policy was "hold what you've got and hit them when you can." For the time being the hitting was to be done by the submarines and the carriers. Immediately after the Pearl Harbor disaster, the *Yorktown* had been ordered from the Atlantic to the Pacific. Her arrival brought the American carrier strength in the Pacific up to four, but on January 11 the *Saratoga* was torpedoed by a Japanese submarine 500 miles southwest of Oahu. She was able to make port, but repairs kept her out of the war for five critical months.

Fortunately for the Allies, the Japanese did not make the most effective use of their carriers during that interval. Upon Nagumo's return from Pearl Harbor his force was sent to support operations in the South. To cover the left flank of their advance the Japanese had already occupied the British Gilbert Islands in early December 1941, and in the latter part of January they sent their carriers for an unnecessary softening up of Rabaul, at the northern end of New Britain, in preparation for a landing on the 23rd.

Meanwhile there was considerable apprehension at Pearl Harbor that the Japanese might move from the Marshalls and Gilberts against Samoa. Accordingly reinforcements were dispatched to that group, and two carrier forces were sent to hit the Japanese bases. While Rear Admiral Fletcher's *Yorktown* group

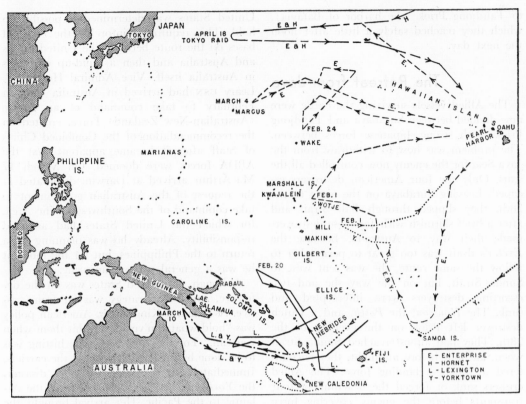

EARLY RAIDS BY UNITED STATES CARRIER FORCES

on February 1 raided Makin in the northern Gilberts and Jaluit and Mili in the southern Marshalls, Vice Admiral William F. Halsey's *Enterprise* group penetrated farther into the Marshalls to attack Wotje, Malœlap, and Kwajalein. Admiral Nagumo's carriers had just returned from Rabaul to Truk, the major Japanese base in the Carolines, when news of the attacks sent them on a futile chase after the Americans. Damage done by the American raids, particularly that on Kwajalein, was severe enough to make the Japanese concerned for the safety of Japan itself. Accordingly they detached the *Shokaku* and *Zuikaku* from Nagumo's group for a defensive patrol of Japanese waters, thus immobilizing one third of their most effective striking force.

At the time of the fall of Singapore in mid-February both the United States and Australian governments were apprehensive that the Japanese might advance from Rabaul to attack New Caledonia and the New Hebrides. Consequently Vice Admiral Wilson Brown's *Lexington* group was temporarily assigned to Leary's Anzac force and undertook an attack on Rabaul. But on his approach on February 20 the force was attacked by Japanese planes. With surprise lost, Brown abandoned the strike.

The critical situation in the Southwest Pacific was responsible for an attempt to divert the Japanese by an attack on Wake. Admiral Halsey, whose ready courage in undertaking such risky missions endeared him to Nimitz, struck Wake with planes of the *Enterprise* group on February 24, then pressed on to attack Marcus Island, less than a thousand miles from Tokyo.

By the time of the raid on Marcus, Allied naval forces had abandoned Java. Japanese bombing of points in New Guinea, including Port Moresby, and of Tulagi in the lower Solomons seemed to portend a further advance to the south or southeast. To check any such move, Admiral Brown was given a force built around the *Lexington* and *Yorktown* to make another attempt against Rabaul, which the Japanese were rapidly developing into a major base. But a report of Japanese landings on March 8 at Lae and Salamaua on the northern side of the New Guinea tail caused Brown to shift his attack to those points. Launching from south of Papua, he achieved surprise by sending his planes over the Owen Stanley Mountains and scored some successes against the few Japanese vessels still present.

While the United States and Anzac forces were thus attempting to check Japanese expansion to the south and east, the British were facing a similar problem in the west. In mid-January the Japanese had advanced from Thailand to begin their invasion of Burma. By early March Rangoon, the capital and key to lower Burma, had fallen, leaving the British the difficult task of withdrawing from upper Burma into India. In the latter part of March the Japanese protected the left flank of their advance by occupying the Andaman Islands, which put them in a position to threaten India. (See map page 818.) Then to render their sea route to Burma doubly secure they sent Nagumo's force to hit the British in the Indian Ocean.

When Vice Admiral Sir James Somerville, the former commander of Force H at Gibraltar, arrived in Ceylon at the end of March to replace Admiral Phillips, he had at his disposal carriers *Indomitable, Formidable,* and *Hermes,* five battleships, and a number of cruisers and destroyers. On paper this was a respectable force, but the carriers were of limited capacity and the battleships old and slow. Shortly after his arrival, Somerville received a warning that the Japanese would attack Ceylon about April 1. He at once concentrated his force to the south of Ceylon, searched for three days, and then on April 2 retired to a secret base in the Maldive Islands.

Meanwhile Nagumo had entered the Indian Ocean with virtually the same carrier force that had raided Pearl Harbor. On Easter Sunday, April 5, his aircraft raided the British base at Colombo, Ceylon and shortly afterward sank H.M. heavy cruisers *Dorsetshire* and *Cornwall,* which had sailed the day before to join Somerville. Four days later Nagumo raided Trincomalee, Britain's other base in Ceylon, and that same afternoon sank at sea the carrier *Hermes* and an accompanying de-

stroyer. At both places the Japanese easily overwhelmed the weak British air opposition with negligible losses to themselves.

Vice Admiral Takeo Kurita had in the meantime entered the Bay of Bengal with six heavy cruisers and a light carrier and pounced upon merchant shipping. In the first nine days of April 1942, Japanese air, surface, and submarine forces sank four British warships and 135,000 tons of merchant shipping.

After this disaster Britain practically abandoned the Indian Ocean. Somerville sent his four slowest battleships to east Africa, while with the *Warspite* and his two remaining carriers he covered sea communications between India and the Persian Gulf. But there was serious apprehension that his base at Bombay might not long remain secure, for it appeared that a Japanese invasion of Ceylon and India might be imminent. Churchill asked that the United States Navy undertake some action that might force the Japanese to draw their carriers back into the Pacific, and arrangements were made for American vessels to join the British Home Fleet so that reinforcements might be sent to India.

It was only coincidence that the British plea for a diversion in the Pacific was followed by the most daring of the series of United States carrier raids, the Halsey-Doolittle raid on Tokyo on April 18. The plan was for the newly-arrived carrier *Hornet,* accompanied by the *Enterprise* and a cruiser-destroyer screen, under the over-all command of Admiral Halsey, to carry 16 Army B-25's to within 500 miles of Japan. The planes, manned by volunters, were to hit targets in Tokyo, Nagoya, Osaka, and Kobe, cross Japan, and land on friendly airfields in China. But while the carriers were still 650 miles from Japan they encountered Japanese picket boats that reported their presence. Rather than abandon the raid, Colonel James H. Doolittle USA decided to launch at that distance. Waves were breaking over the *Hornet*'s bows and the carrier was pitching badly when Doolittle led his planes off. Not one of the pilots had ever taken off from a carrier deck before; yet somehow every one succeeded in getting his big, heavily-loaded plane into the air.

There was only scattered opposition, and none of the American aircraft was lost over

Japan, but on arriving over China in the dark, 15 of the planes were lost in crash landings or when their crews abandoned them by parachute. The only plane to land safely was impounded by the Russians at Vladivostok. Of the 80 men who left the carrier, 71 survived the raid.

The physical effect of the raid on Tokyo was slight. Few of the Japanese public even knew that the city had been bombed, but Japan's rulers knew and were disturbed. The raid was to have an important effect on strategic developments.

None of the early raids inflicted really significant damage, but their moral effect on both sides was important. They seriously alarmed the Japanese rulers, while for the Americans they did much to dispel the gloom and defeatism engendered by the Pearl Harbor attack and to create a feeling that the United States was fighting back.

Japanese Strategic Decisions

The conquest of the Philippines, the Netherlands East Indies, Burma, and Malaya, completed by the spring of 1942, had required only about half the time the Japanese had anticipated and had cost them only a few thousand casualties. In the entire campaign they had lost no naval vessel larger than a destroyer.

The rapidity with which the Japanese had achieved their main objectives left them without a decision as to their further strategy. Apart from consolidation of conquests to date, the three possibilities were to move westward against Ceylon and India, to move southward against Australia, or to move eastward against Hawaii. The first two were advocated by elements of the Naval General Staff, while Yamamoto and his Combined Fleet Staff espoused the third course. But the Japanese army, with its eyes upon the continent and Russia, objected to committing the large number of troops necessary for either of the first two. Hence the Naval General Staff worked out a more modest plan for isolating Australia by moving from Rabaul into Eastern New Guinea and down the Solomons and the New Hebrides to New Caledonia, the Fijis, and Samoa.

The first steps of this new Naval General Staff plan had already been taken with the landings at Lae and Salamaua in early March, and preparations for the capture of Port Moresby and Tulagi were under way by April. But Yamamoto and his staff, arguing that the destruction of the United States carriers was essential to Japanese security in the Pacific, insisted on early operations against Midway and the Aleutians that would be sure to draw out American naval forces. In early April they secured the reluctant consent of the Naval General Staff. The date and other details of the Midway operation were still in dispute however when the Doolittle raid seemed to prove the soundness of Yamamoto's argument. On the recommendation of the Naval General Staff the Imperial General Staff on May 5 ordered the Midway operation for early June.

Thus through compromise the Japanese had adopted two concurrent strategies which were destined to over-extend their forces. The first, the Naval General Staff's campaign to isolate Australia, was to lead to the Battle of the Coral Sea and eventually bring American marines to Guadalcanal, while Yamamoto's thrust toward Hawaii was to result in the Battle of Midway.

The Battle of the Coral Sea

The occupation of Port Moresby and Tulagi had originally been planned for March, but the appearance of United States carrier forces in the southwest Pacific had caused the Japanese to delay the operation till early May so that the Fourth Fleet might be reinforced by the carriers *Shokaku* and *Zuikaku* from Nagumo's force and the light carrier *Shoho* from the Combined Fleet.

The Japanese wanted Port Moresby in order to safeguard Rabaul and their positions in New Guinea, to provide a base for neutralizing airfields in northern Australia, and in order to secure the flank of their projected advance toward New Caledonia, Fiji, and Samoa. They wanted Tulagi, across the sound from Guadalcanal in the lower Solomons, to use as a seaplane base both to cover the flank of the Port Moresby operation and to support the subsequent advance to the southeast. To the Allies

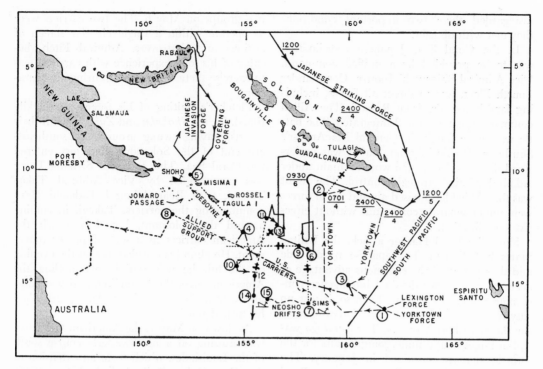

BATTLE OF THE CORAL SEA, MAY 4–8, 1942

1. May 1, 0623: *Yorktown* and *Lexington* meet.
2. May 4, 0701: *Yorktown* launches attack on Tulagi.
3. May 5, 0846: *Yorktown* rejoins *Lexington*.
4. May 7, 1000: Attack group launched.
5. May 7, 1150: *Shoho* sunk.
6. May 7, 0815: Japanese launch attack on Neosho and *Sims*.
7. May 7, 1230: *Sims* sunk.
8. May 7, 1425: Japanese planes attack Support Force.
9. May 7, 1615: Japanese launch night attack group.
10. May 8, 0900: U. S. carriers launch attack.
11. May 8, 0915: Japanese carriers launch attack.
12. May 8, 1118: U. S. carriers under attack.
13. May 8, 1058: Japanese carriers under attack.
14. May 8, 1956: *Lexington* sinks.
15. May 11, 1550: *Neosho* sunk by *Henley*.

the retention of Port Moresby was essential not only for the security of Australia but also as a springboard for future offensives.

In the Japanese plan a Covering Force built around the 12,000-ton carrier *Shoho* was first to cover the landing on Tulagi, then turn back west in time to protect the Port Moresby Invasion Force, which was to come down from Rabaul and around the tail of New Guinea through Jomard Passage. There were close support forces for both landings, and in addition a Striking Force centered on the *Shokaku* and *Zuikaku* was to come down from Truk to deal with any United States forces that might attempt to interfere with the operation. Land-based aircraft were counted upon for scouting and support. Altogether there were six separate naval forces engaged in this dual operation. Such complex division of forces was typical of Japanese strategy throughout most of the war. So far, against a weak and disorganized enemy, it had worked well, and it was not inconsistent with concentration so long as the forces were properly coordinated and sufficiently close together to render mutual support. But when the Japanese disregarded these two important conditions they met with disaster.

In the Coral Sea, Japanese coordination was to be provided by a unified command. Vice Admiral Shigeyoshi Inouye, Commander Fourth Fleet, was to direct all forces, including land-based air, from Rabaul. The Allied command was not so well integrated. The battle was to be fought in General MacArthur's Southwest Pacific Theater, but it was understood that any fleet action would remain under Admiral Nimitz' strategic control. The result was that Allied land-based air and naval forces were under separate commands without effective coordination.

Since the Pearl Harbor attack, the United States had broken the Japanese naval code and thus possessed the enormous advantage of accurate and rather detailed intelligence concerning the enemy's plans. Even so, it was no easy matter to gather sufficient forces to meet the threat to Port Moresby. The *Saratoga* was still in Puget Sound undergoing repairs for the torpedo damage sustained in January. The *Enterprise* and *Hornet* did not return to Pearl Harbor from the Tokyo raid till April 25. Although they were hurried on their way as soon as possible, there was little likelihood that they could reach the Coral Sea in time to play a part. The only carriers immediately available were Admiral Fletcher's *Yorktown* force, which had been in the South Pacific for some time, and Rear Admiral Aubrey W. Fitch's *Lexington* group, fresh from Pearl Harbor. From Noumea, New Caledonia came the *Chicago*, while Rear Admiral J. C. Crace RN brought cruisers H.M.A.S. *Australia* and *Hobart* from Australia. The Japanese, overconfident from their long series of easy successes, assumed that a single carrier division was sufficient to support their new advance.

The two American carrier groups, which had been ordered to join under Fletcher's command, made contact in the southeast Coral Sea on May 1. Two days later Fletcher received a report of the Japanese landing on Tulagi. Leaving the *Lexington* group to complete fueling, he headed north with the *Yorktown* group, and during the 4th made a series of air attacks on the Tulagi area that sank a few minor Japanese naval craft. He then turned back south and formally merged his two groups on May 6. The two carriers were to operate within a single circular screen of cruisers and destroyers. Admiral Fitch, because of his long experience with carriers, was to exercise tactical command during air operations.

Fletcher's uniting of his forces was luckily timed, for the *Shokaku* and *Zuikaku* with their escorts, having swung around the southeastern end of the Solomons, had just entered the Coral Sea. The Japanese Striking Force was commanded by Vice Admiral Takeo Takagi, with Rear Admiral Tadaichi Hara commanding the carriers. Takagi, in coming around the Solomons, hoped to catch the American carriers in a sort of pincer movement. He almost succeeded, for on the evening of the 6th he was rapidly overhauling the American force, then refueling, and was actually within 70 miles of the Americans when he turned north.

At dawn on May 7, the American task force was cruising on a northwesterly course south of the Louisiades, which form an extension of the New Guinea tail. A little before 0700, Fletcher detached three cruisers and three destroyers under Admiral Crace and ordered them to push on to the northwest while the carriers turned north. The detached vessels were to prevent the Port Moresby Invasion Force from coming through Jomard Passage, regardless of the fate of the American carriers, which Fletcher expected would come under attack during the day. In sending Crace forward however, Fletcher was depriving a part of his force of carrier air cover and at the same time further weakening his already weak carrier antiaircraft screen.

Thus far neither Takagi nor Fletcher was sure that the other was in the area, though Fletcher had information that three Japanese carriers were involved in the operation. Takagi was depending on land-based searches which actually sighted the American carrier force but failed to get word through. Fletcher's air searches were defeated by bad weather to the northeast, where the two Japanese heavy carriers were operating.

To the northwest however the weather was clear, and early on the 7th reports began to come in from American scout planes searching in this direction. At 0815 a pilot reported "two carriers and four heavy cruisers" not far north of Misima Island, whereupon Fletcher ordered attack groups launched from both his carriers. The 93 planes were well on their way before the scout returned and it was discovered that the report was an error due to improper coding—that the scout had meant to report two cruisers and two destroyers.

Fletcher made the courageous decision to let the attack proceed, probably thinking that with the Japanese Invasion Force nearby there must be some profitable targets. His boldness was rewarded at 1022 by a report which placed an enemy carrier with several other vessels only 35 miles southeast of the point toward which the strike had been sent. The attack group had to alter course only slightly for the new target.

The Americans came upon the *Shoho* about 1100 and, in the first attack ever made by American pilots on an enemy carrier, smothered her with 13 bomb and seven torpedo hits, which sent her down within a few minutes. Upon their return, Fletcher decided to withhold a second strike until the other two enemy carriers were located. Moreover, he suspected that the enemy knew his position, and it seemed likely that he would soon come under attack.

The Japanese failed to attack Fletcher on the 7th only because of a series of errors which by evening reached the fantastic. Before 0900 on the 7th, Inouye, directing the Japanese operation from Rabaul, had reports of two American carrier forces. One was Fletcher's; the other, some 45 miles to the west, was in fact Crace's cruiser-destroyer force. Then came a report from Takagi of a third American carrier in the eastern Coral Sea. This last was actually the oiler *Neosho,* which had been detached from Fletcher's force the evening before and was proceeding with the destroyer *Sims* toward a rendezvous.

At 0950 Japanese navy planes took off from Rabaul to attack the westernmost of the United States forces. The Japanese pilots returned with reports that they had sunk a battleship and a cruiser. Actually Crace's force survived without damage both this attack and another by B-26's from Australia, which mistook his vessels for Japanese.

The identification of the *Neosho* as a carrier had a serious effect on Japanese operations, for

Hara at once launched a full attack upon the hapless oiler and her escort. The *Sims* with three hits went down with most of her crew. The *Neosho* took seven but remained afloat until her crew was taken off four days later.

This erroneous attack left Tagaki and Hara facing a critical situation. As night approached, the weather closed in, but Hara was determined to destroy the American carriers before they could further damage the Invasion Force. Selecting 27 pilots best qualified in night operations, he sent them out at 1615 in the direction in which he estimated the American carriers lay.

It was not a bad gamble, for in the bad weather and poor visibility the Japanese actually passed near Fletcher's force. The American combat air patrol, vectored out by radar, intercepted the Japanese planes and shot down nine. An hour later several of the returning Japanese, mistaking the American carriers for their own, actually attempted to join the *Yorktown*'s landing circle until American gunners shot down one and drove off the others. The *Lexington*'s radar showed planes circling as if for a landing about 30 miles to the east, which seemed to indicate that the Japanese carriers were very close indeed. Of the Japanese striking group, ten had been shot down, and eleven others went into the water in attempting night landings on their carriers. Hara recovered only six of his 27.

The pilots of these planes reported the American carriers only 50 or 60 miles away. Thus each of the opposing commanders was aware of the proximity of the other. Both seriously considered a night surface attack, and both abandoned the idea because they hesitated to weaken their screens with an enemy near. Thus the main action of the Battle of the Coral Sea was postponed another day.

Actually the distance between the two forces was greater than either commander imagined, for postwar plots show that they were never closer than 95 miles.

The Battle of May 8

Thus far the antagonists had been together in the Coral Sea for two days, and had twice come within a hundred miles of each other without exchanging blows. On the evening of

May 7 each of the opposing commanders felt that the enemy was uncomfortably close. There was every likelihood that a decision would be reached the next day. During the night Fletcher withdrew to the south and west, while Takagi moved north. For both commanders everything depended on locating the enemy as promptly as possible on the morning of the 8th. Both launched searches a little before dawn, and the scouts of each reported the other almost simultaneously a little after 0800.

The contest of May 8 started on curiously even terms. Each force contained two carriers. Fitch had available 121 planes, Hara 122. The Americans were stronger in bombers, while the Japanese enjoyed a preponderance in fighter and torpedo planes. The Japanese pilots had more combat experience, and their torpedoes were better. In another respect the Japanese enjoyed a significant advantage. By moving south through the night Fletcher had run out of the bad weather area in which he had been operating, and on the 8th his force lay exposed under clear skies, while the Japanese remained within the frontal area, under the protection of clouds and rain squalls.

Essentially the battle consisted of a simultaneous exchange of strikes by the two carrier forces. Between 0900 and 0925 both American carriers launched their attack groups. That of the *Yorktown,* consisting of 24 bombers with two fighters, and nine torpedo planes with four fighters, departed first. About 1030 the dive bombers found the Japanese carriers with their escorts in loose formation. While the pilots took cloud cover to await the arrival of the torpedo planes, the *Zuikaku* disappeared into a rain squall. Hence the attack fell only on the *Shokaku.*

When the torpedo planes approached, the SBD's began their dives. Although the attack was well coordinated, it was only moderately successful. The slow American torpedoes were easily avoided, but the dive bombers succeeded in planting two bombs on the *Shokaku.* Of the *Lexington* group, which departed about ten minutes later than the *Yorktown*'s, the 22 dive bombers failed to find the target. Only the eleven torpedo planes and the four scout bombers found the enemy. Again American torpedoes were ineffective, but the bombers

succeeded in adding another hit to the two already sustained by the *Shokaku.* These three hits put the *Shokaku* out of action for the time being; because the damage to her flight deck prevented her recovering planes, Takagi detached her, ordering her to proceed to Truk.

The Japanese had sent off their group of 70 attack planes and 20 fighters at about the same time as the American launching. Although the American radar picked them up at 70 miles away, only three fighters succeeded in intercepting them before the attack. At a distance of 20 miles, still having met no interference by American fighters, the Japanese planes divided into three groups, two of torpedo planes and one of bombers.

The two American carriers were together in the center of their circle of screening vessels, but evasive maneuvers gradually drew them apart. The screen divided fairly evenly, but this breaking of the circle undoubtedly contributed to the Japanese success.

The *Yorktown,* which came first under attack, successfully evaded the torpedoes launched at her and took only a single bomb hit, which did not significantly impair her fighting effectiveness. But the *Lexington,* larger and less maneuverable, fell victim to an "anvil" attack on both bows simultaneously and took two torpedoes on the port side, which flooded three boiler rooms. Two bomb hits, received at almost the same time, inflicted only minor damage. The list caused by the torpedo hits was quickly corrected by shifting oil. Her engines were unharmed, and her speed did not fall below 24 knots. To her pilots returning from their strike she appeared undamaged.

As the American force began to recover its planes it appeared that they had won the battle. Both carriers were operational with combat effectiveness essentially unimpaired. On the other hand, the *Shokaku* had been put out of action and was already withdrawing. Because the *Zuikaku* had been unable to take on all the Japanese planes, many had to be jettisoned. Admiral Hara had only nine aircraft fit for further operations, while Fitch could still put into the air 37 attack planes and twelve fighters.

Even had Fletcher and Fitch been aware of their advantage they could not have seized it, for at 1247 there was an explosion deep inside the *Lexington,* caused apparently by vapor from ruptured gasoline lines touched off by a spark from a generator. At first the full danger was not apparent, and the *Lexington* continued landing her planes. But at 1445 there was a more severe explosion. Fires passed rapidly out of control and the carrier was forced to call for assistance. The *Yorktown* took aboard the *Lexington* planes that were in the air, but there was no opportunity to transfer those already on the *Lexington.* With the ship burning furiously and shaken by frequent explosions there was no choice but to "get the men off." Abandonment was orderly, and after it was completed a destroyer was detailed to sink the carrier. She fired five torpedoes to send the *Lexington* down at 1956.

The Japanese pilots who returned from the attack reported sinking both American carriers, and Hara was sufficiently sanguine to forward that estimate to his superiors. This comfortable belief undoubtedly influenced both Takagi's decision to detach the damaged *Shokaku* and Inouye's decision to withdraw the entire Striking Force. But even though he imagined both American carriers had been destroyed, Inouye still deemed it necessary to postpone the Port Moresby invasion, apparently because he felt unable to protect the landing force against Allied land-based planes.

Admiral Yamamoto, Commander in Chief Combined Fleet, did not acquiesce in the Japanese retirement. At 2400 he countermanded Inouye's order and directed the Striking Force to advance and annihilate the remaining American forces. Takagi thereupon put about and searched to south and east. But Fletcher was by this time safely out of reach.

Results

Thus the first carrier battle of the war, the first naval battle in history in which the opposing ships never came within sight of each other, closed with the Japanese holding the field and the Americans in retreat. Tactically the Coral Sea was by a slight margin a victory for the Japanese, for although they lost substantially more planes than the Americans and suffered twice as many casualties, the loss of the 30,000-ton *Lexington* far outweighed the sinking of the 12,000-ton *Shoho,* and the Japa-

nese destroyer and small craft sunk at Tulagi scarcely balanced the loss of the *Neosho* and *Sims.* Strategically however the United States had won. For the first time since war began, Japanese expansion had been checked. The Port Moresby Invasion Force had been obliged to withdraw without reaching its objective.

The battle had other important consequences. The strategic success helped the United States morally by taking some of the sting out of the surrender of Corregidor, which came on May 6, during the battle. More important, the damage to the *Shokaku* and the necessity for reforming the battered air groups of the *Zuikaku* kept those two carriers out of the Battle of Midway, where their presence might well have been decisive.

Summary

Japan had to have oil to carry on her war in Asia. In 1941 the United States cut off the flow from American wells. When negotiations to secure resumption of the flow of American oil proved fruitless, the Japanese attacked Pearl Harbor with carrier aircraft, seized Guam and Wake, invaded the Philippines, and advanced into the East Indies (the "Southern Resources Area"), where oil, rubber, tin, and quinine were to be had in abundance. At the same time they set out to complete a Defense Perimeter, a ring of island air and submarine bases, to cover Japan, the Southern Resources Area, and the line of communications in between. They believed that American naval forces sent against this perimeter could be destroyed faster than they could be built, and that the steady attrition would eventually compel the United States to accept a negotiated peace that would leave Japan in possession of her Asiatic conquests.

The apparent weakness of Allied defenses and the speed of the initial Japanese advance encouraged Japan to plan further advances: into New Caledonia, the Fijis, and Samoa, in order to isolate Australia from the United States; against Midway and the Aleutians, to extend the Defense Perimeter and draw out the weakened U.S. Pacific Fleet for destruction. To secure the flank of the first advance, which was to be via the Solomons and the New Hebrides, the Japanese prepared to seize Port

Moresby. To provide a seaplane base on the flank of the Port Moresby operation, they first seized Tulagi in the lower Solomons.

When the United States in 1922 agreed to a 5:5:3 ratio of capital ships with Great Britain and Japan, Japanese naval tonnage was only half that of the U.S. Navy. By construction in categories not limited by the disarmament treaties, Japan had built up to 73 per cent of American naval tonnage by 1936, when the treaties expired. By December 1941, Japanese naval tonnage was 81 per cent of American. But the U.S. Fleet had to be divided between two oceans, and Japan's resulting naval superiority in the Pacific was greatly increased by the raid on Pearl Harbor and the torpedoing of the *Saratoga*. On top of this, the United States in compliance with the 1922 treaty had refrained from arming its islands in the Pacific while Japan had not. As a result, the Japanese early in World War II exercised command over vast reaches of the Pacific Ocean.

The United States and its allies, committed to employing their main effort against Germany, necessarily went on the defensive in the Pacific until America could generate sufficient power to shift to the offensive. In the meantime the Allied navies employed the means historically used by weaker powers to dispute the enemy's command of the sea: (1) suicide missions to delay the enemy's advance, (2) attacks on the enemy's communications and isolated fleet units, and (3) raids on enemy bases. The first was carried out by the ABDA forces in the Java Sea area; the second, by Allied submarines; the third, by American carrier forces, which raided the Gilberts, the Marshalls, Wake, Marcus, Lae, Salamaua, and Tokyo itself.

It was clear however that such means were not enough, even for defense. The Allies were committed to maintaining communications between Hawaii and Midway and between the United States and Australia. Somewhere, in meeting this commitment, Allied naval forces would have to make a stand to check Japanese expansion. Thanks to intelligence of Japanese plans, and to the overconfidence that caused Japan to commit only two heavy carriers to the Port Moresby operation, the Allies were able to do so in early May 1942, in the Battle of the Coral Sea. Here for the first time they turned back the Japanese, though at the cost of the carrier *Lexington*.

It remained to be seen whether the United States could hold the line against a truly major Japanese effort.

36:

Midway and the Aleutians

On May 5, 1942, Japanese Imperial Headquarters, as we have seen, ordered the Midway operation for some time in June. This strategy bore no relation to the Battle of the Coral Sea, though the *Yorktown* had raided Tulagi the day before the issuing of the order. Nor did the outcome of the carrier battle of May 8 cause any modification of Japanese plans. Although Yamamoto's staff cautiously estimated that there might be two or three American carriers in the Midway area, it seemed more likely that there would be none, for the Japanese believed they had sunk both the *Yorktown* and the *Lexington*, and several days after the battle they sighted Halsey's *Enterprise* and *Hornet* in the South Pacific. The absence of American carriers from the Central Pacific would facilitate the capture of Midway but would partially frustrate the other Japanese objective, the destruction of the remaining United States naval forces.

Japanese Plans

There was nothing petty in Japanese planning. The entire Combined Fleet, under the personal command of Admiral Yamamoto, was to be employed in a vast operation covering the Northern and Central Pacific. A carrier task force would strike in the Aleutians on June 3, after which occupation forces would land on Adak, Attu, and Kiska. This attack, to take place a day before that on Midway, was intended partially as a diversion. There would hardly be time for American forces actually to be pulled out of position, but the attack would at least confuse the American command.

At dawn on June 4 a second and larger carrier force, coming from the northwest, would bomb Midway Atoll, destroy the planes based there, and soften it up in preparation for the landing. Then on the night of June 5 the occupation forces, approaching from the southwest, would put some 5,000 troops ashore to take the island and convert it into a Japanese base.

The Americans, the Japanese believed, lacked the will to fight but would be forced either to defend Midway or to attempt to retake it. When the United States fleet sortied from Pearl Harbor it would cross one or the other of two lines of submarines that the Japanese had placed to the west and north of that base. (See diagram page 670.) These would inflict some losses on the American fleet and would give Yamamoto ample warning. The Japanese carrier force would then attack the Americans and might well maneuver to get between them and Pearl Harbor. At that point Yamamoto's heavy surface ships of the Main Body, hitherto kept safely back to the northwest, would close in for the kill. The work of December 7 would be completed and the United States fleet destroyed before it could be reinforced by new construction. The Japanese had no immediate plan for the occupation of Pearl Harbor. When the American fleet had been eliminated there would be ample time to think of that.

The fixed pattern of Japanese strategic thinking is evident when this plan is compared with that for the Coral Sea. Again there was a dual objective, again a multiplicity of forces, and again the Japanese were obsessed with the notion of pincer movements and envelopments.

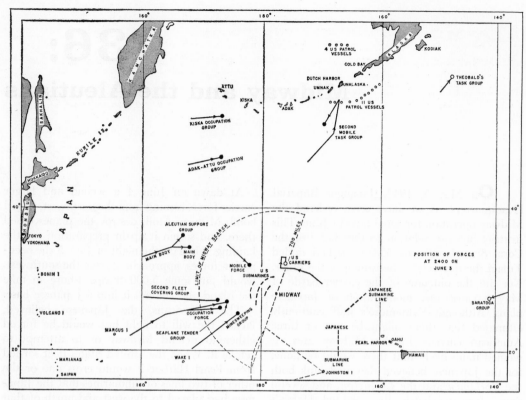

BATTLE OF MIDWAY, POSITION OF FORCES AT 2400, JUNE 3, 1942

The multiplicity of forces is even more striking when one examines the Japanese organization in detail. Vice Admiral Hosogaya's Northern Area Force, destined for the Aleutians, contained three principal groups besides the command-supply group. Rear Admiral Kakuta's Second Mobile Group consisted of the two carriers *Ryujo* and *Junyo,* two heavy cruisers, three destroyers, and an oiler. The Adak-Attu Occupation Group was separate from that destined for Kiska and operated independently.

Vice Admiral Nagumo's carrier force that had raided Pearl Harbor, Darwin, and Ceylon, reappeared in the Midway operation as the Mobile Force. Present were carriers *Akagi, Kaga, Hiryu,* and *Soryu,* screened by 2 fast battleships, 3 cruisers, and 11 destroyers and accompanied by their own oilers. Conspicuously absent were carriers *Shokaku* and *Zuikaku,* left behind in Japan, the one because

of damage and both because of shortage of planes and pilots resulting from the Coral Sea battle.

A little to the south and west of the Mobile Force was the Main Body. It was composed of 7 battleships, including the *Yamato*,[1] flagship of Admiral Yamamoto, one light aircraft carrier, the *Hosho,* 2 seaplane carriers carrying midget submarines, 3 light cruisers, and

[1] The *Yamato* and her sister ship the *Musashi*, each 64,000 tons, were the largest battleships ever built. Their main batteries consisted of nine 18.1-inch guns, firing a 3,200-pound projectile, which was almost 50 per cent heavier than a 16-inch projectile. One of the triple-mounted turrets weighed as much as a large destroyer, and the ships' side armor was more than 16 inches thick. A third vessel of the class was laid down at Yokosuka early in 1940, but after the Battle of Midway the hull was converted into aircraft carrier *Shinano.* Construction was abandoned on a fourth unit of the class. The *Yamato* was completed in December 1941 and the *Musashi* eight months later.

20 destroyers. But even this force was divided. On June 3 the greater part, including 4 battleships and 2 cruisers, turned north to become the "Aleutian Support Group." It was supposed to take a position about half way between the Aleutian and Midway forces, presumably to be able to give support in either area.

The Midway Occupation Force was commanded by Vice Admiral Nobutake Kondo, who as Commander in Chief of the Second Fleet had participated in the conquest of the Philippines and Indies. It consisted of five groups. Its 12 transports were screened by a cruiser, 10 destroyers, and 3 patrol boats. The Close Support Group of 4 heavy cruisers and 2 destroyers was to cover the transports and support the landing. A powerful Second Fleet Covering Group, which Kondo retained under his direct command, was to assist in the same mission. It comprised 2 battleships, the light carrier *Zuiho*, 4 heavy cruisers, and 7 destroyers. A Seaplane Tender Group was intended to set up a base on Kure, to the northwest of Midway. A Minesweeper Group would clear the way for the landings. These forces operated more or less independently. The Second Fleet Group was usually more than 50 miles to the north or northwest of the transports, while the Close Support Group was usually some 75 miles to the northeast.

The Japanese as usual sent an "Advance Expeditionary Force" of submarines to scout ahead of the Combined Fleet. One boat went ahead to scout Midway, while four took positions off the Aleutians and two stationed themselves off Seattle. Most important of the submarine dispositions were two patrol lines designed to cover Pearl Harbor. One line of four submarines lay about 500 miles west of Oahu, while another of seven boats ran athwart the route between Pearl and Midway. These boats were to be on station by June 1.

Why did such a vast armada fail to accomplish its mission? There is no doubt that American intelligence of Japanese plans was a decisive factor. Even with ample warning Nimitz was barely able to get three carriers onto the scene in time. It is difficult to believe that without that warning he either could or

would have done so. So one may say that the most obvious reason for the miscarriage of the plans of the Japanese was their failure to achieve the surprise on which they counted.

Surprise is extremely important in naval and military operations and ought to be exploited whenever possible. Very often the weaker force has no alternative but to rely on surprise to achieve its ends. But the Japanese made the mistake of planning a major operation so that it depended on surprise when there was no necessity for their doing so. Even with the most complete warning, it is inconceivable that the three United States carriers could by any combination of luck and skill have defeated and turned back the 8 carriers, 11 battleships, and immense number of supporting vessels which the Japanese committed to this action *had the Japanese fleet been concentrated.* As it was, June 3, the day of the attack on Dutch Harbor and of the first contact in the Midway area, found the Japanese surface ships in no fewer than ten groups scattered all over the North and Central Pacific. (See chart page 670.)

Concentration does not require the massing of forces in a single group. In what, then, did the Japanese fail? First of all, they failed to pursue a single objective. The two carriers sent to the Aleutians might well have supplied the decisive margin in the Central Pacific. Had the Midway operation succeeded, the Japanese could have taken the Aleutians at their leisure. Without success at Midway the Aleutian operation lost its meaning.

In the Midway area itself the Japanese had some of the elements of concentration. Their forces were grouped concentrically about Midway, which they assumed was the strategic center. They had a unified command under Yamamoto, who could bring about coordinated action. But when the crisis developed Yamamoto found that his forces were too widely separated for mutual support. He found after a vain attempt that he could not bring the scattered groups together in time to retrieve the situation.

Fault may also be found with the more detailed arrangements of the Japanese. The carriers of the Mobile Force were inadequately screened. The vessels scattered elsewhere might profitably have been used to give them better protection. The Main Body after the departure of the Northern Support Group was for all its surface strength an ill-balanced, useless force. The Occupation Force, which approached Midway from the southwest under clear skies, was dangerously exposed. It did not have adequate air protection and might well have become a principal target for American forces. Bringing the Occupation Force forward before the United States fleet had been accounted for bespeaks the callousness of the Japanese command, which was more careful of its battleships than of its transports.

One of the most serious mistakes of the Japanese was in their handling of their submarines. On the assumption that the Americans were not likely to sortie from Pearl before the attack on Midway, Japanese submarines did not take station until June 1. By that date the American carriers had actually crossed their patrol line between Pearl Harbor and Midway, the *Hornet* and *Enterprise* on May 29, the *Yorktown* on the night of May 31. Had the Japanese submarines been on station in time, there would have been no surprise at Midway and again the result might have been quite different.

United States Preparations

Since the United States was intercepting and reading Japanese coded messages, American intelligence of the enemy's plans was remarkably complete. Nimitz' information indicated the Japanese objectives, the approximate composition of the enemy forces, the direction of approach, and the approximate date of attack. It was this knowledge that made the American victory possible, but in view of the meager forces available to meet the threat it must have seemed to the United States command very much like foreknowledge of an inevitable disaster.

The first decision confronting Nimitz was whether to let the Aleutians go by default or to reinforce them at the expense of the Central Pacific. He chose the latter course and sent to the Aleutians a force of only 5 cruisers, 14 destroyers, and 6 submarines. These were under

Rear Admiral Robert A. Theobald, who was also to command land-based air.

As for the Central Pacific, Midway itself was too small to support sufficient forces to repel an attack of the proportions of that impending. Lying at the northwest end of the Hawaiian chain about 1,100 miles from Pearl Harbor, the little atoll consists of two islands surrounded by a reef. Sand Island, the larger of the two, is only about two miles long, while Eastern Island, on which the runways were situated, is little more than half as large. However, everything possible was done to strengthen Midway's defenses. The beaches and surrounding waters were mined. The marine garrison was reinforced and given additional antiaircraft guns. Finally, air strength was increased to the limit of the island's facilities. For search there were some 30 PBY's. There was between Midway and Oahu a constant interchange of B-17's that left 17 on Midway on June 3. The marine squadrons were equipped with planes cast off by the carriers, which had acquired more modern equipment. For defense they had 26 fighters operational on the day of the attack, mostly old Brewster Buffaloes. For attack there were 34 scout bombers, divided between Douglas Dauntlesses and Vought-Sikorsky Vindicators. Most of the pilots for these planes had been rushed out from flight school and had not yet practiced dive bombing. There were four Army B-26's, jury-rigged for a torpedo attack for which they were unsuited. The only really effective planes on the island were six TBF's, the first to reach the Pacific. This motley collection of planes was the best an unprepared country could provide for defense of a vital point.

The marines would undoubtedly have given the Japanese a warm reception had they come in for a landing, but it was clear that the fate of Midway depended in the final analysis on naval support. What could Nimitz assemble for the purpose? The *Lexington* had of course been sunk in the Coral Sea. The *Saratoga*'s repairs had been completed and she was training on the West Coast, but there was delay in forming an escort for her, so that she left San Diego only on June 1 and did not reach Pearl till June 6, too late for the battle.

The *Hornet-Enterprise* force had been hurriedly recalled from the South Pacific and arrived at Pearl Harbor on May 26. There illness compelled Halsey to relinquish command, and his place was taken by Rear Admiral Raymond A. Spruance, who had commanded the cruisers of the task force. Thoughtful, cautious, and modest, Spruance was in personality a striking contrast to the impetuous, colorful Halsey. But his unassuming manner concealed a brilliant mind and sound judgment, as the battle was to prove. The two carriers with a screen of five heavy cruisers, one light cruiser, and nine destroyers put to sea on May 28.

Fletcher's damaged *Yorktown* had also come back posthaste from the South Pacific. Repairs which would ordinarily have taken three months were compressed into three days, so that on the morning of May 30 she was able to put to sea with a screen of two heavy cruisers and five destroyers. The two carrier forces met northeast of Midway on June 2, and Fletcher, as senior, assumed local tactical command.

These three carriers and their escorts were all that could be assembled. The United States had some old battleships on the West Coast, but they were too slow to accompany the carriers, there were no destroyers available to screen them, and they scarcely fitted the "attrition tactics" Nimitz had decided to employ.

To backstop the carriers 19 submarines were assigned positions to cover the approaches to Midway. The *Cuttlefish* was stationed 700 miles west of Midway, where it was thought the Japanese might rendezvous. Three boats patrolled 200 miles to the west of the atoll. Six more 150 miles from the island patrolled an arc stretching from southwest to north, while two more were only 50 miles northwest of Midway. Others were stationed to support the carriers and to cover Oahu. Nimitz retained at Pearl Harbor the over-all command so that he could if necessary coordinate the movements of the submarines, the carriers, and the Midway planes.

The task that faced Fletcher and Spruance was appalling. Nimitz' instructions were: "You will be governed by the principle of calculated risk, which you shall interpret to mean the avoidance of exposure of your force to attack by superior enemy forces without good prospect of inflicting, as a result of such exposure, greater damage on the enemy." To fight cautiously, to meet a superior enemy force without unduly exposing one's own is difficult in the highest degree. That Fletcher and Spruance were able to carry out these orders successfully was due primarily to their skillful exploitation of intelligence, which enabled them to turn the element of surprise against the Japanese. The American command perceived that air power was the key to the situation and correctly concentrated on the Japanese carriers. The position northeast of Midway was well chosen, since it placed the United States carriers on the flank of the Mobile Force, which the Japanese were unable to succor in time because of the wide dispersion of their forces.

The Attack on the Aleutians

Admiral Theobald, like a good many other officers, suspected that the information on which American intelligence estimates were based had been "planted" by the Japanese. He was particularly concerned that the threat of an attack on the western Aleutians might be designed to draw him away from the more important Dutch Harbor-Cold Bay area; hence he decided to concentrate his forces for the defense of the latter. Inasmuch as his surface vessels were completely dependent for air cover on land- or harbor-based planes, the most westerly base for which was the secret field at Otter Point on Umnak, he could scarcely have done otherwise, but this decision meant that his task force was destined never to make contact with the enemy.

Theobald directed his main force of 5 cruisers and 4 destroyers to rendezvous 400 miles south of Kodiak. The last ships did not arrive till the morning of June 3, a few hours after the Japanese had struck Dutch Harbor. At Makushin Bay, Unalaska, he stationed a striking force of 9 destroyers to break up any landing the Japanese might attempt in the Dutch Harbor area.

Since the surface vessels could be used only

if a favorable opportunity arose, the primary burden of defense fell upon the planes, and they were all too few. The Navy had 20 PBY's for search. The Army had about 65 pursuit planes, but little more than half these were at Cold Bay and Umnak, where they were needed. The principal striking power lay in the 20 army bombers (chiefly B-26's) based at Kodiak, Cold Bay, and Umnak.

To provide early warning of the Japanese approach Theobald stationed his 6 submarines in likely positions for interceptions and placed 20 small vessels at a radius of 200 miles from Dutch Harbor, both to the south and in the Bering Sea. PBY's patrolled all the approaches, but their search was limited to 400 miles because of the scarcity of radar-equipped planes.

Somehow Kakuta's two carriers, approaching from the south-southwest, eluded submarines, picket boats, and planes. Although it was only an hour after midnight[2] of June 2–3, there was already a foggy half-light in Alaskan latitudes when the Japanese admiral launched 36 planes from a position about 165 miles south of Dutch Harbor. But the bad weather that had enabled him to escape detection now favored the Americans. The *Junyo*'s planes wandered in the fog and returned to the carrier without finding the target. The *Ryujo*'s group, emerging into locally clear weather over Dutch Harbor, scored almost complete surprise however and were able to inflict considerable damage with the loss of only two of their number.

On their return the Japanese sighted five destroyers of Theobald's force in Makushin Bay. Kakuta at once launched another strike at these targets, but worsening weather prevented the group from joining up. American P-40's from Otter Point shot down two, and none of them ever reached Makushin Bay.

After the attack on Dutch Harbor, American patrol planes made strenuous efforts to discover the Japanese carrier force, but without

[2] In this account both of the Aleutians and Midway, west longitude dates are used and zone-plus-12 time, which is local time for Midway and the central Aleutians.

success. Their failure was in part due to a belief that the attack had come from the Bering Sea, in part to the fact that Kakuta had retired to the southwest after his attempted strike on Makushin Bay. His orders were to attack Adak, but unfavorable weather in that direction forced him to abandon the project and return for a second attack on Dutch Harbor.

Kakuta had already started toward Dutch Harbor when at 0450 on the 4th a PBY reported his position. Thereafter American aircraft maintained intermittent contact and subsequently made a series of sporadic attacks, but none of the planes—PBY's rigged with torpedoes, B-26's, and B-17's—were really suited for operating against ships. Although the pilots attacked with great gallantry, they achieved nothing better than a few near misses at the cost of three planes, one of each type.

Before the American attacks began, Kakuta had launched a striking group, which arrived over Dutch Harbor at about 1600. During the next half hour it bombed and set fire to the new fuel oil tanks with some 22,000 barrels of fuel, the old station ship *Northwestern,* which had to be beached, a warehouse, and an empty aircraft hangar. Afterward the *Junyo*'s planes, making rendezvous over the western end of Unalaska, discovered the Army's secret airfield at Otter Point when American pursuit planes rose to shoot down four of them.

Meanwhile there were indications that the Japanese operations around Midway were going less well than in the Aleutians. Soon after launching his strike, Kakuta had received from Yamamoto the order to join the Mobile Force immediately, and about the same time he was informed that the occupation of Midway and the Aleutians had been postponed. Kakuta waited till he recovered his planes more than two hours later before setting course to the south to join Nagumo. By that time Yamamoto, at the urging of his staff, had changed his mind about the Aleutian landings and authorized the occupation forces to proceed according to plan. However, Hosogaya, Commander of the Northern Force, made one modification. He canceled the landing on

Adak. Apparently he considered it too risky to land only 350 miles from the newly discovered American airfield at Otter Point.

Soon after noon on June 6, about 1,250 men of a Special Naval Landing Force went ashore on Kiska, where they took prisoner the personnel of a small United States weather station. In the early hours of the following morning 1,200 Japanese troops landed on Attu, "capturing" 39 Aleuts and an American missionary and his wife. It was not till June 10 that American patrol planes discovered the Japanese on the two islands.

Midway Area— First Contacts, June 3

The PBY's based on Midway departed before dawn each morning to search the western sector to 700 miles. That distance was calculated to prevent any force which might be just out of range from reaching a launching position before the next day's search. During the last days of May and the first days of June coverage was excellent except in the critical area beyond 350 miles to the northwest, where weather was bad.

The first contact of the battle was made on the morning of June 3 when a patrol plane reported "six large ships in column" about 700 miles to the southwest. American commanders both on Midway and in the carriers surmised correctly that this was part of the

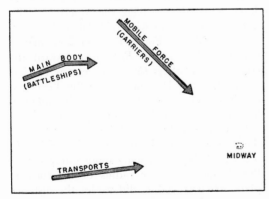

JAPANESE APPROACH TO MIDWAY, JUNE 3

Japanese Occupation Force. Since the main attack was expected from the northwest, the American carriers kept their position some 300 miles north-northeast of Midway, and the island forces for a while held their attack. Finally, a little after noon, when no new contacts had been made, nine B-17's with bomb-bay fuel tanks took off from Midway. Their attack, delivered about 1630, was ineffective. First blood of the battle was to be drawn by four radar-equipped PBY's which took off that night with torpedoes and hit and slightly damaged a Japanese oiler. Before these planes returned, Midway was under attack.

The Attack on Midway, June 4

As the American commanders expected, the Japanese carriers were approaching from the northwest under cover of the weather front. At 0430 on the 4th, half an hour before sunrise, at a distance of 240 miles from Midway, Nagumo sent off an attack group of 108 aircraft, made up of equal numbers of fighters, bombers, and torpedo planes. Weather was clear with scattered clouds and good visibility, and a southeast wind permitted him to hold his course while launching.

At Midway in the meantime patrol planes had as usual taken off at 0415, followed by the B-17's, which were put into the air to prevent their being surprised on the ground. At 0545 a PBY pilot reported in plain English, "Many planes heading Midway, bearing 320, distance 150." Five minutes later the Midway radar picked up the approaching planes at a distance of 93 miles. But where were the Japanese carriers? The answer for which American commanders both on Midway and in the carriers were waiting came just two minutes later when a PBY pilot reported two carriers and their escorts, bearing 320° from Midway, distant 180 miles. This report placed the Japanese about 40 miles southeast of their true position, an error which was to cause difficulty for the American carrier planes. The B-17's, then in the air, were at once directed to the enemy carriers, while the marine attack planes, the four B-26's, and the six TBF's, already warmed up and manned, took off to attack the same targets.

By this time the Japanese planes were approaching Midway. The marine fighters met them 30 miles out. "Each pilot made only one or two passes at the bombers and then spent the remainder of the time trying to shake from one to five Jap fighters off his tail," for the Zeke easily outperformed the American fighters.[3] Midway antiaircraft opened up as the Japanese formation came within range. The first bomb fell at 0630. Within the next half hour almost everything above ground was damaged; the power house was hit, the fuel tanks set afire, a hangar destroyed. Only the runways escaped injury. When it was all over, the marine fighters were told to land. "Pitifully few" responded. Of the 26 planes, 16 were missing, and only two of the survivors were fit for further combat. Only half a dozen of the Japanese planes failed to return to their carriers.

Midway Strikes Back, June 4

Midway's attack on the Japanese carriers was executed with high courage, but it was piecemeal, uncoordinated, and ineffective. It did however serve a useful purpose, for it distracted the Japanese at a critical moment, prevented their launching, and thus helped make possible the success of the American carriers.

The B-26's and TBF's attacked at low altitude separately but simultaneously just after 0700. The Japanese ships made smoke, maneuvered radically, and threw up a heavy antiaircraft fire, while Zekes intercepted. The American planes scored no hits. Five of the six TBF's and two of the four B-26's were shot down, while the three planes that returned were too badly damaged for further use.

Almost an hour later Major Lofton R. Hen-

[3] Report of Major Verne McCaul USMC, Group Executive Officer, Aircraft Group 22, Second Marine Aircraft Wing.

The famous Japanese aircraft was called Zero until 1943. Thereafter Zeros with rounded wingtips were called Zekes and those with square wingtips were called Haps. Zeke however was the general term applied to all Zeros after 1943.

derson's marine scout bombing squadron attacked the enemy force. Since the pilots were fresh from flight school, untrained in dive bombing, they were forced to make a more dangerous glide bombing attack. They scored no hits on their target, carrier *Hiryu,* and only eight of the 16 planes returned to Midway. Six of these were badly shot up.

About 15 minutes later fifteen B-17's arrived. Bombing from 20,000 feet, the Fortresses suffered no casualties and inflicted none. They were just departing when the second marine group arrived. Making a high speed approach at low level, they encountered such heavy antiaircraft and fighter opposition that they were unable to reach a carrier but dropped at a battleship instead. Again they scored no hits, and two planes made water landings before reaching Midway.

The first round of the Battle of Midway had clearly gone to the Japanese. They had pretty thoroughly smashed Midway. The island had sacrificed half its planes without damaging any enemy vessels in return. As Nimitz observed, "Most of Midway's fighters, torpedo planes, and dive bombers—the only types capable of making a high percentage of hits on ships—were gone." It was at this point that the United States carriers entered the battle.

The United States Carriers Intervene

When the Midway scout first reported the Japanese carriers at 0552 the American striking force was approximately 200 miles E by N of the Mobile Force. Fletcher immediately sent the *Hornet* and *Enterprise* toward the contact with orders to "attack enemy carriers when definitely located," while the *Yorktown* continued on an easterly course in order to land the planes of her morning search.

Spruance in the *Enterprise* decided to close the range for an hour before launching in order to bring the enemy more safely within the 175-mile combat radius of his torpedo planes. It was well he did so, for the distance was actually 25 miles greater than the report indicated. Finally, about 0700, when he estimated that he was 150 miles from the enemy and when there seemed a good chance of catching the Japanese refueling the planes which had struck Midway, he ordered launching.

In preparation for action the two carriers had separated, dividing the screening vessels between them. This was to avoid the error of the Coral Sea, where the *Lexington* and *Yorktown* had drawn apart under attack and had split the screening formation. The *Enterprise* put into the air 33 dive bombers, 14 torpedo planes, and 10 fighters. The *Hornet* group consisted of 35 bombers, 15 torpedo planes, and 10 fighters. To expedite the attack Spruance ordered the *Enterprise* bombers to proceed before the torpedo squadron was fully launched, and the *Hornet* bombers and torpedo planes, flying at different altitudes, became separated. Thus the attack force soon after its departure at approximately 0800 fell into four separate groups.

The *Yorktown* meanwhile had completed recovery of her search planes at about 0630 and turned to follow the *Enterprise* and *Hornet*. Because Fletcher had expected four or five carriers in the enemy force and only two had thus far been reported he hesitated to commit the *Yorktown*'s air group until the other enemy carriers had been accounted for. Finally, a little after 0830, in the absence of any further reports, he decided to launch half the *Yorktown*'s planes. In the next half hour the carrier launched 17 dive bombers, 12 torpedo planes, and 6 fighters. Then, still concerned about the two or three enemy carriers that had not yet been sighted, Fletcher launched a search to the north and west a little after 1100.

Nagumo had up to this time been acting with admirable caution. Although his intelligence led him to expect no naval opposition, he had sent only about half his available planes against Midway and had kept the rest on deck, armed with torpedoes, ready for action should any American vessels appear. Then, after his planes had departed for Midway, he had ordered his cruisers to catapult seven planes for a search to the east and south. These had departed at intervals through the next half hour, with the *Tone*'s plane last to take to the air.

At 0700 Nagumo's strike commander, then returning from Midway, reported that another strike at the island was necessary. Midway's torpedo attack, which came in almost immediately afterward, seemed to emphasize the point. By that time Nagumo's cruiser search planes had been gone for from 2 to 2½ hours and should have reached a radius of at least 200 miles. It seemed safe now to relax his precautions. At any rate, the planes from the Midway strike would soon be landing and would require servicing.

Therefore at 0715 Nagumo issued the fateful order, "Planes in second wave stand by to carry out attack today. Re-equip yourselves with bombs." It was just 13 minutes later that the *Tone*'s scout reported ten American ships about 200 miles to the northeast. It is easy to imagine how different the Battle of Midway might have been had the *Tone*'s plane been launched promptly so that this report might have come in half an hour earlier. Surface vessels 200 miles away did not constitute an urgent problem, but at 0745 Nagumo sent his carriers the order, "Prepare to carry out attacks on enemy fleet units. Leave torpedoes on the attack planes which have not yet changed to bombs." It was not till 0820 that the *Tone* scout reported that one of the American ships appeared to be a carrier.

Nagumo was undoubtedly aware of the desirability of striking first, even though a single United States carrier against his four did not seem particularly dangerous. But he could not launch immediately because of the necessity of re-arming his planes. Moreover he was under attack by Midway planes from 0705 to 0830, taking evasive action which would have interfered with launching. Another distraction was provided by submarine *Nautilus*, which had intercepted the Midway scout's first report of the Japanese carriers and had headed toward them. Between attacks by Midway planes she stuck up her periscope in the midst of the Mobile Force and fired two torpedoes to set off a grand confusion of circling destroyers and exploding depth charges. This turmoil had scarcely subsided before Nagumo

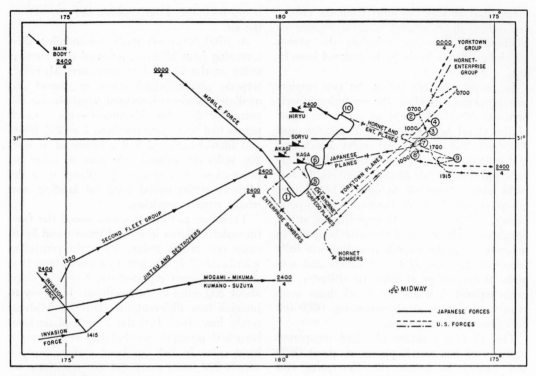

BATTLE OF MIDWAY, JUNE 4

1. 0705-0830: Midway planes and *Nautilus* attack Japanese carriers.
2. 0705: *Enterprise* and *Hornet* begin launching attack groups.
3. 0806: *Enterprise* and *Hornet* planes depart.
4. 0838: *Yorktown* begins launching.
5. 0920-1025: U. S. carrier planes attack Japanese carriers.
6. 1115: *Hiryu* attack group departs.
7. 1208: Japanese dive bombers attack *Yorktown*.
8. 1500: *Yorktown* abandoned.
9. 1530-1615: *Enterprise* and *Hornet* launch attack group.
10. 1701: *Hiryu* bombed.

had to recover the planes of his Midway strike, which began to arrive about 0830. After the last of these had been taken aboard at 0918, he withdrew to the north to reorganize his force while he struck them below and brought up fresh planes for an attack on the American naval vessels. By that time it was too late, for the United States carrier planes were on him.

The *Enterprise-Hornet* planes had broken into four groups, while the *Yorktown*'s made a fifth, so that whatever coordination was achieved in the ensuing attack was entirely accidental. The *Enterprise* fighters, which were supposed to protect their carrier's tor-

pedo squadron, had by mistake joined the *Hornet*'s instead. Climbing to 20,000 feet en route, these fighters were above the Japanese force when both the *Hornet* and the *Enterprise* torpedo planes made their ill-starred attacks; but, not receiving the pre-arranged signal for help, they circled until their fuel ran low, then returned to the carrier without having engaged in the battle.

Because of the scout's error in reporting the Japanese position, aggravated by Nagumo's change of course to the north, the Mobile Force was not where the American pilots expected to find it. The *Hornet*'s dive bombers, flying at high altitude, failed to sight the Japanese and continued on to the southwest. However, "Torpedo 8," beneath the clouds, sighted the enemy carriers to the northwest at 0920 and immediately began its approach. Japanese fighters, which had been brought down to lower levels to counter the attacks by Midway planes, met them well out, and the veteran Japanese pilots easily overwhelmed the slow and clumsy torpedo planes. All 15 were shot down before they were able to drop their torpedoes. Only one pilot survived. He escaped strafing or capture by hiding under a floating seat cushion till dark. The *Hornet*'s dive bombers continued to the southwest until their fuel ran low. Then 21 returned to the carrier, while the remaining 14 headed for Midway, where three crashed. All the accompanying fighters, which had shorter ranges, landed in the sea when their fuel was exhausted.

The *Enterprise* torpedo squadron arrived ten or 15 minutes after the *Hornet*'s. Like Torpedo 8, it was without fighter protection, and it fared little better. The squadron split in an attempt to make an attack on both bows of the Japanese carriers, but the enemy turned to keep the planes on their quarter and to prolong their approach. Zekes swarmed over them and shot down ten of the 14. Again there were no hits. But the sacrifice of the torpedo squadrons was not in vain, for their attacks drew the Zekes down to low altitudes, and in their preoccupation with the torpedo planes the Japanese forgot to look up.

The *Enterprise* dive bombers, like the *Hornet*'s failed to find the enemy in the position expected, but Lieutenant Commander Clarence McClusky, Jr., the Air Group Commander, making "one of the most important decisions of the battle," turned north to fly the first leg of an expanding square. A little after 1000, setting his course by a straggling Japanese destroyer, he was rewarded by a view of the Mobile Force. The four carriers were in a sort of diamond formation with the *Hiryu* somewhat off to the north. (See following diagram.) McClusky divided his attack between the two carriers in the southwest portion of the formation, which happened to be the *Akagi* and *Kaga*. Just as Spruance had hoped, their decks were covered with planes

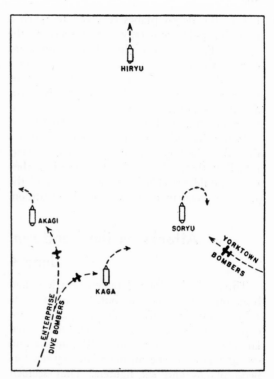

DISPOSITION OF JAPANESE CARRIERS AT TIME OF BOMBING ATTACK BY ENTERPRISE AND YORKTOWN PLANES, 1020, JUNE 4

which they had been refueling and which they were now endeavoring to launch. Into the midst of these the American pilots dropped their bombs. There was no fighter opposition until after they pulled out of their dives. By that time both carriers were burning. Off to the east the *Soryu* was also on fire, for the *Yorktown* planes had made a simultaneous attack.

The *Yorktown* air group had been launched more than an hour later than those of the *Enterprise* and *Hornet*, but rapidly clearing weather aided it both in joining up en route and in finding the enemy. Consequently its attack, without either group's being aware of it, coincided with that of the *Enterprise* dive bombers. Coming in from the east, the *Yorktown* planes concentrated on the nearest carrier, which was the *Soryu*. The torpedo squadron was slightly ahead. Despite the efforts of the six accompanying fighters, only five of the dozen planes survived to reach a dropping point, and only two returned to the carrier. They scored no hits. But the bombers, diving in from the sun, encountered no fighter and little antiaircraft opposition. By the time the first 13 had completed their dives the *Soryu* was so completely aflame that the four remaining planes turned to other targets.

It was indeed fortunate for the Americans that they had caught the Japanese carriers refueling their planes, for the few hits they made would scarcely have been fatal had the Japanese been in a less vulnerable condition.

Attacks on the *Yorktown*, June 4

Three of the four Japanese carriers had been put out of action, but the fourth, the *Hiryu*, standing off to the north, had escaped unscathed. A little after 1000 she started launching an attack group of 18 bombers and six fighters, followed an hour later by ten torpedo planes and six fighters. That seemed adequate to take care of the one American carrier which had thus far been reported to the Japanese command. In the meantime Nagumo had with difficulty been persuaded to transfer from the flaming *Akagi* to a cruiser, while Kondo was bringing his powerful Second Fleet Group from the transports, which did not seem to be threatened, to reinforce the screen of the Mobile Force.

The *Yorktown* had just completed launching her search planes and was refueling fighters of her combat air patrol and preparing to recover her striking group when about noon her radar picked up the *Hiryu*'s planes at a distance of less than 50 miles. Refueling was hastily abandoned, planes on the flight deck were quickly launched with orders to clear the area, and returning bombers were waved away. The carrier's screen was in the standard circular disposition with a cruiser on either bow as the attack came in.

The combat air patrols of the *Enterprise* and *Hornet* had joined that of the *Yorktown* to make a total of 28 fighters. So effective was their interception that the Japanese attackers were split into small groups, and only about eight bombers succeeded in reaching the *Yorktown*. These scored three hits. One holed the flight deck, while another exploded on the fourth deck and forced flooding of the magazines in the vicinity. A third hit ruptured the uptakes, disabled two boilers, and extinguished the fires in all but one.

Repairs did not take long. Fires were quickly brought under control, the hole in the flight deck was covered, and boilers were relighted. The carrier was steaming at 20 knots and again refueling fighters when at about 1430 her radar picked up the *Hiryu*'s torpedo group only 40 miles away. Again refueling was suspended and the combat air patrol vectored out, but the *Yorktown* was still launching fighters when the attack developed.

The American fighters shot down a few of the Japanese before they came within range of the ships' guns. The *Yorktown*'s screen, which after the first attack had been reinforced by two cruisers and two destroyers from Spruance's force, threw up a formidable barrage, but a few planes succeeded in penetrating it. The carrier avoided two torpedoes by maneuvering, but two more caught her amidships on the port side. Three fire rooms were flooded, and white smoke issued from her stacks as she slowed to a stop with a heavy list to port.

There was no power for shifting fuel or for counter-flooding, and as the list increased to 26 degrees there seemed to be imminent danger of the ship's capsizing. So at 1500 her captain ordered Abandon Ship, and destroyers took off the crew. That evening the screening vessels departed, leaving only the destroyer *Hughes* standing by to sink the carrier, if necessary to prevent her capture.

Elimination of the *Hiryu*

Just as the attack on the *Yorktown* was drawing to a close, one of her scouts launched three hours earlier reported the *Hiryu* force approximately a hundred miles WNW. Spruance thereupon ordered a strike, and the *En-*

terprise at once began launching an attack group of 24 bombers of which ten were *Yorktown* refugees, while the *Hornet* launched 16. Both groups departed about 1600. There was no fighter escort, because Spruance felt that all fighters were needed for protection of the carriers.

The *Enterprise* group sighted the *Hiryu* at 1700. Off to the south three columns of smoke marked the other three Japanese carriers. There were a few Zekes in the air, and they shot down three of the bombers, but the others succeeded in planting four hits on the carrier. By the time the *Hornet* planes arrived half an hour later, the *Hiryu* was burning so fiercely that she was no longer a profitable target; so they attacked the escorting vessels instead.

Spruance meanwhile had reported the attack on the *Hiryu* to Fletcher, who had transferred from the *Yorktown* to heavy cruiser *Astoria*. He added: "Have you any instructions for further operations?" "Negative," replied Fletcher. "Will conform to your movements." He thus transferred the tactical command of both forces to Spruance. This was a wise decision, for carrier operations can best be controlled from a carrier, where the admiral can immediately question his returning aviators. Spruance, with an experienced staff and with his flagship *Enterprise* undamaged, was fully prepared to take control.

On the bridge of the Japanese flagship *Yamato* news of the disabling of the *Akagi*, *Kaga*, and *Soryu* had caused consternation, but Yamamoto saw no reason to abandon his plans, for he believed that the attack had been made at least in part by land-based planes. He still supposed that there was only one American carrier present, and the *Hiryu* was dealing with that. Consequently he decided to proceed with the occupation of Midway with only a few changes in the disposition of his fleet. Kondo's Second Fleet, which was already on the way, would reinforce the Mobile Force. Midway transports were to retire to the northwest till the situation became clearer. The Aleutian Support Group was to rejoin the Main Body.

It was not till 1300 that Yamamoto learned that the American force contained three carriers. He had just received a report that the *Hiryu*'s planes had left one of these burning, but that still left two against the single *Hiryu*. It was on the receipt of this news that Yamamoto temporarily canceled both the Midway and Aleutian landings and recalled Kakuta's Second Mobile Force from Alaskan waters. With his forces united he would have three fleet carriers to deal with the two remaining American carriers.

The *Hiryu* was meanwhile preparing to get off an evening strike with all her remaining planes—five bombers, five torpedo planes, and ten fighters. She had turned into the wind and was just commencing to launch when the *Enterprise* bombers attacked at 1701. Half an hour later Yamamoto learned that his fourth carrier was burning.

By this time there was little hope of saving any of the other three. The American submarine *Nautilus*, which had doggedly trailed the Mobile Force most of the day, at about 1030 sighted on the horizon three columns of smoke from the burning carriers. In the early afternoon she closed the *Kaga* and fired three torpedoes. Two missed and the third was a dud. But the *Kaga* was doomed nevertheless; she went down at 1925 as a result of internal explosions. The *Soryu* sank about the same time. The *Akagi* and *Hiryu* remained afloat till next morning, when Japanese destroyers sank the burning hulks with torpedoes.

Midway, Night of June 4

The *Yorktown* had been abandoned, and all the American air groups had suffered severely. The torpedo squadrons had been wiped out, and losses of both bombers and fighters had been heavy. Yet there were no enemy planes left to dispute the control of the air, and with it the control of the sea, now exercised by the weary aviators of the *Enterprise* and *Hornet*. The action of June 4 had decided the Battle of Midway. But this was not immediately evident to most of the principals of the action, and indeed, had Spruance shown a little less judgment the battle might yet have moved on to a new climax and to another dramatic reversal of fortune.

On Midway itself the defenders awaited developments with considerable apprehension through the afternoon and evening of the 4th. They had received no clear reports of the success of the American carriers and knew only that the Midway planes had been so badly shot up that it was doubtful that they had inflicted any significant damage. Through the afternoon B-17's were dispatched, in small groups as they became available, to attack elements of the Mobile Force, but they scored no hits. On the report of a burning carrier 200 miles to the northwest, the eleven surviving marine dive bombers took off about 1900. They encountered rain squalls and failed to find the target. Eleven PT boats that left about the same time on a similar mission had the same experience. Meanwhile refueling of planes by hand and preparations for repelling a landing continued through the night. When a Japanese submarine shelled Midway about 0130 it looked as if zero hour might be drawing close.

Yamamoto Tries to Retrieve the Battle

Aboard the Japanese flagship Yamamoto clung doggedly to his plans of conquest. At 1915 he sent a message to his commanders: "1. The enemy fleet, which has practically been destroyed, is retiring to the east. 2. Combined Fleet units in the vicinity are preparing to pursue the remnants and at the same time occupy Midway. . . . The Mobile Force, Second Fleet, and Submarine Force will immediately contact and attack the enemy." Yamamoto may have been confused as to the real situation, or he may have been whistling in the dark to sustain Japanese courage, but it was evident that he was determined to carry on the fight. An hour later he ordered the submarine *I-168* to shell Midway till 0200, when it would be relieved by a cruiser division from the Occupation Force.

Nagumo did not share his chief's offensive frame of mind. While things had been going well he had shown high competence, but since the bombing of his flagship he had revealed signs of shock and failing judgment. Now at 2130 he reported to Yamamoto: "The total strength of the enemy is 5 carriers, 6 cruisers, and 15 destroyers. These are steaming westward. . . . We are offering protection to the *Hiryu* and are retiring to the northwest at 18 knots. . . ." Obviously Nagumo intended to continue his retreat. After a second communication in the same vein Yamamoto replied with the order: "Commander in Chief Second Fleet Kondo will take command of the Mobile Force excepting the *Hiryu, Akagi,* and the ships escorting them." Kondo, who had shown both good judgment and initiative in the crisis, was even then well on his way toward joining the remnant of the Mobile Force. He at once sent out orders for concentrating his force for a night surface action. For this he would have 4 battleships, 9 cruisers, and 19 destroyers.

But this engagement, by which Yamamoto might yet have restored his situation, was not destined to take place. Spruance, now in tactical command of the American naval forces, had decided to set course to the east for the night. As he subsequently explained, "I did not feel justified in risking a night encounter with possibly superior enemy forces, but on the other hand, I did not want to be too far away from Midway in the morning. I wished to have a position from which either to follow up retreating enemy forces or to break up a landing attack on Midway. At this time the possibility of the enemy having a fifth CV somewhere in the area, possibly with his occupation force or else to the northwestward, still existed."[4]

By midnight Yamamoto had to face the facts. There were at least two American carriers still operational. They were retiring to the east, so that there was very little likelihood of their being forced into a surface action. Rather, his own vessels, if they persisted on their present courses, would almost certainly be caught by air strikes at dawn. Consequently

[4] Admiral Spruance's report on the Battle of Midway.

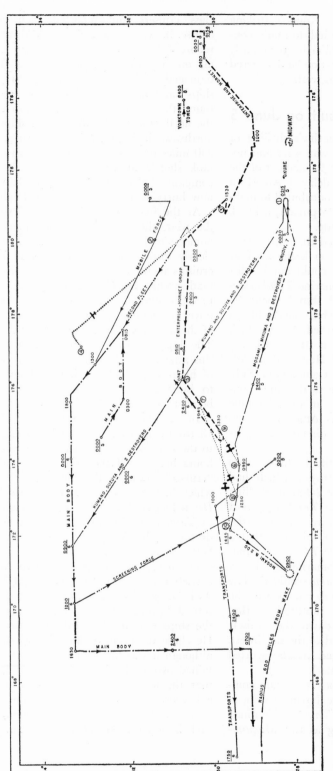

BATTLE OF MIDWAY, JUNE 5-6

JUNE 5

1. 0215: *Tambor* sights Crudiv. 7; *Mogami* and *Mikuma* collide.
2. 0719: Midway patrol planes report burning carrier (*Hiryu*), two
   battleships, cruisers and destroyers in this position.
3. 1500-1530: *Enterprise* and *Hornet* launch search-attack groups.
4. 1830: *Enterprise-Hornet* groups attack destroyer *Tanikaze*.

JUNE 6

5. 0757: *Hornet* launches attack group.
6. 0950: *Hornet* group attacks *Mogami*, *Mikuma*, and two destroyers.
7. 1045: *Enterprise* launches attack group.
8. 1250: *Enterprise* group attacks.
9. 1330: *Hornet* launches attack group.
10. 1445: *Hornet* group attacks.

at 0015 Yamamoto ordered Kondo's striking force, which had not yet united, to rendezvous with the Main Body. At 0255 he reluctantly canceled the Midway operation and ordered a general withdrawal to the west.

Pursuit on June 5

So it was that the submarine's shelling of Midway was the Japanese swan song and not the prelude to invasion. But an incident of the early morning of June 5 delayed American recognition of the fact and contributed to making the 5th a day of fruitless pursuit, a blank day in the midst of the battle.

Spruance had not believed that the enemy would attempt a landing after losing his four carriers, but the possibility could not be disregarded. At 0215 the submarine *Tambor* reported "many unidentified ships" about 90 miles west of Midway. "This looked like a landing," as Spruance reported, "so we took a course somewhat to the north of Midway at 25 knots." Back at Pearl Harbor Rear Admiral Robert H. English, Commander Submarines Pacific Fleet, came to the same conclusion and pulled his boats in to a five-mile radius from Midway. Thus American forces were moving in the wrong direction for pursuit.

The *Tambor*'s "unidentified ships" were four cruisers and two destroyers which had been ordered to relieve the *I-168* in shelling Midway. Not long after the *Tambor*'s report they received Yamamoto's retirement order and put about. It was after this turn that a Japanese lookout sighted the *Tambor*. In maneuvering to avoid the submarine the heavy cruisers *Mogami* and *Mikuma* collided. The *Mogami*'s bow was damaged, and one of the *Mikuma*'s fuel tanks was ruptured so that she streamed oil. Before dawn the cruisers *Kumano* and *Suzuya* retired to the northwest, leaving the slower, damaged vessels escorted by two destroyers on a westerly course.

Not till dawn could the American commanders be certain that the Japanese were in retreat. About 0600 the *Tambor* identified the vessels she was trailing as two *Mogami*-class cruisers and reported their westerly course. Between 0630 and 0800 Midway planes reported the few Japanese vessels within range, all on retirement courses. Besides the two damaged cruisers, mis-identified as "battleships" and now 125 miles to the west, they found the *Kumano* and *Suzuya* 175 miles to the northwest, and finally several ships to the northwest, including a burning carrier about 250 miles distant. This was the *Hiryu*, which sank shortly afterward, momentarily in the company of elements of Kondo's striking force, now hurrying to join Yamamoto to the west.

At the first report of the "battleships" to the west, the twelve remaining marine dive bombers took off from Midway. Following the clearly visible oil slick, they found the two cruisers about 0800 and attacked at once. They made no hits, but Captain Richard E. Fleming USMC, commanding one of the two sections, dove his flaming plane into the after turret of the *Mikuma*, causing considerable damage. The Japanese were so engrossed in repelling this attack that they failed to notice a group of high-flying B-17's until their bombs began to burst around the vessels. Even so, the bombers scored no hits.

In the early afternoon twelve B-17's took off from Midway to attack the burning carrier to the northwest. It had of course gone down hours before. All the bombers found was a "cruiser"—actually the destroyer *Tanikaze*, which had been sent to ascertain whether the *Hiryu* had sunk and was now scurrying back to Yamamoto. In two attacks the Fortresses dropped eighty 500-pound bombs with nothing better than a few near misses.

Dawn of the 5th found the two American carriers about 130 miles northeast of Midway. As it became clear that the Japanese were in retreat, Spruance had to select his targets from the ships reported by Midway patrol planes. He chose the group to the northwest, which, although it was farther away, reportedly contained two battleships and a carrier. Knowing that the attack would have to be made at extreme range, Spruance ordered the bombers armed with only a single 500-pound bomb each in order to enable them to carry maximum fuel, and held the strike till about 1500 in order to close the distance as much as possible. Delaying the launching till that hour meant that the planes could not return before dark and that the carriers would have to illuminate to receive them, but Spruance, believing that he was in pursuit of the fourth Japanese carrier, accepted the risk.

All that the carrier planes found was the little *Tanikaze*, which they attacked with no more success than had the army B-17's. When they returned, the *Enterprise* turned on both deck and search lights, and the *Hornet* followed suit. Although there was a possibility that an enemy submarine might be lurking in the area, Spruance was considerably more concerned about the recovery of his pilots, most of whom had never before landed on a carrier at night. All came in safely, however, except for one plane, the crew of which was rescued by a destroyer.

Spruance had ascertained that there were no Japanese forces for more than 250 miles ahead, and the carriers were approaching the bad weather area, into which it was futile to follow. Consequently he altered course to the west for the night and slowed to 15 knots to save fuel for his destroyers and to avoid overtaking any enemy battleships in the dark.

Last Contacts, June 6

June 6 dawned clear with a smooth sea and good visibility. *Enterprise* planes flying a dawn search to the west soon discovered the *Mogami* and *Mikuma* approximately 130 miles southwest of the American force. A southwest breeze facilitated launching and recovery as the carriers moved toward the contact.

In three successive attacks American planes made repeated hits on the two cruisers and put one bomb on the stern of each of the two accompanying destroyers. By the time of the third strike the carriers had closed to 90 miles, so that pilots could see both forces simultaneously. Despite a terrific battering the *Mogami* was able to stagger off to Truk, but she was out of the war for more than a year. The *Mikuma* went down a few hours after the

last attack, taking a thousand men with her.

On the evening of the 6th Spruance abandoned the pursuit. He had detached destroyers as their fuel ran low, so that he now had only four left. That was too few for safety in waters in which Japanese submarines had been reported. His aviators were exhausted from three days of continuous operations. Finally, it seemed unwise to come within air range of Wake, where he believed the Japanese had concentrated planes to be transferred to Midway. Consequently he turned back to the northeast toward a rendezvous for the first refueling of his force since May 31.

Again Spruance's caution was the highest wisdom, for Yamamoto, fleeing to the west with his scattered forces, had not yet given up hope of salvaging something from the operation. The attacks on the *Tanikaze* on the 5th and on the *Mogami* and *Mikuma* on the 6th told him he was being pursued and gave him some indication of the movements of the American force. At about noon on the 6th he dispatched a force of seven cruisers and eight destroyers to the south with the dual object of protecting the *Mogami* and *Mikuma* and of destroying the American carrier force. The commander of this "Screening Force" made preparations for an engagement during the night of the 6th, and the chart shows that he would probably have had it if Spruance had continued west. Meanwhile Yamamoto's Main Body was also moving south to join in the engagement, and planes were coming north from the Marshalls to reinforce Wake's striking power. Everyone was there except the victim.

End of the *Yorktown*, June 7

After the abandonment of the *Yorktown* on the afternoon of June 4, her screening vessels withdrew, leaving only the *Hughes* to stand guard over the carrier, which was then stable with a list of about 24 degrees. On the morning of the 5th the firing of a machine gun from the port side of the *Yorktown* caught the attention of a lookout on the *Hughes*. An investigating party rescued two wounded men and discovered three secret coding devices that had been overlooked in the hasty abandonment of the vessel. But no one that morning noticed somewhere in the distance a Japanese cruiser-type plane, one of two that the fleeing Nagumo had that morning sent out for a search to the east. It reported the position of the abandoned carrier.

About noon the minesweeper *Vireo* arrived from Pearl and Hermes Reef, where she had been on patrol when Nimitz ordered her to go to the assistance of the *Yorktown*. She soon had the carrier under tow toward Pearl Harbor at about three knots, but that was more than the little vessel could maintain, and by morning of the 6th she was scarcely making steerageway. In the meantime five more destroyers had joined, and at daylight on the 6th the *Hammann* went alongside the carrier to put aboard a salvage party of *Yorktown* officers and men.

During the day the party made considerable progress. They reduced the list by two degrees and were lowering the water level in some of the flooded compartments. The *Hammann* was secured forward along the *Yorktown*'s starboard side to supply foamite for fighting fires and power for the pumps. The other destroyers were circling the carrier as a precaution against submarines.

At 1335 the wakes of four torpedoes were sighted to starboard. These had been fired by the *I-168,* which after shelling Midway on the early morning of the 5th had received orders to go after the carrier reported by Nagumo's plane. After searching for a day and a half she had just found the *Yorktown*. There was no time for the *Hammann* to pull clear. One torpedo broke her back, while the other two passed under her to explode against the carrier. The *Hammann* went down at once, and underwater explosions killed many of her crew in the water. Some of the destroyers picked up survivors while others went after the submarine. They succeeded only in damaging the boat, which later limped back to Kure for repairs.

The *Yorktown* remained afloat for some time, riding low in the water but with her list

partially corrected. In the early morning of June 7 she rolled over to port and went down.

Summary

The Japanese in early June 1942 set out to seize Midway and points in the western Aleutians as observation posts, and to lure out the U.S. Pacific Fleet for destruction. Admiral Nimitz, informed of Japanese intentions through cryptanalysis, sent his three available carriers, *Yorktown, Enterprise,* and *Hornet,* and their escorts to operate under the command of Admiral Fletcher in the waters northeast of Midway. To the Aleutians he sent only submarines and a cruiser-destroyer force. As a result, the Japanese were able to damage the American naval base at Dutch Harbor with two carrier air attacks and to occupy the Aleutian islands of Attu and Kiska, but at Midway they met disaster.

The Japanese naval forces approaching Midway under command of Admiral Yamamoto were in three widely separated groups: the Mobile Force of four carriers without adequate antiaircraft escort, coming down from the northwest; the Main Body of surface vessels without adequate air cover, coming in from the west; and the Occupation Force, coming up from the southwest. The Japanese counted on taking Midway by surprise and thereafter having plenty of time to redeploy their forces for a fleet engagement. They expected submarines patrolling between Pearl Harbor and Midway to give early warning of the approach of the American naval forces. When the submarines reached position on June 1 however, the American carriers had already crossed their patrol line.

PBY's from Midway sighted the approaching Occupation Force on June 3. That night torpedo-rigged PBY's from Midway damaged an oiler in the same group. Other PBY's early on the 4th sighted both the Mobile Force and numerous planes heading for Midway. These planes bombed Midway installations and either shot down or damaged most of Midway's defending fighter aircraft. Bombers and torpedo planes from Midway attacked the Mobile Force without success and took heavy losses. Torpedo planes from the American carriers also attacked the Japanese carriers with equal lack of success and even heavier losses, those from the *Hornet* being entirely wiped out.

The turning point in the Battle of Midway, and in the whole Pacific war, was brought about by dive bombers from the *Enterprise* and the *Yorktown,* which quite by accident attacked the Japanese carriers simultaneously from different directions. At that time the Japanese Zeke fighters could offer little resistance because they had been drawn down close to the surface by the torpedo attacks. Moreover, partly by chance and partly through calculation, the American bombers arrived just as the enemy carriers were rearming and refueling aircraft that had just returned from the Midway strike. As a result, the American bombers were able to set carriers *Akagi, Kaga,* and *Soryu* fatally ablaze.

Carrier *Hiryu,* escaping to the north, now launched an attack which so damaged the *Yorktown* that in mid-afternoon she was abandoned by her crew. Admiral Fletcher, having lost his flagship, now transferred tactical command of the American forces to Admiral Spruance, who had already launched an air attack that sank the *Hiryu.*

Yamamoto, seeking to retrieve the battle, ordered Kondo's Second Fleet to detach itself from the Occupation Force, collect the remains of the Mobile Force, and seek a night engagement with the American fleet. He also sent in a cruiser-destroyer force to shell Midway. Kondo was foiled by Spruance, who turned east for the night. At 0255 on June 5, Yamamoto canceled the Midway operation, whereupon the cruiser-destroyer force going against Midway reversed course. In maneuvering to avoid an American submarine, two of the cruisers, *Mogami* and *Mikuma,* collided, receiving damages that slowed them down.

Spruance turned back west before dawn. Through June 5 he pursued the retreating Japanese without overtaking them. On the 6th his planes sighted and attacked the *Mogami* and the *Mikuma,* heavily damaging the former and sinking the latter. That evening Spruance abandoned the pursuit—wisely, as it turned out, for Yamamoto was again gathering forces to entrap him.

Meanwhile, it appeared that the damaged *Yorktown* might be saved. When she refused to sink, a salvage party was put aboard her and she was taken in tow. But a Japanese plane had sighted her and broadcast her position. A Japanese submarine approached the injured carrier on the 6th and fired a spread of torpedoes that further damaged her and sank a destroyer alongside. Early on the 7th, the *Yorktown* herself rolled over and sank.

Midway was essentially a victory of intelligence. In attempting surprise, the Japanese were themselves surprised. But in addition they made serious errors which the American command skillfully exploited while making few of its own. Like the Coral Sea, the battle was entirely a contest of air power. The Japanese were never given an opportunity to employ their immense superiority in surface ships.

The American performance, while not without faults, showed a more professional touch than at the Coral Sea. Better tracking by scouts and more rapid communications would have paid handsome dividends. The pursuit phase of the battle could have been immensely more profitable had there been an earlier realization that the Japanese were in retreat. Prompter and more determined damage control might have saved the *Yorktown.* The poor performance of American torpedoes and the inferiority of American planes were again demonstrated.

For the Japanese it was the first major defeat since that at the hands of the Korean Yi Sun Sin at the end of the 16th century. Against the *Yorktown* and *Hammann* they had to list four carriers and a heavy cruiser sunk. The United States lost 150 planes, but the Japanese carriers took down with them their entire complement, bringing Japanese aircraft losses to 322. While 307 Americans died in the battle, 3,500 of the Emperor's subjects, including a hundred first-line pilots, lost their lives. This loss of experienced pilots was not the least important consequence of the battle, for it began a process of attrition that was eventually to prove fatal to Japan.

The battle marks a turning point in the war. It removed the margin of superiority that had enabled the Japanese to take the offensive at will. For the United States it ended the purely defensive phase of the war and introduced a period in which American arms could take some initiative.

The Japanese concealed their defeat not only from their public but even from officials in responsible positions. They deleted mention of it from war diaries and reports, but they could not undo its effects.

37:

Guadalcanal

The Battle of Midway jarred the Japanese out of their faith in their own invincibility. A week after the battle, Imperial General Headquarters canceled the bold plan for the invasion of New Caledonia, Fiji, and Samoa, originally scheduled for July 1942. The immediate and imperative task was strengthening the defense perimeter.

To the Bismarcks came Vice Admiral Gunichi Mikawa with a force of cruisers and destroyers. More planes and equipment arrived to buttress airdromes in New Guinea, the Bismarcks, and the Upper Solomons. Yet there still remained the Allied base at Port Moresby. The Imperial Navy had signally failed to eliminate that threat. Now the army would have a try, striking from the north coast of Papua across the Owen Stanley Mountains. To cover the flank of this operation, work was begun on a bomber strip on Guadalcanal, 20 miles south of the Japanese seaplane base already operating at Tulagi.

To the Allies the results of Midway spelled opportunity. Now that the enemy was off balance, his preponderance of strength cut down, the time had come to seize the initiative and block his expansion by an offensive-defensive move.[1] Where to strike depended upon probable future enemy thrusts. As early as February 1942, Admiral King had pointed out the growing Japanese base at Rabaul as a likely springboard for the next enemy advance. To counter any move from this quarter and also to provide a jumping off place for an Allied drive through the Solomons and the Bismarcks, he ordered a base constructed

[1] *Tactically* offensive because the move would require seizing points not already held; *strategically* defensive because the immediate purpose was to thwart an enemy effort.

on Efate in the New Hebrides. He then set up a separate command in the South Pacific, subordinate to Admiral Nimitz' Pacific Ocean Areas, and appointed Vice Admiral Robert L. Ghormley Commander South Pacific Force and Area. Ghormley established headquarters at Aukland, New Zealand and promptly began work on a second New Hebrides base on Espiritu Santo. (See map page 690.)

The Navy's plan called for a carrier-supported initial landing in the southeast Solomons by the amphibiously trained 1st Marine Division. Here the Americans would construct airfields to provide land-based air cover for capture of islands farther up the chain. On these islands they would build additional airdromes to advance their bomber line still closer to the main target. Thus in a series of steps, each new landing covered by land-based air, they would at length bring Rabaul itself under intensive air attack. Each step would have to be less than 300 miles, the extreme operational radius of American fighter planes in 1942, because fighters would be needed over the target to protect both the bombers and the expeditionary force from enemy aircraft.

After Midway, both Admiral Nimitz and General MacArthur were of the opinion that the counteroffensive should be launched as quickly as possible, but there were difficulties. Nimitz, as Commander in Chief Pacific Fleet and Pacific Ocean Areas, controlled the marines, the transports to carry them to the beachhead, and the carriers and gunnery vessels needed to support them. The Solomons however were all within General MacArthur's Southwest Pacific Area. Accordingly, Nimitz and MacArthur each, with some reason, insisted that the entire campaign should be under his command. The latter moreover had his

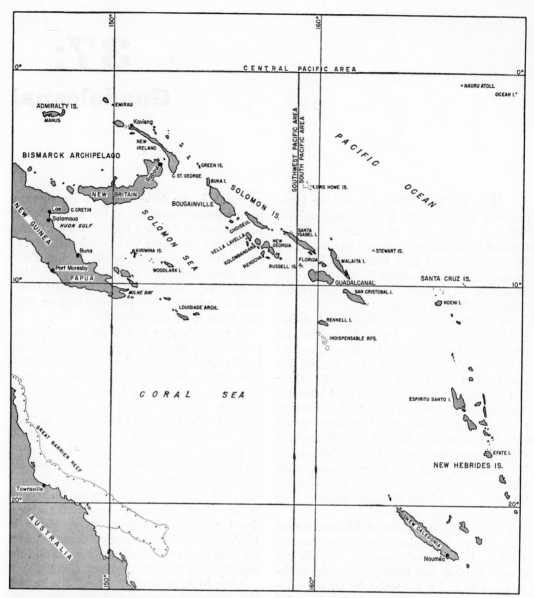

SCENE OF EARLY OPERATIONS IN THE SOUTH AND SOUTHWEST PACIFIC THEATERS

own idea about how to attain the objective. Give him the fleet and its carriers and the 1st Marine Division, said MacArthur, and he would go in and recapture Rabaul in a single uninterrupted operation.

There is much to be said for MacArthur's bold strategy. Rabaul was growing steadily more formidable. With each month of delay it would be harder to capture. Once it was in Allied hands, the Japanese in the Solomons and on Papua would be hopelessly cut off, the threat to Australia and United States-Australia sea communications would be entirely removed, and the way would be open for an Allied advance on the Philippines. But the Navy was unalterably opposed to sending scarce carriers and its single division of amphibious troops across the reef-strewn, virtually uncharted Solomon Sea into the teeth of a complex of enemy air bases. Later on, with more carriers and more amphibious troops at their disposal—and more experience in using them—naval strategists could afford to be more daring. They would in fact stage amphibious assaults on the most strongly defended enemy positions using air support from carriers only. But in the present circumstances they favored the step-by-step approach as the more likely to achieve success and avoid disaster. They insisted moreover that Pacific Fleet forces should remain under naval control.

Here was an impasse that could be settled only in Washington, for Nimitz and MacArthur was each supreme in his own area. Here also was another of the many difficulties resulting from divided command within a single theater. Should the entire Pacific have been put under a single officer? There were convincing arguments for such a move. There were equally strong arguments that with a military front extending from the Aleutians to Australia, the strategic problems of the various areas were on too large a scale for one officer to grasp. Proponents of the latter view decried uncritical adherence to unified command. These advocated unified command only within a geographic entity that gives coherence to operations. Their opinion prevailed, and for better or worse MacArthur's Southwest Pacific Area and Nimitz' Pacific Ocean Areas remained separate and independent commands, responsible only to the Joint Chiefs of Staff.

It was within the Joint Chiefs that the differences were resolved. In a series of conferences, General Marshall and Admiral King reached agreement and on July 2, 1942 issued a directive that substantially followed the Navy's proposals. The opening operations, seizure and occupation of the Santa Cruz Islands, Tulagi, and adjacent positions, would be under the strategic control of Admiral Nimitz. To facilitate command problems in this first step, the boundary between the South Pacific and the Southwest Pacific Areas was shifted westward to 159° East Longitude, just west of Guadalcanal. As soon as a suitable base had been secured in the Tulagi area, the strategic command would pass to General MacArthur, who would coordinate a move up the Solomons with a second thrust—up the Papuan Peninsula to Salamaua and Lae. The two Allied advances would then converge on Rabaul. Target date for the initial invasions, called Operation WATCHTOWER, was set for August 1.

Planning "Operation Shoestring"

Admiral Nimitz, anticipating the Joint Chiefs' directive, had almost completed basic planning for Operation WATCHTOWER by the first week in July. Vice Admiral Ghormley, as Nimitz' deputy in the South Pacific Area, would exercise strategic control, with Vice Admiral Frank Jack Fletcher, of Coral Sea and Midway fame, in tactical command of the Expeditionary Force. From King's staff, where he had headed the War Plans Division, came Rear Admiral Richmond Kelly Turner to command the Amphibious Force. The 1st Marine Division, which would make the assault, was to be commanded by Major General Alexander A. Vandegrift, who had learned the business of fighting in the jungles of Nicaragua and the theory of amphibious warfare on the staff of the Fleet Marine Force.

A month was of course an uncomfortably brief period in which to assemble forces, work out details, and complete training and rehearsals for so complex an operation as an amphibious assault. Moreover, adequate reinforcements and proper air and surface support were hard to come by. The invasion of North Africa, planned for November, had top priority for everything. MacArthur's three divisions, assigned to the protection of Australia, could not be touched. South Pacific bases would have to be stripped of part of their defense forces to provide garrison troops to follow up the marines. Little wonder the somewhat baffled participants in Operation WATCHTOWER soon began calling it "Operation Shoestring."

While Fletcher and Turner were conferring with Nimitz at Pearl Harbor, there came the startling news that an American patrol plane had sighted an airstrip under construction on Guadalcanal. This information put a more urgent complexion on the WATCHTOWER project. Obviously Guadalcanal would have to be included in the Tulagi-Santa Cruz plan, but King and Nimitz would allow no more than one additional week to prepare for the expanded operation. D-day was set definitely for August 7. The airfield had to be captured before the Japanese could complete it. Whoever first put it into operation might well be the victor.

In the latter part of July the situation took

another turn when a Japanese convoy landed 1,800 troops near Buna, on the Papuan Peninsula directly opposite Port Moresby. This invasion was a source of grave concern to MacArthur, particularly as the Southwest Pacific Forces had been on the point of occupying the Buna area themselves. But in the South Pacific the news was received with a certain measure of relief. Japanese attention was focused on the old target of Port Moresby, not upon the end of the Solomons chain. Rabaul was looking southwest instead of southeast. Surprise was possible.

The Allied Invasion

Steaming from points as widely separated as Wellington, Sydney, Noumea, San Diego, and Pearl Harbor, the various components of the WATCHTOWER Expeditionary Force, some 80 vessels in all, met at sea on July 26 south of the Fijis. Here Admiral Fletcher held council aboard his flagship, carrier *Saratoga*. Admiral Ghormley, then shifting his headquarters to Noumea, could not be present. He neither saw the fleet over which he exercised a distant control nor met all his top commanders to discuss operation plans. After a less than satisfactory landing rehearsal in the Fijis, the fleet steamed westward. In the Coral Sea it shaped course due north and headed for Guadalcanal through rain squalls that grounded all aircraft, including Japanese search patrols.

Guadalcanal, part of the drowned volcanic mountain range forming the Solomons, rises steeply in the south from a narrow coastal flat. Only on the north side of the island are there plains broad enough to provide level ground for airfields. Here on Lunga Plain, mostly rain forest traversed by numerous creeks and small rivers and broken here and there by coconut plantations and grassy fields, the Japanese had landed and begun their airdrome. This was the main Allied objective. The secondary objective was the Japanese seaplane base in the Tulagi area, 20 miles to the north.

Under a clearing sky in the early hours of August 7, the *Saratoga*, *Enterprise*, and *Wasp* carrier groups moved into position south of Guadalcanal while Turner's Amphibious Force slipped up the west coast, split into two groups around little Savo Island, and entered Ironbottom Sound.[2] The surprise of the Japanese was complete. After a brief naval bombardment and a strike by carrier aircraft, Higgins boats, LCM's, and LCPR's headed for the beach. Here they met no opposition.

By nightfall 10,000 marines were on Guadalcanal, and the beach was cluttered with supplies. One combat team had advanced west along the shoreline, while a second was penetrating the jungle in a southwesterly direction. Most of the 2,000 or so Japanese on the island, chiefly construction workers, had fled westward during the bombardment, but a few determined warriors had remained behind to snipe and to man machine guns. These the marines encountered and destroyed on the second day of their advance. In mid-afternoon of the 8th, one marine team had entered the main Japanese base, taking possession of machine shops, electric power plants, and considerable stores of provisions, firearms, and ammunition. A little later the other team occupied the airstrip, the future Henderson Field.[3]

On the north side of Ironbottom Sound, operations did not proceed so smoothly. Here the objectives were three small islands lying inside a bight of the larger Florida Island: Tulagi, a two-mile-long ridge rising abruptly from the Sound, and Tanambogo-Gavutu, a pair of islets joined by a narrow causeway. In this area, despite naval bombardment and bombing and strafing by carrier aircraft, which quickly knocked out all the enemy seaplanes, the marines ran into trouble.

On Tulagi, by picking an unlikely beachhead, the invaders got ashore easily enough. It was only when they reached high ground that they found an enemy so well dug in that they had to dislodge him with machine guns, mortars, and grenades. Gavutu had to be taken by amphibious assault in the face of heavy small-arms fire, for this island, rising sheer out of a broad coral shelf, could be invaded only by way of the seaplane ramp. An attempt to take Tanambogo on August 7 was thrown back.

[2] Or more alliteratively, if inaccurately, Ironbottom Bay. So called in memory of the many vessels sunk there in 1942 and 1943.

[3] Named in honor of Major Lofton Henderson, commander of the marine bombing squadron in the Battle of Midway.

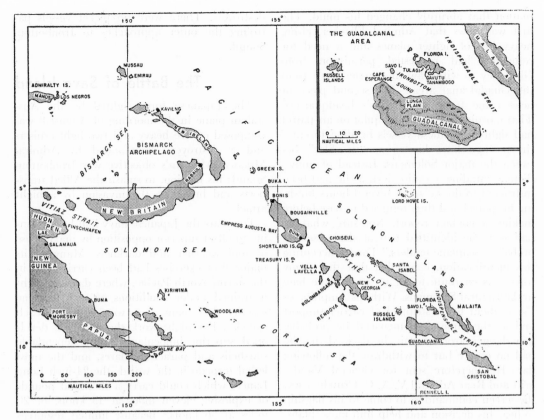

THE APPROACHES TO RABAUL

Before these three little islands could be secured on the 8th, Vandegrift had to double
the 1,500 marines he had originally sent
against the 780 defenders. This used up all his
reserves and meant that the Santa Cruz phase
of Operation WATCHTOWER would be postponed and eventually abandoned.

A few hours after the first landing, enemy
bombers and fighters from Rabaul appeared
over Ironbottom Sound. Alerted by a coast-
watcher,[4] the American carriers sent in a

[4] The Australian coastwatchers manned a network
of small radio stations along the coasts of the
Bismarcks and the Solomons. Established before
the war and incorporated into the Australian navy
in 1939, some remained after the Japanese invasion;
others returned later. Operating in concealment
usually with portable radio equipment and assisted
by loyal natives, they were of inestimable value in
warning Allied commands of enemy ship, troop,
and plane movements. A similar New Zealand network operated in the Gilberts, the Ellices, the Fijis,
and the more easterly islands. Many coastwatchers
were captured or killed by the advancing Japanese.

strong combat patrol of fighter aircraft which
soon decimated and routed the intruders.
Warned the following morning of approaching
torpedo planes, Turner had his transports and
screening vessels in cruising formation and
maneuvering at top speed when they arrived.
Caught between the devastating fire of more
than 50 vessels and the air patrol sweeping
down from above, the torpedo planes were
almost wiped out.

The Expeditionary Force came through the
air attacks rather better than many would have
ventured to predict—18 carrier aircraft lost
from all causes, two destroyers damaged, a
transport set fatally ablaze. But the long absence of the cargo vessels from their anchorages
had utterly confused an already critical logistics problem. By the evening of August 8 some
of the vessels were no more than 25 per cent
unloaded, so Turner accepted the necessity
of remaining in Ironbottom Sound at least
two more days. Then came two bits of infor-

mation that abruptly changed his mind. The first was news that Admiral Fletcher, citing heavy loss of fighter planes and a need for refueling, had requested permission from Ghormley to withdraw the carrier force from the Guadalcanal area.[5] The second piece of news came from MacArthur's headquarters. That morning an Australian pilot on air patrol had sighted Japanese vessels heading to enter the passage—later known as "the Slot"—between the major Solomons. Instead of immediately sounding a radio alert, as he had been instructed to do, he spent several hours finishing his patrol and then returned to base before making a contact report. Not sure what he had seen, he identified two of the vessels as probably "seaplane tenders." Turner, accepting this identification, concluded that the enemy force was en route to set up a seaplane base in the Central Solomons. With his Amphibious Force about to be stripped of carrier support and at the same time menaced by probable new dangers from the air, he decided that he had no choice but to withdraw the following day. He therefore sent for General Vandegrift and Rear Admiral V. A. C. Crutchley RN, the screen commander, to come to his flagship to hear his decision and help him make plans.

Crutchley, speeding to the rendezvous in the cruiser *Australia,* had drawn up no battle plan for countering a surface attack and had designated no one to the over-all command of the cruisers and destroyers in his absence. These vessels, in second condition of readiness, were divided several ways, in groups too far apart for quick mutual support. Light screens of destroyers and minesweepers covered the Guadalcanal and Tulagi beachheads, where the transports were anchored. One cruiser-destroyer group patrolled the passage between Savo and Florida Islands, another patrolled the passage between Savo and Guadalcanal, while a third patrolled the east channels. Just northwest of Savo was a radar patrol of two

destroyers. There were no picket vessels patroling the outer approaches to Ironbottom Sound.

The Battle of Savo Island

The Japanese force sighted by the Australian plane in the morning of August 8 was composed of five heavy and two light cruisers and a destroyer, commanded by Admiral Mikawa. Mikawa's objective was Ironbottom Sound; his mission, to smash the Allied transports and break up the invasion by a night attack.

For years the Japanese navy had been training to offset superior opposition by making use of foul weather and darkness. Many of its major fleet exercises had been carried out in the stormy North Pacific, where day and night it trained under conditions of such extreme severity that many men were killed in each exercise. For night work the Japanese developed superior binoculars, highly dependable starshells and parachute flares, and the most lethal torpedo in the world—the 24-inch Long Lance, which could carry a thousand pounds of explosive eleven miles at 49 knots, or 20 miles at 36 knots.[6] Because limited resources made Japan a weak base for naval operations, the Japanese counted on surprise coupled with adverse forces of nature to give them the advantage over better-based adversaries.

After he had been sighted from the air, Mikawa entered the Slot and headed directly for Guadalcanal. Late in the evening two of his cruisers launched float planes, which proceeded ahead to report the location of ships in Ironbottom Sound and to provide illumination when needed. Some Allied vessels saw the aircraft and tried to warn the flagship but were defeated by static; others assumed, since no general alarm had been sounded, that the planes must be friendly. A few minutes after 0100, when Mikawa's force was heading for the passage between Savo and Cape Esperance, Japanese lookouts dimly made out the

[5] Fletcher, having already lost two carriers since the outbreak of war, was understandably loath to risk further losses, but opinion is divided as to whether his situation off Guadalcanal was as critical as he implied, for he still had 83 fighter planes. Nimitz, calling Fletcher's withdrawal "most unfortunate," suggested that he might have solved his fuel problem by sending the carrier groups southward one at a time for refueling.

[6] The contemporary American torpedo was 21 inches in diameter and carried a 780-pound charge three miles at 45 knots, 7.5 miles at 26.5 knots. Through the first two years of the war the exploder and depth regulating mechanisms remained notoriously undependable, particularly when the torpedoes were launched from submarines.

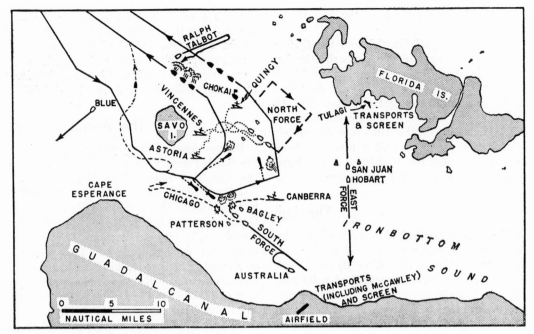

THE BATTLE OF SAVO ISLAND, AUGUST 9, 1942

hull of picket destroyer *Blue.* Promptly the entire force prepared for action, training all guns. But there was no reaction from the picket, which steamed tranquilly away, having observed nothing. Mikawa, puzzled, suspecting trickery, detached his destroyer to watch the *Blue* and engage her if she should attempt to follow him. Then he entered the Sound.

Not since the Pearl Harbor attack had American or allied forces been taken so unaware. As the Japanese planes overhead eerily illuminated the area with parachute flares, Mikawa's cruisers dashed past the South Patrol Force firing torpedoes and shells. Destroyer *Patterson* had sounded the alarm by voice radio: "Warning! Warning! Strange ships entering harbor!" but it was too late. Before the Allied vessels could bring their guns to bear or the surprised torpedomen could insert firing primers, Japanese torpedoes had blown a chunk out of the bow of American heavy cruiser *Chicago* and crushed in the side of Australian heavy *Canberra,* which lost way and began to blaze under a hail of enemy shells. Still unscratched, the attacking column split into two divisions and wheeled north, three cruisers passing across the van of the North Patrol Force and four steaming across the rear,

searchlights open, guns blazing. In a matter of minutes all three cruisers of the North Force, the American heavies *Vincennes, Astoria,* and *Quincy,* were afire and listing. The *Quincy* managed to get a couple of shells into the Japanese flagship *Chokai,* smashing the staff chart room and killing 34 men. Hits made by the other American cruisers did only trifling damage. At 0220 Mikawa ordered "All ships withdraw," and his attack force headed back up the Slot. North of Savo Island one of his cruiser divisions encountered the second picket destroyer, the *Ralph Talbot,* and concentrated upon her a massed fire that left her superstructure a shambles.

Mikawa, mindful that he had not completed his mission, considered returning to Ironbottom Sound to blast the transports. He rejected the idea because he was sure that Fletcher's carriers were already pursuing him and that they would attack at first light. The farther he could get to the northwest, the better the chances would be for a successful counterattack by aircraft out of Rabaul. But there was neither attack nor counterattack. Fletcher had received his permission to withdraw and was moving in the opposite direction. By dawn the carriers were far to the southeast. The Japanese attack force retired up the Slot unmolested.

In the waters off Guadalcanal the *Quincy* and the *Vincennes* had gone down shortly after the battle. The *Canberra,* helpless, unable to leave the Sound, was sunk by an American destroyer at 0800 the next morning. The *Astoria* lingered until noon before she plunged. The attack had cost the Allies four desperately needed heavy cruisers and a thousand lives. It had vindicated the confidence of the Japanese in their night-fighting techniques.

The Lull

The roar of battle had scarcely died away before the American sailors and marines resumed unloading cargo. After dawn, alarms of air raids that never materialized twice sent all ships into the open Sound for evasive maneuvers. Hence when the transports and cargo vessels weighed anchor that afternoon, they carried away more than half the supplies they had brought. The last ship of Turner's Amphibious Force cleared Ironbottom Sound just before dark. The 16,000 marines left behind on Guadalcanal and Tulagi would be limited to two daily meals of B and C rations eked out with captured rice.

For several days the Japanese limited their offensive against the new American positions to light aerial bombings and to bombardments by surfaced submarines. During this relative lull, marine engineers, using hand shovels and captured steam rollers and trucks, got the airstrip in good enough shape to receive light planes. On August 15 four American destroyer-transports darted into Ironbottom Sound bringing aviation gasoline, bombs, ammunition, and ground crews. On the 20th an escort carrier approached Guadalcanal from the southeast and flew in twelve dive-bombers and 19 fighters. Fletcher's carrier force meanwhile patrolled the waters between the Solomons and Espiritu Santo, guarding the sea communications.

Despite their apparent inactivity, the Japanese were not idle. They were gathering forces to recapture Guadalcanal and also to reinforce their campaign in Papua. By mid-August, the whole Combined Fleet had moved to Truk, and 17,000 troops had arrived in the area or were on the way. Because the Japanese,

through a monumental misestimate, believed that no more than 2,000 Americans had landed in the Solomons, 11,000 of the new arrivals were promptly dispatched to Papua. The rest were assigned to the first of four attacks aimed at regaining Guadalcanal and its airfield.

The August Attack

Because most of the Japanese transports in the South Pacific were assigned to reinforcing the campaign against Port Moresby, only a few hundred troops at a time could be sent to Guadalcanal. Even the first Reinforcement Group, commanded by Rear Admiral Raizo Tanaka, split into two sections. One section, comprising six destroyers, left Truk at dawn on August 16, proceeded to Guadalcanal at 22 knots, and landed 900 troops two nights later west of Henderson Field. The second section, which left Truk shortly after the first, could make only 8½ knots because its 1,300 troops were carried in three slow transports. Escorting the transports was light cruiser *Jintsu,* Tanaka's flagship, and four patrol boats.

While Tanaka was still at sea with his slow convoy, he and Japanese headquarters received three reports that changed the whole strategic picture. The first report, on August 20, was that Fletcher's carrier task force was cruising southeast of Guadalcanal. The second, also on the 20th, was that American planes were operating from Henderson Field. The third, on August 21, was that the 900 troops put ashore on Guadalcanal had attacked prematurely and had been wiped out almost to a man. The Japanese would have been even more shocked had they known that this action, known as the Battle of the Tenaru River, had cost the marines only 25 lives.

As a result of the first of these reports, Rabaul radioed Tanaka orders to reverse course. The following evening he was told to resume his advance toward Guadalcanal. Vice Admiral Nobutaka Kondo was bringing down the Combined Fleet to support his landing and, if possible, to destroy Fletcher's task force. This decision led to the second naval battle of the campaign, the Battle of the Eastern Solomons.

Dawn on August 24 saw the Japanese sea forces emerging on a southerly course from an

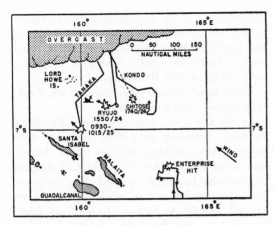

BATTLE OF THE EASTERN SOLOMONS,
AUGUST 24–25, 1942

overcast that had concealed their advance—
Tanaka 250 miles north of Guadalcanal, with
Kondo, his main air strength concentrated in
the sister-carriers *Shokaku* and *Zuikaku*, 40
miles to the east covering his flank. Far in
advance was a third group centered about
light carrier *Ryujo*, whose aircraft were assigned the task of neutralizing Henderson
Field.

When Fletcher, cruising 150 miles east of
Guadalcanal, learned from patrol planes of
the presence of the *Ryujo*, he was taken aback.
Not anticipating fleet action, he had sent the
Wasp group southward to refuel. Though this
left him only two carriers to oppose to an
enemy of undetermined strength, he decided
to seize the initiative. Retaining his entire
combat air patrol of 53 F4F Wildcat fighters
to defend his fleet from attack, in the early
afternoon he sent 30 bombers and eight torpedo planes against the *Ryujo*. These found
the little carrier shortly after she had launched
the bulk of her aircraft against Henderson
Field. In a well-coordinated attack the Americans sent her down.

When American patrol planes located the
big Japanese carriers to the north, Fletcher
promptly made preparations for an attack
from that quarter. He turned fighter-plane
direction over to Rear Admiral Thomas Kinkaid's *Enterprise* group and, hoping to divide
the enemy, withdrew with the *Saratoga* group
ten miles to the southeast. When radar detected aircraft approaching from the north, he
ordered the remaining bombers and torpedo

planes of both American carriers to take to
the air and seek out the hostile fleet, while
the fighters stacked themselves over the American groups and on the line of approach of
the enemy planes. Kinkaid's Wildcats quickly
broke the enemy formations and shot down
half a dozen bombers before they could begin
their dives. The rest of the enemy aircraft,
ignoring the *Saratoga*, swooped down upon the
Enterprise group, where they ran into blistering
antiaircraft fire which no torpedo planes and
few bombers penetrated.

Three determined bomber pilots however
bored through the fire and made direct hits
in quick succession on the flight deck of the
Enterprise, killing 74 men, knocking out two
elevators, wrecking compartments, and blasting holes in her side. Six minutes after the first
attack on the carrier, the battle was over, and
a small remnant of the attacking squadrons
was fleeing northward with the Wildcats in hot
pursuit. The Americans had lost only 15
planes. Within an hour damage control parties
aboard the *Enterprise* had corrected her slight
list and she was steaming south at 24 knots
landing aircraft. The American air attack
squadrons meanwhile had missed the main
enemy carrier force and instead struck a detached group, sending the seaplane carrier
Chitose flaming out of action.

At midnight Kondo, having lost a carrier
and 90 planes, withdrew toward Truk. But
Tanaka's Reinforcement Group, accompanied
by destroyers, steamed doggedly southward
through the night to become the morning target of Henderson Field bombers, which severely damaged the *Jintsu* and sank a transport. Not long afterward B-17's from Espiritu
Santo struck the Reinforcement Group and
sank a destroyer. Rabaul thereupon acknowledged the failure of this first attempt to recapture Guadalcanal by recalling Tanaka and
canceling the operation.

The September Attack

Tanaka, though shaken by his experiences
in the Battle of the Eastern Solomons, had
scarcely reached the naval staging base in the
Shortland Islands before he was busy with his
inadequate transport facilities pushing more
troops into Guadalcanal. In a sunset attack

on August 28, Henderson Field bombers sank a troop-carrying destroyer and damaged two others. Thereafter the Japanese timed their approaches more cautiously. Hovering up the Slot until dark, destroyers and small transports darted into Ironbottom Sound by night so regularly that the marines began to refer to them as the "Tokyo Express." After putting men and supplies ashore they would lob a few rounds of shells at the airstrip and be back up the Slot out of reach of marine bombers before light. Allied vessels, after the night sinkings of two destroyer-transports by Japanese destroyers, shunned the Sound after nightfall as conscientiously as the enemy shunned it after dawn. Thus the Americans, under protection of Henderson Field aircraft, commanded the waters around Guadalcanal by day, and the Japanese commanded these waters by night. Every surface action in Ironbottom Sound resulted from contacts made when Allied warships outstayed the sun or ventured into the waters north of Guadalcanal after dark.

By September 10, the Japanese had 6,000 troops on Guadalcanal, divided between positions east and west of the American perimeter. The time had come for a second drive to recapture the airfield. The Imperial Army commander ashore, accepting the official underestimate of American forces, reported that he had sufficient strength for an attack. Thereupon Kondo's Combined Fleet again departed Truk to lend support and to fly planes in to the airstrip as soon as it was captured. The Japanese troops, after chopping a trail through the jungle, at nightfall on September 12 struck with their main force along the high ground, subsequently known as Bloody Ridge, that led from the south directly to Henderson Field. But their move had been anticipated, and marines were waiting for them with mortars and machine guns backed by 105-mm. howitzers. The American lines held through the night and the next day. When darkness came on the 13th, the marines opened and maintained a continuous barrage of shells which the Japanese for lack of artillery could not counter. Just before midnight Imperial Army troops launched a final attack that carried them perilously close to the airfield before collapsing under withering massed fire. By first light the

Japanese were in disorderly retreat. Planes taking off from Henderson Field peppered the jungle with strafing fire, helping to bring enemy losses to 1,500. American casualties were 40 dead and 103 wounded.

Once more Kondo's fleet retired on Truk. The second attack had failed.

In the Coral Sea however, where Fletcher's carriers continued to patrol, Japanese submarines were taking a grievous toll of American naval strength. On the last day of August, a submarine had fired a torpedo into the *Saratoga*, putting her out of action for the three crucial months to follow. Two weeks later, the *Wasp*, new battleship *North Carolina*, and destroyer *O'Brien* were all torpedoed within a quarter of an hour. The two torpedoes that struck the *Wasp* ignited open fuel lines and at the same time broke her water mains so that effective fire fighting was impossible. Captain Forrest P. Sherman, her commanding officer, after vainly attempting to confine the flames by turning her undamaged stern into the wind, at length ordered Abandon Ship, and a destroyer sent her down with torpedoes. The *North Carolina*, with a 32-foot underwater rip in her hull, made Pearl Harbor for repairs, but the *O'Brien* broke up and sank before she could reach drydock.

That day's series of calamities left the Allies with only one operational fleet carrier, the *Hornet,* and one undamaged new battleship, the *Washington,* in the whole Pacific. Luckily, the convoy that the *Wasp* and the *Hornet* had been supporting reached Guadalcanal safely. Aboard were 4,200 troops, Turner's last marine reserves, which he had withdrawn from the defense of Samoa.

The October Attack

The crushing defeat of the Imperial Army forces in the Battle of Bloody Ridge had a profound effect upon Japanese strategy. It shocked Tokyo into realizing that the Americans were on Guadalcanal in considerable force and that Japan was likely to lose the island for good unless stronger measures were taken to recapture it.

Over in Papua, the troops based on Buna had penetrated a 6,500-foot-high pass in the Owen Stanley Mountains, descended the southern slope, and come almost within sight of Port Moresby in spite of courageous resistance by MacArthur's Australians. On September 18 Imperial General Headquarters ordered the Japanese troops to cease their advance and withdraw back across the mountains to Buna, where they were to take a strong defensive position and hold it until Guadalcanal had been recaptured. Everything was now to be subordinated to that objective. In line with the new emphasis, the Tokyo Express stepped up operations until by October 1 it was transporting as many as 900 troops a night down the Slot. Meanwhile a fresh Japanese division moved to the Shortlands for transfer to Guadalcanal.

In an attempt to counter this formidable enemy buildup, Admiral Ghormley stripped his New Caledonia garrison of 3,000 United States Army troops and embarked them to reinforce Vandegrift's marines. Task forces built around the *Hornet* and the *Washington* cleared the way for the convoy, and a force of four cruisers and five destroyers under Rear Admiral Norman Scott advanced to derail the Tokyo Express.

In preparation for their October offensive,

the Japanese planned a series of naval bombardments of Guadalcanal which, together with intensified air attacks, were calculated to put Henderson Field out of operation. The first bombardment group, three cruisers and two destroyers from Rabaul, came to grief when it blundered head-on into Scott's cruiser-destroyer force just north of Cape Esperance toward midnight on October 11. For once Japanese cat eyes had not penetrated the darkness, and the American force was almost equally blind because Scott had chosen as his flagship the *San Francisco*, which was not equipped with the new SG surface-search radar. But good fortune was with the American cruisers. They had just reversed course by column movement. This is a dubious maneuver in disputed waters because it masks one's batteries and provides the enemy with a stationary point of aim, but as luck would have it, the move carried the American cruiser column on a T-capping course directly across the head of the oncoming Japanese column.

At length becoming aware of the enemy, the Americans opened fire, sinking a cruiser and a destroyer and setting another cruiser ablaze. In the subsequent pursuit of the surviving

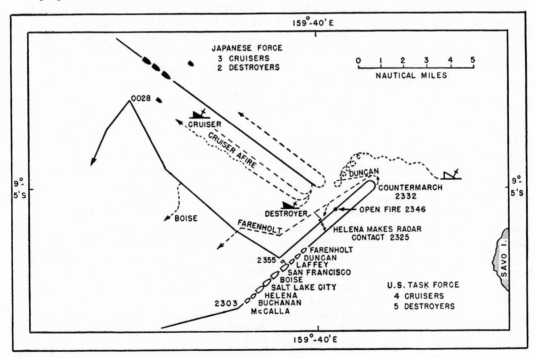

BATTLE OF CAPE ESPERANCE, OCTOBER 11–12, 1942

Japanese vessels, Scott's force battered the previously undamaged enemy cruiser with shellfire, but one of his own cruisers was put out of action and another was damaged by two hits. The American van destroyers had no luck at all. The initial countermarch, led by the cruisers, threw them out of line. As they raced to regain the head of the column, they were caught between the opposing forces. One of the destroyers was holed by two American shells; another, furiously battered by friend and foe, caught fire and sank.

This action, known as the Battle of Cape Esperance, temporarily lifted flagging Allied spirits in the South Pacific, particularly as the Americans greatly overestimated the damage they had done the enemy. The situation looked still brighter on the 13th when the convoy from New Caledonia reached Guadalcanal, discharged soldiers and cargo, and got safely away. But that night two Japanese battleships entered Ironbottom Sound and systematically pounded the Henderson Field area for an hour and a half with hundreds of high-capacity shells, churning up the landing strips and destroying half the aircraft on the island. Two air raids the next day and a bombardment by heavy cruisers the following night added to the destruction. Only a few planes were left to oppose a convoy of six transports which in the early hours of October 15 brought in some 4,500 Japanese soldiers. The new arrivals raised the enemy garrison to 22,000, the majority fresh troops, to oppose 23,000 Americans, mostly battle-worn, malaria-ridden marines. As the Imperial Army forces confidently prepared for what they regarded as the inevitable recapture of the airdrome, Admiral Kondo brought down from Truk the most powerful battleship-carrier fleet assembled since the Battle of Midway.

In the face of these vast enemy preparations, morale in the South Pacific took a new plunge. Part of the general lack of confidence grew out of command problems that had haunted the Guadalcanal operation from the beginning. Now Turner was finding fault with Vandegrift's perimeter defense, insisting that the American troops should go on the offensive from a number of points along the coast of Guadalcanal. Vandegrift for his part felt that he was getting inadequate support from the fleet. Ghormley, who from the beginning had had his doubts about the invasion, seemed able neither to resolve these differences nor to instill confidence in his subordinates. Nimitz therefore relieved Ghormley of the South Pacific command, replacing him with the confident and aggressive William F. Halsey.

Halsey promptly called a conference at Noumea and settled the disagreement on strategy in favor of Vandegrift, to whom he said, "Are we going to evacuate or hold?" "I can hold," said Vandegrift, "but I've got to have more active support than I've been getting." "All right," replied Halsey. "Go on back. I'll promise you everything I've got."[7] Backing up his word, he directed the *Washington* force to put a halt to the enemy reinforcement and bombardment of Guadalcanal. He then daringly ordered Kinkaid, who had recently relieved Fletcher, to take the two carrier forces, one centered around the *Hornet* and the other around the hastily-repaired *Enterprise,* to the waters northeast of Guadalcanal.

The Japanese army launched its drive on October 23. It quickly became apparent however that this was to be no easy march to Henderson Field. The well-entrenched Americans refused to give ground. The three lines of the Japanese advance got out of phase. After the army command had thrice notified Kondo's carriers that they might approach and send in planes, and each time postponed the hour, Admiral Yamamoto, at Truk, lost patience. He warned the army that the fleet was running out of fuel and would have to retire unless Henderson Field were soon captured.

In the early hours of the 26th, PBY's from Espiritu Santo reported that Kondo was heading northward, away from the Guadalcanal area. Kinkaid's two carrier forces had by this time reached the vicinity of the Santa Cruz Islands, within striking range of the Japanese fleet. Admiral Halsey noted all this on his operations chart at Noumea and just before dawn flashed the electrifying order: "Attack—Repeat—Attack." Search planes promptly left the deck of the *Enterprise* and began the day

[7] From William F. Halsey and J. Bryan III, *Admiral Halsey's Story* (New York: McGraw-Hill Book Company, Inc., 1947), 117. Copyright, 1947, by William F. Halsey. Copyright, 1947, by The Curtis Publishing Company.

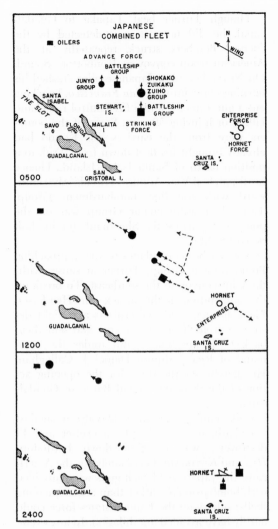

BATTLE OF SANTA CRUZ ISLANDS, OCTOBER 26, 1942

auspiciously by locating the major enemy carrier group and with a pair of 500-pound bombs blasting a hole in the flight deck of the light carrier *Zuiho*.

Thereafter events worked increasingly to American tactical disadvantage. Kinkaid, whose experience prior to Operation WATCH-TOWER had been with battleships and cruisers, adopted Fletcher's plan of controlling all fighter-direction from the *Enterprise*, but with less precision and certainly with less luck. Because the Japanese got the jump on him by putting a strike in the air 20 minutes before the Americans launched, Kinkaid had to accept battle over his own decks before his

fighters attained altitude; and as ill fortune would have it, the enemy concentrated on the *Hornet* force while the *Enterprise* was ten miles away. Five bombs struck the *Hornet*'s flight deck, some penetrating deep into the hull before detonating. Two torpedoes exploded in her engine spaces, severing electric cables and water mains and flooding fire rooms. Listing, ablaze, without power or communications, the carrier went dead in the water. Meanwhile, far to the northwest, the *Hornet*'s bombers were exacting vengeance by fighting their way through strong Japanese air patrols to cripple heavy cruiser *Chikuma* and put carrier *Shokaku* out of the war for several months.

An hour later a second Japanese air strike found the *Enterprise* force unready and in a state of some confusion because a submarine had just torpedoed destroyer *Porter*. Accuracy and volume of antiaircraft fire, especially from new battleship *South Dakota*, limited damage this time to three bomb hits on the flight deck of the *Enterprise*. After a third morning attack had damaged two more of his ships, Kinkaid ordered the *Porter* scuttled, and the *Enterprise* force retreated to the southeast.

Left thus without fighter cover, the *Hornet* became the target of repeated afternoon air attacks. When another torpedo and two more bomb hits made her blaze afresh and heel over dangerously, the force commander ordered the carrier abandoned. He then withdrew, leaving two destroyers behind to sink her. These expended all their torpedoes and more than 400 shells without producing any effect except to start new fires. After dark, when the American destroyers had departed, ships of Kondo's fleet approached the burning derelict. Unable to take her in tow, they sent her down with four Long Lances.

Though tactically the Americans had got the worse of this action, known as the Battle of the Santa Cruz Islands, in the long run it worked to their strategic advantage. Kondo had lost 100 planes; Kinkaid, 74. This disparity was more one-sided than the bare numbers indicate, for the Japanese were to be quickly outmatched by the upsurging American pilot training and aircraft construction programs.

Though the fleet at a heavy price had won

important long-term gains, it was the American soldiers and marines on Guadalcanal who saved the immediate situation. They held firm while the enemy attack rose to a crescendo and finally died out on the 26th. Henderson Field remained in American hands, and Japanese casualties were roughly ten times the American losses. Enemy ground forces would no longer pose a serious threat.

The November Attack

Convinced that they had barely missed recapturing Guadalacanal, the Japanese in early November duplicated their October preparations, but at a swifter pace. The night-running Tokyo Express sped up operations until Imperial Army forces on Guadalcanal outnumbered the Americans by several thousands. These piecemeal reinforcements however were merely a preliminary to the 13,500 troops which the persistent Admiral Tanaka was about to bring down from the Shortland Islands in a Reinforcement Group of 11 transports escorted by 11 destroyers. Exactly as in October, a battleship group and a cruiser group would bombard Henderson Field on successive nights, and bombers would raid by day. To provide some air cover for Tanaka's transports, Kondo's carriers would maneuver north of the Solomons, but they were under orders to avoid a fleet engagement.

Arrival of fresh troops from New Zealand and the United States enabled Halsey to strip the remainder of his island garrisons and rush 6,000 soldiers and marines to Guadalcanal escorted by Turner's surface forces. By direct intervention of President Roosevelt, additional cruisers, destroyers, and submarines were ordered to the South Pacific; bombers and fighter planes were flown in from Hawaii and Australia. Finally, as the November showdown became imminent, Admiral Kinkaid set out from Noumea with the *Enterprise* force, now including the *Washington* as well as the *South Dakota,* taking along a tender so that repair to the damaged carrier could continue at sea. The Battle of the Santa Cruz Islands had taught Halsey caution also, for he directed Kinkaid under no circumstances to take the *Enterprise* into the waters north of the Solomons.

Though Turner beat Tanaka to Guadalcanal, he did not arrive undetected by the enemy. Bombers struck repeatedly at the American troop convoy in Ironbottom Sound. On November 12, a Japanese pilot crashed his burning plane into the *San Francisco,* knocking out a gun director and a fire control radar and killing or injuring 50 men. Some of the bombers were from the carriers, for Kondo had already brought his fleet down from Truk to a position north of Santa Isabel Island. Thence he dispatched Vice Admiral Hiroaki Abe southward with the first Bombardment Group. Tanaka's Reinforcement Group was on the point of departing the Shortlands for its dash down the Slot.

Notified by scout planes of the approaching Bombardment Group, Turner at sunset withdrew his convoy to the southeast. To break up the impending night attack on Henderson Field, he detached five cruisers and eight destroyers from his convoy escort and sent them back to Ironbottom Sound under the command of Rear Admiral Daniel J. Callaghan. He thereby set the stage for the opening action of the three-day Naval Battle of Guadalcanal.

Callaghan's force was a David sent against a Goliath, for Abe, besides a cruiser and 14 destroyers, was bringing down battleships *Hiei* and *Kirishima.* Fortunately for the Americans, the Japanese 14-inch guns were provided with bombardment rather than armor-piercing shells; otherwise the United States force could hardly have avoided annihilation. In any event, it was little prepared for the sort of battle it was about to fight. Callaghan neither issued a battle plan nor provided for any means of scouting ahead. In imitation of Scott in the Battle of Cape Esperance, he disposed his vessels in a single column, cruisers in the center, destroyers divided between van and rear. Also like Scott, he chose for his flagship the *San Francisco* with her inferior radar. Scott, now second in command, led the cruisers in the *Atlanta,* which also lacked SG radar.[8]

Under a moonless but starry sky, Callaghan's force passed back through the eastern channel and re-entered Ironbottom Sound. His vessels

---

[8] Cruisers *Portland, Helena,* and *Juneau* and destroyers *O'Bannon* and *Fletcher* carried long-range SG radar.

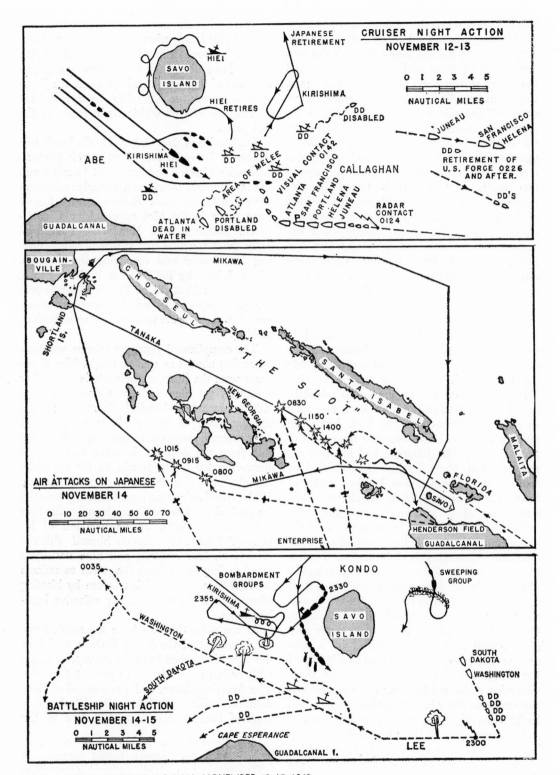

CRUISER NIGHT ACTION
NOVEMBER 12–13

JAPANESE
RETIREMENT

SAVO
ISLAND

HIEI

HIEI
RETIRES

KIRISHIMA

DD
DISABLED

0 1 2 3 4 5
NAUTICAL MILES

DD

JUNEAU

SAN
FRANCISCO

HELENA

ABE

KIRISHIMA
HIEI

DD

VISUAL CONTACT
0142

DD

CALLAGHAN

DD

RETIREMENT OF
U.S. FORCE 0226
AND AFTER.

DD's

AREA OF MELEE

DD

ATLANTA
SAN FRANCISCO
PORTLAND
HELENA
JUNEAU

RADAR
CONTACT
0124

GUADALCANAL

ATLANTA
DEAD IN
WATER

PORTLAND
DISABLED

BOUGAIN-
VILLE

MIKAWA

CHOISEUL

SHORTLAND
IS.

TANAKA

"THE SLOT"

SANTA ISABEL

NEW GEORGIA

0830

1150

1400

MALAITA

1015

M 0915

0800

MIKAWA

FLORIDA

SAVO

AIR ATTACKS ON JAPANESE
NOVEMBER 14

0 10 20 30 40 50 60 70
NAUTICAL MILES

ENTERPRISE

HENDERSON FIELD

GUADALCANAL

0035

BOMBARDMENT
GROUPS

KONDO

SWEEPING
GROUP

KIRISHIMA

2355

2330

WASHINGTON

SAVO
ISLAND

SOUTH
DAKOTA

WASHINGTON

SOUTH DAKOTA

DD

DD

DD
DD
DD
DD

BATTLESHIP NIGHT ACTION
NOVEMBER 14–15

0 1 2 3 4 5
NAUTICAL MILES

CAPE ESPERANCE

GUADALCANAL

LEE

2300

NAVAL BATTLE OF GUADALCANAL, NOVEMBER 12–15, 1942

had almost reached the waters north of Lunga Point, when Abe's Bombardment Group, without radar, entered the sound through the passage south of Savo with a pair of detached destroyers scouting out ahead. The two forces were thus speeding toward each other almost on a collision course when cruiser *Helena* detected the enemy 14 miles away and warned the flagship by voice radio. Callaghan thereupon ordered two successive column movements to the right which put him on course due north. He apparently hoped by this maneuver to reproduce Scott's capping position of the month before. But the leading destroyer *Cushing,* suddenly espying enemy scout destroyers dead ahead, swung out of line and threw the van into disorder. Callaghan's cruisers then wheeled left to avoid their own destroyers, and Japanese and American ships intermingled.

There followed a half-hour melee which for confusion and fury is scarcely paralleled in naval history. All formations broke and the engagement became a series of individual ship duels with each side at one time or another firing on its own vessels. From this midnight brawl the contending forces at length managed to extricate themselves, but both had been desperately hurt. Dawn revealed the extent of their injuries. The Japanese had lost two destroyers; and Abe's flagship *Hiei,* riddled by more than 50 shells, was helpless north of Savo, where aircraft from Henderson Field struck her again and again until she sank. Admirals Callaghan and Scott and most of the members of their staffs had been killed. Four American destroyers had been lost. Cruiser *Portland* and a destroyer were unnavigable. Cruiser *Atlanta,* flame-gutted, and shelled by friend and foe, had to be sunk. All but one of the other American vessels were damaged. Cruiser *Juneau,* while retiring from battle with a weakened keel, was torpedoed by a submarine and went down, carrying nearly 700 of her crew. Yet the Americans, despite overwhelming odds, had by sheer valor carried out their mission. Abe's battleships had been turned back; Tanaka's transports returned to base.

The frustration of their intended battleship bombardment interrupted the Japanese schedule scarcely at all. Down came Mikawa from the Shortlands with his Cruiser Bombardment Group and in the early hours of the 14th carried out his bombardment of Henderson Field, achieving considerably less damage than Abe might have done with his 14-inch guns. The fortunes of war were turning against the Japanese however, for Kinkaid's *Enterprise* force had at last arrived within flight range of the Solomons.

Daybreak on November 14 disclosed two Japanese forces to American search planes—Mikawa's Cruiser Bombardment Group south of New Georgia Island on a westerly retirement course and Tanaka's Reinforcement Group once more in the Slot approaching Guadalcanal. Bombers from Henderson Field and from the *Enterprise* first struck Mikawa, sinking one cruiser and damaging three others. Then, joined by B-17's from Espiritu Santo, they struck repeatedly at Tanaka's lightly-protected transports. By evening seven of them, carrying about 1,000 troops each, were sunk or sinking.

The complicated Japanese scheme was now becoming absurd as well as tragic. The transports were the heart of their whole November offensive, yet they had come down the Slot shielded by a mere handful of destroyers and a meager cover of fighter planes operating at near extreme range out of the Upper Solomons and from the decks of Kondo's carriers maneuvering far to the north. In his extremity Tanaka now rose to a sort of magnificence. With remarkable if perhaps foolhardy tenacity he pushed on toward Guadalcanal with four damaged transports, all he had left of his convoy.[9] Meanwhile, Kondo himself with the *Kirishima,* four cruisers, and nine destroyers was heading down from the north to redeem Abe's failure of two nights before by blasting Henderson Field with a really effective bombardment.

At the same time up from the south came the *Washington,* the *South Dakota,* and four destroyers, detached from the *Enterprise* group with orders from Halsey to protect the field. The American force, under command of Rear Admiral William A. Lee in the *Washington,* reached Guadalcanal first, and late in the

[9] For Tanaka's own description of his convoy under attack, see "Japan's Losing Struggle for Guadalcanal," *U.S. Naval Institute Proceedings,* August 1956, 821–23.

evening under a setting moon passed into Ironbottom Sound through the passage north of Savo. Though Lee had detected nothing, Kondo had seen Lee and divided his force into three groups, two to attack and the third to keep the Americans under observation. (See diagram page 703.)

As Lee's force, in column with the destroyers leading, turned west toward Cape Esperance, the battleships made radar contact with the sweeping group and chased it away with a series of salvos. But one of the attack groups, a light cruiser leading several destroyers, had passed west around Savo so that it could not be detected by American radar. This group now attacked Lee's van with shells and torpedoes, sinking two of his destroyers and putting the other two out of action. To avoid colliding with the disabled vessels the *Washington* shifted to port and the *South Dakota* swung to starboard toward the enemy. This accidental separation of the American battleships occurred at a critical moment, for Kondo was about to strike again. His main attack group, the *Kirishima*, two heavy cruisers, and two destroyers, which had been maneuvering northwest of Savo, emerged from behind the island and took the nearby *South Dakota* under fire, so wrecking her superstructure that she was obliged to retire.

The *Washington* was thus left to face the entire Japanese force. Lee, with the advantage of radar fire control, at which he was expert, accepted the challenge and quickly evened the score. With his 5- and 16-inch guns, he concentrated on the *Kirishima*. Seven minutes and 50 shell hits later the Japanese battleship was helpless and turning in circles. Lee continued for a while to the northwest to attract the enemy away from his cripples and then withdrew to the south.

Kondo now gave up, ordered the *Kirishima* and a disabled destroyer scuttled, and left the area. But "Tenacious Tanaka," who had steamed unflinchingly through the embattled waters, continued on to Guadalcanal, where he beached his four remaining transports. After dawn American planes and ship and shore artillery quickly smashed them to pieces —but not before the surviving troops had landed.

Japan's final attempt to recapture Guadal-canal had ended in failure like all the rest. Thereafter Yamamoto risked no more capital ships in the Solomons campaign.

The Battle of Tassafaronga

Following the collapse of their November attack the Japanese went entirely on the defensive, maintaining their garrison on Guadalcanal merely as a holding force to keep the Americans occupied while they prepared a new defense line by constructing a pair of airfields on Kolombangara and New Georgia in the Central Solomons. In the meantime Admiral Tanaka contrived a streamlined Tokyo Express of fast destroyers to keep the garrison precariously alive by dropping floating drums of food and medical supplies offshore and then darting back up the Slot before daylight. To derail this new express Halsey assigned to Admiral Kinkaid a force of cruisers and destroyers.

Kinkaid, an able tactician with surface forces, prepared a detailed battle plan designed to secure him from the errors his predecessors had made. Not for him was the blind approach or the single unbroken column. In night engagements he would use float planes for early warning and for parachute flare illumination when needed. His destroyers were to speed ahead to make a surprise torpedo attack and then turn away. His cruisers, holding off at 12,000 yards, out of visual range of the enemy, were to open with their guns the moment the torpedoes hit. But Kinkaid was detached for duty elsewhere and it fell to his successor, newly-arrived Rear Admiral Carleton Wright, to execute this plan.

Warned that Tanaka was about to begin operations, Wright approached Guadalcanal on November 30 and that evening took his force through the east channel—four destroyers in the van, followed by five cruisers. Two additional destroyers, which joined too late for briefing, were stationed at the rear of the column. Forming line of bearing inside Ironbottom Sound, the cruisers swept westward with the destroyers on their flanks. Meanwhile Tanaka with eight destroyers had entered the Sound from the opposite direction; but of this Wright was unaware, for the float planes that were to give him warning had been unable to rise from the water because of the dead calm.

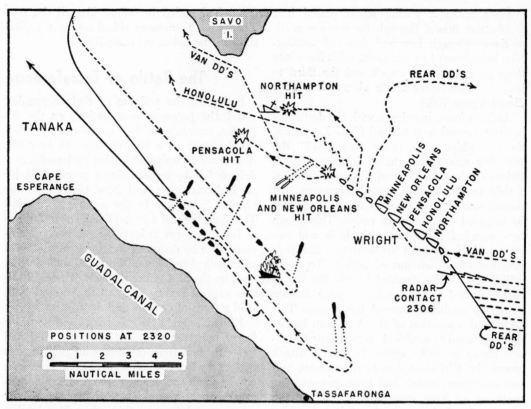

BATTLE OF TASSAFARONGA, NOVEMBER 30, 1942

At 2306 Wright's flagship made radar contact with the Japanese, whereupon the cruisers promptly resumed column formation and wheeled to parallel the enemy. Now was the moment to release the van destroyers, but Wright hesitated because he could get no clear radar data; Tanaka's force, speeding past on an opposite course, merged with the nearby shoreline. When at last Wright ordered his van destroyers to launch torpedoes, the moment of opportunity had passed. The range was opening rapidly and none of the torpedoes found a target. The cruisers however opened fire on a destroyer, somewhat nearer than the others, and sent her down in flames.

The other Japanese destroyers had now reversed course by divisions. Since the Americans had no flashless powder, their gun flashes provided Japanese torpedo directors with a point of reference. Tanaka's well-drilled team released a score of deadly Long Lances at the extended American track. Because they were well aimed and ran true, and Wright's cruisers maintained course and speed, the torpedoes inevitably found their targets. Every one of the cruisers except the *Honolulu* took one or more hits. The *Minneapolis* and the *New Orleans* had their bows ripped away. The *Pensacola,* her after engine room flooded, three of her turrets knocked out, was quickly wreathed in oil fires. Worst hit of all was the *Northampton*; as water poured into her gashed-in side and blazing oil drenched her decks, the crew abandoned ship and she heeled over and sank. By that time Tanaka's seven surviving destroyers, virtually undamaged, were far up the Slot. This brief battle, which besides vitally needed cruisers cost the Americans 400 lives, provided a sort of textbook, later well studied, on how not to combat the powerful and accurate Japanese torpedo.

Wright's battered force was obliged to withdraw from the Guadalcanal area. Its retirement seemed to open the way for Tanaka's Express, which was scheduled to come down the Slot at four-day intervals, covered until dark by Zekes from the Shortlands. The Americans however found ways to complicate Tanaka's problem. As his ten destroyers started down the Slot on December 3, aircraft from Henderson Field flew out to meet them. They damaged one destroyer slightly, shot down three Zekes, and lost two of their own planes. Tanaka's force nevertheless pressed on and dumped 1,500 drums of supplies off Tassafaronga. Such was the exhausted and weakened state of the Japanese garrison however that the troops succeeded in hauling only 310 of these ashore by dawn. American fighter planes then sank the rest of the drums with machine gun fire.

The Tokyo Express in its December 7 approach came under a more severe air attack that left one Japanese destroyer so damaged that she had to be towed back to base under escort. Hence only a portion of the Express reached Ironbottom Sound, and here they were met by torpedoes and machine gun fire from eight PT boats out of Tulagi. None of the torpedoes found a target and one PT boat was heavily damaged, but the Express was constrained to retire without delivering any supplies. Tanaka led the December 11 Express in person, flying his flag in Japan's newest and best destroyer, the 2,500-ton *Teruzuki*. His force passed unscathed through the usual sunset air attack and dropped 1,200 drums off Cape Esperance. As the destroyers were withdrawing however, the American PT boats found them and put a torpedo into the *Teruzuki*, which caught fire. Her after powder magazine blew up, and Tanaka was among the wounded. Two other Japanese destroyers stood by to remove survivors from the sinking vessel. They rescued Tanaka and a few others, but before they could complete their task they were driven away by the arrival of more PT boats. Following this repulse, Tokyo at last concluded that Guadalcanal would have to be abandoned.

Guadalcanal Secured

In December the malaria-ridden veterans of the 1st Marine Division together with their commander, General Vandegrift, were evacuated to Australia, and Major General Alexander M. Patch USA took command of the Guadalcanal garrison, which was soon raised to corps strength by the arrival of an additional army division directly from the United States. In January 1943 Patch had 50,000 soldiers and marines[10] under his command. Unaware that the enemy had already conceded defeat, he began an all-out offensive in mid-January, driving westward from the American defense perimeter toward the area where all the enemy were now concentrated.

The Japanese, using cleverly sited artillery, gave ground stubbornly, fighting for time to carry out their evacuation. This they achieved by means of a neatly-timed stratagem. While transports and destroyers assembled at Rabaul and in the Upper Solomons, Admiral Kondo brought the Combined Fleet once more to the waters north of Guadalcanal. As the Japanese had expected, all this activity caught Halsey's attention. What did it portend? Was the enemy, after failing four times, about to make a fifth attempt to recapture the island? If so, the South Pacific at long last had power aplenty to turn him back. Halsey promptly dispatched to Guadalcanal an additional troop convoy supported by five task forces, including two large and two escort carriers and three battleships. But no fleet action ensued, for Kondo had brought his ships down not to do battle but merely to create a diversion. Instead, the Japanese struck from the air. At night, using parachute flares and floating lights, torpedo planes from the recently-constructed airfield on New Georgia succeeded in sinking the cruiser *Chicago*. Evidently the enemy had developed yet another technique for turning the night to his advantage.

As the main body of Patch's troops advanced westward along the north coast of Guadalcanal, a battalion was ferried around to a new beachhead west of Cape Esperance. The newly-landed troops then advanced eastward to meet the approaching main body in order to nip off the enemy's communications with the coast and seal him up in the jungle for annihilation. But when the American forces made contact on February 9, they found that the quarry had slipped through their fingers. While American attention had been diverted elsewhere, a score of destroyers in three high speed night runs down the Slot had carried away the 12,000 half-starved survivors of the Imperial Army

[10] Of the 2nd Marine Division.

garrison. Thus on a note of mingled frustration and triumph for both sides, the Guadalcanal campaign came to an end.

Papua Secured

While the Americans were tightening their grip on Guadalcanal, Allied forces a thousand miles to the west were with equal difficulty and equal success wresting from the Japanese the peninsula of Papua. As Australian troops pursued the retreating enemy via the direct route across the Owen Stanley Mountains, American and Australian forces crossed the mountains by a roundabout trail or were flown to airfields on the north coast in areas not held by the enemy. All Allied forces then converged on the Buna area and in mid-November 1942 began a coordinated offensive to capture it from the Japanese defenders.[11]

The Allied situation on Papua was now the reverse of that on Guadalcanal, for on Papua it was the Allies who were assaulting a well fortified perimeter defense—fighting along matted jungle trails, across fields of man-high kunai grass, and through dense mangrove swamps. The Papuan campaign however, unlike that on Guadalcanal, never involved major fleet elements. A strong naval force might quickly have turned the tide either way by repeated bombardment and by supporting rapid waterborne supply and reinforcement. But neither side ventured major ships into this area of uncharted waters and hostile airfields. The sea however did play an important part in the campaign. The Japanese tried first to reinforce and then to evacuate the Buna area by means of night-running barges, but American PT boats made such attempts too costly. And although airdrop and later airlift were an important means of Allied supply, more than three quarters of the material brought in to the investing forces came by luggers and small commercial steamers.

Though MacArthur at length committed nearly 30,000 troops, half Australian and half American, to dislodge some 12,000 enemy from Papua, the Japanese held their bit of coastline until late January 1943. Then at last their

[11] For details see Samuel Milner, *Victory in Papua* (Washington, D.C., Dept. of the Army, 1957).

defenses collapsed, as much from starvation and disease as from outside pressure. In recapturing Papua, 3,095 Allied troops had lost their lives, nearly twice as many as were killed on Guadalcanal.

The long and critical preliminaries were over. South Pacific and Southwest Pacific forces had each captured a base that the Japanese had intended to use as a springboard for further aggression. For the Allies two roads to Rabaul were now open.

Summary

The determined but fruitless drive of the Japanese to recapture Guadalcanal, which precipitated numerous skirmishes and nine major battles, forms one of the most complex campaigns of World War II. The outstanding events of the campaign can perhaps best be summarized in outline form:

August 1942

7   Guadalcanal invaded

9   Battle of Savo Island (night surface action)

The main attack:

21   Battle of the Tenaru River (land action)

24-25   Battle of the Eastern Solomons (carrier action)

September 1942

The main attack:

12-14   Battle of Bloody Ridge (land action)

No sea battle

October 1942

11-12   Battle of Cape Esperance (night surface action)

The main attack:

23-26   Battle of Henderson Field (land action)

26   Battle of Santa Cruz Islands (carrier action)

November 1942

The main attack:

No land battle

Naval Battle of Guadalcanal:

12-13 Cruiser Night Action (night surface action)

14 Air attacks on Japanese transports and support

14-15 Battleship Night Action (night surface action)

30 Battle of Tassafaronga (night surface action)

February 1943

9 Guadalcanal secured

Until the Battle of Midway the Japanese had been superior in the Pacific, but at the time of the invasion of Guadalcanal the opposing forces, all elements considered, were roughly equal. Guadalcanal moreover lay exactly equidistant from Rabaul, the nearest Japanese base, 560 miles to the northwest, and Espiritu Santo, the nearest Allied base, 560 miles to the southeast. What, then, enabled the Allies to win the victory?

In the first place, before August 7, 1942 the Japanese had held the island too lightly. With a whole division of crack troops and the advantage of surprise, the Americans easily wrested Guadalcanal from the few hundred combatants defending it. Thereafter the situation favored the Americans, for it is enormously more difficult to capture a strongly defended position than to hold it.

The retirement of Fletcher and Turner on August 9 left the Japanese in potential command of the sea around and the air over Guadalcanal, but they were not prepared to make their control permanent by seeking out and destroying the Allied fleet in the Coral Sea. Their experience at Midway made them wary of this classic means of isolating the target. Instead they chose to begin by putting troops ashore by one means or another to defeat the American occupation force and recapture the airfield. As the plan gradually evolved, carriers would then approach and send in planes to operate from the captured airfield and seize command of the air over the island. Under cover of this air power, now land based, fleet units could move in to take command of the waters around Guadalcanal.

This plan of reconquest was destined to fail-ure because the Japanese, grossly underestimating the number of Americans on Guadalcanal, for two months directed their main strength against Papua. When they learned the truth, it was too late. In the reinforcement race they could never get a sufficient preponderance of manpower on the island, with the necessary artillery, ammunition, and supplies, to wrest the airfield from the entrenched Americans.[12] By November the Japanese situation was hopeless because superior Allied training and construction programs were beginning to make themselves felt, particularly in the vital areas of manpower and airpower. True, the Japanese at that time had three heavy carriers, the *Zuikaku, Junyo,* and *Hiyo,* to oppose damaged u.s.s. *Enterprise,* but that bald statement fails to take into account the severe losses in aircraft they had suffered in the Battles of the Eastern Solomons and the Santa Cruz Islands, their inability to replace these losses quickly, and the growing power of the Henderson Field airdrome. The Japanese moreover were coming to realize that they had achieved maneuverability in the air at high cost. Their fragile planes quickly disintegrated in the face of massed American antiaircraft fire. Yamamoto was well advised not to expose his carriers to close support of the November attack. Japanese carriers did not in fact go into action again until the middle of 1944.

One of the greatest weaknesses of the Japanese counterattack lay in the field of command. The Imperial Army and Navy, which were

[12] The following table gives approximate troop strengths on Guadalcanal on important dates:

	AMERICAN	JAPANESE
Aug. 7	10,000	2,200
Aug. 20	10,000	3,600
Sept. 12	11,000	6,000
Oct. 23	23,000	22,000
Nov. 12	29,000	30,000
Dec. 9	40,000	25,000
Feb. 1	50,000	12,000

On August 7 there were also 780 Japanese in the Tulagi-Tanambogo-Gavutu area. Some 6,000 United States marines landed on these islands, and a garrison of around 5,000 Americans was maintained in this area throughout the campaign. Of about 60,000 American soldiers and marines who fought on Guadalcanal, 1,600 were killed and 4,200 wounded. Of more than 36,000 Japanese on Guadalcanal, about 15,000 were killed or missing, 9,000 died of disease, and 1,000 were captured.

supposed to be cooperating in the Guadalcanal campaign, not only failed to coordinate planning but worked together, if at all, with ill-concealed hostility. Even within the services, commands overlapped and were at odds with one another. The result was a kind of grudging, improvised collaboration that looked to the Allies like a single grandiose, inflexible plan of operation repeated four times.[13] On the Allied side also there was some lack of coordination, particularly between the Southwest Pacific and South Pacific commands. But there was never any doubt that General MacArthur was in full command in the Southwest Pacific; and after Admiral Halsey arrived in Noumea, there was no question of who was running the show in the South Pacific.

The one real and continuing advantage the Japanese had over the Americans in the Guadalcanal campaign was superiority in night

[13] For sharply expressing his opinion of the way his superiors were conducting the war, Admiral Tanaka was relieved of his seagoing command. His opinions, frankly expressed, are in "Japan's Losing Struggle for Guadalcanal," U.S. *Naval Institute Proceedings,* July-August 1956.

surface tactics. This was of course a Japanese specialty, emphasized to make fullest use of the superb Long Lance torpedo. The new SG radar, then being installed in American vessels, could have offset enemy binoculars and night training had more American commanders understood its capabilities. But the fact was that the Americans were not well prepared for night surface action; that was not the sort of warfare they had anticipated. The dreadful example of the Battle of Savo Island, together with the scratch teams and impromptu commands that characterized all Allied surface action in 1942, constrained commanders to adopt a single-column, defensive formation in which destroyers, attached to the van and rear, could not scout ahead, readily use their torpedoes, or reach the enemy with their 5-inch guns. Admiral Kinkaid's battle plan pointed the way toward better night tactics, but his ideas would not reach fruition until late 1943, with the development of the Combat Information Center and the establishing of surface forces with some permanence of composition and command.

38:

The Limited Offensive

Following the Allied capture of Guadalcanal and of Buna, there was a pause in military operations in the Pacific theater. This was a period of planning and preparation for both the Japanese and the Allies.

As noted on page 582, the Combined Chiefs of Staff at the Casablanca Conference of January 1943 had allocated a greater percentage of men and material to the Pacific in order to keep the offensive rolling in that theater. At the Washington Conference of the following May they assigned the general conduct of the war in the Pacific to the American Joint Chiefs of Staff. They also accepted in principle the Joint Chiefs' "Strategic Plan for the Defeat of Japan." This plan assumed that the Japanese were to be defeated (1) by blockade, especially through cutting off Japan's access to the oil of the East Indies; (2) by sustained aerial bombing of Japanese cities; and (3) possibly by actual invasion of the Japanese home islands. To provide a base for carrying out these operations, all major lines of Allied advance were to converge on Hong Kong and the China coast. The British army, with Chinese and American help, was to invade Burma and reopen the Burma Road in order to supply the Chinese army, which would drive in from the west. Even if the Chinese did not reach Hong Kong, they would at least draw Japanese forces from the coast, making Allied invasion from the sea less hazardous. The British fleet was to penetrate the Straits of Malacca and advance to the Celebes Sea. Here it would be joined by MacArthur's Southwest Pacific forces, advancing from the east, and together they would recapture the Philippines and seize Hong Kong by amphibious assault. Meanwhile, Nimitz' Central Pacific forces would have advanced westward across the center from Pearl Harbor via the Marshalls and the Carolines and reached Hong Kong by way of Formosa.

This complex program had to be drastically curtailed because the British found that they could not disengage enough forces from the Mediterranean campaign to carry out their part of the plan and because the Japanese launched an offensive in China that eliminated the possibility of Chinese participation. The drive on Japan would have to be carried out by the Americans, aided only by such limited forces as Canada, New Zealand, and Australia could provide. The program actually put into effect included intensified submarine attacks on Japanese sea power and three ground-air-surface offensives:

1. North Pacific forces to eject the Japanese from the Aleutians.
2. Central Pacific forces to advance westward from Pearl Harbor.
3. South Pacific and Southwest Pacific forces to cooperate in a drive on Rabaul. Southwest Pacific forces then to press on westward along the north coast of New Guinea.

Because No. 2, the Central Pacific drive, was given priority in men and materials, No. 1 and the first phase of No. 3, with which this chapter deals, were necessarily limited offensives. The best in new naval construction, especially carriers, battleships, and attack transports, was deliberately hoarded at Pearl Harbor for the drive across the center, which was to begin as soon as the build-up permitted. The Japanese, noting this growing concentration of power, also held back their capital ships. But they recklessly expended their naval aircraft without setting up an adequate training program for replacement of pilots. That, as we shall see, proved their undoing.

In March 1943, Admiral King had clarified

naval organization by inaugurating a numbered fleet system whereby United States fleets operating in the Atlantic and Mediterranean would bear even numbers, and those in the Pacific would bear odd numbers. Under this plan, the principal naval forces in the Pacific were designated as follows:

CENTRAL PACIFIC. The Central Pacific Force, based at Pearl Harbor, would become the U.S. Fifth Fleet.

SOUTH PACIFIC. Halsey's South Pacific Force became the U.S. Third Fleet, with Halsey in direct command; and Turner's amphibious team became the Third Amphibious Force.

SOUTHWEST PACIFIC. MacArthur's miniature Naval Forces Southwest Pacific became the U.S. Seventh Fleet, under Vice Admiral Arthur S. Carpender (later succeeded by Vice Admiral Kinkaid), with amphibious craft and support designated as Seventh Amphibious Force, under Rear Admiral Daniel E. Barbey. Unlike the Third and Fifth fleets, the Seventh Fleet and its components were not part of the U.S. Pacific Fleet and hence were not subject to control by Admiral Nimitz.[1]

The Reconquest of Attu and Kiska

For nearly a year following the Japanese occupation of Attu and Kiska, Allied operations in the Aleutians were limited to harassing and isolating the enemy-held islands by air and submarine action. In August 1942, an American cruiser-destroyer force finally penetrated the Aleutian fog to give Kiska its first pounding from the sea. For several months thereafter the job of harassment was left in the hands of Canadian and U.S. Army air forces, which raided the islands whenever the weather permitted. During the winter of 1942-43, the Americans occupied Adak and Amchitka, the latter only 65 miles east of Kiska. On these islands they constructed airfields in record time so that fighters could escort bombers in stepped-

[1] The fleets would be divided into task forces, task groups, and task units as operations required. Thus TU 31.2.3 would be a component of TG 31.2, which would be a component of TF 31, which would be a component of the Third Fleet. For logistic purposes, ships of the same type requiring the same sort of equipment and services continued to be organized (on paper at least) into squadrons and divisions.

up attacks which soon cut off Kiska from all surface contact with Japan.

In order to isolate the more westerly Attu, Rear Admiral Charles H. McMorris in mid-February 1943 bombarded the island, then led his cruiser-destroyer group to the southwest to patrol the enemy supply line. Here he had the satisfaction of sinking an ammunition ship en route to Attu and sending two accompanying transports fleeing back to the Japanese base at Paramushiro in the northern Kurils. Vice Admiral Boshiro Hosogaya, realizing that Japanese surface supply to the Aleutians could not much longer be maintained, early in March rushed to Attu a convoy escorted by his entire North Area Force, unloaded, and got safely back to Paramushiro. Later the same month he tried it again, but this time McMorris's group of two cruisers and four destroyers was patrolling in an intercepting position south of the Russian Komandorski Islands. Contact between the two forces resulted in the Battle of the Komandorskis, last of the classic daytime surface actions.

An hour before sunrise on March 26, the American task group made radar contact with the Japanese convoy to the north, and McMorris promptly gave chase, little guessing that he was in pursuit of a force considerably stronger than his own. As Hosogaya made out the approaching American vessels in the first light of dawn, he ordered his two transports to retire to the northwest and hastened to put his four cruisers and four destroyers between the Americans and their Aleutian bases. The pursuer now became the pursued. The three-hour westerly chase that followed is chiefly remarkable for how little the Japanese accomplished with superior speed and firepower. They lost their speed advantage by zigzagging in order to use their after turrets, which would be masked in a bows-on approach; and the Americans avoided serious damage by making smoke and by expert salvo chasing. At length however cruiser *Salt Lake City* took a hit that flooded an engine room. Her engineers, in attempting to correct a resulting list, inadvertently let sea water into a fuel line, thereby extinguishing her burners and bringing her temporarily to a standstill. In this desperate situation, McMorris retained one destroyer to

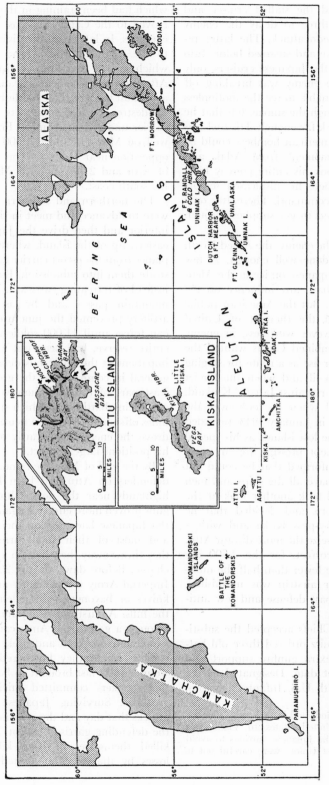

THE ALEUTIAN THEATER OF OPERATIONS

make smoke around the stalled cruiser and ordered the other three to delay the enemy with a suicide torpedo attack. The latter reversed course at once and steamed boldly into the blazing guns of the Japanese cruisers, only to observe that the enemy was breaking off action. Hosogaya, unable to see the motionless *Salt Lake City* through the smoke, felt that he had stretched his luck far enough. His fuel was running low, and American bombers could be expected at any moment from Adak and Amchitka. So he took his entire convoy back to Paramushiro, where his displeased seniors relieved him of his command. Thereafter only submarines attempted to get supplies through to Attu and Kiska.

In thus isolating the enemy, the Allied North Pacific forces had done well enough. A few thousand starving Japanese on ice in the Aleutians could hardly have any influence on the outcome of the war. But the American public remained uneasy at the thought of United States territory, however worthless, in enemy hands, and the Combined Chiefs wanted the Aleutians cleared for use as a route for staging aircraft into Siberia—if and when the Soviet Union joined the war against Japan.[2] Kinkaid, still a rear admiral when he took over the Aleutians command in January 1943, regarded the reconquest of the lost islands as his special responsibility and kept pressing for an early assault on Kiska. Informed that he could not for several months have all the ships and men he needed, Kinkaid took another look at the reconnaissance reports and decided that he could temporarily by-pass Kiska and with a much smaller force seize the more distant Attu. His estimate was correct, for the 2,600 defenders of Attu were fewer than half the number on Kiska, their airstrip was unfinished, and they had no coast defense and few antiaircraft guns.

When the Joint Chiefs accepted the substitution, Admiral Nimitz ordered three old battleships north for extra gunfire support and set May 7 as target date. Designated as the landing force, the 7th U.S. Infantry Division,

[2] Soviet vessels carried lend-lease goods from the west coast of the United States to Vladivostok throughout the war. The Japanese, anxious to avoid trouble with the Soviet Union, were careful not to interfere.

which had been training in the Nevada desert, moved to the California coast for amphibious exercises. In late April the division sailed away to the Aleutians and a kind of warfare for which it had had little realistic preparation. After two postponements because of heavy surf, an assault force of three battleships, six cruisers, 19 destroyers, five transports, and an escort carrier under Rear Admiral Francis W. Rockwell on May 11 landed 1,000 troops without opposition near Holtz Bay on the north coast of Attu and 2,000 more at Massacre Bay on the south coast.

The northern and southern invasion forces were to advance and meet in the mountainous interior and then drive the Japanese into the eastern tip of the island, where fleet guns and planes from the escort carrier could pound and strafe them into submission. But the Japanese, instead of retreating eastward, holed up in the mountain passes and by use of concealed artillery prevented the juncture of the American forces until 11,000 soldiers, including the entire reserve, had been put ashore. Kinkaid, impatient at the numerous delays, relieved the general in command of the ground forces. At least part of the fault however lay with the supporting battleships, which stood six to eight miles offshore delivering a neutralizing fire that drove the enemy temporarily to cover but left his positions largely intact.

By the end of May the remnant of Japanese defenders on Attu had been forced into the highlands near the north shore, where fleet guns proved more effective against them. When the Japanese had used up their store of shells and most of their small arms ammunition, they threw away their lives in a massive banzai charge. Before dawn on the 29th, a thousand Imperial Army troops, many armed only with knives or bayonets, came silently down from the hills. At first light they hurled themselves through a gap in the American lines, overran two command posts, and broke into a medical station, where they butchered the sick and wounded. At last brought to bay, some 500 of the attackers committed suicide with hand grenades. Surviving Japanese made further attacks that day and the next morning until all the defending garrison except 28 captives had killed themselves or been killed. American losses by that time amounted to about 600 killed and 1,200 wounded. Nearly 1,500 more had been put out of action during the campaign because their shoes and clothing, not to speak of their training, had been ill-suited to the cold, damp climate of the Aleutians.

The only attempt of the Japanese to support their troops on Attu was by submarines, which made no hits, and by aircraft from Paramushiro, which were generally defeated by fog. The Combined Fleet never intervened because the Commander in Chief was at Tokyo looking three ways at once. Worried over Allied offensive preparations at Pearl Harbor and in the New Guinea-Solomons area, he could not bring himself to commit major naval forces to the Aleutians.

In preparing for the assault on Kiska, set for mid-August 1943, the North Pacific command put to good use the hard lessons learned at Attu. In six weeks Eleventh Air Force planes dropped 1,200 tons of bombs on the island. Battleships, cruisers, and destroyers bombarded the main camp and harbor. At Adak 29,000 United States and 5,300 Canadian troops under Major General Charles H. Corlett USA, equipped to a man with tested arctic gear, practiced landings and maneuvered across the muskeg. This huge force, carried in numerous transports and supported by nearly a hundred men-of-war, left Adak August 13. Before dawn on the 15th, gunnery support vessels were off Kiska thundering away at enemy positions. At first light, LST's, LCI's, and LCT's moved to the beach and disgorged their troops. There followed the greatest anticlimax of the war. The Japanese escape artists had carried out another evacuation. Three weeks before, while fog covered the area and the American blockading force had temporarily withdrawn to refuel, cruisers and destroyers had slipped in and carried away the entire Kiska garrison.

Some officers now urged using the recovered islands as jumping off points for an advance on Japan via the Kurils, but the Combined Chiefs never took such suggestions very seriously. The cold, fog, and foul weather of the North Pacific forbade proper logistic support for such a drive, and even if it had been logistically feasible, it was strategically unsound because it would leave intact Japan's principal external source of strength, the oil-rubber-rice shipping line from the East Indies, which

Japan had gone to war with the United States to establish. The North Pacific forces lapsed back into their former patrol functions, and Kinkaid, promoted to vice admiral, went south to assume command of the U.S. Seventh Fleet under MacArthur.

Preliminaries to the Dual Advance on Rabaul

With the expulsion of the Japanese from Guadalcanal and Papua early in 1943, the Allies completed Task One of their campaign against Rabaul. During the pause in the Allied offensive that preceded Task Two, the coordinated advance via the Solomons and via New Guinea, both the Japanese and the Allies set out to strengthen their own positions and to weaken the enemy.

The Japanese drew in the defenses of Rabaul to a line running from their new airfield at Munda Point on New Georgia to Salamaua in New Guinea. The Imperial Navy, with assistance from army infantry, assumed the responsibility of guarding the Central Solomons; the Imperial Army, with the assistance of naval ships and aircraft, would defend the Northern Solomons and New Guinea. In command of the defense forces were Vice Admiral Jinichi Kusaka and General Hotishi Imamura. There was no unified joint command nearer than Tokyo.

The night-running Tokyo Express again went into high gear, pouring troops into the Central Solomons. Reinforcing the Lae-Salamaua area in New Guinea was more risky, for this involved passage over open seas partly by daylight. Early in March a convoy of eight Japanese transports escorted by eight destroyers met disaster while carrying 7,000 troops from Rabaul to Lae. Medium and light bombers out of Papua attacked it persistently almost at masthead level, using slow-fused bombs that permitted them to pull out of range of the explosions. The Battle of the Bismarck Sea continued for three days, until all of the transports and four of the destroyers had been sunk and about 25 planes of the Japanese combat air patrol had been shot down by Allied fighters. Some of the surviving troops made their way to New Guinea in boats and on rafts, but

RABAUL NEUTRALIZED AND BY-PASSED

at least 3,600 were lost. After additional sinkings of Japanese vessels in the next few days, Imperial General Headquarters forbade sending more convoys to New Guinea. Any further reinforcements or supplies would have to go by submarine or barge.

Alarmed by the deteriorating situation, Yamamoto himself came to Rabaul to direct an all-out air offensive which he counted on to snarl up Allied plans. By stripping some 200 planes from the Imperial Third (Carrier) Fleet and adding them to his 100 land-based naval aircraft, he built up the most powerful Japanese air armada of the war and sent it first against the shipping in Ironbottom Sound and then against targets in Papua. Its achievements were by no means negligible: a destroyer, a corvette, a tanker, and two transports sunk, 25 Allied planes destroyed. But these results had been attained at the cost of 40 aircraft and a heavy loss of first-line carrier aviators which rendered the Japanese carrier force considerably less battleworthy than before.

In preparation for further aerial offensives, Yamamoto set out with his staff on an air tour of the Upper Solomons to inspect installations and raise morale. Unfortunately for the Japanese, the Americans had decrypted radio messages from which they inferred that Yamamoto would arrive by air at a certain time in southern Bougainville. Counting on his known passion for punctuality, a squadron of long-range P-38's took off from Henderson Field and shot him down precisely on schedule as his plane was coming in for a landing. To the Japanese navy the loss of its most able and colorful commander was the equivalent of a major defeat.

Yamamoto's successor, Admiral Mineichi Koga, directed frequent air raids against Guadalcanal but with steadily diminishing success, for the Imperial Navy had expended its best flyers. The ineptitude of the new, hastily-trained aviators was spectacularly demonstrated in mid-June, when 24 Japanese bombers and 70 Zekes struck at transports in Ironbottom Sound. All but one of the attacking planes were shot down, at a cost of six Allied fighters.

While the Japanese were in general weakening themselves in their attempts to shore up their defenses, the Allies were emphasizing preparations for their coming offensive. Be-

cause General MacArthur proposed to advance along the northern New Guinea coast by a series of waterborne leaps, the Southwest Pacific command set out to build up the tiny Seventh Fleet into a respectable force. The South Pacific meanwhile was training the 43rd Infantry Division to operate amphibiously while the 1st and 2nd Marine Divisions were undergoing rest and rehabilitation from the rigors of the Guadalcanal campaign.

Henderson Field was expanded into a complete bomber base surrrounded by three fighter strips. Five miles to the east, Carney Field, a bomber base bigger than Henderson, went into operation on April 1, 1943. By this time there were on Guadalcanal more than 300 aircraft of every variety.[3] Operating together were bombers and fighters of the Royal New Zealand Air Force and of the United States Army, Navy, and Marine Corps. To this heterogeneous but closely-integrated force, known as Air Command Solomons—Airsols for short—was to fall the major burden of knocking out Rabaul. Equally powerful were the mutually supporting Allied army airfields on New Guinea—at Dobodura near Buna, at Milne Bay, and at Port Moresby.[4] From these fields operated General George C. Kenney's U.S. Fifth Air Force, to which Royal Australian Air Force squadrons were attached. Airsols and the Fifth Air Force were destined within a few months to win command of the air over the whole Eastern New Guinea-Solomons-Bismarcks area.

Meanwhile the pair of Japanese airfields in the Central Solomons, on Munda Point and at the mouth of the Vila River on nearby Kolombangara Island, proved a continuing nuisance and threat to Guadalcanal. As a step preliminary to seizing or neutralizing these fields, Admiral Turner's Third Amphibious Force put troops and Seabees ashore in the Russell Islands, 65 miles northwest of Henderson Field. Here small craft bases were established, and a pair of airstrips was constructed to extend the reach of Airsols bombers a little

[3] By June 30, when the Allied offensive was resumed, Airsols had 213 fighters, 170 light bombers, and 72 heavy bombers ready to fly. By then the Fifth Air Force had operational about 220 fighters, 100 light and medium bombers, and 80 heavy bombers.

[4] Supplemented in late July by a fighter strip at Marilinan, just 40 miles inland from Salamaua.

farther up the Slot. Before and after the Russell Islands occupation, Allied ships and aircraft mined the waters around New Georgia and southern Bougainville, Airsols bombed the Munda and Vila fields by day and by night, and a pair of cruiser-destroyer task forces under Rear Admirals Stanton Merrill and Walden L. Ainsworth took turns making night runs to subject the airstrips to prolonged naval bombardment.

Merrill's and Ainsworth's task forces were a far cry from the usually ill-prepared, often hastily assembled scratch teams that had fought in Ironbottom Sound during the Guadalcanal campaign. Naval forces operating in the Solomons in 1943 were better equipped and much better organized to meet the night-fighting Japanese. Dependable radar had now become generally available on Allied vessels, and fleet personnel had learned to use it effectively. The scopes were housed in a special compartment known as Radar Plot, where contacts were plotted and analyzed. Gradually other information, from radio and lookouts, began to be correlated here, and Radar Plot became the Combat Information Center (CIC). Possession of the CIC gave the Allies an enormous advantage over the Japanese, whose radar, still primitive by American and British standards, had at this time been installed in only their largest vessels. Equally important to the improvement of Allied night fighting tactics was the comparative permanence of the new surface task groups and task forces. Operating regularly together, commanders and crews developed the skills and the confidence that eventually enabled them to expel the Japanese night fighters and their Long Lances from the Solomons. In this exacting school of tactics, three names stand out: Commanders Frederick Moosbrugger and Arleigh Burke and Rear Admiral Merrill, who were to fight three of the most skillfully conducted battles of the war.

At the end of March 1943, the Joint Chiefs of Staff issued a directive covering Task Two of the campaign against Rabaul. MacArthur's assignment was to control the Huon Gulf and Peninsula and to invade New Britain. Halsey's was to invade Bougainville Island and there establish airfields whence fighter-escorted bombers could strike regularly at Rabaul. Before either commander could move upon his assigned objective however, he would have to seize intermediate positions. MacArthur would occupy Kiriwina and Woodlark Islands; simultaneously Halsey would invade the Central Solomons. The purpose of this intermediate step was to deny these positions to the enemy, to extend the Allied bomber radius to cover the final step, and to afford air staging and mutual support between the two Allied lines of advance.

Since the dividing line between Halsey's and MacArthur's areas of command lay just west of Guadalcanal, Task Two would see South Pacific forces penetrating the Southwest Pacific Area. This led to a curious command situation, with Halsey planning the details of his own operations but looking to MacArthur for general strategic directives and to Nimitz for ships, troops, and aircraft to carry them out.

The Central Solomons Campaign

Getting at Munda airfield, the South Pacific's first major objective in Task Two, presented a tricky problem, for the only New Georgia beaches in the vicinity were within easy artillery range of Rendova Island, five miles to the south. But the Japanese, failing to appreciate their advantage, had no artillery and only 120 troops there. So on June 30, 1943 Turner's Third Amphibious Force put ashore on Rendova 6,000 soldiers and marines who wiped out the enemy garrison and turned American guns on Munda. Then, under artillery cover, they began ferrying troops over to New Georgia for the drive on the Japanese airfield. Airsols fighters chased enemy aircraft away whenever they appeared. Only one Allied vessel, Turner's flagship *McCawley*, was seriously damaged. Put out of action by a Japanese airborne torpedo, she was subsequently sunk by an American PT boat that mistook her in the darkness for an enemy.

So far the operation had gone according to schedule, but once the assault forces entered the New Georgia jungle, the optimistic picture changed abruptly. Some 4,500 Japanese, well-entrenched behind a strong defensive perimeter and sporadically reinforced, held off the attackers for a month. The Americans once more faced the problem of seizing a well defended position from a determined enemy under diffi-

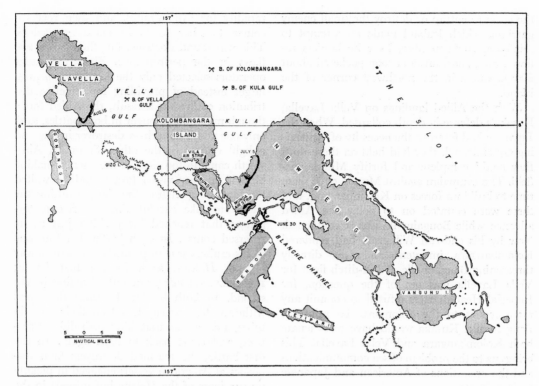

OPERATIONS IN THE CENTRAL SOLOMONS, 1943

cult natural conditions. As at Buna and on Attu, there was a shake-up in the U.S. Army command, and all available reserves had to be committed—32,000 soldiers and 1,700 marines. Even after the airfield had been captured, the invaders had to spend several more weeks dislodging and pursuing enemy defense forces, who, when counterattack proved hopeless, generally succeeded in working their vanishing act, slipping away by water to nearby Kolombangara.

Halsey's original plan had called for a continuation of the "island hopping" campaign, which would bring Allied forces next against Kolombangara and Vila airfield. Admiral Kusaka, who suspected and indeed hoped that this would be the next Allied target, had been reinforcing Kolombangara for weeks, making an assault on that island an increasingly unattractive prospect. Halsey, noting the build-up of enemy strength, decided not to play Kusaka's game. He would by-pass Kolombangara and invade lightly-held Vella Lavella beyond. Such a move would be distasteful to an army general engaged in continental warfare, for it

would leave an enemy force in position to intercept his supplies and attack his rear. But, as Kinkaid had recently demonstrated in going past Kiska to take Attu, the naval commander can sometimes outflank the enemy with impunity provided that in doing so he can isolate him, cut his communications, and leave him to "wither on the vine."

On August 15 the Third Amphibious Force, now headed by Rear Admiral Theodore S. Wilkinson, began putting some 6,000 Americans ashore on Vella Lavella under cover of Airsols fighters operating from the newly captured strip at Munda. Despite persistent enemy air attacks, the assault forces suffered only a few casualties and slight material damage. Wilkinson avoided the high costs and delays of the Munda drive by invading the southern tip of the island, where there were no enemy forces. Here the invaders established a defense perimeter within which Seabees began constructing a new airstrip. When it became apparent that there was to be no counterattack on the American position, troops moved out of the perimeter in both directions along the coast to entrap or destroy the small enemy garrison, which Rabaul made no attempt to reinforce. In September, New Zealanders relieved the Americans and soon pocketed about 600 Japanese in the northwest corner of the island.

With the Allied landings on Vella Lavella, Kusaka's defense in depth collapsed. When the Japanese had foreseen the necessity of evacuating Guadalcanal, they had held on there until they could complete and fortify Munda airfield. The campaign against Munda gave them time to build up forces on Kolombangara, and these were counted on to delay the Allied advance while Bougainville was strengthened. Now by his end-run Wilkinson had rendered Kolombangara impotent and was directly threatening Bougainville. A last-ditch fight for Vella Lavella was out of the question, for Imperial Headquarters refused to commit any more troops to the Solomons. To reinforce Bougainville, Kusaka would have to evacuate both Kolombangara and Vella Lavella. This brings us to the problem of sea communications and the operations of American and Japanese surface forces.

Besides bringing invasion forces to the beachheads, transporting supplies and reinforcements, and bombarding enemy positions, the U.S. Third Fleet had the responsibility along with Airsols of cutting the enemy's communications with his rearward bases. Interception of the Tokyo Express was assigned to Ainsworth's and Merrill's cruiser-destroyer forces. Merrill made no contact with Japanese surface forces during the Central Solomons campaign, but while the Americans were driving on Munda, Ainsworth twice met the enemy in the same waters a little after midnight and fought the almost identical night battles of Kula Gulf (July 6) and Kolombangara (July 13) with similar tactics and similar results. Allied achievements and shortcomings in these battles demonstrate how far American night-fighting tactics had progressed since 1942—and how far they yet had to evolve to offset Japanese training and skill.

Ainsworth entered both battles in the favored nighttime formation, a single column with cruisers in the center and destroyers in the van and rear. In both, his cruisers closed the enemy, fired with almost machine-gun

rapidity for five minutes, and then reversed course together to avoid enemy torpedoes. This was sound doctrine, but there were two flaws in the performance. First, the radar operators selected only the largest or nearest target instead of providing for effective distribution of fire; as a result, the Allied force, though much the stronger in both battles, sank only one vessel in each—a destroyer in one and a light cruiser in the other. Secondly, Ainsworth came in too close to the enemy, making himself an easy visual target, and he waited too long to open fire, thereby permitting the enemy to take careful aim and release torpedoes that reached his position just as he reversed course. In each battle therefore one of his cruisers was torpedoed on the turnaway —U.S.S. *Helena*, sunk in the first battle; H.M.N.Z.S. *Leander*, put out of action in the second. In both battles, Japanese destroyers withdrew temporarily to reload their torpedo tubes, a capability that Ainsworth did not suspect, and came back to fight again. In the first battle, the rearmed destroyers fired torpedoes at American vessels engaged in picking up survivors of the *Helena* but missed; in the second, the returning Japanese torpedoed two cruisers and a destroyer. The cruisers were not severely damaged, but the destroyer could not be saved. In the Battle of Kolombangara, Ainsworth, in addition to turning away after opening fire, released his van destroyers for a torpedo attack, and it was these that sank the Japanese cruiser, *Jintsu*, already put out of action by shellfire. In short, the Americans at this stage showed considerable advance in tactical doctrine over the preceding year but still fell short in battle efficiency and in intelligence of enemy capabilities.

Convinced that Ainsworth's force was smashed, Rear Admiral Shoji Nishimura came steaming down the Slot a few nights after the Battle of Kolombangara with a strong cruiser-destroyer force looking for Merrill. Merrill's ships were not out that night, but a PBY "Black Cat" picked up Nishimura by radar and flashed the word back to Guadalcanal, whence came bombers that sank two of his destroyers, damaged a cruiser, and sent the rest of his force reeling back to the Shortlands. The Japanese, after this sample of the new American aerial night-fighting techniques, steered clear of the Kula Gulf route to their base at Vila, choosing rather to thread the ticklish passage south of Kolombangara. Here American PT boats sank one enemy barge and battered several others but proved no barrier to the Tokyo Express of heavier types.

Admiral Wilkinson decided early in August to put larger craft on the new enemy reinforcement route. Because Merrill's force was too far away and Ainsworth's was depleted by the July battles, he ordered to the area what he had available—Commander Burke's division of six destroyers. Burke, most vocal proponent of independent action for destroyers, had worked out an ingenious plan for just such a mission, but on the eve of battle he was detached to assume a higher command. Luckily, his successor was Commander Moosbrugger, who adopted the essential features of Burke's plan and carried them out with such skill and sense of timing that in the Battle of Vella Gulf he achieved a little classic of naval warfare.[5]

Warned by a search plane that the Express was en route, Moosbrugger's destroyers entered Vella Gulf from the south at 2200, August 6, two columns in line of bearing, and advanced northward, hugging the coast to avoid radar

[5] One of the distinctive features of Burke's battle plan (dated August 1, 1943) was the use of two mutually supporting columns. This concept, Admiral Burke tells us, was based upon his study of the Punic Wars. "The tactics of Scipio Africanus particularly interested me as being sound, simple of execution, and adaptable to naval employment. The plan was based on hitting the enemy with one sudden surprise after another. This was accomplished by putting two destroyer divisions in parallel columns. One division would slip in close, under cover of darkness, launch torpedoes and duck back out. When the torpedoes hit, and the enemy started shooting at the retiring first division, the second half of the team would suddenly open up from another direction. When the rattled enemy turned toward this new and unexpected attack, the first division would slam back in again. Of course, the Solomon Islands area was ideally suited to this type of tactic, with the many islands helping prevent radar detection of the second column.

"Surprise is one of the fundamentals of successful tactics, and successful military leaders throughout history have developed their tactics to insure this vital ingredient. It is usually the decisive increment in battle. These old tactics, adapted to modern tools of war, are still valid. A study of them can provide many clues for increased effectiveness of our own weapons." Letter to W. H. Russell, January 27, 1956.

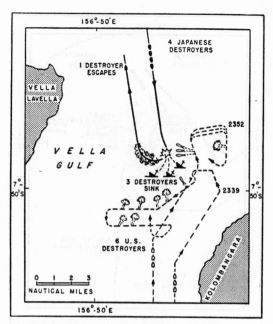

BATTLE OF VELLA GULF, AUGUST 6–7, 1943

or visual detection. A little before midnight, four enemy destroyers, three of them crowded with troops for Vila, entered the Gulf from the north and soon registered themselves on American radar scopes. Moosbrugger's first division thereupon raced past the enemy column on a parallel and opposite course, launched torpedoes, and then promptly turned away together. The other division meanwhile came about on a T-capping course across the van of the enemy column. Just as the torpedoes struck their targets, both American divisions opened up with gunfire. Under this neatly-timed triple blow, the three troop-carrying destroyers exploded, hurling 1,800 soldiers and sailors into the water and creating such a pyrotechnical display that PT boatmen 30 miles away in Kula Gulf thought a volcano had erupted on Kolombangara. The escorting enemy destroyer escaped only because the torpedoes that slid under her hull failed to detonate. None of the American vessels were damaged. The Battle of Vella Gulf provides a perfect example of tactical concentration achieved by divided but mutually supporting forces. Americans at last had outperformed the Japanese at their own specialty.

As usual, the Japanese proved more adept at evacuation than at reinforcement. After the

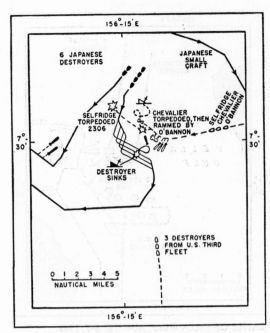

BATTLE OF VELLA LAVELLA, OCTOBER 6–7, 1943

Japanese division of four destroyers missed a chance to cross his T and then masked its own fire by approaching in line of bearing. The Americans fired 14 torpedoes and a hail of shells at the nearest enemy vessel, which burst into flames and presently blew up. By this time the Japanese had turned away under a smoke screen. Walker might properly have turned away also to avoid the inevitable Japanese torpedo attack. Instead, he chose to maintain course in order to keep his guns bearing. As a result, the *Chevalier* and the *Selfridge* both had their bows blown off by torpedoes, and in the confusion the *O'Bannon* rammed the *Chevalier*. The timely arrival of three more Third Fleet destroyers obliged the enemy to retire, but while the Americans were looking after their crippled vessels and sinking the helpless *Chevalier*, the Japanese small craft proceeded to Vella Lavella and carried out still another evacuation.

The Japanese had completed their mission and won the battle, but this was the last battle they were to win in World War II. And their victory did not alter the fact that the Allies now held the Central Solomons, with air fields close enough to support a jump to Bougainville.

The Bougainville Campaign

The scheduled Allied invasion of fiddle-shaped Bougainville, northernmost and largest of the major Solomons, would permit construction of bomber and fighter strips from which Airsols could bring Rabaul under continuous attack. On and near Bougainville there were 33,000 Japanese—mostly in the south, at Kahili and Buin and in the nearby Shortland Islands, and in the north, at Buka and Bonis. Profiting by lessons learned at Munda and on Vella Lavella, Admiral Halsey planned to by-pass the concentration of Japanese strength in the southern bases and invade half way up the weakly defended west coast at Cape Torokina in Empress Augusta Bay. Here the Allies would establish a powerful perimeter, lay out their airstrips, and let the Japanese come to them, over rough mountains and primitive jungle trails.

For so formidable an operation, Halsey had barely enough troops—some 34,000, including

American invasion of Vella Lavella, they waited until late September and the dark of the moon before sending destroyers, submarines, and swift barges to evacuate Kolombangara. American destroyers sent out to intercept succeeded in damaging a destroyer and sinking a submarine and about a third of the barges. Nevertheless three quarters of the garrison of 12,400 got safely away. Obviously the Allies, though they had by-passed Kolombangara, had not truly isolated it.

After the Battle of Vella Gulf, the Japanese had generally avoided surface action, but during their evacuation of Vella Lavella, which closely followed that of Kolombangara, a force of Japanese destroyers found themselves at such a numerical advantage that they disdained to turn tail and run from the Americans. The resulting Battle of Vella Lavella brought little tactical credit to destroyermen on either side.

Warned by search planes of the approach of six Japanese destroyers escorting small craft, Captain Frank R. Walker took destroyers *Selfridge*, *Chevalier*, and *O'Bannon* into the waters northwest of Vella Lavella to intercept. As Walker advanced to attack, the nearer the 3rd Marine Division, the 37th Infantry Division, and a brigade group[6] of New Zealanders, which together made up the I Marine Amphibious Corps, commanded by General Vandegrift. Naval forces were even more scarce because of the concurrent Mediterranean campaign and because Nimitz was about to unleash the U.S. Fifth Fleet in the Central Pacific. Wilkinson would have to cram his first echelon landing force into a dozen transports, escorted by eleven destroyers. Support would be provided by Task Force 39 (Merrill's cruiser-destroyer force) and by Rear Admiral Frederick C. Sherman's carrier task group, including the *Saratoga* and the light carrier *Princeton,* on loan from the Fifth Fleet.

In preparation for the new assault, the Fifth Air Force began a series of massive raids on Rabaul, while Airsols bombed out Japanese airfields on Bougainville. On October 27, 6,000 New Zealanders seized the Treasury Islands for a small-craft staging base, and that night 725 marines landed on Choiseul to attract Japanese attention away from the main Allied invasion area. A little after midnight on D-day, November 1, Merrill's TF 39 provided further diversion by bombarding Buka and Bonis airfields; then while Merrill raced back south to bombard the Shortlands at first light, Sherman's carriers sent in planes to continue the pounding of Buka and Bonis.

While Japanese attention was thus diverted in several directions, Wilkinson's amphibians entered Empress Augusta Bay at dawn on the 1st. Despite determined resistance from about 300 Japanese at the beachhead and an air attack from Rabaul, which Airsols fighters soon scattered, the invasion progressed rapidly. By nightfall the Third Amphibious Force had put ashore 14,000 troops and 6,000 tons of supplies. In the early evening the transports pulled out, and four minelayers began laying a mine field off the beachhead.

The Imperial Eighth Fleet reacted to the new landing much as it had 15 months before when the marines had landed on Guadalcanal. Down from Rabaul came a hastily organized cruiser-destroyer force under Rear Admiral

[6] Comparable to a U.S. regimental combat team. For a definition of regimental combat team, see page 730, *note.*

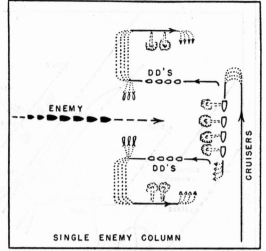

SINGLE ENEMY COLUMN

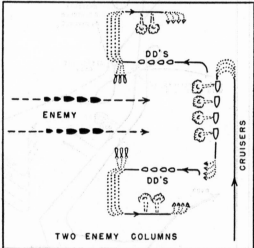

TWO ENEMY COLUMNS

MERRILL'S BATTLE PLAN FOR NIGHT ATTACK

Sentaro Omori to smash the American transports. This attack force was early spotted by Airsols patrol planes, which promptly and accurately reported their find to South Pacific headquarters and continued tracking. By 0200, November 2, Omori in intense darkness under a rain squall, was approaching the Torokina beachhead, his two heavy cruisers *Myoko* and *Haguro* flanked to starboard and port by light cruisers *Agano* and *Sendai,* each leading three destroyers.

The only force available to stop Omori was TF 39. Though the crews were exhausted after having carried out two bombardments in the past 16 hours, Admiral Halsey had no choice

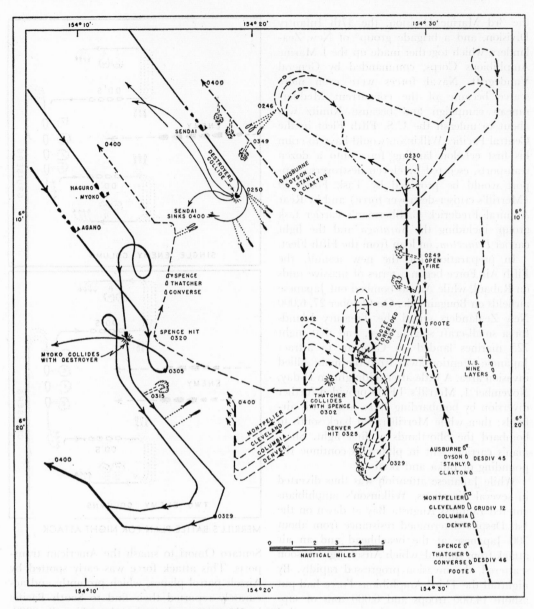

BATTLE OF EMPRESS AUGUSTA BAY, NOVEMBER 2, 1943

but to order them to Empress Augusta Bay. Caution was imposed on Merrill by the fact that TF 39 was now the principal Allied surface force in the whole South Pacific. Instead of risking scarce cruisers in a battle of annihilation, he would have to limit himself to repulsing the attackers from the beachhead. In accordance with an oft-rehearsed plan, he intended to release his destroyer divisions for

torpedo attacks on the flanks of the enemy. With his four light cruisers he would block the entrance to the bay and, by continuous fire from his six-inch guns and a series of simultaneous reversals of course, gradually force the enemy out to sea. Merrill was fortunate in having Arleigh Burke, now Captain Burke, as commander of his Destroyer Division 45, for the two had operated together and saw eye-to-eye in tactical matters. But Desdiv 46, his other four-destroyer division, would be at a disadvantage, for it was so new as a unit that Commander Bernard Austin had not yet had an opportunity to exercise his vessels in formation.

At 0227, as TF 39 neared Empress Augusta Bay on course 345° with the three divisions in line of bearing north to south, flagship *Montpelier* detected the enemy 18 miles away, coming down from northwest. Merrill thereupon shifted to course due north, which brought his divisions into the usual American single column formation for night action. As soon as the enemy appeared on his radar scopes, Burke, in the van, swung left and led Desdiv 45 toward the flank of the northern enemy group. The American cruisers then reversed course together, and Merrill detached Desdiv 46 to strike the southern enemy group.

At 5,600 yards on the *Sendai*'s port bow, Desdiv 45 fired half salvos of torpedoes and turned away together. None of the torpedoes found targets, for the Japanese had changed course. The *Sendai* had seen the American cruisers and launched torpedoes, warning Omori, who ordered his divisions to wheel south to form a line of battle.

"My guppies are swimming!" Burke had reported at the moment he launched. Merrill then began to count off the six minutes it would take the torpedoes to complete their run, but when his CIC reported the enemy change of course, he at once ordered his cruisers to open fire. Forty-eight guns promptly began to roar, taking as their target the nearby northern group, which replied with shells that fell forward and short. Two of the Japanese destroyers collided while maneuvering to avoid the concentrated 6-inch American fire, and the *Sendai* began to blaze and fell out of line with a jammed rudder. The Americans had handily won the first round, but Desdiv 45 had become separated on the turnaway. It would take Burke an hour to locate and reassemble his vessels and bring them back into the battle.

Because of Omori's change of course, the TF 39 cruisers at 0251 turned together to course 200° in order to close the range. It now appeared that Austin's destroyers had been released prematurely, for Merrill's advance to the southwest brought them within the cruisers' line of fire. Moreover, destroyer *Foote* had become separated.[7] In racing west to rejoin Desdiv 46, she cut across the path of the oncoming cruisers so that the *Denver* had to sheer left to avoid a collision.

To clear Desdiv 46 and close on the *Sendai* group, the cruisers at 0302 turned north. Almost at once they had to swing right to avoid hitting a vessel dead in the water. It was the *Foote* again. Still heading west she had been struck by one of the *Sendai*'s torpedoes, which had demolished her stern.

At 0310 Merrill turned south once more, thus completing the first loop of a huge figure eight. The waters of the South Pacific were now witnessing a new high in ship handling. Barking his orders by TBS through the roar of gunfire, Merrill kept his cruisers in perfect order—zigzagging and swinging back and forth across the enemy's line of fire to present him constantly changing problems in range and deflection. Through 30 minutes of rapid maneuver Merrill managed always to be somewhere else when the enemy's shells or torpedoes arrived.

To take advantage of his 8-inch guns, Omori, like Merrill, wanted to fight at long range, but he was having difficulty locating the Americans. So he began a complete loop, thereby sadly confusing the *Agano* group, which vaguely tried to conform. Then as he steadied again on a southerly course, American 6-inch shells began to fall all around him. One of the *Agano* destroyers, while dodging, collided with the *Myoko* and had a piece of her bow sheared off. Then six shells, including four duds, hit the *Haguro*. By this time Japanese planes arriving over the American cruisers were dropping red and white parachute flares. These, reflecting off the low cloud ceiling, combined with star shells to turn the night into an eerie twilight and thereby rob Merrill of some of his radar advantage.

Now at last Omori saw Merrill and advanced southeast to close the range a little. The *Myoko* and the *Haguro* launched torpedoes and fired salvos of shells. Three shells

[7] When Desdiv 46 had countermarched to conform to the cruisers, the *Foote* had turned at once instead of following around in column.

hit the *Denver,* whereupon Merrill turned away, making smoke. Omori, under the illusion that he had sunk several heavy cruisers, also turned away and presently ordered a general retirement. In so doing he abandoned his assigned mission of sinking the American transports. But, greatly overestimating the force opposing him, he thought he had done well enough, and he wanted to be out of easy range of Airsols by dawn.

While Merrill and Omori were dueling it out, Austin's division was suffering one unlucky break after another. The *Foote,* as we have seen, was early put out of action. Then, while the other three destroyers were maneuvering frantically to avoid being silhouetted by starshell and to clear the line of fire of their own cruisers, the *Spence* sideswiped the *Thatcher.* Though both vessels suffered heavy topside damage, Desdiv 46 proceeded westward at high speed until it was 6,000 yards on the port bow of the enemy center group, in perfect position to carry out a torpedo attack against the Japanese heavy cruisers. At that moment the *Spence* was temporarily slowed down by a shell hit at the water line. Immediately afterward, the CIC evaluator became disoriented and reported to Austin that the *Myoko* and *Haguro* were American ships. With no time to check, Austin turned north to go after the *Sendai,* which was turning in circles but still firing. A couple of his destroyers launched torpedoes and apparently made hits, but the cruiser was still afloat as he headed northwest in pursuit of her two collision-damaged destroyers.

Burke, after having cruised far and wide to reassemble his scattered division, now sped in from the east and sent the *Sendai* down at last in a hail of shells. Then, because radar recognition was working badly that night, he set out in hot pursuit of Austin. Presently Austin's division opened fire on the Japanese destroyers, one of which caught Burke's attention. "We have a target smoking badly at 7,000 yards, and we are going to open up," Burke warned by TBS. "Oh-oh, don't do it," replied Austin, "that's us." And so the two Japanese destroyers got away, and Burke turned his fire on the *Spence.* "Hope you are not shooting at us," said Austin. "Sorry," Burke responded, "but you'll have to excuse the next four salvos. They

are already on their way." After such loss of opportunity and near disaster the two division commanders at length located each other and with special satisfaction joined forces in sending down the last of the Japanese cripples in the area, the destroyer whose bow had been ripped off by the *Myoko.* Except for the lost *Sendai* the remainder of Omori's force was making best speed for Rabaul.

Because dawn was breaking, Merrill ordered his divisions to leave off the chase and to rendezvous for better defense against the inevitable air attack. Leaving three destroyers behind to salvage the torpedoed *Foote,* he headed south with the rest of TF 39. At 0800 the Japanese struck with a hundred carrier bombers and fighters from Rabaul. By a combination of accurate antiaircraft fire and deft ship handling, the Americans shot down 17 attacking planes and avoided all but two rather inconsequential bomb hits. Before the enemy planes could come in for a second strike, Airsols fighters arrived and chased them away, shooting down eight more.

The American performance in the Battle of Empress Augusta Bay was not without flaws, particularly in the accuracy and distribution of radar-controlled gunfire, but Merrill had brilliantly carried out his mission of repulsing the enemy from the beachhead. His night victory demonstrated the soundness of the tactical doctrine and practice that his predecessors had been groping for.

Incensed at Omori's poor showing, Admiral Koga promptly relieved him of his command. He then ordered Vice Admiral Takeo Kurita south from Truk with a stronger, better integrated cruiser-destroyer force to redeem Omori's failure. And to bolster the air defense of the Bismarcks, he once more stripped his carriers, sending down 173 fleet aircraft.

On November 4, Airsols planes sighted Kurita approaching Rabaul to refuel and flashed a timely warning. Kurita's force was too strong for Merrill, even if Merrill's cruisers and destroyers had been within reach and his crews fresh. In this desperate emergency Halsey did what the Navy had recoiled from doing 16 months before when MacArthur had suggested it. He sent Sherman's carrier group into the Solomon Sea for an attack on the ships at Rabaul. At the same time he directed

Airsols to lend Sherman all the help it could.

Halsey's perilous resort succeeded beyond the most sanguine hopes of anybody in the South Pacific command. On the morning of November 5, as Sherman maneuvered under a concealing cloud cover 60 miles southwest of Empress Augusta Bay, Airsols fighters from Vella Lavella arrived and took over combat air patrol. The carriers were thus able to send nearly a hundred planes against the target. Striking from clear skies over Rabaul, Sherman's bombers bored in through a steel curtain of antiaircraft fire. Their objective was Kurita's force, which had anchored in Rabaul's Simpson Harbor just two hours before. At a cost of ten aircraft, the American dive bombers and torpedo planes put Kurita out of business, damaging six cruisers and two destroyers.[8] There would be no surface attack on the amphibious shipping in Empress Augusta Bay.

Elated at the success of his experiment, Halsey tried it again on a larger scale. From the Fifth Fleet he borrowed an additional carrier group, including the *Essex,* the *Bunker Hill,* and the *Independence,* under Rear Admiral Alfred E. Montgomery. On November 11 he sent both Sherman and Montgomery against Rabaul. Sherman attacked first from the waters north of Bougainville but was thwarted by foul weather. Montgomery had better luck. Striking from south of Bougainville under Airsols fighter cover, his carriers launched 185 planes, which thrust aside defending Zekes to hit shipping once more in Simpson Harbor. Kurita had prudently departed, but there were other targets. The Americans sank a destroyer, torpedoed another, sheered off the stern of a light cruiser, and played havoc among transports and cargo vessels.

This time Admiral Kusaka located the source of his attackers and struck back. In the afternoon, 120 Japanese planes swooped down from the north and headed for Montgomery's carriers. Their raid cost them 35 aircraft without damaging a single ship. American losses in both attack and defense were limited to eleven planes. The opposition of carrier fighters plus land-based combat patrol plus intense VT-fused antiaircraft fire was simply too formi-

dable for the hastily trained Japanese aviators who now replaced the veterans expended in the defense of the Solomons.

Sherman's and Montgomery's carrier groups now steamed away to participate with the Fifth Fleet in opening the drive across the Central Pacific. Their contribution to the campaign against Rabaul, though potent, was not the most lasting of their achievements. They had settled once and for all the long-debated question as to whether carriers could be risked against powerful enemy bases. Moreover they had paralyzed the Combined Fleet at a crucial stage in the war. The Central Pacific forces would meet no fleet opposition at the outset of their offensive, for Koga was obliged to send his carriers to Japan to train new flyers to replace his losses.

With the departure of the carriers, the conduct of the Solomons campaign once more devolved upon local forces. In the afternoon of November 24, Captain Burke, then heading for Bougainville with a squadron of five destroyers, received a message from Admiral Halsey's headquarters: "Thirty-One-Knot Burke, get athwart the Buka-Rabaul evacuation line. . . . If enemy contacted, you know what to do."[9]

The Japanese army command at Rabaul, believing that the Americans were about to assault Buka, had requested the navy to rush more soldiers to the area and bring away the airmen. A Tokyo Express of two destroyers and three destroyer-transports was told off to do the job. This was the movement that Halsey wanted stopped, and Burke knew very well what to do. Here at last was an opportunity to make personal use of his destroyer battle plan.

The Battle of Cape St. George, which occurred that night, was in essence a duplication of the Battle of Vella Gulf, followed by a chase. Reaching the interception point a little before 0100, Burke made radar contact with the two vessels of the enemy screen. Then while Commander Austin with two destroyers

---

[8] Included was the heavy cruiser *Mogami.* Newly repaired from her battering at Midway, she had to return to Japan for another major repair job.

[9] By this message Halsey's operations officer, Captain Harry R. Thurber, conferred upon "31-knot Burke" the nickname that soon became known around the world. The prefix, from an old destroyer shipmate, was a gentle gibe at Burke's repeated reports that he was "making 31 knots" with a force previously reported as capable of no more than 30 knots sustained speed.

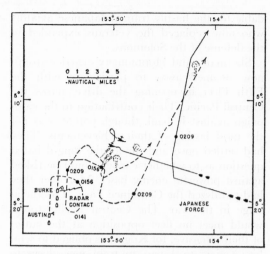

BATTLE OF CAPE ST. GEORGE, NOVEMBER 25, 1943

The New Guinea Campaign

We now have to backtrack a few months and follow the operations of Southwest Pacific forces. It will be recalled that MacArthur's assignment in Task Two of the campaign against Rabaul was to control the Huon Gulf and Peninsula and to invade New Britain. But, like Halsey, he was obliged first to seize positions nearer his established airfields.

On June 30, 1943, timed to coincide with South Pacific landings on Rendova and New Georgia, Southwest Pacific forces began putting troops ashore without opposition on Kiriwina and Woodlark Islands off the Papuan Peninsula and at Nassau Bay 17 miles southeast of Japanese-held Salamaua. Admiral Barbey's Seventh Amphibious Force staged the island invasions, proceeding from Townsville and Milne Bay with destroyers, transports, and beaching craft. But because no one was yet ready to risk such valuable vessels in the inner reaches of the Solomon Sea, the Nassau Bay operation was a mere 40-mile run up the coast with elements of the 41st U.S. Infantry Division carried in PT's and landing craft. Four such night runs established a beachhead.

The main purpose of the Nassau Bay operation was to secure a coastal position to ease the problem of supplying the 3rd Australian Division in the Bulolo Valley. Here at the site of a small pre-war airstrip just 30 miles southwest of Salamaua, Australian troops had been isolated since the Japanese invasion of New Guinea. Meagerly supplied and reinforced by air, they had successfully held off all enemy attacks for more than a year. Once the Bulolo Valley veterans had joined hands with the newly-arrived Americans however, MacArthur had a special assignment for the combined forces. He ordered them to make a diversionary attack on Salamaua, which he was about to by-pass by sea and by air. In preparation for the by-pass, surveys of the dangerous offshore reefs went on apace, and General Kenney's Fifth Air Force planes ranged as far west as Madang and Wewak destroying enemy aircraft. The diversionary attack, which thrust back the defenders of Salamaua to within six miles of the town, put the Japanese in the Huon Gulf area into a quandary. Cut off from Rabaul by Allied aircraft and barge-hunting

maneuvered to take them under fire at the appropriate moment, Burke led his other three toward the enemy's flank, launched 15 torpedoes at his extended track, and turned away. The Japanese destroyers, having seen nothing, plowed unsuspectingly ahead. Both blew up as Burke's torpedoes reached them at the calculated point. Austin thereupon opened fire and swung in to finish them off. By that time Burke was away after the loaded transports. He sank one with shellfire and chased the other two to within 60 miles of Rabaul before turning away to clear the area while it was still dark.

Meanwhile Vandegrift's soldiers and marines on Bougainville had moved steadily forward despite increasing opposition from Japanese forces filtering through the jungles. Airsols lent close, effective air support and, together with the Third Fleet, kept the Tokyo Express from resuming operations. The Third Amphibious Force, despite vicious and damaging air attacks out of Rabaul, in two weeks brought 34,000 men and 23,000 tons of supplies to the expanding perimeter. The I Marine Amphibious Corps in another month of hard fighting pushed the defense line inland and laterally along the coast until it enclosed 22 square miles. Within this area Seabees and a New Zealand engineering brigade constructed a fighter and a bomber strip by the end of 1943. These airfields, just 220 miles from Rabaul, extended Halsey's bomber line to include the Bismarcks. The South Pacific forces had completed their assignment in Task Two.

PT boats, they were obliged to reinforce threatened Salamaua by drawing troops from Lae—exactly what MacArthur hoped they would do.

In the night of September 3–4, Barbey's Amphibious Force at last penetrated the Solomon Sea, moved across the Huon Gulf past Salamaua, and after dawn put nearly 8,000 Australians ashore east of Lae in the face of an enemy air attack, which the Fifth Air Force quickly dispersed. The next day, army transport planes from Port Moresby, escorted by fighters from Marilinan, flew over the jungle and dropped 1,700 American paratroops, who quickly seized a Japanese airstrip west of Lae. The 7th Australian Division was then flown in to the captured field and began advancing on Lae from one side to meet their seaborne compatriots moving in from the other. The Japanese thereupon abandoned Salamaua and attempted to take a stand at Lae, which however soon became untenable under the pounding of American destroyer guns. So, as the pincers closed, the Imperial Army evacuated Lae also. The 7,500 defenders took to the jungle and began a starving, month-long march northward across the Huon Peninsula to the coastal town of Sio. (See map page 716.)

From captured Lae, Barbey in late September carried a brigade group of Australians by sea 82 miles around the tip of the peninsula for pre-dawn landings north of Finschhafen. This invasion took the enemy completely by surprise. Expecting the Allied forces to march overland, they had deployed most of their troops south and west of the town. Only a handful of Japanese guarded the northern approaches. These the Australians quickly pushed aside and, after a series of skirmishes, took possession of Finschhafen on October 2. The local defenders thereupon pulled out to a nearby mountain range to await a Japanese division coming overland from Madang. But the Australians, using water transportation, could be supplied and reinforced more rapidly than their antagonists. They shattered a Japanese counterattack in mid-December and by early January were pushing 7,000 enemy survivors along the coastal road toward Sio. Meanwhile, the 7th Australian Division had outflanked Sio by way of the river valleys and was advancing on Madang from the interior.

In a series of quick strokes MacArthur had conquered all of the Huon Peninsula except the Sio area. He thereby completed his conquest of the northeast coast of New Guinea from Milne Bay to Vitiaz Strait. The quick acceleration of the Southwest Pacific advance, in such striking contrast to the painful march on Buna, resulted in part from a touch of sea power in the form of Barbey's makeshift amphibious force. It was also made possible by the diversion of Japanese strength in the vain attempt to stop Halsey's march up the Solomons.

Admiral King had early in the year questioned the wisdom of expending time and lives to capture Fortress Rabaul. At far less cost, once airfields were operational on Bougainville, Rabaul could be bombed into impotence while Southwest Pacific forces broke through the barrier of Bismarck-based air and sea power and captured the Admiralty Islands on the far side. In the Admiralties was ample level ground for airfields and base installations, and here also was Seeadler Harbor, a finer anchorage than Rabaul's Simpson Harbor. In August the Combined Chiefs, then meeting at Quebec, concurred with King in deciding that Rabaul was to be neutralized and by-passed rather than captured.

Nevertheless, MacArthur decided to go ahead with the invasion of New Britain. Before advancing westward through Vitiaz Strait, he wanted both shores in Allied hands to secure his sea communications from air or surface attack. By late December the stepped-up Fifth Air Force and Airsols offensives had brought the whole Bismarck defense system to the verge of collapse. But MacArthur, not realizing that the door to the west stood open before him, went ahead with his original plan and ordered the 1st Marine Division into New Britain. An Army invasion at Arawe on the south coast in mid-December provided a small-craft staging base that was never used. Then on December 26 the Guadalcanal veterans, supported by Seventh Fleet guns and Fifth Air Force planes, stormed ashore near Cape Gloucester on the north coast. Fighting through swamps in the monsoon rain, the marines captured the nearby enemy airfield in less than a week. Then they shattered the local defense forces and chased the 17th Imperial Division back to Rabaul.

Meanwhile, Barbey on January 2 had used his Cape Gloucester task force to rush an American regimental combat team of 7,000 troops[10] to a landing at lightly-held Saidor, a village on the New Guinea north coast. Meeting only slight resistance, the soldiers quickly took possession of a prewar airfield nearby. The sorely reduced Imperial Army Air Force did not react until mid-afternoon, after all Allied vessels had got clean away. Subsequent echelons of troops and engineers soon turned Saidor into an important Allied naval and air staging base.

The occupation of Saidor became something of a model for subsequent Southwest Pacific amphibious operations. It by-passed the 12,000 fugitives from Lae and Finschhafen now at Sio, cutting them off from the rest of the Japanese Eighteenth Army at Madang and Wewak. It provided an excellent base for covering Vitiaz Strait and for supporting the concurrent Cape Gloucester operation, the scheduled assault on the Admiralties, and the planned westward advance along the New Guinea coast. Moreover it was a classic example of what Admiral Wilkinson, in baseball parlance, had called "hitting 'em where they ain't."

The Japanese at Sio, cut off from supply by

[10] The 126th Regimental Combat Team of the 32nd Infantry Division.

A *regimental combat team* (abbreviated RCT), or simply *combat team*, was defined as follows in the Army Field Manual in use at that time: "The infantry regiment may be grouped with a battalion of light artillery and units of other arms in suitable proportion. Such tactical groupings are called *combat teams*, and their composition may be prescribed in standard operating procedure." For amphibious operations the combat team was subdivided into (usually three) *battalion landing teams*, or simply *landing teams*.

The combat team system was the ground forces' counterpart to the Navy's task force system. For administration and training, the army or marine corps division segregated its elements by type. A typical division would be administratively organized into three regiments of infantry, each comprising three battalions, an artillery regiment, an engineer regiment, and battalions of special and service troops (tank, special weapons, transport, medical, and so on). For specific tasks such as amphibious assaults, the division (usually reinforced) was divided into combat teams of size and composition suitable to the task. The troops were carried to the combat area in teams so that the sinking of a single transport would not mean the loss of all the division's artillery, tanks, or other element.

land and sea and too weak to attack the growing Allied garrison at Saidor, abandoned Sio to the Australians on January 15, turned inland, and set out on foot for Madang by way of the jungle. Two thousand of them, starved and diseased, died on the way. Hardly had the survivors arrived when the 7th Australian Division, attacking from the interior, obliged the whole Madang garrison to fall back to Wewak.

Neutralizing Rabaul

Though Rabaul had been stunned by the Allied air offensive in the fall of 1943, it remained far too powerful either to be invaded or entirely by-passed. The 90,000 Japanese there began to go underground, scooping out subterranean barracks, shops, and hangars. Though the fleet had left, Kusaka retained some small craft and more than a thousand seagoing barges. All carrier planes had been withdrawn, but as late as mid-December there were at Rabaul and at other Japanese bases in the Bismarcks nearly 300 serviceable aircraft. This was more striking power than either MacArthur or Nimitz cared to have athwart his communications as his forces advanced westward.

So with the completion of the new Airsols fighter strip on Bougainville in mid-December, Halsey launched an all-out air offensive to pound the Bismarcks into final impotence. Then and later enemy aircraft were to be the principal targets. In January, when the bigger fields at Torokina became operational, Airsols bombers operating directly from Bougainville stepped up the raids to one or more a day. A month later they were averaging a thousand sorties a week. For a while Admiral Koga kept rushing additional planes to Rabaul. But in mid-February the U.S. Fifth Fleet, advancing rapidly across the Central Pacific, made a devastating raid on Truk. Koga thereupon abandoned Rabaul as indefensible and began pulling aircraft out of the Bismarcks to areas where they could be used more profitably. U.S. Third Fleet destroyer squadrons now moved freely along the coasts of New Britain and New Ireland, demonstrating Allied control of the sea and air by bombarding Japanese shore installations.

Fortress Rabaul had been knocked out. But

to make sure that the Japanese should not again make use of their extensive facilities in the Bismarck Archipelago, Halsey and MacArthur completed their ring of steel around the enemy stronghold.

In February 1944, Wilkinson's Third Amphibious Force placed nearly 6,000 New Zealand and American troops ashore in the Green Islands 115 miles due east of Rabaul. After the invaders had defeated the small Japanese garrison, Seabees built a fighter strip on the main island, thereby bringing the entire Archipelago within the radius of fighter-escorted Airsols bombers.

At the end of February, MacArthur ordered a thousand-man American reconnaissance-in-force on Los Negros, easternmost of the Admiralties. Though there were 4,300 Japanese on the islands, Allied fleet guns and air support enabled the invaders to turn the reconnaissance into a regular invasion. They seized part of the airdrome and drew around it a tight perimeter into which poured fresh echelons of troops with artillery and Seabees with bulldozers. These quickly expanded the beachhead and made the airstrip operational.

In mid-March, the Third Fleet put the 4th Marine Regiment ashore on Emirau, 70 miles northwest of Kavieng. Soon 18,000 men had gone ashore on this island which the Japanese had never occupied, and work was underway on a PT base and another airstrip.

The boxing in of Rabaul was complete, but this time there was scarcely a pause in Allied offensive operations. As the marines occupied Emirau, MacArthur's soldiers were invading Manus, main island of the Admiralty group. By the end of March 3,300 Japanese had been killed or captured in the Admiralties, as against 300 Americans killed, and work on the naval and air base was under way—not merely to help keep Rabaul neutralized but to support further operations westward.

Development of the base facilities in the Admiralty Islands (or simply Manus, as they came collectively to be called) was the last cooperative effort of the South and Southwest Pacific commands. The South Pacific Area, left far behind by the war, was being gradually reduced to garrison status. Its army forces, plus a few warships, were allotted to MacArthur; its marine and most of its naval forces

went to Nimitz. MacArthur had hoped to enlist Halsey to command his Seventh Fleet, but Admiral King had other plans. Halsey was ordered to Pearl Harbor for a seagoing command under Nimitz.[11]

For MacArthur, the capture of Manus marked the end of one campaign and the beginning of another. Even before the Admiralties were secured, he was planning a tremendous 400-mile leap westward to Hollandia, a movement not inappropriately named Operation RECKLESS. Beyond Hollandia he would leap forward again and again until at length he reached the Philippines, in fulfillment of his promise: "I shall return."

Summary

As noted at the beginning of the chapter, 1943 saw Allied offensives underway in the North, Central, and South Pacific. The table on pages 732–3 shows concurrent Allied operations from early 1943 to the end of the campaign against Rabaul in March 1944.

Operations in the North Pacific were not only of little importance in themselves; they had little influence on events elsewhere. The 20-month campaign against Rabaul, on the contrary, was of enormous significance. Among the numerous advantages accruing to the Allies from this campaign, five stand out: (1) it enabled MacArthur to break through the Bismarcks barrier of enemy air and sea power and advance toward the Philippines, (2) it bypassed and put out of the war more than 125,000 Japanese troops, (3) it reduced Japanese air power to the point where it was no longer a serious threat, (4) it forced the Japanese to withdraw their carriers from the Pacific, and (5) it gained for the United States time to provide ships, weapons, and trained manpower for a swift advance across the Central Pacific in 1944.

Japan lost nearly 1,000 naval aircraft trying to recapture Guadalcanal and about 1,500 more defending the Upper Solomons and

---

[11] The plan that brought Halsey and MacArthur into close cooperation during the advance on Rabaul was given the code name ELKTON, after the small Maryland town famous for quick marriages. At the same time, the tentative plan for operations westward after the reduction of Rabaul was prophetically named RENO.

1943	NORTH	CENTER*	SOUTH	
			South Pacific	Southwest Pacific
March	26—Battle of the Komandorskis			2-5—Battle of the Bismarck Sea
April			18—Death of Yamamoto	
May	11—Assault on Attu	30—First of new carriers joins U.S. Pacific Fleet		
June			The Dual Advance on Rabaul	
			30—Invasion of New Georgia Group	30—Invasion of Kiriwina, Woodlark, and Nassau Bay
July			6—Battle of Kula Gulf 13—Battle of Kolombangara	
August	15—Occupation of Kiska		6-7—Battle of Vella Gulf 15—Invasion of Vella Lavella	
September		1—Raid on Marcus I. 18-19—Raid on Gilberts		16—Capture of Lae
October		5-6—Raid on Wake I.	6-7—Battle of Vella Lavella	2—Capture of Finschhafen
November		20—Assault on the Gilberts	1—Invasion of Bougainville 2—Battle of Empress Augusta Bay 5 & 11—Carrier Strikes on Rabaul 25—Battle of Cape St. George	
December				26—Assault on Cape Gloucester

1944	NORTH	CENTER*	SOUTH	
January			South Pacific	Southwest Pacific
				2—Occupation of Saidor 15—Capture of Sio
February		1—Assault on the Marshalls	15—Occupation of the Green Is.	
		17—Assault on Eniwetok 17-18—Raid on Truk 22—Raid on the Marianas		
				29—Assault on the Admiralties
March			20—Occupation of Emirau	

* Operations in the Central Pacific are covered in Chapter 39.

Rabaul. Exact figures for Japanese army aircraft lost in the defense of New Guinea are unavailable but they must have been almost as great.[12] When Airsols, the Fifth Air Force, and U.S. Pacific Fleet carriers combined efforts in support of the Bougainville invasion, they very nearly wiped out the Japanese carrier planes committed to the defense of Rabaul. With the Combined Fleet stripped of half its fighters, 85 per cent of its dive bombers, and 90 per cent of its torpedo planes, Admiral Koga had no choice but to send his carriers back to the home islands to train new flyers. This fruitless draining away of Japanese air power left Japan's defenses vulnerable everywhere. It enormously facilitated Nimitz' drive across the center, and this in turn allowed the Japanese at most six months to train new fleet aviators before they were forced into battle against American flyers who had generally two years' training and a minimum of 300 hours flying time.

[12] Japanese naval aircraft loss figures are from U.S. Strategic Bombing Survey, *Interrogations of Japanese Officials*, Nav. Nos. 50, 86, and 97. Noted above are combat losses only; these were greatly exceeded by operational losses. The estimate of Japanese army aircraft losses is based mainly on USSBS, *The Fifth Air Force in the War against Japan*, 59–61.

Task Two and subsequent joint operations against the Bismarcks are best referred to as the "Dual Advance on Rabaul"—to avoid confusion with the far more powerful Dual Advance on the Philippines, with which it eventually merged. Advancing simultaneously along more than one line toward an objective undeniably risks defeat in detail, but a dual or multiple drive also confers the advantages of exterior position: it can keep the enemy off balance and under continuous pressure, it obliges him to divide his own forces and leaves him in doubt where the next attack will come, and it is a means of achieving strategic concentration by bringing one's main strength against part of the enemy forces while the enemy is held at other points.

No one has adversely criticized the concept of the Dual Advance on Rabaul. True, the Japanese gained some of the advantages of interior position in that they, at least theoretically, could strike with the same forces from New Britain against either line of Allied advance, but the great merit of the Allied plan was that the South Pacific and the Southwest Pacific offensives were mutually supporting. For the Allies to have advanced exclusively via the Solomons or exclusively via New Guinea would have meant leaving a flank uncovered.

39:

Beginning the Central Pacific Drive

From the beginning of Operation WATCHTOWER in 1942, General MacArthur had in mind a fairly complete strategic plan for defeating the Japanese. Early in 1943 he spelled it out and laid it before the Joint Chiefs of Staff. He proposed that, once Rabaul had been captured or neutralized, the transpacific advance on Japan should be via New Guinea and the Philippines by forces under his command. This drive, along what he called the New Guinea-Mindanao Axis, would be mainly an army offensive, with troops carried forward by naval forces in a series of coastal leaps and landed under cover of army aircraft. The Navy, besides transport and convoy, would carry out such supporting functions as shore bombardment, guarding communications, and securing the flank of the Army's advance by neutralizing enemy-held offshore islands.

MacArthur argued that his proposed line of advance made use of bases already established in the South Pacific and Southwest Pacific Areas, that it would maintain a defensive shield between Australia and the enemy-occupied Central Pacific islands, that it was the only feasible route along which land-based air support could be provided all the way, and that the large land masses in the southwestern and western Pacific would enable Allied forces to by-pass enemy strong points and seize relatively unopposed beachheads.

Opponents of the New Guinea-Mindanao Axis argued that it was a roundabout approach to Japan, uneconomical of force and requiring long and vulnerable communication lines; that it was a slow means of approach, with each successive advance limited to the attack radius of fighter aircraft and of fighter-escorted bombers; that, once begun, it was obvious and predictable, permitting the enemy to mass his strength in the path of the oncoming Allied forces; that it exposed troops to malaria and other diseases of the tropical jungles; that it was by way of close and mutually supporting enemy strong points; and that the successive beachheads of this line of advance would be subject to attack by troops moving overland, and its flank, rear, and communication lines, to attack from the Japanese-held islands of the Central Pacific.

The United States Navy, faced since 1898 with the problem of defense or recovery of the Philippines, had long ago concluded that the best line of advance was directly across the Central Pacific. Here there were no large land masses, only hundreds of small islands and atolls, providing a choice of numerous targets. An Allied advance in the Central Pacific would be construed by the enemy as a potential threat to his whole island empire, obliging him to fragmentize his strength all over the Pacific to defend each position. Allied forces coming against such tiny points of land would of course have to assault defended beachheads, but only so many troops could occupy any one small island or group of islands. Because of the vast distances between the island groups, they could not in general be mutually supporting and, once isolated by America's growing carrier air power, they could not be reinforced. The advance across the center, through an area where the climate was healthful and the communication lines short, would be economical of troops and shipping. It would cut Japan's communications to the South Pacific and establish shorter Allied lines to the same theater. It would speedily bring the war into Japanese waters and force out the enemy fleet for a decision that presumably would leave Japan itself open to attack.

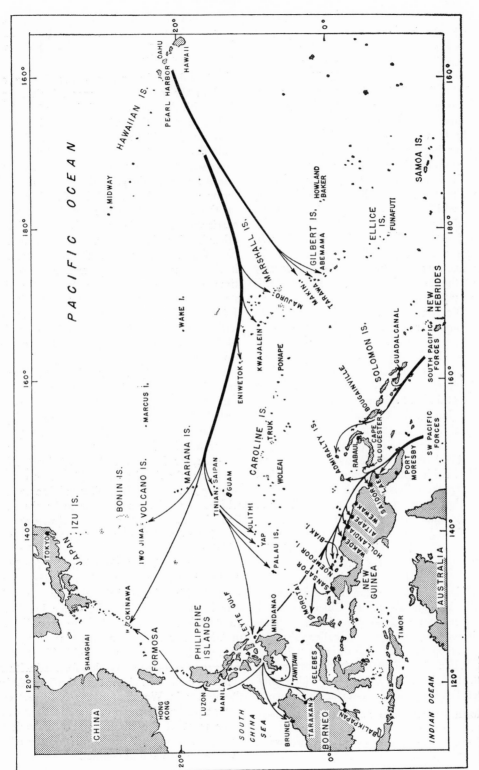

ACROSS THE PACIFIC

In anticipation of the eventual opening of a Central Pacific Axis, the United States Navy, just before and after the declaration of war, had ordered 22 new fleet carriers, and these were becoming available in 1943. Used in support of the New Guinea-Mindanao Axis they would be largely wasted, but freed from a merely auxiliary role they could be used continuously to win command of the sea over ever-increasing areas. Central Pacific forces, spearheaded by these mobile arifields, could eventually dispense with land-based air support and make tremendous leaps, invading any point to which reasonably secure communications could be established.

The Joint Chiefs of Staff and their subcommittees, after carefully weighing all the arguments, reached a compromise that largely favored the Navy's plan. Over MacArthur's vigorous protests, they decided to open a Central Pacific Axis as the main line of advance against Japan. In deference to Australian fears however and because Allied forces in the south were already in contact with a retreating enemy, the chiefs did not propose to reorient the fighting front entirely but to continue along the New Guinea-Mindanao Axis as a supporting operation for the Central Pacific Axis.

Admiral King had tentatively brought up the idea of a new line of advance at the Casablanca Conference in January 1943. The startled British Chiefs protested that thus broadening the offensive against Japan might reduce the scale of operations in Europe, which was and remained the primary theater. General Marshall won British assent however with assurances that the new drive could be carried out with resources already assigned to the Pacific. The Joint Chiefs thereupon developed their "Strategic Plan for the Defeat of Japan," which the Combined Chiefs endorsed at the Washington Conference in May. This plan, it will be remembered, called also for early participation of British and Chinese forces. When these were not forthcoming, the final strategic plan for 1943–44 provided only for the following ground-air-surface offensives:

1. North Pacific forces to eject the Japanese from the Aleutians.

2. Central Pacific forces to advance westward from Pearl Harbor.

3. South Pacific and Southwest Pacific forces to cooperate in a drive on Rabaul. Southwest Pacific forces then to press on westward along the north coast of New Guinea.

No. 1 and the first phase of No. 3 were covered in the preceding chapter. This chapter deals with the opening of Offensive No. 2.

The combination of Nos. 2 and 3 would form another dual advance, on a much larger scale than the Dual Advance on Rabaul. The proposed Allied westward drive along two parallel lines again gave the Japanese an interior position, but the Joint Chiefs counted on the power and mobility of America's new carrier power to offset this advantage. On the other hand, a dual advance would protect the New Guinea-Mindanao Axis from attacks on its flanks and communications and at the same time oblige the Japanese to divide their strength. Because of the many possibilities, the Joint Chiefs kept the plan flexible by not settling details far in advance. Opportunities as they arose would determine how the strategy would be executed.

Because a dual drive must be closely coordinated in order to attain maximum effectiveness and mutual support, certain naval officers suggested that it had at last become mandatory for the entire Pacific theater to be placed under Admiral Nimitz. This proposal was well founded, for the Joint Chiefs had clearly stipulated that the Southwest Pacific forces were to operate in support of the Central Pacific Axis, which, as we have seen, was to be the main line of advance. But the proposal was not followed for a variety of reasons, not the least of which were the military reputation and towering stature of MacArthur himself, for MacArthur had captured the imagination of the world by his defense of the Philippines and his promise to return. On the other hand, the Joint Chiefs would not give the over-all command to MacArthur, at least at this stage, because they did not agree with his strategy. Thus the two offensives rolled forward with no common command closer than the Joint Chiefs themselves in Washington. As it turned out, instant worldwide radio communications overcame most of the disadvantages of such an arrangement—at any rate until the two offensives came into actual contact.

Power for the New Drive

The Central Pacific drive was unique in the history of warfare. Nothing in the past gave any sure clue as to how armed forces could advance in great leaps across an ocean studded with hostile island air bases. Carrying out the new offensive required new methods of training, new techniques of combat, support, supply, and maintenance, and a whole arsenal of new weapons. Yet when the drive began in the autumn of 1943, less than two years after the attack on Pearl Harbor, the means were at hand. That perhaps was the most remarkable achievement of World War II.

The main combat arm of the Central Pacific forces was the U.S. Fifth Fleet, a complex of men, ships, and aircraft organized for the purpose of projecting power at a distance.[1] It began to take form with the arrival at Pearl Harbor of the first of the new 27,000-ton, 32-knot *Essex* class of heavy carriers in the spring of 1943. The first of the equally swift new 11,000-ton *Independence* class of light carriers soon followed. By autumn there were in the Fifth Fleet six heavy and five light carriers, eight escort carriers, five new and seven old battleships, nine heavy and five light cruisers, 56 destroyers, 29 transports and cargo vessels, and large numbers of landing and beaching craft. Commanding this considerable and growing fleet was Vice Admiral Raymond A. Spruance, a man of outstanding intellect and an austere and exacting officer. His work on the staff of the Naval War College had won him a reputation as a strategist. The Battle of Midway had demonstrated his brilliance as a tactician. Since then, as Admiral Nimitz' chief of staff, he had assisted in planning the operations he was to lead.

Spearheading the Fifth Fleet was the Fast Carrier Task Force, whose specific task was to support amphibious operations—by distant strikes to isolate the beachhead, by pre-invasion raids on the target area, by tactical support of the assault troops, and by interception of air

and surface threats to the amphibious forces. The Fast Carrier Task Force operated normally in four task groups, each of which at full strength typically contained two heavy and two light carriers surrounded by an escort of one or two fast battleships, three or four cruisers, and 12 to 15 destroyers. While the group was cruising, the destroyers formed an outer screen for submarine detection, but when air attack was imminent they joined the inner circle of battleships and cruisers. Highly flexible, the carrier groups could operate together or independently, and they could detach vessels to form surface striking forces or to carry out special missions. Such was the floating air base that was to lead the way across the Pacific to the shores of Japan. The Fast Carrier Task Force commanded by Rear Admiral Charles A. Pownall in 1943 was however only a miniature version of the armada that later wiped out Japanese air power and shattered the Combined Fleet.

The amphibious component of the Fifth Fleet was the Fifth Amphibious Force, organized and commanded by Rear Admiral Richmond Kelly Turner. In an invasion this force controlled transports, cargo vessels, landing and beaching craft, and LSD's (landing ships, dock), and also the destroyers, escort carriers, cruisers, and old battleships assigned for close support. The Amphibious Force was normally split into two or more Attack Forces, and it often detached elements for special missions. Some fast gunnery vessels operated either with the carrier groups or with the amphibious groups as the tactical situation required. With growing experience and specialization, a Support Force of escort carriers and gunnery vessels of the Amphibious Force tended to take over tactical support of the troops, leaving the fast carriers and their escorts as a Covering Force for interceptions.

Troops assigned to the Fifth Amphibious Force, both army and marine, were designated V Amphibious Corps. Commanding the Corps was Major General Holland M. Smith USMC, whose typical reaction to an inept or slovenly performance had won him the nickname "Howling Mad Smith." Though "Howling Mad Smith" was as stubborn and outspoken as "Terrible Turner," the two made an effective

[1] The Central Pacific Fleet did not officially assume the title Fifth Fleet until early in 1944, but for simplicity this narrative follows the informal practice of calling it the Fifth Fleet from the beginning of operations in 1943.

team, for both were amphibious experts and each recognized and appreciated the special qualifications of the other.

Finally, the Fifth Fleet had its own land-based air force, composed of army, navy, and marine corps planes under the operational control of Rear Admiral John H. Hoover. At first, Hoover's Defense Force and Shore-based Air supplemented the carriers by pre-invasion photographic reconnaissance and by raids on or about the target. But as the Fast Carrier Task Force and the Fifth Amphibious Force acquired power and experience to support invasions unsupplemented by shore-based air, Hoover's command changed its title to Forward Area Central Pacific, with the responsibilities of air reconnaissance, neutralization of enemy bases, and defense of newly-acquired Allied bases.

To thrust rapidly across the Central Pacific, seizing command of the sea as it went, the Fifth Fleet had to have mobility and strategic momentum to an unprecedented degree. It could not, like fleets of the preceding hundred years, be closely tied to rearward bases for supply, refueling, and upkeep. The Fast Carrier Task Force had to remain at sea or in the forward area in order to keep the enemy from attacking positions already won and to deal him blow after blow to pave the way for further assaults. As we have seen, the key to the endurance of the Fifth Fleet was quickly-established advanced bases—largely afloat, in the lagoons of atolls or in other protected anchorages. As the war progressed, the advanced bases were more and more supplemented by replenishment at sea.

Service Force's mobile service squadrons of tenders, repair ships, and floating drydocks made it possible to supply all ships in the forward area and to repair all but those so extensively damaged as to require the facilities of a completely equipped navy yard. Elements of the Fifth Fleet periodically visited the advanced bases, set up ashore and afloat by Service Force, for a few days of maintenance and repair for the ships and rest for the crews, before again picking up the burden of the war. As operations progressed westward, the mobile service squadrons would move to another suitable anchorage in order to establish a new advanced base nearer to the operating area.

Visits of the Fast Carrier Task Force to the advanced base were kept to a minimum by underway replenishment groups which delivered essential material to the ships at sea. Late in the war one carrier task group would leave the operating area each day for a rendezvous with an underway replenishment group, the other carrier groups continuing operations against the enemy. On meeting the replenishment group, the carrier group would refuel, take on replacement ammunition, food, stores, aircraft, and personnel, receive mail from home, and evacuate its serious casualties to a hospital ship. The carrier group would then return to the operating area to relieve another group, which would repeat the process the next day. The underway replenishment group, after servicing the whole carrier force, amalgamated cargoes and sent its empty ships back to the advanced base to fill up again, while freshly laden ships from the base replaced them. This whole elaborate bucket brigade system was only a facet of the planning, construction, procurement, training, transportation, and maintenance that brought together the integrated forces to strike the swift and powerful blows that carried decisive military power from Pearl Harbor to the Philippines in less than a year.

Plans and Preliminary Operations

Early plans provided for opening the Central Pacific drive with an invasion of the Marshall Islands. But the more the staff planners in Washington and at Pearl Harbor studied the strategic and logistic picture, the less enthusiastic they became about such a beginning.

Like most island groups in the Central Pacific, the Marshalls are an archipelago of atolls, each a perimeter of flat coral islets surrounded by a fringing reef and enclosing a lagoon. Included are some 35 atolls, most of which contain one or more islands large enough for an airfield. Within aircraft support radius are the Gilberts, the eastern Carolines, and Wake. The Marshalls, under Japanese mandate since World War I, had been closed to foreigners since 1935. In the years of privacy thus afforded, Japan had had ample opportunity to fortify and make them as impregnable

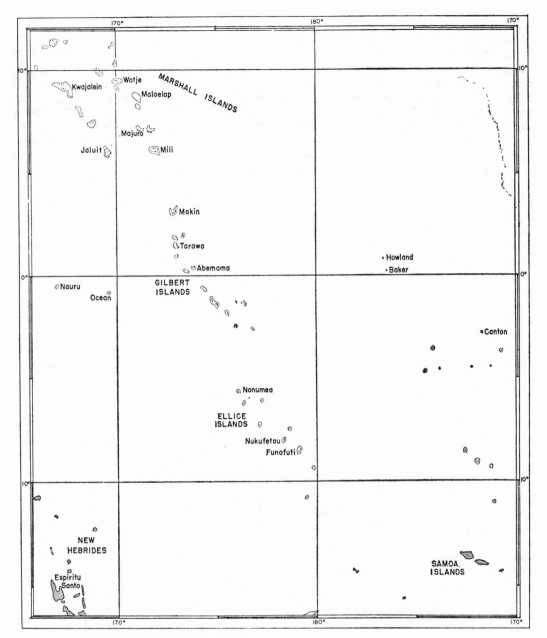

MARSHALLS-GILBERTS-ELLICES-SAMOA CHAIN

as natural conditions permitted. Allied intelligence correctly estimated that they contained at least half a dozen air bases. But no one could be sure, for no Allied military force had visited the area since Halsey's hit-and-run raid early in 1942, and there were no Allied airfields close enough from which to take them under reconnaissance.

To the planners, weighing all the available evidence, it became increasingly obvious that the Central Pacific forces had neither the power nor the experience to go in and take the Marshalls in 1943. Most of the Allied troops then available in the Pacific were assigned to defending bases, to the Aleutians campaign, or to the South-Southwest Pacific drive on Rabaul. Though the U.S. Fifth Fleet was steadily growing more formidable, it was far from being up to planned strength. Besides, no one in mid-1943 knew how well carriers could stand up to land-based air in the proximity of fully developed enemy strong points. Lastly, the Americans still lacked adequate amphibious experience, for in mid-1943 all their invasions of any magnitude had been carried out over undefended or lightly defended beaches. In the circumstances, the Washington and Pearl Harbor staffs concluded that the conquest of the Marshalls, like the drive on Rabaul, had to be achieved by means of a step-by-step approach that would permit land-based Allied planes to make adequate photographic reconnaissance and supplement carrier air.

There was an island route to the Marshalls, just as there was to Rabaul. Like the Bismarcks, the Marshall Islands stand at the northwest end of a chain of islands. At the southeast end are the British-American Samoa Islands. In between are the British Gilberts and Ellices. The Allies had airfields in Samoa, and on Canton Island, another British-American possession some 800 miles north of Samoa and 800 miles east of the Gilberts.

The Marshalls-Gilberts-Ellices-Samoa chain, roughly paralleling the Solomons, had early attracted the attention of the Japanese, who at the outbreak of war had invaded the Gilberts and set up a seaplane base on Makin Atoll to keep the islands to the southeast under observation. They correctly assessed the Halsey attack as the one-shot affair it was, but saw a prelude to full-scale invasion in a subsequent raid on Makin by a battalion of United States marines who arrived by submarine.[2] Following the marine raid, the Japanese quickly strengthened Makin and occupied the atolls of Abemama and Tarawa, turning the latter into the most formidable small bastion in the Pacific.

To counter the Japanese move into the Gilberts, American forces meanwhile had advanced up the chain from Samoa into the adjacent Ellices and dredged out an anchorage and constructed a bomber base at Funafuti Atoll, 700 miles from Tarawa. When the Japanese decided to make their initial advance against United States-Australia communica-

[2] Details of this raid are given in Chapter 42.

tions not via the Marshalls-Gilberts-Ellices-Samoa chain but via the Solomons and the New Hebrides, Funafuti fell into neglect while the Americans rushed forces southward to join their allies in stopping the enemy at Guadalcanal and forcing him back on Rabaul.

On receiving orders after the Casablanca Conference to prepare for a Central Pacific drive, Nimitz reactivated Funafuti. In mid-June 1943 he received further orders from the Joint Chiefs of Staff to prepare for operations against the Gilberts. The following month, marines and Seabees occupied and began building bomber strips on Nukufetau and Nanumea in the upper Ellices. Early in September, an aviation engineer battalion landed on Baker Island, an American possession 480 miles east of the Gilberts, and constructed a fighter strip there to supplement the bomber base on Canton.

Into the anchorage at Funafuti moved the first of the mobile service squadrons to be formed, and into Funafuti, Nukufetau, Nanumea, Canton, and Baker moved Admiral Hoover's Defense Force and Shore-Based Air, its main striking power concentrated in 90 Seventh Army Air Force B-24 heavy bombers operating out of the Ellices. Meanwhile the 2nd Marine Division in New Zealand and the 27th Infantry Division in the Hawaiian Islands, alerted for the Gilberts operation, were undergoing amphibious exercises and training.

The new fast carriers *Essex, Yorktown, Lexington, Bunker Hill, Princeton, Belleau Wood, Cowpens, Monterey,* and *Independence* had by this time joined the veteran *Enterprise* and *Saratoga* in the Pacific, and with them came supporting vessels of all sorts fresh from shipyard and shakedown. As the new men-of-war arrived at Pearl Harbor, they had been formed into task groups and sent against live targets for warm-up and training. In early September a three-carrier group struck Marcus Island, doing great damage to installations and destroying several Japanese bombers. On September 18–19, another three-carrier group joined Seventh Air Force bombers from Canton and Funafuti in a raid on the Gilberts. The main purpose of this joint attack was to ease enemy pressure on the American air bases in the Ellices, which had been bombed by planes from Tarawa and Makin. This aim was more than fulfilled, for the Japanese immediately evacuated all air units from Tarawa and left at Makin only four amphibious planes for reconnaissance. Equally important, the defenders shot off a great deal of ammunition that they were unable to replenish, and the attackers succeeded in getting some excellent photographs of both Tarawa and Makin. Eighteen days later, a six-carrier force, the largest yet organized, staged a massive raid on Wake, so denuding the base of aircraft that the Japanese had to send up additional planes from the Marshalls. Lastly, in early November, as we have seen, carrier groups under Admirals Sherman and Montgomery assisted Halsey's Bougainville campaign by raiding Rabaul.

A major result of the considerable increase in carrier strength was the decision to abandon the practice of operating each carrier in a separate formation. Maneuvering several carriers within a single ring of escorts was not an easy technique and it sacrificed some flexibility, but these handicaps were more than offset by the defensive advantages of concentrated combat air patrols and massed VT-fused anti-aircraft fire.

Alarmed by the carrier raids, Admiral Koga in September and again in October took the main strength of the Combined Fleet to the Marshalls, but failing to make contact with the American task forces, he returned each time to Truk. From there in early November he dispatched most of his carrier aircraft to the defense of Rabaul. While thus engaged, they came under attack by Airsols and by Sherman's and Montgomery's carrier groups, which destroyed two thirds of the planes and more than half the flight crews. During the same period, Koga lost the use of most of his cruisers, sunk or damaged at Rabaul or in the Battle of Empress Augusta Bay. Thus on the eve of the launching of the Central Pacific drive, Allied operations against Rabaul paralyzed the Combined Fleet, rendering it impotent to oppose the invasion of the Gilberts or, subsequently, of the Marshalls.

The Americans, unaware of the paralysis of the enemy fleet, took elaborate care to achieve surprise, in order to gain a foothold in the Gilberts before Koga could strike. So as not to disclose the target, Hoover's B-24's delayed regular raids on the invasion area until mid-November, when the Fifth Fleet was already at sea en route to the assault.

Reconquest of the Gilbert Islands

The objectives of the U.S. Fifth Fleet were, from north to south, the atolls Makin, Tarawa, and Abemama. To assault Makin Atoll came a Northern Attack Force from Pearl Harbor, bringing a regimental combat team of the 27th Infantry Division. The rest of Admiral Turner's Fifth Amphibious Force, designated the Southern Attack Force, picked up the 2nd Marine Division at Wellington, New Zealand, rehearsed landing operations in the New Hebrides, and then headed for Tarawa Atoll. The submarine *Nautilus*, carrying a single company of marines, set out to scout lightly-held Abemama, which was to be invaded after Makin and Tarawa had fallen. The Gilberts invasion, like all operations against Japan in the Central Pacific until the final stages of the war, was carried out exclusively by United States forces.

At appropriate moments in the intricate pattern of approach, the four task groups of the Fast Carrier Task Force set out for their assigned supporting and covering positions—two from Pearl Harbor and the two from the South Pacific that had just completed their raids on Rabaul. While the carrier groups were pounding away at the Gilberts and nearby enemy strong points, the Northern and Southern Attack Forces made contact at sea and moved on parallel courses toward Makin and Tarawa, prepared to land troops simultaneously on the morning of November 20, 1943.

Though Tarawa was known to be the strong point of the Gilberts, both Admiral Turner and General Holland Smith gave their personal attention to the assault on Makin, for Makin lay only 190 miles from the nearest enemy base in the Marshalls—a hundred miles closer than Tarawa. Because of Makin's exposed position, a one-day conquest here was deemed essential so that the supporting fleet could be quickly withdrawn. Accordingly 6,500 assault troops were assigned to seize little Butaritari, main island and headquarters of the atoll, which was known to be lightly forti-

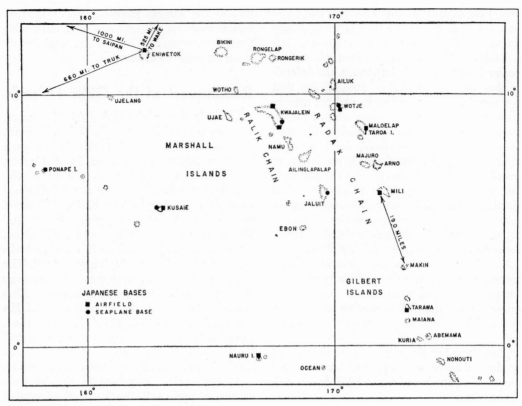

THE MARSHALLS AND THE GILBERTS

fied and defended. The occupation forces on Butaritari in fact amounted to no more than 800 men, comprising 284 naval infantry commanded by a junior grade lieutenant, and an assortment of non-combatants, including ground crewmen of the recently departed seaplanes, Japanese construction troops, and Korean laborers.

Division plans called for an initial landing on the head of hammer-shaped Butaritari to draw the Japanese out of their main defensive area about a third of the way down the narrow handle. This was to be followed two hours later by a second landing, against the stronghold itself, in order to put the enemy between two fires. Unfortunately for the success of this plan, the Japanese generally remained in their defenses and let the Americans come to them. Fleet guns and carrier aricraft prepared the way so well that the scheduled landings were made against only minor opposition. Once ashore however, the invaders aroused the wrath of Holland Smith by losing momentum

and bogging down. Instead of clearing the island in a single day, they spent two days dislodging the enemy from his main defenses and nearly two more pushing him the full length of the handle.[3]

Responsibility for the slowdown has been attributed to poor leadership and faulty indoctrination of the 27th Division, which after long garrison duty in Hawaii was seeing combat for the first time. Over-age officers had unrealistically trained the division in the continental-style warfare typical of World War I, a combat method whereby troops advance deliberately and methodically under a barrage and do not proceed until the enemy's fighting potential has been shattered by artillery. Such tactics are out of place in island warfare where a quick victory is essential in order to release the fleet from support. Moreover, when the area to be conquered is small and the dangers

[3] For details, see Philip A. Crowl and Edmund G. Love, *Seizure of the Gilberts and Marshalls* (Washington, D.C., Dept. of the Army, 1955), 75–126.

of physical exhaustion and outrunning supply are not excessive, speed is especially desirable to keep the enemy off balance, permitting him little opportunity to dig in. In such a tactical situation, isolated pockets of resistance should be by-passed and left to the rear echelons to clean up.

In view of their inexperience and inadequate training, it is not surprising that whole companies of the invading regiment were held up for hours by a few snipers or a machine gun or two, or that they gave away their positions at night by nervously firing at anything that moved or rustled. By November 23 however, sheer numbers had conquered the island at the cost of 64 American soldiers killed and 152 wounded. All of the defenders were wiped out except one Japanese infantryman and 104 construction troops and laborers taken prisoner. In view of the 23-to-1 superiority of American to Japanese combatants on Butaritari, the American casualty rate must be considered excessive.

By far the heaviest losses of the battle for Makin were suffered not by the troops ashore but by personnel of the supporting fleet. During the naval bombardment on November 20, a turret explosion aboard the old battleship *Mississippi* killed 43 men and wounded 19 more. On the 24th, when the fleet should already have been withdrawn from the exposed waters off Makin, a torpedo from a newly arrived Japanese submarine struck escort carrier *Liscome Bay,* which simply blew apart as the blast set off her stored aircraft bombs. Of her crew of about 900, nearly 650 were killed by the explosion or in the flaming oil that spread out from her shattered hull. Nowhere has the Navy's insistence upon speed in amphibious assault been more sharply vindicated.

The demands of the defense of Rabaul had so drained Japanese aircraft from the Central Pacific that the American carriers were able to shield the Gilberts invasion forces from all effective air attacks. Not a single enemy plane appeared over Makin during the fighting there, and the two minor strikes against Tarawa were ineffective. The only important enemy air raid during the first six days was by 16 torpedo bombers out of the Marshalls, which in the evening of the 20th attacked Admiral Mont-

gomery's Southern Carrier Group, then 30 miles west of Tarawa. Eleven of the attacking aricraft were shot down. One of them however succeeded in putting a torpedo into light carrier *Independence*. With 17 killed and 43 wounded, her magazine, fireroom, and after engine room flooded, the *Independence* retired to Funafuti for temporary repairs that enabled her to proceed under her own steam to Pearl Harbor. In the evening of the 25th, aircraft reinforcements from Truk struck from the Marshalls at Admiral Turner's Northern Attack Force and at Rear Admiral Arthur W. Radford's Northern Carrier Group, both off Makin. Turner completely foiled the enemy by radical maneuvering. Radford's ships broke up the attack of the 25th with antiaircraft fire. In another attack the following evening, Radford's carrier group made history and threw the enemy into confusion by launching against him a newly organized, radar-equipped night combat patrol of three fighters. In none of the attacks of November 25–26 was a single American ship hit.

Meanwhile, a company of marines and a submarine were making history of another sort at tiny Abemama Atoll. The capture of Abemama was not expected to present much of a problem, but nobody foresaw that the atoll would fall into American hands without preparatory bombardment and even without a regular assault. When the marine scouts put ashore from the *Nautilus* found only 25 defenders, they called on the submarine for gunfire support and went ahead and captured Abemama themselves.

Interest in the Gilberts operation centers chiefly on Tarawa, where at the cost of heavy casualties the Americans learned the techniques that were to carry them across the powerfully defended beaches of the Central Pacific. The storming of Tarawa proved a bitter school for amphibious assault, completing the lessons of the Solomons and New Guinea operations and the prewar exercises of the Navy and the Fleet Marine Force.

The main target for Rear Admiral Harry Hill's Southern Attack Force was narrow, two-mile-long Betio, only fortified island in Tarawa Atoll and strong point and administrative center of the Japanese-held Gilberts.[4] On Betio

[4] Pronunciations: TA-ra-wa, BAY-shio.

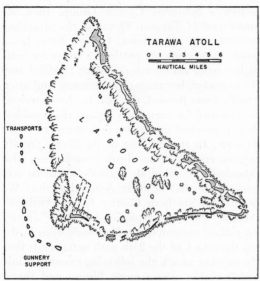

TARAWA ATOLL

0 1 2 3 4 5 6
NAUTICAL MILES

TRANSPORTS

GUNNERY
SUPPORT

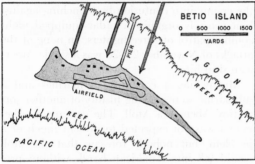

BETIO ISLAND

0 500 1000 1500
YARDS

PIER

LAGOON

REEF

AIRFIELD

REEF

PACIFIC OCEAN

THE ASSAULT ON TARAWA, NOVEMBER 21, 1943

there were about 2,600 Japanese naval infantry, elite troops corresponding somewhat to marines in other navies. There were also 1,000 Japanese construction troops (comparable to Seabees), and 1,200 Korean laborers. Since some of the construction troops were trained and equipped for combat, a fair estimate would place the combat effectives on the island at about 3,000. The American landing force was to be drawn from Major General Julian C. Smith's reinforced 2nd Marine Division, comprising some 16,000 men, mostly veterans of Guadalcanal. One regimental combat team was assigned to corps reserve, to be used on either Makin or Tarawa as needed. The other two combat teams were assigned to Tarawa. Of these, three battalion landing teams would make the assault landings. The remaining three would constitute the follow-up forces of the regimental and division reserves. Since the

landing teams averaged only about 900 infantry each, the invaders were going in short-handed, for it is a military axiom that assault troops should outnumber defenders by at least three to one.

For this assault the marines needed every advantage in numbers and support that could be made available to them, for Betio presented problems never faced before by any sea-borne invader. The strength of the island lay not only in the quality and number of its defenders but also in the difficulty of its approaches and the nature of its fixed defenses. It was surrounded by a wide shelf of coral, barely submerged at low tide. On this shelf the Japanese had laced together concrete, coral, and metal obstacles with barbed wire to force approaching craft into lanes covered by shore-based artillery. Along the beach at the high-water line ran a four-foot-high sea wall of tough, green coconut logs, almost impervious to anything but heavy caliber fire. Directly behind the wall and forming a part of the barrier was a series of gun emplacements, interconnected by trenches and protected by logs and sandbags and in some places by steel and concrete. From these positions antiboat guns and machine guns were sited to fire over the wall or through ports so as to command the beach and the seaward approaches. At points along the shore were pillboxes containing field guns, emplacements for antiaircraft guns, and a number of coast defense guns up to 8 inches in caliber. Inside the sea wall, particularly in the area of the airstrip and taxiways, were half-submerged bombproof shelters built of double layers of green coconut logs braced together with angle irons and having six-foot-thick roofs of logs and corrugated iron piled high with sand so that they resembled igloos. Interspersed among these were steel-reinforced concrete blockhouses with six-foot-thick roofs and walls, to be used as command posts. Having thus thoroughly fortified his island, Rear Admiral Keiji Shibasaki, commanding the defense force, boasted that Betio could not be conquered by a million men in a hundred years.

Against a small island so strongly manned and defended, the possibility of an unopposed or even a lightly opposed landing was of course out of the question. Invading adjacent islets to set up supporting artillery was ruled out by the requirement of speed to release the fleet quickly. The marines would have to go in and seize a foothold by sheer frontal assault. Hence the planners gave careful consideration to the choice of a beachhead. Photographic reconnaissance had revealed no weak spots in Betio's defenses, but there was an option of difficulties. The slight concavity of the south shore permitted enfilade defense fire from the flanks. The west shore was considered too narrow for the initial assault. Both seaward beaches were somewhat more strongly defended and more heavily barricaded with underwater obstacles than those inside the lagoon. For the assault landings therefore the planners selected a 1,500-yard strip of beach on the lagoon side.

Essential for an amphibious assault is correct hydrographic intelligence, but the invaders had only conflicting information regarding the tidal conditions at Betio. At least four feet of water was needed to float standard landing craft, but the time chosen for the assault was a period of neap tides when even at best there might not be more than two or three feet of water over the reef. At the various American command levels, there was hope up to the last moment, but no certainty, that there would be enough water at Betio to float the LCM's and LCVP's up to the beach. In the circumstances, the Navy did what it could to obtain scarce amphibian tractors, familiarly known as amtracs, that operate as easily ashore as afloat.[5] By D-day however only 125 amtracs were available for Betio, not nearly enough to carry all the assault waves across the reef.

The American commanders, studying reconnaissance photographs, concluded that to avoid prohibitive losses and achieve sustained momentum, the attacking forces would have to destroy most of Betio's defenses before the landing took place. Experienced officers did not count heavily on the effectiveness of a week of bombing by Hoover's B-24's or of raids by the Fast Carrier Task Force immediately preceding D-day. They pinned their hopes mainly on close-range pre-invasion gunfire from Hill's three old battleships and five cruisers.

At 0400 on November 20, the Southern Attack Force was off Betio with buglers sounding "Boats away!" Half an hour later, most of

[5] Official designation: LVT (Landing Vehicle, Tracked).

the transport-carried landing craft were circling in the water or transferring marines of the first waves to the amtracs, which had been brought to the area by LST's. Shortly after 0500, shore batteries on Betio opened up, whereupon Hill's gunnery vessels replied with counterbattery fire that knocked out coastal guns, blew up ammunition dumps, and ignited wooden barracks. At dawn the American guns ceased fire to permit aircraft from Montgomery's Southern Carrier Group to take over, but no planes appeared. For some reason, Hill had not been notified that the air strike had been postponed until 0610, sunrise, and he could not contact Montgomery because radio aboard Hill's flagship, the *Maryland*, had been temporarily knocked out by the jar of the ship's own first salvo. During the cease fire, near misses by Japanese shells obliged the transports to haul farther out to sea. At sunrise the aircraft arrived on schedule, gave Betio seven minutes of scattered bombing, and then departed.

At 0620 the pre-invasion bombardment began. In two and a half hours, Hill's battleships and cruisers, using the best gunfire-support doctrine developed up to that time, poured nearly 3,000 tons of projectiles into little Betio. At ranges varying from 15,000 down to 2,000 yards, they worked methodically over the island for 75 minutes with destruction fire—intended to knock out the enemy's defenses and smash his emplacements, pillboxes, shelters, and blockhouses. Then the gunnery vessels shifted position to enfilade the beachhead and delivered 45 minutes of high-speed neutralization fire, to drive the enemy to cover and leave him dazed. Five minutes before the first wave landed, the gunners were to lift fire inland while fighter aircraft strafed the beaches. This treatment was supposed to render Betio virtually defenseless.

The massed bombardment was extraordinarily spectacular. The whole island appeared to be aflame and an enormous pall of dust and smoke billowed into the air. Betio was hurt, no question about that, but it was not hurt badly enough. A good many Japanese were killed; some of the coast-defense, antiaircraft, and antiboat guns were knocked out; most of the above-ground structures were destroyed; camouflage screens were burned off; and, most important, the network of telephone wires on which the Japanese depended for coordination was completely disrupted. On the other hand, few of the enemy's blockhouses, pillboxes, shelters, or protected gun emplacements were seriously damaged. The defenders were still prepared to sweep the beachhead and its approaches with light artillery, machine guns, and rifles.

Just as the naval bombardment was getting under way, two minesweepers advanced under a smoke screen and swept a channel into the lagoon. While one remained inside to mark the line of departure for the assault waves, the other turned back to escort in two destroyers, which took the beachhead under fire. One of the destroyers was hit by a pair of duds, but there were no other damages to the four vessels, which were soon joined by a dock landing ship (LSD) bringing tanks.

The landing craft, now making their way from the rendezvous area outside the lagoon to the line of departure inside, were so delayed by head winds, a choppy sea, a receding tide, and breakdowns among the amtracs that Ad-

miral Hill was obliged to postpone H-hour, the scheduled landing time. Beginning at 0825 the first three assault waves, amtracs carrying troops, crossed the line of departure at three-minute intervals and headed for the beach some 6,000 yards away. The fourth, fifth, and sixth waves, LCM's and LCVP's carrying troops, tanks, and light artillery, soon followed. Each wave carried elements of three battalion landing teams, each assigned to a 500-yard stretch of beach designated from west to east Beach Red 1, Beach Red 2, and Beach Red 3.

Just as the first waves were leaving the line of departure, fighters from the carriers passed over the beach for the final strafing that should have immediately preceded the landing. Because the *Maryland*'s radio was again inoperative, they had received no word of the postponement. Delays in the run to the beach, which for the first waves took more than three quarters of an hour, obliged Admiral Hill to postpone H-hour once more. At 0845, fearful of hitting the landing craft, which were invisible to the fleet through the dense smoke, he ordered all ships outside the lagoon to cease

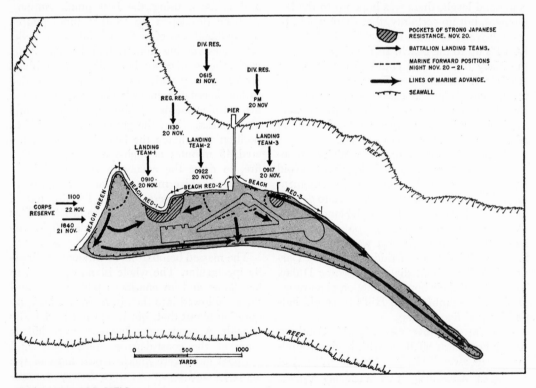

THE BATTLE FOR BETIO

fire. The first wave was then still 15 minutes from the shore.

During this period of respite, the Japanese left their shelters and their emplacements on other beaches and massed behind the sea wall on the beach toward which the assault waves were moving. Apparently because of the threat of the gunnery ships off the west coast and the continued firing of destroyers and minesweepers inside the lagoon, the defenders bunched in two major pockets of resistance, leaving relatively undefended the extreme right and the left center of the beachhead. These "weak spots" were to prove the key to the conquest of Betio.

From the moment they left the line of departure, the amtracs came under scattered enemy fire. The reef, as many had feared, was under only two or three feet of water, but the tracked craft merely lumbered onto and across it. As they did so, they ran into a crescendo of machine gun, rifle, and antiboat fire that threw the waves into confusion. Worst hit during the approach across the reef were the troops of the battalion heading for Beach Red 1, for these had to enter a deep cove where they were raked by fire from the more westerly enemy pocket. Here many of amtracs were hit and disabled while still in the water, and of those that reached the beach few were able to retire.

Far heavier casualties were suffered by troops of the fourth, fifth, and sixth waves, whose conventional landing craft grounded on the edge of the reef. Some of the troops jumped out into deep water and were pulled down by their heavy gear. Others were ferried in by returning amtracs of the first waves. Most got out into the shallow water and waded 600 yards to the beach through withering machine gun and rifle fire. A few Sherman tanks, discharged by LCM's onto the reef, made the shore; but LCVP's bringing in 37- and 75-mm. guns had no choice but to retract and wait for the tide to rise.[6]

The low water that held up the landing craft

[6] The most vivid account of this walk to the beach is that in *Tarawa, the Story of a Battle* (New York, 1944), by Robert Sherrod, a newspaper reporter who came in with the fifth wave. For details of the assault as a whole, see Capt. James R. Stockton USMC, *The Battle for Tarawa* (Washington, D.C., U.S. Marine Corps Headquarters, 1947).

proved a blessing in that it left a stretch of sandy beach on which the marines who reached the shore could assemble with some protection afforded by the sea wall. At the far right of Beach Red 1, marines quickly seized the northwest tip of the island. At the right center of Beach Red 3, there was a break in the wall some 200 yards east of a pier jutting out into the lagoon. Through this opening plunged two amtracs, carrying about 50 marines. Other marines followed and, despite heavy flanking fire, expanded their salient west and south. Along the more heavily defended stretches of beach, those adjacent to the two enemy strong points, casualties were extremely heavy. The marines in these areas could do little except huddle against the wall with their dead and wounded. Even to stand erect made one the target of deadly fire from several directions. Yet after the first shock, marines even here began climbing the wall and clearing out gun emplacements and rifle pits with charges of TNT.

While still boated, the assault commander, Colonel David M. Shoup, ordered his regimental reserve committed without delay. He then radioed General Julian Smith, in the *Maryland*, for immediate gunfire and air support. The division commander not only saw that Shoup got the support he requested but also committed half the division reserve to reinforce the decimated marine left flank. As further reports of the critical situation ashore reached him, Julian Smith radioed General Holland Smith, then off Makin, requesting and receiving permission to commit the corps reserve.

Nearly a third of the 5,000 Americans who reached Betio before dark on November 20 were casualties. At nightfall most of the marines who had been able to land near the strong enemy defense areas were either dead or still pinned to the beach, but nearly half of the western shore was in American hands to the depth of 150 yards, and at the base of the pier the marines had established a perimeter 300 yards deep and 500 yards wide. During the hours of darkness, the invaders maintained remarkable fire discipline—scarcely a shot was fired. The expected enemy counterattack never came, apparently because Admiral Shibasaki could establish communications with only a small portion of his troops. The principal nocturnal activity of the Japanese was by individuals who prepared for sniping the next day by concealing themselves in suitable positions ashore or by wading out to disabled amtracs and tanks on the reef. Through a peculiarity of the time and place, the tide continued too low to float in the landing craft stalled at the edge of the reef, but enough amtracs had survived the first day to bring some of the light artillery to the beach, whither additional tanks also made their way.

During the next day, D plus 1, call strikes from the carriers and call fire from the gunnery vessels developed steadily increasing accuracy. On the marine right flank, a naval gunfire spotter called destroyer fire so accurately on enemy positions that the invaders were able to advance with little opposition the whole length of Betio's western shore. Over this beach, designated Beach Green, poured a battalion of the regiment that had been released from corps reserve. By the end of the day, the marine perimeter at the base of the pier had also expanded across to the south shore.

On November 22, D plus 2, a second reserve battalion landed at Beach Green. As the assault phase came to an end, General Julian Smith came ashore and took command. His immediate objectives were to clean out the enemy pocket at the boundary between Red Beaches 1 and 2 and to begin an advance to the east. In both offensives the principal task was clearing out enemy-occupied pillboxes and shelters. Tanks and artillery were useful in this perilous business, but generally the job had to be completed by infantrymen with flamethrowers and hand-delivered charges of TNT.

During the night of November 22–23, the Japanese who had been squeezed into the narrowing tail of the island made three counterattacks. The attempts ended in such heavy losses for the attackers that the marines were able the next day to penetrate swiftly to the eastern end of the island. By that time the Japanese position between Red Beaches 1 and 2 had been eliminated by a steady drive from all directions, including a frontal infantry-artillery assault across the beach.

When Julian Smith announced the end of organized enemy resistance in the afternoon of

the 23rd, the defenders had been practically wiped out. More than a hundred Korean laborers had been captured, but of the Japanese, only one officer and 16 enlisted men had surrendered as prisoners of war. Of the 18,300 Americans, marine and naval, ultimately committed to the capture of Tarawa, more than 3,000 were casualties. Of these, more than a thousand were killed or died of wounds.

A nation shocked by the cost in lives of the brief Gilberts campaign could not be expected to understand at once that here was a new kind of warfare, in which lasting control over a large area was purchased at the price of heavy losses compressed into a few days. The casualties suffered in the quick conquest of the Gilberts were not nearly so high as those incurred in the six-months campaign to capture Guadalcanal, yet the advantages gained were closely similar. Each of the captured bases safeguarded established and potential communication lines, and each provided airfields for bombing and photographing the next objective. The conquest of the Gilberts removed a menace to American communications with the South, Southwest, and Central Pacific, and it provided an essential base for air support of the forthcoming invasion of the Marshalls.

Equally important were the tactical lessons the Americans learned in the Gilberts—especially at Tarawa. It was discovered that a few hours of bombing and bombardment are not enough to knock out the numerous strong points of fortified positions like Betio. What was needed was precision bombing and accurately controlled gunfire delivered over a much greater period of time, with frequent checking of fire to permit smoke to subside in order to assess the progress of destruction. More plunging fire, using major-caliber armor-piercing shells, was needed to penetrate the overheads. Rapid shifting of fire, designed originally to confuse moving targets, was found merely to hamper fire control when directed against stationary targets. Armored amtracs were shown to be essential for carrying troops across reefs, and the need was demonstrated for close-range neutralizing fire against the beachhead right up to the moment of landing. Experiences at Tarawa again showed the need for special amphibious command ships like those already in use in the Mediterranean, with no responsibility for gunfire support, and for improved radio equipment ashore and afloat. Had these lessons not been learned at Tarawa, they would have had to be learned elsewhere, at similar or greater cost.

On the other hand, the conquest of the Gilberts provided some evidence that carrier planes could gain command of the air over enemy atolls and proved that the fleet could operate against such positions with acceptable losses, that, with naval air and gunfire support, well trained, resolute troops could cross reefs under even the most adverse conditions and seize strongly fortified islands. There was a strong indication moreover that the Japanese fleet was not prepared to sortie and offer powerful resistance to thwart an invasion anywhere in Japan's island empire.

Invasion of the Marshall Islands

Planning for the Marshalls invasion was well under way before the assault on the Gilberts. The first formal operation plan, issued by Admiral Nimitz in mid-October 1943, called for simultaneous assaults on Maloelap and Wotje Atolls, the two Marshallese bases nearest Pearl Harbor, and on Kwajalein Atoll, Japanese headquarters at the center of the archipelago.

After the shock of Tarawa, General Holland Smith recommended that the Marshalls plan be reconsidered, contending that not enough troops and support were available to capture three major bases at the same time. Admirals Spruance and Turner concurred. They favored a two-step operation: Maloelap and Wotje to be captured first and developed into American bases to support a later assault on Kwajalein. To their surprise and consternation, Nimitz proposed instead that Maloelap and Wotje be by-passed and that the forthcoming assault be carried out against Kwajalein alone.

Spruance, Turner, and Smith argued strongly against Nimitz' proposal, pointing out that Kwajalein in American hands would be subject to air attack from Japanese bases at Maloelap, Wotje, Mili, and Jaluit, which were also in position to intercept communications from Pearl Harbor or the Gilberts, while an air pipeline back to Japan through Eniwetok

Atoll would be left intact.[7] When Nimitz insisted upon by-passing the more easterly bases, Spruance requested and received permission to occupy undefended Majuro Atoll in the eastern Marshalls. Occupation of this atoll would provide a protected fleet anchorage in the area of operations, for use until Kwajalein was secured, and a base whence aircraft could cover communications between Kwajalein and the Gilberts. Included in the final plan also was a tentative proposal for the capture of Eniwetok, the date and the forces to be used contingent upon the success and speed of the Kwajalein operation.

The decision to go directly to the heart of the Marshalls took the Japanese as much by surprise as it did Nimitz' commanders. The chief question in the minds of the Imperial High Command was whether the next assault would come against Mili and Jaluit from the Gilberts or against Wotje, or possibly Maloelap, from Pearl Harbor. Accordingly, these outer atolls were given priority in defense materials and personnel. As Admiral Nimitz correctly estimated, the fortification of Kwajalein remained comparatively light, certainly nothing on the order of what the marines had found on Betio. Though the occupation forces on Kwajalein numbered in excess of 8,000, fewer than 2,200 of these were trained combat troops. The rest were technicians, mechanics, laborers (many Korean), grounded aviators, marooned sailors, and the miscellaneous spinners of red tape found at any military headquarters. How effective these non-combatants proved as defenders is difficult to assess. All of the Japanese were probably given arms of one sort or another, and most of them appeared determined to avoid capture and to sell their lives as dearly as possible.

The attack on the Marshalls was begun early in January 1944 by Admiral Hoover's land-based planes operating from the Ellices and from the new American airfields in the Gilberts. On January 29, an expanded Fast

[7] Paraphrased from Admiral Spruance's letters quoted in Lt. Col. Robert D. Heinl, Jr. USMC and Lt. Col. John A. Crown USMC, *The Marshalls: Increasing the Tempo* (Washington, D.C., U.S. Marine Corps Headquarters, 1954), 11, and in Crowl and Love, *Seizure of the Gilberts and Marshalls*, 168.

Carrier Task Force, now designated Task Force 58, arrived in the Marshalls under the command of Rear Admiral Marc A. Mitscher with 750 planes to step up the destruction. While Hoover's aircraft concentrated on neutralizing Jaluit and Mili, one carrier group attacked Maloelap, another hit Wotje, and the other two struck Kwajalein, destroying every plane on the atoll in a single raid. That night TF 58 gunnery vessels moved in and bombarded airfields to keep the Japanese from flying planes in from Eniwetok. At dawn on the 30th, one carrier group hit Eniwetok, destroying the aircraft banked up there. On the 30th also, two carrier groups worked over the defense installations on Kwajalein, and one kept both Maloelap and Wotje under attack. This series of strikes completely eliminated Japanese air power in the Kwajalein area and went far toward destroying the shore defenses in the Marshalls.

Meanwhile the attack forces of the Fifth Amphibious Force were on the way: nearly 300 vessels bringing 53,000 assault troops—of whom half were soldiers and half were marines —and 31,000 garrison personnel. As this armada approached the Marshalls, a Special Attack Group under Rear Admiral Hill was detached to occupy Majuro. Into Majuro's lagoon followed a mobile service squadron prepared to look after the needs of the naval forces. Thus was set up another of the series of temporary forward bases which freed the fleet from immediate dependence upon Pearl Harbor and extended its reach step by step across the Pacific.

On January 30 the Northern Attack Force, under Rear Admiral Richard L. Conolly, and the Southern Attack Force, under Admiral Turner's direct command, reached Kwajalein Atoll and added their guns and escort carrier planes to the fast carrier planes to step up the three-day intensive preparation. The Navy's meticulous study of the Tarawa assault now paid off. The primary invasion targets, Roi and Namur, a pair of islands connected by a causeway at the north end of Kwajalein lagoon, and Kwajalein Island, 44 miles to the south, were pounded with four times the weight of bombs and shells that had been hurled against Betio. Aircraft picked their tar-

gets and bombed precisely. Gunnery ships varied range and trajectory, and shifted from high-capacity to armor-piercing shells as the situation required.

On January 31, troops seized islets near Roi-Namur and near Kwajalein Island to permit entry of amphibious and close-support vessels through the narrow passes into the relatively calm lagoon and to site artillery to cover the main landing beaches. That day and the following night, newly organized underwater demolition teams of swimmers, protected by naval gunfire, reconnoitered the approaches to the beachheads. They found no offshore mines or obstructions and reported reef and surf conditions not too hazardous.

All through the night, destroyers wore down the resistance of the enemy troops with harassing fire. Then, shortly after dawn on February 1, the pre-invasion softening up began, climaxing the preceding two days of bombing and bombardment. Fleet guns blasted Roi-Namur and Kwajalein from close range;[8] artillery on the adjacent islands added enfilading fire; from above the trajectory of the shells, Gilberts-based B-24's dropped 1,000- and 2,000-pound bombs on Kwajalein Island. While the guns paused, carrier aircraft came in to dive-bomb and strafe. Coordinating all this destruction, and other phases of the assault as well, were new amphibious command ships (AGC's), carrying the force, corps, and division commanders and their staffs. Conolly ran the northern operation from AGC *Appalachian* off Roi-Namur; Turner and Holland Smith, the southern operation, from AGC *Rocky Mount* off Kwajalein Island.

There were still not enough amtracs to carry all the assault waves over the reefs, but the amtracs available were all now armored, and armed with machine guns. In the Southern Attack Force moreover they were supplemented by the Army's equally versatile DUKW's, which would bring in supplies. The amtracs were to be carried to the line of departure by LST's, out of which they would crawl fully loaded under their own power. To accompany the first wave were armored am-

[8] Confirming Admiral Conolly's nick-name "Close-in-Conolly," earned for his close support of the assaults on Sicily and at Salerno.

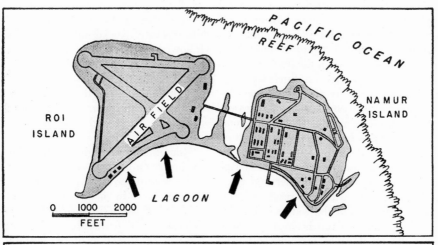

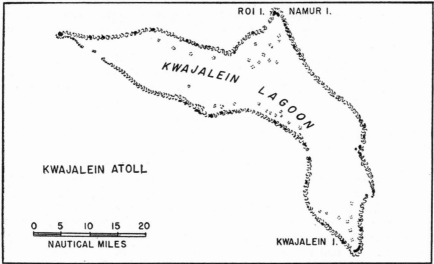

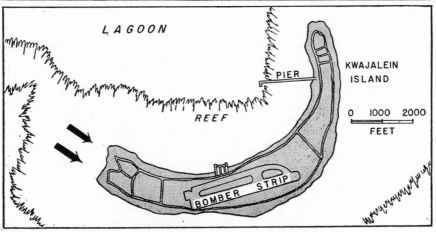

THE ASSAULT ON KWAJALEIN, FEBRUARY 1, 1944

phibians[9] and shallow-draft LCI's converted into amphibious support vessels by the addition of rocket racks and 20- and 40-mm. guns. Air observers were prepared to drop parachute flares to signal the fleet when the leading waves were 500 yards from the beach. Such were the new amphibious weapons and techniques developed in response to the lessons of Tarawa.

Despite the thoroughness of the pre-invasion bombardment, which had knocked out most of the enemy's fixed defenses and killed more than half of the defenders, the assault on Roi and Namur was marred by disorder and poor timing. In part this was the result of the unexpected choppiness of the waters inside the lagoon, from which the northern assault was made. But the chief cause was inexperience, for the invasions in this area were carried out by green troops brought to the line of departure by inexperienced sailors.

The landing force was Major General Harry Schmidt's newly organized 4th Marine Division, untried in battle and lifted directly from the United States to the Marshalls with inadequate opportunity to practice landings. The confusion began on January 31, when one of the division's three regimental combat teams seized the islands adjacent to the main targets. The amtracs that had participated in these operations were supposed to return to their parent LST's, refuel, and take aboard troops of the combat team assigned to make the assault on Namur. At 0900 on February 1, few of the LST's involved had located all their amtracs and none of these LST's had reached the line of departure. Even the fresh LST's, those bringing in the combat team assigned to Roi, failed to reach the line on time and, once there, they encountered unforeseen difficulties in bringing their amtracs down by elevator from the weather decks.

After repeated postponements, the control destroyer finally flagged in the first wave at

1112, though many amtracs were still not accounted for, and others were milling about in the distance. Rocket-firing LCI's led the way, followed by a wave of armored amphibians, two waves of infantry in amtracs, and two waves of tanks in LCM's. After the battleships and cruisers outside the lagoon had lifted fire, nearby destroyers continued to pound the shore as long as they could do so without endangering the marines.

Remarkably enough, though the approach to the beach at Roi was marked by numerous collisions among the amtracs, the assault forces landed here in good order—two battalions abreast, as planned. During the approach, the defenders had fruitlessly fired a few shells in the general direction of the landing craft. As the troops set foot on shore, there was a burst of machine gun fire from the left. At the same time two Japanese soldiers armed only with bayonets rushed down to the water's edge, charging at the invaders in a brave but futile gesture. Without pausing, the marines pushed into the interior, advancing rapidly with considerable spirit but not much coordination and almost no fire discipline. Some troops even wounded each other in their anxiety to get a shot at one of the 300 or so Japanese left alive by the bombardment. Because Roi was mostly airfield, with little room for buildings or installations, the defenders had scarcely any opportunity to take cover or to put up an effective resistance. Before nightfall the island was in American hands.

Because only a fraction of the assault forces intended for Namur had arrived at the line of departure when the first waves were flagged in, the landings on this heavily built-up island were chaotic and piecemeal. Fortunately for the marines, there was no resistance or other impediment at the beach. In the interior however, the invaders were confronted with a wilderness of rubble, undergrowth, and shattered palms that held up tanks and troops and provided concealment for enemy snipers. To maintain momentum through this maze of destruction, the assault forces were obliged to leave behind a great many pockets of resistance for later echelons to clean out with demolition charges and flamethrowers. On this island, explosions of stored Japanese ammunition

---

[9] So called by the Navy and the Marine Corps. The Army called them amphibian tanks. The official designation was LVT(A)(1). Each of these vehicles carried a turret-mounted 37-mm. gun and three .30-caliber machine guns, and some were equipped with flamethrowers. The armored amphibians should not be confused with the light and medium tanks, strictly land vehicles, that were brought to the beach in LCM's.

caused severe casualties. The heaviest explosion was unintentionally set off by the marines themselves when they mistook a blockhouse full of torpedo warheads for an enemy command post. As the blockhouse burst asunder, the island was instantly covered with a pall of acrid smoke, and for minutes afterwards chunks of concrete and metal rained down on invaders and defenders alike. After a night in which the assault troops were harassed as much by trigger-happy marines in the rear as by infiltrating Japanese in front, they pushed rapidly to the north shore. Namur was declared secured in the early afternoon of February 2.

American casualties on the northern islands of Kwajalein Atoll were 196 killed and about 550 wounded. Of the 345 Japanese troops and 3,200 other occupying personnel in the area at the beginning of the bombardment, all were killed except 40 captured Korean laborers and 51 Japanese taken as prisoners of war.

In the Kwajalein Island area, at the southern end of the lagoon, Major General Charles H. Corlett's 7th Infantry Division was carrying out an assault using a plan almost identical with that employed by the 4th Marine Division at the northern end. In the south, as in the north, two regimental combat teams captured the main target; the third, the adjoining islets. The principal difference was that Kwajalein Island was invaded end-on. An assault on Kwajalein's concave lagoon side was ruled out because it would have exposed the invaders to flank fire from the shore. A landing on the ocean side was equally unacceptable because of rough surf and heavy defenses. That left only the narrow western beach, where the two assigned combat teams necessarily went ashore in column of battalions rather than battalions abreast.

In contrast to the confused assault on Roi-Namur, the landings on Kwajalein Island were almost flawless. Mild seas in this area helped, but the efficiency of the operation was mainly the product of the rigorous training and rehearsals that Corlett had put his division through since it fumbled on Attu the preceding May. Taking station west of the line of departure, the LST's discharged their troop-loaded amtracs, and the LSD's launched LCM's carrying medium tanks. These landing craft circled in columns of waves until the transports had launched the LCVP's, which were to bring in the supporting waves. First to head toward the shore were three LCI gunboats that swept the landing beaches with 40-mm. fire and rocket salvos. Control vessels flanking the line of departure flagged the first waves across the line precisely on schedule at 0900. The leading wave, which included 16 amtracs, 16 armored amphibians, and two control craft to keep the line in order, was followed by three more waves at four-minute intervals. The whole parade then moved in at a steady five knots. As the landing craft neared the shore, the distant battleships and cruisers lifted fire inland, while four nearby destroyers continued to pound the beach until the last moment. When the first wave was 200 yards from the shore, the LCI's pulled over to the flanks and stood by to provide call fire. The first wave, still exactly on schedule, touched down at 0930. While the amtracs unloaded and circled back to bring in troops boated in LCVP's from the edge of the reef, the armored amphibians continued inland a hundred yards or so to cover the beachhead. Within twelve minutes, 1,200 troops had landed and begun to organize for advance. Though there was some small arms fire from the enemy on the island, there was not a single casualty among the assault forces. This was as near perfection as any such operation was ever likely to attain.

By the end of the day on February 1, some 11,000 soldiers were ashore on Kwajalein Island. Compared to the marines on the northern islands, they advanced very slowly. The reason for their slower rate appears to be three-fold: they had to defeat a larger defense force, their choice of landing beach obliged them to fight their way the whole length of the island while presenting a narrow front that could be resisted by a relatively small force, and they used infantry tactics inherited from the fairly static conditions of World War I. After three days of typically deliberate advance under a barrage of shells and aerial bombs, the soldiers squeezed a few hundred surviving defenders into Kwajalein's northern tip and began the final mopping up. By the afternoon of February 4, all effective resistance had ended.

American casualties on Kwajalein Island

and the adjacent islets were 177 killed and about a thousand wounded. The enemy occupation force, originally comprising some 1,800 ground troops and about 3,200 other personnel, were all killed except 125 captured Korean laborers and 49 Japanese prisoners of war. Throughout the four-day conquest, the fleet had stood by in support. Except for a few minor hits from coast defense guns, not a ship was damaged.

Because he had not had to commit the 10,000 troops of the corps reserve, Admiral Spruance could push on without delay to the conquest of Eniwetok Atoll. Here he planned to set up another logistic base to support his next westward leap. But Eniwetok, largest of the western Marshalls, was in an exposed position, only 1,000 miles from the Marianas, less than 700 from Truk, less than 600 from Ponape. To prevent interference with the new operation, these Japanese bases had to be neutralized. That was quite an undertaking and might have been considered too risky before American carrier-air power had so brilliantly demonstrated its capabilities by isolating Kwajalein. Now Admiral Nimitz did not hesitate to order the new invasion and all the operations necessary to support it.

When the Japanese high command had been forced to concede that the Bismarcks, the Gilberts, and the Marshalls were no longer tenable, Tokyo had drawn in its defenses to a more restricted perimeter stretching south through the Marianas and the Palaus to western New Guinea. Garrison troops on the islands east of the new defense line were given the suicide mission of delaying and weakening American forces so as to allow Japan time to build up her depleted air power. With the fall of Kwajalein, Admiral Koga felt so exposed at Truk that he prudently withdrew the bulk of the Combined Fleet to the Palaus, leaving behind only two light cruisers and eight destroyers to defend local naval forces and cargo vessels at the base.

Meanwhile training of aviators went on apace in Japan. As soon as crews for land-based aircraft had attained enough skill to fly so far, they took their planes south along the new inner defense chain and to outposts, such as Truk, in the Carolines. In this manner the Japanese began building up power along the restricted perimeter to destroy any invading force that might approach. By mid-February 1944, there were 365 planes at Truk, and 200 more were ready to take off from Japan for the Marianas.

That was the situation when Marc Mitscher's TF 58 sortied from Majuro, and Harry Hill's Eniwetok Expeditionary Group left Kwajalein. Both headed for Eniwetok, and while one group of the Carrier Force remained in that area to support the assault, the other three shaped course southwest for Truk. Bombers of the Seventh Air Force were already reaching out 900 miles from Tarawa to take the fight out of Ponape with a series of sharp blows.

Truk, an archipelago of islands surrounded by a coral reef, provides one of the world's finest anchorages. Its reputation for impregnability while under Japanese mandate had earned it such names as "the Japanese Pearl Harbor" and "Gibraltar of the Pacific." Task Force 58 exploded that reputation and at the same time proved the ability of the carriers to neutralize enemy bases without any assistance from land-based air. While Mitscher's planes hit Truk repeatedly on February 17, Spruance led the 45,000-ton *Iowa* and *New Jersey,* with two heavy cruisers and four destroyers, in a sweep around the archipelago to sink any ships attempting to escape through passages in the perimeter reef. To catch any vessels that might elude Mitscher's planes and Spruance's guns, Nimitz had sent ten submarines to patrol the area. During the night of February 17–18, carrier aircraft, exploiting a newly-developed technique, bombed vessels in Truk lagoon by radar. At dawn the carriers, already beginning to withdraw, launched a final all-out attack. In the course of this two-day strike, the attackers destroyed about 200 enemy aircraft and damaged some 70 more. They sank 15 Japanese naval vessels, including Koga's two cruisers and four of his destroyers, and sent down 19 cargo vessels and five tankers. The cost to the Americans was 25 aircraft lost, and severe damages to the carrier *Intrepid,* which was hit by a night-flying torpedo plane in the only counterattack Truk was able to launch during the entire operation.

"Impregnable Truk" had been proved a myth. Japan's maritime investment during the 20 years of her mandate had gone into her fleet and not, as many had supposed, into building up an oceanic Maginot Line. By smashing the air power of Truk, TF 58 had both isolated Eniwetok and completed the neutralization of Rabaul. Airsols planes on February 18 encountered not a single enemy aircraft over the Bismarcks.

Following the successful raid on Truk, Admiral Mitscher with two groups of TF 58 set out for the Marianas Islands. Detected by a Japanese patrol plane in the afternoon of February 22, Mitscher's force was attacked by aircraft through the night. Rather than lose time by turning into the wind to launch fighters, the Americans defended themselves with gunfire alone. So effective were their radar-aimed, VT-fused antiaircraft shells that not a ship was hit. The speedy approach paid off handsomely, catching the enemy awkwardly off balance. Vice Admiral Kakuji Kakuta, commanding the Marianas Air Base Force, had just moved about 150 torpedo-bombers in from Japan, ahead of the fighter squadrons. After sunrise on the 23rd, TF 58 planes struck at Guam, Tinian, and Saipan and wiped out the bombers before the fighters could arrive to protect them. As important to the Americans as this destruction of Marianas air power were aerial photographs taken of airfields and of beaches suitable for assault.

While Mitscher and Spruance were thus pounding distant enemy bases, Hill's force captured Eniwetok, using techniques similar to those employed at Kwajalein. But whereas the assault troops at Kwajalein had outnumbered the defenders nearly 6 to 1, the ratio at Eniwetok was less than 3 to 1. Hence the three occupied islands of Eniwetok Atoll had to be taken one at a time. The landing force here consisted of the 22nd Marines (a detached regimental combat team)[10] and two battalion landing teams of the 27th Infantry Division, which had also provided the landing force for Makin. Originally assigned to corps reserve, none of these troops had been adequately rehearsed in making assault landings—and none thus far had had any battle experience. The 22nd Marines however had been superbly trained in jungle warfare during 18 months' garrison duty in Samoa, whereas the army troops were drawn from the division that

[10] Nucleus of the future 6th Marine Division.

earlier, in the Gilberts operation, had revealed lack of suitable training.

Predictably enough, the assaults at Eniwetok were marked by considerable confusion. Once ashore however, the marines advanced with the speed and precision of veterans, overrunning the islands of Engebi and Parry each in a single day. But on Eniwetok Island, the soldiers got off to such a slow start that one of the marine landing teams had to be rushed in to take over the brunt of the fighting. Conquest of this island required three days, partly because the invasion force, discovering belatedly that it was defended, had given it too little bombardment, and partly because of the dissimilar tactics of the soldiers and the marines. Individuals of both services showed high courage and determination, but the superior training and leadership of the 22nd Marines gave them a cohesiveness and *esprit de corps* that, here as on Makin, was lacking in elements of the 27th Division.

By now the Americans, moving out from their lodgements on Roi-Namur and Kwajalein Island, had cleared the enemy from all his positions in the chain of islands surrounding Kwajalein lagoon. The invaders were soon moving into the rest of the Marshalls—all except strongly fortified, heavily occupied Wotje, Maloelap, Mili, and Jaluit. These enemy bases were kept neutralized by occasional air raids. Cut off from all supply and reinforcement except by submarine, they could create no serious problem in the rear of the American advance. On the contrary, they proved useful as live targets for newly arrived air reinforcements.

For their achievement in conquering the Marshalls, and in recognition of their increased responsibilities in an expanding fleet, Mitscher, Holland Smith, Turner, and Spruance were each awarded an additional star. In Admiral Mitscher, Nimitz had found a carrier force commander worthy to complete the Smith-Turner-Spruance team. Marc Mitscher, soft-spoken, often reticent, had little of the colorful command personality of Smith or Turner and few pretensions to the intellectual eminence of Spruance, but 30 years of intense devotion to naval aviation had fitted him uniquely to command the Navy's roving air bases of World War II.

Summary

In opening a new, more direct line of advance toward the heart of the Japanese Empire, the Joint Chiefs of Staff and other strategic planners of the Central Pacific drive assumed (1) that capture of small islands and atolls on which the enemy had long been based would require frontal assaults against powerful defenses, and (2) that the Central Pacific Fleet, once it had attained full strength, would be able to support such captures with acceptable losses. They deemed it necessary in the first stages however to rely on support by land-based air as well. The initial attack therefore was directed against the Gilberts, which could be reached by bombers from the Ellices, and this was followed by an invasion of the Marshalls, which could be reached by bombers operating out of the newly captured Gilberts.

One of the most striking facts about the war in the Pacific is that the techniques and weapons of amphibious assault fully matured in the two months between Tarawa and Kwajalein. The assault on Tarawa revealed serious flaws in support, communications, reconnaissance, and ship-to-shore movement. All of these were substantially corrected by improved techniques and timing, by prolonged pre-invasion bombing and bombardment, and by the introduction of amphibious command ships, LCI gunboats, armored amphibians, additional amtracs, special control craft, and underwater demolition teams. Even though future assaults in the Central Pacific were to be against islands and large land masses rather than against atolls, the nearly perfect assault on Kwajalein (south) set the pattern for all subsequent assaults in the theater.

The opening of the Central Pacific drive clearly revealed the advantages of a dual advance. The drive by South and Southwest Pacific forces to neutralize Rabaul had incidentally removed the Japanese Combined Fleet, for the time being at least, as a barrier to the advance across the center. And the Fifth Fleet raid on Truk, incidental to the Marshalls operation, had completed the neutralization of Rabaul.

General MacArthur, who called the invasion of the Gilberts and Marshalls a "diversion," again advocated a single line of advance—along the New Guinea-Mindanao Axis. But the Joint Chiefs of Staff were confirmed in their opinion that the Central Pacific Axis was the most profitable line of advance, certainly not to be canceled or curtailed. It was clear now that fleet surface and air capabilities in the Central Pacific had reached a state where they could support invasions far beyond the reach of land-based air. It was equally clear that Truk and other bases in the eastern Carolines could safely be by-passed. On Admiral Nimitz' recommendation, the Joint Chiefs in March 1944 named the next invasion target for the Fifth Fleet. This entailed nothing less than a breathtaking thousand-mile leap to the Marianas.

40:

The Dual Advance to the Philippines

The Joint Chiefs of Staff early in March 1944 reaffirmed the concept of a dual advance across the Pacific and specified the next objectives for each of the two offensives. MacArthur's Southwest Pacific forces were to continue northwestward along the north coast of New Guinea and in mid-November invade the southern Philippine island of Mindanao. Nimitz' Central Pacific forces, beginning in mid-June, were to occupy the islands of Saipan, Tinian, and Guam in the Marianas. In mid-September they were to begin seizing bases in the Palaus. In November they would provide fleet support and cover for MacArthur's invasion of Mindanao. The dual advance was thus to be a converging movement. (See maps pages 735 and 840.)

The Marianas operation was expected to yield rich dividends. American occupation of islands in this group would cut the main air pipeline from Japan to the Carolines and New Guinea, provide bases for stepped-up submarine attrition of tankers and freighters plying between Japan and the East Indies, and furnish sites for airfields from which the Army Air Forces' new long-range B-29 bombers could strike directly against the Japanese home islands. An invasion so near Japan moreover would almost certainly force out the Japanese fleet for destruction—possibly removing it from the board prior to MacArthur's return to the Philippines.

While the Central Pacific command was planning the Marianas operation, General MacArthur's Southwest Pacific forces were completing their conquest of the Admiralties and preparing to advance westward by sea to Hollandia on the north coast of New Guinea. They would thus by-pass the Japanese Eighteenth Army at Wewak, some 20,000 combat effectives, including survivors of the march from the Huon Peninsula. But the 400-mile leap to Hollandia would carry the Seventh Amphibious Force beyond the radius of efficient land-based air support and at the same time expose it to attack from western New Guinea and the Carolines. So the floating airfields of the Fifth Fleet were called upon to neutralize the Carolines to lend support and cover to the new invasion, and to protect the amphibious shipping of the Seventh Fleet.

Task Force 58 Supports MacArthur

Toward the end of March 1944 three groups of TF 58 departed Majuro and headed for the western Carolines to give the new Combined Fleet base in the Palau Islands the same treatment they had given Truk the preceding month. Detection of this westbound force by patrol aircraft stimulated the Japanese into extraordinary activity. When Admiral Koga had pulled back to the Marianas-Palaus-Western New Guinea line, he had declared that this was to be his last retreat—he would hold the new line at all costs. Estimating that the Americans were now about to attack his new defense perimeter, Koga summoned all available aircraft, including carrier planes, and ordered his surface fleet to sortie from the Palaus and stand by to the northward to await reinforcement and possible action. He then set out with his staff in three planes for new headquarters at Davao in Mindanao. En route they ran into bad weather and two of the planes crashed, including Koga's. The Combined Fleet was once more without a commander in chief.

All the Japanese hustle and bustle was to no

avail. As March was turning into April, TF 58 struck the Palaus, destroying most of the defending aircraft and sinking practically all the ships that had not departed. Before the Combined Fleet could assemble for counterattack, TF 58 had also raided the nearby islands of Yap and Woleai and was well on its way back to the Marshalls. The western Carolines were at least temporarily neutralized; MacArthur's right flank was safe.

In mid-April the fast carriers and their escorts were again at sea, this time in direct support of the Hollandia landing. On the return passage, the carrier aircraft gave Truk another pounding which left it so helpless that bombers from Eniwetok and the Admiralties had no further trouble keeping it neutralized. Before returning to base, TF 58 detached cruisers to bombard the central Caroline island of Satawan, and Vice Admiral Willis A. Lee's battleships, formed into battle line, shelled Ponape in the eastern Carolines.

In the course of these two advances into enemy territory not a single American ship had been damaged, evidence of the decreasing effectiveness of Japanese air power and of the growing efficiency of American air defense measures.

Hollandia and Westward

The Hollandia invasion, which included a subsidiary landing at Aitape to the southeast, was by far the largest amphibious operation undertaken up to then in the Southwest Pacific Area. Assigned to the operation were 84,000 troops, of whom 52,000 were to make the assault. These were carried to three beachheads by 113 ships and supported by the combined striking power of the Fifth and Seventh Fleets.

Admiral Barbey's Seventh Amphibious Force, divided into three attack groups, sortied from Manus supported by eight escort carriers on loan from the Fifth Fleet. After setting a course toward the Palaus to mislead the enemy, the groups split in the evening of April 21 and headed for their separate objectives. The Eastern Attack Group, with the escort carriers, proceeded to Aitape, 125 miles southeast of Hollandia, and put ashore a regiment of American soldiers. The small enemy garrison after negligible resistance fled into the jungle. Engi-

neer battalions quickly began constructing an aircraft staging base, while the assault troops set about plugging the coastal road between Wewak and Hollandia in order to contain the Japanese Eighteenth Army. For the latter task the invaders were eventually reinforced to corps strength—and none too soon, for shortly afterward the enemy advanced from Wewak and attacked. While warfare raged in the jungle, Allied PT boats and aircraft kept the Japanese from using the coastal road or sending supplies by barge; and with the aid of Australian spotting planes, Seventh Fleet cruisers and destroyers bombarded the enemy's inland supply line. Thus deprived of food and ammunition, the initial Japanese counteroffensive at length collapsed with heavy losses. American (and subsequently Australian) forces based on Aitape nevertheless had their hands full until the end of the war. By that time the Eighteenth Army was very nearly wiped out, and the Allies had suffered 4,600 casualties, including 900 killed.

Simultaneously with the invasion at Aitape, Barbey's Central and Western attack groups landed two American infantry divisions 20 miles apart in the Hollandia area. Thanks to a series of massive bomber raids by General Kenney's Fifth Air Force, which had destroyed nearly 500 enemy planes at Hollandia, and to vigorous support by TF 58 and by Seventh Fleet gunnery vessels, these landings also were made virtually without opposition. The Allied objective here was three Japanese airfields south of the coastal Cyclops Mountains. Passing around the ends of the range, one invading division advanced from the west, the other from the east. They closed the pincers on April 26, having taken the fields by double envelopment. Of the 11,000 Japanese in the area, 650 were taken prisoner. Most of the rest fled into the jungle, where all but about a thousand died of starvation or disease before reaching the nearest Japanese base at Sarmi, 145 miles to the northwest. The Americans suffered 1,200 casualties, including 160 killed.

General MacArthur was now launched upon his drive to capture Japanese airstrips and convert them to his own use, ever advancing his fighter-escorted bomber line until it could cover his invasion of Mindanao. Determined to maintain momentum, he issued his next invasion

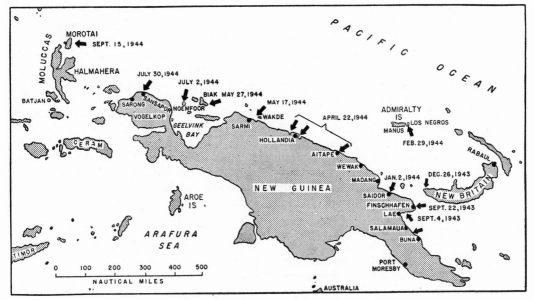

THE NEW GUINEA CAMPAIGN, 1943–1944

order only five days after the Hollandia landings. The new target was Wakde Island just off the New Guinea coast 130 miles northwest of Hollandia. His plan called also for occupation of the adjacent mainland, both to provide sites for artillery support of the assault on Wakde and to secure Wakde from enemy shellfire after it had been captured. This double operation, successfully carried out in mid-May by MacArthur's well-balanced infantry-navy-air force team, demonstrated the contrasting problems of coastal invasion and small island assault. The troops met little resistance on the mainland beach, but over a period of several months they had to defend their positions against repeated enemy counterattacks that eventually took 400 American lives. At Wakde, on the contrary, they had to fight their way ashore, yet they conquered the island once and for all in a little over two days by destroying the 800-man garrison, at a cost of 40 American lives. A week later army engineers had lengthened the Wakde airstrip for use by heavy bombers, just in time to support MacArthur's next westward leap.

This was the invasion of Biak, a large island in the mouth of Geelvink Bay, 190 miles northwest of Wakde. Here, through a misestimate of enemy strength and intentions, MacArthur's swift-moving advance nearly met disaster. The 12,000 American assault troops that landed on Biak on May 27 were expected to achieve a quick conquest, for the island was thought to be lightly held. In fact, however, the garrison numbered over 11,000, a good third of whom were trained combat troops. More ominous than the unexpected strength of Biak was the unforeseen reaction of the Japanese high command.

Early in May, Admiral Soemu Toyoda had assumed command of the Combined Fleet with orders from the Naval General Staff to put an end to the passive policy of Admiral Koga, his predecessor, and actively seek a decision at sea. Toyoda promptly issued a plan, designated Operation *A-Go*, calling for fleet action in the western Carolines area—on the assumption that the Allies were committed to a single line of advance, via New Guinea, and that TF 58 would continue in direct support of MacArthur. He then ordered his best combat vessels to Tawitawi, between the Philippines and Borneo. The force thus assembled was the First Mobile Fleet, newly organized around carriers in evident imitation of TF 58. Commanding this force was Vice Admiral Jisaburo Ozawa, Japan's top naval air officer. Because Operation *A-Go* called for use of land-based air to offset the inferiority of the Mobile Fleet, Biak suddenly assumed new importance in the eyes of the Imperial High Command. Allied or Japanese bombers from here could supplement the striking power of their own naval forces operating in the designated battle area. It was thus essential to the *A-Go* plan that the island be kept out of Allied hands. For this reason MacArthur's invasion spurred the Japanese into drastic action.

First, they drained their Central Pacific bases of much of their air power, rushing planes to New Guinea and Halmahera from Japan, from the Marianas, and from the Carolines. Seventh Fleet antiaircraft fire kept the new arrivals from achieving much on and around Biak, but the hostile planes considerably weakened Biak's air defense by damaging or destroying upwards of 60 Allied aircraft parked on Wakde. They might have done more had not the Japanese aviators from more healthful latitudes to the north quickly succumbed to malaria and jungle fever. Even those who survived were out of action through the crucial month of June.

The air attack was a mere preliminary. From Tawitawi Ozawa released surface units to reinforce the troops on Biak, somewhat in the manner of the Tokyo Express of the Solomons campaign. The first reinforcement group prudently turned back after being sighted by a submarine and by aircraft from Wakde. A second was chased away from the Biak area by a cruiser-destroyer force from the U.S. Seventh Fleet. To support the third attempt, and also in hopes of luring TF 58 into the designated combat area, Ozawa sent his superbattleships *Yamato* and *Musashi* and several cruisers and destroyers under Vice Admiral Matome Ugaki. This formidable force on June 11 assembled at Batjan in the Moluccas, just west of New Guinea, for a quick run to Biak. But the very day that Ugaki reached Batjan, the strategic picture abruptly changed for the Japanese. A thousand miles to the northeast the U.S. Fifth Fleet attacked the Marianas preparatory to invading Saipan. Toyoda at once suspended the Biak operation and activated a modified version of Operation *A-Go*. Ozawa sortied from Tawitawi to do battle; and Ugaki, leaving his transport units at Batjan, headed northeast to join the Main Body of the Mobile Fleet east of the Philippines.

Ozawa's defeat in the great sea-air Battle of the Philippine Sea (June 19–20, 1944) took the pressure off MacArthur. He could proceed unmolested with his conquest of Biak, an operation that required two months of hard fighting and cost the Americans 474 killed, 2,000 wounded, and several thousand incapacitated by disease. By the time Biak was secured, it was already in the rearward area of the Southwest Pacific drive. In early June a regimental combat team had invaded Noemfoor Island, 50 miles farther west. The naval bombardment supporting this landing was so thorough that the surviving Japanese defenders were too stunned to offer any organized resistance. At the end of July, Southwest Pacific forces went ashore at Cape Sansapor near the western end of New Guinea. Here the invaders encountered no enemy at the beachhead but later succeeded in ambushing a few hungry Japanese who were withdrawing westward in hopes of being evacuated.

In a little more than three months, General MacArthur's forces had advanced 550 miles from Hollandia to Cape Sansapor, seizing five enemy air bases en route. Only the Moluccas and the Talaud Islands now stood between MacArthur and Mindanao, 500 miles to the northwest.

We must now backtrack a little in time in order to follow the Central Pacific Axis of the dual Allied advance.

Across the Center

June 1944 saw unleashed the most titanic military effort in history. Almost simultaneously, American forces in the Pacific and predominantly American forces in Europe cracked the inner defense lines of Japan and of Germany. In terms of sheer magnitude, including the follow-up forces, the cross-Channel invasion of France is without rival, but the assault on Saipan nine days later was scarcely less complex, for the Saipan operation required projecting overwhelming power more than three thousand miles westward from Pearl Harbor and a thousand miles from Eniwetok, the most westerly American anchorage in the Central Pacific. Yet whereas planning for the Normandy invasion had been under way for more than two years, Spruance, Turner, and Holland Smith and their staffs had had only

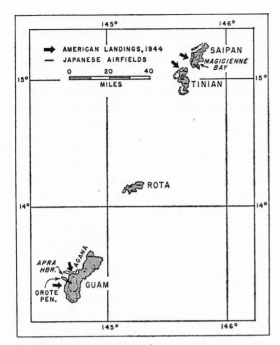

THE SOUTHERN MARIANAS

three months to plan and organize the expedition against the Marianas.

On June 6, Task Force 58, with Admiral Spruance in the *Indianapolis* and Vice Admiral Mitscher in the *Lexington,* left Majuro in the Marshalls and headed northwest, followed at a considerable distance by the amphibious forces, which included 535 ships, carrying more than 127,000 troops, two thirds of whom were marines. During the advance of the Fifth Fleet, army planes from the Marshalls and from the Southwest Pacific Area created a diversion and cut down Japanese air power by striking repeatedly at enemy bases in the Carolines. On June 11, when TF 58 had reached a point 200 miles east of Guam, Mitscher hurled his carrier air groups against the southern Marianas. (See map page 766.) Enemy plane losses were heavy and retaliation was light, partly because, as we have seen, most of the Japanese air power in the Central Pacific had been drained away southward in defense of Biak.

On June 13 Mitscher detached his seven battleships under Vice Admiral Lee to begin the bombardment of Saipan and nearby Tinian. On the 14th he detached two carrier task groups northward under Rear Admiral Joseph

J. Clark to attack landing fields on Iwo Jima and Chichi Jima in order to cut air communications from Japan and thereby complete the isolation of the Marianas. The other two carrier groups steamed around to the west of the island chain to lend direct support to the invasion of Saipan.

The Assault on Saipan

Mountainous, 14-mile-long Saipan could not be bombarded into impotence as the flat islets of Kwajalein Atoll had been. Yet the island had to be seized quickly from its 32,000 defenders because the Japanese were certain to react violently to an invasion so near their homeland. The proposed solution was to strike for a broad, deep beachhead from which the invaders could seize the main airfield and drive straight across the island.

On June 14 the old battleships and other fire support vessels of the amphibious force relieved Lee's battleships off Saipan and began a methodical bombardment. The same day underwater demolition teams reconnoitered the approaches to the beachhead, on the relatively flat southwest coast, and blasted passages through the coral reef. In the early hours of the 15th, transports and LST's bringing the 2nd and 4th Marine Divisions reached Saipan.

After a final two-hour naval bombardment, interrupted by a half hour of air strikes, eight battalions of marines in amtracs advanced toward the beach on a four-mile front. LCI gunboats led the way. Armored amphibians accompanied the first wave. Battleships, cruisers, and destroyers delivered support fire from so close inshore that the landing craft passed between them as they advanced from the line of departure to the beach.

Though 8,000 marines reached shore in the first 20 minutes, it was soon evident that the bombardment had been too brief for a strongly defended island the size of Saipan. Moreover it had been too general, with insufficient fire directed at the immediate beachhead area. Still intact behind the beach and on the flanks were numerous mortar and machine gun nests backed by well-sited artillery in the hills. By nightfall the marines had penetrated inland only about half way to the D-day objective line. Of the 20,000 who had landed during the day, more than ten per cent had been killed or wounded.

The next morning, informed by submarine reports that a Japanese fleet was approaching, Admiral Spruance postponed the intended early invasion of Guam. Admiral Turner thereupon ordered ashore his reserve, the 27th Infantry Division, and directed the Guam Attack Force to stand by in the event even more troops should be needed on Saipan.

By June 17, the American offensive, now amply supported by tanks and artillery, had overcome fierce Japanese resistance and begun to roll. The next day the 4th Marine Division reached the east coast, and the 27th Division captured the main airfield. On the 19th, as the fleets joined battle in the Philippine Sea to westward, the two marine divisions began to pivot for a drive to the north.

Spruance Covers the Beachhead

On June 14 the situation of the U.S. Fifth Fleet superficially but rather startlingly resembled that of the Japanese Combined Fleet two years earlier, when it had advanced on Midway with results so disastrous to itself. The Saipan Attack Force was heading in for the assault. The Floating Reserve and the Guam Attack Force were maneuvering east of the Marianas awaiting the outcome of the Saipan invasion. Half of TF 58, including Mitscher's flagship, was steaming to a covering position west of Saipan; the other half, under Clark, was mov-

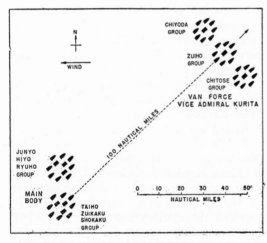

DISPOSITION OF MOBILE FLEET, JUNE 19

ing north for the strike at Iwo Jima and Chichi Jima, 500 miles away. The parallel would have been exact had the Japanese, with advance intelligence of American intentions, brought their whole carrier fleet undetected to the Marianas before the Americans arrived. Then, while the Fifth Fleet was divided several ways, the enemy carriers might conceivably have struck the two task groups west of Saipan before the rest of the Fifth Fleet could come to their support. The Japanese might thus have defeated the two American groups as decisively as the Americans defeated Nagumo's Mobile Force on June 4, 1942.

But the relative state of military intelligence in June 1944 was such that nothing of the sort occurred. The American attack on the Marianas took the enemy completely by surprise, and Spruance knew very well where the Japanese fleet was—at least until June 15. United States submarines were on station off Tawitawi and in the Philippine Sea keeping close watch on the Mobile Fleet and on all approaches to Saipan. Submarine *Redfin* observed and reported Ozawa's sortie from Tawitawi on the 13th. Coastwatchers kept Spruance informed by radio of the progress of the Japanese Main Body as it threaded its way through the Philippines. On the 15th, submarine *Flying Fish* reported it debouching from San Bernardino Strait. Spruance knew then that battle was imminent. Calculating the enemy's rate of advance, he postponed the invasion of Guam, transferred eight cruisers and 21 destroyers from the Saipan Attack Force to TF 58, directed Turner's old battleships to operate 25 miles west of Saipan in order to cover the beachhead, and ordered Clark's two carrier groups to complete their strikes on the 16th and head back south to rejoin the other two groups. Then in the *Indianapolis*, which had been off Saipan, he steamed back to resume his place in the carrier force west of the Marianas. Though Spruance did not take tactical control of TF 58, he told Mitscher that he would "issue general directives when necessary," and he expected Mitscher to inform him in advance of his intentions.

An hour after the *Flying Fish*'s June 15 report, submarine *Seahorse* sighted Ugaki's battleship force on a northeasterly course in the Philippine Sea. The reports of these submarines established that the Japanese fleet was in at least two widely separated divisions; and since the rendezvous of Ozawa and Ugaki on the 16th went unobserved, Spruance remained uncertain whether the enemy had massed his forces or was employing the tricky strategy of divided force which had characterized most of his operations up to that time. Two contacts by submarine *Cavalla* on the 17th indicated that the Japanese were still advancing on the Marianas, but because the *Cavalla* had sighted only part of the Mobile Fleet, Spruance continued to suspect that not all Japanese forces had been accounted for.

At noon on June 18, Clark's two carrier groups rejoined TF 58, whereupon Mitscher ordered his seven fast battleships, plus four heavy cruisers and 14 destroyers, detached from the carrier task groups to form battle line under Lee, ready for a surface engagement should opportunity offer. The five task groups thus formed, all in circular formation, then deployed for safe maneuver with 12- to 15-mile intervals between groups.

During the period of expectant waiting, Mitscher, in compliance with orders from Spruance, maintained a covering position near the Marianas and the Saipan beachhead, advancing westward by day and retiring eastward by night so as to prevent any enemy naval force from passing him in the darkness. Through the daylight hours of the 18th, TF 58 shaped the usual westerly course toward the last enemy contact, feeling out ahead with search planes. The carrier aircraft found nothing.[1] At nightfall, having developed no further intelligence regarding the enemy, Mitscher ordered TF 58, then 270 miles WSW of Saipan, to reverse course and head back east. Two hours later he received from Pearl Harbor radio direction finder bearings that placed the Mobile Fleet 355 miles WSW of his own position.

The situation was not at all to Mitscher's liking. He knew that Ozawa could outreach him, for Japanese carrier planes unencumbered

[1] Fighter aircraft, which had no radar but could elude or fight off Zekes, were used for daylight search. A PBM, operating from a tender off Saipan, made radar contact with the Mobile Fleet at 0115 on June 19 but could not get the word through by radio because of atmospheric conditions.

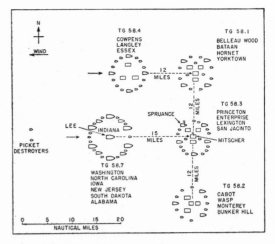

DISPOSITION OF TF 58, JUNE 19

with heavy armor and self-sealing fuel tanks, had an optimum striking radius of more than 300 miles, compared to 200 miles or less for American planes. Mitscher wanted to attack the Mobile Fleet early the next day, but if the direction-finder bearings were correct, he could be close enough to strike only by advancing westward during the remaining hours of darkness. After dawn it would be too late, for flight operations would then oblige his carriers to turn repeatedly into the steady easterly trade wind, thus backing off from the enemy. Mitscher was anxious also to put distance between himself and the Marianas. To remain near enemy airfields would invite simultaneous attacks by enemy land-based and carrier-based planes. It would also enable the Japanese carrier planes to shuttle-bomb him, that is, take off from their decks while the Mobile Fleet was well beyond American reach, attack TF 58, proceed to nearby Guam, there refuel and rearm, hit TF 58 again, and return to their carriers with fuel to spare. With these possibilities in mind, Mitscher proposed to Spruance by voice radio that TF 58 "come to a westerly course at 0130 in order to commence treatment of the enemy at 0500."[2]

After an hour-long discussion with his staff, Spruance a little after midnight rejected Mitscher's proposal. He was just as eager as Mitscher to sink enemy carriers, but his overriding objective—the only one mentioned in

[2] Theodore Taylor, *The Magnificent Mitscher* (New York, 1954), 221.

his orders—was to "capture, occupy and defend Saipan, Tinian and Guam."[3] Everything else had to be subordinated to this paramount purpose. In the circumstances TF 58 was primarily a Covering Force; its dominant mission at that moment was defensive, to shield the beachhead and the amphibious forces at Saipan. Recalling that the Japanese had used flanking forces in the battles of the Coral Sea and Midway and in the actions off Guadalcanal, Spruance sought a position where no enemy units could get behind his back to strike at the invasion forces. He discounted arguments that search planes could readily detect and bombers easily frustrate such an "end run." Up to that time, so far as he knew, American aircraft had utterly failed to locate the enemy. He could not be sure that they would do any better the next day. He distrusted the direction-finder fix as possibly a decoy; this contact however proved nearly exact. On the other hand, a badly garbled transmission from submarine *Stingray* had left him with the impression that the Mobile Fleet was much farther east than it actually was. Through the night therefore he continued to close the Marianas, accepting the risks of placing himself between enemy carriers and enemy airfields—and within range of each. Dawn on June 19 found TF 58 ninety miles SW of Saipan, 80 miles NW of Guam, still with no precise information regarding the location of the Mobile Fleet.

The Advance of the Mobile Fleet

In 1944 Japanese naval leaders, with the tide of war turning ever more against them, became obsessed with a false parallel between the Russo-Japanese War and World War II, and looked to a new Battle of Tsushima to extricate them from their difficulties. This was the spirit and intention of Operation *A-Go,* announced by Admiral Toyoda on assuming command of the Combined Fleet.

The selection of Tawitawi as base for the carrier-centered First Mobile Fleet was dictated chiefly by the chronic fuel shortage that hampered Japanese naval operations more and more with the steady attrition of tankers by

[3] Cincpoa Operation Plan No. 3–44, dated April 23, 1944.

American submarines. Tawitawi was within easy cruising range of the Western Carolines battle area designated in the original *A-Go* plan. It was also near the remarkable wells of Borneo, which produced pure but dangerously volatile oil that in a fuel emergency could be used by ships without processing.

But Tawitawi proved an unfortunate choice after all. When documents captured in New Guinea revealed to the Allies the existence and location of the new carrier fleet, American submarines converged upon the Celebes Sea and the Philippine Islands in such numbers that Ozawa dared not leave port for maneuvers. And since there was no suitable airdrome on or near Tawitawi, his aviators, who had been sent to the carriers with a minimum of basic training, ceased training altogether and merely loafed, losing their fighting edge.

When aircraft from TF 58 attacked the Marianas on June 11, Toyoda, as we have seen, immediately suspended operations for reinforcing Biak and ordered Ozawa and Ugaki to rendezvous in the Philippine Sea. Because there was not sufficient processed oil available for distant operations, oilers accompanying the two segments of the Mobile Fleet carried crude Borneo petroleum. At 1700 on June 16, Ozawa and Ugaki joined forces east of the Philippines and refueled with the dangerous crude. In the early afternoon of the 17th they resumed their advance, with radio orders from Toyoda to "attack the enemy in the Marianas area and annihilate the invasion force."[4]

Ozawa, estimating correctly that TF 58 was nearly twice as strong as the Mobile Fleet on the surface and more than twice as strong in the air, was acutely aware of the inadequate training of his flyers.[5] But he counted on certain advantages—or supposed advantages. He and Ugaki had, for example, selected routes

[4] Quoted in Morison, *United States Naval Operations in World War II*, VIII, 221.

[5] Mobile Fleet: 9 carriers, 5 battleships, 13 cruisers, 28 destroyers, 430 carrier aircraft, 43 float planes. Task Force 58: 15 carriers, 7 battleships, 21 cruisers, 69 destroyers, 891 carrier aircraft, 65 float planes. The Japanese had gathered extensive intelligence about the U.S. Fifth Fleet from captured documents, from daring air reconnaissance over the Marshalls, and from interrogation of downed American aviators.

of advance beyond the range of air reconnaissance from Manus. The trade wind would give him the lee gage, permitting him to launch and recover aircraft while advancing on the enemy. Having appraised Spruance as a cautious man on the basis of his tactics at Midway, he rightly estimated that TF 58 would maintain a close covering position off the Saipan beachhead. That and the long striking radius of his planes gave him all the advantages that Mitscher feared. Ozawa expected aircraft based on Rota and Guam to attack first and achieve at least 33⅓ per cent attrition of TF 58 before the Mobile Fleet went into action. Then he intended to stand off beyond reach of the American carriers and make use of the Guam airfields to shuttle-bomb them into final defeat.

In the afternoon of June 18, planes from the Japanese carriers located TF 58 some 200 miles west of Saipan. Ozawa thereupon began to take disposition for an attack the next morning. Under Vice Admiral Takeo Kurita, a Van Force consisting of three circular groups, each centered on a single light carrier, advanced to a position 300 miles WSW of TF 58, just outside the extreme attack radius of the American planes. A hundred miles to the rear of the Van Force, that is, 100 miles farther from TF 58, was the Main Body under direct command of Admiral Ozawa. This consisted of two circular groups, each centered on three carriers—six carriers in all, five heavy and one light. Most of the heavy surface ships were in Kurita's Van, for this force with its concentration of antiaircraft fire was expected to absorb the first shock, should the aircraft of TF 58 manage to attack. Ozawa's disposition had a certain logic, but as in the Battle of Midway the Japanese divisions were too widely separated for mutual support, and the heavy carriers were poorly protected against possible submarine attack.

"The fate of the Empire depends on the issue of this battle; let every man do his utmost," Admiral Togo had announced to his fleet just before the Battle of Tsushima. And from Japan Admiral Toyoda had repeated Togo's exhortation to the Mobile Fleet, now going into action. As dawn grayed the skies over the Philippine Sea on the morning of June 19, 1944, more than 300 Japanese carrier planes prepared to take off against TF 58, in order to repeat by other means Togo's decisive victory of 39 years before.

The Battle of the Philippine Sea, June 19–21, 1944

Had Ozawa realized that TF 58 had already reduced Japanese air power in the Marianas to no more than 30 operational planes, that Clark had destroyed aircraft reinforcements coming down from Japan, and that the aviators sent to the relief of Biak were in no condition to return, he might have been less sanguine about the approaching battle. Aircraft based on Guam attempted to attack TF 58 early on June 19, but Hellcats pounced on them as they were taking off, shot down a few, and then turned their attention to 19 reinforcements arriving from Truk. In this early morning skirmish, 33 Hellcats destroyed 30 fighters and five bombers. That ended the participation of land-based air in the Battle of the Philippine Sea.

Having at last reversed direction at 0619, TF 58 steamed on a southwesterly course awaiting attack. Finally at 1000 American radars detected aircraft at 150 miles, approaching from the west. This raid, the first of four launched by the Mobile Fleet, consisted of 45 bombers, eight torpedo planes, and 16 Zekes from the three light carriers of Kurita's Van Force. Task Force 58 steamed steadily toward the contact for 20 minutes, then turned into the wind and launched every available fighter, numbering more than 450. Mitscher next ordered into the air all bombers and torpedo bombers. These remained clear of TF 58 while the carriers landed, rearmed, refueled, and again launched the Hellcats. Many of the bombers, at first on their own and later on orders from Mitscher, dropped their bombs on the airstrips on Guam, keeping them generally unusable by the would-be shuttle-bombers from the Mobile Fleet.

While the Japanese planes of the initial attack were regrouping 70 miles from TF 58, American fighter directors operating with superb efficiency vectored out the Hellcats and stacked them at high altitude, whence they swooped down on their ill-trained opponents

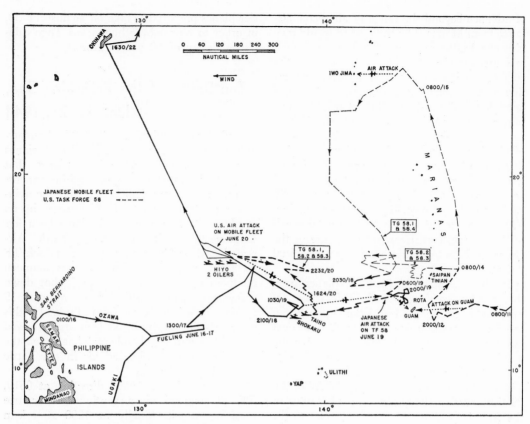

BATTLE OF THE PHILIPPINE SEA, JUNE 19–21, 1944

and shot down about 25. A few Japanese aircraft penetrated as far as the American battle line, where they were blasted with deadly VT-fused ammunition. One bomber made a near miss on the *Minneapolis;* another hit the *South Dakota,* causing numerous casualties but no crippling damage. Only 27 Japanese planes returned to their carriers. All but one of the American planes returned.

The second raid, 128 planes from Ozawa's Main Body, was met by Hellcats 50 miles out and cut down to half size. Survivors took further losses over the battle line and one crashed into the side of the *Indiana,* Lee's flagship. A few reached the carrier groups, where two bombers started fires on the *Bunker Hill* with near misses. Only 31 planes of this raid returned to the Mobile Fleet.

Of the 47 planes of the third raid, most failed to find TF 58. They caused no damage and suffered only seven losses. The 82 planes of Ozawa's final raid became scattered. One

group was intercepted far out and cut in half; another reached the American carriers and did minor damage with near misses, but was very nearly wiped out. The third group headed for Guam, jettisoning bombs. Here Hellcats intercepted them and shot down 30. Nineteen Japanese survivors were wrecked in attempting to land on the cratered runways. Only 11 planes of the final raid returned to their carriers.

During this eight-hour decimation of Japanese naval air power, which American flyers called the "Marianas Turkey Shoot," other disasters were overtaking the Mobile Fleet. Two American submarines had slipped through the weak screen of the Main Body and attacked the heavy carriers. The *Albacore* put a single torpedo into Ozawa's flagship, the new *Taiho.* Three hours later the *Cavalla* fired three torpedoes into the veteran *Shokaku.* From ruptured fuel tanks and bunkers, gasoline fumes and explosive vapors from the crude Borneo petroleum seeped through the vessels. Damage control parties worked valiantly, but they had developed no techniques adequate to deal with such a situation. In mid-afternoon both carriers blew up with tremendous loss of life. Among the survivors were Ozawa and his staff, who transferred from the sinking *Taiho* to a cruiser and thence to carrier *Zuikaku*.

Ozawa ordered a general retirement to the northwest for refueling, intending to resume battle the next day, for he believed reports from his aviators that TF 58 was badly crippled. When the tally was in and he learned that his carrier planes had been reduced from 430 to an even hundred, his only reaction was to postpone the proposed attack till the 21st.

Night was approaching before TF 58, then 35 miles west of Rota, had recovered the last of the planes from the Turkey Shoot. Now that the enemy's wings were clipped, Spruance was ready to advance on the Mobile Fleet. Leaving one carrier group behind to keep Guam and Rota neutralized, Mitscher moved S by W through the night. The choice of course, based on a misestimate of the enemy's position, was unfortunate, for though the Americans were making five knots better speed than the Japanese, they closed the range only slightly. After a fruitless search to westward in the morning of the 20th, Mitscher at noon changed course to NW, but because he was obliged to turn into the easterly wind several times to launch and recover search planes, he ceased to gain on the enemy.

As the day wore on it appeared that the hoped-for counterstroke could not be delivered after all. Not a single American carrier plane had yet seen the Mobile Fleet. Mitscher had received no information on Ozawa's position since the *Cavalla* had reported her attack on the *Shokaku* at noon the preceding day. At last toward 1600 the long-awaited word came in. A search pilot had sighted the Mobile Fleet, which he reported on a westerly course 220 miles WNW of TF 58.

This was considerably beyond the optimum attack radius of American carrier planes. If Mitscher launched a strike so late in the day at such a distance, the flyers would have to return in darkness and make night landings, for which they were untrained. With feelings of almost paternal affection for his aviators,

Mitscher had always sought to minimize the risks of their dangerous calling. Yet now, with the enemy at last within his reach, he felt he had no alternative but to attack. "Launch 'em," said he firmly.[6]

The flyers were quickly briefed, with orders to concentrate on the Japanese carriers. Then they raced for their planes. The first deckload strike—85 fighters, 77 dive bombers, 54 torpedo bombers—was in the air by 1630. Thereupon TF 58, having turned into the wind for launching, resumed course toward the enemy in order to close the range for recovery of its returning aircraft. Then came a shock. The search pilot who had reported the location of the Mobile Fleet had made a mistake. His corrected report placed the enemy 60 miles farther away.[7] Mitscher considered recalling the planes already launched, then, after restudying the charts, decided against it—merely canceling the second deckload.

Shortly before sunset the aviators from TF 58 sighted the Japanese oilers. While a few planes attacked these, sinking two, the rest went after the enemy carrier groups, now scattering fanwise to the northwest. In a series of uncoordinated but otherwise neatly executed attacks, the American bombers ripped up the flight decks of and set fire to carriers *Chiyoda* and *Zuikaku* and damaged a battleship and a cruiser. The only combat vessel actually sunk was the victim of torpedo planes. Avengers, dropping out of a cloud, succeeded in releasing their torpedoes at low altitude, one, possibly two, of which found their mark in carrier *Hiyo*. Ablaze and racked by internal explosions, the *Hiyo* gradually settled at the bow and went down.

Ozawa managed to get 75 planes airborne, and these survivors of the Turkey Shoot gave a good account of themselves. Antiaircraft

---

[6] J. Bryan III and Philip Reed, *Mission beyond Darkness* (New York, 1945), 15.

[7] The *Lexington* received the correction at 1605, but radio traffic was then so heavy that by the time the communicators had copied, decoded, and rushed the corrected report to Mitscher, the strike was on its way. Because TF 58 had to turn east for launching while the Mobile Fleet continued west, the American air groups had to fly more than 300 miles to make their attack. Task Force 58, by heading at maximum speed toward the enemy fleet, considerably shortened the return flight.

guns and swift-darting Zekes shot down 20 American planes, but Japanese losses were much heavier. When the sun set on June 20, the Mobile Fleet had left only 35 carrier aircraft.

The American air groups, their mission completed, headed back toward TF 58. Fuel gauges in a few of the bombers and torpedo planes were far below the half-full mark; some showed perilously close to empty. Pilots with badly damaged aircraft were among the first to go down. Those who had neglected fuel-conserving measures soon followed. Others wasted fuel in a vain attempt to outspeed nightfall. One group took a vote by radio to ditch together instead of each continuing until his fuel was exhausted. "O.K.," said the chairman, "here we go."[8]

Mitscher had spread out his three carrier groups to allow more maneuvering room for recovery operations. As the minutes ticked past he prowled restlessly between Flag Plot and Flag Bridge. A little after 2000 Air Plot announced the approach of the first of the returning planes, whereupon the task force turned into the east wind to take them aboard. Mitscher went back into Flag Plot, took a seat, and puffed thoughtfully on a cigarette. If he lighted up the task force, he would save many a desperate pilot who otherwise must make a water landing, but he would also expose his fleet to possible submarine and aircraft attack. Still, he knew what he had to do—not only for humanitarian reasons but because a carrier stripped of its planes is a liability rather than an asset. To his chief of staff, Captain Arleigh Burke, he said, "Turn on the lights."[9] Then he went back to the bridge. On went running lights, truck lights, and glow lights to outline the flight decks, while 5-inch guns of the screen fired star shell, and searchlights pointed straight upward as homing beacons.

8 Bryan and Reed, *Mission beyond Darkness*, 64.
9 *Ibid.*, 73. Mitscher had ample precedent for his action in Spruance's daring illumination for night recovery in the Battle of Midway, when the U.S. Navy had no carriers to spare. (See page 685, above.) In that battle Mitscher commanded U.S. carrier *Hornet*. Arleigh ("31-Knot") Burke, who had made his reputation with the destroyers in the Solomons campaign, had joined TF 58 just before the raid on the Palaus.

Landing signal officers, gesturing with fluorescent batons, waved in the first few planes smoothly enough, but as the newly-arrived aircraft swarmed into the landing circles, the officers were obliged to wave off far more than they landed. When planes exhausted their last drops of fuel and went down, destroyers moved busily through the fleet seeking survivors. Pilots, ordered to land wherever they could find a flight deck, shopped through the fleet for an uncrowded landing circle. One desperate pilot disregarded a wave-off from the *Lexington* and crashed into six newly-landed planes, killing two men and injuring half a dozen others. Two aircraft in quick succession disregarded signals and crash-landed on the *Bunker Hill*, killing two men and injuring four. Aboard the *Enterprise* a fighter and a bomber landed at the same time and incredibly did not crash, the fighter's tail hook catching the second cable and the bomber's, the fifth.

Since the battle over the Mobile Fleet, 80 American aircraft had ditched, or crashed on landing. After completing recovery of planes at 2232, TF 58 shaped course toward the scene of the twilight battle, proceeding at 16 knots through the night and the next day along the path of the returning flyers. By this means destroyers and float planes rescued all but 49 of the 209 aviators who had participated in the battle of June 20.

Spruance estimated that the two hours the American force had spent on an easterly course recovering planes plus the subsequent slow speed to facilitate rescues had permitted the fleeing enemy to get beyond reach of a second air strike. This opinion was confirmed early on the 21st when long-range Avengers found the Mobile Fleet making 20 knots on a NW course 360 miles away. All that day Hellcats searched fruitlessly for possible enemy cripples. An hour after sunset Spruance ordered the search abandoned, and TF 58 turned back east.

Since submarines *Albacore* and *Cavalla* had not stayed to observe the results of their marksmanship on June 19, and reports from TF 58 aviators were conflicting, American evaluators could assume with confidence only that one Japanese heavy carrier had been sunk and two or three light carriers damaged. To many naval officers this was a disappointment, falling far short of the overwhelming victory they felt they had a right to expect. And though Admirals Nimitz and King both applauded Admiral Spruance's decision to remain close to Saipan until the enemy's wings had been clipped, Spruance himself regretted that his primary responsibility had kept him tethered to the beachhead. But if Mitscher had moved westward to attack the Mobile Fleet on June 19, his planes would have encountered the heavy antiaircraft fire of Kurita's Van Force while the Japanese heavy carriers were still a hundred miles away. By remaining on the defensive near the Marianas, TF 58 had all its fighter planes available for interception. These aircraft, with able assistance from Lee's battle line and the carrier groups, shot down most of the Japanese planes at or near the limit of their attack radius and destroyed the planes on Guam as well. Thus TF 58 on the 19th was at the optimum position to hurt the enemy.[10] True, most of the Japanese carriers got away, but they had lost nearly all of their trained aviators.

Conquest of the Southern Marianas

Until the Japanese Mobile Fleet had been defeated and repulsed, the U.S. Fifth Fleet was unable to give its full support to the assault on the Marianas. Saipan, as we have seen, received only two days of pre-assault bombardment, and during the Battle of the Philippine Sea all amphibious forces not absolutely essential to the operation retired from the area to await the outcome. The American naval victory at once altered this situation. Since there was no longer any serious danger from enemy naval forces, Fifth Fleet carrier aircraft and gunnery vessels could devote their full attention to supporting the American troops on Saipan and to preparing for the forthcoming assaults on Tinian and Guam.

As the two marine divisions on Saipan pivoted for their drive to the north, Holland Smith ordered the 27th Infantry Division to the center of the new front. But the tardy compliance and deliberate tactics that had

[10] Morison, *Naval Operations*, VIII, 315–6.

slowed down elements of this division on Makin and on Eniwetok now brought it so nearly to a standstill that the inner flanks of the advancing marine divisions became more and more exposed. His patience exhausted, General Smith, with the concurrence of Turner and Spruance, summarily replaced the 27th Division's commanding general.

Thereafter, well supported by naval guns and aircraft, the Americans advanced together up the narrowing north peninsula, where the enemy was deeply entrenched in a network of fortified caves and underground defenses. At the end of the first week in July, some 3,000 Japanese, finding themselves being forced into an ever-diminishing perimeter, struck out in a desperate early morning banzai charge. They broke through a gap in the 27th Division front and surged forward more than a mile before the greater part of them were killed and the rest repulsed, at a cost of 400 American lives. Holland Smith now withdrew most of the army troops into reserve. Three more days of fighting carried the marines to the northeast tip of the island. That ended organized Japanese resistance on Saipan, but several thousand enemy troops in by-passed caves and ravines still remained to be captured or destroyed before Admiral Spruance could declare the island secured.

The capture of Saipan had cost 16,500 American casualties, including 3,400 killed—mostly during the first few days. The subsequent conquests of Tinian and Guam were much less costly, partly because these islands were more lightly garrisoned than Saipan but chiefly because they received more sustained and more systematic bombardment.

All through the Saipan campaign, naval bombers and guns had intermittently softened up nearby Tinian. As the campaign came to an end, most of the artillery on Saipan, nearly 200 field pieces, was placed hub to hub on the southwest shore to take over the bombardment of the northern half of Tinian, while the ships and aircraft continued working over the rest. Because Tinian's two best landing beaches, one in the southwest and one in the east, were heavily mined and fortified, Admiral Turner, after exchanging views with Generals Harry Schmidt and Holland Smith and Admirals Hill and Spruance, decided to invade over two very narrow beaches on the northwest coast. Achieving a secure landing through these restricted corridors required surprise, speed, and new logistic techniques. On July 24, while the 2nd Marine Division staged a mock assault on the southern beach to bemuse the defenders, the 4th Marine Division was transported from Saipan to the area off Tinian's northwest beaches. From LST's amtracs carried the invaders ashore in 15 closely spaced waves, which quickly crossed the beaches and fanned out. This was, as it were, the Saipan invasion turned sidewise, making up in momentum what it lacked in breadth. Because the canefields of generally flat Tinian offered little opportunity for the Japanese to take protective cover, the marines abandoned their usual rushing tactics for a methodical advance behind artillery barrages. Now for the first time aircraft used the deadly napalm fire bomb to destroy pockets of enemy resistance. At the end of a week the 2nd and 4th Marine Divisions, late victors of Saipan, had reached the southern end of Tinian.

The conquest of Guam took longer because this island was considerably larger and more heavily garrisoned. Thirteen days of sustained, methodical bombardment however demoralized the defenders and knocked out most of their artillery. In the morning of July 21, Rear Admiral Conolly's Southern Attack Force arrived off the west coast of Guam bringing the new III Amphibious Corps, commanded by Major General Roy S. Geiger USMC. Advancing shoreward in amtracs under rolling naval barrages, the 3rd Marine Division landed north of Orote Peninsula, and the 1st Provisional Marine Brigade,[11] followed by the 77th Infantry Division, landed south of Orote. From the two beachheads, the invaders forced their way to a meeting in the hilly interior, sealing off the Peninsula, which the Marine Brigade soon captured. The Americans were thus early enabled to use Orote airfield and nearby Apra Harbor. (See map page 761.) The 3rd and 77th Divisions then advanced together to the north, with the fleet providing call fire by day and harassing fire and star

[11] Including the 4th and 22nd Marine Regiments, a further step toward the formation of the 6th Marine Division. See footnote page 755.

shell illumination by night. On August 10 Guam was declared secured, though as on Saipan and Tinian a great many Japanese troops were still at large.

The successful landings in the Marianas revealed the increasing efficiency of American amphibious techniques, and the invasion of Tinian provided a striking demonstration of their flexibility. Ship-to-shore movement as practiced by the Central Pacific forces had evidently reached maturity. At Guam American fleet support had attained similar efficiency. It should be noted however that the pre-assault bombardment that neutralized Guam was stretched over many days. Saipan after two days of bombardment was far from neutralized. With the weapons available in 1944, no means could be devised for softening up a strongly defended position quickly.

Conquest of the southern Marianas cost more than 5,000 American and nearly 60,000 Japanese lives. Japan had lost its direct air staging line to the Carolines. The United States had acquired logistic bases for further conquests westward, submarine bases for stepping up attacks on Japanese communications with the Southern Resources Area, and air bases from which the new long-range B-29's could blast the industrial concentration in and about Tokyo. The loss of the Marianas was the beginning of the end for Japan. Yet not all Allied officials saw it that way. The general refusal of Japanese troops to surrender even when hopelessly overpowered, and the wholesale suicide of Japanese civilian residents of Saipan in order to avoid capture led many to the chilling conclusion that Japan could be conquered only by direct invasion and the virtual extermination of her armed forces and population.

This assumption was incorrect. The Emperor and other high Japanese officials knew very well that they must soon capitulate. The Tojo government fell and was succeeded by a cabinet to whom the Emperor made known his desire for early peace negotiations. Yet so binding was the Japanese military code, so rigid the demands of Oriental "face," that for a whole year no official in Japan could bring himself to initiate steps for ending hostilities. On the Allied side, the goal of "unconditional surrender" set by Roosevelt and Churchill at Casablanca forbade the proffering of terms which might have served as bases for negotiation.

Preliminaries to the Invasion of the Philippines

While the Spruance-Turner-Smith team was busy conquering the Marianas, Nimitz ordered Halsey up from the South Pacific to relieve Spruance in command of the Central Pacific Force and to plan for participation in the forthcoming invasion of the Philippines. As preliminary operations, beginning September 15, 1944, the forces under Halsey were to capture staging and support bases in the western Carolinas—Peleliu and Angaur islands in the Palaus, and Ulithi Atoll and Yap Island between the Palaus and the Marianas. Halsey was also to support MacArthur's Southwest Pacific forces, which would invade Morotai, half way between New Guinea and Mindanao, on September 15; the Talaud Islands, half way between Morotai and Mindanao, on October 15; Mindanao, southernmost of the Philippines, on November 15; and Leyte, in the central Philippines, on December 20. The date for the contemplated invasion of Luzon, northernmost of the Philippines, was to be contingent upon the success and speed of the earlier invasions. (See map page 778.)

Such was the plan. But the Joint Chiefs of Staff, King in particular, had begun to question the desirability of approaching Japan by way of the Philippine archipelago. Such a step-by-step approach would be costly, and it would inevitably slow down the tempo of the war. It would mean more "island-hopping," the sort of warfare the Allies had abandoned since the Fifth Fleet had demonstrated its capacity for by-passing and isolating Japanese positions with thousand-mile leaps. After MacArthur had conquered a foothold on Mindanao, suggested the Joint Chiefs, let him establish air bases there to reduce enemy air power on Luzon; then let him join forces with Nimitz' Central Pacific command in an invasion of Formosa and the China coast. This by-passing strategy would give the Allies a base quite as good as Luzon for blockading

Japanese communications with the East Indies, and it would in a single stroke provide a convenient staging area for invading Japan itself. Japan would thus be defeated sooner and the Filipinos liberated earlier, so ran the argument, than by means of a time-consuming campaign through the Philippines.

General MacArthur reacted strongly against the Joint Chiefs' suggestion. At a July 1944 conference in Honolulu, he pointed out to President Roosevelt that thousands of Filipino guerrillas were already harassing the Japanese occupation forces, that nearly the entire Filipino population could be counted on to join the American campaign of liberation, that to by-pass and seal off these friendly people and the American prisoners in the islands would expose them to frightful privations and to mistreatment at the hands of their Japanese captors, that for the United States to fail to honor its promise to liberate the Filipinos at the earliest possible moment would be construed in the Orient as a second American abandonment of the Philippines. The President found these arguments convincing, but a final decision had not been reached when the Combined Chiefs of Staff met with Roosevelt and Churchill at the second Quebec conference on September 11.

By this time, Spruance, Turner, and Smith had returned to Pearl Harbor to rest and to plan future operations. Their places in the Pacific Fleet command echelon were taken by Admiral Halsey, under whom the Central Pacific Force was designated U.S. Third Fleet; by Vice Admiral Theodore Wilkinson, Commander Third Amphibious Force; and by Major General Geiger, to whose III Amphibious Corps all the Central Pacific invasion troops were now assigned.[12] Vice Admiral Mitscher, by his own choice, remained in command of the Fast Carrier Task Force, now called Task Force 38. This change of titles accompanying successive changes of command incidentally led the Japanese to suppose that

[12] Because General Geiger was detained too long by the Guam operation to participate fully in planning the western Carolinas campaign, over-all command of the amphibious corps for the conquest of the Palaus, Ulithi, and Yap was assumed by Major General Julian C. Smith, of Tarawa fame.

two mighty fleets, the Third and the Fifth, were alternately opposing them in the Central Pacific.

Just as the Combined Chiefs were assembling at Quebec, Halsey in his flagship *New Jersey* joined TF 38 and carried out air strikes against the central Philippines in strategic support of the impending invasions of Morotai and Peleliu. The results were startling. At the cost of eight planes and ten aviators, TF 38 destroyed about 200 enemy aircraft and sank a dozen freighters and a tanker. Convinced that the central Philippines were "a hollow shell with weak defenses and skimpy facilities,"[13] Halsey sent Nimitz an urgent radio dispatch recommending that the planned seizure of Yap and the Palaus be abandoned forthwith and that the ground forces for these operations be turned over to MacArthur for an invasion of Leyte at the earliest possible date. Nimitz, willing to by-pass Yap but insisting upon the capture of the Palaus, forwarded Halsey's suggestion to Quebec. The Joint Chiefs thereupon radioed for MacArthur's opinion. When MacArthur concurred in the speed-up plan, they canceled the proposed landings on Yap, the Talauds, and Mindanao, and ordered MacArthur and Nimitz to combine forces for an invasion of Leyte on October 20, 1944—two months ahead of schedule.

Nimitz now ordered the Eastern Attack Force, then en route to Yap with the XXIV Army Corps, to shape course instead for Manus and report to General MacArthur's Southwest Pacific command. This transfer at sea of command of a mixed force from one theater commander to another is indicative of the flexibility of planning and of the cooperation of the theater commanders. The Western Attack Force continued on toward the Palaus with the warning that fire support vessels, escort carriers, transports, and escorts of this force also would report to MacArthur as soon as they could be released from the Palau-Ulithi operation. The U.S. Third Fleet was thus to be stripped down virtually to TF 38. Practically everything else would be transferred to the Southwest Pacific forces in

[13] W. F. Halsey and J. Bryan III, *Admiral Halsey's Story* (New York, 1947), 199.

preparation for the assault on Leyte.[14] Meanwhile the four groups of TF 38 deployed to support the landings on Morotai and Peleliu.

These concurrent mid-September invasions by the Southwest Pacific and the Central Pacific forces provide a study in contrasts. Except for the hazard and inconvenience of natural beach obstacles, the capture of Morotai proved to be one of the easiest conquests of the war; while overcoming the intricate defenses of Peleliu cost the attackers the highest combat casualty rate (nearly 40 per cent) of any amphibious assault in American history.

By-passing heavily garrisoned Halmahera, the Seventh Amphibious Force, with 28,000 army troops aboard, took Morotai by surprise. While Third and Seventh Fleet carrier planes and Fifth Air Force planes from Biak and Noemfoor isolated the target, a two-hour naval bombardment sent the few hundred defenders scurrying to the hills. Despite delays caused by an almost impassable reef, mud flats into which troops sank to their hips, torrential rains, and absence of coral suitable for surfacing, engineers had two bomber fields and a fighting strip ready on Morotai in time to cover the left flank of the Philippines invasion.

The conquest of much-smaller Peleliu, 500 miles to the northeast, was a very different story. In this area, the attack force by-passed Babelthuap, largest of the Palaus with a 25,000-man garrison. But on four-mile-long Peleliu there were more than 10,000 Japanese, about half of whom were combat troops of the crack 14th Army Division. Moreover, the Peleliu garrison had diligently complied with a July directive from Imperial General Headquarters setting forth a new defense doctrine.

Formerly, orders issued to Japanese island commanders anticipating an amphibious attack by Allied forces had specified that the defenders were to "meet and annihilate the invaders at the beachhead." Against the power-packed American ship-to-shore movement and support, this doctrine had every-

[14] The stripped-down Third Fleet also included TG 30.8 (At Sea Logistic Group Third Fleet), comprising oilers, escort carriers with replacement aircraft, fleet tugs, ammunition ships, and attached screening vessels (destroyers and destroyer escorts). Elements of TG 30.8 met, refueled, and replenished TF 38 at designated points.

where proved disastrous. The new Japanese plan employed a carefully calculated defense in depth. Expendable forces at the beach were intended merely to delay the invaders. The main line of resistance was to be far enough inland to escape the full power of the naval bombardment. This line would be backed by a defense fortress that took full advantage of irregularities in the terrain, made as impregnable as possible by every device that human ingenuity could contrive. Troops were to be held in reserve for counterattack when opportunity offered. There were to be no useless banzai charges; every defender was to sell his life dearly.

The three-day naval bombardment of Peleliu completely wiped out all visible defenses on the beach and on the plain behind it. When the 1st Marine Division headed for the shore, most of the casualties to their landing craft were caused by artillery fire from the reverse slopes of the "fortress," a system of ridges to the northeast. Despite continuing fire from these ridges and a series of counterattacks from the main Japanese defense line, the marines quickly made good their beachhead and captured the airfield. When they penetrated the northeast ridges however, they ran into a new sort of resistance. Here the Japanese had withdrawn into a labyrinth of more than 500 natural and artificial caves, mostly interconnected, some fitted with steel doors, all skillfully camouflaged or concealed by vegetation.

By this time, regiments of the 81st Infantry Division, which had been standing by as a floating reserve, had proceeded to invade nearby Angaur Island and distant Ulithi Atoll. Fortunately for the Americans, Angaur proved to be lightly defended and Ulithi not defended at all. General Geiger was able to detach one regiment from the Angaur operation and rush it across to Peleliu to join the hard-pressed marines. Bazookas, demolition charges, and tank-mounted long-range flamethrowers provided an eventual answer to the new Japanese defense techniques, but clearing the enemy off Peleliu was a slow, costly process lasting until February of the following year.

Long before then, American planes were operating from airfields on both Angaur and Peleliu, and Allied ships were using Kossol

Passage at the northern end of the Palaus as an emergency anchorage. While it might be questioned whether these advantages offset the cost, 10,000 American casualties, including nearly 2,000 killed, there can be little doubt that the Palaus left entirely in Japanese hands would have been a real threat to MacArthur's advance to the Philippines. The advantages of the bloodless occupation of Ulithi are beyond question, for Ulithi provided the Pacific Fleet with an anchorage and logistic base of major importance, largely replacing Majuro, Kwajalein, and Eniwetok. Every subsequent operation of the Central Pacific forces was at least in part launched from here.

While the invasion forces were assembling at Manus and Hollandia, Allied air and sea power staged a campaign to isolate Leyte. From bases in the South and Central Pacific, aircraft attacked Japanese-held islands in the Marshalls and the Carolines. From western China, B-29's of the 20th Bomber Command and medium bombers of Major General Claire L. Chennault's Fourteenth Air Force operated against Formosa and the China coast. General Kenney's Far Eastern Air Forces, based on New Guinea, Biak, and Morotai, hit the southern flank, striking repeatedly at Japanese airfields in Mindanao and the East Indies.

The Third Fleet, assigned the mission of neutralizing the northern flank, struck Okinawa on October 10, attacked airfields on Luzon on the 11th, and on the 12th began a three-day campaign against bases on Formosa. Here the carrier planes destroyed shipping and airdrome installations and quickly shot down more than 200 fighter aircraft. When Japanese torpedo bombers from the home islands began reaching Formosa via the hastily repaired Okinawa airfields, they too took heavy losses. They succeeded however in torpedoing cruisers *Canberra* and *Houston*,[15] which had to be taken in tow. The Japanese aviators, elated by this moderate success and supposing that they had achieved a great deal more, flashed word back home that they had sunk eleven carriers, two battleships, and three cruisers. They thereby set off victory celebrations in

[15] The second cruisers in World War II so named. U.S.S. *Canberra* was the first American warship to be named for a foreign city.

Japan, and Radio Tokyo broadcast the fictitious triumph to the world. Taking advantage of the enemy's delusion, Halsey set a trap. He temporarily withdrew the bulk of the Third Fleet from Formosan waters, leaving behind the damaged cruisers and a single task group to lure out the Japanese fleet and thus precipitate a sea battle.

Admiral Toyoda took Halsey's bait. He sent all his better trained carrier air squadrons to help the land-based torpedo bombers complete their supposed victory, and he ordered his Second Striking Force of cruisers and destroyers to sortie from Japan "to mop up remaining enemy elements." But long-range Japanese search planes, quartering the seas for a final check, at length found all the groups of the U.S. Third Fleet and reported none noticeably impaired. So Halsey's trap was exposed, and the Second Striking Force prudently retired to the Ryukyus. The Japanese aircraft got in the last lick however, firing another torpedo into the battered *Houston.* That ended the battle. Both damaged American cruisers, saved by efficient damage control, at length reached Ulithi under tow. The rest of the Third Fleet, having wiped out the greater portion of Japanese land-based air power and the only effective part of Japanese carrier air power, proceeded to station off Leyte to support the invasion of the Philippines. Between October 11 and 16, Halsey's carrier squadrons had destroyed about 350 aircraft and lost 89.

The Invasion of Leyte

The main elements of the Leyte attack forces sortied from Manus and Hollandia in several echelons between October 10 and 15. On the 17th and 18th the advance units put Rangers ashore on the islands guarding the entrance to Leyte Gulf in order to secure the flanks of the oncoming invasion forces. On the 18th minesweepers and underwater demolition teams began their important preparatory work off the Leyte beachheads, while fire support ships and escort carriers came in for a two-day pounding of Japanese coastal defenses.

In the early hours of October 20, the transports entered the Gulf and steamed to position for the assault—those of Admiral Barbey's Seventh Amphibious Force off Tacloban, capital of Leyte; those of Admiral Wilkinson's Third Amphibious Force off Dulag, 17 miles south of Tacloban. At the same time one regimental combat team was lifted down to Panaon Island to seize a base whence PT boats could patrol the southern entrance to Surigao Strait, gateway into Leyte Gulf from the south. After a final bombardment of the shoreline, troops headed for the marshy beaches in a variety of craft, including amtracs, which had been loaded in Third Amphibious Force LST's for the canceled invasion of reef-surrounded Yap.

Conforming to their new defense doctrine, most of the Japanese retreated to prepared positions in the hilly interior, leaving behind only enough troops to harass and delay the landings. The Japanese at the beachheads caused some casualties with rifle, machine gun, mortar, and artillery fire. A single torpedo plane, attacking in the late afternoon, heavily damaged light cruiser *Honolulu.* Compared to most invasions in the Pacific however, the landings on Leyte were easy. By sunset on the 20th more than 60,000 assault troops and more than 100,000 tons of supplies and equipment were ashore, both Leyte beachheads had expanded more than a mile inland, and the Tacloban airstrip was in American hands.

A few hours after the first landings on Leyte, General MacArthur came ashore accompanied by Sergio Osmeña, President of the Philippines. Stepping up to a signal corps microphone, the General broadcast his speech of liberation for all Filipinos to hear: "This is the Voice of Freedom, General MacArthur speaking. People of the Philippines! I have returned. By the grace of Almighty God our forces stand again on Philippine soil—soil consecrated in the blood of our two peoples. . . . Rally to me. Let the indomitable spirit of Bataan and Corregidor lead on. As the lines of battle roll forward to bring you within the zone of operations, rise and strike. Strike at every favorable opportunity. For your homes and hearths, strike! For future generations of your sons and daughters, strike! In the name of your sacred dead, strike!"

Summary

Operations in the Pacific theater during 1944 have been described in several ways. Some officers thought of the series of landings along the coast of New Guinea as the principal line of advance toward the Philippines and Japan. They regarded the conquests of Nimitz' Central Pacific forces as useful chiefly for clearing the right flank of the Southwest Pacific drive, and hence were critical of the leap from the Marshalls to the Marianas while the Carolines were left in Japanese hands. The drive across the Central Pacific was officially designated as the main line of advance, but in practice this designation was meaningless, for in the allocation of men, supplies, and weapons neither advance was favored over the other. Yet there were officers who considered MacArthur's operations as useful principally for clearing the left flank of the Central Pacific forces and for protecting Australia. The truth lies between these two extremes. The Allied advance to the Philippines was along two distinct but mutually supporting lines, enjoying the advantages and running the risks of the exterior position.

The campaign against Rabaul, by greatly weakening Japan's carrier air power, enabled the Fifth Fleet to seize the Gilberts and Marshalls without having to fight off any significant counterattack. The Fifth Fleet raid on the Palaus removed the Japanese fleet from MacArthur's path. MacArthur's invasion of Biak pulled out of the Central Pacific land-based aircraft that otherwise might have resisted the Fifth Fleet assault on Saipan. The Fifth Fleet, by invading the Marianas, drew Ugaki's battleships away from their intended attack on MacArthur's forces at Biak and attracted the Mobile Fleet into the Philippine Sea, where the "Marianas Turkey Shoot" stripped it of planes. The Third Fleet raids on Okinawa, Luzon, and Formosa so weakened Japan's air power that it could make no immediate resistance of any consequence to MacArthur's invasion of Leyte.

The two Allied forces advancing across the Pacific operated as a team, each relieving the other of a portion of its burden. The Allied forces attained strategic concentration by
holding part of the enemy in one quarter while bringing their main attack against the enemy in another. Such concentration may be achieved, among other means, by either interior or exterior position (or interior or exterior lines of advance), but the exterior position, being more risky, is best avoided by the weaker power. Suppose for example Ozawa had had the strength to defeat Spruance in the Battle of the Philippine Sea. The Mobile Fleet might then have taken advantage of its interior position by turning south and advancing directly through the Japanese-held Carolines to smash MacArthur's forces at Biak before a weakened Fifth Fleet could come the long way around east of the Carolines to lend support.

Those who question the wisdom of opening the Central Pacific drive point to the high costs of capturing such positions as Saipan or the Palaus, each of which cost more casualties than MacArthur's entire advance from the Admiralties to the Philippines.[16] These critics however fall into the common fallacy of assuming that the Japanese would have acted as they did even had the Allies acted otherwise than as they did. Ukagi's advance from Tawitawi to Batjan and his subsequent shift from Batjan to the Philippine Sea is sufficient evidence that, had there not been a Central Pacific drive to attract and hold Japanese forces elsewhere, the Southwest Pacific forces would have met far greater resistance in the New Guinea area.

Spruance's controversial tactics in the Battle of the Philippine Sea have led some critics to assert that he failed to make best use of fleet mobility, that in fact he was using TF 58 as a fortress fleet. Such a criticism raises again the old question of whether the commander of armed forces should, in the Nelsonian or Clausewitzian tradition, regard the destruction of enemy armed forces as his primary objective, or whether he should make all tactical decisions in the light of ultimate and par-

[16] Saipan: 3,426 killed in action, 13,099 wounded in action. Palaus: 1,950 killed in action, 8,515 wounded in action. Aitape, Hollandia, Wakde, Biak, Noemfoor, Sansapor, Morotai, and associated operations: 1,648 killed in action, 8,111 wounded in action. Figures given in the text are round figures.

amount objectives, strategic and national. It also raises the question whether at that time, and in the light of all that followed, it was more to the Allied advantage to destroy trained Japanese aviators and Japanese aircraft or to sink Japanese carriers. Certainly Spruance could not have destroyed both enemy planes and enemy carriers without risking heavy losses to his fleet and assault forces.

By mid-1944 the success of American amphibious assaults varied with the degree of systematic, sustained pre-landing bombardment, particularly in the beachhead area. But when this relationship had been clearly established, the Japanese developed a new doctrine that placed the focus of their defense not at the beachhead but in the interior, where the main line of resistance was to be backed by a defense "fortress," ingeniously taking advantage of irregularities in the terrain. The Iwo Jima and Okinawa campaigns were thus foreshadowed. Clearly, the Americans and their allies would have to develop new techniques to cope with Japanese ingenuity.

41:

The Battle for Leyte Gulf

The Battle for Leyte Gulf, touched off by the American invasion of the Philippines, is for complexity and magnitude without parallel in naval history. Lasting four days, it was actually a series of battles and subsidiary actions hundreds of miles apart. The most important were the Battle of the Sibuyan Sea on October 24, and the Battle of Surigao Strait, the Battle off Cape Engaño, and the Battle off Samar on October 25, 1944. When the long-drawn-out conflict at length subsided, the Imperial Japanese Navy no longer existed as an effective fighting force, and the United States Navy commanded the Pacific.

Activating *Sho-Go*

When the Americans broke Japan's inner defense perimeter by seizing the southern Marianas, the Imperial High Command readjusted its strategy in preparation for last-ditch defense. The home islands had of course to be defended, but almost equally vital to Japanese security were the Philippines, Formosa, and the Ryukyus. Behind the screen of these offshore islands, the dwindling tanker fleet could still transport vital supplies of oil from the East Indies to Japan. Hence the new Japanese defense plan, called *Sho-Go* ("Victory Operation"), was worked out in four variations: *Sho* 1 for the Philippines; *Sho* 2 for Formosa, the Ryukyus, and southern Japan; *Sho* 3 for central Japan; and *Sho* 4 for northern Japan. Like the *A-Go* plan, which came to grief in the Philippine Sea, *Sho-Go* anticipated massing sea and air power against the next American assault, with land-based planes striking a first, devastating blow.

Whatever chance *Sho-Go* had of working was spoiled in advance of the Philippine invasion. The U.S. Third Fleet in its series of air attacks on the Philippines, the Ryukyus, and Formosa in September and October had reduced Japanese air power by more than 1,200 planes. American submarines, by giving high priority to the destruction of Japanese tankers and thereby nearly shutting off the flow of oil to Japan, had rendered the Mobile Fleet incapable of operating as a unit out of home ports. In this critical situation Admiral Toyoda had no choice but to divide the fleet. Retaining his carriers in Japan for repairs and pilot training, he sent the bulk of his surface vessels to operate in the Singapore area, where fuel was plentiful.

On October 17, when the Rangers landed in Leyte Gulf, the Mobile Fleet was dispersed as follows: (1) A force of battleships, cruisers, and destroyers commanded by Vice Admiral Kurita was at Lingga Roads, near Singapore. (2) A force of cruisers and destroyers under Vice Admiral Kiyohide Shima was at Amami in the Ryukyus. This was the group that sortied from Japan on October 15 to mop up the "remnants" of Halsey's Third Fleet, and then hastily retired when the over-optimistic reports of the Japanese aviators proved false. (3) A force of carriers and screening vessels under Vice Admiral Ozawa was in the Inland Sea, between the Japanese home islands of Honshu and Shikoku.[1]

[1] The Japanese called the forces under Kurita, Shima, and Ozawa respectively the First Striking Force, the Second Striking Force, and the Mobile Force. That part of the Mobile Force which Ozawa led out of the Inland Sea was called the Main Body. The Americans, as they made contact with the various segments of the Mobile Fleet, called them the Center, Southern, and Northern forces.

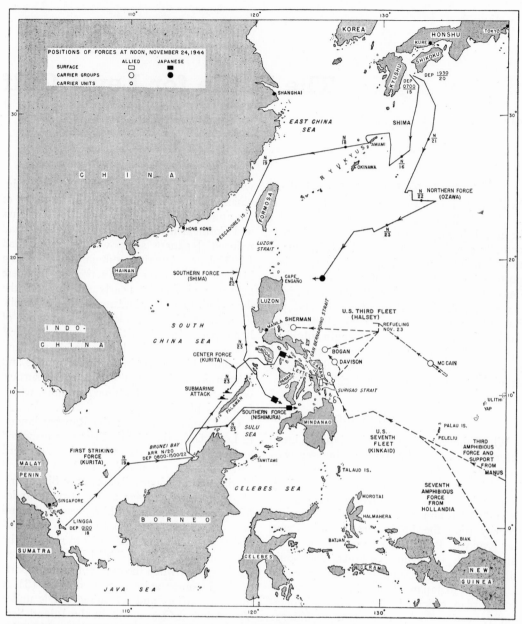

APPROACH OF ALLIED AND JAPANESE NAVAL FORCES TO LEYTE GULF
Unless otherwise indicated, the daily positions are as of 1200 hours.

With the landing of the Rangers, Toyoda promptly activated the naval phase of *Sho* 1. Though he knew that his forces were vastly outnumbered on the sea and in the air, he had no thought of not putting up a fight. For if the Japanese lost the Philippines, they would lose everything. The lifeline between Japan and the East Indies would be severed, the Mobile Fleet would be permanently divided, and there would be no means of supplying Kurita's force with ammunition or Shima's and Ozawa's with fuel. The fleet could be defeated in detail and Japan blockaded.

Kurita's force departed Lingga in the early

morning of October 18, with orders to head for Leyte Gulf—eluding the U.S. Third Fleet if possible, engaging and defeating the U.S. Seventh Fleet if necessary—in order to attack the American amphibious shipping off the beachhead. On October 20, just as MacArthur was gaining a foothold on Leyte, Kurita entered Brunei, Borneo, and began to refuel. Early on the 22nd, he led out the greater part of his force (the two superbattleships *Yamato* and *Musashi*, three older battleships, ten heavy cruisers, two light cruisers, and 15 destroyers) and shaped course for Palawan Passage. This segment became known to the Americans as the Center Force. With it Kurita planned to cross the Sibuyan Sea, south of Luzon, penetrate San Bernardino Strait, and enter Leyte Gulf from the north at dawn on the 25th.

Vice Admiral Shoji Nishimura sortied from Brunei in the afternoon of the 22nd with the rest of Kurita's force (two old battleships, heavy cruiser *Mogami,* and four destroyers). This segment was to be the southern arm of a double envelopment. Nishimura, after a swing to the north to elude enemy submarines, headed via the Sulu and Mindanao Seas for Surigao Strait in order to strike at Leyte Gulf from the south in coordination with Kurita's attack from the north.

On receiving Toyoda's order activating *Sho 1*, Shima's force (two heavy cruisers, a light cruiser, and four destroyers) headed for the Pescadores, west of Formosa, and thence shaped course southward with orders to cooperate with Nishimura in the attack through Surigao Strait. Nishimura's and Shima's forces became known to the Americans as the Southern Forces.

A few hours after Nishimura departed Brunei, Ozawa sortied from the Inland Sea with the Northern Force (heavy carrier *Zuikaku*, flagship; light carriers *Zuiho*, *Chitose*, and *Chiyoda*;[2] the *Hyuga* and the *Ise*, converted battleships with flight decks aft but never actually used as carriers; and a screen of three light cruisers and eight destroyers). This force

---

[2] Ozawa sortied with enough carriers to make an attractive bait but left his less expendable carriers in Japan for future use. Left behind were four large new carriers, the *Shinano*, the *Amagi*, the *Unryu*, and the *Katsuragi*, and two older 28,000-ton carriers, the *Junyo* and the *Ryuho*.

was not expected to provide much direct assistance in the impending battle, for the loss of Japanese carrier pilots over Formosa had been so severe and the training of new pilots was so far from complete that there remained in the Imperial Navy few pilots with enough skill to land on flight decks. The mission of the Northern Force was to decoy the Third Fleet away from the vicinity of Leyte Gulf, leaving the transports open to attack by Kurita, Nishimura, and Shima. Toyoda, who had correctly guessed that Spruance would not let himself be drawn away from Saipan, now estimated that Halsey, presented with an opportunity to sink carriers, might well be lured away from Leyte. He assumed that the Northern Force, serving as bait, would be annihilated.

Thus at one time four separate Japanese forces were converging on Leyte Gulf. The success of so complex an operation depended upon teamwork and perfect timing. These in turn depended to a large extent upon good radio communication, but time and again during the battle the widely scattered segments of the Mobile Fleet failed to get crucial information through to the other segments.

First Blood

Kurita's Center Force soon ran into trouble. An hour after dawn on October 23, it was attacked off Palawan by the *Darter* and the *Dace*, two of the American submarines assigned to patrol the approaches to the Philippines. Kurita's flagship, heavy cruiser *Atago*, hit by four torpedoes from the *Darter*, sank in 18 minutes. Two more torpedoes so severely crippled heavy cruiser *Takao* that she was obliged to head back toward Brunei escorted by a pair of destroyers. Just after the *Atago* went down, the *Dace* put a spread of torpedoes into a third heavy cruiser, the *Maya*, whose exploding magazines blew her apart in a series of searing blasts.

From the *Atago* Kurita and his staff managed to escape to a destroyer and transferred thence to the *Yamato*, which became the new flagship. Early on the 24th the surviving vessels of the Center Force passed south of Mindoro Island into the Sibuyan Sea. Kurita, shaken by his experience of the day before, realized that the presence of his force was now known to the

Americans and that he was coming within easy attack radius of Halsey's carriers east of the Philippines.

Nearly 200 miles to the south, in the Sulu Sea, Nishimura, with Shima trailing some 60 miles behind, was also coming within striking radius of Halsey's carrier planes. The main phase of the battle was about to begin.

Disposition of the Allied Forces

During the first stages of the Leyte invasion, Allied naval forces, almost entirely American, were disposed in several layers off the beachhead.

Inside Leyte Gulf was the greater part of the enlarged Seventh Fleet, including the two amphibious forces of transports, cargo vessels, and amphibious craft, and also a Bombardment and Fire Support Group composed of six old battleships and of cruisers and destroyers, commanded by Rear Admiral Jesse B. Oldendorf. Here also were Commander Seventh Fleet Vice Admiral Kinkaid in the AGC *Wasatch* and General MacArthur in the cruiser *Nashville*. To the east, just outside Leyte Gulf, were three Seventh Fleet carrier task units commanded by Rear Admiral Thomas L. Sprague. These units, which initially included 18 escort carriers screened by destroyers and destroyer escorts, were on antisubmarine, antiaircraft, and ground support patrol.

East of Luzon were the combat vessels of Admiral Halsey's Third Fleet, temporarily stripped down to TF 38 in order to build up the Seventh Fleet for the Leyte invasion. The four task groups making up TF 38 were at this time commanded by Vice Admiral John S. McCain and Rear Admirals Gerald F. Bogan, Frederick C. Sherman, and Ralph E. Davison. These groups, though not uniform, averaged about 23 ships each—two heavy carriers, two light carriers, two new battleships, three cruisers, and 14 destroyers. Halsey, in the *New Jersey*, was with Bogan's group; Mitscher, in the *Lexington*, was with Sherman's. Because as a combat force Third Fleet and TF 38 were now identical, Halsey exercised direct tactical command.

When the landings on Leyte were carried out without hindrance from the Japanese fleet, Halsey seized the opportunity to refuel

and rearm his ships and to give his tired crews a little rest. Intending to replenish one task group at a time, he had already dispatched McCain's group toward Ulithi when he received the *Darter*'s report of Kurita's approach from the west. Evidently the Japanese fleet was about to strike after all. Halsey let McCain's group continue southeastward but at once ordered his other three groups to rendezvous with oilers for refueling and then to head in closer to the Philippines. Fanning out during the night, the groups by dawn on October 24 had reached positions 125 miles apart—Sherman's off Luzon, Bogan's off San Bernardino Strait, Davison's off Leyte Gulf. Before 0630 scout planes were away from all three groups, searching west, northwest, and southwest.

The Battle of the Sibuyan Sea

A little after 0900 on the 24th, scout planes from Davison's group discovered Nishimura's force, van of the Southern Forces, in the Sulu Sea and attacked at once, slightly damaging the old battleship *Fuso* and a destroyer, without however cutting down the speed of either. Later in the morning a Fifth Air Force bomber sighted Shima's rear echelon, also in the Sulu Sea. Kinkaid, assuming that these two groups were divisions of a single force and correctly estimating that their destination was Leyte Gulf via Surigao Strait, prepared to strengthen Seventh Fleet defenses in that quarter.

Halsey's interest in these small Southern Forces was overshadowed by news of much bigger game farther north, for at 0810 one of Admiral Bogan's flyers had sighted Kurita's Center Force about to enter the Sibuyan Sea. Leaving the Southern Forces to Kinkaid and the Seventh Fleet, Halsey ordered Davison and Sherman to close at best speed on Bogan, at the center, and to concentrate their full air power upon stopping Kurita. At the same time he directed McCain to reverse course and to refuel at sea in order to be available for whatever might develop.

From the carrier decks of the Third Fleet task groups, five air strikes attacked Kurita on October 24 as, virtually without air cover, the Center Force doggedly plowed across the Sibuyan Sea toward San Bernardino Strait. By mid-afternoon four of Kurita's battleships had been hit, heavy cruiser *Myoko* had been put out of action and was retiring westward, and superbattleship *Musashi*, struck repeatedly by torpedoes and bombs, had fallen far astern of the formation. The final attack of the day concentrated on the *Musashi* which, after being hit by 19 torpedoes and 17 bombs, at length capsized, carrying down 1,100 men, half her complement.

Complaining bitterly by radio about the lack of air support that had left him open to crippling attack, Kurita at length ordered his Center Force to reverse course and head back west.

Attacks on Sherman's Task Group

Kurita lacked air support because the Japanese air command on Luzon had concluded that it could best assist the Center Force by attacking the American carrier groups. The hastily-trained Japanese pilots, it was believed, had a better chance of hitting the enemy's ships than of hitting the enemy's planes over their own ships. Hence when a searching Luzon-based pilot sighted and reported Sherman's task group early on October 24, the Japanese launched against it every plane they could muster.

Sherman's group detected the oncoming enemy aircraft just as the carriers were about to launch a strike of their own against the Center Force. Sherman postponed his strike, returned his bombers and torpedo planes to the hangar decks, and scrambled (ordered into the air) every fighter, while his task group retired under a rain squall. As in the Marianas Turkey Shoot, the highly trained, experienced American pilots decimated their inexperienced opponents. During the air battle not a single Japanese aircraft got close enough to Sherman's carriers to attack. A little after 0930 however, when the air had apparently been cleared of hostile planes and the task group was emerging from the overcast to take the fighters aboard, a lone bomber dived out of a cloud and bombed light carrier *Princeton*. Gasoline from shattered planes spread fires through the hangar deck, where six torpedoes, loaded in Avengers for the postponed strike, went off one at a time, blowing out both elevators and ripping up much of the flight deck.

In the circumstances Sherman did not close on Bogan as Halsey had directed. Instead he left several cruisers and destroyers standing by the burning carrier and maneuvered the rest of his group within support range. Late in the morning his three remaining carriers at last got off their strike against Kurita.

Search planes from Ozawa's Northern Force, now maneuvering off Cape Engaño, the northeast tip of Luzon, had by this time also located Sherman. At 1145 Ozawa launched a strike of 76 planes, which included most of the operational aircraft he had left. An hour later American radar detected their approach, just as Sherman was about to launch a second attack against the Center Force. This time he launched the strike at once and then scrambled his fighters to ward off the new attack. So successful were Sherman's Hellcats that the Japanese in this raid achieved nothing at all. Of Ozawa's attacking aircraft, some 20 fled to Luzon. The rest were lost.

Fire fighters aboard the *Princeton* meanwhile were apparently getting her fires under control. But in mid-afternoon one stubborn blaze reached the torpedo stowage, setting off a tremendous explosion that blasted off most of her stern and after flight deck. The *Birmingham*, then alongside, was swept by debris and chunks of steel which killed more than 200 of her crew and injured nearly twice as many others. Shortly afterward the captain of the *Princeton* ordered Abandon Ship.

Halsey Uncovers the Beachhead

Though the Leyte invasion brought Central Pacific and Southwest Pacific forces together in a single operation, no provision was made for an over-all commander at the scene of action. Admiral Halsey, as Commander Third Fleet, was responsible to Admiral Nimitz at Pearl Harbor, and Admiral Nimitz was responsible to the Joint Chiefs of Staff in Washington. Admiral Kinkaid, as Commander Seventh Fleet, was responsible to General MacArthur in Leyte Gulf, and General MacArthur was responsible to the Joint Chiefs. Though Halsey and Kinkaid were thus operationally independent of each other, no serious difficulties were anticipated. Both were seasoned commanders and could be expected to cooperate

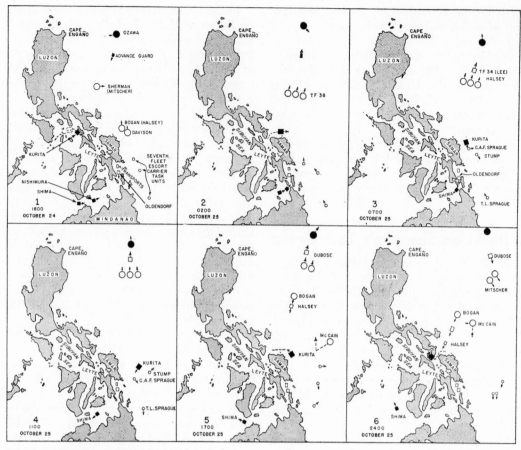

FLEET MOVEMENTS, BATTLE FOR LEYTE GULF

and to coordinate their efforts. Yet seeds of trouble were present, for the two fleet commanders went into battle with differing conceptions regarding the specific mission of each.

It was clear that the Seventh Fleet, which had escorted the invasion forces to Leyte, was to furnish close support for the assault. But which fleet was to provide cover, that is, fend off hostile naval forces from the beachhead? Nimitz' Operation Plan directed Halsey to "cover and support forces of the Southwest Pacific,"[3] from which Kinkaid assumed that it was the business of the Third Fleet to protect Seventh Fleet amphibious shipping. The task of the Seventh Fleet, said he, ". . . was to land troops and keep them ashore. The ships were armed accordingly with a very low percentage

of armor-piercing projectiles. The CVE's carried anti-personnel bombs instead of torpedoes and heavy bombs. We were not prepared to fight a naval action."[4]

But Nimitz' Plan also directed: "In case opportunity for destruction of major portion of the enemy fleet offer or can be created, such destruction becomes the primary task." From this, Halsey concluded that the mission of the Third Fleet was offensive, not defensive. "It was not my job to protect the Seventh Fleet," he later wrote. "My job was offensive, to strike with the Third Fleet."[5]

Kinkaid early on October 24 assumed the task of blocking Surigao Strait, adjacent to the beachhead area, against the approach of the

[3] Cincpoa Operation Plan No. 8–44, dated September 27, 1944.

[4] Quoted in Walter Karig *et al.*, *Battle Report*, IV (New York, 1948), 422.

[5] *Admiral Halsey's Story*, 219.

Japanese Southern Forces. Halsey meanwhile massed all his available air strength against Kurita's formidable Center Force. In mid-afternoon, while Kurita was still boring steadily eastward evidently intent upon breaking through San Bernardino Strait, Halsey made provision for possible surface action. At 1512 he sent his subordinate commanders a radio message, headed "Battle Plan," in which he stated that four battleships, including flagship *New Jersey,* three heavy cruisers, three light cruisers, and 14 destroyers from Bogan's and Davison's task groups "will be formed as Task Force 34" under Vice Admiral Lee. "This dispatch, which played a critical part in the next day's battle," said Halsey, "I intended merely as a warning to the ships concerned that if a surface engagement offered, I would detach them from TF 38, form them into TF 34, and send them ahead as a battle line."[6]

Kinkaid, though not an addressee, intercepted Halsey's 1512 dispatch and read it with considerable satisfaction. Not intercepting further modifying messages, he assumed that Halsey had carried out his intention as expressed in the preparatory dispatch and that San Bernardino Strait was being guarded by a strong surface force. "It was inconceivable," said he, "that Halsey would have scrapped a perfect battle plan."[7]

The movement of Kurita's force in the Sibuyan Sea and of Nishimura's and Shima's forces in the Sulu Sea suggested a pincer attack of surface forces on Leyte Gulf. But what about the Japanese carriers? Surely in a naval attack of such magnitude the enemy would use his carrier force. Since it was almost certain that the carriers had been in Japanese waters at the time of the Leyte invasion, it could be inferred that they were now at sea, coming down from the north to cooperate with the Japanese Southern and Center forces in their grand convergence on Leyte Gulf.

Ozawa's carrier force was indeed to northward, as we have seen. It was doing its utmost to attract American attention—making smoke, breaking radio silence on various frequencies,

[6] Fleet Admiral William F. Halsey, Jr. USN (Ret.), "The Battle for Leyte Gulf," *United States Naval Institute Proceedings,* May 1952, 488.
[7] Letter to E. B. Potter, August 15, 1959.

and even sending forward an advance guard of surface vessels in a fruitless attempt to contact and engage the Third Fleet. Through the morning and early afternoon Sherman, whose responsibility it had been to search to the north, had sent out no scout planes because he was preoccupied with warding off air attacks and with covering the burning *Princeton.* At last, late in the afternoon, his scout bombers found the Japanese carrier force only 190 miles away to the NNE and flashed back the word. Mitscher passed the information to Halsey, and Sherman sent in a cruiser to sink the derelict *Princeton* with torpedoes.

Now that Halsey had at last located all the pieces of the Japanese puzzle, the picture seemed to confirm his first impression—that the Southern Forces heading for Surigao Strait, the Center Force heading for San Bernardino Strait, and the Northern Force coming down from Japan were all moving toward a rendezvous in the vicinity of Leyte Gulf. This massing of hostile forces he was determined to thwart. He felt he could ignore the weak Southern Forces, leaving them to Kinkaid. According to his pilots, the Center Force had received so much damage to guns, fire-control instruments, and communications that it too could be left to Kinkaid. Moreover latest reports indicated that it had reversed course and was retreating to the west. That left the carrier-centered Northern Force, fresh and undamaged, with a combat radius hundreds of miles wider than the others. In the circumstances, Halsey selected destruction of the Northern Force as his primary objective. How best to meet this antagonist offered him a choice of alternatives.

He could guard San Bernardino Strait with his whole fleet and wait for the Northern Force to approach and strike. This he rejected because it left the Third Fleet between Japanese carriers and Japanese airfields, subject to attack from both and to shuttle-bombing by the carriers. In the Battle of the Philippine Sea, Mitscher's bombers had forestalled such attacks by keeping the airfields on Guam neutralized, but neutralizing all the enemy airfields in the Philippines was manifestly impossible.

He could guard San Bernardino Strait with TF 34 while striking the Northern Force with his carriers. This he rejected because, overestimating the enemy's land-based and carrier air power, he believed that together they might inflict far more damage on a divided fleet than on the Third Fleet intact. He wanted all his available antiaircraft fire to protect his carriers and all his carrier air cover to protect his surface vessels.

He could leave San Bernardino Strait unguarded and strike the Northern Force with his whole fleet. Although this alternative involved also leaving his covering position off the American beachhead, he accepted it for, as he said, "It preserved my Fleet's integrity, it left the initiative with me, and it promised the greatest possibility of surprise. Even if the Central Force meanwhile passed through San Bernardino and headed for Leyte Gulf, it could only hope to harry the landing operation. It could not consolidate any advantage, because of its reported damage. It could merely hit-and-run. I felt Kinkaid was amply strong to handle this situation if it should develop."[8] His decision made, Halsey went into Flag Plot just before 2000, put his finger on the charted position of the Japanese Northern Force 300 miles away and said to Rear Admiral Robert B. Carney, his chief of staff, "Here's where we're going. Mick, start them north."

Carney promptly sent off a series of radio messages: to McCain, ordering him to close the other Third Fleet carrier groups at best speed; to Davison and Bogan, to shape course due north; to Sherman, to join the Davison and Bogan groups at midnight as they dashed past; to Mitscher, to re-assume tactical command of TF 38 at that time and strike the Northern Force early on the 25th. To Kinkaid he radioed in Halsey's name: "Am proceeding north with three groups to attack enemy carrier force at dawn."[9]

Kinkaid, believing that TF 34 had been formed, interpreted this latest dispatch to mean that Halsey was sending three *carrier* groups north. Kinkaid had already sent most of the Seventh Fleet gunnery vessels south to block Surigao Strait and destroy the approaching Japanese Southern Forces. Though he felt safe

[8] Halsey, "Battle for Leyte Gulf," 490.
[9] All dispatches are quoted verbatim from the appropriate message files.

in his assumption that TF 34 was blocking San Bernardino Strait, he took the routine precaution of ordering searches to the north, by night-flying PBY's after dark on the 24th and by his escort carrier aircraft at first light on the 25th. He did not order Seventh Fleet planes over the Sibuyan Sea to locate and trail Kurita lest they tangle in the darkness with Third Fleet planes presumably doing the same job. As it turned out, the one PBY that flew through San Bernardino Strait passed over the area a little too early to detect anything, and the escort carrier planes were launched a little too late.

Of his decision to attack the Japanese Northern Force, Admiral Halsey afterward wrote: "Given the same circumstances and the same information as I had then, I would do it again."[10] Hostile carriers were, in Halsey's opinion and in the opinion of practically all naval commanders at that time, the principal threat to any operation involving ships or shipping. Sherman's search planes had reported only a few enemy carriers to the north, but Halsey could not be sure that they had seen the entire Northern Force—and of course he had no way of knowing that Ozawa's carriers had come south as decoys or that Ozawa had already expended most of his aircraft. Weighing immediate objectives against the long-range objective of bringing Japan to defeat, Halsey had concluded that his best contribution to the war as a whole was to seize the opportunity, now apparently within his grasp, of destroying Japan's naval aviation capability. With this point of view his staff was in entire agreement.[11]

Admiral Halsey believed that it was within Admiral Kinkaid's capacity to handle both the Japanese Southern Forces heading for Surigao Strait and also Kurita's damaged Center Force should it attempt to sortie from San Bernardino Strait to attack in Leyte Gulf.[12] Never-

[10] Halsey, "Battle for Leyte Gulf," 490.
[11] Letter, Fleet Admiral Halsey to E. B. Potter, July 27, 1959. Letter, Admiral Robert B. Carney to E. B. Potter, July 31, 1959.
[12] Comparative strengths available for combat at sunset 24 October: Kurita, Nishimura, and Shima combined—4 new and 2 old battleships, 8 heavy cruisers, 3 light cruisers, 19 destroyers. Kinkaid—6 old battleships, 4 heavy cruisers, 4 light cruisers, 21 destroyers; also 39 PT boats and 16 escort carriers screened by 9 destroyers and 12 destroyer escorts.

theless Halsey was taking a risk and he knew it, but most of his military successes up to that time had been based upon calculated risks. Moreover, he interpreted that part of his orders specifying as his primary task "destruction of major part of the enemy fleet" as a mandate to do exactly what he was doing.

So convinced was Halsey that he was doing the right thing that he was undeterred by reports sent in by night-flying aircraft from the carrier *Independence* that Kurita's Center Force had turned back east and was heading again for San Bernardino Strait and that navigation lights in the Strait, long blacked out, had now been lighted. He was similarly undeterred by messages from Bogan and Lee implying doubt as to his course. He heard nothing from Mitscher, who vetoed a suggestion of his staff that he urge Halsey to turn back south with the battle line. "If he wants my advice, he'll ask for it," said Mitscher.[13] Sherman's task group joined Bogan's and Davison's at 2345, October 24. An hour later the Japanese Center Force emerged from San Bernardino Strait into the Philippine Sea behind Halsey's back.

Kurita had turned back east shortly before sunset. His renewed advance toward the Strait was spurred on not long afterward by a peremptory order to the Mobile Fleet from Admiral Toyoda in Tokyo: "Trusting in Divine Assistance, all forces will advance to the attack." By this Toyoda meant that the raid on Leyte Gulf was to be carried out in spite of any obstacles and at any sacrifice.

On reaching the Pacific, Kurita fully expected to run into an ambush, but he found nothing there. The only vessels standing between him and the thin-skinned American transports and supply shipping were the small Seventh Fleet carrier task units operating eastward of Leyte Gulf. His sortie was not detected by the Third Fleet because the *Independence* night flyers had been recalled from tracking the Center Force in order to search ahead of TF 38 for the Northern Force.

Though Toyoda's decoy scheme had succeeded, Kurita did not know it then or later. Ozawa's dawn radio announcement that Hal-

[13] Theodore Taylor, *The Magnificent Mitscher* (New York, 1954), 262.

sey was hot on his trail was not received by the other commanders of the Mobile Fleet.

The Battle of Surigao Strait

Since October 20, an antisubmarine picket of seven American destroyers had been patrolling the northern end of Surigao Strait, where it opened into Leyte Gulf. These had later been supplemented by PT boats that patrolled inside and at the southern end of the Strait. On October 24, after the approaching Japanese Southern Forces had been sighted, all available PT's in Leyte Gulf were sent south, bringing the total of patrolling torpedo boats to 39. In sections of three boats each, these took station at intervals from a little below the destroyer picket line to positions far out in the Mindanao Sea. At noon on the 24th, Admiral Kinkaid alerted the Seventh Fleet to prepare

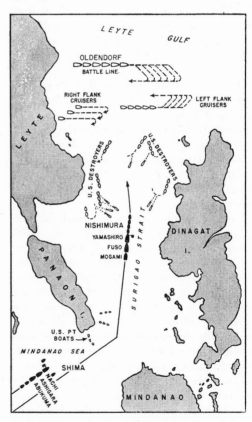

OLDENDORF'S TRAP, BATTLE OF SURIGAO STRAIT, POSITIONS AT 0330, OCTOBER 25, 1944

for a night attack by enemy surface forces, and three hours later he ordered Admiral Oldendorf to block the northern exit from Surigao Strait with gunnery vessels. Confident that Halsey's Third Fleet was guarding the approach from the north, Kinkaid assigned to the task the entire Seventh Fleet Bombardment and Fire Support Group, consisting of six old battleships, four heavy and four light cruisers, and 21 destroyers.

In view of his immense superiority of force, Oldendorf determined not merely to repulse but to destroy his antagonists. To that end, and also because he was somewhat short of armor-piercing projectiles, he planned for a short and decisive action at close ranges. His battleships, mostly veterans of the Pearl Harbor attack, he placed cruising back and forth across the upper end of the Strait a little north of the destroyer picket line. In this position he had ample sea room for maneuver, while any enemy approaching from the south would be restricted within the confines of the Strait; and from here, if necessary, he could quickly transfer his battle line to cover the eastern entrance to Leyte Gulf. He extended the flanks of the battle line with his cruisers, and stationed his destroyers also on or ahead of his flanks for high-speed torpedo runs on the enemy as he approached. Any hostile force entering Surigao Strait from the south would thus have to run a gantlet of torpedo fire, first from PT boats and then from destroyers, and at last come under T-capping shellfire from battleships and cruisers.

Across the Mindanao Sea toward this perfect ambush sped Nishimura's force, with Shima's force 40 miles behind. Though these two Japanese forces had been ordered to cooperate, the commanders at no time communicated with each other directly. Shima, unaware that he had been sighted by the army bomber, hoped through maintaining radio silence to surprise the Americans by bringing his reinforcement into Leyte Gulf unexpectedly. He avoided making radio contact with Nishimura moreover because Shima was the senior of the two. Had he notified Nishimura of his presence, the ironbound Japanese rules of seniority would have required him to assume tactical command of both forces. That, Shima felt, would only lead to confusion since he was a newcomer, unacquainted with the details of the battle plan. Nishimura, with ideas of his own on how to make the attack, was content to operate independently.[14]

Late in the afternoon Nishimura was notified that the Center Force had been delayed in the Sibuyan Sea by air attacks and could not arrive in Leyte Gulf on schedule. He thereupon advanced his own time of arrival in order, apparently, to reach the Gulf under cover of darkness. From 2300 October 24 until after 0200 October 25, he ran the gantlet of American PT boats, hitting three with gunfire and so damaging another that it had to be beached. The PT's, long without experience in torpedo work, did no damage at all, but they performed an invaluable service in keeping Oldendorf advised of Nishimura's arrival and of his progress up the Strait.

The main action of the battle was opened at 0230 by five of the picket destroyers. Warning the PT's to stand aside, they went speeding down Surigao Strait in two divisions, fired 47 torpedoes from east and west, turned away making smoke, and cleared the area without sustaining damage despite heavy enemy fire. In this remarkable attack, the Americans hit both of Nishimura's battleships, sank a destroyer, and put two more destroyers out of action. Battleship *Fuso* sheered out of line and presently blew apart into two burning halves. Nishimura's flagship, battleship *Yamashiro*, though struck by one torpedo, pressed on to the north accompanied by heavy cruiser *Mogami* and destroyer *Shigure*.

Now in quick succession Oldendorf struck first with his right flank destroyers and then with his left flank destroyers. These put three more torpedoes into the *Yamashiro* and sank one of the destroyers disabled by the pickets. Meanwhile, at 0351, as the remnant of Nishimura's force came within 23,000 yards of the American battle line, Oldendorf's cruisers opened up, followed a minute later by all of his battleships that could find a target. In 18 minutes they fired nearly 300 rounds of 14- and 16-inch and more than 4,000 rounds of 6- and 8-inch projectiles. Under this hail of

[14] Letter, Kiyohide Shima to William Frazer, *Los Angeles Sunday Examiner*, December 28, 1958. *Interrogations of Japanese Officials*, Nav. Nos. 58 and 79.

shells the *Yamashiro* began to sink, the *Mogami* blazed up and came almost to a stop, and the *Shigure* sheered to the right, hit by a dud and further damaged by numerous near misses. At 0409 Oldendorf, informed that his retiring left flank destroyers were under fire, stopped the shelling. Destroyer *Albert W. Grant,* hit 19 times by friend and foe, had been put out of action with a loss of 34 of her crew. This was the sole damage suffered by the Americans during the battle.

Shima's force had by this time fought its way past the PT boats, which however put a torpedo into light cruiser *Abukuma,* slowing her down to ten knots. To the north lay a dense pall of smoke through which Shima could discern arching tracers and the flash of gunfire. At 0410, as the firing ceased, he passed the burning halves of the *Fuso,* which he took to be both the *Fuso* and the *Yamashiro.* Ten minutes later he saw the burning *Mogami* ahead and to starboard, apparently dead in the water. Immediately afterward his radar detected targets ahead. Ordering his destroyers forward to attack, he at once turned his cruisers 90 degrees right so that they could fire torpedoes short of the *Mogami,* where they would not be silhouetted by her flames. On the new course, Shima's flagship, heavy cruiser *Nachi,* collided with the *Mogami,* which was actually moving south at eight knots.

Shima now recalled his destroyers and withdrew down the Strait, accompanied by the crippled *Shigure* and the burning *Mogami.* Obviously Nishimura had run into a deadly trap. Shima saw no reason why he should offer his own ships for similar fruitless destruction. The last word he had from the Center Force was that it was retiring westward. He had no information at all from the Northern Force. In the circumstances, Shima decided that his best course was to retire also and await a better opportunity to close the pincers on Leyte Gulf in coordination with Kurita and Ozawa.

Oldendorf, having detected Shima's retiring force by radar, set out in pursuit with cruisers and destroyers. In the dim light of early dawn, he at length made visual contact with the enemy column, trailed by the *Mogami.* After shelling the damaged cruiser until she was once more ablaze, he temporarily turned away to evade enemy torpedoes. A little later a part

of his force encountered and sank the last of Nishimura's disabled destroyers. The rest of the Japanese fugitives, four cruisers and five destroyers, fought their way back past the PT boats and regained the Mindanao Sea. Here planes from the southernmost of the Seventh Fleet escort carrier units attacked them, finally stopping the die-hard *Mogami,* which the Japanese themselves sank after removing the crew. Of Nishimura's force, only battered destroyer *Shigure* was left, but Shima still had all his ships, and of these only the *Abukuma* was seriously damaged.

In the midst of the American mopping up operations, there came an electrifying report: Kurita's Center Force had penetrated San Bernardino Strait and was off Samar attacking the northernmost of the Seventh Fleet escort carrier units. Oldendorf at once called off his pursuit and hastened to reassemble his forces. The planes that had attacked the *Mogami* refueled at Tacloban and went after Kurita.

Admiral Kinkaid was in a quandary. He knew now that the whole Third Fleet was far to the north, unable for many hours to answer his calls for help. He knew that Shima had escaped and, given an opportunity, might return through Surigao Strait and attack the American shipping. Kinkaid's solution was to order Oldendorf to lead his force back into Leyte Gulf where it could cover both the southern and eastern entrances, then to divide the force into two equal groups and take one group some 25 miles eastward where it would be in position to sortie in support of the embattled escort carrier unit. This was a measure of desperation, for even if Oldendorf could reach the combat area in time to be of help, which was doubtful, his ships were now too low in armor-piercing ammunition to fight a running battle.

The Battle off Cape Engaño

In the dark early hours of October 25, while Kurita was debouching from San Bernardino Strait and Nishimura and Shima were advancing into Surigao Strait, Halsey and Mitscher, with Bogan's, Davison's, and Sherman's task groups, were speeding north in pursuit of Ozawa. A little after 0200 *Independence* search planes scouting ahead of TF 38 made radar contact with two separate enemy surface groups. These were the advance guard and the main body of Ozawa's Northern Force, which the day before had split apart in the frustratingly difficult task of attracting American attention, and were now heading on converging courses for a 0600 rendezvous. On receiving word of this contact, Halsey at last formed TF 34, enlarged to include all six of the battleships attached to the Third Fleet. With this force he set out in advance of the carrier groups, intending to complete the work of Mitscher's planes by sinking cripples and stragglers and any other Japanese vessels he could overtake.

As dawn was breaking, search planes followed by a deckload strike of 180 aircraft took off from the American carriers. An hour later the TF 38 scouts regained contact with the Northern Force, now united and comprising one heavy and three light carriers, two carrier-battleships, three light cruisers, and eight destroyers. The American attack groups, quickly vectored in, arrived in sight of the enemy fleet a little after 0800. Hellcats shot down most of the dozen or so fighter aircraft that came out to meet them, while the American bombers and torpedo planes bored in through intense antiaircraft fire to drive home their strike. The attacking air groups promptly sank a destroyer, bombed light carriers *Zuiho* and *Chitose,* and torpedoed heavy carrier *Zuikaku.* The *Chitose,* holed below the waterline, soon went down. The *Zuikaku,* steering erratically, began to fall behind, obliging Admiral Ozawa to shift his flag to a cruiser in order to direct the defense of the main body. A second American air strike at 1000 found the Northern Force widely scattered. One group of bombers worked over cruiser *Tama* and slowed her down to ten knots. Another group left light carrier *Chiyoda* dead in the water, afire and listing.

By this time Admiral Halsey, forging ahead with TF 34, scanning the horizon for masts of Japanese stragglers, was having his attention diverted more and more from the impending surface action. At 0412 that morning Admiral Kinkaid had informed him by radio that Seventh Fleet surface forces were engaging enemy surface forces in Surigao Strait. Then, to reassure himself, he added a question: "Is TF 34 guarding San Bernardino Strait?" It is part of

the bad radio communications bedeviling this whole battle that Halsey did not receive Kinkaid's message until 0648. He then promptly radioed back: "Negative. TF 34 is with carrier groups now engaging enemy carrier force"—a reply that dumfounded Kinkaid.

At 0800 Halsey received the much-delayed news that the enemy had been repulsed in Surigao Strait. From this he assumed that the Seventh Fleet was now free to give Leyte Gulf whatever cover it might need. Twenty minutes later he received a radio call for help, also delayed, from Rear Admiral Clifton A. F. Sprague, commanding one of the three small escort carrier task units off Leyte Gulf. Kurita's Center Force had suddenly appeared and was attacking Sprague's little carriers, then cruising near Samar Island. Halsey was not alarmed. "I figured," he said, "that the sixteen little carriers had enough planes to protect themselves until Oldendorf could bring up his heavy ships."[15]

On the heels of Sprague's call for help Halsey received a whole series of messages from Kinkaid, one in plain English, requesting air strikes and support by fast battleships. Kurita, listening in, was rattled by the plain language dispatch, concluding from it that powerful forces were close enough to lend Sprague prompt assistance. Halsey was exasperated. "It was not my job to protect the Seventh Fleet," said he. "My job was offensive, to strike with the Third Fleet, and we were even then rushing to intercept a force which gravely threatened not only Kinkaid and myself, but the whole Pacific strategy."[16] In the circumstances, he took what he deemed to be the only appropriate action. He radioed McCain's task group, then fueling to the southeast, to go "at best possible speed" to the aid of Sprague and notified Kinkaid that he had done so. Then with TF 34 and three groups of TF 38 he pressed on to the north, away from Leyte Gulf.

At Pearl Harbor, Admiral Nimitz, who had been listening in on all radio communications and watching the progress of the battle on the

[15] Halsey, "Battle for Leyte Gulf," 491. Two of the original 18 escort carriers had departed for Morotai the day before to bring back replacement aircraft.
[16] *Admiral Halsey's Story,* 219.

operations chart, at length felt compelled to intervene. He sent Halsey a sharp and laconic message: "Where is, repeat where is, Task Force 34?" When Halsey received this dispatch a little after 1000, he was annoyed, for he recognized it as a prod. He was further displeased to note that Admiral King and Admiral Kinkaid had been cut in as information addressees. He was enraged when his eyes ran past the end of the message to the final padding, which he took to be part of the text. With padding included, the dispatch seemed to be couched in insulting language: "Where is, repeat where is, Task Force 34. The world wonders."[17]

The more Halsey thought about Nimitz' message and its curious ending, the angrier he became. At length, a little before 1100, he took a step he afterward regretted. He ordered TF 34 to change from course 000 to course 180—from due north to due south. "At that moment," says Halsey, "the Northern Force, with its two remaining carriers crippled and dead in the water, was exactly 42 miles from the

[17] The ensign who encrypted the message at Pearl Harbor, following normal procedure, added random phrases ("padding") at both ends to increase difficulty of enemy cryptanalysis. He violated regulations by using end padding that could possibly be read as part of the text. On being queried later, he professed not to have recognized his mistake. "It was just something that popped into my head," said he.
In the New Jersey the communicators had orders than when an urgent operational dispatch came in they were not to take time to copy the message on a dispatch form but were to rush the decode tape directly from the decoding machine to Admiral Halsey or Admiral Carney—after first tearing off the padding. When Nimitz' message came off the machine, the padding was plainly separated from the text by double letters, as regulations prescribed. But the end padding was so plausible that the communicators decided not to remove it, on the chance that might be part of the message. The strip of paper handed Halsey read as follows: "FROM CINCPAC [Nimitz] ACTION COM THIRD FLEET [Halsey] INFO COMINCH [King] CTF SEVENTY SEVEN [Kinkaid] X WHERE IS RPT WHERE IS TASK FORCE THIRTY FOUR RR THE WORLD WONDERS."
Because the repeat (RPT) device was used by communicators to repeat important words that might be lost in garble as well as by senders for emphasis, it has been deleted in most official files, which record the message simply as "Where is Task Force 34?"

muzzles of my 16-inch guns. . . . I turned my back on the opportunity I had dreamed of since my days as a cadet. For me, one of the biggest battles of the war was off, and what has been called the 'the Battle of Bull's Run' was on. I notified Kinkaid. . . ."[18] At 1115 Task Force 34 came about and headed south. As it passed the still-northbound TF 38, Halsey picked up Bogan's carrier task group to provide air cover and detached four cruisers and ten destroyers under Rear Admiral Laurance T. DuBose to provide additional surface support for the carriers remaining under Mitscher.

Mitscher, with Sherman's and Davison's carrier groups and DuBose's surface group, continued to the north to launch further air attacks on the Northern Force. The third strike of the day, more than 200 planes, took off a little before noon with instructions to sink the enemy's two remaining operational carriers. The Zuiho was heavily damaged but managed to stay afloat. Three torpedoes finished off the Zuikaku, last survivor of the carrier attack on Pearl Harbor and veteran of every carrier battle of the Pacific war except Midway. The fourth air strike in mid-afternoon at last sank the die-hard Zuiho. The fifth and final attack, carried out by aviators who had been almost constantly at battle for two days, concentrated on the converted battleship Ise but achieved only a succession of near misses.

Around 1400 Mitscher, deciding that his carriers were getting too close to the enemy for safety, turned east with Sherman's and Davison's groups, and detached DuBose's cruisers and destroyers north to finish off the enemy cripples. This last was no casual mission, for Ozawa still had his two converted battleships —and Halsey had taken all six Third Fleet battleships south with him. DuBose's group, pausing to sink the derelict Chiyoda, last of Ozawa's bait carriers, was outsped by most of the retreating Northern Force. After dark however DuBose overtook a group of three destroyers and sank one in a running gunfire-torpedo battle. Farther to the north, cruiser Tama, limping home alone, was sunk by one of the numerous submarines that Vice Admiral Charles A. Lockwood, Commander Submarine

[18] Admiral Halsey's Story, 220–1. Halsey was often referred to in the press (but not by his intimates) as "Bull" Halsey.

Forces Pacific Fleet, had ordered to cover all likely escape routes.

Ozawa, minus his bait carriers but with ten of his 13 surface vessels, returned to Japan. His decoy mission had succeeded beyond his most hopeful expectations. He had not only saved Kurita from annihilation but extricated a good portion of his own suicide force as well. Yet the Japanese failed to attain the ultimate object of Ozawa's mission, for Ozawa was unable to establish radio communication with Kurita, who faltered when the amphibious shipping in Leyte Gulf was almost under his guns.

The Battle off Samar

On arriving in the Pacific, a little before 0100 on October 25, Kurita's Center Force, by then reduced to four battleships, six heavy cruisers, two light cruisers, and eleven destroyers, went to General Quarters and steamed cautiously eastward in a night search disposition. At 0300 the force wheeled to starboard and proceeded southeast down the coast of Samar. On this course Kurita received Nishimura's final radio report, stating that he was under attack in Surigao Strait. An hour later, he received word from Shima that he was "retiring from the battle area." From these two messages, Kurita correctly surmised that the southern Japanese attack had met with disaster. He heard nothing at all from Ozawa, to the north.

At sunrise Kurita began to deploy his force from search disposition, with ships in several columns, to circular antiaircraft formation. Hardly had he given the signal for deployment when a lookout in the crow's-nest of flagship *Yamato* reported masts looming over the horizon to the east. Presently the masts and then the hulls of carriers and escorting vessels became visible from the *Yamato*'s bridge. The consensus of Kurita's staff was that they had come upon a task group of Halsey's Third Fleet, that the vessels dimly visible on the horizon were fleet carriers, cruisers, destroyers, and perhaps a battleship or two. Halsey however was then 300 miles to the north engaging Ozawa. What Kurita and his staff saw in the morning haze was the task unit of six little 18-knot escort carriers, three destroyers, and four destroyer escorts commanded by Rear

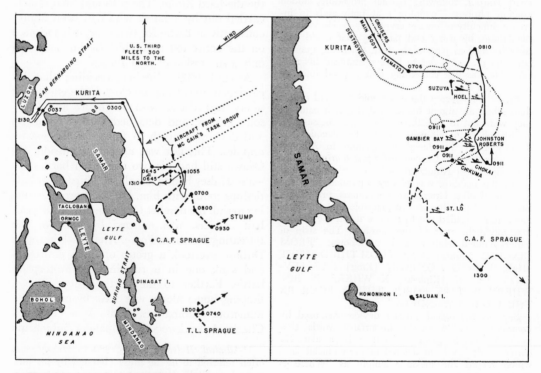

BATTLE OFF SAMAR, OCTOBER 25, 1944

Admiral Clifton A. F. Sprague. This was one of the three Seventh Fleet task units stationed off Leyte Gulf. A second, of similar composition, under Rear Admiral Felix B. Stump, was just over the horizon to the southeast. The Third, under the group commander, Rear Admiral Thomas L. Sprague, was 130 miles to the south, off Mindanao. These vessels alone were available to contest Kurita's entrance to the Gulf to attack the vulnerable amphibious shipping.

Some of the Japanese were elated at the prospect of attacking what they took to be a major carrier force rather than expending themselves and their ships to sink cargo vessels and transports. Kurita felt otherwise. He knew now that he could not expect air support, and he had lost confidence in his antiaircraft gunners. But battle was now unavoidable. In the circumstances he should have formed his battleships and heavy cruisers into battle line and sent his destroyers and light cruisers forward for a torpedo strike. Instead he made the fatal mistake of ordering "General Attack" while his fleet was still in the midst of the complicated maneuver of deploying to circular formation. That threw the fleet into confusion as each division turned independently toward the enemy and the faster ships forged out ahead. At 0658 Kurita opened fire.

Clifton Sprague was no less surprised than Kurita. On receiving an aircraft contact report and immediately afterward sighting Japanese pagoda masts to the west, he changed course to due east in order to open the range and at the same time steer close enough into the northeast wind to launch aircraft. He next ordered his planes into the air, armed with whatever they had on board. Then, as 14-, 16-, and 18-inch shell splashes began walking up on his carriers, he directed all ships to make smoke and headed at flank speed for the cover of a nearby rain squall. In plain language he radioed for help, knowing well that his little carriers and his thin-hulled escort vessels were by no stretch of the imagination a match for the swift Japanese surface vessels. "It did not appear," said he, "that any of our ships could survive another five minutes of the heavy-caliber fire being received."[19]

[19] C. Vann Woodward, *The Battle for Leyte Gulf* (New York, 1947), 168.

There followed one of the most extraordinary chases of naval history—climaxed by a surprise ending. Concealed by rain, Sprague's unit turned south and headed toward Leyte Gulf in the hope of meeting Seventh Fleet surface vessels which Sprague presumed would soon be on their way to assist him. Presently, the American force passed out of the squall and again became visible to the Japanese, but Kurita refrained from cutting across the angle and heading directly for his quarry. Instead he continued for some time on his original easterly pursuit course, intent upon getting ships to windward of the Americans so that the carriers could not turn into the wind for further air operations.

By 0800 Sprague had battleships and heavy cruisers overtaking him from astern, while more heavy cruisers crept up on his port flank, gradually forcing him around to course southwest and threatening to cut off his retreat. Toward 0900 a squadron of four destroyers and a light cruiser, which had been trailing the battleships, advanced on Sprague's starboard quarter. Evidently he was about to be boxed in.

Shortly after the battle opened, Sprague's three destroyers, later joined by three of his destroyer escorts, began making a series of suicidal attacks with shells and torpedoes on elements of the pursuing Japanese fleet. As the commander of one of the destroyer escorts announced to his crew upon heading for the enemy, this was "a fight against overwhelming odds from which survival could not be expected."[20] Plowing forward under a hail of heavy-caliber fire, the little ships resolutely pressed home their attacks—chasing salvos, making smoke, and dodging into rain squalls.

In the first attack, destroyer *Johnston* put heavy cruiser *Kumano* out of action with a single torpedo. It is possible that others of the escort vessels then or later also torpedoed heavy cruisers *Chokai* and *Chikuma*. Heavy cruiser *Suzuya*, already slowed to 20 knots by an aerial bomb, came alongside the *Kumano* to remove the division commander and his staff and never again caught up with the running battle. But, as events were to prove, the most important result of the first attack by Sprague's escorts was that flagship *Yamato*,

[20] *Ibid.*, 175.

accompanied by another battleship, turned north to evade torpedoes and fell far behind in the chase. Kurita thus lost sight of the carriers and was not again able to get a clear picture of the tactical situation.

As the attacks on the Japanese fleet continued, destroyer *Hoel,* hit more than 40 times, went dead in the water and was abandoned by her crew. Stationary, she became the target of every enemy ship within gun range. These pumped shells into her until she went down. A few minutes later, destroyer escort *Samuel B. Roberts,* her side ripped open by 14-inch shells, rolled over and sank. Destroyer *Johnston,* badly damaged, her torpedoes expended, presently observed a squadron of four Japanese destroyers and a light cruiser coming in to attack the carriers. These were the vessels that threatened to complete the boxing in of the American force. The *Johnston* promptly advanced and took the whole squadron under such furious, close-range fire that the Japanese ships launched their torpedoes prematurely, too far short of the carriers to be effective. They then turned on the *Johnston* and circled her, firing into her until she went down. By this time two of the surviving vessels of Sprague's carrier screen had been damaged by shellfire. In the annals of naval warfare few men-of-war ever performed their duty more gallantly or against heavier odds than Sprague's little escorts.

The six American carriers, forced by Kurita's heavy cruisers to steam before the wind, could no longer be adequately covered with smoke. They began to take hits, at first from the heavy cruisers coming up on their port quarter and then by two battleships which soon plowed the cruisers' wake. That the carriers were not all sunk can be attributed to poor Japanese gunnery, expert American damage control, and the fact that the attackers were using armor-piercing shells that passed through the unarmored carriers without exploding. However, carrier *Gambier Bay* at length took more hits than her engineers and damage control parties could handle. She lost power, began to list, and at 0907 capsized and sank.

The really decisive attack on the Center Force was carried out by aircraft. Torpedo planes, bombers, and bomb-carrying fighters from Clifton Sprague's and Felix Stump's task units were gradually reinforced over the Japanese fleet by aircraft from Leyte and from Thomas Sprague's unit, including those returning from the strike on the *Mogami.* The planes kept up an almost continuous attack. When they exhausted their ammunition, they made dry runs to divert the enemy, or they landed on Stump's nearby carriers or on the more distant Tacloban airstrip to rearm. Under this unremitting pressure, heavy cruisers *Chokai,* *Chikuma,* and *Suzuya* were battered into sinking condition. The rest of the widely dispersed Center Force, following Japanese doctrine for each ship to maneuver independently under air attack, fell into increasing confusion. The Japanese commanders overestimated their rate of advance and were confirmed in their belief that they were chasing fast fleet carriers.

Kurita, who had lost touch both with Clifton Sprague's carriers and with most of his own force, concluded that his prey had escaped and that the time had come to bring order out of chaos. So at 0911 he headed north at 20 knots, summoning his ships by radio to converge on the *Yamato.* Thereupon the two Japanese heavy cruisers still in action reversed course—almost within point-blank range of the carriers. So did the two battleships that had been following the cruisers. The destroyer squadron that had advanced into the battle lingered a little longer to finish off the *Johnston* before retiring.

Sprague's task unit, bewildered by the sudden retreat of the enemy vessels, which a few minutes before seemed to have every advantage on their side, again shaped course for Leyte Gulf, 25 miles away.

The Kamikazes Strike

With Kurita's turnaway, the Seventh Fleet escort carriers escaped annihilation by what at the time seemed a miracle, and remained until after the war a profound mystery to the Americans. The hazards of the day were by no means ended however, for on October 25 the Japanese also carried out the first successful operations of the newly-organized Kamikaze ("Divine Wind") Special Attack Corps, composed of suicidally-inclined aircraft pilots and taking its name from the typhoons that in 1273 and 1279 saved Japan by scattering Kublai Khan's invasion fleets.

When word of Kurita's advance toward Leyte Gulf reached the Japanese air forces in the Philippines, Vice Admiral Takijiro Onishi, commanding the 1st Air Fleet, decided that the time had come for his aviators to take similarly desperate measures. Evidently, ill-trained flyers piloting bombers were not elusive enough to penetrate American air defense and turn back the Allied attack, but the inexperienced Japanese aviators might yet prove effective if they flew highly-maneuverable Zeke fighters armed with light bombs directly into their targets. Onishi personally put the proposition before his aviators at Clark Field on Luzon and received immediate and whole-hearted acceptance. Thus at last, when it was too late, the Japanese began improvising a new and terrifying means of disputing America's growing command of the sea.

Following the invasion of Leyte, the Special Attack Corps sortied four successive days but because of bad weather, or out of sheer ineptitude, failed to find a target. On the 24th, the limited success of the conventional attack against Sherman's carrier task group off Luzon underlined the growing necessity for better methods and more certain results. Clearly, if the kamikazes had a better method, the time to demonstrate it had arrived. The next morning they staged their first successful attacks.

At dawn on October 25, six Special Attack planes took off from Davao, Mindanao and, winging almost due north, discovered Thomas Sprague's carrier task unit. Out of an overcast at about 10,000 feet the Zekes dived directly, some almost vertically, at the escort carriers just as they were launching planes for a strike against Kurita's Center Force, then engaging Clifton Sprague's task unit to the north. The Zekes heading for carriers *Petrof Bay* and *Sangamon* were deflected by antiaircraft fire, but the other two carriers in this unit, the *Suwannee* and the *Santee*, were both struck by aircraft whose exploding bombs tore gaping holes in their flight and hangar decks. In the midst of the ensuing confusion, the *Santee* was also torpedoed by an undetected Japanese sub-

marine. Despite these attacks, the damaged carriers kept station in the formation and by means of quick emergency repairs resumed flight operations within a couple of hours.

Later in the morning, after Kurita had broken off action, kamikazes from Clark Field went after Clifton Sprague's battered carriers. One of the suicide pilots, diving at the *Kitkun Bay*, succeeded in striking her only a glancing blow, but his bomb exploded and did considerable damage. Two more kamikazes crashed into the *Kalinin Bay*, already scarred by 14 shell hits, and started fires. One rammed through the flight deck of the *St. Lô*, caught fire, and detonated bombs and torpedoes on the hangar deck. The resulting series of explosions nearly blew the *St. Lô* apart. She sank a little before noon.

Leaving his remaining escort vessels to pick up the *St. Lô*'s survivors, Clifton Sprague withdrew toward Manus with his carriers. "We had been through so much by then," said he, "that it didn't seem to matter whether we had escorts with us or not."[21]

Kurita's Retirement

Kurita meanwhile, having reassembled the remnant of his Center Force, was steaming off Samar on various courses trying to decide what to do next. Despite his losses, he thought he had done a good morning's work by sinking, as he supposed, three or four fleet carriers, two heavy cruisers, and several destroyers. Once he shaped course again for Leyte Gulf but presently thought better of it and turned away. By now, he reasoned, the transports and cargo vessels would surely have been unloaded, and with plenty of warning they must have withdrawn from the Gulf. On the other hand, radio intercepts left him with the impression that powerful air forces were assembling on Leyte and that Third Fleet carrier groups were converging on him from all directions. Though the horizon was empty, he felt surrounded. In the circumstances Leyte Gulf might easily prove a trap instead of an opportunity. At any rate, he definitely preferred fighting the next battle in the open sea.

[21] Gilbert Cant, *The Great Pacific Victory* (New York, 1945), 307.

Kurita's orders, like Halsey's, gave him the option of engaging enemy carrier forces if opportunity offered. From Manila that morning had come a radio report of American carriers to the northeast of Samar. After due consideration, Kurita and his staff concluded that these nonexistent carriers were their most profitable objective. With the aid of planes from Luzon, the Center Force might yet win a decision—or at least go down gloriously, fighting capital ships. A little before 1300, as the American escort carrier aircraft came in for their final attack, Kurita headed north in search of enemy carriers.

Not long afterward came the first of several attacks by carrier planes coming in from the northeast. These were from McCain's group, which was speeding toward Samar in response to Halsey's summons. McCain's aircraft, because they had to strike from extreme range, were hampered by wing tanks and carried bombs instead of heavier torpedoes. They inflicted no important damage, but they did confirm Kurita in his decision to avoid Leyte Gulf.

At Kurita's request, nearly every operational plane on Luzon made rendezvous with his force in the late afternoon for a coordinated attack on the supposed American carrier group. This was the sort of support Kurita had been trying to get for two days, but now that he had it, no trace of enemy ships was to be found. By this time the Japanese destroyers were low in fuel, and Kurita and his staff were utterly exhausted after three days under attack from surface, subsurface, and air. In the circumstances Kurita saw retirement from the field of battle as his only alternative. Toward dusk the Center Force headed for San Bernardino Strait, which it entered at 2130. One vessel, destroyer *Nowake,* having stopped to remove the crew of the doomed *Chikuma,* trailed far behind the others.

By this time the massed power that Halsey had assembled off Luzon the night before was split four ways. Mitscher's forces in the north were divided, with DuBose's cruiser-destroyer group advancing ahead of the carrier groups to pick off cripples and stragglers from Ozawa's Northern Force. In an attempt to beat Kurita to San Bernardino Strait, Halsey had further divided the Third Fleet by detaching from his southbound vessels his two fastest

battleships, the *Iowa* and the *New Jersey,* together with three light cruisers and eight destroyers. With this detachment he raced ahead, but the race was futile, for when Halsey arrived off the Strait a little after midnight the only ship of the Center Force that had not already passed through was the *Nowake.* This lone vessel Halsey's cruisers and destroyers quickly sank with gunfire and torpedoes. The fast battleships of the Third Fleet had steamed 300 miles north and then 300 miles back south between the two major enemy forces without quite making contact with either.

Through the night the Japanese Center Force made best possible speed across the Sibuyan Sea. After dawn on the 26th it passed through Tablas Strait on the far side and shaped a southerly course west of Panay. Here it came under attack by planes from Bogan's and McCain's groups, which had made rendezvous off Luzon. The carrier planes sank the light cruiser *Noshiro* and further damaged the straggling heavy cruiser *Kumano.* That ended four days of attack on the much-battered Center Force. Kurita escaped with four battleships, two heavy cruisers, a light cruiser, and seven destroyers—not a powerful force for offensive action but a fleet-in-being that MacArthur and Kinkaid would have to take seriously into account in planning further operations in the Philippines.

Summary

The main conditions affecting the Battle for Leyte Gulf were the greatly superior power of the United States Navy, supplemented by a few Allied combat vessels; the immense superiority of American air support; the division of the Japanese fleet, caused by Allied submarine attacks on the Japanese oil supply and augmented by Japanese dispersion tactics; and poor radio communications and generally inadequate exchange of information among the segments of both fleets. The American naval forces were undoubtedly hampered by lack of unified command in the theater of operations; but the Japanese fleet, despite unified command in the person of Admiral Toyoda, was even less successful than the Americans in achieving coordination and mutual support. Out of these conditions developed the most complex and far-flung naval battle in history, a battle notable on both sides for remarkable achievements as well as for lost opportunities.

The Japanese, without attaining their main objective of sinking the amphibious shipping in Leyte Gulf, lost 306,000 tons of combat ships—three battleships, four carriers, ten cruisers, and nine destroyers. The Americans not only saved their amphibious shipping but also destroyed the enemy's capacity to fight another fleet battle, at a cost of 37,000 tons of ships —one light and two escort carriers, two destroyers, and a destroyer escort. The Battle for Leyte Gulf was thus an overwhelming victory for the United States. Yet the Americans, as well as the Japanese, failed to employ their naval power with optimum efficiency.

Admiral Kurita, though under the most unremitting attack of any naval commander in history, fought his way without air support across the Sibuyan Sea and passed unobserved through San Bernardino Strait into the Pacific. Once there however he failed to recognize or to profit by his opportunities. He made a disorderly attack on a small American escort carrier unit, became confused, lost touch with the enemy and with his own ships, took heavier losses than he inflicted, and retreated back the way he had come. Admiral Nishimura, advancing ahead of schedule via Surigao Strait to cooperate with Kurita in Leyte Gulf, ran into an ambush and sacrificed his force in vain. Admiral Shima, for reasons he considered sufficient, failed to cooperate with Nishimura, but prudently withdrew from Surigao Strait when he perceived that Nishimura had met with disaster. Admiral Ozawa sacrificed his bait carriers, as he expected, but succeeded in decoying the U.S. Third Fleet away from Leyte Gulf and preserving most of his surface force as well. Another Japanese success, limited but ominous for the future, was achieved by the new kamikaze suicide corps that on October 25 made the first of many attacks on Allied ships.

The individual segments of the American naval forces performed brilliantly, but the Third and Seventh fleets, misled by a series of unconfirmed assumptions, also failed to co-ordinate. Admiral Halsey concentrated upon and battered the Japanese Center Force into temporary retreat in the Sibuyan Sea; he then abandoned that target and uncovered San Bernardino Strait and the American beachhead on the assumption that the Seventh Fleet was prepared to cover the northern approach to Leyte Gulf. Admiral Oldendorf, in possibly the last line battle of naval history, overwhelmed the Japanese in Surigao Strait with a perfect ambush and an almost flawless attack. Oldendorf could hardly have failed to win a victory, for Admiral Kinkaid had given him nearly all the Seventh Fleet surface combat strength, assuming that the Third Fleet was covering the northern approach to Leyte Gulf. Admiral Mitscher, with his usual resolution and effective employment of air forces, worried the Japanese carriers to destruction; yet elements of both the Northern and Center Japanese forces were able to escape because Halsey carried the main American surface strength fruitlessly north and then south through the most crucial hours of the battle, leaving inferior forces to deal with the enemy in two areas. The most memorable achievement of the battle was the combination of American forces off Samar that turned back the Japanese Center Force within a few miles of Leyte Gulf. Here Admiral Clifton Sprague, backed by Admiral Stump and Admiral Thomas Sprague, squeezed every possible advantage from wind, rain, smoke, interior position, and air and surface attack to confuse and repulse an immensely superior enemy. Overhead, the escort carrier planes, untrained for attacking ships, performed like fast carrier aircraft at their best. On the surface, Clifton Sprague's little screening vessels, steaming boldly into battleship and cruiser fire, dodging through smoke and rain, chasing salvos, opposing 14- and 16-inch shells with 5-inch when they had expended their torpedoes, provided the slender margin that enabled the air attack to succeed and most of the escort carriers to escape. The history of the United States Navy records no more glorious two hours of resolution, sacrifice, and success.

42:

Submarines in the Pacific

There was a grim symbolism in the fact that on December 31, 1941 Admiral Nimitz took command of the Pacific Fleet on the deck of a submarine—the *Grayling*. Though the new Cincpac was an old submariner, the choice was not a matter of sentiment. The hard fact was that at this time the suitable surface combatant ships were on the bottom or en route to the West Coast for repairs. None but submarines were available for the brief and businesslike assumption-of-command ceremony.

Since the Pearl Harbor disaster none but submarines had been available to carry the attack to Japan. On December 7 the U.S. Chief of Naval Operations had ordered unrestricted submarine warfare against the Island Empire. The little-publicized, unremitting campaign of attrition by the "dolphin Navy"—though dogged by bad luck and faulty equipment in the early months—was to sever Japan's logistic jugulars, and virtually to starve Japan into submission. The American submarines were to be second to no other service branch in their contributions to victory.

The singular success of the U.S. submarines would derive not merely from exemplary command and crew performance, but also from a sound doctrine—always well-directed, but sufficiently flexible to be improved in the light of combat experience and the changing nature of the war. Japan's brave and well-trained submariners on the other hand would be largely wasted, hampered by a faulty doctrine and a myopic high command.

It is often forgotten that the attack on Pearl Harbor began, not with carrier planes, but with Japanese miniature submarines attempting to penetrate the harbor. As we have seen, one was sunk by an American destroyer seventy minutes before the first air strike. These midgets, five in all, had been carried to the scene on specially converted I-class submarines as a part of the force of 27 boats intended for reconnaissance, for intelligence information on the carrier force, and for attacks on ships escaping from the harbor. Although the midgets accomplished nothing, their abortive attack illustrates a key aspect of the Japanese submarine doctrine. In spite of the records of U-boats in World War I and in spite of the Allied losses in the Battle of the Atlantic in World War II, the Japanese persisted in discounting the value of the submarine as a commerce raider. Not only did they have no plans for employment of their submarines against Allied shipping; they had no plan for convoying their own merchant ships. Their primary submarine doctrine was to use their boats in support of fleet operations. The Japanese, moreover, so underestimated the potentialities of the American submarines that their striking force made no substantial attack on the U.S. Submarine Base at Pearl Harbor.

The Japanese Drive into the Southern Resources Area

Simultaneously with the attack on Pearl Harbor, the Japanese forces, as we have seen, embarked on their real goal in the war—the rich resources of oil, rubber, tin, copper, and rice in the Netherlands East Indies, Borneo, Celebes, Halmahera, Malaya, and Indo-China. The American embargo of July 1941 had obliged the Japanese to begin expending their 6,450,000-ton oil reserve. Unless they could win the East Indies, they would be oil starved. Hence all else depended on the seizure of the

Southern Resources Area oil fields, on their proper exploitation, and on the transport of their products to the home islands. The weak Allied forces in the Far East could do nothing to prevent Japan's attainment of the first two requirements, but submarines could and did strike at the third, the transport of oil and other strategic resources to Japan.

American submarines in the Pacific Theater were divided between the Asiatic Fleet Submarine Force, based at Cavite in Manila Bay, and the Pacific Fleet Submarine Force at Pearl Harbor. The Asiatic Force at this time consisted of six S-class boats, 23 larger fleet types, three tenders, and one rescue vessel. The old S-class boats were small and uncomfortable, with a relatively short cruising radius. They were numbered, not named. As rapidly as replacements became available, they were withdrawn from combat service and assigned to training commands. The fleet boats, named for fish and other marine creatures, were much more battle-worthy. The *Gato,* built in 1941, was the archetype. It displaced 1,500 tons on the surface, was 312 feet in length, had a cruising radius of 12,000 miles, and carried 24 torpedoes and ten tubes, six forward and four aft. A 3-inch gun and up to four light automatic weapons mounted topside completed the armament. The complement was approximately eight officers and 80 men. This was the type of boat that carried the war to Japan.

The first American submarines to engage the Japanese had the mission of helping protect the Philippines from invasion. They operated under instructions to proceed cautiously, feeling out the Japanese defense and anti-submarine measures. Forming a defensive cordon around Luzon, they watched and waited. Meanwhile the *Sealion,* undergoing refit at Cavite, was destroyed in the first Japanese air attack. She was the first of 52 American submarines to be lost during the war. At this time every single combat vessel counted importantly in the hopelessly outnumbered Allied fleet in Asiatic waters. For the simultaneous loss of the *Prince of Wales* and the *Repulse* left a surface force with no vessel larger than a cruiser.

The submarines struck back, but in vain. During December the 28 boats made 31 determined attacks on warships and transports bringing the Japanese landing force to the Philippines. Expending 66 torpedoes, the submariners suffered the bitter disappointment of sinking only two Japanese vessels. From perfect attack positions the torpedoes missed or fired prematurely. The U.S. Navy had a defective torpedo design which caused the loss of priceless opportunities to destroy enemy shipping and to delay the Japanese campaign.

Because of equipment difficulties, no submarine guarded Lingayen Gulf in northern Luzon as the Japanese expeditionary force landed on December 21 to begin its march on Manila. The Japanese were heavily escorted and, once in the Gulf, they skillfully took advantage of shoal water and protective reefs to frustrate belated attempts of American submarines to disrupt the landing. Only the *S-38,* in a daring penetration, managed to sink a transport at its anchorage, while the *Seal* torpedoed a small freighter en route to the landing area.

The threat to their bases near Manila forced a retreat of the Allied naval forces. The Asiatic Fleet Submarine Force, under command of Captain John Wilkes, moved its base first to Darwin, and later to Fremantle, Australia. Only the tender *Canopus* remained in Manila Bay to service submarines there as long as possible.

While continuing their patrol missions, submarines began a series of evacuation runs, removing civilians, key military personnel, and treasure from besieged Bataan and Corregidor, and at the same time delivering food, medical stores, and ammunition to the ever-diminishing numbers of defenders. On the first of these runs, the *Seawolf* took in 37 tons of .50-caliber ammunition and brought out 25 army and navy aviators, a selection of submarine spare parts, and 16 torpedoes from the *Canopus.* The *Trout,* requesting 25 tons of ballast to replace the cargo brought in, received two tons of gold, 18 tons of silver, and five tons of U.S. mail and negotiable securities. On her way back, the *Trout,* not allowing her cargo to interfere with essentials, torpedoed a freighter and a submarine chaser.

Although no submarine sinkings occurred during the Java Sea campaign, Americans were establishing their patrol zones and improving their tactics. Early doctrine called for daylight submerged attack, with periscope observations kept brief and infrequent in order to avoid detection. Attack doctrine also limited the use of sonar equipment to its listening component, lest the pings of its echo-ranging feature reveal the presence of the attacking submarine. Since early periscopes lacked precise range-finding equipment, and since use of sonar solely as a hydrophone could give only the bearing of a target, skippers preferred to attack with a zero or 90-degree gyro angle. For there was no means of exact calculation of the range factor in the torpedo problem.[1] In time, periscopes were equipped with stadimeter range finders. Commanding officers also learned that a single range-finding ping on the sonar was unlikely to alert the enemy. Thus, with accurate ranges, a submarine was able to employ any gyro angle with some assurance of hits. For a considerable while, despite German successes with night surface attacks, daylight submerged attack continued to be standard practice in the U.S. Navy. The solid black American hulls, so painted to conceal a submarine from air observation, offered poor camouflage to a submarine on the surface at night, and lack of a good night periscope precluded successful submerged attacks after dark. Later experiments proved that a light gray color on the sides gave good camouflage qualities at night, and the development of an effective night periscope made possible submerged night attack. But before the American submarines could become really flexible day-or-night weapons for combating Japanese ships, they had to be provided with a reliable torpedo data computer (TDC),[2] more effective radar, and—above all—more reliable torpedoes.

As the Japanese extended their conquests, they exposed their shipping more and more to submarine attack. Nevertheless in the period between the Pearl Harbor raid and the Battle of the Coral Sea, they managed to keep their losses well within bounds. Allied submarines during this phase of the war sank only three surface warships, none larger than a destroyer,

[1] In 1941 U.S. submarines had "banjos"—markings on their periscope cross wires to aid in range estimation. Even with such crude equipment, many hits were scored.

[2] The Bennehoff computer had been developed before the war. It was installed in all the fleet boats after Pearl Harbor.

two submarines, and 35 merchantmen. But American submariners were beginning to learn Japanese traffic patterns, with fruitful results in the months to come.

Japanese use of submarines in support of fleet operations is well exemplified in the Battle of Midway, in which boats were sent out individually or positioned in cordons to scout and intercept American fleet movements. It will be recalled that the two cordons between Pearl Harbor and Midway took position too late to observe or intercept the American carriers. The only Japanese submarine that accomplished any positive results in this battle was the *I-168*, which sank the *Yorktown* and the destroyer *Hammann*.

American submarines, stationed on the western approaches to Midway, achieved even less. During the carrier battle, the *Nautilus* fired a harmless dud at the carrier *Kaga,* and thought she had sunk the *Soryu*. That night heavy cruisers *Mogami* and *Mikuma* collided while maneuvering to avoid submarine *Tambor*. Thus crippled and slowed, the *Mikuma* later became a victim to American carrier planes.

Between the Battle of Midway in June and the invasion of Guadalcanal on August 7, 1942, the chief American submarine operations were attacking Japanese merchant ships, sinking about 60,000 tons during the period. The Japanese during the same period concentrated a large measure of their submarine efforts in the Indian Ocean, sinking ships as far west as Mozambique Channel, between Madagascar and Africa. Other Japanese submarines operated around Australia, New Guinea, and Samoa. Total sinkings for this period amounted to some 30 Allied ships.

The Makin Raid

Early in August 1942, the *Nautilus* and the *Argonaut,* two of the largest American submarines (more than 370 feet long and displacing 2,700 tons), operated together in one of the most unusual special missions of the war. At Pearl Harbor they took aboard Lieutenant Colonel Evans F. Carlson and two companies of marines for a commando raid on Makin in the Gilbert Islands. This was at the time of the Guadalcanal invasion, and the Makin operation was intended as a diversion—to attract Japanese forces away from the Solomons. The marines got ashore without opposition at dawn on August 16. Soon however they began to encounter Japanese troops arriving by foot, on bicycles, and by truck. On request from the marines, the *Nautilus* opened fire in the general direction of the fighting, but lacking spotters to pinpoint targets in this area, she shifted fire to the lagoon and sank a 3,500-ton merchant ship and a patrol boat.

Japanese aircraft forced both submarines to submerge several times during daylight hours, but on two successive nights they took aboard what were presumed to be all the surviving marines. Nine however were left behind. Captured by the Japanese, they were taken to Kwajalein, where they were beheaded.

The landing party had wiped out the small garrison on Butaritari Island, destroyed installations, and picked up useful intelligence material. Though this operation boosted Allied morale, from the strategic point of view it was a failure. Not only were the Japanese not diverted from Guadalcanal; they began to build up formidable defenses in the Gilberts, especially on Tarawa, which were to cost the lives of many Americans a little more than a year later.

The Solomons Campaign

When the United States assumed the offensive-defensive with the landings on Guadalcanal, American S-boats from Brisbane were assigned by Rear Admiral Charles A. Lockwood, Commander Southwest Pacific Submarine Force, to regular patrol areas in the vicinity of the Bismarcks and New Guinea to attack Japanese ships. The S-boats were also to cover and, insofar as possible, blockade bases at Rabaul, Kavieng, Buin, Lae, and Salamaua, in order to keep the Japanese from reinforcing the lower Solomons. Meanwhile boats from Pearl Harbor established a close blockade on Truk, the so-called "Gibralter of the Pacific." In addition to sinking 79 merchant ships for a total of 260,000 tons during the Guadalcanal campaign, American undersea craft sank light cruiser *Tenryu,* an old destroyer, and one of the big I-class submarines. They also accounted

for heavy cruiser *Kako,* one of the victors of the Battle of Savo Island, fought on the night of August 9, 1942. Returning with her sisters in triumph to Rabaul the next morning, the *Kako* fell victim to four torpedoes from the *S-44* which was patrolling the entrance to the harbor. This successful attack in some small measure compensated the Americans for their crushing defeat at Savo, and, more important, it caused the Japanese to adopt more cautious measures in employment of their surface ships for the Tokyo Express.

Japanese submarines too operated in support of the Solomons campaign. As usual, they made little effort to interfere with American logistic shipping but concentrated rather on warships. Their mere presence in the area however forced the Americans to take extensive anti-submarine measures, employing forces that might otherwise have been used elsewhere. On a run from Espiritu Santo to Guadalcanal, an American convoy, escorted by a close screen and supported by the *Wasp, Hornet,* and *North Carolina,* on September 14 ran into a group of Japanese submarines. It would not be correct to call these boats a wolf pack, for they were not making a concerted attack, nor were they under any sort of common tactical command. The *Wasp,* the *North Carolina,* and the escorting destroyer *O'Brien* were all heavily hit by torpedoes in the space of ten minutes. The battleship received very serious damage. The *Wasp,* afire, had to be abandoned and sunk. The *O'Brien* broke up and sank before she could reach dry dock. The important point to remember about this attack however is that the Japanese made no effort to attack the convoy itself, for Japanese commanders believed that only warships were worthy targets for sea warriors. The loss of the *Wasp,* combined with heavy damage sustained by the *Saratoga* two weeks earlier, brought American carrier strength in the Pacific down to two, the *Hornet* and the *Enterprise.* In the remainder of the Solomons campaign, the Japanese submarine force sank only two more American warships, destroyer *Porter* during the Battle of the Santa Cruz Islands, and light cruiser *Juneau* following the Cruiser Night Action of the Naval Battle of Guadalcanal.

Participation by American submarines in the

Solomons campaign took the form of strategic support. Submarines took up their patrol stations near the bases from which the Japanese ships operated against the Solomons—Truk, the Palaus, and Rabaul. In addition they covered the straits in and about the Bismarck Archipelago and gave support to MacArthur's drive up the Papuan Peninsula of New Guinea. These assignments kept the submarines well clear of the operating area and minimized the risk that American boats might be attacked by their own surface forces.[3] One exception to this practice took place when, during the October crisis on Guadalcanal, the *Amberjack* delivered a load of aviation gasoline to Tulagi, the only time during the war that an American submarine was employed as a tanker.

The most famous story of this period of operations concerns the *Growler*, which was patrolling near the Bismarcks in February 1943. At 0110 on the 7th she sighted an enemy ship and began a surface run. As the range closed, the target, a 2,500-ton Japanese gunboat, sighted the submarine, reversed course, and rushed at her. The *Growler*'s radar operator below decks noted the enemy's change of course promptly, but her skipper, Commander Howard W. Gilmore, and the other six men on the bridge did not see the maneuver in the darkness. The command "Left full rudder!" came too late to avoid collision; the *Growler* plowed into the Japanese gunboat at 17 knots. All hands were knocked down by the impact. As the submarine, which had heeled far over, righted herself, the gunboat sprayed the bridge with machine gun bullets. The junior officer of the watch and one of the lookouts were instantly killed; Commander Gilmore was severely wounded. Clinging to the bridge frame, he made his voice heard: "Clear the bridge!" The four other living men scrambled through the hatch. Unable to follow, Commander Gilmore gave his last command: "Take her down!"

For this "distinguished gallantry and valor," Commander Gilmore was posthumously awarded the Medal of Honor.

In January 1943 Rear Admiral Robert English, who had commanded the submarines of the Pacific Fleet under Admiral Nimitz, was lost in a plane crash. Admiral Lockwood was ordered to assume Admiral English's job, while Rear Admiral Ralph W. Christie took over Lockwood's Southwest Pacific submarine command. Lockwood immediately set about establishing a submarine base nearer than Pearl Harbor to the submarine patrol areas. At this time the logical forward base for American submarines was Midway Island, which was equipped with submarine tenders and with a minimum shore installation. This base saved a submarine 2,400 miles of travel on each patrol. The chief disadvantage was Midway's unpopularity with submariners. On the islands, submariners complained, were nothing "but sand and gooney birds." To sustain morale, Lockwood arranged schedules so that boats returned to Pearl Harbor periodically.

To give maximum rest and relaxation to submarine personnel, when a boat returned from patrol, its crew, officers and men alike, would be removed to recuperation camps or hotels while a relief crew took over. Thus the sea-going crew would have no responsibility for their boat until she was ready to leave on her next assignment. Even the commanding officer would be temporarily relieved so that he had no legal responsibility during the time. Submarine squadron commanders, who had no regular combat assignments,[4] supervised and executed this program. On completion of the upkeep period, the reassembled crew would take their boat out for a few days of refresher training and then depart on patrol. This system proved of great benefit to the morale of submariners, who were thus kept in top form for the performance of their primary duties.

Torpedo Troubles

The blame for the malfunctioning of torpedoes which beset the U.S. Navy in World War II can be laid in some measure to im-

---

[3] This was an important consideration: air and surface forces were inclined to shoot first and ask questions afterward. Because of failure or misunderstanding of recognition signals, no less than 28 U.S. submarines were strafed or bombed by U.S. aircraft. Five others were shelled by U.S. surface craft. The *Dorado* and the *Seawolf* were sunk with all hands by "friendly" forces. Nine others were more or less severely damaged.

[4] But who did on occasion serve as "wolf pack" commanders on special assignment.

proper design and a stubborn confidence in the magnetic exploder. Yet defects in design would have been more quickly revealed had the sufficient funds been available for testing. With the limited funds provided, peacetime tests with live torpedoes were out of the question, since to explode a single live torpedo would cost a substantial fraction of the torpedo facility's annual budget. Hence tests were made with exercise heads and with the torpedoes set to pass under rather than to hit the target. These trials thus tested nothing but the gyro steering mechanism and the steam propulsion units. The critical warhead had to be taken on faith. And the faith was misplaced.

The Mark 6 exploder, highly secret before the war, contained a magnetic impulse device, activated by a sharp change in the earth's magnetic field, such as that caused by the steel hull of a ship. Doctrine called for torpedoes employing Mark 6 exploders to pass ten feet beneath the target so that the explosion would rupture bottom tanks and perhaps break the keel. In practice many torpedoes failed to explode, even though they passed directly beneath the target. Reports such as that from the *Sargo*, which suffered 13 misses out of 13 easy shots, caused Lockwood to conduct a series of tests. Eight shots fired through a fish net ran an average of 11 feet deeper than set. The Bureau of Ordnance finally conceded that the torpedoes with heavy warheads (750 lbs of TNT) *did* run 10 feet deeper than set. However, when set to allow for this error, another serious problem was introduced, for the torpedo often ranged up and down in a kind of sinusoidal wave. If it happened to be at the top of its cycle when it passed under the target, it would go off; otherwise the change in the magnetic field was not great enough and the torpedo passed harmlessly beneath.

Premature explosions, which often deceived the submariner into believing that he had obtained hits, now redoubled. Near the magnetic equator, the horizontal component of a ship's magnetic field is often stronger than the vertical component, with the result that the Mark 6 exploder frequently went off some 50 yards from the target. The resultant explosion, shower of water, and heel of the target led to many reports of hits which were in fact prematures. In view of these findings, Lockwood in June 1943 ordered the inactivation of the magnetic component in order to rely on the contact exploder built into the Mark 6 for use in case the magnetic exploder failed.

An outbreak of duds followed. The contact device too was faulty, but its weaknesses had been concealed by the deep running and the premature firing of the torpedoes. The discovery of the defects of the contact feature of the Mark 6 came as a result of the frustrations of Lieutenant Commander L. R. Daspit, commanding the *Tinosa,* which encountered a mammoth 19,000-ton tanker west of Truk on July 24, 1943. The *Tinosa* had 16 torpedoes remaining and fired four at long range from an unfavorable track angle. Two torpedoes hit and went off near the stern, and the huge tanker stopped. Two more hits were scored on her port quarter. Daspit then worked the *Tinosa* into an ideal firing position on the target's beam and fired nine thoroughly checked torpedoes at her, deliberately, and in single shots. Nine hit and nine failed to explode. The exasperated but clear-thinking Daspit took his one remaining torpedo back to Pearl Harbor for examination.

This move resulted in the final cure. Lockwood ordered the contact feature of the mechanism to be thoroughly tested. The results indicated that the firing pin assembly was too weak to withstand a square hit. On a glancing hit, at an angle of 45° or less, the firing pin would function, but on the so-called "perfect hit," the delicate mechanism would jam and the torpedo would fail to go off. This bore out the *Tinosa*'s experience perfectly, for the four torpedoes which had exploded had all hit at the curve of the stern, while the nine duds had all hit from the perfect right-angle track. Corrective modifications were accomplished at Pearl Harbor, and American submarines finally had a reliable weapon. Thus at long last was overcome the effect of misguided "super secrecy" and insufficient testing of material before the war.

The electric torpedo began to appear soon after the steam torpedo had been brought to satisfactory performance. Its low speed (28 knots vs. 46 knots for the steam torpedo) made the electric torpedo tardy in winning acceptance, but its wakeless feature came to offset its slowness in the minds of submarine officers. At length the majority of torpedoes employed were electric.

The Gilberts and Marshalls

For the invasion of the Gilbert Islands in November 1943, Admirals Nimitz, Spruance, and Lockwood worked together as a team. They decided that enemy surface opposition to the landings must emanate from Truk, that it would probably swing north to avoid land-based air searches from Guadalcanal, and that it would have to refuel in the Marshalls. So three submarines took station off Truk, three more patrolled the Marshalls, and two patrolled the line between. A ninth was stationed 300 miles west of Tarawa to send daily weather reports.

Because no Japanese surface forces went to the Gilberts, the submarines had little to do except attack whatever convoys or unescorted merchantmen came their way. Nevertheless two of the boats were lost. The *Corvina*, off Truk, was sunk on November 16 by a Japanese submarine—probably the only American submarine so destroyed during the war. The *Sculpin*, between Truk and the Marshalls, was detected on the 19th while closing in on a convoy. She underwent a depth charge attack from the convoy escorts, receiving damages that forced her to the surface, where her crew fought her deck guns as long as they could and then scuttled her. Thirteen officers and men rode the *Sculpin* down. Among these was Captain John P. Cromwell, whom Admiral Lockwood had sent to take command of a wolf pack, should one be formed. Because Cromwell possessed important information about war plans, he had elected to go down lest the Japanese extract his information through torture or "truth serums." For his decision he was posthumously awarded the Medal of Honor. Of the members of the *Sculpin*'s crew that abandoned ship, the Japanese picked up 42. One of these, badly wounded, was callously tossed back overboard by his captors. The rest were taken to Truk, where they were transferred to escort carriers *Unyo* and *Chuyo* for transportation to Japan.

Now came one of the most tragic and ironic coincidences of the war. Approaching Japan was U.S. submarine *Sailfish*, on her tenth war patrol—her first under Lieutenant Commander Robert Ward. Her crew often referred to her as the *Squailfish* because she had formerly been the famous *Squalus*, which had gone down off Portsmouth, New Hampshire, in 1939. It was the *Sculpin* that had then located her on the bottom, making possible the rescue of her crew and her subsequent raising. Now, four years later, Ward, in common with other American submarine commanders, was keenly aware that no large Japanese warship had been sunk by a submarine in 16 months. He was anxious for the *Sailfish* to break this run of bad luck. She did, but from the American point of view there was a tragic irony in her success.

Just before midnight on December 3 in typhoon weather, the *Sailfish* made radar contact with several large targets. Despite the gale and near zero visibility, Ward soon reached firing position and fired four tubes. One torpedo scored a hit on a carrier, which managed to limp away through heavy seas. Despite depth charge attacks that drove him down, Ward regained contact with his quarry and stalked her through the night. At dawn he fired three more torpedoes and made another hit, this time leaving the carrier dead in the water. At 0940 he fired a spread from his stern tubes and got a third hit. Eight minutes later the carrier went down, unobserved by the submarine, which had been driven deep by the Japanese escorts. The *Sailfish* had sunk escort carrier *Chuyo*. The *Chuyo* had 21 *Sculpin* survivors aboard, all but one of whom were lost.

The deployment of submarines for the Gilberts operation impressed Admiral Spruance so favorably that he advocated the same pattern thereafter. Instead of having a scouting line at sea, he requested that the submarines be stationed in waters, particularly straits, through which the enemy was likely to pass in order to approach the scene of action.[5] Unlike the Japanese at Midway, he got his submarines to their stations early enough for them to be of value.

[5] Submarines remained under operational command of the type commander. Joint plans were agreed on in conference between Admiral Lockwood and the fleet commander concerned.

By this time submarine doctrine had come to include several distinct missions:

1. Submarine concentration to cut the enemy's supply lines to the target areas.
2. Submarine photographic reconnaissance of beachheads marked for amphibious landings and enemy military or naval installations marked for future reference.
3. Submarine lifeguarding during air strikes.
4. Submarine scouting duty in the target area and off enemy bases to report enemy movements and intercept and attack enemy forces which emerged to oppose the attacking United States forces.
5. Submarines stationed to intercept and attack fugitive shipping attempting to flee the target area.[6]

For the Marshalls landings of January 1944 four submarines performed photo-reconnaissance. Again three submarines took station off the approaches to Truk, and this time two of the three sank destroyers. The deployment of the other available submarines for this operation was patterned on that of the Gilberts operation.

For the three big carrier strikes at Truk, Saipan, and the Palaus in early 1944, the pattern varied somewhat, since Spruance believed that his opposition would come not from surface units but from the enemy's land-based air, while the surface units and the merchant ships present would flee the areas. Consequently he requested submarines where they might intercept the fugitives. Off Truk the *Skate* sank light cruiser *Agano,* and the *Tang* got a cargo ship. At Saipan the *Sunfish* sank two merchantmen; the *Tang,* four. Off Palau the *Tullibee* was sunk by her own circling torpedo,[7] and apparently most of the Japanese ships escaped through the area assigned to her. It was on this occasion however that the *Tunny* put two torpedoes into superbattleship *Musashi.*

The Marianas

Before the American invasion of the Marianas in June 1944 Admiral Lockwood, of the

[6] Theodore Roscoe, *United States Submarine Operations in World War II* (Annapolis, 1949), 361.
[7] Reported by a survivor picked up by the Japanese and released from prison camp at the end of the war.

Pacific Fleet, and Admiral Ralph Christie, of the Seventh Fleet, both positioned their submarines at the request of Admiral Spruance. Three boats scouted the Tawitawi area as the Japanese fleet assembled at Tawitawi; others operated off the principal straits through which it would have to pass to reach Saipan; four more patrolled the Philippine Sea in 90° arcs inside and centered on the corners of a great square. Still others were in motion, relieving patrollers or returning to base after relief; two of these transients played major roles in the development of the battle. There was also a wolf pack on routine patrol—the *Shark II,* the *Pilotfish,* and the *Pintado*—called Blair's Blasters after group commander Captain L. N. Blair.

On May 31, 1944, submarine *Silversides,* patrolling an adjacent area, informed the Blasters that a convoy was coming their way, apparently heading from Honshu to Saipan. By the time the *Silversides* had joined forces with the wolf pack, two more convoys had appeared in the area. Early on June 1 the *Pintado* picked off a freighter from the first of the three convoys. All that day and for several days thereafter the wolf pack chased the third convoy, but the *Silversides,* her torpedoes expended, had to withdraw. The *Shark* sank a cargo ship late on June 2 and another on the morning of June 4. On the evening of June 5 she got two more, one a passenger-cargo vessel of 7,000 tons. That same night the *Pintado* sank two ships. As a result of these sinkings, half a division of Japanese reinforcement troops was drowned, and many other soldiers reached the Marianas without guns or battle gear. The Japanese commander on Saipan had to ration munitions. Blair's Blasters had greatly lessened the opposition the American assault troops would have to overcome.

From June 6 through June 9 submarine *Harder,* under Commander Samuel D. Dealey, set a remarkable record in the vicinity of Sibutu Passage, between the Sulu Archipelago and Borneo, sinking three destroyers and damaging at least two more. On the morning of June 10, as the *Harder* was patrolling in the Sulu Sea off Tawitawi, she witnessed the sortie of Admiral Ugaki's battleship force for the relief of Biak and radioed a timely warning to Allied commands.

When planes from the U.S. Fifth Fleet began their preliminary bombing of the Marianas on June 11, 1944, the Japanese high command realized that an invasion of Japan's inner defenses was imminent. Admiral Toyoda suspended the Biak operation and ordered the two segments of the Mobile Fleet, under Admiral Ozawa and under Admiral Ugaki, to rendezvous in the Philippine Sea and "attack the enemy in the Marianas area."

As this movement got underway, Christie's and Lockwood's careful positioning of their submarines began to pay off. Submarine *Redfin* saw the carrier force, under Ozawa, sortie from Tawitawi on June 13 and flashed a warning. In the early evening of the 15th, submarines *Flying Fish* and *Seahorse* sighted the two segments of the Mobile Fleet 300 miles apart in the Philippine Sea. Early on the 17th, the *Cavalla* made contact with an oiler convoy, and Admiral Lockwood ordered her to follow, on the chance that the oilers would lead her to the Japanese combat vessels. The *Cavalla* soon lost the oilers, but that evening she sighted the Mobile Fleet, now united and heading for the Marianas. As a result of these sightings, Admiral Spruance postponed the invasion of Guam and prepared for the Battle of the Philippine Sea. Admiral Lockwood now shifted the four submarines, patrolling from the corners of a square, southward a hundred miles. Now that the approximate location of the Japanese fleet was known, Lockwood gave his submarines permission to shoot first and transmit contact reports afterward. Thus it was that the *Albacore,* assigned to the southwest corner of the new square, found herself in the right place with the right orders to enable her to sink carrier *Taiho.* Three hours later the ubiquitous *Cavalla* put three torpedoes into carrier *Shokaku* and sent her down.

In contrast to the precision with which Christie and Lockwood had stationed their submarines, the Japanese had theirs all in the wrong place. MacArthur's landing on Biak had led them to expect that the next Fifth Fleet operations would be against the Palaus instead of the Marianas, for it was the Palaus that Spruance had hit in support of MacArthur's invasion of Hollandia. Confident that the Americans would come that way again, the Japanese sent submarines to operate north of the Admiralties. In setting up their screen they not only selected the wrong area; they also failed to allow for improvements in American anti-submarine warfare. By mid-1944 the war in the Atlantic against the U-boat had been won, and escorting vessels were bringing the weapons and experience of the Battle of the Atlantic to the Pacific. Of some 25 I-boats and RO-boats operating in connection with the Marianas campaign, 17 were sent to the bottom by American destroyers, destroyer escorts, and aircraft.

The exploits of U.S. destroyer escort *England* (Lieutenant Commander W. B. Pendleton) in May 1944 demonstrate the impotence of Japanese submarines against the new type of attack. Alerted by the news that an American destroyer division had sunk a submarine near the Green Islands, destroyer escorts *England, Raby,* and *George* proceeded from Ironbottom Sound off Guadalcanal to the Bismarcks area. The next day the group made contact north of the Solomons with the *I-16* on a cargo-carrying mission out ahead of the main line of Japanese submarines. The *England* attacked with hedgehogs, ahead-thrown bombs that explode on contact with the submarine. She obtained five hits, whereupon she was rocked by a terrific explosion as the I-boat blew apart. Proceeding northwest, the group ran into the main defense line of seven RO-boats. Here on three successive days, May 22, 23, and 24, the *England* sank RO-boats *106, 104,* and *116.* Proceeding to Manus to take on more hedgehog ammunition, the group toward midnight on the 26th made radar contact with *RO-108.* The group commander gave the *Raby* first chance at this submarine, but she lost contact, and the *England* made another kill. Joined by a fourth destroyer escort bringing the needed ammunition, the *England*'s group returned to the hunting grounds, where they were integrated into a hunter-killer group of destroyers and an escort carrier. When this combined group made contact with the *RO-105* in the early hours of May 31, the officer in tactical command deliberately ordered the *England* to stand aside in order to give the other ships an opportunity to score.

When their attacks failed, in came the *England* once more and destroyed the boat with another hedgehog salvo. When the report of this action reached Washington, Admiral King signaled: "There'll always be an *England* in the United States Navy."

The Palaus and the Philippines

Before the invasion of the Palaus in September 1944, the *Burrfish* made a combined photographic and landing-party reconnaissance of Peleliu and Yap. Because four of the men put ashore on Yap failed to return to the submarine, the landing-party reconnaissance mission, rarely employed by the United States Navy, was abolished.

Admiral Halsey's ideas for submarine deployment differed somewhat from those of Admiral Spruance. Though Halsey agreed that the narrow seas should be patrolled, he placed considerable reliance on use of a scouting line in the open ocean. Hence he requested that while four boats watched important straits, nine form a double scouting line between the Philippines and the Palaus. Two submarines from each of three wolf packs formed a first line of six, and the third boat of each pack formed a second line, in safety position. Because these submarines, called "Halsey's Zoo," made no important contacts during the operation, the submarine scouting line was not used again by the Americans during the war.

The story of submarine operations at the time of the Battle for Leyte Gulf has already been told in some detail. Southwest Pacific submarines *Darter* and *Dace,* it will be recalled, on October 23, 1944 gave the first warning of the approaching Japanese Center Force, and directly afterward sank two of Admiral Kurita's heavy cruisers and put a third out of action. During the same morning, submarine *Bream* severely damaged heavy cruiser *Aoba* off Manila Bay. On the morning of the 25th, while TF 38 was pursuing Ozawa's carrier group northward in the Battle off Cape Engaño, Lockwood ordered two wolf packs, Clarey's Crushers and Roach's Raiders, into an intercepting position. It was the *Jallao* of Clarey's Crushers that sank Ozawa's damaged light cruiser *Tama.*

Other Operations Against the Japanese Navy

In operations less closely associated with the surface fleet, American submarines achieved several more successes against large warships. The most noteworthy were the sinkings of battleship *Kongo* and carrier *Shinano.*

The 31,000-ton *Kongo,* which went down in November 1944, was the only battleship sunk by an American submarine. On November 21, the *Sealion II* (Commander Eli T. Reich) encountered her victim 40 miles north of Formosa. The first radar contact showed the target so far distant that the officer of the deck mistook it for land, but when a further contact showed the target moving nearer, he called the captain. It was just past midnight, with the sky overcast but visibility fair. Identifying the contact as comprising at least two battleships, two cruisers, and several destroyers heading for Japan, Reich elected to make a surface approach, using radar. By the time he had gained the desired attack position and made visual contact with the enemy, the sea was rising, whipped by a night wind. At 0256 Reich fired six bow torpedoes at the leading battleship, at a range of 3,000 yards. Throwing the rudder hard right, he brought his stern tubes to bear on the second battleship and got away three more torpedoes at 0259. Then he took the *Sealion* away at flank speed. To his great disappointment, the task force continued on course at 18 knots. Taking water over the bridge and a good deal down the conning tower hatch, the *Sealion* gave chase. At 0450 the battleship at which the bow tubes had been fired slowed to twelve knots and dropped astern of the task force with two destroyers standing by. Shortly afterward this ship, the *Kongo,* went dead in the water. As the *Sealion* maneuvered into attack position, a flash of light, presumably from the explosion of the battleship's magazines, illuminated the entire area, and the *Kongo* sank. The *Sealion* immediately began to pursue the other battleship but was unable to overtake her in the now heavy seas. Only after the war did the *Sealion*'s crew learn that one of its sterntube torpedoes fired at

0259, missing its intended battleship target, had sunk a destroyer.

Even this achievement was overshadowed about a week later when the *Archerfish* (Commander J. E. Enright) sank the *Shinano*. The *Shinano* was of 68,000 tons displacement, one of the largest warships in the world. Begun as a sister ship to the superbattleships *Yamato* and *Musashi,* she had been converted into an aircraft carrier. She was commissioned on November 18, 1944 and sunk ten days later. When the *Archerfish* found her 150 miles south of Tokyo, she was on her way to the Inland Sea for fitting out in comparative safety from air attack. The submarine made radar contact with the carrier and her four escorts at 2048. A stern chase ensued, which the *Archerfish* must inevitably have lost had the target not zigzagged. At 0300 a radical change in the Japanese base course put the submarine ahead of the carrier, and a zig at 0316 made the position perfect except for a rather large gyro angle. At 0317, with range 1,400 yards and a 70° starboard gyro angle, Enright fired a spread of six torpedoes, all of which probably hit and at least four of which certainly took effect.

The *Shinano* probably would not have sunk, but the crew was inexperienced and the ship unready for sea. Doors that should have been watertight had no gaskets; water poured through them and through unsealed conduits. Steam pumps had not yet been installed, and piping was incomplete. There were too few hand pumps. When the morale of the crew failed also and discipline broke down, the loss of the ship was inevitable. It is fitting that an American submarine should climax the undersea campaign against Japanese warships by sending down the new queen of the Imperial Navy before she had an opportunity to come into action. It is also ironic because Japan no longer had any use for such a vessel. She had freely expended four of her remaining fast carriers as mere decoys in the Battle for Leyte Gulf because she lacked trained pilots for carrier aircraft.

The Lifeguard League

While American submarines were decimating the Japanese navy, they were simultane-ously performing a mission of lifesaving. When planning was in progress for the Gilbert Islands invasion, Admiral Lockwood received the suggestion that submarines might well be employed to rescue downed fliers. He agreed at once, and thus was born the successful Lifeguard League, which rescued 504 airmen before the end of the war. Submarines were stationed in appropriate positions, and airmen were briefed on their locations. The pilot of a crippled plane would set it down as near the submarine as possible, and then he and the crew would take refuge aboard. Lifeguarders also performed notable service for army flyers, especially crews of B-29's shot down while engaged in operations against Japan from bases in the Marianas. These rescues were by no means always easy or free of danger. The *Harder,* for example, went into the shoals of Woleai Island and brought out a navy fighter pilot from the shore by means of a volunteer crew in a rubber boat, all the time under sniper fire. The most dramatic story however is that of the *Stingray,* under Lieutenant Commander S. C. Loomis, which in June 1944 received a report of a downed aviator near Guam. When the *Stingray* got to the position, she found the pilot in his rubber raft acting as involuntary target for a Japanese shore battery. Not daring to surface, Loomis raised both periscopes, one for observation, and the other for the pilot to employ as a cleat for a line from his raft. The pilot at first seemed not to understand, and the *Stingray* made three unsuccessful approaches in the midst of numerous shell splashes. At last on the fourth try, Loomis ran the periscope into the pilot, and he hung on. When the *Stingray* had towed him well out of range of the guns, she surfaced and took the aviator aboard. "We are on speaking terms now," Loomis noted, "but after the third approach I was ready to make him captain of the head."

Further Japanese Submarine Operations

Like the Americans, the Japanese often sent their submarines on special missions, some of them peculiar to the Imperial Navy. Such was the practice of "piggy-backing" small attack devices into effective range. These included midget submarines, aircraft, and outsize torpedoes, called *Kaitens,* steered by a one-man suicide crew. Midgets carried out several attacks early in the war, achieving their most notable success by damaging H.M. battleship *Ramillies* at Madagascar. Thereafter the Japanese dropped them from use, replacing them later in the war with the newly-designed *Kaitens* as a kind of naval equivalent of the kamikazes. Unlike the kamikazes however, the *Kaitens* achieved nothing.

Submarine-launched aircraft carried out some successful photo-reconaissance missions, and one of them dropped several incendiary bombs in the forests of Oregon. Difficulties of launching and recovery precluded widespread use of aircraft-carrying submarines. The war was ending when Japan began to commission the *I-400*-class of 3,500-ton monsters, each of which was intended to bring three planes to within range of the Panama Canal.

The Japanese sometimes used their submarines for nuisance raids of little strategic value. Occasionally the boats refueled seaplanes to extend their radius of attack. In 1942 submarines caused some alarm along the Pacific Coast of North America by sinking a few ships and shelling Vancouver Island, Astoria, and an oil installation near Santa Barbara. Several boats tried to establish liaison with Germany, but only the *I-8* made the round-trip successfully.

The poor showing of the Japanese submarines in contrast to the remarkable success of the American boats invites analysis. The opposing underwater forces were about equal in numbers at the outbreak of war.[8] (The Japanese had a few more submarines than the Americans, but submarines of the Netherlands Navy also were operating in Far Eastern waters.) The small, obsolete Japanese RO-class was greatly inferior to the corresponding American S-boat, but the modern I-class was fairly comparable to the U.S. fleet boat. The Japanese submarines, like their destroyers, were armed with an oxygen-fueled, high-speed, long-range torpedo which was superior to the American

type. Technical deficiencies of the Japanese boats themselves of course account to some extent for their comparative ineffectiveness. Until late in the war they had no radar, and their sound gear was extremely inefficient, leaving them far more vulnerable to countermeasures than German U-boats. The main trouble however was simply strategic blindness on the part of the Japanese high command. The Imperial Navy never used its submarines in a regular campaign against merchant shipping, apparently failing to realize the central place of logistics in modern war.

When the Germans pointed out the extraordinary effectiveness of the submarine as a weapon against cargo carriers and urged Japan to use her underwater fleet against Allied merchant ships, the Japanese invariably replied that they would risk their submarines only against warships. So while American submarines were wearing down Japan's fighting potential by unremitting attacks on her cargo ships, the Japanese disregarded the vulnerable tankers and freighters on which the Allied fleets depended, and sent their boats after well-screened fleet units.

With the inauguration of the Allied bypassing strategy, the desperate Japanese sidetracked even this objective. To supply their isolated garrisons, they began at the insistence of the army to use their submarines as cargo carriers. Gradually their best boats were pressed into such unsuitable service. Hence even while the Allied forces were operating at ever-increasing distances from their continental bases, and closer to Japanese bases, the effectiveness of the Japanese submarines steadily declined. Seldom in the long history of warfare has a primary weapon been used with less grasp of its true potential.

The Assault on Japanese Merchant Shipping

While Japan's submarines were achieving less and less, American submarines, as we have seen, were sinking increasing numbers of Japanese warships. Even more significant in the outcome of the war was the achievement of American submarines against the cargo ships of Japan, which carried the life blood of her

[8] Actually in effective, battleworthy boats, the Japanese had a near 2–1 advantage. U.S. submarines on the east coast in 1941 were small, obsolescent craft useful only for training purposes.

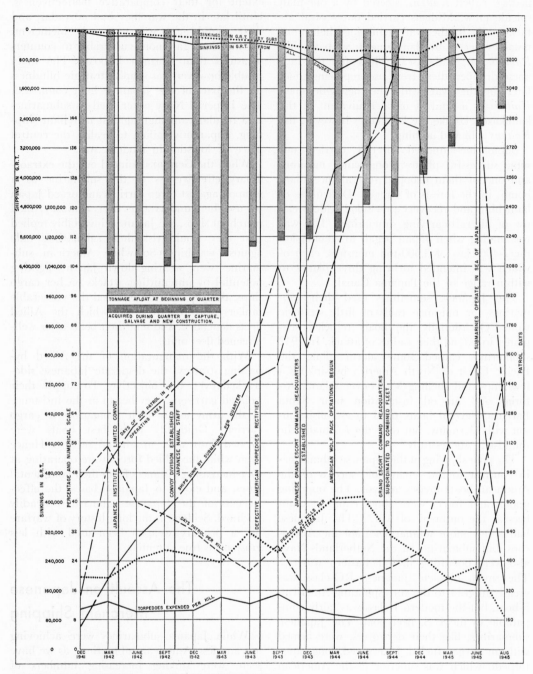

ATTRITION OF JAPANESE SHIPPING IN WORLD WAR II

existence. Japan's shipping problem was complex, for having no industry in her resources areas and no resources in her industrial area, she had to bring all raw materials to Japan for manufacture and then distribute them to the ultimate consumers which, in war, were the forces in the field. Basically there were two main routes required by these circumstances: across the Sea of Japan or the Yellow Sea to Japan to bring iron and coal from Manchuria, and, more important, the route from the Southern Resources Area past Formosa and the Ryukyus to the home islands. So long as these were the principal routes, Japan had little difficulty, for ships could travel loaded in both directions. But as military operations ceased in the Southern Resources Area, the requirements there fell off, and Japan was forced to send many ships down partially loaded or in ballast. In addition, when Japan extended her operations into the South Pacific, it became necessary for her to send ships from Japan directly to that area. One main route ran from Osaka to the Palaus, another from Tokyo-Yokohama to the Bonins, Saipan, Truk, and Rabaul, later continuing down into the Solomons. Ships unloaded in these areas were forced to undertake the long voyage back to Japan empty. The Japanese never established a triangular routing by which loaded ships would proceed from the Southern Resources Area to Japan, and after discharging cargo, reload for the southern Pacific, there deliver military supplies, and then proceed in ballast to the Resources Area for a repetition of the process. In this manner, each ship would be empty only one third of the time, while as the traffic was actually established, each ship spent approximately half her cruising time empty or lightly loaded. In other words, Japan's shipping pattern took the form of an inverted V with the apex in the home islands, whereas a delta-shaped pattern would have resulted in a more efficient use of available ships. The only exception to this V pattern was a secondary route from Balikpapan to the Palaus, Truk, and Rabaul for oil delivery to advanced elements of the fleet.[9] Thus Japanese ships were needlessly exposed to attack by

[9] In addition to these major routes, minor ones connected the islands in the Resources Area and served as feeders to the principal convoys.

American submarines and their carrying capacity was reduced by eight to ten per cent.

When the American order for unrestricted submarine warfare against enemy shipping was issued a few hours after the Japanese attack on Pearl Harbor, it was a break with tradition for American submariners, who had been trained for operations in accordance with international conventions. After all, the United States had entered World War I in protest against the German use of unrestricted submarine warfare. American officers and men had to readjust their thinking as a result of these orders from Washington. Yet the order was realistic. In modern total war, there is no effective distinction between contraband and non-contraband. All the shipping of a country is enrolled in the war effort, and the tankers and cargo ships of Japan, bringing in vital oil, rice, tin, rubber, iron, and coal, were as much a part of Japan's war machine as her battleships and aircraft carriers.

In the early months of the war, American submarine effort was largely limited to areas around the Philippines, to the waters east of Japan, and to the straits between the home islands—Bungo Suido between Shikoku and Kyushu, and Kii Suido, between Shikoku and Honshu. A few boats attacked ships on the Manila-Formosa-home islands run. The British and Dutch had a limited number of submarines operating and achieved considerable success in the Straits of Malacca against ships sailing between Rangoon and Singapore, sinking in all 16 warships and 39 merchant vessels, totaling 30,000 and 110,000 tons respectively.

Until April 1942 Japanese shipping sailed independently, without benefit of convoy escort. Growing losses however caused the Japanese to establish limited convoys at that time and to organize the First Convoy Escort Fleet in July with headquarters on Formosa. This force had the responsibility for escort of convoys in the East China Sea, or between Formosa and Japan, although later the convoys were extended into the South China Sea, to Manila, Saigon, and Singapore. These Japanese convoys were small in comparison to those of the North Atlantic, consisting of only six to ten ships escorted by a single old destroyer or smaller vessel. The reasons for Japanese neglect of convoy were similar to those of the British in late 1916 and in the 1930's. First, the Japanese underestimated the potential threat of Allied submarines. Second, they looked on convoy escort as defensive, and both the army and navy were offensive-minded, having contempt for defensive operations. In contrast, the Allies had come to regard escort of convoy as both defensive and offensive, offering the best chance for killing submarines. So long as the Japanese believed that convoy work was defensive, their convoys received little support from Combined Fleet headquarters, which even refused to permit fleet destroyers on the way to operating areas to serve en route as convoy escorts. Such assignment, said Combined Fleet, would interfere with the warships' basic missions. And escort vessels in any case were in short supply.

As the Japanese ultimately established their convoy system, they sacrificed the advantages of a strong offensive screen around a large convoy in favor of retaining as much of the flexibility of independent shipping as possible. This compromise was efficient neither in protecting ships nor in killing the attacking submarines, which could readily avoid a single escort. If the Japanese had employed convoys of 30 to 50 ships with five or six escorts, they would have given their ships greater safety at no loss in carrying capacity and with no increase in the number of ships allocated to escort work. In addition, these multiple escorts would have been much more dangerous to the attacking submarines than a single one could be. When the Japanese in November 1943 established a Grand Escort Command Headquarters and adopted more sizable convoys, the Americans resorted to wolf-pack operations as a counter. Yet in spite of all the weaknesses of Japanese convoys, sinkings of independently routed ships were two and a half times as numerous as those of ships in convoy. Furthermore the U.S. Navy lost more submarines to convoy escorts than they lost to patrols, mines, aircraft, or any other single agency. The inference is clear: Japan might have severely curtailed the effectiveness of the American submarines, if she had employed convoys earlier and more efficiently.

By the end of 1943, most Japanese shipping was provided with some kind of escort protection. In view of the small size of Japanese convoys, American wolf packs rarely comprised more than three submarines, a practice that promoted close-knit cooperation. Initial wolf-pack tactics called for a boat on each flank of the convoy and a third behind to get stragglers. Such station keeping on a sharply maneuvering convoy proved so difficult however that doctrine gave way to improvisation on the spot, and American skippers made themselves virtuosos of undersea warfare. They made kills at all hours, from all depths and angles, including "down the throat" and "up the kilt"—difficult shots from dead ahead and dead astern. The curve of sinkings soared.

With the increasing destruction of Japanese shipping, especially of vital tankers, the efficiency of Japan's war machine declined even more sharply. On the eve of the Philippine Sea battle, it will be recalled, scarcity of oil in the home islands forced the Mobile Fleet to base at Tawitawi. After the battle Admiral Ozawa took his fleet to Japan for repairs and ammunition, but there he found an acute shortage of fuel. So the fleet had to be divided, and Admiral Kurita took most of the surface vessels back south where there was oil aplenty but repair facilities and ammunition were lacking. The Imperial Fleet was thus caught in two widely separated parts when the Americans invaded the Philippines, precipitating the last great clash of fleets in the Battle for Leyte Gulf. Even then the Japanese might have achieved something had they been able to use their carriers as combatant ships rather than as mere decoys. But the carriers were powerless to strike because Japan, largely for lack of aviation fuel, could never train enough replacement pilots to offset the heavy losses which began with the Battle of Midway. Thus American submarines, patiently tracking and destroying oil-bearing ships from the East Indies,[10] divided the enemy's sea power and rendered him incapable of maintaining his air power.

Operation Barney— The Sea of Japan

By the spring of 1945, Japan was almost completely cut off from the Southern Re-

[10] One hundred and ten Japanese tankers were sunk by U.S. submarines.

sources Area, but she was still able to draw supplies from the mainland of Asia, especially Manchuria, across the Sea of Japan. Because all entrances to this sea were heavily mined, American submarines had not as a rule been able to operate in these waters. The *Wahoo* had made two daring penetrations into the Sea of Japan, but she had defective torpedoes on her first patrol and did not return from her second. Until some method could be found of avoiding the mines at the entrances, the Sea of Japan remained, as the submariners called it, "Hirohito's Lake," and the blockade of the islands could not be complete.

The answer came in a new electronic sonar device, FMS, which gave a visual presentation of objects in the water all around a submarine and which had sufficient powers of resolution to indicate mines as well as ships. Beset with growing pains, the device won slow acceptance by submariners, but eventually it proved the key to unlock the barred passageways into the Sea of Japan.

In possession of this device, Lockwood planned a penetration in force called Operation BARNEY. It involved nine submarines, *Sea Dog, Crevalle, Spadefish, Tinosa, Bonefish, Skate, Tunny, Flying Fish,* and *Bowfin,* which were to pass through Tsushima Strait in relays between June 3-6, and to commence operations against Japanese ships on the 9th. The *Sea Dog* leading the way, all boats got through successfully. Once in the Sea of Japan, all commanding officers had a hard time holding themselves in check until the official starting time, for the many Japanese ships they sighted were sailing on a peace-time basis singly, with no escort, and with running lights burning.[11] Operating in three wolf packs, but under such freedom as to be almost on individual patrols, the boats struck hard when the time came at last. They sank the submarine *I-122* and 28 merchant ships for a total of 55,000 tons. The *Bonefish* was lost, but the remaining eight submarines passed successfully out of La Perouse Strait north of Hokkaido on the night of June 24.[12]

[11] As one cynical torpedoman put it, "The skipper almost couldn't wait to open his packages."

[12] The successful completion of Operation BARNEY was the fulfillment of a naval tactician's dream. As far back as the Class of 1923 at the U.S. Naval

Summary

Because the Japanese looked upon the submarine primarily as an adjunct to fleet operations, they made little effort to interdict Allied shipping in the Pacific and no effort at first to protect their own shipping. It is ironic to consider that Japan's chief war aim in 1941 was to win control of the Southern Resources Area, yet she neglected the only means of bringing the rewards of conquest to Japan. When the Americans embarked on unrestricted submarine warfare, they found great opportunities against the unescorted ships of Japan but were hindered for some time by failures of their own torpedoes. By the time the torpedo defects were remedied in mid-1943, Japan had instituted a limited convoy system.

In contrast to the Atlantic, where the convoy had proved the key to Allied success in two World Wars, it failed the Japanese for several reasons. The escorts were ill-equipped, not suitable for convoy escort operations, and manned by ill-trained crews. Far too few escorts were provided for each convoy, the Japanese preferring to send six ships with one escort rather than 30 escorted by five, which would have given far greater protection. An attacking submarine could keep track of and avoid a single escort, but was immediately forced on the defensive by the presence of several. Hence escort of convoy failed for Japan, but even these weakly escorted convoys proved more difficult to attack than independent ships.

The story of the decline of the Japanese merchant marine is told graphically on page 808. Submarines sank 1,113 merchant vessels of over 500 tons, with an additional 65 "probables," for a total of 5,320,094 G.R.T. In addition they accounted for 201 sure and 13 probable naval ship kills, for a total of 577,626 displacement tons. This they achieved at a loss to themselves of 52 boats, all but seven in action against the Japanese. Before Japan could be invaded, before the atomic bombs

War College, Newport, R.I., the students concluded that only when Japan was completely isolated from the Asiatic Mainland could Japan be forced to surrender. Operation BARNEY served that purpose. [Footnote by Admiral Nimitz.]

were dropped, the Japanese were making surrender overtures, starved into defeat.

On 24 November 1945, Admiral Nimitz again stood on the narrow deck of a submarine in a change of command ceremony, this time to relinquish to Admiral Spruance the responsibilities of Cincpac and Cincpoa he had borne so long and so well. This time there perhaps was a concession to sentiment on the part of the commander of the greatest fleet in the world's history, for surely there were available plenty of more commodious decks than that of U.S.S. *Menhaden*. Every submariner in the fleet recognized the significance of the fact that a great commander deliberately carried out his last official duty in that command aboard a submarine. It was his salute to all of them for a job well done.

43:

The Defeat of Japan

As the war in the Pacific moved toward its inevitable conclusion, Allied leaders propounded various theories as to how Japan could most quickly and economically be made to surrender. Many submariners held the view that submarines could do the job alone, as U-boats had twice nearly defeated Britain. The scientists and military men involved in the Manhattan Project were convinced that once they produced the atomic bomb Japan could not long hold out—especially after the development of the B-29, capable of carrying the bomb, and the American conquest of the southern Marianas, providing airfields from which the target could be reached. Others pointed to the coming defeat of Germany or the promised invasion of Manchuria by the Russians as the final blow that would convince Japan that further resistance was futile. There was undoubted merit in all these views, yet the majority of Allied military leaders and statesmen adhered to one or a combination of three other theories. For convenience we may call these the Army Theory, the Navy Theory, and the Air Forces Theory, provided we understand that none of the three was advocated exclusively by any one service or branch.

The Army Theory regarded the invasion of Japan as a necessary step in breaking the Japanese will to resist. Military history supported this view, for in the past nations generally had capitulated only after invaders had occupied a substantial portion of their territory, usually including the capital. The Army Theory gained wider acceptance after the American conquest of Saipan, for here even Japanese civilians had committed suicide in wholesale numbers rather than surrender. This sort of fanaticism convinced many officers that nothing short of physical seizure of their home islands could make the Japanese stop fighting.

The Navy Theory, as old as naval history, proposed defeating Japan by means of blockade. Like England, Japan was peculiarly vulnerable to attacks on her sea communications. An island nation, overpopulated and lacking internal resources for carrying on modern warfare, she was absolutely dependent upon imports. She had gambled all she had won in Asia by warring on the United States to obtain unimpeded access to the essential oil, rubber, and other products of the East Indies. With the recapture of the Philippines and the virtual destruction of Japanese sea and air power, Allied air, surface, and subsurface forces operating from Luzon would be able to interdict the flow of materials from the Southern Resources Area and thus gradually render Japan incapable of fighting.

The Air Forces Theory was that Japan could be defeated by continuous bombing of her cities and industries until she lacked the will and means to make war. Though bombers from the Marianas could reach Tokyo, airfields still nearer Japan would have to be captured for such strategic bombing to achieve maximum effect.

In line with the American policy of "unremitting pressure" on Japanese military and naval power, the Joint Chiefs of Staff directed operations to put into effect all means of defeating the enemy—and all except actual invasion of the Japanese home islands were carried out.

The Navy Finds New Objectives

The Battle for Leyte Gulf was the Trafalgar of World War II. Halsey and Kinkaid in 1944, like Nelson in 1805, had finally wiped out the Japanese fleet as an effective fighting force. There would be no more stand-up battles at sea in this war. Moreover the United States Navy in bringing the Army to the Philippines had apparently assured the success of the Navy's primary objective of cutting Japan's communications with the Southern Resources Area.

After Trafalgar the Royal Navy had been at loose ends, not quite knowing what to do with its fighting fleets. In consequence it had spent several years engaging in all sorts of eccentric operations before it found its true function. While continuing to control the sea, the Royal Navy put the Army on the Continent and kept it supplied and reinforced where it could come actively to grips with Napoleon.

After Leyte Gulf the United States Navy had no doubts regarding its further function. It had entered World War II with a well-established tradition of cooperating closely with the sister service. After the Navy had attained its own major objective in the fall of 1944, it continued to assist the Army and the Army Air Forces to attain theirs. The 21st Bomber Command, based on the Marianas, was hampered because fighter planes lacked sufficient range to support the B-29's in the long flight to Japan and back. So following the Battle for Leyte Gulf Admiral Halsey prepared to take the Third Fleet north for a joint raid on Tokyo. He did not make the move however, for it soon appeared that the Sixth Army still required the support of the Third Fleet in the Philippines campaign.

The Leyte Campaign

The Japanese High Command had correctly estimated that the two transpacific lines of Allied advance would converge on the Philippines, and the operations of the U.S. Third Fleet in the fall of 1944 convinced them that an invasion was imminent. From Manchuria in early October Imperial Headquarters transferred Japan's ablest army commander, General Tomoyuki Yamashita, conqueror of Singapore, to command the Japanese army in the Philippines. Uncertain where the impending invasion would come, Yamashita kept his

387,000 troops distributed through the islands. As a result, when the Americans landed on October 20, there were only 22,000 Japanese troops on Leyte. The High Command nevertheless decreed that here the decisive battle for the Philippines must be fought. Hence Yamashita began rushing reinforcements to Leyte, and the Mobile Fleet began converging on Leyte Gulf. The crushing defeat of the Imperial Navy in the battle of October 23–26 did not alter the basic Japanese plan.

Torrential rains brought by the monsoons soon turned Leyte into a quagmire that minimized the American superiority in numbers of troops and in motorized equipment. The invaders had found only one usable airstrip on the island, that at Tacloban. Efforts by U.S. Army Engineers to improve or construct others were for a long time defeated by a combination of continuing rain and unsuitable subsoil. At the same time the Japanese were staging in fresh planes from Formosa and the home islands and operating from the all-weather airfields of Luzon. A few days after the Battle for Leyte Gulf, General MacArthur directed the Army Air Force to relieve the Seventh Fleet escort carriers of responsibility for air operations in the Leyte area. When the little carriers departed however, the Air Force proved unable to take over. It did not have enough planes available, it did not have enough usable airfields, and its aviators were not trained to provide the sort of support that was needed at Leyte. As a result, the U.S. Third Fleet was obliged to return to Philippine waters. At the end of October, Admiral McCain assumed temporary command of TF 38 in order to give Admiral Mitscher a much-needed rest.

In late October and November 1944 Third Fleet aviators, striking chiefly at Luzon airfields and at enemy shipping in the Luzon area and en route to Leyte, destroyed about 700 planes and sank three cruisers, ten destroyers, and numerous transports and other auxiliaries. They sent one complete convoy to the bottom, drowning about 10,000 Japanese. Further to supplement his inadequate land-based air power, General MacArthur in November ordered marine air groups up from the Solomons to provide close air support for his troops and borrowed other marine groups from Peleliu to cope with the wily Japanese night bombers.

Despite all efforts the Americans could not regain command of the air in the Leyte area. Kamikazes struck repeatedly at the Third and Seventh Fleets. In Halsey's fleet they damaged six carriers. In Kinkaid's they hit two battleships, two cruisers, two attack transports, and seven destroyers, one of which, the *Abner Read*, sank. After a particularly severe suicide attack on TF 38 on November 25, the Third Fleet temporarily ceased operating in Philippine waters. It had been at sea and in combat almost continuously for three months.

The Japanese, in spite of severe losses, by mid-November had 70,000 troops on Leyte to resist the 100,000 Americans then on the island. Joining the campaign to cut down Japanese reinforcements, PT boats occasionally slipped around west of Leyte, where they sank a number of troop-carrying barges, two freighters, two small transports, and two patrol craft. After the departure of the Third Fleet, Kinkaid had minesweepers clear the passage between Leyte and Bohol. (See map page 790.) He then sent small groups of destroyers around for night sweeps, chiefly off Ormoc, the principal port on the west coast. The first destroyer sweep sank a surfaced submarine. The second sank a freighter. The third, sent to attack a Japanese convoy approaching Ormoc, was itself furiously attacked by aircraft and by a pair of destroyers. The Americans sank one of the Japanese destroyers, but the other succeeded in putting a torpedo into u.s. destroyer *Cooper,* which broke in two and went down in less than a minute.

By December 1 Japanese casualties were far exceeding reinforcements. By the same date the number of American troops on Leyte had increased to 183,000. Nevertheless American combat operations, supplied over muddy, primitive roads, had slowed down. The U.S. 1st Cavalry Division was making a hotly contested advance through the mountains toward Ormoc from the north. The U.S. 7th Infantry Division was making a similarly contested coastal drive toward Ormoc from the south. To accelerate operations and shorten the campaign, Lieutenant General Walter Krueger, Commander

Sixth Army, decided to divide the enemy by landing troops between the Japanese fighting the U.S. 1st Division in the north and those fighting the U.S. 7th Division south of Ormoc. On December 6 two regimental combat teams of the 77th Infantry Division embarked in beaching craft and destroyer-transports and were escorted around to the western side of Leyte by twelve Seventh Fleet destroyers. At sunrise on the 7th they began landing three miles south of Ormoc. Because the Japanese defenders had been drawn away from the Ormoc area in an attempt to stop the simultaneous American advances down from the north and up from the south, the landing was virtually unopposed. Only after the troops were safely ashore did the Japanese react. Then the naval force, still off the beachhead, came under fierce attack by kamikazes that outnumbered the combat air patrol of U.S. Army fighters. Crashing suicide planes so damaged destroyer *Mahan* and destroyer-transport *Ward* that both had to be abandoned and sunk. A few days later kamikazes hit the second resupply convoy to the new beachhead, sinking destroyer *Reid* and heavily damaging destroyer *Caldwell.* The evident improvement in the techniques used by the suicide pilots boded increasing peril to Allied naval operations against the Japanese.

The American landing on the Leyte west coast proved decisive. The 77th Division promptly took Ormoc and then moved up Ormoc Valley, making contact on December 21 with the southward advancing 1st Division. Though destroying the Japanese survivors, most of whom were now sealed off in the northwest peninsula, was to require four more months, General MacArthur could declare on Christmas Day that all organized resistance on Leyte had ended. American troops and Filipino guerrillas had already liberated nearby, more lightly held Samar. On December 26 Lieutenant General Robert L. Eichelberger relieved General Krueger, taking over the command of the American troops in the Leyte area, who were now designated U.S. Eighth Army—a change of command and force designation similar to that of the U.S. Third-Fifth Fleet the preceding August. By the time the army under Eichelberger completed the conquest of Leyte, about a thousand Japanese had succeeded in escaping from the island, 400 had surrendered, and about 68,000 had been killed or died of starvation or disease. American casualties ashore for the entire campaign were 12,000 wounded and 3,500 killed.

The Return to Luzon

Long before Leyte was secured, General MacArthur's staff had begun planning for the recapture of Manila. First however airfields would have to be secured nearer Luzon and on the western side of the Philippines, outside the monsoon rain belt. So on December 13 the Third Fleet, after two weeks' rest at Ulithi, again stood to east of the Philippines and began operations against Luzon airfields in preparation for an Allied landing on Mindoro Island, 300 miles northwest of Leyte. Meanwhile a Seventh Fleet invasion convoy, the Mindoro Attack Force, carrying 12,000 combat, 9,500 Air Force, and 6,000 service troops had set out for Mindoro via Surigao Strait and the Mindanao and Sulu seas. Admiral Kinkaid also sent along a covering force of six escort carriers, with battleships, cruisers, and destroyers in the screen. Further cover and support would be provided by the Fifth Air Force, operating from Leyte.

Detected by the Japanese during the approach, the Mindoro Attack Force became the target of numerous kamikazes, one of which hit the convoy flagship *Nashville,* killing 133 officers and men, wounding 190, and obliging the cruiser to return to Leyte. Another suicide plane severely damaged a destroyer, which also had to turn back. However, with tactical cover by planes from the escort carriers and from Leyte and strategic support from Halsey's fast carriers, the invaders went ashore on December 15 without opposition. Only after the assault troops were ashore did the kamikazes succeed in making a D-day strike, which cost the expeditionary force two LST's.

All the aircraft that attacked Mindoro and the Mindoro Attack Force between December 14 and 16 were from the Central Philippines. The Third Fleet was keeping the airfields on Luzon blanketed, maintaining an umbrella of fighters over them around the clock to prevent planes from taking off. In the process the

Third Fleet planes destroyed nearly 200 enemy aircraft, mostly on the ground. This achievement was the result of one of several innovations that Admiral McCain had introduced into TF 38 to meet the threat of the kamikazes. He had cut the number of dive bombers aboard his heavy carriers to less than half, and more than doubled the number of fighters. The change actually increased the striking power of the carriers because the Hellcat and Corsair fighters had been modified to carry 2,000 pounds of bombs and thus became dual-purpose planes.

During the same period not a single enemy plane reached TF 38. McCain as a further countermeasure had reduced the number of task groups from four to three in order to concentrate his antiaircraft fire and combat air patrol. Moreover while strikes were in progress, radar picket destroyers were stationed 60 miles from the task force on the flanks of the target-bearing line to give early warning of approaching enemy planes. The pickets had their own combat air patrol, and American planes returning from a strike were required to make a turn around a specified picket so that the destroyer's air patrol could weed out any kamikazes that had joined the returning planes as a means of locating the carriers. Aircraft approaching the task force from a direction other than that of the designated picket destroyer were assumed to be enemy and were treated accordingly.

On December 17, TF 38 withdrew eastward to refuel, but worsening weather obliged Halsey to discontinue fueling a little after noon. On the morning of the 18th, a small, tight typhoon, which the aerologists had not detected, struck the task force in full fury. The commanding officers of destroyers *Hull, Monaghan,* and *Spence,* hoping to take on much-needed fuel, waited too long to reballast their partly empty tanks with sea water. As a result all three destroyers capsized at the height of the storm and went down. Seven other ships were heavily damaged; 186 planes were jettisoned, blown overboard, or collided and burned; and nearly 800 officers and men were lost. The task force was as badly battered as if it had fought a major battle.

Because of the typhoon and the delay in fueling, TF 38 could not carry out strikes on

Luzon scheduled for December 19–21. On the 21st the strikes still could not be carried out because the typhoon was then passing over Luzon. So the Third Fleet returned to Ulithi, where the crews got some much-needed rest, and Service Squadron 10 repaired the storm-damaged ships. During the short respite at Ulithi, Admiral McCain and his staff devised more means for increasing the Third Fleet's combat efficiency. Some of the carriers were assigned a still higher proportion of the dual-purpose fighters, including two squadrons of Marine Corsairs, the first marine planes to operate from carriers. A special duty task group, comprising the *Enterprise* and *Independence* with a screen of six destroyers, was organized in TF 38 to specialize in night operations, including bombing, search, combat air patrol, and special missions. On December 30 the Third Fleet departed Ulithi to support the impending invasion of Luzon with a strike at Formosa.

Meanwhile, Allied operations on Mindoro and on the Mindoro supply line continued under sporadic enemy attack. Kamikazes on December 21 struck the first resupply convoy, sinking two more LST's. On Christmas Eve a Japanese cruiser-destroyer force—the one that Admiral Shima had commanded in the Battle of Surigao Strait—departed Camranh Bay, Indo-China, and set out eastward across the South China Sea. Concealed by foul weather, this force was within 200 miles of Mindoro when it was sighted by a Leyte-based navy reconnaissance plane. There were at that time no Allied naval vessels in the area larger than PT boats. Arriving off Mindoro in the night of December 26–27, the Japanese ships briefly bombarded an airfield but were driven off by air attack. While they were retiring a PT boat sank one of the destroyers with a spread of torpedoes. At the end of the year a resupply convoy to Mindoro, attacked by Japanese aircraft, lost four ships, including an ammunition vessel that blew up and sank with her entire crew. In the same convoy, kamikazes damaged four more ships. Off Mindoro in the next few days three cargo vessels were bombed from the air, and a kamikaze rammed into an ammunition ship, which instantly exploded, killing another entire crew. The attacks on Mindoro then abruptly ended, for the Japanese shifted

their attention to the Allied forces heading for Luzon. By that time there were on Mindoro three operational airfields. These proved invaluable in supporting the Luzon invasion.

The assault on Luzon was to be north of Manila inside Lingayen Gulf, where the Japanese had landed three years before. The expeditionary force, scheduled to make the assault on January 9, 1945, was about the same as for the invasion of Leyte: the Sixth Army and the Seventh Fleet supplemented by the Third Amphibious Force from the Pacific Fleet. The Army Air Force, operating from Morotai, Leyte, and Mindoro would cover the convoys and operate against airfields in southern Luzon. Further cover was to be provided by escort carriers accompanying the invasion forces. Halsey's Third Fleet, still stripped down to TF 38, would interdict airfields on Formosa and northern Luzon.

The Lingayan assault was spearheaded by a support force of 164 ships, including 6 old battleships, 12 escort carriers, 10 destroyer-transports carrying underwater demolition teams, and 63 minesweepers. This force, commanded by Vice Admiral Oldendorf, was to proceed to Lingayen Gulf to sweep mines, search the beach approaches, and give shore defenses three days of bombardment before the amphibious forces arrived. As it turned out, the principal contribution of the support force was to serve as bait for the kamikazes, which very nearly expended themselves on Oldendorf's advance echelon before the transports arrived.[1]

In the late afternoon of January 2, as Oldendorf's leading group debouched from Surigao Strait, it was seen and reported by a Japanese lookout in a church steeple on high ground on the northeastern point of Mindanao.

[1] Beginning with the American invasion of Peleliu, as we have seen, the Japanese defenders took the preparatory naval bombardment as a signal to withdraw from the beachhead area to strong positions inland. In Europe, on the contrary, the bombardment continued to attract defending reinforcements to the beachhead area. As the reader will recall, Allied army commanders in the European theater, anticipating this, at first insisted on night landings, with no naval bombardment at all. Later, to avoid the confusion inevitable in a night assault, they staged daylight landings but generally limited the preparatory naval bombardment to a brief period between dawn and sunrise.

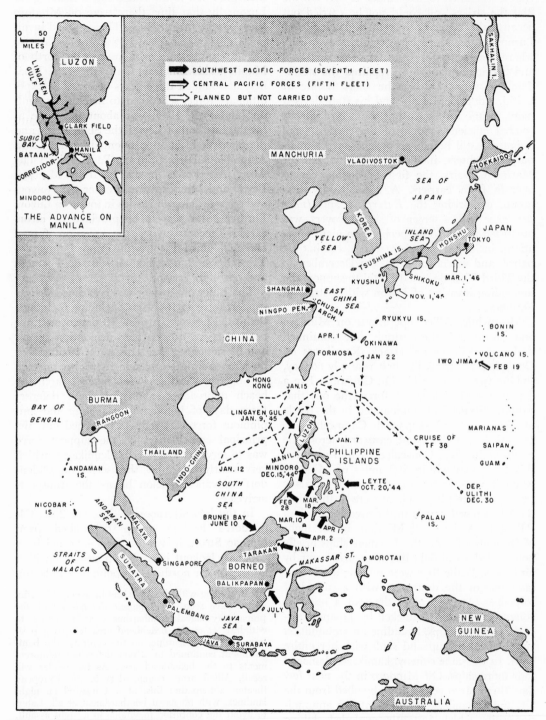

FINAL OPERATIONS OF THE WAR AGAINST JAPAN

The next morning in the Mindanao Sea, a Japanese bomber made a suicide crash on an oiler in the group, doing little material damage but killing two men. This was the ominous beginning of a kamikaze campaign that, in proportion to numbers of planes committed, was the most effective of the war.

When Oldendorf's force reached the Sulu Sea, the Japanese, as we have seen, terminated operations against shipping at Mindoro and went after the new and fatter targets. In the afternoon of January 4, as the Lingayen support force was passing to westward of Panay, a two-engine bomber dived into the flight deck of the *Ommaney Bay*. The carrier, aflame and torn by internal explosions, had to be abandoned and sunk. The next day, as the force stood off Manila, 16 kamikazes succeeded in penetrating the combat air patrol. Suicide planes crashed into u.s. heavy cruiser *Louisville*, H.M.A. heavy cruiser *Australia*, u.s. escort carrier *Manila Bay*, a destroyer escort, and an LCI gunboat, and caused damage to four other vessels with near misses. It began to appear that the Special Attack Corps had indeed found the long-sought-for means of repelling Allied invasions.

On January 6, as the heavy ships were entering Lingayen Gulf preceded by the minesweepers, the kamikazes began a series of furious attacks that between 1145 and sunset damaged eleven ships and sank one. Suicide planes crashed into battleships *New Mexico* and *California,* cruiser *Columbia,* three destroyers, a destroyer-transport, a seaplane tender, and a minesweeper. Cruisers *Louisville* and *Australia* were each hit a second time. Minesweeper *Long,* hit twice, her back broken, capsized and went down. Since leaving Leyte Gulf Oldendorf's force had suffered 325 men killed and nearly 800 wounded by enemy aircraft. Nevertheless both minesweeping and shore bombardment proceeded on schedule.

The attacks on the Lingayen support force might have been even more severe if the Third Fleet, despite murky weather, had not hit Formosan airfields on January 4 and again on the 5th. As a result of these strikes, no reinforcements of aircraft reached Luzon from the north. Halsey's planes struck Luzon airfields on the 6th, according to schedule, but continuing foul weather made blanketing of the fields impossible. On the 7th, at Kinkaid's request, Halsey again struck Luzon, canceling a scheduled strike on Formosa. This time the combination of Third Fleet carrier, Seventh Fleet escort carrier, and Army Air Force planes very nearly put Luzon airfields out of operation. Only a few enemy planes appeared over Lingayen Gulf that day, and most of these were shot down. Two more minesweepers were sunk however, one by aerial bombs, the other by an airborne torpedo. The Japanese had now decided to evacuate what planes they could from the Philippines. After January 7 there were no more organized air attacks on the Allied forces, but individual pilots struck at the Allied shipping from time to time on their own initiative.

The amphibious forces, bringing elements of the Sixth Army from various points in the South and Southwest Pacific Areas, were now en route to Luzon. In Leyte Gulf General MacArthur, in light cruiser *Boise,* joined Admiral Barbey's Seventh Amphibious Force (TF 78), which carried the I Corps (6th and 43rd Infantry Divisions); and Admiral Kinkaid, in AGC *Wasatch,* joined Admiral Wilkinson's Third Amphibious Force (TF 79), which carried the XIV Corps (37th and 40th Infantry Divisions). Barbey's force then led the way toward Lingayen Gulf, using the same route that Oldendorf had taken. Use of the shorter route, via San Bernardino Strait, was out of the question so long as the Japanese had airfields in southern Luzon.

As Admiral Barbey's force was passing via Mindoro Strait into the South China Sea early on January 7, it came under air attack, and a bomb narrowly missed the *Boise.* That afternoon a kamikaze penetrated intense antiaircraft fire and crashed into an LST. The next morning, as Barbey's force stood off Luzon, a bomb-carrying Japanese fighter dived into escort carrier *Kadashan Bay,* putting her out of action. Shortly afterward another kamikaze crashed into a troop-filled transport. Wilkinson's force also came under attack on the 8th, a little before sunset. In this force escort carrier *Kitkun Bay* was crashed by a suicide plane and extensively damaged. Inside the Gulf that day, the *Australia* was hit twice more, but refused Admiral Oldendorf's offer to relieve her of further duties.

Despite the air attacks, the amphibious forces arrived in Lingayen Gulf on schedule, and at sunrise on January 9 all transports were in position for a landing. A few minutes later three kamikazes appeared. One knocked down the mast of a destroyer escort; another crashed into the *Columbia,* already heavily damaged by her earlier hit. In the afternoon a kamikaze dived into battleship *Mississippi,* causing heavy casualties, and the luckless *Australia* took her fifth hit.

Meanwhile the assault troops had made their landings with no opposition except from Japanese batteries in the hills on the north flank of the beachhead. Oldendorf's heavy and prolonged bombardment had not been necessary, for the Japanese were employing their new tactics of contesting the beaches, if at all, only with delaying forces. General Yamashita with the bulk of his army was already withdrawing northward to make a stand in the mountains. By sunset on the 9th the invaders had penetrated inland as deep as three miles.

That night, while the ships in Lingayen Gulf lay under a blanket of smoke to conceal them from air attack, some 70 plywood powerboats, manned by Japanese troops and carrying depth charges, headed for the fleet. Most were repelled by gunfire and nearly all were destroyed, but a few managed to release their explosives against the sides of Allied vessels and then speed away. In this manner an LCI was sunk, and a transport, an LCI, and four LST's were damaged.

On the night of January 9–10 also, Halsey boldly led the Third Fleet through Luzon Strait and penetrated deep into the South China Sea. In the absence of McCain's carrier planes to keep the northern Luzon airfields neutralized, individual kamikazes began to appear over Lingayen Gulf in greater numbers, striking at arriving and departing Allied convoys. The suicide planes damaged two ships on January 10, nine on the 12th, and three on the 13th. The kamikaze attacks on the Seventh Fleet then sputtered out. Since January 3, Japanese aircraft, mostly kamikazes, had damaged 43 Allied vessels, 18 seriously, and sunk 4; and they had killed 738 men of the Allied forces and wounded nearly 1,400.

Halsey had entered the South China Sea to safeguard the Mindoro-Lingayen supply line by attacking a Japanese fleet, including battleships *Ise* and *Hyuga,* presumed to be in Camranh Bay. On January 12 McCain's carrier aircraft flew nearly 1,500 sorties over the Indo-China coast without finding any signs of the enemy fleet, which had prudently departed for Lingga Roads some time before. But there was shipping aplenty, and the TF 38 planes sank 44 ships, including a dozen tankers and light cruiser *Kashii.* They also destroyed more than a hundred enemy aircraft. On the 15th the carrier squadrons hit Takao on the southwest coast of Formosa. Here they were hampered by low ceilings but managed to sink a destroyer and a transport, to disable a tanker, and to wreck 34 planes. The next day they struck the China coast, concentrating on the Hong Kong area, but again they were partially defeated by bad weather, and they lost 22 planes from intense antiaircraft fire. Their score in this attack was a freighter and a tanker sunk, four more ships heavily damaged, and 13 planes destroyed. On January 17 TF 38 began refueling from a fast fueling group that had followed it into the waters west of Luzon. Then while Radio Tokyo was announcing to the world that the U.S. Third Fleet was bottled up in the South China Sea, Halsey slipped back through Luzon Strait at night under an overcast and re-entered the Pacific.

Before returning to Ulithi to turn his fleet over to Spruance in accordance with the plan for alternating commands, Halsey struck again at Formosa, sinking five tankers and five freighters and destroying at least 60 planes on the ground. This time Japanese aircraft succeeded in striking back. A bomb hit light carrier *Langley,* and suicide planes crashed into heavy carrier *Ticonderoga* and picket destroyer *Maddox.* The *Langley,* only moderately damaged, was able to continue operations, but the kamikaze victims had to retire to Ulithi under escort. The rest of TF 38 moved northeast for photo-reconnaissance of Okinawa in preparation for an impending American assault. On January 25 the Third Fleet steamed back into Ulithi Lagoon, having completed its mission of supporting MacArthur's Southwest Pacific forces in their invasion of the Philippines. Halsey was well satisfied. "I am so proud of you," said he in his farewell message to the Fleet, "that no words can express my feelings. . . . Superlatively well done!"

With the return of the Third Fleet to Ulithi, the lines of advance of the Central Pacific forces and of the Southwest Pacific forces diverged. Most of the ships on loan to the Seventh Fleet came again under Nimitz' command for operations northward, in the direction of Japan. At the same time, MacArthur was planning a drive southward for recovery of the rest of the Philippines and of the East Indies.

The Liberation of the Philippines

While the I Corps contained Yamashita in the hills northeast of Lingayen Gulf, the XIV Corps advanced on Manila. On January 29, 1945, the Seventh Amphibious Force put 30,000 troops ashore without opposition on the Luzon west coast near Subig Bay, both to prevent the Japanese from withdrawing into Bataan Peninsula and to provide additional punch for the drive on Manila from the north. Two days later, 8,000 Americans landed south of Manila Bay for an advance on Manila from the southwest. The XIV Corps' final drive from the north was assisted and expedited by two Marine Air Groups that dispelled the skepticism of army commanders by successfully providing close air support for the ground forces. On February 4 the XIV Corps reached Manila, which was defended by 16,000 naval troops and 5,000 soldiers. There followed a solid month of fighting, street by street and house by house, until the last of the Japanese garrison had been killed or captured, and the city was a shambles.

Before Manila fell, operations were initiated to secure the bay and harbor. (See map page 369.) On February 15 a regimental combat team went ashore at the tip of Bataan Peninsula against negligible opposition. The next day the island fortress of Corregidor was assaulted by a regimental combat team of paratroops from the air and a battalion landing team of infantry from the sea. The conquest of Corregidor proved an unexpectedly costly and time-consuming operation, partly because Intelligence had estimated the enemy garrison at 850, whereas there were actually nearly six

times as many Japanese on the island. The Rock was finally secured in early March. Conquest of the other islands at the mouth of the Bay extended into April. Commodore William A. Sullivan, who had played a major part in clearing the ports of Casablanca, Palermo, Naples, Cherbourg, and Le Havre, was by then busy directing operations to clear the harbor of Manila. This proved Sullivan's hardest task of the war, for here the Japanese had sunk hundreds of ships. By the time the port was in regular use, troops put ashore at Legaspi (see map page 655) had secured Luzon's southeast peninsula, thereby easing the problem of supplying the American forces on Luzon by opening San Bernardino Strait to Allied communications.

While General Krueger's Sixth Army was pursuing General Yamashita's 170,000 surviving troops into the mountains of Luzon, Admiral Kinkaid's Seventh Fleet, now stripped of the Third Amphibious Force, cooperated with General Eichelberger's Eighth Army in clearing the enemy out of the rest of the Philippines. This operation was contrary to the intention of the Joint Chiefs of Staff, who had expected the Filipinos to complete the job of liberation by themselves. But since the forces under General MacArthur were not immediately needed elsewhere, the Joint Chiefs raised no objections.

Between late February and mid-April 1945, Admiral Barbey's Seventh Amphibious Force staged no fewer than 38 landings in the Central and Southern Philippines. These were all minor operations compared to the assaults on Leyte and Luzon. Though some of the islands were fairly heavily garrisoned, the defenders had almost no aircraft; and no naval forces came to their aid, for Japan had written the Philippines off. Moreover, in accordance with current doctrine, the Japanese defenders never seriously opposed the landings. They held the cities as long as they could, wrecked them with demolition charges when forced out, and then withdrew to the mountains, where far more died from starvation and disease than as a result of military operations. Usually only a small fraction of the original garrison survived till the general surrender at the end of the war.

The first of the new series of landings were carried out on February 28 against Palawan Island and on March 10 against Zamboanga, the tip of the western tail of Mindanao. Allied aircraft operating from these positions could intercept enemy naval units approaching the Central Philippines from the Celebes and South China seas. The Americans then invaded Panay, Negros, Cebu, Bohol, and a number of smaller Central Philippine islands. At the same time they advanced southwest from Zamboanga, landing without opposition on the islands of Basilan, Tawitawi, and Jolo in the Sulu Archipelago. These islands, along with Palawan, provided airfields for close support of MacArthur's planned assault on Borneo. Lastly, the Americans staged a series of invasions of the mainland of Mindanao. Here the purpose was to complete the work of a 25,000-man guerrilla army that already controlled 95 per cent of the island and had confined the Japanese garrison of 42,000 to the cities and a few other strong points. From beachheads on the west, north, and south coasts, the invaders advanced, splitting the Japanese forces and preventing them from achieving a united front. The Americans then ousted the enemy from the cities into the countryside, where the Filipino guerrillas kept them under attack until the end of the war.

The Royal Navy

After the surrender of the Italian fleet in September 1943, the Royal Navy was at last able to release some ships to the Indian Ocean. By the following January the British Eastern Fleet, commanded by Admiral Sir James Somerville, was again operating out of Ceylon. At British request, Admiral Nimitz loaned Admiral Somerville u.s. carrier *Saratoga* to teach the Eastern Fleet American methods of carrier operations. In the spring of 1944 Somerville's fleet with the *Saratoga* and H.M. carrier *Illustrious* raided Japanese bases on and around Sumatra and Java.

With the defeat of the U-boat and the successful invasions of France, the Royal Navy by the late summer of 1944 was virtually without employment in the Atlantic and Mediterranean theaters. The U.S. Joint Chiefs of Staff therefore pressed the British to employ their naval forces against Borneo, relieving the U.S. Seventh Fleet in support of Australian troops under General MacArthur. Recapture of Borneo would deprive the Japanese of their principal oil wells and refineries and at the same time provide British and American fleets in the Far East with a handy source of fuel at an enormous saving in tankers.

The British Chiefs of Staff agreed and began planning for a return to Borneo. When the Americans announced their intention of invading Japan in 1945 however, Prime Minister Churchill felt that the British should participate—as American forces had participated in the invasions of North Africa, Italy, and France. Accordingly he offered the British fleet for operations under American command in the Pacific Ocean, and President Roosevelt accepted the offer. Admirals King and Nimitz were at first dismayed over this decision. As they saw it, the British ships could be used to best advantage in the East Indies, while in the Pacific they were not needed. Second, British fleet carriers were neither constructed nor trained to support large-scale amphibious assaults. Lastly, the facilities of Nimitz' Service Force were already stretched to the limit in meeting the logistic needs of the U.S. Pacific Fleet. King insisted that if the Royal Navy joined the operations against Japan, it must provide its own service force, a stipulation to which the British agreed. In the end however most of the service vessels attached to the British Pacific Fleet had to be supplied by the United States, and the British carriers had to be provided with American planes since their own were too short-ranged for distant operations.

As a result of Churchill's offer and Roosevelt's acceptance, the reconquest of Borneo was left to the Australian army and the Seventh Fleet, under the over-all command of General MacArthur. The fastest and best ships of the Royal Navy proceeded via the Indian Ocean to join the forces under Admiral Nimitz. En route, during December 1944 and January 1945, the British Pacific Fleet made three carrier attacks on the oil refineries of Sumatra—both to cut down the supply of aviation fuel reaching Japanese air forces in Burma and to gain the sort of combat experience needed for the war against Japan. Left behind in the Indian Ocean were the older and slower British and allied ships, now called the East Indies Fleet.

The first task of the East Indies Fleet was to support the British campaign in Burma by covering the sea approaches and by staging an amphibious assault in early May 1945 on the port of Rangoon. But so rapidly was the situation ashore turning in favor of the British that the Japanese had evacuated Rangoon before the assault could be launched. A little later however five destroyers operating in support of the Burma campaign had their hour of glory. Pursuing a Japanese vessel reported damaged by an escort carrier plane, they overtook her in darkness off the Strait of Malacca and found they were confronting a heavy cruiser—actually the *Haguro*, which had fought with Kurita's Center Force in the Battle for Leyte Gulf. The destroyers nevertheless attacked, eluded the cruiser's superior fire, surrounded her, and sent her down with torpedoes.

The Borneo Campaign

MacArthur's Borneo campaign opened with an assault on Tarakan Island off the east coast, with the objective of capturing oil fields and airstrips. Eschewing surprise, elements of the Seventh Amphibious Force spent several days sweeping mines and clearing obstacles off the beachhead. On April 30, 1945, troops went ashore on an adjoining island and emplaced artillery to support the main landing. At dawn on D-day, May 1, an attack group, including American and Australian cruisers and destroyers, under Rear Admiral Forrest B. Royal USN, arrived off Tarakan and began landing 18,000 troops, mostly Australian but including some American and Dutch. The 2,300 Japanese defenders, as usual at this stage of the war, offered no opposition at the beach, but in the interior they put up stubborn resistance, requiring the invaders to call for destroyer gunfire support for nearly a month. A small remnant of the Japanese garrison held out on Tarakan till the end of the war.

On June 10 Admiral Royal's task group took more Australian troops around to the opposite coast for a series of landings in the Brunei Bay area. All the invasions were monotonously similar—extensive minesweeping followed by unopposed landings, which in turn were generally followed by increasing resistance in the interior. The sole novelty was the appearance of a few Japanese planes which did no damage. North Borneo was declared secured on July 1.

On the same date a Seventh Fleet attack group, including three American escort carriers, eight cruisers (five American, two Australian, and one Dutch), and nine destroyers, commanded by Rear Admiral Albert Noble, USN, put a reinforced division of Australian troops ashore near the oil-rich port of Balikpapan on Makassar Strait. This invasion was unique in several respects: it was carried out against the most formidable beach defenses that the Southwest Forces encountered during the entire war; it was preceded by 16 days of naval bombardment, the longest for any amphibious assault of the war; and it was the final invasion of the war.

Balikpapan's defensive strength was based on natural conditions similar to those at Omaha Beach on the Normandy coast—shallow approaches and hills behind the beaches. For many months the Allies themselves had been inadvertently contributing to Balikpapan's defenses by dropping acoustic and magnetic mines from the air into the harbor in an effort to cut down the outflow of oil to Japanese forces elsewhere. The defenders had sown more mines and constructed obstacles in the shallows and had emplaced numerous guns in the hills. Even though the Japanese here could count on no surface and little air support, they appeared prepared to make any would-be invader pay dearly.

But Allied amphibious forces had by now attained such power and precision that apparently no beachhead could hold out against them. Allied air forces, correctly estimating the situation at Balikpapan, attacked the new beachhead prior to invasion for a solid month, expending 3,000 tons of bombs. On June 17 the Seventh Fleet support vessels arrived off Balikpapan and began their bombardment. By D-day they had fired at the shore defenses 38,000 rounds of shell, 114,000 rounds from automatic weapons, and 7,300 rockets. Meanwhile motor minesweepers had swept the approaches, and underwater demolition teams had blasted holes through the obstructions. The minesweepers, working in water too shallow for close gunfire support, took the brunt of the Japanese fire. Only three sweepers were hit, but three others, in dodging enemy shells, ran into mines and were blown up.

So thorough and effective was the preparation for the Balikpapan invasion that on July 1 the assault troops, in 17 waves, went ashore without suffering a single casualty. In the high interior however the invaders as usual met stiffening resistance. For a week the cruisers remained off shore to provide fire support, expending 23,000 more rounds of shell. There followed two additional weeks of attack and counterattack before the last of the Japanese defenders had been killed or had fled the area. By that time the invasion forces had advanced some 50 miles to the north, seizing oil wells and refineries. Australian losses for the entire operation were 229 killed. Seventh Fleet losses were seven killed in the damaged and destroyed minesweepers.

With the completion of the Borneo campaign, General MacArthur planned to advance on Java. This time however the Joint Chiefs of Staff called a halt to his southward drive. All available Allied strength was to be concentrated for an invasion of Japan, for which MacArthur was to command the ground forces.

The Capture of Iwo Jima

We must now backtrack a few months to observe the activities of Nimitz' Central Pacific forces, which were again operating independently of MacArthur's Southwest Pacific forces.

In late November 1944, B-29's of the 21st Bomber Command, based on Saipan, had begun raiding the Tokyo area. The results from the Allied point of view were less than satisfactory because the big bombers were operating under severe handicaps. The 3,000-mile round trip required them to cut their bomb loads from a possible ten to three tons. Lack of fighter support obliged them to make fuel-consuming climbs to around 28,000 feet, an altitude from which precision bombing was impossible. Enemy bases in the Volcano and Bonin Islands, lying midway between the southern Marianas and Japan, further cut down the effectiveness of the bombers by warning Tokyo of their approach and by sending

up fighters to attack them en route. Capture of an island in the Volcano-Bonin group would not only enable American aircraft based there to put an end to this nuisance but would also provide a base for fighter planes and medium bombers within attack radius of Japan, a way station for B-29's in need of refueling, a refuge for damaged bombers, and a base for air-sea rescue. To obtain these obvious advantages, the Joint War Planning Committee in Washington began drawing up plans for the capture of Iwo Jima in the Volcanoes almost as soon as the decision was made to invade the Marianas. In early October 1944 the Joint Chiefs directed Admiral Nimitz, after providing fleet cover and support for MacArthur's invasion of Luzon, to proceed in early 1945 with the capture of Iwo Jima, and also of Okinawa in the Ryukyus.[2]

Because the situation on Leyte had obliged MacArthur to postpone his invasion of Luzon from December 20, 1944 to January 9, 1945, Halsey was not able to deliver the Fast Carrier Task Force to Spruance at Ulithi until near the end of January. As a consequence, the Iwo assault was deferred till mid-February, with the invasion of Okinawa to follow six weeks later. This was tight scheduling, but further delay was out of the question because planning was already under way for a massive invasion of Japan in the fall, and the success of this invasion depended in large measure upon long-sustained air operations involving both Iwo Jima and Okinawa.

To direct the new operations, Nimitz, newly promoted to fleet admiral, shifted from Pearl Harbor to advanced headquarters on Guam. Under Admiral Spruance, the Central Pacific Force again became U.S. Fifth Fleet. Vice Admiral Marc Mitscher resumed his command of the Fast Carrier Task Force, back to its old title of Task Force 58. The Fifth Fleet now had two amphibious forces, the Third and the Fifth, with Vice Admiral Richmond Kelly Turner in over-all command as Commander Amphibious Forces Pacific Fleet. Lieutenant General Holland Smith was in over-all com-

[2] To allow Nimitz some freedom of action, the Joint Chiefs' directive specified only "one or more positions" in each of the two island groups, but it was understood that Iwo and Okinawa were the preferred targets.

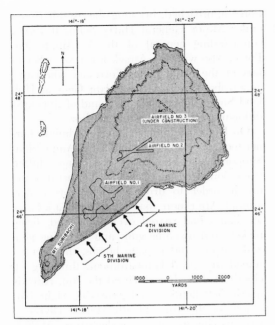

IWO JIMA

ridge between. On the high ground he set up more than 400 pillboxes and blockhouses, interconnected by passages tunneled through the lava.

For 74 consecutive days, B-24's of the Seventh Air Force, also operating out of the Marianas, raided Iwo in preparation for the coming assault. The raids however achieved no important effect other than to stimulate the defenders to greater exertions in their underground burrowing. Pinpoint precision was required to hurt Kuribayashi's type of defenses, and high-level bombing was not noted for precision, particularly where, as in the Bonin-Volcano area, haze or cloud cover is almost continuous. In an effort to isolate Iwo, marine-operated B-25's made day and night sorties against shipping in the area. Despite all this aerial activity, the Japanese brought in supplies to Iwo as before, maintained two airfields on the island, and began construction on a third.

Even hard-bitten marine commanders were startled by what air photo-reconnaissance revealed about Kuribayashi's preparations. Assigned to make the assault on Iwo, they asked for no less than ten days of preparatory naval bombardment. They, like the Navy, had learned in the school of experience that rapid expenditure of shells, with resultant clouds of obscuring smoke and dust, could not knock out well-built defenses. The fleet had to take its time, locate actual targets, and using a variety of shells and trajectories, endeavor to pinpoint fire at close range from different angles. Unfortunately, the speeded-up timetable of the war could allow only a three-day bombardment and, as events were to prove, this was not enough.

The delay in opening fire on Iwo Jima stemmed partly from the necessity of isolating the island by a carrier strike on the Tokyo area. Because of Halsey's late return to Ulithi, TF 58 could not rest its crews, rearm and replenish its ships, and reach Japanese waters before mid-February. On the 16th, the Fast Carrier Task Force, with Spruance and Mitscher aboard, arrived off Tokyo and sent in planes for the first fleet attack on Japan since the Halsey-Doolittle raid of early 1942. In the strikes of February 16 and 17, bad weather limited destruction to 40 or 50 enemy planes

mand of the corresponding III and V Amphibious Corps, with the title General Fleet Marine Force Pacific.

After the Fifth Fleet invasion of the Marianas in the summer of 1944, the Japanese had taken for granted that the Americans would eventually try to capture one of the islands of the Volcano-Bonin group and had selected Iwo Jima as the probable target because it provided the best terrain for airfields. So on this tiny volcanic ash heap they established a garrison of 14,000 army and 7,000 naval personnel, nearly all highly trained combat troops. Able Lieutenant General Tadamichi Kuribayashi, in over-all command of the island's defenses, set out to make Iwo the most formidably defended eight square miles in the Pacific. In achieving this goal he was abetted by the terrain. The broad northeast end of the island was a plateau of lava, for the most part tortured into fantastic hills and ravines and falling off into steep escarpments at the shoreline. At the opposite end stood an extinct volcano, 550-foot-high Mt. Suribachi. These two heights flanked the only possible landing beaches, along the tapering waist, and on the heights Kuribayashi concentrated his artillery where it could enfilade the beaches and the and minor damage to the airfields. The raids did however distract Japanese attention briefly away from Iwo, on which Rear Admiral William H. P. Blandy's Amphibious Support Force of gunnery vessels and escort carriers opened fire on the 16th.

Despite rain and mist over the island, the Support Force performed extraordinarily well in the limited time allowed. Each of the gunnery vessels, six old battleships and five cruisers, was assigned a specific area of responsibility. The known targets had been mapped in advance, and each was checked off as it was destroyed. Others were added to the control map as they were discovered. Though the Japanese had from the beginning returned the American fire and early on February 17 hit a battleship and a cruiser, Kuribayashi's heaviest coast defense batteries were holding their fire until the actual invasion in order not to reveal their location. But when, in mid-morning of the 17th, underwater demolition teams moved toward the east coast beaches accompanied by twelve LCI gunboats, the defenders must have assumed that the assault had begun. At any rate, the heavy batteries now opened up, putting nine gunboats out of action and damaging the other three. The old *Nevada* began counterbattery fire against the new targets at once, and the other gunnery ships soon followed suit. On the 18th the Support Force shifted fire so as to concentrate on the landing beaches, but this was probably a mistake, for the Japanese, in conformity with current doctrine, had left the beaches and the area between the two citadels only lightly defended.

Throughout the naval bombardment, the escort carrier aircraft did valuable service in spotting gunfire and in dropping napalm bombs to burn off concealing vegetation and camouflage. Neither their 500-pound general purpose bombs nor their 5-inch rockets had the power to knock out the heavier Japanese emplacements, but the latter because of their accuracy proved formidable weapons against less well protected enemy positions. High-level bombers from the Marianas joined the softening-up operations but were generally defeated by cloud cover and achieved negligible results.

Following the raids on Tokyo, TF 58 turned back to join the bombardment of Iwo. At the same time Rear Admiral Harry Hill's Attack Force approached, bringing the assault troops under Major General Harry Schmidt USMC, commanding general of the V Amphibious Force. Also with the Attack Force were Secretary of the Navy James Forrestal, who came as an observer, and Lieutenant General Holland Smith, in over-all command of the expeditionary troops, including garrison.

On D-day, February 19, Vice Admiral Turner took personal command of the Amphibious Support Force. The gunnery vessels now shifted from slow destructive fire to fast neutralizing fire in order to drive the defenders underground. After more than a hundred Task Force 58 planes had roared over the island, firing rockets and machine guns and dropping general purpose and napalm bombs, the fleet resumed the naval bombardment, throwing up clouds of dust that obscured the sun. Already nearly 500 landing craft, carrying eight battalions of the 4th and 5th Marine Divisions, were moving to the line of departure. At 0830 the first wave, 68 armored amphibians, headed for the beach. The naval guns thereupon shifted fire to provide a rolling or box barrage ahead of and on the flanks of the landing force, while more than 50 LCI gunboats advanced to furnish close support.

The momentum attained by this powerful assault was expected to carry the first waves well beyond the beach, but at the shoreline they were brought to a virtual halt by an unforeseen obstacle. The shore, rising steeply from the water, was composed of volcanic ash so soft that the treads of many of the amphibians sank in without taking hold. Succeeding waves of landing craft could not be beached at all. Many were thrown broadside to the shore and swamped. Newly arriving craft had their screws damaged or their bottoms stove in by the wreckage of earlier arrivals.

The marines who succeeded in scrambling ashore began crawling up a series of terraces toward the island's spiny ridge. For a while the heavy fleet bombardment kept the Japanese relatively quiet. But after the barrage had passed over, the defenders gradually recovered, opening fire first with machine guns and mortars and then with heavier guns. As the marines reached the first terrace, they came under intense rifle and machine gun fire from pillboxes on the central ridge. Nevertheless they doggedly climbed the second terrace, taking heavy losses, and advanced from shell crater to shell crater. Tanks and heavy weapons were slow to arrive in support, chiefly because many of the LST's, LSM's, and other craft bringing them in, unable to beach themselves or to find purchase with their anchors in the soft ash, collided and added to the confusion at the shore line.

The marine right wing, nearest the northeast plateau, remained pinned down through the 19th. The center, after putting several pillboxes out of action with flamethrowers and 75-mm. tank guns, got as far as Airfield No. 1. The marine left surged across the narrows, isolating Mt. Suribachi. All this the invaders accomplished under continued heavy fire from the flanks, and with no other cover than sparse vegetation and depressions in the churned up ash. The cost was high; of the 30,000 marines put ashore the first day, more than 2,400 were casualties by nightfall.

On February 20, marines of the center captured Airfield No. 1, those on the right began to penetrate the high ground to the northeast, and the regimental combat team on the extreme left began the assault on the mountain. The capture of Suribachi required nearly three days of blasting or burning out pillboxes and sealing up interconnected caves with grenades, flamethrowers, rockets, and demolition charges. On the morning of the 23rd the volcano was surrounded, and a patrol reached the summit and raised the American flag.[3] Meanwhile the 4th Division and two regiments of the 5th Division had pivoted to the right and begun the assault on the plateau. As the battalions that had suffered the most casualties were relieved, the 3rd Marine Division, in reserve, began to be committed, moving in between the other two divisions.

Throughout the advance into the northeast plateau area, which involved fighting among crevices, gullies, ledges, and caverns, the fleet added call fire to the barrage from the American artillery ashore. In the course of the cam-

[3] Toward noon the marines raised a second and larger flag, visible to the entire island and a source of inspiration to all the Americans. Newspaper photographer Joe Rosenthal took a picture of the second raising, producing the most frequently copied and reproduced of all war photographs.

paign, the support ships fired nearly 300,000 rounds of shell, with a weight of more than 14,000 tons. At night the ships reduced opportunities for Japanese infiltration by starshell and searchlight illumination. Carrier air support was unusually effective, particularly during the first four days while TF 58 stood off Iwo Jima. Coordination of the various supporting arms reached a new high, reflecting improved communication procedures and sound training based on experience. Nevertheless most of Kuribayashi's well concealed strong points had to be taken one at a time by infantry with close-range tank support.

The expected counterattack from Japan came in the late afternoon of the 21st, when some 20 kamikazes escorted by fighters appeared over Iwo Jima and struck at the carriers of the Amphibious Support Force, to which heavy carrier *Saratoga* was attached for night operations. The suicide planes crashed into five ships. Three were only moderately damaged, but the *Saratoga*, hit by three aircraft and as many bombs, was wreathed in flames and had a huge underwater hole in her hull. Though she was at length saved by expert fire fighting and damage control, she suffered nearly 300 casualties and was out of action for the rest of the war, undergoing extensive repairs. The two kamikazes that struck escort carrier *Bismarck Sea* started fires that set off her ammunition in a series of rending explosions, one of which blew off her stern. Abandoned, she rolled over and sank. Of her crew, 350 were lost.

Instead of the estimated five days, the capture of Iwo Jima required nearly a month of vicious fighting and mutual slaughter. The island was declared secured on March 16, but on the 25th hidden Japanese troops came forth and made a final attack. At length however all the enemy garrison except 200 prisoners of war were killed. This time casualties among the assault forces exceeded losses among the defenders; on the island and in the fleet 19,000 Americans were wounded and nearly 7,000 were killed or died of their wounds. "Among the Americans who served on Iwo Island," said Fleet Admiral Nimitz, "uncommon valor was a common virtue."

The stepped-up campaign against Japan got under way even before the captured airfields on Iwo were usable, for on February 25 bombers and fighters from Task Force 58 cooperated with 200 B-29's in a massive raid on Tokyo. The B-29's succeeded in burning out two square miles of the enemy capital, while the carrier aircraft, attacking military targets, destroyed about 150 Japanese planes. From off Tokyo TF 58 shaped course southwest to raid and photograph Okinawa. It then proceeded to Ulithi to replenish for the next invasion.

The Okinawa Campaign

Shortly after the American conquest of Saipan, Admiral Spruance had suggested the capture of Okinawa, 350 miles southwest of Japan. Okinawa in American hands, he pointed out, would provide airfields to supplement the bomber bases about to be established in the Marianas. The Joint Chiefs of Staff at that time rejected Spruance's offer because plans were being drawn up for an invasion of Formosa. The plan for Formosa however was canceled by the decision to invade the Philippines because there were not enough troops in the Pacific theater to occupy both. But whereas Luzon was as good as Formosa as a base for interdicting Japanese communications with the Southern Resources Area and for staging an invasion of the home islands, it was too far away from Japan to provide airfields for effectively bombing Japanese industrial centers. So the Joint Chiefs, reverting to Spruance's proposal, decided that they had enough troops to capture Okinawa. In October 1944, as we have seen, they issued orders for the capture of both Iwo Jima and Okinawa.

To support and cover the new assault, TF 58 departed Ulithi in mid-March 1945, with Spruance in strategic and Mitscher in tactical command. Spruance knew that the fast carriers would not return to base for many weeks. The conquest of Okinawa, much the largest island invaded by the Central Pacific forces, would entail an extended campaign involving many troops. The supply problem would be formidable, requiring a steady stream of shipping into an area that was within easy attack range of Japanese airfields on Formosa, in China, in the Ryukyus, and in Japan. Large-scale kamikaze attacks could be expected. American airfields would of course be estab-

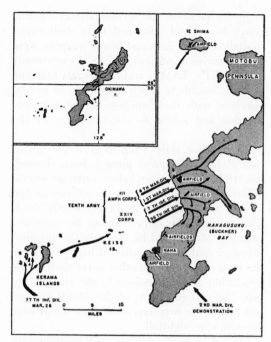

OKINAWA

lished as quickly as possible on Okinawa, but flyers operating from these would have their hands full supporting the troops. They could not also protect the logistic shipping. That would be the main task of aircraft from the big carriers, which accordingly would have to remain off Okinawa until the island was secured or the threat from the air had been greatly lessened.

To pave the way for the invasion, Task Force 58 on March 18 and 19 launched a series of massive raids on the airfields of Kyushu, southernmost of Japan's home islands, and on the dwindling Japanese fleet in the Inland Sea. This time Japanese aircraft counterattacked, bombing carriers *Enterprise, Yorktown, Franklin,* and *Wasp.* Only the *Franklin* was seriously damaged. Two bombs penetrated to her hangar deck while she was launching aircraft and set off fires and explosions that took the lives of more than 800 of her crew. No other ship in World War II, and possibly in history, suffered as extensive injuries and yet remained afloat. Saved by an extraordinary feat of damage control, the battered *Franklin* headed under her own power for the United States and a major repair job. These preliminary raids also cost the Americans 116 planes, but they damaged several enemy warships and did so much damage to installations and communications on Kyushu that the Japanese were unable to strike back again in force for nearly three weeks.

On March 23, after refueling, TF 58 began the pre-assault air strikes on Okinawa. On the 24th Rear Admiral Morton L. Deyo's Gunfire and Covering Force of old battleships, cruisers, and destroyers and Vice Admiral Lee's new battleships from TF 58 began the preparatory naval bombardment. Deyo's force in its support capacity was a part of Rear Admiral Blandy's Amphibious Support Force, but Admiral Spruance, suspecting that the Japanese might attempt a surface counterattack, had organized it as a detachable command to counter any such threat.

While the softening up of Okinawa was in process, an amphibious attack force including troops of the 77th Infantry Division carried out an inspired piece of planning by seizing the Kerama Islands, 15 miles west of southern Okinawa. These tiny islands were lightly held, for the Japanese considered them of little use to an invader. But to the Americans the Keramas were invaluable because they provided a sheltered anchorage where a seaplane and a logistic base could be set up. Into the Kerama anchorage on March 27 steamed the first of the tenders, oilers, repair ships, ammunition ships, and other auxiliaries of Service Squadron 10 to begin servicing the fleet. Thus was established a floating base for replenishment and light repairs right in the area of operations, supplementing Service Squadron 6, which remained underway to the southeast. The Kerama attack force also unexpectedly removed a serious threat to shipping by capturing some 350 depth-charge-carrying powerboats such as had menaced the fleet at Lingayen Gulf. Following the invasion of the Keramas, a field artillery group landed on the Keise Islands, still nearer Okinawa, and emplaced 155-mm. guns on the Japanese flank.

During the preliminary operations, aircraft from TF 58 and from escort carriers in Blandy's Amphibious Support Force flew 3,000 sorties in the Okinawa area, and the gunnery vessels fired 5,000 tons of shell. As minesweepers cleared 3,000 square miles off the Okinawa coast, the support ships moved in ever closer, achieving increasingly effective results. After the mines were cleared, underwater demolition teams reconnoitered the selected invasion beaches on the west coast and blew out of the water about 2,900 wooden posts that the defenders had set up as obstacles to landing craft. Involved in the final preparations, besides the gunfire and rocket vessels and the carrier aircraft of the Fifth Fleet, were bombers from the Marianas, the Philippines, and Western China. Task Force 58 covered the approaches from Japan, and at the other end of the line the British Pacific Fleet, designated Task Force 57, covered the approaches from Formosa and kept the intervening islands neutralized by cratering the airfields.

Newly arrived via Sydney and Manus under the command of Vice Admiral Sir Bernard Rawlings RN, the British fleet included four carriers, two battleships, five cruisers, and ten destroyers—about the strength of one task group of TF 58. Though the British carriers had nearly the same displacement as American *Essex*-class carriers, they could accommodate only about half as many planes, their logistic force was not designed to service them in long-sustained campaigns,[4] and their closed-in hangars slowed operations and proved uncomfortable in tropical waters. In the Okinawa campaign however their armored flight decks gave them a special advantage, rendering them less vulnerable to kamikaze attack than the contemporary American carriers with wooden flight decks and armored hangar decks.

Admiral Turner's Joint Expeditionary Force, assembled from such distant points as Espiritu Santo, Guadalcanal, San Francisco, Seattle, Oahu, Leyte, and Saipan, arrived off Okinawa on schedule in the early hours of D-day, April 1. In the force were 1,300 ships bringing 182,000 assault troops. These included the III Amphibious Corps, composed of the 1st and 6th Marine Divisions; and the XXIV Army

---

[4] From April 20 to May 3, at the height of the Okinawa campaign, the British fleet was obliged to retire to Leyte for replenishment. During its absence, escort carriers of Blandy's Amphibious Support Force took over the task of covering the southwest approaches to Okinawa. For details of the British operations, including a frank comparison of British and American material and techniques, see Admiral of the Fleet Sir Philip Vian, *Action This Day* (London, 1960).

Corps, comprising the 7th and 96th Infantry Divisions. These two corps made up the U.S. Tenth Army, commanded by Lieutenant General Simon Bolivar Buckner, Jr., USA. Three more infantry divisions were available as reserve forces: the 27th, as floating reserve; the 81st as area reserve; and the 77th, after it had captured the Keramas and Ie Shima off the Okinawa west coast.

Awaiting the invasion on Okinawa were about 100,000 defenders, of whom 67,000 were regular Imperial Army troops and the rest were naval personnel and Okinawan draftees. Lieutenant General Mitsuru Ushijima, the army commander, had prepared his defenses in accordance with current Japanese doctrine. All Okinawans whose services could be spared by the armed forces had been transported to Japan or ordered into northern Okinawa. The main defense force took position in a natural citadel of steep hills and narrow ravines in southern Okinawa northeast of Naha. This position they rendered even more defensible by siting mutually supporting artillery to cover all approaches and by linking pillboxes, caves, blockhouses, and other strong points together with trenches and tunnels. About the main citadel they established smaller outlying bastions in concentric rings to slow down the invader's advance. On Ushijima's orders, the Japanese guns held their fire throughout the American preparatory bombardment so as not to disclose their positions to naval gunners. On his orders also, no troops were to be wasted in any attempt to stop the Americans at the beachhead, which he correctly estimated would be on the west coast north of Naha. A regiment of Okinawans would man the hills overlooking the beach, but these were to serve only as a delaying force, retreating before the invaders and joining the rest of the defenders in their prepared positions. The general plan was to maintain the defense as long as possible, exposing the invasion forces on land and sea to a prolonged period of attrition, chiefly by Japanese air power.

On the morning of April 1, after the heaviest neutralizing fire unleashed on any beach in the Pacific, the Tenth Army began going ashore. At the same time, in a needless attempt to draw defending forces away from the beachhead, a Demonstration Group including the 2nd Marine Division staged a mock landing on the southeast coast.

The Tenth Army met only sporadic small-arms and mortar fire. In the course of the day, 50,000 soldiers and marines went ashore, and advance elements seized two airfields. By noon of April 2 the invaders had thrust across to the east coast. Then, while most of the XXIV Corps wheeled right for an advance to the south and the 1st Marine Division secured the area opposite the beachhead, the 6th Marine Division advanced up the long northeast axis of the island. In northern Okinawa the marines met only scattered resistance until they entered the rugged hills of the Motobu Peninsula. Here the enemy fought back for several days. Capture of the peninsula provided high elevations for bombardment in support of an assault on nearby Ie Shima, which the 77th Division invaded in order to obtain another airfield. By April 18 the marines had secured all of northern Okinawa but continued to patrol the coasts on the lookout for possible counterlandings.

Meanwhile the XXIV Corps, reinforced by the 27th Infantry Division, had penetrated the outer defenses in the south and had come up against the main Japanese citadel. This they attacked on April 19 but were bloodily repulsed. Thereafter the battle remained relatively stalemated for several days while American fleet guns and shore artillery blasted away in vain against the enemy stronghold. Around May 1, the American front was reorganized to put fresh troops in the line. The 27th Division relieved the 6th Marine Division in northern Okinawa, and the III Amphibious Corps took over the west flank in southern Okinawa. The 77th Division, having completed its conquest of Ie Shima, relieved the 96th Division, which rested for ten days and then relieved the 7th Division for ten days of rest. The Japanese, who had had neither rest nor relief, counterattacked on May 4 but were thrown back. Toward the end of May, the Americans, closely supported by fleet guns, began to outflank the enemy citadel by advancing down both coasts. The defenders, to avoid being surrounded, thereupon began withdrawing under cover of rain to a new defense position in the southern tip of the island.

Because planning for the Okinawa operation

was largely completed before heavy kamikaze raids developed in the Philippines, the Fifth Fleet commanders had not anticipated large-scale Japanese suicide attacks at Okinawa. They nevertheless took due precautions. Admiral Mitscher stationed radar picket destroyers for early warning around TF 58. Admiral Turner set up around Okinawa a double ring of radar picket stations, patrolled early in the campaign typically by a destroyer and two well-armed amphibious vessels. On Okinawa, the Keramas, and Ie Shima the army emplaced antiaircraft batteries as quickly as possible, and from captured airfields marine fighter groups soon began to operate.

From the beginning, Japanese bombers and suicide planes made sporadic attacks on the American ships off Okinawa. On March 31 a kamikaze crashed into Spruance's flagship *Indianapolis,* releasing a bomb that penetrated several decks and blew two holes in her hull. While Spruance transferred his flag to old battleship *New Mexico,* the *Indianapolis* was patched up in the Kerama anchorage and then headed for Mare Island for extensive repairs. On April 4 a crashing kamikaze so mangled a destroyer-transport that she had to be sunk. By April 5 Japanese bombers and suicide planes had succeeded in damaging 39 naval vessels, including two old battleships, three cruisers, and an escort carrier. These raids however were mere preliminaries to the general counterattack which the Imperial Army and Navy, acting for the first time in really close concert, launched on April 6. On the morning of the 6th a Japanese reconnaissance plane sighted TF 58 east of Okinawa. Shortly afterward 355 kamikaze pilots in old aircraft rigged for suicide attack began taking off from airfields in Kyushu. Some headed for TF 58, others for the shipping off Okinawa.

First and most persistently attacked by the kamikazes were the outlying picket vessels, which early in the campaign generally had only their own guns to protect themselves. In mid-afternoon of the 6th, suicide planes swarmed down on destroyer *Bush* on picket patrol north of Okinawa and made three hits. Destroyer *Colhoun,* patrolling the adjacent station, rushed to support the damaged *Bush* and was herself crashed by three kamikazes. Both destroyers began to sink. An alert combat air

patrol and long-practiced countermeasures prevented the enemy aircraft from reaching TF 58 that day, but about 200 reached the Okinawa area. Here most of the attackers were disposed of by fighter planes and by antiaircraft fire so intense that a hail of falling shell fragments caused 38 American casualties. Nevertheless the enemy planes damaged 22 naval vessels, sank a destroyer-transport and an LST, and demolished two loaded ammunition ships, leaving the Tenth Army short of certain types of shell.

Meanwhile the second phase of this wholesale suicide attack got underway as the giant battleship *Yamato,* light cruiser *Yahagi,* and eight destroyers emerged from the Inland Sea propelled by the last 2,500 tons of fuel oil in Japan—just enough for a one-way passage to Okinawa. Due to arrive at the island at dawn on the 8th, they were to beach themselves there and fire at the American forces until all the Japanese ships had expended their ammunition or been destroyed. But two American submarines patrolling off Kyushu sighted the Japanese force before dark on the 6th and flashed a warning. Admiral Spruance thereupon alerted Admiral Deyo's battleship force to prepare to carry out its covering function. Deyo was to let the Japanese ships come south, too far for retreat into a Japanese port and

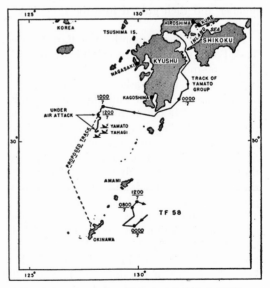

LAST SORTIE OF THE IMPERIAL JAPANESE FLEET, APRIL 6–7, 1945

beyond easy protection from Kyushu airfields. Then at the appropriate time on April 7 Deyo's force was to advance and take them under fire. But Admiral Mitscher had no intention of leaving the enemy ships to be dealt with by the surface forces. Before dawn on the 7th he began leading TF 58 northward for the kill. A little after 0800, his search planes relocated the enemy force steaming westward, and Kerama-based PBM's kept it under surveillance as it changed to a southerly course. At 1000 Mitscher launched his air groups. Two hours later the carrier planes struck the enemy in overwhelming force, sending down the *Yamato,* the *Yahagi,* and two destroyers and so damaging two other destroyers that the surviving vessels sank them before returning to base.

On April 7 a kamikaze at last penetrated the TF 58 air patrol and crashed into the deck of carrier *Hancock,* killing 43 men. By nightfall, suicide planes had damaged four more naval vessels. The April 6-7 raid was only the first of ten general kamikaze attacks launched against the fleet and shipping off Okinawa. Smaller-scale suicide and conventional air raids occurred nearly every day. An additional suicide device used in the April 12-13 raid and in subsequent attacks was the *Oka* (cherry blossom),[5] a winged, rocket-propelled bomb that was released from the undercarriage of a bomber and then guided into the target by a pilot.

For nearly three months the Fast Carrier Task Force remained east of Okinawa patrolling a 60-mile-square area, while its planes supported the troops ashore, combated enemy aircraft, and executed antisubmarine patrols. Task groups left the patrol area from time to time to refuel. They also moved north six times to strike at Kyushu airfields, but blanketing the fields as had been done at Luzon was out of the question because there were too many, they were too scattered, and they were too well protected by antiaircraft batteries.

Though the kamikazes continued to find most of their victims among the radar pickets and the ships off Okinawa, the fast carrier force took its share of hits. Admiral Mitscher lost a large part of his staff and had to shift

[5] Called *Baka* (foolish) bomb by the Americans.

flagships twice in three days as carriers *Bunker Hill* and *Enterprise* were successively hit and put out of action by crashing kamikazes. Southeast of Okinawa the British task force also came under persistent kamikaze attack. Four of the British carriers were hit, but all were able to continue operations.

The American aviators and ships' crews obtained some relief as vessels were sent back to Ulithi or elsewhere for repair, upkeep, or overhaul. The Fifth Fleet commanders however remained at the scene of operations until the strain they were under became almost unendurable. At last Admiral Nimitz, toward the end of May, took the unprecedented step of changing the command in the midst of a campaign. Halsey relieved Spruance, McCain relieved Mitscher, and Hill relieved Turner, whereupon the Fifth Fleet again became the Third Fleet. Halsey was not happy to remain off Okinawa in what appeared to him a purely defensive role, but he quickly perceived that he had no choice. He continued the tactics inaugurated by Spruance, but urged that American air power based on Okinawa be built up as rapidly as possible so that the Fast Carrier Task Force, now again called TF 38, could be relieved of its covering and support duties.

At the time of the change of command, the Americans, steadily improving their techniques, had got the kamikaze menace nearly under control. They had supplemented their surface radar pickets with picket planes, strengthened the surface pickets with additional destroyers and amphibious vessels, and provided the more exposed picket stations with their own combat air patrols. They had set up radar stations in northern Okinawa and on offshore islands that they seized for the purpose. The smaller and more maneuverable American ships had learned to present their beams to diving kamikazes for maximum fire power and to work up speed in order to present a difficult target problem to diving suicide planes, which generally came down so fast that air pressure froze their controls.

The kamikazes, on the contrary, could develop no body of data on which to base improvements because none who went into a final dive ever returned to base to report his experiences. Moreover the nature of the Special Attack Corps had undergone change. All the willing glory seekers had been expended, and Japanese aviators were now being coerced into giving up their lives. Among these unwilling suicides there was a growing feeling that they were making a useless sacrifice because Okinawa was already obviously lost. Pilots began returning to base claiming that they could not locate any enemy ships. One pilot vented his resentment at being sent to his death by strafing his commanding officer's quarters as he took off.

By June 10 the decline in kamikaze attacks, coupled with the build-up of air power on Okinawa and the successes of B-29's operating against Kyushu out of China and the Marianas, had created a situation that permitted TF 38 at last to be released from Okinawan waters. When the fast carrier force arrived at Leyte Gulf on the 13th to prepare for a series of July attacks against Japan, it had been at sea 92 days.

Gunfire support ships and escort carriers remained off Okinawa till the Japanese southern bastion had been taken. The island was declared secured on June 21. The next day General Ushijima and his chief of staff acknowledged defeat by ceremoniously committing suicide. Mopping-up operations continued however until the end of the month. By then practically all the defending forces except 11,000 prisoners of war had been killed. American naval guns, shore artillery, and aircraft had also killed some 24,000 Okinawan civilians who had the misfortune to be near Japanese troops or installations. For the invaders too the campaign had been costly. Nearly 13,000 Americans had been killed, of whom 3,400 were marines and 4,900 navy. In the fleet most of the casualties among ships and men were the result of enemy air attack, chiefly by suicide planes. By air attack alone 15 naval vessels were sunk, none larger than a destroyer, and more than 200 were damaged, some beyond salvage. This costly sacrifice had purchased a position for bringing air power to bear heavily upon the industrial centers of southern Japan and a base for completing the blockade of the home islands and for supporting an invasion of Kyushu.

The Japanese Surrender

On June 22, 1945 Emperor Hirohito of Japan at a meeting of his Supreme War Council gave utterance to what others in authority had been unwilling or afraid to state officially: Japan must find a way to end the war. It was high time. Clouds of American bombers were turning Japan's cities into ashes. The strangling blockade was bringing the nation's production of war materials to a standstill. In April the Soviet Union had made the ominous announcement that it would not renew its Neutrality Pact with Japan. In May the surrender of Germany had dispelled the vain hope that some decisive weapon might yet be obtained from that quarter, and at the same time released the combined forces of the Allied world for operations against Japan. Okinawa, the last Japanese outpost, had fallen to the Americans.

Ending the war was not simple. Powerful factions in Japan and in the armed forces abroad favored a war to the bitter end, and neither the rulers nor the people would accept a peace that did not preserve the imperial system. Negotiations therefore had to be carried out in secret, and terms short of "unconditional surrender" had to be obtained. Since of the major powers only Russia was even ostensibly neutral with respect to the Pacific war, it was appropriate that peace feelers be extended through Moscow. The Supreme Council hoped also by bringing the Soviet government into the negotiations to obtain a new neutrality commitment from Russia in exchange for concessions in Manchuria. But when the Japanese ambassador in Moscow approached the Soviet foreign office on the subject of peace terms, he found the Russians disposed to stall. At the July conference of the victors over Germany held at Potsdam, Premier Stalin at first said nothing to President Truman or to Prime Minister Churchill about Japan's request for mediation.[6] The Russians evidently had no intention of helping the Japanese get out of the war until they them-

[6] Clement Attlee replaced Churchill as British prime minister before the end of the Potsdam Conference.

selves could get into it and thereby share the fruits of victory.

But President Truman knew about the peace feelers, for American intelligence was reading the coded radio messages passing between the Japanese foreign minister in Tokyo and the Japanese ambassador in Moscow. On July 26 the governments of the United States, Britain, and China gave Japan her answer in the Potsdam Proclamation, which specified that for Japan "unconditional surrender" was to apply only to the armed forces. The Proclamation further stated that Japan was to be stripped of all her territorial gains and possessions except the four home islands, and that points in Japan would be occupied until a "peacefully inclined and responsible government" had been established in line with the people's desires expressed in a free election. Nothing was said about the fate of the Emperor or the imperial system because the Allied governments had not yet made up their minds on that point. Two days after the Proclamation was issued, Stalin at last informed his colleagues of the Japanese request for terms.

The Potsdam Proclamation came a little too suddenly for the Japanese Cabinet, for they had not taken steps to prepare the Japanese people for surrender, they had not received the hoped-for commitment from the Soviet Union, and they had not settled disagreements among themselves. The chief stumbling block however was the failure of the Proclamation to spell out what the Allies intended to do about the Japanese Emperor.

While the Russian leaders were stalling and the Japanese leaders were procrastinating, the Americans and the British were actively planning an invasion of Kyushu for November 1945, with an assault on Honshu and an advance into the Tokyo Plain to follow in March 1946. On July 16, 1945, the world's first manmade atomic explosion was set off at Alamogordo, New Mexico, and within a few hours the erstwhile Fifth Fleet flagship *Indianapolis*, newly repaired from the battering she received off Okinawa, was en route from San Francisco to the Marianas with the first military atomic bomb. Bombers from Okinawa and the Marianas were now appearing over Japan in waves of 500 or more, burning out vast areas in Japan's major cities. On July

10, Task Force 38 had raided airfields near Tokyo. From this date on, with a single break, the Third Fleet carrier force paraded up and down the Japanese coast till the end of the war, bombing and bombarding with virtual impunity while Japan hoarded her aircraft to throw back the expected invasion. On July 17, Halsey's 105 men-of-war were joined by 28 British warships, designated Task Force 37. This combined fleet, the most powerful striking force in history, then raided the naval bases at Yokosuka on Tokyo Bay and at Kure on the Inland Sea, sinking or heavily damaging the remnants of the Imperial Japanese Fleet. On July 30, the Third Fleet ended the first phase of its intensive operations against Japan with a raid on airfields and factories in central Honshu. On this date also, the *Indianapolis*, having delivered her bomb to Tinian, touched at Guam, and then headed for Leyte, was sunk in the Philippine Sea by a Japanese submarine with the loss of nearly 900 lives.

Japan waited a little too long for a commitment from the Soviet Union, for the Americans at length interpreted the continued Japanese silence as a rejection of the Potsdam Proclamation. On August 6, a B-29, taking off from Tinian, flew over Japan and dropped an atomic bomb that seared and flattened most of the city of Hiroshima. The Russians now realized that if they were to get into the war at all, it must be soon. On August 8 the Soviet foreign minister at Moscow handed the Japanese ambassador his long-awaited answer. It was a declaration of war. Within a few hours the Red Army marched into Manchuria. On the 9th another air-borne atomic bomb devastated the city of Nagasaki. Also on the 9th the Third Fleet, having ridden out a typhoon, returned to Japanese waters and raided airfields in northern Honshu and Hokkaido. On the 10th Russian forces entered Korea.

These startling events both ended the procrastination of the Japanese government and solved one of its most difficult problems. Until then the imperial councilors had been at a loss how to present the facts to a nation long deluded with propaganda. There was a strong chance that any attempt to surrender would precipitate mutiny in the armed services and civil war among the people. But the power and mystery of the new bomb, the swift advance of the Red Army, and the resumption of Third Fleet raids persuaded all but the most hot-headed that further resistance was useless. Shortly after midnight in the morning of August 10, Emperor Hirohito rose with deep emotion before his Supreme Council and advised immediate acceptance of the Potsdam Proclamation. The Cabinet unanimously agreed but only on the condition that the imperial system remain unimpaired. This decision they forwarded via Switzerland and Sweden to Washington, London, Moscow, and Chungking. On receipt of the Japanese decision, America Secretary of State James Byrnes, acting on behalf of the Allied governments, drafted a reply accepting the condition but imposing two stipulations: that during the occupation the Emperor must submit to the authority of the Supreme Allied Commander in Japan, and that the Japanese people should decide the Emperor's ultimate status through free election.

While the Allies were considering the Japanese condition and the Japanese were considering the Allied stipulations, the Third Fleet raided northern Honshu again and struck at the Kurils. It then turned south and on August 13 once more attacked Tokyo. On the 14th the Japanese Cabinet, again on the Emperor's advice, accepted the Allied stipulations. On August 15, when one carrier strike was already over the Tokyo area and another had just been launched, the Third Fleet received the order to "cease fire."

On September 2 aboard battleship *Missouri* in Tokyo Bay, with ships of the Third Fleet standing by, the Japanese foreign minister, acting for the Emperor, the Government, and Imperial General Headquarters, signed the instrument of surrender. General of the Army Douglas MacArthur then signed the acceptance as Supreme Commander for the Allied Powers. Fleet Admiral Chester Nimitz next affixed his signature as Representative for the United States. He was followed by Representatives for the United Kingdom, China, the Soviet Union, Australia, Canada, France, the Netherlands, and New Zealand.

Soon afterward General MacArthur moved into headquarters in Tokyo to direct the occupation of Japan.

Summary

When the United States denied Japan the oil she needed to conduct her war of aggression in China, the Japanese, after fruitless negotiations, on December 7, 1941 raided the U.S. Pacific Fleet at Pearl Harbor with carrier aircraft, eliciting a declaration of war. The Japanese then proceeded to invade the Philippines and Thailand, to seize Guam and Wake, and to advance into Malaya and the Netherlands East Indies. The East Indies region they designated the Southern Resources Area, a source of oil and other materials necessary to the conduct of war. At the same time they set out to complete a defense perimeter of air and naval bases that would serve as a barrier protecting Japan, the Southern Resources Area, and the line of communications ("the oil line") connecting them. Establishing the perimeter entailed Japanese occupation of the north coast of New Guinea, the Bismarck Archipelago, the upper Solomons, and the Gilbert Islands.

Because the American declaration of war on Japan had automatically involved the United States in war with Japan's allies, Germany and Italy, the Americans had to retain a large part of their fleet in the Atlantic and remain on the defensive in the Pacific. The best that the United States armed forces could do to slow the Japanese offensive was to participate in the military defense of the Philippines, combine the small U.S. Asiatic Fleet with British, Dutch, and Australian ships for the naval defense of the East Indies, send out submarines with faulty torpedoes to attack Japanese shipping, and launch carrier raids on Japanese bases in the Gilberts, the Marshalls, and New Guinea, and on Tokyo.

The Japanese offensive advanced at a greater speed than the Japanese themselves had anticipated. By early March 1942, forces moving around the east and west coasts of Borneo had clamped the pincers on Java, cutting off the escape of the remaining ABDA ships, fugitives from defeat in the Battle of the Java Sea (February 27-28, 1942).

The quick success of their advance decided the Japanese to extend their perimeter, a decision reinforced by the American raid on Tokyo, which revealed a wide gap in the northern flank of Japan's outer defenses. In the south

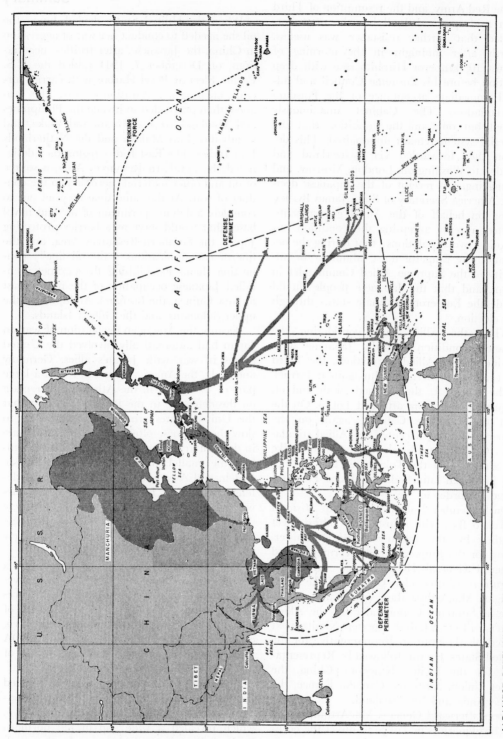

JAPANESE OFFENSIVE, DECEMBER 1941–APRIL 1942

the Japanese planned to seize Port Moresby on the southern coast of New Guinea, Tulagi in the eastern Solomons, and later New Caledonia, Fiji, and Samoa, where they would establish air and naval bases to attack ships plying between the United States and Australia. To provide observation posts covering the gap between the Marshalls and the Kurils (inadequately covered by Wake and Marcus), they expected to capture the Midway Islands at the center and some of the Aleutian Islands in the north.

The Japanese sea-borne advance on Port Moresby was stopped by an American carrier force in the Battle of the Coral Sea (May 4-8, 1942). The Japanese advance at the center was stopped by American carrier forces in the Battle of Midway (June 3-6, 1942). The Battle of Midway proved a major turning point in the war. The Americans, by destroying four Japanese carriers, so reduced Japan's preponderance of naval power in the Pacific that the United States and her Australian, New Zealand, and Canadian allies could abandon the purely defensive. Only in the north did the Japanese succeed in carrying out their plan. Here they occupied the Aleutian islands of Attu and Kiska.

The Allies shifted to the offensive-defensive with a landing on Guadalcanal in August 1942 and an advance northward from Port Moresby the following month. By January 1943, the Americans had made good their hold on Guadalcanal, ejecting the Japanese, and Americans and Australians had penetrated across and around the Papuan Peninsula of New Guinea and seized Buna from the Japanese.

The next phase of the war against Japan was a limited offensive which began in the north with an American assault on Japanese-held Attu in May 1943 and resulted in ejecting the enemy from the Aleutians by mid-August. In the south the limited offensive took the form of a dual advance on Rabaul ("the little dual offensive"), via the Solomons and via the north coast of New Guinea. The advance up the Solomons was carried out by forces from Admiral Halsey's South Pacific Area, a subdivision of Admiral Nimitz' Pacific Ocean Areas. The New Guinea advance was made by forces of General MacArthur's Southwest Pacific Area. By March 1944, the South and Southwest Pacific forces had surrounded and neutralized Rabaul and other, nearby Japanese bases, thus assuring MacArthur a safe supply line for further advances to the west. Equally important, the dual drive had cut so deeply into Japanese naval air power that the Combined Fleet was unable for some time to oppose a new American drive that was now advancing across the Central Pacific.

The South Pacific forces ended their advance with the neutralizing of Rabaul. The continued drive of the Southwest Pacific forces together with the drive of the Central Pacific forces constituted a new dual advance ("the big dual advance"), which was to merge at the Philippines. The Southwest Pacific forces, making a series of amphibious leaps along the north coast of New Guinea, occupied Aitape and Hollandia in April 1944 and the offshore islands of Wade and Biak in May. In July they seized Noemfoor Island and landed at Sansapor near the western end of New Guinea.

Meanwhile Admiral Spruance's U.S. Fifth Fleet, spearhead of the Central Pacific forces, in November 1943 had captured the atolls of Makin, Abemama, and Tarawa in the Gilberts, with assistance from bombers based on the Ellices. In February 1944 the Fifth Fleet captured the atolls of Majuro, Kwajalein, and Eniwetok in the Marshalls, with assistance from bombers based on the Gilberts. In June 1944 the Fifth Fleet, having proved that carrier aircraft were entirely adequate to provide air support for amphibious assaults, went far beyond the operational radius of land-based American planes to stage an invasion of the island of Saipan in the Marianas.

The invasion of the Marianas at last brought out the Japanese fleet, which engaged the Fifth Fleet's fast carrier force (Task Force 58), then covering the landing on Saipan. The resultant Battle of the Philippine Sea (June 19-21, 1944) cost the Japanese three carriers, sunk by American submarines and carrier planes, and most of their naval aircraft. The Americans could then proceed without interference to assault Tinian and Guam in the southern Marianas. Capture of bases in the Marianas provided airfields from which the new B-29 long-range bomber could raid the industrial centers of Japan.

JAPANESE OFFENSIVE, MAY–JULY 1942

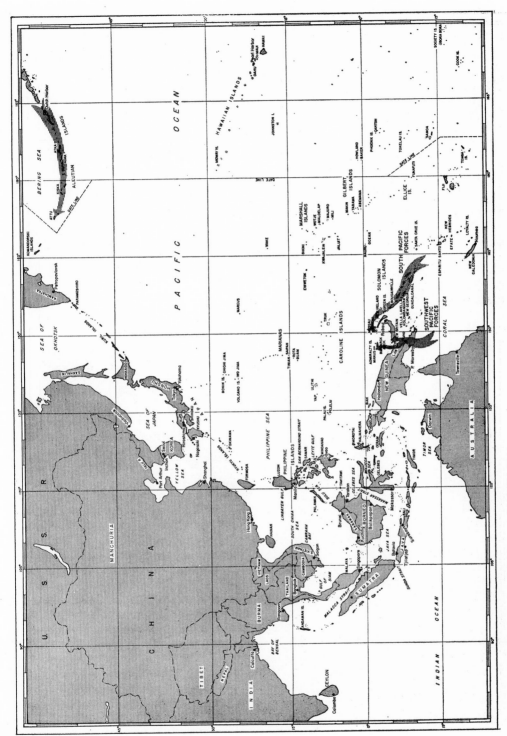

ALLIED LIMITED OFFENSIVE, AUGUST 1942–MARCH 1944

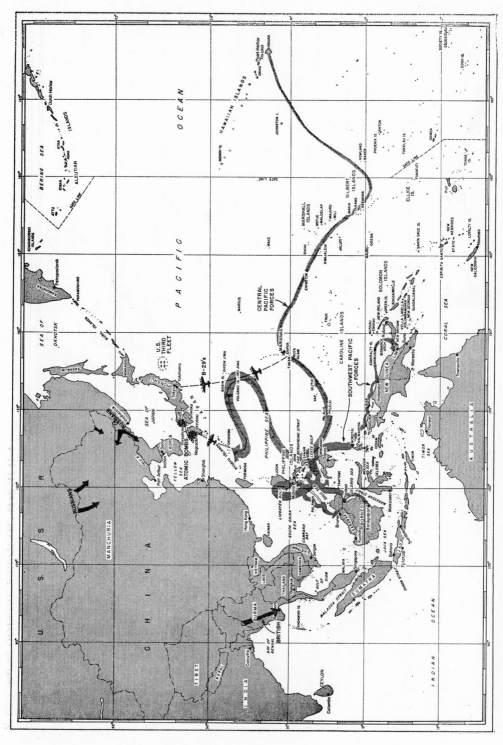

ALL-OUT ALLIED OFFENSIVE, NOVEMBER 1943–AUGUST 1945

After the Marianas campaign, Admiral Halsey replaced Admiral Spruance in command of the Central Pacific fleet, which was then called the U.S. Third Fleet, with the fast carrier force now designated TF 38. In September 1944 the Third Fleet staged an invasion of Angaur and Peleliu in the Palau Islands, while the U.S. Seventh Fleet (naval component of the Southwest Pacific forces) staged an invasion of Morotai Island. These positions were captured to cover the flanks of an American invasion of the Philippines, which took place in October 1944 at the central Philippine island of Leyte.

The invasion of the Philippines brought the Southwest Pacific and the Central Pacific forces together in a single operation. The amphibious forces of the Third Fleet were temporarily added to the Seventh Fleet to land troops on Leyte, while TF 38 stood off the beachhead area providing cover. Again the Japanese attacked at sea, and in the resultant Battle for Leyte Gulf (October 23-26, 1944) the Japanese fleet was so decisively defeated that it ceased to exist as an effective fighting force.

The Third Fleet continued in support of the Southwest Pacific forces until they had captured the Philippine islands of Leyte and Mindoro and had invaded Luzon. American occupation of these islands insured interdiction of shipping between the Southern Resources Area and Japan, a major objective of the U.S. Navy. Thereafter the Southwest Pacific forces turned south to liberate Manila and the rest of the Philippine Islands and to capture the oil ports of Borneo, operations that carried them past the middle of 1945. The Central Pacific forces

(again designated Fifth Fleet, under Admiral Spruance) turned north to assault Iwo Jima in mid-February and Okinawa in early April 1945, moves toward stepping up the bombing of Japanese industry and shipping. In June 1945 U.S. submarines penetrated into the Sea of Japan to complete the isolation of Japan's home islands.

The defeat of Germany in May 1945 and the American capture of Okinawa in June, coupled with growing shortages, severe bombing of Japanese cities, and attacks on Japan by the Third Fleet, at length decided the Japanese government to capitulate. While the Cabinet was considering terms put forth in the Allied Potsdam Proclamation and at the same time seeking mediation through the Soviet Union, the dropping of two atomic bombs on Japanese cities by American planes and the invasion of Manchuria by a Russian army quickly brought the war to an end.

In contrast to the war against the European Axis, in which navies operated chiefly in support of armies and army-controlled air power, the victory in the Pacific was achieved by balanced power—land, air, surface, and subsurface—often navy controlled. This balancing of power proved the correct solution to the special problems posed by the geography of the Pacific theater. It enabled the Allies to advance on the enemy homeland by more than one route while seizing numerous strongly defended positions, to by-pass large enemy garrisons, to deprive Japan of sea control and of supplies from her newly-won empire, and at length to force her to surrender while large Japanese armies in Asia and the home islands remained still undefeated.

44:

The Uneasy Peace

Even before the surrender of the Imperial Japanese forces the War and Navy Departments of the United States began to feel pressure "to bring the boys home." The American public, negligent of requirements for occupation forces, and unaware of other vast commitments inevitable in a postwar world, forced upon the Congress a swift demobilization which in a few months reduced the vast fighting forces of the United States to near impotence. The Navy hastily arranged "Operation Magic Carpet," employing all types of ships in transport service. Cots and hammocks were rigged on the hangar decks of carriers, which ran shuttle services across both the Atlantic and the Pacific. In one such crossing, the *Lake Champlain,* crowded with troops, set a speed record for the Gibraltar-New York crossing, but even that seemed too slow to the troops aboard and to the American people at home.

Soviet Expansion and the United Nations

While the United States and her allies disarmed, the Soviet Union resumed the offensive in its ceaseless war against capitalism. The temporary wartime alliance with the West had been only a tactical maneuver. Russia's strategic goals remained unchanged.

The United States, possessing a world monopoly of the atomic bomb, and having few post-war strategic objectives, depended on the good faith of the victors to maintain the principles enunciated in the Atlantic Charter. As after World War I, the victorious allies banded together to establish a world organization to settle international disputes. Planning for such

an organization had been going on for more than a year; the United Nations officially came into existence in San Francisco on June 26, 1945. While the details of the United Nations Charter are outside the scope of this book, a few points need to be made clear in view of their importance in connection with the Korean War. Two representative bodies, the General Assembly and the Security Council, were established. The General Assembly provided for one vote for each of the member states and was designed to be a guiding and advisory rather than a policy-making body. The real strength of the UN was vested in the Security Council of eleven members. Five of these members, the United States, the Soviet Union, Great Britain, France, and China, were permanent, the other six being elected in rotation. Each of the five permanent members possessed veto power over any action proposed by the Security Council, which might employ a wide variety of measures for the settlement of international disputes, ranging from mediation and conciliation at one extreme to "such action by air, sea, or land forces as may be necessary to maintain or restore international peace."

America's hopes for the UN sped her process of demobilization and slashed her military budgets. But the Soviet Union, making only a token demobilization, still had power to move into areas which could not be contested by the United States other than by diplomatic protest or by the use of the atomic bomb. Short of these extremes there was no practicable way to oppose Soviet expansion or to hold the U.S.S.R. accountable for violations of agreements reached in conferences at Yalta and Potsdam. Already a limitation in American strategy was becoming apparent, a limitation which for several years was to hamper the

United States in its international relations. To be effective, particularly against an expansionist state, diplomacy must be backed up with power in order to enforce the will of the protester, or at least to bring about a reasonable compromise, which is, of course, a partial defeat for the expanding nation. By the spring of 1946, the United States had too few men under arms to supply its garrison forces and have any force left as a support for diplomacy. American public opinion was solidly against more war, even in the face of outrageously bold Soviet violations of wartime agreements. A good many people in the United States were suffering pangs of conscience over the use of the atomic bomb against Hiroshima and Nagasaki. Hence, the Soviet's calculated risk that the United States would not employ this terrible weapon against its former ally was shrewdly judged, and the United States was nearly impotent to take any effective steps to hold Russia to the terms of the wartime agreements or to keep her from territorial expansion.

Russia's Strategic Picture

A study of the globe will reveal that in the over-all strategic picture, Russia enjoys the advantage of interior position with respect to the areas that were to come into dispute. On both littorals of the Eurasian land mass exist countries over which Russia sought control. These countries were, generally speaking, weakened from the efforts of World War II, and occupation or partial occupation had disrupted the governments and the economies of these countries. Germany, France, Finland, Belgium, Norway, the Netherlands, and Italy on the Atlantic side had all undergone defeat and occupation, and the consequent instability of these countries seemed a natural opportunity or series of opportunities for Russia. On the Pacific side, the Kremlin saw its opportunity in China and Korea. Korea had been under Japanese rule for years; China had not been defeated by Japan, but large areas had been occupied; a Communist movement was already making headway in China, and the Nationalist Government of Chiang Kai-shek was losing the support of the masses. Into both these coastal

areas the Soviet Union planned to extend its control, but was prepared apparently to draw back when opposed by significant force or when there seemed to be the risk of global war.

Immediately off both the Atlantic and the Pacific shores of this vast continent are situated island powers which in hands unfriendly to Soviet expansion could serve as great dangers to any Russian military operation against the littoral areas. The British Isles in the Atlantic had already proved their usefulness as air and naval bases in the war against Germany and Italy. Japan, in a similar position off the Pacific coast of Eurasia, controls the sea entrances to Russia's only Pacific ports; hence bombers based on Japan would offer a serious threat to the Soviet lines of communication between European Russia and the coastal cities of Siberia. Both of these island groups off the continental mass were under the control of powers which the Soviet Union deemed unfriendly to her national aims. However, lacking a navy which could compete with that of either the United States or Great Britain, the Soviet Union could not readily threaten these island groups as it could the continental nations of Europe and Asia.

Another opportunity for Russia existed in the Middle East. The large deposits of oil in Iran and Iraq offered tempting bait to any nation whose civilian or military components were large oil consumers. Again however these areas are coastal in a large sense. They lie within the reach of the Mediterranean Sea, the Red Sea, and the Persian Gulf, and at a somewhat greater distance from the Indian Ocean.

The Weakness of the Western World

In this strategic situation, with the Soviet Union in firm and expanding control over the center of the largest land area in the world, with the littoral countries weakened in military power and torn by internal dissension, the Western Powers—especially the United States and Great Britain—sought a means of living with this new threat. It was not however immediately recognized as a threat. Large numbers of people both in and

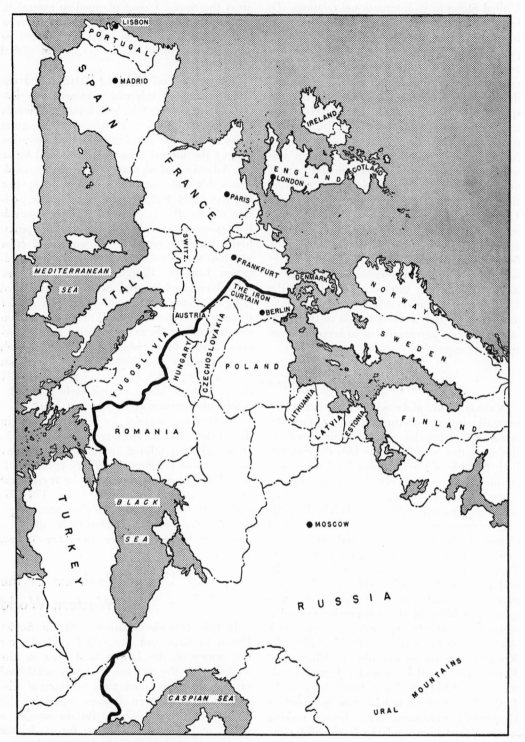

EUROPE AS SEEN FROM THE KREMLIN

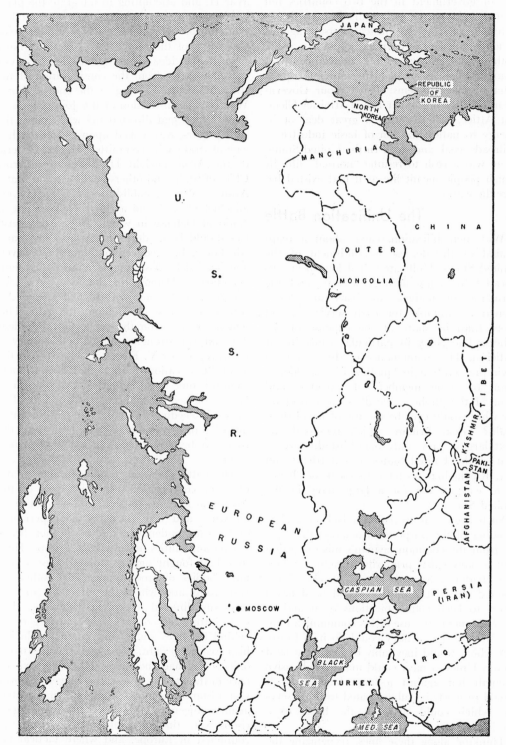

ASIA AS SEEN FROM THE KREMLIN

out of government in the two countries felt that Russia was merely pursuing legitimate defensive policies to protect herself against "encirclement" by unfriendly powers. Also, both countries were more concerned with domestic policies than with large, complex, international problems. The Labour Government in England, under Prime Minister Clement Attlee, was devoting a great deal of its energy to nationalization of basic industries— railroads, coal, and steel. In the United States, there was a rush to resume "normal" life, by which people meant life as it had existed before the war.

The Unification Battle

With demobilization, came about a reappraisal of the defense establishment of the United States. Unification had long been advocated by many military leaders, and the shrinking of budgets to peace-time levels caused a scramble for each service to get more than its share at the expense of the others. The Navy in particular came in for criticism. The maintenance of ships, or even their preservation in "mothballs" was looked upon by some members of Congress and some of the public as needlessly extravagant, for what would ever be the use of naval ships again? Great Britain, which possessed the next largest navy—only one-third the size of that of the United States—was a friend and ally. Russia had no navy to speak of; hence there was no use for a large navy in the United States.

Such arguments revealed a lack of understanding of the purposes of a navy; they suffer from the common layman's misconception that a navy exists primarily to fight another. The better informed critics of the Navy pointed out that while we would need naval forces to keep communications open and to deny an enemy the use of his communications, this was all that a navy could do in a future war which would inevitably be against a land power. Unless a navy could make its offensive strength felt against a large land mass, it should properly be subordinated to those services which could strike at the heart of a continent.

Thinking along these lines, recognizing the role played by the Army Air Forces in World War II, and attempting to integrate the place of the atomic bomb in strategic and tactical planning brought about a desire for the reorganization of the armed forces of the United States. The idea of reorganization received special impetus from the consideration of the strategic picture existing at the end of World War II. The institution of the Joint Chiefs of Staff, which had directed the war against the Axis powers, was looked upon as too much a case of strategy by committee. Hence, General of the Army Dwight D. Eisenhower, Army Chief of Staff, and others in the United States Army sought the establishment of a single overall chief of staff and a single Department of National Defense in which the existing services should be made three, Army, Navy, and Air Force, but reduced to subordinate levels and headed by Assistant Secretaries—Assistant Secretary of Defense for the Army, Assistant Secretary of Defense for the Navy, and Assistant Secretary of Defense for Air. This scheme, which won the support of President Truman, was strongly opposed by Secretary of the Navy James V. Forrestal. Thus began the great "Unification Battle" that was to rage from this time until the outbreak of the war in Korea pushed it into the background. The story is exceedingly complex, and unfortunate intrusion of personalities sometimes caused the issues to be forgotten in a spate of namecalling.

The battle grew out of two fundamentally different concepts of war. The view of the Army was in many respects close to that of its air wing, and was based on the experiences of the army leaders who had borne their heaviest responsibilities in the war in Europe. Here they had fought against a land mass where large bodies of troops faced each other on vast fronts and where the effort by air was primarily directed to strategic bombing, that is, to hitting the enemy's industrial targets far behind the lines and in this manner reducing his capacity to fight. Most high-ranking naval officers had had their most important experience in the Pacific, in a war of movement over vast distances against an island empire and against objectives whose area and whose garrisons were tiny in comparison to those encountered in Europe, and where tactical air support played an enormous part.

This is not to say that either group was too narrow to be able to appreciate and understand the war as it had been fought on the other side of the globe, but intellectual understanding is one thing and wholehearted acceptance is another. All were convinced that the most likely—indeed, the only possible—enemy was Soviet Russia, or a Russian inspired satellite, but methods proposed for countering the threat differed. The Army and its air component, the Army Air Forces, felt that the only realistic possibility was to plan on the basis of an all-out war with Russia. The United States obviously could not hope to match the number of soldiers that Russia could place in the field, but the advantage in troops could be neutralized by strategic bombing, for if the factories behind the lines could be knocked out, the huge armies of the Soviet (200 divisions or more) could not long be supported in the field. This strategic bombing concept was based largely on the fact of American possession of the atomic bomb which, it was believed, would prove a powerful deterrent to war.

The Navy's point of view, shared by Secretary Forrestal and the Chief of Naval Operations, Fleet Admiral Chester W. Nimitz, was that strategic bombing, even with the atomic bomb, could not alone win a major war. Sooner or later, ground forces would have to move in, and they would require support of two kinds: direct air support in battle, usually called tactical support, and logistic support, which would require shipping and protection of shipping. The navy men also felt that the danger was not so much that a big war would break out in the immediately foreseeable future, but that the United States would be unable to oppose the piecemeal taking over of countries on the littorals of Eurasia, having nothing between protest and the atomic bomb as a counter to this kind of move. Mr. Forrestal opposed the idea of the single Chief of Staff on the grounds that the officer who filled this post would be in the position of being oversold on the potentialities of one service only, and that the consequent loss of flexibility would embarrass or even cripple the war potential of the United States.

Out of these different concepts came differing methods of planning for another war.

The airmen were convinced of the deterrent effect of the atomic bomb and of the effectiveness of strategic bombing. They prepared to assume the Navy's traditional role of the First Line of Defense, even though almost all of their planning was offensive or at least retaliatory in nature. They pinned their faith in the B-36 bomber, which was capable, they said, of delivering an atomic bomb anywhere in the world and of bombing from 40,000 feet. In their opinion the major portion of the defense funds of the United States should be devoted to the air arm with the other services substantially reduced.

The view of Secretary Forrestal was that there should be "balanced forces." This phrase, unfortunately, was subjected to almost immediate misunderstanding. His critics leaped to the conclusion that he meant each service should get an equal part of the defense budget. This was far from Forrestal's thinking. By "balanced forces" he meant balanced in capability, so that each would be able to function capably and to coordinate with the others. In this manner, he hoped to achieve flexibility and the capability of responding to threats in ways of the nation's own choosing, without having to depend on the all-out destructiveness of atomic warfare.

Inter-service rivalry aggravated, and in some ways obscured, the points at issue between the armed forces. Air Force enthusiasts sought control over all aviation, no matter how used. Whether their view was the simple one that each service should have control of all weapons in its particular field—the Air Force, all air; the Army, all ground troops; and the Navy, all ships—or whether they feared that air expenditures by the Navy and the Army would offer budgetary competition or needless duplication and expense, their view found widespread support both in Congress and among the public.

The idea of relying on the Air Force to win the next war by strategic bombing was as appealing to the public as it was appalling to the navy leaders. The Navy felt that such a rigid strategic plan would invite disaster and that it would also make it impossible for the naval establishment to carry out its mission. The Navy needed to duplicate or at least adapt two types of military force which would come under the control of other services if the

Air Force view prevailed. It needed a highly mobile body of troops, trained in sea-to-land operations, which could be used to seize, protect, and garrison bases needed for naval operations, and to protect American lives and interests in troubled areas in the world. To this end, the Marine Corps had been formed and its achievements had become a part of the national heritage of the United States. The other requirement of the Navy was for an air arm which would be under naval control and which could be used to support the naval mission.[1]

At least in the mind of the general public, there was never any idea of entirely doing away with the Marine Corps. But it was felt that there should not be two land armies in the United States with identical missions. This criticism resulted from the widespread employment of marines on the division scale in the Pacific and on the multidivision scale on Iwo Jima and Okinawa. Army leaders tended to feel that such employment of marines was a usurpation of the Army's proper function. In the same way, Air Force enthusiasts felt that the air arm properly belonged to them and that the Navy was stepping out of line in its employment of air. Although the Navy perhaps had the need of carrier-based air for its antisubmarine operations in mid-ocean, the Air Force argued that it should not have control of land-based air, whatever its mission, or of combatant air, even carrier-based, that was not directed against strictly naval targets.

To understand the Navy's objections, we must review its three main functions—to defend American territory against sea-borne attack, to protect merchant ships against enemy warships, and to carry the attack with its logistic requirements across the sea to an enemy. Each of these missions requires a degree of command of the sea; at times this command may be tenuous and strictly limited in area, as in the case of a convoy whose escort commands only the water through which the convoy is passing; at other times it is much broader. However if significant strategic use is to be made of the oceans of the

world, and if they are to be used as highways of attack, it follows that the nation desiring to employ these weapons must exercise a substantial degree of command of the sea.

To a large extent since World War I, and to some extent even earlier, command of the sea has become three-dimensional. When Farragut reportedly damned the torpedoes in Mobile Bay, he was at least recognizing an effort to dispute command of the sea by means of underwater attack from moored mines. Blake, St. Vincent, Decatur, Nelson, and the rest had to contend only with the surface. But mines, torpedoes, and especially submarines have greatly complicated the problem of the navy that seeks command of the sea in wartime, for command must also extend to the sub-surface. In the same way, the airplane has extended the problem to the air, and the air and sub-surface may be exploited on a hit-and-run basis by a force that does not command the surface. But a nation wishing to use the sea for large-scale transport of strategic materials *must* command the surface, the sub-surface, and the air above the surface to such a degree that the losses the enemy can inflict are kept to an acceptable minimum. This command not only requires a high degree of flexibility in the employment of naval weapons, but also requires that it adopt weapons traditionally assigned to other services, notably troops and aircraft, if it is to accomplish its role. It needs troops to seize and hold bases required for operations, and it needs aircraft to be able to dispute the enemy's command of the air. In addition, the airplane is one of the best instruments for detecting submarines. To this end, not only carrier-based air is needed, but also land-based air for detection of submarines and for searching for other naval targets. To hold a carrier near a coast to do a task that might be accomplished by shore-based planes is to negate the chief advantage of the carrier: its mobility.

For these reasons the Navy opposed the unification bill being pushed by the Army and its air component. Yet there were many things to be said for unification. Even as recently as World War II there had been difficulties arising from lack of unified command. Presumably the new bill would preclude such experiences. It was possible through unification moreover

[1] The Navy had fought this battle during World War II when the Army sought to control antisubmarine patrols flown from the east coast of the United States. (See Chapter 30.)

to eliminate considerable waste and duplication among the services.

The National Security Act of 1947

After a long and sometimes bitter debate, Congress passed the National Security Act of 1947, which became law on July 26. The Act specified a sweeping reorganization of the defenses of the United States. It provided for three super-military policy boards. It established the National Military Establishment[2] with three basic components: the Department of the Army, the Department of the Navy, and the Department of the Air Force. It specified the functions and responsibilities of the Joint Chiefs of Staff and provided for interservice staffs and boards for coordinated planning.

Under the Act the National Security Council became the nation's top policy body. Its membership consisted of the President, the Vice President, the Secretary of State, the Secretary of Defense, and several other officers of policy boards. Its duties were:

(1) to assess and appraise the objectives, commitments, and risks of the United States in relation to our actual and potential military power, in the interest of national security, for the purpose of making recommendations to the President in connection therewith; and

(2) to consider the policies on matters of common interest to the departments and agencies of the Government concerned with the national security, and to make recommendations to the President in connection therewith.[3]

The Central Intelligence Agency, also provided in the Act, placed high-level strategic intelligence under a single direction. The National Security Resources Board[4] was established to coordinate plans for use of the nation's natural and industrial resources in time of war.

[2] Replaced in 1949 (Defense Reorganization Act) by a regular executive department, the Department of Defense.
[3] National Security Act of 1947, Washington, 1953, 2.
[4] Replaced in the Reorganization of 1953 by the Office of Defense Mobilization, which in 1958 merged with the Federal Civil Defense Agency to form the Office of Civil and Defense Mobilization.

By the terms of the National Security Act, the National Military Establishment (later Department of Defense) was to be headed by a Secretary of Defense, who would sit in the President's Cabinet. Heading the sub-departments were the Secretaries of the Army, of the Navy, and of the Air Force, who would not be of Cabinet rank. The Act further specified that the Air Force be given responsibility for strategic bombing and for combat operations in support of land armies. The Navy retained not only its carrier aviation but also its land-based reconnaissance wing and a Marine Corps of limited size. The Army was left its traditional functions virtually unchanged.

Secretary of the Navy Forrestal became the first Secretary of Defense and set about administering the law that he had helped to keep within reasonable bounds despite the efforts of extremists.

"The Great Debate"

Matters rested in fairly peaceable fashion until bitter acrimony again broke out among the services in 1948. The quarrel seems to have originated in the projected budget, which was set at $16 billion for defense. Air Force spokesmen charged that the Navy was attempting to edge its way into the field of strategic bombing by requesting new, larger carriers and carrier planes capable of transporting the atomic bomb. Naval supporters responded with an attack on the B-36, on which the Air Force was basing its strategy. A series of articles in the popular magazines succeeded in selling the public the idea of an easy victory through strategic atom bombing. In the naval view, this projected plan was not only inflexible but was nearly suicidal. Tempers flared. The B-36 was attacked as lacking the capability to press home an attack. Air Force supporters retorted that the aircraft carrier was obsolete, that it was too vulnerable to land-based air, to submarines, and to weather conditions. So the argument raged. Secretary of Defense Louis Johnson, who had succeeded Forrestal, accepted the Air Force view in the main and added fuel to the flames by his decision to cancel the 60,000-ton carrier *United States*, then under construction at Newport News. Tempers grew so hot in this so-called "Great Debate" that it seemed to many that the whole affair was out of hand. The debate was ended, as far as the public was concerned, with the dismissal of the Chief of Naval Operations, Admiral Louis Denfeld, and his replacement by Admiral Forrest P. Sherman, but the dispute was effectively ended only by the outbreak of war in Korea, with its immediate problems and more liberal budgets.

The Truman Doctrine
and the Marshall Plan

It is now time to back-track in order to examine in detail the strategic picture of the world. Even before the end of World War II it was apparent that there would be every prospect of trouble with Russia, conceivably leading to war between the United States and the Soviet Union. The United States had stood by helplessly as the Soviets expanded to the Baltic and into the Balkans and threatened the Middle East. The first major trouble came over Iran, but serious consequences were averted through the action of the United Nations. In the spring of 1947 President Truman proclaimed a new policy in regard to United States relations with Russia, a policy of helping free peoples everywhere "against aggressive movements that seek to impose upon them totalitarian regimes" and "of supporting peoples who are resisting attempted subjugation by armed minorities or by outside pressures."

Although the Soviet Union was not mentioned by name, there was no doubt that this policy was directed against her. At this time, Greece and Turkey were both threatened by Soviet aspirations. In Greece civil war was in progress, the rebels receiving substantial aid from Yugoslav sympathizers across the border and even aid from the Yugoslav government itself. At that time Yugoslavia was considered to be a Russian puppet government acting with the approval of and in support of the Russian Politburo. Russia also demanded of Turkey the rights to—indeed complete control of—the Dardanelles. The Truman Doctrine effectively served notice on the Soviet Union that the United States would clearly support

Greece and Turkey against any expansion by Communist forces into their territory. American supplies and munitions and American military advisers were sent to aid the Greek government. Visits of American naval forces to the Mediterranean, begun in 1946, were stepped up to serve as a diplomatic show of force. Again serious trouble was avoided.

In early June 1947 Secretary of State George C. Marshall, speaking at Harvard University, proposed a scheme for reconstruction of European countries through their own efforts, supported by American economic aid. This program came to be called the Marshall Plan, and was translated into the European Recovery Program. This plan, which at first met with enthusiastic response, was later viewed with a certain degree of hostility in Congress. The Soviet Union denounced the plan as American economic aggression and not only refused to participate but also kept any of its satellites from accepting American assistance.

Coup in Czechoslovakia

Ever since the end of World War II Czechoslovakia had been governed by coalition governments, which despite Soviet influence had maintained respect for civil liberties. Then in a sudden *coup d'état* in 1948, the Communist party under Prime Minister Klement Gottwald seized complete control of the Czech government. This coup, the first seizure *after World War II* by Communists of a country not under Red Army domination served to awaken many people to the ferocity and determination of Communist aggression.

Because of this action and because of deteriorating relationships with Russia, American defense officials began to press for a revival of Selective Service and also for universal military training. These two proposals touched off bitter Congressional debate. At length, in June 1948, the Selective Service Act was passed, but Congress balked at universal military training. The Selective Service Act was later rewritten to act as a substitute for universal military training by providing obligatory service in the reserve components in addition to prescribed tours of active duty.

The Berlin Blockade

The most dangerous situation to confront the United States since the end of World War II occurred in June 1948, when to all intents and purposes, the Soviet Union clamped down a blockade on Berlin, preventing all material from entering or leaving by road, rail, or canal. This blockade resulted partly from the division of Germany into four zones of occupation after World War II. The Russian Zone surrounded all of Berlin, but the capital itself was under quadripartite rule in a manner similar to that of occupied Germany itself. Hence, the three western powers, France, Great Britain, and the United States, held their Berlin garrisons as on an island surrounded by Soviet-held territory and by Soviet troops. The Soviet Union obviously had as its aim the complete ousting of the Western Powers from Berlin. The ostensible reason given for the blockade was the imminence of a western currency reform in the western zones, which the Russians said was sure to disorganize the East Zone currency. The blockade became so tight that no land or canal traffic was allowed to flow between the western zones and Berlin.

This situation presented United States leaders with a grave problem. Russia, obviously making a major bid for supremacy in Germany, was forcing a show of strength. On the reaction of the Western Powers depended not only the fate of Germany but also that of the free world. It was clear that if the free nations backed down now, Russia would assume they were acting from fear and would proceed to further and even more serious aggression. The challenge was clear. How could the West respond? In his diary, Secretary Forrestal outlined the alternatives:

1. Decide now to withdraw from our position in Berlin, in concert with the other Western powers, at an appropriate time in the future, presumably when a constituent assembly for a Western German government is called on September 1, and plan accordingly.

2. Decide at this time to retain our position in Berlin by all possible means, including supplying Berlin by convoy or using force in some other manner, such action to be only as a last resort after utilizing all diplomatic and other means without force to avoid war, but accepting the possibility of war as a consequence if necessary.

3. To maintain our unprovocative but firm stand in Berlin, utilizing first every local means, and subsequently every diplomatic means, to obtain recognition and assertion of our rights while postponing ultimate decision to stay in Berlin or withdraw.[5]

The second of these alternatives was adopted, but rather than resort to force by sending an armed train or escorted truck convoy overland, an airlift was attempted. This proved successful. Soon large quantities of foodstuffs, coal, and other supplies were being delivered to the former German capital on a round-the-clock schedule by British and American planes. The Russians did not oppose the airlift in any serious way although Russian fighters occasionally made dry runs on airlift planes. The American and British pilots were careful to stick to the routes prescribed in the original agreement on Berlin in 1945. The Soviets clearly did not wish to resort to force unless the Western Powers used it first, as would be inevitable if an armed convoy were sent through. United States Navy as well as Air Force planes were used in the airlift to supply foodstuffs, medical supplies, and coal. The blockade came to an end early in May 1949, when the Western Powers and Russia agreed to hold another session of the Council of Foreign Ministers to reconsider the German problem. In the 11 months of the blockade the Anglo-American airlift transported 2,343,-315 tons of supplies.

The North Atlantic Treaty Organization

As the cold war progressed from insult and vilification to such dangerous phases as the Berlin Blockade, the United States and several of the western European nations began to realize that their national security was at stake and that military cooperation between free countries was essential to combat the Soviet threat. Hence in 1949 the United States and

[5] Walter Millis, editor, *The Forrestal Diaries* (New York, 1951), 453.

eleven other nations agreed upon a treaty, the North Atlantic Pact, by which it was provided that the member nations would consider an attack on any one of them as an attack against them all. The signatory nations were Belgium, Canada, Denmark, France, Iceland, Italy, Luxembourg, the Netherlands, Norway, Portugal, the United Kingdom, and the United States. The year after its inception the North Atlantic Treaty Organization (NATO) invited Greece and Turkey to become members.

The language of the treaty had to be very carefully chosen in order to keep within the limitations of the United Nations Charter, especially Article 53, which provides for United Nations action in times of aggression. When Russia later charged that the North Atlantic Pact violated Article 53, Secretary of State Dean Acheson pointed out the provisions of Article 51 and 52 which allow each member state to take whatever action it deems necessary in self-defense. Another hurdle that the pact had to face was ratification procedure in the United States Senate. Some members charged that the decision on declaring war would no longer be up to Congress but would rest with any of the signatories who fancied themselves attacked. In spite of this opposition, the Senate gave its consent to the treaty in July 1949, by a vote of 82-13.

The teeth of the pact are in Article 5, which states:

The parties agree that an armed attack against one or more of them in Europe or North America shall be considered an attack against them all. And consequently they agree that, if such an armed attack occurs, each of them, in exercise of the right of individual or collective self-defense recognized by Article 51 of the Charter of the United Nations, will assist the party so attacked by taking forthwith, individually and in concert with the other parties, such action as it deems necessary, including the use of armed force, to restore and maintain the security of the North Atlantic area.

Provisions of the treaty called also for a command organization of military forces to be made available for military operations as necessary. The employment of this force was to be directed by a council known as the North Atlantic Council, which would sit permanently in Paris. This council represented the political planning level and was to be responsible for grand strategic direction. Below the council came the military level, which was to be directed by the Military Committee through its executive agency, the Standing Group. The Standing Group, composed of representatives of the chiefs of staff of France, The United Kingdom, and the United States, would coordinate and integrate defense plans originating in the major NATO commands. The basic commands were Allied Command Europe, Allied Command Atlantic, Allied Command Channel, and the Canada-United States Regional Planning Group.

To implement the program, the United States passed a billion dollar grant-in-aid for military equipment needed under the proposed arrangement. At a meeting in London in May 1950, it was agreed that in order to avoid duplication of effort, each member nation should concentrate on a part of the defense machinery. Great Britain, for example, was to concentrate on jet tactical aircraft and naval vessels; France, on light artillery and infantry weapons; and the United States, on strategic bombers and naval forces. In December 1950, General of the Army Dwight D. Eisenhower was appointed Supreme Allied Commander Europe (Saceur), and in January 1952, Admiral Lynde D. McCormick USN was named to command the naval forces and to become Supreme Allied Commander Atlantic (Saclant). The actual operation of setting up a military force met with considerable difficulty because of national pride and national rivalries and because of the economic impact of armament budgets on countries still trying to recover from the economic disruptions of World War II.

The Far East

At the end of World War II, the victorious allies seemed to have nothing to fear. Japan was badly beaten; the other eastern powers were allied to the common effort. Yet within five years, all of China was shut off from the Free World behind a "Bamboo Curtain" like the Iron Curtain in Europe, and outright war was in progress in the Far East. China was gradually lost through civil war. Step by step the Communists won territory until at length the Nationalists fled to Formosa and established a "temporary" government seat there. Similar civil war broke out in Indo-China in 1946. In Korea, the artificial division of the country at the 38th parallel led to open warfare in June of 1950.

China

The government of Chiang Kai-shek, which had fought the war against Japan, came under severe criticism both inside and outside China. Charges of corruption and mismanagement were loud and severe. Local unrest bred by uneven distribution of food and other consumer goods was seized upon by Chinese Communists. As time went on, the Communists under Mao Tze-Tung became well organized and were armed with surrendered Japanese weapons, with captured Chinese Nationalist weapons, and with American weapons originally supplied to Chiang but sold by unscrupulous persons, some of them inside the Nationalist government itself. In the course of events, sporadic guerrilla fighting spread into organized civil war between the Nationalists and the Communists.

Attempting to halt the deterioration of the situation in China, the United States supplied more money and arms to the Nationalists and sent a special representative to strive to resolve the conflict. General of the Army George C. Marshall was chosen for this mission; his instructions were to attempt to bring about a coalition government of the Nationalists and the People's Party—as the Communists called themselves. The efforts of Marshall met with very little success. American marines, which had been in China since the end of the war, were withdrawn, and the Communists gained strength as time went on. By October 1948, they had occupied all of Manchuria, and during 1949 and 1950 took over the rest of the country. The Nationalist Government moved to Taipeh, Formosa in December of 1949.

Mao immediately established a *rapprochement* with Soviet Russia, and a 30-year pact of "friendship, alliance, and mutual assistance" was signed by the two Communist powers on February 15, 1950. Thus, within five years, nearly 500 million persons came under the domination of the Communist world. An American "White Paper" issued late in 1949 pointed out American efforts to stem the tide, noting that equipment for 39 divisions and over two billion dollars in aid had been given to the Chinese Nationalists and that most of the arms and money had gone ultimately into the hands of Mao and his followers. The loss of arms and money was serious enough, but loss of China behind the "Bamboo Curtain" was to have consequences of the utmost gravity.

Korea

At the Potsdam Conference it had in effect been decided that on a temporary basis Russia would occupy North Korea and the United States South Korea. The actual line of demarcation, the 38th parallel, was decided on the spot as a convenient division line for the acceptance of the Japanese surrender. No one on the non-Communist side thought of it as an actual boundary. In the last four days of World War II, Russian forces moved into North Korea and seized Japanese forces there. Immediately the Soviets began organizing Socialists and Communists in their zone and set up the Korean People's Interim Committee as the basis of a government in opposition to the Democratic Party of Kim Koo and Syngman Rhee. Much political maneuvering ensued, with the Russians refusing to recognize Rhee and his party or even to allow the United States and, later, United Nations officials to visit north of the 38th parallel. In September 1947, the Soviet Union, having organized the North Korean government and army to its liking, proposed that all occupation forces be withdrawn by January 1948. This proposal was rejected. The United Nations named a commission to hold free elections in all of Korea in 1948, but the members of that commission were summarily refused permission to enter North Korea. Making the best of a bad situation, South Koreans established in South Korea the Republic of Korea with Syngman Rhee as president and the capital at Seoul. This government was elected in July 1948, and on August 15, the United States turned the government over to the Republic. American troops were withdrawn by the end of June 1949.

In May 1948, the Communists of North Korea proclaimed the People's Democratic Republic of Korea with its capital at Pyongyang. Shortly after this the Russians withdrew, leaving behind them a well organized and trained North Korean army. The United States had left South Korea with nothing more than a police or constabulary force to keep order but lacking the organization, equipment, and training for fighting against an army. Thus, the situation was ripe for the North Korean attack on South Korea in June of 1950.

Indo-China

As early as 1941, a nationalist movement had begun to gather strength in French Indo-China, but Japan's occupation of that territory during World War II prevented any fulfillment of the Indo-Chinese desire for independence. When Japan's forces were withdrawn in 1945, the Nationalist drive was renewed, and met with some degree of sympathy in Paris. The French government recognized the Vietnam Republic of Annamese Nationalists in 1946, but following a series of Communist-inspired guerrilla raids, withdrew its recognition. The Viet Minh Communist forces under General Ho Chi Minh had early sought to exploit the power vacuum caused by the withdrawal of Japanese troops, and these activities caused the French to station an expeditionary force there, including elements of the famed French Foreign Legion, almost as soon as the Japanese moved out. When France recognized the new anticommunist Provisional Government of Vietnam in June 1948, civil war broke out. The French diverted a large proportion of their national income to maintaining forces in Indo-China and were thereby weakened in fulfilling their commitments to the European Army. The United States extended economic aid to the French in Indo-China without producing decisive results. The issue was further clouded by the fact that many anticommunists are also anti-French. Further, because there was no distinct territorial division as in Korea, no well-defined battle lines could be drawn.

Japan

Unlike Germany, Japan was not divided between occupying powers at the end of the war. The Allied Command named the United States as the occupying power and General of the Army Douglas MacArthur as Supreme Commander. By the terms of the surrender, Japan agreed to a democratic government and to free elections. Under the direction of General MacArthur, a cabinet headed by Baron Kijuro Shidehara granted the franchise to women, lowered the voting age from 25 to 20, and dissolved the vast family and corporate trusts that had constituted much of Japan's economic and military strength. A new constitution was ratified and became effective May 3, 1947. Under it Japan renounced her right to wage war and the idea of the divinity of the emperor, and also abolished the House of Peers. A new Diet became the "highest organ of state power and sole law-making authority."

In American strategic planning for the Far East, Japan was established as one of a series of key positions running from Japan through Okinawa and Formosa to the Philippines. Areas of friction with the Russians developed over the Kurile islands and fishing rights in the waters between Japan and Siberia. Further friction developed from Russia's efforts to organize a Communist party in Japan. Although small, the party was well organized and so active that on June 6, 1950, General MacArthur ordered the government to ban Communist members of the Council from public activities "for perversion of truth and incitation to mass violence."

Naval Developments

With the deterioration of relations between the Western Powers and Russia following World War II, it became necessary for military planners in the West to consider Russia as the most likely future enemy and to base plans and policies on that assumption. Accordingly, heads of naval forces set in motion plans and programs to counter Russia's known or suspected capabilities. It was perfectly obvious that no nation could challenge the sea power of the United States, for her navy in terms of tonnage was larger than that of the rest of the world combined. However, Russia could choose the traditional role of an inferior naval power, that of commerce raiding, depending largely on submarines. At the end of the war,

Russia secured not only several of the latest German hydrogen peroxide U-boats, but also the persons and services of several top designers responsible for the type. The hydrogen peroxide U-boat had been developed too late to be of war service to Germany, but its menace was real. It was a limited submersible, not requiring surface air for its propulsion unit and capable of high speed submerged, if only for a short period.

War planners among the non-Communist powers had to assume that in a future war, Russia would embark on wide scale submarine operations, not only against commerce but against naval forces as well. In 1950 Russia was known to have about 350 operational submarines in contrast to the 56 with which Germany started World War II. Armed with new acoustic torpedoes and equipped with the snorkel, even the conventional boat was a threat, while the probability of encountering hydrogen peroxide boats or improvements on them presented Western naval planners with very grave problems.

To meet these problems required much imagination and boldness in a time when national feeling was concentrated on peace. Officers and men of the United States Navy were being released from active duty so fast that it was sometimes difficult to get ships to ports where they could be decommissioned. The first step taken in the United States to prepare for possible future trouble was to organize a strong reserve of both ships and trained personnel. Some ships that had outlived their usefulness or whose cost of maintenance would exceed their replacement value were disposed of by sale or transfer. Others were sold outright to private citizens. Some were scrapped. A few were used as target ships in atomic tests at Bikini Atoll in the Marshall Islands. Most ships which were worth retaining in the fleet but which had to be decommissioned for want of funds and personnel were put in "mothballs."[6]

The establishment of an adequate, well-

trained Naval Reserve was of utmost importance. Drilling units were set up in the various naval districts, some with drill pay for 48 drills a year. The Organized Reserve consisted of units with authorized complements of 200 enlisted men and 15 officers. In addition there were many volunteer specialized units in electronics, intelligence, base construction (Seabees), aviation, and many others. Fourteen days' paid training duty afloat or ashore annually was authorized for reservists in these programs. Some of these cruises were on fleet ships, others on district ships, usually destroyer escorts assigned to the various naval districts and kept in partial commission with a skeleton crew aboard. The reservists would fill out the crew and help take the ship to sea.

The active fleet operations were extended to include the Navy's traditional role of implementing diplomacy. Beginning in 1947 the U.S. Sixth Fleet remained on continuous duty in the Mediterranean, showing the flag and helping to support Western interests. One large carrier—the *Midway*, the *Franklin D. Roosevelt*, or the *Coral Sea*—was always on duty there; a second carrier, several cruisers and destroyers completed the carrier task force. In addition there was maintained an amphibious force of transports carrying the Fleet Marine Force. Logistic supply was handled primarily from the United States on a simulated wartime basis. This force existed not only as an arm of diplomacy but as a force to strike offensively in time of war, to protect American lives and interests, to act as goodwill ambassadors, and to keep control of all that vital waterway, essential for western communication lines. With the establishment of NATO, joint naval operations came into increasing prominence. NATO signals and tactics were developed for joint operations of ships of NATO navies and joint manuevers were successfully held on several occasions.

The American navy spent much time and effort in combating the submarine menace for future operations. Hunter-killer groups, sonobuoys, high frequency radio direction

---

[6] "Mothballing" was intended to preserve ships from the deterioration usually considered inevitable in long periods of idleness. Gun mounts were covered in a moisture-proof "cocoon" of vinylite plastic. Machinery spaces were sealed and electrically dehumidified. Ships' records were transferred intact

to storage, and propulsion machinery was greased and otherwise protected from moisture. The success of the program became apparent with the outbreak of war in Korea when the mothballed ships were returned to full service in a matter of a few weeks.

finders, sonar, and other devices were refined and improved.

Developments were also extensive in naval aircraft design and operation. The jet fighter completely replaced the old propeller-driven types. Jet bombers became common, and the speed of aircraft, both fighter and bomber, far outstripped anything available in the war years. *Essex*-type carriers gradually received strengthened flight decks to accommodate jet planes and heavier bombers. One of the most radical changes in design was the angled carrier deck, which was developed by the British and was installed in u.s.s. *Antietam* and other United States carriers. The landing section of the deck was angled about eight degrees to port so that a plane coming in for a landing would not crash through the barriers into planes parked on the forward part of the flight deck. This kind of angling also permitted simultaneous landing and launching operations from one carrier, planes being sent off forward at the same time others are landing aft.

Changes in munitions were also of prime importance. Depth charges and ahead-thrown antisubmarine weapons were redesigned to speed sinking time so that a submarine would not be able to twist away while these projectiles were dropping through the water. Automatic 6- and 8-inch guns were developed and installed on cruisers. Automatic 3-inch guns began to replace 40-mm. mounts as antiaircraft weapons. In the field of rocket weapons both the Army and the Navy conducted extensive developmental programs.

The helicopter was another important development in the Navy's aircraft program. Its flexibility of operation and the small space needed for landing and take-off meant that it could operate successfully from cruisers and battleships as well as carriers. It made a good scout and was able to relieve destroyers of some of the more onerous mail-delivering duties as well as the duty of plane guard in carrier operations. In Korea these craft were to play many other important roles from air strike control planes to rescue missions. Supply or evacuation of isolated positions was but one of the vital services they performed. The lives of many wounded were saved by these "whirlybirds" operating from hospital LST's and hospital ships, for they were able to pick a wounded man up from an advance dressing station and fly him directly to the hospital ship. Most important of all, the Marine Corps began experiments in the use of helicopters for ship-to-shore movements in amphibious operations.

The Atomic Bomb

After the dropping of the atomic bombs on Hiroshima and Nagasaki in the closing days of the war, it became imperative for military leaders to have more exact knowledge of this weapon. They needed to know how to use it effectively in offense and they needed to know its capabilities and limitations so that some countermeasures might be taken to minimize its effects in the event that an enemy used it. For this purpose Operation CROSSROADS was scheduled as a test of the atomic bomb against naval ships. The venture became a joint experiment of the War and Navy Departments. Under the command of Vice Admiral William H. P. Blandy usn, tests were conducted at Bikini Atoll in the Marshall Islands. Over 200 ships, 150 airplanes, and 42,000 men were involved in the test. Seventy-five ships were placed in the target area to provide data for study of blast damage and radiation contamination. The target ship, the *Nevada*, was in the center with four other battleships, the *Pennsylvania*, the *Arkansas*, the *New York*, and the Japanese *Nagato*, ranged around. Two carriers, the *Saratoga* and the *Independence*, were included as well as the cruisers *Pensacola*, *Salt Lake City*, the German *Prinz Eugen*, and the Japanese *Sakawa*. In addition there were other cruisers, destroyers, attack transports, submarines, and various smaller vessels. Each of the ships contained scientific instruments, an assortment of equipment, and live animals to measure or reflect the effects of the blast and subsequent radiation. Drone airplanes were prepared to fly through the cloud and send back scientific data. Drone boats were to take samples of the water after the explosions.

Test Able, a drop from a B-29, took place on July 1, 1946 at 0900 Bikini time. The damage was summarized by an evaluation board set up by the Joint Chiefs of Staff. A destroyer and two transports sank at once, and another destroyer capsized and sank later. The Japanese cruiser *Sakawa* sank the next day. The *Independence* was wrecked and gutted by fire. The submarine *Skate*'s superstructure received extensive damage. The superstructures of the *Nevada, Arkansas,* and *Pensacola* were badly wrecked. Casualties would have been very high among exposed personnel, but the animal survivors indicated some measure of protection from radiation would be afforded crew members below decks.

Test Baker, held at 0825 on July 25, 1946, was an underwater explosion. The bomb was suspended below *LSM 60,* which disintegrated from the blast. Also sunk were the *Arkansas,* the *Saratoga,* an LST, an LSM, and an oiler, while the destroyer *Hughes* and the transport *Falcon* were beached to prevent them from sinking. One submerged and three surfaced submarines went permanently to the bottom. The Japanese battleship *Nagato* sank five days later. The water of the lagoon was so dangerous from radioactivity that four days after

Test Baker it was unsafe for personnel to spend any "useful length of time" on the target vessels. Subsequent tests were held at a new test area in Eniwetok Atoll.

The United States did not long enjoy the monopoly on the atomic bomb. Partly as a result of the work of traitors and partly as a result of Soviet scientific knowledge, the Russians developed an atomic bomb of their own several years ahead of the time Western scientists thought possible. They successfully exploded the prototype somewhere in the Caucasus area in September 1949. Detection of radioactive particles in the stratosphere led to American knowledge of this explosion, an event confirmed by the Russians a short time later. The fact of Soviet possession of atomic weapons caused military and political leaders to take another look at the world strategic picture. They had scarcely begun this process when a new development brought war from a hypothetical to an actual condition. The militarized North Koreans recklessly flung down the gauntlet; the response was up to the free world.

45:

The Korean War

The uneasy peace ended abruptly on the morning of June 25, 1950 when North Korean troops crossed the 38th parallel in an invasion of the Republic of Korea. Unlike previous border skirmishes, this was invasion—full scale and without warning. Nothing, it seemed, could save free Korea.

The Communist leaders had, they thought, chosen shrewdly in their efforts to fill the gap in their holdings in Asia. The invasion of South Korea would point a dagger at the heart of Japan, where General Douglas MacArthur prevented their customary subversion. Incidentally it would test the determination of the Western world to resist Communist aggression. Spokesmen for the U.S. State Department had publicly intimated that Korea was not important to American strategic defense. The implication seemed clear: the United States would not seriously oppose the invasion of South Korea.

North Korean troops, well trained in conventional infantry tactics, excelled in camouflage, infiltration, and night operations. Even if the forces of the United Nations should intervene, the physical aspects of Korea and the primitive but effective North Korean logistic organization were of a kind greatly to hinder a force that put great emphasis on the use of machines, both for supply and for attack, and whose striking power could most quickly be brought to bear through sea and air power. The mountainous terrain and the extremes of heat and cold, mud and dust, typhoon and rainy season would limit the effectiveness of mechanized warfare. In logistics, North Korea had an organization almost invulnerable to United Nations forces; it later proved nearly impossible to interdict the flow

of supplies without physical possession of the supply routes or the supply bases. The North Korean soldier could practically live off the land. Conscripted peasants could carry supplies, ammunition, and other requisites over back roads while giving the appearance of harmless refugees. The 1,500-mile-long Korean coastline offers many places for concealment, but not many beaches suitable for amphibious landings. The east coast of Korea has adequate harbors, but these have limited access to the interior. The west coast is protected in many areas by vast mud banks and tide ranges. The mountainous terrain would assist a foot-borne and foot-supplied army by offering easy cover, opportunities for ambush, and protection from air attack. The same mountainous terrain would greatly handicap a mechanized army, adding immeasurably to its vastly greater logistic problem.

The United Nations Intervene

Some such reasoning process as this may well have formed the basis for the North Korean—or Communist Chinese or Russian—"Enemy Capabilities" section of their Estimate of the Situation. If this is true, events soon proved the soundness of many of their conclusions. They miscalculated however in several important respects. On June 25 (New York time), the day after the Reds crossed the border, an emergency meeting of the United Nations Security Council convened in New York. Without a veto, by grace of a Russian boycott, the Security Council condemned the North Korean act as a breach of world peace and forthwith ordered military sanctions. The United States undertook the direction of mili-

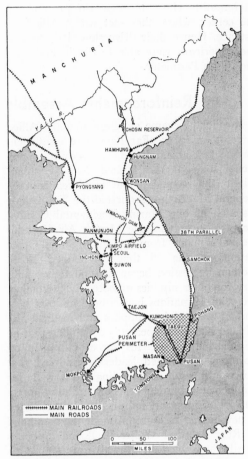

KOREA

in South Korea, later at targets located in North Korea as well.

Naval Operations

Early naval operations in Korean waters included evacuation of civilians and Americans at Inchon and Pusan. Merchant freighters, protected by American and South Korean naval forces, picked up thousands of refugees at both ports. The u.s. destroyers *Mansfield* and *De Haven* stood by off Inchon, and Korean patrol craft looked after Pusan. Meanwhile on the east coast, the North Koreans executed amphibious landings at Kangnung and Samchock, putting 10,000 troops ashore. The *De Haven* saw further action in a counter attack at Samchok shortly afterward.

The first ship-to-ship action of the war took place off Pohang. Three South Korean ships, two YMS's and one PC, discovered what turned out to be a North Korean troop transport attempting to seize the port of Pohang. The strange vessel flew no colors and refused to answer repeated challenges. Searchlight illumination revealed her identity, and she was sunk after a short gun battle.

As the days passed, it became evident that South Korean ground forces and Allied naval and air forces alone could not stop the advance of the North Korean armies. Because Allied ground forces also were needed, General MacArthur was authorized to strip Japan of occupation forces to furnish troops for the action in Korea. Transportation of these men from Japan to Korea was handled for the most part by air and by LST's. During this operation two aircraft carriers in the area, u.s.s. *Valley Forge* and h.m.s. *Triumph,* sent interdiction and air support strikes over Korean territory.

The air operations reveal a striking difference in troop support doctrine between the U.S. Air Force on the one hand and the U.S. Navy and Marine Corps on the other. Planes from the two carriers were supporting the Army and came under control of Air Force airborne controllers who ordered attacks well distant from the lines under the theory of interdiction of the battlefield. In contrast, planes from escort carriers *Sicily* and *Badoeng*

tary operations. President Truman, who had courageously taken the lead in opposing the Communist aggression, delegated responsibility for the "police action," as he later called it, to the American Joint Chiefs of Staff. The Joint Chiefs in turn named General of the Army Douglas MacArthur to have operational control in the Far East in addition to his responsibility as Supreme Commander, Occupied Japan. On June 27, President Truman ordered the United States Seventh Fleet, based on Japan, to neutralize Formosa—to prevent the Chinese Communists from attacking that island and to prevent the forces of Generalissimo Chiang Kai-shek from attacking the mainland. In addition the Seventh Fleet was to operate under the orders of General MacArthur in attacks on military targets, at first

Strait, which supported the marines, were controlled from the ground. Their marine pilots, well trained in close air support, often attacked strong points within a few yards of their own men. Although the escort carriers could provide only 55 per cent of the number of sorties flown by the larger carriers, their planes accomplished as much in slowing the North Korean advance.

Escort of supply ships to Pusan became advisable in face of reported submarine sightings in Korean waters. Speculation over Russian intentions with their Vladivostok-based submarines caused deep concern in the early days of the war. Commitment of submarines would very certainly mean great difficulty in support and reinforcement of ground forces already in Korea, and it might well mean that World War III was at hand. Fortunately this menace never materialized, for submarines, although occasionally spotted in the area, never engaged in any offensive actions.

The Reds Drive South

The South Koreans, lacking tanks and combat aircraft, fell back before the invaders in a hopeless rout. Smashing past Suwon, the Reds sent flanking drives to the east just as the first American troops, two battalions of the 24th Infantry Division, arrived from Japan. Digging in, falling back from one road block to another, the American troops managed to slow the Red drive and caused the Communists to overestimate American strength. As a result the invaders deployed across the country instead of smashing through to Pusan as they well might have done.

As the Americans retreated from Taejon to Kumchon, an important rail and road junction, they received strong support on their right flank from the Republic of Korea army which had somewhat recovered from its early reverses and was fighting effectively in the east. In the west however defenses were nonexistent, and in a few days the Red invaders had reached the southwestern corner of Korea, where they wheeled and began a drive east to Pusan. In sight of Masan, only 30 miles from the vital port of Pusan, they were stopped by a small, determined force of the 24th Infantry. Instead of reinforcing this drive, the

Communists chose to maintain pressure on the center, where they met strong Allied resistance. Hence their drive slowed down and the Americans were able to dig in and hold the Pusan Perimeter.

Reinforcements Assemble

It quickly became apparent that the Allied forces then in the Far East were insufficient for the task at hand. Unless speedy reinforcements arrived, the United Nations troops might well be pushed out of Korea entirely. General MacArthur requested the "immediate dispatch of one Marine Regimental Combat Team with comparable Marine Air Unit for tactical support" from the United States. Other nations of the 53 that condemned North Korean aggression began to send either military forces or supplies or both. By the end of the year, 19 nations had offered military help and 21 were giving supplies and medical aid. Chiang Kai-shek repeatedly demanded that he be allowed to use his forces currently on Formosa, but Allied leaders considered that this would result in spreading the war. By far the heaviest burden for both military forces and logistic support fell on the United States. A new carrier task group under the command of Rear Admiral Walter F. Boone USN was hastily assembled in Hawaiian waters. This group included, besides heavy carrier *Philippine Sea,* cruisers *Toledo* and *Helena,* ten destroyers, five submarines, and four oilers.

Manpower became an increasing Allied problem; many ships were not only short of wartime complements but were not even up to authorized peacetime strength. General MacArthur's request for a Marine Regimental Combat Team was followed by requests for a full Marine Division. He received assurance from Washington toward the end of July that one would be forthcoming. On its timely arrival depended whether the United Nations could hold in Korea. To fill manpower shortages personnel of the Army, Navy, Air Force, and Marine Corps were pulled out of duty stations in the United States and rushed to Korea. Their places were taken by reservists who either volunteered or were recalled to active duty. Many reservists too found themselves Korea-bound.

Already boxed within a small perimeter around the port of Pusan, the United Nations forces could no longer trade space for time. Taejon had fallen; Taegu was threatened. Driving to Mokpu, the North Koreans, as we have noted, had reached the southwest tip of Korea. They then began to close to the eastward and the southward, compressing still further the narrow field of operations around Pusan. In an attempt to reinforce the armies in the field, and because of the port congestion at Pusan, on July 18, the United States 1st Cavalry Division was ordered to make an amphibious landing at Pohang, 70 miles north of Pusan. So rapidly were the Reds driving south, no one was sure until the last moment whether or not the Americans would have to fight their way ashore. As it turned out, the landings were unopposed. Approximately 10,000 men, 2,000 vehicles, and 2,800 tons of bulk cargo were put ashore. The newly landed troops got into action two days later, assisting the badly battered 24th Infantry Division.

The Pusan Perimeter, as finally established, was enclosed by a line beginning on the south coast of Korea at Tongyong, about 25 miles west of Pusan, proceeding northerly for approximately 80 miles, around Taegu, and thence easterly to a point south of Pohang, which had to be given up after the 1st Cavalry Division's landing there. The situation grew so desperate that General MacArthur ordered the 1st Provisional Marine Brigade directly to Pusan, canceling its plans for landing first at Japan for reorganization. The marines reached Pusan on August 2, preceded by a day by the Army's 2nd Infantry Division and the 5th Regimental Combat Team. Since the United Nations did not have sufficient force to hold the perimeter at all points, the marines were employed as a mobile reserve to counterattack quickly at the scene of any breakthrough. There are few clearer examples of an inferior force taking advantage of an interior position.

Planning Operation Chromite

By the end of the third week in August, the North Korean drive seemed to have lost its push. Hence on the 23rd General MacArthur called a conference in Tokyo to discuss the possibilities of an amphibious assault on Inchon. To attend this meeting, the Chief of Naval Operations, Admiral Forrest C. Sherman, and the Army Chief of Staff, General J. Lawton Collins, flew from Washington. Representing United States naval forces in the Far East were Vice Admirals C. Turner Joy and Arthur D. Struble.

MacArthur had first directed planning for a landing in the Inchon area in the early days of the war, but the deteriorating situation on the Korean mainland had forced cancellation of these plans. Now, in August, they were revived. Determined to take advantage of the mobility afforded him by his sea power, MacArthur pointed out that a landing well up the peninsula would cut off supplies for the bulk of the North Korean army, 90 per cent of which was engaged in South Korea. Inchon, the port of Seoul, very nearly the only possible port for a large-scale amphibious landing, presented almost insurmountable difficulties. In the first place, the only approach to the area is through Flying Fish Channel, a long, narrow, tortuous channel with irregular three-to-five knot currents. The approaches to the harbor itself are commanded by the island fortresses of Wolmi-do and Sowolmi-do. The difficulties of the harbor meant that the reserve ships would have to stand off 30 miles from the assault vessels, approximately three times the distance customarily considered the maximum. Greater than all these difficulties loomed the matter of the tide. The tidal range at Inchon—one of the greatest in the world, 29 feet on the average and on occasion rising to 36 feet above low water—nearly precluded the proposed landing, yet paradoxically made it possible because it afforded deep water over the mud flats that make up a large part of Inchon's waterfront. LST's need 29 feet of water for proper maneuvering, and this depth of water could be assured only for a period of about three days once a lunar month. Hence the moon set the date for the Inchon landing. The proper tide conditions would obtain on the three days beginning September 15; such conditions would not again be encountered until the middle of October—too close to the Korean winter. Accordingly September 15 was set, leaving just over three weeks for planning an operation more difficult than most of those encountered in World War II, when preparation for amphibious operations had customarily taken months. In view of the short period of time remaining, planning for Operation CHROMITE was begun without delay.

At once, Lieutenant General Walton H. Walker USA[1] was warned that the Marine Brigade would be withdrawn from the Pusan area in the immediate future for an amphibious landing. General Walker was understandably reluctant to let it go since it was in combat and he had no replacement. The brigade was released however by the personal order of General MacArthur and became the nucleus for the 1st Marine Division which was to spearhead the Inchon landing. No replacements were offered General Walker because none were available. The risk of weakening the Pusan Perimeter was foreseen, but nothing could be done about it; the risk had to be taken if the Inchon landing was to succeed. Only the command of the sea exercised by the United Nations naval forces made such a speedy redeployment possible and the risks acceptable.

The marines from Pusan were to be reinforced by others coming from the United States, and from these two sources the 1st Marine Division was organized. The division, with the 7th Infantry Division, the 187th Airborne Regimental Combat Team, and a Korean Marine Corps regiment, comprised the X Corps, which was to make the assault. The operation was placed under the tactical direction of Vice Admiral Struble, Commander Joint Task Force Seven. The Attack Force, TF 90, was under the command of Rear Admiral James H. Doyle USN. Escort carriers were to fly close support missions, while the cruisers and destroyers of the Covering Force supplied artillery assistance. Deep support air strikes were to be flown from carriers *Philippine Sea, Valley Forge,* and *Boxer,* under the command of Rear Admiral Edward C. Ewen USN in the *Philippine Sea.* Logistics were the responsibility of Captain Bernard L. Austin USN, Commander Task Force 79.

One of the pressing needs was for intelligence information on the landing area. Air

Force, Marine, and Navy planes flew photo-reconnaissance missions, but on-the-spot information was vital. Accordingly an intelligence team led by Lieutenant Eugene F. Clark USN landed near Inchon. His reports, especially on the feasibility of the landing beaches and on the strength of the defenses on Wolmi-do, played a important part in the planning.

It seemed that all the work of preparation was to be lost when a typhoon boiled up through Japan, hitting Kobe especially hard, where the 1st Marine Division had debarked three days earlier. The typhoon, with winds up to 110 knots, not only imperiled ships but, worse, cost 24 hours of the precious time needed for the arduous tasks of unloading mixed cargoes and combat-loading assault vessels. Another delay like this would postpone the landing until the middle of October, the next period of flood tide. Anxious weather observers carefully checked for disturbances. A few days later, they spotted a depression about 200 miles west of Saipan. By September 8, this depression had blown up into another typhoon whose predicted track crossed that of Joint Task Force Seven. As if this were not bad enough, a new danger loomed: a South Korean patrol vessel on station near Inchon sank a North Korean minelayer. Had it already laid its mines? No one knew. Mines in Flying Fish Channel would make Operation CHROMITE nearly impossible. Not only would detection be difficult in the muddy water, but even a small ship sunk in the channel would effectively block it.

On September 11, the second typhoon began a slow turn to the north. Taking a chance that the northerly curve would continue, Admiral Doyle ordered the Transport and Advance Attack Groups to get underway from Kobe, one day ahead of schedule. Because rough weather impeded the passage, the extra time was all to the good.

Capturing the Harbor Islands

The first job to be done at Inchon was to neutralize the islands of Wolmi-do and Sowol-mi-do. The plan as finally carried out was to send a cruiser-destroyer force to draw fire from Wolmi-do in order to reveal batteries and to knock them out. This effort was to be

[1] General Walker had replaced Major General William F. Dean in command of the Eighth Army in Korea after Dean had been captured in the defense of Taejon.

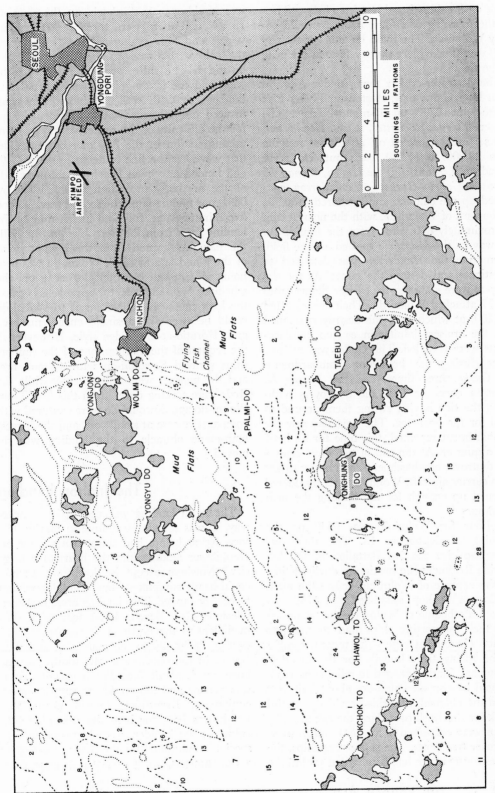

THE APPROACHES TO INCHON

made on D-minus-2 and D-minus-1 days. Then on the morning of D-day, marines would occupy Wolmi-do. The main landing on the city itself would take place that evening at the peak of the tide.

The destroyer-cruiser force, under Admiral John H. Higgins USN, started up Flying Fish channel at 0730 on D-minus-2 day. The cruisers *Toledo, Rochester,* H.M.S. *Kenya,* and H.M.S. *Jamaica* peeled off at stations ranging from 20,000 to 14,000 yards out. Destroyer Squadron 9, *Mansfield, De Haven, Lyman K. Swenson, Collett, Gurke,* and *Henderson,* continued up the channel and anchored in a line to the west of Wolmi-do, with the nearest ship approximately 800 yards from the island. On the way in, the *Mansfield* spotted a mine field, whereupon the *Henderson* was detached to investigate and destroy the mines. As the destroyers were standing in, carrier planes from TF 77 attacked Wolmi-do. Their strikes lifted at 1300, at which time the destroyers opened fire, the cruisers joining in as gun emplacements were revealed. The *Collet* was hit five times during the hour-long bombardment, the *Gurke* three times, and the *Lyman K. Swenson* once. At 1400 the destroyers withdrew, the tide having swung them around to head for the open sea. The next day saw the bombardment repeated, this time for an hour and a quarter. At the end of two days' cruiser and destroyer bombardments, and heavy strikes from carrier aircraft, Wolmi-do was considered softened up enough for the landing the next morning.

H-hour for Wolmi-do was 0630 on the morning of September 15. The time was chosen to give the 3rd Battalion of the 5th Marine Regiment the maximum daylight time for the capture of Wolmi-do before the main landing at Inchon scheduled for 1730. To arrive on schedule at Wolmi-do the transports and their supporting ships had to navigate Inchon channel at night—the moonless night of the spring tide. Luckily for the invaders Lieutenant Clark managed to relight the navigational beacon on Palmi-do, about half way down the channel, and this provided a useful check for the 19 ships making the assault. The troops were embarked in an LSD and in three destroyer transports. The supporting ships, the six destroyers which had bombarded Wolmi-do,

were making their third trip up the channel. In addition there were three rocket landing vessels and four cruisers. The *Mansfield* led the column in, navigating without difficulty by radar. The ships were all in position by 0500 and the landing force was ordered into the boats at 0540. At 0545 bombardment commenced and proceeded without incident except for the difficulty of the rocket vessels in maintaining station in the 3½-knot current. The first wave left the line of departure at 0627½ and landed on Green Beach on the west side of the northerly projection of the island at 0631, one minute late. The second wave landed five minutes later, followed in ten minutes by landing craft from the *Fort Marion.* By 0701, the flag was hoisted from the highest point of the island and at 0807, Wolmi-do was pronounced secured. Sowolmi-do, next on the schedule, was difficult to approach because the long causeway connecting it to Wolmi-do could be swept by a single enemy machine gun, Horatio-at-the-bridge style. However, at the request of the marines, one of the support ships sprayed Sowolmi-do with 40-mm. fire, and the marines were able to cross while the Reds were seeking cover from this fire. Thus, Wolmi-do and Sowolmi-do were captured with comparative ease at small cost, and the biggest man-made obstacle to the landing was removed.

The Inchon Landing

The main landing was next to get underway. It was something unique in marine history. Never before had the marines made an amphibious landing into the heart of a large city.[2] Nowhere except in downtown Inchon could heavy equipment—tanks, bulldozers, and trucks—be landed. Two landing areas had been selected: Red Beach, 1,000 feet wide, immediately to the north of the causeway connecting Wolmi-do to the mainland, and Blue Beach, in the outskirts to the south. No one knew much about Blue Beach except that it was narrow and too muddy to support heavy equipment. Everything known about Red Beach was bad, for here the potential difficulties of the invaders were increased by two special conditions. In the first place, tidal

[2] In 1946 Inchon had a population of 216,000.

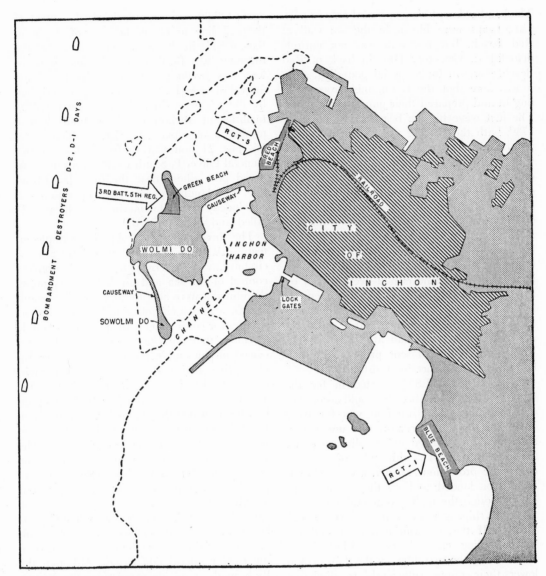

THE ASSAULT ON INCHON

conditions at Red Beach made it as easy for the defenders as for the invaders to figure out the time of landing. It had to be no later than 1730 so that the area might be secured before the LST's came in at high water, approximately an hour later. It could not be earlier, for then the tide would not be high enough to allow the landing craft to get ashore. In the second place, the very word "beach" was a misnomer, for at Red there was no beach whatever, only sea walls designed to keep out the highest tides. The landing craft would not be able to discharge over these walls. All carried scaling ladders, but there was no way of knowing in advance whether the ladders and grappling equipment were the right sort for the task.

The preliminary bombardment began at 1645, a combination of cruiser and destroyer guns, rockets, and carrier aircraft strikes. Task Force 77, the fast carrier force, flew deep support and interdiction strikes. Close support for the landings came from marine flyers based on escort carriers *Sicily* and *Badoeng Strait*.

The bombardment was successful only in part. Large gaps were blown in the sea wall at Red Beach, but the wall was not entirely demolished. Cemetery Hill, in back of Red Beach, came in for a special pounding, since it was here that the Communist troops had dug in and prepared their gun emplacements. The first wave hit the beach on schedule at 1730, with the landing unopposed except for natural obstacles over the rubble of the sea wall. Not until the fourth wave was landing did the defenders open up with any serious opposition, but by that time, the troops already ashore were becoming effective in seizing enemy strong points. There was some confusion as the marines tried to make their objective line, about 1,000 yards inland, including Cemetery Hill and Observatory Hill next to it. Although the officers had been briefed on the layout of Inchon's streets, some men got lost and all were in danger from snipers and falling rubble. However by 2000, when darkness fell, the marines had attained their objective line and had sent probes 500 yards beyond it without meeting resistance.

At 1830, eight LST's started in for the beach; the 1,000-foot breadth could accommodate no more. The situation was far from ideal, for the landing area was under fire, and the LST's carried oil, gasoline, napalm, and ammunition. The thin sides of an LST offer little protection for such a cargo, but it had to be landed to keep the marines supplied through the night. Remarkably enough, all eight ships got safely in and began unloading. If the sea wall had hampered the small landing craft, it nearly blocked the LST's. Only the two ships on the flanks could lower their ramps sufficiently to discharge cargoes through the bows. The ramps of the others slammed down on the wall with their outboard ends six feet above the ground on the far side. The situation improved as bulldozers from the LST's at each end of the line knocked down parts of the sea wall to enable the other ships to unload. The bulldozers also took care of pillboxes and other defensive emplacements, so that with the marine advances the beach rapidly became a safer place for unloading.

At Blue Beach the 1st Marines went ashore against light resistance and seized control of the rail line to Seoul. Because of the mud flats, LST's in this area had to wait for the morning tide. By that time the logistic problem was becoming simplified, first, by the arrival of more LST's at Red Beach, and then by the discovery that the conventional port facilities of Inchon could be used with a minimum of repair. At 1730 on September 16, just 24 hours after the landing, Major General Oliver P. Smith USMC set up his command post ashore near the force beachhead line. The landing phase of the operation was concluded, with total marine casualties of 21 killed and 186 wounded.

The invasion was a superb example of teamwork and adaptability under adverse circumstances. American forces had complete control of the sea and air and by exploiting these media were able to land a major assault against a major city offering excellent opportunities for concealment. In spite of the ample warnings that the Communist forces had received of the imminence of a landing in Inchon, they had not given sufficient thought or care to the disposition of troops in the city. The few mines encountered in Inchon harbor had been outside the channel routes, although natural conditions determined that United Nations ships must use the channels. The sporadic mining merely indicated that the North Koreans had not been effectively prepared for the possibility of an amphibious assault.

On D-plus-2 day, the two assault regiments began the advance on Seoul. They met with only scattered resistance, so effective had been the carrier interdiction strikes. Although the Reds made a suicide stand near the Kimpo Airfield, this did not seriously delay the marines. On September 21 the amphibious phase ended, and over-all command passed from Admiral Doyle, commanding TF 90, to the Commanding General X Corps, Major General Edward M. Almond USA.

Pusan Breakout

On D-plus-1 day, the Eighth Army under General Walker began a major offensive in the area of the Pusan Perimeter. This offensive, together with the landings at Inchon, placed the North Korean forces in an impossible military situation. The mountainous terrain, on which they had counted, now worked to their disadvantage, for the mountain ranges determined that adequate supplies could be brought to the Perimeter area only via the Seoul-Taejon road or via the east coast road. The Inchon landing brought the former under fire, while Allied naval forces interdicted use of the latter.

Cut off from their sources of supply, attacked both in front and behind, the North Koreans literally had no way to turn. The situation was true military surprise. Even though the Inchon landing could have been and probably was foreseen by the Reds, there was nothing they could do. Their forces were in a position from which they could not extricate themselves. When the advance forces of the Eighth Army coming up from Pusan made contact with elements of the X Corps 25 miles south of Seoul on September 26, the war between the United Nations and North Korea was over. Not that the fighting had ceased, but the North Korean troops were finished; they had no hope of victory. Those below the line of junction of the two United Nations forces were cut off; those above were disorganized and were only a small proportion of the total number of North Korean soldiers. The landing had "pulled the drawstring" on Korea, cutting off the last hope of a North Korean victory; short of Chinese intervention, all that remained was mopping up.[3]

Nowhere is there a better illustration of General MacArthur's dictum that four times out of five a force is defeated when its main supply line is cut, or, as Alfred Thayer Mahan put it 60 years earlier, that "communications dominate war."

[3] The strategic similarity of the Inchon invasion to the Anzio invasion of January 1944 is obvious. A commander less bold than MacArthur might have been deterred from undertaking in Korea the type of amphibious end-run that had so signally failed in Italy. On the other hand, the unqualified success of the Inchon operation leads one to suspect that had the invaders at Anzio pushed promptly to the Alban Hills as the invaders at Inchon pushed on to Seoul, they might with equal success have cut off supplies to the enemy's main front, with similar results.

Even before the success of military operations in South Korea became apparent, political questions began to loom very large. The question of the intent of the United Nations directive in regard to the Korean War came to be paramount. Were the United Nations forces simply to liberate South Korea? Were they to proceed into North Korea to punish the aggressor? Were they to occupy all of North Korea? If they did the last, would the Red Chinese intervene? These questions caused concern not only at Lake Success, New York—at that time the United Nations Headquarters—but also in the American State Department, the British Foreign Office, and in ministries of the 53 nations that had condemned Communist aggression in Korea.

The 38th parallel had long ceased to be a dividing line as far as naval and air operations were concerned, but the decision to cross it with ground troops was not made lightly. Most of the non-Communist nations in the United Nations believed that sanction had been given to drive North Korean troops as far as necessary to insure that South Korea would be safe from future attack. For this purpose, it was necessary to move into North Korea to prevent North Korean forces from regrouping and rearming and launching an attack at some later date.

The Russian group, of course, opposing any operations at all in Korea, attempted to deny United Nations forces permission to cross the 38th parallel. In this attempt, Andrei Vishinsky received support from Prime Minister Pandit Nehru of India, who argued against crossing the parallel, but for different reasons. First, he thought that by this action, United Nations troops might become aggressors themselves and that crossing the line might bring Communist China and even Russia into the war. He further showed in the course of debate that he had no great love or admiration for Syngman Rhee, the President of South Korea. At length the United Nations authorized the crossing of the 38th parallel in order to attempt to end the capability of North Korea to remount an aggressive drive to the south.

While the Eighth Army, breaking out of the old perimeter in all directions, mopped up the liberated countryside, ROK (Republic of Korea) troops advanced into North Korea via the east coast road.

Driving North

The Eighth Army, advancing north from Seoul toward Pyongyang, capital of North Korea, met strong resistance and was temporarily brought to a standstill. On the United Nations right flank however, the ROK's met little more than token resistance. Racing up the east coast, they advanced a hundred miles beyond the 38th parallel in ten days. In order to exploit the enemy's weakness in the east, MacArthur prepared to shift General Almond's X Corps from the Seoul area around to the opposite coast of Korea to begin a second line of advance on Pyongyang. To spearhead this move the 1st Marine Division moved by sea from Inchon on the west coast for an amphibious assault on Wonsan on the east coast.

The situation was so fluid however that plans were not able to keep up with events, for the Eighth Army captured Pyongyang on October 19, while the marines were not able to land at Wonsan until the 26th, after it had been taken from the rear by the ROK's. Mines had caused the delay. The North Koreans had mined Wonsan harbor as they should have mined Inchon. Instead of the five days of minesweeping operations allowed in the operation plan, the job had taken 15 days. During the extra time, the transports had steamed up and down off Wonsan in what the marines called "Operation Yo-yo." It was somewhat anticlimactic for them to land quietly, especially when they found that the First Marine Air Wing was already there and had been entertained the previous night by a USO show featuring Bob Hope.

The rest of the X Corps soon arrived at Wonsan and proceeded to clear the area of enemy and to push on to Hamhung. Meanwhile, on October 29, a battalion of the 7th Infantry Division executed an amphibious landing at Iwon, 60 miles northeast of Hamhung.

The New War

With the advance of United Nations forces into North Korea, there came increasing hints that the Red Chinese might intervene. But General MacArthur's intelligence chief, Major General Charles A. Willoughby, estimated that the Chinese would not enter the war in significant numbers, even though they might send "volunteers." He argued that if they had intended to intervene in force, they would have done so while the Allies had their backs to the sea. On the strength of this estimate, MacArthur sent General Walker's Eighth Army northward from Pyongyang and General Almond's X Corps north from Hamhung. As these two forces drove toward the Yalu, they were separated from each other by 80 miles of mountainous terrain, so that liaison between them had to be handled through Tokyo.

Into this breach, on November 24, 1950, the Chinese hurled their armies, though their own territory was not threatened. The bitter cold of late November found both American drives in full retreat after efforts at mutual support had failed. The Eighth Army fell back, trading space for time, past Pyongyang, past the 38th parallel, and past Seoul, until it managed to stabilize a new line across Korea. In the meantime, Almond's X Corps retired in the direction of Hungnam.

During the drive toward the Yalu, elements of the 1st Marine Division, X Corps, had reached the Chosin Reservoir. There the Chinese surrounded them, threatening them with total extinction. The marines, as at Guadalcanal and Bougainville, depended on their perimeter defense and held their position until they could organize for retirement southward. This retreat, through difficult terrain, through snow and cold, under constant attack and harassment, has come to be known as one of the great retreats of history. The marines, skillfully supported by carrier aircraft from the U. S. Seventh Fleet, fought their way through eight Chinese divisions, brought out most of their equipment and the survivors of three army battalions which had also been cut off in the Reservoir area. On December 11, sixteen days after the Chinese had first attacked the Eighth Army in force and 13 days after they had swept down upon X Corps positions, Almond's forces had reached Hamhung and Hungnam, where they were safe under the protection of Seventh Fleet guns and planes. In the long march the marines had suffered more than 7,000 casualties, nearly half from frostbite and exposure. Enemy losses probably amounted to 25,000 killed and half as many wounded.

Hungnam—An Amphibious Operation in Reverse

The Hungnam evacuation or embarkation —it was called both, depending on the optimism of the speaker at the moment—had as its aim the saving of life and the orderly retirement from an impossible military situation. Unlike Dunkirk, Hungnam represented no military rout, for the retirement was carried out with a minimum of confusion and loss. Task Force 90, reconstituted for the operation under the command of Rear Admiral Doyle, included 76 transport vessels—navy transports and cargo ships, USMT's and chartered merchant vessels. The Gunfire Support Group consisted of two heavy cruisers, the *Saint Paul* and the *Rochester,* eight destroyers, and three LSMR's. Close support strikes were again flown from escort carriers *Sicily* and *Badoeng Strait,* joined by light carrier *Bataan.* The *Missouri* employed her big guns to support the Gunfire Group and she also operated with TF 77, the fast carrier task force, now increased to include four attack carriers, the *Leyte, Philippine Sea, Valley Forge,* and *Princeton.*

The first phase of the Hungnam operation was the limited evacuation of Wonsan, where the 3rd Infantry Division was waiting. In addition, it seemed to observers on the spot that the entire population of Wonsan—about 75,000, and another 20,000 from the outlying districts—was attempting to get aboard the transports in Wonsan harbor. Of course only a few could be accommodated, and when the ships left, approximately 20,000 were still milling around the waterfront area.

The "amphibious operation in reverse" at Hungnam lasted two full weeks, from December 10 to 24. Gunfire and carrier strikes kept the Reds back, actually creating a "no man's land" troops could not penetrate. Transports were loaded not only with men but also with heavy equipment of all sorts—trucks, tanks, bulldozers, ammunition, artillery, stores, and great numbers of civilian refugees. Altogether in that two-week period, Task Force 90 evacuated approximately 100,000 troops, 90,000 Korean refugees, 17,500 vehicles, and 350,000 tons of bulk cargo. During this time the Fast Carrier Task Force flew strikes at the Red supply lines, operating in conditions of great difficulty because of icy decks, molasses-thick lubricating oil, and freezing winds that made carrier operations all but impossible. In spite of such difficulties, the Hungnam operation was brought to a successful close on Christmas Eve as the Underwater Demolition Teams blew up port facilities and waited for stragglers before embarking in the *Catamount,* the last ship out of Hungnam.

Other Naval Operations

We have outlined the land operations from the time of the Chinese intervention through the Hungnam evacuation. At sea nothing very dramatic was going on, yet the operations of the United Nations naval forces during this time were of great significance. Repeated bombardment of coastal roads forced the Reds to rely on inland roads and trails. Carrier strikes successfully interdicted use of the inland trails, roads, and railroads by day, so that the Red advance was considerably held up as they were forced back on night operations and infiltration tactics.

Perhaps the most significant naval air operations came about as a result of the complex political situation. In spite of the open intervention of Communist China in the Korean war, General MacArthur received orders that Manchurian territory was to be immune from attack or even territorial violation. Shortly after the Chinese intervention, the Reds had begun to use aircraft in a militarily significant way, employing Russian-built MIG-15 jets, which flew from bases in Manchuria. The denial of permission for United Nations planes to fly over Manchuria, even for a moment, meant that the MIG's had a sanctuary; if they were attacked by Allied jets, they broke contact and streaked across the Manchurian border while Allied planes had to break contact about ten miles from the border to have room to turn so that they could avoid inadvertent crossing. Repeated requests for permission to cross the Yalu in "hot pursuit" were refused. The question of "hot pursuit" came to play an important part in later political discussions and activities.

As soon as the Red Chinese intervened, an important question arose concerning the bridges across the Yalu. General MacArthur had previously regarded the southern bank of the river as the limiting line for his operations. Yet to leave the Yalu bridges intact was to invite disaster by affording unimpeded passage of Chinese troops across the river. He made the decision to destroy the bridges, but his political directives were unchanged. He now assumed however that the mid-point of the river was the dividing line and set out to destroy only the Korean half of the bridges, thereby preserving Manchurian territorial integrity and also achieving his objective of denying the bridges to the Reds. How to destroy the bridges presented a problem. It had to be done by air, for there were no demolition teams in the area. Yet the Fifth Air Force pilots were not trained in the type of precision bombing required for this kind of operation. The task was given to the navy carrier pilots. It was no easy one. A bridge is a difficult target to hit and a more difficult one to destroy. A hole in the bridge roadway can be patched easily. It is necessary to hit one of the main supporting members. When there is only half a bridge to aim at, the task is even more difficult. Moreover, only two routes of approach to the bridges could be used, from either side, exactly parallel to the river bank. Any other route of approach would result in crossing the border either on the run-in or the pull-out. This limitation of mobility imposed on the planes meant that the Red defenders could concentrate their antiaircraft weapons along the north bank of the Yalu, and put up extremely heavy fire that the Allied planes would have to penetrate.

Seven bridges spanned the Yalu, all of them ruggedly built. Against the odds mentioned above, against fire from the Manchurian side of the river, and against MIG attacks, dive bombers from the *Philippine Sea*, the *Leyte*, and the *Valley Forge* in ten days of strikes knocked down three of the Yalu bridges, including the main railroad bridge at Manpojin.

Another operation of carrier planes in the Korean War is of interest. In mid-spring 1951, the decision was made to destroy Hwachon Dam on the Yalu in order to flood the valley below it and also to knock out Manchurian hydroelectric plants. Several unsuccessful strikes were flown by conventional bombers, but even their largest bombs could not successfully penetrate the concrete of the dam. When the problem was put up to the Navy, it was solved very quickly and simply —torpedoes. Using a weapon new to the Korean War, navy attack bombers dropped torpedoes into the lake above the dam, aiming them at the flood gates. A single strike succeeded in penetrating the dam and releasing the pent-up waters.

The Dismissal of General MacArthur

When the Red Chinese intervened, the Korean War became, as General MacArthur later called it, a new war. Once the position of the Eighth Army had become fairly stabilized south of Seoul, the X Corps was integrated into the new line. The United Nations land forces were at last placed under a unified command in the person of Lieutenant General Matthew B. Ridgway USA, who had succeeded General Walker, killed in a jeep accident.

MacArthur pressed for new instructions, new directives to enable him to cope with the changed situation. But pressure from European allies, especially France and Britain, who were fearful of expanding the war, was received with sympathy in the United States State Department, and their view prevailed with the President. No new directives were forthcoming except to reinforce the old ones regarding the sanctity of the Manchurian border.

So General Ridgway began Operation KILLER, with the announced aim not of capturing or recapturing territory, but of inflicting maximum casualties on the Reds. Operating along the new line the United Nations army, better supplied with weapons, with superior air power, and using superior tactics, began methodically chewing up the Communist army. In the process Ridgway pushed his line again toward the 38th parallel, at length attaining a new stabilized line above Seoul on the west and thence northeasterly to a point well above the parallel on the east.

General MacArthur, chafing at the limitations imposed upon his freedom of action, sought the right to cross the Manchurian border in "hot pursuit," to bomb Red supply bases and airfields in Manchuria, to institute blockade of the China coast, and to use the troops of the Chinese Nationalists on Formosa, either in Korea or against China itself in order to take the pressure off Korea.

The fact that General MacArthur was out of sympathy with the policy of the United States in regard to the Korean War was well known, and he was particularly reminded of a presidential order that all statements by him must be cleared with the Joint Chiefs of Staff. This reminder was dated March 24, 1951. However on the 20th General MacArthur had written in answer to a letter from Joseph W. Martin, Jr., Minority Leader in the House of Representatives, a statement of his own views, which Martin read in the House. This letter reveals his views so well that excerpts from it are worth quoting.

My views and recommendations with respect to the situation created by Red China's entry into war against us in Korea . . . are well known and clearly understood, as they follow the conventional pattern of meeting force with maximum counter-force as we have never failed to do in the past. . . .

It seems strangely difficult for some to realize that here in Asia is where the Communist conspirators have elected to make their play for global conquest, and that we have joined the issue thus raised on the battlefield; that here we fight Europe's war with arms while the diplomats there still fight it with words; that if we lose the war to communism in Asia the fall of Europe is inevitable, win it and Europe most probably would avoid war and yet preserve freedom. As you pointed out, we must win. There is no substitute for victory.

Nothing MacArthur said later was more than an amplification of the ideas contained in this letter. Its release appeared to the President to be a violation of orders on the part of the General. Summarily, Mr. Truman ordered MacArthur's immediate relief from all his duties in the Far East, replacing him with General Ridgway. The President's dispatch was released to the press in advance of delivery to General MacArthur, so that the General first heard of it on a news broadcast.

On his return to the United States MacArthur received a tremendous ovation from the public everywhere he went. Public opinion, not fully aware of the dangers of Russian involvement under the Sino-Russian mutual defense pact of 1950, was strongly sympathetic with the General's point of view. He was invited to address a Joint Session of Congress, at which time he elaborated the views already presented in his letter. A committee to investigate the relief of General MacArthur held lengthy hearings. The inquiry broadened its scope into an investigation of the conduct of the Korean War and agreed that the President had a right to remove the General, but that the method of removal was unwise, that the General had never violated directives, that there was no serious disagreement between him and the Joint Chiefs of Staff, that the Secretary of State had assumed military functions, his advice overruling that of the Joint Chiefs of Staff, and that there had been a lack of adequate support from the other nations involved in the United Nations effort. The conclusion reached was that cessation of hostilities based on a restoration of the *status quo* at the 38th parallel would be a victory for aggression.

Truce Talks

Despite this conclusion, when Russia's Jacob Malik proposed in June 1951 that armistice talks might profitably be held, United Nations leaders agreed. Admiral Joy was named chief delegate for the United Nations forces; North Korean General Nam-Il led the Communist truce party. The Communists soon tried to twist the situation to their advantage, making it appear that the United Nations forces had been defeated. But skilled diplomacy and a rigid insistence on United Nations rights brought an end to such attempts.

The truce talks revealed more clearly than any previous conferences the Communist methods of negotiation. The Reds showed no conception of give and take or of compromise. To them a concession was a sign of weakness and a signal for making increased demands. Negotiating with Communists, it became clear, was merely entering another battlefield where the weapons were steadfastness of policy, infinite patience, and complete firmness.

During the long-drawn-out discussions, the fighting continued on land, the Navy devoted major efforts to attacking the enemy's lines of supply, and seapower continued to maintain United Nations forces in the field. Carrier aircraft knocked out bridges and wrecked rail lines but could not decisively disrupt North Korean communications because the Communists were able to draw on huge numbers of people to repair roads and railroads and to fill in ravines once spanned by bridges. During this period the carrier planes encountered increasing numbers of Russian-built MIG jet aircraft, which they were forbidden to pursue to their bases in Manchuria.

In an effort to cut the principal east coast road and rail lines, Allied naval forces laid siege to the port of Wonsan. This siege, which lasted a record 861 days, involved clearing mines from the harbor so that gunfire ships could get in position to shell gun emplacements and to interdict the road and railroad. Battleships, cruisers, and destroyers expended more than 4,000,000 rounds of ammunition, laying waste to half the city and eventually cutting the supply along the east coast to a trickle.

Neither during the truce talks nor earlier could the war in Korea have been conducted without the sea transport that carried men, weapons, and supplies to the peninsula. Eighty-six percent of all Allied personnel who went to Korea traveled there by ship. Ships carried thither 54,000,000 tons of dry cargo and 22,000,000 tons of oil, gasoline, and aviation fuel—99.63 per cent of all cargo transported there. For every ton delivered by air, ships had to provide four tons of aviation fuel.

For more than two years the peace talks dragged on, involving discussion and haggling over the line of demarcation between the two forces. Was it to be the 38th parallel? So the Communists said. The Allies insisted on a militarily defensible line based roughly on the then existing battle zone. The issue of the return of prisoners of war held up the discussion for many months. Eventually however agreement was reached, and the armistice was signed at Panmunjon on July 27, 1953.

Hostilities ceased twelve hours later, troops withdrawing from an agreed buffer zone. Thus ended the third largest war in American history, with no clear-cut victory on either side and with neither side completely satisfied with the situation, but willing to accept it as the end of a conflict unprofitable to the policies of both the Communist and the non-Communist worlds.

Summary

The Korean War came about as a result of the Communists' miscalculation that the Western Powers would not fight in defense of South Korea. It was the first occasion after World War II that the Communists attempted to implement their expansion program through military attack. Crossing the 38th parallel on the morning of July 25, 1950, the North Korean forces quickly seized the South Korean capital of Seoul and drove south. Meanwhile the United Nations Security Council, meeting at Lake Success, denounced the aggression and authorized military action to assist the Republic of Korea in repelling the invasion. Direction of the war was entrusted to the United States, and President Truman appointed General of the Army Douglas MacArthur to supreme command.

There followed a race for time as American forces hastily thrown in from Japan attempted to halt the North Korean drive to the south. While the defenders fell back, reinforcements from all over the free world began to move toward Korea. For a time it seemed that the United Nations forces might be driven out of Korea altogether, but at length they managed to stabilize a perimeter around Pusan.

On September 15, U.N. forces employed the mobility of sea power to stage an amphibious assault at Inchon. Despite enormous tides and the difficulty of invading the heart of a city, the landing was completely successful. Cut off from their source of supply, the North Korean armies collapsed, and a U.N. drive north from Pusan soon joined hands with the troops landed at Inchon.

Military action now had to wait until political leaders could decide on their war aims. At length General MacArthur received permission to proceed north of the 38th parallel, and he drove north amid increasing threats of Red Chinese intervention. On November 24, 1950, with United Nations patrols reaching the Manchurian border, the Chinese struck, forcing Allied troops back south. The 1st Marine Division, cut off at the Chosin Reservoir, managed to force its way back to Hungnam where, along with 90,000 Korean refugees, it was evacuated by the navy.

The Eighth Army, farther west, fell back past Seoul before it could call a halt. Meanwhile General MacArthur was vainly requesting authority to attack the Chinese Red bases in Manchuria from the air. British and American political leaders concluded that this move would risk Russian intervention and bring about World War III. At length the divergence of opinion between General MacArthur and President Truman grew so marked that the President relieved MacArthur, replacing him with General Matthew B. Ridgway USA.

In Korea meanwhile United Nations troops began Operation KILLER, designed not so much to capture ground as to kill Red troops. Carrier aircraft and surface ships supported this operation by attacks on roads, rail lines, and storage facilities. Gradually the line was pushed back to just north of the 38th parallel, whereupon the Russians suggested truce talks, and the belligerents agreed. The talks dragged on for two years, the Reds seeking every opportunity to gain military, political, or propaganda advantages. Skill and determination on the part of United Nations representatives kept the Communists from gaining their objectives, and on July 27, 1953 the armistice was signed, bringing to an end the most unpopular war in American history.

Clausewitz' dictum that war is an extension of state policy by other means inexorably suggests an analogue—that a nation must have a clear and decisive policy if war is to be prosecuted successfully. When no clearly defined policy is stated, military operations become aimless. Twice during the Korean War military operations were stalled by political indecision. When MacArthur sought to cross the 38th parallel after the recapture of Seoul, he had to wait several days for a policy formulation. Hence he lost momentum, while the Reds had time to improve their defenses. Again, on the entry of the Communist Chinese into the war, MacArthur had to wait for a decision on bombing Manchurian bases. Had the policy of immunity of Manchurian territory been known to him in advance, and had he sufficiently recognized the danger of Chinese intervention, he unquestionably would have exercised more caution than he did in his advance to the Chinese border. There can be no question that policy must emanate from the government and not from the commander in the field, but the failure of the government to make timely enunciations of policy can vitiate the results of military success.

46:

The New Navy

The end of the war in Korea brought no real peace to an apprehensive world. In Indo-China the French resisted the advance of the Red forces of Ho Chi Minh. Mao Tse-tung, with hordes of Chinese troops blooded in Korea, threatened the island of Formosa. Russia, blowing hot and cold in the war of nerves with the West, alternated protestations of peaceful intentions with denunciations, threats, and verbal attacks. People lived their daily lives amid local wars and under the constant threat of a global war of annihilation.

Russia had apparently decided to shift the emphasis from Europe to Asia. The period before the Korean War had, as we have noted, been disturbed by threats to the peace in Iran, Greece, Turkey, and Germany. The outbreak of war in Korea marked the beginning of the new Red emphasis on the Far East. There Russia saw her opportunity for extensive territorial gains for world Communism by using the armed forces of other nations. Stirring up discontent through well indoctrinated native agents in key places, training military forces in troubled countries, and equipping them with arms and munitions were Soviet tactics both before and after Korea. The Korean Truce left the Communists in a position of strength vis-à-vis the West. The United Nations had shown that they feared beyond all things any extension of the Korean War, in which they had not used atomic weapons. Any effort that they might make against further aggression would be at worst on a pattern with Korea, which had left the Reds no worse off than before and which their propaganda extolled as a victory for Communism, even though it was the United Nations and not the Communists who attained their original objectives. Seizing on the hated word "colonialism," Red spokesmen identified

the United States with the worst imperial practices of the 19th century. Allying themselves with the nationalist causes, the Reds were soon ready to undertake further expansion.

In the midst of all of their planning of directed subversion, the Reds had a new reason for caution when the United States exploded a hydrogen bomb. On November 1, 1952 United States Joint Task Force 132 set off the most violent blast ever made by man. The target island in Eniwetok Atoll completely disappeared, and the explosion was visible from 50 miles away. The bomb was estimated to have an explosive force of five megatons, equivalent to five million tons of TNT, or, to put it another way, to be 25 times as powerful as the original atomic bomb dropped on Hiroshima. In March 1954, two more hydrogen bombs were set off at Eniwetok. One of these so contaminated a Japanese fishing boat some 75 miles away that the crew was in a critical condition for a considerable time, and one man died as a result of the radioactivity. A B-29 flying about 20 miles from ground zero was flipped over on its back by the force of the blast. On the basis of figures released concerning this bomb, which had an explosive force of 40 megatons, we can deduce that the area of total destruction would be bounded by a circle with a radius of twelve miles, that serious damage would extend up to 40 miles and dangerous radiation over 100 miles from the explosion, while windborne radioactive fallout would extend even farther.

The United States did not long enjoy a monopoly of this fearsome weapon. The Russians had sources of information within the atomic energy program itself—notably the British physicist Klaus Fuchs, who supplied Soviet scientists with vital information. At the end of August 1953, the Atomic Energy Commission announced that Russia had exploded a hydrogen bomb.

The new defense establishment of the United States had to take into consideration developments in political as well as military fields. A NATO conference which convened in Lisbon in February 1952 considered means of realizing plans for developing Western strength, and adapted a "firm and vigilant" policy to discourage Russia from aggressive war. The Lisbon conference set as its goal the organization and equipping of 4,000 tactical aircraft and 50 divisions for use by the end of 1952 and laid plans for further expansion in later years. Specific quotas were allocated to each country in the number and kind of troops and equipment. The conference also approved the use of West German troops in the projected European army, but this decision led to difficulties, particularly with France, which feared any move to rearm the Germans. An effort was made between 1952 and 1954 to establish a European Defense Community, which in cooperation with NATO would supply an effective ground force for the defense of Western Europe. This scheme was finally vitiated by the unwillingness of the French to cooperate closely with the Germans, though the French did agree to let Germany rearm as a member of NATO.

Meanwhile, with the election of President Eisenhower, new direction had come to the United States Departments of State and Defense. The members of the Joint Chiefs of Staff who had directed the war in Korea completed their terms, and their replacements took a new look at the world strategic situation.

The vastly expanded scope of American military commitments and the need of developed military power to cope with limited war threats as well as the danger of unlimited war imposed hard choices on American policy makers, for even the wealthy United States was unable to afford maximum development of all types of weapons systems. American leaders came increasingly to lean on the concept of "massive retaliation." The United States Strategic Air Command (SAC) was strengthened, and the Joint Chiefs of Staff and the Administration, reversing their predecessors' decisions, permitted the Navy to build new aircraft carriers, partly to help counter the ever-increasing Russian submarine threat, and partly to share in the strategic bombing role. The performance of aircraft carriers during the Korean War had helped to quiet many critics, and the obvious flexibility of the carrier at sea and the difficulty of pinpointing it as a missile target made it particularly suited to share the role of massive retaliation with SAC. Policy makers realized that rather than rivaling SAC, the carriers supplemented it. The carriers became increasingly valuable as rising nationalism, particularly in Africa, threatened the existence of SAC bases abroad. The newly designed carriers of the *Forrestal* class, displacing 60,000 tons, by 1955 were beginning to take their place in the fleet, ready to assume the role of supporting and coordinating with SAC in the event of all-out war. The dependence on massive retaliation probably kept all-out war from materializing, but it suffered from the very lack of flexibility which Defense Secretary Forrestal had foreseen as early as 1946.

One of the first results of the failure of the United States to press the Korean War to a clear-cut victory was an increase in the intensity of the war in Indo-China in the spring of 1954. The siege of Dienbienphu, in which the beleaguered French forces of General de Castries held out against hordes of Red attackers, won the sympathy of the Western world. But sympathy was not enough. The United States, which was already supplying generous military aid to France, seriously considered intervening, but reluctance to engage in more "little wars," particularly in one closely identified with French colonialism, led the National Security Council to reject the idea.

Apparently emboldened by the Red success in Indo-China, the Chinese Communists began to show further signs of belligerence. Their leaders made open threats to invade the island of Formosa, which was under protection of the guns of the United States Seventh Fleet. Actual bombardment of Nationalist-held islands off the coast of China stirred up a near-crisis in American military policy over the issue of whether the United States was also committed to fight for the preservation of such places as Quemoy. Again the decision was for inaction, but the commitment to guard Formosa and the Pescadores Islands was confirmed by a pact signed in November 1954 with Chiang Kai-shek. Red Chinese reaction to the announcement of the pact was a further statement that Formosa was a part of China and a warning to the United States of the gravest consequences if she opposed "legitimate" efforts of the Reds to seize that island.

With America seemingly committed to a policy of war of words and diplomatic notes in the Pacific, the Reds began to stir up further trouble in Indonesia, Thailand, Malaya, and elsewhere. External pressure and internal sedition were the methods used with the aim of bringing these territories into the Communist orbit. In Korea itself the Communists openly defied the West, violating the Korean Peace Treaty by bringing additional combat aircraft and airmen into North Korea, by blocking the work of United Nations Inspection Teams, and by holding Allied prisoners of war in spite of agreements for their return. The Reds apparently felt that the United Nations, particularly the United States, would not again open the war over such peace treaty violations.

When Red China announced that she was holding as spies 13 American airmen, some captured during the Korean War and some shot down by her planes during routine patrol missions over the ocean, a new challenge was presented to the United States. One vocal party in Congress, led by the Republican Majority Leader, Senator William F. Knowland, proposed that the United States institute a blockade of Communist China. A majority of the members of the Joint Chiefs of Staff also favored blockade, but the proposal was rejected by President Eisenhower, who was unwilling to accept the obvious risk of war. Instead, negotiations for the release of the Americans were put up to the General Assembly of the United Nations.

About this time, Russia entered an apparently new phase in her international diplomacy. Less belligerent since the death of Stalin, Russia espoused the policy of "peaceful coexistence" and began to talk more pleasantly to foreign diplomats. Many observers interpreted this as Russia's two backward steps in her strategic manner of advancing three steps

and then backing up two. The peaceful face was particularly apparent in Europe; tension remained in Asia.

Formosa Again

In mid-January 1955 the Red Chinese launched a successful amphibious assault on the tiny island of Yikiangshen, about 215 miles north-northwest of Formosa and about 20 miles off the coast of China. This seizure was accompanied by threats directed toward the nearby Tachen Islands and by renewed promises on the part of the Reds that they would capture Formosa in spite of the protective cover of the U.S. Seventh Fleet. President Eisenhower, taking cognizance of the threat to peace, sent a message to Congress asking for authority to use American military forces as he saw fit in the defense of Formosa and the Pescadores Islands and such other areas as were considered necessary for the defense of Formosa. After a brief debate Congress granted this power.

The immediate concern became the evacuation of the Tachen Islands, and the larger question again was whether such islands as Matsu and Quemoy would be defended by the armed forces of the United States. During the operations around the Tachen group several skirmishes took place between ships and aircraft of the Chinese Nationalists and Communists. In an attempt to stop these clashes, several nations proposed a cease-fire agreement, but Chou En-lai, Premier of Red China, flatly rejected the idea and reiterated his challenge to the United States, promising to "liberate" Formosa. Under such ominous conditions, the Seventh Fleet successfully carried out the evacuation of the Tachens.

Suez Crisis and Hungarian Revolt

In 1955 Colonel Gamal Abdel Nasser, the fanatically nationalist dictator of Egypt, who cherished dreams of heading a pan-Arab bloc, had mortgaged Egypt's cotton crop (her principal export) far into the future in order to purchase arms from Czechoslovakia. The first of these, which included new Russian jets, were accompanied by the inevitable Soviet "technicians."

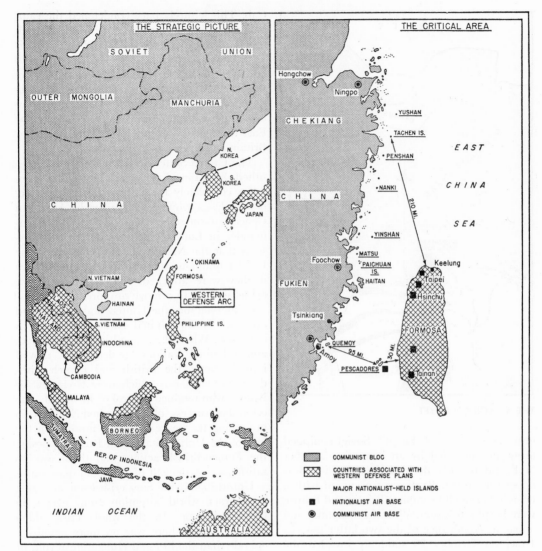

THE STRATEGIC PICTURE IN THE FAR EAST

As a result both of Egypt's *rapprochement* with the Soviet bloc and of the compromising of Egyptian credit, the United States in mid-July 1956 rescinded its offer of a loan to construct the Aswan dam, intended to contribute immensely to Egypt's economic development. A week later Nasser retaliated by seizing the internationally-owned Suez Canal, with the announced intention of using its tolls to build the dam. The British and French, who were the principal stockholders in the Suez company and whose economic life depended upon Middle Eastern oil brought largely by tanker through the canal,[1] at once began considering military action to protect their rights, but at the urging of the United States merely undertook diplomatic negotiations, which were destined to drag on futilely for two months.

In the meantime Israel, which saw herself threatened by Arab encirclement and by the

[1] The rapid development and exploitation of the French oil resources in the Algerian Sahara will lessen British and French dependence upon Middle East oil.

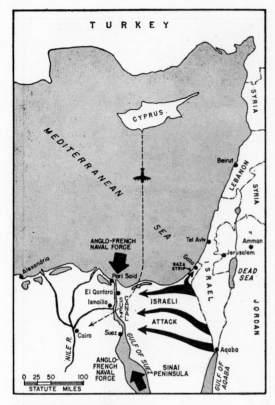

THE ATTACK ON EGYPT

Cab. This leisurely pace condemned the campaign to failure. Had the British and French seized the canal suddenly and quickly, it would have been difficult to challenge the *fait accompli*. As it was, Russia, anxious to preserve her hold on Egypt and to extend her power in the Middle East, threatened to send troops "to crush the aggressors and restore peace in the East through the use of force" and to destroy Britain and France by rocket attack.

The United States, which had not been consulted by France or Britain and had been taken completely by surprise by their action, nonetheless approved a statement by American General Gruenther, Supreme Allied Commander in Europe, pointing out to the Russians that the NATO alliance committed the United States to support Britain and France if they were attacked. On the other hand, being anxious to remove any pretext for Russian intervention, the United States supported attempts by the United Nations to secure a cease fire. When this was ultimately achieved, and a United Nations "police force" moved into the zone, the British and French withdrew, but on terms which were a victory for Nasser, who retained control of the canal. The ostensible success of the United Nations in preserving the peace in reality arose from the fact of the United States and Russia opposing the Franco-British action, and there was no satisfactory settlement of the canal question.

Unfortunately the Suez crisis came at a time to distract world attention from events in Central Europe. In the whole crisis-ridden postwar period there was no more agonizing episode than the ill-fated Hungarian revolt, or one more deserving of the world's attention. Inspired by news of important Soviet concessions to Polish nationalism, students and workers rioted in Budapest and other Hungarian cities on October 23, 1956. The Soviet-dominated government collapsed. Imre Nagy, the "national Communist" leader, was recalled from oblivion and became premier. A National Front cabinet, which included prominent non-Communists, was formed. Soviet forces temporarily withdrew from Budapest, but Russia obviously could not permit a Hungarian success which might lead to the crumbling of her satellite empire. Throwing pretense to the winds, she sent massive armored forces which

growing strength of Egypt's Soviet-equipped army and harassed by an increasing number of Egyptian raids, decided that the time was opportune to act. Russia was occupied with a crisis in her satellite empire; Britain and France were hostile to Nasser. With the sympathy and apparent connivance of the two latter powers, Israel on October 29 suddenly invaded the Sinai Peninsula. She efficiently eliminated the Egyptian forces there in the first three or four days, and within a week substantially controlled the area.

On October 30 the British and French, who had gathered forces on Cyprus, issued a twelve-hour ultimatum to the Israelis and Egyptians to cease fighting, and announced that they would occupy the canal zone. Next day British and French planes began bombing Egyptian military bases and destroyed a considerable quantity of the new Czechoslovakian equipment. At length on November 5 the Allies began to land troops at Port Said, and occupied the Canal Zone as far south as El on November 4 began a bloody suppression of the Hungarian revolt. Though the General Assembly of the United Nations condemned the Russian action, the Western governments realized that nothing effective could be done short of committing humanity to World War III. Although the brutal suppression of Hungary did more than any other event to reveal to the world the true nature of Russian Communism, the moral effect was vitiated by the simultaneous events in Egypt.

Space

In the fall of 1957 the Russians scored an outstanding propaganda success. As part of the International Geophysical Year, they launched the first man-made satellite, *Sputnik,* on October 4, 1957, followed a month later by *Sputnik II,* which carried a dog into space. Although the armed forces of the United States had long been working on satellites of their own, the undertaking had not been a "crash" program, and the first American satellite was not launched till January 31, 1958. The Navy was soon in the program with its *Vanguard,* which put a satellite into orbit on March 17. By the end of 1959 the United States had put 15 satellites into orbit, as compared with only three Russian *Sputniks.* The case with lunar and space probes was similar: the Russians scored the first successes, but by the beginning of 1960 the United States had launched four to the Russian three, and had two still in orbit compared to the Russian one.

An impressive aspect of Russia's performance was the power of her rockets. The first *Sputnik* weighed 184 pounds, while the first American satellite weighed only a little over 18. On the other hand, it was clear that the United States was far ahead in miniaturization and refinement of instruments, and that the scientific value of the American satellites was proportionately greater.

Although all these space efforts were made in the name of science, it required no great insight to recognize that rocket engines which could lift a ton and a half into orbit were capable of powering an Intercontinental Ballistic Missile (ICBM), and the Russian moon shots had proved the accuracy of their guidance systems. Thus space programs and military rocketry were inextricably mixed, despite allegations to the contrary. But if Russia held a clear advantage in the thrust of her rockets, America's system of overseas bases, many bordering Russia, reduced her need of extremely heavy rockets.

Lebanon and Quemoy

Certain events of the summer of 1958 constitute a dramatic case study of the continuing value of sea power expertly handled and a vindication of current U.S. naval policy.

Since World War II the entire Middle East, like most of the underdeveloped regions of the world, had been a tinder box. Nasser's precipitation of the Suez crisis had been simply one example of the unrest in the area. Again in 1958 this troubled region was in the headlines. A coup d'état in Iraq upset the local balance of power, and Communist agents from Syria, now a part of Nasser's United Arab Republic, fomented revolution in Lebanon. Lebanese President Chamoun appealed to the United States for direct military aid, in accordance with the "Eisenhower Doctrine,"[2] pending a lawful election in his country.

The United States government acted promptly. On July 15, twenty-seven hours after Chamoun's appeal, American marines were coming in by air. Within a week 10,000 troops with heavy equipment were landed near Beirut, and the Sixth Fleet carriers were deployed to offer air support if the police action turned into a shooting war. French warships reinforced the strength of the Sixth Fleet, and the British sent 2,000 airborne troops to Jordan, also threatened. Thanks largely to this prompt and decisive show of strength, the explosive situation was stabilized, the Lebanese election was peaceably held, and an orderly transition to a new government occurred in September. All American forces were withdrawn by October.

At this very time however a potentially even more dangerous situation was developing on the other side of the world. The Red Chinese

[2] The American President had pledged intervention in any Middle Eastern state that was invaded, if such action was requested by the lawful government. Chamoun claimed his "revolutionists" were mainly trouble-makers from Syria.

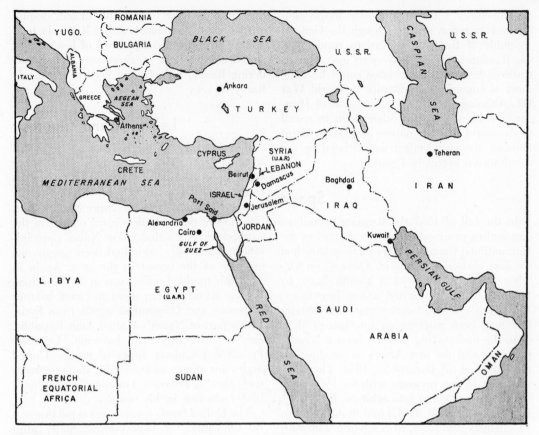

THE NEAR EAST

had made ominous new preparations which appeared to presage an amphibious attack on Quemoy, still held by the Nationalists. New military airfields near Amoy, and a semicircle of siege guns mounted on the mainland opposite the island made its position seem precarious, for all Quemoy's 60,000-man garrison of well trained troops.[3]

Though the United States had a treaty commitment to defend Formosa itself, as noted earlier there was no firmly enunciated U.S. policy on the so-called "offshore islands." It seemed all too likely to the U.S. Chief of Naval Operations, Admiral Arleigh Burke, that the time when the Sixth Fleet was deeply committed in the Eastern Mediterranean would be the very time Red China would try a probe of United States intentions in the Far East. Consequently, he immediately put the Pacific

Fleet[4] on a four-hour alert, and prepared for major operations on the China coast.

In accordance with the General Emergency Operations Plan (GEOP), designed to prevent a repetition of the Pearl Harbor disaster, the major units put to sea and with gratifying smoothness took positions of maximum strategic advantage. These positions enabled the fleet to support Formosa if attacked (the most likely contingency), to reinforce the Sixth Fleet via the Indian Ocean if need be, or to take an immediate offensive if Russia precipitated a general war over the Lebanese intervention.

Probably the prompt and successful action in Lebanon discouraged an immediate Chinese move in the Far East. In any event tensions were relaxed in the Mediterranean, and, more

[3] Matsu, to the north, also threatened, had an additional 25,000.

[4] Consisting of the Seventh Fleet in Far Eastern waters, and the First Fleet based on the U.S. West coast.

temporarily, in the Far East as well. The fleet stood down from GEOP readiness in late July. The United States Navy had demonstrated its capacity for full readiness for simultaneous war on opposite sides of the globe.

But in the Far East, this was only the first round. After sporadic fighter plane combat near Formosa in early August, the Red Chinese on August 23 opened a tremendous artillery barrage on Quemoy, apparently preliminary to invasion. Although there had been no announcement on whether the U.S. Navy should actively intervene to protect Quemoy and the other offshore islands, the Seventh Fleet striking force was rapidly reinforced by carrier *Hancock* out of Hong Kong, carrier *Shangri-La* from Yokosuka, and carrier *Midway* from Pearl Harbor. Carrier *Essex* was detached from the Sixth Fleet in the Mediterranean and raced 8,000 miles to join up. By late September six attack carriers and a 150-ship fleet were on a war footing in Formosan waters. Three squadrons of marine all-weather fighters, and several U.S. Air Force squadrons from the Philippines and Japan were on Formosan fields.

The demonstrated fighting capacity of Chiang Kai-shek's well trained air force and small-craft navy counted for much, but it is probable that the quick assembly of the U.S. Navy's Pacific power was the factor most responsible for averting a general war. The "Sidewinder" air-to-air homing missile, supplied by the U.S. Navy to the Nationalist Chinese fighters, proved itself magnificently in operation and may have been a weight in the balance. The very fast new American jets—carrier-borne F8U's and Skyrays (F4D's) and Air Force Lockheed F-104's—though never committed, patrolled the straits at speeds and altitudes that must have given pause to the Red Chinese command as their radar images streaked across the search scopes. The U.S. Navy also supplied expert schooling to Chiang's little navy in the vital task of resupplying the beleaguered garrison across beaches under fire, and furnished the screen of fighting ships off Quemoy when this successful task was carried out.

The battle threats subsided, with the Nationalists more firmly entrenched than ever. Subsequently Quemoy was armed with well protected batteries of 8-inch howitzers to provide formidable counterbattery fire against any Red attack.

The U.S. Navy's demonstrated readiness to support America's Far Eastern allies brought a new prestige to the United States in that whole area, and a corresponding loss of face to Red China. As a consequence it undoubtedly improved the bargaining position of the United States in its dealings with Allies and neutralist countries alike.

Ships and Weapons

The most revolutionary weapon in America's New Navy—possibly the capital ship of the future—was the missile-firing submarine, combining to an unparalleled degree a potentiality for secrecy and surprise. The first nuclear-powered vessel of any type, submarine *Nautilus,* was developed by a crash program under the direction of the Navy's own hard-driving, irascible, creative genius, Captain Hyman G. Rickover and a devoted research and development team. The *Nautilus,* launched in January 1954, became the prototype of a growing fleet of sister craft. Its submerged cruising capacity was dramatically demonstrated in the summer of 1958 by Commander William R. Anderson, who commanded her in a voyage from Pearl Harbor to England under the polar ice pack and over the North Pole. In the spring of 1960 the nuclear-powered *Triton,* under Captain Edward L. Beach, circumnavigated the earth without surfacing.

While the atomic submarine was in the development stages, the Navy had experimented gingerly with intermediate-range ballistic missiles (IRBM) of the *Jupiter* variety, first developed by the Army. As a shipboard operational weapon however the *Jupiter* presented appalling problems. It stood as high as an eight-story building, all 55 tons of it. Its liquid oxygen fuel component was a frightful fire hazard. Fortunately some experiments in 1956 demonstrated the feasibility of a solid propellent. Soon thereafter the Atomic Energy Commission devised means of greatly reducing the weight and size of a thermonuclear warhead. The Navy immediately wedded the new warhead and a solid-fuel body to create the *Polaris,* an IRBM 28 feet long, weighing 15 tons, to be fired from a submerged submarine.

Adapting the nuclear submarine concept to *Polaris* was a logical next step, realized in the *George Washington,* commissioned at the end of 1959. A new weapons system was born.

The *George Washington* was the culmination of the age-long search for the highest order of security combined with a maximum of offensive power. Enormous for a submarine, she displaced 6,700 tons submerged, with a length of 380 feet, a 33-foot beam, and a surface draft of 28 feet. In her three decks she carried a conventional torpedo battery and 16 launching tubes to accommodate *Polaris* missiles. A newly devised startracker periscope and three inertial navigation systems as well as all the conventional methods for pinpointing position were installed to insure accuracy of aim on targets within the range of her missiles. Two complete crews were provided to enable her to remain at sea indefinitely. Thus the navy found an answer to the ICBM with *Polaris*-equipped submarines which could fire on any target behind the Iron Curtain from completely unpredictable positions under the sea.

In the program for fiscal 1960, seven more nuclear-powered *Polaris* submarines were authorized, with twelve more scheduled for the following year, to build up to a total of 40. Such a force, armed with sufficient thermonuclear missiles to devastate every production center in any enemy country, complementing SAC and ground-launched missiles, became a major hope of the United States as she faced the 1960's.

To complete America's arsenal of retaliatory weapons, the U.S. Air Force in the spring of 1960 produced an ICBM that outdistanced anything the Soviet Union had produced. On May 20 an Atlas missile streaked up from Cape Canaveral, Florida and dropped its warhead less than an hour later at a pre-selected target in the Indian Ocean 1,000 miles southeast of the Cape of Good Hope. This 9,000-mile flight exceeded by 140 miles the longest surface-to-surface rocket flight claimed by the Russians. The new Atlas ICBM was capable of reaching every part of the Soviet Union from the United States.

Carriers continued to be regarded as a major weapon in any atomic war. By virtue of their mobility, they would avoid the danger of being overwhelmed by a sudden surprise onslaught by ICBMs. With their 720-foot angled landing decks, the big *Forrestal*-class carriers could accommodate planes carrying atomic bombs, and such more recent fighters as the F4H, capable of a speed of Mach 2. In early 1960, four of the big carriers were in commission, and three more were on the ways. One of these last was the nuclear-powered *Enterprise,* which the Navy planned as the prototype of seven more sister ships. As the new carriers joined the fleet, the *Essex*-class carriers of World War II vintage were retired one by one to the mothball fleet or were transferred to antisubmarine warfare duty. Though valuable in any nuclear war, the carriers continued to have the principal function of projecting power quickly to threatened regions and in backing up the marines in amphibious operations in limited wars—the role they played so well in Korea and in Lebanon.

The problem of defense at sea from aircraft and missile attack engaged the serious attention of the Navy's policy-makers. Guided missile cruisers such as the *Boston* and *Canberra* were supplemented by the nuclear-powered *Long Beach,* launched in the summer of 1959. All three of these vessels were equipped with launchers for surface-to-air missiles of the Talos-Terrier type. In quantity, these weapons, with their remarkable guidance systems, could be expected to provide a task force with a reasonable degree of invulnerability to attack by manned aircraft.

New amphibious troop carriers also appeared on the ways, notably the Amphibious Transport, Dock, an improvement on the LSD, and capable of floating craft out of the well in her open stern. Able to carry a 900-man assault team, she was equipped with a carrier-type half deck which could accommodate big Piasecki helicopters. Vessels of this kind were scheduled to join the amphibious forces in 1962.

Amphibious Doctrine

Following World War II and the Korean War, U.S. Marine Corps planners set about updating amphibious doctrine. Though of course still capable of the massive, concentrated beach landings of the Iwo Jima variety, the Marine Corps also became capable of occupying large stretches of enemy territory by vertical envelopment. In unlimited nuclear war it is essential to avoid bunching of personnel and equipment as is inevitable in a beach landing. To avoid this the marines planned to employ helicopter lifts and airborne troops to seize a large number of positions simultaneously, including many well away from the beaches. This would make it impossible for an enemy to use thermonuclear weapons without destroying a good deal of his own force, while tactical atomic weapons used by the enemy would lose much of their effectiveness because of the wide dispersal of targets.

Successful implementation of the new marine doctrine required discipline, and initiative, and superlative training on the part of small unit leaders, right down to the squad level. It also demanded almost ideally dependable communication equipment. It has always been a major concern of the marines to maintain their excellence in the first of these requirements, and to foster rapid progress in the second.

Apart from the more spectacular developments in weapons systems and tactics, the U.S. Navy quietly devoted some of its best talents to research and development in a wide variety of fields. It supported oceanographic research on a substantial scale. A Navy expedition sent a manned bathysphere to the remotest depths in the Marianas Trench. Anti-submarine equipment and tactics became far more sophisticated and effective than the relatively primitive techniques of World War II.

Objectives of the Naval Policy

What must be the objectives of U.S. Naval policy? This question must be answered by the Navy's planners before allocations can be made from the $11-$12 billions at which the Navy's budget stabilized during the 1950's. By this time American naval policy included the following points: (1) A rapidly expanding *Polaris*-armed nuclear submarine force as the Navy's principal contribution to deterring major, all-out, or unlimited war. (2) A more gradual but substantial addition to its large carrier force (with emphasis on nuclear-powered vessels), as part of its striking force in nuclear war, but particularly as its principal weapon in limited wars. (3) A stepped-up program of anti-submarine preparedness, including suitable specialized vessels and aircraft as well as continuing research and development of improved detection and attack devices. (4) A well devised ship replacement program to overcome the "block obsolescence" faced between 1960 and 1966 as World War II construction (which in 1960 still constituted four fifths of the Navy's active vessels) reached the end of the 20-year period conventionally assumed to constitute the useful life of a ship of war. (5) A comprehensive procurement and training program for officers, enlisted men, civilian experts, for regulars and reserves, which would maintain an immediate mobilization readiness in event of war.

The Alliance System of the United States

In spite of the commitment of much of the best brain power of the nation, and in spite of huge defense budgets, the state of preparedness seemed never quite adequate to the leaders ultimately responsible for the safety of the United States. The continuing threat of the hostile Communist world was only partly responsible. The multiplicity of commitments accepted by American diplomacy vastly enlarged the area of responsibility of the American armed forces in a very specific way.

In the history of United States foreign policy, the bomb explosions of Pearl Harbor marked the end of isolationism. During and after World War II, America made herself the center of elaborate alliance systems which committed the nation to the defense of half the land areas of the world.

The North Atlantic Treaty Organization, established in 1949, is the best known of several regional groupings in the interest of mutual security. The 15 member-nations are the United States, Canada, the United Kingdom, France, Italy, West Germany, Iceland, Norway, the Netherlands, Denmark, Belgium, Luxembourg, Portugal, Greece, and Turkey. The terms of the treaty specify that "the parties agree that an armed attack against one or more of them in Europe or North America shall be considered an attack against them all, and . . . each of them . . . will assist the . . .

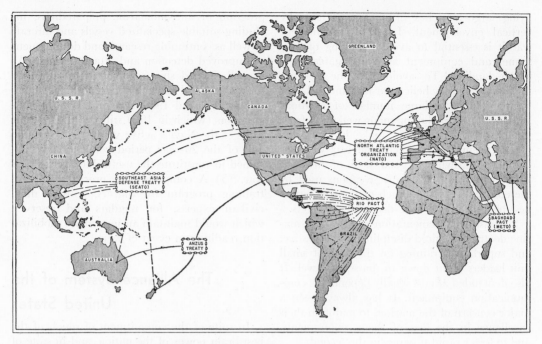

UNITED STATES COLLECTIVE DEFENSE ARRANGEMENTS

attacked by taking forthwith, individually and in concert with the other parties, such action as it deems necessary including the use of armed force."

The ANZUS Treaty (1951), to which the United States, Australia, and New Zealand are signatories, though its protocol is not quite so definite and unequivocal, is the corresponding agreement for the Southwest Pacific. The ANZUS treaty was broadened by the Southeast Asia Treaty (SEATO), signed in 1954. Besides the ANZUS nations, the United Kingdom, France, Thailand, Pakistan, and the Philippines engaged to meet "the common danger in accordance with [each nation's] constitutional process."

The earlier Rio Treaty (1947) had already committed the United States and the 20 independent Latin American nations to mutual defense. And in addition America made bilateral treaties with the Philippines, Nationalist China, South Korea, and Japan. All told, the United States by 1960 was committed to the defense of some 45 sovereign nations besides her own territories. Even this total does not completely reflect the magnitude of the total defense problem for the United States armed

forces. There were in addition less-formalized commitments such as that embodied in the "Eisenhower Doctrine," pursuant to which the Lebanon intervention was made.

It was thus in the context of worldwide involvement that American defense policy in general and naval policy in particular had to be developed. Inexorable circumstance made America the champion of free men everywhere, and its armed might the principal guardian of the culture and the liberty of the Western World.

Summary

After Korea a consistent pattern emerged in the Cold War still being waged between the Communist world and the West. Communist policy was committed to nibbling at the fringes of the free world, as in Indo-China, and exploiting nationalist unrest wherever found, as in Iraq and Lebanon. The Western powers would be obliged to accept a succession of losses, fight a series of peripheral wars, or run the risk of nuclear war. Although the United States and her allies aimed at greater flexibility, their policy remained in essence that of containment, first enunciated during the Truman administration. In the various skirmishes around the globe, the Communists commonly won when the conflict point was deep in the hinterland (e.g., Hungary, Tibet). The Western democracies won when their naval superiority could be thrown in the balance (e.g., Lebanon, Quemoy).

Through the decade of the 1950's, while the United States lagged in the race with Russia to develop an operational Intercontinental Ballistic Missile (ICBM), the Navy was planning and forging the new instrumentalities of sea power. In 1960 a New Navy was about to emerge—atomic-powered, nearly invulnerable to air attack, equipped with fighter aircraft flying at twice the speed of sound, operating missile-firing submarines able to cruise submerged for thousands of miles and to keep the seas indefinitely. Equipped with both conventional and atomic weapons, carrying battle-ready marine combat teams, the U.S. Navy would continue to be capable of all-out or limited war—the flexible weapon required by a flexible national policy.

To the vocal minority who insist that sea power has come to the end of its usefulness as a military weapon, there are clear and unequivocal answers. If by sea power, we mean the ability to keep ships moving between distant areas of the world, there is no doubt that sea power can and must continue to fulfill this vital mission. If by sea power we mean the ability to carry attack to the enemy shore, to land armed forces in the face of atomic and thermonuclear weapons and to deliver those weapons against a large land mass, there may be a different answer. However, as long as sea power has the capacity to control surface, subsurface, or air in tridimensional war at sea, then it can make its force felt at long distances from its point of origin, over water or over land; and its point of origin can move rapidly from one point to another to concentrate force. With thermonuclear weapons however war has become so absolute that perhaps no weapon can be decisive. Sea power offers flexibility in projection of force and for swift retaliation in attack. Where land bases may well be neutralized by enemy bombs or by political decisions, the carrier force at sea at the beginning of hostilities can hope to evade detection and be in position to launch a devastating counterattack. Fleets of submarines carrying guided missiles with atomic warheads may cripple a nation whose defenses are concentrated merely against attack from the air. The navies of the world may yet prove to be decisive.

Bibliography

The Age of Galley Warfare (Chapter 1)

Gravière, Edmond Jurien de la, *La Guerre de Chypre et la Bataille de Lepante,* 2 v.; Paris: E. Plon, Nourrit, et Cie., 1888. Grundy, George B., *The Great Persian War;* New York: Charles Scribner's Sons, 1901. Lewis, Archibald R., *Naval Power and Trade in the Mediterranean, A.D. 500–1100;* Princeton: Princeton University Press, 1951. Rodgers, Vice Admiral William L., USN (Ret.), *Greek and Roman Naval Warfare;* Annapolis: U.S. Naval Institute, 1937, and *Naval Warfare under Oars;* Annapolis: U.S. Naval Institute, 1939. Rose, J. Holland, *The Mediterranean in the Ancient World;* Cambridge: Cambridge University Press, 1933. Shepherd, Arthur M., *Sea Power in Ancient History;* Boston: Little, Brown & Company, 1924. Starr, Chester G., *The Roman Imperial Navy, 31 B.C.–A.D. 324;* Ithaca: Cornell University Press, 1941. Tarn, William W., *Hellenistic Military and Naval Developments;* Cambridge: Cambridge University Press, 1930. Thiel, J. H., *A History of Roman Sea-Power Before the Second Punic War;* Amsterdam: North-Holland Publishing Co., 1954, and *Studies on the History of Roman Sea Power in Republican Times;* Amsterdam: North-Holland Publishing Co., 1946. Torr, Cecil, *Ancient Ships;* Cambridge: Cambridge University Press, 1894. Also the works of the classical historians and commentators, available in various editions and translations; for GREECE: Arrian, Diodorus Siculus, Herodotus, Polybius, Quintus Curtius, Thucydides, and Xenophon; for ROME, including the Eastern Empire: Appian, Dio Cassius, Julius Caesar, Livy, Polybius, Suetonius, and Tacitus.

The Rise of English Sea Power (Chapters 2–9)

GENERAL

Navy Records Society, London (the nearly 100 volumes are invaluable collections of source and authoritative materials on the British navy). Albion, Robert G., *Forests and Sea Power: The Timber Problem of the Royal Navy, 1652–1862;* Cambridge: Harvard University Press, 1926. Baker, J. N. L., *History of Geographical Discovery and Exploration;* London: George G. Harrap & Co., Ltd., 1931. Branch, W. J. V., and Brook-Williams, E., *A Short History of Navigation;* Annapolis: Weems School of Navigation, 1942. Brendon, J. A., *Great Navigators and Discoverers;* London: George G. Harrap & Co., Ltd., 1929. Clowes, Sir W. L., *et al., The Royal Navy: A History from the Earliest Times to the Present,* 7 v.; London: Sampson Low, Marston & Co., Ltd., 1897–1903. Corbett, Sir Julian S., *England in the Mediterranean: A Study of the Rise and Influence of British Sea Power within the Straits, 1603–1713,* 2 v.; London: Longmans, Green & Company, Ltd., 1904; ed., *Fighting Instructions, 1530–1816;* London: Navy Records Society, 1905, and *Signals and Instructions, 1776–1794;* London: Navy Records Society, 1908. Fortescue, Sir John, *A History of the British Army,* 13 v.; London: Macmillan & Co., Ltd., 1899–1920. Gravière, Edmond Jurien de la, *Guerres Maritimes sous la République et l'Empire,* 2 v.; Paris: Plon, 1853. Hakluyt, Richard, *The Principal Voyages, Traffiques, & Discoveries of the English Nation,* 12 v.; New York: The Macmillan Company, 1903. Hewson, J. B., *A History of the Practice of Navigation;* Glasgow: Brown, Son, & Ferguson, 1951. Jouan, René, *Histoire de la Marine Française;* Paris: Payot, 1950. Lewis, Michael, *The Navy of Britain: A Historical Portrait;* London: George Allen & Unwin, Ltd., 1948. Mahan, Alfred T., *The Influence of Sea Power upon History, 1660–1783;* Boston: Little, Brown & Company, 1890, 1918, 1935, and *The Influence of Sea Power on the Wars of the French Revolution and Empire,* 2 v.; Boston: Little, Brown & Company, 1901. Marshall, John, *Royal Naval Biography,* 12 v.; London: Longman, Rees, Orme, Brown, & Green, 1823–

1825. Montross, Lynn, *War Through the Ages;* New York: Harper & Brothers, 1946. Oman, Sir Charles W. C., *The Art of War in the Middle Ages;* Ithaca: Cornell University Press, 1953. Richmond, Sir Herbert W., *The Navy as an Instrument of Policy, 1558–1727;* Cambridge University Press, 1953, and *Statesmen and Sea Power;* Oxford: The Clarendon Press, 1946. Rivera y Casares, P. D. de, *Historia de la Organizaciones Navales de España y Francia;* Madrid: Editorial Alhambra, 1932(?). Tramond, J., *Manuel d'Histoire Maritime de la France;* Paris: Challamel, 1916.

EARLY PERIOD (CHAPTER 2)

Beadon, Roger, *Robert Blake;* London: Edward Arnold & Co., 1935. Beazley, C. Raymond, *Prince Henry the Navigator;* New York: G. P. Putnam's Sons, 1895. Clark, G. N., *The Dutch Alliance and the War against French Trade, 1688–1697;* Oxford: Oxford University Press, 1934. Corbett, Sir Julian S., *Drake and the Tudor Navy, with a History of the Rise of England as a Maritime Power,* 2 v.; New York: Longmans, Green & Company, Ltd., 1898; *The Navy during the Spanish War, 1585–1587;* London: Navy Records Society, 1894. Duro, Cesario Fernandez, *La Armada Española,* 9 v.; Madrid, Sucesores de Rivadeneyra, 1895–1903. Graham, Gerald S., *Empire of the North Atlantic: The Maritime Struggle for North America;* Toronto: University of Toronto Press, 1950. Laughton, Sir John Knox, ed., *State Papers Relating to the Defeat of the Spanish Armada,* 2 v.; London: Navy Records Society, 1894. Mattingly, Garrett, *The Armada;* Boston: Houghton Mifflin Company, 1959. Morison, Samuel Eliot, *Admiral of the Ocean Sea: A Life of Christopher Columbus;* Boston: Little, Brown & Company, 1942. Owen, John H., *War at Sea under Queen Anne, 1702–1708;* Cambridge: Cambridge University Press, 1938. Penn, C. D., *The Navy under the Early Stuarts, and Its Influence on English History;* London: J. Hogg, 1920. Richmond, Sir Herbert W., *The Navy in the War of 1739–1748,* 3 v.; Cambridge: Cambridge University Press, 1916. Tedder, Arthur W., *The Navy of the Restoration;* Cambridge: Cambridge University Press, 1916. Williamson, James A., *The Age of Drake;* London: A. & C. Black, Ltd., 1938, *Maritime Enterprise, 1485–1558;* Oxford: Oxford University Press, 1913, and *Sir John Hawkins: The Time and the Man;* Oxford: Clarendon Press, 1927.

THE SEVEN YEARS' WAR (CHAPTER 3)

Corbett, Sir Julian S., *England in the Seven Years' War: A Study in Combined Strategy,* 2 v.; London: Longmans, Green & Company, Ltd., 1918. Pitt, William, First Earl of Chatham, *Correspondence,* Kimball, G. S., ed., 2 v.; New York: The Macmillan Company, 1906. Richmond, Sir Herbert W., *The Navy in India, 1763–1783;* London: Ernest Benn, Ltd., 1931. Sherrard, O. A., *Pitt and the Seven Years' War;* London: Bodley Head, 1955. Stacey, C. P., *Quebec, 1759—The Siege and the Battle;* New York: The Macmillan Company, 1960. Tunstall, Brian, *Admiral Byng and the Loss of Minorca;* London: Philip Allen & Co., Ltd., 1928. Willson, Beckles, *Life and Letters of James Wolfe;* London: Heineman, 1909.

THE WAR OF THE AMERICAN REVOLUTION (CHAPTERS 4–5)

GENERAL

AMERICAN NAVY

Allen, Gardner W., *A Naval History of the American Revolution,* 2 v.; Boston & New York: Houghton Mifflin Co., 1913. Knox, Commodore Dudley W., USN (Ret.), *The Naval Genius of George Washington;* Boston: Houghton Mifflin Co., 1932. Maclay, Edgar S., *A History of American Privateers;* New York: D. Appleton, 1899. Middlebrook, Louis F., *History of Maritime Connecticut during the American Revolution 1775–1783,* 2 v.; Salem: The Essex Institute, 1925. Paine, Ralph D., *Ships and Sailors of Old Salem;* New York: Outing Publishing Co., 1909. Paullin, Charles O., *The Navy of the American Revolution, its Administration, its Policy, and its Achievements;* Cleveland: The Burrows Brothers Co., 1906. Rogers, Ernest D., ed., *Connecticut's Naval Office at New London,* 2 v.; New London: New London County Historical Association, 1933. Stewart, Robert A., *The History of Virginia's Navy of the Revolution;* Richmond, Va.: Mitchell & Hotchkiss, 1934.

BRITISH NAVY

James, Captain William M., *The British Navy in Adversity;* London: Longmans, Green & Company, Ltd., 1926. Mahan, Alfred T., *The Major Operations of the Navies in the War of American Independence;* London: Sampson Low, Marston & Co., Ltd., 1913. White, Thomas, *Naval Researches, or a Candid Inquiry into the Conduct of Admirals Byron, Graves, Hood, and Rodney in the Actions off Grenada, Chesapeak, St. Christopher's, and of the Ninth and Twelfth of April 1782, Being a Refutation of the Plans and Statements of Mr. Clerk, Rear Admiral Ekins, and Others: Founded on Authentic Documents or Actual Observation;* London: Whittaker, Treacher & Arnett, 1830.

FRENCH NAVY

Chevalier, E., *Histoire de la Marine Française Pendant la Guerre de l'Independance Américaine;* Paris: Librairie Hachette et Cie., 1877. Doniol, Henri, *Histoire de la Participation de la France à l'Établissement des États-Unis d'Amérique, Correspondance Diplomatique et Documents,* 5 v. and supplement; Paris: Imprimerie Nationale, 1886–1892. Lacour-Gayet, G., *La Marine Militaire de la France sous le Règne de Louis XVI;* Paris, Librairie Spéciale pour l'Histoire de la France, 1905. Loir, Maurice, *La Marine Française;* Paris, 1893. Perkins, James B., *France in the American Revolution;* Boston and New York: Houghton Mifflin Co., 1911. Scott, James B., *De Grasse à Yorktown;* Paris: Editoriale Internationale, 1931. Troude, O., *Batailles Navales de la France,* 4 v.; Paris: P. Levot, 1867–1868.

OTHER

Landers, H. L., *The Virginia Campaign and the Blockade and Siege of Yorktown 1781, Including a Brief Narrative of the French Participation in the Revolution Prior to the Southern Campaign;* Washington: USGPO, 1931 (Senate Document No. 273, 71st Congress, 3rd Session).

BIOGRAPHIES, MEMOIRS, DIARIES

Anderson, Troyer S., *The Command of the Howe Brothers During the American Revolution;* New York and London: Oxford University Press, 1936. Barnes, John S., ed., *Fanning's Narrative, Being the Memoirs of Nathaniel Fanning, an Officer of the Revolutionary Navy, 1778–1783;* New York: The Naval History Society, 1912. Barrow, Sir John, *The Life of Richard Earl Howe, K.G., Admiral of the Fleet and General of the Marines;* London: John Murray, 1838. Burgoyne, Lieutenant General John, *A State of the Expedition from Canada as laid before the House of Commons by Lieutenant-General Burgoyne and verified by evidence with a collection of authentic documents;* London, 1780. Calmon-Maison, *L'Amiral d'Estaing;* Paris, Calmann-Lévy, 1910. Cornwallis-West, G., *The Life and Letters of Admiral Cornwallis;* London: Robert Holden & Co., Ltd., 1927. Cunat, Charles, *Histoire du Bailli de Suffren;* Rennes: A. Marteville et Lefas, 1852. De Koven, Mrs. Reginald, *The Life and Letters of John Paul Jones,* 2 v.; New York: Charles Scribner's Sons, 1913. Fitzpatrick, John C., ed., *The Diaries of George Washington 1748–1799,* 4 v.; Boston and New York: Houghton Mifflin Co. for the Mount Vernon Ladies' Ass'n. of the Union, 1925. Freeman, Douglas Southall, *George Washington, A Biography,* 7 v.; New York: Charles Scribner's Sons, 1948–57. Hannay, David, *Rodney;* London and New York: MacMillan and Co., 1891. Hennequin, T. F. G., *Essai Historique sur la Vie et les Compagnes du Bailli de Suffren;* Paris: Librairie de Paytieux, 1824. Keppel, Rev. Thomas, *The Life of Augustus, Viscount Keppel, Admiral of the White, and First Lord of the Admiralty in 1782–3,* 2 v.; London: Henry Colburn, 1842. Lewis, Charles L., *Admiral de Grasse and American Independence;* Annapolis: U.S. Naval Institute, 1945. Lorenz, Lincoln, *John Paul Jones, Fighter for Freedom and Glory;* Annapolis: U.S. Naval Institute, 1943. Morison, Samuel E., *John Paul Jones, a Sailor's Biography;* Boston: Little, Brown & Co., 1959. Mundy, Godfrey B., *The Life and Correspondence of the Late Admiral Lord Rodney,* 2 v.; London: John Murray, 1830. Ralfe, J., *The Naval Biography of Great Britain, Consisting of Historical Memoirs of those Officers of the British Navy who Distinguished Themselves during the Reign of His Majesty George III,* 4 v.; London: Whitmore and Fenn, 1828. Stone, William L., trans. and ed., *Memoirs and Letters and Journals of Major-General Riedesel during his Residence in America,* 2 v.; Albany: J. Munsell, 1868. Thiéry, Maurice (Agnew, Anne, trans.), *Bougainville, Soldier and Sailor;* London: Grayson and Grayson, 1932. Weelen, Jean-Edmond (Lee, Lawrence, trans.), *Rochambeau, Father and Son, A Life of the Maréchal de Rochambeau by Jean-Edmond Weelen, and the Journal of the Vicomte de Rochambeau;* New York: Henry Holt & Co., 1936.

SOURCES

Barck, Dorothy C., ed., *Letter-Books and Order-Book of George, Lord Rodney, Admiral of the White Squadron 1780–1782,* 2 v.; New York: The Naval History Society, 1932. Barnes, John S., ed., *Logs of Serapis—Alliance—Ariel under the Command of John Paul Jones 1779–80;* New York: The Naval History Society, 1911. The Bedford Club, *Operations of the French Fleet under the Count de Grasse in 1781–2, as Described in Two Contemporaneous Journals;* New York: The Bedford Club, 1864. Barnes, G. R., and Owen, J. H., eds., *The Private Papers of John, Earl of Sandwich, First Lord of the Admiralty 1771–82,* 4 v.; London: Navy Records Society, 1932–38. Chadwick, French E., ed., *The Graves Papers and Other Documents Relating to the Naval Operations of the Yorktown Campaign, July to October 1781;* New York: The Naval History Society, 1916. Fitzpatrick, John C., ed., *Writings of George Washington,* 39 v.; Washington: USGPO, 1931–44. Hannay, David, ed., *Letters Written by Sir Samuel Hood (Viscount Hood) in 1781–2–3;* London: Navy Records Society, 1895. Institut Français de Washington, ed., *Correspondence of General Washington and Comte de Grasse, 1781 August 17–November 4;* Washington: USGPO, 1931 (Senate Document No. 211; 71st Congress, 2nd Session, 1931). Johnson, Amandus, trans. and ed., *The Naval Campaigns of Count de Grasse during the American Revolution 1781–1783, by Karl Gustaf Tornquist;* Philadelphia: Swedish Colonial Society, 1942. Keim, De B. Randolph, ed., *Rochambeau; Army of de Rochambeau on Land and Naval Exploits of de Ternay, des Touches, de Barras, and de Grasse in American Waters 1780–81;* Washington: USGPO, 1907 (Senate Document No. 537, 59th Congress, 1st Session, 1907). Laughton, Sir John Knox, ed., *Letters and Papers of Charles, Lord Barham, Admiral of the Red Squadron, 1758–1813,* 3 v.; Navy Records Society, 1907–1911. *The Naval Miscellany,* Vol. I, Navy Records Society, 1902. *Log of the Bon Homme Richard;* Mystic: Marine Historical Association of Mystic, Conn., 1936. Neeser, Robert W., ed., *Letters and Papers Relating to the Cruises of Gustavus Conyngham, a Captain of the Continental Navy 1777– 1779;* New York: The Naval History Society, 1915. *The Despatches of Molyneux Schuldham, Vice-Admiral of the Blue, Commander-in-Chief of British Ships in North America January– July 1776;* New York: The Naval History Society, 1913. Paullin, Charles O., ed., *Out-Letters of the Continental Marine Committee and Board of Admiralty, August 1776–September 1780,* 2 v.; New York: The Naval History Society, 1914. Sparks, Jared, ed., *Correspondence of the American Revolution, Being Letters of Eminent Men to George Washington, from the Time of His Taking Command of the Army to the End of his Presidency,* 4 v.; Boston: Little, Brown & Co., 1853. Stevens, Benjamin F., *The Campaign in Virginia 1781, The Clinton-Cornwallis Controversy,* 2 v.; London: 4 Trafalgar Square, 1888. *Facsimiles of Manuscripts in European Archives Relating to America 1773–1783,* 25 v.; London: 4 Trafalgar Square, 1889–1898.

THE WAR OF THE FRENCH REVOLUTION (Chapter 6)

Bryant, Arthur, *The Years of Endurance;* London: Collins, 1942, and *The Years of Peril;* London: Collins, 1944. Burne, Alfred H., *The Noble Duke of York;* London: Staples Press, 1949. Closmadeuc, G. Thomas de, *Quiberon, 1795;* Paris: Plon, 1899. Debrière, Edouard, *1793–1805 Projets et Tentatives de Débarquement aux Îles Britanniques,* 4 v.; Paris: Chapelot, 1900–1902. Jackson, T. S., *Logs of the Great Sea Fights,* 2 v.; London: Navy Records Society, 1899–1900. James, Admiral Sir William, *Old Oak: The Life of John Jervis;* London: Longmans, Green & Co., Ltd., 1950, and *The Naval History of Great Britain from the Declaration of War by France in 1793 to the Accession of George IV*, 6 v.; London: Richard Bentley, 1837. Mahan, Alfred T., *Types of Naval Officers;* Boston: Little, Brown & Company, 1901. Pellew, George, ed., *Life and Correspondence of Henry Addington, Viscount Sidmouth*, 3 v.; London: John Murray, 1847. Rose, J. Holland, *Lord Hood and the Defence of Toulon;* Cambridge: Cambridge University Press, 1922. Smith, D. B., *The St. Vincent Papers*, 2 v.; London: Navy Records Society, 1921 and 1926. Tonnèle, Jean, *L'Angleterre en Méditérranée;* Paris: Charles-Lavauzelle, 1952.

NELSON AND BONAPARTE (CHAPTER 7)

Anderson, R. C., *Naval Wars in the Baltic during the Sailing Ship Epoch;* London: Gilbert Wood, 1910, and *Naval Wars in the Levant, 1559–1853;* Princeton: Princeton University Press, 1952. Barrow, John, *Life and Correspondence of Admiral Sir William Sydney Smith*, 2 v.; London: Richard Bentley, 1848. Bruun, Geoffrey, *Europe and the French Imperium, 1799–1814;* New York: Harper & Brothers, 1938. Bunbury, Sir Henry (Fortescue, Sir John, ed.), *Narratives of Some Passages in the Great War with France;* London: Peter Davies, Ltd., 1927. *The Cambridge Modern History*, Chapters 2–13 seriatim. Carlan, J. M., *Navios en Secuestro: La Escuadra Española del Oceano en Brest (1799–1802)*; Madrid: Instituto Historico de Marina, 1951. Corbett, J. S. and Richmond, H. W., eds., *The Spencer Papers*, 4 v.; London: Navy Records Society, 1913–1914 and 1923–1924. Garcot, Maurice, *Kléber;* Paris: Berger-Levrault, 1936. *Histoire de l'Expédition Française en Égypte*, 10 v.; Paris: Denain, 1830–1836. Hoskins, H. L., *British Routes to India;* New York: Longmans, Green & Company, Ltd., 1928. James, Admiral Sir William M., *The Durable Monument: Horatio Nelson;* London: Longmans, Green & Company, Ltd., 1948. Maurice, Sir J. F., ed., *The Diary of Sir John Moore*, 2 v.; London: Longmans, Green & Company, Ltd., 1904. Napoleon I, *Correspondence*, 28 v.; Paris: Plon avec Dumain, 1857–1859. Nicholas, Sir Harris, ed., *Dispatches and Letters of Lord Viscount Nelson*, 7 v.; London: Henry Colburn, 1846. Puryear, V. J., *Napoleon and the Dardanelles;* Berkeley: University of California Press, 1951. Warner, Oliver, *Victory: The Life of Lord Nelson;* Boston: Little, Brown & Company, 1958.

THE CAMPAIGN OF TRAFALGAR (CHAPTER 8)

British Admiralty Bluebook, *The Tactics of Trafalgar;* London: H. M. Stationer's Office, 1913. Corbett, J. S., *The Campaign of Trafalgar;* London: Longmans, Green & Company, Ltd., 1910. Désbrière, Edouard, *Trafalgar;* Paris: Chapelot, 1907. Leyland, John, ed., *The Blockade of Brest, 1803–1805*, 2 v.; London: Navy Records Society, 1898 and 1901. Mahan, Alfred T., *The Life of Nelson*, 2 v.; Boston: Little, Brown & Company, 1907. Marliani, M. de, *Combate de Trafalgar;* Madrid: Impreso de Orden Superior, 1850. Thomazi, A., *Trafalgar;* Paris: Payot, 1932.

THE DECLINE AND FALL OF THE FRENCH EMPIRE (CHAPTER 9)

Creswell, John, *Generals and Admirals;* London: Longmans, Green & Company, Ltd., 1952. Hamilton, Sir R. V., ed., *The Byam Martin Papers*, 3 v.; London: Navy Records Society, 1898, 1900, and 1902. Napier, W. F. P., *History of the War in the Peninsula, 1807–1814;* Philadelphia: Carey & Hart, 1842. Parkinson, C. N., *War in the Eastern Seas, 1793–1815;* London: George Allen & Unwin, Ltd., 1954. Ross, John, *Admiral Lord de Saumarez*, 2 v.; London: Richard Bentley, 1838.

The Beginnings of the United States Navy (Chapter 10)

Ferguson, Eugene S., *Truxton of the Constellation;* Baltimore: The Johns Hopkins Press, 1916. Knox, Commodore Dudley Wright USN (Ret.), *A History of the United States Navy;* New York: G. P. Putnam's Sons, 1948, and ed., *Naval Documents Related to the Quasi-War between the United States and France*, 7 v.; Washington: USGPO, 1935–38, and *Naval Docu-*

ments Related to the United States Wars with the Barbary Powers, 7 v.; Washington: USGPO, 1939–45. Smelser, Marshall, The Congress Founds the Navy, 1787–1798; South Bend: University of Notre Dame Press, 1959. The Autobiography of Charles Morris; Annapolis: U.S. Naval Institute, 1880.

The War of 1812 (Chapter 11)

Adams, Henry, The War of 1812; Washington: The Infantry Journal, 1944. Brackenridge, H. M., History of the Late War, between the United States and Great Britain; Baltimore: Cushing and Jewett, 1818. Davies, Godfrey, Wellington and His Army; London: Basil Blackwell, 1954. James, William, Naval Occurrences of the Late War between Great Britain and the United States of America; London: Thomas Egerton, 1817. Mahan, Captain A. T., Sea Power in Its Relation to the War of 1812; Boston: Little, Brown & Company, 1905. Roosevelt, Theodore, The Naval War of 1812; New York: G. P. Putnam's Sons, 1903. Smith, W. H., Life and Services of Captain Philip Beaver; London: John Murray, 1829.

Navies in Transition (Chapter 12)

TECHNOLOGY

Bathe, Greville, Ship of Destiny; St. Augustine, Fla.: n.p., 1951. Baxter, James Phinney, Introduction of the Ironclad Warship; Cambridge: Harvard University Press, 1933. Bennett, Frank M., The Steam Navy of the United States; Pittsburgh: Warren and Co., 1896. Brodie, Bernard, Sea Power in the Machine Age; Princeton: Princeton University Press, 1941. Bushnell, David, letter to Thomas Jefferson, Transactions of the American Philosophical Society, IV (Old Series), 303–312. Chapelle, Howard I., History of American Sailing Ships, and The History of the American Sailing Navy; New York: W. W. Norton & Company, Inc., 1935, 1949. Cowie, J. S., Mines, Minelayers and Minelaying; London: Oxford University Press, 1949. Dahlgren, J. A., Shells and Shell Guns; Philadelphia: King and Baird, 1856. Preble, George Henry, and Hammersley, L. R., A Chronological History of the Origin and Development of Steam Navigation; Philadelphia: L. R. Hammersley, 1883. Robertson, Frederick Leslie, The Evolution of Naval Armament; London: Constable & Company, Ltd., 1921. Tennent, Sir J. Emerson, The Story of the Guns; London: Longmans, Green & Company, Ltd., 1864.

THE MEXICAN WAR

Bancroft, Hubert Howe, History of the Pacific States, XXII; San Francisco: The History Company, 1886. Bayard, S. J., A Sketch of the Life of Commodore Robert F. Stockton; New York: Derby and Jackson, 1856. Conner, P. S. P., The Home Squadron under Commodore Conner in the War with Mexico; Philadelphia: n.p., 1896. Report of the Secretary of the Navy, 1846; Washington: USGPO, 1847. Senate Executive Document 33, 30th Congress, 1st Session; Washington: USGPO. Smith, Justin A., The War with Mexico, 2 v.; New York: The Macmillan Company, 1919.

THE CRIMEAN WAR

Bazancourt, Baron C. de, The Crimean Expedition to the Capture of Sebastopol, 2 v.; London: Sampson Low, Son, and Co., 1856. Daly, Robert W., "Nakhimov: Black Sea Admiral," Marine Corps Gazette, April 1953, 54–61. Furse, Col. George Armand, Military Expeditions beyond the Seas, 2 v.; London: William Clowes & Sons, Ltd., 1897. Heath, Sir Leopold George, Letters from the Black Sea during the Crimean War, 1854–1855; London: Richard Bentley and Son, 1897. Kinglake, William, The Invasion of the Crimea, 8 v.; Edinburgh: William Blackwood & Sons, Ltd., 1863–1887. Russell, William Howard, General Todleben's History of the Defence of Sebastopol: a Review; New York: D. Van Nostrand Company, Inc., 1865, and The War, 2 v.; London: George Routledge & Sons, Ltd., 1856.

The American Civil War (Chapters 13, 17)

GENERAL

Johnson, R. U., and Buel, C. C., eds., *Battles and Leaders of the Civil War,* 4 v.; New York: The Century Co., 1887–1889. *Official Records of the Union and Confederate Armies in the War of the Rebellion,* 128 v.; Washington: USGPO, 1880–1902. *Official Records of the Union and Confederate Navies in the War of the Rebellion,* 128 v.; Washington: USGPO, 1894–1922. Porter, D. D., *Naval History of the Civil War;* New York: Sherman Publishing Co., 1886. Moore, F., ed., *The Rebellion Record,* 11 v.; New York: George Putnam's Sons, 1861–1864, and Van Nostrand, 1864–1868. *Report of Joint Committee on the Conduct of the War,* 9 v.; Washington: USGPO, 1863–1866. Scharf, J. T., *History of the Confederate States Navy;* New York: Rogers and Sherwood, 1887. Thompson, R. M. and Wainwright, R., *Confidential Correspondence of G. V. Fox,* 3 v.; New York: The Naval History Society, 1918–1919. Welles, G., *The Diary of Gideon Welles,* 3 v.; Boston: Houghton Mifflin Company, 1911. West, R. S., Jr., *Gideon Welles: Lincoln's Navy Department;* Indianapolis: The Bobbs-Merrill Company, 1943, and *Mr. Lincoln's Navy;* New York: Longmans, Green & Company, 1957.

THE BLOCKADE AND THE CRUISERS (CHAPTERS 13 AND 17)

Bradlee, F., *Blockade Running during the Civil War and the Effect of Land and Water Transportation on the Confederacy;* Salem: Essex Institute, 1925. Bulloch, J. D., *The Secret Service of the Confederate States in Europe,* 2 v.; New York: George Putnam's Sons, 1883. Ellicott, J. M., *The Life of John Ancrum Winslow;* New York: George Putnam's Sons, 1902. King, J. E., "The First Fort Fisher Campaign, 1864–65," *U.S. Naval Institute Proceedings,* v. 77 (August, 1951); 843–855. Owsley, F. L., *King Cotton Diplomacy;* Chicago: University of Chicago Press, 1931. Robinson, W. M., *The Confederate Privateers;* New Haven: Yale University Press, 1928. Semmes, R., *Memoirs of Service Afloat;* New York: P. J. Kenedy & Sons, 1869. Soley, J. R., *The Blockade and the Cruisers;* New York: Charles Scribner's Sons, 1883. Schwab, J. D., *The Confederate States of America, 1861–1865: A Financial and Industrial History;* New York: Charles Scribner's Sons, 1901. Watson, William, *The Adventures of a Blockade Runner;* London: T. Fisher Unwin, 1892.

The New Technology: Ironclads in Action (Chapter 14)

Bennett, F. M., *The Monitor and the Navy under Steam;* Boston: Houghton Mifflin Company, 1900. Church, W. C., *The Life of John Ericsson,* 2 v.; New York: Charles Scribner's Sons, 1891. Daly, Robert W., *How the Merrimac Won;* New York: Crowell, 1957. Lewis, Charles L., *Admiral Franklin Buchanan;* Baltimore: The Norman, Remington Company, 1929. Wells, W. S., ed., *The Original U.S. Warship Monitor;* New Haven: C. S. Bushnell Memorial Association, 1899. Worden, J. L., *et al., The Monitor and the Merrimac;* New York: Harper & Brothers, 1912. (See also Baxter, *Introduction of the Ironclad Warship, supra,* Chapter 14.)

The Mississippi Campaign (Chapters 15 and 16)

Butler, B. F., *Autobiography and Personal Reminiscences;* Boston: A. M. Thayer, 1892. Farragut, L., *The Life of David Glasgow Farragut;* New York: D. Appleton Co., 1879. Fiske, John, *The Mississippi Valley in the Civil War;* Boston: Houghton Mifflin Company, 1900. Lewis, Charles L., *David Glasgow Farragut, Our First Admiral;* Annapolis: U.S. Naval Institute, 1943. Mahan, A. T., *Admiral Farragut;* New York: D. Appleton Co., 1892. Mahan, A. T., *The Gulf and Inland Waters;* New York: Charles Scribner's Sons, 1883. Walke, H., *Naval Scenes and Reminiscences of the Civil War;* New York: F. R. Reed & Co., 1887. West,

R. S., Jr., *The Second Admiral: A Life of David Dixon Porter;* New York: Coward-McCann, 1937.

Naval Developments of the Late 19th Century (Chapter 18)

Long, John D., *The New American Navy,* 2 v.; New York: The Outlook Co., 1903. Mahan, Alfred T., *From Sail to Steam;* New York: Harper & Brothers, 1907. Parkes, Oscar, *British Battleships, 1860-1950;* London: Seeley Service, 1957. Sprout, Harold and Margaret, *The Rise of American Naval Power;* Princeton: Princeton University Press, 1944. Westcott, Allan, ed., *Mahan on Naval Warfare;* Boston: Little, Brown & Company, 1948. Wilson, H. W., *Ironclads in Action,* 2 v.; Boston: Little, Brown & Company, 1896. (See also Bennett, *The Steam Navy of the United States, supra,* and Brodie, *Sea Power in the Machine Age, supra.*)

The Rise of Japanese Naval Power (Chapter 19)

GENERAL

Ballard, R. N., *The Influence of the Sea on the Political History of Japan;* New York: E. P. Dutton & Co., Inc., 1921. Falk, E. A., *Togo and the Rise of Japanese Sea Power;* New York: Longmans, Green & Company, 1936.

RISE OF, TO 1870

Brown, D., "The Impact of Firearms on Japanese Warfare, 1543-1598," *Far Eastern Quarterly* (May, 1948). Clowes, W. L., *The Royal Navy, A History,* VI-VII, *supra.* Cole, A. B., ed., *With Perry in Japan;* Princeton: Princeton University Press, 1942. Dennett, T., *Americans in Eastern Asia;* New York: Barnes & Noble, Inc., 1941. Dulles, F. R., *China and America;* Princeton: Princeton University Press, 1946. Eldridge, F. B., *The Background of Eastern Sea Power;* Melbourne: Georgian House, 1945. Hansard, A. C., "Early Days in Japan," *U.S. Naval Institute Proceedings,* XXXVII (March, 1911); 141. Marder, A. J., "From Jimmu Tenno to Perry: Sea Power in Early Japanese History," *American Historical Review,* LI (October, 1945); 1. *Narrative of the Expedition of an American Squadron to the China Seas and Japan;* Washington: USGPO, 1856. Paullin, C. O., "Early Naval Voyages to the Orient," *U.S. Naval Institute Proceedings,* XXXVII (March, 1911: 239, 255; June, 1911: 387). Sadler, A., "The Naval Campaign in the Korean War of Hideyoshi, 1592-1598," *Asiatic Society of Japan Transactions* (June, 1937). Underwood, H. H., *Korean Boats and Ships;* Seoul: Chosen Christian College, 1934. Walworth, A., *Black Ships Off Japan: The Story of Commodore Perry's Expedition;* New York: Alfred A. Knopf, Inc., 1946.

SINO-JAPANESE WAR

Marble, F., "The Battle of the Yalu," *U.S. Naval Institute Proceedings,* XXI (1895), No. 3; 479. McGiffin, P. N., "The Battle of the Yalu," *Century Magazine,* L (August, 1895); 585. Porter, R. P., *Japan, The Rise of a Modern Power;* London: Oxford University Press, 1914. Wallach, R., "The War in the East," *U.S. Naval Institute Proceedings,* XXI (1895), No. 21; 691. Wilson, H. W., *Battleships in Action,* 2 v.; New York: Little, Brown & Company, 1928. "Vladimir" (pseud. Volpicelli, C.), *The China-Japan War;* London: Sampson Low, Marston & Co., Ltd., 1896.

RUSSO-JAPANESE WAR

"Battle of the Sea of Japan," *Journal of the U.S. Artillery,* XXIV (July-August, 1905); 72. Cotten, L. A., "The Naval Strategy of the Russo-Japanese War," *U.S. Naval Institute Proceedings,* XXXVI (March, 1910); 41. Fuller, J. F. C., *Decisive Battles: Their Influence on*

Civilization and History, chap. 24; New York: Charles Scribner's Sons, 1940. Great Britain, Committee of Imperial Defence, Historical Section, *Official History of the Russo-Japanese War,* 3 v.; appendix, 3 map cases; London: H. M. Stationery Office, 1910–1920. Hoadley, W. T. (trans.), "The Battle of the Yellow Sea: Official Version of the Japanese General Staff," *U.S. Naval Institute Proceedings,* XL (September-October, 1914); 153. Jane, F. T., *Heresies of Sea Power;* London: Longmans, Green & Company, Ltd., 1906, and *The Imperial Russian Navy;* London: Thacker, 1899, and *The Imperial Japanese Navy;* London: Thacker, 1899. Klado, N., *The Battle of the Sea of Japan;* London: Hodder & Stoughton, Ltd., 1906. Kladre, N., *The Russian Navy in the Russo-Japanese War;* London: Hurst and Blackett, 1905. Lloyd, A., *Admiral Togo;* Tokyo: Kinkodo, 1905. Mahan, A. T., "Retrospect upon the War between Japan and Russia," *Naval Administration and Warfare;* Boston: Little, Brown & Company, 1918. Mizuno, H., *This One Battle;* Tokyo: Daitoa Shuppan Kabushiki Kaisha, 1944. "Naval Attacks upon Port Arthur," *Journal of the U.S. Artillery,* XXVII (January-February, 1907); 54. Nebogatoff, "Battle of Tsushima," *Journal of the Royal United Service Institution,* L (October, 1906); 1262. Nojine, E. K., *The Truth about Port Arthur;* London: John Murray, 1908. Novikov-Priboy, *Tsushima;* London: George Allen and Unwin, Ltd., 1936. Ogasawara, N., *Life of Admiral Togo;* Tokyo: Saito Shoin, 1934. Semenoff, V., *Rasplata;* London: John Murray, 1909, and *The Battle of Tsushima;* London: John Murray, 1906. Theiss, F., *The Voyage of Forgotten Men;* Indianapolis: The Bobbs-Merrill Company, 1937. White, R. D., "With the Baltic Fleet at Tsushima," *U.S. Naval Institute Proceedings,* XXXII (June, 1906); 597. Whitton, F. E., *The Decisive Battles of Modern Times;* London: Constable & Company, Ltd., 1923.

The Spanish-American War (Chapter 20)

GENERAL

Annual Report of the Secretary of the Navy, 1898; Washington: USGPO, 1898. *Annual Report of the Secretary of War, 1898;* Washington: USGPO, 1898. *Appendix to the Report of the Chief of the Bureau of Navigation, 1898;* Washington: USGPO, 1898. U.S. Naval Intelligence Office, *Information from Abroad: Notes on the Spanish-American War;* Washington: USGPO, 1898–1900. Chadwick, French E., *The Relations of the United States and Spain: The Spanish-American War;* New York: Charles Scribner's Sons, 1911. Mahan, A. T., *Lessons of the War with Spain and Other Articles;* Boston: Little, Brown & Company, 1899. Mayo, Lawrence S., ed., *America of Yesterday, As Reflected in the Journal of John Davis Long;* Boston: Little, Brown & Company, 1923. West, Richard S., Jr., *Admirals of American Empire;* Indianapolis: The Bobbs-Merrill Company, 1948. Wilson, Herbert W., *The Downfall of Spain;* London: Sampson Low, Marston & Co., Ltd., 1900. (See also Long, *The New American Navy, supra.*)

PHILIPPINES CAMPAIGN

Dewey, George, *Autobiography of George Dewey;* New York: Charles Scribner's Sons, 1913. Fiske, Bradley A., *From Midshipman to Rear-Admiral;* New York: The Century Company, 1919. Sargent, Nathan, *Admiral Dewey and the Manila Campaign;* Washington: Naval Historical Foundation, 1947.

CARIBBEAN CAMPAIGN

Record of Proceedings of a Court of Inquiry in the Case of Rear-Admiral Winfield S. Schley, U.S. Navy; Washington: USGPO, 1902. Alger, Russell A., *The Spanish-American War;* New York: Harper & Brothers, 1901. Clark, Charles E., *My Fifty Years in the Navy;* Boston: Little, Brown & Company, 1917. Evans, Robley D., *A Sailor's Log, Recollections of Forty Years of Naval Life;* New York: D. Appleton-Century Company, 1901. Goode, William A. M., *With Sampson through the War;* New York: Doubleday and McClure Company, 1899. Schley, Winfield S., *Forty-Five Years under the Flag;* New York: D. Appleton & Co., 1904. Sigsbee,

Charles, *The "Maine," An Account of Her Destruction in Havana Harbor;* New York: D. Appleton-Century Company, 1899.

The United States Becomes a Naval Power (Chapter 21)

Bywater, H. C., *Navies and Nations;* Boston: Houghton Mifflin Company, 1927. *The Complete Book of Submarines;* New York: The World Publishing Co., 1958. Davis, G. T., *A Navy Second to None;* New York: Harcourt, Brace, & Co., 1910. Marder, Arthur J., *The Anatomy of British Sea Power, 1880–1905;* New York: Alfred A. Knopf, 1940. Morison, E. E., *Admiral Sims and the Modern American Navy;* Boston: Houghton Mifflin Company, 1942. O'Gara, G. C., *Theodore Roosevelt and the Rise of the Modern Navy;* Princeton: Princeton University Press, 1943. (See also Brodie, *Sea Power in the Machine Age,* Bennett, *The Steam Navy of the United States,* Long, *The New American Navy,* and Sprout, *Rise of American Naval Power, supra.*)

World War I: Opening Operations (Chapter 22)

GENERAL

History of the Great War, Based on Official Documents: Corbett, Julian S., and Henry Newbolt, *Naval Operations,* 5 v. (London: Longmans, Green & Company, Ltd., 1920–1931); Fayle, C. Ernest, *Seaborne Trade,* 3 v. (New York: Longmans, Green & Company, 1920 and 1923); Hurd, Archibald, *The Merchant Navy,* 3 v. (New York: John Murray, 1921–1929). Bingham, Barry, *Falklands, Jutland, and the Bight;* London: John Murray, 1919. Churchill, W. S., *The World Crisis, supra,* 4 v.; New York: Charles Scribner's Sons, 1923–27 (available also in condensed one-volume edition). Dreyer, Frederick C., *The Sea Heritage: A Study of Maritime Warfare;* London: Museum Press, 1957. Keyes, Roger, *The Naval Memoirs of Admiral of the Fleet Sir Roger Keyes;* New York: E. P. Dutton & Co., 1934. May, Ernest R., *The World War and American Isolation, 1914–1917;* Cambridge: Harvard University Press, 1959. Raeder, Grand Admiral Erich, *My Life;* Annapolis: U.S. Naval Institute, 1960. Scheer, Reinhard, *Germany's High Seas Fleet in the World War;* London: Cassell & Co., Ltd., 1920. (See also Wilson, H. W., *Battleships in Action,* II, *supra.*)

CRUISER ACTIONS

Fisher, John A., *Memories and Records,* 2 v.; New York: George H. Doran Company, 1920. Hirst, Lloyd, *Coronel and After;* London: Peter Davies, Ltd., 1934. Milne, A. Berkeley, *The Flight of the 'Goeben' and the 'Breslau';* London: E. Nash, 1921. Pocchammer, Hans, *Before Jutland;* London: Jarrolds, Publishers, Ltd., 1931. Raeder, Erich, *Cruiser Warfare in Foreign Waters,* 2 v.; Newport: U.S. Naval War College, 1923–1935. Scott, Percy, *Fifty Years in the Royal Navy;* London: George H. Doran Company, 1919. Tirpitz, Alfred, *My Memoirs,* 2 v.; New York: Dodd, Mead and Company, Inc., 1919. Verner, Rudolf, *The Battle Cruisers at the Action of the Falkland Islands;* London: J. Bale, Sons & Danielsson, 1920. Young, Filson, *With the Battle Cruisers;* London: Cassell & Co., Ltd., 1921.

The Campaign for Constantinople (Chapter 23)

Ansel, Walter C., "Naval Gun Fire in Support of a Landing," *Marine Corps Gazette,* XVII (May, 1932), 23; and "Naval Gunfire in Support of Landings," *U.S. Naval Institute Proceedings,* LVIII (July, 1932), 1001. Aspinall-Oglander, Cecil, *Roger Keyes;* London: Hogarth Press, 1951, and co-author with Becke, A. F., *Official History, Military Operations, Gallipoli,* 4 v.; London: William Heinemann, Ltd., 1929. Bacon, R. H., *The Life of Lord Fisher of Kilverstone,* 2 v.; New York: Doubleday & Company, Inc., 1929. Dardanelles Commission, *First Report;* London: H.M. Stationery Office, 1917. DiBona, C. J., "The Asiatic Road System to Gallipoli in 1915," typescript in U.S. Naval Academy Library, Annapolis, Maryland,

1956. Hamilton, Ian, *Gallipoli Diary,* 2 v.; New York: George H. Doran Company, 1920. Keyes, Roger, *The Fight for Gallipoli;* London: Eyre and Spottiswoode, Ltd., 1941. Marder, Arthur J., *Fear God and Dread Nought, The Correspondence of Admiral of the Fleet Lord Fisher of Kilverstone,* 2 v.; Cambridge: Harvard University Press, 1952, and *Portrait of an Admiral: The Life and Papers of Sir Herbert Richmond;* London: Jonathan Cape, Ltd., 1950. Mason, A. T., "An Introduction to the Gallipoli Campaign," *Marine Corps Gazette,* XX (February, 1936, and May, 1936). Moorehead, Alan, *Gallipoli;* London: Hamish Hamilton, 1956. Oxford and Asquith, Herbert Henry Asquith, Earl of, *Memories and Reflections,* 2 v.; Boston: Little, Brown & Company, 1928. Liman von Sanders, Otto, *Five Years in Turkey;* Annapolis: U.S. Naval Institute, 1927. Wester-Wemyss, Rosslyn, *The Navy in the Dardanelles;* London: Hodder & Son, 1924. (See also Churchill, *The World Crisis, supra.*)

The Battle of Jutland (Chapter 24)

Bacon, R. H., *The Life of John Rushworth, Earl Jellicoe;* London: Cassell & Co., Ltd., 1936. Bellairs, C. W., *The Battle of Jutland;* London: Hodder & Stoughton, Ltd., 1920. Bywater, H. C., "Gunnery at Jutland," *U.S. Naval Institute Proceedings,* LI (September, 1925); 1780. Chalmers, W. S., *The Life and Letters of David, Earl Beatty;* London: Hodder & Stoughton, 1951. Chatfield, A. E. M., *The Navy and Defence;* London: William Heinemann, Ltd., 1942. Cruttwell, C. R. M. F., *A History of the Great War, 1914–1918;* London: Oxford University Press, 1936. Fawcett, H. W., and Hooper, G. W. W., eds., *The Fighting at Jutland;* London: Hutchinson & Co., Ltd., 1920. Frost, H. H., *The Battle of Jutland;* Annapolis: U.S. Naval Institute, 1936. Frothingham, T. G., *The Naval History of the World War,* II; Cambridge: Harvard University Press, 1924. Gibson, L., and Harper, J. E. T., *The Riddle of Jutland;* New York: Coward-McCann, Inc., 1943. Gill, C. C., *What Happened at Jutland: the Tactics of the Battle;* New York: George H. Doran Company, 1921. Groos, O., *Der Krieg in der Nordsee,* V; Berlin: E. S. Mittler & Sohn, 1925. Liddell Hart, B., *A History of the World War, 1914–1918;* New York: Little, Brown & Company, 1935. Von Hase, G. O. I., *Kiel and Jutland;* London: Skeffington & Son, Ltd., 1921. Jellicoe, J. R., *The Grand Fleet, 1914–1916;* New York: George H. Doran Company, 1919. Macintyre, Donald, *Jutland;* New York: W. W. Norton & Co., Inc., 1958. Pastfield, J. L. R., *New Light on Jutland;* London: William Heinemann, Ltd., 1933. Rawson, G., *Earl Beatty, Admiral of the Fleet;* London: Jarrolds, Publishers, Ltd., 1930. Von Schoultz, G., *With the British Battle Fleet: War Recollections of a Russian Naval Officer;* London: Hutchinson & Co., Ltd., 1925. Waldeyer-Hartz, H., *Admiral von Hipper;* London: Rich and Cowan, Ltd., 1933.

Warfare Against Shipping (Chapter 25)

SUBMARINE AND ANTISUBMARINE WARFARE

Carnegie Endowment for International Peace, *Official German Documents Relating to the World War,* 2 v.; New York: Oxford University Press, 1923. Gayer, A., "Summary of German Submarine Operations in the Various Theaters of War from 1914 to 1918," W. P. Beehler, trans., *U.S. Naval Institute Proceedings,* LII (April, 1926); 621. Gibson, R. H., and Maurice Prendergast, *The German Submarine War, 1914–1918;* New York: Richard R. Smith, Inc., 1931. Jellicoe, John R., *The Crisis of the Naval War;* London: Cassell & Co., Ltd., 1920, and *The Submarine Peril;* London: Cassell & Co., Ltd., 1934. Michelsen, Andreas, *Der U-Bootskrieg, 1914–1918;* Leipzig: K. F. Koehler, 1925. Spindler, Freiherr, "The Value of the Submarine in Naval Warfare," *U.S. Naval Institute Proceedings,* LII (May, 1926); 835.

BLOCKADE

Bacon, Reginald, *The Dover Patrol 1915–1917,* 2 v.; New York: George H. Doran Company, 1919. Guichard, Louis, *The Naval Blockade, 1914–1918;* New York: D. Appleton Co., 1930. Tupper, Reginald G. O., "The Blockade of Germany by the Tenth Cruiser Squadron," *Journal of the Royal United Service Institution,* LXVII (February, 1923); 1.

MINELAYING

Belknap, Reginald R., *The Yankee Mining Squadron;* Annapolis: U.S. Naval Institute, 1920.
Cowie, J. S., *Mines, Minelayers, and Minelaying;* London: Oxford University Press, 1949.

U.S. NAVY IN THE WAR

Annual Report of the Secretary of the Navy, 1914–1919; Washington: USGPO, 1914–1919.
Gleaves, Albert, *A History of the Transport Service;* New York: George H. Doran Company,
1921. Kittredge, Tracy B., *Naval Lessons of the Great War;* New York: Doubleday, Page
& Company, 1921. Sims, William S., and Hendrick, Burton J., *The Victory at Sea;* New
York: Doubleday, Page & Company, 1920.

Disarmament and Rearmament (Chapter 26)

Atwater, E., *American Regulation of Arms Exports;* New York: Columbia University Press,
1941. Buell, R. L., *The Washington Conference;* New York: D. Appleton Co., 1922. Bywater,
H. C., *Navies and Nations;* Boston: Houghton Mifflin Company, 1927. Davis, F., *The Atlantic
System: the Story of Anglo-American Control of the Seas;* New York: Reynal & Hitchcock,
1941. Davis, H. I., ed., *Pioneers in World Order: An American Appraisal of the League of
Nations;* New York: Columbia University Press, 1944. Engely, G., *The Politics of Naval
Disarmament;* London: Williams and Norgate, Ltd., 1932. Grew, J. C., *Report from Tokyo:
a Message to the American People;* New York: Simon and Schuster, Inc., 1944. Johnstone,
W. C., *The United States and Japan's New Order;* London: Oxford University Press, 1941.
Levine, I. D., *Mitchell, Pioneer of Air Power;* New York: Duell, Sloan & Pearce, Inc., 1943.
Miller, H. B., *Navy Wings;* New York: Dodd, Mead & Company, Inc., 1937. Perkins, D.,
America and Two Wars; Boston: Little, Brown & Company, 1944. Rippy, J. F., *The Carib-
bean Danger Zone;* New York: G. P. Putnam's Sons, 1940. Sprout, H. and M., *Toward a
New Order of Sea Power;* Princeton: Princeton University Press, 1940. Strakhovsky, L. I.,
Intervention at Archangel; Princeton: Princeton University Press, 1944.

World War II (Chapters 27–44)

HISTORIES: BRITISH

British Official History Series, *Grand Strategy,* 3 v. projected, Butler, J. R. M., ed. United
Kingdom Military Series, *History of the Second World War,* Butler, J. R. M., ed.; London:
H. M. Stationery Office (included in the series are: Roskill, Captain S. W., *The War at Sea,*
3 v. projected, 1954– ; and Playfair, Major General I. S. O., *et al., The Mediterranean
and Middle East,* 6 v. projected, 1954–). Bryant, Arthur, ed., *The Turn of the Tide;*
New York: Doubleday & Company, Inc., 1957. Churchill, Winston S., *The Second World
War,* 6 v.; Boston: Houghton Mifflin Company, 1948–1953. Creswell, Captain John, *Sea
Warfare, 1939–1945;* New York: Longmans, Green & Company, 1950. James, Admiral Sir
William R., *The British Navies in the Second World War;* New York: Longmans, Green &
Company, 1947. Kemp, P. H., *Victory at Sea;* London: Frederick Muller, Ltd., 1957.
Morgan, Lieutenant General Sir Frederick, *Overture to Overlord;* Garden City: Doubleday &
Company, Inc., 1950. Richards, Dennis, and Saunders, Hilary St. George, *Royal Air Force
1939–1945,* 3 v.; London: H. M. Stationery Office, 1953–1954. Wheatley, Ronald, *Operation
Sea Lion;* Oxford: Clarendon Press, 1958.

BRITISH NAVAL ENGAGEMENTS

Grenfell, Captain Russell, *The Bismarck Episode;* New York: The Macmillan Company, 1949,
and *Main Fleet to Singapore;* New York: The Macmillan Company, 1952. Pope, Dudley,
The Battle of the River Plate; London: William Kimber, 1956, and *73 North;* London:
Weidenfeld and Nicolson, 1958.

HISTORIES: FRENCH

Auphan, Admiral Paul, and Mordal, Jacques, *The French Navy in World War II;* Annapolis: U.S. Naval Institute, 1959. De Belot, Rear Admiral Raymond, *The Struggle for the Mediterranean, 1939–1945;* Princeton: Princeton University Press, 1951. Kammerer, Albert, *La passion de la flotte française;* Paris: Librarie Arthème Fayard, 1951. Mordal, Jacques, *La bataille de Casablanca;* Paris: Librairie Plon, 1952.

HISTORIES: GERMAN

U.S. Office of Naval Intelligence, *Fuehrer Conferences on Matters Dealing with the German Navy,* 3 v.; Washington: USGPO, 1946. Dönitz, Grand Admiral Karl, *Ten Years and Twenty Days;* New York: World Publishing Company, 1959. Lohmann, W., and Hildebrand, H. H., *Die Deutsche Kriegsmarine, 1939–1945,* 3 v. projected; Bad Nauheim: H. H. Podzun, 1956– . Martienssen, Anthony T., *Hitler and His Admirals;* New York: E. P. Dutton and Co., 1949. Raeder, Grand Admiral Erich, *My Life, supra.* Ruge, Vice Admiral Friederich, *Der Seekrieg, The German Navy's Story 1939–1945;* Annapolis: U.S. Naval Institute, 1957.

HISTORIES: ITALIAN

Bragadin, Commander Marc' Antonio, *The Italian Navy in World War II;* Annapolis: U.S. Naval Institute, 1957. Fioravanza, Giuseppe, *La Marina Italiana Nella Seconda Guerra Mondiale,* 12 v. projected; Rome: 1952.

HISTORIES: U.S. ARMY

U.S. Department of the Army, Office of the Chief of Military History, *The United States Army in World War II,* 96 v. projected; Washington: USGPO, 1947– (relevant works include: Greenfield, Kent Roberts, ed., *Command Decisions* (New York: Harcourt, Brace and Company), 1959; Howe, George F., *Northwest Africa, Seizing the Initiative in the West,* 1957; Matloff, Maurice, and Snell, E. M., *Strategic Planning for Coalition Warfare, 1941–1942,* 1953; Matloff, Maurice, *Strategic Planning for Coalition Warfare, 1943–1944,* 1959; and Vigneras, Marcel, *Rearming the French,* 1957.

HISTORIES: U.S. ARMY AIR FORCES

U.S. Office of Air Force History, *The Army Air Forces in World War II,* 7 v., Craven, W. F. and Cate, J. L.; Chicago: University of Chicago Press, 1948– . *U.S. Strategic Bombing Survey;* Washington: USGPO, 1945–1947. (Students of naval history will be particularly interested in *Interrogations of Japanese Officials,* 2 v., *Campaigns of the Pacific War,* and *The Allied Campaign against Rabaul.*)

HISTORIES: U.S. MARINE CORPS

U.S. Marine Corps, Historical Section, *Operational Narratives of the Marine Corps in World War II;* Washington: USGPO, 1947– (this Marine Corps monograph series when completed will cover all operations in which United States Marines participated, from Guadalcanal to Okinawa). U.S. Marine Corps, Historical Branch, G-3, *History of U.S. Marine Corps Operations in World War II,* 5 v. projected; Washington: USGPO, 1958– . (See also U.S. Amphibious Doctrine bibliography *ff.*)

HISTORIES: U.S. NAVY

Karig, Walter, and others, *Battle Report,* 5 v.; New York: Rinehart and Co., 1944–1949. Connery, Robert H., *The Navy and the Industrial Mobilization in World War II;* Princeton: Princeton University Press, 1951. Morison, Samuel Eliot, *History of United States Naval Operations in World War II,* 14 v.; Boston: Atlantic, Little, Brown & Company, 1947– . Roscoe, Theodore, *United States Destroyer Operations in World II;* Annapolis: U.S. Naval Institute, 1953. U.S. Naval War College, *Strategical and Tactical Analyses* (Confidential);

Washington: Bureau of Naval Personnel, 1947. (See also *U.S. Strategic Bombing Survey, infra,* "Air Forces.")

BIOGRAPHIES, MEMOIRS

Cunningham, Admiral of the Fleet Viscount Andrew B., R.N., *A Sailor's Odyssey;* New York: E. P. Dutton & Co., Inc., 1951. *The Forrestal Diaries,* Millis, Walter, ed.; New York: Viking Press, Inc., 1951. Eisenhower, Dwight D., *Crusade in Europe;* Garden City: Doubleday and Company, Inc., 1948. Kesselring, Field Marshal Albert, *A Soldier's Record;* New York: William Morrow & Co., 1954. King, Fleet Admiral Ernest J. USN, and Whitehill, Walter M., *Fleet Admiral King: A Naval Record;* New York: W. W. Norton & Company, Inc., 1952. Montgomery, Field Marshal Viscount Bernard, *El Alamein to the River Sangro;* London: Hutchinson & Company, Ltd., 1948, and *The Memoirs of Field Marshal Montgomery;* Cleveland: The World Publishing Company, 1958. *The Rommel Papers,* Liddell Hart, B. H., ed.; New York: Harcourt, Brace & Company, 1953.

NORWEGIAN CAMPAIGN

Derry, T. K., *The Campaign in Norway;* London: H.M. Stationery Office, 1952. Hubutsch, Walther, *Die Deutsche Besetzung von Dänemark und Norwegen;* Göttingen: "Musterschmidt" Wissenschaftlicher, 1940. Macintyre, Donald, *Narvik;* London: Evans Bros., 1959.

THE BATTLE OF THE ATLANTIC

Admiralty, *The Battle of the Atlantic;* London: H.M. Stationery Office, 1946, and *German, Italian, and Japanese U-boat Casualties during the War;* London: H.M. Stationery Office, 1946. Assmann, Kurt, "Why U-boat Warfare Failed," *Foreign Affairs* (July, 1950); 659. Baxter, James Phinney, III, *Scientists Against Time;* Boston: Little, Brown & Company, 1948. Brennecke, Jochem, *The Hunters and the Hunted;* New York: W. W. Norton & Co., 1957. Chalmers, William S., *Max Horton and the Western Approaches;* London: Hodder and Stoughton, Ltd., 1954. Creighton, Kenelm, *Convoy Commodore;* London: William Kimber, 1956. Dönitz, Grand Admiral Karl, *Essay on the Conduct of the War at Sea;* Washington: Office of Naval Intelligence, 1946, and *Memoirs: Ten Years and Twenty Days;* London: Weidenfeld and Nicolson, 1959. Frank, Wolfgang, *The Sea Wolves;* New York: Rinehart & Co., Inc., 1955. Gallery, Daniel V., *Twenty Million Tons under the Sea;* Chicago: Henry Regnery Co., 1956. Herzog, Bodo, *Die Deutschen U-boote, 1906–1945;* Munich: J. F. Lehmann, 1959. Lane, Frederic C., *et al., Ships for Victory: A History of Shipbuilding under the U.S. Maritime Commission in World War II;* Baltimore: Johns Hopkins Press, 1951. Riesenberg, Felix, *Sea War; the Story of the U.S. Merchant Marine in World War II;* New York: Rinehart & Co., Inc., 1956. Slessor, John, *The Central Blue;* New York: Frederick A. Praeger, Inc., 1957. Stimson, Henry L., and Bundy, McGeorge, *On Active Service in Peace and War;* New York: Harper & Brothers, 1947.

U.S. AMPHIBIOUS DOCTRINE

Hough, Lt. Col. Frank O., USMCR, Ludwig, Major Verle E., and Shaw, Henry I., Jr., *Pearl Harbor to Guadalcanal;* Historical Branch, G-3, U.S. Marine Corps, 1958, *supra.* Isely, Jeter A., and Crowl, Philip A., *The U.S. Marines and Amphibious War;* Princeton; Princeton University Press, 1951. Potter, E. B. *et al., The United States and World Sea Power;* Englewood Cliffs: Prentice-Hall, Inc., 1955. Russell, W. H., "The Genesis of FMF Doctrine: 1879–1899," *Marine Corps Gazette,* (March-July, 1951). Smith, Holland M., "Amphibious Tactics," *Marine Corps Gazette,* (June, 1946 through March, 1947). Smith, Holland M., and Finch, Percy, *Coral and Brass;* New York: Charles Scribner's Sons, Inc., 1949.

U.S. CARRIER DOCTRINE

Morrow Aircraft Board, *Hearings before the President's Aircraft Board,* 4 v.; Washington: USGPO, 1925. Paine, Ralph D., *The First Yale Unit,* 2 v.; Cambridge: The Riverside Press, 1925. Sherrod, Robert, *History of Marine Corps Aviation in World War II;* Washington:

Combat Forces Press, 1952. Turnbull, Archibald D., and Lord, Clifford L., *History of United States Naval Aviation;* New Haven: Yale University Press, 1949. Wilson, Eugene E., *Air Power for Peace;* New York: McGraw-Hill Book Company, Inc., 1945; *Slipstream;* New York: McGraw-Hill Book Company, Inc., 1950; and *Kitty Hawk to Sputnik to Polaris;* Barre, Massachusetts: Barre Publishing Co., 1960. (See also Fiske, *Midshipman to Rear-Admiral, supra.*)

U.S. LOGISTICS DOCTRINE

Ballentine, Duncan S., *U.S. Naval Logistics in the Second World War;* Princeton: Princeton University Press, 1949.

PEARL HARBOR ATTACK

Pearl Harbor Attack, Hearings before the Joint Committee, 79th Congress, 40 v.; Washington: USGPO, 1946. *Narrative Statement of Evidence at Navy Pearl Harbor Investigation,* 3 v.; Washington: Navy Department, 1945. Kimmel, Rear Admiral Husband E. USN (Ret.), *Admiral Kimmel's Story;* Chicago: Henry Regnery Co., 1955. Kittredge, Captain Tracy B. USNR (Ret.), "The Muddle before Pearl Harbor," *U.S. News & World Report* (December 3, 1954).

THE WAR IN THE PACIFIC

Beach, Edward L., *Submarine;* New York: Henry Holt and Company, Inc., 1952. Bryan, Joseph, and Reid, Philip, *Mission Beyond Darkness;* New York: Duell, Sloan and Pearce, Inc., 1945. Butow, Robert J. C., *Japan's Decision to Surrender;* Stanford: Stanford University Press, 1954. D'Albas, Emmanuel E. A., *Death of a Navy; Japanese Naval Action in World War II;* New York: Devin-Adair Co., 1957. Field, James A. Jr., *The Japanese at Leyte Gulf;* Princeton: Princeton University Press, 1947. Fuchida, Mitsuo, and Okumiya, Masatake, *Midway, the Battle that Doomed Japan;* Annapolis: U.S. Naval Institute, 1955. Halsey, Fleet Admiral William F., USN, and Bryan, J. III, *Admiral Halsey's Story;* New York: McGraw-Hill Book Company, Inc., 1947. Hashimoto, Mochitsura, *Sunk: The Story of the Japanese Submarine Fleet, 1942–1945;* London: Cassell & Co., Ltd., 1954. Horikoshi, Jiro, and Okumiya, Masatake, *Zero;* New York: E. P. Dutton & Co., 1956. Inoguchi, Rikihei, Nakajima, Tadashi, and Pineau, Roger, *The Divine Wind: Japan's Kamikaze Force in World War II;* Annapolis: U.S. Naval Institute, 1958. Johnston, Stanley, *Queen of the Flat-tops;* New York: E. P. Dutton & Co., 1942. Jones, K., *Destroyer Squadron 23;* Philadelphia: Chilton Co., 1959. Kenney, George C., *General Kenney Reports;* New York: Duell, Sloan and Pearce, 1949. Lockwood, Vice Admiral Charles A., USN, *Sink 'Em All;* New York: E. P. Dutton & Co., Inc., 1951, and co-author, with Adamson, Colonel Hans Christian, *Hellcats of the Sea;* New York: Greenberg, 1955. Merillat, Herbert L., *The Island, a History of the First Marine Division on Guadalcanal;* Boston: Houghton Mifflin Company, 1944. Sherman, Frederick C., *Combat Command: the American Aircraft Carriers in the Pacific War;* New York: E. P. Dutton & Co., 1950. Sherrod, Robert, *Tarawa: The Story of a Battle;* New York: Duell, Sloan and Pearce, 1944. Taylor, Theodore, *The Magnificent Mitscher;* New York: W. W. Norton & Co., Inc., 1954. Willoughby, Charles A., and Chamberlain, John, *MacArthur, 1941–1951;* New York: McGraw-Hill Book Company, Inc., 1954. Woodward, C. Vann, *The Battle for Leyte Gulf;* New York: The Macmillan Company, 1947. (See also *U.S. Strategic Bombing Survey, supra,* "Air Forces," and numerous articles in the *Naval Institute Proceedings* and the *Marine Corps Gazette.*)

The Korean War (Chapter 45)

Cagle, Commander Malcolm W., USN, and Manson, Commander Frank A., USN, *The Sea War in Korea;* Annapolis: U.S. Naval Institute, 1957. Geer, Andrew Clare, *The New Breed: the Story of the U.S. Marines in Korea*; New York: Harper & Brothers, 1952. Karig, Walter, *et al., Battle Report,* VI; New York: Rinehart and Co., Inc., 1952 (a continuation of the World

War II series). Marshall, S. L. A., *The River and the Gauntlet;* New York: William Morrow and Company, 1953. Thomas, R. C. W., *The War in Korea, 1950–1953;* Aldershot: Gale and Polden, 1954. Truman, Harry S., *Memoirs,* 2 v.; New York: Doubleday & Company, Inc., 1955. U.S. Army Department, Historical Division, *Korea—1950;* Washington: USGPO, 1952.

The New Navy (Chapter 46)

Britannica *Book of the Year.* Collier's *Annual.* Dinerstein, H. S., *War and the Soviet Union;* New York: Frederick A. Praeger, Inc., 1959. Furniss, E. S. Jr., *American Military Policy;* New York: Rinehart & Co., Inc., 1957. Jackson, J. H., *The World in the Postwar Decade, 1945–55;* New York: Houghton Mifflin Company, 1957. Kissinger, H. A., *Nuclear Weapons and Foreign Policy;* New York: Harper & Brothers, 1957. Miksche, F. O., *Failure of Atomic Strategy;* New York: Frederick A. Praeger, Inc., 1959. Riggs, F. W., *Formosa Under Chinese Nationalist Rule;* New York: The Macmillan Company, 1952. Ropp, Theodore, *War in the Modern World;* Durham: Duke University Press, 1960. U.S. Department of State, *Soviet World Outlook;* Washington: (State Department Publication No. 6836), 1959. Taylor, General Maxwell D., *The Uncertain Trumpet;* New York: Harper & Brothers, 1960. Vagts, Alfred, *Defense and Diplomacy;* New York: Columbia University Press, 1956.

INDEX

Instructions

INTRODUCTORY NOTE

With the exception of very early ships, all ships mentioned in this index are noted as to rate and nationality. In the days of sail, the rated number of guns is given, as for example, *Victory* (100). Following appears the nationality and then the page references in the text. Later ships are indicated by type.

All military units are American unless otherwise noted. Task Force 38 thus is an American force, while the British Force H would be listed "Force H (Br)."

In general, officers are listed with the highest ranks associated with their names in this book, but grades within ranks are not supplied. Thus the term "admiral" is used for all grades of that rank.

THE FOLLOWING ABBREVIATIONS ARE USED:

Nationalities

Am	American	Conf	Confederate	Fr	French	Mex	Mexican	Ru	Russian
Aust	Austrian	Ch	Chinese	Ger	German	Nor	Norwegian	Sp	Spanish
Austr	Australian	Dan	Danish	It	Italian	NZ	New Zealand	Tur	Turkish
Br	British	Du	Dutch	Jap	Japanese	Pol	Polish	U.S.	United States
Can	Canadian								

Ships

AC	Armored cruiser	CB	Battle cruiser	LCI	Landing craft, Infantry
AGC	Amphibious command ship	CL	Light cruiser	LCM	Landing craft, Mechanized
AKA	Attack cargo ship	CLC	Cruiser command ship	LCT	Landing craft, Tank
AM	Minelayer	Cr	Cruiser	LCVP	Landing craft, Vehicles and Personnel
AMS	Minesweeper	CV	Aircraft carrier, heavy	LSD	Landing ship, Dock
APA	Transport	CVB	Aircraft carrier, large	LST	Landing ship, Tank
APD	Destroyer transport	CVE	Aircraft carrier, escort	LVT	Landing craft, Tracked (amtrac)
AR	Repair ship	CVL	Aircraft carrier, light	LVTA	Landing craft, Tracked, Attack
ARS	Repair ship, Submarines	DD	Destroyer	mer	Merchant ship
AV	Seaplane tender	DE	Destroyer escort	Pr Cr	Protected cruiser
BB	Battleship	DL	Destroyer leader	SS	Submarine
CA	Heavy cruiser	IX	Unclassified ship		

Aircraft

B-17	Flying Fortress, Army heavy bomber	MIG	Russian Army fighter
B-24	Liberator, Army heavy bomber	P-47	Thunderbolt, Army fighter
B-25	Mitchell, Army medium bomber	PBM	Mariner, Navy patrol bomber
B-26	Marauder, Army medium bomber	PBY	Catalina, Navy patrol bomber
B-29	Superfortress, Army heavy bomber	SB2C	Helldiver, Navy dive bomber
B-36	Army heavy bomber	SBD	Dauntless, Navy dive bomber
F4F	Wildcat, Navy fighter	TBF	Avenger, Navy torpedo bomber
F4U	Corsair, Navy fighter	TBM	Avenger, Navy torpedo bomber
F6F	Hellcat, Navy fighter	Zeke	Japanese Navy fighter
Hap	Japanese Army fighter	Zero	Japanese Navy fighter

Ranks

Abbreviations of ranks follow common military usage, and are preceded in index listings by the nationality of the officer, e.g., "(U.S. gen)." In the case of the rank of captain however naval captains are distinguished as follows: "U.S.N. capt," "R.N. capt."

Index

A

"ABCD's," 344
"ABC-1 Staff Agreement," 549, 647
ABDA Command, 656-67, 835
Abdiel (AM) (Br), 449
Abe, Hiroaki (Jap adm), 702, 704
Abemama, captured, 743
Abercromby, James (Br gen), 55
Abercromby, Sir Ralph (Br gen), 147, 148; assault on Aboukir, 140-42, 184, 232; Helder Expedition, 138
Abner Read (DD) (U.S.), 815
Aboukir, Bay and Point, 139
  amphibious assault on (1801), 140-42
  compared to Gallipoli assault, 430
  diagram, 141
Aboukir (Cr) (Br), 232, 403, 456
Abukuma (CL) (Jap), 787
Acheson, Dean, 852
Achilles (CL) (NZ), 493-95
Acre, siege of, 139; *map*, 139
Across the Pacific, *map*, 139
Actium, Battle of, 13-14, 19, 20; *diagram*, 13
Activity (CVE) (Br), 561
Adamant (50) (Br. razee), 125
Adams, Charles Francis, 258
Adams, John, 71, 195
Addington, Henry, 147, 149, 167
Admiralty Islands, invaded, 731
Advanced Base Operations in Micronesia, 630
Affondatore (turret ram) (It), 328, 330, 331
Africa, *map*, 538
Afrika Korps, 526, 528, 531-32, 540, 583
Agamemnon (64) (Br), 112, 119, 145, 166
Agamemnon (screw ship) (Br), 328
Agano (CL) (Jap), 723, 725, 803
AGC, *defined*, 578
A-Go operation, 759, 760, 764
Agrippa, 13-14, 20
Agrippina (collier) (Conf), 259
Aguinaldo, Emilio, 386
Ainsworth, Walden L. (U.S. adm), 718, 720
Air Command Solomons (Airsols), 717, 719, 722, 723, 726-31, 733, 741
Air Corps Act of 1926, 636
Aircraft carrier development, 635-39
Aix, Island of, captured, 53
Aitape, invasion of, 758
Aix-la-Chapelle, Treaty of, 46
Aix Roads, 175-76, 185
Ajax (74) (Br), 166
Ajax (CL) (Br), 493-95
Akagi (CV) (Jap), 650, 670, 679-82, 683

Alabama (raider) (Conf), 257-61, 407; Battle with *Kearsarge*, 260-61
"*Alabama* Claims," 257
Alamogordo, 834
Alanbrooke, Lord (Br. field marshal), 552 n., 594, 605
Albacore (SS) (U.S.), 766, 768, 804
Albatross (gunboat) (U.S.), 304
Albemarle, Earl of (Br gen), 61-63, 65; quoted, 63
Albemarle (ironclad) (Conf), 273
Albert, Prince Consort of England, 254
Albert W. Grant (DD) (U.S.), 787
Aleutian Islands, in Battle of Midway, 673-75
  reconquest of, 712-15
  Theater, *map*, 713
Alexander I, Czar of Russia, 147
Alexander, Sir Harold R. (Br gen), 539, 584-85, 594, 600-01, 604
Alexander of Macedon (The Great), 10, 139
Alexandria, Egypt, 417, 421, 536
  British capture of, 142
  founding of, 10
  French capture of, 132
Alfred (24) (U.S.), 71, 73
Alger, Russell, U.S. Secretary of War, 367
Algeria:
  invasion of, 578-80
  map, 567
  U.S. war with, 226
Algiers, 566, 567, 571, 597
  Exmouth's attack, 228
  map, 567
  tribute system, 188, 226
  U.S. war with, 226
Algonquin (mer) (U.S.), 465
Ali Pasha, 16-18
Ali Rashid, 531
All-big-gun ship, 388-89
Allemand, Zacharie Jacques (Fr adm), 175
Allen, Ethan, takes Ticonderoga, 67
Allied Mined Areas and German Barred Zones (WWI), *map*, 459
Allied Offensive, All-out, Nov. 1943-Aug. 1945, *map*, 840
Allied Offensive, Limited, Aug. 1942-March 1944, *map*, 839
"Alligator," swamp vehicle, 634
Almond, Edward M. (U.S. gen), 866, 868, 869
Altmark (AKA) (Ger), 493, 495-96
Amagi (CV) (Jap), 779 n.
Amberjack (SS) (U.S.), 800
Amboina, taken by Japanese, 656
Amelia Island, 253
American Nautical Almanac, 628 n.

American Revolution, 35, 66-107
  and the West Indies, 75, 79, 82-84, 88, 97-104, 105-06
  British strategy, 67
  Campaigns (1775-76), *map*, 67; (1777-82), *map*, 70
  ended by the Treaty of Paris, 105-06
  French entry into, 75
  Netherlands entry into, 87
  Spanish entry into, 81
American Turtle (SS) (U.S.), 236
Amherst, Lord Jeffrey (Br gen), 55-58, 63-64
Amiens, Peace of, 148; broken, 149
Ammonoosuc (screw cruiser) (U.S.), 339
Amoy, 880
Amphibious command ship (*see* AGC)
Amphibious doctrine, 426, 427, 430, 431, 629-35
Amphibious operations:
  Abemama, 743
  Aboukir, 140-42
  Admiralty Is., 731
  Algeria, 567-68, 578-80, 583
  Anzio, 600-02
  Attu, 714-15
  Betio, 744-49
  Bougainville, 723
  Cape Gloucester, 729
  Central Solomons, 718-20
  Corsica, 119
  Daiquiri, 373, 376
  Dardanelles-Gallipoli, 420-27
  Dunkirk (1793), 111
  Egypt, 132
  Eniwetok, 755
  Finschhafen, 729
  Fort Fisher, 322
  France (World War II), 614-18, 621-23
  French Morocco, 571-78
  Gilbert Is., 741-49
  Guadalcanal, 692
  Guam, 770
  Guantanamo (1898), 373
  Havana, 61-63
  Helder, 137-38
  Hollandia, 758
  Inchon, 864-66
  Iwo Jima, 824-28
  Kiska, 715
  Kwajalein, 749-53
  Lae, 729
  Leyte, 774
  Lissa, 328-31
  Louisburg, 55
  Makin, 741-43
  Manus, 731
  Marathon, 5
  Marianas, 769-71
  Marshall Is., 749-54
  Martinique (1794), 113-14
  Morocco, 569-78, 583

187th Airborne Regimental Combat Team, 862
Oneida (18), 217
Oneida (gunboat) (U.S.), 287, 294, 318, 320
Onishi, Takajiro (Jap adm), 793
Onslow, Richard (Br adm), at Battle of Camperdown, 126
"Open Door" Policy in China, 387
Operation *Achse* (Ger plan for disarming Italy, 1943), 597
Operation *A-60*, 759, 760, 764
Operation Anvil-Dragoon (Southern France), 606-07, 621-23; *maps,* 607, 621
Operation Barbarossa (Nazi invasion of Soviet Union), 506, 526
Operation Barney, 810-11
Operation Battleaxe (Wavell's unsuccessful attack on Rommel's forces, 1941), 532
Operation Chromite (Inchon), 861-62
Operation Crossroads (Atomic bomb test), 856
Operation Felix (Hitler's abortive plan for capture of Gibraltar), 526
Operation Hat (redistribution of Br Mediterranean Fleet, 1940), 524
Operation Hercules (Axis plan to seize Malta, 1942), 537
Operation Husky (Sicily), 582-83, 584-94, 596; *maps,* 586, 589
Operation Ironclad (Madagascar Operation, 1942), 539; *map,* 538
Operation Juno, 502
Operation Killer (Korean drive), 870, 873
Operation Magic Carpet, 842
Operation Mulberry (for artificial harbors in Normandy invasion), 617-18; *diagram,* "Mulberry A," 617
Operation Neptune (Cross Channel Naval Operation), 611 *ff.; maps* and *diagrams,* 613, 617
Operation Overlord (Normandy), 605 *ff.; maps* and *diagrams,* 613, 617, 619
Operation *Pakenschlag*, 552-53
Operation *Rösselsprung*, 555-56
Operation Roundup (France planned), 565
Operation Sea Lion (German Invasion of England), 505-07; *map,* 506
Operation Shoestring, 691
Operation *Sho-Go*, 777, 778
Operation Sledgehammer (planned invasion of Europe), 565-66 n.
Operation Torch (North Africa), 566-81, 582-83; *map,* 567
Operation Trickle, 556
Operation Watchtower (Guadalcanal), 691, 693, 701, 734
Operation *Weserübung*, 496-99
Operation Yo-yo (Wonsan), 868
Operations research, British, 557
Opium War, 227, 229, 238
Oporto, 178
Oquendo (gunboat) (Sp), 374
Oran, 566-67, 570, 579-80, 583, 597
Orange, Prince of, 138
Orders in Council (Br), 170, 185, 187, 188, 456; revoked, 209
Ordnance, change from shot to shell, 240-41
Orde, Sir John (Br adm), 156

Oregon (BB) (U.S.), 344, 367, 372, 374, 376, 383
Oregon forests, incendiary bombing of, 807
"Oregon" gun, 240
Orel (BB) (Ru), 362-63
Orient (120) (Fr), 133, 134
Orion (CL) (Br), 529, 531
Oriskany, Battle of, 74
Orleans, Isle of, 56
Orne River, 606, 614
Ormoc, 815
Osliabia (BB) (Ru), 359, 360, 362
Osman Pasha, 233
Osmeña, Sergio, 774
Ossipee (gunboat) (U.S.), 318
Ostend, 457, 471-72; *map,* 471
Ostfriesland (BB) (Ger), 636
Otranto Mine Barrage, 470
Otranto (aux Cr) (Br), 404-05
Otway (R.N. capt), 145-46
Outer Bay of Biscay, 561
Ozawa, Jisaburo (Jap adm), 777, 804-05, 810; at Battle for Leyte Gulf, 778, 781, 785, 788-790, 795, 805; in Battle of the Java Sea, 657; in Battle of the Philippine Sea, 759, 760, 763-67, 775

P

P-51 aircraft, 596
Pacific Ocean Areas, World War II, *map,* 653
Pact of Steel (1939), 519
Page, Walter Hines (Am. ambass.), 464, 467
Paixhans, Henri-Joseph (Fr gen), 241
Paixhans gun, 241
Pakenham, Sir Edward (Br gen), 222
Palau Islands, 841
captured, 772-73
TF 58 raid, 758, 803-05
Palawan, 822
Palermo, 592
Palestro (gunboat) (It), 330, 331
Pallas (32) (Fr), 73
Palliser, Sir Hugh (Br adm), 76-77
Palmetto State (ironclad) (Conf), 313
Pamplona, 179
Panama Canal, building of, 383-84; opened, 406; threats to, 807
Panama Canal Zone, acquired by U.S., 383
Pan-American Republics, 548
Panay, 822
Panhellenic Congress, 6
Panhellenic League, 9
Panmunjon, 872
Papua, secured, 708
Paris, liberated (World War II), 620
Paris, Treaty of, (1769), 64; (1783), 105-06, 108; (1898), 375
Parker, Richard, 125
Parker, Sir Hyde (Br adm), 143; at Battle of Copenhagen, 145-47; *quoted,* 144
Parma, Duke of, 28-30
Parrott rifle, 241
Pas de Calais, 606, 614
Passaic (monitor) (U.S.), 313, 314
Passes of the Mississippi, 553
Patapsco (gunboat) (U.S.), 314
Patch, Alexander M. (U.S. gen), 622, 623, 625, 707
Pathfinder (Cr) (Br), 403, 456
Patrick Henry (gunboat) (Conf), 268-69, 272

Patrick Henry (Liberty Ship), 644
Patterson (DD) (U.S.), 695
Patterson, Daniel T. (U.S. naval officer), 222
Patton, George S. (U.S. gen), 569-70, 575, 581, 585, 587, 591-92, 603-04, 619, 621, 623-25
"Paukenschlag," Group, 552
Paul, Czar of Russia, 138, 142, 147
Paulding, Hiram (U.S. commo), 246, 265
Paul Jones (DD) (U.S.), 389 n.
Pawnee (sloop) (U.S.), 246, 252 n.
Pax Romana, 14
PBY, 558, 673-76
"Peacemaker" guns, 240, 271 n.
Peacock (18) (Br), 212, 223
Pearl Harbor:
attack, 551, 552, 637, 649-51, 796, 798; *diagrams,* 649, 650
naval base begun, 388, 640
submarine base, 796
Pearson, Richard (R.N. capt), 73-74
Peary (DD) (U.S.), 657
Peleliu, 805
invasion, 772-73
Pellew, Sir Edward (R.N. capt; *see also* Exmouth, Viscount), 152
Peloponnesian War, 10
Pemberton, John C., 298, 305
Pembroke Lighthouse, 405
Penang, 406
Pendleton, W. B. (U.S. naval officer), 804
Peninsular War, 148, 172-75, 177-79, 185; *map,* 173
Penn, Sir William (Br adm), 32
Pennsylvania (120) (U.S.), 226
Pennsylvania (BB) (U.S.), 389, 651, 856
Penobscot Expedition, 71-72
Pensacola (sloop) (U.S.), 286, 287, 289
Pensacola (CA) (U.S.), 706, 856, 857
Pensacola, Naval Air Station, 244, 248, 251 n., 254, 391
Pepys, Samuel, 35
Pericles, 9
Perier, *defined,* 27
Periscope, night, 798
Permanent Fighting Instructions, 40, 41, 45, 48, 50, 51, 65
Perry (DD) (U.S.), 389 n.
Perry, Matthew C. (U.S. commo), 251; commands *Fulton II,* 237; opening of Japan, 237 n., 347-48; operations in Mexican War, 232; at Vera Cruz, 232
Perry, Oliver Hazard (U.S. naval officer), 228 n.; at Battle of Lake Erie, 217, 218; in West Indies Squadron, 226
Persano, Count Carlo di (It adm), 328, 329, 330, 331
Persian Expeditions against Greece, 5-9, 20
Persian Gulf, 412; *map,* 413
Perth (CL) (Austr), 657-59
Pescadores Islands, under U.S. protection, 876
Pétain, Philippe (Fr marshal), 504-05, 568, 579
Peter III (Czar of Russia), 64
Petrel (gunboat) (U.S.), 369
Petrof Bay (CVE) (U.S.), 793
Petropavlovsk (BB) (Ru), 354
Phidias, 9

Philadelphia, Pa.; taken by Brit., 1777, 74; evacuated by Brit., 1778, 77; Amer. army passes thru, 1781, 91
Philadelphia (36) (U.S.), 196, 197, 198, 200, 201, 202
Philadelphia (CL) (U.S.), 576, 592, 598-99
Philip II, King of Macedonia, 10
Philip II, King of Spain, 24-25, 27; and the Sp. Armada, 27-30
Philippeville, bombardment of, 398
Philippine Insurrection, 370
Philippine Islands, 63-64 *n.*, 346
  as U.S. defense problem, 628
  dual advance on (World War II), 757-76 *n.*; *maps*, 735, 840
  Leyte, U.S. invasion, 774, 841
  U.S. acquisition of, 370, 375
  U.S. problems, 377
Philippine Sea (CV) (U.S.), 860, 862, 869, 870
Philippine Sea, Battle of, 760, 765-69, 775, 803-04, 810, 837; *diagram*, 766
Phillips, Sir Tom (Br adm), 654
Philosophy and Conduct of Maritime War (D. W. Waters), 541 *n.*, 546 *n.*
Phoebe (38) (Br), 214
Phoenicians, early developers of sea power, 4
"Phoenicians" in Normandy invasion, 617-18
"Phony War" (1940), 548
"Piggy-back" Submarines, 806-07
Pillsbury (DE) (U.S.), 562
Pilotfish (SS) (U.S.), 803
Pink (corv) (Br), 558
Pinola (gunboat) (U.S.), 287, 288
Pintado (SS) (U.S.), 803
Pitt, William (The Elder), 46, 65, 153, 190
Pitt's Plan, 51-52, 64, 148, 397; World War I British version of, 432, 565; warns Lord North, 67
Pitt, William (The Younger), 150, 162, 236-37 *n.*; death, 168; Prime Minister, 153; and Second Coalition, 135; strategy of, 169, 183
Pittsburg (ironclad) (U.S.), 276, 280
Pitzuo, 355
Pius V, Pope, 16, 24
Plan Z (Ger. naval constr. program), 492, 541
Platt Amendment, 380, 385
Pleasant Hill, battle of, 307
Plum Point Bend engagement, 293
Plunger (SS) (U.S.), 390
Plymouth (sloop) (U.S.), 348
Pocock, George (Br adm), 59-65
Pohang, 859, 861
Pohl, Hugo von (Ger adm), 410, 457
Point Lévis, 56, 58
Pola (CA) (It), 529
Polaris, armed nuclear submarine force, 883
Polaris, IRBM, 881-82
Polaris (gunboat) (U.S.), 340
Polk, Leonidas (Conf gen), 275, 277, 280
Pomerania, 180
Pompey, Sextus, 12, 13
Ponape, 403, 758
Pondicherry, 60, 104, 105
Pontoon causeways, *developed*, 588, 590
Pope (DD) (U.S.), 280

Popham, Sir Home Riggs (R.N. capt), at Buenos Aires, 169; at Cape Town, 169; at Walcheren, 177
Portal, Sir Charles (Br air marshal), 552
Port Arthur, 365
  ceded to Japan, 353
  Japanese attack on, 352, 354-55
  Russian lease of, 353
  surrender to Japan, 356
Porter (DD) (U.S.), sunk, 701; 799
Porter, David (U.S.N. capt), 226 *n.*; Commander in Chief of Mexican Navy, 227; commands *Essex* (War of 1812), 214; court-martial, 227
Porter, David Dixon (U.S. adm), 227 *n.*, 245, 285, 286, 287, 290, 294, 295, 296, 299, 302, 303, 304, 306, 307, 339; commands Mortar Flotilla (New Orleans), 288; commands Mississippi Squadron, 298; at Fort Fisher, 322-24; in Red River Campaign, 306; *quoted*, 307; at Vicksburg, 305
Port Hudson, 297, 304
  surrenders, 306
Portland (CA) (U.S.), 702 *n.*, 704
Port Lyautey, 572, 576
  capture (1942), 577, 584
Port Mahon, 48
Porto Farina, Blake's raid on, 32
Port Royal (gunboat), 318
Port Royal Operation, 252-54, 262, 370; *map*, 252
  tactical lessons, 253-54
Portsmouth (Va), burned by Brit. (1779), 80; Br. base, 88-89, 272
Portsmouth (N.H.), 251 *n.*
Portsmouth, Treaty of, 382
Port Said, 878
Port Stanley, 403, 405-06
Portugal, 63
  established as oceanic power, 346
  expelled from Asia, 347
  grants bases in Azores, 561
  loss of trade to Dutch, 347
  Napoléon threatens, 169
  Peninsular War in, 173-75, 177-79
Potomac, Army of the, 255, 262-63, 266, 272
Potsdam Conference, 833-34, 842, 853
Potsdam Proclamation, 834, 835, 841
Pound, Sir Dudley (Br adm), 552, 555
Powder, slow-burning, 332; smokeless, 332, 338
Powhatan (frigate) (U.S.), 245, 258, 283
Pownall, Charles A. (Am adm), 737
Prado Porto Carrero, Don Juan de (Sp gen), 62
Prairie (Cr) (Am), 386
Pratt, William V. (U.S. adm), 637
Praxiteles, 9
Preble (sloop) (U.S.), 220
Preble (U.S.) (Civil War), 283
Preble, Edward (U.S. naval officer), 192, 198, 199, 200
"Preble's Boys," 199, 203
President (44) (U.S.), 191, 196, 203, 208, 222 and *n.*
Pressburg, Treaty of, 168, 176
Prevost, Sir George (Br gen); in War of 1812, 220
Pridham-Wippel, H. D. (Br adm), 528-29

Prien, Gunther (Ger naval officer), 544, 546-47
Primauguet (CL) (Fr), 575-76
Prince (98) (Br), 165
Prince Henry the Navigator, 22
Prince of Wales (98) (Br), 159, 163
Prince of Wales (BB) (Br), 509-11, 536, 648, 654, 797
Princess Royal (Br ship of line), 78
Princess Royal (CB) (Br), 401, 408-09, 438
Princeton (CV) (U.S.), 869
Princeton (CVL) (U.S.), 723, 740, 781; sunk, 783
Princeton (sloop) (U.S.), 238, 240, 265, 271 *n.*
Principal Allied Convoy Formations, World War II, *diagram*, 543
Prinz Eugen (CA) (Ger), 508-09, 512-14, 856
Privateers, *defined*, 44; American: in American Revolution, 72
  in War of 1812, 213-14
Prize money, 32, 63
Providence (Amer. sloop), 71; (Amer. frigate), 73
PT boats:
  Central Solomons, 721
  Guadalcanal. 707
  Leyte, 774, 785-87, 815
  Mindoro, 817
  New Guinea, 758
Puerto Rico, 60, 62, 371-72, 375, 377
  American accession of, 375, 377
  occupation of, 380
Puccini, Giacomo, 382
Punic Wars, 11-12, 19
Pusan, 350, 859-62, 867, 872
Pusan Perimeter, 860-62, 866-68, 872
  breakout, 866-68
Pyongyang, Korea, 854, 868

Q

"Q-Ships," 462, 553
Quadrant, 22
  reflecting, 22
Quallah Battoo, 227
Quasi-War with France, 191, 192
  Convention of Peace, 195
Quebec, 55-59, 64, 65
  assaulted by Montgomery and Arnold (1775), 67
  Campaign, 55-59
  Siege of, 56-59; *map*, 56
Queen Charlotte (100) (Br), 116-17
Queen Charlotte (21) (Br), 219
Queen Elizabeth (BB) (Br), 389 *n.*, 392 *n.*, 536
Queen Mary (CB) (Br), 401, 438-39
Queen of the West (ram) (U.S.), 294, 296, 303
Quemoy, 876, 879-81, 885
Quiberon Bay, battle, 54-55, 64-65; *map*, 54
Quick-firing guns, 338, 352, 358
Quincy (CA) (U.S.), 614, 618, 695-96
Quisling, Vidkun, 496
Quota Act of 1795, 124

R

Rabaul:
  advantages of campaign against, 731; approaches, *map*, 693
  campaign against, 799
  decision to by-pass, 729

Suez Canal, 383, 566, 877
   mined by Germans, World War II, 527, 539
Suez Crisis, 876-79
Suffolk (CA) (Br), 509-10
Suffren, Pierre André, Bailli de (Fr adm), 104-05
Sullivan, John (U.S. gen), 78
Sullivan, William A. (U.S. commo), 821
Sultan of Turkey, 229
Sulu Sea, 803
Sumter (ram) (U.S.), 296
Sumter (Conf), 257-58
Sunderland, planned bombardment of, 434
Sunfish (SS) (U.S.), 803
Supermarina, It., 588
Supreme Allied Commander Atlantic, 852; Europe, 852
Suribachi, Mt., 825, 827
Surigao Strait,
   Battle of (*see* Leyte Gulf, Battle for)
Susquehanna (frigate) (U.S.), 348
Sussex (mer) (Fr), 458, 460
"Sussex Pledge," 458, 465
Suvorov (BB) (Ru), 360-62
Suvorov, Alexander Vasilievich (Ru fld mar), 135, 136, 138
Suvla Bay, 428-29; *map*, 423, 427
Suzuya (CA) (Jap), 684, 791-92
Sweden, in Napoleonic Wars, 64, 179, 181, 182
Sword Beach, 607, 611, 616
Sydney (CL) (Austr), 407, 524
Syracuse, Sicily, 585-86, 591-92
Syria, 879

T

Tachen Islands, 876
Tactics (*see also* Breaking, Doubling, Massing, Fighting Instructions)
   bait and kill (ASW), 558
   breaking the line, 39, 101, 103
   changes wrought by steam, 242
   chase, 41, 50, 54, 65
   defined, 3
   five basic questions, 45
   Formal school, 34, 39, 45
      diagram, 38
   for galleys, 3
   grappling and boarding, 11, 13, 25
      dropped after Spanish Armada, 30
   line of battle, *defined*, 95; Graves memo. on, 95
   Melee school, 34, 36, 39, 45
      diagram, 37
   Nineteenth Century development, 336-37
   ramming, 3
   sideswiping, 3
Tactique Navale, by Bigot de Morogues, 75, 82
Taegu, 861
Taejon, 860, 861, 862 n.
Taft, William Howard (U.S. President), 383
Tagus River, 177
Takagi, Takeo (Jap adm), 664-67
Takao (CA) (Jap), 779
Taiho (CV) (Jap), 766-67, 804
Taipeh, Formosa, 853
Talavera, Battle of, 178
Talien Bay, 352
Talleyrand, 162, 191, 195
Talos-Terrier (U.S. rocket), 882
Tama (CL) (Jap), 788-89, 805

Tambor (SS) (U.S.), 683, 798
Tanaka, Raizo (Jap adm), 696-97, 702-06, 710 n.
Tang (SS) (U.S.), 803
Tangier, 358
Tanikaze (DD) (Jap), 685-86
Tarakan Island, 823
Taranto, 596
   British carrier attack, 525-26
Tarawa, 599, 623
   capture of, 743-49
   map, 744
Task Force G (Br), 611
Task Force J (Br), 611
Task Force O, 611, 614
Task Force S (Br), 611
Task Force U, 611, 614
Task Force 34, 783
   in Mediterranean, 567-78, 585-92
   in Pacific, 784, 788, 789
Task Force 38, 771, 772, 780, 816-17, 820, 832-34
   at Battle for Leyte Gulf, 787-89, 805
Task Force 39, 723-26
Task Force 57, 829, 834
Task Force 58, 750, 754-55, 758-60, 824-32, 837, 841
   in Marianas operation, 761-69, 775
   disposition of, *diagram*, 763
Task Force 77, 864-65, 869
Task Force 78, 819
Task Force 79, 819, 862
Task Force 90, 862, 866, 869
Task Force, U.S. Joint, 132, 874
Tassafaronga, Battle of, 705-06, 709
   diagram, 706
Tassigny, Jean de Lattre de (Fr gen), 623
Tatnall, Josiah (Conf naval officer), 272
Taussig, Joseph (U.S. naval officer), 467
Tawitawi, 762, 764, 803-04, 810, 822
Taylor, Richard (Conf gen), 307
Taylor, Zachary (U.S. gen), 230-31
TBD (U.S. aircraft), 638
TBF (U.S. aircraft), 559, 638, 673, 677
Tecumseh (Indian chief), 209, 219
Tecumseh (monitor) (U.S.), 318, sunk, 319
Tedder, Arthur W. (Br air marshal), 584, 587-88, 591, 594, 599
Tegetthoff, Wilhelm von (Aust adm), 328-31
Teheran Conference, 601 n., 605
Teller Amendment, 368
Téméraire (98) (Br), 165
Tenaru River, Battle of, 696, 708
Tendency of windward ships to come singly into action
   diagram, 40
Tenedos Island, 417; *map*, 423
Tennessee (ironclad) (Conf), 317-19
   capture of, 320-21
Tennessee (BB) (U.S.), 650-51
Tenryu (DD) (Jap), 799
Tentative Manual for Landing Operations (1934) 631-34
Tenth Air Fleet (Ger) (*see* Fliegerkorps X)
Tenth Army, 830-31
X Corps, 862, 866, 867, 868-70
Tenth Cruiser Squadron (Br), 456
Tenth Fleet, 558-59
"Ten-Year Rule," 541
Terminal point, *defined*, 44
Terrible (74) (Br), 95
Terry, A. H. (U.S. gen), 324-25

Teruzuki (DD) (Jap), 707
Test Able, 856
Test Baker, 857
Texas (BB) (U.S.), 344, 374, 472, 577, 614, 616, 618, 621
Texas navy, 229
Text for Landing Operations, 631
Thailand, 653, 876
Thames, Battle of, 219
Thatcher (DD) (U.S.), 726
Themistocles, 6-9
Theobald, Robert A. (U.S. adm), 673-74
Thermopylae, Pass and Battle of, 6-7
Thermonuclear Weapons, 883
Thiery, Captain de (Fr army officer), 240
III Amphibious Corps, 770-71, 825, 829, 830
Third Amphibious Force, 712, 717-19, 728, 771, 774, 817, 819, 821, 824
Third Army, 619-21, 623-25
3rd Infantry Division (Canadian), 616
Third Coalition, 153-54, 168
   War of, 184
3rd Division (Br), 618
Third Fleet, 712, 720, 728, 730, 731, 771-75, 777, 779-83, 814, 815, 816, 817, 819, 820, 821, 832, 834, 835, 841
   at Battle for Leyte Gulf, 784, 785, 786, 794-95
3rd Infantry Division, 601, 869
3rd Infantry Division (Austr), 728
3rd Marine Division, 723, 770, 827
38th Parallel, 858, 867, 871, 872, 873
37th Infantry Division, 723, 819
Thomas (DE) (U.S.), 562
352nd Division (Ger), 615
Thucydides, 4, 9
Thurber, Harry R. (U.S. naval officer), 727 n.
Tibet, 885
Ticonderoga,
   taken by Ethan Allen (1775), 65
   taken by British (1775), 74
Ticonderoga (14) (U.S.), 220
Ticonderoga (CV) (U.S.), 820
Tiger (CB) (Br), 408-09, 438
Tilghman, Lloyd (Conf gen), 277
Tilsit, Treaty of, 171, 184
Timby, Theodore R., 242
Ting Ju Chang (Ch adm), 350, 351, 353
Ting Yuen (BB) (Ch), 350, 351, 353
Tinian, 770
Tinosa (SS) (U.S.), 801, 811
Tippecanoe, Battle of, 209
Tirpitz (BB) (Ger), 492, 515, 517, 555-56
Tirpitz, Alfred von (Ger adm), 378-79, 396, 456, 458
Tobago (Is. W. Indies),
   retained at Peace, 105
   taken by Fr (1781), 88
Tobruk, 526, 532, 537, 540
Togo, Heihichiro (Jap adm), 354, 765; in Battle of Tsushima, 360-64; in Battle of August 10, 355-57; quoted, 360; tactical plan, 360
Tokyo, 868; TF 58 raid, 825
Tokyo Express, 698, 702, 799
Toledo (CA) (U.S.), 860, 864
Tone (CA) (Jap), 677
Tongyong, 861
Tonnage warfare, *defined*, 547, 552, 558, 564
Tonnante (ironclad) (Fr), 236, 239

Y

Yahagi (CL) (Jap), 831-32
Yalta Conference, 842
Yalu River, 868, 870
  Battle of the, 350-52
    diagram, 350
Yamamoto, Isoroku (Jap adm), 649,
    662, 667, 700, 705, 709;
    at Midway, 669, 672, 675,
    681-87; death, 717
Yamashiro (BB) (Jap), 786-87
Yamashita, Tomoyuki (Jap gen), 9,
    814, 820-21
Yamato (BB) (Jap), 670, 760, 779,
    790-92, 806, 831-32
Yangtze Patrol, 476
Yap, 805

Yarmouth (64) (Br), 73
Yazoo Pass Expedition, 301
Yeo, Sir James Lucas (R.N. capt),
    217
Yellow Fever, toll in West Indies op-
    erations, 63
Yikiangshen, 876
Yi Sun Sin (Korean adm), 239, 346
York, Duke of, 138
York (Toronto), raid on, 217
Yorktown Campaign, 90-96; *map*, 91
Yorktown, Va., 272
Yorktown (CV) (U.S.), 638-39, 647,
    659-60, 664-67, 673-74, 677-
    81, 685, 686, 687, 740, 798,
    826
Young, Walter (Br capt), 82 *n.*, 83
"Young Turks," 416

Z

Zama, Battle of, 12, 19
Zamboanga, 822
Zamzam (mer) (Egyptian), 549
"Zaunkönig" torpedo, 560, 562, 564
Zealand, 172
Zeebrugge, 457
  raid, 471-72
    map, 471
Zeke, 676, 793
Zeppelin, Count von, 392
Zeppelin, 635
  development, 392
Zimmerman Note, 465
Zuiho (CVL) (Jap), 647 *n.*, 672,
    701, 779, 788-89
Zuikaku (CV) (Jap), 650, 660, 662-
    67, 670, 697, 709, 767, 779,
    788-89